CANADIAN EXPEDITIONARY FORCE
1914–1919

CARLETON LIBRARY SERIES

The Carleton Library Series publishes books about Canadian economics, geography, history, politics, public policy, society and culture, and related topics, in the form of leading new scholarship and reprints of classics in these fields. The series is funded by Carleton University, published by McGill-Queen's University Press, and is under the guidance of the Carleton Library Series Editorial Board, which consists of faculty members of Carleton University. Suggestions and proposals for manuscripts and new editions of classic works are welcome and may be directed to the Carleton Library Series Editorial Board c/o the Library, Carleton University, Ottawa K1S 5B6, at cls@carleton.ca, or on the web at www.carleton.ca/cls.

CLS board members: John Clarke, Ross Eaman, Jennifer Henderson, Laura Macdonald, Paul Litt, Stanley Winer, Barry Wright

191 *A Wampum Denied*
Procter's War of 1812
Sandy Antal

192 *The Blacks in Canada: A History*
(Second edition)
Robin Winks

193 *A Disciplined Intelligence*
Critical Inquiry and Canadian Thought in the Victorian Era
A.B. McKillop

194 *Land, Power, and Economics on the Frontier of Upper Canada*
John Clarke

195 *The Children of Aataentsic*
A History of the Huron People to 1660
Bruce G. Trigger

196 *Silent Surrender*
The Multinational Corporation in Canada
Kari Levitt

197 *Cree Narrative*
Expressing the Personal Meanings of Events
Richard J. Preston

198 *The Dream of Nation*
A Social and Intellectual History of Quebec
Susan Mann

199 *A Great Duty*
Canadian Responses to Modern Life and Mass Culture, 1939–1967
L.B. Kuffert

200 *The Politics of Development*
Forests, Mines, and Hydro-Electric Power in Ontario, 1849–1941
H.V. Nelles

201 *Watching Quebec*
Selected Essays
Ramsay Cook

202 *Land of the Midnight Sun*
A History of the Yukon
Ken S. Coates and William R. Morrison

203 *The Canadian Quandary* (New edition)
Harry Johnson

204 *Canada and the Cost of World War II*
The International Operation of the Department of Finance, 1939–1947
Robert B. Bryce
Edited by Mathew Bellamy

205 *Lament for a Nation* (Anniversary edition)
George Grant

206 *Confederation Debates in the Province of Canada, 1865* (New edition)
P.B. Waite

207 *The History of Canadian Business, 1867–1914*
R.T. Naylor

208 *Lord Durham's Report* (New edition)
Based on the Abridgement
by Gerald M. Craig

209 *The Fighting Newfoundlander*
A History of the Royal Newfoundland Regiment
G.W.L. Nicholson

210 *Staples and Beyond*
Selected Writings of Mel Watkins
Edited by Hugh Grant and David Wolfe

211 *The Making of the Nations and Cultures of the New World*
An Essay in Comparative History
Gérard Bouchard

212 *The Quest of the Folk*
Antimodernism and Cultural Selection in Twentieth-Century Nova Scotia
Ian McKay

213 *Health Insurance and Canadian Public Policy*
The Seven Decisions That Created the Canadian Health Insurance System and Their Outcomes
Malcolm G. Taylor

214 *Inventing Canada*
Early Victorian Science and the Idea of a Transcontinental Nation
Suzanne Zeller

215 *Documents on the Confederation of British North America*
G.P. Browne

216 *The Irish in Ontario*
A Study in Rural History
Donald Harman Akenson

217 *The Canadian Economy in the Great Depression* (Third edition)
A.E. Safarian

218 *The Ordinary People of Essex*
Environment, Culture, and Economy on the Frontier of Upper Canada
John Clarke

219 *So Vast and Various*
Interpreting Canada's Regions in the Nineteenth and Twentieth Centuries
Edited by John Warkentin

220 *Industrial Organization in Canada*
Empirical Evidence and Policy Challenges
Edited by Zhiqi Chen and Marc Duhamel

221 *Surveyors of Empire*
Samuel Holland, J.F.W. Des Barres, and the Making of The Atlantic Neptune
Stephen J. Hornsby

222 *Peopling the North American City*
Montreal, 1840–1900
Sherry Olson and Patricia Thornton

223 *Interregional Migration and Public Policy in Canada*
An Empirical Study
Kathleen M. Day and Stanley L. Winer

224 *How Schools Worked*
Public Education in English Canada, 1900–1940
R.D. Gidney and W.P.J. Millar

225 *A Two-Edged Sword*
The Navy as an Instrument of Canadian Foreign Policy
Nicholas Tracy

226 *The Illustrated History of Canada*
25th Anniversary Edition
Edited by Craig Brown

227 *In Duty Bound*
Men, Women, and the State in Upper Canada, 1783–1841
J.K. Johnson

228 *Asleep at the Switch*
The Political Economy of Federal Research and Development Policy since 1960
Bruce Smardon

229 *And We Go On*
Will R. Bird
Introduction and Afterword by David Williams

230 *The Great War as I Saw It*
Frederick George Scott
Introduction by Mark G. McGowan

231 *The Canadian Oral History Reader*
Edited by Kristina R. Llewellyn, Alexander Freund, and Nolan Reilly

232 *Lives in Transition*
Longitudinal Analysis from Historical Sources
Edited by Peter Baskerville and Kris Inwood

233 *W.A. Mackintosh*
The Life of a Canadian Economist
Hugh Grant

234 *Green-lite*
Complexity in Fifty Years of Canadian Environmental Policy, Governance, and Democracy
G. Bruce Doern, Graeme Auld, and Christopher Stoney

235 *Canadian Expeditionary Force, 1914–1919*
Official History of the Canadian Army in the First World War
G.W.L. Nicholson
With a new introduction by Mark Osborne Humphries

Reproduced by permission of the National Gallery of Canada

"OVER THE TOP"

From a painting by Lieut. Alfred Bastien

Men of the 22nd Battalion assaulting east of Arras during the Canadian Corps' advance to the Drocourt-Quéant Line, August 1918

Canadian Expeditionary Force, 1914–1919

Official History of the Canadian Army in the First World War

G.W.L. NICHOLSON

Carleton Library Series 235

McGill-Queen's University Press
Montreal & Kingston • London • Chicago

© McGill-Queen's University Press 2015

First published in 1962
by Queen's Printer and Controller of Stationary, Ottawa
Reprinted with corrections in 1964

ISBN 978-0-7735-4617-2 (cloth)
ISBN 978-0-7735-4618-9 (paper)
ISBN 978-0-7735-9790-7 (ePDF)

Legal deposit fourth quarter 2015
Bibliothèque nationale du Québec
First paperback edition 2016

Printed in Canada on acid-free paper

McGill-Queen's University Press acknowledges the support of the Canada Council for the Arts for our publishing program. We also acknowledge the financial support of the Government of Canada through the Canada Book Fund for our publishing activities.

Library and Archives Canada Cataloguing in Publication

Nicholson, G.W.L. (Gerald William Lingen), 1902–1980, author
Canadian Expeditionary Force, 1914–1919: official history
of the Canadian Army in the First World War / G.W.L. Nicholson.

(Carleton library series; 235)
Reprint, with new introduction. Originally published: Ottawa : R. Duhamel,
Queen's Printer and Controller of Stationery, 1962.
Includes bibliographical references and index.
Issued in print and electronic formats.
ISBN 978-0-7735-4617-2 (bound). – ISBN 978-0-7735-4618-9 (paperback). –
ISBN 978-0-7735-9790-7 (ePDF)

1. Canada. Canadian Army. Canadian Expeditionary Force – History.
2. Canada. Canadian Army – History – World War, 1914–1918. 3. Canada –
Armed Forces – History – 20th century. 4. World War, 1914–1918 –
Regimental histories – Canada. 5. World War, 1914–1918 – Canada.
I. Title. II. Series: Carleton library series; 235

D547.C2N52 2015 940.4'1271 C2015-905575-X
C2015-905576-8

The new material in this book was typeset by Interscript in 10.5/13 Baskerville.

CONTENTS

APPENDICES

MAPS
(in Colour)

SKETCHES
(in Black and White)

ILLUSTRATIONS

Every effort has been made to identify, credit, and obtain publication rights from copyright holders of illustrations in this book. Notice of any errors or omissions in this regard will be gratefully received and corrections will be made in any subsequent editions. Unless otherwise indicated, archival photographs appear courtesy of the George Metcalf Archival Collection, © Canadian War Museum.

Introduction to the Carleton Library Series Edition

THE ORIGINS OF NICHOLSON'S *CANADIAN EXPEDITIONARY FORCE, 1914–1919*

MARK OSBORNE HUMPHRIES

On the 1962 publication of Colonel G.W.L. Nicholson's *Canadian Expeditionary Force, 1914–1919*, an old soldier of the C.E.F. noted that an official history of the First World War was long overdue. "In the hearts and minds of Canadian veterans of the First World War there has lurked a resentment, or at the least a slightly cynical feeling of hurt, over the fact that no official history of the performance of the half million men in the Canadian Expeditionary Force was ever produced," wrote Gregory Clark. "There have been of course a large number of commercial books published about the war, about various aspects of it; battalion histories have been privately printed; there have been a few Canadian novels on it. But it seemed to us old soldiers, sailors and airmen that it was a queer thing that our own nation, whom we helped to waken to consciousness as a nation, our fellow countrymen, did not think we were worth a history we could give our grandsons."[1] In reviewing Nicholson's work in early 1963, the distinguished British historian Cyril Falls – who had himself been an official historian on Britain's series of histories – wrote that "the reasons why" no Canadian history had been completed to that date "are fairly well known and need not be discussed."[2] That may have been true in 1963, but it is certainly not the case today. While Nicholson's book remains the bedrock of modern Canadian scholarship on the First World War, many readers might not be aware that it was almost never written at all.

Between 1918 and 1962, there were three abortive attempts to write Canada's official history of the Great War, but successive historians found it impossible to escape backroom intriguing, personal rivalries, and funding cuts. Although ordinary Canadians were anxious to learn about a conflict that killed 58,000 young men and left another 170,000 wounded, it was also an explosive political subject for men like Sir Sam Hughes, Sir Arthur Currie, Sir Richard Turner, and Lord Beaverbrook who were anxious to control the official story in order to protect their own reputations. Documents disappeared, historians were hired and fired, and eventually the whole official history project was cancelled after two decades of work produced only one published volume. Although now largely forgotten, it was briefly the stuff of national scandal. Nicholson's one-volume history was, as we will see, a work of compromise that was written to appease veterans and their families who, despite the passage of almost fifty years, were as interested as ever to learn about the war that took their youth.

Like any scholarly or literary work, Nicholson's official history has to be considered within the peculiar historical context and circumstances in which it was written. What it says (and does not say), its emphasis on military operations over personalities, and the accessible style in which it was written, reflect a half-century-long struggle for control of the official memory of the Great War. After the guns fell silent, all the warring nations committed to writing multi-volume official histories, and when Nicholson's work was published, Canada was the last country to meet that commitment. In the intervening years, politics, money, and incompetence conspired to ensure that an originally planned eight-volume history was never completed. Several times this failure became the object of scandal as veterans and historians publically lamented both a lack of scholarship on Canada's most costly war and the absence of a textual memorial to its participants. It was only the approach of the fiftieth anniversary of the war and the insistence of the Second World War official historian Charles P. Stacey that allowed Nicholson an opportunity to employ a team of historians to research and write a single-volume history as a compromise.

Official history is a controversial subject in the twenty-first century. The writing of sanctioned campaign histories began with the formation of the general staff system in nineteenth-century Prussia, which was gradually adopted by other Western armies thereafter. Military history was then written by soldiers for soldiers as detailed and thorough campaign histories that were intended to serve as case studies for officers training to fight the "next war." Stylistically bland, early official histories resembled Victorian taxonomic tomes with their emphasis on rational classification and meticulous attention to operational and administrative detail. They were histories of decision-making, staff work, logistics, and operational command from the perspective of the general staff rather than the experience of war at the sharp end. They also shared a common basic assumption: by creating an encyclopaedic rendering of past campaigns and laying bare the facts, future generals could actually converse with historical actors and learn why battles and campaigns unfolded as they did. In this sense, they embodied German historian Leopold von Ranke's claim that history must be written to show history as "it actually happened" (*wie es eigentlich gewesen*).[3]

Few historians would now agree that it is possible or even desirable to only write "what happened" and to let the evidence speak for itself. We now agree that the writing of any history, no matter how voluminous, detailed, or well-researched, must necessarily omit details, ignore themes, and discard whole lines of inquiry while emphasizing others, which, of course, introduces bias – and this is acceptable because there is simply no way to avoid it. Instead, we must read history with a keen awareness of the forces that act upon its authors. This is especially important when reading a work of official history written long ago that purports to impart a single, objective truth.[4]

When reading an official history, we must be conscious of the fact that the text itself is not only a secondary source describing "what happened" during the Great War, but also a primary source that sheds light on what members of the establishment believed and wanted others to believe about the conflict at another particular moment in history. While this does not diminish the importance of the research or its usefulness as a historical source, this caveat should give us pause. As Jonathan Vance has noted, official histories present politically acceptable versions of the past; they are usually the first word on a subject, usually written several decades before un-vetted historians and the general public are allowed access to official records.[5] This makes them especially powerful and important works because they set the tone for all subsequent inquiry. So in addition to being histories by soldiers for soldiers, official works could also become tools of propaganda and censorship, controlling potential sources of dissent and protecting reputations.[6] If, as Jay Winter and Antoine Prost observe, "the [popular] history of battle … is the lens through which readers are invited to re-examine the national character of their own country," then official histories only allow light to shine on certain places and in certain ways, highlighting portions of the past that are useful in the present while hiding others that are at odds with official aims.[7]

While readers should be critical thinkers, it is equally important to understand that the Great War's official historians were not engaged in a conscious conspiracy to defraud the public – far from it. They were writing in the spirit of their times and they genuinely believed in the viability of their methodology as well as the objectivity of their work. Perhaps naively, they thought that if all the facts could be elucidated and described, the truth would become self-evident. What we would say today, though, is that their truth was only one among many possible versions of history. In the years after the Great War, the overarching concern of most Western governments was to ensure that the sacrifices and accomplishments of the men who fought were properly recognized, and that war aims and the terms of peace were either properly supported or refuted. In essence, the belligerents refought the war on paper as much to justify the present order as to protect the reputations of those who oversaw the bloodletting. This process of assembling and deploying facts represented a new front where former enemies (and often allies) traded blame for casualties, poor decision-making, and responsibility. Indeed, every nation involved in the war produced an official history to justify and explain what happened – as did Switzerland and the Netherlands, which chose to remain neutral.[8]

The war itself had been a battle of *materiel* and the war of reputations was similar in scope as historical sections amassed documents just as the armies had stockpiled shells. Between 1922 and 1938 the French Ministère de la Guerre's Service Historique produced a 106-volume official history of the Great War titled *Les Armées françaises dans la Grande Guerre* (The French Armies in the Great War). In the twenty-one narrative tomes, which were authored by a team of 130 researchers, neutral statement of fact follows neutral statement of fact, each supported by footnotes to sources that were not buried in the archive, but actually reprinted in dozens of additional volumes of appendices.[9] It remains a staggering work of scholarship: the narrative volumes alone comprise 14,790 pages. Germany's salvo from the general staff historians was about half as long as France's. The first two books in its series, *Der Weltkrieg* (The World War), appeared in 1925 and the remaining fourteen volumes (including a history of wartime railways and the German economy) were written over the next two decades until the final books, though drafted in 1943 and 1944, were published by the Bundesarchiv in 1956. Not to be out-done by France, Germany also produced a thirty-six-volume series of popular battle histories titled *Schlachten des Weltkrieges* (Battles of the World War), which were all in print by the early 1930s. These shorter books (each between 120 and 350 pages) were supplemented by dozens of official divisional and regimental histories. If the purpose of the French series was to emphasize that wartime sacrifices had not been made in vain, then the similarly sized team of German historians tried to show that while the war had been lost, frontline soldiers had served nobly and bravely – an exculpatory narrative that was easily co-opted in the 1930s by the Nazis and others on the right wing of German politics. If these histories were written with a specific political purpose, they were also narrowly confined to military operations and questions of grand strategy – largely avoiding issues of culpability, morality, and politics that suited the statesmen who sponsored them.[10]

In Great Britain, the writing of official military history was the purview of the historical section of the Committee of Imperial Defence, which, in the decade before 1914, had produced studies of the South African War as well as the Russo-Japanese War. During the 1914–18 conflict, the historical section was tasked with collecting records from the front, compiling them, and producing an index that would later be used in writing the official history. According to Andrew Green, the committee established as early as August 1915 three inter-related aims to guide its work: the history would be written "to provide a popular and authoritative account for the general reader; for the purposes of professional reference and education; and to provide 'an antidote to the usual unofficial histories which besides being generally inaccurate, habitually attribute all naval and military failures to the ineptitude of the Government.'"[11] This, he suggests, created an inherent contradiction that the British official historian, Brigadier-General James Edmonds, would have to struggle to resolve: a history that was accessible to the general reader and defended the reputation of war leaders could not also be an accurate, soul-searching work useful to students of military science.[12] Indeed, although most would agree that Edmonds's history was a work of serious scholarship, the series has also been criticized for its uncritical treatment of Sir Douglas Haig, particularly his handling of the Somme and Passchendaele campaigns. But once the context in which Edmonds's work is understood, and the constraints it placed on certain aspects of his analysis considered, critical readers can easily see past the work's limitations. It remains the most detailed and accurate account of the war in English, even if it is dry and sometimes slanted towards the senior members of the B.E.F.

At the hundredth anniversary of the war, most British military historians would probably agree that Edmonds's history is no less and no more objective than any other; he has also outlasted his chief critics J.F.C. Fuller and Basil Liddell Hart. This speaks to the real value of an official history: because they are written by teams of historians with significant funding, time, and unimpeded access to the archival record, they are generally more encyclopaedic and comprehensive than any subsequent works. In the case of Germany's and Britain's histories, official accounts have additional value because they were written before many of the original archival records were destroyed in bombing raids or purged from collections to save on storage costs.[13]

Because of the size of the available body of source material, official historians had to research and write in highly systematized ways. Edmonds and his historical section had to retrieve, manage, organize, and examine more than twenty-five million separate documents, some of which are several thousand pages long.[14] Following an initial examination of official unit war diaries, related appendices, operational orders, administrative arrangements, and personal accounts, a sketch outline for the whole series was produced complete with prospective tables of contents organized by topic. In contrast with Germany's and France's historical sections, which opted for institutional authorship, Britain assigned lead authors to each volume and "narrators" to each subtopic. The former were the more senior historians like James Edmonds, Cyril Falls, and Wilfrid Miles whose names appeared on the books' dust-jackets while the latter junior colleagues – the men who actually sorted through the documents and drafted monographs or narratives – usually went uncredited. When complete, the manuscripts were submitted to the lead historian who edited the monograph and revised it to fit stylistically and analytically with the rest of the volume and series. Draft histories were then circulated to surviving senior officers who had participated in the operations under question and the text was then revised again (if necessary) to address their comments. Narratives from French, Belgian, and German perspectives also had to be generated and the text checked for accuracy by the foreign historical sections. In total, between 1922 and 1949, Britain's historical section produced a thirty-three-volume history of military operations in Africa, France and Belgium, Gallipoli, Italy, Persia, the Rhineland, and Salonika. This number does not include the multi-volume histories of the navy, air force, supply and logistics, seaborne trade, or munitions, all of which were written by separate research teams under separate direction.[15]

Edmonds's approach served as a model for the imperial historical sections. In Canada and the other so-called white settler Dominions of the British Empire, the production of official histories became an important part of the myth-making process that followed the war. Australia, Canada, Newfoundland, New Zealand, and South Africa had all fielded national forces of various sizes, roughly in proportion to their own populations, and their sacrifices had been significant. So on the one hand, while it was essential that participation in the war be acknowledged and explained for returned soldiers and the general public, the very act of writing a war history raised questions about the nature of each Dominion's relationship to Great Britain and what Dominion status actually meant. Each Dominion's force, regardless of size, had served under British command as part of the British or Mediterranean Expeditionary Forces. They had played an important part in the fighting, but not in strategic decision-making or even operational level command above that of the corps – and there were twenty-six corps in the British Army. Whereas Edmonds's history had been concerned with explaining, critiquing, and more often defending the actions of Haig and wartime government leaders, Dominion historians had the awkward task of writing national histories in which their subjects merely carried out orders from British commanders.

When politicians in Canberra or Ottawa decided to write an official history they were engaging in a conscious process of nation-building that necessarily differentiated the Dominion and its people from Britain. In these narratives, Britain necessarily was depicted as a foil that thwarted and diluted colonial efforts rather than as a partner or superior. Reflecting on the process of writing a colonial official history in 1938, Australian historian Charles Bean noted that he began his own twelve-volume work by asking several questions:

> how did the Australian people – and the Australian character, if there is one – come through the universally recognised test of this, their first great war? Second was the question: what did the Australian people and their forces achieve in the total effort of their side of the struggle? Third: what was the true nature of that struggle and test so far as Australians took part in it? How well or ill did our constitution and our preparations serve us in it? What were their strengths and

> weaknesses? And what guidance can our people or others obtain from this experience for future emergencies?[16]

Many of the assumptions embedded in the answers to these questions are no different than those which informed the writing of Britain's history, and later, Canada's volumes. But at the periphery of empire, the very existence of a separate Dominion history of the war gave Bean's work a single overarching thesis: Australia's war effort was distinct from Britain's; the war had forever changed the people of Australia as well as the Dominion's relationship to the mother country, making it essential to have a unique history explaining that process of change.

Australia's official history of the war was completed in 1943 while the narrower histories for South Africa and New Zealand were completed in 1924.[17] The story of Canada's and Newfoundland's histories is more complex because neither one was complete until G.W.L. Nicholson published *Canadian Expeditionary Force* and *The Fighting Newfoundlander* in 1962 and 1964 respectively. Why did the writing of official history in Canada prove so problematic? In short, Canadian politicians and those entrusted with writing war history could never agree upon what that history should be, what purpose it would serve, and how the narrative could be squared with difficult political questions related to language and ethnicity.

Work on an official history began in Canada following the Second Battle of Ypres in April 1915 when Max Aitken (soon-to-be Lord Beaverbrook, who was a friend of Canada's minister of militia, Sir Sam Hughes, and an ally of the Borden government), was allowed to create a Canadian War Records Office (C.W.R.O.) in London. Beaverbrook had a grand vision for the memorialization of Canada's war effort, which included a war art program funding more than 100 Canadian artists, taking documentary photographs and films of the battlefield, and producing official histories for a public audience rather than a military one. In this respect, he was the Canadian counterpart to Bean, who went overseas in 1915 with a similar vision for Australia. After the war Bean would spearhead the creation of the Australian War Memorial museum and archive while personally writing much of the official history, but Beaverbrook seems to have gradually lost interest in the memorial project as, unlike Bean, he was pulled in a myriad number of directions by his Canadian and British political connections. During the first years of the fighting, Beaverbrook personally authored two books in the three-volume series *Canada in Flanders*, which was labelled "official history," but more accurately is unabashed wartime propaganda. As Tim Cook argues, Beaverbrook's lasting legacy is the C.W.R.O., which obtained, preserved, and then organized the body of records that is now unparalleled in terms of scope, depth, and completeness for any other belligerent nation except Australia.[18]

Beaverbrook's appointment set the tone for the early writing of official history in another way. He was a well-connected newspaper man, a Conservative Party loyalist, and his appointment as guardian of Canada's war records ensured that from the start the writing of official history would be enmeshed in politics. As a meddlesome ally of Sir Sam Hughes – some regarded him as the minister's eyes and ears in Britain – it was clear that his office could make or break the reputations of wartime officers and politicians. No one understood this more clearly than Victoria, BC, real-estate salesman Sir Arthur Currie who began the war as a brigade commander and after June 1917 headed the Canadian Corps as Canada's first lieutenant-general.[19]

It is sometimes forgotten that Currie played an important role in shaping official history in Canada. Currie was undoubtedly a brilliant commander – perhaps one of the best British corps commanders of the war – but he was also vain, petty, and, perhaps for good reason, prone to paranoia. Before leaving for the Canadian training camp at Valcartier in August 1914, as a colonel in the Victoria militia Currie embezzled $10,883 from his regimental fund to pay off real-estate debts he had incurred during the collapse in housing prices the previous year.[20] This rash crime would cast a long shadow over Currie's life and career. After all, the Canadian militia was an integral part of the patronage system that dominated the Canadian political landscape and the Canadian Corps during the first years of war. Although he went overseas as a friend of Sir Sam Hughes, by the time Currie became a corps commander, Hughes had been ousted from the Borden cabinet and was itching for a way to strike back. Whether Currie was eager to please his political masters or just acted rashly, that summer he poisoned his relationship with the former minister: Currie not only refused to give Hughes's son Garnet command of a division, but also gave him a public, prolonged dressing down that reduced the man to tears.[21] This left Currie vulnerable to a counterattack as, at around the same time, the news of his theft was apparently beginning to spread both in Ottawa and overseas, although it is impossible to know how many people learned the details. Late that summer, Currie was forced to turn to two of his friends – who were also Hughes's cronies and generals in the Canadian Corps – 11th Brigade commander Victor Odlum and the commanding officer of the 4th Canadian Division, David Watson, to help him pay off his debts in Victoria.[22]

Currie was sure that Hughes knew about the theft and seems to have believed that Hughes was only waiting for an opportune moment to mount a smear campaign against him.[23] Whether Hughes in fact knew Currie had taken the money or not will never be known, but what matters is that the general's paranoia soon became all-consuming. His letters and diaries suggest that with each victory he achieved on the battlefield he became more frightened, convinced that Hughes was about to oust him as a fraudster. Although Currie's crime would remain a secret until the 1970s when two historians accidentally stumbled across the scandal in the papers of Prime Minister Robert Borden, Currie's fears were stoked by repeated and vitriolic attacks from Hughes in the House of Commons. The great irony is that these were based in pure fiction: the former minister accused Currie of intentionally slaughtering Canadian soldiers during the final Hundred Days campaign, wasting lives in order to heap glory on himself in the race to capture the symbolic city of Mons on 11 November 1918. Although patently unfair, Currie refused to take the bait, perhaps fearing that if he did respond, personal revelations would follow.[24]

Meanwhile in England, Beaverbrook's *Canada in Flanders* series reached the end of the Battle of the Somme with publication of the third volume, penned by poet Charles G.D. Roberts. From his headquarters in France, Currie attacked the accuracy and credibility of the books, strenuously objecting to any further work on the latter phases of the war. As Jack Hyatt notes, Currie's real issue with the series was "Beaverbrook's continual intriguing at army headquarters"[25] – long before Hughes began his attacks in the House of Commons, Currie had already come to the conclusion that Beaverbrook was acting as a cipher for the former minister and that his C.W.R.O. was out to destroy his reputation.[26] To counter the threat – real or perceived – on 20 December 1918 Currie established the Canadian War Narratives Section (C.W.N.S.), which operated out of his own headquarters under the direction of machine-gun tactician Brigadier-General Raymond Brutinel.[27] Brutinel was tasked by the corps commander with recording the story of Canada's victories during the final year of war and writing a history in the form of an objective report to be submitted the next spring to the Ministry of Overseas Forces. Currie felt that a comprehensive study would speak for itself, countering all of Hughes's attacks with evidence while blunting any counterthrusts from Beaverbrook's C.W.R.O. The battle for control over official narratives was now the frontline in the new Canadian war of reputations.

To write the official history for Currie, Brutinel employed a method similar to Edmonds's. First, the official records were borrowed from (or in other cases, never sent to) the C.W.R.O. in London and then the task of researching and writing each division's role in the campaign was assigned to a different narrator. These junior historians were told that they should try to achieve clarity and accuracy but that "no adverse comment need be made respecting the leadership or conduct of formations."[28] Of course, by taking the records away from Beaverbrook's office, Currie had effectively crippled the C.W.R.O. Writing the report was as much about controlling sources of information and limiting opportunities for dissent as establishing a specific narrative. The report was eventually published in May 1919 under Sir Arthur Currie's name.[29] It was a bland, straightforward account focused on military planning and the results obtained from battle rather than the fighting itself but it did the trick. However, as Tim Cook argues, the report was not meant to be an entertaining read; it was intended to make Currie the "final arbiter" over what would and would not be considered fact, allowing him to lay "the groundwork for conceptualizing the conflict."[30]

The government of Prime Minister Robert Borden was not prepared to assign the official history to either Beaverbrook's C.W.R.O. or Currie's new office. Another serving soldier, Ernest Alexander Cruikshank, a militia officer and an amateur historian of the War of 1812, was recruited to write the official, multi-volume history of Canada's Great War. Cruikshank, though, was probably never up to the task. Less a historian than an antiquarian, he was known for compiling long, idiosyncratic collections of historical documents rather than detailed, exacting histories of military operations.[31] In November 1918 he was made director of the new Historical Section of the Canadian General Staff and over the next two years he quickly compiled and published three volumes on the military history of Canada from the arrival of Europeans to the outbreak of the Great War, believing that the story of Canada in France and Flanders had to be properly contextualized. While Cruikshank may have had a vision, his books were strange: like the earlier histories of the War of 1812 and Upper Canada they were comprised of a few dozen pages of summary followed by hundreds of pages of documents – some important, others not so much, some entirely irrelevant.[32] Little progress was made on the war histories and by the time he retired in 1921, Cruikshank had only just reached the Great War. Although fully drafted and laid out, the remaining volumes of his military history of Canada were never published.[33]

In 1921, there were three agencies competing for authority over official history in Canada. The C.W.R.O. had possession of films, photographs, war art, and most of the documents covering the 1914–17 period, but no mandate. The C.W.N.S. had a sizable staff of researchers who were continuing to work on drafting narratives related to the later stages of the war and more than twelve tons of documents, but it was a wartime entity due to stand down when the final peace treaties were signed and the provisions of the War Measures Act rescinded. On 1 June 1921, the government took the logical step of merging the two offices with the Historical Section of the soon-to-be renamed Department of National Defence, which would have responsibility for managing all the Canadian records as well as writing the official history.[34]

The first head of the new Historical Section was a former artillery officer, Archer Fortescue Duguid, who had served on the general staff of the 3rd Canadian Division later in the war. Born in Aberdeenshire, Scotland, on 31 August 1887, Duguid immigrated to Canada in 1906 for health reasons, studying civil engineering at McGill University.[35] Duguid had no formal historical training but learned the craft on the job as a narrator for Currie's *Interim Report* in late 1918 and early 1919; a few months after the report was completed in the spring of 1919, he was transferred to the permanent staff of the C.W.N.S.[36] Duguid's subsequent appointment as official historian was a victory of sorts for Currie because it kept the official history in the hands of his former friends at Canadian Corps headquarters and out of the grasp of his enemies. This meant, though, that Duguid now found himself at the head of the Historical Section thanks in large measure to politics and a war of attrition between competing offices rather than any particular skill or qualifications.

Duguid's history was probably doomed from the start. How could an officer who owed his position to wartime connections, trained only to avoid criticizing leaders or formations, ever expect to write a history that would satisfy very different political, military, and civilian masters? In 1922 the new head of the Historical Section nevertheless proposed an ambitious eight-volume series of operational histories supplemented by four additional books covering the engineering, medical, chaplain, and nursing services.[37] While Duguid began by compiling records and sorting through location tables, the first volume in the series, the medical history, was quickly written by Sir Andrew Macphail, a prominent Canadian author and physician who had served overseas with a Canadian field ambulance during the war. Macphail's history illustrated the twofold problem at the heart of Canada's Historical Section: there were clear divisions between those who served in the C.E.F. and the Canadian politicians of the Overseas Ministry; there were also camps divided in support for either Currie or for Sir Richard Turner among the serving officers. As an overseas partisan of the old school, Macphail launched a polemical attack on the political management of the war, and the Canadian Army Medical Corps in particular, while lauding doctors' work at the front. Although Macphail was a member of the Currie camp, the medical history did not touch on the contentious Currie–Turner issue.

The reaction to his book is telling. Across the country, reviewers in medical journals and newspapers dismissed it as a confused compendium of facts and figures interspersed with anecdotes and lacking narrative cohesion – a sustained and unnecessary rant.[38] Yet Arthur Currie told the chief of the General Staff in 1926 that he felt it to be "very excellent" and an example for the official historians in the proper exercise of "selection and judgement" as well as the writing of "accurate," "fair," and "unbiased" history.[39] When it came to the C.E.F., everything was politics.

As if the political pressure were not enough, Duguid was already beginning to drown in a sea of minor tasks unrelated to the writing of his history. Battle honours had to be awarded to Canadian regiments, parliamentary queries responded to, while a myriad of requests from the general public poured in.[40]

Meanwhile, Edmonds was making steady progress on Britain's official history and, as official historian, Duguid was constantly asked to respond to and correct drafts related to the Canadians. As Wes Gustavson has observed, Duguid personally took on all of these tasks, determined not only to write an official history, but also act as guardian of the memory and reputation of the Canadian Corps.[41] It was more than any one man could master – even without the politics.

While it is certain that Duguid was at times stunned by the enormity of the task before him, it was the politics of actually writing his history and necessarily taking sides in the war of reputations that became truly paralyzing. At first glance, Duguid's aims were hardly different than those of Bean or Edmonds. As he stated in a preface to the first volume of the series, he wanted the book to be a memorial to the fallen, a source for historians, and a guide to soldiers preparing to fight future wars.[42] Could he reasonably achieve all three outcomes? While the other official historians declared similar intentions, they seemingly were able to emphasize one aspect of the task over the others when it was necessary to do so. For example, when faced with conflicting evidence or loyalties, Bean certainly always felt free to emphasize the memorial task that gave his history a certain nationalistic and narrative flair. Edmonds, on the other hand, reconciled the paradox by seeking to protect the reputation of the senior-most leadership, which gave rise to criticism, but was also the nature of writing contemporary history. In contrast, Duguid seems to have been unwilling or unable to manoeuvre in the face of controversy.

Duguid seems to have genuinely believed that a thorough and complete search of the documents would produce a form of pure history that would, by its very truthfulness, nullify any criticism from within or without. As Gustavson suggests, Duguid approached military history in a systematic fashion, first establishing what he called a series of "control points" from which orders emanated and then tracking down why they were followed, misinterpreted, or disobeyed. This was a problematic approach for several reasons. First, it assumed that operations (and people) always followed logical, cogent patterns of cause and effect when the reality was often more confused and complicated. Second, it meant that he often spent months following chains of correspondence and orders into dead-ends. The most significant problems arose when he tried to square postwar testimony from his friends and former superiors with contradictory documentary evidence from the time. Duguid's problem was that he never fully accepted that the two might never converge.[43]

In addition to the political problems he shared with Macphail, Duguid also had to contend with the postwar struggle between the rival camps represented by Currie and Turner. The depth of the problem became clear early in the process when James Edmonds sent Duguid his chapters on the Second Battle of Ypres – the 1st Canadian Division's baptism of fire that was both a point of pride for the Canadian public and a secret source of consternation for many of the senior officers of the former Canadian Corps. As T.H.E. Travers relates, Edmonds was highly critical of Canadian performance at the battle, and in particular the actions of Currie who was then the brigadier in command of 2nd Canadian Infantry Brigade. British researchers had uncovered "inconsistencies," reported Edmonds, between British and Canadian records and, to make matters worse, the original war diaries from 1st Canadian Division headquarters, Currie's 2nd Brigade, and Richard Turner's 3rd Brigade had seemingly been destroyed and replaced with positive narrative reports that presumably covered up poor decision-making. Currie in particular was roundly criticized for attempting to withdraw units from the line at a critical point in the battle and leaving his headquarters in search of reinforcements. Edmonds's drafts were circulated not only to Duguid, but also to Currie, Turner, and other surviving senior officers who were understandably dismayed at what they read. Duguid responded by mounting an ardent defence of Currie's actions while, according to Travers, he also intentionally concealed evidence supporting the view that some of the war diaries had been deliberately altered. He simultaneously covered up the actions of Richard Turner who had arguably made worse decisions than Currie during the battle by sending conflicting orders to retreat and advance, ordering rash counterattacks, and ultimately deciding to withdraw to an unfortified position known as the G.H.Q. line without notifying neighbouring units. The episode is revealing because while Duguid proved himself loyal to both men, it is also clear that he genuinely failed to see any way of reconciling the documents with the divergent memories of the participants.[44]

Duguid seems to have come to an unsettling conclusion: the Historical Section's job was to limit the spread of information and to dampen its political effects. His successor, C.P. Stacey, later recalled Duguid believed that armies would naturally cleave into political camps and that the Historical Section had to save itself by not aligning with one side or another – even if that meant doing nothing![45] And this was precisely what Duguid proceeded to do. While at first he proposed to write a history that would entirely refrain from discussing relations between officers, he began to wonder whether any history should be written at all until after Turner, Currie, and the other key participants had died.[46] Given these self-imposed constraints, an eight-volume history proved to be an impossible task. This might also explain why Duguid was willing to take on any and every request for information – no matter how obscure and distracting – that came to his department. Doing so allowed him to dither, dally, and repeatedly assure politicians, the press, and former comrades that a first volume would be in print very soon when in reality little progress was being made.[47] It is telling that Duguid would later internalize his own rhetoric, claiming he had orders "that nothing should be published until at least twenty years after the event" in order to protect the reputations of those involved. This was not the case.[48]

Duguid's overambitious aim had been to "produce a history second to none ever written in any language."[49] Instead, the first and only volume published in the projected eight-tome series went to press in 1938, less than a year before the outbreak of the Second World War. Reviews were mixed. Although C.P. Stacey was favourable to it at the time, he later recalled (after gaining experience as an official historian himself) it was exaggerated praise: "history is better written by historians than civil engineers," he snidely remarked in his own memoirs.[50] While some historians rightly continue to praise the first volume's detail and promise, it is worth pausing to reflect on its limitations. While it is possible to use the accompanying appendices to read between the lines and find fault with Richard Turner's actions during the battle, the same cannot be said for Arthur Currie's controversial performance. In describing Currie's decision to leave his headquarters in the middle of the Second Battle of Ypres, Duguid merely said, "[he] risked his military career by going back personally to find some troops wherewith to stop the gap. He was not successful in his quest."[51] In reality, Currie was out of contact with his brigade for several hours and received a severe dressing down from Major-General T.O. Snow, the commanding officer of 27th Division, who would later say that if he had been a British officer, Currie would have been shot.[52] The truth, of course, lies somewhere between, but Duguid steered clear of all controversy and he selected the evidence that allowed him to do so. For example, other serious issues with command and control (such as one Canadian battalion commander, J.A. Currie – no relation to Sir Arthur – who was found drunk behind the lines after abandoning his headquarters) were similarly ignored or glossed over.[53]

There are many reasons why the Historical Section failed to produce more volumes. While it is true that Duguid's staff never approached the numbers available to Edmonds, the Reichsarchiv, or the Service Historique, his task was also exponentially smaller. It was also no greater than that faced by Charles Bean, who had just as little historical training and faced similar obstacles and controversies, yet still managed to complete his series for Australia. More than once, Canadian governments considered replacing Duguid but ultimately kept him in place to save on the expense and time of finding a replacement.[54] In the end, Duguid failed to produce a complete history because he set himself an impossible task and then personally tried to master it. He spent nearly three decades pursuing contradictory and competing aims that only took him in circles. This does not mean that he was necessarily incompetent, but he was certainly naïve.

Between 1939 and 1946, the writing of the First World War official history was put on hold as the Army Historical Section worked to document the experience of Canadian soldiers fighting in the Second World War. Anxious to avoid a repeat of the Duguid fiasco, General Harry Crerar, who had served as a young officer in the Great War, appointed a new historian to gather documents and write a history of the 1939–45 conflict.[55] C.P. Stacey was everything that Duguid was not. A professional historian trained at the University of Toronto, Oxford, and Princeton, Stacey was also a serving militia officer and that rare type of team player capable of independent thought. Most importantly, he had the confidence, drive, and force of personality to press forward with the writing of contemporary history, fully understanding that nothing he would write could ever be entirely without controversy.[56]

In the summer of 1945, C.P. Stacey was appointed head of the Army Historical Section while Duguid was rebranded chief at the new sub-office of C.E.F. Historian.[57] The details of Stacey's fascinating career, first as chief historical officer at Canadian Military Headquarters, London, and later as director of the Army Historical Section, has been well covered by Tim Cook in *Clio's Warriors*.[58] Stacey also gives us his own account in his memoirs, *A Date with History*.[59] For our purposes, though, it is important to note that Stacey was a realist determined to avoid Duguid's fate. For the official history of the Second World War, he planned a modest four-volume series to be proceeded by a one volume sketch-history or summary. This would, he argued, provide the Canadian public with a thorough account of the war at an early date, allowing the Historical Section to later expand on the text in more detail through subsequent volumes on the Canadian experience in England, the campaigns in northwest Europe and Italy, and a separate work on the political direction of the war.[60] Unlike Duguid, Stacey was prepared to accept that no work of history can ever be the final word on a subject – and he wrote the summary history with the full understanding that it would be surpassed as new documents became available from both sides.[61] As all historians must do, Stacey strived to provide as accurate and authentic an account of operations as possible; he and his team of historians wrote objectively and dispassionately but were never silenced by controversy or contradiction. While he undoubtedly chose sides when faced with contradictory evidence, he produced results and his books still stand up as examples of good official history today.

Stacey also understood that leaders have to delegate. To write the history of the Italian campaign, he selected Gerald "Gerry" William Lingen Nicholson, an English-born high school principal from Saskatchewan.[62] Nicholson was thirty-nine when he joined the army in 1942 at Prince Albert, where he served as an adjutant for the next year. In a confidential report on his character, the assessing officers described him as "a confident, inspiring leader, poised, reasonably aggressive and self-assured ... He is an excellent lecturer, which is backed up by a fine educational background and educational training as a High School

Principal. He is a hard and conscientious worker and a good learner. Quite original, resourceful, and has an excellent ability. He has a charming, agreeable personality, optimistic nature, cheerful outlook … An artistic nature, rather than practical; is sympathetic, tactful, diplomatic, loyal, co-operative, high spirituality and sense of duty."[63] Based in large part on his experience as a teacher as well as this assessment, in 1943 A.F. Duguid asked for Nicholson's transfer to the Historical Section in Ottawa; later he was sent overseas to work for Stacey.[64] A few years after the war, Nicholson was appointed deputy director of the Historical Section and selected to write the official history of the Italian campaign.[65]

Stacey approached the history of the Second World War much differently than Duguid approached the First. As a starting point, he had detailed surveys made of the available primary sources stored on site at the A.H.S., in the files of various departments, at the national archives, and in private hands. From these surveys, they made estimates of the range of possible topics from which they could produce detailed outlines complete with sub-headings. These outlines were then assigned to individual researchers who re-examined the evidence, referenced the relevant source material and produced short, summative "monographs" usually including lengthy quotes. The senior historian named on the dust jacket would later work from these to write the complete volume, synthesizing and quoting as necessary. Surviving senior officers and the historical sections of the other allied armies then checked circulating drafts for accuracy and bias.[66]

Working under Stacey, Nicholson learned that "an official history must be the last word in accuracy and completeness."[67] Perhaps most importantly, he also learned the importance of clearly defining one's intended audience because, by the late 1940s, the purpose of official history was beginning to change. "What is an official war history?" Nicholson asked a public audience during an October 1956 lecture. He answered his own question, saying,

> In the past such histories had been written primarily for the soldier and the military student. Thus the histories reached a comparatively small circle of readers and existed mainly as a work of reference. This situation has now been changed and in no country has the change been more significant than in Canada. We had always prided ourselves on being an unmilitary people – no Prussian militarism here – but in the space of one generation we have sent our young men into two bloody wars. We have become at least a "middle" power in world affairs. We have found ourselves obliged to increase our peacetime military commitments very materially. Is it not high time that we, as a people, begin to be better informed than we have been in the past on military matters?[68]

The men working in Stacey's historical section became acutely aware of the fact that although their histories might be used for training purposes, they had to be aimed at a general public anxious to understand a complex war.[69] This also changed the underlying emphasis of the narrative and analysis – it was no longer about teaching soldiers to fight more effectively, but reproducing ideal citizens instilled with common values.

This shift towards commemorative official histories reflected both the financial constraint of the postwar period as well as the changing nature of warfare itself. The multi-volume histories of the First World War produced in Britain, France, and Germany were no help at predicting the questions future campaign commanders would need to answer, nor did they adequately address the overarching strategic problems that plagued commanders in both wars. Their real value had been in justifying the methods and ideas used to direct the war and so became textual memorials to the fallen. Following the Second World War, Britain's official histories of the conflict were similarly scaled down and addressed to a less specialist audience. The German military only began working on its official history of the 1939–45 war in the late 1990s, not to help German soldiers fight future wars, but to demonstrate the folly of the Third Reich's military programs. If official histories had any practical purpose in the immediate postwar period, it was to reflect and articulate the values for which nations claimed they fought. As Nicholson said in the mid-1950s, reflecting on the purpose of his own history of the Italian campaign, "Canadians will have to go on forming judgements on [foreign policy] for many years to come and if they are to form judgements worthy of an intelligent democracy, they must surely have available, for their guidance and consideration, authentic accounts of recent military history in a form comprehensible by the ordinary citizen."[70] Nicholson's history of the Italian campaign was published in 1956 and was well-received by readers and historians alike.[71]

Following the Second World War, Duguid seems to have cheerfully accepted Stacey's promotion and agreed to continue work on the Great War history, but it was about to die an ignoble death. Promising that the second volume would be ready for publication soon, he returned to work with a team of seven officers and eleven other ranks plus several civilian researchers.[72] Duguid was as optimistic as ever. In a schedule drafted that first winter of peace, he promised volume II, covering minor operations in the Ypres Salient during 1915–16 including the St Eloi Craters and Mount Sorrel, would be ready to go to the printer by July 1946. Projecting forward, he committed to having volume III (The Somme, 1916) ready for May 1947, volume IV (Vimy, 1917) for December 1947, volume V (Passchendaele, 1917) for January 1948, volume VI (Amiens, 1918) for March 1948, volume VII (Arras to Mons) for August 1948, and volume VIII (Armistice, secondary fronts, and demobilization) for January 1949.[73] But by September 1946, almost no progress had been made on volume II and Duguid was forced to revise his own target date for completion to 1953. An additionally discouraging point was that the single published volume had cost nearly $200,000 to produce and generated only $540 in sales by 1947. With no end in sight and little progress made, officials at the Department of National Defence wondered again whether it was worth continuing work on the series. "I cannot see what advantage there can possibly be to this Department or to the country as a whole by allowing this matter to drag on even until January, 1948," concluded Major-General C.C. Mann, vice-chief of the General Staff, in a damning report on the C.E.F. history. "It seems to me that, without recriminations, the production of the History of the First World War has 'missed the boat' completely and I am of the opinion that it would be a wiser and bolder course to take the bull by the horns now."[74] As a consequence of Duguid's lack of progress, the C.E.F. history was officially abandoned at the end of March 1947.[75]

The next year, though, Stacey's office began to publish the new series of official histories on time and on budget. Soon the decision to cancel the Great War history would be revisited, but despite Duguid's protests to the minister of National Defence, the Massey Commission, and anyone else who would listen, his work on the series was through. By the fortieth anniversary of the war, it was clear that veterans and their families were still anxious – perhaps more so than ever – to read about the conflict that consumed their youth. So, in 1956, Stacey was given the task of producing a one-volume history of that war to satisfy public demand, organized in a similar way to his own one-volume summary history of the Second World War. However, Stacey was then working on the more detailed multi-volume official history of the Second World War, specifically *The Victory Campaign*, and was looking forward to starting the final volume *Arms, Men, and Government.*[76] Stacey asked G.W.L. Nicholson to write a new and condensed First World War history. In this task, he was assigned narrators Frank McGuire, who had worked on the official history of the Korean War, and John Sweetenham, an officer in the Royal Engineers who had written a book titled *The Tragedy of the Baltic States* in 1952. They were joined eighteen months later by A.M.J. Hyatt, a young graduate of the Royal Military College and the University of Toronto.[77] As Hyatt recalls, Stacey and Nicholson had probably both read Duguid's voluminous reports in which the older historian claimed that most of the research for the remaining seven volumes had already been completed with most of the narratives drafted; it was first thought that the new team would work from Duguid's notes. However, when they went to the files, they soon discovered that almost nothing of the sort had been done. According to Hyatt, the only valuable thing left from the Duguid years were the handwritten notes he made on key documents and the copious number of cross-references he provided between sources. Stacey recalled that almost nothing of value was found in the files. In essence, Nicholson's team had to begin from scratch.[78]

Each narrator was assigned a portion of the history that they then had to research and write, ultimately producing a monograph draft to submit to Nicholson. Like the Italian campaign history, the narrators started with the war diaries and worked their way outwards through the appendices, orders, administrative records, and private papers that still form the core base of sources for military historians to this day. By the late 1950s, the records were no longer housed at the Historical Section but had already been transferred to the National Archives. As Hyatt remembers, the team were given unfettered access to all the records they needed, working in the stacks themselves where they were able to retrieve the necessary files at will.[79] As chapters were completed they were forwarded to Nicholson who made comments, asked questions, and sent them back for revision. They were also circulated to surviving members of the C.E.F. officer corps including General Andrew McNaughton, Lieutenant-Colonel D.E. MacIntyre, and Sir Richard Turner who had outlived Currie by nearly thirty years. C.P. Stacey was also sent drafts as was Colonel A.F. Duguid who fittingly did not return his sometimes scathing comments until after the book had already been published.[80]

What type of history would it be? Nicholson took a broad view of military history, at least in comparison to some of his contemporaries. In a 1965 lecture he discussed his approach to the subject, saying "I assume that the term 'military history' in general means to most of us the study of some particular war or wars, the political situations and events leading up to the outbreak of hostilities … the raising of armies and navies, and perhaps air forces, and the battles in which they were engaged; the kind of generalship displayed by the opposing commanders; the territorial or strategic gains or losses resulting from each encounter; the balance sheet of the casualties; and finally the terms of the peace treaty." Although he also conceded that the study of various technological developments was important and that it would always be "rewarding to go back into the past to see how the fighting men of earlier days lived," he did not believe that these topics deserved special attention in an official history. Instead, he maintained that pure military history's real purpose was to promote the development of good concepts of citizenship, which meant demonstrating to readers that individual actions had real meaning and providing role models that young people could emulate. As he concluded, "In these days when patriotism has too often become a word of little significance, and one that is heard only – and with some embarrassment – around November 11 – understanding of the contribution made in service and sacrifice for what men believed was for the security and welfare of their country, if not its very survival in freedom, such an understanding would surely help to combat the force of disunity abroad today."[81]

In this vein, Nicholson conceived *Canadian Expeditionary Force* primarily as a memorial to the men who fought as part of the Canadian Corps. It was a teaching tool, not for soldiers but average Canadians. If the book did have an overarching thesis, it was that the Great War had been Canada's coming of age. "The First World War brought Canada to maturity," he told the United Services Institute on 23 March 1960.

> And this maturity came not alone in the growth of industry, the increase in the national wealth, the greater readiness for Canadian statesmen to be listened to in the Councils of the World. Beyond this material evidence are the intangible contributions of her fighting men – their skill and determination, their devotion to duty, and their spirit of high sacrifice … For the battalion which fought at Vimy Ridge, and at the Somme, and at Passchendaele, were manned by soldiers from every part of Canada. And those who returned brought back with them to Canada a heritage, bought at great price – a heritage of endurance, self-sacrifice and loyalty – a heritage indeed of nationhood.[82]

Of course, this view of the war as a nation-building event could be traced back to the war itself and Robert Borden's belief that sacrifices on the battlefield would yield a greater voice in imperial affairs. In *Death So Noble*, Jonathan Vance argues that when this war aim failed to bear fruit, Canadian families still had to find meaning to the deaths of loved ones and they did so by constructing a myth of purposeful sacrifice. Christ-like Canadian soldiers had died, went the narrative, in order to preserve Christian civilization. In this respect, Nicholson was both reflecting and reinforcing an old, familiar theme: as Duguid told the Canadian Historical Association in 1935, it was at Vimy that the Canadian Corps "was consolidated into one homogeneous entity; the most powerful self-contained striking force on any battle-front." It had been, he said, an important national accomplishment and he believed that it was the duty of historians to preserve "the tradition of self-sacrifice, and the transmission of posterity of that precious heritage so dearly bought in battle overseas during the most momentous years in Canadian history."[83]

In this respect, Duguid should have been happy with Nicholson's work. *Canadian Expeditionary Force* subtly argues that the Great War was the crucible in which modern Canadian identity was formed. As such, it emphasizes the war's unifying effects over the divisions caused at home by conscription, labour unrest, as well as the 1917 election. As a military history, the emphasis is instead on operations rather than politics with little discussion of the experience of military service beyond technological questions surrounding the Ross rifle and other elements of a soldier's kit. It also downplayed the divisive internal politics that dominated the relationship between the Overseas Ministry and Currie's headquarters. It told the story of the Canadian experience overseas in an authoritative, accurate and necessarily brief way. Casualty figures are all there, as well as the context for important operational decisions, but it really reads like a summary and, as a result, is different in tone from the other official histories of the conflict.[84]

It is interesting here to note Duguid's criticisms because, while they were received late, they illustrate both the limitations of Nicholson's work as well as the genre itself. "It is the type of super-regimental history common to the period," he wrote. "Narrow in sympathy, one-sided, limited to treating the war as a series of heroic episodes ... the principal persons – namely Hughes, Currie, Turner – and Haig and French – are not treated definitively; this book does not offer an opinion about their historical role or their personal character. It offers little or no comment on the tactical problems of the war ... it does not consistently set the Western Front in the larger operational or strategic framework of the World War from the German point of view."[85] Duguid was clearly envisioning a much grander history that would deal comprehensively with all aspects of the conflict – indeed many of the so-called short-comings he identified would develop into major historiographical themes over the next half century. The real difference was that while Duguid may have had a clear vision, he also saw no way of achieving it. When Nicholson's history was published in 1962, the Department of National Defence advertised it to Canadians with perhaps understandable overstatement, saying that it provided "in a single volume an authentic and comprehensive account of the achievements of the Canadian Expeditionary Force in the War of 1914–1919 against Germany and the other Central Powers."[86] Of course Nicholson's single-volume history of a conflict that saw the mobilization of almost 20 per cent of Canada's male population necessarily meant that some things had to be left unsaid.

Nicholson's history was received with near universal acclaim. "It has taken the Department of National Defence 44 years to produce the history of the Canadian Expeditionary Force of the 'Great War,'" wrote W.H.S. Macklin, a veteran of the C.E.F. "Perhaps it was worth waiting so long to get the book that Colonel Nicholson has written. I suppose it might be possible to find some faults in any work so massive and comprehensive. In the space allotted for this review I find room to mention none. The author has discharged his task with scrupulous care for accuracy, great literary skill, and above all a sympathetic understanding of the gigantic sacrifice he was called upon to record."[87] The strength of Nicholson's work is that he wrote it with the full understanding that it would function as a one-volume summary history that would have to be expanded by further scholarship. Over the next five decades, historians of the C.E.F. have indeed refined and expanded on *Canadian Expeditionary Force*, but it has withstood the test of time and remains the standard reference work for Canada's First World War.[88]

The publication of this single-volume, summative history of the Great War has had a profound effect on the development of the literature on Canada's

Great War. Until 1962, little of a scholarly nature was produced on the conflict. In large measure, this was because most of the primary documents were still locked away in the Public Archives of Canada, but it also reflected the fact that in the two decades after the Second World War, public attention focused more on the latter conflict.[89] Nicholson's history really does act as a coda along a broken line of first-wave scholarship that began at Arthur Currie's headquarters. Even though Nicholson's history was published nearly a half-century after the First World War's end it served a purpose similar to Currie's original report to the Overseas Ministry. In subtle ways, the commemorative impulse at the heart of the book has set the tone for every historian working on the Great War in Canada.

Nicholson's book is narrowly focused on military events and jumps to the home front only when events in Canada intrude on the operational narrative. This isolation of what happened overseas from what happened at home is an artificial construction: in reality home front and battle front were intimately and inseparably linked. Separation was necessary, though, to sustain the nation-building narrative that is at the heart of Nicholson's book. For this thesis to hold together, the war must be seen as having unified Canadians behind a common cause, bringing them together rather than driving them apart. As social and political historians have shown over the last half century, the war was undoubtedly more divisive than the nation-building thesis allows.[90] The War Measures Act of 1914 introduced censorship and suspended civil rights, leading to the internment of German and Ukrainian Canadians as enemy aliens, often without cause. Although urban Canadians and Canadians who were British-born were quick to sign up in 1914 and 1915, others were more reluctant and by 1917 the voluntary spirit that Borden believed would sustain Canada's overseas commitments failed. In response, a Union government, which secured its grip on power by making significant alterations to the electoral franchise, introduced conscription. The Military Service Act of 1917 was as much about supporting English imperial views of duty and citizenship as it was about generating manpower for the Canadian Corps. Conscription and later the cancellation of exemptions divided the country and in Quebec City, English-speaking soldiers from Ontario opened fire on French-Canadian protestors with machineguns. Violence and disaffection were not only confined to French-speaking parts of the country. In the summer of 1918, there were labour riots in Toronto while a general strike vote was taken at Calgary and over the next year, rioting and labour unrest rocked the country. When the war ended, Canada was a far more violent, radicalized, and internally divided country than it had been in 1914. Not surprisingly, C.P. Stacey told Nicholson to deal with divisive measures like conscription as little as possible. They did not fit the narrative.[91]

The idea that Canada came of age during the Great War, that the Dominion figuratively became a nation at Vimy or somewhere else in France or Flanders, was an easy way of bringing meaning to a conflict that at least in hindsight served little purpose – it did not stop the German threat and it did not bring lasting peace.[92] As such it follows an archetypal hero narrative. In the first act of *Canadian Expeditionary Force*, Canadian troops are inexperienced colonials, well-intentioned and eager, but largely untrained. Mistakes are made and lessons learned. Over the next four years, Canadians gradually proved themselves on the battlefield and Nicholson charts this "progress" with the milestones of Vimy Ridge, the ascension of Arthur Currie to corps command, the taking of Passchendaele Ridge, all the way to the war's last hundred days when the Canadian Corps spearheaded the advance to victory. Along the way Canadians learn that they do things differently than their stubborn, backwards British masters and, by the end, have become their betters.[93]

As in any myth there are important kernels of truth. The Canadian Corps did begin the war as an inexperienced formation and did become a respected, efficient fighting force – one of the elite formations of the British Expeditionary Force. Arthur Currie was also one of the best corps commanders of the war. Yet in the conventional nationalist telling, we lose much of the nuance to the story. The Canadian Corps was never an autonomous formation capable of independent action just as battle planning and staff work were often done at higher levels or by British officers attached to corps headquarters. For those who fought between 1914 and 1918, the war was not about national independence or a coming of age: this claim is an historical imposition. Canadians were doing their bit for King and Empire because it was ultimately an Imperial war effort to safeguard a British Empire that most believed was indestructible. In the 1950s and early 1960s, though, as Canada moved further away from Britain's sphere of influence and the winds of change blew across Africa and the Middle East, Empire was no longer a sufficient explanation. History always leads to the present.

Nicholson's book is like any other: it is a product of its time. It is simultaneously a detailed and authoritative history of military operations and a reflection of the world in which it was written. Today it can be read as both a source on what happened on the battlefield between 1914 and 1918 and the ways in which Canadians have tried to make sense of that conflict in the decades after the guns finally fell silent. In both respects, it remains an important, indispensable source to understanding Canada's Great War.

A NOTE ON THE TEXT

Canadian Expeditionary Force was reprinted in 1964 with textual corrections that were proposed to the Army Historical Section and approved by Nicholson prior to the second printing. This Carleton Library Series edition reproduces the text from the corrected 1964 printing by means of an optical character recognition scan. No additional corrections have been made for this new edition, but two areas of the text were not corrected despite Nicholson's short list of emendations.[94] In the caption for the top-right photograph facing page 531 the beginning of the second sentence reads "In this picture Captain Al Plunkett," but it should read "In this picture Captain J.A. Plunkett." Consequently, the index on page 607 should read "Plunkett, Capt. J.A.: illustration 531," followed by a separate entry for "Plunkett, Capt. M.W.: 135, 529*n*."

NOTES

1 Gregory Clark, "The Packsack," Clipping, 1962, G.W.L. Nicholson Papers, MG31 G19, Volume 6, File C.E.F., 1914–19, Library and Archives Canada (LAC).

2 Cyril Falls, "Review of Canadian Expeditionary Force, 1914–1919," *International Journal* 18, no. 2 (Spring 1963): 229.

3 Mark Humphries and John Maker, *Germany's Western Front: Translations from the German Official History of the Great War, 1915* (Waterloo: Wilfrid Laurier University Press, 2010), xxix–xxxi.

4 For example, see R.G. Collingwood, *The Idea of History* (Oxford: Oxford University of Press, 1966), 282–3.

5 Jonathan F. Vance, *Death So Noble: Memory, Meaning, and the First World War* (Vancouver: UBC Press, 1997), 163–98.

6 See Keith Wilson, "Historical Engineering," in *Forging the Collective Memory: Governments and International Historians through Two World Wars*, ed. Keith Wilson (Providence, RI: Berghahn, 1996), 1–28, and Holger H. Herwig, "Clio Deceived: Patriotic Self-Censorship in Germany after the Great War," *International Security* 12, no. 2 (1987): 14–17.

7 Jay Winter and Antoine Prost, *The Great War in History: Debates and Controversies, 1914 to the Present* (New York: Cambridge University Press, 2006), 62.

8 Humphries and Maker, *Germany's Western Front*, xxxi–xxxiii.

9 Andrew Green, *Writing the Great War: Sir James Edmonds and the Official Histories, 1915–1948* (London: Frank Cass, 2003), 16.

10 Humphries and Maker, *Germany's Western Front*, xv–xvi. On the writing of the German official history see Markus Pöhlmann, *Kriegsgeschichte und Geschichtspolitik: Der Erste Weltkrieg. Die amtliche deutsche Militärgeschichtsschreibung, 1914–1956* (War History and History's Politics: The First World War and the Official German History, 1914–1956) (Schöningh: Paderborn, 2002).

11 Green, *Writing the Great War*, 6.

12 Ibid., 14.

13 Tim Cook, *Clio's Warriors: Canadian Historians and the Writing of the World Wars* (Vancouver: UBC Press, 2006), 201–3.

14 Green, *Writing the Great War*, 16.

15 Ibid., 17.

16 C.E.W. Bean, "The Writing of the Australian Official History of the Great War – Sources, Methods and Some Conclusions," *Journal and Proceedings of the Royal Australian Historical Society* 24, part 2 (1938): 91.

17 Ian McGibbon, '"Something of Them Is Here Recorded': Official History in New Zealand," in *The Last Word?: Essays on Official History in the United States and British Commonwealth*, ed. Jeffrey Grey (Westport, CT: Praeger, 2003), 56.

18 Cook, *Clio's Warriors*, 17–19.

19 On Currie see Tim Cook, *The Madman and the Butcher: The Sensational Wars of Sam Hughes and General Arthur Currie* (Toronto: Allen Lane, 2010), and Mark Osborne Humphries, ed., *The Selected Papers of Sir Arthur Currie: Diaries, Letters, and Report to the Ministry, 1916–1933* (Waterloo: LCMSDS/Wilfrid Laurier University Press, 2008).

20 R. Craig Brown and Desmond Morton, "The Embarrassing Apotheosis of a 'Great Canadian': Sir Arthur Currie's Personal Crisis in 1917," *Canadian Historical Review* 60, no. 1 (1979): 51.

21 A.M.J. Hyatt, *Sir Arthur Currie: A Military Biography* (Toronto: University of Toronto Press, 1987), 70–2.

22 Brown and Morton, "The Embarrassing Apotheosis of a 'Great Canadian,'" 58.

23 Ibid., 58–9.

24 Humphries, *The Selected Papers of Sir Arthur Currie*, 66–81.

25 Hyatt, "Official History in Canada," 94.

26 Beaverbrook to Currie, 22 January 1918 and Currie to Beaverbrook, 27 January 1918, MG30-E100, Volume 1, File 1, LAC.

27 Cook, *Clio's Warriors*, 28–9.

28 Quoted in ibid., 34.

29 The report's full title is *Interim Report on the Operations of the Canadian Corps during the Year 1918*, and is reprinted in *The Selected Papers of Sir Arthur Currie: Diaries, Letters, and Report to the Ministry, 1917–1933*, ed. Mark Osborne Humphries (Waterloo: LCMSDS/Wilfrid Laurier University Press, 2008), 211–324.

30 Ibid., 35.

31 Mark Humphries, "Ernest Alexander Cruikshank," *Dictionary of Canadian Biography*, volume 16, http://www.biographi.ca, forthcoming.

32 A.M.J. Hyatt, "Official History in Canada," *Military Affairs* 30, no. 2 (Summer 1966): 93–4.

33 Cook, *Clio's Warriors*, 42–3.

34 Government of Canada, *Report of the Department of Militia and Defence, 1923* (Ottawa: House of Commons, 1924), 23–4.

35 Wesley C. Gustavson, "Missing the Boat?: Colonel A.F. Duguid and the Canadian Official History of World War I" (Unpublished Master's Thesis: University of Calgary, 1999), 44–5.

36 Hyatt, "Official History in Canada," 94.

37 Ibid.
38 Cook, *Clio's Warriors*, 55–6.
39 Currie to J.H. MacBrien, c. 1926, quoted in Humphries, *The Selected Papers of Sir Arthur Currie*, 358–9.
40 Cook, *Clio's Warriors*, 62–70.
41 Gustavson, "Missing the Boat?," 34–5.
42 A.F. Duguid, *Official History of the Canadian Forces in the Great War, 1914–1919, Volume 1, Part I* (Ottawa: King's Printer, 1938), vii.
43 Wes Gustavson, '"Fairly Well Known and Need Not Be Discussed': Colonel A.F. Duguid and the Canadian Official History of the First World War," *Canadian Military History* 10, no. 2 (Spring 2001): 46–8.
44 T.H.E. Travers, "Allies in Conflict: The British and Canadian Official Historians and the Real Story of the Second Ypres," *Journal of Contemporary History* 24, no. 2 (April 1989): 301–13.
45 C.P. Stacey, *A Date with History: Memoirs of a Canadian Historian* (Ottawa: Deneau, 1982), 127–8.
46 Gustavson, "Missing the Boat?," 51.
47 See for example R.B. Bennett to Arthur Currie, 10 April 1933, MG30 E100, Volume 6, Folder 18, LAC.
48 A.F. Duguid to Vincent Massey, c. 1950, A.F. Duguid Fonds, No. 200110, Folder E, File 21, Directorate of History, Ottawa.
49 Ibid.
50 Stacey, *A Date with History*, 66.
51 Duguid, *Official History of the Canadian Forces in the Great War, 1914–1919*, 306–7.
52 Tim Travers, "Currie and 1st Canadian Division at Second Ypres, April 1915: Controversy, Criticism and Official History," *Canadian Military History* 5, no. 2 (1996): 9.
53 Andrew Iarocci, *Shoestring Soldiers: The 1st Canadian Division at War, 1914–1915* (Toronto: University of Toronto Press, 2008), 28.
54 S.F. Wise, "Canadian Official Military History," in *The Last Word?: Essays on Official History in the United States and British Commonwealth*, ed. Jeffrey Grey (Westport, CT: Greenwood, 2003), 11.
55 Cook, *Clio's Warriors*, 94.
56 Anon., "Biography: Colonel CP Stacey," Directorate of History and Heritage, http://www.cmp-cpm.forces.gc.ca/dhh-dhp/adh-sdh/bio/index-eng.asp.
57 Cook, *Clio's Warriors*, 135.
58 Ibid., 93–161.
59 Stacey, *A Date with History*, 169–228.
60 Ibid., 180.
61 C.P. Stacey, *The Canadian Army, 1939–1945: An Official Historical Summary* (Ottawa: King's Printer, 1948), viii.

62 Stacey, *A Date with History*, 178–9.

63 D.W. MacKendrick and J.C. Hedson, "Confidential Report, Administrative Wing, CSAA," 29 January 1943, MG31 G19, G.W.L. Nicholson Papers, Volume 6, File: "Personal Correspondence, 1972–75," LAC.

64 Stacey, *A Date with History*, 178–9.

65 C.P. Stacey, "Obituary: Colonel G.W.L. Nicholson, CD," *Historical Papers, Canadian Historical Association* (1982): 230–1.

66 Mark Osborne Humphries personal communication with A.M.J. Hyatt, 26 March 2015.

67 G.W.L. Nicholson, "The Writing of an Official History," unpublished lecture, 26 October 1956, MG31 G19, G.W.L. Nicholson Papers, Volume 6, File: Speech, LAC.

68 Nicholson, "The Writing of an Official History."

69 Stacey, *A Date with History*, 214.

70 Nicholson, "The Writing of an Official History."

71 Stacey, *A Date with History*, 214.

72 Ibid., 172.

73 A.F. Duguid, "Official History of the Canadian Forces in the Great War, 1914–1918: Tentative Dates for Publication," 15 January 1946, A.F. Duguid Papers, Series 200110, File 2: 'Official History Volume II – Generally,' DHH.

74 C.C. Munn, "Official Histories," 16 September 1946, A.F. Duguid Papers, Series 200110, File 2: "Official History Volume II – Generally," DHH.

75 Memorandum of Interview between Brigadier Megill and Colonel Guguid, 17 January 1947, A.F. Duguid Papers, Series 200110, File 2: "Official History Volume II – Generally," DHH.

76 Cook, *Clio's Warriors*, 201–2

77 Ibid.; Mark Osborne Humphries personal communication with A.M.J. Hyatt, 26 March 2015.

78 Mark Osborne Humphries personal communication with A.M.J. Hyatt, 26 March 2015; C.P. Stacey to D Hist, 30 July 1962, MG 31 G19, Volume 1, File C.E.F., 1914–19, LAC.

79 Mark Osborne Humphries personal communication with A.M.J. Hyatt, 26 March 2015.

80 "C.E.F. Distribution Lists," G.W.L. Nicholson Papers, MG31 G19, Volume 6, LAC.

81 G.W.L. Nicholson, "Approaches to the Teaching of Military History," c. 1965, G.W.L. Nicholson Papers, MG31 G 19, Volume 6, LAC.

82 G.W.L. Nicholson, "Some Second Thoughts on the First World War," 23 March 1960, G.W.L. Nicholson Papers, MG31 G 19, Volume 6, LAC.

83 A.F. Duguid, "Canadians in Battle, 1915–1918," *Report of the Annual Meeting of the Canadian Historical Association* 14 (1935): 42, 50.

84 Cook, *Clio's Warriors*, 202–6.

85 A.F. Duguid, "C.E.F. – Comment," c. 1962, MG31 G19, Volume 6, File Misc. Drafts, Comments …, LAC.

86 Advertisement Proof, c. 1962, MG31 G19, Volume 6, File C.E.F. 1914–19, LAC.

87 W.H.S. Macklin, "A Belated War History Does Canada Justice," *Ottawa Citizen*, 26 January 1963.

88 For an analysis of the subsequent historiography, see Mark Osborne Humphries, "Between Commemoration and History: The Historiography of the Canadian Corps and Military Overseas," *Canadian Historical Review* 95, no. 3 (September 2014): 384–97.

89 Cook, *Clio's Warriors*, 202.

90 On the development of the Canadian literature on the Great War over the past fifty years see Humphries, "Between Commemoration and History," 385–7 as well as the other historiographical essays in the same special issue of the *Canadian Historical Review*. Tim Cook provides a thorough overview of the development of military history writing in Canada in general from the 1960s to the recent past in *Clio's Warriors*, 200–52.

91 Amy Shaw, "Expanding the Narrative: A First World War with Women, Children, and Grief," *Canadian Historical Review* 95, no. 2 (September 1914): 398–406.

92 G.W.L. Nicholson, "Some Second Thoughts on the First World War," 23 March 1960, G.W.L. Nicholson Papers, MG31 G 19, Volume 6, LAC.

93 Humphries, "Between Commemoration and History," 387. For another view, see Tim Cook, "Battles of the Imagined Past: Canada's Great War and Memory," *Canadian Historical Review* 95, no. 2 (September 1914): 417–26.

94 G.W.L. Nicholson Papers, MG31-G19, Volume 1, File: "C.E.F., 1914–1919 – Correspondence re Publication of Book, 1961–62," LAC.

FOREWORD

THE PUBLICATION of the official account of the Canadian Expeditionary Force in the Great War is a welcome occasion for a tribute not only to Colonel Nicholson, the author, but also to his predecessor in this field, Colonel A. Fortescue Duguid.

Colonel Duguid's plan to write an eight-volume history of the Canadian Forces in the Great War was never realized. The quality of that part which was published makes clear how great this loss was, to the veterans of the Expeditionary Force and to Canada at large.

In 1956 the government decided that there should be a completed account of Canada's Expeditionary Force and authorized a one-volume work. Colonel Nicholson, Deputy Director of the Historical Section at that time, was assigned the task and, assisted by a devoted team of researchers, completed it during his term as Director, 1959-1961. He and his staff found both the published and the unpublished work of the earlier Historical Section of great value to them in many ways.

As one who has had nothing to do with either Colonel Duguid's work or with Colonel Nicholson's I am happy to speak a word of tribute linking the military scholarship of two generations. I hope the earlier historians and their fellow veterans of the Great War will find in the present work a worthy memorial of Canada's first great expeditionary force.

G. M. C. SPRUNG, Colonel,
Director Historical Section.

PREFACE

THIS BOOK has been written to provide in a single volume an authentic and comprehensive account of the achievements of the Canadian Expeditionary Force in the War of 1914-1919 against Germany and the other Central Powers. It is directed primarily to the general reader, but it will, it is felt, be of special value to the military student. The author ventures to express the hope that the book will be read with particular interest by surviving members of the C.E.F.

After the war, work began on the preparation of a definitive eight-volume series bearing the title *Official History of the Canadian Forces in the Great War, 1914-1919.* Volume I, written by Colonel A. Fortescue Duguid, D.S.O., Director of Historical Section, General Staff, was published in 1938, together with a volume of appendices and maps. It covered the period from August 1914 to September 1915. A volume entitled *The Medical Services,* by Sir Andrew Macphail, appeared in 1924.

After the Second World War work on the official history of the former conflict was discontinued and it was decided to abandon the project. The great mass of documentary material dealing with the war was turned over to the Public Archives of Canada for the use of bona fide students of military history. Following this decision the Canadian Government began to receive from individuals and veterans' organizations requests for the completion of an official history of the First World War; and when work on the history of the 1939-1945 war was well advanced, the Historical Section was directed to produce a one-volume account of the earlier struggle.

This volume deals primarily with operations in France and Belgium. In general it has been possible to describe these events only in broad outline, for the limitations imposed by the covers of a single book have ruled out the inclusion of much detail. The same reason has prevented individual treatment of the contribution made by many arms and services who provided the necessary tactical and administrative support for the units which were fighting in the front line. Two chapters have been devoted, however, to consideration of problems of organization and administration, particularly the controversial question of the introduction of conscription in 1917. A further chapter summarises the activities of Canadian forces who served outside the Canadian Corps, some of them in theatres far removed from the Western Front.

The main sources used in writing this history have been the contemporary records of the campaigns. These include the war diaries, planning papers and operational reports of the participating formations and units, as well as a multiplicity of files and other documents originating with Militia Headquarters in Ottawa, Headquarters Overseas Military Forces of Canada, in London, and the headquarters of formations in the field. Particularly valuable were collections of private papers held by the Historical Section or in the custody of the Public Archives of Canada, including those of Sir Robert Borden, Lieut.-General Sir Richard Turner, Sir George Perley, Lieut.-General Sir Arthur Currie and Sir Edward Kemp. Permission was graciously given by Earl Haig of Bemersyde to consult the complete text of his father's diary, and by Mr. Henry Borden for examination of Sir Robert Borden's personal diary. Among the many published sources of which the author has made extensive use are the official histories of the First World War produced by participating countries on both sides, and the regimental histories of Canadian, British and German units. He would particularly acknowledge his indebtedness to Colonel Duguid's first volume of the Canadian Official History, from which he drew extensively for the account of the mobilization of the C.E.F. and its early operations. He has further profited by the research carried out by Colonel Duguid and his staff for subsequent volumes that were projected. For the benefit of students and others who may wish to pursue their research further, it has been considered desirable to document this volume fairly extensively, though such references have been placed unobtrusively at the end of the book. Care has been taken to use the most reliable statistics available. Those in the tables which appear as appendices to the volume are based on data prepared by the Machine Records Section, Adjutant General's Branch, National Defence Headquarters. Permission to include the extract from Laurence Binyon's "For the Fallen" has been granted by the Society of Authors and Mrs. Cicely Binyon.

While the author did not serve in the First World War, he has had the benefit of the advice of a number of senior officers who were participants in the events described. These have been kind enough to read the draft of the text, in whole or in part, and the writer is much indebted to them for their helpful criticism and comments. In this connection he is glad to acknowledge also the assistance of the Historical Branch of the Cabinet Office in London. In the year 1959 he made an extensive tour of the battlefields of France and Belgium in order to study the topography of the areas in which Canadian troops were engaged.

Many members of the Canadian Army's Historical Section, past or present, have contributed in varying degrees to the production of this book. To all of them the author expresses his grateful appreciation. Particularly would he acknowledge the work of three officers, Captain F. R. McGuire, C.D., Captain J. A. Swettenham and Lieut. A. M. J. Hyatt, who performed the major part of the research for this volume and prepared the preliminary drafts of many of the chapters. The present writer must, however, take full responsibility for the chapters as now printed, for all have undergone considerable revision at his hands. Captain L. R. Cameron, C.D., has given valuable assistance with research on the administrative side and in preparing the appendices. The book owes much to the painstaking work of Mr. A. G. Steiger on German sources, and to maps compiled by Major C. C. J. Bond, C.D., and drawn by Sergeant E. H.

Ellwand. A special word of thanks to Staff-Sergeant R. C. Wellstood, C.D., and Sergeant A. A. Azar, C.D., for their help in the exacting task of checking references and preparing the index, and to the various members of the Section's staff who at one stage or another assisted in typing the successive drafts of the book. Last but not least the author would express his warm appreciation to Lt.-Col. T. M. Hunter, C.D., who was charged with the onerous responsibility of seeing this volume through the press.

G.W.L.N.

Historical Section (G.S.),
Army Headquarters,
Ottawa, Canada.

CANADIAN EXPEDITIONARY FORCE
1914–1919

CHAPTER I

CANADA AT WAR

The Outbreak of War

ON 28 JUNE 1914 an assassin's bullet struck down the Archduke Franz Ferdinand, heir to the Austro-Hungarian throne. The incident, occurring at a time when a dangerous tension strained the relations between the two armed camps into which the great powers of Europe had grouped themselves, precipitated the devastating conflict which we have come to call the First World War.

The slaying took place at Sarajevo, capital city of Bosnia, a Balkan province which Austria after thirty years of occupancy had formally annexed in 1908. The plotters were allegedly agents of a Serbian secret society, and on 23 July Austria, seizing the opportunity to end the "Greater Serbia" movement which she saw as a threat to the prestige, if not the very existence, of the Dual Monarchy, presented a harsh ultimatum whose demands Serbia could not possibly accept and retain her national sovereignty. Austria hoped to crush Serbia in a purely local war, but in view of Russia's known encouragement of Serbian ambitions, she had taken the precaution of obtaining Germany's assurance of support in the event of a wider conflict. With only forty-eight hours allowed for her answer Serbia immediately appealed to Russia for help, at the same time seeking advice from France, Britain and Italy. She replied to the ultimatum in most conciliatory terms, proposing that the matter be settled by arbitration. But Austria found in the reply enough reservations to break off diplomatic relations at once, and three days later, on 28 July, she declared war.

One by one the major powers were drawn into the conflict—although there is strong evidence that not one of them wanted a general war, and Britain in particular made genuine efforts to prevent one. Germany, committed by the defensive alliance in which she had joined Austria-Hungary in 1879 (which the addition of Italy three years later had made the Triple Alliance), must bear the responsibility of initially giving Austria a free rein. A week after the assassination an Austrian emissary seeking advice in Berlin had received a "blank cheque" from the German Emperor. The decision to enter hostilities was left to Vienna, but the Kaiser assured the Austrian ambassador that in the event of war Germany would stand by Austria's side "with her accustomed faithfulness as an ally".[1] Subsequently Germany, believing that the Austro-Serbian conflict could be localized, made belated efforts to bring Austria to mediation as Russia moved towards mobilization. These attempts, if indeed they were genuine, proved ineffective. Although Russia was not anxious to fight, in keeping with her frequent encouragement of her Slav protégé she took the momentous decision on 30 July of ordering a general mobilization—a measure which by European states was considered tantamount to a declaration of war. A German demand that these warlike preparations cease brought no reply, and on 1 August Germany declared war on Russia. Five days later Austria followed her ally's lead; but Italy, the remaining partner of the Triple Alliance, remained neutral until May 1915, when she entered the war on the opposing side.

Since 1894 Russia had been linked with France in a defensive pact directed against the Central European powers. Britain had no actual alliance with either country. Early in the twentieth century, however, she had been led to forsake her "splendid isolation" when the German Fleet Law of 1900 called for "a battle fleet of such strength that even for the most powerful naval adversary a war would involve such risks as to make that Power's own supremacy doubtful".[2] The resulting Anglo-French Convention of 1904 (the *entente cordiale*) and a similar agreement with Russia in 1907 had set the stage for close political cooperation between the three nations. Although the Triple Alliance was thus confronted by a "Triple Entente", German statesmen in July 1914 believed that their war plans need take into account only Russia and France. These plans, as we shall see, called for simultaneous hostilities against both countries, with an initial offensive in the west. Accordingly the German ultimatum to Russia was matched by a demand that France declare her intentions. The reply was given before the deadline on 1 August: "France will act in accordance with her interests."[3] Each nation issued mobilization orders that afternoon, and at 6:15 p.m. on the 3rd, alleging several hostile French acts, Germany declared war on her ancient rival.

During the critical days that followed the Sarajevo assassination, Great Britain had made repeated efforts to preserve peace. Her Foreign Secretary, Sir Edward Grey, successively proposed direct conversations between Vienna and St. Petersburg; mediation in those capitals by Germany, Italy, France and Britain if Austria and Russia should mobilize; and a conference of the ambassadors of these four powers in London to seek a peaceful settlement. All these proposals came to nothing, as in each case the various powers, with the exception of Britain and Italy, either gave an outright rejection, or countered with alternative proposals, or delayed answering until too late. Even after Austria's declaration of war on Serbia there was considerable opposition within the British Cabinet to participation in a European war; but on 30 July Grey received from the German Chancellor, Dr. Theobald von Bethmann-Hollweg, a proposal that did much to change the Government's "overwhelmingly pacific" attitude.[4] This was a strong bid for Britain to remain neutral, accompanied by a virtual admission that Germany intended to violate Belgium's neutrality—to respect which Germany, France and Britain were pledged as signatories of a treaty of 1839.

The proposal was summarily rejected, but on 2 August the German Minister to Brussels presented an ultimatum demanding agreement to a German advance against France through Belgian territory. The Belgian Government "firmly resolved to repel by all means in its power every attack upon its rights", and King Albert asked for French and British aid. The British Government was now assured that the House of Commons would support a policy of resistance to Germany, and on the morning of the 4th, as news came of a German violation of Belgian soil, Sir Edward Grey sent an ultimatum giving Berlin until midnight to withdraw her demands on Belgium. In an interview with the British Ambassador Bethmann-Hollweg deplored the terrible step taken by His Majesty's Government, that "just for a scrap of paper Great Britain was going to make war on a kindred nation who desired nothing better than to be friends with her."[5] The time limit passed without a satisfactory reply.

Britain was at war with Germany.

Canada Supports Great Britain

When a quarter of a century later the Second World War broke out, the Canadian Government was firmly committed to a policy of not involving the country in hostilities without first consulting Parliament. As a result, in 1939 Canada formally remained "neutral for one week after the declaration of war by Britain".[6] In 1914, however, seventeen years before the enactment of the Statute of Westminster, Canada's constitutional position within the Empire gave her little share in formulating foreign policy and none in declaring war or making peace. She found herself at war through the action of the British Government. "She had not been consulted; she had herself made no declaration of war; and she had in no way taken part in the diplomatic exchanges which had led to the final catastrophe."[7] Like her sister Dominions, however, Canada reserved the right of deciding what form her participation should take. That her contribution would be whole-hearted and generous there was never any doubt. Thus it was possible on 1 August for the Governor General, Field-Marshal H. R. H. the Duke of Connaught, to cable the Secretary of State for the Colonies his Government's firm assurance

> . . . that if unhappily war should ensue the Canadian people will be united in a common resolve to put forth every effort and to make every sacrifice necessary to ensure the integrity and maintain the honour of our Empire.[8]

Canada's position had been made clear on various recent occasions by her leading statesmen. In January 1910 Sir Wilfrid Laurier, then Prime Minister, declared in the House of Commons, "When Britain is at war, Canada is at war. There is no distinction."[9] The Leader of the Opposition at the time, Sir Robert Borden, had expressed himself in similar vein, and now on the eve of war pronouncements in the daily press made it clear that the whole country accepted this view.

The Canadian Parliament was not in session, having been prorogued on 12 June. On 30 July members of the Cabinet still in Ottawa met to consider the

European situation and on 31 July the Prime Minister, Sir Robert Borden, returned to Ottawa from an interrupted holiday in Muskoka. Other Cabinet Ministers who were away reassembled in the capital without delay. During the tense days which preceded the fateful decision preliminary steps were taken for safeguarding the country and for ensuring the most effective means of furnishing aid to the Empire. A second cablegram to the Colonial Office on 1 August sought "any suggestions and advice which Imperial Naval and Military authorities may deem it expedient to offer" and intimated that "a considerable force would be available for service abroad". Word that war had broken out with Germany was received in Ottawa at 8:45 p.m. on the 4th, and published in a *Canada Gazette* extra next day. Although Canada had not needed Parliamentary consent to be at war, her law provided, as her Minister of Militia and Defence, Sir Frederick Borden, had put it at the Colonial Conference of 1907, "that if it is desirable to contribute a force to Imperial defence abroad, Parliament shall be called together. . . ."[10] Accordingly Parliament was immediately summoned to meet in emergency session on 18 August.

With the tension of uncertainty past a great wave of loyal demonstrations surged across Canada. The enthusiasm of crowds in the Montreal streets singing "La Marseillaise" and "Rule Britannia" was matched by the stirring spectacle of the impromptu parades, waving of flags, processions of decorated automobiles, and impassioned speeches with which every western city from Winnipeg to Victoria received the news of war.[11] This outward display of patriotism quickly passed, as thoughtful Canadians, facing the grim realities of war, foresaw the awful possibilities that lay ahead. Yet it had been no idle outburst of sentiment. A statement in the Toronto *Telegram* of 6 August was to be proved remarkably correct: "The men who have cheered the loudest will be among the first to offer their services." From all parts of the country came applications from officers, men and whole regiments volunteering for active service, so that a considerable force was assured even before war was declared.

The importance of taking full advantage of this national enthusiasm was fully realized. On 4 August the Governor General cabled London:

> Great exhibition of genuine patriotism here. When inevitable fact transpires that considerable period of training will be necessary before Canadian troops will be fit for European war, this ardour is bound to be damped somewhat. In order to minimize this, I would suggest that any proposal from you should be accompanied by the assurance that Canadian troops will go to the front as soon as they have reached a sufficient standard of training.

The Canadian Militia before 1914

What was the nature of the resources from which an unmilitary nation like Canada could furnish an organized body of troops for service overseas? She had a small Permanent Force of regular soldiers. Its statutory strength, set at 750 in 1883, had been increased from time to time until in 1905, when the decision to abandon Halifax and Esquimalt as Imperial naval bases led to the withdrawal of the last British troops in Canada, it reached a maximum of 5000. This quota, however, was never fully recruited. A limited establishment was set each year, its numbers determined by the amount of the annual Parliamentary vote, but even with this reduction it was often found difficult, because of more attractive conditions in the labour market, to obtain sufficient recruits.[12] For the fiscal year beginning 1 April 1914 the total authorized establishment of the force was 3110 all ranks and 684 horses.[13] It then comprised two regiments (each of two squadrons) of cavalry—the Royal Canadian Dragoons and Lord Strathcona's Horse; the Royal Canadian Horse Artillery with two batteries, and the Royal Canadian Garrison Artillery with five companies; one field company and two fortress companies of engineers; one infantry battalion—The Royal Canadian Regiment; together with detachments of the various service and administrative corps. The Permanent Force's main peacetime functions were to garrison the fortresses on either coast and assist in training the militia.

Although lacking a large standing army ready for immediate action, in her Non-Permanent Active Militia Canada had the basis of the contingents that she must mobilize when the need should arise. The past decade had seen a steady increase in the strength and efficiency of this force of citizen soldiers. Between 1904 and 1913 the number of men undergoing annual training had grown from 36,000 to 55,000, an expansion that had been matched by marked improvement in organization and training. Just before the end of the previous century Major-General E. T. H. Hutton, one of the last British soldiers to serve as General Officer Commanding Canadian Militia, had reported that the condition of the militia force of Canada was "unsatisfactory in the extreme", it being "but a collection of military units without cohesion, without staff and without those military departments by which an army is moved, fed, or ministered to in sickness".[14]

That was in 1898, and General Hutton and his successors had set about creating a "militia army"—a balanced force of all arms with the necessary administrative services, sufficiently well trained and equipped to make a worthwhile contribution in emergency. The South African War provided the occasion for Canada for the first time to send a military contingent overseas. A battalion was raised from volunteers supplied by 82 different militia units, and about 150 men of the Permanent Force. It sailed for Cape Town in October 1899 as the 2nd (Special Service) Battalion, Royal Canadian Regiment of Infantry (which became The Royal Canadian Regiment on 1 November 1901), and performed creditably at the Battle of Paardeberg. It was closely followed by a second Canadian Contingent consisting of two battalions of Mounted Rifles and a brigade of field artillery. Other units were sent later, the total Canadian contribution numbering more than 8000 (including a battalion provided for garrison duty at Halifax). The participation of these troops in the war spurred the interest of the Canadian public in its military forces. There was justifiable pride in the award of four V.Cs. to Canadians.* Not only did the militia benefit from the experience gained in South Africa, but a precedent had been set for Canadian military participation in future conflicts beyond her shores.

Following the South African War an improved system of administration brought reforms and development. The increasing government support given to Sir Frederick Borden as Minister of Militia (1896-1911) and his successor, Sir Sam Hughes, is demonstrated by the rise in the Militia expenditures from three millions at the turn of the century to $11,000,000 for the fiscal year ending 31 March 1914.[15] An Army Service Corps was set up in 1901, to be followed within three years by the organization of a Corps of Engineers, an Ordnance Corps, a Signalling Corps and a Medical Corps.

In 1904 the post of General Officer Commanding the Canadian Militia, which (by law) had been held by officers of the British Regular Army since 1875, was virtually abolished after the Canadian Government had relieved Lord Dundonald of his position at the instance of the Minister of Militia. A new Militia Act (1 November 1904) continued to provide for a Commanding Officer of the Militia but on an optional basis—though the provision remained on the Statute books for the next forty-six years the position was never filled.

Considerable though the contribution by the eight British commanders had been, serious differences of opinion had arisen between at least two of the G.O.Cs. and the Minister of Militia. Most of the trouble may be attributed to the absence of a clear-cut division between the responsibilities of the civil and military branches of the Militia Department. The Militia Act entrusted the G.O.Cs. with the "military command and discipline of the Militia", and the British Generals were inclined to place a more liberal interpretation upon this clause than the Ministers. Having come to Canada owing allegiance to neither political party, the former considered that their role was to bring about the greatest possible improvement in the organization and training of the Militia. And so they issued orders and made decisions on their own responsibility, giving no heed to the possible effect on domestic politics. Inevitably friction occurred with certain Ministers who felt that the G.O.Cs. were exceeding their powers and should subordinate themselves to the Government they were temporarily serving.

The void left by the abolition (in practice) of the G.O.C. was filled by the 1904 Militia Act's establishment of a Militia Council, composed of the Minister as President; four Military Members (the Chief of the General Staff, Adjutant General, Quartermaster General and Master General of the Ordnance); a Civilian Member (the Deputy Minister); a Financial Member (the Accountant of the Department of Militia and Defence); and a civilian Secretary. Its duties were "to advise the Minister on all matters relating to the militia which are referred to the Council by the Minister".[16] Unlike the Army Council in the United Kingdom on which it was based, which assumed the powers previously

* One of these was won by Lieutenant R. E. W. Turner, who in the First World War rose to the rank of Lieutenant General and the command of all Canadian forces in the British Isles.

exercised by the Secretary of State for War or the Commander-in-Chief,[17] the Militia Council was purely advisory. The Minister was now supreme, the Government's senior military adviser, normally the Chief of the General Staff,* becoming the first Military Member of the Council. With this change in the management of Militia affairs public quarrels between the Ministers of the day and their principal military officers became a thing of the past, and a period of at least outward tranquillity began.

Imperial Military Ties

We have already noted that Canada had not bound herself by any formal commitment to furnish troops for Imperial defence overseas. Yet it was never in question that she would send forces to the aid of the Mother Country in an emergency, and the need of preparing to meet this demand was to stimulate the growth of her militia and direct the course of its development. From the Imperial viewpoint it was obviously desirable that there should be a high degree of co-ordination within the Empire's military forces, and much was accomplished in a series of Imperial Conferences. The representatives of the various parliaments quickly made clear their opposition to any "departure from the principle of Colonial self-government"; the Colonial Conference of 1902 decisively rejected a War Office proposal that Dominions should maintain local contingents ear-marked for Imperial wars (Canada's quota would have been one brigade of field artillery and one infantry brigade—a total of 3000 men).[18] An important step forward was taken when the 1907 Conference proposed the creation of an Imperial General Staff selected from the forces of the Empire as a whole. It would study military science and disseminate to the various governments military information and intelligence, prepare schemes of defence, and "without in the least interfering in questions connected with command and administration" give advice, when requested, on matters of training and organization.[19]

Two years later, delegates to a special Imperial Defence Conference, meeting in London with the shadow of war upon them, proceeded to lay "the foundation of a workable system which will enable us, should necessity arise, to employ the potential military strength of the Empire for a common Imperial purpose".[20] They agreed on a number of measures to secure general uniformity throughout the Empire in such matters as war organization, administration, training, armament and equipment. The organization of units of the Dominion forces was to be modelled as far as possible on the War Establishments† of the Home Regular Army; any contingent despatched by a Dominion for Imperial service overseas would be accompanied by a due proportion of administrative units; as far as

* There was one exception. Maj.-Gen. P. H. N. Lake (C.G.S. 1904-8) was Chief Military Adviser to the Government from November 1908 to October 1910 in addition to performing the duties of Inspector General. Brig.-Gen. W. D. Otter, a Canadian, was C.G.S. at the time; he held this appointment from April 1908 to October 1910.

† Tables showing the authorized composition of a unit upon mobilization, expressed in numbers and ranks of personnel, and numbers and types of weapons and transport.

practicable each Dominion would take into use the Field Service Regulations and training manuals issued to the British Army (and would be consulted with respect to amendments in subsequent editions); and Dominions would adopt as far as possible Imperial patterns of arms, equipment and stores.

The Conference approved the principle of an Imperial General Staff with branches in all self-governing Dominions; except for a few special cases, only Staff College graduates were to be eligible to hold appointments on this General Staff. During 1909 the War Office suggested that, as a temporary measure, the Canadian Section of the Imperial General Staff should consist of six military positions, including the Commandant and two officer-instructors at the Royal Military College (which had been established at Kingston in 1876 to provide a military education to young men desiring to obtain Commissions in the Canadian Militia). In the meantime, despite the objections raised by the War Office, Canada decided to proceed with the formation of a purely Canadian General Staff from which officers would be selected to form the Canadian Section of the Imperial General Staff. Although appointment to the Canadian General Staff was not dependent upon the attainment of any definite standard of military qualifications, it was ruled that no officer would be posted to an appointment on the Canadian Section of the Imperial General Staff unless he was a Staff College graduate or had served with credit on the staff of a force in the field.

The Conference of 1909 had other practical results for the Canadian Militia. More officers went to the United Kingdom to qualify as General Staff Officers at the Camberley Staff College; an interchange of officers began with Great Britain, Australia and India; Militia Headquarters undertook to organize the additional Corps and Line of Communication services required to complete divisional establishment; and mobilization schemes were prepared for the defence of Canada and for an Overseas Expeditionary Force.

Further progress followed the visits, at Canada's invitation, of two eminent British soldiers—in 1910, Sir John French, Inspector General of the Imperial Forces, and in 1913 Sir Ian Hamilton, Inspector General of the Overseas Forces. On the recommendation of the former officer the Militia in Eastern Canada was reconstituted on a divisional basis, to provide for ready conversion to a wartime footing. The ten eastern Military Districts became Divisional Areas,* in which were organized six infantry divisions and four cavalry brigades. The Districts in Western Canada continued to exist, and provided for three cavalry brigades. It was necessary to obtain six General Staff Officers from the United Kingdom for appointment to the new Divisional Areas (as well as one for all Western Canada), for Canada was still sadly short of officers thus qualified, having only twelve Staff College trained officers of her own when war broke out in 1914.

Sir Ian Hamilton's chief concerns were with bringing the actual strength of the Active Militia (43,000 in 1913) closer to its peace establishment (60,000); raising the general standard of training; and building up stocks of equipment,

* The Divisional Areas were renamed Military Districts by a General Order dated 1 March 1916.

clothing, ammunition and reserve stores for issue on the outbreak of war. Though Sir Ian found some improvement in training since Sir John French's inspection, he insisted that there was no room for relaxation of effort. The chief limitation was the brevity of the annual training. The period authorized for city corps of the Active Militia was sixteen days, of which at least four days had to be spent in summer camp. Rural units, however, did all their training in twelve days at camp, and Sir Ian urged that this should be supplemented by four days of concentrated local training. Furthermore, the increase in personnel had outstripped the provision of the tools of war, so that it had been necessary to equip new regiments from the stores intended for use in the mobilization of older units. The 200 modern guns available in Canada would arm the artillery of only two divisions, and motor vehicles and horsedrawn transport wagons were almost entirely lacking. There was insufficient clothing for even the Militia's peace strength, and much of this was old and obsolete.[21]

The prospect of increasing artillery stocks in the near future was not good, for being dependent upon English sources of supply Canada had to compete with the War Office in getting her orders filled from British factories. She had long since taken steps to correct a similar situation with respect to small arms. In 1900, when arms manufacturers in the United Kingdom were working at capacity to make good in the British Army the wastage of the South African War, the Canadian Minister of Militia had found it impossible to place an order for 15,000 .303-inch Lee-Enfield rifles—to supplement 40,000 of these arms purchased in 1896. The Government therefore decided that Canada should make her own rifles; and when attempts to have a British company manufacture the Lee-Enfield in Canada failed, a contract was signed for the production in the Dominion of a .303 rifle designed by Sir Charles Ross—even though this meant a departure from the principle of uniformity of armament within the Commonwealth. A factory was built by the Ross Rifle Company on ground adjoining the historic Plains of Abraham at Quebec City, and the Militia received the first 1000 rifles in 1905.* Defects natural in a new and unproved weapon soon appeared, and the rifle underwent a number of modifications (more than eighty in the Mark II pattern alone). Although successes gained by Canadian marksmen at Bisley using the Ross brought the rifle a high reputation as a target weapon, complaints of defects continued to come in from the training camps and the relative merits of the Ross and the British Lee-Enfield for service in the field became the subject of a widespread controversy in Press and Parliament. By the time that manufacture of the Mark III pattern began late in 1911, the barrel had increased from 28″ to 30½″ in length and the total weight of the rifle from 7½ to 9½ pounds. This was the pattern authorized for the Canadian Militia when war broke out. By 30 July 1914 12,200 had been delivered out of orders totalling 30,000. Production was stepped up to capacity, and another 30,000 rifles were ordered on 10 August.

* For the detailed story of the Ross rifle see Appendix 111 to Colonel A. F. Duguid, *Official History of the Canadian Forces in the Great War, 1914-1919*, General Series, Vol. I (Ottawa, 1938).

On the Eve of War

Although all the recommendations of the British Inspectors General were not implemented immediately, their timely reports contributed to the outburst of activity that took place in the Militia organization in the three years before the outbreak of war. The man chiefly responsible for this upsurge was Colonel (afterwards Honorary Lieutenant-General Sir Sam) Hughes, who on the defeat of the Laurier administration in 1911 had taken over the portfolio of Militia and Defence from Sir Frederick Borden. Continually warning the Canadian parliament and people of the grave threat of war with Germany, he secured an increase in the defence budget of three and a half million dollars between 1911-12 and 1913-14. An enthusiastic champion of Imperial defence, he is reported as telling a Vancouver audience in 1912: "Germany has to be taught a lesson, and the lesson to be taught her is that Canada, South Africa, Australia and New Zealand are behind the Mother Country."[22] In 1912 and again in the following year he conducted a party of Canadian militia officers to Europe to tour north-western France and attend the annual manoeuvres staged by the British, French, German and Swiss armies. In the summer of 1914 he ordered a mixed force of more than 10,000 militiamen to concentrate at Petawawa, Ontario (which had been acquired as a central training camp in 1905). There they carried out combined manoeuvres which more closely achieved active service conditions than any held in Canada since the Fenian disturbances half a century before. In all 59,000 troops carried out training in Canada that year, and but for the outbreak of war the total would have reached 64,000.[23]

The authorized establishment of the Canadian Militia in July 1914 (as distinct from actual strength) was 77,323 all ranks, distributed as shown in the following table:[24]

Arm of Service	Permanent Active Militia		Non-Permanent Active Militia	
	Personnel	Horses	Personnel	Horses
Cavalry	346	265	12,146	10,615
Artillery, Horse and Field	254	267	4,172	2,481
Artillery, Heavy	—	—	602	388
Artillery, Garrison and Siege	656	53	1,554	6
Engineers and Signals	314	6	2,196	523
Corps of Guides	—	—	499	379
Officers Training Corps	—	—	595	—
Infantry	793	12	47,691	690
Army Service Corps	164	55	1,927	937
Army Medical Corps	101	26	2,136	607
Other Corps and Services*	482	—	695	100
Totals	3,110	684	74,213	16,726

* Included in the "Other Corps and Services" were veterinary, ordnance, pay and postal personnel, together with a number of miscellaneous detachments employed in instructional and administrative duties.

But if the years immediately before the war found Canada's land forces progressing under the direction of an enthusiastic Militia Department, the condition of her naval service was far less satisfactory. (There was no air force; in 1909, the year of the first aeroplane flight in Canada, the Militia Council had witnessed demonstration flights at Petawawa, but a very limited Canadian military flying service was not organized until after war broke out.) The naval defence of Canada had suffered from a failure of the political parties to agree on a common policy. In the early years of the twentieth century, when other members of the Commonwealth were contributing increasing amounts to the support of the Royal Navy, the government of Sir Wilfrid Laurier, opposing such subsidies as contrary to the "principle of Colonial self-government", gave nothing. At the Colonial Conference of 1902 Laurier announced that the Dominion was "contemplating the establishment of a local Naval force in the waters of Canada".[25]

Yet from 1902 to 1909 nothing was done to implement this policy. In the latter year the Canadian House of Commons unanimously passed a resolution approving "the speedy organization of a Canadian naval service in co-operation with and in close relation to the Imperial Navy". The Naval Service Act of the following year authorized a Canadian Navy, to be controlled by a Minister of Naval Service who was also Minister of Marine and Fisheries. Two old cruisers, H.M.C.S. *Niobe* (1897) and H.M.C.S. *Rainbow* (1891), were purchased from the Admiralty to be used as training ships, and tenders were invited for the construction of four light cruisers and six destroyers for the Royal Canadian Navy. In 1909 the Leader of the Opposition, Sir Robert Borden, supported Laurier's resolutions, and in 1910 he claimed that he still favoured a Canadian Navy as a long-term policy. The defeat of the Laurier administration in the 1911 general election, however, produced a reversal in policy.

Nevertheless the growing crisis in Europe changed Borden's views and led him to take emergency measures. Inspired by a secret Admiralty opinion "that no step which Canada could take at the present time would be so helpful to the British Navy, or so likely to put a stop to dangerous naval rivalry, as the provision of capital ships for general Imperial service",[26] he forced through a bill voting up to $35,000,000 for the construction of three Dreadnoughts for the Royal Navy. The measure did not pass the Liberal-controlled Senate—which suggested an appeal to the country. As a result nothing was done about an Imperial contribution and very little about the rudimentary Canadian naval organization founded by Laurier. The contracts for the additional warships had never been awarded, and at the end of 1912 all recruiting for the Royal Canadian Navy stopped and men were allowed free discharge before their term of engagement was completed. By 3 August 1914 the strength had sunk to 393 officers and ratings (including members of the newly formed Royal Naval Canadian Volunteer Reserve and personnel on loan from the Royal Navy). H.M.C.S. *Rainbow*, on the west coast, had not raised steam since March 1913, and *Niobe*, which had stranded on Cape Sable in July 1911, had been caught by the new naval policy before being completely repaired and had not put to sea again.

Mobilization Plans and Defence Preparations

For some years after its institution the Militia Council, occupied with the task of enlarging and reorganizing the Militia, had found neither the funds nor the trained personnel to undertake the arduous and intricate work of drawing up a plan for mobilizing its armed forces. Eventually there emerged almost simultaneously two different schemes—one for the general mobilization of the Militia, and one for providing a limited force for service abroad. In 1911 a British General Staff Officer, Colonel W. G. Gwatkin, was secured from the War Office to head a mobilization committee which had begun drafting the previous year under the chairmanship of the Chief of the General Staff, Brig.-Gen. W. D. Otter. By 1914 plans were well advanced for transferring from a peace to a war footing the six divisions of the militia so far as their incomplete organization and deficiencies in arms and equipment would have permitted. At the same time, under instructions from Otter's successor, Major-General C. J. Mackenzie, a British officer, Gwatkin drew up plans for mobilizing for active service overseas a Canadian contingent consisting of a division and a mounted brigade.

Under this scheme each divisional area and district would contribute its quota of troops, in general the six divisional areas in Eastern Canada furnishing the units for the infantry division and the three western military districts providing the mounted brigade. Service in the contingent would be voluntary, with preference given to men with previous service or military training. Divisional and district commanders—upon whom the plan placed much responsibility—selected their own "places of assembly" (to be approved by Militia Headquarters), whence the troops after partial mobilization would move to Petawawa, which was chosen as the "place of concentration". If mobilization should take place in winter, units would be fully mobilized at their place of assembly and thence proceed direct to the port of embarkation. One of the principal defects of the scheme was its failure to provide for adequate mobilization stores. We have already noted the difficulty in obtaining sufficient stocks for the existing Militia, and it was ruled that there should be no accumulation of reserve supplies for the use of an entirely problematical overseas force. Notwithstanding this and other deficiencies (no Line of Communication units were included), the scheme did supply a considered plan for the provision of troops on a fair ratio throughout the Dominion for a contingent of the same strength as that subsequently mobilized in 1914.[27]

The preparation of mobilization plans formed only a part of the concern of those charged with the responsibility of ensuring Canada's readiness for war. The military action to be taken when war threatened had been prescribed in a defence scheme drawn up in 1898 and elaborated in local mobilization plans. In that year the British Government, acting upon a request made by the Canadian Government, appointed a defence commission to investigate the Dominion's defence problems, prepare a defence scheme, and make recommendations as to the military organization best suited to Canadian conditions. The commission was composed of an officer of the Royal Navy, three British Army officers (including Major P. H. N. Lake, who in 1904 was to become Canada's first Chief of the General Staff) and two Cabinet Ministers representing the Canadian Government.[28] During its five-month tour of duty the commission consulted forty prominent Militia officers,[29] and at the end of the year submitted two comprehensive reports, "No I—Defence Scheme", and "No II—Recommendations". Although never formally approved by the Canadian Government (in April 1903 the Governor General admitted to the Colonial Office that pressure of work during the past three years had deferred consideration of the reports by the Privy Council),[30] "Report No I" remained the accepted Defence Scheme for Canada until after the First World War. It does not appear ever to have been formally revised, though the Colonial Defence Committee in London had suggested that this be done annually and a revised Defence Scheme passed to it for information and comments. Despite this omission there is little doubt that the existence of the Scheme was of great assistance to officers charged with the responsibility of mobilization planning. From 1908 defensive measures affecting both the Department of Militia and Defence and the Department of Marine and Fisheries (e.g., the regulation of traffic of defended ports and the construction of floating defences) were dealt with by an Interdepartmental Committee representing these two ministries. (The new Department of the Naval Service was added after 1910.)

In the non-military field arrangements for coordinating the defensive action to be taken by the several Government departments in the event of war were completed much later. At the beginning of August 1912 the two service chiefs, reminding their respective ministers that it had "become increasingly apparent during the past two years that the machinery for the Defence of Canada lacks a directing head", presented them with proposals for setting up a Canadian Defence Committee. These recommendations pointed to the dependence of other ministries upon the Naval and Militia Departments, and stressed the importance of having "a practical organization to coordinate the often conflicting claims of strategy, commerce and finance". The proposed committee would be headed by the Prime Minister and would include the Secretary of State for External Affairs, the Ministers of Militia and Defence, Naval Services, and Finance, as well as the Chief of the General Staff and the Director of the Naval Service. Among the questions which the Government could refer to such a committee would be those dealing with the whole military and naval defence policy of the Dominion; cooperation with the Imperial Forces; the strategical location of fortresses and dockyards, the construction of railways and canals, and the conservation of national resources; and coordination of action between the Government Departments in times of emergency.[31]

These recommendations however did not pass the two ministers, in spite of the urgings of their senior officers. Indeed, as late as 1 July 1914 Colonel Gwatkin, who had become C.G.S. the previous October, wrote (apparently to the Governor General's office—the file copy of the letter bears no address), "With a little persuasion the Premier, I think, would take a step in the right direction and appoint himself President of a Canadian Defence Committee; but I give you solemn warning that unless you stimulate us into activity, we shall merely drift."[32] Many years later another C.G.S., holding similar views, was more successful. In August 1936 there came into being a Canadian Defence Committee (subsequently referred to as the Defence Committee of the Cabinet) whose composition and functions closely followed the proposal which had been shelved almost a quarter of a century before.[33]

Action was finally taken as a result of a strong recommendation received in March 1913 from the Overseas Defence Committee in the United Kingdom that Canada, in common with the other self-governing Dominions, should compile a "War Book", similar to the one drawn up by the Imperial Government, showing the precise steps to be taken in time of emergency by each Department of State.[34] An Interdepartmental Conference at which seven departments were represented held its first meeting in January 1914, and with commendable energy completed its assignment in six months. The War Book defined the tasks to be undertaken by each department in the "Precautionary Stage"—when relations with any foreign power had become so strained that measures against a possible surprise attack were necessary—and for the further measures required upon the declaration of war. The delay in establishing the Interdepartmental Conference had left so little time for its work of compiling the War Book that its final deliberations were interrupted on 29 July by the arrival from London of the warning telegram ordering the adoption of the Precautionary Stage.

Fortunately preparation of the individual War Books of the Departments of Militia and Defence, Naval Service and Customs—the Departments most concerned at the time—had been completed, and the action outlined in them was taken "without delay or hitch of any kind—everything working smoothly".[35] Prearranged measures were put into effect without delay. Immediate steps were taken to guard wireless stations and cable landings, man the fortresses at Halifax, Quebec and Esquimalt, and establish an examination service at these three ports. To perform these tasks the Royal Canadian Garrison Artillery and The Royal Canadian Regiment were placed on active service, and in each of the two coastal military districts details of infantry and garrison artillery were called out from the Non-Permanent Active Militia. On 2 August the Minister of Militia took over control of cables and the Minister of the Naval Service control of wireless telegraphy; both these channels of communication at once came under a strict censorship. A personal letter from Colonel Hughes to the Press of Canada appealing for the exercise of "wise reticence upon matters affecting military operations" was followed by formal instructions on security sent to all newspapers by the Deputy Chief Censor. Without waiting for Parliament to meet, the Governor General in Council enacted a number of emergency measures to regulate finance, trade and commerce, and to preserve good order throughout the country.

The Department of the Naval Service in keeping closely in touch with the Admiralty followed the British lead by placing the Canadian permanent naval forces and the Naval Volunteer Force on active service on 4 August. On the same day H.M.C.S. *Niobe* and *Rainbow* were put at His Majesty's disposal "for general service with the Royal Navy",[36] a disposition that was to continue throughout the war, with all charges being borne by Canada. At the Admiralty's request the 3600-ton *Rainbow* had steamed bravely out of Esquimalt early on the 3rd "to guard trade routes north of the Equator", and specifically to escort to safety two British sloops without wireless (*Algerine* and *Shearwater*) which were working north from San Diego. After her long period of neglect the *Rainbow* was in no condition to engage in hostilities. She had barely half her proper complement (many of whom were untrained), and no high explosive shells. The main enemy threat came from the modern light cruiser *Leipzig,* which was reported in Mexican waters. The *Rainbow* reached San Francisco on 7 August but was compelled to return to Esquimalt to refuel, luckily without having encountered the German warship. The *Shearwater* was found on the 13th and the *Algerine* on the following day and both were brought safely to Esquimalt.[37] Their crews went by train to Halifax to join H.M.C.S. *Niobe,* which by 1 September had completed a hasty refit and was ready for duty with other units of the Royal Navy on the Atlantic Patrol.

Speedy action to augment Canadian naval strength at the outbreak of war took place on the west coast, where between 29 July and 5 August negotiations to purchase two submarines were initiated and completed, and delivery of the vessels effected—all within a week. The acquisition of the submarines, which had been privately built at Seattle for the Chilean Government, owed much to the initiative of the Premier of British Columbia, Sir Richard McBride, who, while Ottawa was urgently seeking the Admiralty's advice on whether or not to buy, on his own responsibility provided the purchase price of $1,150,000 from provincial funds, which the Federal Government repaid three days later.* The two craft, redesignated C.C.1 and C.C.2, were based at Esquimalt for nearly three years, carrying out patrol work and training duties. In 1917 they moved by way of the Panama Canal to Halifax, where they remained until the war ended.

Apart from calling out the military units and detachments referred to above there was no large-scale mobilization while the outbreak of hostilities was still in the balance. On the fateful 4th, a few hours before word of the declaration of war reached Ottawa, the Canadian Government was advised by London that there seemed to be "no immediate necessity for any request on our part for an expeditionary force from Canada", although it would be wise "to take all legislative and other steps" which would enable such a force to be provided without delay if required later.[38] Two days later a signal brought the grateful acceptance of His Majesty's Government of the Canadian offer to send a force, and asked that it "be despatched as soon as possible". On 7 August the Army Council advised that "one division would be suitable composition of expeditionary force".[39]

* The intriguing story of this unusual transaction is related in detail in the Navy's official history, G. N. Tucker, *The Naval Service of Canada,* Vol. I, Chapter 13.

CHAPTER II

FORGING THE WEAPON

(See Sketches 1, 2 and 3)

Mobilization

As soon as British acceptance of the Canadian offer was received, the Cabinet authorized the "raising and equipment of such units" as might be determined by the Governor General in Council, "to be composed of officers and men who are willing to volunteer for Overseas service under the British Crown".[1] An Order in Council of 10 August set the strength of the contingent at 25,000.

As we have seen, a scheme for mobilizing just such a force had been drawn up in 1911. In the summer of 1913, however, shortly after Colonel Hughes had given instructions for certain revisions to be made in the plan initiated by his predecessor, all action appears to have been abandoned. The Minister of Militia had other ideas about mobilization—what he later described as "really a call to arms, like the fiery cross passing through the Highlands of Scotland or the mountains of Ireland in former days".[2] It will be recalled that the 1911 plan (referred to as Memorandum C.1209) had placed upon the commanders of divisional areas and districts the responsibility of raising the units required from their respective commands in the event of mobilization. On 31 July 1914, however, by direction of the Minister, these Officers Commanding received secret instructions to regard "as purely tentative" the scheme outlined in Memorandum C.1209, and to "consider what procedure you would adopt on receiving orders that troops were to be raised in your command for service overseas".[3] This inquiry seems to have been only academic, for on 6 August, giving immediate effect to the Cabinet's order, the Minister of Militia had the Adjutant General send a night lettergram direct to 226 unit commanders of the Canadian Militia. Ignoring normal channels of communication Hughes by-passed the Officers Commanding Divisions and Districts, who received a copy of the message only for information. Units were instructed to prepare and forward direct to Militia Headquarters not later than 12 August "descriptive rolls" of volunteers, between the ages of 18 and 45, who could meet prescribed physical standards. A high standard in musketry and general proficiency was required, and in addition to members of the Active Militia, reserve officers and others with military experience who could meet the necessary requirements were eligible. After the rolls had been examined in Ottawa each Commanding Officer would be told the number to be enlisted from his unit.

The impracticability of selecting 25,000 individuals by this cumbersome process was soon realized, and on 10 August Districts regained their normal position in the pattern of command when they were told the divisional formations and units that each must furnish. This enabled district headquarters to allot recruiting quotas to Militia unit commanders; but three days later, as though determined to keep matters confused, Ottawa modified its instructions. Since the exact allotment would "necessarily depend on the numbers volunteering", the table showing the divisional composition and the areas from which units were to be drawn "should be looked upon in the light of a general guide only.[4] Instructions, often conflicting, continued to flow from Militia Headquarters not only to commanders of Divisions and Military Districts but direct to other levels of command down to units. When a divisional commander protested "that orders have so far been given out not only by wire, but also apparently through the telephone, by Heads of Departments at Headquarters to myself as well as to Heads of Departments of this Division",[5] he was voicing the concern of those who repeatedly found that military activities of which they had no knowledge were taking place within their commands on instructions from Ottawa.

"In a short time", proudly declared the Minister of Militia, "we had the boys on the way for the first contingent, whereas it would have taken several weeks to have got the word around through the ordinary channels . . . The contingent was practically on the way to Europe before it could have been mobilized under the ordinary plan."[6] This disparagement of the "ordinary plan" was scarcely justified; normal military channels of communication properly used could have carried the warning in a matter of hours, not weeks. Indeed, once the confusion caused by the first dramatic but irregular "call to arms" subsided, most of the volunteers joined through existing militia units in virtually the manner prescribed by the pre-war scheme.

While the troops for the first contingent were being recruited, the British Government had "gratefully accepted" an offer of four additional Canadian units of a thousand men each.[7] The proposal had been enthusiastically, if somewhat prematurely, relayed to London by the Governor General after attending a meeting of the Cabinet during which the Minister of Militia referred to offers received from three Provinces to provide battalions. These failed to materialize, Sir Robert Borden reporting to the Acting Canadian High Commissioner in London, Mr. George Perley: "New Brunswick entirely repudiates having made any such offer and Manitoba and Calgary find themselves financially unable to undertake what was suggested rather than offered."[8] The proposal that stood was that by Captain A. Hamilton Gault, a Montreal veteran of the South African War, to raise an infantry battalion of ex-soldiers and to contribute $100,000 towards the cost. The battalion, named Princess Patricia's Canadian Light Infantry after Her Royal Highness, the daughter of the Governor General, was speedily recruited in Ottawa, its ranks being filled by veterans from all parts of Canada. Lt.-Col. F. D. Farquhar (Coldstream Guards), Military Secretary to the Governor General, was appointed Commanding Officer. As will be seen, this unique venture in mobilization was to pay high dividends. In three weeks from the date of its authorization the regiment was ready to sail, and it embarked at Montreal on 28 August. Admiralty convoy restrictions held the unit impatiently in Canada, and it crossed with the First Contingent late in September. The Patricias landed in France on 21 December and entered the line as part of the 80th Brigade, 27th Division, on the night of 6-7 January 1915—eight weeks before the 1st Canadian Division was committed to action.

No further offers of formed units were entertained, for having learned that it cost a million dollars to equip and maintain a regiment of a thousand men for a year in active service, the Government (as pointed out by the Prime Minister to Mr. Perley) decided "absolutely to reject all such offers in the future unless the person, city or province making the offer is prepared not only to equip but maintain the proposed force".*[9] When the War Office ventured to inquire about the Governor General's offer, it was informed that two of the battalions "have been absorbed by the Division; and two have meantime been merged in The Princess Patricia's Canadian Light Infantry, now in process of being formed."[10]

The First Contingent at Valcartier

The summons sent out on 6 August 1914 by the Minister of Militia had named the place of mobilization as Valcartier, sixteen miles north-west of Quebec City. The first group of volunteers reached the new camp on 18 August, and by 8 September the influx, carried in one hundred special trains, had raised the strength to its maximum of 32,665.

The new campsite lay along the east bank of the Jacques Cartier River. From a belt of woodland beside the stream sandy flats reached back some two miles to a tree-covered ridge rising abruptly a thousand feet above the valley. Occasional patches of swamp and timber intruded on the open fields of small farms, granted originally to British soldiers after the capture of Quebec. The transformation of this area in less than a month into an organized military establishment accommodating more than 30,000 men was a striking testimonial to the foresight and unbounded enthusiasm and driving power of the Minister of Militia—who having fathered the project personally saw it through to completion. In 1912 he had taken steps to acquire the site for a central training area for the Militia of the province; and his decision to concentrate the Canadian Expeditionary Force there necessitated the purchase of additional land after war broke out, the eventual area of the camp reaching 12,428 acres.

* Not quite within this category was the acceptance of $150,000 subscribed by fifteen public-spirited Canadian citizens for the purchase in the United States of machines and vehicles to equip the Automobile Machine Gun Brigade No. 1, a unit of nine officers and 114 other ranks.

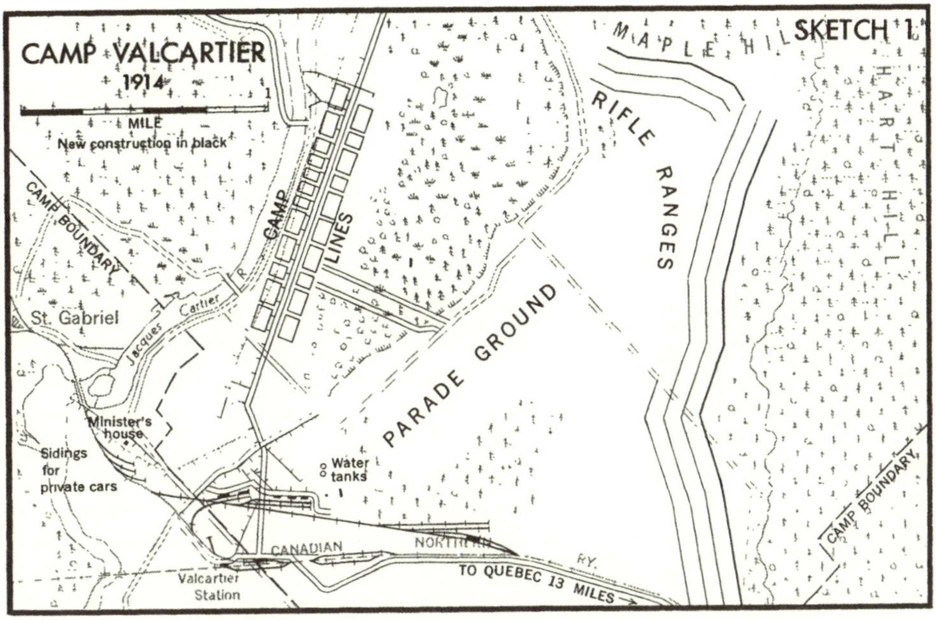

Teams of lumberjacks at once began clearing the section by the river for the camp lines, and the central area for a parade ground. A contracting firm engaged in building the Connaught rifle range near Ottawa moved its full complement of men and equipment by special train to work on the new site. Progress was spectacular. Afterwards Colonel Hughes was able to point out with the pride of achievement:

> On Saturday, the 8th [of August], Valcartier was taken over, and on Monday the 10th, ranges and waterworks were begun. By the 20th, three and a half miles of ranges were completed, and 1,500 targets were put in position. Up to the same date, 12 miles of water mains had been laid in, and 15 miles of drains, open and covered had been located. Army Service Corps and Ordnance buildings were constructed, railway sidings laid in, fences removed, crops harvested, ground cleared, streets made, upwards of 200 baths for the men put in, water chlorinated, electric light and telephones installed . . . and 35,000 men got under canvas in less than three weeks from the acceptance of the call.[11]

During the second week in August militia detachments and units not slated for the Expeditionary Force began arriving at Valcartier to take over administrative and instructional duties in the camp. The Permanent Force supplied the R.C.H.A. Brigade, the Royal Canadian Dragoons and Lord Strathcona's Horse, together with ordnance personnel. From the Non-Permanent Active Militia a field company of Canadian Engineers, four companies of the Army Service Corps, three field ambulances of the Canadian Army Medical Corps, a veterinary section and a postal detachment were called out on active service to assist in these utilitarian tasks. A camp staff of 25 officers, and the necessary other ranks, was headed by the Adjutant General, Colonel V. A. S. Williams, whose transfer from the army's highest administrative post at so critical a time is hard to justify.

Incoming volunteers were assigned to provisional battalions according to their place of origin. A Camp Order of 22 August listed twelve such battalions (each representing from four to as many as seventeen Militia units); but ten days later, when the enrolment far exceeded the war establishment of twelve battalions (plus ten per cent reinforcements), an entirely new infantry organization appeared. Camp Orders of 1 September gave the composition of sixteen provisional battalions in four provisional brigades. There were further reshufflings during the month, and the organization which finally emerged differed widely from the divisional allotments of 10 August. The 1st (Provisional) Infantry Brigade, comprising the 1st, 2nd, 3rd and 4th Battalions, all from Ontario, was commanded by Lt.-Col. M. S. Mercer. The 2nd Brigade, from the west (5th, 6th, 7th and 8th Battalions), was commanded by Lt.-Col. A. W. Currie. The 3rd Brigade, commanded by Colonel R. E. W. Turner (above, page 8), who had served with the Royal Canadian Dragoons in the South African War, was composed of the 14th Battalion from Montreal and the Maritimes and three Highland battalions from across Canada (the 13th, 15th and 16th). The 4th Brigade, Lt.-Col. J. E. Cohoe, consisted of three Prairie battalions (9th, 10th and 11th) and one (the 12th) from the Maritimes. When it was decided on 21 September that regardless of numbers all who were medically fit should proceed to England (see below, page 29), the 17th Provisional Battalion was formed to handle the surplus infantry. The 18th Provisional Battalion was authorized for the same purpose, but was disbanded on 27 September without being filled.

Organization of other arms and services for the Expeditionary Force followed more closely the pattern presented in the preliminary mobilization instructions. Artillery units were mobilized at local headquarters in Eastern Canada under instructions issued by the Director of Artillery. Here they received most of their uniforms direct from the manufacturer and drew upon Militia stores for their equipment. Horses were purchased locally, so that organization was well advanced by the time the artillery reached Valcartier on 29 and 30 August. There were three field artillery brigades, each of three batteries of 18-pounders and an ammunition column; a heavy 60-pounder battery with its ammunition column; and a divisional ammunition column. (Because of a lack of howitzers, the 4.5-inch howitzer brigade normal to a divisional establishment was not formed.) Camp Orders of 1 September appointed Lt.-Col. H. E. Burstall to command the Divisional Artillery.

Detachments from each of eleven Militia engineer units sent enough volunteers to Valcartier to form the two field companies in the original divisional establishment as well as a third company which was added to conform with a new British establishment. The technical ability required in the Divisional Signal Company was met by enlisting skilled personnel from the Permanent Force and from Militia signal units, and from commercial telegraph and telephone companies. Organization of the Divisional Train—with its four companies drawn mainly from Ottawa, London, Montreal and Winnipeg—was interrupted by a request from the Army Council that the Canadian Expeditionary Force should include certain Line of Communication units. It became necessary to reassign personnel to fill the four Army Service Corps units required—a Divisional Ammunition Park, a Divisional Supply Column, a Reserve Park and a Railway Supply Detachment. A small Postal Corps detachment was manned from N.P.A.M. detachments across Canada.

Mobilization of the medical services was carried out under the Director General of Medical Services, Colonel G. Carleton Jones. Volunteers concentrated at Toronto and Winnipeg as well as at Valcartier. When all had assembled at Valcartier Camp the British request for Line of Communication units made a general reorganization necessary. Sufficient medical personnel were found in camp to form the required units which, in addition to the three divisional field ambulances, included a casualty clearing station, two stationary hospitals (each of 400 beds), and two general hospitals (1040 beds each). The casualty clearing Station and No. 1 Stationary Hospital took over from N.P.A.M. units the operation of the two camp hospitals at Valcartier. Hospital admissions for the whole period until embarkation numbered only 856, for in general the health of the troops was excellent. An order to mobilize nursing sisters was issued on 16 September, and by the end of the month 98 had reported at Quebec, where they were billeted at the Immigration Hospital.* Provision of veterinary sections, called for at the last minute by the War Office, was not completed until after the First Contingent had sailed.

Early plans for the Contingent did not include any units of the Permanent Force. We have noted that the two regular cavalry regiments and the R.C.H.A. Brigade were employed at Valcartier in administration and training. The only cavalry authorized for the Expeditionary Force was the Divisional Cavalry Squadron, of 196 all ranks (furnished by the 19th Alberta Dragoons of the non-permanent Militia), which together with a cyclist company, drawn from all arms and services in the camp, formed the divisional mounted troops. When the War Office accepted a tentative offer made on 7 August of "one regular cavalry regiment and two regular horse artillery batteries", the Minister of Militia at first asked permission "to retain them for a short time for instructional and other purposes at Valcartier Camp".[12] On 26 August the Camp Commandant was ordered to mobilize the two R.C.H.A. batteries and a composite cavalry regiment from the two regular units. On 14 September, however, the Prime Minister approved a proposal by Hughes to mobilize and embark with the army troops two complete cavalry regiments, "one to be called Royal Canadian Dragoons, and the other Lord Strathcona's Horse".

While Permanent Force units were thus unexpectedly finding overseas destinations, the only regular infantry battalion, The Royal Canadian Regiment, was given a role which though carrying the honour of being the first Canadian unit to serve outside the Dominion in the First World War was nevertheless to keep it out of active operations for another year. On 6 September the regiment embarked

* Details of the mobilization of the medical forces are in Sir Andrew Macphail, *The Medical Services* (in the series *Official History of the Canadian Forces in the Great War 1914-19*) (Ottawa, 1925).

at Quebec and sailed under escort of H.M.C.S. *Niobe* for guard duty in Bermuda, where it relieved a British unit, the 2nd Battalion, The Lincolnshire Regiment. The following March and April saw No. 6 Company of the Royal Canadian Garrison Artillery (123 all ranks) off to St. Lucia, in the Windward Islands; there it was to man four 14-centimetre and two 6-inch guns, operate a 70-ton steamship on examination service, and sweep the entrance of Port Castries for mines.*

The Beginning of Training

Though most of the 1500 officers assembled at Valcartier had qualified for their ranks at military schools of instruction, there was a wide diversity in the men's standard of training. The requirements prescribed in the lettergram of 6 August had not been met; many were without military training or experience. Yet the Minister's desire to send the contingent to England as quickly as possible[13] limited the time for training at Valcartier, and this was further shortened by frequent interruptions. Having arrived with no unit organization, the men had to be medically examined, inoculated and attested, and issued with clothing and equipment—the last a protracted affair dependent upon deliveries from the manufacturers. All these processes played havoc with training programmes, which were further disrupted by repeated changes in the composition, location and command of the units to which the troops were assigned. All arms and services engaged in elementary squad and foot drill and rifle exercises. Route marches and physical training began the necessary hardening process. With the instructional staff of eighty spread thinly throughout the entire force much depended upon the initiative of unit commanders in arranging their own training programme. They used as their basic manual a "Memorandum for Camps of Instruction, 1914".

By 22 August 1500 targets were in position on the new ranges, which stretched for more than two and a half miles† along the foot of the eastern ridge. Target practice using the Ross rifle began with seven battalions simultaneously on the ranges, and by 19 September practically all infantrymen had fired the prescribed classifications, which totalled 50 rounds at distances of up to 300 yards. Some repeated the course several times before qualifying. This range practice, carried out under the supervision of the Commandant of the School of Musketry, from Ottawa, and a staff of thirteen, was given priority in the training programme. "I want, first of all, men who can pink the enemy every time", Colonel Hughes told the troops at Valcartier.[14] He was pleased with the standard which they attained, and he enthusiastically declared later that the men at Valcartier had been "trained to handle a rifle as no men had ever handled it before".[15]

There was little time for advanced or specialist training. Two barrel pier bridges thrown over the Jacques Cartier River by the engineers were put to

* This unit plus attached services remained in the West Indies for the duration of the war. The R.C.R. was relieved in August 1915 by the 38th Battalion, which in turn handed over to the French speaking 163rd Battalion in May 1916. Relieved six months later by a British battalion, the 163rd went to England, where it provided reinforcements for French-Canadian battalions in the field.

† The distance given by the Minister, 3½ miles (above, p. 21), is incorrect.

PRINCIPAL CIVIL AND MILITARY LEADERS OF THE CANADIAN EXPEDITIONARY FORCE

Lt.-Gen. Sir Sam Hughes

Sir G.H. Perley

Sir A.E. Kemp

Maj.-Gen. S.C. Mewburn

Maj.-Gen. W.G. Gwatkin

Sir Robert Borden

Lt.-Gen. Sir R.E.W. Turner

Lt.-Gen. Sir E.A.H. Alderson

Lt.-Gen. Sir J.H.G. Byng

Lt.-Gen. Sir A.W. Currie

TRAINING AT VALCARTIER

Artillery of the First Contingent C.E.F. crossing the log-filled Jacques Cartier River on a pontoon bridge constructed by the Engineers.

THE SHORTAGE OF UNIFORMS

Members of the 24th Battalion C.E.F. in training in Montreal in the early winter of 1914-1915. Only one recruit in about ten has been issued a uniform.

practical use when units crossed to take part in field manoeuvres in the rough wooded area beyond. On two occasions the Governor General was an interested observer of these tactical schemes. His Royal Highness reviewed the troops three times during September, the marching columns being led past the saluting base by the Minister of Militia in uniform.

Equipping the Force

We have already noted (above, p. 11) that in spite of recommendations by the Inspector General of the Overseas Forces, Canada had produced in peacetime only sufficient war materials to maintain her Militia forces—indeed, members of the N.P.A.M. had been required to provide their own boots, shirts and underclothing. The outbreak of war thus found the country without the large stocks of equipment, clothing, or stores required for the mobilization of an overseas contingent. The tremendous task of clothing and equipping at short notice both the expeditionary force and the troops on home defence was undertaken with the utmost dispatch and vigour. Without waiting for Privy Council authority the Minister of Militia began approving requisitions for large orders; contracts to complete the clothing of 50,000 troops were let on 10 August for delivery in full by 21 September. Within this short space of time the wool for the garments had first to be woven into cloth, and the leather procured from which boots and harness could be manufactured. Subsequent orders covered every required item of equipment, the contracting firms being enjoined to meet the prescribed deadline "even though you have to work night and day until then".[16] There were protests from the Auditor General at the independent action taken by the Militia Department, though such purchases made in August and September were subsequently authorized, the Quartermaster General and the Director of Contracts having vouched that the system had brought "good and satisfactory service in respect of deliveries, and at fair and reasonable prices throughout".[17] Early in October the Cabinet appointed a sub-committee to advise the Minister of Militia in respect to contracts—a stricture which, according to Hughes, resulted in the Contract branch of his department being "very much hampered and practically blockaded... Indeed the most ardent agents of the German Government could scarcely have been more successful in holding up the proper equipment of our forces, had they been in control".[18]

With the Ross Rifle Company's factory producing at capacity, it was possible to arm with the Mark III rifle and bayonet all but one infantry unit (the 15th Battalion, which took the long Mark II to England). To equip the Automobile Machine Gun Brigade and provide the two machine-guns authorized for each infantry battalion fifty Colt .303-inch automatic guns were ordered from an American factory, but only twenty weapons arrived before sailing time. These were issued to the Machine Gun Brigade, the infantry taking with them four obsolescent Maxims that had been used for instruction at Valcartier. When the War Office was unable to supply light Vickers guns ordered by Canada for delivery in the United Kingdom, 51 more Colts were shipped across the Atlantic in November and December and issued to the C.E.F. Artillery units had brought their full armament from the Districts—twelve 13-pounder guns for the two R.C.H.A. batteries, fifty-four 18-pounders for the three field brigades, and four 60-pounders for the heavy battery.

Provision of vehicles for the force required extensive purchasing, for only a comparatively few horse-drawn vehicles were available from Militia sources. The Minister of Militia appointed special purchasing agents, giving them honorary commissions, so that "if I found any sharp work going on . . . I could put them through Court Martial".[19] To obtain sufficient horse transport meant buying farm wagons (455 heavy and 398 light) of eight different makes, a diversity of pattern which was later to bring serious maintenance problems. A similar difficulty was to arise with the mechanical transport which the War Office had asked should accompany the contingent to England, for which no detailed specifications appear to have been provided. The Minister's special agent had to depend on five separate makes of motor truck to meet the requirement of 133 vehicles for the 1st Division's Supply Column and Ammunition Park (infantry units used horse transport only).[20] Complete transport (including eight armoured cars) for the Automobile Machine Gun Brigade was bought in the United States on behalf of the donors by the commanding officer, Major R. Brutinel, a former French Army officer.

In order to acquire the more than 7000 riding, artillery and draught horses authorized for the Division and its added units, fifty Militia and five civilian purchasing agents were appointed by the Director of Veterinary Services, whose designation as Remount Officer cancelled an arrangement under the 1913 Mobilization Regulations which made procurement of horses a district responsibility. Only artillery units which had mobilized at local headquarters brought their horses with them. The promptness and zeal with which the purchasing agents went about their duties created accommodation problems at Valcartier, and on two nights horses broke out from temporary corrals and stampeded through the camp. Altogether 8150 horses were bought, at an average cost of $172.45; some 480 which were found unfit for service were later auctioned off at Quebec for an average price of $54.[21]

An item of personal equipment for the troops in which Colonel Hughes took a special interest was the "MacAdam" shovel, an implement modelled upon a pre-war Swiss invention and patented by the Minister's woman secretary, whose name it bore. Designed to serve as a combined shield and entrenching tool for the infantryman, it had a blade 8½ by 9¾ inches made of three-sixteenths inch steel (said to be capable of stopping a bullet at 300 yards). When used as a shield, it was stuck into the ground on a four-inch handle which formed an extension of the blade, two loopholes being provided, a large one for shooting and a smaller for sighting through. Twenty-five thousand MacAdam shovels, purchased in Philadelphia at $1.35 each, were taken to England, where even with the addition of a special folding handle they proved unsatisfactory. The

Commander of the 1st Canadian Division reported that they were not effective as shields, were too heavy for the men to carry and were awkward to dig with. The issue of entrenching tools of War Office pattern to the Division brought prompt instructions from Hughes to "hold a tight hand on all that improper work over there" and to cancel the order for the English implement, which he termed "absolutely useless for any purpose".[22] Nevertheless, the 1st Division proceeded to France without their MacAdam shovels, and when trials in the field by the 2nd Division brought more adverse reports,[23] all were withdrawn from use and eventually sold for $1400 as scrap metal.

With so much determination and effort put into the tremendous task of equipping the First Contingent, it is distressing to have to record that much of it turned out to be lost labour. Many of the items issued to the Canadians were not of the pattern prescribed for the British army, and after strict scrutiny in England by War Office inspectors and selected officers of the 1st Division, certain articles were ordered to be replaced from British Ordnance Stores. The boots supplied to the force had been manufactured from a pattern that had been found satisfactory by Canadians in the South African War and with some improvements had been used by the Permanent Force ever since. As late as April 1914, when consideration was being given to strengthening the soles, about which there had been many complaints, the Director General of Clothing and Equipment had reported that "the British army boot appears much too heavy for wear in Canada". But after the First Contingent moved to the United Kingdom it soon became apparent that the Canadian boots would not stand up to the hard marching on metalled roads and the continual soaking in the mud of an exceptionally bad English winter. It was the harshest kind of testing, for with only one pair available per man, there was no chance to dry them and waterproof them with dubbin, and stitching quickly rotted. The arrival in November of a shipment of 48,000 pairs of overshoes from Canada helped but little—some lasting only ten days. On the recommendation of the Commander of the Canadian Contingent British regulation boots were issued, and before the Division moved to France each unit commander was required to render a certificate "that every man is in possession of a service pair of Imperial pattern Army boots".

Only five battalions took web equipment to England. The obsolescent Oliver pattern brought by the remainder had to be rejected because it carried only 50 to 80 rounds of ammunition instead of 150; it had no pack or any facilities for carrying the entrenching tool; and it cut the wearer under the arms. It became necessary for the War Office to issue web equipment to seven Canadian battalions.

Canadian vehicles, both motor and horse-drawn, came under criticism from the War Office, the main objection being the difficulty of supplying spare parts in the field for so many different makes, particularly since these parts would in most instances have to come from North America. Two of the types of motor truck brought over by the First Contingent had developed serious defects, and it was decided to hold these in England for use by subsequent Canadian forces. They were replaced by 51 British lorries (somewhat surprisingly—in view of the earlier strictures by the War Office—representing no less than six different makes!). Further shortcomings were found in the horse-drawn wagons. Their serviceability was questioned and they were not suited for ride-and-drive work with the British service pattern harness—a breast harness that was considered much better for military purposes than the Canadian type (which used a collar requiring individual fitting and had no means of quick release). New British general service wagons for the Division were shipped direct from factories in the United Kingdom, a change that necessitated the substitution of British harness for the Canadian pattern. Water carts and a number of other vehicles of special type were issued from British stocks to replace Canadian patterns or to complete establishment.

To the Minister of Militia the rejection of a considerable amount of the equipment in providing which he had expended so much personal energy and enthusiasm came as a bitter blow. He blamed the fact that Canada at that time "had practically no control of her forces Overseas", and he saw no justification for the British substitutions. "Our transport, our rifles, our trucks, our harness, our saddles, our equipment, our shovels, our boots, our clothing, our wagons", he told a Toronto audience late in 1916, "those were all set aside and in many cases . . . they were supplanted by inferior articles."[24] The findings of a court of inquiry appointed by the Militia Department that the Canadian-made boot was of unsuitable style and shape for active service were modified by a special Parliamentary Committee, which while absolving Canadian manufacturers of any fraudulence or negligence, reported that the pattern could be improved in several particulars. The Committee's findings greatly pleased Hughes, and his special representative in England received a long cable "congratulating us all very heartily on the results of the boot investigation and muster parades".[25] Henceforth specifications issued to Canadian manufacturers conformed closely to the British standard and resulted in a much improved product, though Canadian forces overseas continued to draw the British boot on moving to France.

The Move Overseas

While the work of organizing the Canadian Expeditionary Force was proceeding at Valcartier Camp, the selection of a commander had been the subject of discussions between Ottawa and London—principally between Colonel Hughes and Lord Kitchener, Secretary of State for War. The possibility of a Canadian being chosen was not entertained for long, but it was the Canadian Government that made the final selection. On 14 August the Prime Minister told Perley, "Hughes has no intention of going in command but would probably do so if convinced that he would command Canadian division after arrival and be in fighting line." The Minister of Militia had under consideration for the appointment three senior British officers with whose services during the South African War he was familiar. On the 18th Perley replied to this trial balloon, "Have consulted highest authority. Thinks mistake change Minister of Militia at this juncture". In between these messages Lord Kitchener gave Mr. Perley, on request, the names of three Canadian-born officers serving in the British Army (none over the rank of Brigadier General), pointing out that if the Canadian Government considered none of these sufficiently senior or suitable for high command there were many non-Canadian officers from whom a selection could be made. The three men whom Hughes had been considering were Lieut.-General the Earl of Dundonald (G.O.C. Canadian Militia from 1902 to 1904), Major-General Sir Reginald Pole Carew, and Major-General E. A. H. Alderson.[26] Of these the Minister thought the last named "best qualified by far".[27]

On 5 September Lord Kitchener informed Mr. Perley that "as the Canadian Government show a preference for General Alderson to command the Canadian Division, I am glad to be able to designate him for that command". Official notification of the new appointment was made on 25 September, and effective 14 October (the day the First Contingent arrived in the United Kingdom) Alderson was promoted to the rank of Lieutenant General.[28]

From the outset it was the intention of the Militia Department and the War Office that the Canadian Contingent should lose no time in moving to England, where preparations were being made for training on Salisbury Plain. Delay in completing the issue of clothing and equipment held the Force at Valcartier until the end of the third week in September, and embarkation for mounted units began at Quebec on the 23rd. At a conference held on the 21st in the Minister of Militia's house at Valcartier Camp, attended by the Prime Minister and other members of the Cabinet, it had been decided to send all effective men overseas—a total of 31,200. The sudden increase by more than 6000 invalidated a plan which the Director of Supplies and Transport had produced on 17 September allocating troops and horses to the 25 vessels already chartered, and even with the necessary revisions it was rejected by the Minister. He placed in charge at Quebec as Director General of Embarkation Lt.-Col. William Price (who had been granted an honorary commission on undertaking responsibility for installing water and electrical services at Valcartier Camp). At the same time he instructed his Naval Transport Superintendent (obtained from the Department of Marine and Fisheries) to engage any additional ships required, utilizing transports already engaged to the "greatest extent possible consistent with health and safety of men and horses". All this was to be accomplished "without reference to Headquarters or to previous schedule".[29] The Director of Supplies and Transport thus passed out of the picture. No provision had been made for a staff to work with Colonel Price, and his efforts to draw sufficient experienced officers from Valcartier Camp failed. "Apparently", he reported later, "the embarkation of this force was considered a matter of little importance and much ease."

It is small wonder that, in the words of one of Price's assistants, "chaos reigned supreme."[30] The new Director General quickly improvised a working organization, and somehow the job was done in spite of many obstacles, which included a notable tendency on the part of some units (not of the Permanent Force) to disregard regulations. For instance, much unnecessary congestion on the docks was caused by the failure of the 1st and 2nd Artillery Brigades to wait as instructed at a rendezvous camp set up at the Exhibition Grounds. In the absence of any loading plans units were brought successively into Quebec as vessels arrived with reputedly the appropriate space for them. Mounted units came from Valcartier Camp by march route to the rendezvous camp; all others moved by rail direct to shipside. An example of the method of "trial and error" employed was the loading on the *Bermudian* (one of the smallest transports) of the 1161 troops of the 8th Battalion with their wagons and baggage. Only when all were aboard was it realized that there was insufficient room, and all had to be transferred to a larger vessel—the *Bermudian* eventually sailing with but 562 on board.

Getting vehicles and baggage on board created special problems. The official in charge reported: "No one had any idea of what was to be loaded on the vessels." In some cases transports arrived from Montreal with their holds filled with non-military freight—including a large shipment of flour that Canada was giving to the Mother Country. It was discovered that hatchways were too small to take the Ammunition Park's crated motor-trucks, and an additional vessel, the *Manhattan,* had to be chartered from New York.[31] Much space was unnecessarily wasted when guns and limbers were shipped without first removing their wheels, and as a result some vessels were forced to take on water ballast to complete their load. After half the transports had pulled out into the river, tugs had to ferry ammunition to them in order to comply with a belated order that each vessel should carry an allotted number of rounds. With these complications it is hardly surprising that few units embarked with their full complement of horses, vehicles and baggage in the same ship, and that little heed was paid to a War Office request for camp equipment (other than tents) to accompany each unit so as to avoid "serious inconvenience" on disembarking. Mounted units were dismayed to find that in many cases they were separated from their mounts, and because of limited passenger accommodation on the horse-boats attendants had to look after as many as sixteen animals instead of the four prescribed by military regulations.

By nightfall on 1 October thirty loaded transports had moved out into the St. Lawrence. There remained only the *Manhattan,* which took on board 90 motor vehicles, 863 horses and a considerable amount of miscellaneous cargo left out of the other vessels. When she sailed independently late on the 5th, Colonel Price's hardworking staff could report that "not a single package of any kind belonging to the Expeditionary Force was left on hand". The main body proceeded downstream and dropped anchor in Gaspé Harbour, to await rendezvous with escorting British warships. There it was joined by a troopship bearing the 2nd Lincolns, which the R.C.R. had relieved in Bermuda. The thirty-second and last vessel to join the convoy was to meet it outward bound off Cape Race, with the Newfoundland Contingent aboard.

Protection of the Canadian Contingent during its passage to England had been planned by the Admiralty originally for a convoy estimated to be fourteen transports, and when this number was more than doubled the provision of additional escort strength caused a delay in sailing from Gaspé. The visible escort was the Royal Navy's 12th Cruiser Squadron of four light cruisers commanded by Rear-Admiral R. E. Wemyss, all of them nineteen or more years old; and on 2 October Colonel Hughes, who had come to Gaspé to see the Contingent on its way, wired the Prime Minister, "Escort altogether inadequate, should increase strength." This concern was relayed to the Admiralty by the Governor General, who was promptly reminded of an assurance given to the Minister of Militia two weeks earlier that the four cruisers would be reinforced en route by two battleships (H.M.S. *Glory* and *Majestic*), and that the whole of the Grand Fleet would cover the escort "from all attack by any large force of the enemy". Besides having the Grand Fleet block off intervention from the enemy's home ports, and the North American Squadron (which included H.M.C.S. *Niobe*) watch German armed liners in New York and Boston, the Admiralty had given orders for the 26,000-ton battle cruiser *Princess Royal* (launched in 1911) to join the convoy in mid-Atlantic. This detachment from the Grand Fleet of one of its best warships at such a time, observes the British official naval historian, "was dictated not so much by military considerations as to afford testimony of how highly the Canadian effort was appreciated by the Mother Country".[32] Be that as it may, nothing of this was known to the Canadian Government. Concerned at the publication in the Canadian press and the cabling "in clear" of details of the convoy and the force it carried, the Admiralty exercised the most rigid security about the intended employment of H.M.S. *Princess Royal,* keeping the matter secret from even Admiral Wemyss.[33]

On 2 October, while the convoy was still at anchor in Gaspé Harbour, the Minister of Militia passed through the lines of waiting transports in a launch distributing to the troops bundles of his 900-word valedictory, "Where Duty Leads". In stirring language the message reviewed the achievements of the past six weeks in producing an "army of free men" from "peaceful Canadian citizens", and praised their high motives in setting forth "to do duty on the historic fields of France, Belgium and Germany for the preservation of the British Empire and the rights and liberties of humanity."* At 3:00 p.m. next day the flotilla sailed. It took three hours for the line of ships, more than twenty-one miles long, to steam through the harbour's narrow exit into the Gulf of St. Lawrence. Once in the open the great armada reformed in fleet formation—three lines ahead, fifteen cables (3000 yards) apart, each led by a cruiser, the fourth cruiser bringing up the rear.

The crossing, which was uneventful, lasted twelve days. The sea was smooth, and there was little demand for 20,000 boxes of a secret mal-de-mer remedy in the medical stores.[34] The troops were kept occupied with routine cleaning tasks and such physical exercise and training as were possible on shipboard. Concerts in the evenings, a Saturday sports day and church parades on Sundays rounded

* The Minister's valedictory is reproduced in full in Duguid, *Official History of the Canadian Forces in the Great War 1914-1919,* Volume of Appendices, Appendix 149.

out the programme. On 8 October the convoy said good-bye to the cruiser *Lancaster,* flagship of the North American Squadron, which with H.M.S. *Glory* had been guarding the southern flank, and daylight on the 10th disclosed the *Princess Royal* and the *Majestic,* which had been waiting at the rendezvous for two days. The troops gave the great *Princess Royal* a warm ovation on the 12th, when she dropped back to the convoy and steamed at 22 knots in full review past the cheering troopships. Reports of German submarines in the English Channel changed the intended destination at the last minute from Southampton to Plymouth. Ploughing through heavy seas on the final lap of the voyage, the first transports entered Plymouth Sound at 7:00 a.m. on 14 October, and thirty-six hours later the Admiralty reported all safe in harbour. Dock and rail facilities at Plymouth and adjacent Devonport fell far short of those at Southampton; but since the Channel was not yet free of danger Admiral Wemyss was ordered to proceed with disembarkation. Late on the 14th Colonel V.A.S. Williams, who had brought the Contingent across the Atlantic, handed over command to General Alderson, and next morning the force began landing.

It was an historic occasion, this arrival in Britain of the first large contingent from one of her overseas Dominions. "Canada sends her aid at a timely moment", cabled the First Lord of the Admiralty, Winston Churchill, to the Government in Ottawa. "The conflict moves forward and fiercer struggles lie before us than any which have yet been fought."[35] There were messages of welcome from Lord Kitchener and the Mayor of Plymouth. The people of Plymouth greeted the Canadians wholeheartedly with cheers, handshakes and kisses, plying them freely with cigarettes and drinks. A seven-hour train journey followed by a march of eight or ten miles brought them into camp on Salisbury Plain, their home for the next sixteen weeks.

Back at the docks the confusion which was an inevitable result of the unorthodox loading at Quebec had been aggravated by the last-minute switch in the port of debarkation. It took nine days to complete disembarkation, the last unit going ashore on 24 October. Few units managed to claim their equipment or stores at the quayside. In general it was found best to ship the great bulk of miscellaneous material by trainloads to be sorted out at railway stations near camp.

On Salisbury Plain

At the turn of the century the War Office had acquired an area of some ninety square miles on Salisbury Plain as a military training ground. Extensive artillery and rifle ranges were constructed, and permanent accommodation was provided in barracks begun during the South African War. The tented camps to which the Canadians now came were on sites where the Territorial Forces had done their summer training for many years.

Like the rest of Salisbury Plain the War Office's acquisition spread over a broad, undulating plateau, the expanse of upland pasture broken only by occasional

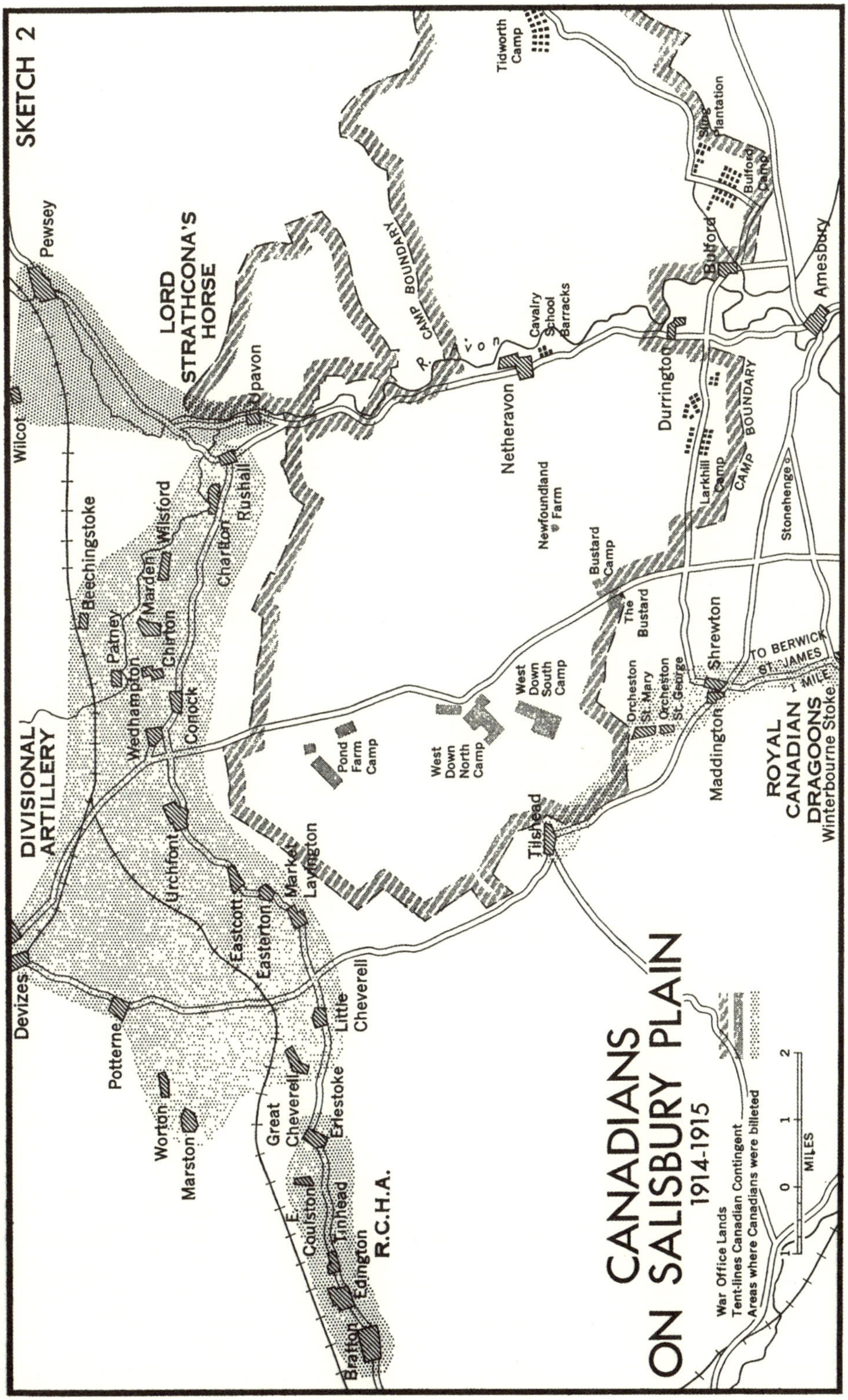
SKETCH 2
CANADIANS ON SALISBURY PLAIN
1914-1915
War Office Lands
Tent-lines Canadian Contingent
Areas where Canadians were billeted
MILES
0
1
2
1
LORD STRATHCONA'S HORSE
DIVISIONAL ARTILLERY
R.C.H.A.
ROYAL CANADIAN DRAGOONS
CAMP BOUNDARY
CAMP BOUNDARY
TO BERWICK ST. JAMES
1 MILE
Pewsey
Wilcot
Beechingstoke
Wilsford
Marden
Chirton
Patney
Wedhampton
Conock
Charlton
Rushall
Upavon
Netheravon
Cavalry School Barracks
Tidworth Camp
Sling Plantation
Bulford Camp
Bulford
Amesbury
Durrington
Larkhill Camp
Stonehenge
Newfoundland Farm
Bustard Camp
The Bustard
Shrewton
Maddington
Winterbourne Stoke
Orcheston St. Mary
Orcheston St. George
West Down South Camp
West Down North Camp
Pond Farm Camp
Tilshead
Market Lavington
Easterton
Eastcott
Urchfont
Devizes
Potterne
Worton
Marston
Little Cheverell
Great Cheverell
Erlestoke
E. Coulston
Tinhead
Edington
Bratton

belts of trees planted as sheep shelters in days gone by. In the deep valley of the River Avon, which crossed from north to south, several hamlets of ivy-covered cottages clustering around a small stone church and the inevitable wayside tavern formed little civilian islands in the military area. British engineers had put the sites in readiness for the Canadians. The task of setting up thousands of bell tents, marquees, and kitchen shelters had been done by fatigue parties from the Territorial Force assisted by a group of New Zealand troops recently enlisted in England. In the hot dry weather which prevailed in the early autumn of 1914 the countryside was at its best. An officer in the small Canadian advance party reported from Salisbury at the beginning of October: "I must say that the camp sites are beautifully situated and the turf is excellent, and will be quite an agreeable change from the sand plains which our boys have been accustomed to."[36]

Divisional Headquarters were established at "Ye Olde Bustard", an isolated inn three miles north-west of Stonehenge. The bulk of the Contingent was distributed in four camps extending for five miles near the west side of the military area. Bustard Camp, beside General Alderson's headquarters, was given over to the 1st Infantry Brigade, the Divisional Mounted Troops and Princess Patricia's Canadian Light Infantry; two miles to the north-west the 2nd and 3rd Brigades were in West Down South Camp; a mile beyond in West Down North were all the artillery and the Divisional Supply Column; while two miles farther north the 4th Brigade, the cavalry, the 17th Battalion and the Newfoundland Contingent occupied Pond Farm Camp.

In common with British formations encamped on Salisbury Plain, the Canadian Division formed part of the Southern Command, Lieut.-General Alderson being directly responsible to its General Officer Commanding-in-Chief, and through him to the War Office. The War Office was the sole channel of communication with the "Colonial authorities". When Alderson by-passed this channel in replying directly to cables sent to him from Ottawa, he was expressly informed that "direct communication between the General Officer Commanding 1st Canadian Division and the Canadian Civil or Military Authorities in Canada is not permissible".[37] Yet Alderson's responsibilities were obviously wider than those of a British commander of one of the infantry divisions of the British Expeditionary Force, and the restrictions were relaxed pending the setting up of appropriate liaison between the Government of Canada and the Canadian forces in the field.

A preliminary, if informal, move in this direction had already been taken by the Minister of Militia, who was anxious to retain in England as much as possible of the personal control over the Canadian forces which he had exercised in Canada. While the Contingent was still on the Atlantic, he had crossed by fast ship from New York in order (as the Prime Minister signalled his High Commissioner in London) to brief General Alderson "respecting officer and other important matters". Sir Robert stipulated that Colonel Hughes would be going in an "unofficial capacity for a holiday"; he was "not to assume any military command or interfere in military matters".[38] Hughes visited the Secretary of State for War,

Lord Kitchener, and, according to his biographer, agreed with him that the war would last at least three years.[39] During his stay in England his promotion to the rank of Major General was announced.[40] When he returned to Canada at the end of October he left behind as his "special representative" Colonel J. W. Carson, who had led the small advance party which preceded the Contingent to England.

There is an account by a Canadian officer that while Hughes was in England he defied an order by Kitchener that the Canadian regiments were to be broken up and the men redistributed among British units.[41] The story was recorded only in June 1934, almost twenty years later, and no evidence can be found in contemporary files or in the Borden or Perley Papers to corroborate it. Colonel Hughes himself, who in the course of Parliamentary debates was never reluctant to recount his exploits as a champion of Canadian rights, is not reported in Hansard as making any mention of the incident; nor did he mention the matter in a letter written to the Prime Minister regarding his visit to England.

On 7 January 1915, however, Colonel Carson reported to the Prime Minister that he had been asked by Lord Islington (Under Secretary of State for the Colonies) whether the Canadian Government would agree to having selected Canadian battalions or brigades sent to the front. The intention seems to have been no more than to place these temporarily with British units to get them indoctrinated into trench warfare—a plan that was eventually carried out. But when Carson brought the matter to Hughes' attention, the Minister firmly opposed the scheme, insisting that the Canadians should go into action as Canadian Divisions.[42] Borden appears to have taken no action on Carson's letter, and on 14 January Perley informed Sir Robert that Lord Kitchener had advised him of his intention to send the Division across the Channel in the first week of February.[43]

Before the last Canadian unit to disembark reached Salisbury Plain the weather had broken. A quarter of an inch of rain fell on 21 October, and a full inch in the next five days. It was the beginning of a period of abnormally heavy precipitation which brought rain on 89 out of 123 days; the fall of 23.9 inches between mid-October and mid-February almost doubled the 32-year average. There was no escape from the ever pervading dampness, and conditions steadily deteriorated. Temperatures were unusually low, on some nights dropping below the freezing point. High winds pierced the light fabric of the unheated tents, and twice in three weeks gales flattened much of the Division's canvas. Mud was everywhere. An impervious layer of chalk a few inches below ground-level held the rain water at the surface, and wherever wheels rolled or men marched the "excellent" turf quickly became a quagmire. All attempts at drainage were fruitless; scraping the mud from the roads only exposed the treacherously slippery chalk.

There were no permanent barracks available for the Canadians, and a programme of building huts begun in October 1914 was overtaken by the arrival of winter. The contractors had taken on more work than they could handle, so that commitments by Lord Kitchener to have all the Canadians in huts before the end of November could not be met.[44] First to move under a roof were the units of the 4th Canadian Infantry Brigade, which on 9 November took over newly completed hutments at Sling Plantation, north-east of Bulford. To push the work forward the Canadian Contingent was called on to supply an increasing number of carpenters, bricklayers and unskilled labourers. At the beginning of January some 900 Canadians were under employment to a civilian contractor, drawing besides working pay an extra daily ration of a quarter of a pound of meat. But great as was the need for dry accommodation, the need for training was even greater, and after 8 January demands for labour were made only on the 4th Infantry Brigade, which furnished working parties of 250 men per battalion.

By 17 December the Engineers and the 2nd and 3rd Infantry Brigades had gone into huts at Larkhill, between Bulford and Bustard Camp; but Christmas found 11,000 Canadians still under canvas. From the beginning of the war, the War Office had sought to solve its accommodation problems by billeting a large part of the "New Armies" recruited by Lord Kitchener.* Now, as the continual exposure to the wretched weather threatened the health of the Canadians on the open plain, billets were requisitioned for as many as possible in the adjoining villages. Moves into private houses began at the turn of the year, and the names of numerous little Wiltshire communities entered the annals of Canadian regiments—villages between Wilton and Tilshead for the Royal Canadian Dragoons, between Upavon and Pewsey for Lord Strathcona's Horse; to the north the artillery were spread out between Market Lavington, Rushall and Devizes; farthest west, between Bratton and Erlestoke, were the Royal Canadian Horse Artillery. Only the 1st Infantry Brigade remained throughout the winter in tents. Of greater significance to the mounted units than their own move into billets was the fact that at the same time their horses were put under cover and on dry standings. During November and December the condition of the animals had deteriorated seriously through their being forced to stand outside in mud to their hocks, their rain-soaked blankets providing little protection from the elements. Grooming was impossible, nor could sodden leather be kept clean. The change of accommodation worked wonders, and before January ended horses, harness and saddlery were reported restored to their proper condition.

The general health of the troops was remarkably good, and only after the move into crowded huts were there serious outbreaks of respiratory and intestinal ailments. There were 39 cases of meningitis, 28 proving fatal. Of the four thousand admissions to hospital in the fourteen weeks on Salisbury Plain, 1249 were cases of venereal disease.

The training begun at Valcartier was resumed during the first week of November and continued for thirteen weeks under the direction of Southern Command. For the infantry a period of basic training, devoted principally to physical training (which included route marches of progressive length thrice

* On 7 August 1914 posters and notices in newspapers announced Lord Kitchener's immediate call to arms of 100,000 recruits to form the first New Army of six divisions. This contingent, "the First Hundred Thousand" was raised in a few days.[45]

weekly), musketry instruction, foot and arms drill and entrenching, was followed by five weeks of company training, two of battalion and two of brigade training. Except for two officers and five N.C.Os. loaned by the War Office, all instructors were members of the Contingent. British regular divisions in France had amazed the enemy by the speed at which they could deliver their rifle fire, and with this standard before them Canadian infantrymen daily practised charger-loading and rapid fire with dummy cartridges. In comparison with the extensive array of targets at Valcartier, range facilities were limited, and cold weather hampered shooting, but each infantryman fired an allotment of 155 rounds. The artillery ranges also proved inadequate; with six British Divisions competing with the Canadians for their use, the Canadian batteries managed only one week of range practice, firing fifty rounds a battery. The Engineers found plenty to do, supplementing their technical training with practical work on construction projects about the various camps. Tactical exercises were held at all levels of command, but these were frequently interrupted by heavy storms of wind and rain.

Indeed the miserable weather turned training into a drudgery. There were no means of drying clothing, and men who ploughed through ankle-deep mud all day had to let their rain-soaked uniforms dry on their backs. Describing conditions of camp life as "simply appalling", with the whole camp grounds from Salisbury to Pond Farm "just one sea of mud", Colonel Carson reported to the Minister on 7 December that he had learned from a large number of medical officers that "the general consensus of opinion is that another two or three months of present conditions in England will have a serious effect on the general health and well-being of our troops". He felt that "they would have been a thousand times better off in Canada than they are at Salisbury Plains".[46] The plight of the Canadians had been studied with no little concern by the Australian authorities, and as a result of the conditions on Salisbury Plain the combined Australian and New Zealand contingents, 29,000 strong, on their way to train in English camps, had been halted at Suez and diverted to training grounds in Egypt.[47] Carson's proposal to Lord Kitchener that the Canadian Contingent should also move to Egypt to train was turned down.

It is surprising that in such deplorable circumstances the Canadian troops maintained a good standard of morale. The enthusiasm with which they had flocked to Valcartier persisted, and in general they bore their adversities with admirable patience, regarding them as the inevitable consequences of war. Officers and men did their best to improve conditions. Welfare agencies helped to ameliorate the lot of the soldier in his off-duty hours. Welcome parcels of food, knitted goods and tobacco came from the Canadian War Contingent Association, an organization of Canadians in England and their friends. The Y.M.C.A. supplied reading material and stationery and operated refreshment centres. The Canadian Field Comforts Commission, organized from voluntary women workers by two Toronto ladies, who on the Minister of Militia's authority had proceeded overseas with the First Contingent, looked after the distribution of gifts received from Canada.[48]

Regulations for the Canadian Militia dating back to 1893 prohibited alcoholic liquor in camps, and Valcartier had been "dry". But almost immediately upon taking over command of the Canadians General Alderson had seen the need for establishing wet canteens in the camps. He reported that the controlled sale of beer under military supervision would put a stop to troops going to the neighbouring villages where they "get bad liquor, become quarrelsome and then create disturbances". In spite of protests from temperance organizations in Canada, the new arrangements proved wise. Nearby villages were placed out of bounds except to men with passes. A rebate of 7½ per cent on sales of beer enriched unit funds by $7,500 during November and December. Undoubtedly one of the most important factors contributing to the maintenance of morale was the allowance for all ranks of up to six days' leave, with a free ticket to anywhere in the British Isles. While many flocked to London (where the disorderly conduct of some cut down the number granted leave), others found their way into English homes to form permanent friendships and to enjoy the warm hospitality extended to the visitors from overseas.

The Division Goes to France

As the troops trained on Salisbury Plain, the suitability of their Canadian equipment was being debated between London and Ottawa, and by the end of January the Force had embarked on the extensive programme of substitutions to which we have referred (above, page 27). By that time the Division had adopted the final establishment with which it was to proceed to France—with certain exceptions that of a regular division of the British Expeditionary Force. The question of whether the eight-company battalion of Colonial establishments should be retained instead of the Imperial four-company organization had produced considerable confusion. After the War Office had changed its mind several times—which had the effect of converting battalions from an eight to a four-company basis and back again—it ruled that the British system would stand. As a result every Canadian battalion lost three officers from its headquarters, in addition to the eight subalterns that each had been carrying supernumerary to establishment.[49] While authority was given to augment brigade staffs by a staff captain and two orderly officers, the net increase in the number of surplus Canadian officers was to cause General Alderson considerable concern.

In the 18-pounder artillery brigade the three 6-gun batteries were reorganized into four 4-gun batteries, the surplus guns and personnel going to form brigade depot batteries for supplying reinforcements. The revised establishments brought increases in the Cyclist Company and the Divisional Column, added a sanitary section to the medical units, and produced a new Army Service Corps unit—the 1st Canadian Motor Ambulance Workshop. There had been one change in the infantry order of battle. On 15 December the 10th Battalion was transferred from the 4th to the 2nd Brigade, replacing the 6th Battalion (Fort Garry Horse), which became a reserve cavalry regiment (or depot). The 4th Brigade was disbanded in mid-January. Its three remaining battalions and the 17th Battalion became reinforcing units forming part of the Canadian Training Depot, which was established in Tidworth Barracks on Salisbury Plain.[50] The Depot, together with artillery depot batteries in the Devizes area, furnished drafts of 1077 early in February to bring the Division up to strength.

On 2 February advance and billeting parties left for France, and two days later a review by His Majesty King George V and Lord Kitchener gave warning of approaching embarkation. An all-day rain on the 7th provided a fitting climax to the Canadian stay on Salisbury Plain as the first units boarded the troop trains which were to take them to Avonmouth on the Bristol Channel. This west country port had been chosen, with St. Nazaire in the Bay of Biscay as the port of disembarkation, when announcement of Germany's intention to establish around the British Isles a zone of unrestricted submarine attacks on shipping ruled out the usual Southampton-Havre route. For the majority of the troops, packed in the holds of small cargo vessels, it was a thoroughly unpleasant voyage. A rousing gale caused wholesale sea sickness, and tedious delays at either end of the journey meant that some were on board for five days. But there was little complaining, for present inconveniences were offset by the general feeling of relief at leaving the misery of Salisbury Plain. Two divisions of destroyers escorted the various groups of transports, and the whole movement was completed by the 16th without enemy interference.

There were few port facilities at St. Nazaire, and the vessels had to anchor in the outer harbour waiting their turn to berth. At the dock most of the unloading was done by work parties furnished by the units themselves. As the troops marched through the streets of St. Nazaire to the railway station, they were given a warm welcome by the French people. Unit by unit entrained in the small box-like cars, labelled "Hommes 40, Chevaux 8", and then commenced the long, circuitous 500-mile journey to the front.

When the Canadian Division sailed from England, it parted company (in some cases only temporarily) with the units which had come with it from Canada. It has been noted that the P.P.C.L.I. was already in France. The battalion had joined the 80th Brigade on 16 November 1914, and after completing training at Winchester had embarked at Southampton for Le Havre on 20 December. Early in December the Newfoundland Contingent went north to train at Fort George, in the Scottish Command; as a battalion of the 88th Brigade, 29th Division it was to serve with distinction in Gallipoli and later on the Western Front. The first day of February saw the formation of the Canadian Cavalry Brigade from the Royal Canadian Horse Artillery, the Royal Canadian Dragoons, Lord Strathcona's Horse, and the 2nd King Edward's Horse—the second regiment of a unit of the British Special Reserve whose pre-war role had been to train officers and men from the Dominions. The Cavalry Brigade concentrated near Uckfield, Sussex, under a British officer, Colonel J. E. B. Seely—whose appointment by Lord Kitchener so displeased Sir Robert Borden (in whose judgement there were

Canadian officers more capable of filling the position) that he declared: "I shall see to it that the next Mounted Corps that goes from Canada is placed in command of one of our own men as Brigadier."[51] The Automobile Machine Gun Brigade was attached to the South Eastern Mounted Brigade, and for the next five months was employed in a home defence role at Ashford, Kent.

Of the Line of Communication medical units which accompanied the Contingent to England, No. 2 Stationary Hospital landed at Boulogne on 8 November —the first Canadian unit to see service in France and the only one whose personnel were eligible* for the 1914 Star. No. 1 Stationary Hospital and No. 1 Canadian Casualty Clearing Station crossed the Channel on 2 February 1915, No. 2 General Hospital on 13 March, and No. 1, which had been left in charge of the Division's sick, on 13 May. Most of the L. of C. supply units followed the Division to France in February.

Six months had passed since the Canadian Contingent had begun to assemble at Valcartier Camp. During that time much had been accomplished. The Division had been provisionally organized and equipped, and partially trained; it had crossed an ocean, it had to a considerable extent been re-equipped and had completed its organization and training. The fact should not pass unnoted that all this had been achieved in as little time as British pre-war planning had calculated would be required to place in the field the Territorial Divisions. The British divisions which preceded the Canadians across the Channel were all regular formations; the first British Territorial Division to go to France did not arrive until 24 February 1915, while the first of Kitchener's New Army divisions crossed early in May.

The Early Battles on the Western Front

The battle front to which the 1st Canadian Division came had stood virtually unchanged since mid-October, when the opposing sides had found themselves in deadlock along an entrenched line that stretched five hundred miles from Switzerland to the North Sea. Although Canadians had not fought in the opening battles on the Western Front, a brief account of those operations may be helpful as a background to what followed.†

The strengths of the Western belligerents at the outbreak of war, in terms of infantry divisions available or being formed, gave the enemy a slight advantage on paper. Against 87 German divisions France could put 62 in the field, and Belgium and Great Britain six each.[52] Britain, being primarily a sea power, had no firm military plan other than to assist France or Belgium if needed. The Belgian plan was a defensive one. Both France and Germany, however, contemplated an immediate offensive.

* The only other Canadian troops to reach France in 1914, the Patricias, arrived a month too late to qualify for the Star, for which the closing date was midnight 22-23 November.

† For a more detailed treatment see The Historical Section, General Staff, A.H.Q., *The Western Front, 1914* (Ottawa, 1957).

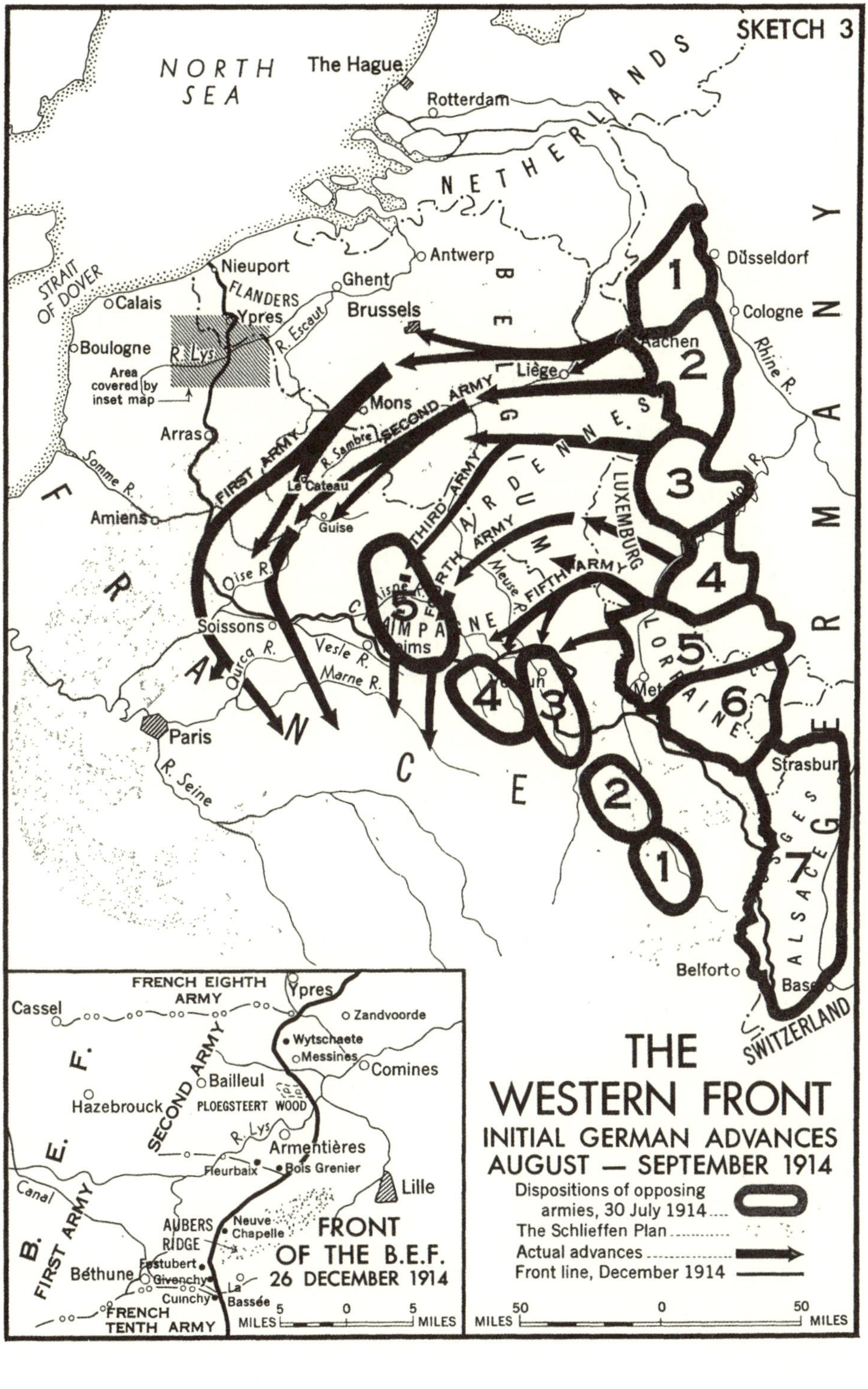
SKETCH 3
NORTH SEA
The Hague
Rotterdam
NETHERLANDS
STRAIT OF DOVER
Nieuport
Antwerp
Düsseldorf
Calais
Ghent
FLANDERS
Ypres
Brussels
Cologne
Boulogne
R. Lys
R. Escaut
Aachen
Area covered by inset map
Liège
Rhine R.
BELGIUM
Mons
SECOND ARMY
ARDENNES
Arras
FIRST ARMY
R. Sambre
Le Cateau
THIRD ARMY
LUXEMBURG
Amiens
Somme R.
Guise
FOURTH ARMY
FIFTH ARMY
Oise R.
Meuse R.
Soissons
CHAMPAGNE
Reims
LORRAINE
Metz
Ourcq R.
Vesle R.
Marne R.
Paris
R. Seine
FRANCE
GERMANY
Strasburg
VOSGES
ALSACE
Belfort
Basel
SWITZERLAND
THE WESTERN FRONT
INITIAL GERMAN ADVANCES
AUGUST — SEPTEMBER 1914
Dispositions of opposing armies, 30 July 1914
The Schlieffen Plan
Actual advances
Front line, December 1914
50 MILES 0 50 MILES
FRENCH EIGHTH ARMY
Cassel
Ypres
Zandvoorde
Wytschaete
Messines
Comines
B. E. F.
SECOND ARMY
Bailleul
Hazebrouck
PLOEGSTEERT WOOD
R. Lys
Armentières
Fleurbaix
Bois Grenier
Lille
Canal
FIRST ARMY
AUBERS RIDGE
Neuve Chapelle
FRONT OF THE B.E.F.
26 DECEMBER 1914
Festubert
Béthune
Givenchy
La Bassée
Cuinchy
FRENCH TENTH ARMY
MILES 5 0 5 MILES

The French preparations were in accordance with "Plan XVII", adopted by the Chief of the French General Staff, General Joseph Jacques Joffre, the seventeenth of a series prepared between 1875 and 1907. It called for French attacks in Alsace-Lorraine and in the Ardennes. It recognized the probability of a German invasion of Belgium and an attack on the French left wing, but this appreciation was marred by an underestimation of the enemy's capabilities—it was believed, for example, that for lack of troops the German front would not extend west of the Meuse. The whole plan suffered from an overemphasis on French offensive action (particularly to regain Alsace-Lorraine) at the expense of other military considerations. When war broke out five French armies were disposed along the German frontier, ranged in order from the First, opposite Alsace, to the Fifth, covering Reims.

German intentions were based on the doctrine formulated by Field-Marshal Count Alfred von Schlieffen, Chief of the Prussian General Staff from 1891 to 1905. In successive plans von Schlieffen had prescribed that in a war on two fronts Germany was to open hostilities by a powerful attack against one opponent while holding the other one at bay with a minimum of forces.[53] First to be dealt with was France; the blueprint for the operation was Schlieffen's December 1905 memorandum, "War against France".[54] Execution of this plan would have required 96 divisions, many more than were available in 1905. In this respect the plan was actually a programme for the expansion of the Army.[55] But even by 1914 the German forces available for the West did not amount to more than 87 divisions,[56] and in the meantime both France and Russia had significantly increased their military strengths. Yet while failing to provide the forces demanded in the 1905 plan, the Germans had retained the plan itself, though modified greatly and perhaps fatally. Von Schlieffen had intended the main effort to be a powerful attack through Belgium and the Netherlands by 79 divisions wheeling on Metz to envelop the French left wing.[57] But when his successor, General Helmuth von Moltke, launched the 1914 offensive, it was on a reduced frontage, both in order to conserve troops and to keep the Netherlands neutral.

Originally only nine German divisions had been assigned to guard the frontier from Metz to the Swiss border; for loss of some ground in Alsace-Lorraine was acceptable since a French offensive here would render the French left all the more vulnerable. Nevertheless, von Moltke increased the German left wing to 25 divisions at the expense of his right, where only 53 divisions remained available for the main offensive.* The opening of hostilities found these grouped in five armies, numbered in order from north to south. The Sixth and Seventh Armies formed the German left wing on the Western Front; the Eighth Army, of nine infantry divisions under General von Prittwitz, held the Eastern Front. In pursuance of each side's plans, the Germans began crossing the Belgian frontier with elements of three armies on 4 August, and three days later farther south a corps of the French First Army made a limited advance towards Mulhausen. Thus

* The German Official History places the strengths of the two deployment wings in the ratio 7:1 in Count Schlieffen's last draft, and 3:1 as a result of General von Moltke's changes.[58]

commenced the series of operations along the Western Front known collectively as the Battle of the Frontiers. A week after Joffre's opening move the First and Second French Armies set out to attack Lorraine. On the 21st, the Third and Fourth Armies were ordered to strike north-eastward into the Ardennes forests. All these French offensives failed.

In the meantime the Germans, despite unexpected delay at the Liège forts, had all but crushed active resistance by the Belgians; most of King Albert's army had withdrawn to Antwerp. General von Bülow's Second Army had already passed the Sambre; General von Hausen's Third Army was soon to cross the Meuse. Nevertheless, until he saw all his forces of the centre and right in retreat, General Joffre still had hopes of extending his offensive northward across the whole front. By 17 August the first four infantry divisions of the British Expeditionary Force, plus the Cavalry Division, had landed in France and were now preparing to advance on the left of the French Fifth Army (General Lanrezac). Only on the 22nd, as the British lined up along the Mons canal, did their C.-in-C., Field-Marshal Sir John French, realize from the strength of the forces opposing him that the coming battle would be a defensive one.

The Battle of Mons, fought on 23 August, imposed a 24-hour check on General von Kluck's First Army. On the same day farther east General Lanrezac's forces managed to hold up the German Second Army south of the Sambre and to recapture a bridgehead won by von Hausen's Third Army over the Meuse. But reverses in the centre, and the threat of a major German advance through a gap between the Fourth and Fifth French Armies, compelled the latter to begin retiring on the morning of the 24th. The B.E.F., with both its flanks already insecure and its right soon to be further exposed by Lanrezac's withdrawal, had to conform, and to begin its fighting "retreat from Mons" towards Paris. Now, with all his forces falling back, Joffre could abandon the near-disastrous Plan XVII in favour of a more realistic course of action.

Although the Schlieffen Plan seemed to be working remarkably well for the Germans, it had already undergone further modification, and other changes were about to come. Both from above and below, von Moltke had received protests against losses of territory in Alsace-Lorraine and East Prussia (where following a German withdrawal he had called the 68-year old General Paul von Hindenburg out of retirement to replace von Prittwitz).[59] Moltke had been compelled to sanction premature defensive battles and local counter-offensives. As a result, forces which might have been employed more effectively on the right wing were retained on the left—which was still not strong enough to break through Joffre's eastern fortress system—and two corps were soon to be transferred to the Eastern Front.

During the last week of August and the first few days of September, the French and British continued to retire, but in relatively good order, occasionally striking back and causing considerable delay and confusion. Such an action was the stand at Le Cateau on the 26th, when in Britain's biggest battle since Waterloo, General Sir Horace Smith-Dorrien's 2nd Corps inflicted an estimated 9000 casualties on von Kluck's First Army, against nearly 8000 British losses. Three days later at

Guise on the River Oise Lanrezac struck von Bülow's flank a blow which though losing much of its effectiveness because of Sir John French's refusal to co-operate[60] nevertheless halted the enemy's Second Army for 36 hours. German hopes of outflanking the Allies steadily faded. The machine was losing some of its efficiency, as unforeseen problems of administration arose. Von Moltke was finding that seven armies were too many for one man to control effectively; but the day of the permanent army group had not yet arrived. From time to time he placed one army under command of another. But such arrangements often suffered from professional rivalry between the commanders concerned, the subordinate sometimes finding that the task originally assigned his force had been relegated to a secondary role. Furthermore, a system which permitted considerable freedom in staff circles led to cases in which a staff officer might make a major decision without referring to his own commander.

Eventually the German advance—scarcely ever a pursuit—became less orderly than the Allied withdrawal. On 31 August von Kluck, believing that the B.E.F. was retiring westward to the Channel and was out of his reach, on his own initiative turned south-eastward so as to catch the French Fifth Army in flank and rear. The movement took him across the front of the Sixth Army, which was guarding Paris. No longer were German operations in accordance with the Schlieffen Plan. On 4 September, after von Moltke and most of his army commanders had deviated from it at least once, it was finally discarded in favour of a frontal attack by the three central armies (Third, Fourth and Fifth) to drive the French south-eastward from Paris. The right flank, which originally was to have invested and passed beyond Paris, now became a mere protective force facing the French capital.

Throughout the Allied retreat General Joffre had been able to regroup and reinforce his armies as the situation required. The general distribution of the German forces, however, had been governed by the Schlieffen Plan until its abandonment, and only hasty, piecemeal adjustments were possible. Thus in the centre, where von Moltke now attempted to break through, he had only 25 divisions against 21½; while on the Allied left 43½ French and British faced 25½ German divisions.[61] On 4 September, as German forces crossed the River Marne, Joffre gave the order for his armies to turn and attack.

The four-day Battle of the Marne began on 6 September, as von Kluck, hurriedly turning to face west, and pulling back his left wing some twenty miles, was engaged by the French Sixth Army at the River Ourcq. But while von Kluck's move secured the German right flank, it opened a gap between the First and Second Armies through which the B.E.F. pushed forward across the Marne. Unfortunately the British did not receive expected support from the French Fifth Army, which became involved in the new Ninth Army's (General Foch) frontal attack on von Bülow's forces. With their supply lines over-extended and their communications disorganized, the German armies were unable to deal effectively with the crisis caused by the threat to their right wing. Von Moltke appears to have accepted defeat on the 8th, and from his remote headquarters in Luxembourg he sent his Chief of Intelligence on a strange and fateful mission to sound out the various army headquarters. No one commander seems to have ordered a general withdrawal; it was largely arranged on a staff level. Some formations of the First and Second Armies began falling back on the afternoon of the 9th, and by nightfall the retirement was spreading to the armies of the centre. Operations in the Lorraine sector, where the German Sixth and Seventh Armies had launched an unsuccessful attack towards the Moselle, were suspended at about the same time.

The defeat at the Marne ended German hopes of quickly winning the war. General Erich von Falkenhayn, formerly Prussian Minister of War, who replaced von Moltke, declared the situation serious, though not to be looked upon with pessimism. The German forces withdrew to the general line Soissons-Reims-Verdun, with the First Army digging in north of the Aisne River, and the Second and Third behind the Vesle. A wide gap between Kluck's and Bülow's forces was filled by the Seventh Army, brought over from Alsace. On 13 September pursuing Allied forces gained bridgeheads over the Aisne, but enemy resistance in the next two days produced a deadlock. The Allies dug in, and the era of trench warfare descended upon the Western Front.

Then began the "race to the sea", as each side engaged in a series of left or right hooks in an attempt to cut around the other's seaward flank. Neither was successful, and by the second week of October the opposing trenches had been extended from the Oise northward to the Belgian coast at Nieuport. During the remainder of the year each side made repeated bids to break through the other's line. Each operation inevitably began as a frontal attack, and ended either in complete failure or in the capture of a pitifully small piece of ground at great cost. The lesson that mobile warfare could not be waged under conditions of trench warfare had yet to be learned. The B.E.F., which had moved north from the Aisne into Flanders early in October, was heavily engaged in the month-long series of operations known as the Battles of Ypres, 1914. The line fluctuated but remained unbroken. In mid-December a French offensive near Arras achieved only heavy casualties, as did the costly operations in Champagne, which dragged on fruitlessly into mid-March.

The line which existed at the beginning of 1915 was to stand for the next two years without varying as much as ten miles in either direction. At the coastal end, adjoining a French detachment holding Nieuport, was the Belgian Army, which had taken up a position on the Allied left flank when Antwerp fell on 10 October. In the Ypres sector was the French Eighth Army entrenched on a seventeen-mile front.[62] On its right, British forces defended the Flemish plain as far south as Givenchy. French armies held the remainder of the line, which continued generally southward through Arras to the Aisne, thence turning eastward to Verdun and finally southward again through the Vosges mountains to the Swiss border. On the enemy side the northern sector of Flanders was guarded by the German Fourth Army (Colonel-General Duke Albrecht of Württemberg); in the southern sector was the Sixth Army (Crown Prince Rupprecht of Bavaria).

As 1914 ended the B.E.F. had been reinforced to eleven regular infantry and five cavalry divisions; these were formed into two armies on 26 December.

By 18 February 1915 General Sir Douglas Haig's First Army (1st, 4th and Indian Corps) was holding a trench line eleven miles long which centred on Neuve Chapelle. On the left the Second Army (2nd, 3rd and 5th Corps), commanded by General Sir Horace Smith-Dorrien, held a seventeen-mile front across the valleys of the Lys and the Douve, extending northward from Bois Grenier to just beyond the Ypres-Comines railway, where it joined the French Eighth Army defending the Ypres salient. Fifteen miles behind the Second Army's front was Hazebrouck. East of the town was the billeting area to which the 1st Canadian Division came in mid-February, to form a reserve to the British 3rd Corps.

Future Allied Strategy

The winter of 1914-15 gave the belligerents a breathing space in which to review the general situation and consider plans for the coming year.

In the fighting so far each side's carefully prepared schemes had miscarried. The German plan for quickly crushing France and then turning east to overwhelm Russia had not survived the Marne and the Aisne. The French design of attacking north and south of Metz had played into the enemy's hands. Austria's dream of easy subjugation of Serbia had been rudely dispelled. Although the Russians had had some success against Austria, they had accomplished nothing against Germany. An invasion of East Prussia, hastily improvised to take German pressure off France, had come to a bad end in late August at Tannenberg.

In the west the deadlock was complete by sea and land. The German fleet lay static in fortified harbours; and with no way of drawing it out the British Admiralty pinned its faith to the blockade. On land the 500-mile front from the North Sea to the Alps offered no flank which could be turned. If the Allies decided to adopt the "forlorn expedient of the frontal attack"[63] they would place themselves in the unfortunate position of losing ground before they had fully mastered the conditions, and then having to attempt its recapture after the defensive had been developed into a fine art.

The Eastern and South-Eastern Fronts presented a different picture. Here the Central Powers had to defend a line nearly 2000 miles long. While in summer the defenders could hold wide marshlands which were virtually impassable, the winter frosts rendered this ground traversable by an opponent, at the same time making it too hard for entrenching. Furthermore, to provide an adequate garrison for this extensive front would mean drawing on races hostile to Austria-Hungary. For the Allies the main weakness in the east was that the Russian armies, though possessing an overwhelming advantage in manpower, were short of arms and ammunition. To supply these deficiencies it would be necessary to establish "intimate and continuous contact" between Russia and the Western Allies.[64] There was need for prompt action. The transfer of large numbers of German troops late in 1914 from the Western to the Eastern Front brought the threat of a major Russian defeat which would leave the Central Powers free to resume the offensive in Flanders with great numerical superiority. Yet the deadlock in the west gave the

Allies little hope of assisting Russia by seeking a decision on that front. On 2 January Lord Kitchener expressed the belief that "the German lines in France may be looked on as a fortress that cannot be carried by assault and . . . that the lines may be held by an investing force, whilst operations proceed elsewhere".[65]

In Britain the War Council (which had been formed in November 1914 as an augmented committee of the Cabinet) was already considering where such alternative operations might be most advantageously conducted. Unlike the Allied Commanders in France it recognized that, as a maritime power, Britain's best strategy for 1915 lay not in throwing armies against the impregnable positions in the west but in turning a flank by sea so as to achieve union with Russia. The conflict between the "Easterners" and the "Westerners" had begun.

At the beginning of September the first Lord of the Admiralty, Mr. Winston Churchill, had directed that a plan be prepared for seizing the Gallipoli Peninsula and securing a passage through the Dardanelles in order to gain direct contact with Russia. Greece was ready to supply the ground forces for the enterprise; but since Turkey had not yet entered the war, and it was hoped to keep her neutral, the scheme was held in abeyance and the Greek offer was declined. While keeping the Gallipoli plan alive, Churchill propounded an alternative scheme to dominate the Baltic by a seaborne invasion of Schleswig-Holstein, to be followed by the seizure of the Kiel Canal. British naval control of the Baltic would enable Russian armies to land within ninety miles of Berlin. Implementation of this plan would require several months of the closest cooperation. Prospects seemed much brighter in South-East Europe, where the early restrictions had been removed late in October by Turkey's entry into the war on Germany's side.

Turning the Southern flank would not only be less hazardous than the Baltic enterprise, but the project held other inducements beside providing direct contact with Russia. There was less threat of formidable resistance from Germany, as Serbia lay across her communications with Turkey. Possession of the Gallipoli peninsula would eliminate Turkey from the war and pave the way for directing against Austria the combined efforts of four Balkan states (Serbia, Greece, Bulgaria and Rumania), mustering between them armies of more than a million men. On New Year's Day, 1915, Mr. David Lloyd George, Chancellor of the Exchequer (who as Prime Minister was to be the leading Easterner), proposed to the War Council two operations in the Eastern Mediterranean. The main one, a drive through Salonika or the Dalmatian coast against the Austrians, was intended to rally the Balkan armies to the Allies. The second, a subsidiary venture, was a landing on the Syrian coast to cut off Turkish forces advancing against Egypt.

Early in January, Turkish operations against Russia in the Caucasus brought a request from Grand Duke Nicholas to Lord Kitchener for "a demonstration of some kind against the Turks elsewhere, either naval or military" which would compel a withdrawal of some Turkish forces from the Caucasus.[66] Kitchener discussed this request with Churchill, who was opposed to a demonstration in the Dardanelles that might jeopardize any subsequent attempt to force the Straits.

In any event no troops were available, and Kitchener's reply to the Grand Duke, while assuring him that a demonstration would be made, held out little hope that it would seriously influence the strength of the Turks in the Caucasus.[67] The Admiralty reached the opinion that the Straits could be forced by naval action alone, though a large number of ships in "extended operations" would be required. Sir John Jellicoe, Commander-in-Chief of the Grand Fleet, was opposed to the Baltic venture, and on 28 January the War Council, having consulted Russia and France, decided in favour of the naval attack on the Dardanelles. On 16 February a decision was taken to make available military forces to support the naval operation if needed.[68] Thus was born the ill-fated Gallipoli campaign.

In contrast to the strategy approved by their governments, both the British and French Commanders-in-Chief in France held the view that the Allied effort should be made in the west. They argued that the demands of the Russian front had weakened the western German armies in manpower and material. Sir John French felt that breaking through the German lines was largely a question of having more ammunition, particularly high explosive. General Joffre agreed, welcoming the opportunity of liberating French territory by reducing the great German salient between Reims and Amiens, which at one point reached within 55 miles of Paris. Thus it happened that while the War Councils in London and Paris were exploring the possibilities of compaigning in some new theatre, their General Staffs at St. Omer and Chantilly were actively planning an early offensive on the Western Front. This divergence of aims violated one of the basic principles of warfare. Events were to prove that in 1915 Allied resources in men and munitions were insufficient to sustain with any hope of success large-scale offensives in two widely-separated theatres.[69]

CHAPTER III

THE BATTLES OF YPRES, 1915

(See Map 1 and Sketches 4–14)

The 1st Division Enters the Line

THE CANADIANS' entry into active operations was not long delayed; but before taking over a sector of the front line the Division was given a brief period of indoctrination into trench warfare.

Between 17 February and 2 March each infantry brigade, accompanied by a field artillery brigade and engineer, signal and service corps personnel, was attached for a week to one of two British divisions holding the line in front of Armentières. The 1st and 3rd Canadian Brigade groups, commanded respectively by Brig.-Gen. M. S. Mercer and Brig.-Gen. R. E. W. Turner, went successively to the 6th Division on the right, and the 2nd Brigade group (Brig.-Gen. A. W. Currie) to the 4th Division on the left. The indoctrination was practical and thorough. From company commanders down to private soldiers everyone was associated with a corresponding member of the host unit for 48 hours of individual training. Then followed 24 hours of platoon training, during which each Canadian platoon was made responsible for a definite length of trench as part of the company forming the regular garrison. Throughout the week battalion commanders and their staffs learned from their opposite numbers the many details of battalion administration in trench warfare. Artillery officers spent some time at the gun emplacements and then occupied by day and night the exact positions which would be theirs when their own units were in action.

On the 20th the Commander-in-Chief of the British Expeditionary Force, Field-Marshal Sir John French, inspected units of the Division in their rear area. He reported from what he "saw of them that they were well trained, and quite able to take their places in the line of battle"—an opinion which he later found to be "thoroughly justified".[1]

Before the tour ended, orders came for the 1st Division to take over a section of the First Army's front. The relief of the 7th British Division began on the last day of February, and at 11:00 a.m. on 3 March General Alderson assumed responsibility for 6400 yards of line in front of Fleurbaix. Here the Canadians formed the left wing of Lieut.-General Sir H. S. Rawlinson's 4th Corps; on their immediate left the inter-army boundary ran three and a half miles south of Armentières. Each infantry brigade employed two battalions in the front line, and its affiliated field artillery brigade had three of its four batteries in action some 2500 yards to the rear, the fourth being in reserve. Operating with each infantry brigade were a field company of engineers and a field ambulance.

Because the water level came close to the surface of the ground, the trenches were shallow and built up with breastworks of sod and sandbags. They looked out upon an area of flat fields between which the rows of pollarded willows that lined the intervening ditches provided German snipers with concealed points of vantage. About three miles to the east the low Aubers Ridge, rising in a few places 70 feet above the plain, barely hid from view the city of Lille, seven miles from the front line. The Canadian role was in general defensive—the "cardinal principle" being "a determination to hold the front trenches at all costs". General Alderson, however, impressed on all ranks the necessity for maintaining the initiative over the enemy, convincing him by means of "bold patrolling, persistent and accurate sniping and prompt enterprises against any sapheads . . . that the Canadian Division is his superior".[2] In the event of a German attack reserves would man the "G.H.Q. 2nd line"—a partly constructed position 2000 yards to the rear. For an uneventful week the Canadians accustomed themselves to the routine of trench warfare. Then, on 10 March, came a more exciting role as the British front on their right flared into action.

Neuve Chapelle, 10-12 March 1915

The plan of operations proposed by General Joffre for a 1915 campaign in France was with little change to remain the main Allied purpose in the West until the summer of 1918. It called for a three-fold offensive designed to cut the long German supply lines through the occupied territory of Northern France: in the north an advance eastward from Artois* against German communication centres in the Douai plain; in the south a northward thrust from Reims to sever the German lateral running north-westward through Mézières to Valenciennes; and with these having succeeded an advance northward from the Verdun-Nancy front to cut the enemy's line of retreat across the Rhine. The main blow in the north would be delivered by the French Tenth Army, striking eastward between Arras and Lens to capture the heights of Vimy and dominate the whole Douai region. In a memorandum to Sir John French on 15 February Joffre suggested that the British should participate on the left by attacking in the direction of La Bassée and the Aubers Ridge. The successful completion of this joint offensive on a seventy-mile front would pave the way for an advance into the Douai plain.[3]

This combined Anglo-French effort, however, was not to materialize. At a meeting at Chantilly on 21 January, the two Commanders-in-Chief had formally

* The former province of Artois (capital, Arras) formed the greater part of the present *Département* of the Pas-de-Calais.

MAP 1

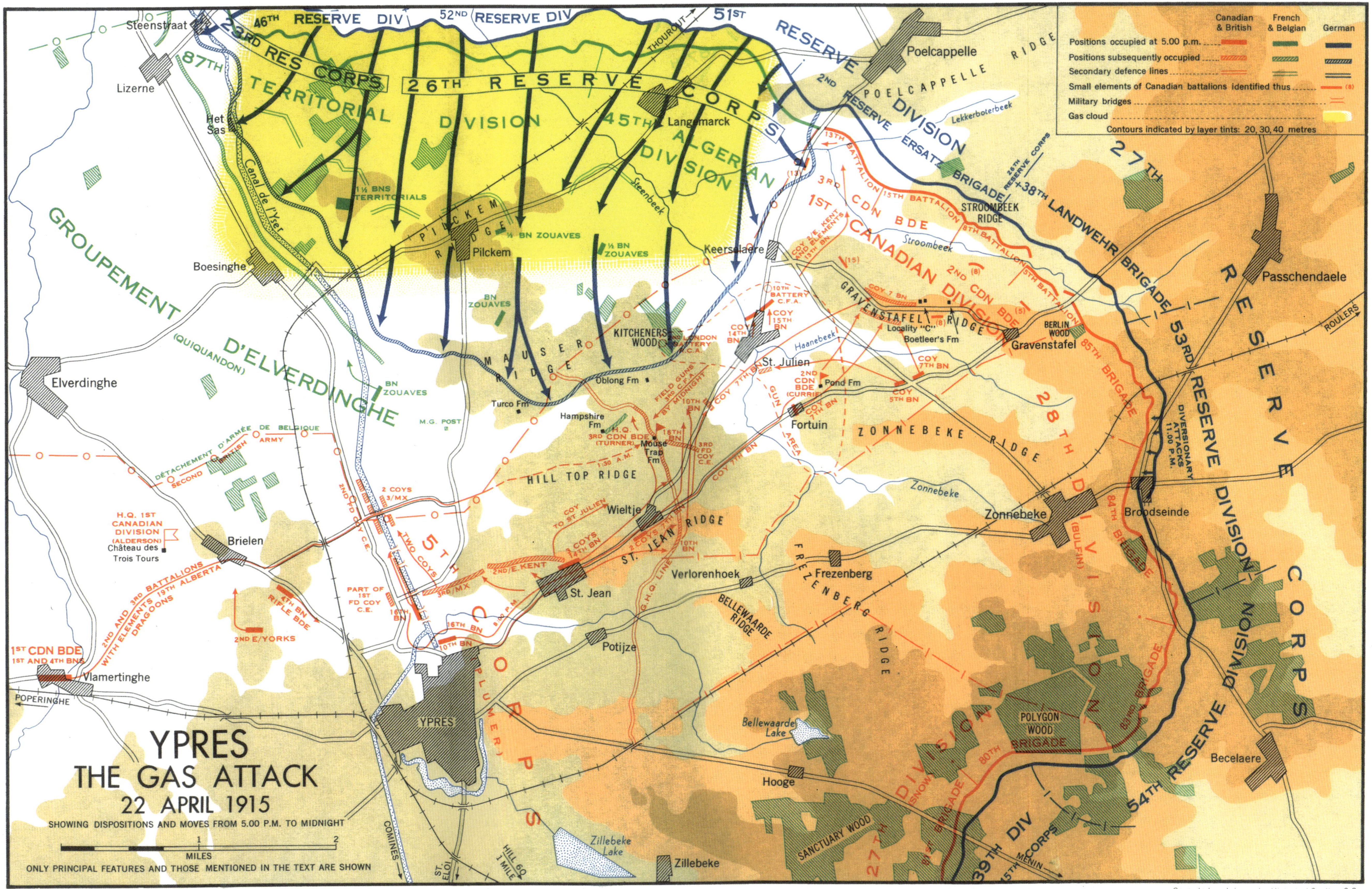

Reproduced by Army Survey Establishment

Compiled and drawn by Historical Section G.S.

agreed that as soon as the arrival of additional British troops in France permitted, Sir John French would relieve the 9th and 20th Corps of the French Eighth Army, which held the Ypres sector. The 20th Corps would be used to extend the Tenth Army's front northward across the La Bassée Canal by taking over the sector of the 1st British Corps; the 9th Corps was required to strengthen the projected French attack. Field-Marshal French had counted on the arrival of the 29th British and 1st Canadian Divisions to enable him to carry out the agreed reliefs. But the 29th Division—it was the last of the Regular divisions, having been formed from units brought from overseas stations—was diverted to Gallipoli, and its Territorial replacement would require additional training before it could be put in the trenches. On 18 February he told Joffre that he could not both mount the La Bassée attack and relieve French forces in the Ypres Salient.[4] He held firmly to his decision during further correspondence in which Joffre pointedly compared the lengths of front held by British and French forces. Finally on 7 March Joffre told the British C.-in-C. that while he had commenced offensive operations in Champagne in mid-February, "the troops at my disposal do not allow me to undertake the attack with the Tenth Army at present".[5] The British attack thus became an independent operation.

General Sir Douglas Haig's first objective was the straggling village of Neuve Chapelle, which lay opposite the centre of the First Army's front, less than half a mile from the forward trenches. Following a preliminary bombardment to smash the German breastworks and wire, four divisions of the Indian Corps and the 4th Corps, acting as a "battering-ram", were to "carry the Germans off their legs" and push forward to the Aubers Ridge, about three miles distant. The assaulting force would be in preponderant strength: forty-eight battalions would be opposed by only three German battalions manning the defences, and not more than four additional enemy battalions were expected to be available as reinforcements on the day of attack. On the British left the Canadian Division (which on 8 March had come directly under command of the First Army) was to make a demonstration with fire along its entire front in order to prevent German reinforcement of the battle area from that sector. If a British break-through developed, the Canadians would be ready to advance on orders from the First Army.[6]

When the bombardment began at 7:30 a.m. on 10 March, the Canadian divisional artillery shelled enemy positions opposite, and as the assault went in thirty-five minutes later, riflemen and machine-gunners opened bursts of rapid fire which continued at fifteen-minute intervals throughout the day. The main attack took the enemy completely by surprise, and within twenty minutes a breach 1600 yards wide had been opened in the German line. By nine o'clock British troops had cleared Neuve Chapelle, and with virtually no resistance in sight were halted on a pre-arranged line, awaiting orders from their corps headquarters to resume the offensive. Never were the disadvantages of a rigid control from a high level more disastrously demonstrated. With telephone and telegraph lines broken by enemy shelling, transmission of information to the rear and the

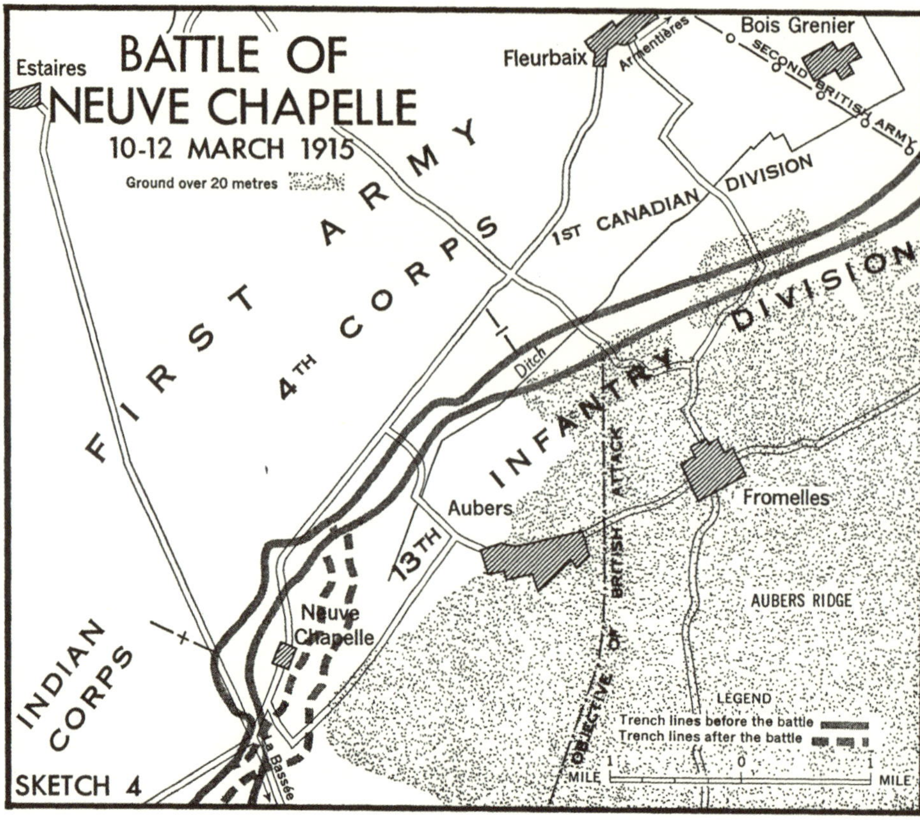

return of orders to the forward troops proved a slow and cumbersome process, taking an hour or more in each direction. Each corps commander, failing to realize the golden opportunity for rapid exploitation in the centre, waited for his flank (where progress had been slower) to get forward; and then the 4th Corps waited for the Indian Corps, so that both might move simultaneously. It was 2:50 p.m. before orders were issued for both corps to resume the advance at 3:30. Yet the time taken to relay these successively through division, brigade, and battalion headquarters meant that the companies in the front line did not begin moving until after half-past five, as dusk was falling. In the meantime the enemy had had at least five uninterrupted hours in which to bring up reinforcements and prepare new defences, so that the British attack was opposed by double the strength which it had faced that morning.[7]

This time there was no surprise, and artillery preparation was inadequate. Heavy fire from well-sited German machine-guns inflicted damaging casualties on the infantry as they crossed the flat fields. The advance came to a halt. During the night the Germans closed the breach with a well-wired rallying line linking up strongpoints armed with machine-guns, and brought forward new batteries. The Allied artillery, unable to determine the location of either the German guns or the new entrenchments, could not usefully support the infantry's early-morning renewal of the attack. It was quickly checked by the enemy's fire, and an afternoon attempt to advance was equally fruitless and costly. Throughout the day the Canadian Division repeated its role of the 10th, though to little effect, for a shortage of ammunition limited the artillery to a daily allotment of from ten to fifteen rounds a gun, unless enemy batteries should disclose themselves, when ammunition was to be "expended freely".[8]

Early on 12 March, after a pre-dawn bombardment of the Allied positions, the Germans counter-attacked with twenty battalions. British unit commanders were well prepared and the full force of their rifle and machine-gun fire threw back the enemy with very heavy losses. Previous orders by Sir Douglas Haig for a renewal of the British advance at 10:30 a.m. kept the forward troops from immediately exploiting the German setback, and there was a further postponement of two hours because of a thick haze which hindered artillery observation. The attack brought only further British losses, and at 10:40 p.m. orders from Haig to establish a new defensive line on the ground gained ended the battle.* For a while during the afternoon reports of sweeping British gains had caused the 3rd Canadian Brigade to be alerted for an advance; and towards evening the Army Commander asked Sir John French for a division from general reserve to relieve the 1st and 2nd Canadian Brigades for participation in the expected break-through. But the reports of success proved unfounded, and the Canadians remained in their trenches.

Neuve Chapelle cost the First Army 12,892 casualties (including one hundred in the 1st Canadian Division—which was no more than the normal wastage for that period in the line). German losses, estimated at twelve thousand, included 1687 officers and men taken prisoner. Though the tactical gains were disappointing, this first planned British offensive had certain useful results. The realization that neither the Germans nor their defences were invulnerable contributed much to the morale of the Allied soldiers. The B.E.F. was now held in greater respect, both by the enemy, who would not again dare to thin out to a minimum his defensive forces on a British front, and by the French High Command, who would no longer relegate the British role to taking over additional frontage so as to relieve French troops for offensive action.[10] Although many of the lessons that the operation had to teach were to be disregarded far too long by Allied commanders, at least one received immediate attention. A General Staff "Memorandum on Operations" issued by Sir Douglas Haig's headquarters on 14 March stressed the importance of displaying "enterprise and initiative" in the attack. It criticized the "inexcusable" inaction of officers who would not advance because they had "not received specific orders to do so from their immediate superiors".

The Canadians' remaining stay in the Fleurbaix sector was uneventful. Their 24-day tour in the front line ended on 27 March when they were relieved by

* In a wire to Lord Kitchener early next day, the C.-in-C. blamed the cessation of the advance on "the fatigue of the troops, and, above all . . . the want of ammunition".[9]

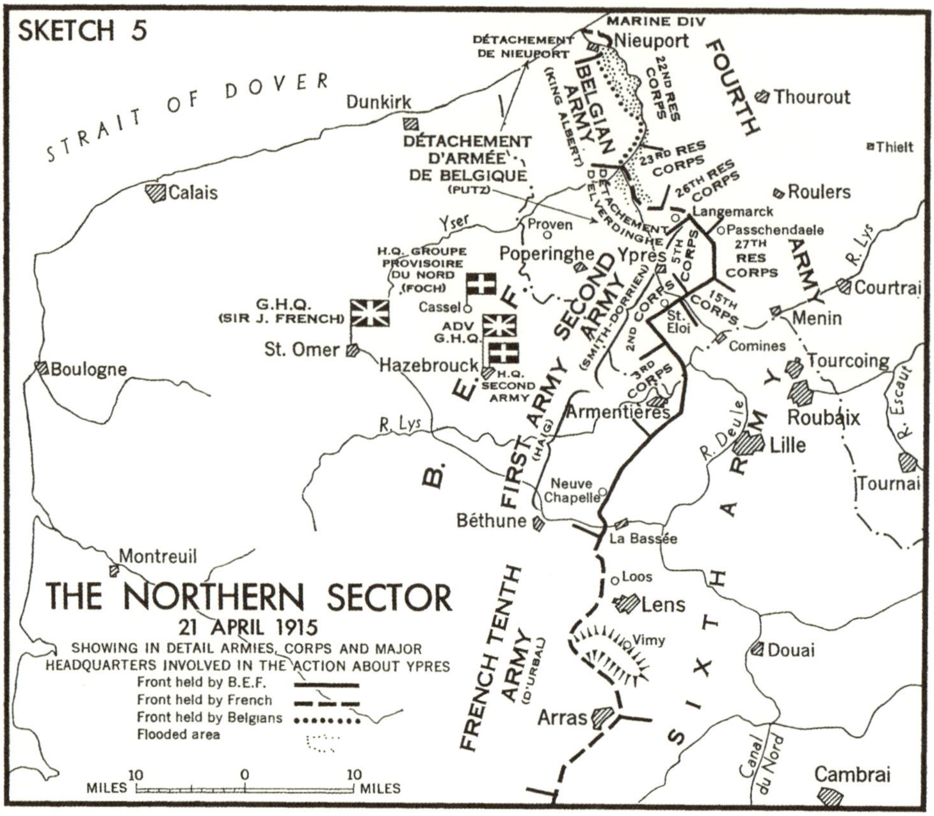

the British 8th Division and went into army reserve at Estaires, five miles behind the line. Almost immediately demands for working parties broke in on the relative calm of life in billets. Units of all three brigades took their turn at trench-digging, and this, combined with a number of training schemes rehearsing the attack, pointed to an early return to action. On 1 April orders from Sir Douglas Haig returned the Canadian Division to the Second Army,* placing it under command of the 5th Corps, which had been formed in mid-February under Lieut.-General Sir H.C.O. Plumer. On the 5th and two succeeding days the Canadians marched across the rolling Flanders countryside to the Cassel area—about seventeen miles west of Ypres, to begin a week of preparation for new tasks.

The Canadian move formed part of the approaching relief—long advocated by General Joffre—of the French 9th and 20th Corps in the Ypres Salient. On 1 April Sir Douglas Haig, deciding that the first three Territorial divisions—46th (North Midland), 47th (2nd London) and 48th (South Midland)—which reached France in February and March, had received sufficient training to replace regular divisions in the field, notified Joffre that he was extending his front north-

* It was not the first time that the Army Commander, General Smith-Dorrien, had had Canadians under his command. During the South African War he had commanded the 19th Brigade, which included the 2nd (Special Service) Battalion, Royal Canadian Regiment.

ward five miles to the Ypres-Poelcappelle road. Responsibility for the new sector was given to General Plumer, who between 2 and 17 April relieved three French divisions with, from south to north, the 27th, 28th and 1st Canadian Divisions.

These moves placed two-thirds of the Ypres Salient within the Second Army's boundaries. Only the northern flank, extending westward five miles from opposite Poelcappelle to the Yser Canal at Steenstraat, remained in French hands. It was manned by two divisions—the 45th (Algerian), adjoining the Canadians, and on its left the 87th (Territorial), next to the sector held by the Belgian Army. These two divisions and a detachment of cavalry made up the Groupement d'Elverdinghe (named from a town four miles north-west of Ypres), commanded by the G.O.C. 45th Division. This group together with the Groupement de Nieuport between the Belgians and the coast formed the Détachement d'Armée de Belgique, under General Putz; while all French forces from south of Arras to the sea (including in addition to the foregoing the Tenth Army in the Arras-Vimy-Lens sector) constituted the Groupe Provisoire du Nord, under the command of General Ferdinand Foch, with headquarters at Cassel. As General Joffre's representative he was responsible for coordinating the operations of these French formations with those of the British and Belgians.[11]

The Ypres Salient

At the conclusion of the unsuccessful German attempts to break the deadlock in Flanders in the late autumn of 1914 the Allied line in front of Ypres formed a deep curve seventeen miles long, extending from Steenstraat (on the Yser Canal, five miles north-west of the town) around to St. Eloi (nearly three miles south of Ypres). Throughout the winter this perimeter had remained unchanged.

At the focal point of the Salient was the ancient moated town of Ypres, which the Canadians first saw in April 1915. By that time German bombardment had damaged the stately 500-year old Cloth Hall and Cathedral, but many streets were still unharmed, and most of the inhabitants were still living at home. War had not yet devastated the fertile, densely populated area of the Salient. The network of roads which spread out across the Flanders plain linked Ypres with villages, hamlets and farms to north, east and south still tenanted though many were within two miles of the firing line. The largest of these communities, proceeding clockwise around the perimeter, were Langemarck (in the north-east angle of the Salient), St. Julien (on the Poelcappelle road), Zonnebeke (about half-way down the eastern flank), and Zillebeke (two miles south-east of Ypres).

A number of physical features were to have an important bearing on the tactics employed by both sides. The low sandy ridge which ran in a north-easterly direction from Messines to Passchendaele, rising no more than 200 feet above sea level, or 150 feet above Ypres, marked the south-eastern flank of the Salient. From it the land fell away gradually to the north-west, a series of subsidiary spurs at right angles to the main ridge forming the watershed of the muddy little streams feeding the Steenbeek, which flowed sluggishly through St. Julien to be joined south of Langemarck by the Lekkerboterbeek. Another series of four ridges running east and west, just high enough above the plain to overlook Ypres from the north, lay between the Steenbeek and the Yser Canal. The most northerly of these, named from the hamlet of Pilckem on its slopes, was to be the enemy's first objective in the Battles of Ypres, 1915. A feature which was to impose a limitation on the movement of Allied reserves and otherwise affect the battle was the barrier presented by the Yser Canal, which passed behind Ypres and ran in a generally northerly direction through Steenstraat to the sea. The canal's normal road bridges, augmented by a number of military bridges north of Ypres, constituted defiles constricting the movement of troops and became the targets of German artillery fire.

The 1st Canadian Division's relief of the French 11th Division took place between 14 and 17 April, General Alderson assuming command at 10:00 a.m. on the 17th. The Canadian sector, 4500 yards in length, lay obliquely astride the valley of the Stroombeek, northernmost of the Steenbeek's tributaries within the Salient. Between 1000 and 2000 yards to the rear was the Gravenstafel Ridge, which took its name from the hamlet lying just inside the Canadian boundary with the 28th Division. On the left the junction with the 45th (Algerian) Division lay 1000 yards south-west of Poelcappelle on the road leading to Ypres. The Canadian front was held by the 2nd Brigade on the right and the 3rd on the left, each with two battalions in the line, one in support, and one in divisional reserve on the northern outskirts of Ypres. The 1st Brigade was in corps reserve at Vlamertinghe, two and a half miles west of Ypres.[12] French artillery remained in position while the infantry was taking over, and was relieved section for section on the two succeeding nights by batteries of the 2nd and 3rd Brigades, Canadian Field Artillery. Reports on the divisional relief pay tribute to the courtesy and helpfulness of French officers and men in making the handing over as easy and methodical as possible.

The Canadians immediately found that French and British methods of conducting a war differed considerably. This was most noticeable with respect to the forward defences, where the British policy (as set forth in the Scheme of Defence issued by General Alderson) was "to hold the front trenches at all costs". The French, however, believed in manning the front line only lightly; if attacked the infantry would retire, allowing the artillery's effective 75-millimetre field guns to come into action to stop the enemy. It was an early example of the doctrine of "defence in depth" which, as we shall see, within the next two years the enemy was to adopt and practise with considerable success. In view of these different standards, it is hardly surprising that the state of the French front line came as a great shock to the men of the 1st Canadian Division. They found unconnected lengths of field works without the customary traverses for protection against enfilading fire. Because the closeness of water to the surface prevented digging to a depth of more than two feet, there was a need for building up the parapets into breastworks of sod, mud or sandbag four feet or more high, but these were flimsily constructed, and seldom thick enough to stop bullets; in some places they did not exist. There was no parados to give protection from the rear. Besides these serious shortcomings from the standpoint of security and safety, the trenches were sadly deficient in the matter of sanitation. A report to the C.R.E. 1st Canadian Division by one of his officers described the 2nd Brigade's sector of the line as being "in a deplorable state and in a very filthy condition, all the little broken down side trenches and shell holes apparently being used as latrines and burial places for bodies". The 3rd Brigade's sector was equally bad. The trenches and the ground behind them were littered with dead, buried and unburied, and the numerous shallow graves greatly hampered digging.[13]

A "subsidiary line" named in the 5th Corps instructions was shown on French tactical maps as being under construction or projected along the crest of the Gravenstafel Ridge. It was far from complete, and existed merely as a series of unlinked strongpoints or shelter trenches. One group of shelter trenches was at Locality "C", a position on the sky-line opposite the centre of the Canadian sector; another covered Gravenstafel, and one was midway between these at Boetleer's Farm. Considerably stronger was the G.H.Q. Line,* which ran northward from Zillebeke Lake (a mile and a half behind the front) to a point on the Poelcappelle road half a mile east of Wieltje, turning thence north-west to link up with defences intended to cover the village of Boesinghe and its bridges over the Yser Canal. This well-sited position consisted of a number of redoubts, 30 yards across, about a quarter of a mile apart, protected by a continuous belt of wire six yards wide and three feet high. There was one major drawback—being passable at only certain road and track crossings, the G.H.Q. Line was, like the Yser Canal, seriously to restrict the forward movement of reserves. Each brigade holding the front trenches was assigned a section of the G.H.Q. Line to occupy in the event of a withdrawal, and all regimental officers were required to familiarize themselves with the position without delay.[14] In addition to its responsibilities in manning posts in the "subsidiary line", the brigade on the divisional left was charged with the defence of St. Julien, a key point covering the bridge by which the Ypres-Poelcappelle road crossed the Steenbeek.

The Canadians immediately began converting the front line into a defensive position more in keeping with British standards. Every available man in the forward companies went to work rebuilding breastworks, deepening existing trenches where possible and adding traverses and communication trenches, linking all into a continuous work guarded by an unbroken belt of barbed wire. While this construction was in hand, reserve companies improved the positions in the subsidiary line. Some reliefs took place during the first week and there were minor boundary adjustments. By the morning of 22 April the 2nd Canadian Brigade was holding the division's right sector with the 5th Battalion (next to the 28th

* This position corresponded to the G.H.Q. 2nd Line in the Fleurbaix sector and elsewhere (above, p. 50); but northward from Fleurbaix to Ypres there was no G.H.Q. 1st Line.

Division) and the 8th Battalion. The 3rd Brigade had the 15th Battalion on the right and the 13th on the left. Each of these units had detachments of from two platoons to a company manning posts on or near the Gravenstafel Ridge. St. Julien was garrisoned by two and a half companies drawn from battalions of the 3rd Brigade. The 1st Brigade had been moved from Vlamertinghe to Proven, north-west of Poperinghe, and placed in Second Army Reserve for employment if needed in an operation by the 2nd Corps against Hill 60, just across the inter-corps boundary.

Hill 60 (designated by its altitude in metres) was an artificial mound of earth thrown up by the excavation of a cutting on the adjacent Ypres-Comines railway. Its position on the crest of the Messines-Passchendaele ridge made it the highest point overlooking the Salient, and one to be denied to German observers if possible. The 2nd Corps' assault was made by the 13th Brigade of the 5th Division on the evening of 17 April, after five mines containing in all five tons of explosives had been fired under the German positions. The enemy reacted vigorously with heavy shelling and repeated infantry counter-attacks. Bitter fighting continued for the next four days as British battalions strove to retain the battered mound. Early on the 21st the 1st Canadian Brigade, commanded by Brig.-Gen. M. S. Mercer, which had returned to Vlamertinghe the previous day, was placed under orders of the 5th Division and put on one hour's notice to move to Hill 60.[15] The morning of the 22nd found the 2nd and 4th Battalions standing by, their commanders having reconnoitred routes forward to the battle area.

But the move to Hill 60 did not take place. Before the day ended the 1st Brigade was to find itself committed to action closer at hand.

German Dispositions and Plans

The Germans were holding the perimeter opposing the six Allied divisions within the Salient with seven divisions and two independent brigades, all grouped in four army corps of Duke Albrecht's Fourth Army. Next to the Ypres-Comines Canal the 30th and 39th Divisions* of the 15th Corps faced the British 5th and 27th Divisions. Farther north was the 27th Reserve Corps, with its 54th and 53rd Reserve Divisions confronting the 28th Division, and the 38th Landwehr Brigade on the Corps right flank, opposite the 2nd Canadian Brigade. Then came the 26th Reserve Corps, which had the 2nd Reserve Ersatz Brigade under command of the 51st Reserve Division opposing the 3rd Canadian Brigade, while the 101st Reserve Brigade of the 51st Reserve Division and the 52nd Reserve Division were facing respectively the 45th Algerian Division and the right of the French 87th Territorial Division. The 51st Reserve Division had its 102nd Reserve Brigade in reserve, and the 37th Landwehr Brigade was in corps reserve nearby. The north-west shoulder of the Salient, opposite the Franco-Belgian boundary, was held by the 23rd Reserve Corps with the 46th and 45th

* German divisions and regiments not otherwise described are regular infantry formations.

Reserve Divisions, the latter facing the Yser. On the rest of the Fourth Army's front were the 22nd Reserve Corps along the Yser Canal and the Marine Division on the Belgian coast. In army reserve were the Guard Cavalry Division, the 43rd Reserve Division (from the 22nd Reserve Corps) and the 4th Ersatz Division.[16]

Ever since the Battles of Ypres, 1914, the existence of the Allied-held Salient had remained a challenge to the Fourth Army. But no major operation to reduce it could be contemplated, for by the end of March the German G.H.Q. had reached a decision to stand on the defensive in the west while making a determined effort in the east "to annihilate the offensive power of the Russians for all time".[17] By mid-April Austro-German armies were concentrating for the great offensive in Galicia which was to carry them 250 miles eastward by winter. To draw attention from these troop movements German forces on the Western Front were directed to engage in lively activity "combined with attacks, in so far as the modest numbers remaining there permitted".[18] An enterprise of this kind, which entailed the gaining of no major objective, was particularly suitable for testing new techniques or new weapons. "The battles of Ypres which began on the 22nd April", states the *Reichsarchiv*, "had their origin on the German side solely in the desire to try the new weapon, gas, thoroughly at the front."[19]

With the introduction of trench warfare conventional means of attack had proved largely ineffective. We are told by General von Falkenhayn that the Germans' adoption of chemical warfare (contrary to the provisions of the Hague Conventions of 1899 and 1906)* arose from their need for finding a weapon capable of preparing "for assault those positions which were constructed with all the modern methods of the art of fortification."[22] Early in 1915 a 15-centimetre shell containing a gas charge was tried out against the Russians. It proved unsuccessful because of the great cold and a shortage of the guns required to obtain the necessary mass effect.

A decision was taken to use chlorine gas as a cloud, propelled towards the enemy by a suitable wind. The gas was readily available at low cost—it was used in the famous German dye industry—and could be easily transported in cylinders already made for industrial use. Germany produced 37 tons of chlorine a day (less than five days' production would be used on 22 April) against a trivial amount manufactured in Britain. A heavy gas, chlorine was not easily dissipated, and clung to the ground as the cloud rolled forward. It attacked the lungs, immediately incapacitating those exposed to it; sometimes it proved fatal. Since it left no noticeable residue, attacking troops could move forward behind the easily visible cloud.[23]

By the end of January 6000 cylinders of chlorine gas were ready for use by the Fourth Army, the High Command having ordered Duke Albrecht to employ

* In attempting to justify this infringement of the rules of war, the German War Ministry and High Command in 1917 charged the French Army with having used a rifle grenade filled with bromic acid, and a hand grenade filled with ethyl bromo-acetate—a lachrymatory liquid.[20] The German Official History brands the French use of gas shells and gas hand grenades from the end of February 1915 as "the first breach of international agreement in the sphere of gas warfare".[21] These charges were unproved. It should be noted that the Hague agreements barred the use of such projectiles only when their *sole* object was the diffusion of asphyxiating gases.

the new weapon against the Ypres Salient. At first part of the 15th Corps' sector opposite the south-east face of the Salient was selected for the attempt, and by mid-February newly organized pioneer companies had finished digging in the cylinders. But the choice of location reflects little credit on the German meteorologists, for though by 10 March the line of cylinders had been extended to cover the whole of the 15th Corps' front, the wind consistently failed to blow from the south or south-east. On the 25th the Army Commander ordered cylinders not yet installed to be moved to the northern flank of the Salient, in the sector held by the 26th Reserve Corps and the 46th Reserve Division. By 11 April a line of 5730 cylinders extended from 1200 yards west of Poelcappelle to just east of Steenstraat. For ten days there was no wind from the right direction, and postponements of the attack did little to increase the enthusiasm of the troops for the new device. "Almost throughout the forces", records the German Official History, "both leaders and troops regarded with mistrust the still untried means of offence, if they were not entirely inclined against it."[24] Von Falkenhayn was urging the earliest possible execution of the attack, as he intended to transfer to the Eastern Front the 15th Corps and the 26th Reserve Corps (as well as the 4th Ersatz Division in army reserve).[25] On 21 April conditions were considered favourable enough for the undertaking to be ordered for 5:45 the next morning. But the 22nd dawned clear and calm; and at half-past five the attack was put off until evening.

The Allies had not been without warnings that the Germans were contemplating the use of gas. The 5th Corps' "Summary of Information" of 15 April, issued through divisions down to battalion level, reported the interrogation of a deserter from the 51st Reserve Division who had surrendered to the French 11th Division before its relief by the Canadians. The prisoner* revealed the planned attack and gave details of the preparations that had been made to release asphyxiating gas through pipes fitted to cylinders buried deeply in the German forward trenches.[27] An agent of the Belgian Army independently reported that the attack would be made in the Ypres area on the night of 15-16 April. These disclosures corroborated earlier statements about German preparations south-east of the Salient given by prisoners from the 15th Corps and reported in the *Bulletin* of the French Tenth Army on 30 March. On 16 April a Belgian Army information bulletin published an agent's report of a German rush order placed in Ghent for 20,000 mouth protectors, "to protect the men against the effects of asphyxiating gas". The report stated specifically that the gas attack would come on the front of the 26th Reserve Corps—where it actually did come.[28]

Little attention seems to have been paid to these various reports. There was incredulity either that the German High Command would sanction the use of gas, or that if gas were used it could be effective over more than a very limited area. The commander of the 11th Division later declared that when he issued

* Publication of the deserter's name in a post-war article by the former commander of the French 11th Division[26] led to an investigation in Germany which culminated in 1932 in a sentence by the Reich Supreme Court to a ten-year prison term and loss of civil rights.

orders for special measures to be taken to meet a gas discharge he was told by the French General Headquarters, "All this gas business need not be taken seriously."[29] There was no great concern in the Canadian Division over these warnings (though the artillery had orders to search the German line and look out for explosions), perhaps because instructions from the Second Army published on 15 April called for reticence in dealing with "secret" or "confidential" matters, and because the night of 15-16 April (when the 2nd Canadian Infantry Brigade was already in the line) passed without a German attack. By 22 April, as we have noted, the fighting at Hill 60 was about to draw in Canadian forces. Attention was further diverted from the scene of the forthcoming battle by the bombardment of Ypres. On the afternoon of the 20th a 42-centimetre howitzer had begun dropping 2000-lb shells into the city with devastating results.

Von Falkenhayn had emphasized to the Fourth Army that it was more important to launch the gas attack at an early date than to obtain a deep penetration. He rejected Duke Albrecht's request for an extra division to be held in readiness to exploit possible success, not only because he had none to spare (particularly with the prospect of postponements because of the weather), but because he had doubts as to what the gas would accomplish. Accordingly the operation was planned with the limited objective of the Pilckem Ridge. On the 26th Reserve Corps' front the 51st Reserve Division would take Langemarck and the 52nd Pilckem. On the German right the 45th Reserve Division (of the 23rd Reserve Corps) was to seize Steenstraat, while the 46th Reserve Division secured the line of the Yser Canal, with bridgeheads at Het Sas and Boesinghe. The Fourth Army believed that the attainment of these objectives would force the Allies to abandon the Ypres Salient. Subsequent objectives specified the capture of the Yser Canal south to and including Ypres.[30]

The Battle of Gravenstafel Ridge—The First Gas Attack, 22 April

The morning and early afternoon of Thursday, 22 April, a bright sunny day, brought no variation from the daily routine of the troops of the 1st Canadian Division. The 2nd and 3rd Brigades were in the line, and at Vlamertinghe the 1st Brigade, alerted for possible action at Hill 60, continued training. Shortly before 3:00 p.m. the 3rd Brigade received notification of one hundred mouth organs waiting to be picked up at Divisional Headquarters.[31] The Salient had been under fairly heavy shelling since the 19th, the German fire being directed mainly on roads and bridges north and east of Ypres. There was a lull during the afternoon, but soon after four o'clock the French front line on the north of the Salient came under a violent bombardment, which gradually shifted to the Canadian sector. At five o'clock the Germans opened the valves of the gas cylinders* for from six to eight minutes, releasing more than one hundred and sixty tons of chlorine into a light north-east wind.[32]

The first warning to the Canadians was the sound of small-arms fire and the rapid discharge of French 75s coming from the northern flank. Almost simultaneously the 3rd Brigade reported "a cloud of green vapour several hundred yards in length" between the French trenches and the enemy's front line.[33] The chlorine drifted southward at five or six miles an hour, producing an initial concentration about half a mile in depth. It caught in its deadly embrace the Tirailleurs and African Light Infantry holding the Langemarck sector and the Territorials of the 87th Division farther west. Half suffocated, and with eyes streaming and nose and throat burning, their morale broken by this unexpected terror, many abandoned their positions and fled, leaving behind large numbers of dead.

The Canadian sector had escaped the gas concentration, and at all levels of command steps were taken to deal with the serious situation that was developing on the northern flank. General Alderson and his C.R.A. were at the crossroads 1000 yards north-east of St. Julien when the attack started. They made their way on foot back to their horses at Wieltje and then rode back to Divisional Headquarters, in the Château des Trois Tours, west of Brielen. From here the first order was issued just before six. Shortly before 9:30 p.m. the C.R.E. reported the canal bridges prepared for demolition.[34] Meanwhile in the front line the left company of the 13th Battalion sent two platoons to line the ditch of the Poelcappelle road in support of a small party of Tirailleurs, who from their original trench were exchanging fire with Germans occupying a parallel hedge. Some 600 yards nearer Ypres, covering the culvert over the Lekkerboterbeek, two more platoons of the 13th Battalion manned the ditch, their numbers increased by Algerian riflemen driven back by the gas. The battalion commander, Lt.-Col. F.O.W. Loomis, who was also Commandant, St. Julien, ordered his small garrison there into battle positions, placing one company on each side of the road north of the village, and holding the remaining two platoons in reserve. These dispositions left unguarded a stretch of more than a mile of the road north of St. Julien, except for the 10th Battery C.F.A. south of Keerselaere.

West of St. Julien there was a still wider gap, which, lying nearer the centre of the German attack, presented a greater danger. A British 4.7-inch battery in Kitcheners Wood,† half a mile from the village, was the only manned position between the former French line and the 3rd Brigade Headquarters at Mouse Trap Farm, 1000 yards north of Wieltje. At six o'clock Brig.-Gen. Turner ordered the 14th Battalion, in reserve at St. Jean (with one company in St. Julien), to occupy a portion of the G.H.Q. Line from the Ypres-St. Julien road to beyond Mouse

* Of the 5730 cylinders used (above, p. 60) 1600 were of the large, commercial type, containing 41.5 kilograms of gas; and 4130 of a specially prepared smaller type, containing 20 kg. of gas. The total weight in all cylinders was 149,000 kg.

†Named not from Lord Kitchener, but from the French *Bois des Cuisiniers.* The French, who had occupied this sector before the Canadians, may have found the wood a good hideout for unit cooks.

Trap Farm. On its left a group of 500 Zouaves extended south-westward to Hampshire Farm (about 600 yards west of Brigade Headquarters), while on its right the 3rd Field Company C.E. covered the Wieltje-St. Julien road. By that time German rifle fire was coming from Mauser Ridge, which ran westward from Kitcheners Wood. Not until 8:00 p.m. did Turner receive a delayed message releasing to him from divisional reserve his fourth battalion, the 16th Battalion, which had meanwhile lined the west bank of the Yser Canal. Elements of the 1st and 2nd Field Companies C.E. were left to guard the vulnerable canal bridges. Brig.-Gen. Currie did not wait for a parallel message releasing the 10th Battalion from reserve. He took control of the battalion and had it moving forward shortly after six o'clock.[35]

With telephone lines broken by enemy shelling, information reaching brigade and divisional headquarters was slow and frequently inaccurate. A series of messages dispatched by hand from 3rd Brigade Headquarters between 6:45 and 7:10 p.m. erroneously reported that the left of the Canadian front line had been "forced back towards St. Julien", and then "forced back on G.H.Q. line". The 1st Canadian Division at once relayed this faulty intelligence to the 5th Corps, and ordered the 2nd Brigade "to hang on and take care of your left".[36] Currie, whose headquarters were at Pond Farm, south-east of St. Julien, immediately ordered the 10th Battalion's C.O. to report to the commander of the 3rd Brigade. To secure his own sector he concentrated the whole of the 7th Battalion about Locality "C" on the Gravenstafel Ridge.

Reports of the German attack began reaching Second Army Headquarters at Hazebrouck at 6:45 p.m., and during the next two hours a disturbing picture developed of both French divisions having been driven from their first and second lines of defence with the loss of all their guns, and of virtually no formed bodies of French troops remaining east of the Yser Canal. This meant that except for the hasty dispositions made from within the resources of the 1st Canadian Division the Second Army's left flank lay open for 8000 yards. A successful German attack through this gap would not only threaten Ypres but would take in the rear the three divisions still holding the Salient.

One of General Smith-Dorrien's first moves towards establishing a new line was to release the 1st Canadian Infantry Brigade from army reserve at Vlamertinghe. This enabled the 5th Corps at 8:15 p.m. to hand over the 2nd and 3rd Battalions to General Alderson; they were immediately sent forward under the 3rd Brigade, marching across 3000 yards of open front under an escort of the Divisional Cavalry.[37] At the same time General Plumer put at Alderson's disposal the 2nd East Yorks, who were in the 28th Division's reserve a mile north-west of Ypres. This was the first of thirty-three British battalions to come under General Alderson's command during the battle.

Other reserves of the 27th and 28th Divisions were already on the move. The 27th Division had called forward the 4th Battalion, The Rifle Brigade to the St. Jean area. Earlier two battalions of the 28th Division—the 2nd Buffs (East Kent Regiment) and the 3rd Battalion, The Middlesex Regiment—had moved out from

St. Jean to the ridge north of the village, where they deployed westward as far as the Yser Canal. In front of them only a solitary French machine-gun post guarded the 3000-yard gap between Hampshire Farm and the canal.

Fortunately, however, the advance by the German centre and right had halted. Except on the canal flank both enemy corps had speedily gained their initial objectives. For some reason a number of the gas cylinders at the western end of the line had not been discharged, and Steenstraat was able to hold out against the 45th Reserve Division until late evening. The 46th Reserve Division crossed the canal north of Het Sas, but strong French resistance kept the division's left wing from reaching the eastern bank. The most rapid and deepest penetration was made by the 26th Reserve Corps, whose 52nd Reserve Division reached its initial objective, the Pilckem Ridge, by 5:40 p.m. Farther east the 51st Reserve Division was temporarily checked at the long, straggling village of Langemarck, where the garrison had escaped the full effects of the gas cloud. By six o'clock, however, the village ruins were in German possession, and the division was ordered to cross the Steenbeek, and if possible take St. Julien. Before nightfall forward troops had passed the Franco-British boundary and overrun Kitcheners Wood, capturing the four British guns there. Units of the 52nd Reserve Division had meanwhile occupied Mauser Ridge and were near the east bank of the canal overlooking the Boesinghe railway bridge. Orders came for the infantry to dig in at their present positions, and the 37th Landwehr Brigade was brought up from reserve to form a support line along the Pilckem Ridge.[38]

In recording the difficulties encountered by the 51st Reserve Division at Langemarck and farther east, the German Official History blames the fact that the gas "had not had a decisive effect, or else the troops had not followed it up immediately. So it was that the extreme right wing of the French and the Canadians adjoining on the east could offer an obstinate resistance."[39] The two isolated platoons of the 13th Battalion's No. 3 Company at the Lekkerboterbeek crossing fought with mounting casualties until overwhelmed by superior numbers. Farther north, at the left of the Canadian front line, the Algerian detachment was forced back to the Poelcappelle road, where the 13th Battalion's detachment, reinforced by two more platoons drawn from other companies, maintained a stalwart defence against the attackers' heavy rifle fire. South of Keerselaere guns of the 10th Field Battery, in action since early evening, halted a body of Germans marching on St. Julien. To cover the battery in its exposed position, within 500 yards of the enemy, the Commandant of the St. Julien garrison sent forward a party of 60 infantrymen of the 14th and 15th Battalions and a machine-gun detachment of the 13th Battalion.

This manoeuvre, which contributed to the safe withdrawal of the 10th Battery's guns, owed much of its success to the skill and daring of Lance-Corporal Frederick Fisher in working his Colt machine-gun forward under heavy fire and bringing it into effective action against the Germans. Fisher, who was awarded the Victoria Cross, was killed next day.[40]

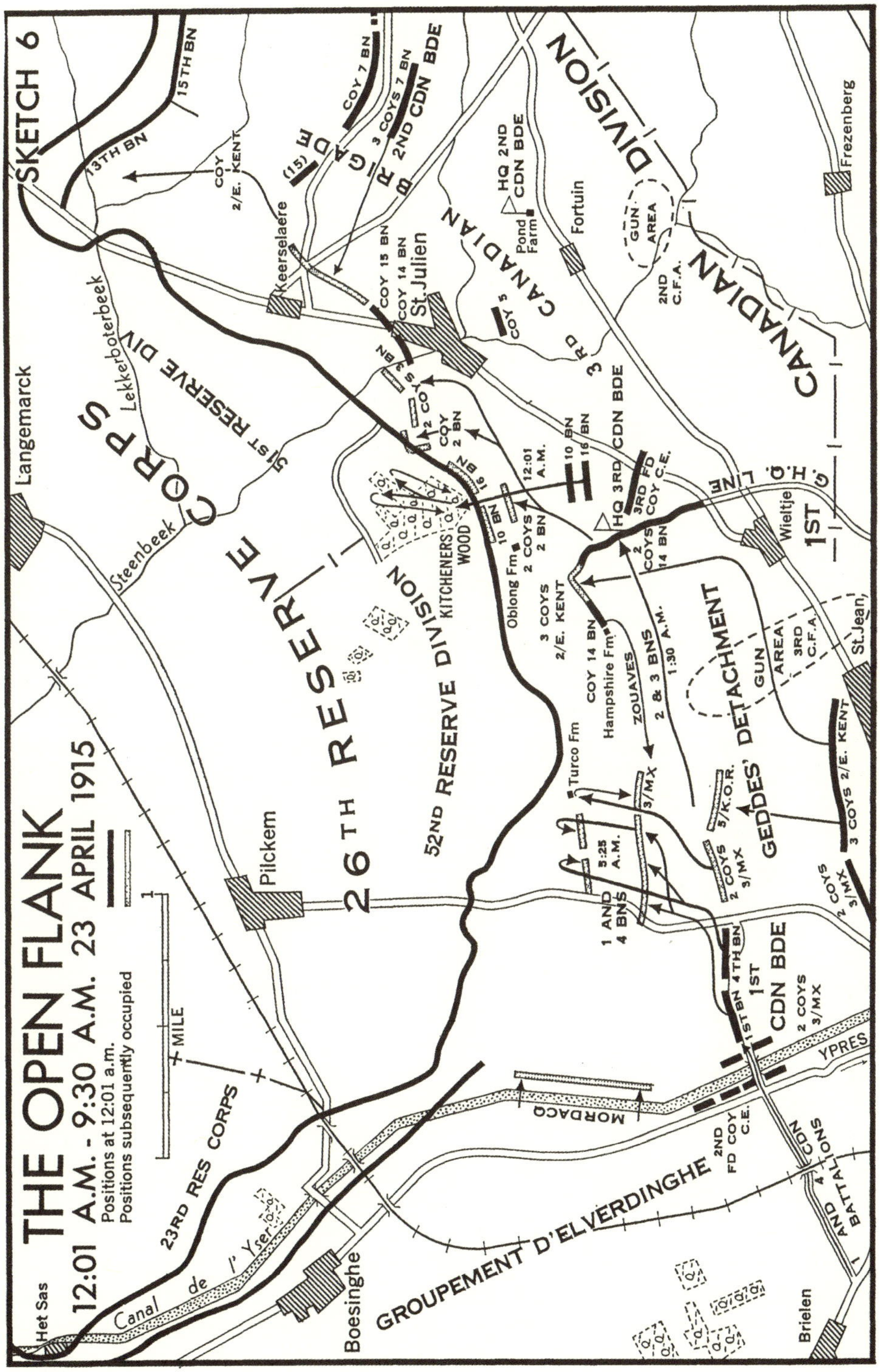
SKETCH 6
THE OPEN FLANK
12:01 A.M. - 9:30 A.M. 23 APRIL 1915
Positions at 12:01 a.m.
Positions subsequently occupied
MILE
Het Sas
Canal de l'Yser
Boesinghe
Pilckem
Langemarck
Steenbeek
Lekkerboterbeek
Keerselaere
St. Julien
Pond Farm
Fortuin
Frezenberg
Wieltje
St. Jean
Brielen
YPRES
Kitcheners Wood
Oblong Fm
Turco Fm
Hampshire Fm
23RD RES CORPS
GROUPEMENT D'ELVERDINGHE
MORDACQ
26TH RESERVE CORPS
52ND RESERVE DIVISION
51ST RESERVE DIV
GEDDES' DETACHMENT
ZOUAVES
1ST CDN BDE
3RD CDN BDE
2ND CDN BDE
CANADIAN DIVISION
G.H.Q. LINE

The Counter-Attacks of 22-23 April

About 8:00 p.m. on the 22nd a French liaison officer asked General Alderson for Canadian cooperation in a counter-attack that the 45th Division was preparing to launch towards Pilckem. The G.O.C. promptly ordered the 3rd Brigade to counter-attack with two battalions toward Kitcheners Wood. The attack was made about midnight from an assembly area east of Mouse Trap Farm, by the 10th Battalion (of the 2nd Brigade) and the 16th, which after its release from divisional reserve reached Brig.-Gen. Turner's Headquarters shortly before ten. The two battalions, with the 10th in the lead, advanced in "column of half battalion"— six waves of men marching shoulder to shoulder on a two-company front, the ranks of the forward battalion spaced at 30 paces, the rear at 20. One hundred bombers from the 2nd and 3rd Infantry Brigades accompanied the attack. Artillery support was provided by a British battery and the 9th and 12th Batteries of the 3rd Brigade C.F.A., firing on the northern part of the wood and beyond. The prescribed task was to "Clear wood C.10.d", but beyond this the hasty arrangements detailed no objectives nor did they provide any plan for consolidation.[41]

There was enough moon to silhouette the dark shape of Kitcheners Wood, and moving briskly the closely massed infantry, 1500 strong, covered half the 1000 yards to the objective before the alarm was given. Then heavy machine-gun and rifle fire burst from the trench which the Germans were holding south of the wood, and many of the Canadians fell. The final stretch of ground was covered on the run, and quickly taking the trench with bayonet and rifle butt, the two battalions pressed on. At 2:45 a.m. the 3rd Brigade reported to the 1st Division that the wood had been carried and the four captured British guns recovered. But success was short-lived. During the advance in the darkness over unknown ground companies and platoons had lost cohesion, many officers having become casualties, and the lack of a preconceived plan made consolidation difficult. The expected French attack on the left had not materialized. Rifle fire from that flank indicated that the Germans were still holding the north-west corner of the wood. Others were strongly entrenched with machine-guns at the south-western extremity. They were also in force on the opposite flank, east of Kitcheners Wood. In the circumstances it was decided to fall back to the trench originally held by the enemy south of the wood. As teams to remove the British guns had not yet arrived, these were abandoned, but not before their ammunition had been destroyed. The retirement was completed by four o'clock, as fewer than 500 survivors of the 10th and 16th Battalions having reversed the parapet began digging in on a line extended to 750 yards.[42]

While the assault on Kitcheners Wood was still in progress, the 2nd and 3rd Battalions had reported to Brig.-Gen. Turner. Ordering the 3rd Battalion to a position facing north behind the G.H.Q. Line, Turner sent the 2nd Battalion to aid the counter-attack. One company unsuccessfully assaulted the German strong-point south-west of the wood; a second occupied Oblong Farm to the left of the 10th Battalion; while a third dug in on the 16th Battalion's right flank. To fill the 500-yard gap west of St. Julien, Turner then moved up two companies of the 3rd Battalion. Meanwhile north-east of the village, in response to the 3rd Brigade's urgent appeal for help, Brig.-Gen. Currie shortly after 2:00 a.m. had ordered the 7th Battalion (less one company) to move westward from Locality "C" to extend the right flank of the St. Julien garrison to the end of the Gravenstafel Ridge. Thus by 5:30 on the morning of the 23rd a continuous though tenuous line had been established reaching south-westward from the crossroads east of Keerselaere to Oblong Farm. But from Keerselaere northward to the original front line the Allied flank still lay open for nearly a mile. In its stubborn defence of the Salient's new apex the 13th Battalion had received welcome reinforcement in the arrival, shortly before dawn, of its two platoons from the St. Julien garrison, and a company of the 2nd Buffs which the battalion commander, Colonel A. D. Geddes, had placed at the disposal of Lt.-Col. Loomis.

The second counter-attack of the night was hurriedly improvised to be carried out by the meagre forces available, and like many impromptu schemes it suffered from hasty planning and faulty coordination. Shortly after one o'clock the G.O.C. 5th Corps made available to General Alderson a composite brigade of four battalions of the 28th Division under the command of Colonel Geddes. This infantry group, which as "Geddes' Detachment" was to operate under the Canadian Division for the next five days, was ordered to fill the dangerous gap between the 3rd Canadian Brigade's left and the French right, "driving back any enemy that may have penetrated".[43] It appears to have been almost 3:00 a.m. when these orders reached Geddes, who, hampered by lack of staff, had difficulty in putting them into effect. Leaving two battalions uncommitted, he placed at the right edge of the gap his own battalion (less the company sent to reinforce the 13th Battalion), and at the left edge two companies of the 3rd Battalion, The Middlesex Regiment (the other two companies being left to guard the Brielen bridge over the Yser Canal).

In the meantime as a precautionary measure the 1st and 4th Battalions of the 1st Canadian Brigade were ordered to move east of the canal. They crossed opposite Brielen shortly after three o'clock, and at 3:47 Alderson ordered them to attack northward in cooperation with a projected French attack timed to begin at five. The French effort was to be made by two battalions of the 45th Division striking north-eastward from the Yser Canal against Pilckem; the Canadians were to attack on the east side of the Ypres-Pilckem road.[44] This was in the same area assigned to Geddes, whose weak force was preparing to advance on two widely separated axes. While the Canadians had been advised of his intended movements, it came as a surprise to Geddes when his left unexpectedly made contact with the 1st Battalion.

The two Canadian battalions had deployed on a 200-yard frontage just below the crest of Hill Top Ridge. Daylight disclosed the enemy busily digging in on Mauser Ridge, 1500 yards to the north. When no sign came of any French attack, the Commander of the 4th Battalion, Lt.-Col. A. P. Birchall, whose four companies were in front, assuming that the French movement was hidden by intervening hedges, at 5:25 gave the order to advance. As the leading waves moved down into the shallow valley, they were met by heavy rifle and machine-gun fire, which was soon supplemented by the enemy's artillery. On the right the two Middlesex companies steadily kept pace, and reinforced by a reserve company of the 1st Battalion occupied Turco Farm within 300 yards of the German position, only to be shelled out again by our own artillery.

This was the farthest point of advance. Casualties were heavy, for the supporting artillery—eight 18-pounders of the 10th and the composite 2nd-3rd Field Batteries and eight 4.5-inch howitzers of two British batteries—could not silence the fire from a mile of enemy trench. Beside the Pilckem road the 1st and 4th Battalions were pinned down in the valley bottom with an uncertain left flank, for though an assuring message had come from the French of three and a half battalions east of the canal and two more about to cross, nothing had been seen of any attack.[45] At 8.30 a.m. Brig.-Gen. Mercer ordered both Canadian battalions to dig in, and a request went to the French attack headquarters to fill the gap on the 1st Brigade's left.[46] During an uncomfortable morning, in which the Canadians and the Middlesex were severely harassed with tear gas shells,[47] a battalion of Zouaves moved up to the Pilckem road, and established contact with Mercer's left shortly after midday. Meanwhile reinforcements had reached Mouse Trap Farm with the arrival of two battalions of the 27th Division from General Smith-Dorrien's already depleted corps reserve—the 2nd Duke of Cornwall's Light Infantry and the 9th Royal Scots. It was now apparent that the French counter-attack would not take place until new batteries arrived to replace the guns lost in the gas attack. It had already been postponed until nine o'clock, and an operation order issued at 1.20 by General Quiquandon set the new time for 3:00 p.m.

The situation in the Ypres Salient had been under careful scrutiny at General Headquarters, where air reconnaissance reports confirmed that the Germans were rapidly consolidating their gains. During the morning Sir John French visited General Foch and was assured that reinforcements were arriving and that the territory lost by the 45th and 87th Divisions would be regained. In agreeing to cooperate in any counter-attack, Sir John reserved the right to withdraw his troops from the threatened Salient if the French position were not soon re-established.[48] On returning to his advanced headquarters at Hazebrouck the Commander-in-Chief ordered General Smith-Dorrien to assist the French attack, and made available to the Second Army the infantry of the 50th Division, and later the whole Cavalry Corps. Shortly after midday the 1st Cavalry Division reached the Ypres area, and with it the 13th Infantry Brigade, the latter much reduced in numbers by its ordeal at Hill 60 (above, p. 58).

At 2:40 p.m. the Army Commander issued orders to the 5th Corps for a general attack between Kitcheners Wood and the Yser Canal. General Alderson's detailed instructions called for the 13th Brigade to cross the Brielen bridge and attack towards Pilckem on a two-battalion front with its right on the Ypres-

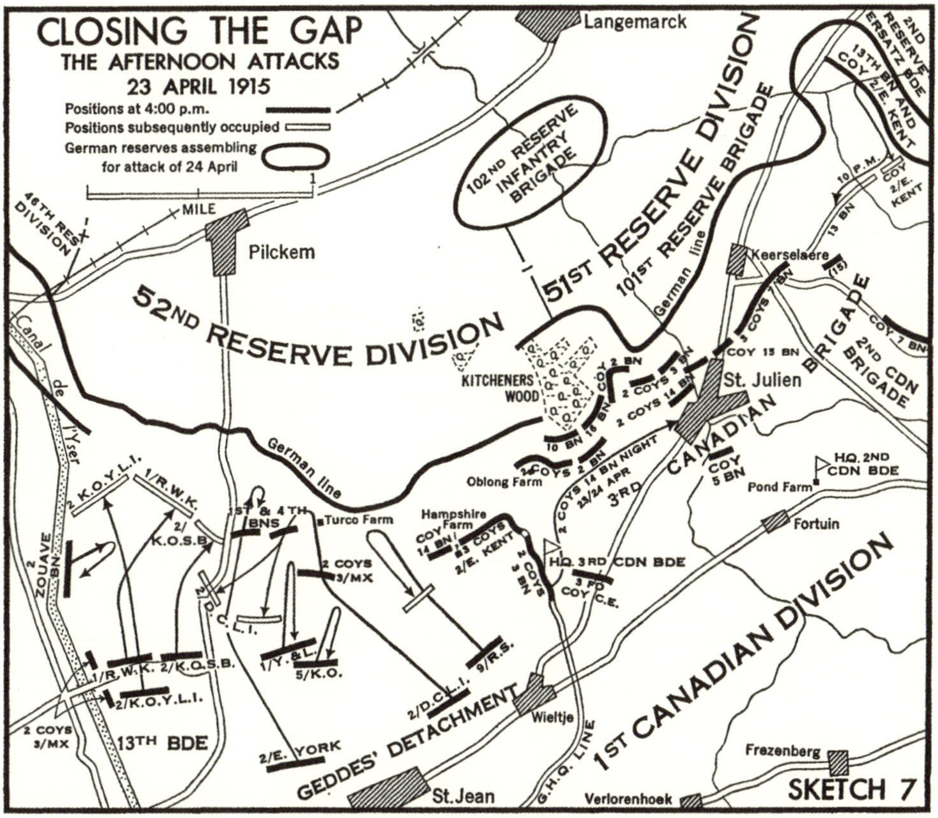

Pilckem road. The effort on the east side of the road would be made by the two uncommitted battalions of Geddes' Detachment (the 5th King's Own and the 1st York and Lancaster), together with the two battalions of the 27th Division.[49] The 13th Brigade would thus attack in an area already allotted to the Algerian Division's 90th Brigade, which General Quiquandon, mistakenly giving the British objective as Langemarck, had ordered to advance northward between Boesinghe and the Ypres-Pilckem road.[50] The British brigade, marching from Vlamertinghe, swung too far to the north and entered the French area, and the resulting confusion caused a postponement of the attack until 4:25 p.m.[51] Each battalion moved off on a front of 500 yards, advancing in five or six widely-spaced ranks.

Unfortunately British and Canadian supporting batteries which had not been informed of the postponement opened fire at 2:45, giving the Germans ample warning of the attack. When the actual assault did go in, a shortage of ammunition prevented another preliminary bombardment. This mishap, coming on top of the general lack of preparation, the absence of any reconnaissance by battalions and the uncertainty as to the enemy's exact location, doomed the attack to failure before it started. As the advancing battalions came into German view they were met by heavy fire from Mauser Ridge. There were many casualties, especially among the officers, with the result that little information came back and direction of the battle broke down. A sudden eastward advance from the canal by a battalion of Zouaves cut across the 13th Brigade's front, temporarily halting the 1st Royal West Kent and the 2nd King's Own Scottish Borderers and forcing them to veer to the right. In the centre, as the leading troops of Geddes' Detachment reached the positions which the 1st and 4th Canadian Battalions and the 3rd Middlesex had been holding under fire since the failure of the 1st Brigade's early morning attack, the survivors of all three units joined in, to carry the advance to within 200 yards of the German trenches. On the right the 9th Royal Scots dug in short of Hampshire Farm, the Duke of Cornwall's doing better by recapturing Turco Farm, though they were to hold it only briefly.[52]

This was the high tide of the counter-attack. The approach of darkness brought the task of sorting out units and establishing a new line about 600 yards south of the German trenches. This furnished a continuous manned position from the 3rd Brigade's holdings in front of Mouse Trap Farm to South Zwaanhof Farm beside the canal, where a battalion of the 13th Brigade reinforced the junction with the French right flank. Except for the uncoordinated effort on its right by the Zouaves, the 45th Algerian Division had achieved little; and farther north attempts by the 87th Division to retake the canal crossings at Het Sas, and by reinforcements from the Groupement Nieuport to recapture Steenstraat had failed.[53]

Casualties had been heavy, running in each British battalion from 200 to 425. In their two efforts that day the 1st Canadian Battalion had lost 404 all ranks; the 4th Battalion's losses of 454 included the C.O., who was killed. Of the survivors it was reported that some were so confused "that daylight found them digging in facing the wrong way."[54] Once more the enemy's advance had been stopped, and at a cost perhaps justifiable. For while it seems probable that a simple night advance might have secured the same ground with few casualties, there is little doubt that the determined Allied counter-offenisve caused a change in the German plans. In the first flush of success following the gas attack on the 22nd, the Commander of the Fourth German Army had broadened his objectives and had ordered the attack to be pressed westward across the Yser Canal in the direction of Poperinghe, in order to drive a wedge between the Belgians and the French. On the morning of the 23rd he ordered the 26th Reserve Corps to regard "the undertaking against Poperinghe as the main operation" and its own advance as only secondary. But later that day, when Allied counter-attacks had brought the Corps' forward movement to a standstill, the German High Command intervened, telling the Fourth Army "that Poperinghe did not primarily enter the question at all as an objective for the operation, and that it was strictly a matter of cutting off the Ypres Salient".[55]

For the time being General Alderson's fear of a German advance down the canal to Ypres had been removed by the gallant action of the 13th Brigade in sealing the gap on the left flank. To the Brigade Commander he wrote, "Words cannot express what the Canadians owe the 13th for their splendid attack and the way they restored confidence."

The Battle of St. Julien—The Second Gas Attack, 24 April

To implement the German High Command's intention of "cutting off the Ypres Salient" Duke Albrecht ordered a discharge of gas to be made on the 26th Reserve Corps' front early on the morning of 24 April, to be followed by a converging attack on the Canadian-held apex. The German formations concerned formed the Corps' left wing, consisting of the 51st Reserve Division with the 2nd Reserve Ersatz Brigade under command. Behind that Brigade was Brigade Schmieden, a strong *ad hoc* formation organized from battalions of the 27th Reserve Corps for the purpose of exploiting any progress on the left wing of the 26th Corps. Adjoining the Ersatz Brigade was the 38th Landwehr Brigade, the extreme right wing of the 27th Reserve Corps. The attack was intended to crush the Canadian old and new lines, capture St. Julien and strike into the heart of the Salient as far as the Zonnebeke Ridge (a mile south of the Gravenstafel Ridge). At the same time the 23rd Reserve Corps (which had captured Lizerne at 1:30 a.m. on the 24th) would continue its operations west of the Yser Canal, circling southward to cut off the line of retreat at Vlamertinghe while the Salient was being driven in. On the east side of the Salient the 27th Reserve Corps would stand ready to join in the advance as the 26th Reserve Corps swept southward.[56]

Along the Canadian front preparations were made to meet the inevitable attack. The line north-east of St. Julien had been shortened. After dark on the 23rd the 13th Battalion and the company of the 2nd Buffs, which together had held the narrow apex all day long under continual fire from front and rear, retired and dug in on a line running south-westward from the 15th Battalion's left to the 7th Battalion's positions east of Keerselaere. The entire line from the Canadian boundary with the 28th Division near Gravenstafel round to Kitcheners Wood was now manned by the equivalent of eight battalions. These were to be attacked by at least three times their number of German battalions.[57] The 5th and 8th Battalions (of the 2nd Brigade) and the 15th Battalion held the original front on the east side of the Salient; from the new apex to St. Julien were in order "B" Company of the 2nd Buffs, the 13th, 7th and 14th Battalions; west of the Steenbeek the 3rd and 2nd Battalions were dug in near the southern face of the wood. The work of entrenching went on all night, and telephone linemen toiled at repairing and extending communications. Each man in the 8th Battalion's trenches was issued with a makeshift respirator—a cotton bandolier to be wetted and tied over his nose and mouth if a gas cloud approached.*

* Manufactured respirators came later. The smoke helmet, an impregnated bag to fit over the head, was introduced in June. The small box respirator was issued in August 1916 and remained in use to the end of the war.

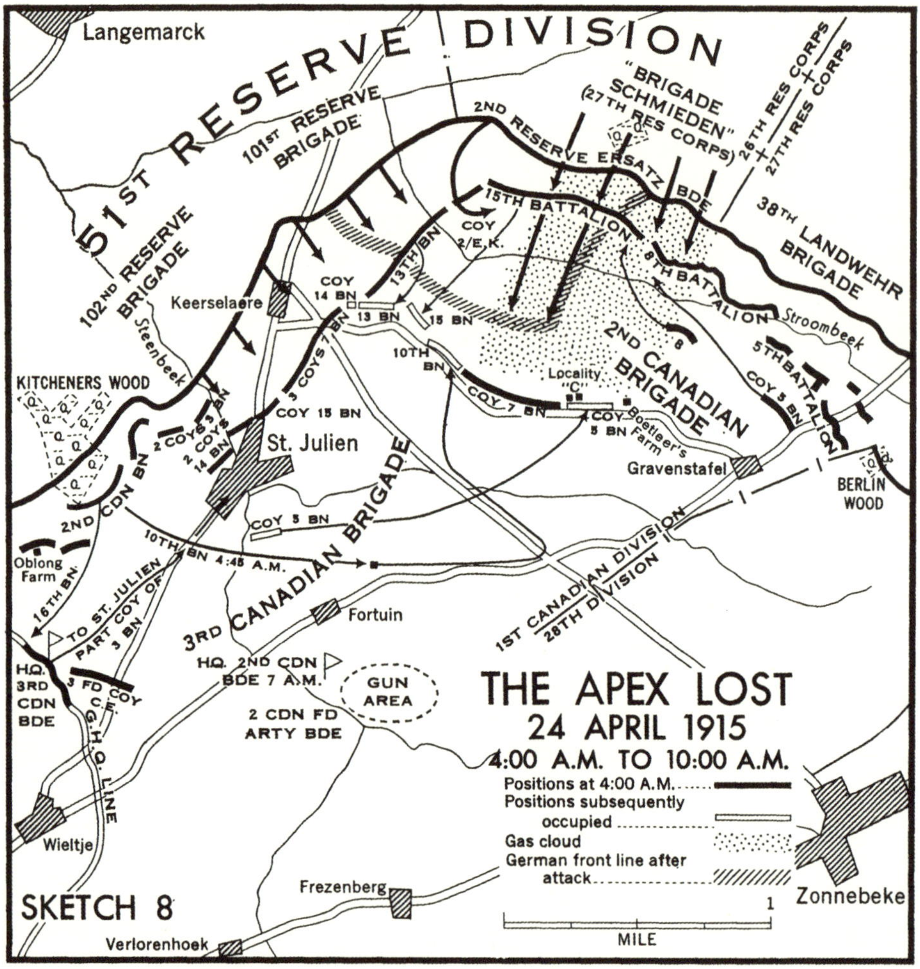

SKETCH 8

THE APEX LOST
24 APRIL 1915
4:00 A.M. TO 10:00 A.M.

At four o'clock in the morning of 24 April the Germans opened up a heavy ten-minute bombardment, at the same time releasing chlorine gas on a 1200-yard front opposite the junction of the 8th and 15th Battalions. As the greenish yellow cloud rolled in across no man's land hurried calls for artillery support brought prompt aid to the 8th Battalion.[58] But on the left there was no help for the 15th Battalion, for the 3rd Field Artillery Brigade (assigned to support the 3rd Infantry Brigade) had to admit that its guns had been moved back behind the G.H.Q. Line, and were out of range.[59] The deadly gas enveloped the whole of the 15th Battalion's right company and most of the 8th Battalion's left one, as well as part of each unit's centre company. The damp cloths over their mouths and nostrils, untreated with any chemical, helped but little against the chlorine, and with eyes blinded and throats burning men collapsed on the floor of the trench in suffocating agony.

Behind the gas cloud came the German infantry wearing their mouth protectors. On the 8th Battalion's front they were met not only by the 2nd Field Artillery Brigade's shrapnel barrage but with steady enfilading small-arms fire from the right rifle company, which had escaped the gas. The men of the centre and left companies who were still able to fight manned the parapet and emptied their Ross rifles into the advancing enemy, desperately jarring loose with boot heel or entrenching-tool handle stubborn rifle bolts that repeatedly jammed with the rapid fire (below, p. 156). In the face of this unexpected resistance the attackers halted. The 2nd Brigade's line had held. But the 15th Battalion's right-hand company, which met the full force of the chlorine, was not only without artillery support but had no enfilading fire; for the platoons to the west, outside the gassed area, could not see the front of the attack. The few members of the company who had escaped death from shelling and gas fell back to the Stroombeek, where they joined survivors of the adjacent platoon from the centre company. Having broken through the 15th Battalion's line to a depth of some 700 yards the Germans mounted further attacks to reduce the apex. By 6:30 a.m. they had overrun the little band at the Stroombeek and were within 300 yards of Locality "C".[60]

The initial attack against the north-western face of the apex, unaccompanied by any effective discharge of gas, had been repelled by determined rifle and machine-gun fire from across the entire front. Then the German guns came into action again and, aided by excellent observation from the Poelcappelle houses and without drawing any countering fire from Allied batteries, systematically shelled up and down the length of the trenches north-eastward from St. Julien. Casualties mounted rapidly amid the wreckage of the shallow trenches. At 8:30, when a lull in the bombardment presaged a renewed German assault, the 13th Battalion, whose position next to the apex was now vulnerable from both front and rear, was ordered back to the Gravenstafel Ridge. The three companies on the left fell back in good order; but of the exposed company on the right, only a dozen men reached the ridge. The Buffs' company at the tip of the apex, cut off and lacking a written order to retire, fought on alongside the remnants of the 15th Battalion's left company. Finally, surrounded on three sides by enemy, the surviving Buffs surrendered shortly after nine o'clock.[61]

As soon as the initial German attack was reported, the commanders of both brigades concerned had taken steps to reinforce the threatened front. Brig.-Gen. Turner, having received an erroneous report that the 2nd Brigade's left had been driven in, promptly released what remained of the 10th Battalion from its trenches south of Kitcheners Wood, with orders to move to Locality "C". At the same time Brig.-Gen. Currie placed under the command of the 8th Battalion a reserve company from each of the 5th and 7th Battalions. The platoons of the 8th Battalion's own reserve company were moved by the battalion commander to his left, first

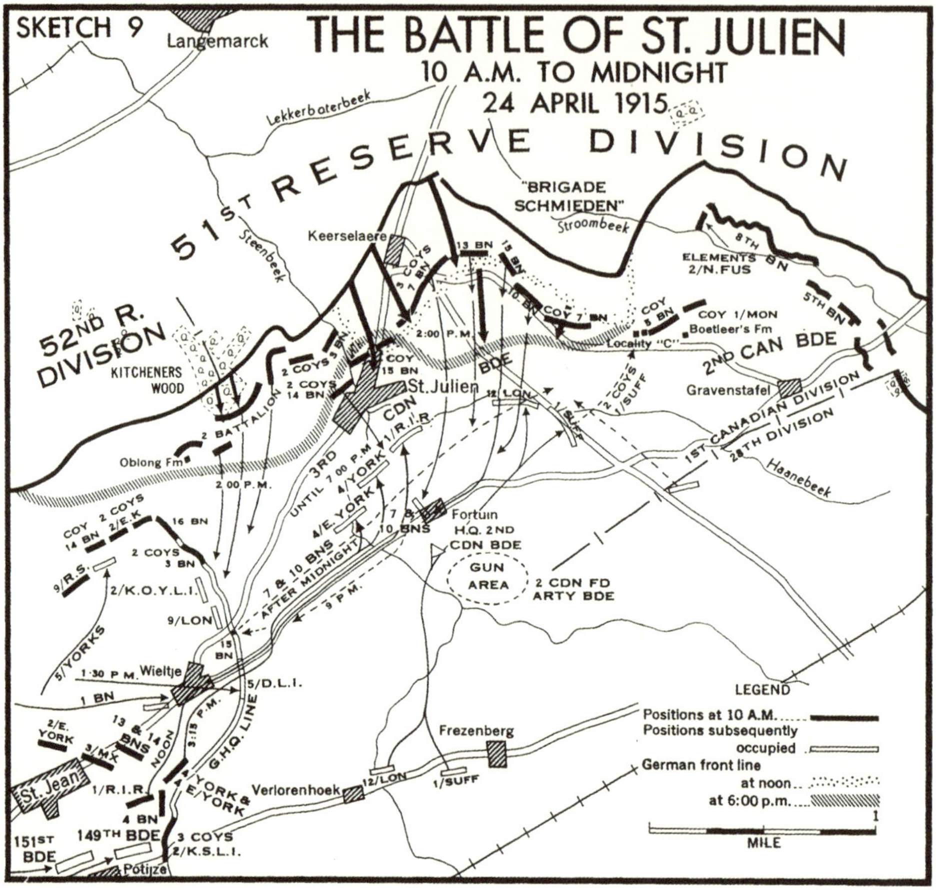

to help the 15th Battalion, and then in an attempt to seal his open flank. During the move Company Sergeant Major F. W. Hall was killed when he went out under heavy machine-gun fire into no man's land a second time to bring in a wounded comrade after two others had fallen in the first attempt. He was awarded the Victoria Cross.[62] Little help could come from higher levels of command, where reinforcements were just as hard to come by. At Corps Headquarters General Plumer could only promise that on arrival in the Ypres area the 4th Division's 10th Brigade would be made available to the Canadians. The 150th (York and Durham) Brigade (of the 50th Division), commanded by Brig.-Gen. J. E. Bush, was already under General Alderson's orders west of the Yser Canal, and between 7:40 and 8:45 a.m. he sent its four battalions forward to the G.H.Q. Line. He hoped to use this brigade to relieve the 3rd Brigade that evening, and at 10:35 a.m. through a staff officer he urged Brig.-Gen. Turner not to "call on Brigadier York and Durham . . . unless absolutely necessary".[63] An hour later, however, Divisional Headquarters assigned Turner two of these battalions "for a counter-attack to restore situation on your right".[64] What that situation was we shall now examine.

The Loss of St. Julien, 24 April

Throughout the early hours of the 24th the left of the 3rd Brigade's line, from Keerselaere to Kitcheners Wood, had been under continual pounding by German artillery. An attempt by enemy infantry shortly after five o'clock to advance up the Steenbeek to St. Julien had been repulsed by rapid fire, as had a more general attack across the whole front about 8:30 a.m. About mid-morning the enemy returned to the attack, heralding his advance with a crushing bombardment of the entire Canadian position. The renewed assault fell on the battle-worn units of the 3rd Brigade, which was virtually without reserves. Near Keerselaere the enemy's progress was checked by the heroism of the 7th Battalion's Machine Gun Officer, Lieutenant Edward Bellew, who, though wounded and cut off from his battalion, kept his last gun firing with telling effect until out of ammunition. Then, having destroyed it, he met his opponents with fixed bayonet, and fought on until overpowered. Bellew remained a prisoner of war until 1919, and only then learned of his award of the Victoria Cross—the first won by an officer of the Canadian Expeditionary Force.

Shortly after 11:00 a.m. the commanders of the 7th and 15th Battalions, and the second-in-command of the 14th, out of touch with 3rd Brigade Headquarters, conferred on the St. Julien-Gravenstafel road and decided to evacuate their exposed position and withdraw 300 yards to a new line south of the Gravenstafel Ridge. The right half of the line, consisting of the survivors of the 15th and 13th Battalions, fell back without great loss, but so closely were the Germans pressing the left that two companies of the 7th Battalion were overrun 500 yards north-east of St. Julien, the majority being taken prisoner. Yet the new position was equally untenable, for from the captured Canadian trench the enemy could sweep with fire the south side of the Ridge. At 12:30, after another consultation, the three commanders agreed on a further withdrawal, this time of 1000 yards to a line north of the Wieltje-Gravenstafel road. It was a fighting retirement, carried out by small parties falling back in a succession of short bounds while their comrades kept up a punishing fire that caused the troops of the 51st Reserve Division temporarily to abandon the attack until reinforced.[66]

These reinforcements had been swarming westward from the 27th Reserve Corps' front, and shortly after midday, when the Canadian withdrawal had exposed the right of the St. Julien garrison, regiments of the 51st Reserve Division infiltrated into the village on three sides. Under frequent admonition to hold St. Julien to the last, the majority of the small garrison fought on until overwhelmed, the Germans entering the outlying houses about 3:00 p.m. At one o'clock Divisional Headquarters, having learned that the enemy was massing troops east of St. Julien, had ordered General Turner not to counter-attack with the two battalions assigned to him from the York and Durham Brigade, but instead to utilize them "to strengthen your line and hold on".[67] Turner, understanding this to mean the G.H.Q. Line (an interpretation that a telephone conversation with Alderson's

General Staff Officer seemed to confirm), at 1:40 issued an order to the two British units and the six Canadian battalions under his command to hold the G.H.Q. Line from the St. Jean-Poelcappelle road southward.[68]

Over towards Kitcheners Wood the 2nd and 3rd Canadian Battalions had taken a heavy toll of the lines of German infantry advancing up the Steenbeek, while themselves under continual attack. Only the 2nd Battalion, on the left, was able to comply with the order to retire. Part of its right company and the two companies of the 3rd Battalion were under such intense fire from front and flank that they could only hold on to their positions, hoping for a counter-attack, and in the meantime continuing to kill Germans with machine-gun and rifle.

Brig.-Gen. Turner's misinterpretation of General Alderson's instructions was but one instance of the wide-spread misunderstanding and confusion which developed, as broken communications and delayed and often faulty reports spread a dense "fog of war" across the battle area, keeping the 2nd and 3rd Brigades at cross purposes for several hours. At nine that morning General Plumer had given the G.O.C. 27th Division, Major-General T.D'O. Snow, command of all troops in corps reserve, though notification of this appointment does not seem to have reached subordinate commands. At noon General Snow moved the 1st Royal Irish Regiment to a position north of Fortuin. Fortuin, a scattered group of farms and cottages centred half a mile south-east of St. Julien, was being held by 200 survivors of the 7th and 10th Battalions. Having no other reinforcements available, Snow next commandeered two battalions from the 28th Division's reserve and sent them to join the Irish, at the same time directing General Turner to take command of the three units and drive the enemy north-eastward, adding the admonition, "Act with vigour."[69] But the Canadian brigadier, unaware that General Snow's powers of command had been extended, and satisfied that his own actions accorded with General Alderson's designs, paid no attention to the message, other than to walk across (at 5:30 p.m.) and order the Irish Regiment to withdraw from the Fortuin area to the G.H.Q. Line at dusk. He saw no sign of the two battalions from the 28th Division.[70]

Other British reinforcements were on the way. Two of the 150th Brigade's battalions—the 4th East Yorkshire and the 4th Green Howards (Yorkshire Regiment)—having "received a good many different orders", finally found themselves marching towards Fortuin, and they occupied positions on the left of the Royal Irish, facing St. Julien. Thus while the exhausted units of the 3rd Canadian Brigade were pulling back into the G.H.Q. Line, five British battalions had fortuitously and most fortunately intervened in the gap through which a resolute German advance could have cut off the 2nd Canadian Brigade and the neighbouring 28th Division. But lack of coordination was to dissipate their effectiveness.

As daylight on the 24th faded, General Currie's 5th and 8th Battalions were still holding firm in the original front line. But he had been much disturbed about his open left flank, where a company of the 5th Battalion at Boetleer's Farm and the survivors of the 7th Battalion's company at Locality "C" held the only remaining positions of the "subsidiary line" along Gravenstafel Ridge. All morning he

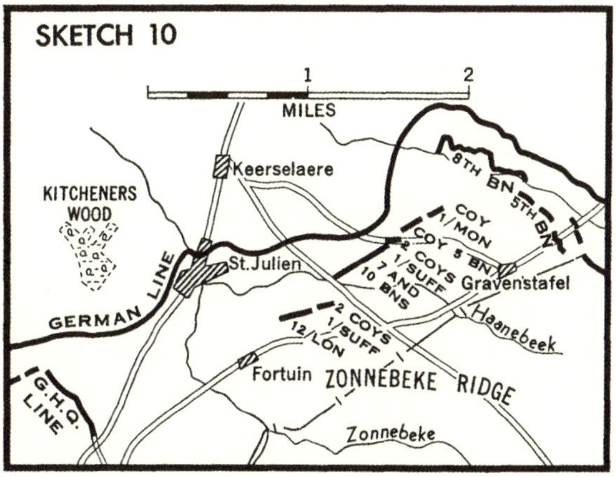

THE SECOND BRIGADE HOLDS FIRM

2.00 A.M. 25 APRIL 1915

had anxiously awaited the planned counter-attack by the two battalions of the York and Durham Brigade, and at about 1:00 p.m., when efforts by his rear headquarters staff at Wieltje had failed to urge these forward from the G.H.Q. Line, Currie took the extreme course of leaving his command post (which had been moved to 400 yards south of the Fortuin road junction) and going back himself, "it being thought", he writes, "that they might move for me when unlikely to move for officers of lesser rank".[71] Before he went he left provisional instructions for his two front line battalions to fall back to the Gravenstafel Ridge, if necessary—an order which was not put into effect.[72] Having failed to persuade Brig.-Gen. Bush (who had now received General Alderson's order cancelling the counter-attack), Currie personally saw General Snow (about 3:30 p.m.) and gave him an appreciation of the situation, but could obtain no assistance from him.[73] The best he could do was to induce some stragglers from the 7th Battalion, who had lost their officers, to go forward and join the 8th Battalion.

Meanwhile, the 2nd Brigade's situation had improved with the arrival of the two units of the 28th Division—the 1st Suffolks and the 12th London (Rangers). South of Fortuin the two battalions had been diverted from their original mission by Currie's brigade major. Continuing their march north-eastward they ran into increasingly heavy fire and finally entrenched just south of the Haanebeek, facing Locality "C", which the Germans had at last captured. During the evening two Suffolk companies occupied the crest immediately west of Boetleer's Farm. After midnight these were joined on the left by the weary remnants of the 7th and 10th Battalions, each about 150 strong, led forward personally by General Currie from the G.H.Q. Line, where they had been taken back in the late evening for a long overdue meal. With these reinforcements and other detachments provided by units of the 28th Division in response to the urgent appeals of the 8th Battalion's C.O. (Lt.-Col. Lipsett), a tenuous defence line was established along the 2nd Brigade's left flank. Shortly before dawn the 8th Durham Light Infantry (of the 151st Brigade), sent forward by General Snow to reinforce the 85th Brigade, relieved the two gassed companies of the 8th Battalion in the front line, but daylight came before Lipsett's right company could be replaced.

The bitterest fighting of the afternoon of the 24th took place south of St. Julien, where the two Yorkshire battalions had arrived in time to meet the fifth German attack of the day. As these Territorial units counter-attacked, they were aided by small-arms fire from the 3rd Brigade troops at the northern end of the G.H.Q. Line, and by the 18-pdrs. of the 5th and 6th Canadian Batteries, shooting over open sights. The enemy was driven back on the village, which, according to the German Official History, he was forced to evacuate. But the counter-attack had come too late to save the stubborn detachments left by the 2nd and 3rd Battalions between St. Julien and Kitcheners Wood; their magnificent resistance had ended an hour before when, with few survivors unwounded and their last machine-gun silenced, their isolated trench had been overrun by the 102nd Reserve Infantry Brigade. Yet this desperate stand and the appearance of the fresh British battalions were sufficient to prevent the execution of an order from the 26th Reserve Corps to retake St. Julien that night. This was most fortunate, for the gap had been partly reopened at seven o'clock when the two Yorkshire units, acting on instructions from General Turner relayed to them by the 1st Royal Irish Regiment, retired with that battalion to the G.H.Q. Line.

It was not until four o'clock that word of the complete withdrawal of the 3rd Brigade and its attached battalions reached General Alderson at the Château des Trois Tours. He had planned on using the 10th Brigade and the uncommitted part of the York and Durham (150th) Brigade to relieve Brig.-Gen. Turner and Geddes' Detachment that evening. In the changed circumstances he promptly ordered Turner to employ six and a half battalions that were "in and around Wieltje" to prevent a German break-through.[74] The message admitted "no exact knowledge of your situation at the present moment"—indeed two of the units referred to were the Yorkshire battalions which were then hotly engaged south-west of St. Julien. Meanwhile Sir John French had told General Smith-Dorrien to make every effort "to restore and hold line about St. Julien or situation of 28th Division will be jeopardised".[75] Sir John hoped that with the Germans being "a bit tired by now, and . . . numerically inferior to us as far as we can judge", it would not be necessary for the 28th Division to evacuate its positions.[76] For the time being the understanding reached with General Foch (above, p. 68) remained in force. General Headquarters was continuing to receive from that commander assurances of an imminent and vigorous French offensive across the Yser Canal; a fresh division, the 153rd, was arriving, and a second would be near Poperinghe early next morning.[77]

Complying with G.H.Q.'s orders, at half-past six General Plumer instructed General Alderson to launch the strongest possible counter-attack to retake St. Julien and "re-establish our trench line as far to the northward as possible", employing the 10th and 150th Brigades and six other battalions,* or such of them

* The 2nd King's Own Yorkshire Light Infantry and the 9th London (Queen Victoria's Rifles) of the 13th Brigade; the 4th Canadian Battalion; the 1st Royal Irish Regiment (27th Division); and the 12th London (Rangers) and 1st Suffolk (28th Division).

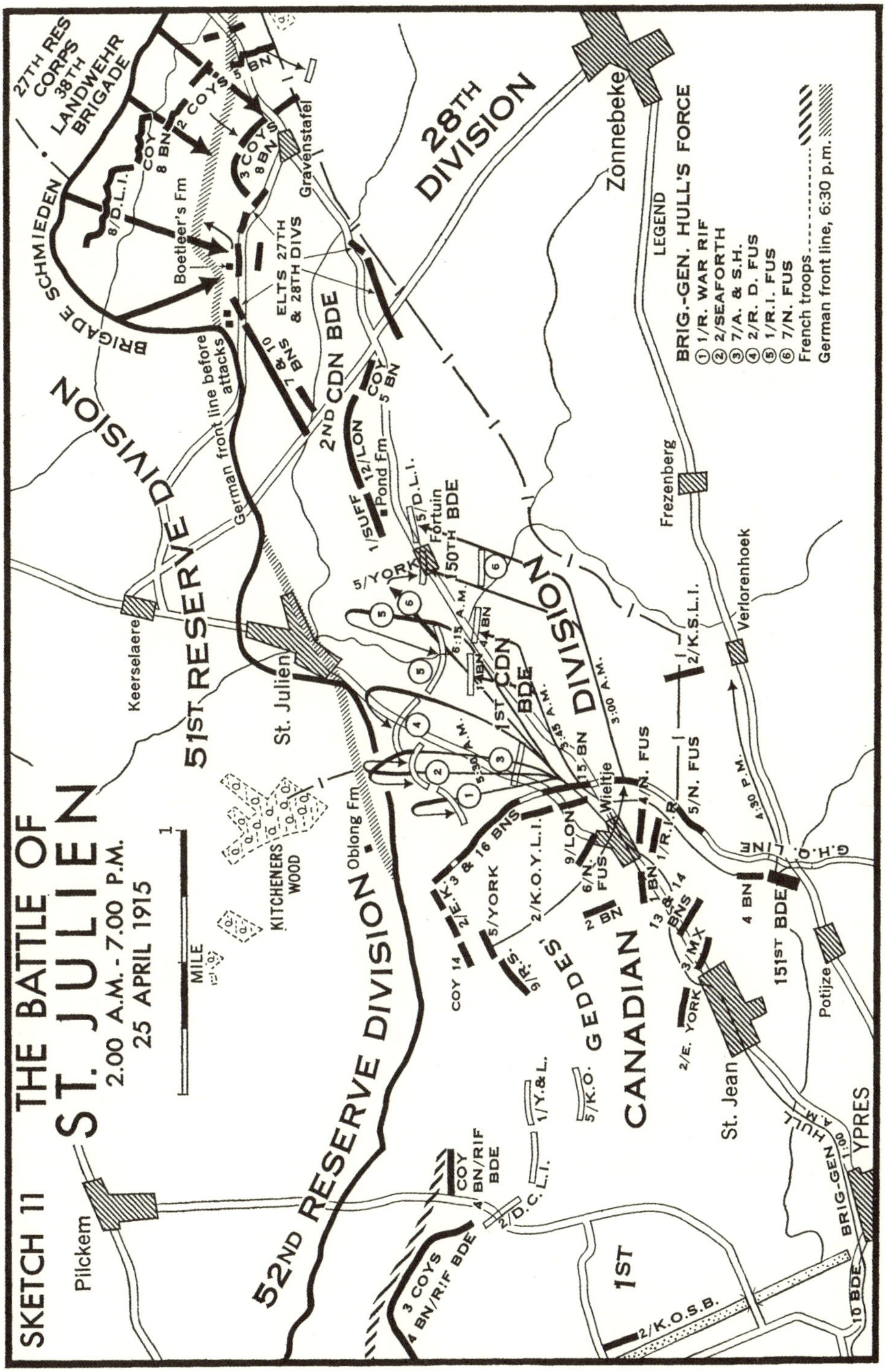
SKETCH 11
THE BATTLE OF
ST. JULIEN
2.00 A.M. - 7.00 P.M.
25 APRIL 1915
MILE
Pilckem
Keerselaere
St. Julien
Kitcheners Wood
Oblong Fm
Boetleer's Fm
Gravenstafel
Zonnebeke
Fortuin
Pond Fm
Frezenberg
Verlorenhoek
Wieltje
St. Jean
Potijze
YPRES
52ND RESERVE DIVISION
51ST RESERVE DIVISION
BRIGADE SCHMIEDEN
27TH RES CORPS 38TH LANDWEHR BRIGADE
28TH DIVISION
50TH DIVISION
CANADIAN DIVISION
GEDDES'
1ST
2ND CDN BDE
1ST CDN BDE
150TH BDE
151ST BDE
German front line before attacks
G.H.Q. LINE
LEGEND
BRIG.-GEN. HULL'S FORCE
① 1/R. WAR RIF
② 2/SEAFORTH
③ 7/A. & S.H.
④ 2/R. D. FUS
⑤ 1/R.I. FUS
⑥ 7/N. FUS
French troops
German front line, 6:30 p.m.

as could be assembled, under a selected commander. He might also call on the Northumbrian Division's other two brigades (the 149th and 151st), which were due to arrive that night about Potijze in corps reserve.[78] Alderson nominated Brig.-Gen. C. P. A. Hull (10th Brigade), and cancelled the relief of the 3rd Brigade and Geddes' Detachment. Allowing as much time as he dared for the complex task of marshalling the force (which was indeed more widely scattered than either he or Hull realized), and arranging for an artillery programme involving the guns of the Canadian and the 27th and 28th Divisions, in formal orders issued at 8:00 p.m. Alderson set the hour of assault at 3:30 a.m. on 25 April. The fifteen battalion commanders (the 10th Brigade had a Territorial battalion attached) were instructed to report to General Hull at his headquarters north-west of Ypres at nine o'clock.[79] But the delay in transmitting these orders—some units, as we have seen, had been taken from their own formations and attached to others, and at least two did not receive their orders till next day—and an ambiguity about the site of the rendezvous, resulted in only one battalion commander showing up. Hull therefore postponed the attack to 4:30 a.m. and went over to Wieltje to try and round up the rest of his force. At three o'clock he moved his headquarters to Mouse Trap Farm, and because of traffic congestion and the fact that his troops would have to defile through two gaps in the wire of the G.H.Q. Line, he put off the attack another hour, when it would be light.

Meanwhile the confusion brought about by contradictory and often misinformed reports was growing worse. When 5th Corps Headquarters received General Snow's appreciation of the situation, it dispatched a wire to General Alderson shortly before midnight sharply criticizing the order sending the troops of the 3rd Brigade and its attached units back to the G.H.Q. Line, "thus giving up all the ground for which such a struggle has been made today and leaving the second bde. in the air". It ordered an immediate re-establishment of the line as far forward as possible, and if necessary the appointment of an officer to take command.[80] The directive made no reference to the forthcoming attack by Brig.-Gen. Hull (whose resources it was likely to affect). Alderson at once sent forward a senior staff officer with plenary powers. Brig.-Gen. Turner, however, at a loss to understand the attitude of General Snow and the apparent inconsistency between his instructions and those received from General Alderson, was on his way back to the Château des Trois Tours on a motor-cycle pillion, to ascertain exactly from whom he was supposed to take his orders. Unfortunately the resulting interview still left Alderson and Turner each convinced that the other did not understand what was happening.

The Counter-Attack by the 10th Brigade, 25 April

At 3:15 a.m., a little more than two hours before the time now scheduled for the attack, Brig.-Gen. Hull found himself with only the five battalions of his own 10th Brigade. Of the other ten units originally allotted to him, three were on their way back, two were near Mouse Trap Farm in an exhausted state, two had been committed since early afternoon and the remaining three had been removed from Hull's command. Hull placed his four Regular battalions in front, and his Territorial unit (the 7th Argyll and Sutherland Highlanders) in support to the left. Shortly before half-past five, shielded by an early morning mist, the assaulting troops marched out in fours from the G.H.Q. position, forming up to advance against Kitcheners Wood and St. Julien. Supporting artillery fire was inadequate, for not only had the batteries of the 2nd and 3rd Brigades C.F.A. and of the 27th and 28th Divisions, ignorant of the postponements of the time of attack, fired their preliminary bombardment two hours earlier, but a warning had been issued not to shell St. Julien because of a mistaken report by the 3rd Brigade that 200 Canadian infantry were still in the village.[81] When early morning patrols of the 51st Reserve Division found the place abandoned, the Germans promptly set up machine-guns in the outlying houses.

As the British troops moved forward they encountered first sniping and then a rapidly increasing volume of rifle and machine-gun fire which halted and then cut down the leading waves, leaving the dead and wounded lying in long rows. On the right the 1st Royal Irish Fusiliers and the 2nd Royal Dublin Fusiliers were held 200 yards short of St. Julien; next to them the 2nd Seaforth Highlanders, though reinforced by the Argylls, were stopped 500 yards from Kitcheners Wood; and on the left the 1st Royal Warwickshire failed to reach Oblong Farm. Two battalions of the 149th (Northumberland) Brigade, ordered forward to add impetus on the right, lost direction and gained only casualties. By seven o'clock the attack had stalled and survivors were withdrawing in search of cover. At 9:15 a.m. on the 25th a message to the Canadian Division reported failure.[82] A new line was consolidated extending from the G.H.Q. Line by Mouse Trap Farm to south of Fortuin, whence the two York and Durham battalions linked up with the entrenchments of the Suffolks and the London Rangers facing Locality "C". The operation had cost Hull's brigade 73 officers and 2346 other ranks. But though it had not gained its objectives it had at last blocked the gap at St. Julien. The Germans made no attempt to exploit their gains; indeed for the next ten days their progress on this part of the front was stayed.

The 10th Brigade's heroic effort on this Sunday morning, 25 April, had seriously disrupted the plans of Duke Albrecht, who having abandoned as unprofitable the offensive across the Yser Canal was concentrating on a southward thrust through St. Julien by the 26th Reserve Corps, with subsidiary attacks by the 27th Reserve Corps' right wing. But the striking power for the main blow was expended in stopping Hull's attack, and the only German gains that day were in the north-eastern part of the Salient.[83] There the enemy had planned converging attacks—one from the east against the face of the Salient at Broodseinde, the other southward against the Gravenstafel Ridge. At 9:00 a.m. a heavy bombardment on the trenches held by the 84th and 85th Brigades (28th Division) heralded the former assault, which was delivered about one o'clock on a quarter-mile front north of Broodseinde by a regiment of the 53rd Reserve Division. Of the ground initially lost an immediate counter-attack recovered all but sixty yards of the front line, a portion which remained in German hands despite subsequent efforts to regain it.

Throughout the morning the same artillery bombardment had pounded the 2nd Brigade's front line and the ridge behind, while from Locality "C" German machine-gunners swept the Stroombeek valley with enfilading fire. By mid-afternoon large bodies of infantry were seen advancing from the direction of Poelcappelle, and soon the three companies holding the left end of the line were heavily engaged from front and flank. The attackers gained a footing at Boetleer's Farm and penetrated behind the two Durham companies before being stopped by rifle fire from the 8th Battalion's reserve companies and the various British detachments on the crest of the ridge. "Strong reinforcements" promised Brig.-Gen. Currie by Divisional Headquarters[84] did not materialize, and efforts to reinforce with detachments gathered locally were driven back by the withering fire that swept the open valley. The German shelling increased in fury and shortly after five o'clock the commanders of the three companies, cut off from communication with their battalions, agreed on withdrawal—about the same time that Currie was issuing orders for the evacuation of the front line at dusk. He had learned that the 151st Brigade would come under his tactical command and would occupy a switch-line from Gravenstafel to Fortuin and that one battalion for this task was already on the way.[85] He judged from this that the ridge was to be abandoned, and that therefore the retention of his exposed positions was hopeless. At about 6:00 p.m. the survivors of the two Territorial companies at the apex fell back through the left of the 8th Battalion's company. Only two of the Canadian platoons had retired when the Germans closed in and overran the rest of the company and a few Durhams who had remained behind to help cover their comrades' withdrawal.[86] The 5th Battalion's two front line companies began to fall back over the Gravenstafel Ridge, whence their reserve companies and those of the 8th Battalion had already retired. Later, however, the two battalion commanders, learning that the 85th Brigade on their right had received no orders to give ground, took some of their men forward again to cover Gravenstafel until replacements should arrive. To the west of Boetleer's Farm the two detached Suffolk companies withdrew soon after midnight, followed by the remnants of the 7th and 10th Battalions, which Currie reported as "simply blown out of their trenches by artillery fire".

The relief of the 2nd Canadian Brigade was not completed until early next morning, 26 April, when the last troops reached Wieltje. At 2:30 p.m. on the 25th General Plumer had ordered a redistribution of the forces holding the front line, which air reconnaissance, mistaking German-held trenches for British positions, had described as continuous and intact. The order, effective at 7:00 p.m., reduced the Canadian sector—which had been more than five miles long—to the two miles between Turco Farm and the Fortuin-St. Julien road, allotting responsibility east of the road to Major-General E. S. Bulfin, G.O.C. 28th Division. To hold his left flank Bulfin was given the fresh 11th Brigade (4th British Division), which had reached his Vlamertinghe headquarters at noon, and pending its arrival in the line the 2nd Canadian Brigade would be under his command. Alderson's subsequent orders sent the 1st and 3rd Canadian Brigades out of the line for much-needed rest.[87] The 11th Brigade was delayed in moving forward; dawn was only an hour away when its right battalion dug in west of Berlin Wood, allowing the Canadian companies to complete their withdrawal. The main body of the 11th Brigade deployed along the Zonnebeke Ridge behind the 1st Suffolk and the 12th London (Rangers).

Daybreak of the 26th found the Germans in possession of the ridge westward from Gravenstafel; for the next seven days Berlin Wood was to mark the new apex of the Salient. There was a sorting out of units west of Fortuin as the readjustments ordered by General Plumer took effect and brigades resumed their normal composition. The 1st and 3rd Canadian Brigades had gone into reserve, each having sustained 1500 casualties.* The 10th Brigade took over the Corps flank from Fortuin to Mouse Trap Farm, and the 13th Brigade from there to the boundary with the French. The 2nd Canadian Brigade was still under the orders of General Bulfin, who moved it forward from Wieltje during the morning of the 26th to support the 28th Division's left. In this role it remained south of Fortuin suffering casualties until after dark on the 27th, when it crossed the canal into bivouac, having served thirteen days in the Salient.

The Lahore Division's Attack, 26 April

The events of the past four days had shown that hasty, isolated counter-attacks by infantry with insufficient artillery support could not stop the enemy's steady encroachment on the Salient, much less dislodge him from the ground he had gained. By the evening of 25 April, however, the arrival of three fresh Allied divisions made it possible to plan a counter-offensive of sufficient power to hold some promise of success.

An inter-Allied conference that afternoon agreed upon a joint scheme of attack, for which later in the day General Smith-Dorrien received the approval of the Commander-in-Chief, whose policy was still to hold the Salient if possible, provided the French regained all or a good part of the ground they had lost. General Putz planned to strike with six divisions, using one of his previously uncommitted formations on each flank. The 152nd Division with part of the battle-worn 5th Division would attack from the east side of the canal towards Pilckem at the same time as a British advance; on the left the newly arrived 18th Division, assisted by an assortment of French and Belgian units, would recapture Lizerne, Steenstraat and Het Sas and drive the Germans back over the canal; while in the

* The 3rd Brigade's Headquarters at Mouse Trap Farm was shelled and set on fire on the afternoon of the 25th. For his devotion in succouring the wounded on this occasion the 14th Battalion's Medical Officer, Captain F. A. C. Scrimger, was awarded the Victoria Cross.[88]

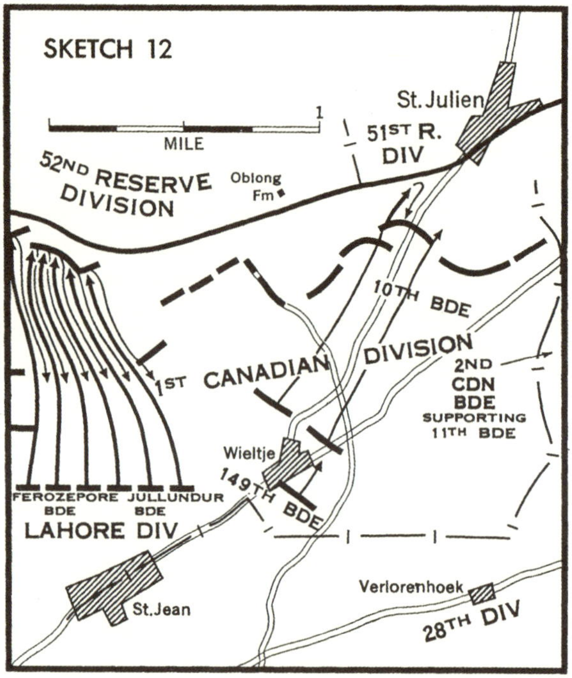

SKETCH 12

THE ATTACK BY THE LAHORE DIVISION

26 APRIL 1915

centre the remainder of the Algerian Division and the 87th Territorial Division would stand west of the canal ready to cross at Boesinghe and join in a successful advance by the right.

The British attack would be made immediately east of the Ypres-Langemarck road by the Lahore Division, which had marched over from the Neuve Chapelle sector and at noon on the 25th was within five miles of Ypres. Its objective was the German line between the Langemarck road and Kitcheners Wood. The Indian division would remain directly under the Second Army, and General Smith-Dorrien's operation orders called on the 5th Corps to coordinate artillery support and to launch an attack on the immediate right.[89] General Alderson accordingly directed the Northumberland Brigade to assault towards St. Julien astride the Wieltje road, and ordered the 10th Brigade to detail a battalion to advance between these two diverging efforts. Geddes' Detachment, in reserve at St. Jean, was to move to the G.H.Q. line to support the attack.[90] Except for the 3rd Brigade, placed in divisional reserve south of Wieltje, active participation by Canadian troops would be limited to the field artillery. The 1st Brigade C.F.A., west of the Yser Canal, was detailed to support the French; the Lahore Division's attack was supported by its own artillery, also west of the canal; and the remaining Canadian batteries covered the 5th Corps' front from St. Julien to west of Kitcheners Wood.

Unfortunately the time of the French attack, originally set for 5:00 p.m. on the 26th, was advanced three hours, thereby curtailing the already limited period available for the Lahore Division's preparations. Nevertheless by one o'clock the two assaulting Indian brigades (each consisting of one British Regular, one

British Territorial and three Indian battalions) were formed up side by side west of Wieltje in the valley behind Hill Top Ridge. They had already suffered casualties from enemy shelling, for their movements had been closely followed by German airmen. The objective was that of Geddes' Detachment three days before—the enemy trenches on Mauser Ridge—and as on that disastrous occasion the leading lines became targets for the German machine-gun and artillery fire as soon as they crossed Hill Top Ridge. Whole platoons were knocked out by single 5.9-inch howitzer shells and soon the valley between the ridges was heaped with the fallen. The British Regulars on either flank gallantly pressed forward through the 13th Brigade's forward positions to within 120 yards of the enemy line, the four battalions between them keeping up to a varying degree. The forward troops went to ground short of the German trenches.

West of the Langemarck road the French had made some progress; but the attack on their northern flank had been postponed an hour because the artillery was not ready. Then at 2:20 p.m. the Germans released chlorine north-west of Turco Farm—the first time it had been used defensively. As the poisonous cloud rolled eastward across the front it swept over the Lahore Division. All except the foremost British detachment fell back in confusion. After the gas had cleared the French attempted a counter-attack, which achieved nothing. By the end of the day the Lahore Division's reserve brigade had relieved the assaulting formations, whose six front line battalions had suffered 1829 casualties, including five battalion commanders.[91]

It is not surprising that the 5th Corps' attack on the right had also failed. Against a strong, well-positioned enemy with overwhelming artillery support there had been little effective coordination with the Lahore Division's effort. The Canadian Division's order for the operation reached both the C.R.A. and the 149th Brigade ten minutes or more after the artillery's and infantry's respective tasks were due to begin. Geddes' Detachment did not receive its final orders until 4:30 p.m. Having made no reconnaissance, the assaulting units (three battalions of Northumberland Fusiliers) lost time in getting through the narrow gap in the G.H.Q. Line and thereby missed what little artillery support there was. As the Fusiliers advanced astride the Wieltje-St. Julien road, German machine-guns to the front and left mowed them down. Among the killed was the brigade commander. Calls for reinforcements went unanswered, for the units of Geddes' Detachment, having received no briefing, were not at hand. Nor did the proposed battalion attack on the Lahore Division's immediate right take place, the 10th Brigade having received its orders too late to take action. At 7:30 p.m. on the 26th the Northumberland Brigade was ordered back to Wieltje, its three attacking battalions having suffered 1200 casualties.

A French report to General Joffre blamed their lack of success on the difficulties of command arising from a committal of newly-arrived brigades and units under commanders who, besides not knowing their troops, were also unfamiliar with the ground. Like the British reinforcements, their movements had been seriously restricted by the canal, where crossings were easily shelled by the

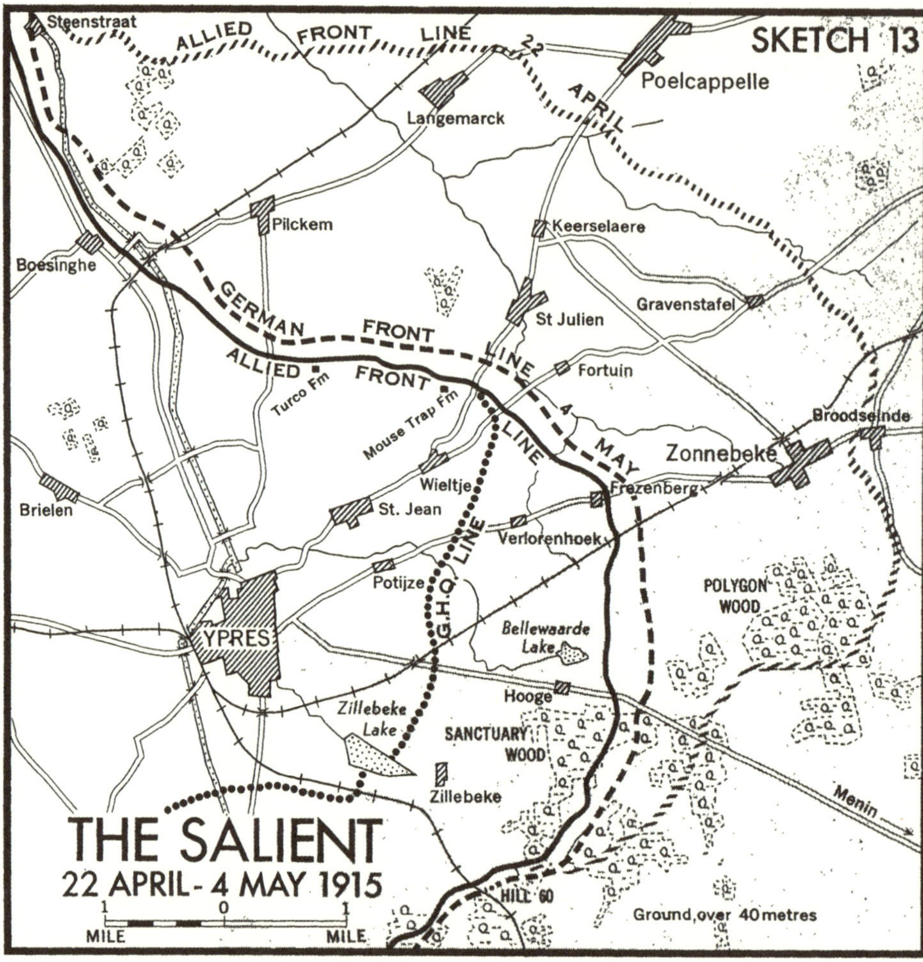

Germans. Their only gain had been on their northern flank, where most of Lizerne had been captured.[92] General Putz's orders for a renewal of the offensive on 27 April designated almost the same objectives, the same commanders and the same plan. It met with virtually the same negligible results. On his right the Lahore Division was called on to attack again, employing two brigades east of the Langemarck road. The assault was made at 1:15 p.m., but as on the previous day German shelling and small-arms fire halted the attackers well short of Mauser Ridge, taking a heavy toll.[93] General Smith-Dorrien, directed by Sir John French "to act vigorously with the full means available" in assisting the French, ordered the attack to be renewed at 6:30 p.m., reinforcing the Indian Division with a composite "brigade" formed from four casualty-ridden British battalions in the 5th Corps reserve.[94] Canadian artillery repeated its bombardment of the German trenches, but the devastating enemy fire broke up the composite "brigade's" attack with no gain. An earlier French attempt on the east side of the canal had also failed. Once again the only gleam of encouragement came from General Putz's northern flank, where the French left wing completed the capture of Lizerne and regained Het Sas and the line of the canal northward to Steenstraat.

The operations on 27 April marked the last attempts by British infantry to regain the ground captured by the Germans on the 22nd and the following days. In an appreciation to G.H.Q. after the Lahore Division's unsuccessful attack of the 26th the Army Commander wrote, "I am doubtful if it is worth losing any more men to regain this French [*sic*] ground unless the French do something really big."[95] He pointed out that the German artillery's domination of the whole area as far back as Poperinghe (where he had his advanced headquarters) meant that the only position that the British could hold permanently would be the G.H.Q. Line from Wieltje to Potijze and thence a switch-line curving south-eastward through Hooge and behind Sanctuary Wood. He suggested a preliminary withdrawal of about 2500 yards from the eastern face of the Salient.

Sir John French's reply, as we have noted, was an order to intensify the British effort, and at 4:35 p.m. on the 27th he directed Smith-Dorrien to hand over the command of all troops engaged in the operation in the Ypres area to General Plumer, who would be responsible directly to G. H. Q.[96] The British C.-in-C. fully realized the precarious position of the troops in the Salient. His instructions from Lord Kitchener had emphasized that he must exercise "the greatest care . . . towards a minimum of losses and wastage".[97] Yet he had been told also that "every effort must be made to coincide most sympathetically with the plans and wishes of our Ally", and he was under considerable pressure from General Foch (who was imbued with the French pre-war doctrine of the offensive on all occasions) to continue to attack. Both commanders, however, were alive to the danger of prolonged large-scale operations at Ypres weakening the proposed Artois offensive, which was then planned to start at the end of April. On the morning of 28 April orders reached the new "Plumer's Force" to take preliminary measures for a possible withdrawal from the Salient. General Foch protested vigorously, and in an interview at Cassel persuaded the British Field Marshal to postpone any move until the night of the 29th. (To General Joffre he reported, "I painted the picture of the consequences of withdrawal blacker than they appeared to me.")[98]

A French attack on the 28th achieved little, however, and an operation planned for next day was postponed to allow time for newly arrived artillery to register. Sir John agreed to delay the British retirement one more day, and when the 30th brought no French success, yet another 24 hours. This was the last postponement, for on 1 May Joffre overruled Foch, ordering that all resources be reserved for the coming attack on the Arras front and that he should "act on the defensive about Ypres". That evening General Plumer was ordered to begin the first stages of withdrawal preparatory to occupying a new line on the night of 3-4 May.

On the afternoon of the 2nd a shift of wind enabled the Germans to launch a strong attack with gas between St. Julien and Berlin Wood, on a three-mile front held by the three brigades of the 4th Division, all under General Alderson's command. But the trenches were far apart here and the fitful breeze dispersed the gas cloud so that only the trenches west of Mouse Trap Farm were affected; and Allied guns, which included all the Canadian field batteries, drove back the German infantry. The three Canadian infantry brigades, west of the canal, were alerted but were not required. In spite of another German attack on Berlin Wood the following afternoon, the 27th and 28th Divisions and the right of the Canadian Division carried out their planned withdrawal that night without the loss of a man. General Plumer's new line, a modification of that proposed earlier by General Smith-Dorrien, followed the recently manned front line from Turco Farm to Mouse Trap Farm,* continued south-eastward to Frezenberg and thence south to pass in front of Hooge and along the east edge of Sanctuary Wood, rejoining the old line 1000 yards north-east of Hill 60. At ten next morning the relief of the Canadian Division was completed as General Alderson handed over to the G.O.C. 4th Division. Only the Canadian Divisional Artillery remained in position attached to the British Division and covering the front between Mouse Trap and Turco Farms. Though the 4th Division's C.R.A. took over on 9 May, ten more days elapsed before the last Canadian batteries were withdrawn.

The P.P.C.L.I. in the Salient

The Battles of Ypres, 1915 were to continue for three more weeks, but in these later phases the only Canadian battalion engaged was Princess Patricia's Canadian Light Infantry. The unit had crossed to France as part of the 80th Brigade of the 27th Division, and from 7 January to 23 March 1915 had served in the St. Eloi sector. In this period its most significant operation had been a small local attack carried out by upwards of 100 Patricias on 28 February. At a cost of sixteen casualties (five of them fatal) they inflicted an unknown number of casualties on the Germans and destroyed thirty yards of enemy trench.[100] On 9 April, as the division relieved the French 17th Division in the Ypres Salient, the Patricias occupied positions in front of Polygon Wood, three miles south of the 2nd Canadian Brigade's right at Berlin Wood. During the bitter fighting on the northern flank the battalion was under repeated bombardments, and suffered 80 casualties. On the withdrawal of Plumer's Force on the night of 3-4 May the Patricias fell back to Bellewaarde Ridge, half a mile north-east of Hooge on the Menin Road. Here on 4 May, before there was time to develop their unfinished, shallow trenches, they suffered 122 casualties in the shelling and machine-gun fire that accompanied the enemy's follow-up.

* On the moonlit night of 28-29 April three battalions of the 1st Canadian Brigade, with the 2nd Battalion acting as a covering party, had dug a traversed trench 1200 yards long between Hampshire and Turco Farms. By this achievement important ground was gained without a casualty.[99]

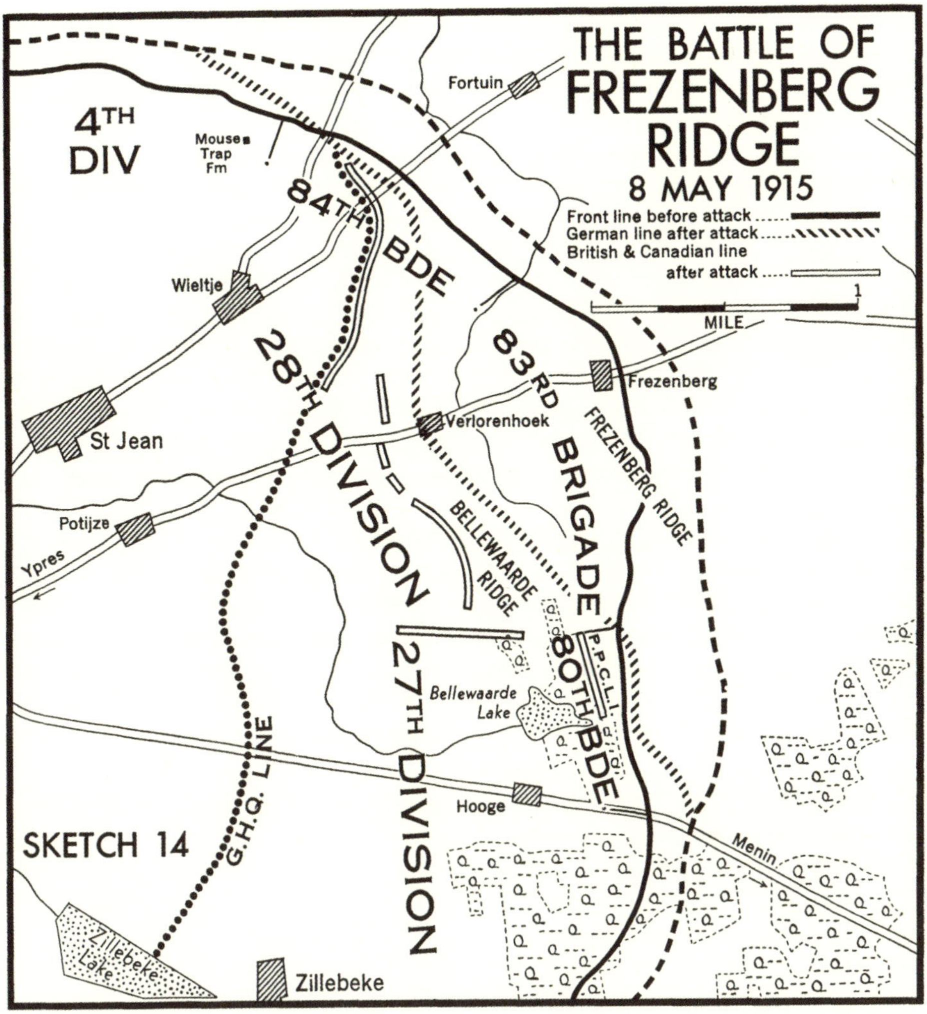

On 8 May a violent bombardment of the whole 5th Corps front heralded a major German assault. Duke Albrecht had ordered three converging attacks to reduce the Salient—the 26th Reserve Corps to advance from the north against the sector Mouse Trap Farm to Frezenberg; the 27th Reserve Corps to make the central and main attack westward between Frezenberg and Bellewaarde Lake; and the 15th Corps to break through north-westward between Bellewaarde and Zillebeke Lakes. The 27th and 28th British Divisions were thus under attack by at least six German divisions.[101] As a preliminary, in three gas attacks on 5 May the 15th Corps had captured Hill 60.

The brunt of the main onslaught on the 8th fell on the 28th Division's 83rd and 84th Brigades holding Frezenberg Ridge. Two assaults were beaten back, but the third overwhelmed the front line, and by mid-morning Frezenberg had fallen. Before noon the Germans had penetrated nearly a mile and were in Verlorenhoek. They advanced no farther, but by mid-afternoon they had widened their breach of the Salient to a gap of two miles and had begun rolling up the British line on either flank.

In their positions on Bellewaarde Ridge at the 27th Division's extreme left the Patricias with the 80th Brigade's other front-line battalion, the 4th King's Royal Rifle Corps, on their right, held the southern shoulder of the gap. The devastating fire that the enemy concentrated on the British trenches from the Menin Road to Frezenberg obliterated whole sections of the P.P.C.L.I. front line on the forward slope of the ridge. Two of the unit's four machine-guns were put out of action and casualties were so heavy that Major Hamilton Gault, who had taken over command of the regiment on 5 May, ordered signallers, pioneers, orderlies and batmen forward into the support trenches. When the Germans launched their main assault at 9:00 a.m., the Patricias' steady rifle fire drove them back on the left; but on the right the enemy gained a footing, compelling a retirement to the main defence line on the crest. Here the battalion, reinforced by a company from the 4th Rifle Brigade, stood unflinchingly for the rest of the day, enduring repeated bombardments and beating back every German attempt to advance from the captured trenches.[102] During the afternoon the left flank, drawn back to face the danger from the north,* was extended by reserve battalions of the 80th and 81st Brigades. These units linked up with counter-attacking battalions of the 85th Brigade in the centre to seal off the German encroachment. East of Mouse Trap Farm a heroic stand by the 2nd Northumberland Fusiliers, when the remainder of the 84th Brigade's front-line battalions were annihilated, held firm the northern shoulder of the gap. On the 4th Division's front west of Mouse Trap Farm British artillery (including eight Canadian field batteries) broke up the infantry attack which followed the early morning bombardment.

When the Patricias were relieved shortly before midnight, their total trench strength was four officers and 150 men. The day's casualties totalled 392. For the last few days of the Battle of Frezenberg Ridge (which ended on 13 May) they formed a composite unit with the 4th King's Royal Rifles, which had shared their valiant stand on Bellewaarde Ridge. On 24 May, when the Fourth Army again attacked the 5th Corps, releasing a heavy concentration of chlorine along a front of 4½ miles (the largest scale yet attempted), the 27th Division was in corps reserve. The Germans captured Mouse Trap Farm and Bellewaarde Ridge, breaking through on both sides of Bellewaarde Lake. Late on the 24th the 80th Brigade made an unsuccessful counter-attack, the Patricias being held in brigade reserve. This operation, named the Battle of Bellewaarde Ridge, ended the Battles of Ypres, 1915. A successful counter-thrust by the French on 15 May had driven the Germans back over the canal about Steenstraat.[104] But the Allies regained no more ground. For the next two years the opposing lines around the Salient were to remain virtually unchanged.

*Remnants of the 83rd Brigade's two right-hand battalions, cut off when the enemy broke through the centre, continued to fight from isolated positions on the Patricias' left.[103]

The successful defence of the Ypres Salient in the spring of 1915 stands as a triumph for the common soldier and his commanders at the regimental and brigade level. At this stage of the war commanders of formations larger than brigades could very rarely exercise effective control of large-scale defensive operations. The absence of adequate air observation and aerial photography made it impossible to determine accurately the enemy's dispositions (or indeed those of our own troops, who had as yet no means of communicating with aeroplanes). The problem presented by this dearth of information was intensified by the deficiencies in signal communications—to the extent that divisional and corps commanders could do little more than pass on the Army Commander's instructions for counter-attacks to be made and try to keep what reinforcements were available moving to the battle area, leaving the tactical employment of these forces almost entirely to the subordinate commanders on the spot. The failure to commit these reinforcements as complete brigades under their own headquarters imposed on the staffs of the formations to which individual units were attached an almost impossible task in the exercise of control and the passage of information and orders. In some cases staffs found their brigades increased by these attachments to twice their normal strength or more.

With no corresponding increase in the administrative services the problems of supply and evacuation reached almost insuperable proportions. An examination of the tactical situation after the first gas attack reveals the dilemma that faced General Plumer. The main pressure had come down on the flank of the Canadian Division, constricting the divisional area to half its normal width. Alderson had to fight along the whole six miles of this front-to-a-flank, moving his reinforcements and supply up through the long narrow sector which ran across the front of the enemy. In this situation Plumer can be criticized for making no change of divisional boundaries throughout the whole of the Battle of St. Julien, during which the 27th and 28th Divisions enjoyed relative quiet. An extension of the 28th Division's front to include the Gravenstafel-St. Julien sector would have greatly facilitated command and supply by sharing the load. As it was, confusion increased when, unknown to the brigade commanders fighting in the line, the corps reserve was placed in the hands of the G.O.C. 27th Division, who was unfamiliar with the sector of the attack and the troop dispositions there. That break-through succeeded break-through at the apex is not surprising. What does surprise is that Currie and his 2nd Brigade hung on so long. In spite of an apparent lack of sound thinking at Corps level, the day was saved by the improvisation of the leaders on the spot—Alderson, Turner and Currie, Snow, Geddes and Hull—that, and the extraordinary slowness of Duke Albrecht's men to capitalize on their early successes.

The movement of substantial reserves into the threatened area was opposed by both the French and British commands, for General Foch did not wish to weaken the projected Artois offensive, and Sir John French would not sanction a further expenditure of British troops unless the French first regained the lost shoulder of the Salient. But these decisions were not immediately known to the hard-pressed defenders of the Salient. Their task was clear—"hold the line at all costs". And hold it they did, in the face of an enemy who by employing superior numbers of infantry supported by a preponderance of heavy artillery and machine-guns was attempting to exploit the advantage gained by his introduction of poison gas into modern warfare. Fortunately the Germans had wasted the potentialities of their new weapon, and the "paralyzing surprise" of its first appearance could never be repeated.

The significance of the Canadian effort lies in the determined stand made during the first three days of the battle. By 25 April enough British and French reinforcements had arrived to end the danger of a German break-through and to make possible an orderly withdrawal to a shorter line of defence. "The Canadians had many casualties", announced a War Office communique, "but their gallantry and determination undoubtedly saved the situation."[105]

Once again Ypres had been held. To our Belgian allies the retention of the city and the Salient meant above all that there was still Belgian territory untrodden by the Prussian heel; to the strategic planners Ypres in Allied hands blocked a German advance to the Channel ports and maintained the threat of an Allied drive towards Lille and Brussels. The cost had been high. The B.E.F.'s total losses at Hill 60 and in the battles of Ypres, from 22 April to 31 May, numbered 59,275 all ranks.[106] During the 1st Canadian Division's period in the line (15 April-3 May), Canadian casualties (not including those of the P.P.C.L.I.) numbered 208 officers and 5828 other ranks, infantry losses being almost equally distributed between the three brigades. The P.P.C.L.I., in their longer period in action with the 27th Division (10 April-21 May), suffered 678 casualties.[107] Against these losses must be set the immense gain in stature which their achievements had brought the Canadians. Henceforth their morale would be high, for they had proved themselves more than a match for the enemy and not less than the equal of their Allied comrades in arms. In their first major operation of the war Canadian soldiers had acquired an indomitable confidence which was to carry them irresistibly forward in the battles which lay ahead.

CHAPTER IV

FESTUBERT AND GIVENCHY, 1915

(See Map 2 and Sketches 15-22)

The Artois Offensive Begins

WHILE the Second British Army was still fighting in defence of Ypres, and possession of Frezenberg Ridge remained in doubt, on the B.E.F.'s right wing the First Army, in cooperation with the French, had begun the long-planned offensive in Artois.

The main effort was to be made in the French Tenth Army's sector, south of the La Bassée Canal. Here, between Lens and Arras, where the eastern edge of the Artois plateau sloped down into the Douai plain, the German Sixth Army was holding a salient seven miles wide and four deep. The principal target was Vimy Ridge, which formed a barrier five miles long across the salient. A five-day bombardment preceded the French attack, which was made by eight assaulting divisions at mid-morning on 9 May, after bad weather had postponed it two days. In the centre a corps of three divisions under General Henri-Philippe Pétain, aided by subsidiary attacks on either flank, broke through the German defences to a depth of two and a half miles, and almost gained the crest of the Ridge. But reserve formations, held seven miles to the rear, came forward too late to exploit this success, and the arrival of German reinforcements turned the battle into an inconclusive struggle which brought the French only heavy losses.[1] The wearing-down process continued until 15 May, to be resumed a month later for another four days unproductive of results. By that time French casualties numbered more than 100,000, the Germans having lost about three quarters of that number.

The nature of the British contribution to the offensive had been settled between General Foch and Sir John French during April. The latter's orders to General Haig called for the First Army to breach the German defences at two points 6000 yards apart, north and south of Neuve Chapelle, to be followed by converging advances to the Aubers Ridge, 3000 yards distant. From there the attack would continue across the La Bassée-Lille road to the line of the Haute Deule canal, six miles from the start line.[2] Unlike the French, who had abandoned the short bombardment in favour of a prolonged artillery preparation of the enemy's positions, the British decided to preface their attack with an intense bombardment of only forty minutes. The choice was influenced partly by the shortage

THE FRONT FROM YPRES TO ARRAS

9 MAY 1915

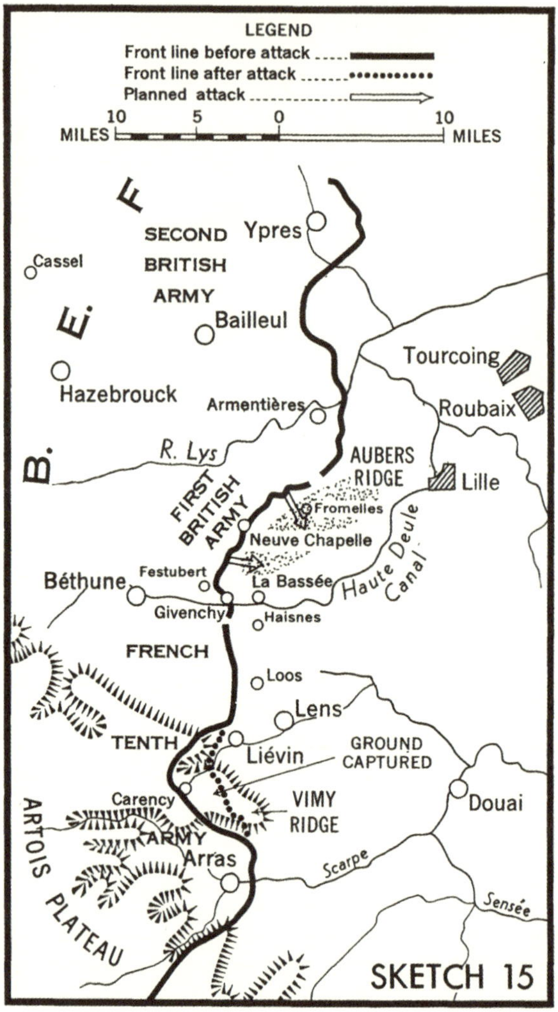

of heavy artillery and ammunition (a deficiency intensified by the operations at Ypres), and also by the hope of gaining maximum surprise for the assaulting infantry. At the battle of Neuve Chapelle, British guns had failed to give rapid and accurate support to the infantry when they were held up by enemy strong-points; it was hoped to remedy this situation by providing "infantry artillery", consisting of batteries of trench mortars and 3-pounder mountain guns carried in lorries or armoured cars. Much preliminary work went into giving the infantry suitable assembly trenches and jumping-off places, and supplying them with assault equipment and adequate reserves of ammunition, rations and engineer stores; for after Neuve Chapelle G.H.Q. had expressed confidence that "by means of careful preparation as regards details and thorough previous registration of the enemy's trenches by our artillery, it appears that a sector of the enemy's front line defence can be captured with comparatively little loss".[8]

But the Germans too had been busy. On the opposing front formations of the Sixth Army's 7th Corps had strengthened their foremost breastwork considerably and more than doubled the width of their barbed wire entanglement. Carefully sited to cover these were each battalion's two machine-guns, placed to fire through steel-rail loopholes close to ground level. Two hundred yards to the rear, at the base of a second breastwork nearing completion, were dug-outs each holding twenty to thirty men ready to garrison the front line immediately the Allied bombardment stopped. Half a mile behind the front trench were concrete machine-gun nests, 1000 yards apart, which would serve as rallying posts in case of a break-through.[4]

The Battle of Aubers Ridge, 9 May 1915

At 5:00 a.m. on the 9th six hundred guns burst into a furious bombardment across the First Army's front. Forty minutes later the assaulting infantry began crossing the 200 yards of no man's land, the men extended to an interval of three paces, and in six lines about fifty yards apart. On the right the Indian and the 1st Corps each attacked with one division: the northern assault was made opposite Fromelles by a division of the 4th Corps. Neither succeeded. The short British artillery preparation, its effectiveness impaired by worn out gun-barrels and faulty ammunition, had failed to destroy the German defences, so that many of the garrison had returned to their forward positions before the bombardment ended.[5]

In the southern attack the first three lines of assaulting troops were mown down by rifle and machine-gun fire from front and flank, and the fourth wave was cut to pieces by German field artillery. At the few points where the attackers did penetrate the front breastwork they were quickly killed or captured. A second attempt made after a new bombardment was equally disastrous. When it ended, the casualties of the nine assaulting battalions of the 1st and Indian Corps exceeded 3100 officers and men.[6]

The attack on the left by the 4th Corps had fared little better. Three of the five assault battalions gained small lodgements beyond the first breastwork but were then cut off as heavy fire from German positions still intact halted all further movement. From army headquarters General Haig, intent on assisting the progress of the French fifteen miles to the south, ordered the assault renewed in both sectors. Once again German riflemen and machine-gunners, seeing no man's land filled with extended lines of men following closely behind one another, took a terrible toll. An Indian brigade lost a thousand men in a few minutes. Only part of the first wave gained a footing in the enemy trenches, and without support these troops were soon overpowered. Survivors withdrew to their own positions after dark. The battle of Aubers Ridge was not renewed. In twelve hours of fighting the First Army had gained no ground and had suffered more than 11,000 casualties.[7] It was a costly demonstration of the futility of pitting unsupported massed manpower against skilfully applied firepower.

Yet Haig recognized the need for continuing the First Army's active operations, if only to meet the demands of General Joffre, who was accusing the British of not "pulling their weight" and thereby upsetting his plans. It seemed the right time to be maintaining pressure on the Western Front, for the enemy's attention was directed to the east, where on 2 May a powerful Austro-German offensive had been launched in the Gorlice-Tarnow sector in Galicia (below, p. 118). For this undertaking von Falkenhayn had withdrawn from opposite the French all the divisions he could spare. When the British struck, the Sixth Army had alerted its only two reserve divisions in the neighbourhood, but the fact that on the evening of 9 May these could be diverted southward from in front of the B.E.F.[8] to reinforce the Arras-Vimy sector increased the urgency of Joffre's appeals for British action. The failure at Aubers Ridge convinced Haig that it was impracticable for the First Army to press two attacks simultaneously on a wide frontage against such strong defences. He therefore abandoned the effort on his left wing in order to concentrate his resources on a three-mile front between Neuve Chapelle and Festubert, a village one and a half miles north of the La Bassée Canal.

General Joffre was anxious that the First Army should either strike at once or extend its front south of the La Bassée Canal so as to relieve a French division for action in the Vimy offensive. In order that General Haig might carry out the attack in his own time, Sir John French agreed to the latter alternative. He was exceedingly short of troops, for the long awaited divisions of the New Armies were being retained in England, ostensibly because Lord Kitchener feared an invasion as soon as the German striking force returned from the Russian front, but in reality because they were deficient in guns, rifles, and above all, ammunition. Sir John named the Canadian Division, which had been reorganizing south of Bailleul, to relieve the French 58th Division on the British right.[9] But the Canadian artillery was still in action at Ypres and at Ploegsteert (where a composite C.F.A. brigade had relieved a brigade of the 4th (British) Divisional Artillery on 10 May), and the French would not leave their own guns behind. Accordingly the relief was carried out by the 1st (British) Division, which on the night of 14-15 May took over 5500 yards of the French line. Holding the front from the canal to Festubert was the 47th Division, and north of this was the 1st British Corps, with which General Haig planned to make his attack.[10]

The disaster of 9 May had brought an important change in British tactics. On the 11th Sir Douglas recorded in his diary:

> The defences in our front are so carefully and so strongly made, and mutual support with machine-guns is so complete, that in order to demolish them a *long methodical bombardment* will be necessary by heavy artillery (guns and howitzers) before Infantry are sent forward to attack.

He purposed using 60-pounder guns in addition to the 15-inch siege howitzers, and accurately observing the result of every shot to ensure that the enemy's strong-points had been demolished before the infantry attacked.[11] In formally approving "a deliberate and persistent attack" in which the enemy would "be gradually and relentlessly worn down by exhaustion and loss until his defence collapses", Sir

John French noted that surprise would be lacking because of the long bombardment and he therefore prescribed only a limited objective, entailing an advance of about 1000 yards—one third the distance contemplated in the battle of Aubers Ridge.[12] The distinction between semi-open warfare and semi-siege warfare had at least been recognized. For the first time in the war British forces were to engage in a battle of "attrition".

The Battle of Festubert, 15-25 May

On the morning of 13 May, 433 howitzers and guns began a systematic bombardment of the German defences on a 5000-yard frontage extending northward from Festubert. The fire was slow and deliberate (50 rounds per howitzer in each 24 hours) in order that the effect upon the German defences might be carefully observed. Six-inch howitzer batteries concentrated on the enemy parapet; 4.5-inch pieces bombarded the support and communication trenches. The field guns went to work on the wire entanglements and harassed enemy troops by spraying the communication trenches with shrapnel. This "wearing-down" preparation continued for the prescribed 36 hours, and was prolonged another 24 hours at the request of one of the assaulting divisions. During the sixty hours the artillery of the 1st Corps expended just over 100,000 rounds of ammunition.

The infantry attacked on the night of 15-16 May. General Haig's plan called for the 2nd Division on the left to launch a midnight assault on a front of 1300 yards: the Meerut Division of the Indian Corps would cover the left flank. At daybreak the 7th Division (which did not know the ground well enough for a night attack) would join in on the right, attacking on a half-mile front, while the 2nd Division advanced to the second objective, the line of la Quinque Rue, which ran north-eastward from Festubert.[13] Both attacks would fall on the German 14th Infantry Division, which was holding the front from south of the La Bassée Canal to the Ferme du Bois, two miles north-east of Festubert, with the 16th, 56th and 57th Infantry Regiments. Farther north the 13th Infantry Division faced the Indian Corps.[14]

The 2nd and Meerut Divisions' use of darkness to gain surprise—it was the first British night attack of the war—was partly successful. The right brigade reached the German breastwork in silence and secured it and the support line as planned. But on the northern flank a preliminary demonstration by the Lahore Division with small-arms fire only alerted the Germans, who drove back the two assaulting brigades on the left with heavy fire. The 7th Division advanced at 3:15 a.m., substituting a field artillery barrage for the surprise which would have attended a silent assault in the dark. The German front breastwork was carried, and the right-hand brigade reached its final objective along la Quinque Rue. Elsewhere the advance was halted by determined fire from unmolested German positions in the gap between the 2nd and 7th Divisions' sectors. Two attempts during the 16th to link the adjacent flanks of the two divisions failed. That night, however, the Germans abandoned any hope of regaining their lost trenches and on orders from the G.O.C. 14th Infantry Division withdrew on a 3000-yard front. Their new line of resistance, which for several days the British were unable to identify accurately, opposite Festubert lay some 500 yards behind la Quinque Rue, but farther north it swung to the west of that road to include their strong position at Ferme du Bois.

Interpreting the German withdrawal as a sign that the enemy's resistance was breaking down,[15] at mid-morning on the 17th the Army Commander ordered the 1st Corps to consolidate a strong front along la Quinque Rue, with brigadiers on the spot pressing on if opportunity offered. At the same time he placed the 3rd Canadian Brigade at the disposal of the G.O.C. 1st Corps, who detailed it as divisional reserve to the 7th Division. The general direction of advance was to swing to the south-east, Sir John French having changed the First Army's ultimate objective from Aubers Ridge to La Bassée, in order to gain access to the area south of the canal.[16] But efforts to get forward failed, and that evening General Haig ordered a fresh infantry attack, preceded by a deliberate bombardment, to take place on the 18th. The Corps Commander named the 3rd Canadian Brigade to assault on the 7th Division's front; immediately on the left the 2nd Division would attack with the 4th Guards Brigade.[17] Because of early morning fog the artillery preparation was postponed and zero hour for the infantry assault was set at 4:30 p.m.

The main attack would be launched at the centre of the 1st Corps front to secure a mile of la Quinque Rue. In a subsidiary effort farther north the Indian Corps was to capture Ferme du Bois. Because the 7th Division's front line was much closer to the road (which angled towards the north-east), the 3rd Brigade was given the additional task of occupying the North Breastwork (a section of the original German line running east and north-east from la Quinque Rue), and at the end of this Breastwork an orchard which was known to be defended.[18] Brig.-Gen. Turner's plan for the Canadian assault called for two companies of the 14th Battalion on the left and one from the 16th Battalion on the right to attack eastward to the road and the orchard beyond. In the meantime another company of the 16th would make a long detour through Festubert village to take the North Breastwork from the south-west and link up with the frontal attack.[19]

General Haig's final orders were not issued until 1:55 p.m., and by the time these had reached the infantry brigades and the supporting artillery, zero hour was fast approaching. A two-hour bombardment scheduled to begin at 2:30 was an hour late in starting,[20] and the Canadian frontal assault did not begin until 5:25 p.m.[21] By that time the Guards Brigade had been halted by machine-gun fire from the new German positions, which because their location was not yet known to the artillery had survived the bombardment without serious damage.

The 14th Battalion's frontal attack across water-logged fields devoid of cover met the same fire from unlocated machine-guns, and was deflected to the south. Then the German artillery opened up, bringing organized forward movement to a halt about 400 yards from the jumping-off trenches. The adjoining company of the 16th Battalion by following a communication trench reached la Quinque Rue and deployed along it. Here they were joined by their flanking company, which had made an encircling two-mile approach through Festubert. It came under heavy shelling at the western end of the North Breastwork—one German salvo caused 47 casualties—and without supporting fire was unable to advance any farther.[22] Although neither the 1st nor the Indian Corps had gained its objectives, the 3rd Brigade's advance had reduced the gap between the 2nd and 7th Divisions. In a downpour of rain relieving companies of the 16th Battalion dug throughout the night to consolidate the gains into a continuous line. The Germans gave full credit to their artillery for stopping the Canadians. "They encountered such an effective barrage", writes the historian of the 57th Infantry Regiment about the 3rd Brigade, "... that the attack collapsed after a few minutes and was not again renewed against the regiment's position".[23]

During the night (18-19 May) the 2nd Canadian Brigade took over positions on the 3rd Brigade's right. This was part of a series of reliefs in which the 2nd and 7th Divisions (less their artillery) were replaced in the line by the 51st (Highland) and the 1st Canadian Divisions. The Army Commander grouped the two relieving divisions and the 2nd and 7th Divisional Artilleries under General Alderson's command "for an active offensive movement", designating the temporary corps "Alderson's Force".[24] Alderson retained operational control of his own division, while the Indian Corps took over the administration of the Canadian and Highland Divisions. But the experimental grouping did not prove successful. With no corps staff Alderson had to use his own chief staff officer, with resulting disorganization of his divisional headquarters.[25] "Alderson's Force" was to last only four days.

In the meantime the enemy had been busy bringing in all available reserves to restore a situation which local commanders regarded as precarious. From the evening of 16 May reinforcing units of company or battalion strength came in piecemeal from the north, some marching, more distant ones by rail. The 2nd Guard Reserve Division, a veteran formation of the 1914 fighting, which had been brought from Alsace on 14 May as reserve for the defenders of Vimy Ridge, marched to La Bassée on the 18th. It gradually relieved the 14th and the left wing of the 13th Divisions, its 55th Reserve and 15th Reserve Regiments taking over the line opposite the Canadians and the 2nd British Division.[26]

General Alderson's first assignment on taking over his new command on the morning of 20 May called for an advance of from 600 to 1000 yards against objectives 3000 yards apart. Later First Army modified these requirements, as the 51st Division's relief of the 2nd Division was delayed. At 3:00 p.m. Alderson ordered the two Canadian brigades in the line to assault at 7:45 that evening. On the right the 2nd Brigade was directed to seize a point (K.5 on the map)* near the junction of the new and old German front lines. At the

* On the trench maps in current use topographical features and other tactical objectives were indicated by a letter and a number, e.g., J.1, J.2, etc. The letters distinguished narrow sectors of the front in alphabetical order from right to left: numbers read consecutively from the British front line out into enemy territory.

same time the 3rd Brigade was to secure half a mile of the enemy's new front line and capture Canadian Orchard (as it came to be called) and an adjoining building (M.10).[27] Farther north the Indian Corps would again try to take Ferme du Bois. The operation would be preceded by a comprehensive artillery programme involving all the guns and howitzers of the First Army.

It was still broad daylight when the attack started, after a bombardment which had begun at 4:00 p.m. In the 3rd Brigade's sector it was the same story of men advancing magnificently against a hail of machine-gun bullets. On the left the two assaulting companies of the 16th Battalion reached the orchard, and quickly clearing it of its surprised defenders dug in within a hundred yards of the main German line. The nearby house at M.10 was found to be well protected by barbed wire and strongly garrisoned, and attempts to cross the intervening open ground had to be abandoned. The 15th Battalion's advance on the right had been made across open fields that gave no cover from the eyes of the German machine-gunners and artillery observers. Casualties mounted rapidly as the two companies of Highlanders pressed forward in short 20-yard dashes. They gained and crossed the North Breastwork, but were halted 100 yards beyond. As night closed in supporting companies came forward to consolidate what had been won.[28]

The 2nd Brigade's attack, which was assigned to two companies of the 10th Battalion, was doomed to failure before it started. In an afternoon reconnaissance Brig.-Gen. Currie had been unable to identify his objective, which was shown as a small circle on the map. (A major disadvantage of this method of designating positions was the use of the same symbol regardless of the nature of the feature to be identified. To confuse matters further, the Festubert trench map was full of inaccuracies, with errors in position amounting to as much as 450 yards. Furthermore, it was printed upsidedown, with the north at the bottom of the sheet and the east on the left.)[29] The assembly trenches were badly breached and under fire, as was a shallow communicating ditch which provided the only semblance of a covered approach to his target. Currie therefore asked for the attack to be postponed until next day, but was refused. Even his expected fire support was reduced. The original artillery plan had included a blasting of K.5 by two 9.2-inch howitzers, but this was cancelled lest the necessary withdrawal of Canadians from the danger zone near such a bombardment should alert the Germans, who from Aubers Ridge could look right into the First Army's positions. The 10th Battalion's attacking party cleared the communication trench of enemy for 100 yards, but as the brigade bombers emerged in single file into the open they came under a storm of fire from machine-guns on built-up positions which had been unharmed by our artillery. Seeing the leaders all shot down, the company commander halted the suicidal advance and ordered the gains made good.[30]

A proposed early morning renewal of the attack on the 21st was postponed till nightfall in order to allow for a more deliberate bombardment. The First Army's order for the operation required "Alderson's Force" to secure

K.5 and M.10 and the intervening 1500 yards of front trench which barred access to the Rue d'Ouvert, leading south-eastward to La Bassée. From K.5 the new German line ran north-eastward along the South Breastwork, forming a sharp salient with the old front line. Enemy records show that the "Stützpunkt" (strongpoint), as the Germans called their redoubt at the tip of this salient, was ordered to be maintained by reinforcement and counter-attack until the new line was completed.[31] K.5 became the principal Canadian target; and since it was opposite the divisional boundary, the 47th (London) Division placed its left forward battalion under General Currie's command for the operation. On Alderson's left, because of the known strength of the fortified house at M.10 and the lack of unexposed assembly area, there were no orders for any advance from the Orchard.

A bombardment of three and a half hours preceded the attack, which was launched at half-past eight, while it was still light. But once again the artillery preparation proved woefully ineffective. Field guns, dispersed thinly across the whole front and forced by ammunition shortages to fire mainly shrapnel, could not compensate for the lack of heavy siege guns. The German strongpoints suffered little damage. With counter-battery work in its infancy, the enemy's guns, superior in calibre and supplies of ammunition, were virtually unmolested. The 2nd Brigade's assault was made by the same two companies of the 10th Battalion, together with the 1st Brigade's grenade company, carrying 500 bombs. From breaches cut in the sides of the approach trench half the force broke out to the left, half to the right. The former, advancing across 200 yards of open ground towards K.5, was quickly cut to pieces by machine-gun fire. The right-hand party, however, attacking the western face of the salient, met less resistance and drove the enemy out of 400 yards of his front line. During the night the Germans attempted several counter-attacks, which the Canadian garrison, reinforced by a company of the 5th Battalion, drove off. Then, with the coming of daylight on the 22nd, enemy guns began a heavy bombardment of their lost position. Large portions of the breastworks were blown away and the occupants wiped out. Before midday Currie withdrew his men from all but 100 yards of the newly occupied line. The 10th Battalion had by then suffered casualties of 18 officers and 250 other ranks.[32]

That same morning General Haig visited General Alderson's headquarters to express dissatisfaction at the failure of the Canadian attacks and to insist that the Germans be driven from the positions.[33] Relinquishing the idea of an "active offensive movement" in favour of a "methodical advance combined with the consolidation of the positions won", he dissolved "Alderson's Force", placing the 51st (Highland) Division under the Indian Corps (whose attempts to take Ferme du Bois had finally been abandoned), and the 1st Canadian Division directly under the command of First Army. At an Army conference next morning he ordered a thorough reconnaissance of the enemy's positions before planning the next attack, which would be a combined effort by the Canadian Division and the 47th Division (of the 1st Corps) on its right to reduce the German salient opposite. From its apex at K.5 this extended 1500 yards north-east to the Orchard and an equal distance south-east to a point opposite Givenchy-lez-la Bassée—a hamlet about half a mile from the La Bassée Canal.[34] The Canadians were to take K.5 and get patrols to the northern part of the Rue d'Ouvert; the British division was to attack towards Chapelle St. Roch, farther south on the same road.[35]

As a preliminary to the main operation the inner brigades of the two divisions made a night assault astride the South Breastwork. Again the 2nd Brigade was entrusted with the Canadian part of the operation. This time there had been opportunity for careful reconnaissance and detailed preparations. The artillery had maintained a slow continuous fire through the night, and at 2:30 a.m. (on the 24th) two companies of the 5th Battalion, led by a party of 30 bombers, assaulted* from the communication trench and the adjoining front line opposite the German redoubt at K.5. Twelve footbridges carried the infantry across a waterfilled ditch ten feet wide, and within half an hour the Canadians had seized K.5 and 130 yards of trench to the north-west. Three companies of the 7th Battalion came forward to reinforce the 5th, which had suffered 250 casualties—including thirteen of its eighteen combatant officers. The 47th Division's attack on the right, half an hour later in starting, reached the near end of the Breastwork but failed to capture any enemy trenches.

On the night of the 24th the Canadian effort shifted to the left flank, where thirty minutes before midnight a company of the 3rd Battalion assaulted from the Orchard in an attempt to capture 300 yards of trench running north from the fortified house at M.10. But a preliminary six-hour bombardment had failed to silence the enemy's machine-guns, four of which caught the attacking troops at ranges of from 50 to 100 yards. Only a few men reached the German trench, and none of these remained alive or uncaptured.[36] The positions along the Orchard's eastern hedge gained by the 16th Battalion four days before remained the farthest points to be reached by the First Army in the Battle of Festubert, and indeed were not to fall into the enemy's hands until his major advance in the spring of 1918.

Before the inconclusive battle ended there was one more Canadian attempt to push the Germans back. The task of cooperating with the 47th Division's attack on the evening of 25 May was given to "Seely's Detachment", which had relieved the 2nd Brigade on the 24th. This dismounted detachment consisted of the headquarters and units of the Canadian Cavalry Brigade. To meet the 1st Division's shortage of infantry after Ypres its personnel had volunteered for service in France and had crossed the Channel on 4 May, approximately 1500 strong, leaving their horses with Yeomanry units in England. Except for 24 hours' instruction given to one squadron of the Royal Canadian Dragoons, Brig.-Gen. Seely's nine squadrons of cavalrymen entered the front line with no experience in trench warfare.[37] They were opposed by the newly arrived 91st Reserve Regiment of the 2nd Guard Reserve Division.

* The battle cry during the attack was "Lusitania". The British liner had been sunk without warning by a German submarine on 7 May, with the loss of almost 1200 lives.

Promptly at 6:30 p.m. the British attacked immediately north of the Givenchy-Chapelle St. Roch road. Within an hour two battalions of the 142nd Brigade had advanced an average distance of 400 yards to capture (at a cost of 980 casualties) the German forward and support trenches on a frontage of 1000 yards.[38] The Canadian contribution began at nine o'clock with a bombing group from Lord Strathcona's Horse working northward from K.5. They carried 200 gas bombs—the first authorized use of gas by the B.E.F.[39]—and they were assisted by bayonet parties from their own regiment. Reports of success coming back soon after midnight indicated that the South Breastwork had been cleared from K.5 to L.8, a point 300 yards to the north-east. Working parties from the 2nd Brigade moved forward to consolidate the new line. But later it was found that L.8 was still in German hands, the attacking party, misled by the unreliable maps and the fact that the ground was "trenched and retrenched in all directions", having occupied positions farther to the west.[40] It was left to the 3rd Brigade, which relieved Seely's Detachment on 27 May, to secure L.8 and link up a continuous line with the 47th Division south of K.5.

On the last day of May 1915 the 1st Canadian Division began shifting to the right to take over the Givenchy sector, immediately north of the canal. The move was part of a reorganization of the First Army's front following a decision by Sir John French on 25 May to halt the Festubert battle and initiate new undertakings to assist the French offensive. "Having attained for the moment the immediate object I had in view", the C.-in-C. reported to the War Office, ". . . I gave orders to Sir Douglas Haig to curtail his artillery attack and to strengthen and consolidate the ground he had won."[41] But French demands could not be ignored. General Foch was pressing for a British offensive south of the La Bassée Canal towards Loos, in cooperation with a renewal of the French effort between Lens and Arras. Yet the serious shortage of ammunition precluded any immediate major offensive, and Sir Douglas Haig argued that the open country west of Loos afforded no cover for artillery positions or for the assembly of troops. He recommended instead a limited operation north of the canal from Givenchy towards La Bassée, possibly to be followed by another small attack south of the waterway towards Haisnes.[42] In concurring, Sir John French ordered the First Army to take over another divisional sector on the French Tenth Army's left so as to enable Foch to reinforce his renewed offensive against Vimy Ridge.

For the 1st Canadian Division, as for the other formations of the First Army taking part in the battle, Festubert had been a frustrating experience. Substantial gains had been looked for but not achieved, and in the lower echelons, where the Army's role of easing pressure on the French was little appreciated, few could readily share the Commander-in-Chief's view of an objective attained. In the course of the battle Canadians had assaulted on five separate days, to advance their line an average distance of 600 yards across a one-mile front. Except for the capture of a bit of German defences at K.5 their attacks had not reached the enemy line. In doing this they had suffered 2468 casualties. The Canadian Division had returned to action a little more than two weeks after losing half its fighting strength at Ypres—far too short a time for units to assimilate their infantry reinforcements (we have noted the inexperience of the dismounted cavalry). Yet no fault can be found with the offensive spirit and the self-sacrifice of the troops, who were called upon to persist in the impossible.

Once again the superiority of the German artillery had decided the issue. The enemy's organized shelling of the front line and support trenches prevented the assembly of troops within reasonable assaulting distance of their objective and kept reinforcements from coming forward to exploit initial gains. Our own guns, outclassed in weight and short of high explosive shell, could neither destroy the enemy's field defences nor silence his batteries. In addition the German defenders held the advantage in machine-guns, trench mortars and their very effective "stick grenades". New tactics were needed to offset the lead thus taken by a nation which had well prepared itself for war; yet so far Allied commanders appeared satisfied that success was merely a matter of persistence—and more guns and ammunition.[43]

The Action at Givenchy, 15 June

On the completion of General Haig's reorganization the 1st Canadian Division found itself forming the right wing of the 4th Corps (Lieut.-General Sir H. S. Rawlinson), which was holding the centre of the First Army's front from the La Bassée Canal northward to Canadian Orchard. Next to the Canadians was the 7th Division, with the 51st (Highland) Division beyond. On the Corps left the Indian Corps had a defensive role on an eight-mile front, while to the south the 1st Corps held six miles of line between the canal and the French Tenth Army with the 1st, 47th and 2nd Divisions.

For a brief period the Canadians enjoyed a respite from fighting. The narrow divisional sector—the 4th Corps' frontage was a little over two and a half miles—required only one brigade in the front line, and units in reserve found relaxation in the pleasant Béthune countryside beside the banks of the canal. The Canadian front extended a thousand yards northward from the canal, crossing the south-westerly tip of the Aubers Ridge to take in the eastern outskirts of the shattered village of Givenchy-lez-la-Bassée—scene of a successful defence by British troops in December 1914. After Festubert it was a welcome change to occupy dry trenches. More important, the higher ground was to permit construction of communication and support trenches that would allow the concealed assembly of troops preparing for an assault. No man's land in the Canadian sector varied from 500 yards wide on the right down to 75 yards east of Givenchy, where a semi-circular sandbagged parapet, known as the Duck's Bill, protruded towards the enemy's line. On the German side, responsibility for the defence of the La Bassée area still rested with the 14th Division. Next to the canal, opposing the Canadians, was the 134th (Saxon) Infantry Regiment, brought in as reinforcement from the 40th (Saxon) Division north of Armentières.[44]

GIVENCHY

15 JUNE 1915

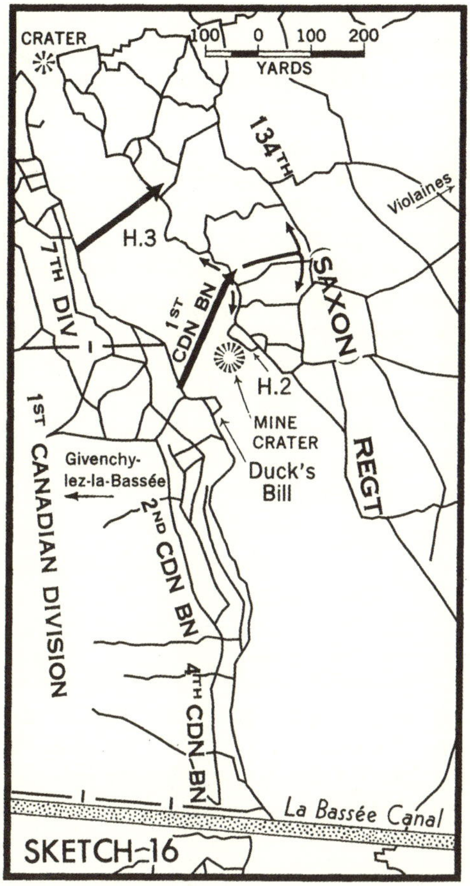

There was not enough heavy ammunition to proceed with the original plan for attacks on both sides of the canal. The project was therefore reduced to an assault by the 4th Corps on a very narrow front towards Violaines, a village 1500 yards north-west of La Bassée; and after several postponements in order to coordinate with the renewal of the French offensive, the date was set at 15 June. General Rawlinson's orders called for an attack by the 7th and 51st Divisions against the line Chapelle St. Roch—rue d'Ouvert, with the Canadian Division "rendering such assistance as may be possible without actually assaulting the enemy's trench line".[45] But the Canadians could not establish the required protective right flank without breaking through the German front line, and General Alderson's orders of 8 and 12 June provided for an assault by the 1st Brigade on two strongpoints—H.2 opposite the Duck's Bill, and H.3 150 yards to the north.[46]

On this occasion the Canadians had time for careful preparation, and the preliminary arrangements which they made were to stand as a model for successful major engagements fought later by the Canadian Corps. The artillery available for the 4th Corps' operation had been divided into five groups. Covering the Canadian front was a group under Brig.-Gen. H. E. Burstall (Commander of the Canadian Divisional Artillery), which included eight 4.5-inch and eight 6-inch howitzers, a group of French 75-mm. guns, and the 2nd and 3rd Brigades C.F.A. (the 1st Brigade C.F.A. was employed in a group supporting the 7th Division's right). The Canadian 18-pounders had the task of destroying the enemy's wire. Determined that there should be no criticism over uncut wire after the battle, General Burstall insisted that the infantry express themselves as satisfied before the assault.[47] The successive postponements prolonged the task, for the enemy was able to repair some of the breaches by night; as a result the artillery was forced to exceed the expenditure of ammunition prescribed by the First Army (six rounds of shrapnel per yard).[48] Afterwards the commander of the 1st Brigade reported that the wire on his front "was found to have been most satisfactorily dealt with".[49]

The experience of Festubert had emphasized the need for neutralizing the enemy's forward machine-guns if the assaulting troops were to be saved from annihilation as they crossed no man's land. To this end three 18-pounders fitted with heavy armour plate shields and with their wheels silenced by rubber tires were secretly dragged forward on the night preceding the attack and placed in position—two (from the 4th Battery C.F.A.) near the Duck's Bill, only seventy-five yards from the German trenches, and one (6th Battery) in a ruined farmhouse within 300 yards' range of H.3.

As mentioned above, the relatively high ground had made it possible for engineers and working parties to construct behind the Canadian front line an assembly trench protected by a parados. By mid-afternoon on 15 June the 1st Battalion, which was to make the Canadian assault, was in position here, its four companies suitably disposed to attack in four successive waves. All were equipped with the short Lee-Enfield rifle, which two days earlier had replaced the Ross rifle throughout the Division (see below, p. 155). A slow artillery bombardment of 48 hours had quickened at six that morning into twelve hours of heavy fire. At 5:45 p.m., fifteen minutes before zero hour, the three forward guns were unmasked, and those near the Duck's Bill began blasting the German parapet over open sights. The third gun, however, did not open fire for fear of hitting our men in the front trenches, and as a result the machine-guns in the twin redoubt at H.3 went unharmed. Unfortunately the wire-cutting programme had shown the enemy exactly where to expect an attack, and his immediate reaction was a heavy artillery concentration upon the Givenchy area. The infantry crowded in the assembly trenches suffered severely and both 18-pounders were put out of action, though not before they had fired some 120 rounds, knocking out three machine-guns and effectively breaching the German parapet.[50]

At two minutes before six British engineers (of the 176th Tunnelling Company, R. E.) exploded a giant mine close to the German line. The plan had been to blow up H.2, but water encountered under no man's land had stopped tunnelling short of this target. In compensation the charge was increased to

3000 pounds of ammonal; yet though the resulting crater was more than forty yards across, the strongpoint was not destroyed. By ill luck the explosion inflicted a number of casualties on bombing parties of the 1st Battalion, and detonated or buried bomb reserves in the Canadian front line. The debris from the eruption had scarcely ceased falling when the 1st Battalion's leading company was on its way, quickly followed by the supporting company with two machine-guns, which were set up in the enemy's front trench. As a covering artillery barrage lifted eastward, both companies went straight through to the German second line and began bombing to right and left and establishing blocks. At 6:10 p.m. the third company crossed no man's land and occupied the German front line, to be joined at seven o'clock by the remaining company.[51]

Early reports from the sector of the main attack, where the 7th and 51st Divisions were each assaulting with two battalions, indicated the capture of the German front line across the whole of the 4th Corps front. But later it was established that the enemy still held H.3. Farther north he was also holding the crater of a mine which the 7th Division had exploded twelve days earlier, and from these two positions his machine-gun fire swept no man's land as far south as the Duck's Bill. Thus he was able to play havoc with the Canadian third and fourth waves, and at the same time cover the reoccupation of his lost trenches. Meanwhile the 1st Battalion's attempts to bomb northward towards H.3 had been halted by German counter-bombing and by the attackers' shortage of grenades. The situation for the Canadians in the enemy's second line became critical, for the 7th Division's failure to advance beyond the opposing front line had left an open flank. To meet a German counter-attack the 1st Battalion's machine-gun officer, Lieutenant F. W. Campbell, took one of his guns forward from the enemy's front line. The tripod had been broken, but the only other surviving member of the detachment, Private H. Vincent, supported the weapon on his back while Campbell kept on firing until he fell, mortally wounded. When the last round had been expended, Vincent, who was later awarded the Distinguished Conduct Medal, crawled back to the Canadian lines, dragging his gun behind him. Lieutenant Campbell received the Victoria Cross.[52]

Bombers of the 2nd Battalion and two reinforcing platoons from the 3rd were carrying on the fight from the mine crater, but a company of the 3rd Battalion sent forward shortly before nine was held at the Canadian front line by the enemy's fire. Cut off from reinforcements and stores the remnants of the 1st Battalion's advanced companies had already been forced to fall back to the German first line, and between 9:00 and 10:00 this position too had to be evacuated. The battalion had suffered 366 casualties; its losses of 20 officers being particularly crippling.

The 3rd Battalion was ordered to renew the attack half an hour after midnight, but because of the uncertain situation on the rest of the Corps front and the time required to mount a fresh artillery bombardment there were several postponements. The new assault was made on all three divisional fronts at 4:45 p.m. on the 16th, after a two-hour bombardment—all that ammunition stocks would allow. Yet again the enemy was fully prepared, and nowhere did the assaulting troops gain a permanent hold on the opposing front line. As soon as the barrage lifted the Germans manned the parapet, and the 3rd Battalion, this time unaided by mine or advanced field guns, met such a hail of rifle and machine-gun bullets that its leading waves could not cross no man's land.[53] Reports of gains by the 51st Division proved unfounded, and arrangements for a new assault at 9:00 p.m. by the Royal Canadian Dragoons were cancelled. That night the 1st Brigade reverted to a role of "passive defensive"; and on 19 June Sir John French instructed General Haig that since the French offensive in Artois had now ended the First Army should make no further attempt to gain ground.[54]

On the 24th the 1st Canadian Division began moving to the Ploegsteert sector, about seventeen miles northward of Givenchy, and some three miles north of Armentières. In returning to the Second Army the Division came under the command of the 3rd Corps (Lieut.-General Sir W. P. Pulteney) and was made responsible for 4400 yards of front line between Messines and Ploegsteert. It was the beginning of a period of three months of relative inactivity along the British front, during which neither side undertook other than local operations.

There was much entrenching to be done. At the direction of the C.-in-C. the Corps Commander ordered the construction of a strong defensive zone immediately behind the front line. As we have seen, while British strength in France had been growing during the first half of 1915, German forces were being transferred to the Eastern Front, so that it no longer seemed probable that the enemy would attack in sufficient numbers to compel a major withdrawal. Accordingly work on such rearward positions as the G.H.Q. line was discontinued.[55] The Corps Commander declared adequate support trenches about seventy yards behind a well maintained front line "to be a matter of the very first necessity", and the early stages of the programme saw 2000 men employed nightly from the 1st Canadian Division.[56] Depth was given to the two forward lines by the construction of a series of mutually supporting defended localities in farm buildings or sandbagged redoubts, each well-wired and sited for all-round defence by a garrison of about platoon strength. In these were mounted eight guns of the 1st Canadian Motor Machine Gun Brigade (the new designation of the former Automobile Machine Gun Brigade No. 1), which had arrived from England on 21 June. Covering these strongpoints was a subsidiary line of trenches and breastworks about a mile behind the front trenches.

From late June to mid-September 1915 a strange tranquillity persisted across the Canadian front. Apart from the activity of snipers on both sides and one small patrol clash in no man's land, the only hostilities were an occasional exchange of light shelling by the opposing artilleries, which in general confined their attention to registering targets. On three occasions the Royal Engineers exploded mines in front of the Canadian trenches, and detachments of the 13th Battalion (on 9 and 13 July) and the 4th Battalion (on 31 August) occupied the resulting craters without difficulty.[57] Mobile anti-aircraft sections formed from the Motor Machine Gun Brigade occasionally engaged enemy aircraft reconnoitring behind the Canadian lines.[58] July brought a visit from Sir Robert Borden; and in August the Minister of Militia, Major-General Sam Hughes, spent two days with the Canadians, witnessing a shoot by three field batteries and reviewing the P.P.C.L.I. and the R.C.H.A.[59]

Before the end of September the arrival of a second division in France had increased Canadian representation in the field into a full army corps. For the decisions and events which led to this expansion we must briefly retrace our steps.

Raising the 2nd Canadian Division

On 6 October 1914, three days after the First Canadian Contingent had set sail, the Governor General telegraphed the Secretary of State for the Colonies an offer by the Dominion Government "to place and maintain in the field a second oversea contingent of twenty thousand men". He explained that since Canada had already parted with nearly all her 18-pounder guns, she could not supply a complete division, but that besides infantry she was prepared to "furnish mounted rifles and units fighting or administrative required for special purposes".[60] Correctly anticipating a favourable reply, Ottawa immediately ordered the mobilization of a second contingent. Fifteen new infantry battalions were to be raised, and to ensure a steady stream of reinforcements it was decided to keep thirty thousand men continuously under arms in Canada in addition to forces required for home defence.[61] In November the Government authorized a number of divisional, line of communication and unallotted units and increased the training quota in Canada to 50,000.[62]

At the end of October 1914 the United Kingdom confirmed its acceptance of a second Canadian contingent, which would form with the balance of the Canadian troops then in England a full division complete with L. of C. units. The War Office warned, however, that if it had to provide guns for the division, these could not be available "for at least 9 months or possibly more".[63] Recruiting had begun in mid-October. Volunteering was brisk, particularly in the west, where quotas were filled as soon as clothing and equipment became available.[64] The new units remained in their respective Military Districts until just prior to embarkation in the spring of 1915. The Minister of Militia had come to prefer local preliminary training under District arrangements to the "call to arms" method employed in the case of the First Contingent; moreover, the lack of adequate winter quarters and training facilities prevented the concentration in Canada of even a brigade. Because of a shortage of accommodation in the United Kingdom, and the demands on shipping space for the movement of reinforcements for the 1st Division, the War Office preferred that the new force should not cross the Atlantic until the 1st Division had gone to France.

We have noted that it was first intended that the existing units of the 4th Infantry Brigade (which had accompanied the First Contingent to England) should form part of the 2nd Division, so that only eight of the new battalions would be required to fill the other two brigades. The remainder would be used as reinforcements. But, as we have previously seen (above, p. 39), the 1st Division was to need all the 4th Brigade's personnel; furthermore three of the battalions newly formed in Canada (the 23rd, 30th and 32nd) sailed in February as additional reinforcements for that division. The other twelve were brigaded as far as possible territorially. The new 4th Brigade had the 18th, 19th, 20th and 21st Battalions, all mobilized in Ontario; the 5th Brigade, from Quebec and the Maritimes, comprised the 22nd (French Canadian),* 24th, 25th and 26th Battalions; the 6th Brigade was made up of the 27th, 28th, 29th and 31st Battalions, all from the west. After December 1914 all battalions, like those of the 1st Division, were organized on a four-company basis. Until the new brigades could be concentrated in the United Kingdom, only temporary commanders, drawn from officers serving in Canada, were appointed.

Troops of other arms and services were drawn from Military Districts across Canada. The 2nd Divisional Cavalry Squadron was formed at the end of March 1915 by detaching "A" Squadron from the 7th Canadian Mounted Rifles—one of thirteen such regiments raised in Canada during November and December. On 26 November the War Office had accepted the Militia Department's offer of the first four C.M.R. battalions, announcing its intention to "use them for service in Egypt", and inquiring how many more such regiments could be mobilized. But neither these four nor any of the other nine regiments ever saw the Middle East. They reached England between June 1915 and July 1916.[66] There the 7th to 13th C.M.R. battalions were broken up as reinforcements. The first six regiments crossed to France in September and October 1915 and were subsequently converted to infantry (below, p. 134).

As had been foreseen, lack of guns delayed completion of the Divisional Artillery. Batteries of the 4th, 5th and 6th Brigades C.F.A. trained in Canada on obsolete 12-pounders. A 7th Brigade was authorized in February when the 6th was sent to England to furnish artillery reinforcements for the 1st Division. Only the 4th Field Brigade, which crossed the Atlantic with the infantry brigades, accompanied the 2nd Division to France; headquarters and the 5th and 7th Brigades, held in the United Kingdom to complete equipment, and the 6th Howitzer Brigade (formed from reserves in September 1915) followed in January 1916. The Divisional Artillery's first commander was Brig.-Gen. H. C. Thacker; but at the end of September he became C.R.A. of the 1st Division and was succeeded by Brig.-Gen. E. W. B. Morrison. Until all its artillery joined it the 2nd Division was supported first by borrowed British units and subsequently (from 4 October) by the 55th (West Lancashire) Divisional Artillery.[67]

* Formation of the 22nd Battalion followed a request made to the Prime Minister on 25 September 1914 by a distinguished delegation from the Province of Quebec for "authorization to levy a French Canadian Contingent to enrol in active service for Great Britain". When it was decided to merge the battalion in an infantry brigade of the 2nd Division, the unit was brought up to establishment by drafting French Canadian recruits from other battalions raised in Quebec.[65]

The Divisional Engineers (the 4th, 5th and 6th Field Companies) were quickly mobilized from Militia field companies. The major medical units, Nos. 4, 5 and 6 Field Ambulances, were formed respectively in Winnipeg, Toronto and Montreal.[68] Following the authorization of the Canadian Army Dental Corps on 17 May 1915, dental surgeons were attached to field ambulances, hospitals and combatant formations.[69] The line of communication units formed surplus to the divisional establishment consisted of eleven Army Service Corps units of various types, four medical units (including No. 3 General Hospital and No. 3 Stationary Hospital), a mobile veterinary section and an infantry base depot.

Public-spirited citizens, such as had already equipped one motor machine gun brigade, wished to provide three more M. G. units. Although the British and Canadian military authorities were then opposed to the inclusion of a motor machine gun battery in the new division, the Minister of Militia was loath to discourage such offers. Three units were formed—Borden's Armoured Battery (recruited chiefly in Ottawa and Northern Ontario), the Eaton Machine Gun Battery (from Toronto), and the Yukon Detachment. They encountered many obstacles. Guns and horses were withheld or even withdrawn according to the needs of overseas units, and cars were not immediately available. The three units went to England in the spring of 1915, with little or none of their equipment, and with their future employment uncertain. The battery named for the Prime Minister, however, on the strong recommendation of General Alderson accompanied the 2nd Division to France in September as the Borden Machine Gun Battery. The two remaining units reached France in 1916 respectively with the 3rd and 4th Divisions.[70]

On 11 March 1915 Lord Kitchener advised General Hughes that the "Second Contingent should be prepared to arrive about the first of May". Instead of sailing in a single large convoy, as had the First Canadian Contingent, it was the wish of the War Office that the force should cross the Atlantic in groups of about 5000, each escorted by a cruiser.[71] On April 18 a group of engineer, medical and service corps units embarked at Halifax in two transports chartered by the Department of Militia. But shipping was so difficult to secure that the Department was forced to request the Admiralty to divert sufficient transports to carry the remainder of the contingent. The Admiralty detailed seventeen vessels, and these were secretly loaded and dispatched singly and without escort. In this manner the bulk of the Division reached England in May and June, several weeks behind schedule.

By the time the foremost elements of the Second Contingent arrived in the United Kingdom, the bulk of the Canadian troops already in the country (with the exception of the Canadian Cavalry Depot at Canterbury) had moved to the Shorncliffe area in Eastern Command. Here they were under Brig.-Gen. J. C. MacDougall, who on the departure of the 1st Division for France had been appointed to the temporary command of all Canadian troops in Great Britain.[72] The 2nd Division also concentrated at Shorncliffe, and to avoid confusion and keep the two commands separate, General MacDougall's was designated the

Canadian Training Division. On 25 May Major-General S. B. Steele assumed command of the 2nd Division. Steele was a veteran officer with long service in the North West Mounted Police whose military career went back to the Red River and North-West Campaigns. During the South African War he had raised and commanded Strathcona's Horse, and after commanding successively Military District No. 13 and No. 10 he had recently been appointed Inspector General for Western Canada. His nomination as G.O.C. by the Minister of Militia was opposed by Lord Kitchener, on the grounds that "to do justice to the troops very experienced officers" were necessary in such positions, and in spite of heated protests General Hughes* had to agree that Steele should not take the Division to France.[74]

Lord Kitchener's offer of the pick of "all unemployed generals on active list" as a successor to Steele[75] was rejected by Hughes, who sent through the Prime Minister a strong recommendation that Brig.-Gen. Turner, then commanding the 3rd Brigade, be appointed to command the 2nd Division. "I would again urge on you", wrote Perley to Kitchener, "the wisdom of giving the appointment to a Canadian Brigadier if on enquiry you find one that is suitable."[76] In replying on 24 June Kitchener expressed his willingness to appoint Brig.-Gen. Currie, who had been recommended by Sir John French as "the most suitable of the three [Canadian] brigadiers".[77] Decision was deferred pending Sir Robert Borden's visit to the United Kingdom, and on 26 July Hughes, who was then in London, cabled Ottawa that Turner was to command the 2nd Division, and that later General Currie would take over the 1st Division.[78]

On 17 August Brig.-Gen. Turner, having relinquished command of his brigade in France to Brig.-Gen. R. G. E. Leckie, took over the 2nd Division with the rank of major-general. By the beginning of September all three infantry brigades of the Division were under the commanders who were to take them to France. Appointed to command the 4th Brigade, at the instance of General Hughes, despite his oft expressed opinion that qualified Canadian officers could be found for almost all positions of command, was Brig.-Gen. Lord Brooke, an Imperial officer who had come to Canada in 1913 at the request of the Minister of Militia to command the 2nd Mounted Brigade in its annual training, and in the summer of 1914 had been in charge of Petawawa Camp.[79] Commanding the 5th Brigade was Brig.-Gen. David Watson, formerly C.O. of the 2nd Battalion. The 6th Brigade remained under Brig.-Gen. H. D. B. Ketchen, the only one of the three temporary commanders appointed in Canada to be given permanent command. General Turner's senior general staff officer was Lt.-Col. H. D. de Prée, an officer of the Royal Artillery who was transferred from the corresponding appointment with the Lahore Division. The new A.A. and Q.M.G. was Lt.-Col. P. E. Thacker, a Permanent Force officer who since April 1912 had

* Yet in a letter to Lord Roberts the previous September Hughes had disparaged Steele's fitness to command the 1st Division on the grounds of age and a lack of "the faculty of thinking and acting rapidly when occasion might demand it".[78]

been attached to the War Office, representing Canada on the Dominion Section of the Imperial General Staff. Most of the remaining staff appointments were held by officers of the Canadian Permanent Force.

Before the 2nd Division left Canada, Ottawa expressed to the War Office its concern that there should not be a repetition of the unfortunate conditions encountered by the First Contingent at Salisbury Plain. The selection of Shorncliffe Camp, near Folkestone, was warmly welcomed, and early in March the Militia Department offered to furnish all tentage required by the Second Contingent. War Office acceptance did not come until the end of July, and it was November before the first shipment of tents was made. By that time the 2nd Division was in France, having been accommodated in England in tents, huts and barracks provided by the War Office without charge.

During June 1915 the Division (still incomplete in artillery) completed its concentration in the Shorncliffe area. Divisional Headquarters, the 4th and 5th Infantry Brigades and the 4th Brigade C.F.A. found accommodation in hutments at St. Martin's Plain, East and West Sandling and Westenhanger. The remaining units were distributed under canvas at Dibgate, Otterpool and New Inn Green. It was a dry summer, and life under canvas presented no hardship. The open fields beside Shorncliffe and the rolling Kentish countryside beyond provided ideal conditions for company and battalion training, and the ranges at Lydd and Hythe were convenient for musketry. Experienced British and Canadian officers attached as special instructors laid special emphasis on the siting and construction of trenches and methods of attacking and defending them. Many officers and men of the 2nd Division attended courses at British schools established primarily to train the rapidly expanding B.E.F. To gain practical experience in the field, staff officers and senior commanders went to France and were attached for seven-day periods to corresponding headquarters and units of the 1st Division. August brought brigade and divisional training. Finally, before sailing, units received written instructions on the trench routine practised by a typical company of the B.E.F.[80]

On 2 September H.M. The King, accompanied by Lord Kitchener, inspected the Division—a sure sign that embarkation would not long be delayed. It crossed the Channel, by night, between 13 and 17 September—Divisional Headquarters and the three infantry brigades from Folkestone to Boulogne, and the remaining units by the route Southampton-Le Havre. On disembarking the troops moved by rail to St. Omer, Cassel or nearby stations, and then marched to the Hazebrouck area, where by 21 September training was once more in progress. It is recorded that both at Folkestone and in France the physical demands of marching in hot weather under full loads and in newly-issued heavy British pattern boots severely tested the endurance of the men, some battalions having 25 per cent stragglers from sore feet and exhaustion.[81]

It was customary for a new division arriving in France to be held for some time in corps reserve to allow further training and a gradual indoctrination into trench warfare. But entry into the front line was to come almost immediately for the combatant units of the 2nd Canadian Division—as a formation of the newly-formed Canadian Corps. Deprived of a preliminary schooling in the ways of semi-siege warfare, they would now have to learn the hard way.

The Canadian Corps is Formed

The creation of a Canadian army corps was a natural but by no means inevitable result of the decision to send the 2nd Division to France. Under British practice the largest permanently organized formation in the field was the division, and the divisions of a corps were subject to frequent interchange; the retention of two or more divisions together under the same corps headquarters, with the same corps troops permanently attached, was a recent Australian-New Zealand innovation.[82]

In a letter written on 1 April 1915 to the Minister of Militia, his special representative in the United Kingdom, Colonel Carson, asked, "Why do you not . . . have our two divisions in the field as an Army Corps with your good self in command?"[83] Further mention of the corps appears in a communication dated 26 April from Hughes to Lt.-Col. J. J. Carrick, the Minister's liaison officer at G.H.Q. It was "the earnest desire of all in Canada", the message read in part, "to increase the existing division in this country [France] into an army corps, first of two, later of three divisions."[84] Carrick showed this to Sir John French, who immediately sent him to London to see Lord Kitchener, at the same time wiring the latter a strong recommendation that Canada's offer be accepted. The C.-in-C. regarded General Alderson as quite capable of commanding an army corps, and referred to the utmost mutual confidence between him and the Canadians. The telegram concluded, "I think best return we can make for splendid service rendered by Canadian Division is to meet their wishes."[85]

Kitchener concurred in the recommendation that Alderson should be Corps Commander,* and on 15 June the Secretary of State for the Colonies informed the Governor General that "the Army Council think that it would be advantageous, when the 2nd Canadian Division takes the field, to join the two Divisions into an Army Corps".[88] Although the initial reply, eleven days later, was non-committal, Ottawa took immediate steps to furnish the necessary Corps Troops. Organization of the Corps proceeded during the summer, when the Prime Minister and Hughes were in England, and was completed by the end of August.[89]

On 13 September 1915 Lieut.-General Alderson opened his Headquarters at Bailleul. His successor as G.O.C. 1st Division was Major-General A. W. Currie, whose former command (2nd Brigade) was taken over by the C.O. of the 8th Battalion, Lt.-Col. L. J. Lipsett.[90] Canada's shortage of staff-trained officers meant that the principal staff appointments in the Corps were given to British officers.

* In a message dated 28 April, criticising the conduct of operations at Ypres, General Hughes informed Carson that "many here demand that if Army Corps is formed I should command it, but this would probably not be satisfactory".[86] On this proposal Sir Robert Borden was to comment in his *Memoirs*, "To remain Minister of Militia and to hold an important military appointment at the Front would have been the ideal situation so far as his outlook was concerned".[87]

MAP 2

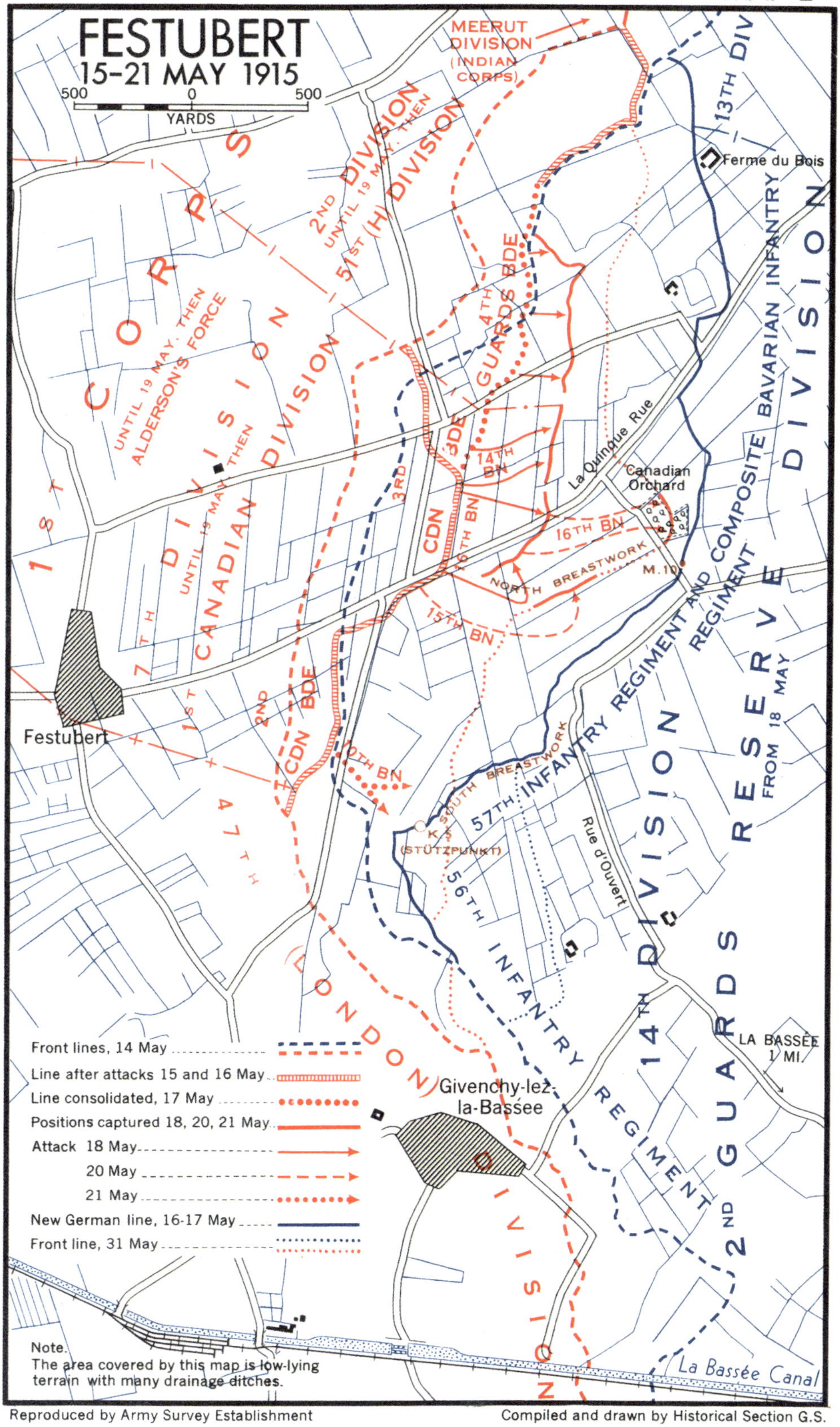

Reproduced by Army Survey Establishment

Compiled and drawn by Historical Section G.S.

The two senior posts went to Brig.-Gen. C. H. Harington, who became B.G.G.S., and Brig.-Gen. T. B. Wood, who was transferred from the 1st Division to be D.A. & Q.M.G. These two officers were succeeded in June 1916 by Brig.-Gen. P. P. de B. Radcliffe and Brig.-Gen. G. J. Farmar. The first G.O.C. Canadian Corps Heavy Artillery, which was formed in April 1916, was Brig.-Gen. A. C. Currie, a British officer. Among Canadians appointed to Alderson's headquarters were Brig.-Gen. H. E. Burstall, G.O.C. Royal Artillery, Canadian Corps, and Brig.-Gen. C. J. Armstrong, Chief Engineer, both of whom moved up from corresponding posts in the 1st Division.

Command of the Corps Troops was given to Major-General M. S. Mercer, who was succeeded in the 1st Infantry Brigade by Brig.-Gen. G. B. Hughes, son of the Minister of Militia. Inauguration of Mercer's command brought together a number of Canadian formations which had been serving separately under various headquarters. The Canadian Cavalry Brigade (Brig.-Gen. J. E. B. Seely) was transferred from its infantry role with the 1st Division, to be rejoined by the R.C.H.A. Brigade, which had been serving as G.H.Q. Troops. Forming part of the Corps Troops was a group of infantry and dismounted cavalry units later to become two brigades of the 3rd Canadian Division. The 7th Brigade would comprise Princess Patricia's Canadian Light Infantry, The Royal Canadian Regiment, and the 42nd and 49th Battalions; the 8th Brigade, made up of the 1st, 2nd, 4th and 5th C.M.R. Battalions, was formed from the six regiments of the 1st and 2nd C.M.R. Brigades. By the end of September 1915 the Canadian Corps, comprising the two infantry divisions and Corps Troops and attached units, had reached a strength of 1354 officers, and 36,522 other ranks.[91]

The front taken over by the new corps on 13 September was that which the 1st Canadian Division had been holding as the left sector of the 2nd Corps, under the Second British Army. From Ploegsteert Wood the line extended 4400 yards north-westward across the valley of the Douve River to the Wulverghem-Messines road. The entire area was under enemy observation from the southern end of the Messines-Wytschaete spur, which rising from the left bank of the Douve, joined the main ridge stretching fifteen miles north-eastward to beyond Passchendaele. Since the 2nd Corps' other forward division, the 28th, needed a rest before taking part in forthcoming operations, the Army Commander (General Sir Henry Plumer) extended the Canadian front some three miles northward to the Vierstraat-Wytschaete road, which formed the boundary with the 5th Corps. Between 19 and 23 September two brigades of the 2nd Division (with the 3rd Brigade, temporarily under command from the 1st Division) relieved British formations. Opposite the Canadian newcomers—at distances varying from 500 down to only a few yards—were regiments of the 2nd Bavarian Corps of the German Sixth Army.[92]

The Canadian Corps was soon to have a role, though a minor one, in active operations. On 23 September General Alderson issued orders setting forth its part in the Allied offensive due to be launched on the 25th—the British share in which was to become known as the Battle of Loos.[93]

THE CANADIAN CORPS IN THE LINE

23 SEPTEMBER 1915

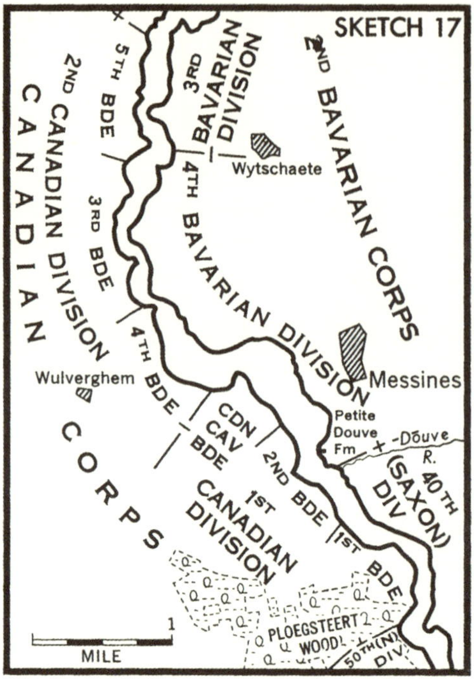

The General Situation

As the summer wore on, the news from the various battle fronts on which the Allies were campaigning had continued to be bad. It was a record of disappointments and defeats that was to make 1915 the most unsatisfactory year of the war for the Allied cause.

High on the list was the disastrous Gallipoli campaign. The decision to support the naval operation by military forces if needed proved to be an unfortunate bit of unsound planning. In the light of events there seems every likelihood that an initial combined operation using both naval and land forces would have achieved surprise and success. Alternatively a purely naval attack, with no land forces nearby to rely on, could undoubtedly have been pressed home to ultimate victory. As it was, the operations fell between these two stools.

A naval bombardment which began on 19 February 1915, had by 2 March destroyed all the outer forts of the Dardanelles. On 18 March the fleet attacked the Narrows in force, silencing almost all the inner forts. But three battleships were lost to undiscovered mines, and although the Turkish command believed defeat was inevitable if the attack was continued next day, the naval attempt to force the Narrows was called off. The British Government now agreed to a landing on the Gallipoli peninsula. What was to have been a mere demonstration to draw off Turkish forces from the Caucasus now became a major operation to open a passage for Allied warships to reach Constantinople and destroy the

THE APPROACHES TO THE BLACK SEA 1915

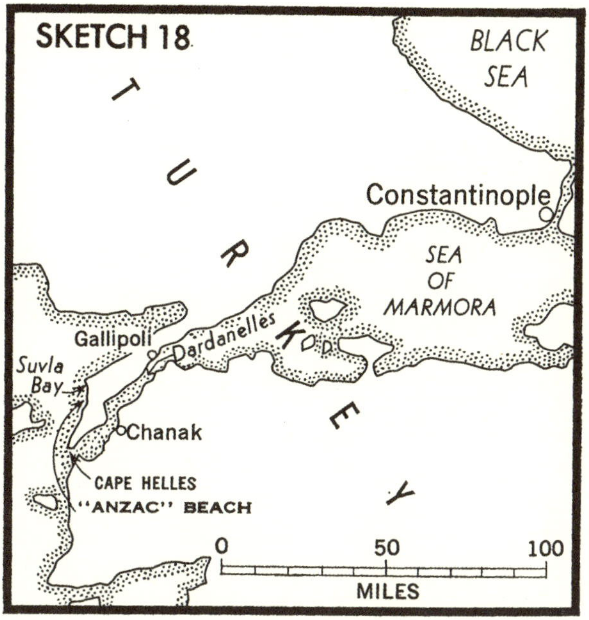

Turkish fleet and the national arsenals, thereby restoring communication with Russia through the Black Sea. Some 250,000 tons of merchant shipping locked up in Russian and Danube ports would be released, and there was hope, as Mr. Churchill emphasized, that "Bulgaria, Greece, and Rumania, perhaps even Italy, might be attracted to the banners of the Entente".[94]

An expeditionary force was organized under the command of General Sir Ian Hamilton, and at dawn on 25 April four British, Australian and New Zealand divisions and a French colonial division began landing at Cape Helles, at the tip of the peninsula and at "Anzac", fifteen miles up the west coast. All the landings were contained by Turkish forces, and three months of trench warfare ensued. Both sides reinforced. By the end of July nine more Allied divisions had been sent to the Mediterranean, while the German commander at Gallipoli, General Liman von Sanders, had increased his defensive force to 22 Turkish divisions.

Then came the fiasco of Suvla Bay, when on the night of 6-7 August two green British divisions (the 10th and 11th) made a confused landing north of Anzac and failed to exploit the surprise they gained. By the time supporting divisions were brought in strong Turkish reinforcements arriving on the heights inland had ringed the British positions. As at the other landings fighting subsided into trench warfare, with all the Allied positions completely dominated by the Turks. Both sides were suffering heavily from exhaustion and disease. The 1st Battalion, The Newfoundland Regiment, which arrived to reinforce the 29th Division on 19 September, saw its first action of the war at Suvla Bay, where it underwent a trying ordeal in the trenches from 16 November until the end of the campaign.[95]

THE EASTERN FRONT 1915

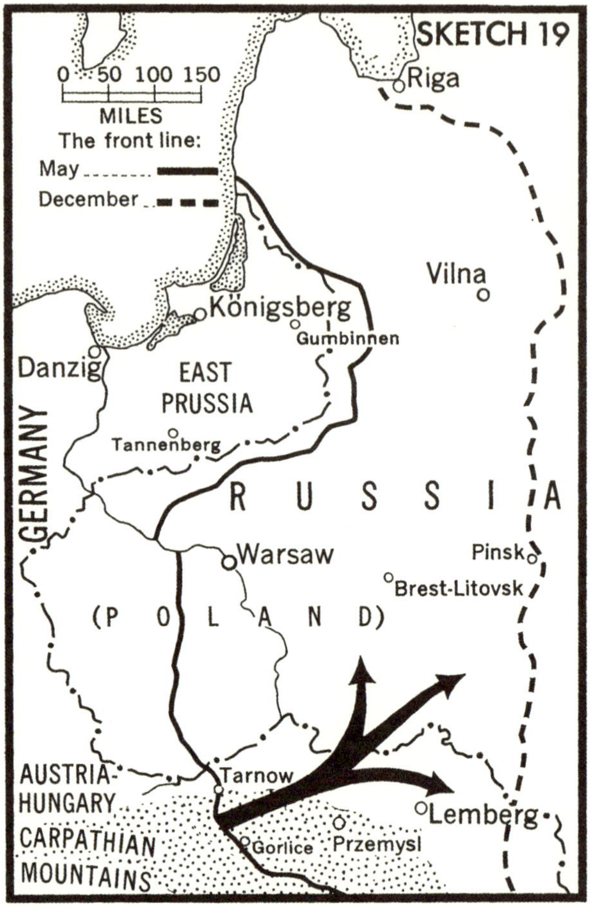

The deadlock continued, and by mid-September the French were recommending a transfer of operations to Salonika. Considerations of prestige, however, kept the Dardanelles Committee (the name taken by the War Committee on 7 June) from reaching a decision to evacuate, and it was not until December, after Lord Kitchener had visited Gallipoli, that a withdrawal was ordered from Suvla and Anzac. Evacuation of the peninsula was finally completed on 9 January 1916. By that time British army casualties had numbered 205,000.[96]

The picture was equally gloomy on the Eastern Front, where von Falkenhayn was putting forth every effort to achieve a complete victory over the Russians that would leave the armies of the Central Powers free for operations elsewhere in 1916. Early in May the Eleventh German Army, flanked by two Austrian armies, had broken through on a thirty-mile front between Gorlice and Tarnow, in Galicia. Gradually the gap was widened, and a renewal of the offensive in July forced a Russian retreat along the entire front from the Baltic to the Carpathians. Warsaw fell on 5 August, and before the end of the month Brest-Litovsk, 110 miles to the east. Towards the end of September von Falkenhayn

NORTH-EASTERN ITALY 1915

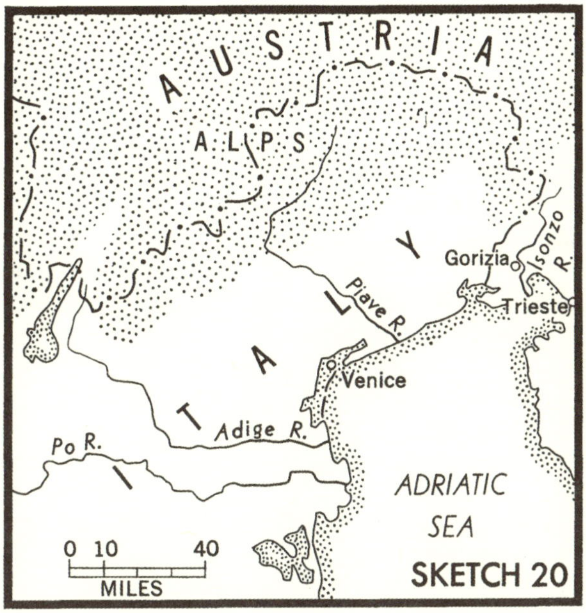

called a halt to the five months' offensive. His armies had outrun their communications, and developments on other fronts were claiming his attention. There was a threat from Italy, which having signed a secret treaty the day after the initial Gallipoli landings to join the Allies had declared war against Austria on 23 May; Italian armies had crossed the Austrian frontier at the head of the Adriatic and fought two indecisive battles along the Isonzo River. Furthermore plans were in the making for a combined German-Austrian-Bulgarian invasion of Serbia; and on the Western Front the Allies were known to be preparing for a September offensive.

In spite of the common danger confronting them, however, France and Britain were still disagreed on a policy for the Western Front. From the beginning of the year the British Cabinet had favoured a strict defensive in this theatre until Kitchener's New Armies could take the field in the spring of 1916. It was in accordance with this design that men and material had been dispatched to the Dardanelles.[97] A Franco-British conference on munitions held at Boulogne on 19-20 June concluded that not until the summer of 1916 would sufficient heavy guns and howitzers and enough shells of all calibres be available to launch an offensive on the Western Front with reasonable hope of success. (It was estimated that such a British undertaking would require a force of at least 36 divisions across a continuous front of 25 miles, supported by 1150 heavy guns and howitzers besides the normal complement of field artillery.)[98] For a while both governments were virtually agreed to postpone an offensive in France until 1916 and to work towards a successful conclusion of the Gallipoli campaign. But General Joffre, who had consistently opposed the Gallipoli enterprise and indeed any undertaking that would hinder operations on the Western Front, persuaded the French cabinet to reverse its stand and to insist on the offensive in the West being carried out that autumn.

The depressing news that came from the Dardanelles and Russian fronts in August so strengthened French arguments for an early offensive and weakened British objections, that following a visit to Joffre's headquarters Lord Kitchener secured the British Cabinet's approval for support of the French plan.[99] On 21 August he instructed Sir John French "to take the offensive and act vigorously".[100] General Joffre's plan was similar to that proposed earlier in the year (above, p. 50). Briefly, the new plan called for two converging thrusts in the direction of Namur, on either side of the large salient which the enemy was holding between the River Aisne and the Scarpe with its apex at Noyon. The southern drive would be made by the French Second and Fourth Armies attacking northward from Champagne against the front of the German Third Army. In the north the French Tenth Army and the British First Army would strike eastward from Artois against the German Sixth Army. Successful offensives would cut off the three German armies (the Second, First and Seventh) holding the Noyon salient, leaving them to be defeated in detail.[101]

At 6:30 a.m. on 25 September the British First Army attacked with six divisions between the La Bassée Canal and Lens on a five-mile front centred on the village of Loos. About six hours later seventeen divisions of the French Tenth Army struck along a front which extended twelve miles northward from Arras to include the area of the unsuccessful May offensive against Souchez and Vimy Ridge. In the meantime the Champagne offensive began with twenty French divisions advancing against six German divisions. The assaults on the French fronts were supported by a considerably greater weight of artillery than in any previous operation. While the British had only 19 heavy guns to each mile of frontage, the French Tenth Army had 35, and the two armies in Champagne 47 per mile.[102] In all, as General Joffre pointed out in a message of encouragement to his forces, the 53 French divisions engaged in the offensive were supported by 2000 heavy and 3000 field guns—as contrasted with the 15 divisions and 300 heavy guns that had been employed in the Artois offensive in May. To make up for the relative British weakness in artillery and ammunition the attack on the First Army's front was preceded by a discharge of chlorine gas.

In the south the French assaults made satisfactory gains on the first day, with advances of 3000 yards in some places—for the enemy, anticipating an attack, had thinned out his forward troops and disposed his reserves for a defence in depth. As a result next day the attackers encountered stiff opposition and could make little further progress. In Artois the Tenth Army achieved only minor gains in the first three days; one division reached the crest of Vimy Ridge on 28 September, but was driven back.[103]

General Haig's First Army did no better. A preliminary four-day bombardment had suffered from a shortage of shells (heavy guns being limited to 96 rounds in 24 hours); and except in a few places unfavourable wind conditions had rendered the gas attack largely ineffective. At first there was some progress, for the Germans had not expected an attack so far north, and many of their foremost defences (including the commanding Hill 70 on the northern outskirts of Lens) fell into British hands. But this success could not be effectively exploited, for in spite of repeated requests from the Army Commander, Sir John French delayed releasing the required divisions from his general reserve until too late. When the assault was renewed the following morning the Germans, who had reinforced their second position with 22 battalions, drove the attackers back with heavy losses.[104]

On Haig's left the Second Army's contribution to the offensive was restricted to subsidiary attacks designed to mislead the enemy as to the direction and frontage of the main British effort. (These included a diversion by the 3rd Corps at Bois Grenier, south of Armentières, in which the 3rd Brigade C.F.A. fired in support of the 8th (British) Division.) Shortly before 6:00 a.m. on the 25th the Canadian Corps staged a feint gas attack from dummy assembly trenches. Six thousand oat sacks and sandbags, filled with damp straw and with a handful of sulphur added, were distributed all along the 10,000-yard front. Though adverse winds prevented all the bags from being ignited, the demonstration induced a German gas-alert and drew artillery fire. Nowhere in the Second Army's sector, however, was the deception taken seriously enough to influence the real battle.[105]

On the 28th General Joffre halted both the Champagne and Artois offensives and ordered preparations for a new general attack. But bad weather and an unsuccessful counter-attack against the British on 8 October interfered, with the result that the new assaults were delivered more or less piecemeal. On the 6th the French captured a village in Champagne; five days later they gained some ground in Artois. On 13 October British forces, attacking north of Loos on a front of four divisions, seized some German trenches but could not hold their gains. (This final effort was the occasion of another demonstration by the Canadian Corps. Some 3500 commercially-prepared chemical smoke bombs and 1500 lbs of phosphorus were discharged, and in addition each division released smoke from 600 home-made bombs which had been fashioned from stovepipe, tallow, gunpowder, coaldust, nitre and pitch by parties of Canadian Engineers working round the clock.)[106] On 4 November the Allied offensives were formally abandoned. The operations which began on 25 September had cost more than 60,000 British, nearly 200,000 French, and about 150,000 German casualties.[107]

For this expenditure the Allies had little to show. The Noyon salient was merely blunted; the German position in the West was as strong as before, if not stronger. The British First Army, having achieved a maximum penetration of two miles on a two-mile front, now held a narrow salient at Loos which, though costly to defend, the higher command insisted must be retained. In Champagne, gains of upwards of three miles had merely moved the French farther into the low ground and exposed them all the more to observation and fire from the adjacent enemy-held heights.[108]

The Battle of Loos had been undertaken against the better judgment of both the British C.-in-C. and the Commander of the First Army. Lord Kitchener gave direct orders to "do our utmost to help France in their offensive, even though by so doing we may suffer very heavy losses".[109] Haig's objections proved well founded—the shortage of heavy artillery and ammunition, the unfavourable ground assigned for the First Army's attack, the strength of the German defences, and the lack of training of the new divisions and the inexperience of the staff officers. Apart from all this the over-all direction of operations at G.H.Q. level left much to be desired. Sir John French was criticized for his general conduct of the offensive, and particularly for his mishandling of reserves; on 19 December he was transferred to the post of Commander-in-Chief Home Forces. His successor in the field was Sir Douglas Haig.

The First Trench Raids

Though major operations for 1915 had come to an end, the higher command was at pains to ensure that the coming winter in the trenches should not be a time of idleness. In contrast to the French, who when not engaged in a major offensive tended to observe an unofficial truce, British G.H.Q. emphasized the necessity for continual aggressiveness in defence.[110] A Second Army directive towards the end of October set down a policy of impressing on all ranks "that the forthcoming winter months are to be utilized not for passive defence but for exhausting the enemy's troops and for training all branches for future operations".[111] There were to be surprise bombardments, sniping was encouraged, and preparations were made to resume trench-raiding—an activity introduced by the British the previous winter. The essence of a raid was that the participants should make a surprise entry into the opposing trenches, inflict as many casualties as possible and return before the enemy could take counter-measures. Sometimes special tasks were added—the capture of prisoners for identification purposes, damaging mine shafts, or the destruction of enemy positions which could not be permanently held. Depending upon the size of the allotted task, raids were made in strengths varying from ten up to 200.[112] It may not be out of place to describe in some detail one or two of the earliest of these ventures.

The first recorded raid by Canadian troops had been staged by Princess Patricia's Canadian Light Infantry on the last day of February 1915 (above, p. 88), less than a week before the 1st Canadian Division entered the line. The first such venture carried out by the Canadian Corps was a joint effort astride the Douve River by parties of the 5th and 7th Battalions (2nd Infantry Brigade) on the night of 16-17 November. There had been a postponement from the previous night because rains had swollen the Douve (at that time of the year usually eight to ten feet wide and three to four deep) to three times its normal width and to a depth of ten feet.[113] The sudden flood precipitated many a hasty move to higher ground, in the course of which some battalion headquarters lost part of their regimental records. But there was a silver lining, as

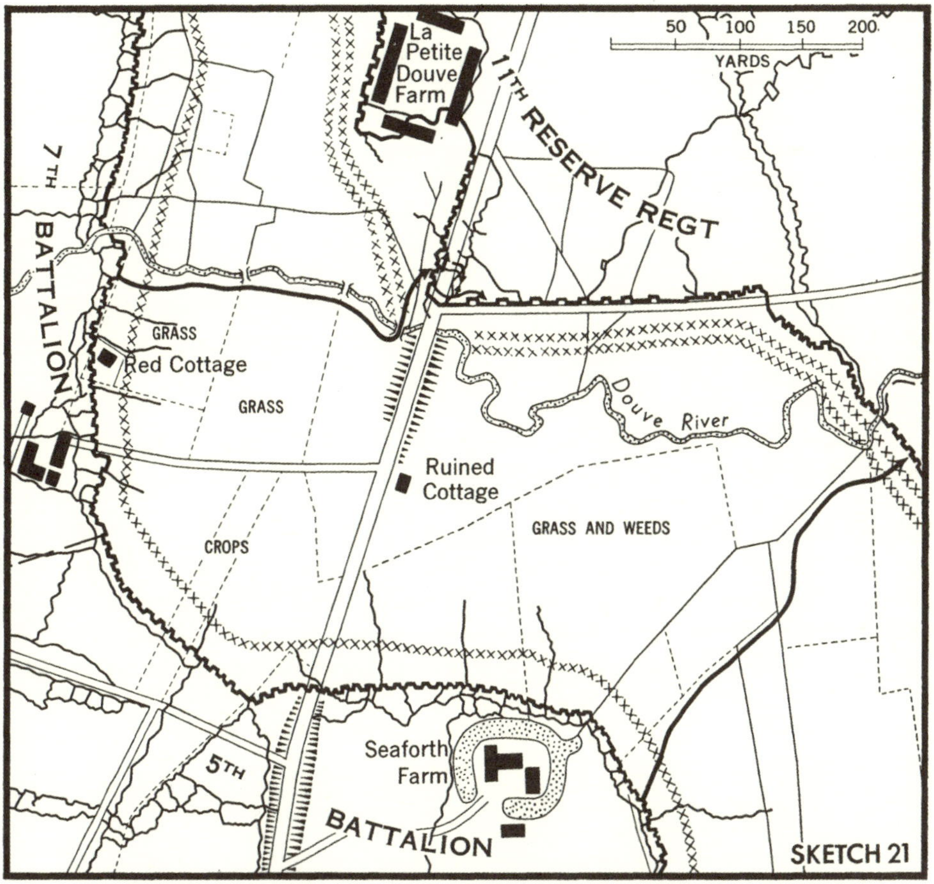

LA PETITE DOUVE: NIGHT RAID, BY 2nd CANADIAN INFANTRY BRIGADE
2.30 A.M. 17 NOVEMBER 1915

one regimental historian points out. Thereafter, whenever a harassed adjutant was asked to furnish "inconvenient information", the relevant document would almost invariably turn out to have disappeared in the flood![114]

The object of the double raid was threefold: to secure prisoners, to induce the Germans to bring up their reserves and so offer a good target for the Canadian artillery, and to lower the enemy's morale. Preparations began ten days beforehand with the selection of five officers and 85 volunteers from the 7th Battalion (including 23 men to be in reserve), and a similar party from the 5th Battalion. Excused all other duties, these rehearsed night and day on ground which closely reproduced the objective and its approaches. Their training included practice with portable bridging ladders and in crossing wire by means of specially prepared "traversor" mats.[115] Immediately north of the river the German line curved outward across the Messines-Ploegsteert road to form a salient 500 yards long which took in the farmstead called La Petite Douve, west of the road. The strongly-held angle of the trenches between the river and the farm was the 7th Battalion's objective. As a diversion the 5th Battalion party would strike some 400 yards to the south-east. Patrolling by the 2nd Brigade had not only served to familiarize battalion scouts with the approaches to the objective, but had been vigorous enough to force the enemy (the 11th Reserve Regiment, of the 117th Division) to abandon listening posts outside his wire.[116]

At 9:00 a.m. on 16 November, 18-pounders of the 1st Canadian Field Brigade and British howitzers joined by the 13-pounders of the R.C.H.A. began shelling the enemy wire, and during the afternoon a trench mortar battery bombarded Petite Douve Farm. That night, while two parties placed 60-pound portable bridges over the Douve, another group completed cutting the wire by hand where the guns had failed in their task.[117]

All identifying marks had been removed from clothing, and the raiders carried no distinguishing Canadian equipment such as the Ross rifle. All wore crepe masks. Attached to their Lee-Enfields were flashlights to be turned on in the enemy trenches so as to dazzle the occupants of the dug-outs. The route up to no man's land was marked by white stakes. So carefully had all details been arranged that "everything and every party", says the official report, "was in its place" to the minute. At 2:30 a.m. on the 17th, about an hour after an almost full moon had set, the two groups crept forward towards the German positions. A setback occurred when leading elements of the 5th Battalion's party became entangled in wire which had been placed in a water-filled moat along the foot of the German parapet. While they were extricating themselves with great difficulty, the enemy opened rifle fire, to which the raiders replied with grenades. Unable either to cross the obstacle or to get around it, the party withdrew shortly before three, surprisingly without having suffered a single casualty.

Meanwhile the 7th Battalion party had reached its objective and caught the enemy completely by surprise, for his sentries had taken cover from the rain which was just beginning to fall. There was virtually no resistance. Canadian blocking parties wired the flanks in anticipation of local counter-attacks which did not materialize. At the end of twenty minutes the raiders withdrew, having killed or wounded an estimated thirty Germans. They had gained useful information about the construction of the enemy trenches, and they escorted with them twelve prisoners, whose new rubber gas-masks were a prize to Canadian intelligence officers. So orderly was the Canadians' return to their own lines that they were able to salvage most of their special equipment, including one of the bridges. German reserves who counter-attacked in strength forty minutes later were promptly engaged with artillery and driven off. The 7th Battalion's only casualties had been one man accidentally shot and killed and another slightly wounded. The success of the whole venture was credited to the thoroughness with which the enemy's position had been scouted in advance, the careful selection of personnel and equipment, the thorough training and rehearsal to meet every contingency, the explicitness of the orders for the operation, and the excellent cooperation which the infantry had received from the artillery. In the eyes of the British Official Historian it was in all respects a model raid.[118]

On the night of 14-15 December the 5th Battalion carried out another raid that resulted in the capture of an advanced barrier which the Germans had placed across the Messines-Ploegsteert road in no man's land, on the Canadian side of the Douve River. Preliminary bombardment on the three preceding days and nights deceived the enemy as to the time of attack, which was put in at four in the morning after an 18-pounder, brought right up to the front line, had fired 26 rounds at point-blank range. The assault went exactly as planned. The obstacle was seized in the face of little opposition. Of those members of the garrison who had not evacuated the position two were taken prisoner and the rest killed. The raiders had only one officer and one man slightly wounded.[119]

Winter in the Line

After the excitement of these raids had passed, the year drew uneventfully to its close. For all the emphasis on aggressiveness and training, the troops devoted much of their energies to trench maintenance and to making themselves as comfortable as possible. They had much to contend with. "The Flanders rain was like no other rain that had ever fallen on earth", comments one regimental historian.

> There was no escape from it. The trenches, which were nothing more than sandbagged breastworks, simply dissolved. The earth within the sandbags liquefied and oozed out. Everything collapsed. Every indentation of the ground filled with water, and, to make things worse, the enemy, being on higher ground, delighted in draining his trenches across No Man's Land into those occupied by the Canadians.[120]

The misery of Salisbury Plain was being repeated, and the troops had no means of shielding themselves against the cold and the wet. Although men stood for days in thigh-deep water, there were not enough high rubber waders* to go round. Trench shelters caved in, leaving no protection from the teeming skies. Conditions were little better back in billets, where roofs leaked and it was all but impossible to coax more than a noxious-smelling smoke out of the damp coke and charcoal that came up with the rations. In the trenches the daily rum ration of half a gill (1/64 of a gallon) helped to ward off the ill effects of wet clothing and exposure to cold. Its distribution was regulated by Trench Orders, which directed that the rum should always be kept under the personal charge of the company commander and issued only in the presence of an officer. Men undergoing punishment for drunkenness would receive no rum for 14 days after the offence, except for medical reasons.[122]

It was inevitable that there should be much influenza and other respiratory ailments. In spite of preventive efforts by the medical authorities, by regimental

* These waders were issued as trench stores (to be used only in the trenches). Late in the previous winter 3500 pairs were ordered for the 1st Division but these did not arrive until the spring floods had subsided. Early in November 1915 the scale of issue was increased to 4000 for each division.[121]

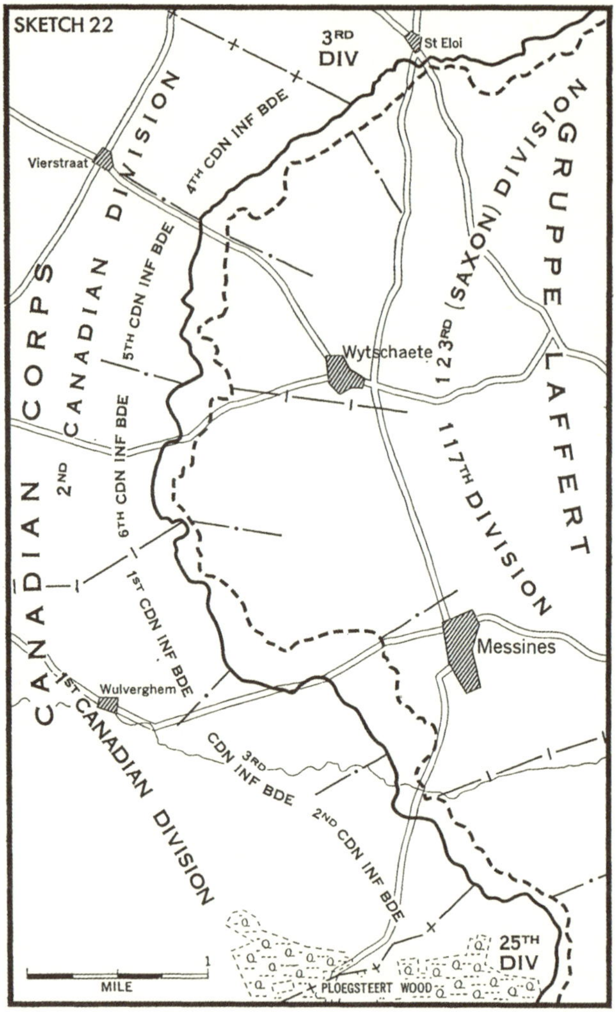

THE CANADIAN CORPS FRONT

23 DECEMBER 1915

officers and by the troops themselves, the number of such cases in the Corps rose from 796 in October to 1198 in November.[123] To reduce the wastage incurred in evacuating men back to a general hospital, minor cases of sickness requiring not more than seven days' treatment were retained at the Corps or one of the Divisional Rest Stations. Each of these had a capacity of about 250 beds, and was operated in turn by the field ambulances during periods of inactivity in the front line. During active operations the rest station closed and the unit would resume its function as a field ambulance.[124]

One environmental ailment which was particularly distressing and hard to cure was "trench feet", resulting from "continued cold wetness . . . with added secondary infection from the soil".[125] This condition, like frostbite (from which it differed only in degree), was characterized by a swelling of the feet and a deterioration of the tissues which soon changed to gangrene if not checked. Preventive measures were the wearing of either rubber boots or well-greased leather boots—in either case, of large size—keeping puttees loose, rubbing feet and legs with whale oil, and frequently changing socks. Failure to prevent trench feet was considered a breach of discipline for which a whole unit might be punished by curtailment of leave; nevertheless 157 cases were admitted during the period 2-5 December 1915 by one hospital alone and before the end of the war nearly 5000 cases had been reported.[126]

For those few who were able to avoid disease and exposure there was the inescapable monotony of static warfare. Enterprising sappers of the 1st Canadian Divisional Signal Company did much to lift the pall of boredom by constructing a long wave receiving set from parts salvaged in the battle area of the previous spring. These men operated "a most successful Press Bureau at Divisional Headquarters", and to them must go the credit for inaugurating the Wireless Service of the Canadian forces in France.[127]

Christmas Day passed quietly. The more fortunate units were those in reserve who could eat their Christmas dinner in billets. There was little activity in the forward trenches. The German artillery was silent and in at least one instance the infantry of both sides walked about in the open behind their forward trenches, without a shot being exchanged. But there was none of the large-scale fraternization that had characterized the unofficial "Christmas Truce" between British and German troops in 1914. The memory of the gas attack at Ypres still rankled, and front-line battalions were instructed that any attempt by the enemy "to bring about a temporary cessation of hostilities" must be met by rifle, and if necessary artillery fire.[128]

On Christmas Day instructions reached Corps Headquarters authorizing the formation of the 3rd Canadian Division. The work of transforming the headquarters of the Corps Troops into the new divisional headquarters began at once, and by the end of December two of the new brigades (below, p. 134) had assembled.[129] The turn of the year thus found the Canadian Corps well settled in and in process of expanding. Since its origin in mid-September the Corps, without having been involved in any major operations, had suffered 2692 casualties, of which 688 were fatal.

When the Canadian Corps and the 2nd Division were organized the shortage of staff-trained Canadian officers had resulted in a number of staff positions being filled by British officers. At the end of November, when command and staff appointments for the 3rd Division were being made, Sir Max Aitken asked the Minister of Militia for "explicit instructions on the whole question of British or Canadian officers filling junior staff posts". He declared, "I have practically exhausted my strength in fighting against selection [of] British officers for artillery commands, brigade artillery and even regimental artillery."[130] Sir Sam's* reply instructed Aitken to "protest most emphatically against staff and other positions in Canadian force being filled by British officers". Hughes assailed

* General Hughes had been knighted (K.C.B.) on 24 August 1915.

what he called "staff college paternalism", asserting that "the men who fought well at St. Julien and Festubert require no staff college theorists to direct them".[131]

The Canadian viewpoint was further impressed on the Colonial Secretary when Sir George Perley showed him a letter from Sir Robert Borden which went so far as to observe that "Apparently there is some movement by the British professional soldiers, or officials of the War Office and British Staff Officers to supersede Canadians in the higher commands of our troops."* Any such attempt would be fraught with the most disastrous consequences to British interest and the interest of the whole Empire. "You may tell Mr. Bonar Law, Lord Kitchener and Mr. Asquith for me that we will not permit anything of the kind."[133] After discussing the matter with Mr. Bonar Law, Perley wrote him a letter, which was referred by Lord Kitchener to Sir Douglas Haig.[134] On 7 January Perley received the Colonial Secretary's assurance that Lord Kitchener "is doing all he possibly can to fill all Canadian appointments with Canadian officers".[135]

It must be concluded that Sir Robert Borden had allowed himself to be unduly influenced by the attitude of Sir Max Aitken and Sir Sam Hughes, and that in trying to meet the increasing demands for qualified officers the British authorities were indeed, as Mr. R. B. Bennett put it, "desirous of treating the Canadians more than well".[136] Yet while it cannot be denied that the War Office supplied the Canadian Corps with good officers, signs were not lacking of understandable British reluctance to relinquish control over the forces from the Commonwealth. Indeed it may be argued that if Hughes, Aitken and Borden had not taken such a strong stand when they did, the Canadian Corps might never have attained its high standard of morale and efficiency.

* In the opinion of Sir Robert Borden's Parliamentary Secretary, Mr. R. B. Bennett, the Prime Minister's strong criticism of the War Office was not justified. Bennett regarded some of Aitken's cables as unwarranted, and accused him of being "at war with what he calls the 'Trade Union' of the soldiers". And he added, "I do fear that we are being used to aid him in that quarrel."[132]

CHAPTER V

THE ST. ELOI CRATERS AND MOUNT SORREL, 1916

(See Maps 3 and 4, and Sketches 23 and 24)

Opposing Plans for 1916

THE SITUATION at the beginning of 1916 offered the Allies little encouragement. In spite of the costly Artois and Champagne offensives large areas of France and Belgium were still in German hands, and in the north the German offensive at Ypres had left the Allies holding only a part of the salient there. Italy, not yet at war with Germany,* had achieved only minor victories over the Austrians. On the Eastern Front the big Austro-German drive had forced the Russians back to a line 215 miles east of Warsaw. Thus encouraged, Bulgaria had joined the Central Powers. Together they had overrun Serbia and Montenegro and compelled the Serbian army to withdraw to the Adriatic coast. When King Constantine of Greece dismissed his pro-Allied Premier Venizelos and repudiated Greek treaty obligations to Serbia, Franco-British troops, brought to Salonika from Gallipoli on the urgings of Veniuzelos, found themselves helpless spectators of Serbia's rout. The Gallipoli campaign had failed and the evacuation of the Dardanelles was nearing completion. In the middle East, the Suez Canal still faced a Turkish threat; an Indian expeditionary force under British command, directed against Baghdad, was shut up in Kut-el-Amara. Another Indian force sent to aid local forces against German East Africa had been defeated, and the enemy was now making raids into British and Belgian colonial territory. The surrender of German South-West Africa in July 1915 marked the only substantial Allied success on land.

It was a disturbing picture, which seemed to indicate that although the Allies still commanded the sea and were far stronger than their adversaries in troops and material resources, they had failed to exploit these advantages properly. There was a real danger that should the Central Powers use their interior lines to transfer large forces from one front to another before the Allies could make their own superiority felt, the war might be lost. Up to this stage the Allied effort had suffered from a want of purposeful, unified direction; conflicting aims

* Italy's declaration of war on Germany came on 27 August 1916.

had resulted in wasteful dissemination of forces, and little attention appears to have been given to studying what courses might be open to the enemy. There was clearly need for a comprehensive Allied policy, and a sound over-all plan.[1]

Early realization of this essential factor in victory prompted General Joffre to convene an inter-Allied military conference at his headquarters at Chantilly in July 1915. The meeting brought home to the commanders and military attaches representing the various powers a recognition of the serious problem confronting the Allies. Because of national susceptibilities the time was not yet ripe to centralize the conduct of the war, but Joffre urged the soundness of a vigorous offensive launched simultaneously by the Allied armies against the Austro-German "bloc". Yet beyond a general agreement "that each national army should be active in its own way", the conference brought no immediate results. In November, however, a meeting of the French and British Prime Ministers adopted "the principle of a mixed permanent committee designed to co-ordinate the action of the Allies". At a second inter-Allied military conference in Chantilly early in December, representatives of the Allied armies unanimously agreed that the war could be decided only in the principal theatres—on the Russian, Franco-British, and the Italian fronts. There would have to be offensives on all these fronts, with every Allied army contributing the maximum in men and material.[2] It was recognized that decisive results would be obtained only if these offensives came simultaneously, or at least at dates near enough together to prevent the enemy from moving reserves in strategically significant numbers from one front to another—a transfer estimated to require at least thirty days. Accordingly the Allied offensives would begin within a month of one another as soon as possible after the end of March 1916. The conference felt that in secondary theatres of war only minimum forces should be employed, and that troops already in these areas were adequate.

The enemy, unlike the Allies, proposed to treat the Eastern Front as a secondary theatre in 1916. There was some disagreement between the Chiefs of the Austro-Hungarian and German General Staffs as to the relative importance of the Western Front and the Italian theatre. In December 1915 the Austro-Hungarian Chief of the General Staff, Colonel-General Conrad von Hötzendorff, requested the loan of nine German divisions for the Eastern Front (in addition to four already with the Austrians) so as to release Austrian troops for an offensive designed to knock Italy out of the war; with this accomplished 400,000 Austrians could be transferred to the Western Front. Von Falkenhayn felt unable, however, to spare sufficient forces for such a purpose, and in a counter-proposal he asked Conrad to replace as many German formations on the Eastern Front as possible with Austrian troops. Maximum German forces would thus be available for operations in France. Unable to reach a compromise, each adopted a course of his own.[3]

On 21 February 1916 the Germans struck at Verdun, near the centre of the Western Front—the first of five major offensives to be launched by one side or the other on all European fronts in the first seven months of 1916. On 14 May two Austro-Hungarian armies attacked in the South Tyrol. According to a document prepared by Falkenhayn "to serve as a basis for a report to H. M. the Kaiser", the German offensive was calculated to bleed the forces of France to death, and thus deprive Britain, the "arch-enemy in this war", of her "best sword".[4] Although neither this nor the Austrian venture succeeded, they limited the scale of the intended Allied offensives and altered their timing.

The Allied Powers had agreed at the Second Chantilly Conference that each would stand ready to repel any offensive against its own front with its own resources, and that the others would assist to the fullest extent the one attacked. Now these new enemy blows brought French and Italian appeals for the British and the Russians, respectively, to strike ahead of schedule. Even before the Verdun offensive Joffre had warned the British Commander-in-Chief (since 19 December 1915, Sir Douglas Haig) that the French armies, which had lost nearly two million men in the offensives of 1914 and 1915, were not capable of making large-scale attacks except to exploit British success. He wanted the British Expeditionary Force to undertake preparatory "wearing down" offensives, whereas Sir Douglas advocated that the French and British forces should attack simultaneously. On 14 February the two commanders reached a compromise (Haig being under instructions to cooperate unless to do so would endanger his armies). Until the French were ready to launch a major attack, the B.E.F.'s operations would be no more extensive than were required to maintain the initiative. After mid-June limited attacks would be made in the Ypres-La Bassée areas; and about 1 July the British and French forces would join in a full-scale offensive astride the Somme.

At the same time the enemy would be under pressure on the Eastern Front, where the Czar, in keeping with his pledge to give effect to the Chantilly agreement, was planning a Russian attack scheduled to begin on 15 June. (The date of the Russian effort was advanced in response to Italian appeals for help against the Austro-Hungarian offensive. On 4 June, in what proved to be the greatest Russian contribution of the whole war, General Brusilov attacked with four armies on a front extending nearly three hundred miles northward from the Rumanian border to the Pripet marshes, driving back five Austrian armies a distance of 20 to 30 miles and capturing 450,000 men and more than 400 guns.)[5]

As the opposing sides drew up their respective plans of action, a comparison of their strengths shows the Allies enjoying a considerable advantage in numbers. According to an intelligence report issued at the end of May, in the West 125 German faced 150 Allied divisions (95 French, 49 British and 6 Belgian). On the Eastern Front the enemy's 90 divisions (48 German and 42 Austrian) were opposed by 141 Russian divisions; in the south the relation was 35 Austrian to 53 Italian divisions; and in the south-east on the Salonika Front sixteen enemy divisions, twelve of them Bulgarian, were holding down an assortment of eighteen Allied divisions.[6] But this Allied numerical superiority of more than 100 divisions (a superiority which was the greater because many Russian divisions contained sixteen battalions to the Germans' nine) was largely offset by the central position of the German and Austrian armies and the homogeneity of the German forces which enabled them to operate on interior lines, concentrating men and guns for an operation more rapidly than could the Allies.

The Germans were well fitted for defensive tactics, on which they intended to rely—except at Verdun—in 1916. Their field defences were much stronger than those of the Allies, whose senior officers, thinking always in terms of advance, tended to treat the defensive as only a temporary measure and did little to improve their own positions. The enemy's wire formed a more formidable obstacle than the Allies'; his deep dug-outs, capable of accommodating most of his front line garrison, had no British or French counterpart; and his superiority (both in quantity and quality) in hand grenades, rifle grenades and trench mortars, far better equipped him for trench-warfare. Thus while the French and British forces sought to retain the initiative and wear down the enemy, the latter in the main continued with great industry to better his defences. Between the middle of December 1915 and the end of May 1916, British (including Canadian) forces carried out 63 raids in strengths of 10 to 200 men, of which 47 succeeded; of 33 German raids on the British front, 20 were successful.[7]

The year 1915 had seen significant developments in the air, and there was promise of further advances in 1916. At first the military aeroplane was primarily a vehicle, armed or unarmed. For serious fighting, however, it had to become a winged machine-gun—as it did when Anthony Fokker, a Dutch designer, designed for the Germans a means of firing through the propeller arc without hitting the blades. Fokker monoplanes so equipped first appeared in the summer of 1915, and their influence began to be felt in October, towards the end of the Loos battle.[8]

"It is hoped very shortly to obtain a machine which will be able to successfully engage the Fokkers at present in use by the Germans", the Royal Flying Corps* announced in mid-January 1916. In the meantime, there was emphasis on flying in formation for protection. The Corps made an inflexible rule that no machine should proceed on reconnaissance unless escorted by at least three other machines. Should one of these become detached from the formation the reconnaissance was not to be continued.[9] The British answer to the Fokker monoplane was the De Havilland "pusher" (propeller in rear), armed with a flexible Lewis gun in front and capable of about 85 miles per hour. The French reply was the Nieuport Scout, a biplane fighter with a semi-flexible Hotchkiss or Lewis gun on the top wing, above the propeller. In February and March several British squadrons were fully or partly equipped with both types, and the "Fokker scourge"—never as serious as was widely supposed—soon abated.[10]

While fighter frequently engaged fighter, the primary role of such aircraft was to attack enemy reconnaissance, artillery observation and bombing planes and protect their own. Aerial reconnaissance included air photography, with which members of the R.F.C. had experimented before the war. Artillery observation

* The R.F.C., formed in 1912, originally consisted of military and naval wings. Shortly before the war the naval wing became the Royal Naval Air Service. On 1 April 1918 the R.F.C. and R.N.A.S. were reunited as the Royal Air Force.

was carried out from both aeroplanes and captive balloons, wireless gradually replacing coloured lights and signal lamps as a means of communication with batteries. In the battle of Loos, British planes fitted with proper bombsights had dropped bombs of up to 112 pounds on German communications.

The 3rd and 4th Divisions Formed

In December 1915 the United Kingdom's War Committee, in line with the decisions at Chantilly, had decided that for the British Empire France was the main theatre of war, and in the months that followed every effort was made to strengthen the British Expeditionary Force. Territorial Force and New Army troops crossed the Channel, and nine divisions were brought home from Egypt. Between Christmas and 1 July the forces under Sir Douglas Haig's command grew from three armies numbering 38 infantry divisions to four armies (and a reserve army) of 49 infantry divisions, the number of cavalry divisions remaining at five. The reserve army became the Fifth Army in October.[11]

Each of these increases reflects an additional Canadian division. Late in June 1915 the War Office had formally inquired whether Canada, in addition to maintaining her present overseas force with some 5000 reinforcements monthly, could see her way to raise "further formed bodies of troops".[12] Although General Hughes, two months earlier, had intimated that a third division could and would be raised (above, p. 114), Sir Robert Borden, the Chief of the General Staff, and others now doubted its feasibility. However, after General Alderson pointed out that in France it was the policy to have army corps of three divisions, with always one being kept in reserve,[13] it was decided to form a new division largely from unallotted units already overseas and to complete the establishment with troops still in Canada.[14] Meanwhile the maximum number of men under arms had been set at 150,000.[15] By September 1915, 56 battalions had been authorized besides the units of the 1st and 2nd Divisions and the 7th and 8th Brigades. Three months later the War Office asked whether Canada would be prepared to provide twelve battalions for service in Egypt—either in addition to completing the 3rd Division, or by deferring the formation of the 3rd Division until the spring. Now confident that they could maintain four divisions in the field, and preferring to keep them all together, the Canadian authorities made the counter-proposal (which was accepted) of both a third and a fourth division for the Western Front.[16]

The 3rd Division came into being towards the end of December 1915. The G.O.C. was Major-General M. S. Mercer, formerly of the 1st Brigade, and at the time Commander of Headquarters Corps Troops. General Mercer was a Canadian, as were also his brigade commanders and a number of his staff officers; by the end of 1916 all staff appointments in the division except three (the G.S.O. I, G.S.O. II and the B.M. Artillery) were held by Canadians. Most of the divisional and brigade staff officers and some of the unit commanders had served in France six months or more; but comparatively few of the regimental officers or other ranks had had previous experience in the field.[17]

The 7th Brigade, formed on 22 December 1915 under Brig.-Gen. A. C. Macdonell, consisted of one veteran battalion and three units with no field experience. From the 27th British Division, after a year's distinguished service in France with the 80th Brigade, came Princess Patricia's Canadian Light Infantry. The Royal Canadian Regiment, at that time the only Permanent Force battalion, had been employed on garrison duty in Bermuda for eleven months; it had arrived in France in November 1915 and trained with the 2nd Brigade. The two remaining units, the 42nd Battalion (from Montreal) and the 49th (Edmonton), had both undergone a tour of non-operational duty in France. The 8th Brigade was organized on 28 December and Colonel Williams, though still holding the appointment of Adjutant General, was placed in command with the appropriate rank. It was made up of the 1st, 2nd, 4th and 5th Battalions, Canadian Mounted Rifles, formed by the conversion to infantry of the six C.M.R. regiments (above, p. 110). The units of the 9th Brigade (Brig.-Gen. F. W. Hill), which joined the division in February 1916, were the 43rd, 52nd, 58th and 60th Battalions. They came from Winnipeg, Port Arthur, the Niagara area and Montreal, respectively, and in the main had reached England in November. Except in artillery, the 3rd Division was complete by late March 1916. Until the middle of July, when its own gunners arrived, it was supported by the artillery of the Indian 3rd (Lahore) Division.

In accepting the offer of a fourth Canadian division, the War Office stipulated that Canada's first obligation was to complete the provision of 18 reserve battalions in England; these were required as a source of reinforcement drafts for the 36 battalions of the three existing divisions. For that reason the 4th Division did not go overseas as such but was formed from units already there, or soon to arrive, on 26 April 1916. A tentative selection was made by representatives of the Canadian Training Depot and the War Office.[18]

Concentration and preliminary divisional training took place at Bramshott, in Aldershot Command. The divisional commander, Major-General David Watson, was brought back from commanding the 5th Brigade in France. Like the 2nd and 3rd Divisions, the 4th did not at first have its own artillery: the 4th Divisional Artillery was formed in June 1917 by a distribution of units in France. Otherwise the new division was complete by August 1916, when it crossed the Channel; though there had been substitutions in the slate of battalions originally proposed.

The 10th Brigade, commanded by Brig.-Gen. W. St. P. Hughes, consisted of the 44th Battalion (from Winnipeg), the 46th (South Saskatchewan), the 47th (New Westminster, Vancouver and Victoria) and the 50th (Calgary). In the 11th Brigade (Brig.-Gen. V. W. Odlum) were the 54th (Kootenay, British Columbia), 75th (Toronto-Hamilton-London), 87th (Montreal) and 102nd (North British Columbia) Battalions. The 12th Brigade was commanded by Lord Brooke, who had previously led the 4th Brigade in France. One of its battalions—the 38th, from the Ottawa district—had previously served in Bermuda, relieving the R.C.R. The other three units were the 72nd, 73rd and 78th Battalions, from British Columbia, Montreal and Winnipeg respectively.[19]

The demands created by the organization of the two new overseas divisions and the necessity of maintaining in the United Kingdom an adequate number of reinforcement battalions (one for every two battalions in France) were met by an increasing flow of infantry units across the Atlantic. Although in the first two months of 1916 a shortage of accommodation in England restricted troop movements from Canada, by the end of June forty-two infantry battalions had sailed. Meanwhile the total establishment of the armed forces had been doubled.[20]

Canadian Operations, January-March 1916

By the end of January there were 50,000 Canadian troops in the field. The Canadian Corps, as part of General Sir Herbert Plumer's Second Army, was holding a six-mile front immediately south of the Ypres Salient, extending from Ploegsteert to north of Kemmel. General Alderson, with headquarters at Bailleul, had his 1st Division on the right and the 2nd Division on the left; during the first three months of 1916 he relieved these on a brigade or battalion basis with troops of the newly formed 3rd Division. The Canadians' first winter in Flanders exposed them to the twin miseries of water-logged trenches and bitterly cold winds. The extensive sector which they were holding meant that no battalion could be out of the front line for long; in general, units served six-day tours successively in the support trenches, in the front line, and in reserve. At their rest billets in the battered little towns behind the lines the weary, muddied men from the trenches found valued refreshment in even the shortest period of relief. There was the luxury of hot baths and laundry facilities improvised by the engineers—and enterprising commanders contrived to have occasional showings of films.[21] The period saw the introduction of the divisional concert parties which were to become famous all over the Western Front. As early as March 1916 the popular "Dumbells", organized by Captain Merton Plunkett, though not yet excused from duty were delighting audiences of the 3rd Division.

In accordance with the policy of "wearing down" the enemy the Canadians carried out their orders to harass the Germans by sniping, raiding, and surprise artillery shoots. The second night of the new year saw some 65 members of the 25th Battalion (5th Brigade) adopt a device only recently introduced into trench warfare. To achieve surprise, the raiding party cut the enemy's wire by hand rather than with the artillery. Ironically enough, the experiment proved too successful. The wire-cutting group completed its task before the assault group was ready to enter the gap; and in the meantime a German wiring party discovered and repaired the damage, making the obstacle much stronger than before. The approach of daylight obliged the raiders to withdraw. Not long after this the enemy introduced tempered steel wire, and hand-cutting became a very slow and difficult process.[22]

In the early morning of 31 January 1916 the 6th Brigade staged a more eventful raid against the enemy's Spanbroekmolen salient, near the centre of the Canadian sector. Brig.-Gen. Ketchen's various objects were to obtain prisoners for identification purposes, to injure the enemy's morale and destroy his works, and to kill Germans—all in the shortest possible time. Picked parties of 30 men from the 28th and 29th Battalions were given special training at the brigade bombing school. After scouts had cut the wire at great risk the two parties, working to a pre-arranged schedule, crossed no man's land shortly before 2:40 a.m. and reached the German trenches at points 1100 yards apart.

As the raiders' bombs burst among them the startled enemy were further unnerved by the terrifying appearance of the Canadians, who had blackened their faces with burnt cork. The Vancouverites (29th Battalion), encountering little resistance, secured three prisoners, bombed the enemy in his dug-outs and in four and a half minutes were on their way back to their front line, which they reached without loss of life. The men of the 28th remained in the German trench for eight minutes, the limit allowed by the brigade staff. A German relief was in progress when they attacked, and the Canadian bombs took terrible toll of the clustering enemy. In the return journey across no man's land their prisoners were killed by enemy machine-gun fire. The raid was considered a marked success and attracted great attention along the entire British front. Three German regiments opposing the 6th Brigade had been identified, the total cost to the Canadians being two killed and ten wounded.[23]

The part played by the 29th Battalion at Spanbroekmolen and by the 7th Battalion in the raid across the Douve in the previous November (above, page 124) received recognition from Sir Douglas Haig. In his first Despatch, dated 19 May 1916, he included these two battalions among 95 units and formations (six of them Canadian) which had been "specially brought to my notice for good work in carrying out or repelling local attacks and raids". The two Canadian raids illustrated the phases through which patrolling in trench warfare had progressed. The casual encounters of hostile parties in the dark, which marked the first stage, had given way to the organized trench raid by night, the pattern of which the Canadians had set.[24] The summer of 1916 was to see the third and final stage—the daylight raid.

Between 8 and 19 February the Germans launched a series of diversionary attacks against French and British positions in preparation for their Verdun offensive. One such attack fell on "The Bluff", a low tree-covered mound on the north bank of the Ypres-Comines Canal, in the sector held by the British 5th Corps. In bitter fighting the enemy captured The Bluff on the 14th, only to lose it seventeen days later to a well-mounted counter-attack.[25] Although not directly involved in the fighting, the Canadian Corps assisted its British neighbours with artillery support and by taking over the southernmost 700 yards of the 5th Corps' front on the 17th—a relief which extended the Canadian sector to the outskirts of the ruins of St. Eloi.[26] The Canadian operations in this period brought distinction to a member of the 1st Brigade. For conspicuous bravery under a heavy bombardment on 18 March, Corporal R. Millar of the 1st Battalion received the Military Medal—the first Canadian to be so honoured. (The M.M., inscribed "For bravery in the field", had been instituted only that month. At first reserved for N.C.Os. and men, it was later awarded also to warrant officers.)

Canadian battle casualties in the first three months of 1916 numbered 546 killed, 1543 wounded, three gassed and one taken prisoner. There were 667 accidents and other non-battle casualties, of which 20 proved fatal. In spite of weather and living conditions the health of the troops was good; though there were cases of influenza, paratyphoid, and—trench feet.

The St. Eloi Craters, 27 March-16 April

By the end of 1915 mine warfare had reached a stage where it was regarded by both sides as an important factor in the siege warfare which now characterized hostilities on the Western Front. Whole sections of the line between Givenchy and Ypres had become the scene of extensive mining operations. German mining and British counter-mining had figured prominently in the fighting for The Bluff, and one of the most elaborate schemes in underground warfare yet undertaken by sappers of the Second Army was now to be the occasion of a costly and frustrating operation by the 2nd Canadian Division.

The German practice had been generally to work between ten and thirty feet underground, driving galleries forward from which to explode mines beneath the British trenches or blow the more lightly charged camouflets which were designed to destroy hostile workings without cratering the surface. At first British counter-mining was carried out at the same shallow level from shafts in the foremost trenches, and was primarily directed towards locating and wrecking the enemy's galleries. In time the British sappers found the answer to the extensive German mining under the front line by sinking their shafts at secluded points well to the rear, going down fifty to ninety feet through sand to reach hard packed strata through which they ran their galleries forward comparatively dry and almost undisturbed by the Germans, who lacked the skill and equipment to compete at these greater depths. So numerous (and on occasion unnecessary) were the local demands for trained tunnellers that in December 1915 a special expert training staff headed by an Inspector of Mines was appointed at G.H.Q., to prepare and supervise mining schemes in connection with major operations and to coordinate, through a controller of mines at each army headquarters, the employment of the more than twenty tunnelling companies (among them the 3rd Canadian Tunnelling Company). The first of a number of mining schools, to give special instruction in mining tactics, listening and mine rescue work, was organized in June 1916.[27]

In retaliation for the German capture of The Bluff (and before its recovery on 2 March) General Plumer ordered the 5th Corps to attack and cut off the enemy-held salient at St. Eloi, about a mile south-west of the Ypres-Comines Canal. The St. Eloi salient, which had been formed by a German attack in March 1915, from a base 600 yards wide penetrated 100 yards northward into the British lines, which in this sector ran due east and west. Part of the salient here was elevated 10 to 20 feet above the surrounding water-logged area. At the western end of this rise was "The Mound"—a clay bank covering half an acre which had been formed by the overburden from a brickfield nearby. Its original height of thirty or more feet had been reduced by much shelling and mining, but as an observation post overlooking the adjacent trenches it was still an important objective for either side. The Mound had unpleasant memories for the P.P.C.L.I., who had had the task of holding it in January 1915, when it was still in British hands. Within this area miners on both sides had waged an almost continuous battle throughout 1915, laboriously driving their sheeted galleries through the shifting quicksands below no man's land and the opponent's trenches. Altogether 33 mines and 31 camouflets had been blown in a space of ten acres.[28]

To offset the enemy's aggressive activity near the surface, British tunnellers had in August 1915 begun sinking three shafts 50 to 60 feet deep, running galleries forward well below the sand. So quietly did they work and so skilfully did they conceal the spoil from the tunnels that the enemy's suspicions were not aroused. Early in March they were under the German positions. On a front of 600 yards six mines (numbered consecutively from west to east), with charges ranging from 600 to 31,000 pounds of ammonal, were in readiness to initiate the British attack by blowing up The Mound and the enemy's front-line trenches. Staffs were confident that the outcome of the mining would ensure the success of the operation, even if the approaching spring weather should fail to improve the deplorable conditions of sticky mud and water-filled shell-holes and craters through which the infantry must assault. Capture of the objectives would reverse the salient by securing a new line which would thrust south into the German position to as much as 300 yards from the existing British trenches.

When the operation against the salient was planned the British 3rd Division had been selected for the assault because it was then still fresh; but by mid-March it was tired and depleted, and its ability to carry out the whole task or even part of it was in question. General Alderson proposed that the Canadian Corps' relief of the 5th Corps, which was about due, should be completed before the operation, and the attack made by the 2nd Canadian Division. But the British force had practised the assault over a course simulating the German front, and there was no time for Canadian troops to undergo similar training, for delay in firing the mines meant the risk of discovery and a counter-explosion by the enemy. Accordingly General Plumer ruled that the 3rd Division should still provide the striking force, but that the Canadians should take over the line as soon as the objectives had been won. The operation would be launched on 27 March; and it was agreed that the relief would be postponed until the new line had been consolidated.[29]

Promptly at 4:15 a.m. on the 27th an opening salvo from 41 guns and howitzers up to 9.2 inches in calibre burst upon the objectives, and the six mines were sprung at intervals of a few seconds. The terrific explosions shook the

MAP 3

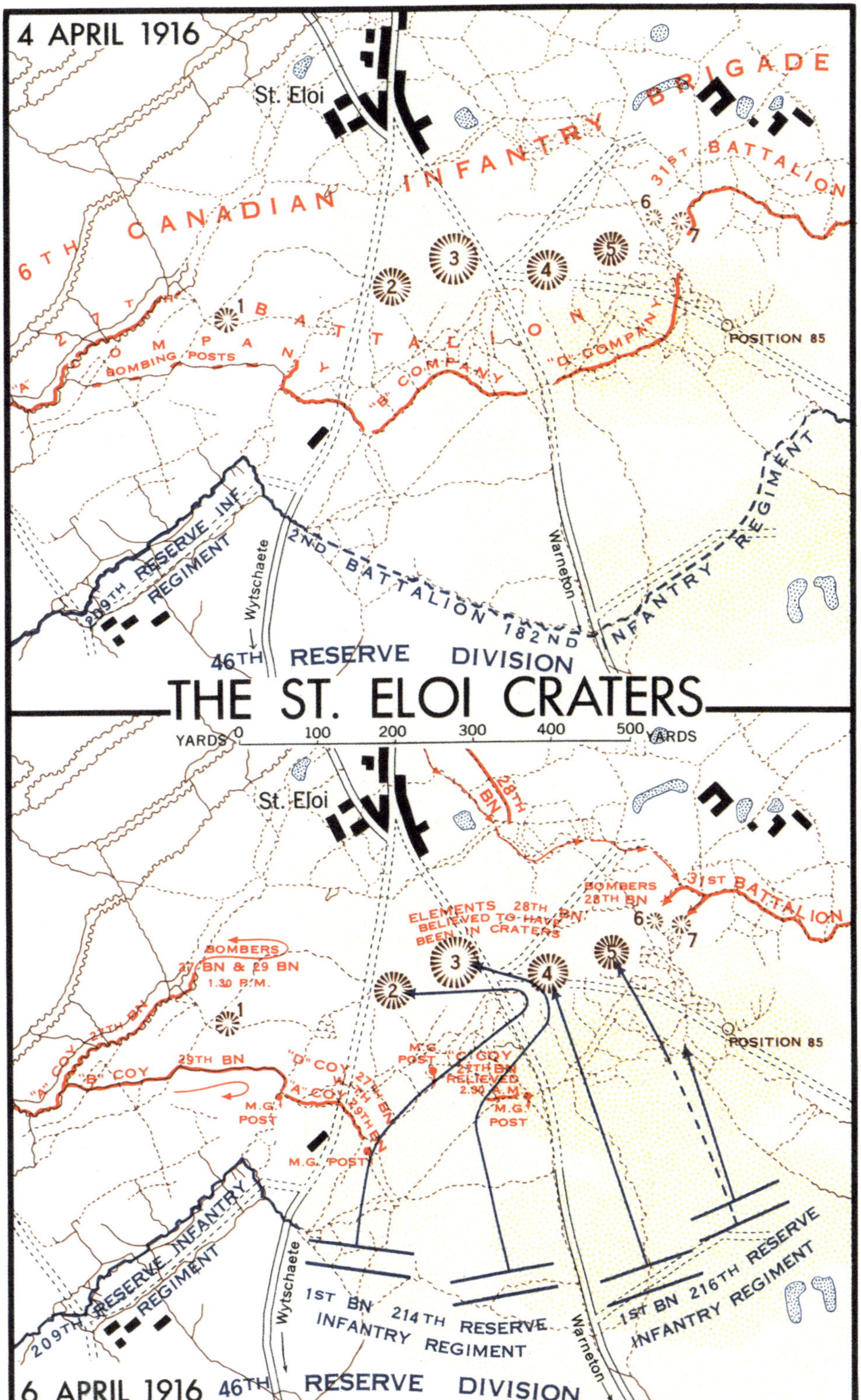

Reproduced by Army Survey Establishment

Compiled and drawn by Historical Section G.S.

MAP 4

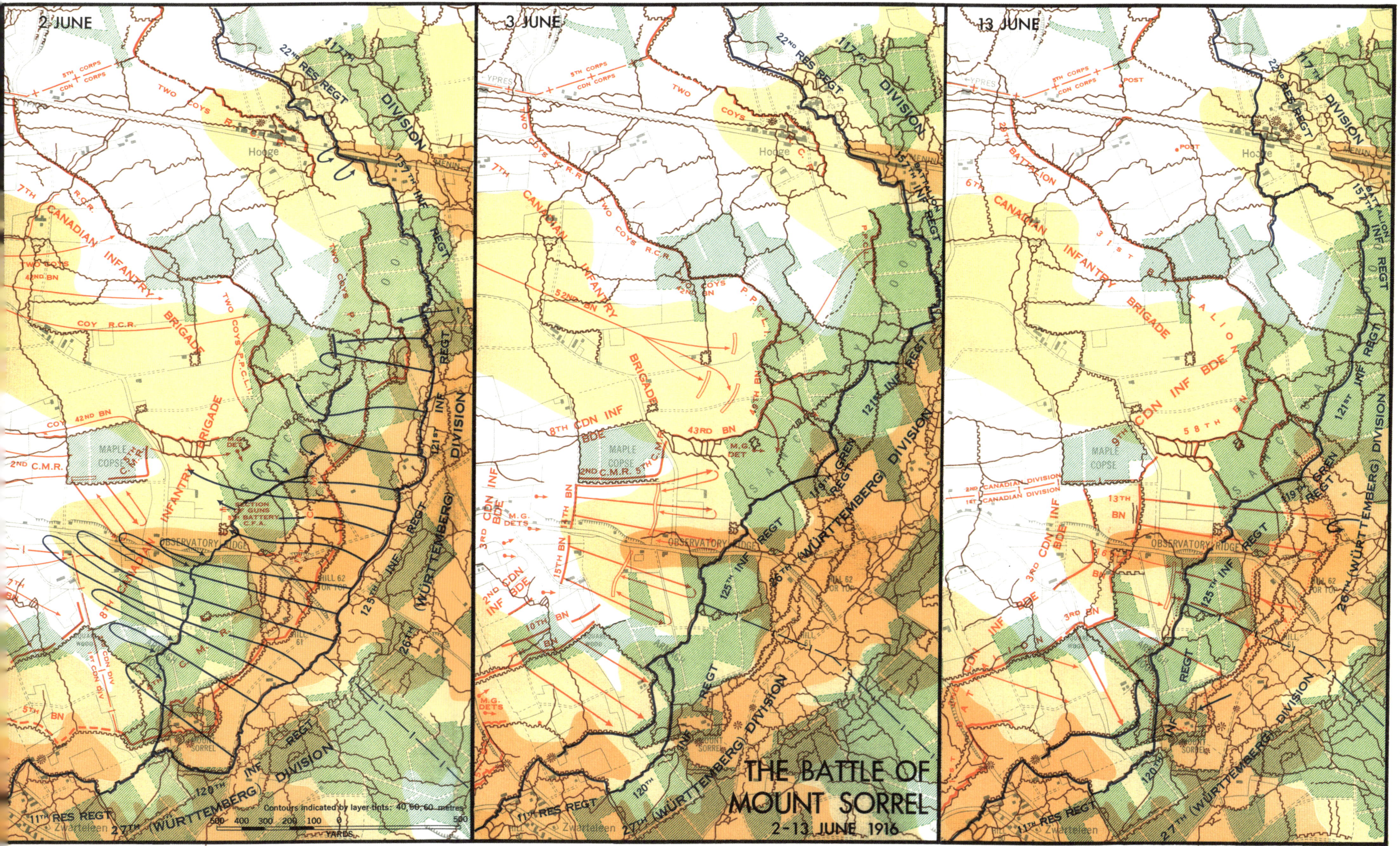

Reproduced by Army Survey Establishment

Compiled and drawn by Historical Section G.S.

earth "like the sudden outburst of a volcano" and the colossal shower of yellow smoke and *debris* that leapt into the heavens could be seen from miles away.[30] The eruption blotted out old landmarks and collapsed trenches on both sides like packs of cards. Two front line companies of the 18th Reserve Jäger Battalion were annihilated by the explosion of Mines 2, 3, 4 and 5 (Mine 3 turning what was left of The Mound into a gaping hole).[31] Mines 1 and 6, being short of the German positions, formed craters in no man's land, which were later to serve as strong points of defence on either flank. While the last clods of earth were falling, the British 9th Brigade, whose troops had spent much of the night lying prone in the chilling mud, assaulted with two battalions. In less than half an hour the right-hand unit had captured the first three craters, and 200 yards beyond had carried its objective, the German third line.

Of the craters on the left, however, only No. 6 and the nearby hole left by an earlier explosion (subsequently labelled Crater 7) were secured. The blowing of the mines had so completely changed the landscape that the occupying troops on this flank believed that they were in Craters 4 and 5, which in reality were held by neither side. For the next three days the 3rd Division failed to realize that a considerable gap existed in its defences. By then the alert enemy (who had continued to man a machine-gun emplacement at a trench intersection, 150 yards to the south-west, identified on battle maps of the period by the number "85") had slipped troops forward to occupy Crater 5. On the same day (30 March) the 3rd Division established a machine-gun post in Crater 4.[32]

For nearly a week the enemy resisted every attempt to dislodge him from his positions on the left. Finally, on 3 April, an assault by the last uncommitted battalion of the 3rd Division won back Crater 5, leaving as the only objective uncaptured Point 85, which had become the key point for mounting the German counter-attacks. By that time the units of the 3rd Division were nearing exhaustion. The enemy losses in the first three days were by German accounts 921, an estimated 300 being killed or buried by the mines. These losses would undoubtedly have been higher but for careless conversation on a British field telephone, loose talk in neighbouring towns and villages, and tell-tale subterranean noises—all of which had prompted the enemy to thin out his front line and alert his rear positions.[33]

The capture of Crater 5 ended a week of fighting during which every battalion of the 3rd British Division had been engaged in the most appalling conditions. The newly-won ground was under constant enemy shelling, and men had been forced to crouch in mud-filled ditches and shell-holes, or stand all day in water nearly to their waists with no possibility of rest. So exhausted and depleted were the British battalions it was decided on 1 April that the relief of the 5th Corps could not wait, as originally intended, for the front to be stabilized. During the night of 3-4 April the Canadian Corps, hitherto occupying the sector to the south, changed places with its British neighbours, command of the new area passing to General Alderson at noon on the 4th. As it seemed unwise to register new guns in the middle of an operation, the British 3rd Divisional Artillery remained in position, as did also the mortars, one Vickers battery and 24 Lewis guns. It had been the practice in the B.E.F. for reliefs to be made on a divisional or lower level; this was the first instance where an entire corps relieved another—and it was carried out on an active battle front. In keeping with Ottawa's wishes it became the rule rather than the exception that the Canadian Corps entered and left the line as a whole.

At three in the morning of 4 April the 6th Canadian Brigade, commanded by Brig.-Gen. H. D. B. Ketchen, wearing steel helmets for the first time (only 50 per company were available), took over from the British 76th Brigade in front of the craters. The 27th Battalion occupied the old trenches next to the corps right boundary, and 1000 yards of the new front line running eastward in front of the first five craters. This line was so badly battered that it was almost impossible to identify it; at best it was little more than a drainage ditch. Along the 250 yards in front of Craters 4 and 5 the incoming Canadians found a machine-gun in only four of the 12 posts that were supposedly held by British Lewis gunners.[34] All that the 27th Battalion could do immediately was to attempt to defend this stretch with small bombing posts insecurely linked by visiting patrols. The 31st Battalion manned the former British trenches on the east side of the salient and a short section of newly-won positions extending to cover Crater 7.[35] The craters themselves had not been manned by the 3rd Division, who considered them too obvious a target for German howitzers and mortars. Being on higher ground, however, they were relatively dry, and Brig.-Gen. Ketchen made plans to fortify them.[36]

There can rarely have been a less advantageous position than the sector taken over by the 27th Battalion. Its limited extent made it an ideal target for German concentrated artillery fire; the whole area lay spread out like a map under the eyes of enemy observers on the Wytschaete ridge, with the sun at their backs through much of the day. There was no such commanding position for British artillery observers. To them the lips of the craters formed the sky-line for the most critical 500 yards, and only when the sun was low was it possible to identify each crater by its shadow; the front line lay invisible in the dead ground 150 yards beyond. The reserve line, which had been the British front line on the day of the original attack, was obliterated and untenable for a thousand yards. The whole system was sodden, with every shell-hole a pond. Long stretches of trenches were from two to three feet deep in water, for all drains had been disrupted by shellfire or the explosion of mines.

To the commander of the 2nd Division the most unsatisfactory feature in the whole grim situation was the complete absence of any communication between the captured line and the rear, except around the flanks of the crater system. The four central craters had been blown so close together that they formed an impassable obstacle—the largest hole was 50 feet deep and 180 feet across,* with a rampart of loose earth (by now rapidly turning to mud) some 12 to 20 feet above ground level extending fifty yards in all directions.[37] As we shall see, this lack of

* Forty-three years later the author found these four craters full of water and well stocked with fish. On the banks of No. 5, which was surrounded by trees, stood a summer cottage, with a row boat moored to a small wharf.

communication through the centre, combined with the difficulties of observation from the rear, was responsible for misconception of the true Canadian positions that was to have disastrous results.

In spite of these disadvantages General Turner felt that, given time, "we could make a pretty good line of the position selected, but that a very great amount of work would be required". The advice of the commander of the outgoing division, based on some experience in crater-fighting, was "to make good the [new] front line and wire it . . . dig a support line in front of the craters and wire it . . . provide communication trenches between old and new front lines . . . make tunnelled dug-outs in the rear exterior slopes of the craters as soon as the earth had consolidated sufficiently . . . make and maintain dummy trenches round the lips of the craters to induce the enemy to waste ammunition by shelling them.[38]

Brig.-Gen. Ketchen was not in agreement with this proposed scheme of developing field works. The 3rd British Division, handicapped by the impossible ground and weather and the enemy's harassing fire, had made little progress on such a programme. Although two communication trenches had been dug, only one was still recognizable by the time of the hand-over. Ketchen was concerned over the extreme vulnerability of the new trench line and wanted instead to occupy and fortify the craters as the main defensive position—which is exactly what the Germans later did. But there was no time to change policy or to arrange for the men and materials required for such a task. The work of consolidation was attacked with energy. During the first two nights the 2nd Canadian Pioneer Battalion, under engineer direction and assisted by large parties drawn from the 4th and 5th Brigades, toiled vigorously to improve the defences. Firing positions in the captured German trenches which formed the front line were reversed, pumping slightly reduced the water level, British wounded were evacuated and the bodies of British and German dead were removed. A support trench running eastward was started south of the line of craters.

Throughout 4 and 5 April the whole of the Canadian front line came under almost continual bombardment. The intensity of the German fire was described by a British artillery officer who had been in the Ypres Salient for the past year as far greater than any he had hitherto experienced.[39] Both battalion sectors were hard hit, and 200 yards of trench in the 27th Battalion's area were completely demolished. The destruction of the sandbag parapet in one of the 31st Battalion's trenches exposed the Canadians to enfilade machine-gun fire from position 85 as well as to sniping from the German lines, only 150 yards away. Although each man dug his own slit trench in the mud, casualties mounted rapidly. By noon on the 4th every second man in one of the 27th's forward companies had been hit. The battalion commander, Lt.-Col. I. R. Snider, was forced to thin out his front line, leaving in front of the craters only bombing parties supplied by battalions of the 5th Brigade and four Lewis gun detachments from the 5th Brigade Machine Gun Company. He had no contact with the 31st Battalion on his left. On the evening of 5 April small parties from the 28th Battalion were sent out to station themselves in the four big craters and act as snipers and observers until these could be trenched and garrisoned. There is doubt that the positions which they occupied were actually the designated craters. Later that same night the 29th Battalion began relieving the badly depleted forward companies of the 27th Battalion.[40]

This relief dragged out interminably. The incoming troops, burdened with extra equipment, had to struggle forward in a long line through the mud and congestion of the same narrow communication trench that was being used by pioneers moving up to work on the craters and by other parties coming to the rear, many of them wounded. The exchange was still in progress when at 3:30 a.m. on the 6th, following an intense barrage, the Germans attacked with two battalions* astride the road which ran from St. Eloi south-eastward to Warneton and before its destruction had passed between the sites of the 3rd and 4th craters. Effective resistance was impossible. West of the road the two relieving companies were not yet in position, having failed to find the positions manned by the 5th Brigade. They could do little more than deflect the tide of the German attack eastward, where it quickly wiped out the machine-gun posts and flowed through the resulting gap in front of the central craters. The eastern wing of the assault was held up momentarily by crossfire from the 31st Battalion's machine-guns, which also repelled attacks against Craters 6 and 7 and the line to the east. Artillery fire on the enemy's lines of approach by all available British field guns failed to stop the attackers, some of whom got through by splitting into small groups. The Germans quickly secured Craters 2 and 3 and from these points of vantage soon spread into Craters 4 and 5. In less than three hours the enemy had regained all the ground taken from him between 27 March and 3 April.[41]

The Canadians launched local counter-attacks with the minimum of delay. The only feasible way to regain the craters seemed to be by bombing, but the element of surprise was missing and the efforts accomplished nothing. On the right bombers of the 27th and 29th Battalions attempting to reoccupy Craters 2 and 3 were caught in the mire and shot down before they could get close enough to fling their grenades. On the left Brig.-Gen. Ketchen ordered the 31st Battalion, reinforced with a detachment from the 28th, to retake Craters 4 and 5. But their unfamiliarity with the ground and the complete absence of recognizable landmarks caused the attackers to repeat the mistake made by British troops ten days earlier. Forced to make their approach from the side, they lost direction and occupied Craters 6 and 7, reporting that they had regained 4 and 5. German shellfire during the remainder of 6 April and on succeeding days isolated the two craters that the Canadians were holding, so that no reconnoitring officer could reach them in daylight. Because of bad weather no air photograph of the positions was taken from the 8th until the 16th. The mistake was to persist throughout that entire period.†[42] The occupants of the two craters could see on their right

* The 1st Battalions of the 214th and 216th Reserve Regiments (46th Reserve Division).

† It is hard to understand why staff officers failed to interpret air photographs correctly. The photo taken on 8 April clearly shows Craters 6 and 7 half full of water and the others comparatively dry. Apparently no use was made of this obvious means of identifying the positions held by the Canadians.

the high edge of what they believed to be Crater 3 (The Mound), but which was in reality No. 5. On the night of 6-7 April the 28th Battalion sent out 75 bombers, supported by two companies, to regain this objective. Enemy shellfire and heavy rain held them up. Losing their way in the darkness they occupied a group of craters north of No. 4, and there captured several small German patrols. They had failed to attain their objective, or even identify it correctly. During the night the 4th Canadian Brigade (Brig.-Gen. R. Rennie) relieved the 6th Brigade, which had suffered 617 casualties in its four days of fighting.[43] For the next week confusion was to persist with respect to the exact positions held by the Canadians.

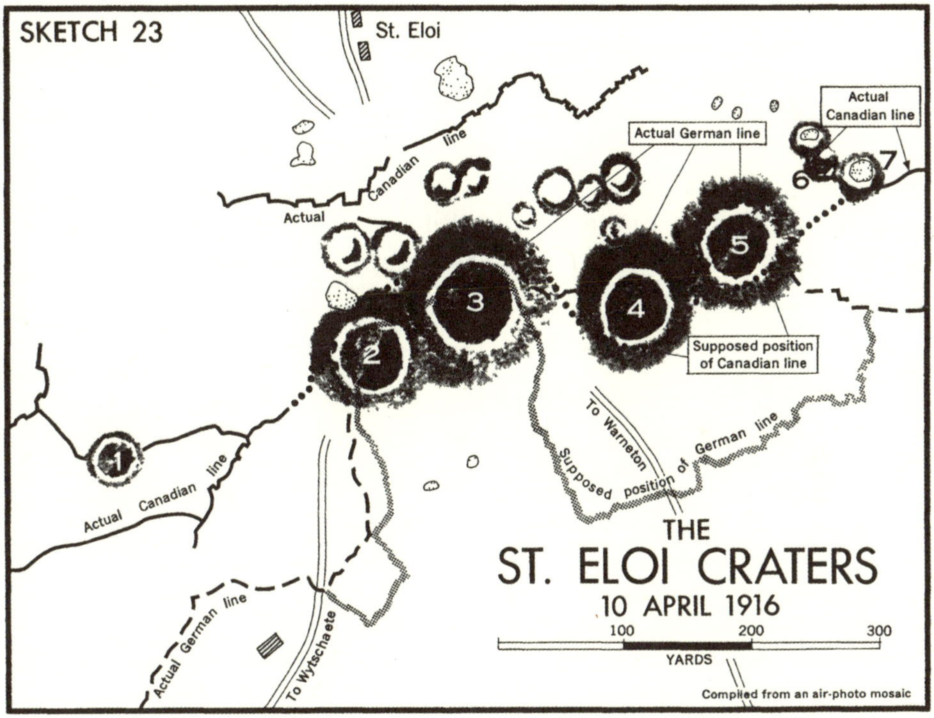

On the 8th General Turner suggested to the Corps Commander two alternatives for clearing up the situation: either to "evacuate the craters, and to shell the Germans out of the line they held, in the same way as they had dealt with us", or to "attack on a wider frontage . . . and to consolidate the ground gained; thus giving the German artillery a wider objective for their retaliation".[44] The former of these proposals seemed the more practicable; a large-scale assault was ruled out by the impossibility of gaining surprise in this disturbed sector and the heavy requirements of men and material for the projected offensive on the Somme.[45] When General Alderson referred the matter to the Army Commander, however, General Plumer, basing his decision on the mistaken belief that only Craters 2 and 3 had been lost, ordered the Canadians to hold their present positions and make every effort to recover these craters. General Turner was told that General Joffre had spontaneously thanked the Army Commander for the present operations at St. Eloi, which he described as "an appreciable help to the French operations at Verdun".[46]

Work on the Canadian trenches was pushed forward by the 4th Brigade and 2000 reserve troops. On the night of the 8th-9th an attempt by the 21st Battalion to seize (the real) Craters 2 and 3 by attacking from the west was repulsed by German rifle and machine-gun fire. Simultaneous attacks on the next night by three battalions (the 18th, 20th and 21st) also failed. The following night it was the enemy's turn to strike, but two attempts to enlarge his holdings were driven off by Canadian bombers. A further attack on the German-held craters, which the 5th Canadian Brigade, relieving the 4th Brigade, was to have carried out on the night of 12-13 April, was cancelled. With the concurrence of the Corps Commander, General Turner decided that for the time being all efforts should be concentrated on improving the existing front line.[47]

Although as early as 10 April one of Turner's staff officers reported having been fired on from Crater No. 4, the belief that only Craters 2 and 3 were in German hands persisted. The 2nd Division's Daily Intelligence Summary for 15 April reported, "At 2:30 a.m., assisted by artillery fire, the enemy made a bombing attack on Craters 4 and 5 . . . . The craters were both in our possession and there are no casualties."[48] Yet on the same night of the 14th-15th, Major J. A. Ross of the 24th Battalion made a personal reconnaissance of Craters 2, 3, 4 and 5 and found all four in the possession of the enemy. This was confirmed on the 16th by aerial photography; and preparations for further Canadian attacks in the area were immediately stopped. The bitter realization came as a heavy blow to the divisional staff. In a sympathetic note on April 16 to the G.O.C. General Alderson wrote: "It seems extraordinary yet if one thinks of it quietly and calmly, it is not only a very likely, but almost a natural outcome of the conditions under which your Division took over the line . . . . Our Army Commander, gallant gentleman as he is, has taken it well, though he is probably the most hit, because the Army originated the situation . . . ."[49]

For nearly two more weeks the St. Eloi area continued to be the scene of heavy bombardment by both sides. The Canadians were now supported by their own guns, the 2nd Canadian Divisional Artillery having relieved the gunners of the 3rd British Division on the night of 12-13 April. Preparations for the Somme were restricting the supply of ammunition for the British heavy artillery, and this meant that the new enemy line covering the craters suffered less severely than the Canadian positions. On the 19th the Germans captured Craters 6 and 7 but did not occupy them. Thereafter both sides reverted to static warfare, glad to end fighting under conditions so indescribably miserable. Enemy records give the German losses in the recapture of the craters and the subsequent fighting as 483;[50] between 4 and 16 April the Canadian casualties numbered 1373.

As is not unusual after unsuccessful operations, inquiries soon began at various levels to determine the responsibility for the St. Eloi fiasco, particularly with respect to the delay in the original capture of Crater 5 and the failure to take position 85, the loss of the craters and the unsuccessful attempts to regain them, and the misinformation about Craters 4 and 5. On 26 April the General Representative of Canada at the Front, Sir Max Aitken (see below, p. 146), cabled Sir Sam Hughes that the British viewed the error as serious "and responsibility wide spreading". A number of changes of appointment followed. The Second Army's Major General, General Staff went to command a brigade; and a brigade major and a battalion commander in the 3rd British Division were replaced, as was the commander of the 27th Canadian Battalion.[51] Ordered by General Plumer (who, according to Sir Douglas Haig, wanted to remove both Turner and Ketchen) to take "severe disciplinary measures", General Alderson initiated an adverse report on the commander of the 6th Canadian Brigade (Brig.-Gen. Ketchen). General Turner however, refused to associate himself with this, and this refusal, aggravating the already strained relations between the divisional and corps commanders (above, p. 80), led to a request by Alderson for Turner's removal. The Commander-in-Chief, however, refused to dismiss Turner. On the 21st Haig noted in his diary the existence of "some feeling against the English" amongst the Canadians; and having weighed "the danger of a serious feud between the Canadians and the British" against "the retention of a couple of incompetent commanders", he had already decided to keep Turner on. He noted that in abnormally difficult conditions—conditions in which mistakes were to be expected—"all did their best and made a gallant fight". Haig's decision, as he learned from Sir Max Aitken two days later, coincided with the views of Prime Minister Borden; the two Canadian officers retained their commands.[52]

Meanwhile steps had already been taken to improve fighting techniques in the 2nd Canadian Division. A memorandum from General Turner to his brigades and units on 12 April listed fourteen "points which may be learnt from our recent operations at St. Eloi". Of these no less than seven dealt with methods of securing and transmitting reliable information, the absence of which had been "one of the greatest obstacles to the success of the enterprise".[53]

The struggle for the craters left an important tactical question unsolved. The operations demonstrated that it was possible in trench warfare, given proper preparations and the help of surprise, to seize a limited objective. But they also proved the impossibility of holding out against the volume of observed artillery fire which such a narrow front invited. Future planners still had to decide the best width of front to attack—"small enough to ensure success but large enough to prevent the enemy's artillery making it impossible to hold the captured ground".[54]

St. Eloi was the 2nd Division's first fight, and from it the troops emerged with a sense of frustration. Fortunately this was only temporary, for the Battles of the Somme were approaching, and in September the Division was to prove its prowess and re-establish its reputation by its sterling performance at Courcelette.

A Change in Command

Four months were to elapse before the Canadians entered the great offensive at the Somme. Before they moved south they were called on to fight a battle in defence of the Ypres Salient which was to bring them a measure of the success which hitherto had too often eluded them.

The sector taken over from the 5th Corps on 4 April extended from half a mile south-east of St. Eloi to 500 yards north-west of Hooge, on the Menin road. During the 2nd Division's fighting for the St. Eloi craters activity in the centre and on the left of the Corps front, held respectively by the 1st and 3rd Divisions, had been confined principally to shelling, patrolling and sniping, as each side strove to improve its own positions despite harassing fire from the opponent. On the night of 26-27 April the Germans exploded two mines on the 1st Division's front and attacked both the 1st and 2nd Divisions—in no great strength, but with formidable artillery support. These incursions were beaten off, and a threatened attack against the 3rd Division failed to materialize. May was quiet. The term is relative only, for the Canadians suffered upwards of two thousand casualties that month. In the continual artillery duel the Germans had an overwhelming advantage in gun power; for the tremendous build-up for the Somme left few extra guns available for other parts of the British line.[55] It was in May, however, that the Canadian Corps first made use of wireless for controlling artillery fire. The experiment was awkward and confused and nearly ended in tragedy, but it marked the beginning of a new system of control which gave more rapid and accurate fire.

On 28 May 1916, in an abrupt change of command, General Alderson was appointed Inspector General of Canadian Forces in England. His removal came as an aftermath of the St. Eloi fighting and the conflict between the Corps Commander and General Turner—although, ironically enough, no censure was attached to either for his conduct of the operation. Sir Max Aitken had arrived in France on 22 April, and on the 23rd he had a long interview with Haig during which the whole matter was discussed. While agreeing to keep Turner and Ketchen the Commander-in-Chief recognized the impossibility of retaining both Alderson and Turner, and indeed had to anticipate the possibility that General Plumer might resign if the recommendation for Turner's removal was not approved. Haig was prepared to attempt to pacify the aggrieved Army Commander but, according to Sir Max, "stipulated that Canada should give him the assistance he required in disposing of General Alderson". Out of the conversations between Haig and Aitken arose a proposal that Alderson should be offered the post of Inspector General of the Canadian Troops in England.

This, noted Haig in his diary on the 23rd, would help meet "the difficulty under which the commander of the Canadian Corps in the field now suffered through having so many administrative and political questions to deal with, in addition to his duties as commander in the field".[56] In recommending to Sir Sam Hughes that the proposal be approved, Aitken cabled "that the loss of

Reproduced by permission of the National Gallery of Canada

"THE CLOTH HALL, YPRES"

Ypres, one of the few Belgian towns that the Germans failed to capture, has given its name to three major battles of the First World War. The ruins of the famous Cloth Hall became a memorable landmark to Canadians who fought in the battles of 1915 and 1917. From a painting by J. Kerr-Lawson.

IN THE YPRES SALIENT

This photograph was taken in July 1916. Among the shell-shattered trees may be seen sandbag shelters, built largely above ground to escape flooding.

THE ORCHARD AT FESTUBERT

The blasted skeletons of a few apple trees were all that remained of the orchard, captured by the 16th Battalion on 20 May 1915. This picture was taken in the spring of 1919.

A ST. ELOI CRATER

A picture taken three years after the explosion of the St. Eloi mines shows one of the water-filled craters, scene of the confused fighting of April 1916. In the background to the west is Mount Kemmel, which the Germans captured in April 1918.

Turner and Ketchen would affect disastrously the Second Division and must be followed by many resignations". He had "reluctantly" come to the conclusion that General Alderson was "incapable of holding the Canadian Divisions together".[57] In Ottawa the Prime Minister and his cabinet gave their assent on 26 April and Alderson's appointment to the post in the United Kingdom followed.[58] For many years, during and after the war, it was widely believed that the immediate cause of Alderson's removal had been the differences of opinion between himself and the Minister of Militia regarding the use of the Ross Rifle (below, p. 158). As we now know,* this was not the case.

General Alderson's new appointment was to be of brief duration; for in November 1916 a reorganization of Canadian command in the United Kingdom terminated his employment. During his eighteen months in command of Canadian forces on both sides of the English Channel he had made an important contribution. It had not been an easy task to organize, equip and train the Canadian Division in the mud of Salisbury Plain, particularly when so often his views had clashed with those of the Minister of Militia. Under his leadership Canadians had sturdily withstood the German onslaught at Ypres†, and to him must go no small part of the credit for building the staunch Canadian force that within a year was to win its spurs as a corps on Vimy Ridge.[59]

The Canadian Government had left the nomination of Alderson's successor in the hands of the Commander-in-Chief. He selected a distinguished British officer and a future Governor General of Canada—Lieut.-General the Honourable Sir Julian H. G. Byng. Sir Julian was a cavalry officer who at the outbreak of war was recalled from service in Egypt to command a cavalry division and subsequently the Cavalry Corps in France. He commanded the 9th Corps in the Dardanelles Campaign, returning to the Western front in February 1916 to take over the 17th Corps.

The Battle of Mount Sorrel, 2-13 June

The beginning of June found the 2nd Canadian Division still in front of St. Eloi. Major-General Currie's 1st Division had two battalions in its front line, which centred on Hill 60, immediately north of the Ypres-Comines railway. The remaining two miles of front on the Corps left were held by the 3rd Division (Major-General Mercer), with four battalions forward. This part of the Canadian line formed the most easterly projection of the Ypres Salient into enemy territory. The challenge to German aspirations presented by this obtrusion was the greater in that the 3rd Division's sector included the only portion of the crest of the Ypres ridge which had remained in Allied hands—a tenure which gave the Canadians observation over the enemy trenches. This advantageous position extended from a point about a thousand yards east of Zwarteleen (beside Hill 60), passing in

* Sir Robert Borden's Papers did not become available for examination at the Public Archives of Canada until 1952.

† Mount Alderson, in Alberta, overlooking the Waterton Lakes, is named after the first commander of the Canadian Corps.

succession over a flat knoll called Mount Sorrel and two slightly higher twin eminences, "Hill 61" and "Hill 62", the latter known also as Tor Top. North of these points the ground fell away to the Menin Road, but from Tor Top a broad spur, largely farm land, aptly named Observatory Ridge, thrust nearly a thousand yards due west between Armagh Wood and Sanctuary Wood. If the enemy could capture Tor Top and advance along Observatory Ridge he would gain a commanding position in the rear of the Canadian lines, and might well compel a withdrawal out of the salient. At the least such an advance might, as the Germans themselves stated, "fetter as strong a force as possible to the Ypres Salient", and thus reduce the number available for a British offensive elsewhere.[60]

Opposite the 1st and 3rd Divisions the enemy's 27th and 26th Infantry Divisions, of the 13th Württemberg Corps, had for the past six weeks been stealthily preparing just such a blow. Warnings were not lacking. During May Canadian patrols reported that German engineers were pushing saps forward on either side of Tor Top. These progressed slowly but steadily in spite of our artillery and machine-guns; and before the end of the month a new lateral trench connected the heads of the saps, now fifty yards in advance of the main front line. The same kind of thing was going on south of Mount Sorrel and at other points beyond. Some weeks earlier observers of the Royal Flying Corps had seen near the Menin Road, well behind the enemy lines, works curiously resembling the Canadian positions near Tor Top. (The history of the German 26th Infantry Division confirms that these were practice trenches used to rehearse the assault.)[61] Other indications of forthcoming action appeared in the bringing up of large-calibre trench mortars, and abnormal activity by the enemy's artillery, aircraft and observation balloons. Weather conditions, however, prevented systematic observation of the German rear areas; and the absence of significant troop movements seemed to signify that the looked-for attack was not imminent. (Actually the only additional enemy troops transferred to the sector for this operation were artillery.) Then on the night of 1-2 June the Württembergers refrained for seven hours from shelling the Canadian trenches, in order, as it subsequently transpired, to avoid interference with their own wire-gapping parties. Later their guns resumed normal activity, and Canadian suspicions were allayed.

At six o'clock on the morning of the 2nd, General Mercer and Brig.-Gen. Williams, commander of the 8th Brigade (which was defending the threatened area about Observatory Ridge), set out to reconnoitre Tor Top and Mount Sorrel. They had just reached the front-line trenches of the 4th Canadian Mounted Rifles on the brigade right when the enemy's preliminary bombardment burst upon them. It was the Canadian Corps' first experience of the terrific violence that artillery preparation was to attain in the summer of 1916. "All agreed", writes Lord Beaverbrook,* "that there was no comparison between the gun-fire of April and of June, which was the heaviest endured by British troops up to that time."[62] For four hours a veritable tornado of fire ravaged the Canadian positions from half a mile west of Mount Sorrel to the northern edge of Sanctuary

* Sir Max Aitken was elevated to the peerage in January 1917.

Wood. The full fury fell upon the 8th Brigade and the right of the 7th Brigade. Hardest hit was Brig.-Gen. Williams' right-hand battalion, the 4th Canadian Mounted Rifles, in front of Armagh Wood. Their trenches vanished and the garrisons in them were annihilated. Of this unit's ordeal a German eye-witness was to write: "The whole enemy position was a cloud of dust and dirt, into which timber, tree trunks, weapons and equipment were continuously hurled up, and occasionally human bodies".[63] "The Tunnel", a gallery dug on the reverse slope of Mount Sorrel by the 2nd Canadian Tunnelling Company (whose sappers were to do stout work in evacuating casualties), afforded some safety until it was blown in; its surviving occupants were captured. In all, the 4th Mounted Rifles suffered 89 percent casualties—of 702 officers and men only 76 came through unscathed.[64]

Neither Mercer nor Williams returned from the Mounted Rifles' area. The latter, wounded, was taken prisoner when the German infantry assaulted. The death of Mercer—his ear-drums were shattered by shellfire, his leg broken by a bullet, and finally he was killed by a burst of shrapnel as he lay on the ground—came tragically at a moment when his new command was entering its first big action.[65] That afternoon Brig.-Gen. E. S. Hoare Nairne, of the Lahore Divisional Artillery, assumed temporary command of the 3rd Division.* Williams' place was taken for the time being by Lt.-Col. J. C. L. Bott, Commanding Officer of the 2nd Canadian Mounted Rifles (then in brigade reserve). For several critical hours, however, both the 3rd Division and the 8th Brigade were leaderless; and the conduct of the defence suffered accordingly.

During the morning the deluge of hostile fire increased in intensity. Our artillery, assisted by two squadrons of British aircraft, accomplished little. Enemy shellfire eventually killed or wounded all forward observation officers and cut all telephone lines. A few minutes after 1:00 p.m. the Württembergers exploded four mines just short of the Canadian trenches on Mount Sorrel, and then attacked—two battalions each of the 121st and 125th Regiments (26th Infantry Division) on the right, and two battalions of the 120th Regiment (27th Infantry Division) on the left at Mount Sorrel.[66] Five other battalions were in support, and six in reserve. In bright sunlight the grey-coated figures advanced in four waves spaced about seventy-five yards apart. Afterwards Canadian survivors spoke of the assured air and the almost leisurely pace of the attackers, who appeared confident that their artillery had blotted out all resistance.

All was methodically planned. The men in the first line had fixed bayonets and carried hand grenades and wire cutters. Those who followed were equipped with entrenching tools, floor boards and sandbags. As they flowed over the flattened trenches along Mount Sorrel and Tor Top they encountered only small, isolated bands of survivors from the 1st and 4th C.M.R. who could offer little effective resistance. There were brief episodes of hand-to-hand fighting with bomb and bayonet, and where sheer numbers were not sufficient to overcome resistance,

* On 16 June Brig.-Gen. Lipsett was promoted to Major General and succeeded General Mercer in command of the 3rd Division.

the enemy used flame projectors. The machine-guns of Princess Patricia's Canadian Light Infantry and the 5th Battalion (1st Division)—on the left and right flanks—raked the attackers. Though they inflicted substantial casualties they could not halt the advance. It remained for the 5th Battalion Canadian Mounted Rifles, holding a series of strongpoints immediately behind the 1st and 4th battalions, to check enemy attacks on the east and south-east sides of Maple Copse with rapid and accurate fire. Exploiting along Observatory Ridge, the Germans captured three strongpoints and overran a section of the 5th Battery C.F.A., killing or wounding all the gunners.* Of this incident a German regimental historian was to write: "It is fitting to stress that here too the Canadians did not surrender, but at their guns defended themselves with revolvers to the last man."[68] Before the Germans began consolidating they had seized most of Armagh Wood and pushed back all but the northernmost 600 yards of our line in Sanctuary Wood.

Credit for temporarily checking the enemy's right wing belongs to the Patricias. One of their two companies in the firing line, next to the 1st C.M.R., had been overrun. But the second had escaped the worst of the bombardment, and as the Germans surged eastward its rifles volleyed into the enemy's right rear. It was to hold out successfully for eighteen hours, isolated from the rest of the battalions and with all its officers killed or wounded. Patricia companies to the rear bore the brunt of the fighting, beating off German attempts to reach the vital support line before it could be reinforced. Resolute detachments held successive blocks in the communication trenches, and the enemy's advance was over the dead bodies of each little garrison in turn. Sanctuary Wood cost the P.P.C.L.I. more than 400 casualties including 150 killed, among them the Commanding Officer, Lt.-Col. H. C. Buller.[69]

Under orders issued before the attack the Germans dug in 600-700 yards west of their former line, though short of "the position to be occupied in the most favourable case". Their formation histories, reporting the road to Ypres open, regret the brake upon exploitation applied in advance by the command. Fortunately for the Canadians no German officer had the initiative to exceed instructions and capitalize on success. Pressure to the north against the weakened defenders might well have rolled up the Canadian left wing, which had been so gallantly held by the Patricia company backed by The Royal Canadian Regiment at Hooge.[70]

By evening of 2 June machine-guns of the 10th Battalion and batteries of the Motor Machine Gun Brigade sent forward by the G.O.C. 1st Division had established a new line sealing off the German encroachment, and at 8:45 p.m. General Byng issued orders that "all ground lost to-day will be retaken tonight". The counter-attack was timed for 2:00 a.m. Because of the 3rd Division's heavy losses two brigades of the 1st Division were temporarily placed at Brig.-Gen. Hoare Nairne's disposal (the 2nd Brigade to operate against Mount Sorrel and the 3rd against Tor Top), and his 7th Brigade (on the left) was strengthened

* This was the only occasion in the war when guns of the Canadian Corps fell into German hands. The two 18-pounders were recovered in the subsequent fighting.[67]

by the addition of two battalions of the 9th Brigade. But because of the distances that had to be covered, the difficulties in communication and the interference by enemy fire, the time allowed for assembly proved inadequate and the attack had to be postponed until after seven o'clock. Then came more trouble. The signal to begin was to be six simultaneous green rockets. Some misfired, and in all fourteen rockets had to be used to send up six. Since these had not burst simultaneously (and at least two battalions saw *no* rockets), units still awaited the starting signal.[71]

As a result the 7th Battalion, on the right, the 14th and 15th Battalions (centre) and the 49th (left) assaulted at different times. The uneven start permitted a concentration of enemy rifle and machine-gun fire that would have been impossible against a whole line advancing at once. The four units suffered heavily as they moved resolutely forward in broad daylight over fairly open ground, and only small parties reached their objectives, to engage the Germans in hand-to-hand fighting. Weakened by casualties they could not overcome the defenders, and many were killed or captured. Before 1:00 p.m. the right and centre units had withdrawn to their start line, though on the left the 49th Battalion remained in possession of some of the trenches just short of the old German line.[72] The Edmonton unit had suffered heavily. Its casualties brought the total losses of the 7th Brigade for the first four days of June to 1050 all ranks.

Although these attacks failed to achieve their purpose, they had nevertheless closed a 600-yard gap from Square Wood across Observatory Ridge to Maple Copse, and advanced the Canadian front about 1000 yards from the scratch positions taken up after the German assault. Work now began on extending this line northward to Hooge, so as to give depth to the 7th Brigade's defences. The enemy, too, had not been idle. Setting himself to defend his important gains he had fortified his new line with machine-guns and barbed wire and constructed eight communication trenches leading forward from his old front line. It would almost seem that the fact of the struggle being between two national corps—Canadian and Württemberger—had strengthened the determination of each to win.

Sir Douglas Haig agreed with General Plumer's desire to expel the Germans from such a commanding position only two miles from Ypres; but in view of the preparations for the Somme offensive he did not wish to divert to the Salient more troops than necessary. He therefore restricted further support from outside the Canadian Corps to artillery and one brigade of infantry, and suggested that the next counter-attack be carried out with few infantry but many guns. This emphasis on artillery—which followed the tactics so successfully employed by the Germans at St. Eloi—brought to the disposal of the G.O.C. R.A. Canadian Corps, Brig.-Gen. H. E. Burstall, one of the greatest arrays of guns yet employed on so narrow a front. The 218 pieces included 116 eighteen-pounders, and ranged in calibre up to two 12-inch howitzers. They represented the Canadian Corps Heavy Artillery, the 1st and 2nd Divisional Artilleries and the Lahore Divisional Artillery; the British 5th, 10th, 11th Heavy Artillery Groups, 3rd Divisional

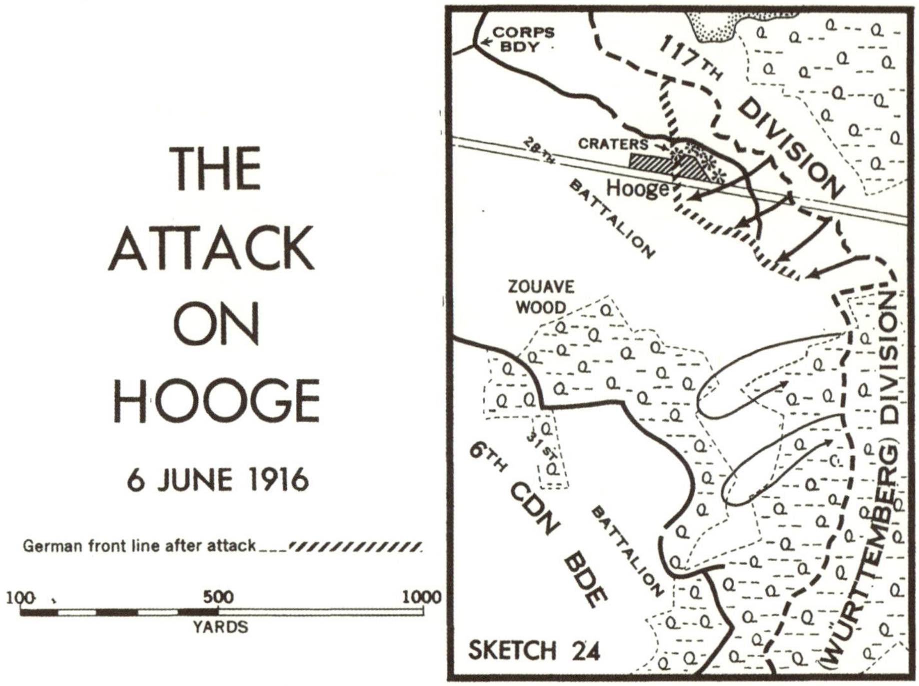

Artillery, 51st Howitzer Battery and 89th Siege Battery; and the South African 71st and 72nd Howitzer Batteries. The "heavies" of the British 5th and 14th Corps, on either flank, were to cooperate.[73]

The main task of the artillery before the counter-attack was to hamper the enemy's consolidation by pounding his front and support lines and seeking out hostile batteries for destruction. German accounts admit the success of this programme. "The losses of the 120th Regiment and the 26th Infantry Division mounted in horrifying numbers . . . What was constructed during the short nights was again destroyed in daytime".[74] But bad flying weather made it impossible to register the heavy guns, and the counter-attack, originally set for 6 June, had to be postponed.

In the meantime the enemy struck again. The target was the spur at Hooge, which had changed hands many times since the Germans first took it in 1914. Their most recent tenancy had been for eight days in the previous August. The spur overlooked Ypres, and its possession would complete the enemy's domination of the salient. In a series of reliefs the 6th Canadian Brigade, brought up from the 2nd Division's reserve, had taken over the 7th Brigade's sector north of Sanctuary Wood, and was thus holding the extreme left of the Corps front. At 3:05 p.m. on the 6th 200 yards of trenches covering the eastern outskirts of the ruins of Hooge were shattered by the explosion of four large mines. Two companies of the 28th Battalion holding these trenches suffered heavily, one being almost wiped out.[75] Determined rifle and machine-gun fire from the remainder of the battalion and the 31st Battalion on the right beat off German attempts to reach the support line. But "Hooge had gone . . . and Ypres remained open to its assailants".[76]

In keeping with the C.-in-C.'s policy of limiting operations in the Ypres Salient so as not to hamper preparations for the Somme offensive, General Byng decided to leave the Hooge trenches in German hands and to concentrate on regaining Mount Sorrel and Tor Top. To guard against further trouble on his left, the British 2nd Dismounted Cavalry Brigade, organized in three battalions, came on loan to the Canadian Corps as a counter-attack force.[77] After further postponement because of bad weather the Canadian operation was set for 1:30 a.m. on the 13th. It was to be carried out mainly by the 1st Division. Because of the casualties suffered by units of two of his brigades in the unsuccessful counter-attack of 3 June, General Currie regrouped his stronger battalions into two composite brigades. Brig.-Gen. Lipsett on the right had the 1st, 3rd, 7th and 8th Battalions, and for the attack on Tor Top Brig.-Gen. G. S. Tuxford (3rd Brigade) commanded the 2nd, 4th, 13th and 16th Battalions. The 58th Battalion (9th Brigade), plus a company of the 52nd, was to assault on the left. The 5th, 10th, 14th and 15th Battalions were placed in a reserve brigade under Brig.-Gen. Garnet Hughes.[78]

Four intense bombardments of 20 to 30 minutes' duration carried out between the 9th and the 12th four times deluded the enemy into expecting an immediate attack; it was hoped that when none materialized he would suppose the artillery preparation for the real thing to be merely another feint. For ten hours on 12 June all German positions between Hill 60 and Sanctuary Wood were shelled unremittingly, particular attention being given to the flanks, from which machine-gun fire might be expected to enfilade the attackers. At 8:30 that evening, after an intense half-hour shelling which proved extremely accurate, the assaulting units moved up to their start lines—in some cases in no man's land. For forty-five minutes before zero there was one more blasting by the heavy artillery, and then the attack went in behind a dense smoke screen and in heavy rain.

Brig.-Gen. Burstall had hoped that with so much artillery support our infantry would be able to advance "with slung rifles", and events proved him very nearly right. In four long lines the battalions pushed forward through the mud, each on a front of three companies—from right to left the 3rd, the 16th, the 13th and the 58th Battalions. There were occasional checks by fire from some machine-gun emplacement which had escaped destruction, or from grenades hurled by isolated pockets of Germans. But the majority of the Württembergers, completely surprised and badly shaken, offered little resistance. Almost 200 were taken prisoner, the survivors falling back to the original German line. In an hour the battle was virtually over. "The first Canadian deliberately planned attack in any force", states the British Official History, "had resulted in an unqualified success."[79] The 3rd Battalion had retaken Mount Sorrel, the 16th now held the northern part of Armagh Wood, the 13th had cleared Observatory Ridge and Tor Top, and the attached 58th Battalion (reporting casualties of 165 all ranks) had recovered much of the old line through Sanctuary Wood. Between 2 and 14 June the Canadian Corps losses numbered approximately 8000; in the same period the Germans in that sector sustained 5765 casualties.[80]

Inability to take effective counter-measures because of the Allied superiority in aeroplanes, artillery (40 batteries to 28 German) and supplies of ammunition was cited by the Germans for their failure to hold their gains of 2 June. They even judged the weather to be in our favour. "For the continual rain contributed to the softening up of the troops, which were exposed to heavy fire day and night."[81] It was a meteorological viewpoint which the Canadian veteran lying in lashing rain in no man's land until the assault or standing knee-deep in water in the assembly trenches might find difficult to share.

Consolidation of the new front line began early on the 13th, as did the enemy's bombardment as soon as he realized the extent of his lost positions. On the morning of the 14th he launched two counter-attacks against Mount Sorrel, both of which were broken up by our artillery. He subsequently advanced his own line to within 150 yards of ours (the average distance which had existed between the forward positions before 2 June) but made no further move to reopen the battle.

Summer in the Salient

The Canadian Corps remained in the Ypres Salient until the beginning of September—its role "stationary yet aggressive". Though holding their positions but thinly the Canadians continued to harry the enemy with bombardment, mining and raids. A German attempt to recapture The Bluff on 25 July by blowing a mine beneath our trenches was frustrated when the 7th Battalion, warned by the 1st Canadian Tunnelling Company of the forthcoming explosion, seized the crater ahead of the enemy. Advanced patrolling entered its third stage on the 29th, when twenty members of the 19th Battalion raided enemy trenches opposite St. Eloi in broad daylight to secure identifications and evidence of mine-shafts or gas cylinders. They killed or wounded an estimated 50 Germans, identified as Württembergers, and found the suspected gas-cylinder boxes; Canadian casualties were only minor. Encouraging as this success was, with complete surprise an essential factor such raids could be carried out at only irregular intervals. On 12 August an enemy attack in company strength at Hill 60 was repulsed by the 60th Battalion, whose "steadiness and tenacity" brought commendation from the Army Commander. There was warm praise for the support given on the occasion by the Canadian Corps Heavy Artillery and the 1st Divisional Artillery.[82]

On the 14th the Canadian Corps played host to King George V and the Prince of Wales. While the royal visitors looked on from Scherpenberg Hill, near Kemmel, 6-inch howitzers of the Corps Heavy Artillery and field guns of the 2nd Divisional Artillery and a Belgian unit under command of the 3rd Divisional Artillery bombarded the St. Eloi craters. Four days later Canada's Minister of Militia and Defence, Sir Sam Hughes, visited Corps Headquarters and the 3rd Division.[83]

As units withdrew into reserve the emphasis was on more advanced training, with new techniques being practised. Demonstrations in artillery-infantry cooperation showed how closely the barrage could be followed without incurring unnecessary casualties. This was the period when cooperation between the air and infantry at last reached a practical stage. There were exercises with the Royal Flying Corps* based on the newly adopted system of "contact patrol". The attacking infantry carried flares, mirrors and special signalling panels, and as they advanced they signalled their positions to aircraft assigned solely to tactical observation. The information thus received was then dropped at formation headquarters or sent back by wireless.[84]

A worthwhile administrative development about this time provided for a supply of reinforcements to be held in close proximity to the fighting units, besides giving reinforcements a less abrupt introduction into active operations. Hitherto replacements for Canadian field units had arrived direct from the Base Depot at Le Havre. Early in August, however, each division was allotted an "Entrenching Battalion"—an advanced reinforcement unit to which infantry and engineer reinforcements were posted pending their assignment to a battalion or field company. During their stay in the Entrenching Battalion personnel were employed in the construction and repair of trenches and roads and in similar maintenance duties. When the 4th Division reached the Corps area in mid-August it followed the pattern set by the 1st Division in attaching its brigades to a division in the line for seven days' training in trench warfare. There was special emphasis on instruction in anti-gas measures, and each battalion of the 4th Division was put through a gas cloud.[85]

After the Corps moved from Flanders to the Somme all formations and units adopted identifying patches. A rectangular patch, sewn on the upper sleeve, denoted the division by its colour—red for the 1st Division, dark blue for the 2nd, black (later changed to French grey) for the 3rd and green for the 4th. It was surmounted by a smaller patch the colour of which indicated the wearer's brigade (in order in each division, green, red, blue), and the shape (circle, semi-circle, triangle or square) his battalion (first, second, third or fourth) within the brigade. Divisional troops wore the divisional patch only or markings peculiar to their particular service.[86]

The Ross Rifle Withdrawn

The summer of 1916 brought the Canadians certain changes in armament. The light trench mortar batteries were reorganized and equipped with the 3-inch Stokes; all 3.7 and 4-inch trench mortars were withdrawn. Owing to difficulty in obtaining spare parts, the Colt machine-gun was replaced by the Vickers, which British factories could now supply in sufficient quantities.[87] By the end of August the 2nd and 3rd Divisions had exchanged their Ross rifles for Lee-Enfields, as the 1st Division had done more than a year earlier. The 4th Division was simi-

* The Royal Flying Corps numbered many Canadians in its ranks. An account of the activities of some outstanding Canadian airmen appears in Chapter XVI.

larly rearmed in September, after which (except for a few snipers who retained the Ross), all Canadian troops in France carried the British rifle. Canadian rifles returned from France, or still held in England, were taken by the British Government in exchange for the Lee-Enfields and issued to British units remaining in the United Kingdom and to the Royal Navy.

The withdrawal of the Ross rifle from the Canadian Corps followed a decision by the British Army Council based on a recommendation from the Commander-in-Chief. It was the culmination of two years of painful controversy which had seen the Minister of Militia uncompromisingly defending the weapon against charges of unsatisfactory performance in the field. As we have seen, the men of the First Contingent went overseas armed with the Ross, but before going into action with a British brigade the P.P.C.L.I. had changed to the Lee-Enfield. In spite of complaints of defects in the Canadian rifle during the training period on Salisbury Plain, the 1st Division (with the exception of the Divisional Cavalry Squadron) took their Ross rifles to France with them. In the spring of 1915, however, the Commander of the Canadian Cavalry Brigade, Brig.-Gen. Seely, arranged with the War Office to have his brigade equipped with Lee-Enfields, claiming that because of its length the Ross was not a suitable weapon for cavalry. The Ross was unpopular with the artillery because the limber brackets, designed for the Lee-Enfield, failed to hold the Canadian rifle securely, with the result that it often slipped sideways and fouled the wheel spokes.[88]

In France the harsh test of trench warfare served to emphasize the new rifle's imperfections. The long barrel struck the overhead struts of the revetting frames as the men moved along the trenches. There were complaints that the backsight was easily broken, or put out of order by the slightest jar. A bayonet jumping off during firing meant a search over the parapet—only practicable after dark. The most serious defect, as reported by Brig.-Gen. Currie to the Divisional Commander, was that after a few rounds of British-made ammunition had been fired "the shells seem to stick in the bore and are not easily extracted, in fact, more than the ordinary pressure must be applied". It is not surprising that many of the 1st Division armed themselves with Lee-Enfield rifles acquired from British casualties; and on 14 March the G.O.C. found it necessary to publish a Routine Order forbidding troops other than the Divisional Mounted Troops to be in possession of Lee-Enfields. After the first gas attack in April twenty-six reports from brigade and battalion commanders varied from accepting the Ross rifle as "a satisfactory weapon" to the condemnation that "it is nothing short of murder to send our men against the enemy with such a weapon". Almost one third of the 5000 troops who survived the ordeal at Ypres had given an unmistakable verdict by throwing away the Ross and picking up the Lee-Enfield. By the time the battle of Festubert had been fought more than 3000 men of the 1st Division had irregularly possessed themselves of Lee-Enfields.[89]

A test made by General Headquarters early in June 1915 brought findings that the only ammunition suitable for rapid fire with the Ross was that manufactured by the Dominion Arsenal. Of the various patterns of .303 ammunition being supplied to the armies in France the Canadian-made cartridge case (the

D.A. 1914 Mark VII) was of smaller calibre (by .010 inches) than the standard British equivalent. The reduced specification had been adopted because the chamber of the Ross rifle was smaller than that of the Lee-Enfield.* At the same time the hardness of the brass in the Canadian case had been increased to lessen the amount of expansion in firing. On orders from the Canadian Master General of the Ordnance, ammunition accepted from the Dominion Arsenal had to conform to narrow limits of tolerance far more stringent than the latitude which Woolwich standards allowed the commercial factories. These precautions were designed to ensure ease of release of the empty case from the Ross, whose "straight pull" system of ejection could not achieve the unseating force exerted by the Lee-Enfield's bolt lever acting powerfully on a screw thread. Not only did the mechanism of the Lee-Enfield give a much more powerful leverage in disengaging the cartridge case swelled by explosion of the propellant, but the weapon's simpler and more exposed action was much less susceptible to clogging by mud and dust.[91]

Unfortunately no one seems to have warned the Canadians before they went into action of these differences and of the danger of using the larger, unhardened British cartridge in the Ross rifle. "As far as I know", wrote General Alderson after tests carried out on the Ross in May 1915, "this is the first occasion that it has been stated that the size of the chamber is smaller than that of the Lee-Enfield".[92] When inspecting the Canadian military forces in 1910 Sir John French had commented on "the difference in armament between the Canadian and Imperial Forces", but had noted "that the most important essential is assured in the similarity of the ammunition used by the Ross rifle and that used in other parts of the Empire".[93] Yet the complete interchangeability which he envisaged had not been achieved, and now five years later, as Commander-in-Chief, when he learned in June that sufficient supplies of Canadian ammunition were not available in France, he had ordered the 1st Division to be rearmed with the Lee-Enfield.[94]

Remedial action was taken in July 1915 when the Militia Council ordered the Ross Rifle Company to adopt the dimensions of the larger Lee-Enfield chamber in future manufacture and to ream out to this size all rifles in stock at the factory. All Ross rifles in the United Kingdom were rechambered, with priority being given to those held by the 2nd Division, which was about to move to France; altogether 44,000 rifles were so treated. Even with the rechambered rifles however instances of jamming continued with certain makes of .303 ammunition; and tests conducted in the field confirmed the superior ability of the Lee-Enfield to handle oversized cartridges. The results of these tests became known to the troops, as did the experiences at St. Eloi, where the mechanism of the Ross had proved more sensitive to mud than its British rival; and even warnings of strict disciplinary measures did not deter men in both the 2nd and 3rd Divisions from continuing to acquire unauthorized Lee-Enfields whenever the opportunity offered. The cause of the trouble was now diagnosed as a variation in the temper of the bolt head and an inadequate surface of impact between the bolt head and the

* The Lee-Enfield chamber measured .339 inches at the neck and .462 inches at the base. Comparable measurements for the Ross were .338 and .460 inches. When modified later the Ross chamber was enlarged to .341 inches at the neck and .464 inches at the base.[90]

bolt stop. Increasing the size of the bolt stop to double this area of engagement proved effective, but the modification came too late.

In the spring of 1916 events marched steadily to a climax. Asked by the C.G.S. in Canada to comment on remarks about the Ross rifle made in a letter from an American serving as a subaltern in the Canadian Ordnance Corps at Shorncliffe, General Alderson replied at length, listing ten reasons for which "85 per cent of the men do not like the Ross". He denied knowledge of any "more or less organized attempt to discredit the Ross rifle", but declared, "I should not be fit for my position if I passed over anything which endangered men's lives or the success of our arms."[95]

The Corps Commander's letter to Major-General Gwatkin drew from the Minister of Militia a strongly worded reply, which contained a spirited defence of the Ross and a series of innuendos regarding General Alderson's criticisms of the weapon. "You seem to be strangely familiar", wrote Sir Sam, "judging from your letter with the list of ten suggestions intended to prejudice the Ross rifle in the minds of the Canadians. . . . Some of them are so absolutely absurd and ridiculous that no one excepting a novice or for an excuse, would be found seriously advancing them." He attacked the "criminality" of permitting "bad ammunition being placed in the hands of soldiers who are risking their lives in defence of the liberties we all hold so dear." And he concluded, "Your emphatic energy concerning what your intentions are, if you will pardon me, might better be directed to having your officers of every grade responsible in the premises to make sure that none of the defective ammunition again finds its way into the Canadian ranks."[96] On the Minister's instructions copies of this letter were sent to all officers down to battalion commanders both in England and France—281 addressees in all.

General Alderson's reaction to this remarkable epistle* was to direct on 2 May, "that a definite and independent opinion be obtained from every Brigade, Battalion and Company Commander" in the 2nd and 3rd Divisions as to the Ross rifle's performance and whether "the men under their command have every confidence" in their weapon.[98] (In relaying a copy of this directive by "reliable messenger" to the Minister's Special Representative in London, the G.O.C. 2nd Division predicted that it would "cause serious trouble to Canada". He suggested that "naturally amongst a large number of officers of British birth, their reply will be in favour of a change of rifle", and he went so far as to write, "action is being delayed too long as regards Alderson".[99]) The answers received from the 2nd and 3rd Divisions to the questionnaire were laid before the Commander-in-Chief. Of 63 officers of the 2nd Division 25 had reported for the Ross, 25 against, and 13 were undetermined. Every unit and formation of the 3rd Division reported adversely. Sir Douglas Haig then recommended to the War Office that the two divisions should be rearmed with the Lee-Enfield.[100] On 6 June

* In writing General Alderson's obituary in 1928, Major-General W. A. Griesbach declared that the Corps Commander's position had been made impossible by the circulation to his subordinates of Sir Sam's offensive letter. "A commander in France", wrote Griesbach, "was faced with the prospect of having his military career blasted if he did not swallow the Ross Rifle lock, stock and barrel."[97]

the War Office was informed of the Canadian Government's readiness to abide by the C.-in-C.'s judgment, and upon General Haig reiterating his recommendation on 21 June the Army Council approved the change. In advising Canada of this decision the Colonial Secretary asked "that no more Ross rifles should be brought to England" and suggested that if the Canadian Government contemplated manufacturing "different rifles suitable for use during war, Army Council think that rifles now being produced in America for British Army on lines of Lee-Enfield Mark III but with improvements would be best."[101] Wartime production of rifles in Canada came to an end. The existing contract with the Ross Rifle Company for the supply of 100,000 weapons was cancelled, and an Order in Council in March 1917 authorized the expropriation of the factory.* Plans to proceed with the manufacture of the new Enfield pattern did not materialize, for two years would be required for the transition, and the needs of the Canadian forces could now be met from British production.

* The Ross rifle stocks remaining in Canada were reconditioned and modified and placed in reserve. At the time of Dunkirk during the Second World War many were sent by fast passenger ship to the United Kingdom, where they were used to arm the Home Guard and other units for whom no weapons were available.

CHAPTER VI

THE BATTLES OF THE SOMME, JULY-NOVEMBER 1916

(See Maps 5 and 6, and Sketches 25-36)

The First Two Months

BEFORE FOLLOWING the Canadians to the Somme it may be useful to survey the situation awaiting them there and to look briefly at the general progress of the war to the end of August 1916.

The Somme offensive had no great geographical objectives. Its purpose was threefold—to relieve pressure on the French armies at Verdun, to inflict as heavy losses as possible on the German armies, and to aid allies on other fronts by preventing any further transfer of Germany troops from the west.[1] (To these motives may be added Sir Douglas Haig's hope of convincing those critics of Allied strategy who advocated offensives only in distant theatres that Germany was not invincible on the Western Front.)[2]

The time and place of the offensive were largely dictated by the demands of Marshal Joffre. Although Haig enjoyed independent command—"unity of command" in France was still almost two years away—it was his practice to meet French wishes wherever possible if the tactical implications were not likely to be seriously disadvantageous to his own forces. He would have preferred to mount an offensive north of the River Lys, in the Messines area, with the possibility of cutting off the Germans to the north and then turning south to roll up the enemy flank.[3] But Joffre's determination to launch an offensive at the Somme (in a sector that held few strategic possibilities) meant that the British effort would take place there, immediately on the French left. There was indeed no other place for a joint attack; the relief of General d'Urbal's Tenth Army in the Arras sector by British forces early in March had left no large body of French troops north of the Somme valley. Left to himself Haig would have postponed his assault until his striking power had been strengthened by the arrival of more men and ammunition, and a new weapon as yet untried in battle—the tank; but, as he recorded in his diary on 26 May, "The moment I mentioned August 15th, Joffre at once got very excited and shouted that 'The French Army would cease to exist if we did nothing till then'."[4] The date was set at 1 July.

Joffre had originally intended a frontal assault by two French armies and one British on a sixty-mile front. But the costly defence of Verdun, coming on top of the staggering French losses in the first two years of war, was to reduce France's initial participation to a single army of only eight divisions. The weight of the offensive would thus be borne by the British, whose contribution was increased to an army and a corps, involving 21 divisions (with eight more, five of them cavalry divisions, in G.H.Q. reserve). The area of attack was shortened to 24 miles. It extended from the Gommecourt sector, midway between Arras and the Somme, to a point four miles south of the river.[5]

From Peronne to Amiens the Somme flows westward through a broad valley cut in the great northern French plain. In contrast to the flat country south of the river, to the north were rolling chalk downs intersected by occasional streams and numerous sunken roads. The most prominent feature in the battle area was the eight-mile long low ridge running from Thiepval to Ginchy and Morval, which rose to a height of 500 feet above sea level, dominating the uplands to the north and east, and forming the watershed between the Somme and its tributary the Ancre. It was sometimes called the Pozières ridge, from the village of that name near the highest part of the crest on the Amiens-Cambrai road. The whole rich countryside was dotted with large villages, and isolated farms were few. The only natural obstacle to the movement of troops was an occasional wooded area and the marshy flats of the two rivers.

At the end of June the front ran generally south from Gommecourt, cutting the Amiens-Cambrai road a mile and a half north-east of Albert; three miles farther south it went eastward for another three miles to skirt the southern slopes of the Thiepval-Morval ridge, before continuing southward to a loop of the marshy Somme flood-bed near Maricourt. The enemy's forward position, which was protected by two great belts of wire entanglement each thirty yards wide, consisted of three trench lines about 150 yards apart. The first of these held a row of sentry groups; the front-line garrison lived in the second; and in the third were the local supports. From 2000 to 5000 yards to the rear a strong second position occupied a commanding site along the Pozières ridge. This was as well wired as the forward defences, and in both of them dug-outs excavated 20 to 30 feet deep in the chalk subsoil, each able to hold 25 men, were designed to give ample protection against artillery bombardment. An intermediate line of strongpoints had been constructed 1000 yards behind the front position.

In accordance with General von Falkenhayn's adherence to the doctrine of the rigid defence of a line, the front position was strongly garrisoned, so that the bulk of each front-line regiment was within 1000 yards of no man's land. (At the beginning of the Somme battles it was customary for a front-line regiment to have two of its battalions in or near the foremost trench system and the third divided between the intermediate strongpoints and the Second Position.)[6]

On the right the French Sixth Army (General Marie Emile Fayolle) was to attack astride the Somme on a six-mile front with two divisions on the north bank and four on the south. North of the inter-allied boundary, which ran through Maricourt, just north of the river, General Sir Henry Rawlinson's new Fourth Army would deliver the main assault with thirteen divisions (plus five in reserve) on a front of sixteen miles. On his left a corps of three divisions from General Sir Edmund Allenby's Third Army was to make a subsidiary attack on Gommecourt in order to hold German forces there and attract enemy reserves to that sector. As an added deception, during the latter part of June the remainder of the Third Army farther north, and the First and Second Armies beyond, had been simulating preparations for an offensive on their fronts.

These activities do not appear to have had the desired effect. On the right wing of the German Second Army, which was holding the sector north of the Somme, preparations for attack had been observed since the end of February, and on the basis of accumulating evidence by 19 June Crown Prince Rupprecht was certain that a big attack here was imminent.[7] The movement of German divisions in early summer to the Fourth and Sixth Armies had been modest attempts to replace first class troops that had been withdrawn for service in the battle of Verdun. But as early as 23 May the High Command had made it possible for General von Below to strengthen the northern wing of his Second Army by inserting the 2nd Guard Reserve Division in the Gommecourt sector. On 1 July von Below had in the line north of the Somme five and two-thirds divisions; south of the river in the sector to come under attack he had three divisions.* These formations were supported by 598 light and 246 heavy pieces of artillery, and 104 aircraft.[8]

The Royal Flying Corps dominated the sky above the Somme with 185 aircraft; but on the ground, even with 471 heavy guns and howitzers (including sixteen 220-mm. howitzers attached from the French), the British superiority in artillery was to prove insufficient. The objectives given by Sir Douglas Haig reflected the optimism caught from General Joffre, who was convinced that a strong initial assault on a wide front could break through both the German front line and Second Position.[9] The Fourth Army was to seize and consolidate a position on the Pozières ridge extending from Montauban, near the boundary with the French, to Serre, two miles north of the Ancre. This meant in effect an advance of about a mile and a half on a front of 22,000 yards, and from Pozières north would involve the capture of nearly five miles of the German second line of defence.

The Allied attack went in at 7:30 a.m. on 1 July. A devastating seven-day bombardment interspersed with repeated discharges of gas over the enemy lines had kept the Germans continually on the alert, but they were expecting trouble only on the north side of the river, in the British sector. Consequently the French forces were only lightly opposed, and reached their initial objectives with comparative ease. General Rawlinson's right wing succeeded in taking the German

* North of the Somme were, from north to south, the 2nd Guard Reserve, 52nd Infantry, 26th (Württemberg) Reserve, 28th Reserve and 12th Infantry Divisions, with two-thirds of the 10th Bavarian Infantry Division distributed at salient points. South of the river in the sector of the Allied attack were the 121st, 11th and 35th Infantry Divisions. Four more divisions completed the Second Army's Order of Battle. In addition, in army reserve were two and one third divisions, and in High Command reserve (placed directly under the Second Army on 1 July) were three more.

forward position, but elsewhere on the British front most of the gains, achieved at tremendous cost, were only temporary and were relinquished before nightfall. Although the million and a half shells fired during the preliminary bombardment and the opening day of the assault had wrought havoc with the German surface positions, it had left many of the deep dug-outs intact—a failure that was blamed upon a shortage of heavy howitzers and a large amount of defective ammunition. As a result the recruits of the Territorial and New Armies (whose valour that day proved itself beyond question), as they pressed forward at a "steady pace" in the then orthodox but inelastic line formation, were mowed down by the German machine-gunners who, having remained safe below ground during bombardment and barrage, had quickly emerged from their dug-outs to man their weapons. British losses in this day's fighting numbered 57,470.[10] It was on this day that the 1st Newfoundland Regiment was virtually annihilated when attacking German trenches south of Beaumont Hamel. (See below, p. 508).

For twelve more days the Battle of Albert continued, as Sir Douglas Haig attempted to exploit the success of his right wing. Then in a great dawn assault on 14 July (the Battle of Bazentin Ridge) the 13th and 15th Corps, attacking midway between the Somme and the Ancre, broke into the German Second Position on a front of six thousand yards. In this operation the Canadian Cavalry Brigade was attached to the 2nd Indian Cavalry Division. (Although the division was not called on for exploitation, a squadron of the Fort Garry Horse* carried out a minor task.)[11] Nine days later the 13th Corps captured most of Delville Wood, a mile west of Ginchy, while the 1st Anzac Corps took Pozières, on the Amiens-Bapaume-Cambrai road. These operations secured a substantial footing on the Thiepval-Morval ridge. During August and the first half of September the British maintained heavy pressure on the Germans. Haig's intention was by "giving the enemy no rest and no respite from anxiety"[12] to wear down his weakening resistance to a point where another powerful attack would break through his remaining defences. By the time Ginchy fell on 9 September most of the Second Position was in British hands, and along the Somme the French had almost reached Peronne. At the point of deepest penetration the line had been advanced about 7000 yards. But the Thiepval end of the plateau was still untaken, and the line to the north stood as at the beginning of the offensive. The two months of ceaseless fighting to the end of August had cost nearly 200,000 British and more than 70,000 French casualties. The Germans, committed to a costly defence by von Falkenhayn's order of 2 July not to abandon one foot of ground, or to retake it at all costs if lost, had suffered an estimated 200,000 casualties. It was being found necessary to replace German divisions after only fourteen days in the line.

One of the Allied purposes had quickly been achieved. Early in July the enemy had abandoned his offensive against Verdun, thereby freeing further forces on both sides for action on the Somme. Meanwhile in the other land theatres,

*This unit had joined the Brigade at the end of February 1916, replacing the 2nd King Edward's Horse.

and on the sea, the war was going reasonably well for the Entente. The Battle of Jutland (31 May-1 June), although claimed as a German victory, had not shaken Britain's naval supremacy; and after one more sortie by the German High Sea Fleet in mid-August the enemy largely restricted his naval activity to submarine warfare. Italy and Russia were both carrying their share of the Allied programme of coordinated operations. The Austrian Tyrol offensive of May having failed, the Chief of the Italian General Staff, General Luigi Cadorna, had been free to renew operations across his north-eastern border into Austria. An attack with 22 divisions over the Isonzo (the Sixth Battle of the Isonzo), begun on 6 August, had resulted in the capture of Gorizia on the 9th. At the same time the Russians, having successfully withstood a German counter-effort south of the Pripet marshes in reply to the June Brusilov offensive, launched a new attack in Galicia on 7 August. They drove the Austrians back in front of Lemberg, and farther south they made substantial progress towards the Carpathians. To meet this threat the enemy brought down all the forces that he could spare from the northern end of his long Eastern Front and, in spite of the demands of Verdun and the Somme, he reinforced from the west. By the end of August ten complete German divisions had moved east, including one for a campaign against the Central Powers' newest adversary, Rumania, which after a long period of sitting on the fence had declared war on Austria on the 27th.[13]

The entry of Rumania, added to the German failure at Verdun and the heavy losses on the Somme, led to the dismissal of von Falkenhayn. One of Germany's ablest leaders, he had restored the confidence of the German armies after their failure under von Moltke at the Marne, and in 1915 had driven the Russians out of Poland and Galicia and brought about the defeat of Serbia. But in 1916, instead of exploiting these successes in the east he had turned to an offensive in the west, where he was now blamed for having underestimated the power of the Allies and for becoming involved at Verdun while Russia was still a formidable antagonist. The new Chief of the General Staff, and soon in effect the Supreme Commander of all the armies of the Central Powers, was Field-Marshal Paul von Hindenburg, who since November 1914 had been Commander-in-Chief in the East. Lieut.-General Erich Ludendorff, who had been closely associated with Hindenburg since August 1914, came with him. Together they had won the battles of Tannenberg and the Masurian Lakes, and devised the great drive against the Russians in 1915. Now, as First Quartermaster-General, Ludendorff was to share joint responsibility with von Hindenburg in the conduct of operations.[14]

Von Falkenhayn's last action before leaving to lead an offensive against Rumania was to reorganize the command of the German forces at the Somme. In mid-July von Below's troops north of the Somme had been formed into a new First Army, under his command; across the river the front remained Second Army, now under General von Gallwitz, who was given temporary charge of the two-army group. On 28 August von Falkenhayn added the Sixth Army (opposite Arras), placing the enlarged group under Crown Prince Rupprecht of Bavaria.

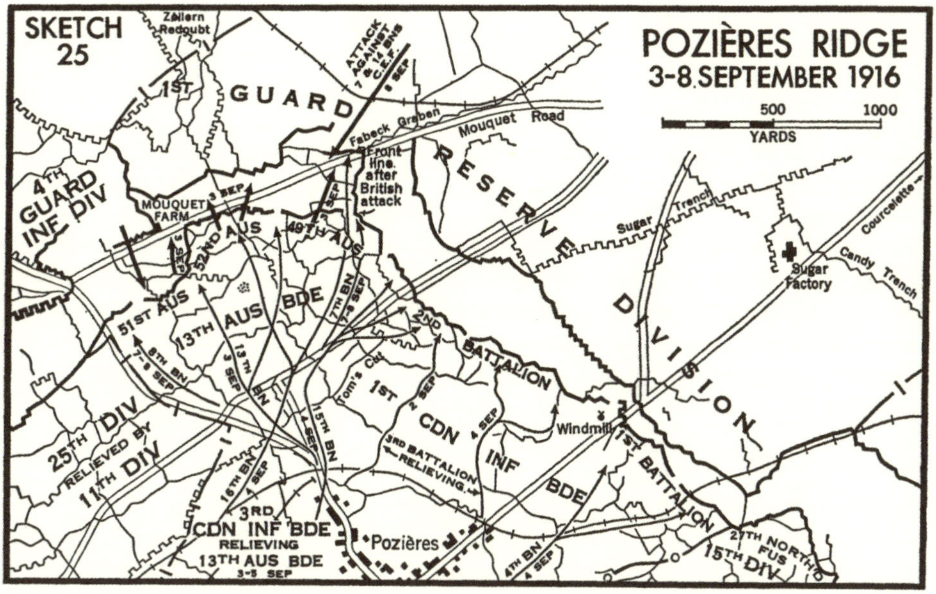

It was the first time on the Western Front that the Headquarters of a Group of Armies had been formed as a separate command, with its own special staff.[15]

Von Falkenhayn's final instructions were to maintain a strict defensive, in order to conserve forces for an emergency. Better than anyone he now realized Germany's perilous shortage of trained troops. "Beneath the enormous pressure which rests on us", he wrote on 21 August, "we have no superfluity of strength. Every removal in one direction leads eventually to dangerous weakness in another place which may lead to our destruction if even the slightest miscalculation is made in estimating the measures the enemy may be expected to take."[16] The Allied decisions taken at Chantilly seemed to be bearing fruit.

Canadians at the Somme

On 30 August the Canadian Corps began relieving the 1st Anzac Corps about Pozières. General Byng assumed command of the new sector on 3 September. It was the first strategical move for the Corps, and involved an exchange of responsibility with the Australians for fronts fifty miles apart. The Corps now formed part of General Sir Hubert Gough's recently constituted "Reserve Army", which on 3 July had taken over from the Fourth Army the northern part of the Somme battlefront.

It was General Sir Douglas Haig's wish that the Canadians should have a chance to settle in before taking part in an offensive. A G.H.Q. directive on 19 August had announced the Commander-in-Chief's intention to deliver a strong attack about the middle of September using "fresh forces and all available resources".[17] This was the role to which the Canadian Corps had been summoned. While the 2nd and 3rd Canadian Divisions prepared for the battle, the 1st Division

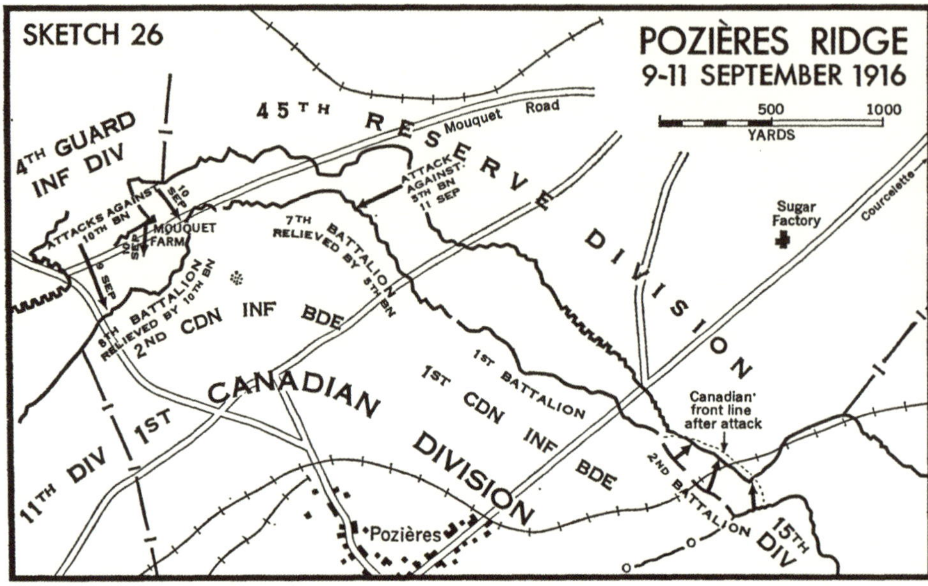

SKETCH 26

POZIÈRES RIDGE
9-11 SEPTEMBER 1916

held the whole of the Corps front—three thousand yards of battered trenches running westward along the Pozières ridge from the boundary with the Fourth Army (just east of Pozières) to a point 700 yards west of Mouquet Farm, a stronghold in the German Second Position based on a nest of deep dug-outs which six bitter Australian assaults had failed to capture. As we shall see, the Division's tour of duty was not as uneventful as Sir Douglas Haig had intended it should be.

The Australians' final attempt to capture Mouquet Farm was made on 3 September by their 13th Brigade, which had the 13th Battalion, of the relieving 3rd Canadian Brigade, temporarily under command. The attack, while failing to secure the farm, gained 300 yards of Fabeck Graben, a German trench running north-eastward towards Courcelette. In attempting to extend this holding two companies of the Canadian battalion suffered 322 casualties. The relief of the Australians was completed on the morning of the 5th, and for three more days the 3rd Canadian Brigade continued to hold under heavy fire and frequent counter-attack more than two thousand yards of line, including the captured portion of Fabeck Graben. The brigade's 970 casualties in this period gave it good reason to remember its first tour of duty at the Somme. Early on 8 September, during a relief by the 2nd Brigade, the Germans regained the now almost obliterated section of Fabeck Graben.[18]

Next day the Canadians slightly improved their positions, when the 2nd Canadian Battalion captured a portion of a German trench about 500 yards long south of the Cambrai road. In gaining and retaining its objective (and thereby earning the congratulations of the Commander-in-Chief) the battalion owed much to the valour of one of its junior N.C.Os.—Corporal Leo Clarke. While clearing a continuation of the newly-captured trench during the construction of a permanent block on the battalion flank, most of the members of his small bombing party were killed or wounded and their supply of grenades was exhausted. Clarke was building a temporary barricade when an enemy party of twenty, led by two officers, counter-attacked down the trench. Coolly the corporal fought them off. Twice he emptied into the Germans his own revolver, and then two abandoned enemy rifles. He shot and killed an officer who had bayoneted him in the leg, and he is credited with having killed or wounded at least sixteen enemy before the rest turned in flight. Then he shot down four more of the fleeing Germans, and captured a fifth—the sole enemy survivor.[19] His courageous action brought Corporal Clarke the first of two Victoria Crosses to be won by his battalion. He was killed five weeks later, before the award was announced.

The Battle of Flers-Courcelette

The Battle of Flers-Courcelette, the two-army assault launched by Sir Douglas Haig on 15 September, was fought on a wider front than its name suggests. The two villages are three miles apart, but the battle area extended for ten miles from Combles, on the French left, to Thiepval, overlooking the east bank of the Ancre. General Rawlinson's Fourth Army, delivering the main attack with three corps, had as objectives Flers and the neighbouring villages of Morval, Lesboeufs and Gueudecourt, all of which were defended by the German Third Position. Work on this strong system had begun in February 1916, and had been completed since the offensive opened on 1 July. It was hoped that a breakthrough here would open the way for cavalry to advance on Bapaume. The Reserve Army's task was to protect the left flank, and to attack with the Canadian Corps to secure in the neighbourhood of Courcelette points of observation over the Third Position. On the left of the Canadians the Second Corps would exert pressure south of Thiepval. Two innovations were expected to give considerable support to the assault—a creeping barrage, which the artillery had only recently adopted*, and the employment of a completely new engine of war, the tank.[21]

The heavy toll exacted in 1915 by German automatic fire had stimulated efforts to invent some form of "machine-gun destroyer" which could negotiate hostile wire and trench. Early in the war an officer of the Royal Engineers, Lt.-Col. (later Major-General Sir) E. D. Swinton, had experimented extensively on such a machine but had failed to interest the War Office in his project. He was helped considerably by the foresight of Mr. Winston Churchill, then First Lord of the Admiralty, who in January 1915 had urged on the Prime Minister the capabilities of "caterpillars"; and in the late summer of that year he won approval for the construction of a prototype of the new machine. A successful secret trial held on 2 February 1916 resulted in an order for 100. To conceal

* Use of such a barrage had been discussed before the war, but because of ammunition shortages it had not been tried before the Somme offensive. Although not very effective in the Battle of Albert by mid-September it had become an accepted factor of the attack.[20]

the nature of the new weapon, the designation "land-cruiser" or "land-ship" used in the experimental stage was changed to "tank", and rumours that these odd creations were water-wagons intended for the Middle East or snow-ploughs for the Russian front were not discouraged.[22]

The model that was soon to appear in battle (the Mark I) was 26½ feet long with a six-foot "tail" (two heavy wheels in rear to minimize shock and aid steering); it was almost 14 feet wide and about 7½ feet high. Fully equipped it weighed 28 tons. A six-cylinder, 105-horsepower Daimler engine gave it a maximum speed of 3.7 miles an hour, a pace that would be reduced to half a mile an hour in heavily shelled ground. It could cross a trench ten feet wide. Tanks were designated "male" or "female" according to armament. The "male" was armed with two six-pounder guns and four Hotchkiss machine-guns for destroying enemy machine-gun posts; the "female" carried only machine-guns —five Vickers and one Hotchkiss—for employment against enemy personnel.[23] The crew, provided by the Heavy Branch Machine Gun Corps (later renamed the Tank Corps), numbered one officer and seven men. The first tanks were shipped to France in mid-August, and early in September a small training centre was set up near Abbeville for the two newly formed companies (each comprising 25 machines) allotted to the forthcoming battle. There was time only for crews to acquire skill in driving and gunnery, and very little opportunity for infantry and tanks to train together.[24]

One other novel feature of the attack on 15 September was that in general (except in the Canadian Corps' sector) it was planned not as a continuous advance to a final line but in limited bounds to a series of successive objectives. The July battles had exposed the fallacy of trusting to the preliminary bombardment to wipe out all opposition. No longer army commanders dared emphasize that "nothing could exist at the conclusion of the bombardment in the area covered by it",[25] and imply that the infantry would be able to walk over at leisure and take possession. Almost invariably the infantry had encountered bitter resistance, so that frequently even if the first wave reached its distant goal it had become too exhausted and reduced by casualties to complete its task; and later waves, following across no man's land at intervals of 100 yards, had found themselves similarly exposed to deadly fire from the uncaptured position. Official doctrine was not as yet ready to accept the idea of advancing by small detachments instead of in waves; infiltration was yet unknown. Once the artillery had done its allotted part the responsibility was the infantry's—and there was supreme faith in numbers. To the end of the Somme battles unit and formation commanders were to be governed by the training instructions issued by General Headquarters in May: ". . . . in many instances experience has shown that to capture a hostile trench a single line of men has usually failed, two lines have generally failed but sometimes succeeded, three lines have generally succeeded but sometimes failed, and four or more lines have usually succeeded."[26]

Although limited, the bounds prescribed at Flers-Courcelette were long enough by later standards, amounting to as much as 1900 yards on the Fourth Army's

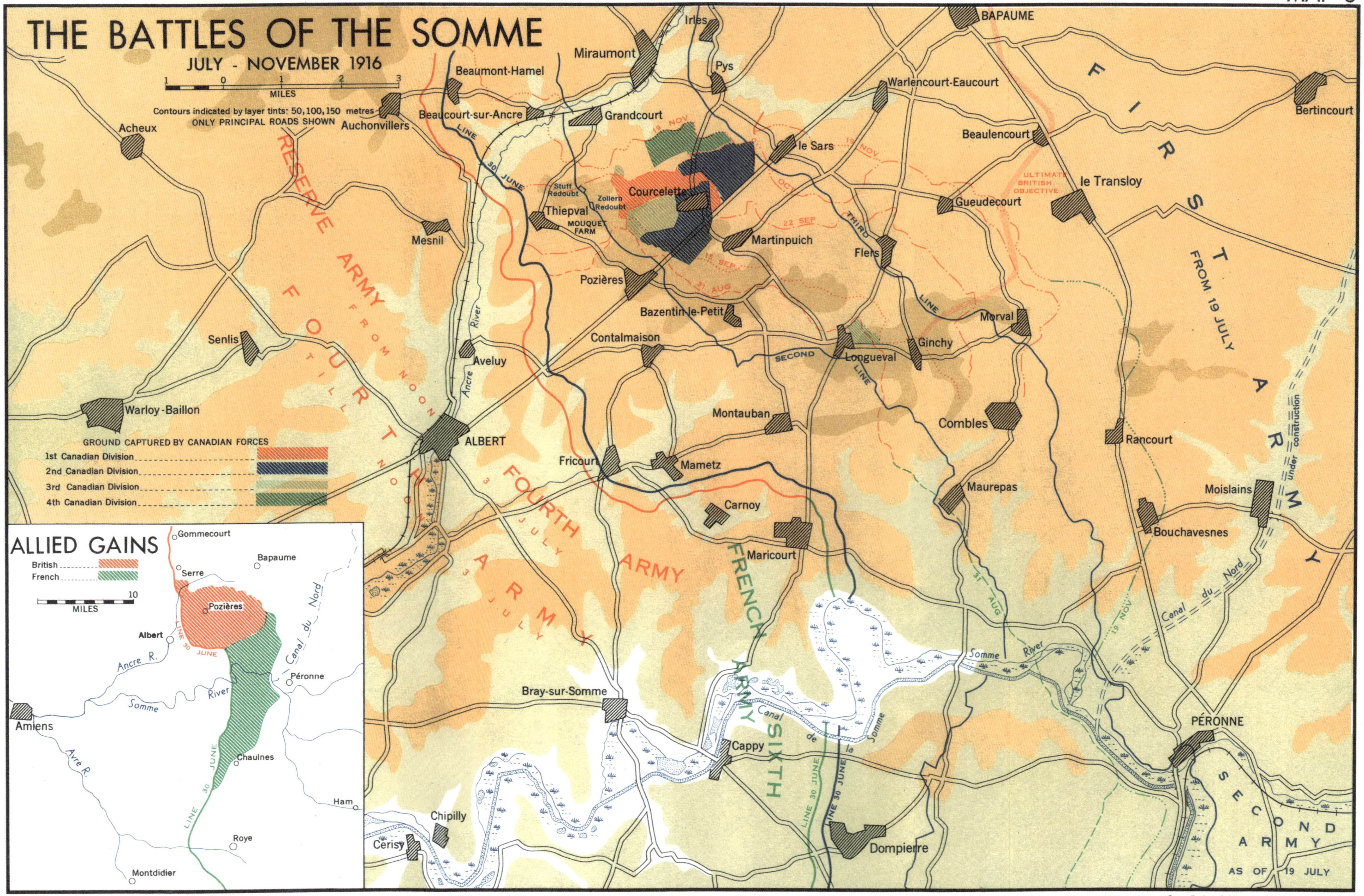

Reproduced by Army Survey Establishment

Compiled and drawn by Historical Section G.S.

front. The Canadian Corps, attacking on the Reserve Army's right flank with two divisions on a 2200-yard front, was to advance in a single bound which from 1000 yards on the right fell away to less than 400 yards on the left. Objectives of the 2nd Division, making the main effort astride the Albert-Bapaume road, were the defences in front of Courcelette. These included Candy Trench (which ran north-west from Martinpuich), the strongly fortified ruins of a sugar factory beside the Bapaume road, and some 1500 yards of Sugar Trench, which cut across Candy. On the left Major-General Lipsett's 3rd Division, its front held by the 8th Brigade, was charged with providing flank protection.

Of the forty-nine tanks available for the operation, the Reserve Army's share of seven were all allotted to General Turner. This Canadian armour was organized in two detachments of three tanks each, one tank being kept in reserve. The right-hand detachment, working with the 4th Canadian Brigade, had orders to advance at top speed astride the Bapaume road through a lane in the artillery barrage, and to engage hostile machine-guns in Martinpuich and at the sugar factory. The tanks supporting the 6th Brigade on the left were to move up behind the barrage and "cover the left flank of the advancing Infantry and assist in mopping up." On reaching the sugar factory they would "attack any machine guns there or in Courcelette that they can deal with".[27] Five infantrymen were assigned to each tank, to walk ahead and remove casualties from its path.

Zero hour was at 6:20 a.m. on 15 September, and promptly the guns standing almost wheel to wheel in Sausage Valley behind Pozières joined in the tremendous bombardment that burst from the mile upon mile of batteries of all calibres massed along the front. The mechanical roar of the tanks as they ground their way forward added an unfamiliar note to the general din. In spite of sturdy resistance (from the 45th Reserve Division) the attack went well. The artillery had crushed opposition in the German front line trenches, which were taken in fifteen minutes. On the Canadian right the three assaulting battalions of the 4th Brigade were on their objectives by seven o'clock, the 21st Battalion taking 145 prisoners out of the ruins of the sugar factory. Half an hour later the 6th Brigade reported success west of the road.

The presence of the tanks encouraged many Germans to surrender, and brought from some of these bitter criticism that it was "not war but bloody butchery".[28] On the whole, however, the armour in its initial action failed to carry out the tasks assigned to it (though one tank, besides inflicting both physical and moral damage on the enemy, laid telephone wire from the forward infantry positions to the rear). All six tanks with the Canadians, either through becoming stuck or breaking down, were put out of action before or during the attack, in four cases as a result of shellfire. One failed to cross the start line; and of the other five, only one reached its objective.[29] Of the 32 tanks on the Fourth Army's start line at zero hour, only ten got fully forward to help the infantry win their objectives.[30] The rest bellied down or failed mechanically (for they had not been designed for such heavily cratered ground, and many miles of trial and demonstration had almost worn them out before the battle), or were destroyed or damaged by artillery fire. The tactical employment of armour had received little study. It seems a questionable procedure to have distributed the machines piecemeal along the battle front, thereby removing them from the tank company commanders' control.* Properly coordinated action of artillery, tanks and infantry was still to be learned.

In reporting on the action General Turner, while forecasting that mopping up "will, in future, be the chief role of these engines", hinted at greater possibilities. "A portion of the tanks", he wrote, "should however be sent through to the final objective with the object of increasing the enemy's demoralization and keeping him on the run . . . Had we adopted some such policy on September 15th . . . Courcelette might well have been in our hands by 10 a.m." The Corps Commander's enthusiasm was similarly restrained: "Tanks are a useful accessory to the infantry, but nothing more."[32] Nevertheless the Commander-in-Chief was highly pleased with the performance of the new weapon, and four days after the battle he asked the War Office for a thousand tanks.[33] Senior German commanders, on the other hand, were so little impressed with the tank that they did not—much to our advantage—immediately attempt to copy it; nor did they give due attention to the problem of anti-tank defence.[34]

Fabeck Graben and Zollern Graben, 15-20 September

Over on the left in front of Mouquet Farm the 8th Brigade had carried out its role successfully. To push home the advantage, less than an hour after the 2nd Division had reached its objectives General Turner directed the 4th and 6th Brigades to establish posts at the south end of Courcelette and along a sunken road which joined Courcelette and Martinpuich. German attempts later in the day to drive in these outposts suffered heavily from British artillery fire. At 11:10 a.m. General Byng issued orders for an attack that evening (the 15th) on Courcelette and on Fabeck Graben, which from the western end of the village ascended the long slope towards Mouquet Farm. To give time for the 3rd British Corps to occupy Martinpuich during the afternoon, the Canadian assault was scheduled for 6:00 p.m. The 5th Brigade (Brig.-Gen. A. H. Macdonell) was brought forward from corps reserve to make the effort on the right; the left-hand objectives were given to the 7th Brigade (Brig.-Gen. A. C. Macdonell).[35]

The second Canadian attack of the day was launched in broad daylight without any jumping-off place, a feature described by the Army Commander as being "without parallel in the present campaign".[36] After ten minutes of "smart bayonet fighting" on the right by the 22nd Battalion and five minutes on the left by the 25th, both units advanced straight through the town while the 26th Battalion began to mop up. Many of the defenders—the 210th and 211th

* Mr. Winston Churchill records that he was shocked when he learned from Mr. Lloyd George of a War Office proposal "to expose this tremendous secret to the enemy upon such a petty scale". He made a fruitless appeal to Mr. Asquith, the Prime Minister, to have the introduction of tanks into operations postponed until they could be employed in tactically profitable numbers.[31]

Reserve Regiments of the 45th Reserve Division—still remained in cellars and dug-outs, whose well-screened entrances made the clearing of Courcelette a two-day operation. Meanwhile, in front of the town, the 22nd and 25th Battalions came under repeated counter-attack—14 in the case of the 22nd, seven during the first night. "If hell is as bad as what I have seen at Courcelette," Lt.-Col. T. L. Tremblay, commanding the 22nd, wrote in his diary, "I would not wish my worst enemy to go there."[37] Between 15 and 18 September, inclusive, the 22nd suffered 207 casualties, the 25th Battalion 222, and the 26th Battalion 224. German losses in the first five days included an estimated 1040 prisoners.[88] The regimental histories of the 45th Reserve Division indirectly pay tribute to the fighting qualities of their Canadian opponents at Courcelette.*

There was difficult fighting in the 3rd Division's sector. On the 7th Brigade's left the 42nd Battalion had gained its portion of the new line without much trouble. The Corps order had given no time for reconnaissance, however, and on the right the Patricias lost their way in broken ground from which all landmarks had been obliterated. Though raked by rifle and machine-gun fire as they struggled forward between the shell-holes, the Patricias reached the Fabeck Graben on their right, making contact with the 5th Brigade in Courcelette. Farther west two platoons linked up with the 42nd Battalion, but a 200-yard stretch of the German trench remained in enemy hands. Before dark the 4th Canadian Mounted Rifles (8th Brigade) on the extreme left, in spite of heavy punishment from the German barrage and enfilade fire from Mouquet Farm, captured a further length of Fabeck Graben and established two blocks to form a firm flank. Shortly after eight the 49th Battalion helped to consolidate the 7th Brigade's holdings by taking some chalk pits beyond Fabeck Graben, though the nearby section of that trench remained in German hands. The Corps report of the day's operations made special mention of the excellent support provided by the 1st Motor Machine Gun Brigade,† whose Vickers had been in almost continual use. Throughout the night engineers of the 4th, 5th and 6th Field Companies directed parties from pioneer battalions working on communication trenches and strongpoints. In the meantime the infantry beat off a number of counter-attacks mounted from German positions north and east of Courcelette.

On the left of the Canadian Corps the 2nd British Corps had advanced its line some 400 yards nearer Thiepval. On the right, however, results had fallen short of expectation. The Fourth Army had broken through the German Third Position on a front of 4500 yards and captured Flers and Martinpuich, but the villages of Morval, Lesboeufs and Gueudecourt were still untaken. Farther south

* In one of the most moving passages of all German war literature the History of the 210th Reserve Regiment describes the annihilation of the Regiment's 2nd Battalion near Courcelette on 15 September 1916. The adjoining 211th Reserve Regiment, which carried the main burden at Courcelette itself, grimly recorded in its History casualties for the period 8-17 September of 59 officers (out of 75) and 1820 other ranks.

† During July and August 1916 the Borden, Eaton and Yukon Batteries had been attached to the 1st Canadian Motor Machine Gun Brigade for tactics. After 19 August Canadian infantry divisions ceased to have a motor machine gun battery on their strength. The entire motor machine gun strength became Corps Troops, being allotted special tasks at the discretion of the Corps Commander.[89]

the French Sixth Army, attacking astride the Somme, had made very little progress.[40]

A thousand yards beyond Mouquet Farm the Zollern Redoubt on the crest of the ridge formed one of the major strongholds of the German Second Position. It marked the midpoint of a long trench, Zollern Graben, which ascended the western slope from Thiepval and from the redoubt continued eastward to join Fabeck Graben about half a mile west of Courcelette. From their commanding position in Zollern Redoubt the Germans could enfilade the adjoining trenches with the most destructive machine-gun fire. Zollern Graben and Redoubt were given to the 3rd Division for a surprise attack on the evening of the 16th. The 7th Brigade would strike northwards from Fabeck Graben to Zollern Graben in order to secure a line from which the 9th Brigade (Brig.-Gen. F. W. Hill) might attack the redoubt from the east. But the first phase failed (for the opening bombardment had overshot the objective) and Brigadier Hill's attack had to be cancelled. In the meantime, bombing parties from the two battalions of the 7th Brigade on either side of the break in Fabeck Graben had worked their way inward on the German stronghold and sealed the gap, taking some sixty prisoners. The end of enemy resistance here was hastened by the action of Private J. C. Kerr (49th Battalion) who, though wounded, ran alone along the top of the trench, firing down upon the defenders and killing several; this heroism earned him the Victoria Cross.[41] The 2nd Canadian Mounted Rifles attacked Mouquet Farm with apparent success. That night troops of the 2nd British Corps began to relieve the Canadians, the 34th Brigade (11th Division) taking over the farm. It turned out, however, that the German garrison, far from being annihilated had taken refuge in tunnels. The 34th Brigade finally secured the troublesome position on the 26th.

The next few days were very wet, and there was only minor activity by both sides. The enemy had brought in fresh troops to hold the maze of trenches immediately east of Courcelette; and on the 17th an attempt by the 5th Brigade to push the line ahead there failed. On the morning of the 18th the 1st Canadian Division took over General Turner's sector, and two nights later the 4th Battalion twice had to fight off German attempts to re-enter Courcelette. Soon after the second of these, in a surprise dawn assault on the 20th, the 43rd and 58th Battalions of the 3rd Division gained a temporary footing in Zollern Graben; but the enemy, employing the newly arrived 26th Regiment of the 7th Division, counter-attacked under a smoke-screen, and after an all-morning struggle recovered most of his losses. Only the eastern end of Zollern, immediately adjoining the junction with Fabeck Graben, remained in Canadian hands. Over on the right the 1st Battalion on the evening of 22 September advanced some 500 yards east of Courcelette on a continuous front of half a mile, and in heavy fighting captured sections of the German front-line trenches.[42]

In its first major operation at the Somme the Canadian Corps had acquitted itself with credit, though the week's fighting had cost 7230 casualties.* "The

* All such figures, except where otherwise noted, refer to total Canadian losses in France and Belgium, and thus include some casualties outside the Corps.

SKETCH 27

THE COURCELETTE SECTOR

20 SEPTEMBER 1916

1000 500 1000
YARDS

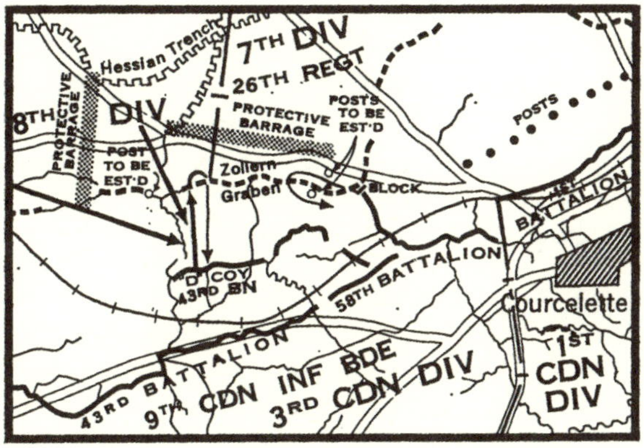

SKETCH 28

THE COURCELETTE SECTOR

22 SEPTEMBER 1916

100 500 1000
YARDS

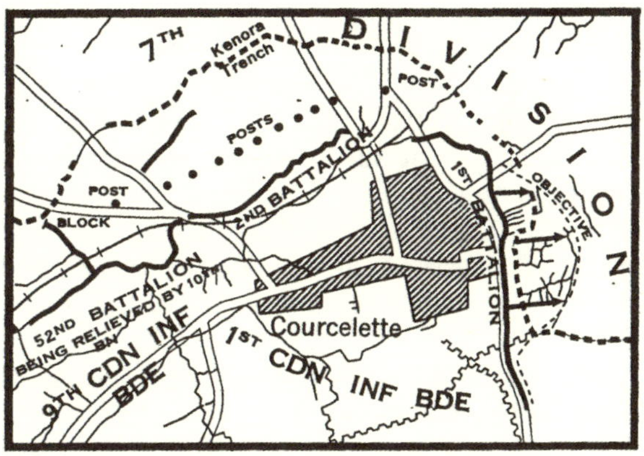

result of the fighting of the 15th September and following days", wrote Sir Douglas Haig in his despatch, "was a gain more considerable than any which had attended our arms in the course of a single operation since the commencement of the offensive." Breaking through two of the enemy's main defensive systems, Allied troops had advanced on a front of six miles to an average depth of a mile and captured three large villages which the enemy had organized for a prolonged resistance.[43] Yet the main objectives were still untaken. The way to Bapaume was blocked by the strongly defended villages of Morval, Lesboeufs and Gueudecourt, and the enemy still held Combles and Thiepval at either end of the ridge. Bad weather and a shortage of ammunition for the French artillery postponed a renewal of the offensive until the 25th. The next phase was to be known as the Battle of Morval on the Fourth Army front, and by the Reserve Army as the Battle of Thiepval Ridge.

General Rawlinson's attack went in shortly after noon on the 25th, following a bombardment of nearly thirty hours. By nightfall Morval and Lesboeufs were in British hands, but Gueudecourt, which lay behind the enemy's fourth main system of defence, held out until the next day. With Morval lost the Germans withdrew from Combles under cover of darkness, and early on the 26th French and British patrols found the ruined village abandoned. The Battle of Morval had gained another belt of ground from Martinpuich to Combles averaging 2000 yards wide. To bring the left flank into line it was now necessary to capture the flattened rubble that had once been the village of Thiepval, and drive the Germans from their strong positions on the ridge above. This was the task given to General Gough's Reserve Army.

Thiepval Ridge, 26-28 September

The orders for the operation emphasized the necessity of driving the Germans from the whole crest-line, both so as to hide from enemy view our rear areas on the southern slopes leading down to Albert, and to give us observation over the valley of the upper Ancre. The 6000-yard front from Courcelette to Thiepval was divided evenly between the Canadian Corps on the right and Lieut.-General C. W. Jacob's 2nd Corps on the left. The British divisions were assigned objectives that had become notorious as German strongholds since the offensive opened at the beginning of July. General Jacob's right had to take Mouquet Farm, and in subsequent stages Zollern Redoubt, and on the crest 500 yards to the rear, Stuff Redoubt, another bulwark of the old German Second Position. His task on the left was to assault Thiepval and then storm the strong Schwaben Redoubt, which overlooked the Ancre from the western tip of the ridge.[44]

The defences which the Canadians were to break lay along a low spur projecting eastward from the main ridge. Linking up with the redoubts in the 2nd Corps' sector were three trench lines which were originally given as successive objectives to the 1st Canadian Division on the Corps left—Zollern Graben, Hessian Trench and Regina Trench, with its branching Kenora Trench. The east end of Zollern was already in our hands, and intelligence maps showed Hessian Trench merging with Regina Trench opposite the 1st Canadian Division's centre. Although low reconnaissance patrols of the Royal Flying Corps had reported on the condition of the German defences in some detail, Hessian Trench, "owing to the uncertainty as to the condition of the wire in front of Regina Trench", was made the limit of General Currie's attack.[45] On the divisional right at the tip of the spur the isolated Sudbury Trench formed an intermediate line to Kenora Trench, which was afterwards described as "one of the deepest and strongest trenches the men had ever seen".[46] Their eastward projection behind Courcelette as far as the Bapaume road became the single objective of the 2nd Division.

For three days the artillery harassed the German positions, 500 tear-gas shells fired on the 24th silencing enemy mortars at Thiepval. The Reserve Army's assault was made with fresh troops, brought into the line between 22 September and the night of the 25th. Zero hour was 12:35 p.m. on the 26th, a warm, sunny day. At 12:34 the massed machine-guns of both the 2nd and the Canadian

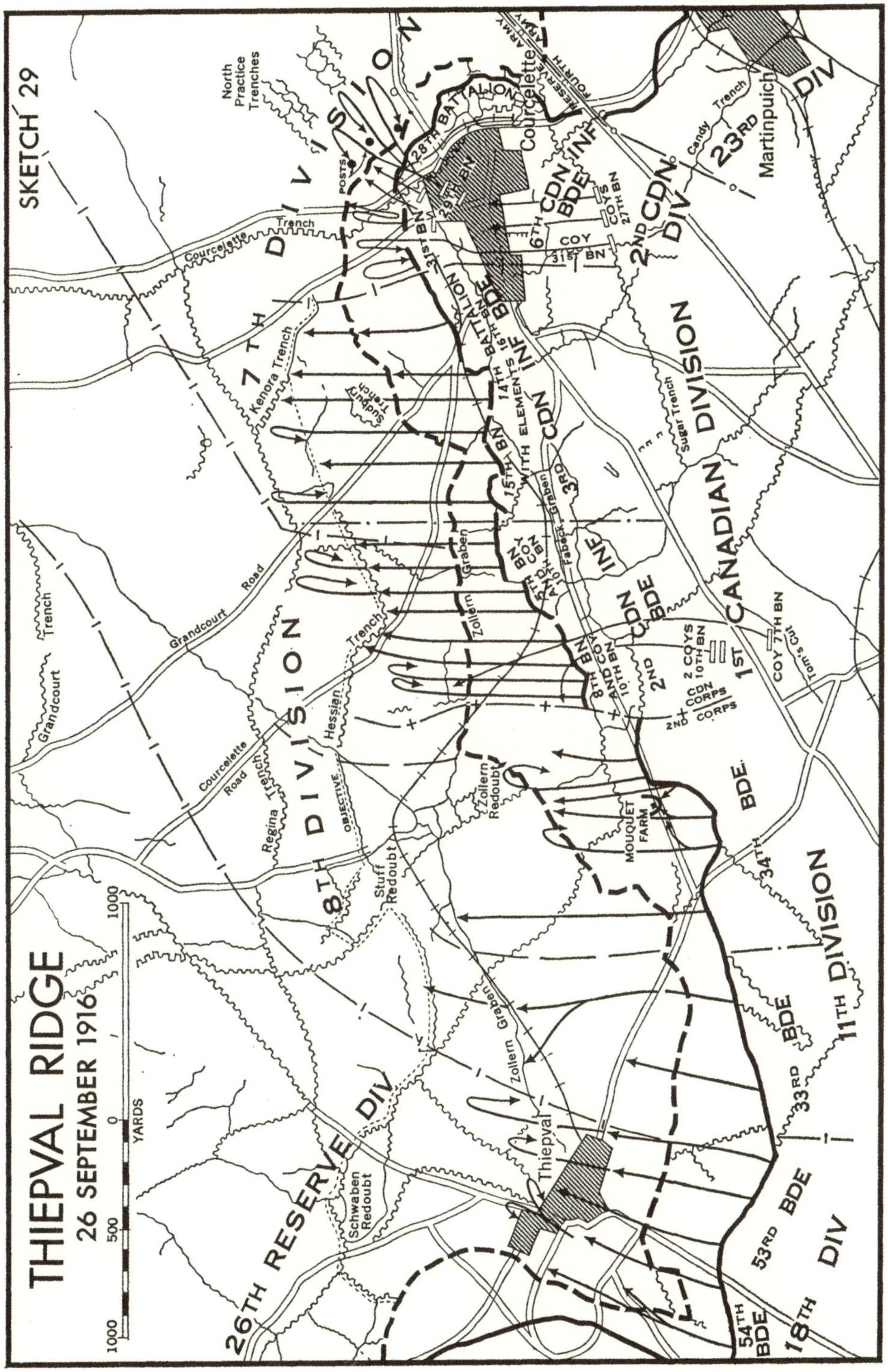
SKETCH 29
THIEPVAL RIDGE
26 SEPTEMBER 1916
1000
500
0
1000
YARDS
26TH RESERVE DIV
8TH DIVISION
7TH DIVISION
CANADIAN DIVISION
2ND CDN DIV
23RD DIV
11TH DIVISION
18TH DIV
Thiepval
Schwaben Redoubt
Stuff Redoubt
Zollern Redoubt
Zollern Graben
MOUQUET FARM
Courcelette
Martinpuich
Regina Trench
Hessian Trench
Kenora Trench
Sudbury Trench
Sugar Trench
Candy Trench
Courcelette Road
Grandcourt Road
Grandcourt Trench
Fabeck Graben
North Practice Trenches
OBJECTIVE
28TH BATTALION
31ST BN
6TH CDN INF BDE
2ND CDN INF BDE
1ST CDN INF BDE
3RD CDN INF BDE
CDN CORPS
2ND CORPS
RESERVE ARMY
FOURTH ARMY
34TH BDE
33RD BDE
53RD BDE
54TH BDE

Corps opened overhead fire. One minute later eight hundred guns, howitzers and mortars put down a mighty barrage of shrapnel and high explosive as the first wave of infantry climbed the parapet. A second wave, a mopping up party, and third and fourth waves followed (in the case of at least one battalion) at intervals of 70 to 100 yards.[47]

Brig.-Gen. Ketchen's 6th Brigade carried out the 2nd Division's attack on the right. North-east of Courcelette the 29th Battalion reached and occupied the enemy's front trenches in ten minutes. On its left the 31st, advancing against heavy machine-gun and rifle fire, encountered a battalion of the German 72nd Regiment (transferred from its parent 8th Division to the centre of the 7th Division's front) and achieved only limited success. On the extreme right, next to the Bapaume road, the 28th Battalion had been charged with making a subsidiary attack supported by the only two tanks allotted to the Canadian Corps. (Of 20 tanks still fit for service, the Fourth Army had twelve in the Morval battle and six were being used against Thiepval by the 2nd Corps.) But one tank broke down before reaching the start line, and the other caught fire when a German shell exploded its ammunition. As a result the battalion remained in its trenches.[48]

In the 1st Division's sector, the 3rd Brigade (Brig.-Gen. G. S. Tuxford) on the right assaulted with the 14th and 15th Battalions. Both immediately met heavy counter-fire from hostile batteries and suffered costly casualties from nests of German machine-gunners, who having survived our barrage caught the second infantry wave as it mounted the parapet. It was a striking demonstration of the improved defensive tactics which the enemy was employing in the later battles of the Somme as he sought an answer to the overwhelming power of the Allied artillery. To escape destruction by our barrage, which was invariably concentrated on known trench lines, forward German troops were ordered to abandon their trenches whenever an assault seemed imminent, and to occupy shell-holes or ditches well in front of where the attacking troops expected to find them. The device was to succeed with heavy cost to the attackers as long as Allied commanders remained wedded to the doctrine of "fire-effect *preceding* movement" instead of putting into practice some form of "fire-effect . . . *combined with* movement".[49]

The 14th Battalion on the brigade right quickly advanced 400 yards to Sudbury Trench, where it took some forty prisoners; shortly after one o'clock it was on its way up the slope to the eastern end of Kenora Trench, its final objective. On its left the 15th Battalion, having met with heavy and unexpected resistance from strong groups in no man's land, was unable to keep pace; and the 31st, as we have seen, was also held up, particularly its left wing. Thus the men of the 14th Battalion on reaching their objective about mid-afternoon came under bitter counter-attack from both flanks. Enfiladed by machine-gun fire they were subject to considerable shellfire during the rest of the day and the following night, and several times had to fight off enemy bombing parties. Kenora Trench was to change hands twice before six o'clock on the evening of 27 September, when the terribly few survivors of a company of the 14th (which

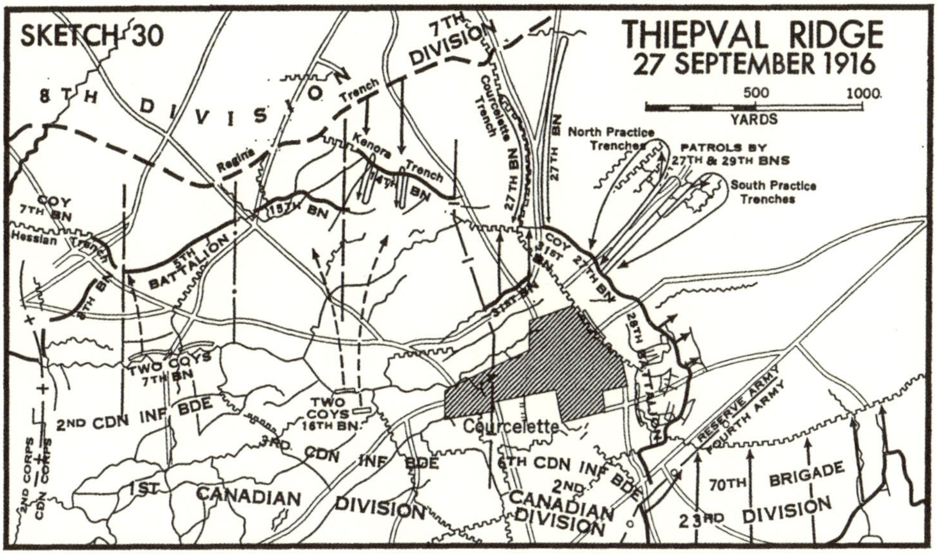

had been reinforced by two companies of the 16th Battalion) fell back half-way towards Sudbury Trench.[50] The 15th Battalion, advancing during the afternoon of the 26th in the open space not covered by Hessian or Kenora trenches, got well up the slope to within 150 yards of Regina Trench before digging in.

In the 1st Division's left sector, the 2nd Brigade (Brig.-Gen. F. O. W. Loomis) had to advance over the highest part of the main Thiepval Ridge. It attacked with the 5th Battalion on the right and the 8th (left), each augmented by a company of the 10th Battalion. Despite heavy machine-gun fire from Zollern and Stuff Redoubts and the Mouquet Farm area, and continual shelling by the enemy's artillery, the troops reached both objectives. Neither one, however, could they completely secure. Enemy pockets remained in Zollern Trench, while the left (German right) of Hessian was still in enemy hands. Not until next day did the Canadians clear both trenches to the corps boundary. In an afternoon counter-attack on the 27th the enemy again occupied part of Hessian Trench, though not for long.[51]

While the Canadian Corps had thus been achieving results which it considered "not unsatisfactory", over on the left the 2nd Corps had taken all but a small corner of Thiepval and most of the western half of Zollern Graben. But the diverging directions of their attacks had left a serious gap between the two corps. The enemy still held the commanding portions of Thiepval Ridge, and in spite of having suffered many casualties he seemed capable of further stout resistance. At 8:45 that evening General Gough called for the completion next day of the tasks of the 26th. Lieut.-General Byng accordingly directed the 2nd Division to secure the German front line north-east of Courcelette and the 1st Division to attack Regina Trench and link up with General Jacob's right.[52]

During the night of 26-27 September the enemy opposite the 2nd Division fell back to Regina Trench. This defence line angled away from the apex of the

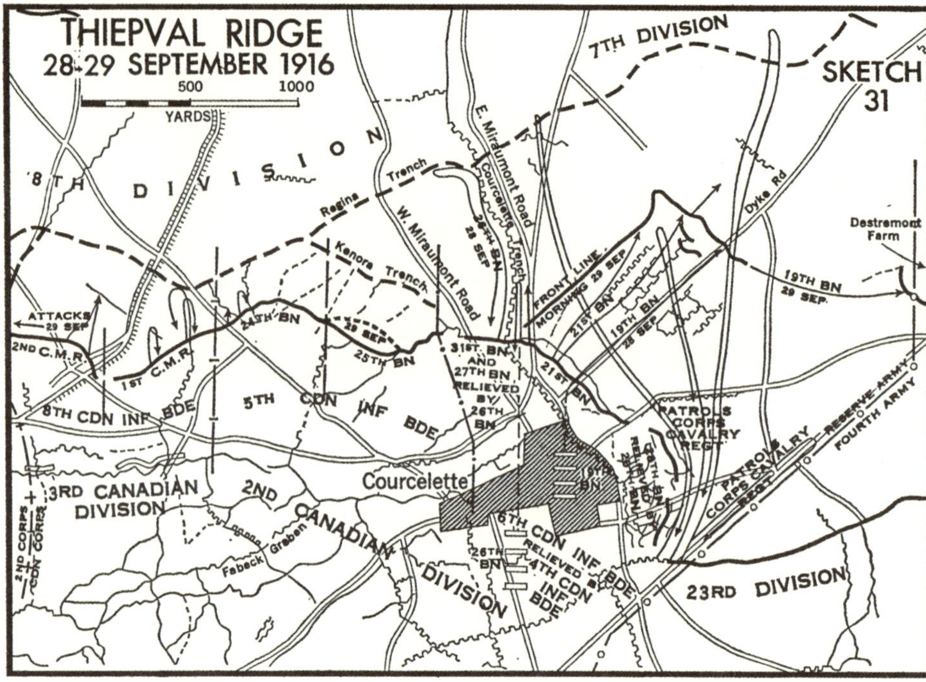

Canadian salient to link up with the German Third Position about 1500 yards north-west of Le Sars, on the Bapaume road. Thus units and companies of the 6th Brigade were able to make satisfactory gains with relatively little fighting. The 28th Battalion seized German positions west of the Bapaume road (the army boundary), while astride the Dyke road the 27th and 29th Battalions patrolled as far as the North and South Practice Trenches. Between the two Miraumont roads, however, the Germans withdraw only gradually, and under pressure. Not until 8:30 p.m. on the 27th did the 31st Battalion link up with the 3rd Brigade west of the West Miraumont road.[53] On the extreme left the 7th Battalion occupied Hessian Trench, putting in a block at the corps boundary. Opposite the 3rd Brigade, however, the enemy stood firm and his counter-attacks continued on the 27th. This made it impossible for the 1st Division to carry out its assault.

General Byng had hoped that both Kenora and Regina Trenches would be in Canadian hands prior to an early relief of the 1st Division by the 2nd Division. But with the second loss of Kenora on the evening of the 27th the chances of this being achieved became very remote. Nevertheless the 14th Battalion, at the insistence of Brig.-Gen. Tuxford—who in turn was under considerable pressure from Divisional Headquarters—made one further attempt.[54] At 2:00 a.m. on the 28th the Battalion, which after forty hours of continuous fighting could only assemble about 75 men, attacked through the mud and rain. As they neared the Kenora position the Canadians were brightly illuminated by enemy flares and became easy targets for the German frontal and flanking fire. After thirty minutes

A VISIT BY THE MINISTER

With Sir Max Aitken (right), General Hughes visits the Canadian Cavalry Brigade in the Amiens area, August 1916. Talking to Sir Sam is the Brigade Commander, Brig-Gen. J. E. B. Seely.

THE PRIME MINISTER IN FRANCE

While attending meetings of the Imperial War Cabinet in the United Kingdom in the spring of 1917, Sir Robert Borden made a four-day visit to Canadian troops in France. Here he is seen, on 9 March, reviewing troops of the 7th Infantry Brigade. With him is the Brigade Commander, Brig.-Gen. A. C. Macdonell, who was later to command the 1st Canadian Division.

THE INFANTRY ATTACKS

Men of the 78th Battalion scaling the parapet in one of the later battles of the Somme, October 1916.

AT THE SOMME

Mud-bespattered Canadian troops marching back from a tour in the trenches meet a mule train carrying ammunition forward, November 1916.

the attack was called off, having brought the 14th Battalion's total casualties in the battle for Thiepval Ridge to ten officers and 360 other ranks. Kenora Trench was not to be taken for five more days. Regina Trench would defy capture until 21 October.

On 28 September a series of Canadian reliefs brought the 4th and 5th Brigades into the line on the right; on the left the 8th Brigade replaced the 2nd, which had linked up with the 2nd Corps back towards Zollern Trench. On orders from General Turner to press the advance, early on the 28th the 19th Battalion moved forward up the Dyke road. It found the Practice Trenches abandoned, and swung eastward. When halted by fire from the strongly-held Destremont Farm,* just north of the Bapaume road, the Canadians succeeded in establishing a position west of the farm.[56]

Meanwhile in the 5th Brigade's sector the 26th Battalion, attacking astride Courcelette Trench (which ran northward from the village ruins), had made two fruitless attempts to gain Regina Trench. Late that afternoon in a coordinating move on the brigade left, the 24th Battalion had embarked on a plan of storming Regina Trench and then bombing its way eastward, while the 25th Battalion assaulted in the centre. The combined effort failed, as leading parties of both battalions ran into wire entanglements uncut by our artillery, and heavy machine-gun fire mowed them down.[57]

The situation was tidied up on the Canadian Corps left, where no contact had existed beyond Zollern Trench between the Canadian and British flanks. Orders issued to the Reserve Army by General Gough on 28 September set deadlines for the reduction of Stuff and Schwaben Redoubts; and at noon on the 29th the 3rd Canadian and 11th British Divisions made a joint attack against the part of Hessian Trench still held by the Germans east of Stuff. The 2nd Canadian Mounted Rifles, already in Hessian, began clearing it westward across the inter-corps boundary in conjunction with a frontal asasult by a battalion of the 3nd Brigade. Bitter hand-to-hand fighting gained three hundred yards of trench. Besides losing many killed and wounded the enemy yielded up sixty prisoners. Two German counter-attacks achieved initial but short-lived success, as Canadian bombers regained ground temporarily lost to the enemy. Two hundred yards of Hessian Trench still in German hands fell the next afternoon to converging attacks by three battalions of the 11th Division, but all efforts failed to expel the enemy completely from the northern part of his two redoubts.[58]

The Battle of Thiepval Ridge had ended (the official dates for the operation are 26-28 September), though the Reserve Army had failed to capture the north-western tip of the blood-soaked feature. North of the main ridge Regina Trench remained an untaken objective of the Canadian Corps as the month ended. Prompted by the Corps Commander's urgings that "no opportunity for gaining ground was to be lost", General Turner had issued orders on the 29th for

* Earlier that morning Canadian cavalry patrols drawn from the 19th Alberta Dragoons and the 1st Canadian Hussars had ridden out of Courcelette to probe deep into enemy territory. Two patrols reached Regina Trench; others moving up the Bapaume road were repulsed by machine-gun fire from Destremont Farm.[56]

the 5th Brigade to seize Kenora Trench and some 1500 yards of the Regina position. Originally planned for the 29th, the operation was twice postponed 24 hours to allow the artillery to deal more effectively with the enemy's defences, and because the 5th Brigade, as reported in appreciations by battalion commanders, was "too exhausted and too few in numbers" (its fighting strength being only 1134).[59]

Across the Reserve Army's front territorial gains had brought a general straightening of the line as had been intended, the greatest progress being on the left, where the 2nd Corps had advanced 2000 yards through Thiepval to Hessian Trench. On General Gough's right, the Fourth Army had taken Destremont Farm and closed on Le Sars (midway between Pozières and Bapaume). The British Commander-in-Chief had handed over Morval on the right of the Fourth Army's line to General Fayolle in order that the French Sixth Army might more easily carry out its next attack.[60] From Combles the French line ran eastward to take in some two miles of the Péronne-Bapaume road before bending back to the south-west to cross the Somme two miles below Péronne.

The Battle of the Ancre Heights Begins

On 29 September, General Haig, deciding that the time was at hand to renew the offensive on an increased scale, instructed the Fourth and Reserve Armies and the Third Army, which was on the left facing eastward, to undertake preparatory operations for a major attack to be launched by 12 October. His goal fell about two miles short of that urged by General Joffre, who was calling for a combined effort by maximum forces to reach a line through Bapaume.[61] The new objectives, capture of which would represent an advance averaging two miles across the front of the Fourth and Reserve Armies, extended from Le Transloy and Beaulencourt (both on the Péronne-Bapaume road) across the valley of the upper Ancre to Gommecourt in the Third Army's sector. One of General Rawlinson's immediate targets, a spur covering the two villages on the Bapaume road, was to give the Fourth Army's operations the name, the Battle of the Transloy Ridges; the Reserve Army's fighting became known as the Battle of the Ancre Heights. General Gough's was to be a two-fold offensive—with a northward attack from Thiepval Ridge (to capture the villages of Pys, Grandcourt, Irles and Miraumont), and on the other side of the Ancre, in the Beaumont Hamel sector, an eastward drive on a three-mile front to converge at Miraumont with the advance of his right.[62]

The immediate task of the Canadian Corps was to capture Regina Trench, in order to secure a jumping-off place for the Reserve Army's attack to the north. The artillery had intensified its shelling of the Regina defences, but General Turner still did not consider that these had been sufficiently reduced. The trench lay just over the crest of the spur, and could not easily be found by our guns. A considerable quantity of concertina wire rolled out by the Germans to supplement the existing entanglements had suffered little damage from bombardment.

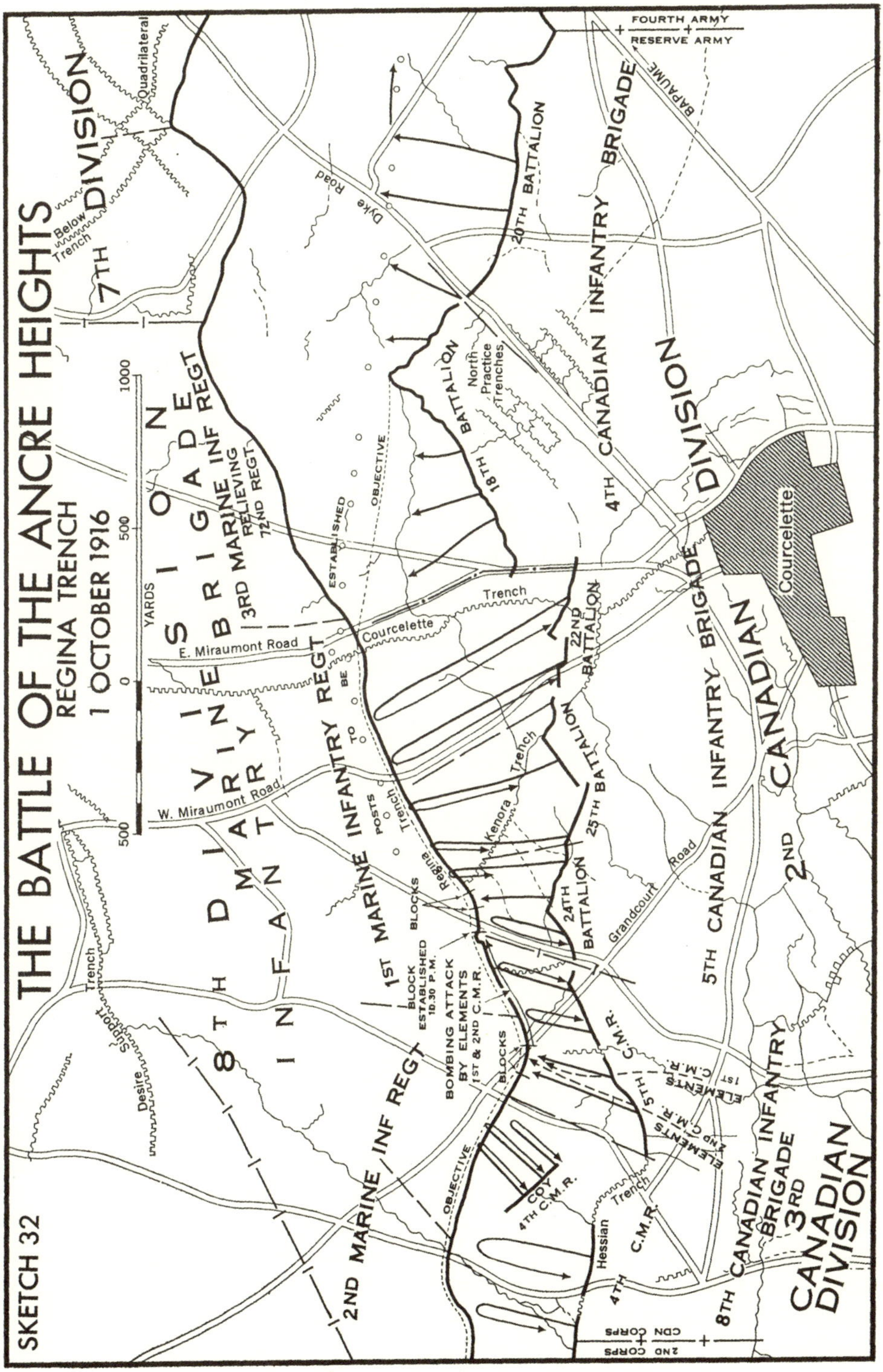
SKETCH 32
THE BATTLE OF THE ANCRE HEIGHTS
REGINA TRENCH
1 OCTOBER 1916
YARDS
500
0
500
1000
7TH DIVISION
8TH DIVISION
MARINE INFANTRY BRIGADE
3RD MARINE INF REGT RELIEVING 72ND REGT
1ST MARINE INFANTRY REGT
2ND MARINE INF REGT
4TH CANADIAN INFANTRY BRIGADE
5TH CANADIAN INFANTRY BRIGADE
8TH CANADIAN INFANTRY BRIGADE
2ND CANADIAN DIVISION
3RD CANADIAN DIVISION
20TH BATTALION
18TH BATTALION
22ND BATTALION
25TH BATTALION
24TH BATTALION
5TH C.M.R.
4TH C.M.R.
COY 4TH C.M.R.
ELEMENTS 1ST C.M.R.
ELEMENTS 2ND C.M.R.
BOMBING ATTACK BY ELEMENTS 1ST & 2ND C.M.R.
BLOCK ESTABLISHED 10.30 P.M.
BLOCKS
OBJECTIVE
POSTS TO BE ESTABLISHED
FOURTH ARMY
RESERVE ARMY
CDN CORPS
2ND CORPS
BAPAUME
Courcelette
Dyke Road
Quadrilateral
Below Trench
Support Trench
Desire
North Practice Trenches
E. Miraumont Road
W. Miraumont Road
Courcelette Trench
Regina Trench
Kenora Trench
Hessian Trench
Grandcourt Road

The garrison which thickly manned the forward position was composed of fresh troops of a Marine Infantry Brigade, brought in at the end of September from the Naval Corps on the Belgian coast. In their rear a deep ravine and several sunken roads afforded covered routes for supplying and reinforcing them. Opposite the Canadian right were the 360th and 361st Infantry Regiments of the 4th Ersatz Division. General Byng agreed to delay the attack "till there is a reasonable chance of getting in", but insisted that "the 2nd Division has got to carry through the operation and will therefore have to stay in until it has completed it".[63] This brought new orders to the 5th Brigade to take the objectives assigned to it on the 29th. On the Corps left the 3rd Division was ordered to attack Regina Trench with one brigade; on the right the 4th Brigade had the subsidiary task of advancing in conjunction with an attack by the Fourth Army's left flanking division.

Regina Trench: (1) The Corps Attack on 1 October

Zero hour was 3:15 on the afternoon of 1 October, and as the Canadians waited in drizzling rain in their advanced positions many were hit by our own shells falling short all along the line. The 8th Brigade attacked obliquely across the Grandcourt road with two battalions of the Canadian Mounted Rifles—the 4th on the left and the 5th on the right. It was the responsibility of one company of the 4th C.M.R. to establish a block in Regina Trench on the extreme left in order to seal off interference from the west. That the enemy had been missed by our barrage was evident in the hail of machine-gun bullets which met the C.M.Rs. the moment they mounted the parapet. As had been feared, the uncut German wire proved a formidable obstacle. One company was practically wiped out in no man's land. Part of another reached its objective, but was there overpowered and perished to the last man. The left forward company of the 5th C.M.R. reached Regina Trench and succeeded in establishing blocks, only to be driven out early next morning by repeated counter-attacks. The other assaulting company was held up by the enemy wire and the blistering machine-gun fire; all but fifteen were either killed or taken prisoner.[64]

The 5th Brigade, attacking on a 1200-yard front which included the two barriers of Kenora Trench and the main Regina position, fared little better. With his strength seriously depleted by earlier battles, Brig.-Gen. A. H. Macdonell was compelled to use three battalions in the assault (from right to left the 22nd, the 25th and the 24th Battalions) and to place the 26th Battalion in support of the 22nd. This left him as brigade reserve only part of the 6th Brigade's decimated 27th Battalion, which had a company detailed to support each of the 24th and 25th Battalions.[65] The French Canadians had an advance of nearly half a mile to their objective—the portion of Regina Trench between the East and West Miraumont roads. Attacking in three waves, each of eighty men extended at five yards' interval, they had advanced a quarter of a mile when they ran into an intense German artillery barrage and heavy rifle and machine-gun fire. Then came the bitter realization that the enemy's wire entanglements were virtually unharmed.

"From this moment," records a regimental account, "the attack failed."[66] Less than fifty men reached Regina Trench, and these could not be reinforced either from support battalion or brigade. After a sharp fight with bayonet and bomb, all survivors were forced to withdraw to their original trenches.[67]

In the centre the 25th Battalion was charged with capturing "at all costs" the greater part of Kenora Trench and the corresponding section of Regina Trench beyond. "To do this", reported the C.O. later, "I had 200 all ranks and 12 M.Gs., counting the Brigade M.Gs."[68] He ordered his two leading waves to push on past Kenora Trench directly to the final objective. Enemy fire cut them down, however, and only thirty reached the wire in front of Regina Trench. Finding what protection they might in shell-holes and hastily dug ditches, they waited out the daylight under steady machine-gun fire. Then they fell back to Kenora, which a following company had secured to within 140 yards of the junction with the main position. Before the day ended more than half the attacking force had become casualties.

It was the same bitter story of defeat on the Brigade left, where the 24th Battalion's objective was some 300 yards of Regina Trench, including the important junction with Kenora. One company gained a footing on the final objective, but with its flank exposed by the 8th Brigade's failure on the left, it was soon annihilated by strong parties of Marines bombing eastward along the trench. The only bit of success came at the junction of Kenora and Regina Trenches, where men of the 24th Battalion managed to establish and maintain a double block fifty yards wide which prevented the Germans from penetrating the newly won sector of Kenora. Meanwhile north-east of Courcelette the 4th Brigade, adjusting the front line, had advanced some 400 yards under spasmodic machine-gun fire and dug in level with the Fourth Army's left flank.[69] Early on 2 October Brig.-Gen. Macdonell handed over to the 6th Brigade. The 5th Brigade had gone into the line on 27 September with a trench strength of 1717 all ranks. It came out five days later with 773.[70]

Bad weather prevented further large-scale operations on either army's front for another week. General Gough left it to General Byng to select his own date for taking Regina Trench, provided this was done and the Canadian Corps in position to attack Pys on 11 October in the opening stages of the proposed three-army offensive.[71] In the meantime Sir Julian handed his left brigade sector over to the 2nd Corps, and on the right the 1st Canadian Division relieved General Turner's battle-worn formations. Preparations for a renewed effort went steadily forward. Working under fire, and further hampered by rain and mud, the Canadians connected advanced posts to form a new jumping-off line which in places came within 300 yards of Regina Trench. The artillery bombarded the German trenches and wire, but though the wire was cut in many places during the day, by night the enemy would fill the gaps with loose concertina. The objectives given to the Corps were somewhat to the east of those of 1 October. They included nearly two miles of Regina Trench from a point 500 yards west of the Kenora junction, and at its eastern extremity the "Quadrilateral" formed

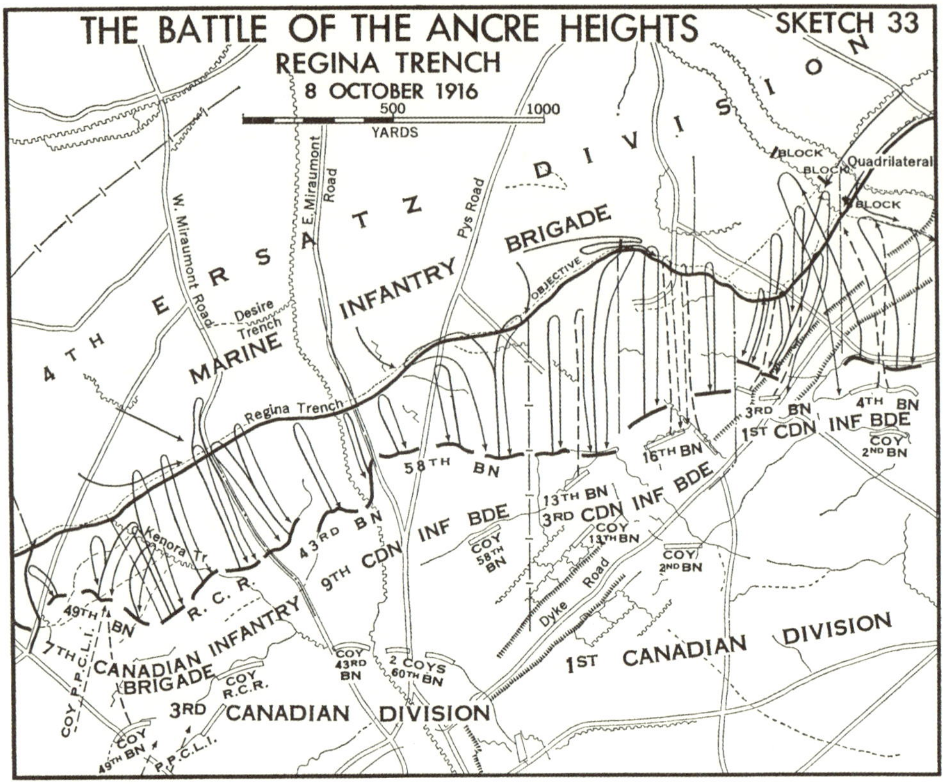

by the intersection of a double row of trenches opposite the Fourth Army's left flank with the dual trench system of the old German Third or Le Sars Position.[72]

Regina Trench: (2) The Corps Attack on 8 October

The Canadian attack was launched on the 8th at 4:50 a.m. It was still dark and a cold rain was falling. In order from right to left across the front were Major-General Currie's 1st and 3rd Brigades, and Major-General Lipsett's 9th and 7th Brigades, each assaulting with two battalions. On the extreme eastern flank the 4th Battalion, advancing behind a creeping barrage in four waves 75 yards apart, with the 3rd on its left, had little difficulty in reaching the first objective, Regina Trench. While the 4th Battalion was held up by wire, the 3rd Battalion pushed forward into the Quadrilateral and took its objectives.

West of the Quadrilateral the two forward waves of the 3rd Brigade's right-hand battalion, the 16th (The Canadian Scottish), were caught at the wire by a storm of rifle and machine-gun fire, not a man being able to get through. In this critical situation 18-year old Piper James Richardson, disregarding the German bullets, "strode up and down . . . playing his pipes with the greatest coolness";[73] thus inspired, about a hundred of the Scottish rushed the wire and somehow fought their way into Regina Trench.* For the 13th Battalion, on the left of the 16th, it was the same story of all but impassable wire. As elsewhere along the front, our barrage helped the attackers across most of no man's land relatively unmolested, but when it had passed on, the Germans, taking advantage of their concave front in the 3rd Brigade's sector, swept the wire with such deadly fire from the flanks that only a small party of the 13th reached the objective. At 7:00 a.m., however, contact aeroplanes sent up to observe the progress of the battle erroneously reported that the 1st Division was on its whole objective.[74]

The 3rd Division, attacking with as much vigour and determination as the 1st, had little success. The assaulting battalions of the 9th Brigade—the 43rd Battalion between the East and West Miraumont Roads, and the 58th on its right—found the wire mostly uncut; and in the darkness of the early-morning attack what gaps had been made could not readily be seen. Only on the flanks did small groups of men fight their way into Regina Trench, and their numbers were too small to withstand the German counter-attacks which quickly developed. A very few got back to the jumping-off trenches; the Brigade's casualties for the day numbered 34 officers and 907 men.[75]

In the 7th Brigade's sector on the Corps' extreme left The Royal Canadian Regiment found the wire well cut and quickly got two companies into Regina Trench east of its junction with Kenora. These took several prisoners from dug-outs reported as being fairly numerous and deep, and while a party advanced 150 yards up the West Miramount Road, bombers began clearing westward along the main trench. Efforts to reinforce the R.C.R. companies were frustrated by the heavy machine-gun fire, and about nine o'clock, after fighting off three counter-attacks, they were driven back out of Regina Trench.[76] On the Brigade left, half the assaulting companies of the 49th Battalion lost direction and became committed in the German end of Kenora Trench. The remainder were stopped short of their objective, for though the wire there had been fairly well gapped, Regina Trench itself had been virtually undamaged by the artillery. Its garrison met the 49th's attack with a considerable volume of rifle fire and bombing, while from the German strongpoint at the Kenora junction machine-guns continually swept the front with enfilading fire.[77]

Over on the 1st Division's front our artillery and machine-guns had helped the 16th Battalion break up a counter-attack and had checked a German threat against the 1st Brigade. But towards mid-afternoon enemy forces advancing in strength down the trenches leading into the Quadrilateral from the north-east and north-west attacked behind a heavy barrage. The 1st Brigade, with all its bombs expended, was gradually forced back to its start line. Soon the enemy's counter-attack spread across the whole front. The few members of the 3rd Brigade in Regina Trench, further reduced by casualties and with no grenades left, had to withdraw or face annihilation. By last light the survivors of the assaulting battalions of both the 1st and 3rd Divisions were back in their original positions.[78]

* Piper Richardson, who was later reported missing and presumed killed, was posthumously awarded the V.C.

The Canadian Corps' casualties on 8 October numbered 1364, more than double those in the fighting on the 1st. The Army Commander called on the Corps for a full report on the attack, to "include your considered opinion as to the reasons for failure".[79] Divisional commanders attributed defeat to various causes. There was strong criticism of the amount of wire remaining intact at the time of the assault. As we have seen, in spite of a deliberate programme of wire-cutting (by the 18-pounders of the Lahore and 1st and 2nd Canadian Divisional Artilleries), results had been disappointing. "Those who were there", writes General McNaughton (who commanded the 11th Brigade, Canadian Field Artillery at the Somme), "will recollect their disheartening task of endeavouring to cut wire with field gun shrapnel".*[81] There had been a tendency for patrols to overemphasize the effect of our guns on the wire, and as we have seen, the Germans were prompt to repair any breaches.

More important (though this was given little prominence in post-operation reports) was the failure of the artillery to destroy or even substantially damage Regina Trench. In the Somme fighting heavy batteries did not attain the high accuracy of fire on unseen targets that came in later battles, and although there was no serious shortage of howitzer ammunition, the expenditure seems frugal when compared with what was used in subsequent operations. Instructions issued by the Corps G.O.C. Royal Artillery had allotted "at least 1 round Heavy or 2 of Medium Howitzer per yard of trench", and the 4.5s of the divisional artilleries (allowed 1000 rounds per division), having completed their other tasks were to expend "any surplus on Regina Trench".[82] After the fiasco of 8 October, however, orders for the deliberate destruction of Regina Trench and the Quadrilateral specified "No limit to number of rounds fired on each spot except that each section of trench must be completely obliterated".[83] And on 14 October the war diary of the Canadian Corps Heavy Artillery reported, "unable without putting guns out of action to fire amount of ammunition received." (The expenditure by the mediums and heavies on that day, principally against Regina and Courcelette Trenches, was 5700 rounds, compared with a maximum of 3300 rounds fired on any day up to and including the 8th.)[84] The situation was well summed up by the O.C. 49th Battalion (Lt.-Col. W. A. Griesbach):

> [The wire] was considered to be passable upon the assumption that the enemy trench had been well battered in and that the garrison had been severely shocked. With the enemy trench in being and the enemy garrison unshocked, the flimsiest wire constitutes an impassable obstacle.[85]

Prevented by the wire from completing a frontal assault overland the troops had sought to bomb their way laterally along the German trench system. This entailed a heavy expenditure of grenades and left the Canadians with few to meet the enemy's counter-attacks. Additional supplies could not be brought forward in daylight save through communication trenches; but communication

* The use of heavy shell was considered undesirable because the resulting craters constituted a fresh obstacle to the infantry.[80]

trenches could not be dug before nightfall. For this reason General Currie felt that zero hour had been too early: "If the attack had been delivered any time after midday I believe we would be there [on the objective] yet."[86] He noted too that though the attacking troops had fought with valour and determination, many were inexperienced reinforcements whose training, especially with grenades, was inadequate, and he observed, "When drafts come to this country they should be already trained."[87]

The Canadian Corps was not destined to take part in further operations on the Somme. The 4th Canadian Division had arrived on 10 October and had successively relieved the 3rd and 1st Divisions. On 17 October the Corps, less the 4th Division and the artillery of the other three divisions, began to move to a relatively quiet sector of the First Army's front between Arras and a point opposite Lens. The Canadians remaining on the Somme came under command of the 2nd Corps (Lieut.-General C. W. Jacob), to whom the task of capturing Regina Trench was now entrusted.

Of the operations planned at the end of September little had been accomplished by mid-October. North of the Ancre the Third Army had not been called on to play an active part. On the immediate left of the Canadians the Reserve Army's 2nd Corps had completed the capture of Stuff Redoubt on 9 October, and on the 14th an attack by three British battalions drove the last Germans out of Schwaben Redoubt. The Fourth Army's Battle of the Transloy Ridges had opened on 7 October with the capture of Le Sars, but thereafter, except for a British advance of 1000 yards north-east of Gueudecourt, the line remained much the same as at the end of September.[88]

Though the prospect of completing this programme was now remote, the British Commander-in-Chief was opposed to any relaxation of the offensive. He felt that the enemy might be close enough to the breaking point for the Allies to achieve a success that would afford "full compensation for all that has been done to attain it".[89] He reported to the War Office that by the end of the first week of October the Germans had employed an estimated 70 divisions on the Somme—40 of these against his own forces*—and had suffered 370,000 casualties. Their new front-line defences lacked depth and the elaborate construction of those which had already fallen. If the winter were normal, Allied operations could continue with profit as long as sufficient reinforcements and greater supplies of ammunition were forthcoming, and if adequate communications and troop accommodation were provided in the devastated areas from which the enemy had been ousted. Haig strongly urged the Chief of the Imperial General Staff that the "utmost efforts of the Empire" should be directed to this end. A G.H.Q. order of 7 October reorganized the British Expeditionary Force so as to make the Fourth and Reserve Armies self-contained forces capable of offensive operations in the coming winter. The Third Army was to remain in reserve, always with three divisions in training. New divisions arriving from the United Kingdom

* The German Official History gives a total of 38 complete divisions engaged with the British to the end of September.[90]

would go to the First and Second Armies; and there would remain in G.H.Q. a spare corps headquarters which in an emergency could intervene wherever required with reserve divisions from the First, Second or Third Army.[91]

On 17 October the plans for the converging advance on both sides of the Ancre (above, page 180) were discarded in favour of separate attacks by the Reserve and Fourth Armies. Then disappointing results of an early-morning assault by the Fourth Army on the 18th led to further revision. The amended programme called for alternate, coordinated blows by the two armies. The Reserve Army was to capture Regina Trench on 21 October, as prelude to an attack astride the Ancre on the 25th; while on the 23rd the Fourth Army, with the French Sixth Army cooperating, would make the first moves towards Le Transloy, the main assault to be delivered three days later.[92] Of these operations, which were recognized as depending on the weather, only the first, in which the 4th Canadian Division was slated to take part, materialized as such.

In the meantime General Joffre, who more than anyone else was responsible for the coordination of all Allied operations in Europe, was becoming impatient about the situation on the Western Front. Elsewhere the overall picture was not bright. In the east the enemy had stabilized his position from the Carpathians to the Pripet marshes. At the head of the Adriatic the Italians, having gained little in two more actions to enlarge their Gorizia bridgehead, were preparing to launch a ninth battle of the Isonzo. Not only had von Falkenhayn thrown back the Rumanian invasion of Transylvania, but a Bulgarian army, stiffened by German and Turkish troops, had defeated Rumanian and Russian forces in the Dobrudja and (on 22 October) captured the Black Sea port of Constanza. A counter-offensive launched in mid-September by General Sarrail's Army of the Orient in an attempt to divert Bulgarian strength to the Salonika front had accomplished little.[93] A major Allied success was needed, and to this end, having learned of the revised British plan, the French Commander-in-Chief on 18 October called on Haig to renew a strong Somme offensive on a broad front as originally conceived (above, page 180). In reply Sir Douglas repudiated the implication that he was wasting time or slackening his efforts and reminded Joffre "that it lies with me to judge what I can undertake and when I can undertake it".[94]

The 4th Division at the Somme

It is necessary now to pick up the story of the 4th Canadian Division, which had landed in France in mid-August and entered the line on the 25th. When the bulk of the Canadian Corps moved to the Somme, the 4th Division remained in the north, and on 3 September became part of "Franks' Force", a temporary formation consisting otherwise of British, Belgian and Australian artillery and some miscellaneous units, and taking its name from its commander, Major-General G. McK. Franks, the Second Army's M.G.R.A.[95] The Division was then holding a 4½-mile front extending from west of Messines to the Ypres-Comines canal. Opposite were the German 26th Division and elements of the 4th Ersatz Division.[96]

Allied patrols found considerable portions of the enemy's front line unmanned—an indication of his willingness to treat the Ypres Salient as secondary to the Somme area and to contain the Allied forces there with a minimum of effort. On many days fire from his artillery and mortars was extremely light, and drew in reply three rounds to one.[97] Activity increased in mid-September, when the Second Army carried out some thirty raids as a diversion to the Fourth Army's assault in the Battle of Flers-Courcelette. Of ten raids on the night of the 16th-17th, seven were conducted by Canadians. In all, 274 officers and men took part, representing the 46th, 47th, 54th, 72nd, 75th and 87th Battalions.[98] In the six raids rated successful the Canadians captured 22 prisoners and killed a known 30 Germans, at comparatively light cost to themselves.[99]

On 18 September the 4th Canadian Division came temporarily under command of the 9th Corps as Franks' Force ceased to exist.* Three days later it went into Second Army reserve in the St. Omer training area. Here the troops learned to handle the newly issued Lee-Enfield rifle, and practised cooperation with aircraft and artillery. There was emphasis on methods of recognition—by ground flares, and chalk marks on helmets—and on advancing behind a creeping barrage at the rate of 100 yards in three minutes. Each man received a new box-type respirator, and tested it with tear gas. On the night of 2-3 October the Division entrained for the Somme.

At the completion of the series of reliefs which attended the departure of the Canadian Corps, Major-General Watson's Division found itself forming the 2nd Corps' right wing, and holding a 2000-yard front from the East Miraumont Road to Below Trench, the forward line of the old Le Sars position.[101] After a few days of fine weather rain began falling steadily, and conditions steadily became worse in the front line trenches. In many places these had been reduced by the rain and the enemy shelling to mere ditches knee-deep with water. In the less damaged trenches the absence of dug-outs had caused the troops to burrow under the parapet to gain protection, and there was a danger of caving in if wet weather persisted. But skies cleared temporarily, and spirits lifted in anticipation of action. The artillery was winning its battle against the wire in front of Regina Trench. Patrols reported that although the enemy persisted in rolling out fresh concertina each night he was unable to fill all the gaps made during the day.[102]

The Battle of the Ancre Heights was resumed on 21 October. It was a cold but clear day as the 2nd Corps launched a renewed attack on Regina Trench in the first of the operations prescribed three days earlier by the Commander-in-Chief. The advance was made on a 5000-yard front, the objectives being the whole of Stuff Trench and all but the most easterly 1000 yards of Regina Trench. Defending this line was the 5th Ersatz Division, which had relieved the Marine Brigade in mid-October. From right to left, the assaulting troops were the 11th Canadian Brigade, commanded by Brig.-Gen. V. W. Odlum, the British 53rd

* A pioneer of the 72nd Battalion, Private A. E. McGubbin, is credited during this period with inventing the "Tommy cooker" out of a pork-and-beans can, using a burning compound of sacking and fat. This miniature improvised stove came into general use on the Somme by this battalion and was adopted by many other units.[100]

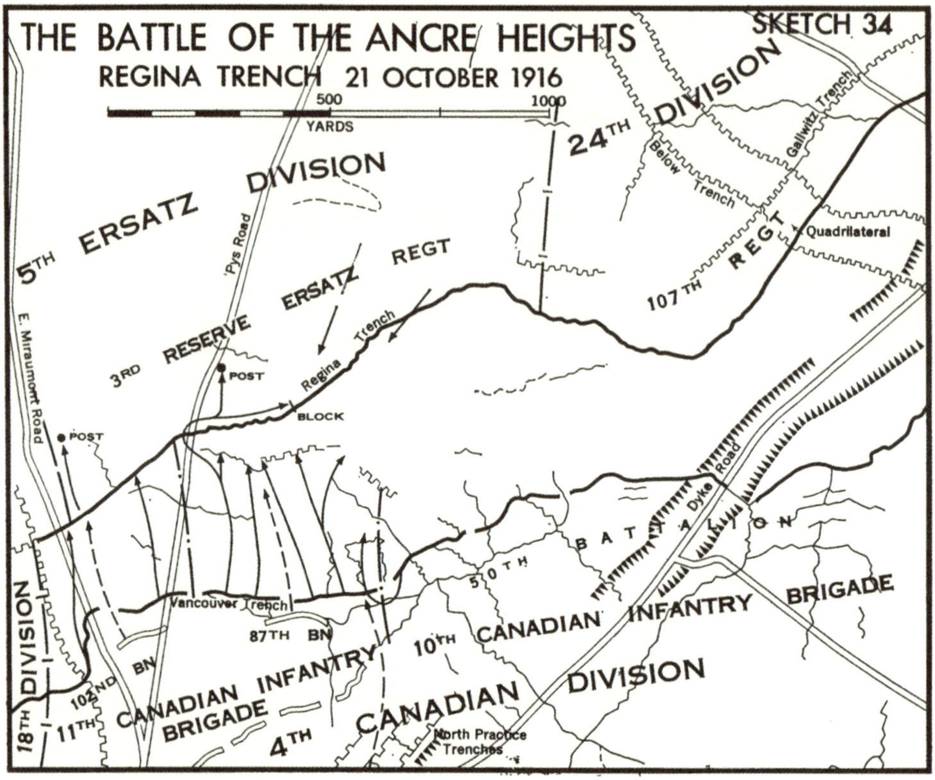

Brigade (18th Division), two brigades of the 25th Division and one brigade of the 39th. In support were seven divisional field artilleries (including those of the 1st, 2nd and 3rd Canadian Divisions) and 200 heavy guns and howitzers.

Regina Trench: (3) The Attacks of 21 and 25 October

The Canadian objective on 21 October was a 600-yard section of Regina Trench immediately east of Courcelette Trench. The 11th Brigade assaulted with the 87th and 102nd Battalions. This time there was no trouble with German wire, which had been broken to bits by systematic bombardment. Using the heavy barrage "like a wall", the two battalions reached Regina Trench by 12:20—less than 15 minutes after zero hour. They found many Germans killed by the barrage, and the survivors quick to surrender. By one o'clock the Canadians were consolidating, having taken some 160 prisoners. At three o'clock the 87th Battalion on the right reported having successfully blocked Regina Trench about 200 yards east of the Courcelette-Pys road.[103] Canadian casualties numbered 200, the majority from enemy shellfire after the objective had fallen. During the afternoon our own artillery broke up a series of counter-attacks against the 102nd Battalion. An all-night howitzer barrage on the untaken portion of Regina Trench guarded the block on the right flank from interference. On the Corps left and centre the success of the British brigades had brought Stuff Trench and the greater part of Regina into Allied hands. When mopping-up operations were complete the 2nd Corps had taken more than 1000 prisoners.[104] The remaining part of Regina Trench was to resist one more Canadian assault before its final capture by the 4th Division.

On 24 October, in preparation for this next attempt, General Watson took over 400 yards of the Fourth Army's left front, thereby extending the 2nd Corps' line eastward to the Le Sars-Pys road. The ease with which the 11th Brigade had seized its objectives on the 21st seems to have prompted the decision to send a single battalion of the 10th Brigade (Brig.-Gen. W. St. P. Hughes) against the same re-entrant 700 yards of Regina Trench that had been the 3rd Brigade's objective in the fiasco of 8 October. The plan of attack followed "Proposals for Minor Operation", circulated on 22 October by 10th Brigade Headquarters (and reproduced for want of other stationery on the back of spare copies of the military "Form of Will").[105] After a postponement had held the attacking troops for 24 hours of pouring rain in jumping-off ditches half full of mud and water, the 44th Battalion assaulted at 7:00 a.m. on the 25th.

Tragedy struck immediately. The barrage, which was being supplied by three field brigades of the 1st and 3rd Canadian Divisional Artilleries, proved woefully light and ineffective. From the Quadrilateral on the right the enemy was able to sweep no man's land with intense enfilading machine-gun fire, and in Regina Trench German riflemen and machine-gunners were seen standing unscathed waist-high at the parapet.[106] With a hail of bullets mowing great gaps in their ranks, the attacking troops soon came under a deluge of shrapnel and high explosive, as a heavy defensive barrage burst relentlessly across the whole front. No one reached Regina Trench. Most of those who were not killed outright sought cover in shell-holes and disused trenches where they lay till darkness, a few managing to crawl back in daylight to their own front lines. From the 11th Brigade's holding on the left the 75th Battalion had managed to push its way 150 yards eastward along Regina Trench, only to be forced back to its original position when the planned junction with the 44th Battalion failed to take place.

In its blackest day of the war the 44th Battalion had suffered close to 200 casualties.[107] The charge of the battalion commander that "the barrage was a flat failure"* is corroborated in numerous reports from infantry and machine-gun officers (including the admission by an artillery observer that the fire was "absolutely insufficient to keep down enemy machine gun fire, their being not enough guns on the zone and the rate of fire was too slow".)[109] Certainly it is a tragic commentary on the planning that, as revealed in the artillery task tables for the operation, the flanks of the attack received little attention in the

* Brig.-Gen. Hughes has recorded that on the eve of the attack he personally advised the Divisional Commander of statements by artillery officers that they had been ordered to move their guns and would not have them all in position for firing at zero hour and that "most of those that could fire would not be registered".[108]

barrage, and not a single shell was directed against the enemy's strong Quadrilateral position.[110]

The weather during the next fortnight brought repeated postponements of further action. Since the 4th Division had entered the line there had been rain on 16 out of 21 days, and the war diary now reported the state of the front trenches as "indescribable". But on 8 November it turned cold and the weather remained dry long enough for the long-delayed offensive at last to seem feasible. The Reserve Army having acquired the extra services and staff to place it on a full army footing had been renamed the Fifth Army. General Gough, whose subordinate commanders were urging that repeated postponements were not fair to the troops, recommended that he should either attack on the 13th or take most of his forces out of the line for a rest. Sir Douglas Haig appreciated the favourable effect that a successful attack would have on the situation in Rumania and Russia. In his diary he suggested that the British position at the forthcoming Chantilly Conference would "be much stronger (as memories are short) if I could appear there on the top of the capture of Beaumont Hamel for instance, and 3,000 German prisoners." He felt "ready to run reasonable risks", and, on the afternoon of the 12th, approved the course proposed by Gough.[111]

Regina Trench: (4) The Capture of Regina and Desire Trenches

The 4th Canadian Division's next operation was a prelude to the new offensive. The objective was still the remainder of Regina Trench. The attack would be made whenever the heavy howitzers had had two successful days of bombarding the enemy's trenches and wire. This happened on 9 and 10 November, and at midnight on the 10th-11th the attack went in. The 10th Brigade, on the right, assaulted with the 46th and 47th Battalions; on the left was the 102nd Battalion, of the 11th Brigade. Each infantry brigade was supported by a full divisional artillery—the 11th Brigade by the 1st Division's four field artillery brigades, and the 10th Brigade by those of the 3rd Division.[112]

This time all went well. The barrage was reported by the infantry as "perfect".[113] By advancing from a start line 150 yards ahead of their own trenches, the Canadians were able to move well inside the enemy's counter-barrage, and aided by a full moon and a clear sky quickly reached and stormed their objective. Taken by surprise the enemy offered little resistance. The 102nd repulsed two counter-attacks, and by 2:20 a.m. consolidation was complete. The enemy left behind some 50 dead and almost 90 prisoners, members of the 58th Division and the 1st Guard Reserve Division. Canadian casualties were light—the 47th had been the only battalion to encounter machine-gun fire.[114] From Major-General Watson went a letter to the artillery commending them for "the very splendid way that your arm of the service co-operated with us."[115]

Thus ended the Battle of the Ancre Heights. Except for a spur immediately west of Pys, all the ground overlooking the low-lying villages of Grandcourt and Miraumont from the south was in our hands. Regina Trench, the capture of which

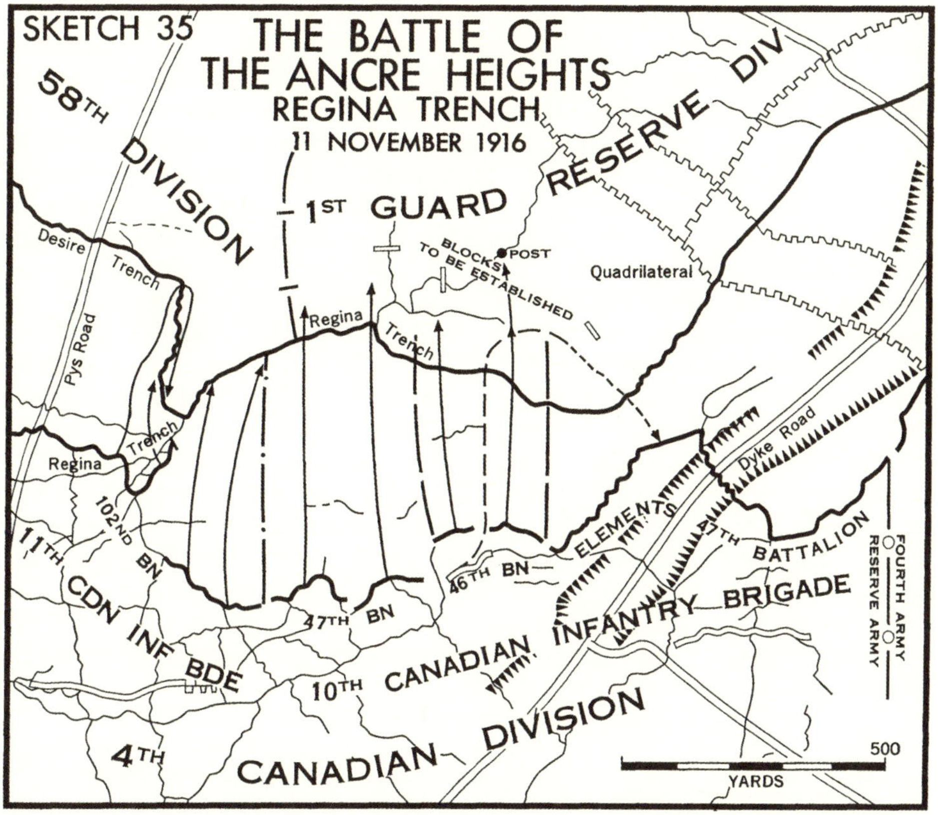

had cost so much blood, was no longer a position of strength. Repeated bombardments had reduced it to a mere depression in the chalk, in many places blown twenty feet wide, and for long stretches almost filled with debris and dead bodies.[116]

On 13 November, when the Battle of the Ancre opened, the Fifth Army's front line encircled the valley on the west and south. On the left, holding a four-mile front which had not changed since the beginning of July, the 13th and 5th Corps faced east towards the ruins of Serre and Beaumont Hamel. Crossing the river just below St. Pierre Divion the line bent eastward and, as we have seen, was held by the 2nd Corps along the northern edge of the Thiepval Ridge as far as the army boundary at the Quadrilateral north-west of Le Sars. General Gough's principal objective was the Beaumont Hamel salient, to be taken by the 5th Corps with four divisions. A division of the 13th Corps was to capture Serre, and in the valley the 2nd Corps was to assault northward from Schwaben Redoubt and Stuff Trench with two British divisions. The artillery support (which included the guns of the 1st, 2nd and 3rd Canadian Divisions) was on a grander scale than for any previous operation, and provided for a 48-hour intense bombardment of all German-held villages and trenches and all enemy approaches to the battle area.[117]

At zero hour (5:45 a.m.) a 30,000-pound mine was exploded near the tip of the German salient and a terrific barrage burst along the whole army front. The operation went best on the right and centre. Astride the Ancre the 2nd and 5th Corps made gains of 1200 to 1500 yards, capturing St. Pierre Divion and Beaumont Hamel. The converging attacks trapped large numbers of Germans in the valley; the total captured for the day was not far short of Sir Douglas Haig's earlier aspirations. General Ludendorff styled the British penetration "a particularly heavy blow, for we considered such an event no longer possible, particularly in sectors where our troops still held good positions."[118] But on the northern flank the attack failed, as battalions advancing through mud in many places waist-deep were hurled back by the enemy's desperate defence of the Redan Ridge and the trenches in front of Serre. Next day, in a thin mist, the forces immediately north of the Ancre advanced another 1000 yards to the outskirts of Beaucourt, a village one mile east of Beaumont Hamel.

The two days which followed saw little action, as the mist thickened, and Haig, who was attending the Chantilly Conference, had ordered any further major operations postponed until his return.[119] But the commander of the 5th Corps was optimistic that more could be accomplished, and General Gough obtained the C.-in-C.'s approval to resume the offensive on the 18th. Intentions changed more than once with varying estimates of the enemy's powers of resistance, and the final plan assigned the main attack to the 2nd Corps. Its left division (the 19th) was to take Grandcourt and cross the Ancre to occupy Baillescourt Farm on the opposite bank. In subsidiary operations on the right, the 18th Division and the 4th Canadian Division were to capture the new Desire (German *"Dessauer"*) and Desire Support Trenches, which lay from 500 to 800 yards north of Regina Trench. On the left there would be no further attempt to reduce the strong Serre defences, but two fresh divisions of the Fifth Corps were given as objectives German reserve trenches farther east running northward from Grandcourt to Puisieux. In spite of uncertain weather and conflicting intelligence reports preparations went ahead with a haste that augured no good for their outcome.[120]

The first snow of the winter fell during the night of 17-18 November, and the operation began shortly after six next morning in blinding sleet which later changed to driving rain. The battle was fought under the worst possible conditions. The infantry, groping their way forward through the freezing mud, had difficulty in identifying their snow-covered objectives and repeatedly lost direction. Deprived of observation the artillery batteries, with little knowledge of the infantry's progress, could only adhere to their pre-arranged programme and hope that the support was effective. The wonder is that in circumstances so desperately bad our troops could make any gains at all. What they accomplished is a tribute to their physical stamina, self-sacrifice and dogged determination.

The Canadian attack took place on a front of 2200 yards, the 4th Division having taken over on 16 November the positions held by the 18th Division's right brigade. General Watson's main effort was on the left, where the 11th Brigade, strengthened with a battalion from the 12th Brigade (Brig.-Gen. J. H. MacBrien), assaulted astride the two Miraumont roads with four battalions (from

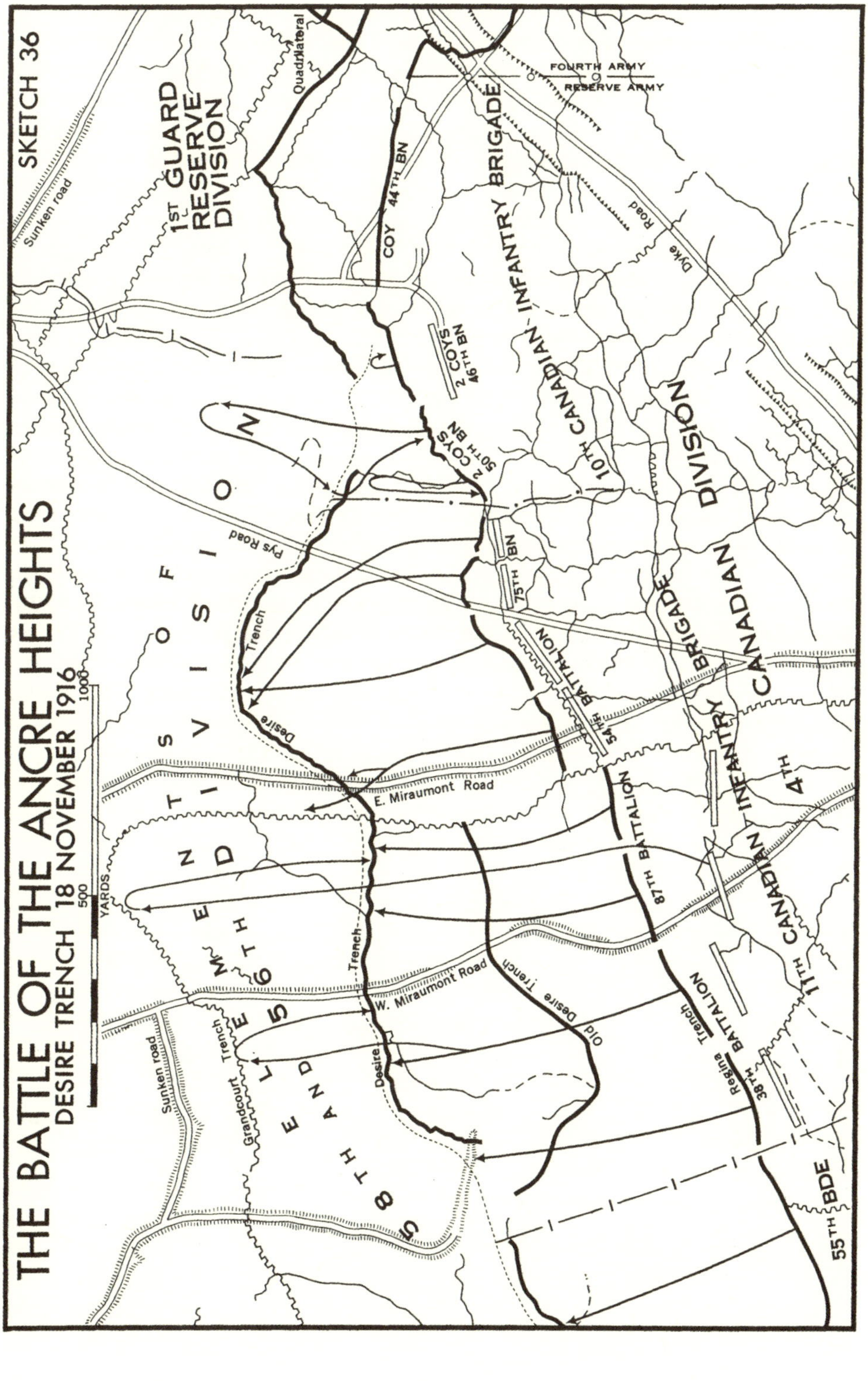
THE BATTLE OF THE ANCRE HEIGHTS
DESIRE TRENCH 18 NOVEMBER 1916
SKETCH 36
YARDS 500 1000
1ST GUARD RESERVE DIVISION
FOURTH ARMY
RESERVE ARMY
Quadrilateral
Sunken road
COY 44TH BN
2 COYS 46TH BN
2 COYS 50TH BN
75TH BN
54TH BATTALION
87TH BATTALION
38TH BATTALION
10TH CANADIAN INFANTRY BRIGADE
4TH CANADIAN DIVISION
11TH CANADIAN INFANTRY BRIGADE
55TH BDE
58TH AND 56TH DIVISION
Pys Road
Dyke Road
Desire Trench
E. Miraumont Road
W. Miraumont Road
Old Desire Trench
Regina Trench
Grandcourt Trench

right to left the 75th, 54th, 87th and 38th). East of the Courcelette-Pys road the 10th Brigade attacked with the 46th Battalion on the right and the 50th on the left. The Division had the support of the 2nd Corps Heavy Artillery, four divisional artilleries (the three Canadian and the 11th British) and the Yukon Motor Machine Gun Battery. A smoke-screen fired by No. 2 Special Company Royal Engineers effectively hid the advance from observation from the front and right flank.[121]

The Canadian task was to seize Desire Support Trench and establish a new line 100-150 yards beyond, exploiting farther if possible. (A late order issued by General Watson's headquarters at 2:30 a.m. directed the 11th Brigade to advance to Grandcourt Trench, some 500 yards beyond Desire Support.) At zero hour, while maintaining a concentrated standing barrage on the enemy trenches, the guns put down a creeping barrage, behind which the infantry companies (two from each battalion except the 46th) advanced in four waves at intervals of 50 yards or less. Fine coordination between artillery and infantry brought excellent results. In less than an hour the 54th Battalion had sent back its first group of prisoners. By eight o'clock both brigades had gained their initial objectives and were hastily digging in beyond Desire Support. Prisoners from the 58th Division were coming back in groups of as many as fifty at a time. A German counter-attack against the 54th Battalion ended suddenly as the enemy threw down their weapons and surrendered; a second threat was broken up by artillery fire. On the left the 38th and 87th Battalions, having overrun both Desire and Desire Support, pushed strong patrols down the slope to Grandcourt Trench, establishing machine-gun posts there and taking more prisoners. The day's total harvest by the 4th Canadian Division was 17 officers and 608 other ranks.[122]

Unfortunately the success achieved by Brig.-Gen. Odlum's troops was not matched on either flank. The situation with the 10th Brigade on the right—never as favourable as it seemed—had changed for the worse. The one assault company of the 46th Battalion had suffered so heavily from small-arms fire that it could not hold the ground it had won. On its left the 50th Battalion, having lost touch with the 11th Brigade, was forced back to Regina Trench by heavy machine-gun fire from both flanks. The 18th British Division, too, had been less successful than early reports suggested. The 55th Brigade (on Odlum's immediate left) seized about 300 yards of the east end of Desire Trench, linking this up with the Canadian-won portion of Desire Support, but the rest of its objective was still in enemy hands. There had been partial success in the valley of the Ancre, where the inner wings of the 2nd and 5th Corps had pushed a salient forward half a mile beyond Beaucourt. But General Jacob's left wing had failed to reach Grandcourt or Baillescourt Farm; and north of the river the 5th Corps had added very little to its gains of 14 November. Both corps had suffered heavy casualties and were in no condition to continue the offensive.[123]

The relief of the German 58th Division by the 56th during the day pointed to the likelihood of a fresh counter-attack in strength against the 2nd Corps' right wing; and as early as 12:30 p.m. General Watson decided to withdraw the patrols from Grandcourt Trench and to shell the position in preparation for making a full-scale assault. At 7:50 p.m., however, in view of the unsatisfactory situation elsewhere on the army front Jacob cancelled any further advance by the 18th or the 4th Canadian Division. There seems little doubt, as the British Official History points out, that the Canadians could not have permanently occupied Grandcourt Trench.[124] Yet even so, their gains had not been inconsiderable. In what proved to be its final action on the Somme the 4th Division had advanced almost half a mile on a 2000-yard front. It had suffered 1250 casualties, in return taking half that number of prisoners and inflicting heavy losses in killed and wounded.[125]

The heavy rain which fell on 19 November would have prevented further attacks even had either of General Gough's corps been capable of renewing the struggle. It ended the fighting at the Ancre—the last of the Somme battles. "The ground, sodden with rain and broken up everywhere by innumerable shell-holes, can only be described as a morass", Sir Douglas Haig informed the Chief of the Imperial General Staff on the 21st.[126] In such conditions, even when there was a lull in fighting, merely to maintain themselves made severe physical demands upon the men in the trenches. For the soldier in the front line existence was a continual struggle against cold and wet, as he crouched all day in the rain and the mud, gaining what protection he could from a rubber groundsheet wrapped around him. Hip boots were issued to help guard against "trench feet", but often these had to be abandoned when their wearer became mired in the clay. For health's sake frequent reliefs were necessary, even though effecting these was an exhausting process. Towards the end of the Canadians' tour on the Somme infantry battalions had as much as eight miles to march to the trenches from their billets in Albert, and at least four miles from the nearest bivouacs at Tara Hill. "With the bad weather", reported General Watson to Canadian Corps Headquarters, "the men's clothing became so coated with mud, great coat, trousers, puttees and boots sometimes weighing 120 pounds, that many could not carry out relief."[127]

Nor did these exchanges bring escape from the continual round of working parties. The demand for nightly carrying parties had to be met alike by units in the line and units at rest. From the point on the Bapaume Road at which German shelling halted the forward movement of wheeled transport, all rations, ammunition and supplies for the front line trenches had to be borne on human backs, or by pack transport. A regimental historian depicts the grim nightly scene.

> Men toil through the darkness under heavy loads, floundering, at times, waist deep in water; climbing wearily over slimy sandbags, stumbling across dismembered corpses—tired, dazed and shaken by the incessant bombardments; clothes soaked and equipment clogged with mud; faces grey from want of sleep.[128]

The main tasks which now faced the Fourth and Fifth Armies were to replace tired and depleted divisions with fresh troops, improve their forward communications and strengthen the new front line for a winter defence. The Fourth Army took over from the French four miles of front line, moving the inter-allied boundary from Le Transloy to within four miles of Peronne. The adjustment freed three French corps as part of the preparation for the spring offensive which

General Joffre was planning.[129] The 4th Canadian Division was not relieved immediately; that it was to complete nearly seven weeks continuously in the front line was recognition that it had satisfactorily won its spurs. Between 26 and 28 November it handed over to the 51st British Division and rejoined the Canadian Corps on the Lens-Arras front.

Canadian battle casualties at the Somme had totalled 24,029.[130]

The Somme Balance Sheet

"The three main objectives with which we had commenced our offensive in July had already been achieved", wrote Sir Douglas Haig in his despatch. ". . . Verdun had been relieved; the main German forces had been held on the Western Front; and the enemy's strength had been very considerably worn down. Any one of these three results is in itself sufficient to justify the Somme battle."[131]

The conclusion thus reached by the British Commander-in-Chief was by no means unanimously accepted either during the war or afterwards. It has continued to be a matter of controversy. The failure to gain much ground and the heavy losses suffered by the Allied forces aroused considerable criticism both in France and the United Kingdom. Especially in question was the extent to which the Allied policy of attrition had succeeded in reducing the enemy's powers of resistance. Writing as late as 1952, the editor of Sir Douglas Haig's private papers declared that it "has probably by now come to be the generally accepted view of the Somme campaign" that it was "a costly failure which did far more damage to the Allied than to the German cause".[132]

Such criticism was based largely on a comparison of the casualties suffered by the German and the Allied armies. How valid is it?

Unfortunately there exist no thoroughly reliable statistics, particularly with respect to German losses. Unofficial figures published shortly after the war gave British and French losses as more than double those of the enemy. In a memorandum submitted to the Cabinet on 1 August 1916, Mr. Winston Churchill charged that during the first month of the Somme offensive British casualties outnumbered German losses by 2.3 to 1. Later (in *The World Crisis, 1911-1918*) he set almost as wide a ratio for the whole of the Somme campaign.[133] In similar vein Mr. Lloyd George asserted in his memoirs that on the Somme "our losses were twice as great as those we inflicted".[134] These comparisons, unfavourable to the Allies, became widely accepted; and it was argued that Haig's intelligence officers in their attempt to balance the cost to each side had grossly overestimated the German losses.

On the other hand, the German casualty figures cited by those who sought to discredit the Allied conduct of the war on the Western Front have been seriously disputed, especially by defenders of Haig. It was charged that the German Government had contrived to conceal from the German public the truth concerning the immense losses suffered by their armies. It is a fact that whereas British casualty figures included as wounded all who passed through a casualty clearing station,

MAP 6

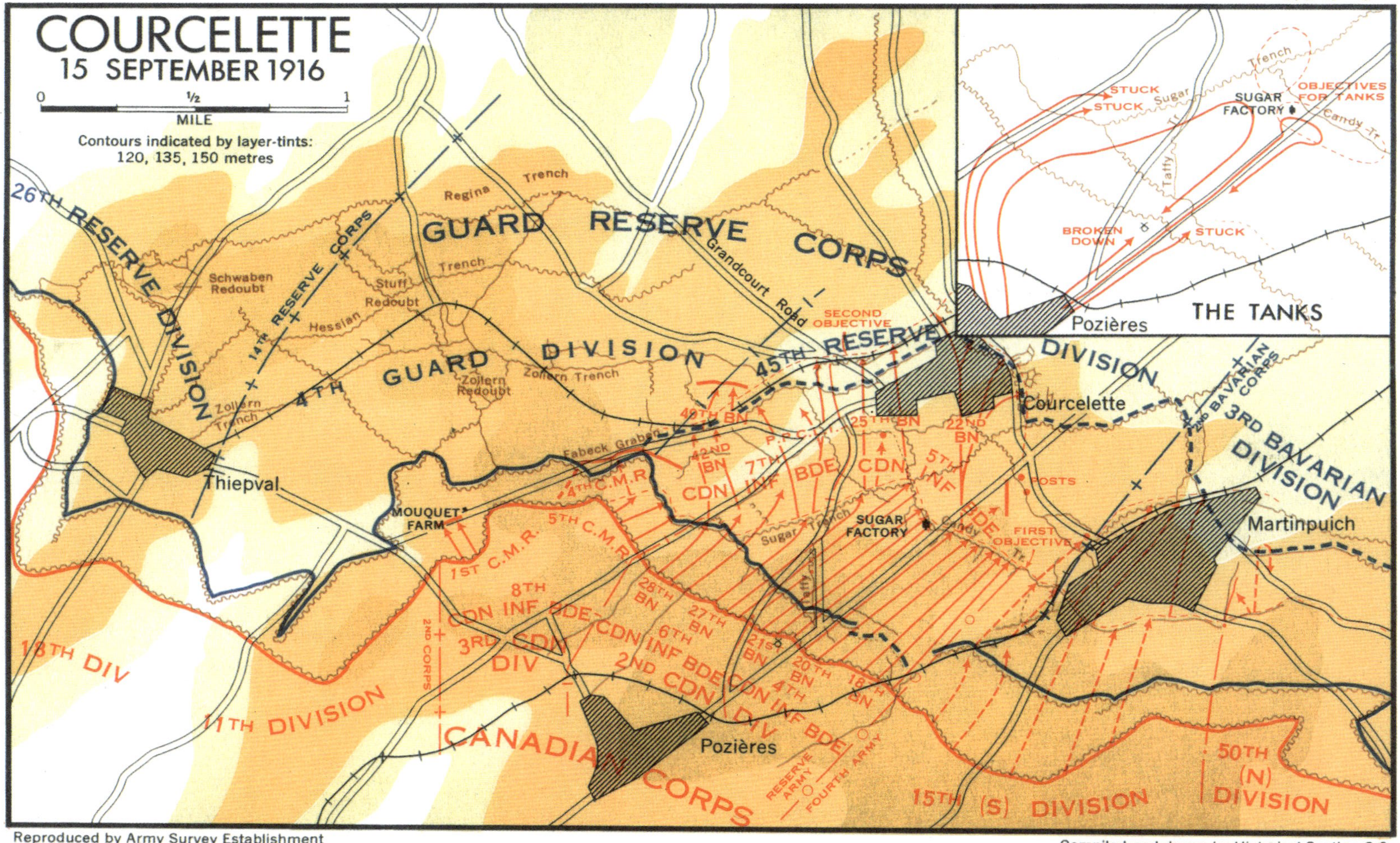
COURCELETTE
15 SEPTEMBER 1916
0
1/2
1
MILE
Contours indicated by layer-tints:
120, 135, 150 metres
26TH RESERVE DIVISION
GUARD RESERVE CORPS
14TH RESERVE CORPS
4TH GUARD DIVISION
45TH RESERVE DIVISION
3RD BAVARIAN DIVISION
2ND BAVARIAN CORPS
Regina Trench
Schwaben Redoubt
Stuff Trench
Stuff Redoubt
Hessian
Zollern Redoubt
Zollern Trench
Grandcourt Road
Fabeck Graben
Thiepval
Mouquet Farm
Courcelette
Martinpuich
Pozières
Sugar Factory
Sugar Trench
Candy Tr.
Taffy
SECOND OBJECTIVE
FIRST OBJECTIVE
POSTS
P.P.C.L.I.
49TH BN
42ND BN
25TH BN
22ND BN
7TH CDN INF BDE
5TH CDN INF BDE
4TH C.M.R.
5TH C.M.R.
1ST C.M.R.
8TH CDN INF BDE
3RD CDN DIV
28TH BN
27TH BN
21ST BN
20TH BN
18TH BN
6TH CDN INF BDE
4TH CDN INF BDE
2ND CDN DIV
2ND CORPS
CANADIAN CORPS
RESERVE ARMY
FOURTH ARMY
18TH DIV
11TH DIVISION
15TH (S) DIVISION
50TH (N) DIVISION
THE TANKS
STUCK
STUCK
STUCK
BROKEN DOWN
OBJECTIVES FOR TANKS
Tatty Tr.
Sugar
Trench
Candy Tr.
SUGAR FACTORY
Pozières
Reproduced by Army Survey Establishment
Compiled and drawn by Historical Section G.S.

German published totals disregarded the less serious cases which were treated in hospitals in the corps areas—a proportion that, by German statistics, averaged 30 per cent of all losses. (Thus in giving figures for "the great losses of the summer of 1916" the German Official History points out that these do not include "the wounded whose recovery was to be expected within a reasonable time".)[135]

The British Official Historian took fully into account the difference in these systems of reporting casualties. In 1931 (in his first volume dealing with the operations on the Western Front in 1916) he estimated that Allied casualties at the Somme were somewhat less than 600,000, and that German losses totalled 582,919.[136] In 1938, however, after Germany had published official figures of 465,525 German casualties (against 700,000 British and French losses)[137] he revised his estimates. He calculated that a fair basis of comparison would show the following gross figures (including prisoners and missing) for the contending armies for the whole of the Somme campaign: German (including the seven-day bombardment at the end of June), between 660,000 and 680,000; British, 419,654; French, 204,253;* or an Allied total of 623,907.[139]

While the objectivity of these figures of enemy losses must be held in question, from the Germans themselves has come ample testimony to the heavy punishment which the Allies inflicted upon them. "The Army had been fought to a standstill and was now utterly worn out", admitted Ludendorff in his memoirs.[140] The Allied offensive had sapped the strength of no fewer than 95 German divisions; 43 of these had been committed twice, and four had been thrown in three times.[141] Unit and formation histories reiterate the story of the liquidation at the Somme of the old German field army. One infantry regiment after another, each nominally 3000 strong, records losses of from 1500 to more than 2800. Among these were the best trained and stoutest-hearted officers, non-commissioned officers and men. Their steadfastness and spirit of sacrifice replacements would never match. No wonder that in January 1917, Ludendorff was to declare at the conference which approved unrestricted submarine warfare, "We must save the men from a second Somme battle".[142] It was largely this realization that caused the Germans, before the Allies could strike again, to renounce their policy of holding and recovering ground at all costs, and to retire to semi-permanent defences fifteen to thirty miles in the rear (below, p. 241).

"In the air the victory had been more complete", the historian of the British flying forces records. "From beginning to last of the battle the air war was fought out over enemy territory."[143] The Royal Flying Corps made the most of its local air superiority—a happy situation which it was to enjoy all too infrequently during the rest of the war—to follow the British naval tradition of "seeking out and destroying the enemy wherever he may be found".[144] The German tendency at this time was to over-emphasize fighters, using them mainly

* These totals are considerably higher than those obtained in an independent analysis by Sir Charles Oman, whose wartime duties included the investigation of German casualties. He produced comparative figures of 523,000 German losses to 490,000 British and French combined.[138]

in a defensive role. The enemy's air policy remained a defensive one, while the R.F.C. continued to wage offensive warfare.[145]

Not the least significant result of the Somme offensive was that, as Sir Douglas Haig had hoped (above, p. 160), it shattered the illusion of German invincibility on the Western Front. Not all the attempts by German writers to disparage the Allied armies' use of their superior weight of war apparatus—"*die Material-Schlacht*"—could hide the fact that German military prestige had been struck a severe psychological blow from which it was not to recover.

Yet after all this has been said in vindication of Haig's achievements at the Somme, we cannot close our eyes to the horror of the mass butchery to which the C.-in-C.'s tactics had condemned the troops under his command. The proof of successful attrition is to be found in convincing casualty figures—and, as we have seen, the casualty figures for the Somme are not convincing. At best the five-month campaign that had opened on 1 July with such high expectations had resulted in a costly stalemate.

CHAPTER VII

BEHIND THE FRONT

FROM THE BATTLEFIELDS of France we turn our attention back to Canada and the United Kingdom to consider briefly some of the major administrative problems which had arisen during the course of the war thus far. First we shall look at the question of the administration and control of Canada's overseas forces in the United Kingdom.

Divided Command in the United Kingdom

We have already noted (above, p. 8) that at the outbreak of war the Canadian Militia was being administered by a Minister presiding over a Militia Council of six members, whose functions, however, were merely advisory. There could be little effective coordinated planning, particularly under a Minister like Colonel Sam Hughes, who virtually ignored the other members of the Council, in whose abilities he appeared to place little confidence.* When war came, no consideration had been given to providing for the administration of a large expeditionary force overseas—indeed the Council's pre-war deliberations towards such an emergency had done no more than set up machinery for mobilization, and this had been discarded by the Minister. To meet a situation without parallel in the history of the Militia it became necessary to resort to improvisation on a large scale. This was to give ample scope to a Minister whose terms of reference allowed him to act without consulting the Militia Council. One restriction was speedily removed. In peacetime, official correspondence between the Canadian and British Governments on military (as on other) matters had been carried on through the Governor General. Now on 10 August 1914 the Secretary of State for the Colonies authorized a direct channel of communication between the Minister of Militia and the Army Council.[1]

We have seen that from the time of the First Canadian Contingent's arrival in the United Kingdom until the 1st Division left for France in February 1915 responsibility for the command and administration of the Canadian troops in Britain rested with Lieut.-General Alderson. In this Alderson was succeeded by

* Witness his shipping the Adjutant General, Colonel V. A. S. Williams, off to Valcartier to act as Camp Commandant (above, p. 21).

his former Military Secretary, Colonel J. C. MacDougall, an officer of the Canadian Permanent Force, who was granted the "local and temporary rank of Brigadier General* while commanding Canadians in England."[2] But the extent of MacDougall's powers was soon to be questioned.

Brief reference has already been made to an officer who was destined to play an important role in the affairs of the Canadian Expeditionary Force. Colonel J. W. Carson, who at the outbreak of war was in command of the 1st Regiment (Canadian Grenadier Guards), a Militia unit localized at Montreal, had headed the First Canadian Contingent's advance party, and had remained in England as the Minister's "special representative" (above, p. 35). An Order in Council passed in January 1915 defined Colonel Carson's status as that of representing "the Militia Department of Canada in the United Kingdom, in connection with supplies and other requirements for the Canadian Overseas Expeditionary Force", and as acting "as agent of the Minister of Militia in maintaining . . . depots . . . for the upkeep and subsistence of the Canadian Expeditionary Force both in the United Kingdom and at the seat of war."[3] Declaring that these restrictions would limit his usefulness to the Canadian Government, Carson urged the Prime Minister to grant him wider powers, suggesting that he be authorized "to advise General Alderson when desired", and appointed as an assistant to Sir George Perley.† But Sir Robert Borden advised the High Commissioner that the Order in Council went "quite far enough".[4]

This did not deter Colonel Carson from giving the British authorities the impression that he had been granted wide powers. Questioned about returning incompetent officers to Canada, he told Southern Command on 18 February, "I am the only officer now serving in the country who would have that power, and I would not hesitate to act if the necessity were unfortunately to arise"—this in spite of the fact that Brig.-Gen. MacDougall had succeeded General Alderson as G.O.C. Canadian Troops in the United Kingdom.[5] Carson showed extreme reluctance to recognize the authority of MacDougall, whom he described as having been "left in the more or less imaginary command of the Canadian troops". (Not included in MacDougall's command at this time were the Canadian Training Depot at Tidworth, commanded by Colonel W. R. W. James, an officer of the Royal Artillery; and the Cavalry Brigade, commanded by Brig.-Gen. J. E. B. Seely.) Carson suggested to Sir Sam Hughes the advisability of appointing "a Senior Canadian Officer", in a rank not below major general, to be in "supreme central command of *all* the Canadian Troops who might be at any time in England".[6]

But any aspirations that Carson may have had towards such an appointment for himself were due for a setback. Early in March Colonel James was given an appointment in France, and on the 19th Hughes bluntly notified Carson, "General

*MacDougall's promotion to major general though effective 21 September 1915 was not approved until August 1916.

†Perley, a Minister without Portfolio in Borden's Cabinet since June 1914, had been Acting High Commissioner for Canada in the United Kingdom. (As a cabinet minister he could not hold full ambassadorial status.) He was created K.C.M.G. on 1 January 1915.

MacDougall is in military command of all Canadian units in Britain except those under Brigadier-General Seely. You will continue as authorized by Order in Council to represent the Defence Minister for Canada in Britain."[7] Although two days earlier the Minister had somewhat forcefully told MacDougall, "You must assume your responsibilities", in continuing to deal directly with Carson on a variety of subjects by no means confined to the provision of supplies and equipment, he kept that officer in a position to pass along instructions to the G.O.C. Canadians.

That Carson was not satisfied to confine his activities to the United Kingdom is illustrated by an incident that occurred in the early summer of 1915, just after the Second Battle of Ypres. This was an attempt by him to have all Canadian battalion commanders in France promoted to the rank of colonel "as some slight reward for their magnificent work during the trying times of the last few weeks". Should considerations of establishment prevent this, he suggested that they be made brevet colonels. Sir Sam Hughes approved this decidedly unusual suggestion, and Carson notified General Alderson of the Minister's authority for a "step in rank to all Lieutenant-Colonels at the Front".[8] In due course the matter reached the War Office, which sent a carefully worded letter to the C.-in-C. British Army in France making no ruling as to whether the promotions should take place but pointing out that such promotions could not "be recognized as affecting in any way the precedence of these officers in relation to that of others in your Command".[9] Alderson did not make the promotions, and despite Carson's efforts to keep the question alive (he wrote Sir Sam seven letters on the matter), the Minister made no demands upon the Divisional Commander to carry out the original instructions.[10]

In May 1915 the formation of the 2nd Canadian Division and the appointment of Major-General Steele as its commander introduced a new complication. There were now two separate Canadian commands in the United Kingdom, though neither the limits of each commander's authority nor the channels of communication he was to use had been clearly defined. It seemed necessary to establish some central control, but this was not done. Instead, on 26 July Sir Sam Hughes (who was then in the United Kingdom) requested the Acting Minister of Militia to "please inform Militia Council that Major-General Steele is promoted to command South-Eastern District including all Canadians in England".[11] MacDougall was to retain his rank of brigadier general while continuing to command the Canadian Training Division at Shorncliffe.[12] On 3 August Steele took over command of the Shorncliffe Area from a British officer, and two weeks later Major-General R. E. W. Turner arrived from France to command the 2nd Canadian Division.

Carson (who had been promoted to brigadier general in May) lost little time in passing on what he described as the Minister's "views and ideas and wishes" as to the relative positions of Steele, MacDougall and Turner. In a letter to Steele, dated 27 August, he spoke of his own "very extended powers" as "Vice-Minister of the Department of Militia and Defence in the British Isles and at the Seat of War". As such, he required that all promotions and appointments of officers were to be referred to him; and he reserved the right to correspond directly upon Canadian matters with the two divisional commanders at Shorncliffe. Steele's command over the two divisions would be exercised through their respective General Officers Commanding, to whose discretion would be left all matters of training. Brig.-Gen. MacDougall's Canadian Training Division was enlarged to include all Canadian Troops in England other than those of the 2nd Division.[13] Steele expressed general agreement with these views, at the same time protesting against any arrangement that would cause him to be by-passed in the chain of command and made the "fifth wheel on the coach".

In November Carson (now a major general), seeking to "do away with all bother and trouble which will always be in existence under present conditions", suggested that the Minister make Steele Inspector General of Canadian forces in the United Kingdom.[14] But this attempt to remove a potential source of disturbance failed, and Steele remained as G.O.C. Shorncliffe area. Before the end of the month another new command had been created. A decision had been reached that complete units arriving from Canada after the departure of the 2nd Canadian Division should be sent to a new camp to be established at Bramshott in the Aldershot area, instead of to Shorncliffe, which had reached its limit in accommodation, and on 19 November Brig.-Gen. Lord Brooke was brought back from France to become G.O.C. "Canadian Division, Bramshott".

More confusion followed. On 3 December General Carson asked the War Office if it would be "at all possible to add the piece of the Aldershot Command which we are now occupying to the Shorncliffe Command." This would enable training at Bramshott to be regulated from Shorncliffe and would obviate the necessity of having "to correspond with, and be under the orders of, two Imperial Commands".[15] Acting on this request the War Office notified the G.O.C.-in-C. Aldershot Training Centre on 12 December that Major-General Steele would be "entirely responsible for the training of the Canadians in your command"—an announcement that greatly pleased Steele but not MacDougall. The latter complained to Carson, who proceeded to explain to a somewhat puzzled War Office that MacDougall was "in command of all Canadian troops in England, under the supervision, however, of Major-General Steele." He went on to emphasize, "at the moment, Lord Brooke, the Commanding Officer in Bramshott, is serving under the orders and instructions of Brigadier-General MacDougall". Carson followed this up with a visit to the War Office, as a result of which he told Steele, a bit optimistically, that everything was "straightened out, and we all know just where we are and in consequence all attend to our own work without treading on anybody's corns". Carson described MacDougall as "responsible for the training and discipline of all Canadians in England"—a statement to which Steele took exception, pointing out that such a situation would prevent him from exercising any supervision in such matters.

The bickering continued. By the end of 1915 Carson had become thoroughly dissatisfied with the situation, and during December he sent the Minister a number of strongly-worded communications urging a clarification of his own status—

MacDougall had charged that Carson was not a member of the C.E.F.—and calling for an organization in the United Kingdom that would be "almost a duplicate of your complete organization in Ottawa". He proposed the establishment of "either a Sub-Militia Council or a Financial Committee" with, in addition to himself "as practically Acting Minister of Militia over here, as your representative, an Adjutant General and Quartermaster General and an Inspector General's Branch".[16]

There was indeed need for coordination in control. Communications from Militia Headquarters were being sent direct to the War Office, to the G.O.C. Canadians at Shorncliffe (Steele), the G.O.C. Canadian Division at Shorncliffe (MacDougall), and to Major-General Carson. In a letter to the Minister the Corps Commander in France complained of "quadruple control", with Carson, Steel, MacDougall and Brooke all dealing directly with his headquarters. Also involved in the conduct of C.E.F. affairs were Sir George Perley and Sir Max Aitken, whose participation added two more to the number of Canadian authorities with whom the War Office found itself corresponding. Perley was indeed in an unenviable position as a result of the Minister of Militia's desire to keep matters firmly within his own control. "When I hear a man say", wrote the High Commissioner to Borden, "that he understands 'There are two Governments in Canada, one of which is represented here by various people sent over by Hughes and is apparently not under control of the others', it makes me squirm." He complained that the Militia Department dealt with his office on routine matters only and by-passed him on anything of importance, and he deplored the fact "that Canadian methods of administration are rather being laughed at over here".[17] Yet Ottawa seemed in no hurry to act. "I am at my wits' end to know how to unravel the tangle which has arisen", Carson admitted to Steele on 1 February.

Early in January an inquiry from the Colonial Secretary as to the "exact position of Carson" gave the C.G.S., Major-General Gwatkin, an opportunity of setting forth his views regarding a better administration for the United Kingdom. In a memorandum to the Deputy Minister of Militia he maintained that Carson was performing functions beyond the scope assigned to him by Order in Council and had in military matters "gradually acquired an influence which is viewed with alarm on both sides of the Atlantic". Gwatkin recommended the establishment of a local Council which would be the medium of communication between the Militia Department and the War Office on matters connected with the administration of the C.E.F.[18] The official Canadian reply to the Colonial Secretary confirmed that Carson's original functions had not been extended and promised that the whole situation would be taken up fully by the Minister of Militia, who was soon to visit Great Britain.

Sir Sam Hughes' "Informal" Council

Nothing had been done in Ottawa about Gwatkin's memorandum when Sir Sam left for England on 9 March 1916, and now Sir Robert Borden was receiving reports from various sources about the unsatisfactory state of affairs in the

United Kingdom. Characteristically the Minister of Militia pursued his own course of action, and on 24 March he informed the Prime Minister, "I am bringing Dave Watson [Brig.-Gen. David Watson, who was commanding the 5th Canadian Infantry Brigade in France] back to England to make him Inspector-General and knock the whole thing into shape".[19] On the 31st Hughes authorized Sir Max Aitken to set up an "informal" Council composed of General Carson, General Watson, an Acting Quartermaster General (Colonel George Murphy), an Acting Adjutant General (Brig.-Gen. MacDougall—"if General Watson would deem it proper"), the Director Medical Services, and Sir Max himself. The Council would meet weekly, and on any non-military question would consult Sir George Perley, the High Commissioner.[20] A few days later, before returning to Canada, Sir Sam added Brig.-Gen. Lord Brooke to the Council.

Meanwhile, back in Canada Sir Robert Borden was proceeding with his own plan for an Overseas Council. A draft report to the Cabinet based upon recommendations from the Deputy Minister of Militia and General Gwatkin (whose earlier memorandum seems to have been carried off to England by Hughes)[21] made submission for a Canadian Overseas Council presided over by Sir George Perley. There would be five members—a vice-president and representatives of the C.G.S., the Adjutant General, the Quartermaster General and the Accountant and Paymaster General—and five associate members, including the Director General of Medical Services and officers representing the Army Council, the G.O.C. Canadian forces in the field and the Master General of Ordnance.[22] Before this draft came before the Cabinet, however, Sir Sam Hughes returned to Ottawa and apparently persuaded the Prime Minister to give his own overseas committee a fair trial.

But its existence was short and its record unimpressive. Two meetings were held at the Hotel Cecil—on 5 and 20 April 1916. The first, described in the minutes as an "Informal meeting of four members of the Committee appointed by the Minister of Militia and Defence", was attended by Carson, Watson, Brooke and Murphy. Among other decisions was one that Brig.-Gen. Watson (whom the Minister had appointed to command the 4th Division, which was about to be formed at Bramshott) should take over temporarily the command of all Canadian troops in England, and that immediate steps should be taken to have Brig.-Gen. MacDougall attached to the Canadian Corps Headquarters in France "for instructional purposes for a definite time". The second meeting decided on the name "Headquarters, Canadian Expeditionary Forces, London, England", but, in the absence of Watson, agreed to hold in abeyance "all matters of importance affecting the Canadian Expeditionary Forces" until he could be present.[23] A meeting called for 27 April was postponed *sine die,* as was a further meeting planned for 4 May.

Sir Max Aitken, who had attended neither meeting, reported to the Minister the failure of his project in a telegram dated 10 May 1916. The stumbling block in the way of carrying out Sir Sam's instructions had been General Watson, who "insisted on Steele and MacDougall being disposed of entirely as the condition of his taking command in England". But MacDougall not unnaturally had refused to be ousted for a temporary post in France "to find on my return that my past year's work has been all pulled to pieces". Aitken was not prepared to head the Council unless he had the cooperation of all its members. He reported to Sir Sam, "I could not now rely on Watson supporting me . . . . I decided on my own account to place every obstacle in the way of the formation of that Committee and this I have done." Watson took command of the 4th Division, "evidently very pleased to be relieved of responsibility for Shorncliffe".[24]

Sir Sam gave a copy of this message to Sir Robert Borden, who passed over what seemed a good opportunity to authorize the formation of his own version of an Overseas Council. The Prime Minister was in an awkward position. The Minister of Militia was involved in a controversy over certain of the Shell Committee's contracts,* and it was well known that Sir Robert was administering Hughes' Department while a Royal Commission investigated the matter.[27] To have put his own drastic reorganization into effect at this time would have brought publicity that would further damage Sir Sam's prestige and add to his troubles. Sir George Perley was expected to visit Canada soon, and the Prime Minister may well have decided to defer action until conferring with him and Hughes. Perley came to Ottawa in July, and on his return to England in September he criticized the existing arrangements in Great Britain as "neither dignified nor effective". He expressed himself in favour of a small committee of about four, "chosen from our most capable and respected men", with a civilian at the head.[28]

The Acting Sub-Militia Council

On the completion of the Shell Committee inquiry Sir Sam Hughes returned to England, having been formally authorized by an Order in Council to make more effective arrangements "for the organization and training of the Canadian Expeditionary Forces now in Great Britain". He arrived in London on 30 July, and on the following day received the following request from Sir Robert Borden: "When you have reached conclusion respecting your proposals for reorganization, please cable them fully as they should be definitely embodied in Order in Council and it would be desirable to consider them before they are actually put in operation."[29] On 16 August and again on the 24th Sir Robert was forced to press Sir Sam for his recommendations.[30] Finally on 6 September the Minister of Militia cabled a rather vague progress report in which he expressed the hope that he would have a full report "ready to mail by the end of week. Meantime everything going splendidly."[31]

Hughes might have elaborated that he had already completed the organization of an "Acting Sub-Militia Council for Overseas Canadians", and that it had held its first meeting on 5 September.[32] On the very day of Sir Sam's

* On 28 March 1916 a Liberal member of Parliament (Mr. G. W. Kyte) referred to enormous profits to American promoters arising from certain fuse and cartridge-case contracts made with the Shell Committee. The M.P. charged that one such promoter, Honorary Colonel J. W. Allison, had used his influence with the Minister of Militia to secure contracts with the Shell Committee.[25] A Royal Commission exonerated Hughes and the Shell Committee but strongly censured Allison for deception in his relations with the Minister and the Committee.[26]

cable to the Prime Minister, Canadian newspapers broke the news that a military council of seven members had already met. Sir Robert immediately questioned Hughes about this "extraordinary press report", repeating his earlier injunction that the proposed arrangements should not be announced until they had been embodied in an Order in Council.[33] Then, on the 8th, Canadian papers republished a London report giving the composition of the new council, which had General Carson as president. Bluntly the Prime Minister cabled Sir Sam: "Greatly surprised that composition of proposed Overseas Council is announced in press this morning. Hope you can return immediately. Kindly cable date."[34] But this demand brought only an evasive reply from the Minister of Militia two days later. He could not understand Borden's "peculiar message"; he had mailed a report on the proposed Council, and he understood absolutely that nothing was settled "until approved by Order in Council"; he was just leaving for an inspection of timber camps at various points which would entail an absence of about a week.[35]

The Acting Sub-Militia Council, thus set up in defiance of the Prime Minister's orders, was destined to last only three months. A memorandum handed by Sir Sam Hughes to the Secretary on 20 September defined its function and membership. The Council was to be an "advisory body," advising generally with respect to the Canadian Expeditionary Force. It was to be composed of Major-General Carson (Chairman), Brig.-Gen. Lord Brooke (Military Representative of the Department of Militia and Defence at the Front),* and ten other designated appointments, including those held by Steele and MacDougall.[36]

From Ottawa the Minister of Militia (who evidently had no intention of delegating any of his authority) sent orders that "all reports of Sub-Militia Council must be carefully prepared and must be endorsed from here before final adoption".[37] At its weekly meetings the Council dealt with numerous matters ranging from the organization of a boys' battalion (22 September) to the question of mounting all military policemen on bicycles instead of horses (27 October). On 13 October it passed a "unanimous resolution" which would allow all men set aside for the as yet unformed 5th and 6th Divisions to be sent to France as reinforcements. At the next meeting, however, it learned that the Minister had not approved this recommendation and had ruled that the two divisions "should be gotten in shape".[38]

Yet though its span of life was short, its terms of reference vague and its status uncertain, the creation of the Acting Sub-Militia Council marked a definite step towards an effective overseas organization. But Sir Sam's efforts to bring about a more businesslike state of affairs were doomed to failure when he chose to ignore the Prime Minister's repeated instructions; it is characteristic of the man that he should not have comprehended what the consequence of his attitude must be.

* Unfortunately Lord Brooke was wounded on 11 September while commanding the 12th Infantry Brigade in France, and was dropped from the Council's membership. Sir Max Aitken continued to act as Canada's Military Representative at the front until January 1917, when Lt.-Col. R. Manly-Sims was appointed Canadian Representative at British G.H.Q.

Formation of the Overseas Ministry

While Hughes remained in the United Kingdom contrary to Borden's expressed wish, in Ottawa Sir Robert was taking action towards establishing an Overseas Ministry. By 2 September a revised draft report for submission to the Cabinet proposed the appointment of a "Minister of Overseas Military Forces of Canada" with wide powers, including those with respect to overseas troops "theretofore exercised by or charged upon the Minister of Militia and Defence". The Overseas Minister would conduct all negotiations between the Canadian and British Governments concerning Canada's overseas forces and would be assisted by an advisory council, to be appointed by the Governor in Council.[39]

The Minister of Militia finally reached Ottawa on 7 October, but not until the 17th* did Borden inform him of the projected Overseas Ministry. "I am not criticizing your suggestions as to the personnel of the proposed Overseas Council", the Prime Minister wrote Hughes next day, "but I am of the opinion that the direction of a member of the Government resident in London is both desirable and essential."[40] Sir Sam, however, was not disposed to have power wrested from his grasp without a struggle. On 23 October he produced a draft Order in Council which would, if approved, have authorized the organization of his own Sub-Militia Council. (It was returned to the Militia Department on 16 November with the note, "Privy Council Referred Back".)[41]

Also on the 23rd Sir Sam wrote at length to the Prime Minister criticizing the proposed changes in overseas administration. He justified the existing organization in the United Kingdom, which had General Carson "surrounded by a sub-militia Council composed of the ablest Officers to be found". He declared that the appointment of an Overseas Minister "would be absurd. There is no more necessity for a resident Minister in Britain than there is for a resident Minister at our Camps in British Columbia, Calgary, Camp Hughes, Camp Borden, Valcartier etc." Having personally established a system "to conduct this war on the basis of proper administration . . . and the perfect harmony between all branches of the Canadian Force and the British Force", he could not "concur in the proposal to destroy these plans".[42] Yet three days later, having realized that Sir George Perley's name did not appear in the draft Order, he indicated that he would support the creation of an Overseas Ministry if Sir Max Aitken were selected as its head.[43] Characteristically on his own responsibility he cabled Aitken asking whether he would accept such an appointment, only to receive a negative reply—Sir Max considered himself "not qualified to fill post".[44] Hughes nevertheless continued to press for Aitken's appointment, suggesting that "Max would be the Canadian representative there for War Purposes under me, while Perley should, as now, be consulted regarding all contracts and purchases not under the fixed charges" (see below, p. 359).[45]

* It so happened that on that date *The London Gazette* announced the appointment of Sir Sam as an Honorary Lieutenant General in the British Army with effect from 18 October 1916.

Meanwhile Borden had presented the draft order to the Cabinet and found that "every one of my colleagues warmly supported the proposal". On 27 October he cabled Perley: "Order in Council signed today creating Military Overseas Forces. Hughes greatly excited and may resign". On the 31st a further Order in Council appointed Sir George Perley "Minister of Overseas Military Forces from Canada in the United Kingdom".[46]

It was a bitter blow to the Minister of Militia. As we have observed, it had always been his practice to retain as far as possible exclusive control over all matters concerned with his Department. On his recent return to Canada, however, he had found many of his former responsibilities distributed among others. Mr. J. W. Flavelle, Chairman of the Imperial Munitions Board, was dealing with the production of ammunition; Mr. A. E. Kemp, Chairman of the War Purchasing Commission, had war contracts largely in hand; Sir Thomas Tait (and later Mr. R. B. Bennett), Chairman of the National Service Boards, was concerned with improving recruiting. A Parliamentary Secretary (Mr. F. B. McCurdy) had been appointed to handle much of the routine work of the Department. Sir Sam appears to have accepted these arrangements without undue concern, realizing the need for allotting to others part of the enormous burden falling upon the Militia Department in time of war. But he was not prepared to accept curtailment of the overseas responsibilities which he had always considered his personal sphere of operations.

On 1 November he expressed his views to the Prime Minister in an unfortunate letter which was to have significant consequences. After defending his actions in setting up the Acting Sub-Militia Council he proceeded to charge Sir Robert with a lack of frankness over Perley's appointment.

> It might be implied from your memorandum that my failing to secure authority by Order-in-Council for this Sub-Militia Council impelled you to the course you are now pursuing regarding Sir George Perley. May I be permitted to say that both you and I know to the contrary. I knew early in August that Sir George Perley had planned something along these very lines. You have, also, admitted that as early as the first week of September you had this matter under consideration by you. I understand that it was under consideration by you and Perley earlier. You incidentally remarked yesterday that you had not consulted any of your colleagues. Of course when I drew your attention to the statement, you corrected yourself.[47]

These were harsh words which no superior could overlook, and they made it clear that as long as Sir Sam was in office there could never be the spirit of cooperation between the Militia Department and the Overseas Ministry upon which the latter's successful operation depended. On the 6th Borden told Perley of having received a letter from Sir Sam "which demands most serious consideration at my hands".[48]

After discussion with his colleagues the Prime Minister reached his decision, and on the 9th he wrote Sir Sam a letter expressing regret "that you saw fit to address to me, as head of the Government, a communication of that nature". Sir Robert recalled the time and energy which he had expended in supporting Hughes in the administration of his department—a very difficult task "by reason of your strong tendency to assume powers which you do not possess and which can only be exercised by the Governor in Council". He criticized Sir Sam's attitude of wanting to administer his department "as if it were a distinct and separate Government in itself", charging that "such an attitude is wholly inconsistent with and subversive of the principle of joint responsibility upon which constitutional Government is based". Finally he took strong exception to the statements and general character of Sir Sam's letter. "You must surely realize", he concluded, "that I cannot retain in the Government a colleague who has addressed to me such a communication. I regret that you have thus imposed upon me the disagreeable duty of requesting your resignation as Minister of Militia and Defence."[49] On 11 November Sir Sam tendered his resignation with "much satisfaction",[50] and on the 23rd Mr. A. E. Kemp was named Minister in his place.

Sir George Perley regarded his new appointment as inferior to his existing post, and the Prime Minister had to convince him as to the relative importance of the two positions that he would now be holding. He told Sir Thomas White (the Minister of Finance, who was visiting the United Kingdom) that he fully understood the relative importance of the two positions, but that if he found himself unable to discharge the duties of both, he preferred that of High Commissioner. Nevertheless, under strong pressure from Sir Robert Borden, in whose judgement Perley's "status as Minister of Overseas Forces altogether outclasses the position of High Commissioner" with duties "infinitely more important than those which devolved upon you as High Commissioner",[51] Sir George began vigorously discharging his new responsibilities. His first major concern was the selection of a commander for the Canadian Forces in Britain. With Sir Thomas White he spent three days in France interviewing senior Canadian officers. The choice fell upon Major-General R. E. W. Turner, G.O.C. 2nd Canadian Division. Like most serving officers in a theatre of operations Turner was reluctant to relinquish the command of his division for a non-combatant position, and in accepting the appointment in the United Kingdom he requested that "in the event of a Canadian General Officer being appointed to the command of the Canadian Corps" his claim as "the senior Major General" should be given priority.[52]

An Order in Council appointing Turner General Officer Commanding Canadians vice Major-General MacDougall was approved on 1 December. MacDougall had recently assumed the command of "Canadian Troops—Brighton" and had moved his headquarters to that city (below, p. 224). But early in January Headquarters, Overseas Military Forces of Canada, took over the functions of the Brighton Command, and MacDougall, for whom there was no suitable position in the new organization "owing to his high rank", returned to Canada in March. For his Adjutant General Sir George Perley asked for and obtained Colonel P. E. Thacker (A.A. & Q.M.G. 2nd Canadian Division); the new Quartermaster General was Colonel A. D. McRae, who had been serving as Acting Overseas Deputy Minister in Sir Sam's Sub-Militia Council. The office of the new headquarters (including the General Staff, Adjutant General and Quartermaster General) was established in London at Argyll House, in Regent Street.

The Acting Sub-Militia Council had continued to function while the new Overseas Ministry was being organized. By unanimous resolution on 16 November its members tendered their resignations to Sir George Perley, who asked them to carry on for the time being. The Council was finally dissolved on 5 December, the day on which the new Headquarters, Overseas Military Forces of Canada came into being. Two days later an Order in Council cancelled Major-General Carson's original appointment as representative of the Militia Department in the United Kingdom. He proceeded on a long leave of absence which was extended from time to time until 31 January 1918, when he was struck off strength in Canada as surplus to establishment.

By the end of 1916 the Overseas Ministry was firmly established in the British Isles. It did not solve completely the problems involved in administering the C.E.F. overseas, and misunderstandings continued to arise between it and the Canadian Corps in France and Militia Headquarters in Ottawa. Yet it was a much better organization than any that had existed since the outbreak of war, and no major changes in its structure were to be made until the spring of 1918. Much of its strength lay in the fact that from now on all Canadian military control in the British Isles was concentrated in a single authority, Turner, who was the Minister's chief military adviser in all matters relating to the organization and administration of the Overseas Forces. As the Minister's delegate he was authorized to discuss with British General Headquarters in France all questions of policy and administration connected with Canadian Forces in the field and to deal directly on such matters with the Corps Commander.

As emphasized by Sir George Perley in a memorandum defining the new Ministry's terms of reference, the appointment held by the G.O.C. Canadian Forces in the British Isles was now "the senior military appointment in the Overseas Military Forces of Canada".[53]

Recruiting in 1914-1915

Another matter that was to cause the Canadian Government no little concern as the war progressed was the provision of manpower to take care of Canada's steadily increasing needs at home and overseas. This is a convenient place to introduce the problem.

For the first year and a half of the war the country found itself faced with no serious recruiting problems. The winter of 1913-1914 had been one of considerable unemployment in Canada, and when war broke out in the following August, conditions pointed to the probability of an increased shortage of jobs during the coming winter.[54] Although fear of being unemployed was, of course, far from being the only motive which impelled men to answer the call to arms in very large numbers, it must be considered a not unimportant factor. As we have seen, supply far exceeded demand, and in the early months of hostilities it was possible to enrol only some 36,000 of those wanting to enlist.

Of the 1500 officers who were appointed to the First Canadian Contingent, two-thirds were Canadian-born, while 29 per cent gave other parts of the Empire as their place of birth. But the enlistments by other ranks told a different story. Less than 30 per cent of the 34,500 accepted had been born in Canada; 65 per cent had come originally from the British Isles or from other parts of the Empire.

There were certain obvious reasons for this, as were noted by the contemporary *Canadian Annual Review*. People born in the United Kingdom were more familiar with what war meant, and they were specially conscious of its nearness "to those living in the country which they still looked upon as home". Many of the men from the British Isles had received some military training, and that experience undoubtedly was a factor in prompting them to volunteer without delay. It is probably fair to say that at first the average Canadian tended to look upon the war as an Imperial war which did not affect his own country directly. It took him some time to recognize as a concrete danger what originally might have seemed a mere abstraction. Furthermore, the Canadian-born was more likely than the recent immigrant to be established in remunerative, congenial and steady employment, and therefore found it harder to tear up the deep roots which held him firmly to his native soil.[55] The first great surge of enlistments was to carry off those men who had come from the British Isles. Once that fruitful source of recruiting had dried up, replenishment was to be much more difficult.

We have noted that the strength of the Canadian military forces authorized to be on active service was periodically increased. When it was decided to form a second contingent in November 1914, approval was given to retain 30,000 men under arms in Canada. In July 1915 the authorized strength was set at 150,000, and on 30 October of the same year this number was increased to a quarter of a million.[56] Still these sizable demands seemed likely to be met without great difficulty. The steady flow of volunteers which had begun coming forward in answer to the Minister of Militia's "call to arms" kept up during 1915, and by the end of that year there appeared every possibility that 250,000 men would be in the C.E.F. within a few more months.

Among the reasons for this gratifying response to the growing demands on Canada's manpower was a relaxation of earlier restrictions. The year 1915 saw the first lowering of medical qualifications for enlistment. In July the required height for all corps except artillery was reduced from 5′3″ to 5′2″ (in the case of artillery from 5′7″ to 5′4″). During the same month the minimum chest measurements were dropped half an inch to a range of 33-34 inches. August brought cancellation of the regulation requiring a married man to produce his wife's written consent before he could be enrolled.

More positive recruiting practices were introduced. After the dispatch of the First Contingent the Militia Department began granting the rank of lieutenant-colonel to certain prominent citizens (generally members of the local Militia unit), authorizing them to raise complete C.E.F. battalions; for it had been found that enlistment into specific battalions, commanded by well-known and respected men, appealed to many who did not want to become general reinforcements. Most cities and larger towns now had recruiting depots which, while enlisting men for all branches of the C.E.F., concentrated upon enrolling specialists for such corps as the Army Service and the Medical. Many communities formed Citizen Recruiting Leagues and Committees, whose functions were to organize recruiting rallies and carry out other activities aimed at stimulating enlistment.

As might be expected, the Minister of Militia took a keen personal interest in recruiting, though the results of his participation were not uniformly beneficial. During 1915 he decided that C.E.F. units while mobilizing need not restrict their recruiting efforts to the Divisional Area or Military District in which they were located. A letter circulated on 1 October by Militia Headquarters permitting more latitude led to encroachments by battalion recruiting officers upon the territorial areas of other regiments and caused considerable ill-feeling.[57] After a heated dispute between the Officers Commanding the 4th Division (with headquarters in Montreal) and the 5th Division (Quebec City), the Adjutant General persuaded the Minister to cancel his earlier instructions, and to restrict recruiting to a territorial basis except in the case of special corps, such as pioneer, tunnelling and forestry units. Among other units permitted to recruit outside their territories were sportsmen's battalions, Scandinavian battalions, a Methodist battalion and an Orange battalion.[58]

Hughes, never one to let the advice of his departmental officers in any way curb his enthusiasm for experiment, was personally the author of the recruiting and billeting policy which was adopted in Canada during the winter of 1915-1916. This scheme provided for men to be recruited and trained not only in cities, where reasonable facilities for the purpose would exist, but also in rural localities. Regulations drafted by the Minister "in his own handwriting" provided for each electoral district to constitute a battalion area (with some districts being combined to form single areas). Each would have a battalion commander or organizer with an adjutant, paymaster and medical officer and the necessary clerical and training staffs. Every centre raising 25 or more men after 1 November 1915 would have such men billeted in homes in the community. The billeting allowance for each man was 60 cents a day, and a married man would also draw 25 cents a day in lieu of the separation allowance for which he could not now qualify. Each recruit would receive a drill book free of charge; qualifying schools for N.C.Os. and men were to be provided at as many centres as possible; and from "the most efficient of the recruits" would be chosen officers and N.C.Os.

But the experiment lasted only one season. Commanders' reports showed that though the scheme had attracted recruits in satisfying numbers, very little training had been accomplished. In October 1916 the Prime Minister was informed that "the experience of the Militia Department last winter with regard to billeting of troops in small detachments throughout the country, while no doubt assisting in recruiting, was not such as to encourage a continuation of this practice."[59]

A Pledge of 500,000 Men

On the whole, then, recruiting moved along in a satisfactory manner into the autumn of 1915. By that time the 2nd Canadian Division had joined the 1st Division in France to form the Canadian Corps. At Ypres, in April, Canadians had fought their first major action, but no serious problem of reinforcements had yet arisen. In November Major-General Sir Eugène Fiset (Deputy Minister of Militia from December 1906 to March 1924) wrote, "so whole-hearted has been the response . . . that the equivalent of a Division [the 3rd] can be added, without difficulty, to the Canadian Army Corps already in the trenches."[60] More striking evidence of the belief (at least on the part of the Prime Minister) that Canada had a considerable pool of manpower available and willing to enlist came on the last day of the year. Without previous warning, Sir Robert Borden, in a New Year's Message to the people of Canada, announced that the authorized strength of the forces was being doubled; commencing on 1 January 1916 the goal was to place 500,000 men in uniform.[61]

It is necessary to define the exact nature of the new commitment. There were many who appeared to believe that the pledge would be fulfilled by obtaining 500,000 *enlistments*. Examination of all the evidence, however, makes it clear that the new figure was to be the actual *strength* at which Canada's military forces were to be maintained. This meant that because of wastage by reason of deaths, discharges, operational casualties, etc., many thousands in excess of half a million would have to be enrolled before the target could be reached. The Senate was warned of the true situation (by Brig.-Gen. the Hon. James Mason on 14 March 1916) in these words: "This large number [500,000], if and when sent to the Front, must be maintained, and it has been estimated that the casualties will not be less than five per cent monthly of the total force. This means that we shall have to provide each month, to maintain our Army's strength, at least 25,000 new men—or 300,000 a year. There can be no question that the additional 250,000 to bring our quota up to 500,000 and the 300,000 if required, annually to keep it at that figure, will not be obtained under the present system of enlistment."

The Senator seems to have faced facts more frankly than some of the officials in the Department of Militia and Defence. A report published by that Department attempted to perpetuate the erroneous impression that the goal of 500,000 was a recruiting figure, towards which almost 400,000* men had been enlisted by the end of 1916.[62] In reality, however, the actual strength of the armed forces on 31 December 1916 was 299,937, or almost 100,000 lower than the total recruited since the beginning of the war.[63] This practice of using unrealistic statistics in an attempt to make the goal appear accessible was

* The report gave the enlistments in the C.E.F. to the end of 1916 as 384,450. To this it added the number of Non-Permanent Active Militia (9646) and the Permanent Force (2451) that had been raised for guard or garrison duty in Canada, thereby reaching a total of 396,547.

criticized by the Canadian Corps Commander, Lieut.-General Sir Arthur Currie, in a letter written in January 1918:

> I know that many people did not understand the urgent need of reinforcements and possibly they were not to blame for their ignorance, because in many published statements they were told the number who had enlisted and were not told the number of enlistments which were of no use to us.[64]

When the initial enthusiasm with which the Prime Minister's announcement had been received died down, there was concern in some quarters as to Canada's capabilities of obtaining such a large number of men by voluntary enlistment. Even before Sir Robert made the decision public his Parliamentary Secretary, Mr. R. B. Bennett, had bluntly warned him, "we cannot possibly look at half a million".[65] The Governor General, who had received no advance notice of the proposal, expressed the fear that "500,000 may be beyond the powers of the Dominion of Canada to provide under voluntary enlistment."[66] Sir Wilfrid Laurier called it "a large contract";[67] and Lord Shaughnessy, President of the C.P.R., did not consider it a "practicable suggestion", and sounded the warning that "if we were to attempt to raise 500,000, or add 225,000 to our present army, we would be making a draft upon the working population of this country that would be seriously felt".[68] The Minister of Militia did not appear to share these misgivings. Publicly he insisted, "We will raise the number now authorized . . . voluntarily and without compulsion or the semblance of compulsion."[69] Indeed, in a speech in Toronto four days after Borden's announcement, he revealed his intention of securing twenty-one additional divisions* "before the snow flies next fall".[70] Privately Hughes assured Borden, "We can easily live up to your offer, if right systems are pursued."[71]

The Prime Minister himself must have been aware of the difficulties involved in placing large numbers of men in uniform. In the previous May he had answered a suggestion that more divisions be recruited by observing that "it is much easier to propose the organization, arming and equipment of a force of 250,000 men than to accomplish it".[72] Now, faced with the task of obtaining and maintaining twice that number, he admitted to the House of Commons in January that it was a large force to raise, but justified his decision on the grounds that it was "fitting that at the opening of the New Year we should announce to the Empire and to all the world that we were not only prepared but willing to do something more".[73] Whatever other considerations there may have been remain obscure.

Apparently Sir Robert took his decision without any serious consultation with his colleagues. Certainly his conclusion was reached without the benefit of any planned study of all that this large-scale commitment of Canada's manpower would involve. Only on the eve of making the formal announcement did he tell three of his cabinet ministers of his decision. On 30 December he wrote in his diary:

> Worked at correspondence all day with Secretary. White [Minister of Finance], Hughes and Reid [Minister of Customs] came and I propounded to them proposal that force should be increased on 1st January to 500,000. They agreed . . . .

* Sir Sam apportioned these divisions as follows: British Columbia, 2; Alberta, 2; Manitoba and Saskatchewan, 3; Toronto and district, 5; Eastern Ontario, 2; Western Ontario, 2; Quebec, 3 and possibly 4; Maritime Provinces, 2. Nothing came of this fantastic scheme.

A scrutiny of Sir Robert's hand-written diary reveals no further reference to this meeting or to the consideration which prompted the Prime Minister's decision. None of the three ministers appears to have been convinced that his leader was doing the right thing. "To more than double this establishment", recorded Sir Thomas White afterwards, "was a most formidable undertaking for a country which less than a year and a half before had considered 50,000 men the maximum it would be able to raise . . . . Not one of us had any clear view as to how so many additional men could be raised . . . ."[74] In July 1916 Sir Sam Hughes was to remind the Prime Minister: "I recommended to you that we could raise as high as four hundred thousand soldiers for the front. Later on you recommended five hundred thousand."[75] And on 30 January 1917 Sir Sam emphasized in the House of Commons that the "offer of" 500,000 had been "made by the Prime Minister—on his own responsibility".*

Borden had received no specific request from the British Government which would require Canada to consider raising a force of the size now authorized, and it is unlikely that his decision could have been based upon any information coming from the United Kingdom authorities. Indeed, on 4 January 1916, he complained to Sir George Perley:

> During the past four months since my return from Great Britain, the Canadian Government (except for an occasional telegram from you or Sir Max Aitken) has had just what information could be gleaned from the daily press and no more. As to consultation, plans of campaign have been made and unmade, measures adopted and apparently abandoned and generally speaking steps of the most important and even vital character have been taken, postponed or rejected without the slightest consultation with the authorities of this Dominion.[77]

Could it have been that Borden felt his announcement of a figure of half a million, besides catching the public fancy, would strengthen his hand in his efforts to obtain from the British Government more information and a greater willingness to consult Canada on general policy in the conduct of the war? It is not without significance that in this same letter to Perley, sent four days after his public announcement, he wrote: "It can hardly be expected that we shall put 400,000 or 500,000 men in the field and willingly accept the position of having no more voice and receiving no more consideration than if we were toy automata."

There remains to be considered the effect of the Prime Minister's decision. The figure of 500,000 became a symbol. Instead of relating Canada's needs in manpower to the number of reinforcements actually required by her forces overseas, it became the fashion to speak of the necessity for Canada to redeem her "pledge" to place 500,000 men in uniform. At first everything looked most promising. The high rate of enlistments during the latter part of 1915 and the first half of 1916 made the prospect of obtaining 500,000 men appear very bright and encouraged

* Hughes had mentioned the figure of 500,000 on at least two occasions, but both of them were casual. On 7 October 1914, during a press interview in New York he had declared, "We can supply the Government with 500,000 picked men. This number will not be required from us, however, nor anything like this number, but they are available." And a year later (25 October 1915), during a recruiting meeting in Toronto, he was quoted as stating that the men at the front must be able to say, "We are coming General Kitchener, 500,000 strong."[76]

those in authority to believe that Canada could provide and maintain additional divisions in the field. As we have seen (above, p. 133), in January a fourth division was offered and accepted; and while visiting England during the summer of 1916 the Minister of Militia committed Canada to raising a fifth division and advanced the possibility of providing a sixth.

Hughes was so carried away by the possibility of obtaining half a million men that he cabled Borden on 15 August to urge that since Australia had five divisions in France and enough troops in England and Egypt for four more (so he had been told), "surely with all our troops we can put at least eight if not ten Divisions in the field".[78] In another message on the same day he asked to have "sixty to eighty thousand troops sent over immediately"; this would still leave "more than one hundred thousand troops in Canada".[79] But a prompt reply from the Prime Minister instructed Sir Sam to take no immediate action, suggesting (quite correctly) that he had overestimated the strength of Australian Forces and also that of the troops in Canada, "which number at present is about 120,000".[80]

Borden's New Year's announcement provided an immediate stimulus to recruiting. Enrolments during January 1916 totalled 29,295, an increase of almost 5600 over the previous month. In March 34,913 enlisted—a figure not to be passed until May 1918, when the operation of the Military Service Act brought in a total for the month of 38,789. By the end of May 1916 the authorized strength of 250,000 decided upon in the previous October had been reached, but still 200,000 men were needed to achieve the new objective. After the heartening initial spurt enlistments began steadily to diminish. May had produced 15,359 men, but June brought only 10,619, and in July the figure dropped to 8389. December 1916 saw only 5279 taken on strength—the smallest number to enrol in any month since the outbreak of war.[81]

Well-meant offers of assistance from various parts of the country had not been lacking. In March 1916 a letter to the Minister of Militia from a gentleman in British Columbia suggested as "a promising field of enlistment not heretofore exploited" the recruiting of Indians from reservations in the four western provinces. He estimated a potential of 12,000 able-bodied males "after deducting the Coast Indians, who are canoemen with large shoulders and small legs, due to excessive use of the former and the sitting posture of the latter". He extolled the fighting qualities of the Indian, who was "accustomed to slaughter daily or to go hungry . . . . The offensive sights, noises and smells incidental to killing does not minimize but excites the primal instinct in them."[82] Other proposals that poured in included an offer from Vancouver of "a full battalion of naturalized Japanese, all British subjects";[83] a suggestion for forming a coloured regiment from the maritime provinces and Western Ontario;[84] and one for raising a Polish battalion.[85]

Failure of the Voluntary System

One of the most serious omissions in whatever calculations Sir Robert Borden may have engaged in before making his momentous announcement was his failure to give due consideration to the adverse effects that it might have on the requirements of industry and agriculture. Seventeen months of war had wrought a tremendous change in Canada's economy. The conditions of stagnation in business and unemployment which had existed at the outbreak of war were being rapidly dissipated during 1915. It should have been readily foreseen that there would be a rapid and continuing expansion in the munitions and other wartime industries and in agricultural production; and that this would inevitably bring increasing demands on Canada's manpower. Wages were bound to rise as employers strove to retain their present employees and augment their labour force. In such circumstances it was to be expected that large numbers of men physically fit for military service would recall their days of unemployment and would hasten to accept positions which provided higher rates of remuneration than the Army could offer.

By the early summer of 1916 this failure to consider the needs of industry and agriculture was bringing the system of voluntary recruiting under criticism. It was charged that indiscriminate recruiting was taking key personnel from industry, while men employed in non-essential work, though of suitable age and medical category, were shirking their duty by failing to enlist. In April a delegation from civilian recruiting organizations in four provinces told the Prime Minister that the existing recruiting arrangements were "expensive, unbusinesslike" and unreliable.[86] An editorial in the *Manitoba Free Press* condemned the aimless methods which had "swept into the battalions plenty of persons who ought not to be there", and urged the setting up of some advisory authority which could protect unsuitable applicants against their feeling that "duty calls them to the fields of Flanders".[87] On 12 April the New Brunswick Legislature passed a resolution recommending that "in order that 500,000 men promised by Canada to the Empire may be speedily raised" the Dominion Government should enact legislation calling to the colours all men of suitable age under an enrolment plan which would consider the requirements of agriculture and industry.[88] On 9 June Sir Thomas White, the Minister of Finance, told the Prime Minister of the strong feeling he had found in Toronto in favour of some system of national registration or compulsory service. Toronto employers felt that Ontario, where large numbers of skilled workers were joining the forces, was suffering more than the other provinces, where recruiting was practically at a standstill.[89]

The Government had indeed made some attempts to correct the matter in an "informal" way rather than by introducing any comprehensive legislation. Recruiting officers had been issued with instructions designed to prevent the enlistment of men employed in certain types of work. Special leave had been granted soldiers who wished to assist farmers during the busy seasons.[90] But these measures were insufficient and ineffective. The country was finding out, in the slow and painful school of experience, that a major war demanded full and effective use of its manpower, and it looked to the Government to give the required guidance and direction.

When Sir Thomas White made his representations the Prime Minister was already examining the possibility of a general registration of Canada's manpower, and 16 August saw the passage of the first of a series of Orders in Council setting up a National Service Board. This civilian organization, which was headed by a Director General at Ottawa and Directors of National Service in the Military Districts, was charged with having "all available labour utilized to the greatest advantage" both for maintaining industry and furnishing men for military service. To this end it was to make an inventory of the labour of the Dominion, the data from which might also be useful in dealing with industrial conditions after the war. The first Director General of National Services was Sir Thomas Tait, President of the English-speaking Citizens' Recruiting League of Montreal, who resigned on 12 October when his choice of a Secretary was not approved by the Prime Minister, and was succeeded by Mr. R. B. Bennett.

The National Service Board's attempt to take an inventory of manpower was made early in 1917 by means of cards* distributed through all post offices in Canada. When the Government overruled the Board's intention of making the completion and return of cards compulsory, extensive publicity was undertaken "to create an atmosphere sufficient to induce the people voluntarily to sign the cards".[91] Of the 1,549,360 cards returned, 206,605 were either blank or only partly completed. The Secretary of the National Service Board estimated that 20 per cent of the total males in Canada between 18 and 65 had failed to send in cards. After deducting cards of serving soldiers, non-British subjects, the physically unfit, personnel with more than three dependents and all others considered unsuitable, the Board reduced the above figure to a total of 470,703 military prospects, of whom 286,976 were not engaged in essential occupations.[92] From the cards in this last category the National Service Board sent Militia Headquarters lists of prospective recruits and these were passed to the appropriate District Recruiting Officers.

But the number of recruits obtained from these lists was negligible. Military District No. 10 (with headquarters at Winnipeg) canvassed 1767 men on its lists without obtaining a single recruit; 4497 names canvassed by M.D. No. 5 (Quebec) furnished only four enlistments.[93] The stock objection to enlisting, as reported by the District Officer Commanding M.D. No. 12 at Regina, was "I will wait and see what the National Service Commission tells me I ought to do"; and from Montreal the D.O.C. M.D. No. 4 observed, "Having filled up the National Service cards, they now claim that their pledge to the Government for industrial service anywhere in Canada exempts them from military service overseas."[94]

An effort to stimulate recruiting in Quebec by bringing back from France a prominent French-Canadian officer achieved little. What was to have been a complete French-Canadian battalion (the 258th) left Montreal for overseas on 2 October 1917 with a strength of only 15 officers and 221 other ranks. Henri Bourassa and other nationalists in Quebec were carrying on a virulent campaign

* The cards asked for the following particulars: name; age; birthplace; parentage and nationality; health, physical condition, sight, hearing, etc.; trade, profession, present occupation; and whether the individual was willing to perform National Service either by enlisting in the C.E.F. or by taking up special employment.

of opposition to Canada's participation in the war; and though they drew little support from leaders in public life, their undoubted influence over the masses was a major deterrent to enlistment. Bourassa's criticism was not directed solely against the Borden administration. He was particularly vindictive against Laurier, whose imperialistic tendencies he blamed for forcing the country towards conscription. "Sir Wilfrid Laurier", he charged, "is the most nefarious man in the province of Quebec, in the whole of Canada."[95]

The military authorities displayed extraordinary lapses of good judgement in handling recruiting in Quebec. When it was decided in August 1916 to appoint a Director of Recruiting in each Military District, the G.O.C. M.D. No. 4 (Headquarters at Montreal) selected Hon.-Major the Rev. C. A. Williams, pastor of St. James' Methodist Church, Montreal. By a strange coincidence the appointee for M.D. No. 2 (Toronto) and the Chief Recruiting Officer for Canada were also named Williams, and both were Methodist clergymen. The appointment of an English-speaking Protestant in a predominantly French-speaking area was unfortunate, though there is evidence that the G.O.C., Major-General E. W. Wilson, has received more blame than he deserved. In a letter which he sent to Sir Edward Kemp on 31 May 1917, General Wilson described his difficulties in attempting to organize a French-Canadian Recruiting Association. (An English-speaking organization had been formed in Montreal shortly after the First Contingent left for England. It had raised a fund of more than $25,000 and had given "most satisfactory results".) Wilson had solicited the assistance of a number of prominent gentlemen without success.* "I had several interviews", he wrote, "with Senator Dandurand, also General Labelle and Colonel Ostell, and urged them to recommend a gentleman to take the active head of the recruiting, and preferred that they would recommend a Priest, and I regret to inform you that they were unable to secure the name of a Priest who would undertake the duties." He further reported that those whom he approached had not been able to raise any funds such as had been done by the English Recruiting Association, and that subsequently the English Organization "did render some financial assistance to French-Canadian Battalions".[96] It may be added that the appointment of Williams was strongly criticized in the House in June, and came under frequent fire from the French press, a section of which indiscriminately confused the records of the three officers of the same name, thereby aggravating a largely imaginary grievance.

Across the country the recruiting situation continued to deteriorate. The total enrolled for April 1917 was only 4761. And this was the month of the Battle of Vimy Ridge, in which Canadian casualties numbered 10,602 in six days (below p. 265). News of the falling off in enlistments had reached the trenches. In December 1916 the G.O.C. 1st Canadian Division wrote to an officer in the Militia Department, "From reports that come from time to time Canada will find

* Major-General Wilson lists the names of the following from whom he sought assistance: Senator Raoul Dandurand, Senator F. L. Beique, Sir Alexander Lacoste, Major Z. Hebert, Brig-Gen. A. E. Labelle, Lt.-Col. J. T. Ostell.

it hard to raise the half-million men as promised. It looks as if Compulsory Service must be introduced."[97] Shortly before Christmas a letter drafted by the C.G.S. for the Minister to send to Sir Robert Borden declared that since the voluntary system was showing signs of collapse, "it would be a risky proceeding to place a 5th Division in the field".[98]

Faced with the Government's reluctance to introduce compulsory service the Militia Department evolved a scheme to call out on a voluntary basis 50,000 members of the Militia for home defence, thereby releasing for overseas the same number of C.E.F. troops in Canada. It was hoped that some of the recruits so obtained would volunteer for overseas service. Though District Officers Commanding with whom the proposal was discussed were less than enthusiastic about its prospects of success, an Order in Council passed on 16 March 1917 set up a Canadian Defence Force of forty-seven battalions. Military District Headquarters were instructed to mobilize designated regiments of the Militia without delay. But the project was a melancholy failure. On 30 April the last in an exchange of depressing telegrams in which the Minister of Militia, now Sir Edward Kemp (above, p. 211), was keeping Sir Robert Borden (then in the United Kingdom) fully posted, informed the Prime Minister, "Enlistments in Home Defence force negligible. Recruiting by voluntary methods almost at an end. Sentiment in favour of some form of compulsion growing."[99] By the end of June 1858 recruits had been obtained; of these 1293 had joined the C.E.F. On 31 July orders were issued to demobilize the Canadian Defence Force.[100]

The Government had at last been forced to recognize the fact that it had reached the limit of the manpower obtainable by voluntary methods. To achieve the goal so optimistically set by Sir Robert Borden in his New Year's Day message, Canada must now turn to conscription.

Reinforcement Establishments Overseas

The means by which Canada adopted compulsory service will be dealt with in a later chapter. For the moment it may be useful to survey briefly the arrangements made to handle Canadian reinforcements in England and France.

It will be recalled that when the First Canadian Contingent arrived in England with more infantry battalions than were required for the three brigades of the 1st Division, one of these surplus units was made into a reserve cavalry regiment, and the other four became infantry reinforcing battalions (above, p. 39). At the same time the personnel made surplus by the reorganization of field artillery brigades were organized into brigade depot batteries for the supply of artillery reinforcements, while the reinforcement needs of other corps were met by forming depots or designating specific units (e.g., No. 2 Veterinary Section).[101] Because accommodation at British bases in France was limited, the Canadian Division's ten per cent first reinforcements remained in England, and were placed in the General and Infantry Base Depots formed at Tidworth in January 1915. These, together with the other reinforcement units, later became part of the Canadian

Training Depot commanded by Colonel W. R. W. James (above, p. 202). The appointment of Brig.-Gen. MacDougall to command all Canadian troops in Britain coincided with the decision to transfer the majority of the Canadian units to the Shorncliffe area. The Canadian Training Depot, the General Base Depot and the Infantry Base Depot were abolished, and MacDougall's command was designated the Canadian Training Division, to distinguish it from the 2nd Canadian Division which was being formed at Shorncliffe.[102]

During March 1915 the four infantry battalions that had been set aside as reinforcement-holding units were joined by three more assigned to a similar role on arrival at Shorncliffe from Canada. Six of these "reserve" battalions (as they became known) were affiliated with formations in the field (two with each brigade), and for a short time the seventh acted as a reinforcement depot for Princess Patricia's Canadian Light Infantry (which, it will be recalled, was serving with a British division). When the 2nd Division was formed, an additional six units were provided to furnish its reinforcements, and towards the end of September 1915 the twelve reserve battalions were organized into four Reserve Brigades.[103]

To meet the 1st Division's reinforcement requirements, which the heavy casualties of the Battle of Ypres had materially increased, the War Office asked, in April 1915, for 6000 infantry to reach England every three months.[104] A call at once went out to every C.E.F. battalion in Canada not earmarked for inclusion in the 2nd Division to furnish a draft of five officers and 250 men.[105] During the last half of 1915 thirty-five infantry battalions in Canada sent such drafts. Some did this more than once—indeed one unit (the 79th Battalion from Brandon) supplied 1020 officers and men before, having refilled its ranks five times, it crossed the Atlantic itself.[106]

Although the demand on these battalions to furnish drafts delayed their own movement overseas, one by one they reached England with a full complement of officers and men. A few of them, as we have seen, became reserve battalions; others, designated as "depot" battalions, were attached to selected Reserve Brigades and were used to replenish the reserve battalions as these sent reinforcements to France. As the depot battalions became depleted of personnel they were absorbed into reserve battalions and lost their identity. Some, however, were to suffer a kinder fate, proceeding to the front as complete units in new divisions.

The decision to raise and dispatch from Canada "draft-giving battalions" at full establishment had been made in preference to a scheme proposed early in the war by the Chief of the General Staff, Colonel Gwatkin, who had recommended organizing depots in Canada for receiving and training recruits preparatory to their dispatch overseas in reinforcement drafts. Unfortunately the method adopted produced in England an accumulation of senior officers who could not be given suitable employment when their own units, depleted of junior officers and other rank personnel, were absorbed into the reserve battalions. Yet the authorities in Canada were reluctant to discontinue this system, for, as the C.G.S. observed in June 1916: "Drafts, for administrative and financial reasons, are to be preferred; but the despatch of complete battalions would gratify the senior ranks and appeal to local sentiment."[107] Not until May 1917 was a policy introduced which required officers of rank higher than lieutenant who were surplus to establishment either to revert to lieutenant's rank as a reinforcement or be returned to Canada.[108] Subsequent to this ruling officers accompanying battalions from Canada were considered to be draft-conducting officers, regardless of rank, and could be retained in England or returned to Canada as decided by Headquarters O.M.F.C.

As we have seen (above, p. 204) limitations on space at Shorncliffe meant that complete units arriving from Canada after October 1915 were sent to the new Bramshott Camp. The Camp became the base reserve depot for supplying the reserve battalions at Shorncliffe with replacements for the reinforcements which they sent to France. In December the Bramshott battalions were organized into four brigades, three of which were used to form the 4th Division in the following May. When the Division left for France and the Somme in August 1916 it was replaced at Bramshott by a new "Canadian Training Division", commanded by Brig.-Gen. F. S. Meighen. At the end of April 1916 all the Canadian Reserve Brigades in England became known as "Training Brigades".[109]

By the end of December 1916 there were 7240 officers and 128,980 other ranks of the Canadian Expeditionary Force in the United Kingdom (as compared with 2467 officers and 49,379 other ranks a year previously). At the same time strength returns showed 2526 officers and 105,640 other ranks in France. To accommodate the steadily growing numbers of Canadians in Britain, in the late autumn of 1916 the War Office placed at Canadian disposal additional camps at New Shoreham, Crowborough, Seaford and Hastings in Sussex. For ease of control the new camps were administered from temporary headquarters set up by Major-General MacDougall at Brighton (above, p. 211), when this was disbanded on 5 January 1917 Headquarters O.M.F.C. took over its functions.[110]

One of the first concerns of the newly formed Headquarters was to overhaul the arrangements for handling Canadian reinforcements in the United Kingdom. Investigation quickly revealed the need for a thorough reorganization, particularly for the infantry (comprising the bulk of the reinforcements), where the situation was "by far the most unsatisfactory of all the Arms". There were in England some seventy infantry battalions (exclusive of casualty units), of various strengths from a mere skeleton cadre up to full establishment. "As an efficient reinforcing machine for battalions at the front", stated the official report of the investigation, "the existing organization was entirely unsuited and inadequate." In taking immediate remedial action, infantry reinforcements were reorganized so as to bring about closer territorial associations between the Canadian provinces and the units in the field. Fifty-seven battalions were absorbed into twenty-six reserve battalions, grouped in six Reserve Brigades. Battalions not absorbed were earmarked for service in the field with divisions yet to be formed.[111]

March 1917 saw the introduction of a regimental territorial system. The reserve battalions in the United Kingdom were grouped with their affiliated battalions in France into Territorial Regiments bearing provincial designations. Later in the summer the scheme was extended to include units in Canada. After the end of 1916, with one exception no overseas battalions were raised in Canada, but in August 1917 one or more "Depot" battalions* were formed in each of the provinces and placed in appropriate Territorial Regiments. A Territorial Regiment now comprised Depot battalions serving in Canada, reserve battalions in England, and battalions in France. By November 1918 the composition of these Regiments was as shown in the table on pages 226 and 227.

Steps had already been taken to ensure that the extent of a province's representation in battalions at the front should be in keeping with its ability to maintain the strength of such battalions. Quebec and British Columbia were the first to be affected. In December 1916 General Turner recommended that in order to remedy somewhat a disproportion at the front among battalions from various parts of Canada, two Montreal and two British Columbia battalions should be absorbed in other battalions from the same section. This would allow Nova Scotia and Ontario to increase their representation in France. In February 1917 the 85th Battalion, which had been recruited in Nova Scotia, and the 116th Battalion, raised in Ontario, were sent to France to replace two Montreal battalions (the 60th and 73rd), which eventually disappeared as their personnel were distributed among other field battalions.[112]

* Not to be confused with the depot battalions which were earlier sent to the United Kingdom (above, p. 223).

COMPOSITION OF TERRITORIAL REGIMENTS, C.E.F.—NOVEMBER 1918

Designation of Regiments (in alphabetical order)	Recruiting Areas in Canada	Designations of Battalions in Territorial Regiments		
		In Canada	In England	In France
Alberta Regiment	Military District No. 13 (H.Q.—Calgary, Alta.)	1st Depot Bn., Alta. Regt.	21st Reserve Bn. (absorbed 9th Res. Bn. in October 1917).	10th, 31st, 49th, 50th Bns.
British Columbia Regiment	Military District No. 11 (H.Q.—Victoria, B.C.)	1st Depot Bn., B.C. Regt. 2nd Depot Bn., B.C. Regt.	1st Reserve Bn. (absorbed 24th Res. Bn. in May 1917 and 16th Res. Bn. in February 1918).	7th, 29th, 72nd Bns.
Manitoba Regiment	Military District No. 10 (H.Q.—Winnipeg, Man.)	1st Depot Bn., Man. Regt.	11th Reserve Bn. (absorbed 14th Res. Bn. in October 1917).	16th, 27th, 43rd Bns.
			18th Reserve Bn.	8th, 52nd, 78th Bns.
New Brunswick Regiment	Military District No. 7 (H.Q.—Saint John, N.B.)	1st Depot Bn., N.B. Regt.	13th Reserve Bn.	26th, 44th Bns.
Nova Scotia Regiment	Military District No. 6 (H.Q.—Halifax, N.S.)	1st Depot Bn., N.S. Regt.	17th Reserve Bn. (absorbed 26th Res. Bn. in October 1917).	25th,85th Bns;R.C.R.
1st Central Ontario Regiment	Military District No. 2 (H.Q.—Toronto, Ont.)	1st Depot Bn., 1st Central Ont. Regt.	3rd Reserve Bn.	4th, 19th Bns; 2nd, 4th C.M.R.
		2nd Depot Bn., 1st Central Ont. Regt.	12th Reserve Bn. (absorbed 5th Res. Bn. in February 1918).	3rd, 15th, 20th, 75th Bns.
2nd Central Ontario Regiment	Military District No. 2 (H.Q.—Toronto, Ont.)	1st Depot Bn., 2nd Central Ont. Regt. 2nd Depot Bn., 2nd Central Ont. Regt.	8th Reserve Bn. (absorbed 2nd Res. Bn. in February 1918).	54th, 58th, 102nd, 116th Bns.
Eastern Ontario Regiment	Military District No. 3 (H.Q.—Kingston, Ont.)	1st Depot Bn., Eastern Ont. Regt. 2nd Depot Bn., Eastern Ont. Regt.	6th Reserve Bn. (absorbed 7th Res. Bn. in February 1918).	2nd, 21st, 38th Bns; P.P.C.L.I.

Western Ontario Regiment	Military District No. 1 (H.Q.—London, Ont.)	1st Depot Bn., Western Ont. Regt.	4th Reserve Bn. (absorbed 25th Res. Bn. in February 1918).	1st, 18th, 47th Bns.
1st Quebec Regiment*	Military District No. 4 (H.Q.—Montreal, P.Q.)	1st Depot Bn., 1st Quebec Regt.	20th Reserve Bn.	13th, 42nd Bns.
			23rd Reserve Bn. (absorbed 22nd Res. Bn. in May 1917).	14th, 24th, 87th Bns; 5th C.M.R.
2nd Quebec Regiment*	Military District No. 5 (H.Q.—Quebec, P.Q.)	1st Depot Bn., 2nd Quebec Regt.		
	Military District No. 4 (H.Q.—Montreal, P.Q.)	2nd Depot Bn., 2nd Quebec Regt.	10th Reserve Bn.	22nd Bn.
Saskatchewan Regiment	Military District No. 12 (H.Q.—Regina, Sask.)	1st Depot Bn., Sask. Regt.	15th Reserve Bn. (absorbed 19th Res. Bn. in October 1917).	5th, 28th, 46th Bns; 1st C.M.R.

*In March 1918 H.Q. O.M.F.C. amalgamated these two Regiments to form the "Quebec Regiment". A proposal to absorb the 10th Reserve Battalion into the 20th Reserve Battalion and distribute French-Canadian reinforcements between the 20th and 23rd Reserve Battalions was abandoned and the 10th Reserve Battalion retained its identity in the newly-organized Quebec Regiment; it became the reinforcing battalion for the 22nd Battalion. The two-regiment organization was retained in Canada, however, the 2nd Quebec Regiment being used to handle French-Canadian reinforcements.

British Columbia's representation at the front was adjusted in a different way. In August 1917 two battalions originally recruited in that province (the 54th and 102nd), which were now being kept up to strength by reinforcements from Ontario, were transferred from the British Columbia Regiment to the 2nd Central Ontario Regiment.[113] While this procedure may have jolted provincial pride, there seems little doubt that the personnel of the battalions concerned found this paper transfer, which kept their unit intact, decidedly preferable to the separation from their comrades that would have come with the disbandment of their battalion and their dispersal among other units.[114] Recalling "the heart-burnings there were when certain Battalions were completely broken up last spring", Lieut.-General Currie, himself a British Columbian, was convinced that the decision to transfer battalions was wise. "We have accomplished the same purpose this time, but we have not broken up the battalions".[115]

University Companies and Battalions

A special group of infantry replacements that went overseas during 1915 and 1916 were the University Companies which were raised to reinforce Princess Patricia's Canadian Light Infantry. The first of these was originally earmarked for a different role. In January 1915 the Department of Militia and Defence granted authority for McGill University to provide a complete overseas company for the 38th Battalion, C.E.F., which was being mobilized in Ottawa. The date of mobilization of the company was arranged to allow undergraduates to complete the College term ending on 1 May. Early in May the company went to Niagara-on-the-Lake to join the summer training of the McGill and Toronto contingents of the Canadian Officers' Training Corps.[116]

While the 38th Battalion was still forming, the War Office, which was concerned about the shortage of officer material in its own forces, made representations to the Canadian Government that the McGill Company should be organized as an officers' training company rather than become part of an infantry battalion.[117] The British suggestion reached the Governor General in June, by which time the Canadian Government had found a new role for the McGill Company—but not that recommended by the War Office. As the United Kingdom authorities were later to be told, the Militia Department was experiencing no difficulty in obtaining officers for the Canadian Expeditionary Force.[118] But the urgent demand made at the end of April for infantry reinforcements had to be met (above, p. 223). On 29 May the McGill Company, now designated No. 1 University Company, with a strength of six officers and 250 men, sailed for overseas as a reinforcing draft for the P.P.C.L.I.[119] The 38th Battalion, as we have seen (above, p. 24 and note) was to serve in Bermuda, England, and France.

Five more University Companies were raised to provide reinforcements for the Patricias. All were mobilized at McGill, but were recruited from a number of Canadian universities. They were composed of "Graduates or Undergraduates of Universities or their friends".[120] Nos. 2 to 5 University Companies proceeded overseas at intervals between June 1915 and April 1916. Thus the first four companies had joined the P.P.C.L.I. in France before the heavy fighting in June 1916. "They saved the Regiment from practical extinction", writes the Patricias' historian, ". . . and it was they who beat the Württembergers in Sanctuary Wood . . ." No. 5 University Company came to the P.P.C.L.I. after Sanctuary Wood, in time to rebuild the battalion's shattered strength.[121] No. 6 University Company was never quite completed; its personnel went overseas in a succession of small drafts.[122]

Besides these University Companies, two C.E.F. battalions were raised and were permitted to include in their designations the names of Universities. They were the 196th (Western Universities) Battalion and the 253rd (Queen's University) Highland Battalion. Recruits for the former came largely from the Universities of Manitoba, Saskatchewan, Alberta and British Columbia, and Brandon College. The 253rd Battalion, however, had little connection with Queen's except for its name, drawing its personnel from the general public. The 196th Battalion reached England in November 1916, and the 253rd in the following May. Both were broken up in the United Kingdom and absorbed into Reserve Battalions.

Undoubtedly it was unsound to use valuable potential officer material in this way.* This fact had been realized earlier by the War Office, but the impact of the shortage of officer material for the Canadian Corps was not realized until later. Unit Commanders found it very difficult to induce their highly educated men to allow their names to go forward for commissions. The great majority preferred to remain in their units with their comrades.

Canadian Base Units in France

The first Canadian administrative unit to be established in France was the Canadian Section, G.H.Q., 3rd Echelon, which began functioning in March 1915 as a section of the Deputy Adjutant General's Office at the Base at Rouen. It was responsible for the preparation of unit Part II Orders, which reflected every circumstance affecting the service or pay of officers and soldiers serving in the field. Acting on reports received from units, the Canadian Section demanded through British Army channels reinforcements from the Canadian Training Divisions in the United Kingdom.

Since, as we have noted, no Canadian Base Depot had been established in France when the 1st Division crossed the Channel, Canadian reinforcements had to pass through the British No. 3 Base Depot at Harfleur (Le Havre) on their way to join units in the field. This arrangement continued until 27 September 1915, when the British Depot was absorbed into the Canadian Base Depot. This Depot though staffed by Canadian personnel remained under British control, and until 1917 the Officer Commanding had no direct communication with the

* This mistake was not repeated in the Second World War.

Canadian authorities in the United Kingdom or at home in Canada. Even the Canadian Section, G.H.Q., 3rd Echelon at Rouen could only deal with the Canadian Base Depot through the Officer Commanding Reinforcements, Le Havre—a British appointment.

By the end of August 1916 the Canadian Base Depot was handling reinforcements for the Canadian Cavalry Brigade, the four Canadian infantry divisions, Corps troops and Line of Communication units. During that month it received 8962 reinforcements from the United Kingdom and dispatched 7567 to units in the field.[123] In the following May the Depot was transferred from Le Havre to Etaples (on the Channel coast, fifteen miles south of Boulogne). For greater efficiency in control and the maintenance of discipline, and because the existing accommodation at Etaples suited such an arrangement, the Canadian Base Depot was reorganized into five independent Depots—the Canadian General Base Depot (to handle all except infantry reinforcements) and Nos. 1, 2, 3 and 4 Canadian Infantry Base Depots. The summer of 1917 saw the institution of a Canadian Corps Reinforcement Camp,* which was to hold near the front reinforcements to the extent of 100 per infantry battalion and ten per cent of other arms.[124] Its existence materially reduced the number of reinforcements retained at the Base. As a result it was possible, in April 1918, to amalgamate the Infantry Base Depots into a single Canadian Infantry Base Depot, the Canadian General Base Depot continuing to deal with non-infantry reinforcements.[125]

The 5th Canadian Division

One of the factors complicating the reinforcement situation was the earmarking of battalions in the United Kingdom for a 5th and possibly a 6th Canadian Division to which the Minister of Militia had committed Canada during the summer of 1916 (above, p. 218). By the autumn of that year most of the infantry battalions for these two divisions had been selected from units in England and the appointment of a divisional and brigade commanders was under consideration.[126] As we have seen, however, in October the heavy losses at the Somme led the Acting Sub-Militia Council to recommend making available as reinforcements all personnel of these battalions except their headquarters, and replenishing them with future drafts from Canada.[127] But Sir Sam Hughes was more concerned with raising new divisions than reinforcing existing ones. "Stand firm", he told General Carson. "Let our Divisions have rest. I cannot comprehend sending troops through undestroyed wire entanglements. Surely Byng cannot repeat June 3rd† every month or two."

There the matter rested until 27 October, when the Chief of the Imperial General Staff, noting that the necessary battalions were available, asked that the

* The Canadian Corps Reinforcement Camp replaced the Canadian Entrenching Group, whose four Entrenching Battalions had been maintained in the forward area to carry out the construction and repair of roads, tramlines, railways, gun positions, dug-outs and similar duties, as well as to furnish drafts to Infantry, Pioneer and Engineer units in the field. These dual functions proved incompatible, and the battalions were disbanded a year after being formed.

† An allusion to the Battle of Mount Sorrel.

Canadian Government authorize the Militia Sub-Council to proceed with mobilization of the 5th Division. But the Cabinet withheld its approval, the Canadian Prime Minister being advised by Sir George Perley that it would be difficult for Canada to reinforce five divisions.[128]

The C.I.G.S. continued to press. In a letter to Perley on New Year's Day 1917 he wrote: "It will be a great pity if this division remains idle in this country while defensive battles are being fought in France." Finally a conference held at the War Office on 12 January brought a compromise. The 5th Canadian Division would not go to France, but its establishment would be completed so that it might assume a role of home defence in the United Kingdom. The War Office asked that no drafts be taken from the Division when other sufficiently trained men were available.[129]

The new division concentrated at Witley, in Surrey, where, on 13 February 1917, Major-General Garnet B. Hughes (promoted from commanding the 1st Canadian Brigade in France) assumed command. Its original composition in infantry was as follows: 13th Brigade, 128th, 134th, 160th and 202nd Battalions; 14th Brigade, 125th, 150th, 156th and 161st Battalions; 15th Brigade, 104th, 119th, 185th and 199th Battalions. In August the Divisional Artillery (the 13th and 14th Field Brigades and four mortar batteries) went to France, where it served until the end of the war as an additional divisional artillery within the Canadian Corps. The Division's Machine Gun Companies (17th, 18th and 19th) subsequently served in France, as did the companies (13th, 14th and 15th) of the Divisional Engineers. On 9 February 1918 Headquarters O.M.F.C. ordered the remainder of the division broken up to provide additional men for units in the field (below, p. 232).[130]

After October 1916 the matter of forming a sixth division in England was dropped. The reluctance of the Canadian Cabinet to send even one more division to the Continent ruled out any thought of raising further field divisions. Yet the possibility of having six Canadian divisions in France did receive brief attention early in 1918, but in different circumstances from the foregoing. In January a serious shortage of reinforcements resulting from the heavy losses at Passchendaele brought an order from the War Cabinet to reduce to three the number of battalions in each British infantry brigade; personnel of the battalion thus made surplus were used to bring the other three battalions up to establishment.[131] A proposal by the Chief of the Imperial General Staff for a similar reorganization in the Canadian Corps in order to form two additional divisions was strongly opposed by the Corps Commander.

In a letter to the Canadian Overseas Minister, Lieut.-General Currie pointed out that the conditions necessitating the change in British formations did not exist in the four Canadian divisions, which were up to strength and had sufficient reinforcements in sight for some time to come. There was therefore no need to break up any units, and a reorganization along British lines would leave twenty surplus battalions. While it was true that with the addition of six battalions from England two new divisions could be formed, the resulting six divisions would be more than a single corps headquarters could handle. It would be necessary to organize into two corps of three divisions each, "with the corollary of a Force Headquarters to command and administer them."[132] Currie agreed that not only would this break up a fighting machine of proved efficiency, but such a reorganization would involve the creation of six new brigade staffs, and headquarters staffs for two new divisions, a new Corps and a Canadian Army. All this, the Corps Commander insisted, would be "increasing out of all proportion the overhead charges" and marked the suggestion as "unbusinesslike", particularly since with this large increase in staff officers the Canadian hitting power would be expanded by only six new battalions from England having an actual fighting strength of 3600* men. Instead of reorganizing along British lines Currie recommended that each of the 48 infantry battalions in the Canadian Corps be authorized to carry 100 men surplus to establishment. Such an arrangement would, he maintained, increase the fighting strength of the Corps by 1200 more men without any increase in staffs, battalion headquarters or transport. Currie concluded his representations to Sir Edward Kemp by expressing his firmest convictions that no good business reason nor "any good military reason" existed for carrying out the reorganization proposed by the British.[133]

The Overseas Minister and General Turner agreed to Currie's proposal, and approval was given by Sir Douglas Haig's headquarters to the plan permitting each infantry battalion in the Canadian Corps to exceed its establishment by 100 men. On 9 February eleven battalions of the 5th Canadian Division were ordered to furnish drafts of 100 men each to the units in the field.[134] Disbandment of the division† followed. This overposting was to continue until the middle of the Second Battle of Arras (26 August-3 September). Even without it Canadian divisions were to hold a marked superiority in manpower over the corresponding British formations—in round numbers relative strengths, including divisional troops, were 15,000 for a British infantry division compared with 21,000 for a Canadian (American divisions had an establishment of 28,000).[136]

Most important of all, the decisions of February, by maintaining the Canadian Corps intact, preserved the excellent esprit de corps that made it a great fighting team, enabling it to operate with continued high efficiency in the decisive battles of the final year of the war.

* Currie estimated that of the six battalions' total strength of approximately 6000 men some 400 men in each unit would not be available for the fighting line because of regimental and other employment.

† Yet a further attempt was made by the War Office about the middle of 1918 to have a fifth Canadian division in France. On 21 June the Canadian Overseas Minister replied negatively to a British proposal to substitute one American for one Canadian battalion in each brigade. Canadian infantry thus made surplus, and/or "A" category men drawn from railway and forestry troops, were to have been formed into a new division.[135]

CHAPTER VIII

THE BATTLE OF VIMY RIDGE, 9-14 APRIL 1917

(See Map 7 and Sketches 37-39)

After the Somme

THE WINTER OF 1916-1917 was for the Canadian Corps a period free from major operations—a time to be used in recuperation, training and strengthening defences while continuing to hold the line.

After its relief on the Somme the Corps moved northward into Artois to take over from the 4th British Corps the right sector of the First Army's front. By the morning of 28 October General Byng was holding a ten-mile sector which extended from two miles north of Arras to the same distance north-west of Lens. Since the 4th Division had stayed at the Somme, Sir Julian was forced to keep all his three remaining divisions in the line.[1] Until their own artillery returned from the Somme towards the end of November the Canadians were allotted the heavy batteries of the 17th British Corps and the field artillery of the Lahore, 24th and 60th Divisions.[2]

A pattern of limited hostilities that was to continue in general throughout the winter was soon established against the opposing enemy formations, the 6th Bavarian Reserve and the 12th Reserve Divisions—a periodic exchange of mortar fire, extensive patrolling, and occasional trench raids. Parties of the 1st Canadian Mounted Rifles, in all more than 400 strong, carried out a particularly successful raid on 20 December near the Corps right boundary. Assaulting from specially constructed galleries leading to craters in no man's land, the Canadians destroyed 26 enemy dug-outs and a machine-gun emplacement, and took almost 60 prisoners.[3]

The largest of a number of raids mounted in January 1917 was one by the 20th and 21st Battalions (4th Brigade) on the 17th. These units were represented by some 860 specially trained all ranks, assisted by sappers of the 4th Field Company. The object was to inflict casualties, take prisoners and booty, and destroy enemy dug-outs three miles east of Lens in the area of the Lens-Béthune railway. Parties of the 18th and 19th Battalions carried out demonstrations on the flank as the assault went in at 7:45 a.m., a time when the enemy usually relaxed his alertness following morning "stand down". Corps and divisional artillery provided adequate fire support in which Canadian machine-gun units joined, while special Royal Engineer units laid down smoke.[4] In one hour the attacking force, operating on an 850-yard front, blew up more than 40 dug-outs, exploded three ammunition dumps, captured two machine-guns and two trench mortars and destroyed several others, taking 100 prisoners of the 11th Reserve Division. Canadian casualties numbered about 40 killed and 135 wounded. The enemy, recording the repulse of "an extraordinarily forceful undertaking" by the Canadians, reported losses of 18 dead, 51 wounded and 61 missing.[5]

On 13 February the 10th Brigade (commanded now by Brig.-Gen. E. Hilliam) carried out a similar operation against the 5th Bavarian Reserve Division. Each of the four battalions (44th, 46th, 47th and 50th) provided a company, 200 strong, and the 10th Field Company and the 67th Pioneer Battalion between them furnished about 70 more men. The raiders inflicted an estimated 160 casualties (including the capture of more than 50 prisoners), and destroyed dug-outs, mine shafts and barbed wire; their own losses totalled approximately 150.[6]

But the most elaborately planned Canadian raid of the winter was an attack on the night of 28 February-1 March by some 1700 all ranks of the 4th Division (representing from left to right the 73rd, 72nd, 75th and 54th Battalions) to reconnoitre and inflict damage on German defences on Hill 145 (see below, p. 258). To achieve surprise the planners ruled out any preliminary bombardment or wire cutting. To aid the attackers cylinders of tear gas and chlorine had been installed along the whole divisional front, but the preliminary discharge of the former served only to alert the enemy (troops of the 16th Bavarian Infantry Division and the 79th Reserve Division), and a changing wind prevented use of the lethal chlorine—indeed the attackers themselves suffered casualties when German shells breached some of the cylinders. The venture was almost a complete failure. While the 12th Brigade parties on the left reached most of their objectives, the enemy discovered those of the 11th Brigade before they were well clear of their own wire, and brought them under withering fire. The Canadians took 37 prisoners: their own casualties numbered 687, including two battalion commanders killed. During the next two days the Germans permitted and even helped our troops to recover their dead.[7]

From 20 March onwards, in preparation for their next major operation (Vimy Ridge, 9 April), the Canadians raided the enemy lines every night. They were costly operations, resulting in some 1400 casualties in two weeks. But this was offset to a great extent by the knowledge which they gained of the enemy's strengths and weaknesses—a knowledge which enabled the Canadians to take their objectives with lighter losses than would otherwise have been possible.

Allied Plans for 1917

The year 1916 had been a costly one for both sides, but for the Entente the tide was turning. The enemy's venture at Verdun had failed and on the Somme Anglo-French forces had dealt the German Army a blow from which it would not recover. On the other side of Europe the Russians had added to

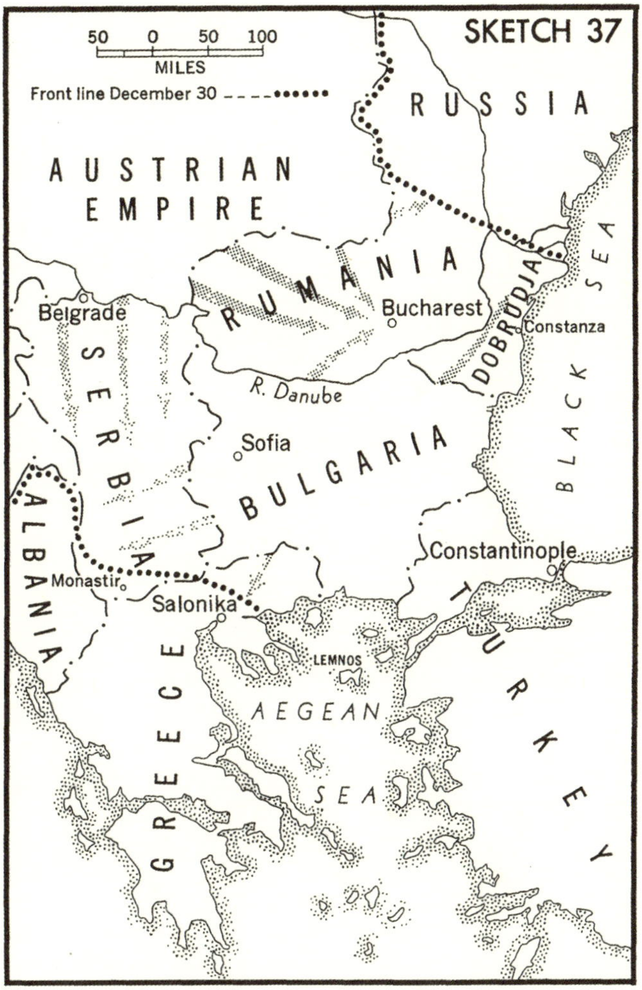

THE BALKAN FRONT 1916

the triumph of the Brusilov offensive by crushing a Turkish invasion of the Caucasus and penetrating 150 miles into Asia Minor. The Revolution, which began on 12 March 1917, did not immediately remove Russia from the war; on the contrary the Russians were destined to launch a further offensive in the summer. At the end of 1916 the Italian Army was pinning down 35 of Austria's 65 divisions, having made some small territorial gains in the autumn battles of the Isonzo (the Sixth, Seventh and Eighth). In Egypt, which throughout 1916 the War Office had declared a defensive theatre, the defeat in July of a Turkish force at Romani, 25 miles east of the Suez Canal, heralded a shifting over to the offensive against Palestine in 1917. The Cameroons and two ports in German East Africa were now in Allied hands.

In Mesopotamia, however, Kut had fallen to the Turks (though it was to be retaken in February 1917), and there had been setbacks in the Balkans. From the Allied "entrenched camp" about Salonika, General Sarrail had launched a Franco-Serbian offensive into western Macedonia which though achieving the recapture of Monastir had fallen short of its main objectives. Rumania had been quickly overthrown by the combined forces of all four enemy powers. As we have noted, the chief German naval activity after the Battle of Jutland had been an intensified submarine campaign. In the final quarter of 1916 U-boats sank a monthly average of well over 50,000 tons of Allied shipping in the English Channel, not counting losses inflicted by submarine-laid mines.

This submarine activity was to increase. The German General Staff was now convinced that the war in the West could not be won on land; the Kaiser's naval advisers had long since despaired of winning it at sea, except by unrestricted submarine warfare. Accordingly, at the beginning of February 1917, all approaches to the British Isles, the French coast and the Mediterranean were proclaimed to be in a state of blockade; any vessel in these waters was liable to be sunk at sight, regardless of type or nationality. Thus Germany hoped before the next harvest—five or six months hence—to crush Britain's will to continue fighting.

On 15-16 November Allied commanders met at Chantilly to approve a plan of action which had as its object "the endowment of the campaigns of 1917 with a decisive character".[8] It was decided that the Armies of the Coalition should carry on such operations as climatic conditions on each front allowed, and would be ready from the first week in February 1917 to undertake coordinated general offensives "with all the means at their disposal". The conference recognized France and Belgium as the principal front. Operations here would take the form of simultaneous French and British attacks—delivered between Lens and the Oise. These would be followed by a secondary French offensive on the Aisne. The whole project was, in effect, a continuation of the Battle of the Somme on a wider front. But within a month of the conference the principal author of these plans, General Joffre, had been supplanted. As Commander-in-Chief of the French Armies he had been the target for parliamentary criticism of Allied reverses (the lack of preparation for the defence of Verdun, the losses at the Somme, and even the defeat of Rumania were cited). On 13 December Premier Briand made him "technical adviser" to the Government, and in his place General Robert Nivelle, who had commanded the Second French Army with conspicuous success at Verdun, was promoted (over the heads of Pétain and Foch) to be General-in-Chief of the French Armies of the North and North-East.[9]

Nivelle immediately produced a new plan, which instead of attrition called for the complete destruction of the enemy's forces. The British and French offensives between the Oise and Lens already proposed would be only preliminary operations designed to pin down the maximum number of Germans. The French would then launch a surprise assault along the Aisne, to secure a break-through between Reims and Soissons. This sudden rupture of the enemy's defences would be accomplished by the same shock tactics (though on a very much larger scale) which Nivelle had employed in capturing Fort Douaumont at Verdun—the exploit which had won him his rapid advancement. Nivelle then visualized a decisive battle in

SKETCH 38

NIVELLE'S PLAN AND THE GERMAN WITHDRAWAL

SPRING 1917

10 0 10

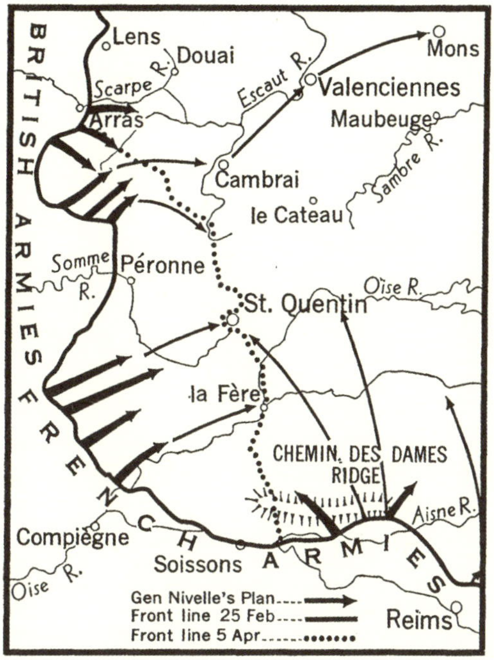

which an Allied "mass of manoeuvre" (or main striking force) would overcome "without chance of failure" all reserves that the enemy might muster. French and British armies would join in "an extremely vigorous exploitation . . . with all the resources at their disposal". Nivelle put the necessary strength of his "mass of manoeuvre" at three armies totalling 27 divisions. To enable him to form a concentration of this size he called for the British to extend their front twenty miles southward to the Amiens-Roye road, thus freeing seven or eight French divisions.[10]

To this plan, which represented a radical change from what had been agreed on at Chantilly, Haig gave general assent. Until he could be sure that the War Office would provide all the necessary additional troops, he undertook to extend his front by no farther than the Amiens-St. Quentin road, a dozen miles short of what Nivelle had asked. He laid down one other condition. The British Admiralty had long urged the capture of Ostend and Zeebrugge, from which German submarines and destroyers were harrying Allied shipping in the Channel; and after the Chantilly Conference Haig had won Joffre's backing for the main Allied offensives to be followed by an Anglo-Belgian advance from the Ypres Salient to clear the whole Belgian coast.[11] Haig now stipulated that should Nivelle's planned operations fail to compel the enemy to abandon the Belgian coast, he would ask for the return of the British divisions which he had supplied on the French left, in order that he might carry out his northern offensive.[12]

It says much for the persuasive powers of General Nivelle that he was able to win the support of Mr. Lloyd George (who on 6 December had succeeded Mr. Asquith as Prime Minister). In the prolonged controversy as to where the enemy should be attacked, the former Secretary of State for War had always been a determined "Easterner", and hence a vigorous opponent of Haig's plans. At an inter-Allied conference in Rome early in January 1917, without consulting his military leaders he had advocated a strong spring offensive on the Austrian front for which the British Government would lend the Italians 250 or 300 heavy guns, with the French being invited to give similar support.[13] But the British Prime Minister's venture into Allied strategy met little support from General Cadorna, and strong opposition from the French delegation, who were ardently backing the Nivelle plan. On Lloyd George's invitation Nivelle came to London in mid-January and gained the War Committee's full support for his project. The attack would be launched not later than 1 April, and Field-Marshal Haig* was instructed to relieve French troops as far as the Amiens-Roye road by 1 March.[15]

Though Haig is on record in his diary as thinking "We are right to comply with the French Government's request", he could not refrain from observing that the conclusions which Nivelle presented for the Conference's approval were but "hastily considered by the War Committee".[16] Neither Haig nor Sir William Robertson, the Chief of the Imperial General Staff, had a high opinion of "our civilian War Committee", and six weeks later the episode of the Calais Conference confirmed Haig's distrust of the British Prime Minister and considerably impaired relations between the British and French Headquarters. The meeting at Calais on 26 February was held ostensibly to deal with the urgent need for improved railway facilities on the British front. But discussion of transportation problems was quickly shelved to allow consideration of a proposal—formulated by Nivelle, Briand and Lloyd George (who had kept it secret from Robertson and Haig)—for the organization of an Allied G.H.Q. in France, commanded by a French Generalissimo (Nivelle). A British Chief of Staff at this headquarters would provide liaison with the British War Committee and would transmit the Generalissimo's operational orders to the British Commander-in-Chief, whose functions would be reduced virtually to those of an Adjutant General—as Haig put it, to "administer the discipline and look after reinforcements".[17]

Both Robertson and Haig were thunderstruck at the proposal and "thoroughly disgusted with our Government and the Politicians". They agreed privately that they "would rather be tried by Court Martial than betray the Army by agreeing to its being placed under the French".[18] After an interview on the 27th with the French War Minister (General Lyautey) and Nivelle, they decided on a compromise. Haig would be subordinate to Nivelle only for the period of the coming offensive, and would have the right of appeal to the British Cabinet against any orders which he considered might endanger the security of his forces. In signing the "Calais Agreement" on 27 February, Sir Douglas made a marginal reservation on his copy: "Signed by me as a correct statement but not as approving the arrangement."

*** Haig's promotion to Field Marshal had been made by the King "as a New Year's gift from myself and the country".[14]**

Having come to terms with the British, General Nivelle was now to run into unexpected trouble at home. The Briand government fell, and the new Minister of War, Paul Painlevé, was hostile to Nivelle and his scheme. There were postponements of the scheduled start of operations, much to the dismay of Field-Marshal Haig, who regarded the forthcoming offensive on the Aisne only as a prelude to his own long-cherished Third Battle of Ypres, which must be launched early in the summer before the rains came to muddy the Flanders plain.

Meanwhile the enemy had been making his own preparations.

The Enemy's New Defensive Tactics

German experience on the Somme had shown that a policy of rigidly defending a fixed line could no longer be relied on, for hostile artillery could not only batter the front trenches out of existence, but could neutralize the entire forward area to a depth of a mile or more. During the 1916 battles, as we have seen, the German First Army's Chief of Staff, Colonel Fritz von Lossberg, had begun moving front line troops into no man's land so as to avoid the opening barrage, which was almost invariably directed on the forward trench lines. Already he had in mind an alternative to fighting in or ahead of the front line, said to be inspired by a French Fifth Army instruction (captured in the summer of 1915), which suggested fighting the main defensive battle at some distance to the rear.[19]

In December 1916 German troops were instructed in a new method of defence described in a booklet, *Principles for the Conduct of Operations in the Defensive Battle in Position Warfare,* written largely by two officers on General Ludendorff's staff.[20] In it the inflexible system of never yielding a foot of ground was abandoned. "In sharp contrast to the form of defence hitherto employed", declared Ludendorff later,

> ...a new system was devised, which, by distribution in depth and the adoption of a loose formation, enabled a more active defence to be maintained.[21]

Instead of conducting a static defence in a succession of trench lines, the defending infantry would fight an elastic defence in a series of zones. Defences were to be laid out with an outpost zone forward of the front trench system or Main Line of Resistance, behind which was a battle zone extending 1500 to 2500 yards back to a Second Line or "artillery protective" position. The less defensible the terrain, or the weaker the defending force, the deeper would be the outpost zone, so as to put the front trench system and the battle zone out of effective range of the attackers' field batteries. Each zone would have numerous strongpoints, with an infantry battalion being responsible for its share of the regimental sector all the way back to the Second Line. Counter-attacks in the battle zone would be delivered by battalions billeted three or four miles to the rear in regimental reserve. If these failed, the leading battalions of counter-attack divisions held in army reserve would be committed from behind the battle zone. Normally such divisions would be stationed several miles behind the front, but the new doctrine provided that prior to an offensive their leading units should be assembled "close behind the Second Line".[22]

With small garrisons in the fortified area too widely dispersed for effective control by battalion or even company commanders, responsibility was decentralized down to the leader of the "group", which (comparable to the British infantry section) consisted of eleven men commanded by an N.C.O. This would be the infantry's tactical unit, and its leader had the right "within certain limits, to retire in any direction before strong enemy fire." No longer, as Ludendorff pointed out in the introduction to his text-book, would the infantryman in the forward positions have to say to himself: "Here I must stand or fall." Under attack the front line would stand firm at some points and yield at others, denying to the enemy the advantage of a uniform rate of advance with constant artillery support. The attacker would thus be able to exploit local successes only by continuing forward without the help of his artillery, and with open flanks. The main battle would follow as counter-attacks were delivered on ground of the defenders' own choice, out of range and view of the attackers' artillery.

When considering these principles of defence, some senior officers expressed concern that the young and half-trained recruits who were replacing the heavy losses at the Somme and Verdun might find an excuse to abandon their posts too readily. In a memorandum, "Experiences of the First Army in the Somme Battles", issued at the end of January 1917, Colonel von Lossberg emphasized the need for a steadfast resistance in every outpost and strongpoint of the forward area.[23] Though this document challenged many of Ludendorff's tactical conceptions, the General authorized its circulation, and incorporated it in a new *Manual of Infantry Training,* which he referred to as "completing" his own text-book.[24] Some conflicting views on detail persisted, but in the main the German Army was to adopt the principle of fighting an elastic defensive battle in depth rather than rigidly holding successive lines of trenches.

While the new doctrine of defence was being demonstrated at special schools of instruction for German staff officers and commanders down to battalion level, the first of five powerful rear positions authorized by Hindenburg and Ludendorff in the previous autumn was nearing completion. This was the *Siegfried-Stellung,* which ran south-east from Arras through St. Quentin to meet the Aisne east of Soissons. It cut a chord across the wide arc of the Noyon salient, and when occupied along its ninety-mile length it would shorten the front between Arras and the Aisne by nearly twenty-five miles. A German withdrawal to the new line would thus effect a considerable economy in manpower, but Ludendorff was at pains to emphasize that no immediate retirement was contemplated. As his instruction issued in November put it, "Just as in time of peace we build fortresses, so we are now building rearward defences. Just as we have kept clear of our fortresses, so we shall keep at a distance from these rearward defences."[25] He opposed suggestions for a withdrawal made by Crown Prince Rupprecht, whose Group of Armies (Sixth, First, Second and Seventh) was holding the

170 miles from the Lys to the Reims area, which included the whole of the sector concerned.

From the end of September more than 65,000 men (including 50,000 prisoners of war, mainly Russian) laboured at building the Siegfried position, or the Hindenburg Line, as it was more popularly called by both the Germans and the Allies. It consisted of two trenches about 200 yards apart, the front one for small sentry garrisons and the second as the main line of defence. Early in February an inspection in the First Army's sector (centred on Cambrai) revealed serious defects in siting, and the Army Commander, General Fritz von Below, and his Chief of Staff, Colonel von Lossberg, gained permission to construct additional defences in accordance with General Ludendorff's doctrine of defence in depth. A new double line of trenches, 200 yards apart, where possible sited on a reverse slope to give concealment from enemy guns, was laid out from 2000 to 3000 yards in front of the original system, which became the support or "artillery-protection" position, known thereafter as the Second Hindenburg Line. Farther north, however, the Sixth Army headquarters failed to take such precautions.[26]

The Withdrawal to the Hindenburg Line

Between 10 January and 22 February the British Fifth Army, in a series of minor but none the less hard-fought engagements preparatory to larger operations, pushed the enemy five miles up the Ancre valley on a four-mile front; and on the night of 22-23 February the Germans fell back three more miles across a front of fifteen miles. The inability of his forces to withstand British pressure in their present positions strengthened Crown Prince Rupprecht's argument for a general retirement to the Hindenburg Line at an early date. On 30 January Ludendorff agreed, not only because the consequent shortening of the front would release thirteen divisions and many artillery units for the projected offensive in Italy, but also because a general retirement could be expected to upset French and British campaign plans. It was in the German interest to delay as long as possible any struggle on the Western Front, in order to allow time for results from the campaign of unrestricted warfare by submarine and cruiser which had begun on 1 February. The deciding factor, however, appears to have been the need for time to replenish supplies of guns and shells, deliveries of which had fallen far short of von Hindenburg's orders and expectations.[27]

On 4 February the High Command issued an order over the Kaiser's signature for a withdrawal of the Seventh Army's right wing, the Second and First Armies, and the left wing of the Sixth Army to the Hindenburg Line between 15 and 18 March. This operation was aptly code-named "Alberich", after the malicious dwarf of the Nibelungen saga,[28] for it called for the devastation of the whole area to be abandoned—nearly 100 miles of front between Soissons and Arras, averaging almost 20 miles in depth. Under this "scorched earth" policy all military installations and useful war material were removed from the existing forward zone, townspeople and villagers were evacuated and their communities razed, livestock were carried away or destroyed, and all wells were either filled in or polluted. To delay an Allied advance the retreating Germans felled trees across the roads, blew large craters at main intersections, and everywhere beset the pursuers' path with ingeniously laid booby-traps. Well organized rearguards covered the German withdrawal, though these received orders not to counter-attack. The skill of the Germans in concealing their plans from the Allies and the success of their delaying tactics helped prevent any effective follow-up. By the morning of 19 March, 29 divisions had completed the withdrawal with a minimum of Allied interference.[29] Four Allied armies found themselves out of contact—from north to south, the right wing of the British Third Army about Arras, the Fifth and Fourth Armies to across the Somme valley, and the left wing of the French between Roye and the Aisne. It took until 5 April to drive in the German outposts and establish a new Allied line in front of the Hindenburg Position.*

The enemy's retirement did not greatly affect the plan of Nivelle's main offensive, which was to be made east of Soissons. But it seriously upset the preliminary offensive in the north, for the Germans in the salient which converging British and French thrusts were to have pinched out had now escaped containment. Time was lacking in which to build new communications across the devastated area, particularly on the French left, where the retreat had been farthest. Accordingly, the northern attack became an all-British operation, the principal aim of which was to outflank the Hindenburg Line from the north and advance towards Cambrai. General Nivelle was forcibly told by Painlevé and Pétain and other high French officers that his scheme was no longer practicable. Army group commanders opposed the plan as a reversion to the discredited pre-war and 1914 overemphasis on offensive action for its own sake. There were also strategic and political objections. Neither the Russians nor the Italians would be able to mount offensives in time to render assistance; and the prospect of America's early entry into the war seemed another good reason for postponing a major French offensive. At one point Nivelle offered his resignation; but this being refused, he continued with his preparations. After various delays the assault on the Aisne was ordered to open on 16 April, the British offensive a week earlier.

The Nivelle Offensive Fails

Although the Nivelle offensive (or the Second Battle of the Aisne as it was named) began later than the British effort, it ended earlier; and since it was the main Allied effort and its outcome greatly affected British operations it will be described first.

* Taking part in the Fourth Army's advance was the Canadian Cavalry Brigade. On 27 March, Lieut. F. M. W. Harvey, Lord Strathcona's Horse, ran into a wired trench and captured a machine-gun, for which daring act he was awarded the V.C.

As we have seen, Joffre had intended to launch his offensive in mid-February. The delays which attended the change of command and the adoption of a new plan, aggravated by unusually cold weather and a crisis in rail transportation, had unfortunate consequences. Nivelle missed a great opportunity to catch the Germans in their withdrawal to the Hindenburg Line; and when he did strike, surprise had been lost. Besides observing the usual signs of an impending attack, the enemy had in mid-February gained possession of the outline plan for the offensive and early in April had captured a French divisional operation order. General Nivelle, knowing this, nevertheless persisted in his plan; the only changes were further postponements of 24 and 48 hours because of bad weather.

By the time the offensive opened on 16 April the enemy had increased his forces in the area from 18 to 42 divisions—fourteen of them made available by the shortening of the front. The French too had benefited by the German withdrawal, which had enabled Nivelle to add eleven infantry and two cavalry divisions to his reserve. The addition of 550 heavy guns gave him a total gun strength of 3800 against the enemy's 2450. Furthermore, he could now attack the Germans north of the Aisne in flank as well as frontally, and enfilade their positions with artillery fire.[80]

The Second Battle of the Aisne brought the French only limited success. Nivelle had hoped to break through the German defences along the Chemin des Dames ridge* in the first two days and then destroy the enemy's reserves in the open. This would have meant advancing more than ten miles in the centre, where the defences were the shallowest. But it quickly became apparent that the artillery preparation had failed to crush the German resistance; the enemy, aware of French plans, had evacuated the forward areas and so escaped bombardment. There were strong counter-attacks, and after a month of fighting the foremost French elements had not moved more than four miles beyond the enemy's front line, while for a twelve-mile stretch north and east of Reims the front remained virtually unchanged.[81] French casualties were enormous; Nivelle reported losses for the first ten days of the battle numbering 96,125, a total which official French sources later raised to 134,000.[82] The German official figures for their own losses for the entire battle were 163,000.[83] Yet, as General Edmonds points out, had the Germans "gained as much ground as Nivelle's Armies did . . . they would have broadcast the battle to the world as a colossal victory".[84] The French Government, disappointed at the failure to achieve a major break-through and dissatisfied with the Commander-in-Chief, did not minimize the seriousness of what they recognized as a defeat, and even allowed the press to exaggerate the losses. On 15 May 1917 Nivelle was transferred to North Africa, and was succeeded by General Pétain.

By this time the French forces, demoralized by heavy casualties, defeatist propaganda and deplorably bad administration, were almost in a state of mutiny. During the summer, particularly in May and June, more than a hundred of what the French Official History calls "acts of collective indiscipline" occurred in 54

* This historic ridge, which had been frequently fought over from the time of Julius Caesar, owed its name to the route travelled by ladies of nobility and the nuns of the Abbey of Soissons.

divisions—infantry units refusing to go into the line, demonstrations against continuing the war, and acts of sabotage and violence. Courts martial convicted 23,385 individuals, but of 412 sentenced to death only 55 men faced the firing squad. The new Commander-in-Chief set about remedying the soldiers' grievances, and by July the situation was largely restored.[35] Meanwhile, thanks to the efforts of more steadfast infantry formations and the artillery—whose fire never slackened—the enemy was kept in the dark. Escaped German prisoners who reported the French mutinies were simply not believed. Had the German High Command realized the gravity of the troubles, it seems probable that in March 1918 Hindenburg might well have attacked the French instead of the British.

Haig's Northern Offensive

Meanwhile the British First and Third Armies had all but completed their offensive about Arras. Though these operations had been ordered by General Nivelle as a diversion to his own effort, changed circumstances were to deprive them of any great strategic significance. Their chief importance now would lie in the extent to which they could subject the enemy to attrition.

The British operations which began on 9 April are known collectively as the Battles of Arras. The opening phase (9-14 April) consisted of the First Battle of the Scarpe—an attack astride that river by the Third Army on an eight-mile front—and the Battle of Vimy Ridge, a simultaneous attack on the adjoining four miles of front by the Canadian Corps and certain formations of the First Army.

While the task of the Canadian Corps was primarily to form a strong defensive flank for the Third Army's effort,[36] the Vimy operation was significant in its own right. The high ground between the Scarpe and the smaller Souchez River, of which the Ridge was the dominant feature, formed a nine-mile barrier across the western edge of the Douai plain. Overlooking Lens to the north, Douai to the east and Arras to the South, Vimy Ridge was tactically one of the most important features on the entire Western Front. In the words of one Canadian observer, from the Lorette spur, north of the Souchez, "more of the war could be seen than from any other place in France".[37] The Ridge was the keystone of the defences linking the new Hindenburg system to the main German lines leading north from Hill 70 to the Belgian coast. Five miles to the east construction of the new *Wotan-Stellung* (known by the British as the Drocourt-Quéant Line) was not yet completed. The Vimy Ridge was therefore a position that the German High Command would not be likely to relinquish without a determined fight.

Together with the Lorette spur, north of the Souchez, the Ridge had fallen to the Germans in October 1914, giving them a secure hold on the industrial area of Lille and the Lens coalfields. During the "race to the sea" the Vimy front became static, but in 1915 French forces recaptured most of the Lorette feature and gained a small, temporary footing on Vimy Ridge. On the whole, however, the enemy not only maintained his position but improved it, and from it his sappers extensively undermined the French positions at the foot of the western slopes. When British forces took over the Vimy sector in March 1916, tunnelling companies of the Royal Engineers forced the Germans to abandon their mining operations. But above ground the enemy still held the upper hand, and in the latter part of May he seized 1500 yards of British front-line and support trenches.[38]

Now the Ridge was to change hands for the last time.

Following a conference of corps commanders held at First Army Headquarters on 21 November, the Canadian Corps drew up plans for a two-corps operation to recapture the whole enemy position from the Arras-Lens road to the Souchez River.[39] The assumption then (December, 1916) was that the Canadians would be assigned the assault on the left, northward from Vimy village.[40] On 19 January 1917, however, the First Army notified General Byng that he would be responsible for capturing the whole of the main crest. His objectives would not include an independent height of 120 metres at the north end of the Ridge, known as "The Pimple", which with the Bois en Hache across the Souchez would be assaulted later by another corps. Active preparations were put in hand for the southern attack, which General Byng would make with his four Canadian Divisions, supplemented by the 5th British Division of the 1st Corps and with Canadian and British heavy artillery in support.

Along the whole German front line it would have been difficult to find terrain better suited to defence, combining the advantages of observation and concealment. The crest of the Ridge was formed by two heights, Hill 135 (measured in metres), immediately north of the village of Thélus, and Hill 145, two miles farther north-west. The western slopes facing the Allied lines rose gradually over open ground which afforded excellent fields of fire for small arms and artillery. (German histories complain, however, that their positions on the narrow forward slope of the Ridge were fully visible to the Canadians.)[41] The reverse slope dropped sharply into the Douai plain, its thick woods providing adequate cover for the enemy's guns. Opposite the Canadian right there was a gradual descent from Hill 135 to the headwaters of the Scarpe, north-west of Arras, with only a few villages and copses breaking the wide expanse of open fields. At its other extremity the Ridge extended beyond Hill 145 to "The Pimple", west of Givenchy*, whence the ground fell quickly to the valley of the Souchez.

The frontage assigned to the Canadians was determined by the objectives requiring early capture. From Hill 135 and Thélus the enemy had unrestricted observation over the area to the south where the Third Army's attack would be made. But the approaches to these objectives were in turn overlooked by Hill 145 and, south-east of it, La Folie Farm, both of which must first be secured. The Canadian attack would therefore be made on a front of 7000 yards, the centre being opposite

* Givenchy-en-Gohelle, not to be confused with Givenchy-lez-la-Bassée, scene of the 1st Canadian Division's fighting in June 1915.

the village of Vimy, which lay on the east side of the Ridge. To enable General Byng to concentrate his forces for this task, early in March the 24th Division of the 1st Corps took over his left from Givenchy-en-Gohelle to Loos, thus setting free the 1st and 2nd Canadian Divisions.

For nearly two years the defenders had been busy constructing fortifications to add to the natural strength of the Ridge. These had been designed in accordance with the old doctrine of a rigid defence, and though the end of 1916 had brought plans for reconstruction on the principles of General Ludendorff's textbook, little had been accomplished by April 1917 to provide the new defence in depth.[42] There were three main defensive lines opposite the Canadian Corps. The advanced field works, five to seven hundred yards deep, consisted of three lines of trench, with deep dug-outs for the foremost garrisons. This forward zone was interspersed by a network of concrete machine-gun emplacements woven about with barbed wire, the whole system being linked by a maze of communication trenches and connecting tunnels.

The German Second Line lay east of the Ridge. On the Canadian left it was a mile to the rear, but because the opposing front lines ran almost due north and south, while the Ridge angled to the south-east, there was a divergence of two miles on the right. It too was well protected by deep belts of wire. Its dug-outs were vast fortified underground chambers, some capable of sheltering entire battalions from hostile shells. From this second position a single-trench Intermediate Line (*Zwischen-Stellung*) reached southward from the village of Vimy through the western edge of Thélus, paralleling the Arras-Lens road. An extension of this line, called by the Germans the *Vimy-Riegel* and by us the Vimy-Lens line, ran north from Vimy to cover the west side of Lens. Still farther east the Third Line snaked its way southward from Lens over the plain, passing in front of the villages of Méricourt and Oppy to join the *Monchy Riegel* east of Arras. In between the First and Third Lines, which at their widest points of separation were more than five miles apart, the Germans had many heavily fortified positions, such as those at Farbus on the east side of the Ridge (2000 yards south of Vimy), and on the western slope Thélus, La Folie Farm (midway between Hills 135 and 145) and the adjacent École Commune. Finally, as noted above, a fourth position—the partly constructed Drocourt-Quéant Line—was intended to contain any Allied success in the Vimy-Lens area.[43]

At the beginning of April 1917 the front from north of Cambrai to north of Lille was the responsibility of General von Falkenhausen's Sixth Army, with 20 divisions forward and the equivalent of six to eight in reserve. In the sector facing the Canadian Corps were the 1st Bavarian Reserve Division, holding Thélus and Bailleul, the 79th Reserve Division, responsible for the Vimy sector, and the 16th Bavarian Infantry Division opposite Souchez.[44] Except for a brief participation in the Somme battles, the 1st Bavarian Reserve Division had been in the Arras area since October 1914. The 79th Reserve Division, raised in Prussia in the first winter of the war, had fought for two years on the Russian front; it was transferred to the Western Front at the end of 1916 and appeared in the Vimy sector at the end of February. The 16th Bavarian Infantry Division, formed in January 1917 from existing Bavarian formations, had so far opposed only Canadian troops—whose raids it had experienced at some cost during February and March.[45]

These divisions had among them only five regiments on the Ridge; and many of their rifle companies were left with only about 75 men each. Each regiment held its portion of the First and Second Lines with its forward battalions and had a second battalion in the Third Line, or immediately to the rear as close support; the third battalions were billeted in rear villages about two hours' march from the battlefield. General von Falkenhausen's five reserve divisions were from ten to twenty-five miles behind the front—as we shall see, too far away to carry out their role of counter-attack. Altogether seven German front-line divisions faced the First and Third Armies, which were preparing to attack with a total of fourteen divisions forward and five in close reserve.[46]

Canadian Plans and Preparations

On 5 March Sir Julian Byng sent General Sir Henry Horne a copy of his "Scheme of Operations", which, with certain amendments made at the direction of the Army Commander, became the plan for the Canadian Corps' attack. The operation would be carried out in four stages dictated by the German zones of defence, the objectives for each being indicated by a coloured line on the map. Each stage would be synchronized with a corresponding advance by the Third Army's 17th Corps, which was attacking on the right of the Canadians.

Attainment of the first objective, the Black Line, at an average distance of 750 yards from the Canadian front trenches, would mean the capture of the German forward defence zone. The Red Line ran north along the *Zwischen-Stellung* on the Canadian right, turning north-westward beyond the crest of the Ridge to include La Folie Farm and Hill 145. It represented the final objective of the formations attacking on the Corps left. On the right, however, two more bounds would be required. The first of these would be to the Blue Line, which included Thélus, Hill 135 and the woods (Bois de Bonval and Count's Wood) overlooking the village of Vimy. The final objective, the Brown Line, covered the German Second Line, running through Farbus Wood, the Bois de la Ville and the southern part of the Bois de Bonval.

A strict time-table governed each stage of the advance. The four divisions of the Canadian Corps, arranged in numerical order from right to left, would assault simultaneously at 5:30 a.m., each with two brigades. They were allowed 35 minutes to gain the Black Line, an advance which on the northern flank should place the 4th Canadian Division on the summit of Hill 145. There would then be a 40-minute pause to allow the troops to re-form, for the Army Commander intended "to guard against the possibility of the barrage running away from the infantry."[47] A further period of twenty minutes was allowed for reaching the Red Line, the final objective of the 3rd and 4th Divisions, whose assaulting units should thus be positioned on the far side of the Ridge by 7:05. The 1st and 2nd Divisions, assisted by the British 13th Infantry Brigade brought in on the left, would then employ their reserve brigades against the remaining objectives. After a pause of two and a half hours on the Red Line they would advance some 1200 yards to the Blue Line, securing the enemy's intermediate position and the village of Thélus and breaching his second-line defences. Finally, after a further halt of 96 minutes, the same brigades would carry the advance beyond the Ridge to their final objectives on the Brown Line.

If this schedule could be maintained, the whole of the eastern escarpment would be in Canadian hands by 1:18 p.m., after an incursion 4000 yards deep into the German defences.[48] While patrols pushed forward a further 500 yards or more to the embankment of the Lens-Arras railway, the final position all along the Corps front would be consolidated against counter-attack by setting up a line of machine-gun posts among the woods on the eastern slope. For this purpose each assaulting battalion would have attached to it two machine-guns, under a machine-gun officer, ready to move forward and participate in the defence of successive objectives. The final outpost line would be backed by a support line just east of the crest and by a main line of resistance, provided with deep dug-outs, 100 yards down the western slope.[49] The plan of operations called for eight tanks to support the 2nd Division's assault on Thélus and its subsequent objectives. Much was not looked for from the use of these new weapons, and infantry and artillery arrangements did not take them into consideration. This was just as well, since in the actual battle the tanks could not negotiate the heavily shelled ground and none got beyond the German support trenches.

Before the infantry attacked, the German defences were to be destroyed by a carefully applied bombardment. The Somme had shown the necessity of thorough artillery preparation against strong positions, and the general principle that "the artillery conquers and the infantry occupies" was held to be particularly significant in the case of the thus far impregnable positions on Vimy Ridge. To this end the First Army strongly reinforced its heavy artillery, making available to the Canadian Corps (in addition to the 1st and 2nd Canadian Heavy Artillery Groups) nine British heavy groups.[50] In all, 245 heavy guns and howitzers were concentrated for the operation. The supporting field artillery, which included seven divisional artilleries and eight independent field artillery brigades, numbered 480 eighteen-pounders and 138 4.5-inch howitzers. Also available to support the Canadians, though at the disposal of the 1st British Corps, were 132 more heavies and 102 field pieces. In addition, a few heavy guns were held under the command of the First Army.[51] The provision of all this fire power gave a density of one heavy gun for every 20 yards of frontage and one field gun for every ten yards.*

The artillery preparation and support was under the direction of Brig.-Gen. E. W. B. Morrison, the Corps G.O.C. Royal Artillery. The preliminary bombard-

* In the artillery preparation at the Somme the proportion had been one heavy gun to 57 yards, and one field gun to 20.

ment would last two weeks. By day the programme called for observed fire on the enemy's trenches, dug-outs, concrete machine-gun emplacements and other strongpoints, and on his ammunition and supply dumps, on road junctions and other key-points in his communications. Both by day and night there would be harassing fire on all known approaches; and machine-guns would engage targets previously dealt with by the artillery in order to prevent or hinder reconstruction. Particular attention was paid to cutting the German wire in the forward areas, in which process a new fuse (No. 106), specially designed for use with high explosive shell where splinter effect was required above ground, was to prove highly satisfactory.[52] On the day of the attack field guns would put down a rolling barrage in front of the infantry in average lifts of 100 yards, while ahead of this a series of standing barrages would be established on known defensive systems by 18-pounders and medium and heavy howitzers. The allotment of artillery ammunition for each of the two corps (the Canadian assaulting, the 1st Corps supporting) was more than 42,500 tons in "bulk", in addition to a daily quota of nearly 2500 tons.[53]

A number of heavy guns detailed for counter-battery work would engage the principal active enemy batteries. The concept of Counter Battery in the British Army was derived from the French, and was initially developed on the Somme by the 5th British Corps from whom the Canadian Corps took it over. The object was to protect the infantry from hostile artillery during critical periods by bringing accurate and effective concentrations on the enemy batteries. Under perfect conditions the task was difficult enough, and required a high state of technical efficiency, good liaison between the artillery and the assaulting troops, and sound intelligence about the enemy. In bad weather each of these factors became critically important. The intelligence organization evolved by the Canadian artillery was an intricate and highly efficient system which could function under practically any conditions. It drew its information from aerial observation and photographs, ground observers, survey and sound ranging sections, and liaison officers. Wireless interceptions, captured documents and the interrogation of prisoners of war made an important contribution. Information from all these sources was rapidly collated and quickly transferred to the gun positions by an elaborate communication system.[54]

Dumps for storing the vast amount of ammunition required for the operation and routes for transporting it and other stores were among the many concerns of the British and Canadian sappers. Within the Canadian forward area more than 25 miles of road had to be repaired and maintained; the construction of new routes included three miles of plank road. A system of twenty miles of tramway in the Corps area was reconditioned and extended. Over these rails light trains drawn by gasoline engines, or more often by mules, hauled forward daily 800 tons or more of ammunition, rations and engineer stores; and there were some 300 push trucks for evacuating wounded. The sudden concentration of 50,000 horses within a restricted area where very little water existed necessitated the large-scale construction of reservoirs, pumping installations and 45 miles of pipe lines in order to meet the daily requirement of 600,000 gallons. In order to ensure good communications in the Canadian zone, signallers added to existing circuits twenty-one miles of cable, burying it seven feet deep to withstand enemy shelling, and sixty-six miles of unburied wire. As the area was in full view of the enemy, most of this work had to be done at night.

The protective tunnelling constructed preparatory to the Battle of Arras, and especially Vimy Ridge, represented one of the great engineering achievements of the war. Tunnelling companies excavated or extended eleven subways of a total length of almost four miles, leading to the Canadian front line. In these electrically lit subways, 25 feet or more underground, telephone cables and water mains found protection from enemy shelling. The subways provided a covered approach for troops moving up for the assault, or in relief, and they allowed a safe and speedy evacuation of the wounded. Chambers cut into their walls housed brigade and battalion headquarters, ammunition stores, and dressing stations; while included in this underground accommodation were several deep caverns, left from chalk-quarrying operations of an earlier day, the largest of which—Zivy cave—had room for an entire battalion.[55]

Unhampered by false notions of security—only the time of the attack was kept secret—Canadian commanders at all levels freely briefed their subordinates and exercised them in their forthcoming role. Under General Byng's personal direction a full-scale replica of the battle area was laid out in a field to the rear, constructed and kept up to date by air photographs supplemented by reports of aerial observers. German trenches were represented by broad white tapes, and flags of various colours identified strongpoints and other special features. While units and formations were in reserve they rehearsed repeatedly on this model from platoon to divisional level, every care being taken to make the exercises realistic. A rolling barrage was simulated by mounted officers with flags moving forward at the appropriate pace. Officers and men carried exactly what they would carry in the attack, and thus loaded practised getting rapidly out of jumping-off trenches, advancing over broken ground, and dealing with various forms of enemy resistance. By the day of the attack all ranks knew just where they would have to go and what to do when they got there.[56]

This emphasis on detailed rehearsals, and indeed the whole nature of the tactics to be used at Vimy, reflect the influence of General Nivelle's successful counter-offensive near Verdun in December 1916. Here eight French divisions, assaulting in two waves on a six-mile front with exceedingly strong artillery support, had recovered ground lost in previous enemy attacks and inflicted very heavy casualties on five German divisions. In preparation for Vimy and Arras, early in January a group of British officers went to Verdun to study the French operation. General Currie was a member of the party, and on his return he delivered at Corps and divisional headquarters a series of profitable lectures on the lessons of Verdun.[57]

The preparatory bombardment began on 20 March; but for the first thirteen days, in order to conceal the full extent of the artillery support, about half the batteries remained silent. Guns of the adjacent 1st Corps on the left and the 17th Corps on the right cooperated in dealing with targets on the Canadian flanks. Then on 2 April the intensive phase started, as from the heavy artillery drawn up in a great arc extending 22,000 yards from Bully Grenay (north-west of Lens) to the outskirts of Arras a crushing bombardment fell on the German positions. One Canadian observer records that the shells poured "over our heads like water from a hose, thousands and thousands a day".[58] Aptly the enemy named this period "the week of suffering".[59] More than a million rounds of heavy and field ammunition, with a total weight of 50,000 tons, battered the limited area on which they fell into a pock-marked wilderness of mud-filled craters. The villages of Thélus, Farbus and Givenchy were systematically destroyed so as to deny them to the enemy. At many points trenches were completely demolished. German ration parties, which had formerly reached the front line in fifteen minutes, now often took six hours to get forward along the broken and shell-swept communication trenches. Rations arrived cold and spoiled, and many of the front companies were without fresh food for two or three days at a time. German accounts afterwards cited this breakdown in the food supply as a major cause of weakness in the defence.[60]

In order to gain accurate information about possible changes in the German dispositions there were nightly raids into the enemy's lines during the bombardment. These varied in size from small patrols to the 600 all ranks sent out by the 10th Canadian Infantry Brigade on 31 March to investigate the defences in front of the Pimple.[61] The artillery depended increasingly upon the Royal Flying Corps to seek out hostile gun positions and perform registration and spotting duties for our batteries. In carrying out these tasks No. 16 Squadron, attached to the Canadian Corps, had to contend with bad flying weather and determined opposition from German fighter pilots. Although outnumbered on the Vimy-Arras front, the enemy had the advantage in both speed and fire-power.* Despite heavy losses the R.F.C. continued its reconnaissance programme and undertook limited bombing operations against German airfields and railway installations. Of an estimated 212 guns opposite the Canadian Corps, 83 per cent were located by various means, including aerial observation.[63]

While much of the air fighting took place over the German lines, Canadian troops noticed and were impressed with the skill and audacity of one of the enemy pilots, identified as Lieut. Baron Manfred von Richthofen.[64] Towards the end of 1916 Richthofen had painted his machine red, a colour later adopted by his entire squadron.[65] In the spring of 1917 gaudy colour schemes became quite common among German fighter units.[66]

It was recognized that the enemy's main defensive strength on Vimy Ridge lay in the immunity of his forward dug-outs to shellfire, even though these shelters were designed and sited according to principles that had become obsolete.

* Germany's 115 m.p.h. Albatros biplane fighter carried two machine-guns. In general, British and French fighters of this period were some fifteen miles an hour slower, though more manoeuvrable, and were armed with a single Vickers or Lewis gun.[62]

French attacks of 1915 had failed partly because of the speed with which the Germans emerged from such shelters after the opening bombardment, and it was here that the Canadians expected the greatest resistance. General Byng's planners therefore sought to achieve a measure of tactical surprise. In the circumstances the only hope of doing this was to keep the enemy in doubt as to the time of the attack. Accordingly, as zero hour drew near the artillery slackened its fire, and the customary final bombardment just before the assault was dispensed with.

Six months earlier General Foch had declared that a "sufficiently accurate and adequate artillery preparation" would be necessary for the capture of the Ridge. By the evening of 8 April, Easter Sunday, this requirement seemed to have been fulfilled. As the firing died down the gunners made final adjustments for the morrow. Ammunition was carefully stacked, shells were fused, and wherever possible barrels of water were made available to cool overheated guns. Fifteen thousand Canadians*, the first wave, waiting to move up for the assault, were confident in the knowledge that everything possible had been done to ensure success.

For once the weather was propitious. A sharp frost on the previous evening had hardened the mud. The day had been fine and clear, but now, as night fell, the barometer was dropping and the air was turning much colder.

The Attack Goes In, 9 April

As darkness gathered, the infantry battalions began moving forward to their assembly areas, guided by stakes marked with luminous paint. Some used the newly completed subways to reach the front lines; others, forced to cross open ground, suffered casualties from the enemy's usual machine-gun and artillery harassing fire. At first the night was bright with a moon just past the full, but the sky clouded later, cloaking the movements of the assembling troops. Through lanes cut in the Canadian wire the forward companies filed into no man's land to occupy the shell-holes and narrow ditches from which they would assault. All ranks had been cautioned to observe strict silence, and the assembly was completed, in some cases to within a hundred yards of the enemy's outposts, with only a few local alarms being given. Enemy signal centres in forward and back areas were special targets in the later phase of the preliminary bombardment. The destruction of most of the German telephone lines by shellfire meant that such reports had to be relayed by runner; and none would reach the rear in time for a general alarm to be raised. All units were in position by 4:00 a.m., every man having received a rum ration and a hot meal.[68]

Shortly before dawn there was a further drop in the temperature and a driving north-west wind swept the countryside with snow and sleet. Consequently

* The attachment of the British 5th Division (in corps reserve) and British artillery, engineer and labour units, had brought the Canadian Corps to a strength of approximately 170,000 all ranks, of whom 97,184 were Canadians.[67]

a bombing programme by the Royal Flying Corps had to be abandoned. Physically discomforting as the storm was to the waiting troops, it gave them the advantage of assaulting with the wind at their backs and in the defenders' faces. It also had the effect of prolonging the darkness beyond zero hour, which had been set to coincide with first light; but so well had the attackers rehearsed their roles that the continued darkness was no serious handicap.

Promptly at 5:30 on the morning of Easter Monday, 9 April, the attack on Vimy Ridge opened with the thunderous roar of the 983 guns and mortars supporting the Canadians. The main field artillery barrage was provided by one gun to every 25 yards of front. These guns, opening at zero hour, fired for three minutes on the enemy's foremost trenches at three rounds a minute, and then lifted 100 yards every three minutes, slowing their rate of fire to two rounds per minute. This was supplemented by 18-pounder standing barrages, 4.5-inch howitzer concentrations, barrages by heavy guns and howitzers, and the continuous fire of 150 machine-guns,* creating a bullet-swept zone 400 yards ahead. This employment of machine-guns for barrage and supporting fire was on a scale unprecedented in military history. Other guns and mortars bombarded German battery positions and ammunition dumps with high explosive and gas shells, while some mortars laid smoke in front of Thélus and Hill 135. This great volume of fire neutralized a large proportion of the enemy's guns, and the response of the remainder to the frantic S.O.S. rocket signals from the German front lines was weak and ineffective, the ill-directed counter-barrage falling well behind the attacking troops.

The ground over which the Canadians had to advance was peculiarly difficult. The heavily laden infantry had to pick their way between deep shell-holes and negotiate a maze of shattered trenches and the torn remnants of wire entanglements. In some places great mine craters from former operations presented insuperable obstacles that had to be by-passed, and everywhere the continuous shelling had pulverized the earth into vast puddles of clammy mud. Nevertheless the long line of twenty-one battalions pushed forward in good order, keeping well up to the barrage. On the right the 1st Division, commanded by Major-General Currie, attacked on a frontage of more than a mile with six assaulting battalions—from right to left the 5th, 7th and 10th Battalions of the 2nd Brigade (Brig.-Gen. F. O. W. Loomis), and the 15th, 14th and 16th Battalions of the 3rd Brigade (Brig.-Gen. G. S. Tuxford). Crossing the devastation of no man's land, the forward companies reached what was left of the enemy's foremost trench while most of the surviving defenders were still in their deep dug-outs. Quickly overpowering the sentries, the leading troops left parties to guard dug-out and tunnel exits until the mopping-up wave arrived. Even at the second trench some of the garrison were caught still underground. As the Canadians pushed on they engaged in some hand-to-hand fighting, but the main opposition came from

* The total number of machine-guns under the Canadian Corps for the operation was 358. Each of the sixteen Canadian M.G. Companies and the four companies of the British 5th Division had 16 Vickers, and the 1st Canadian Motor Machine Gun Brigade had 38. These figures do not include the "liberal" supply of Lewis guns with the infantry battalions.[69]

snipers firing at point-blank range and resolute machine-gun crews manning their strongly-emplaced weapons to the last. About 100 yards beyond the now unrecognizable Arras-Lens road lay the *Zwölfer-Graben*, which marked the southern end of the Black Line objective in the Canadian sector. Here both brigades ran into fire from well-sited machine-guns, and losses were heavy. One by one these enemy strongpoints were attacked with grenade and bayonet and the guns silenced.[70] Among that day's many deeds of heroism was that of Private W. J. Milne, of the 16th Battalion, who when his company was held up by a machine-gun, crawled on hands and knees to within bombing distance, putting all the crew out of action and capturing the gun. He was awarded the Victoria Cross—posthumously, for he was killed later in the day.[71]

In the right centre of the Corps attack, Major-General Burstall's 2nd Division, advancing on a 1400-yard front with four battalions forward (the 18th and 19th Battalions of the 4th Brigade (Brig.-Gen. R. Rennie) and the 24th and 26th Battalions of the 5th Brigade (Brig.-Gen. A. H. Macdonell)), had much the same experience. Walking, running and occasionally jumping across no man's land, the men followed closely the whitish-grey puffs that marked the exploding shrapnel of the barrage. Cooperating aeroplanes swooped low sounding their klaxon horns and endeavouring to mark the progress of the troops in the driving snowstorm. As we have seen, the eight tanks attached to the Division had been unable to negotiate the gripless mud and the deep shell craters and were left behind early in the battle.[72] Opposition stiffened at the second German line, and, as on other sectors of the front, only timely acts of individual daring and initiative kept the advance moving.

Such was the exploit of Lance-Sergeant E. W. Sifton, of the 18th Battalion. Spotting a hidden machine-gun that was causing casualties to his battalion, he leapt into the German trench and overthrew the gun, bayoneting every one of the crew. Then as a party of Germans advanced on him down the trench, he held them off with bayonet and clubbed rifle until his comrades arrived to end the unequal fight. Sifton won the V.C., but like Private Milne he never learned of the award; he was shot down by one of the Germans he had wounded.[73]

Both the 1st and 2nd Divisions were reported at the Black Line by 6:15—forty-five minutes after zero.[74] The 3rd Division's advance encountered only light opposition in the first phase, so completely had the heavy artillery destroyed the enemy's defences. Major-General Lipsett attacked on the right, opposite Bois de la Folie, with Brig.-Gen. J. H. Elmsley's 8th Brigade (1st, 2nd and 4th Canadian Mounted Rifles); on the left, headed for the École Commune, were the assaulting battalions of the 7th Brigade (Brig.-Gen. A. C. Macdonell)—The Royal Canadian Regiment, P.P.C.L.I., and the 42nd Battalion. The first large bag of prisoners was taken by the 2nd C.M.R., who from a tunnel behind the second trench line captured 150 surprised Saxons of a battalion of the 263rd Reserve Regiment (79th Reserve Division).[75] With German trenches obliterated, there were some instances of troops failing to recognize landmarks and running into their own barrage, but in general the attack went like clockwork, and by 6:25 the capture of the Black Line by both brigades had been confirmed.[76] The 4th Division, as we shall see, encountered trouble and could not complete the first phase of its attack for some hours.

After the planned pause, during which it consolidated its first objective, the 1st Division resumed the advance at 6:45, the original rear companies of the forward battalions taking the lead. It was now light enough for them to see the next objective, the enemy's Intermediate Line, which lay 700 yards ahead, along the far edge of a wide, saucer-like depression. The wind had turned, driving snow across the front and carrying smoke southward from Thélus. Thus the Bavarians could not see the attack coming until it was almost upon them. Those who were not captured fled as fast as they could through the hampering mud; within the first five minutes, what appeared to be a full battalion was seen retreating over the sky-line towards Farbus Wood.[77] By shortly after seven o'clock the Division had taken the left half of its second objective, the Red Line, which coincided with the *Zwischen-Stellung,* except for 500 yards on the right where the German trenches turned sharply to the south-east. To capture these a new attack would be mounted by the 1st Brigade (Brig.-Gen. W. A. Griesbach), brought forward from reserve.

In the 2nd Division's sector the Red Line ran just east of the Lens road and included the battered hamlets of Les Tilleuls, immediately west of Thélus. The supporting battalions of the 4th and 5th Brigades had come forward—the 21st Battalion to attack and pass through Les Tilleuls, the 25th to occupy the *Turko-Graben,* which reached northward behind the road. On the way to its objective the 21st Battalion found in a large cave under the shell-torn ruins of the village two German battalion headquarters, and sent 106 prisoners to the rear. At that stage of the advance its own casualties numbered 215.[78] The 25th Battalion quickly seized the Turko-Graben, capturing two 77-mm. guns and eight machine-guns, and with the aid of mop-up parties from the 22nd Battalion took close to 400 prisoners. Its casualty list of more than 250 testified to the strength of the opposition it had encountered.[79] By eight o'clock the 1st and 2nd Divisions were reported on the Red Line, the halfway mark in their advance to the crest at their end of the ridge.[80]

Meanwhile the 3rd Division had reached the crest at 7:30 and occupied the western edge of the Bois de la Folie. The value of sending Vickers machine-guns forward with the assaulting battalions had been amply demonstrated. On the right of the divisional front, two detachments of the 8th Machine Gun Company had reached the Arras-Lens road ahead of the infantry (1st C.M.R.) which they were supporting; between them the two guns inflicted an estimated 100 casualties. One detachment caught an enemy battalion headquarters withdrawing towards the Bois de Bonval. Pursued by the fire of this troublesome gun, reads a German account, the battalion commander, his staff, and twenty men went back along the communication trench, knee-deep in mud, towards the second-line position; but most of the staff and all the men were killed or wounded before reaching it.[81] At the same time the 8th Brigade's centre battalion, still the 2nd C.M.R., had found

La Folie Farm a mass of rubble and overrun it without opposition. In the orchards to the north, however, the 7th Brigade was heavily engaged; here the enemy withdrew from his dug-outs and broken trenches only to launch ineffective local counter-attacks against The Royal Canadian Regiment and its point of junction with the 4th C.M.R. Consolidation began on the east side of the Ridge as engineer detachments arrived and carrying parties of the reserve battalion from each brigade brought forward tools and wire. At about nine o'clock, when it was learned that the 4th Division on the left had not yet captured Hill 145, the 7th Brigade was called on to establish a defensive flank from the Bois de la Folie, through the former German third trench, to the original front line. The P.P.C.L.I. took over part of the front of the 42nd Battalion, which in turn extended to the left to cover the new flank. For the rest of the day both units were harassed by small-arms fire from the top of the hill.[82]

Leaving the 3rd Division on its second and final objective, and before dealing with the 4th Division's operations on the left flank, let us once more follow the fortunes of the lst and 2nd Divisions as they completed their assigned tasks on the Corps right.

The Advance to the Blue and Brown Lines

By half-past nine reserve brigades had moved up to the Red Line, and were ready to advance on the Blue Line objective. In General Currie's sector the 1st Brigade had deployed the 1st, 3rd and 4th Battalions. Because of the 2nd Division's widening front, the 13th Brigade (of the British 5th Division) was brought in on the left of Brig.-Gen. Ketchen's 6th Brigade, which attacked with the 31st, 28th and 29th Battalions.

On the extreme right the 1st Battalion ran into spirited resistance at the *Zwischen-Stellung* before capturing the position and taking 125 prisoners. Elsewhere the leading waves, advancing as if on parade, met remarkably little opposition, and casualties came mainly from shellfire. Capture of the Blue Line was reported by the 1st Division shortly after eleven o'clock, and a little later by the 2nd Division. While the 29th Battalion overran Thélus Trench north of the village and took the south end of Hill 135, the 28th and 31st Battalions, carrying out the attack "in precisely the same manner as it had been worked out on the practice fields", cleared the ruins of Thélus and moved on to the high ground beyond.[83] On the divisional left two battalions of the British brigade advanced around the northern slopes of Hill 135 to occupy Count's Wood, the Bois de Bonval and the Bois de Goulot.[84]

As the men of the 1st and 2nd Divisions neared their third objective, there was an unexpected break in the stormclouds and spring sunshine flooded the air. The enemy was given a sudden view of the high ground about Thélus covered with Canadian troops, some advancing steadily over the Ridge while others worked methodically at consolidating their positions. "Thus for a fleeting moment was revealed the final issue of the day: the Germans saw that the Ridge was lost, the Canadians knew that it was won."[85] Then the weather worsened. Early in the afternoon the sleet began again, and the day closed with intermittent snow flurries driven before a gusty westerly breeze.

After a halt of ninety minutes, during which machine-guns were brought forward, the two divisions began advancing on their final objective, Brig.-Gen. Griesbach keeping his 3rd and 4th Battalions forward, and the 6th Brigade employing the 27th Battalion and a company of the 29th. As we have seen, the Brown Line covered the German Second Position on the eastern slope of the Ridge, and its generally south-easterly direction meant that the 1st Division still had 3000 yards to cover on the right flank, though opposite the 13th Brigade on the left the distance tapered off to nothing. As the British brigade prepared to sweep south-eastward through the still uncaptured portion of the northerly woods, the 1st and 6th Canadian Brigades began wheeling half-left in order to attack their objectives frontally. Of the field artillery maintaining the barrage, the rear batteries were out of range; only the advanced batteries could now be utilized. By firing their barrages in successive lifts from right to left, these gave the troops on the right the additional time required to reach their part of the German wire.[86] The men of the 27th Battalion made sure of receiving due credit for the captured Germans they sent to the rear by displaying their unit designation in green paint on the backs of their prisoners.[87]

Since it had been foreseen that the artillery fire would not have sufficiently reduced the wire on the right, each forward company of the 1st and 3rd Battalions had been issued 24 pairs of wire-cutters, and a number of wire-breakers to be attached to rifles. By this means the men of the 1st Brigade were able to get through both belts of wire without losing the barrage. Beyond the crest they had an excellent view of the Douai plain, and from above Farbus Wood the Brigade's machine-gunners effectively engaged enemy transport on the Willerval-Vimy road. Moving rapidly down the reverse slope the Canadians overran the German batteries, from which the crews had hastily withdrawn. Patrols, crossing the enemy's Second Line trench, set up observation posts on the far edge of the wood. At mid-afternoon Griesbach was called on to throw back his right flank so as to maintain contact with the 51st Division, whose attack at the left of the Third Army front had only partly succeeded.

Farther north the 6th Brigade's final attack was resisted by the enemy in the Bois de la Ville both with machine-guns and with field guns firing point-blank. But the attackers knocked out the machine-guns with rifle grenades, and a downhill bayonet charge by troops of both battalions overran the German gun-pits and trenches.[88] Among the 250 captured were the commander of the 3rd Bavarian Reserve Regiment and his staff. Meanwhile the 13th British Brigade had cleared the Bois du Goulot from north to south. Its capture of nine guns and howitzers brought to a total of 31 the number of pieces taken by the 1st and 2nd Canadian Divisions in the day's fighting.

Earlier in the afternoon, at 2:40, as soon as the capture of the Brown Line seemed assured, General Byng had telephoned the First Army pointing out the possibility of using a cavalry regiment to exploit the success of his two right-hand divisions.[89] Employment of the 1st Cavalry Division to push forward and secure important rail and canal crossings in the Douai plain had been included in an appreciation issued by General Horne twelve days before the battle.[90] Yet in spite of the C.-in-C.'s known predilection for cavalry operations the emphasis had been upon treating Vimy Ridge as a limited objective, and the rigid time-table required for effectively coordinating artillery and infantry in the attack had resulted in the exclusion from the Canadian Corps' scheme and the First Army's artillery plan of any participation by the cavalry.[91] On 5 April an order placing the 1st Cavalry Division under General Horne was cancelled,[92] so that on the afternoon of the battle G.H.Q.'s permission had to be obtained before complying with General Byng's request.[93] A reply was slow in coming; and in any event opportunity had gone by, for (as the British Official Historian points out) "Only by immediate exploitation of the situation on the ridge at 7:15 a.m. could such action on the part of the cavalry have been brought within the realms of possibility".[94] In the late afternoon the 9th Cavalry Brigade was placed at the disposal of the First Army, with one squadron being detailed to reinforce the Canadian Light Horse, which had already seen action.[95]

Shortly after two o'clock the Corps Commander had ordered a Canadian squadron to "push on to Willerval". At 4:20 p.m. two mounted patrols, totalling some twenty men, set out from Farbus for Willerval, a scant mile to the east. One patrol captured ten Germans in the village, but was in turn engaged by a machine-gun and lost half its men and horses; the other was all but wiped out by rifle fire. The main body of the squadron was shelled and half its horses were killed.[96] Nevertheless the action, though costly and unsuccessful, was not without effect on the enemy: German reports that "a strong force of English cavalry had broken through into Willerval" led to orders being issued for a three-battalion counter-attack on the village.[97] Scarcely had the remnants of the Canadian Light Horse patrols returned, when observers on the Ridge reported "enemy advancing in three waves" towards Farbus.[98] The threatened counter-attacks, however, failed to develop.*

With the capture of the Brown Line the three divisions on the Canadian Corps right had taken their objectives on schedule. It is time now to turn back to zero hour and see what had been happening in the 4th Division's sector on the Corps left.

The Fight for Hill 145, 9-10 April

Hill 145, the 4th Division's principal objective, was the highest and most important feature of the whole of Vimy Ridge. As long as it remained in German hands, enemy watchers could observe all movement in the valley of the Souchez

* These were troops of three reserve battalions rushed in from Lille to reinforce the 1st Bavarian Reserve Division and given orders to recapture the southern half of Hill 135 while the 79th Reserve Division counter-attacked from the north. But, according to German sources, regimental commanders, unaware of these instructions, held the new arrivals to fill gaps in their defences.[99]

OUT OF THE TRENCHES

Displaying their souvenirs, Canadians who fought at Courcelette mount a motor truck that will carry them to their rest billets behind the lines.

ON VIMY RIDGE

In this striking photograph, taken on 9 April 1917 during the battle, a detached party of Germans who have been overrun in the initial Canadian assault of the Ridge surrender to follow-up elements.

A REST DURING BATTLE

Vimy Ridge, probably 9 April 1917. As reserves push through to further objectives, Canadian infantrymen take shelter in a machine-gun emplacement which they have captured.

CANADIAN CAVALRY AT VIMY RIDGE

A patrol of the Canadian Light Horse sets out for Willerval on the first afternoon of the battle.

and its southern offshoot, Zouave Valley, which ran behind the 4th Division's front. Once taken, however, Hill 145 would afford its captors a commanding view of the German rearward defences in the Douai plain and on the Ridge itself. It was thus a valuable prize, though the task of attaining it was formidable.

As might be expected, the defences on Hill 145 were particularly strong. The German First Line here consisted of two trenches; the rounded summit of the hill itself was ringed with two more. Though these had suffered severely from the preliminary bombardment, the garrison had comparative immunity in deep mine workings; and on the reverse slope a system of deep dug-outs (the *Hangstellung*) housed the reserve companies. Major-General Watson hoped to overrun the forward slope position by surprise, and by means of artillery and machine-gun barrages to stop any counter-attacks from the *Hangstellung* or from Givenchy during consolidation. But under the enemy's scrutiny surprise was more difficult to achieve here than anywhere else on the Vimy front. The assembly trenches, for instance, had to be dug well forward in order to shorten the distance of the assault; yet any activity in Zouave Valley invited a heavy barrage. Fortunately the enemy was more interested in concealing certain offensive intentions of his own. It was learned later that the 16th Bavarian Division had planned an attack to capture part of the 4th Canadian Division's front-line trenches, with a view to gaining complete command of Zouave Valley. But the operation was based on the use of gas shell, and a persistently unfavourable wind as well as other adverse factors had forced its postponement.[100] With less enemy interference therefore than was expected six subways leading from communication trenches eight to ten feet deep were tunnelled into the eastern slopes of Zouave Valley. Through them troops could reach assembly trenches within 150 yards of the German front line.[101]

General Watson assaulted with the 11th Brigade, commanded by Brig.-Gen. V. W. Odlum, on the right, directed against Hill 145; on the left the 12th Brigade (Brig.-Gen. J. H. MacBrien) was to seize its sector of the German front-line position and cover the northern flank. Each brigade was strengthened by the addition of a battalion of the 10th Brigade (respectively the 47th and 46th Battalions); and the 11th Brigade also had in reserve the 85th Battalion, which had arrived in France two months earlier to replace the 12th Brigade's 73rd Battalion (see above, p. 225).

The 11th Brigade's attack was initially successful on its right, the 102nd Battalion seizing its half of the forward slope and the 54th passing through to consolidate on the summit. Farther north, however, things did not go so well. A portion of German trench had been left undestroyed by the heavy artillery at the request of the commanding officer of the left assaulting battalion (the 87th), who hoped to put it to good use when captured.[102] From this position machine-gun fire cut down half the 87th's leading wave and pinned the right of the supporting 75th Battalion to their assembly trenches. Those who could pressed on, though harassed in flank and rear by machine-gun fire from the uncaptured sector, and from Germans who emerged from mine shafts and dug-outs after the attacking wave had passed. Then came murderous fire from the second trench, whose garrison had been given ample time to man their positions. The entire left wing of the 11th Brigade's attack broke down, and the 54th Battalion, its open flank under counter-attack, was forced to withdraw. Thus for a time the Brigade was left with only the 102nd Battalion on its objective, the south-western slope of the hill. The presence of this unit prevented any artillery bombardment of the German-occupied trench; but at one o'clock bombing parties of the 87th Battalion, supported by Stokes mortars and machine-guns, successfully attacked the troublesome position. Before dark, two companies of the 85th Battalion overran the two remaining trenches on the west side of the summit, silencing the harrying enemy fire from the hill.[103]

An attempted German counter-attack had as little success as the one which had failed to materialize farther south. That morning von Falkenhausen, commander of the Sixth Army, not realizing the extent of the Canadian Corps' success, was still regarding his reserve divisions primarily as a relief, to be kept intact for employment in a long drawn-out defensive battle, and not to be used as a counter-attack force. Accordingly, he first directed resting battalions of the forward divisions to advance to the battle area and mount local counter-attacks.[104] At 6:00 p.m. a reserve battalion of the 16th Bavarian Infantry Division was ordered to regain the northern slope of Hill 145. It was midnight before the troops reached the Pimple, whence the attack was to be launched. In the darkness many of the men lost their way, some abandoning their short field boots in the mud; those who eventually got close to the objective were dispersed by the fire of a single machine-gun. A pre-dawn attempt to reoccupy the first trench east of the summit, which the Germans had abandoned during the night, was forestalled by parties of the 75th and 85th Battalions.[105]

Meanwhile on the division's left the 12th Brigade after an encouraging start had also run into difficulty. Three battalions made the assault—from right to left the 38th, 72nd and 73rd. Two mines exploded at zero hour killed many of the garrison opposite the 73rd Battalion; the survivors fled as the Canadians approached. All three battalions quickly took the German first trench, and here the 73rd consolidated to form a firm left flank. The other two units had to fight hard for the second trench, the 72nd Battalion successfully bombing it from a flank when frontal assault failed. The ground which the 38th had to cross was so badly cut up that the men could not keep up with the barrage; some of the wounded fell into water-filled shell-holes and were drowned. Emerging from dug-outs at unexpected places the defenders put up a spirited resistance, though the Germans too received their share of surprises. Some 75 occupants of a dug-out just over the crest were confronted by an officer of the 38th Battalion, Captain T. W. MacDowell, who called on them to surrender, tricking them into supposing that he had a large force behind him. They were marched out in groups of twelve, only to find that the "large force" consisted of two men! For this intrepid act, which materially aided his battalion to gain its objective, MacDowell (who had already won the D.S.O. at the Somme) was awarded the V.C.[106]

MAP 7

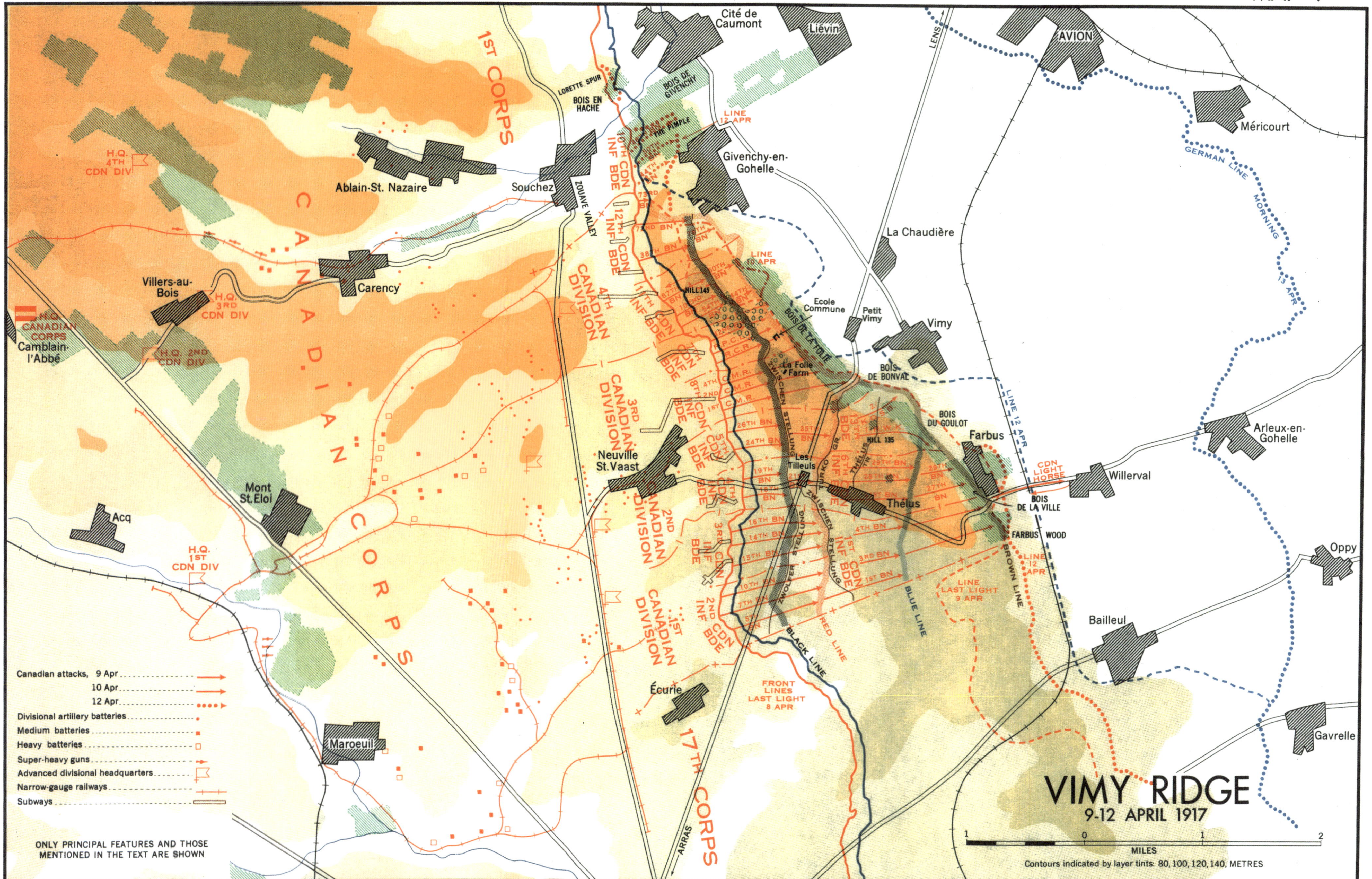

Reproduced by Army Survey Establishment

Compiled and drawn by Historical Section G.S.

Up to this point an effective smoke barrage had combined with the snowstorm to conceal the operations on the left flank from observers on the Pimple. But now the smoke began to clear and soon heavy machine-gun fire from the German-held feature prevented further progress. The survivors of the 72nd Battalion, which had been stricken with casualties, could do no more than gain a footing in the third German trench. The initial setback to the 11th Brigade was adversely affecting the movement of the 12th's right-hand battalion. Passing through the 38th Battalion according to plan, the 78th Battalion had come under fire from Hill 145 and had lost its supporting barrage. About 8:30 a.m. as the few remaining men of the leading companies neared their final objective just outside Givenchy, they were counter-attacked and overpowered by a force of some 200 Germans. But the enemy's attempt to regain his second trench was beaten off with Lewis gun and rifle fire. Late that afternoon, as the 85th Battalion mounted its attack for the 11th Brigade (above, p. 260), two companies of the 46th, which was on loan from the 10th Brigade, came forward to capture a number of craters beyond the disputed second trench. Night fell with the main objectives still untaken.[107]

Since the 12th Brigade could not complete its task until the whole of Hill 145 was secure, at 6:00 p.m. on 9 April General Watson called upon the 10th Brigade (Brig.-Gen. E. Hilliam), which had been standing by in readiness to assault the Pimple, to take the exhausted 11th Brigade's final Red Line objective. By 3:15 next afternoon Brig.-Gen. Hilliam's two uncommitted battalions were in position on Hill 145. The barrage which had been fired on the *Hangstellung* the day before was repeated, and as it lifted the assaulting waves charged down the eastern slope, the 44th Battalion on the right and the 50th on the left. The action was a brilliant success, though the 50th Battalion suffered almost 240 casualties.

Private J. G. Pattison, of the 50th, earned the V.C. by rushing forward under heavy fire to wipe out the crew of a machine gun that was holding up the advance. A quick mopping up of the enemy dug-outs yielded 150 unwounded prisoners and a number of machine-guns. Working forward through the northern end of the Bois de la Folie, parties of the 44th Battalion linked up with the 3rd Division's left flank.[108] On the left all forward battalions of the 12th Brigade improved their positions next morning as German artillery fire dwindled, and at mid-afternoon, when Hill 145 was completely in Canadian hands, they occupied with relative ease the Brigade's final objective, the "Givenchy Line".[109]

So ended the "Southern" operation. The whole of the main part of Vimy Ridge on a length of 7000 yards and to a maximum depth of 4000 yards had been captured. On the right the 51st British Division had advanced to its objectives and was in touch with the Canadian flank at the Brown Line. Canadian casualties in the two days' fighting totalled 7707, of which 2967 were fatal. To these must be added the 13th British Brigade's losses on Easter Monday—approximately 380. Up to midnight on 9-10 April, about 3400 German prisoners had been counted; and more were still coming in.[110]

The Pimple, 12 April

There remained to be captured the northern tip of Vimy Ridge and the Lorette spur west of the Souchez River. The most important objective was the Pimple, with its complete command of the Souchez defile. This German stronghold had withstood many Allied raids. Its surface was a maze of trenches, and below ground German engineers had constructed deep dug-outs and tunnels protected in every way that their ingenuity could devise. Although it was originally intended that the capture of the Pimple would not be a Canadian task (above, p. 245), revised plans by the First Army divided the "Northern" operation between the Canadian Corps and the 1st British Corps.

The attack was to be made within 24 hours of the launching of the "Southern" operation.[111] While the 24th Division (1st British Corps) assaulted the Bois en Hache on the eastern slopes of the Lorette ridge, the 4th Canadian Division would send the 10th Brigade against the Pimple, provided the general situation on the afternoon of 9 April had not required its employment elsewhere.[112] But, as we have seen, General Watson had been forced to commit the 10th Brigade in reducing Hill 145, and time was needed for the participating units to recover, however desirable it would have been to strike while the enemy was still disorganized. The northern attack was therefore postponed 48 hours. In the meantime General von Falkenhausen had belatedly ordered regiments of his "counterattack" divisions to take over the new German front line.* The Canadian attack was to fall mainly on a fresh battalion of the 5th Guard Grenadier Regiment, hastily entrained from the north and thrust into position in front of Givenchy to stem the attack that was bound to come.[114]

On 11 April the weather deteriorated rapidly, and in the early hours of the 12th, as the Canadians moved forward from their rest area behind Zouave Valley, a strong westerly gale was raging, driving sleet and snow towards the enemy's positions. Three battalions divided the thousand-yard frontage of the 10th Brigade's attack—from right to left the 44th, 50th and 46th Battalions.[115] There was strong artillery support from No. 4 (Double) Heavy Artillery Group R.A., five siege batteries of the 1st Corps Artillery, and a "Reserve Divisional Artillery" (which, as the Lahore Divisional Artillery, had more than once supported Canadian operations, and was now taking the place of the as yet non-existent 4th Canadian divisional artillery).[116] On the eve of the attack, heavy and medium howitzers had engaged the enemy's communication trenches and rear areas behind Givenchy, and a special company of the Royal Engineers had fired more than forty gas drums† into Givenchy itself, killing a number of Germans in the cellars.[118]

*Holding the sector between Méricourt and Oppy were, from north to south, the 16th Bavarian Infantry Division with two battalions from the 4th Infantry Division in the line, the 111th Infantry Division and the 17th Infantry Division.[113]

†This was the first use in a Canadian operation of Livens projectors, capable of firing a 50-lb drum containing 30 lbs of mustard gas distances of from 500 to 1300 yards.[117]

Promptly at 5:00 a.m., as nearly a hundred field guns opened fire on the German front trench, the infantry advanced. The benefits of the wind at their backs and the driving snow that blinded the enemy machine-gunners were offset by the heavy mud, which prevented the men from keeping up with the barrage. Nevertheless, so unexpected was an attack in such weather that the 44th and 50th Battalions took the first two trenches, by this time almost obliterated, against little opposition. On the extreme left, however, the 46th came under heavy rifle fire almost from the outset and suffered 108 casualties—about half the strength of the two companies involved in the attack. As the men from Western Canada pushed forward they were engaged by small parties of Guards emerging from scattered shell-holes and the few remaining habitable dug-outs. There was some sharp hand-to-hand fighting, but by six o'clock the right and centre battalions were on their objectives. On the Pimple was the 44th, whose Lewis gunners had cut down 100 of the enemy trying to escape down the hillside into Givenchy. Five hundred yards to the north the 50th Battalion held the shattered stumps of the Bois de Givenchy, and in another two hours the 46th could report the left flank secure with machine-guns sited on the south bank of the Souchez.[119] The sky cleared at daybreak, and the Canadians found themselves overlooking the Douai plain and the south-western suburbs of Lens. Only a small enemy pocket remained on the Ridge—astride the Givenchy-Souchez road, between the 44th Battalion and the 73rd—and it was withdrawn in the next 24 hours. Meanwhile the 73rd British Brigade, successfully attacking the Bois en Hache, had driven the Germans from the edge of the Lorette spur.

On 10 April Crown Prince Rupprecht wrote in his diary: "No one could have foreseen that the expected offensive would gain ground so quickly."[120] The next day, accepting the loss of Vimy Ridge as permanent, he ordered a general withdrawal to the German Third Position, which opposite the Canadians followed the Oppy-Méricourt line and the Avion Switch, encircling the western suburbs of Lens. All villages in the vicinity were completely cleared of civilians, and except for leaving light rearguards and enough guns to simulate normal activity the Germans completed the move on the night of 12-13 April. This was far enough into the level plain to deprive the Canadians of effective observation from the Ridge, and it meant that with respect to terrain defender and attacker would meet on equal terms. The new trenches though not deep were well protected by wire and manned with fresh troops. It would be suicidal to attack such a strong position without intensive artillery preparation; and this would have to wait until the almost obliterated roads had been rebuilt to allow heavy guns and ammunition to come forward. Even with 5000 men working on them, these would not be passable for several days. At the most, the British and Canadian forces could only maintain contact with the retiring enemy; this they did by vigorous patrolling and limited advances, firmly consolidating the additional ground gained.[121]

THE BATTLES OF THE SCARPE

APRIL-MAY 1917

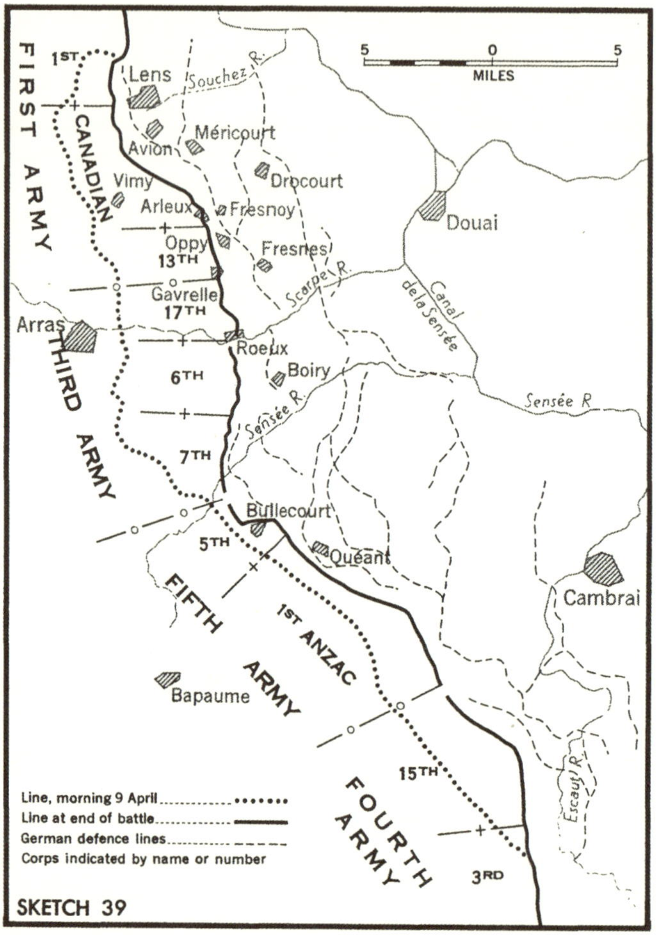

An advance of the Canadian Corps to the line of the Lens-Arras railway, originally ordered by the First Army on the 10th and postponed so as to coincide with attacks by flanking corps, was carried out by the 1st and 2nd Divisions on the evening of the 13th. Similar progress was made on either flank: the 3rd Division reached the line Vimy–Petit Vimy–La Chaudière; the 4th occupied Givenchy; and units of the 1st Corps, on the left of the Canadian Corps, and the 17th on the right, reached respectively Angres and Bailleul. Next day the First Army advanced another thousand yards on a nine-mile front, opposed only by small rearguards. In his retreat (so much more precipitate than his earlier deliberate withdrawal to the Hindenburg Line) the enemy abandoned many guns and much ammunition. During the winter Canadian gunners had been trained in the use of German guns, and now, unable to get their own artillery forward, they were prompt to put these enemy weapons to good effect. By the evening of 14 April nine captured pieces, ranging from 8-inch howitzers to 77-mm. guns, were in action against enemy trenches and batteries, and bombarding the Germans in Avion and Méricourt with their own gas shells.[122] That same afternoon, as patrols confirmed the enemy's occupation of his new positions, General Byng ordered the Canadian Corps to establish a main line of resistance running through Willerval and La Chaudière to the Bois de l'Hirondelle (on the south bank of the Souchez).[123] This line the Corps was to hold virtually unchanged until the autumn of 1918, when the final Allied advance of the war began.

With the completion of this limited exploitation the Battle of Vimy Ridge ended. In six days the Canadian Corps had advanced some 4500 yards and seized 54 guns, 104 trench mortars and 124 machine-guns. It had inflicted severe losses on the enemy, capturing more than 4000 prisoners. The victory had been gained at a cost in Canadian casualties (for the period 9-14 April) of 10,602 all ranks—3598 of them fatal. From His Majesty King George V came a message of congratulations to Sir Douglas Haig: "Canada will be proud that the taking of the coveted Vimy Ridge has fallen to the lot of her troops."

The French press, warmly praising the Canadian achievement, called the Ridge an Easter gift from Canada to France. Just as the planners of the operation had studied the lessons of Verdun, so members of the French General Staff revisited the familiar battlefield on the Ridge to review in detail the whole Canadian action.

The First Battle of the Scarpe, 9-14 April

The Third Army's share in the Arras offensive—the First Battle of the Scarpe—had produced territorial gains about equal to those of the First Army. Easter Monday had seen advances of two to six thousand yards, the Blue Line being reached at a number of points, and that evening General Allenby reported the capture of 5600 prisoners and 36 guns.[124] The enemy had been even more taken by surprise than at Vimy Ridge—as late as 7 April von Falkenhausen had expressed the opinion that any British attack in the German Sixth Army's sector would not take place before the big French offensive in Champagne, which French prisoners revealed was set for about 16 April.[125] The day's tidings spoiled Ludendorff's 52nd birthday. "I had looked forward to the expected offensive with confidence", he wrote, "and was now deeply depressed."[126]

On the 10th German resistance began to stiffen, and the momentum of the attack correspondingly decreased. This was due in part to the arrival of some of the enemy's reserve battalions, and the fact that the attackers had outrun their initial artillery support. Nevertheless on both sides of the Scarpe the British made further advances of up to a mile, adding considerably to their bag of prisoners.[127]

The third and critical day of the battle was marked by a futile attempt of General Gough's Fifth Army, on the Third Army's right flank, to break through the Hindenburg Line just west of its junction with the newly constructed Drocourt-Quéant Switch (or *Wotan Stellung*). In planning such a thrust to assist General Allenby's offensive, Field-Marshal Haig had given orders for the 4th Cavalry Division to be held in readiness to exploit north-eastward so as to link up with the main body of the Cavalry Corps, which was to pass through the Third Army and advance on Cambrai.[128] The attack was made at Bullecourt (eight miles south-east of Arras) by the 4th Australian Division and proved a fiasco. Tanks, called upon to replace the barrage and to smash through broad belts of wire which inadequate artillery preparation had left ungapped, failed in their task; and although the infantry heroically gained a footing in the Hindenburg trenches, they were forced to withdraw, one brigade being almost completely destroyed.[129] The cavalry, committed by the Army Commander on the basis of false reports of the infantry's progress, were halted near the start by artillery fire.[130]

In the Third Army's sector, despite General Allenby's assurance to his troops that they were "now pursuing a defeated enemy", the only gain on the 11th was the capture of Monchy-le-Preux, just north of the Arras-Cambrai road. The 3rd Cavalry Division had an important share in clearing and holding the village, but its intended role of exploitation did not materialize, and that evening General Allenby, recognizing the obvious, withdrew his three cavalry divisions from the battle. Little progress was made during the next three days, and on 15 April Haig, overruling Allenby's desire to continue the offensive, called a halt to allow time for much-needed reorganization, and particularly the restoration of communications, before launching a coordinated attack on a bigger scale. The first three days' fighting had cost the Third Army 8238 casualties—about 700 less than those suffered by the Canadian Corps over the same period. The Army had captured more than 7000 prisoners and 112 guns.[131]

On the German side 11 April saw the removal of the Sixth Army's Chief of Staff as responsible for "this heavy defeat".[132] His place was taken by Colonel von Lossberg, who at once set about organizing the defence of a new position about six miles east of Arras and the same distance in front of the Drocourt-Quéant Line.[133] South of the Scarpe, the new line replaced the fallen Monchy Switch as a continuation of the Méricourt-Oppy line. To ensure that the new position would be strongly held, Prince Rupprecht's headquarters arranged for fortnightly reliefs for the ten or eleven divisions in the line through exchanges with divisions in quiet sectors of the Army Group.[134]

Vimy Ridge in Retrospect

Although the Canadian advance at Vimy and the Third Army's success in front of Arras did not bring the Allies the expected strategic returns, a great tactical victory had been won. The operations had resulted in the capture of more ground, more prisoners and more guns than any previous British offensive on the Western Front. The effective use of artillery in unprecedented strength with adequate supplies of ammunition, coupled with the gaining of tactical surprise, had paid good dividends. The Canadian achievement in taking with relatively light losses what the Germans considered an impregnable position was justly ascribed by the Commander of the First Army to "soundness of plan, thoroughness of preparation, dash and determination in execution, and devotion to duty on the part of all concerned".[185]

The Vimy operation was and remains a classic example of the deliberate attack against strong prepared positions. It was further notable in that the assaulting forces were successful in holding what they had gained, repelling counter-attacks which the enemy had to make in areas dominated by the Canadian guns. In previous operations objectives had been taken at great cost, only to be lost again through failure to consolidate efficiently against the enemy's counter blows. Vimy set a new standard. At last an Allied formation had proved its ability to pass "readily from swift and sustained assault to aggressive and concerted defence".[186]

For Canada the battle had great national significance. It demonstrated how powerful and efficient a weapon the Canadian Corps had become. For the first time the four Canadian divisions had attacked together. Their battalions were manned by soldiers from every part of Canada fighting shoulder to shoulder. No other operation of the First World War was to be remembered by Canadians with such pride—the pride of achievement through united and dedicated effort. Canada's most impressive tribute to her sons is on the Ridge itself. There, on Hill 145, in ground presented in 1922 by France to the people of Canada, is the greatest of Canada's European war memorials. Two majestic white pylons, representing Canada and France, soar high above the summit for which so many Allied soldiers fought and died. Engraved on the walls of the base are the names of more than 10,000 Canadians who gave their lives in the First World War and who have no known grave. The main inscription on the Memorial reads: "To the valour of their countrymen in the Great War and in memory of their sixty thousand dead this monument is raised by the people of Canada."

Yet without taking from the victors rightful credit for their success, one must charge the enemy's loss of Vimy Ridge and so much important ground to the south in large measure to his own inefficiency. Great efforts were made by the German High Command to determine the causes of the defeat. The Sixth Army Commander and his staff were blamed for having misjudged the strength and the frontage of the expected attack, and having failed to take proper measures to meet it. It was found that the opposition offered by the German artillery had been slow and inadequate during the preparatory stages, and heavy batteries available in Douai had not been brought into action against the guns supporting the attack. The resulting breakdown in communications and supply had caused local shortages of shells and machine-gun ammunition.[137] Above all the Sixth Army, ignoring the requirement of Ludendorff's new doctrine to assemble its counter-attack divisions close behind the Second Line, had held them fifteen or more miles from the battlefield to avoid their being shelled.[188] In an appreciation shortly before the battle von Falkenhausen had expressed confidence that his front divisions would not be overrun, planning if necessary to bring forward his counter-attack formations in relief "on the evening of the second day of the battle".[189]

Both Ludendorff and Crown Prince Rupprecht (who were under no delusions as to the Allied intentions) had urged that these reserves be moved close to the battlefield,[140] but neither had seen fit to give the Army Commander a firm order. Even after the battle opened, von Falkenhausen, as we have noted, was in no hurry to commit these divisions, two of which, held near Douai, might have reached Vimy Ridge by rail in the first four hours. He thus failed to take advantage of the opportunity presented him by the inflexible time-table which prescribed that the Canadians should take six hours to gain their final objectives.

A close scrutiny of the evidence however shows that to some extent at least the Sixth Army was criticized beyond its just deserts. One week after being appointed Chief of Staff of that Army, in an outspoken and well founded official report Colonel von Lossberg roundly blamed the Army Group for the initial fiasco at Vimy.[141] Nevertheless, the Army Commander was not long in following his former Chief of Staff. Within a fortnight he was appointed Governor General of Belgium, a post in which, says Ludendorff, he "retained our complete confidence".[142] His successor was General Otto von Below, formerly commanding an Army Group in Macedonia.[143]

CHAPTER IX

THE CAPTURE OF HILL 70, 1917

(See Map 8 and Sketches 40-42)

The Second Battle of the Scarpe and the Attack on the Arleux Loop, 23-28 April 1917

FIELD-MARSHAL HAIG resumed his attacks on the Scarpe on the morning of 23 April, one week after the opening of the Nivelle offensive. His aim was to capture a further section of the Hindenburg position and drive the Germans back to the Drocourt-Quéant Line,* and by this pressure on the enemy to assist the French at the Aisne.

The main British attack was made in the difficult rolling country south of the Scarpe, six divisions of the Third Army advancing on a front of 11,000 yards. Extending this frontage another 5000 yards north of the river to the Arras-Douai road were two more divisions of the Third Army and one of the First. There was to be no action on the Canadian Corps front against the Oppy-Méricourt Line, for bad weather had prevented adequate artillery preparation; but on the Canadians' left the British 5th Division, under General Byng's command, would join with the 46th Division of the 1st Corps in a local attack astride the Souchez River. Its aim was to capture that portion of the Vimy-Lens line (above, p. 246) between the Vimy-Lens railway and Hill 65—a commanding height north of the river overlooking the western part of Lens.[1] This would bite into the salient which the enemy was holding south-west and south of Lens and force a German retirement to the Avion Switch, which ran back to the northern end of the Oppy-Méricourt line.[2]

In some of its hardest fighting of the war so far the Third Army made gains of up to one and a half miles; and north of the river, where the attacks had the support of observed fire from Vimy Ridge, the First Army captured Gavrelle on the Douai road. But the Avion operation failed, mainly because of uncut wire—both divisions were back in their original positions by evening. Next day the Germans launched a series of counter-attacks against the right wing of the Third Army. Before these could develop artillery fire broke up all but one,

* The line ran southward through Drocourt (five miles south-east of Lens) to meet the Hindenburg Line at Quéant (twelve miles south-east of Arras).

and it was repulsed at close quarters. In this Second Battle of the Scarpe the British had suffered 10,000 casualties, while taking 2500 prisoners.[3]

The offensive was renewed five days later—a period used by the Germans to strengthen their new defences; in effect "position warfare" had returned. In addition to the salient at the Avion Switch, the enemy front line bulged westward at the Arleux Loop to cover the village of Arleux-en-Gohelle, which lay at the end of a low spur reaching into the plain from Vimy Ridge. Farther east, extending south across the Scarpe, was the new Fresnes-Boiry switch, a little more than two miles in front of the Drocourt-Quéant Line. This switch line became the next major British objective, and on the morning of 28 April Haig launched a preliminary offensive aimed at eliminating the Arleux Loop and linking together the two salients which had been formed on the 23rd by the advances north and south of the Scarpe. Three divisions of the Third Army attacked astride the river; the British 2nd Division (First Army) assaulted opposite Oppy; and on its left the 1st Canadian Division stormed the Arleux Loop. The six miles of front were being held by four German divisions, the 111th Infantry Division facing the Canadians.[4]

The fairly general repulse of the Allied assault provided an auspicious beginning to General Otto von Below's command of the Sixth Army, which he assumed on that same day, 28 April. In the main the attacks failed because of poor tactics. The Third Army's plan followed an unimaginative pattern of advancing towards successive lines drawn across a map regardless of the enemy's use of reverse slopes and other topographical features favourable to the defence. The preliminary bombardment placed the usual emphasis on the front trench, which was only lightly held. A second trench to the rear (generally behind a crest), with dug-outs for the bulk of the forward garrison, went largely untouched.[5] Thus the main body of the 12th British Division, attacking south of and slightly astride the Scarpe, was halted immediately with heavy losses. On the north bank, two battalions were allowed to advance over a reverse slope just beyond the village of Roeux, where, out of sight of British artillery observers, they were swept by machine-gun fire and then counter-attacked; many were killed and 350 taken prisoner. East of Gavrelle, elements of the 37th Division succeeded in capturing high and therefore important ground. But they were neither supported nor reinforced sufficiently to deal with the inevitable counter-attack; and the Germans soon retook the ground and captured 125 prisoners. Meanwhile in the Oppy sector the British 2nd Division had suffered much the same fate as the 12th Division at Roeux.[6]

The Canadian attack on the Arleux Loop resulted in what the British Official Historian styled "the only tangible success of the whole operation".[7] It was carried out by the 2nd Canadian Brigade, supported by the 1st Brigade, and with a battalion of the 2nd Canadian Division advancing to cover the left flank. Fire support came from the 1st Divisional Artillery and a number of batteries of the Corps Heavy Artillery. There were no illusions about the difficulty of the task. Patrols sent forward on 27 April had reported the

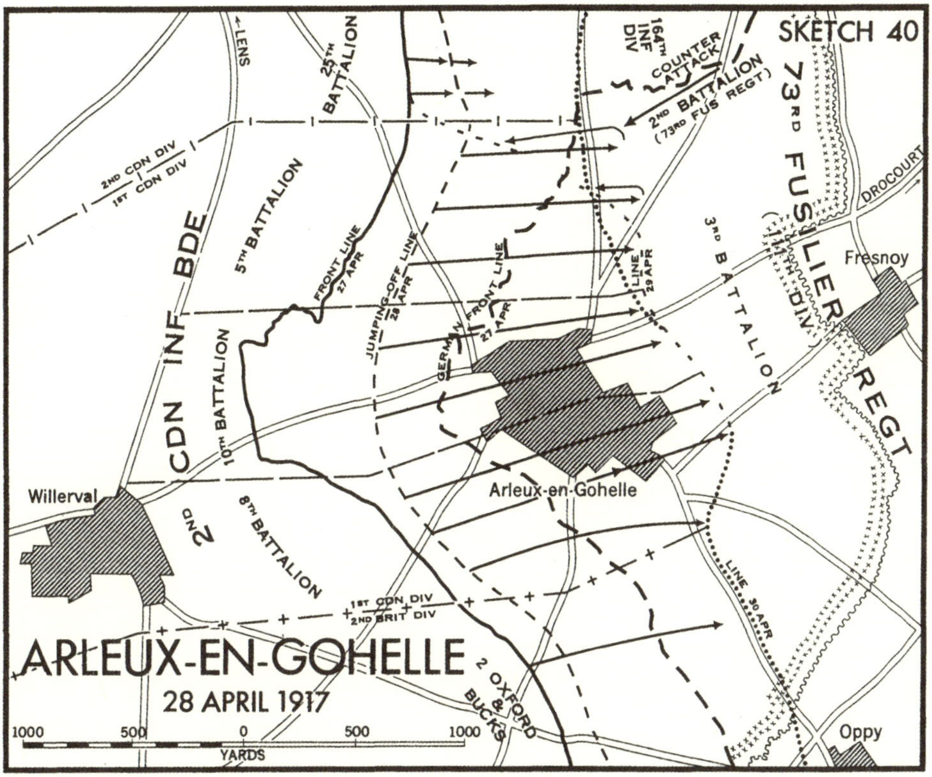

German wire only partially destroyed by our artillery, and it was known that the enemy had an "unusually large number of machine-guns" and was constructing a support line behind the Loop. Defending the Arleux Loop was the 73rd Fusilier Regiment of the 111th Division.[8] Recent operations had demonstrated the German tactics of delivering counter-attacks in great strength within a short time of the assaulting troops' arrival on the objective. Artillery barrages were therefore arranged to meet such a counter-attack, and the 1st Canadian Infantry Brigade, which was in reserve, was ordered to reconnoitre covered approaches for moving up reinforcements. Special patrols of No. 16 Squadron R.F.C. were to watch for signs of a counter blow. At 4:25 a.m. on the 28th three Canadian battalions assaulted on a front of 2600 yards—the 8th on the right, the 10th in the centre, and the 5th on the left.

The 8th Battalion, attacking over a low rise into Arleux, was hit by considerable machine-gun fire from the village and the woods to the south. Although the centre company was held up by wire and lost all its officers, those on the left and right reached their objectives on schedule, a line midway between Arleux and Fresnoy (a village one thousand yards to the east). After repeated efforts to advance, the company in the centre, reinforced by officers and men from the battalion reserve, succeeded in clearing the village. A strong-point was established on the right flank in time to break up a threatened counter-attack against the left of the 2nd British Division. The 10th Battalion, advancing through the northern outskirts of Arleux astride the road towards Drocourt, though held up on the right by fire from the village, cleaned up the opposition and reached its objective in good time. On the brigade left three hard-fighting companies of the 5th Battalion overcame spirited resistance and linked up with the other battalions. Unfortunately the 2nd Canadian Division's 25th Battalion, advancing on the northern flank, had halted before a sunken road only 300 yards from the start line, mistaking it for a more distant objective; as a result the 5th Battalion's left company found itself badly enfiladed by machine-gun fire and was forced to form a defensive flank short of its goal.

Except for this check the 2nd Brigade had gained all its objectives by 6:00 a.m. During the afternoon elements of supporting battalions came forward to reinforce against possible counter-attack. The enemy's movements were in full view of our artillery observers, and two attempts to dislodge the Canadians were broken up by shelling and small-arms fire. Deciding that the exposed Arleux salient would have to be abandoned, the commander of the German 111th Division cancelled further counter-attacks and withdrew his troops to the Oppy-Méricourt line in front of Fresnoy.[9] On the left the 25th Battalion completed its advance. By taking full advantage of ground better suited to an attack than that on the British front the Canadians had turned the Arleux Loop into a small salient facing eastward some 400 yards from the enemy's next line of resistance. Canadian casualties in the operation approached the thousand mark; some 450 Germans had been captured.[10]

The Third Battle of the Scarpe, 3-4 May 1917

By the last week of April the British Commander-in-Chief had good reason to expect that the French offensive on the Aisne would soon be abandoned. If this happened, it would be pointless and even dangerous for him to continue his advance with an open right flank. Yet Haig had not yet attained a "good defensive line",[11] and to suspend all activity on the Western Front would seriously affect the offensive plans of Russia and Italy. The hoped for rupture of the hostile front having failed to materialize, it was a case of returning to wearing-down tactics. Haig decided to maintain limited pressure at the Scarpe until about the middle of May. Whether he would subsequently resume the offensive here on a larger scale,* or open a new one in Flanders, would depend on the outcome of the French operations. In a letter to General Robertson on 1 May, however, Sir Douglas declared his intention of reducing his efforts for the next few weeks, preparatory to beginning preliminary operations in Flanders.[13]

* The Commanders of the Fourth and Fifth Armies were now directed to prepare plans for a major attack towards Cambrai—the genesis of the offensive launched seven months later by the Third Army (below, p. 333).[12]

As we have seen, Nivelle's offensive on the Aisne continued until the second week of May. On 3 May the British resumed their attacks astride the Scarpe, not only to support the French, but also because their present position was not one that could be held securely or economically. The scope of the new operation—an attack by three armies on a front of fourteen miles—seems strangely out of keeping with the C.-in-C.'s declared intention of limiting his efforts. Army Commanders were told that their advance to the "good defensive line" which formed the objective should be deliberate—with consolidation to be completed by 15 May. Attainment of this goal would involve the capture of Lens and the towns and villages on which the Oppy-Méricourt and Fresnes-Boiry positions were based. For the opening attack the First Army's objectives were Fresnoy and Oppy; the line to be taken by the Third and Fifth Armies would require advances of up to a mile from their existing positions.

The operations of the First and Third Armies, known as the Third Battle of the Scarpe, were over in 24 hours; those of the Fifth Army, in the Battle of Bullecourt, lasted two weeks. The results were disappointing and the losses heavy. As usual, surprise was impossible except for concealing the actual timing of the attack, and the enemy was constantly on the alert. Both the artillery preparation and the plan of attack followed conventional lines, ignoring the lessons of recent fighting and the fact that copies of Ludendorff's and von Lossberg's textbooks—prescribing defence of a deep zone rather than a trench line—had been in British hands for some time.[14] In an unfortunate attempt to compromise between his army and corps commanders, some of whom wanted to attack on the night of 3-4 May, others at first light, Haig set zero hour at 3:45 a.m. on the 3rd—too late to offer the advantages of a night operation, and too early for a proper daylight attack.[15] An almost full moon had set only sixteen minutes earlier, silhouetting the assembling troops. Thus warned, the enemy reacted with heavy fire which caused serious loss and confusion before the attack started. As the infantry crossed no man's land they were met by counter-barrages which disorganized movement, inflicted considerable casualties, and cut off the assaulting units from those in support. Machine-gun and rifle fire from between the trench lines raked the leading troops, so that even those who reached their objectives in sufficient strength to wrest them from the enemy were frequently too weak, without reinforcement, to hold them against local counter-attacks.[16]

Except on the flanks of the attacking armies the offensive was a virtually complete failure. On the extreme right the 1st Anzac Corps (Fifth Army) made a small breach in the Hindenburg Line east of Bullecourt, in four days' fighting enlarging it to 550 yards deep and 4000 wide. The Australians routed a succession of determined counter-attacks, smashing the last and largest on the 15th. Failing to regain any of their lost ground, the Germans subsequently left Bullecourt itself in Allied hands. The Third Army's sole gain meanwhile was an advance on 3 May of 500 yards by one brigade on a 1000-yard front immediately south of the Scarpe. North of the river the 13th Corps (First Army) seized and held a narrow strip all along its front, and the Canadian Corps captured Fresnoy—"the relieving feature", writes the British Official Historian, "of a day which many who witnessed it considered the blackest of the War".[17]

The entire period March-April 1917 had been a bad one for the Royal Flying Corps, but May was to see a marked improvement in the air situation. Most writers seek to account for this change in terms of equipment—the arrival of new fighters comparable if not superior to the German Albatros. Yet only a few such machines reached the front before midsummer, and at first these impressed neither their own crews nor the enemy. Part of the reason for the improvement was that British pilots, having survived early encounters with the Albatros, learned how to handle their 1916-pattern machines to the best advantage and so developed confidence in them. Furthermore, at the end of April the enemy began to improvise massed formations of twenty or more fighters, and thus localized his efforts. The immediate answer to the "circuses", as these large brightly coloured formations were called, was to keep aloft increasing numbers of five-man flights. Successive groups of that size, it was found, could exert more influence on the "dogfight" than the same total number involved continuously from the outset; they were more manageable, and their striking power grew while that of the circuses tended to dwindle.[18]

The Fighting at Fresnoy, 3-8 May

The Canadian attack of 3 May was in effect a continuation of the successful assault on the Arleux Loop five days before. Principal target was the hamlet of Fresnoy, which lay, its red-roofed houses little damaged by war, in a slight depression beside the Drocourt road. The well-wired trenches of the Oppy-Méricourt line ran along the western outskirts of Fresnoy, incorporating in the defences a number of strongpoints at the village edge and in the woods to the north and south. These were manned by a battalion of the 25th Reserve Regiment. Three battalions of the 1st Canadian Brigade took part in the operation. While the 2nd Battalion attacked the village itself, the 1st and 3rd Battalions went respectively against the woods on the left and the right. Farther north, in the 2nd Division's sector opposite Acheville, the 6th Brigade was to provide left flank protection for the First Army's attacks by forming a strong front facing north-east. The 27th Battalion was to seize the junction of the northern end of the former Arleux Loop with the main Oppy-Méricourt line (500 yards south of Acheville), while the 31st guarded its left flank. Plans called for generous fire support by the Canadian Corps Heavy Artillery and the 1st, 2nd and 3rd Divisional Artilleries, the Reserve (formerly Lahore) Divisional Artillery, and a number of British heavy groups.[19]

The loss of Arleux had alerted the Germans to the probability of a further attack. In the bright moonlight they detected the Canadians approaching across the open plain from Arleux and began heavily shelling the assembly areas of both brigades. In spite of some confusion and casualties the attack opened on schedule as the thickly emplaced batteries in the general area of the Arras-Lens rail-

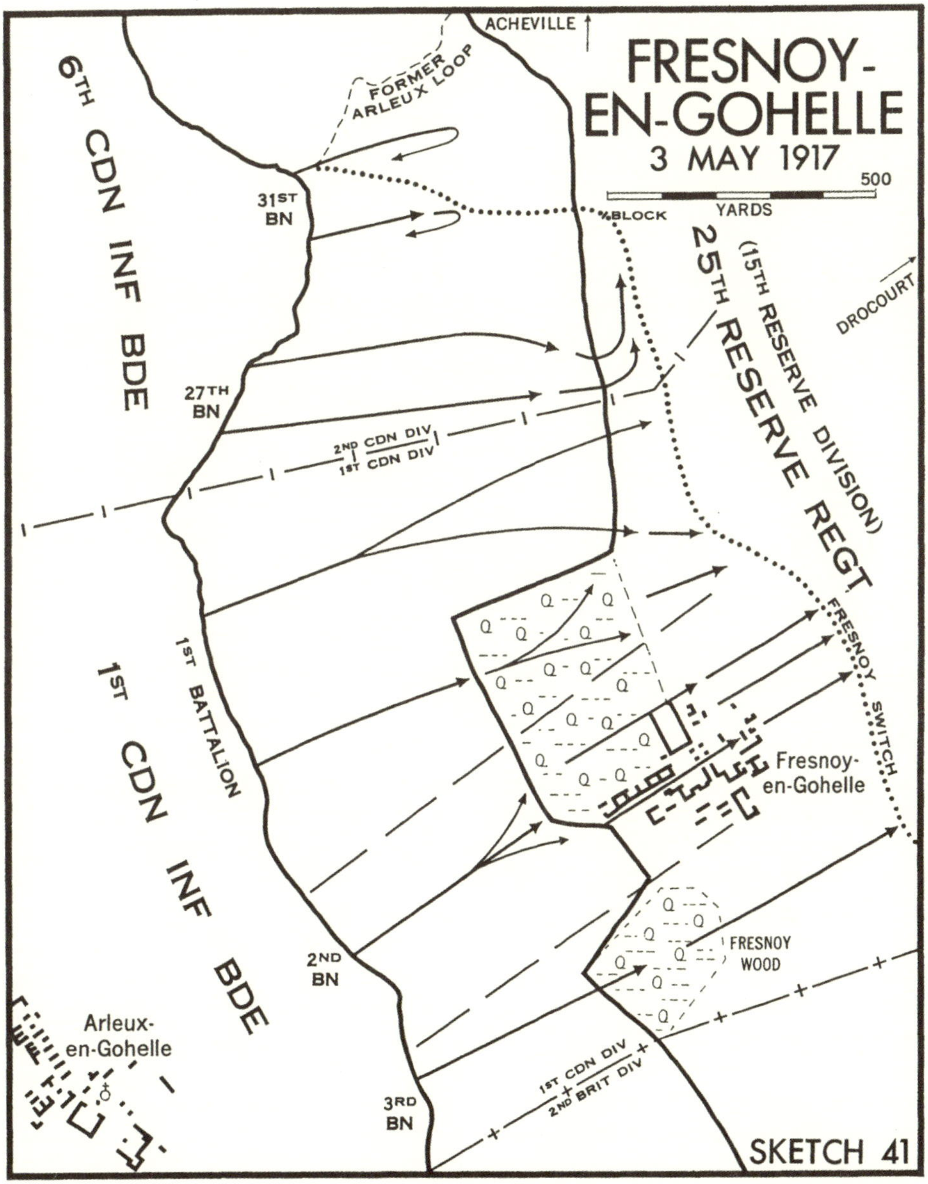

way released a powerful barrage which swept no man's land and rolled in upon the front German trench. Almost immediately the enemy laid down retaliatory fire which harassed the rear waves of the 1st Brigade, while the foremost Canadians were caught in a crossfire from the enemy's machine-guns. Though the wire in front of Fresnoy had been well cut, the gaps were hard to find in the darkness; fortunately the lack of visibility made the enemy's small-arms fire relatively ineffective.[20]

Once through the wire the units of the 1st Brigade made good progress. The 3rd Battalion combed the wood south of Fresnoy like beaters in a pheasant shoot and pushed on to the German support trench, 500 yards beyond. This position —the Fresnoy Switch—fell just before sunrise, but not before one of the assaulting companies had been reduced to 25 men. Meanwhile the 2nd Battalion's leading company stormed and seized the German front trench and knocked out three machine-guns on the western edge of Fresnoy. The battalion had been carefully rehearsed over traced trenches in its training ground on the west side of Vimy Ridge—a preparation which paid good dividends. In the face of rifle fire from outlying houses two more companies passed through and forced their way into the village. Cleaning up small pockets of resistance in houses and dug-outs as they went, both reached the final objective 250 yards east of Fresnoy at about six o'clock. As they set to work with pick and shovel to consolidate their position, they were joined by the fourth company, which had been held in the brigade assembly area with instructions to push straight through to the final goal. German prisoners began carrying the wounded back over Vimy Ridge.[21] In the meantime the 1st Battalion, astride the Drocourt road, had reached its goal without meeting heavy opposition. Well dug in, the battalions around Fresnoy hung on to their gains under heavy German shelling that continued all day.*

The attack of the 6th Brigade was less successful. The 31st Battalion encountered new wire only 300 yards out, half way to the foremost manned defences. This and heavy enfilade fire from the trench junction split the attack, one group seeking to outflank the objective while the other went in frontally. Both failed. The best the battalion could do was to occupy a newly dug German trench immediately east of the wire, and set up a block where this trench joined the old Arleux Loop.[23]

But the day went better on the brigade right. Despite the counter-barrage and the uncut wire, the 27th Battalion's left forward company quickly reached and overran its first objective—the German front trench. The mopping up party lost its way, however, so that there were no following troops to deal with the many Germans who were emerging from their dug-outs. With the enemy at his back and both flanks open—for neither the 31st Battalion nor the 27th's assaulting company on the right had been able to keep pace—the company commander reversed his platoons and attacked the front garrison from the rear, driving the Germans towards the Canadian lines. Thirty German prisoners resulted, but when the company dug in it was short of even its first objective.[24]

Of the right forward company, halted 500 yards short of the front trench by the enemy barrage, only a handful of men under one officer—Lieut. R. G. Combe —had managed to reach the objective. Using enemy grenades as their own supply ran out, they captured more than 250 yards of trench, sending back from eighty to a hundred prisoners and linking up with the 1st Battalion's left. But just as

* Since the Arras battles opened on 9 April the proportion of German to British artillery strength had increased considerably. The total numbers of guns supporting the German Sixth Army and the British First and Third Armies on three significant dates were as follows: 9 April, German 1016, British 2817; 23 April, German 1329, British 2685; 3 May, German 1421, British 2685.[22]

reserves were arriving Combe was killed. He was posthumously awarded the V.C.[25] The reserve company went on to clear 150 more yards of trench and consolidate the position, setting up a Lewis gun in the German support trench, which was found unoccupied. After dark, with help from a party of the 29th Battalion, the 27th, whose casualties that day numbered 267, extended the hold on the support trench. The 6th Brigade had failed to seize the assigned trench junction, but it had captured 400 yards of the Oppy-Méricourt line adjacent to the 1st Brigade's gains.[26]

The Germans made two determined attempts on 3 May to win back what they had lost. About mid-morning a counter-attack by units of the 15th Reserve Division advancing on Fresnoy from the north-east was smashed by our waiting artillery and by machine-gun and rifle fire from the new Canadian front line. A stronger effort was made in the afternoon, using additional units called in from the adjacent 4th Guard Division and the 185th Infantry Division, which was on the point of being transferred from the Vimy sector. But once again the waves of assaulting infantry could not survive our artillery and small-arms fire, while a German bombing party, attempting to work southward from the disputed trench junction, was stopped at the 27th Battalion's block by fire from the unit's Stokes mortars and Lewis guns.[27] By their own accounts the Germans' heaviest losses for the whole front on 3 May were at Fresnoy. One of the 15th Reserve Division's regiments admitted 650 casualties; the other, which had garrisoned Fresnoy village, must have had many more. The Canadian Corps had captured close to 500 Germans: of its own casualties of 1259 all ranks probably a full thousand were incurred by the 1st and 6th Brigades.

In the air there were indications that the enemy would not long continue to enjoy his superiority. The day before the battle fighters of the Royal Flying Corps had destroyed or damaged eight observation balloons opposite the First Army's front.* While the work of contact patrols during the operation was hampered by the incessant bombardment and the confusion of attack and counter-attack, air observers operating with the 13th Corps were able to report preparations for a counter-attack south of Oppy. Elsewhere bombers engaged ammunition dumps and railway junctions and bridges well behind the enemy lines. Meanwhile German artillery observation planes operated over the area of the Canadian attack unmolested.[28]

By the morning of 5 May the First Army had regrouped its forces and drawn new boundaries. The British 5th Division, now under command of the 13th Corps, took over the Fresnoy sector from the 1st Canadian Division, which went into corps reserve. The 2nd Canadian Division remained in position north of the village.[29] It was not to be expected that the enemy would accept the loss of Fresnoy without a determined effort to regain it. Its capture had, as one German regimental historian put it, knocked a stone "out of the German defensive wall

*The observation balloon was a distinctive feature of the sky-line on both sides from the time of the Somme until the end of the war. Raised and lowered by an engine-driven winch, the balloon could carry its observers (usually there were two) to heights of up to 3000 feet, where their mission was to locate targets and direct artillery fire.

which had to be replaced without delay".[80] The long spur which ended at Fresnoy gave its possessors far too commanding a view over flanking sections of the Oppy-Méricourt line and over much of the Wotan defences to the east.

Orders to recapture Fresnoy reached the 5th Bavarian Division, at Douai, on 5 May. Unusually extensive German artillery activity—well over 100,000 rounds between the evening of 6 May and the morning of the 8th—warned of an impending counter-attack. Further signs came shortly before 4:00 a.m. on the 8th, when advanced German troops blundered into the 2nd Canadian Division's lines and interrupted a relief of the 6th Brigade by the 4th Brigade; the incoming 19th Battalion and the outgoing 29th joined forces and quickly ejected the intruders.[81] The main attack, between the Drocourt road and Gavrelle, was launched two hours later by the 5th Bavarian Division's three regiments (the 7th, 19th and 21st Bavarian) and was supported by seventeen heavy and 27 field batteries, besides the artillery of neighbouring divisions. British defensive fire was entirely inadequate to beat off the attack, expected though it was. Some of the guns had been damaged by fire; the crews of others were suffering from the effects of gas shell; and a dense mist prevented the German infantry's rocket signals from being recognized. The battalion holding the village was practically wiped out as it tried to retire. By nightfall the whole of the Fresnoy salient, and with it the 2nd Canadian Division's right flank, had been pushed back almost in line with Arleux.[82]

It seems certain that an immediate British counter-attack would have succeeded; as it turned out, most of the German rifles and machine-guns were by this time so badly clogged with mud that they could not have been fired. But almost 24 hours were allowed to elapse, and the attempt was not made until 2:30 a.m. on the 9th, when it was too late for an immediate counter-attack to be effective, yet too soon for a deliberately prepared operation. The main effort and a parallel advance by the 4th Canadian Brigade to protect the British left flank broke down, owing to poor liaison in the darkness and the heavy shelling that the enemy maintained on the immediate rear of the attacking formations. A British battalion got briefly into Fresnoy, but had to be withdrawn; and shortly after 1:00 p.m. the whole attempt was abandoned, a new line being established midway between Arleux and Fresnoy. The loss of Fresnoy, after it had been held for more than three days, was a serious setback—both because a hard-gained position of advantage had been sacrificed, and because of the blow to the morale of the British troops.[83]

Although local actions extended the Battles of Arras 1917 to mid-August, as a general offensive they ended with the Third Battle of the Scarpe and the Battle of Bullecourt. Indeed, on the second and third days of these operations French and British political and military leaders had met in Paris to consider a new strategy for the Western Front. The policy of attrition would continue. At a conference at Doullens on 7 May, Field-Marshal Haig informed his army commanders that the French and British objective would be to "wear down and exhaust the enemy's resistance by systematically attacking him by surprise". With this end achieved the next "main blow" would be delivered from the Ypres front—beginning with an attack on Messines Ridge early in June—"with the eventual object of securing the Belgian coast and connecting with the Dutch frontier".[34] Further operations in the Arras area would be of a secondary nature, designed to wear down the enemy, misleading him as to British intentions in the north and keeping his attention away from the French front. Chief of these efforts would be threats to Lille and Lens by attacks mounted about the end of June.

Part of the interest in the Belgian coast arose from the enemy's bombing activities against the United Kingdom. Early in 1917 the Germans had begun to turn from the Zeppelin airship to the more effective heavier-than-air Gotha "G IV". The Gotha had twin 260-horsepower engines which gave it a speed of up to 80 miles per hour. Loaded with six 50-kilogram bombs, or the equivalent, it could fly at approximately 16,000 feet by day; at night, when a 10,000-foot ceiling sufficed, it could carry a load of 500 kilograms. On 25 May a squadron of 21 Gothas carried out a daylight raid on the Folkestone-Shorncliffe area, causing nearly 300 casualties. Seventeen of the dead and 93 of the wounded were Canadian soldiers. On 13 June London suffered its first daylight raid, with 162 persons killed and 432 injured—the heaviest casualties inflicted in any one air raid on England in the war.[35] Among the counter-measures recommended by the G.O.C. Royal Flying Corps (Major-General H. M. Trenchard) was the capture of the Belgian coast up to Holland. If this were done German aircraft would have to operate from landing-grounds farther away from England, and their route would either cross the Allied lines or pass over neutral country.[36] Other suggested counter-measures included retaliation in kind. As air power thus became recognized as an independent means of waging war, the R.F.C. and the Royal Naval Air Service were expanded and eventually, as we have seen (above, p. 132), reunited as the Royal Air Force.[37]

Raids Along the Souchez, May-June 1917

The diversionary operation against Lille did not materialize, for the Second Army, which was to have attacked from the north, needed all its strength for the main effort. General Horne planned the First Army's threat to Lens as an advance by three corps along a fourteen-mile front from Gavrelle to Hill 70, on the northern outskirts of Lens. But this scheme, like the design against Lille, was affected by Field-Marshal Haig's coming needs nearer the coast. Faced with the transfer of a quantity of heavy artillery to Flanders,* Horne was forced to reduce the scope of his army's effort. The attack on Hill 70 (assigned to the 1st British Corps) was postponed. In the centre the inner divisions of the Canadian Corps and the 1st Corps would attack astride the Souchez River in an attempt to break into the German salient between Avion and the western outskirts of Lens.[39]

Preliminary Canadian objectives had been detailed in a Corps order issued on 17 May. The 4th Division, holding the left sector of the Corps front, was

* During the latter part of May the Canadian Corps lost to the Second Army five heavy artillery group headquarters, two heavy batteries, ten siege batteries and five brigades of field artillery.[38]

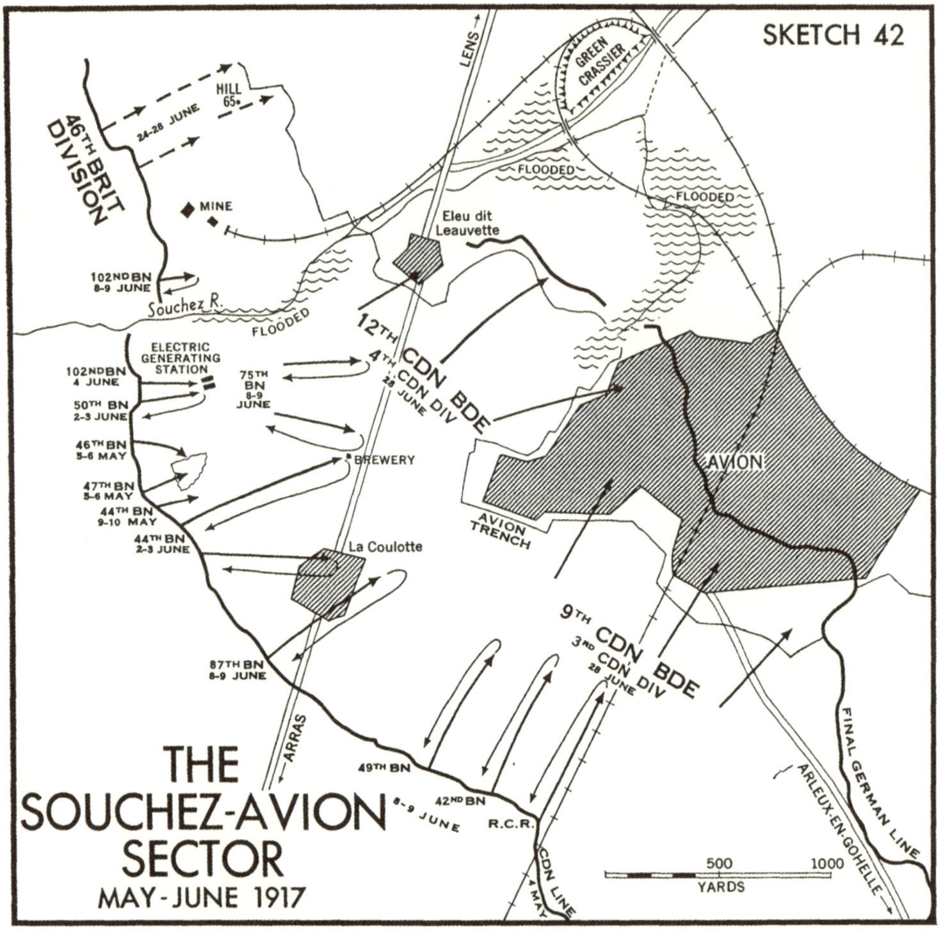

to breach the old Vimy-Lens line and capture a number of fortified positions between Avion and the Souchez. These included the hamlet of La Coulotte on the Arras-Lens road about 1000 yards west of Avion, a brewery 500 yards up the Lens road, and an electric generating station which lay between the brewery and the Souchez. At the river the division would link up with the 1st British Corps, which had been ordered to take Hill 65.[40] It will be noted that these objectives were virtually those of the unsuccessful attack of 23 April by the British 5th and 46th Divisions (above, p. 269).

Preparatory operations had already begun in the Canadian area. On the night of 5-6 May the 46th and 47th Battalions of the 10th Infantry Brigade successfully stormed a triangle of German trenches three-quarters of a mile northwest of La Coulotte: four nights later the 44th Battalion seized 300 yards of the front line and support trench of the Vimy-Lens line immediately south of the triangle. These operations, primarily designed to stir up German reserves so that routes forward would become known to the corps artillery, succeeded in their purpose. Repeated German counter-attacks were broken up by artillery and small-arms fire, but at 3:30 a.m. on the 11th strong elements of the 80th Reserve Division using flamethrowers won back most of the German losses. The setback was only temporary however—late that afternoon the 44th Battalion struck back without artillery preparation and recaptured the position.[41]

At midnight on 2-3 June, after a successful gas bombardment of German positions by more than 600 projectors, the 10th Brigade mounted an attack to take the objectives assigned the 4th Division. The 44th Battalion on the right attacked La Coulotte and the brewery to the north; the 50th's main task was to capture the power station. In heavy fighting both battalions achieved their objectives, but could not hold them. Before dawn on the 3rd the 44th Battalion had been forced back to its start line. The 50th held on all day under unpleasantly accurate shelling which observing enemy aeroplanes directed, only to withdraw early in the evening before a strong counter-attack. The brigade took one hundred prisoners from the 11th Reserve and 56th Divisions. Its own casualties numbered more than 550.[42] Curiously enough, the enemy did not reoccupy the generating station in strength. In an attack two days later the 102nd Battalion (11th Brigade) found it held by only a score of men. These took flight, but were practically annihilated by our Lewis guns.[43]

Short of supporting guns, the Canadians could not keep the enemy from concentrating overwhelming fire on the newly won trenches. The Army Commander therefore, at Currie's suggestion, decided against trying to hold captured ground at great cost, and ordered that operations take the form of large-scale raids in which the assaulting troops would attack in sufficient strength to ensure breaking into the German trenches, but having disposed of the enemy garrison and inflicted the maximum damage on his position, would withdraw under cover of a rearguard.[44] Such a raid was carried out on the night of 8-9 June by strong groups of the 3rd and 4th Divisions on a two-mile front extending from the railway embankment to north of the Souchez. Assaulting in the 7th Brigade's sector on the right were The Royal Canadian Regiment—which, attacking astride the railway, had the heaviest fighting of the Brigade—and the 42nd and 49th Battalions. On the left the 11th Brigade employed the 87th, 75th and 102nd Battalions.

Carefully rehearsed on taped ground, the entire raid went as planned. The two brigades reported more than 150 dug-outs bombed and a number of machine-guns captured or destroyed. A platoon from the 102nd Battalion brilliantly captured and handed over to flanking troops of the 46th Division a concrete machine-gun emplacement on the far side of the Souchez. When the attackers withdrew with some 136 prisoners, they left behind German casualties estimated at more than seven hundred, principally from the 11th Reserve and 56th Divisions.[45] Canadian losses were relatively light—the 7th Brigade, whose claim to have killed 560 Germans seems excessive, reported 335 casualties of its own, 38 of them fatal.[46] The 11th Brigade suffered 374 casualties, including 62 killed.

Twenty-five miles to the north the Second Army's assault on the Messines Ridge had opened auspiciously on 7 June with the capture of all the first day's objectives. It was a triumph for sapper and gunner, using well established tactics of siege warfare. The successful explosion of nineteen huge mines well spaced along the ridge with a total of nearly one million pounds of high explosive, followed by a tremendous artillery barrage, had completely demoralized the defenders. From General Plumer came a message acknowledging the First Army's assistance in diverting the enemy's attention:* "Hope you will let the troops concerned know how much I appreciate their efforts. Your raids last night must have been splendid."[48]

The Battle of Messines, the first phase of the operations planned by Sir Douglas Haig to clear the Belgian coast, ended on 14 June. The completeness of the victory and the speed with which it was attained surpassed that of any previous major operation of the B.E.F. Only the Canadian capture of Vimy Ridge—a lesser operation which the Second Army used as a model—bears comparison. In advancing over the Messines Ridge to a depth of two and a half miles, Plumer's forces had straightened the front line between Ploegsteert and Mount Sorrel, thereby ending German domination of the Ypres Salient from the south. British casualties numbered just under 25,000; German losses probably surpassed this total.[49]

Although the British War Cabinet had not yet approved a continuation of the offensive in Flanders, the Commander-in-Chief was proceeding steadily with preparations for the next phase, which he hoped to initiate in July.[50] He directed the First Army "to hold the enemy to his ground, and prevent his moving troops elsewhere" and to give the impression that the offensive was continuing on that front.[51] To this end, General Horne ordered an advance through the Oppy-Méricourt line and the securing of Lens. Preliminary operations were to begin on 25 June, in such a way as to suggest that the entire 1st, 13th and Canadian Corps were attacking.[52]

On the night of 24-25 June the enemy forces astride the Souchez began falling back before the 46th British Division's attacks. In order to maintain contact, the 1st Corps immediately advanced, the 3rd and 4th Canadian Divisions conforming. The main operation opened at 2:30 a.m. on the 28th, when the 1st and the Canadian Corps attacked respectively north and south of the Souchez River. By morning the 3rd and 4th Canadian Divisions had secured a continuous line on Avion Trench, which angled south-eastward from the river to the outskirts of Avion, and a patrol of the 85th Battalion had reached Eleu dit Leauvette, a hamlet at the junction of the Arras and Givenchy roads.[53]

* Enemy accounts, however, do not admit that the raids affected German troop dispositions. During May the probability, and then the certainty, of a major attack against the Fourth Army had been fully realized. An ever-growing number of divisions and ancillary troops had been placed behind the Fourth Army or close to the inter-army boundary for intervention as required. On the other hand the magnitude of the British underground preparations was not appreciated, and a suggested withdrawal from the forward lines had been turned down by the Fourth Army on the grounds that this would offer no tactical advantages.[47]

The second phase began in a heavy thunderstorm at 7:10 that same evening, after an intense bombardment which utilized artillery on its move north into Flanders. The Germans were completely surprised, and objectives fell quickly. North of the river the 46th Division occupied the whole of Hill 65, and on the Canadian side the 4th Division secured Eleu and most of the village of Avion, the 3rd Division holding a defensive right flank along the Avion-Arleux road. There was little exploitation beyond the Corps objectives, for the heavy downpour had caused the Souchez to flood, and as the enemy recovered from his surprise he fought back fiercely. On the First Army's right two brigades of the 13th Corps assaulted north of Gavrelle and opposite Oppy. Here there was no surprise, yet in spite of hotly contested objectives, all were taken at relatively light cost to the attackers. The new line represented an advance of about half a mile and established British troops in the western outskirts of Oppy.[54]

To complete the encirclement of Lens the First Army had still to capture Hill 70. Yet until the heavy guns available to General Horne could be regrouped, operations against the hill, where strong concrete defences and thick belts of wire called for considerable artillery preparation, had to be postponed. Bad weather brought further delay, and it was mid-August before the attack was finally launched by the Canadian Corps.

A Canadian Corps Commander

The Corps was now under the leadership of Lieut.-General Sir Arthur Currie. On the afternoon of 6 June he had been called to Canadian Corps Headquarters and ordered to assume command, as Lieut.-General Sir Julian Byng was taking over the British Third Army from General Allenby.[55] On the same day the C.-in-C., Sir Douglas Haig, notified the War Office of Byng's new appointment and stated that instructions had been issued for Currie "to take over command of the Canadian Corps". This latter statement was to cause the Canadian authorities in the United Kingdom some concern.[56]

In London the Canadian Overseas Minister, Sir George Perley, was not immediately consulted, and on 9 June, having learned unofficially of the vacancy caused by Byng's promotion, he cabled Sir Robert Borden that he intended "insisting on appointment [of a] Canadian". He set forth the relative suitability of Currie and Major-General Turner for the command of the Canadian Corps, pointing out that "both officers have many strong friends".* He suggested that the "wisest course and one which would cause least friction and difficulty" would be to make Currie Corps Commander and retain Turner as G.O.C. Canadians, giving the latter a certain measure of authority over administrative matters at the front. He would endeavour to get the War Office to promote both officers to the rank of Lieutenant General, thereby preserving Turner's seniority.[57]

* It will be recalled that Turner had foreseen this situation, and upon accepting the appointment of G.O.C. Canadians in November 1916 he had put in his claim for subsequent consideration as Corps Commander (above, p. 211).

The Canadian Prime Minister, occupied with the provisions of the Military Service Bill, which he was to introduce in the House of Commons on 11 June, needed a hastening message from Perley before he replied on the 13th, instructing the Overseas Minister to use his own judgement "and take advice of higher command unless you see strong reason to contrary."[58] Two days later Perley was able to report that the British military authorities would recommend Currie to command the Canadian Corps, and that he had reached a "most pleasant understanding" with Currie and Turner.[59] He had now received a copy of Haig's letter to the War Office of 6 June. In acknowledging this communication he observed, "I should have had to take serious objection to that letter, which reads as though Major-General Currie had already been authorized to command the Canadian Corps, but Major-General Peyton [Haig's military secretary] has explained to me that the word 'temporarily' should have been inserted in the last sentence as that is what was intended and had actually been done." The War Office had made the suggestion (clearly prompted by Sir George himself) that it would be advisable to promote Turner as well as Currie. Sir George found the proposal "most acceptable", and concluded his letter with a gentle reminder of the proper procedure for the War Office to follow: "The Canadian Government is prepared to approve as Commander of the Canadian Corps whichever of these two officers is considered by Sir Douglas Haig to be best fitted for that position, and I shall therefore be prepared to concur in his recommendation when it comes forward."[60]

Currie and Turner were promoted effective 9 June 1917, and it was on that date that the former officially assumed command of the Canadian Corps.[61] Command of the 1st Division passed to Major-General A. C. Macdonell, formerly G.O.C. 7th Infantry Brigade. Sir Robert Borden seized the opportunity to seek further public support for the passage of the Military Service Bill. "As soon as Currie is appointed", he signalled Perley, "I shall send message of congratulations to him. It would be well if in his reply he would make clear the need for reinforcements to maintain Canadian Army Corps at full strength. Liberal Press of Quebec are insisting with great vehemence that no further reinforcements are required."[62] Currie responded by expressing the confident expectation of the troops in the field that "the full fruits of their sacrifice" would not be prejudiced. "It is an imperative and urgent necessity", his statement concluded, "that steps be immediately taken to ensure that sufficient drafts of officers and men are sent from Canada to keep the Corps at its full strength."[63]

The Assault on Hill 70, 15 August

On 7 July the First Army notified the Canadian Corps of orders received from Sir Douglas Haig to capture Lens with a view to threatening an advance on Lille from the south.[64] The centre of the most crowded coal-mining area in France, Lens had suffered heavily from artillery fire and now lay in partial ruin, encircled by a wreath of shattered pithead installations.

General Currie was directed to make plans for breaking through the Méricourt trench south of Lens and advancing to the line of the railway beyond, securing this from Méricourt through the city as far as the Lens-Béthune road. Regrouping for the operations began on 10 July, when General Horne ordered Currie to relieve the 1st Corps opposite Lens and Hill 70. By 16 July the 1st and 2nd Canadian Divisions had taken over three miles of line from the Souchez north to a point opposite the German-held Bois Hugo, a shell-shattered wood one mile north-east of Loos.[65] South of the Souchez the Canadian Corps' right flank, covering the Avion-Méricourt sector, was being held by the 3rd Division.

General Currie was not happy with the objectives assigned to him by the First Army. Lens was dominated from the north by Hill 70 and from the south-east by Sallaumines Hill. He regarded either of these heights as more important, tactically, than the town itself. Merely to occupy the town while the enemy held the high ground would place the attackers in a lower and more exposed position than the recently established British footing on the south-western outskirts of Lens. Furthermore, artillery deployment on the open plain would present serious difficulties. The order as it stood called for a frontal attack, thereby precluding the two hills even as intermediate objectives. At a conference of corps commanders held on the 10th, Currie persuaded the Army Commander to make Hill 70 the "immediate main objective".[66] He hoped to be able to carry out the operation on 30 July. Canadian possession of the hill, giving observation far into the German lines, would be so intolerable to the enemy that he would be compelled to attempt to retake it; and his counter-attacks could be effectively dealt with by artillery. In the meantime minor operations would continue so as to suggest to the enemy a forthcoming attack on the entire First Army front south of La Bassée canal. As part of this programme the G.O.C. 3rd Canadian Division, Major-General Lipsett, was ordered to launch an attack through the Méricourt trench on the night of the 22nd-23rd, with the object of destroying German dug-outs and trench-mortar emplacements behind the railway embankment.[67]

Noting that this preliminary operation was planned as a one-battalion raid, First Army Headquarters drew attention to the Commander-in-Chief's recent injunction that in order to increase the pressure on Lens "all ground must be held, by rifle and bayonet alone if no assistance is obtainable from other arms"[68]. In reply General Currie stressed the tactical unsoundness of trying to occupy permanently the line of the railway embankment, which was commanded from the high ground in front and enfiladed from either flank. His final orders to the 3rd Division were to raid and withdraw.[69]

The assault was delivered at 1:00 a.m. on 23 July by the 116th Battalion (of the 9th Infantry Brigade). In spite of a gas attack launched by the enemy just as our troops were forming up, the operation, adequately supported by the divisional artillery, was completely successful. The 116th quickly took the trench that formed its first objective, killing many Germans. In solid hand-to-hand fighting the attacking companies gained the railway embankment and blew up a number of dug-outs and a tunnel. After thirty-five minutes the main body returned to its original position as planned, leaving outposts who subsequently came under a heavy counter-attack and had to be withdrawn. The Canadian battalion, whose own casualties numbered 74, brought back 53 prisoners from the 36th Reserve Division, one of a number of formations that had been transferred from the Eastern Front earlier in the summer.[70]

We have noted that bad weather was to postpone the attack on Hill 70 until mid-August. In the interval Canadian infantry limited their operations to raiding. The artillery carried out a steady programme of wire-cutting, counter-battery work and gas shelling, which special companies of the Royal Engineers augmented by projecting drums of gas on Lens.* By the 15th of the month more than 3500 drums and 900 gas shells had been sent into the town, and the artillery had neutralized some 40 out of an estimated 102 enemy batteries. On the Corps right the 4th Division had relieved the 3rd Division on 26 July. In the reserve areas troops of the 1st and 2nd Divisions were undergoing special training for their part in the coming venture.[72] These obvious preliminaries to an attack made it impossible to conceal the First Army's general intention or even, as it turned out, the date of the assault. The best that could be done was to try to mislead the enemy with respect to exact time and place. To this end on 14 August the 1st Corps staged demonstration attacks with dummy tanks directly west of Lens.[73]

Hill 70, a treeless expanse of chalk downland standing at the end of one of the many spurs which reached north-eastward from the Artois plateau, dominated Lens and gave a commanding view of the Douai plain beyond. In September 1915, as we have seen (above, page 121), the British had overrun the hill but had not managed to hold it. The Lens-La Bassée highway climbed gently over its upper western slopes, just short of the barren crest. To the north the hill fell away in a steady gradient towards the Loos valley; the descent of the south side was broken by the Cité spur, over which spread the northern suburbs of Lens—Cité St. Edouard, Cité St. Laurent, Cité St. Emile and Cité Ste. Elisabeth. These were brick-built company towns of miners' houses, most of which months of shellfire had reduced to a fantastic maze of ruins across which trenches now meandered. East of the hill, between the La Bassée and Lille roads, was the sprawling Cité St. Auguste. Though much of this extensive built-up area flanking Hill 70 to east and south lay in ruins, the cover it provided the defenders was to present a special challenge to the artillery.

The final Canadian objective was a series of old German trenches which formed an arc around Hill 70's lower eastern slope, stretching for two miles from Cité Ste. Elisabeth to Bois Hugo. This and two forward trench lines on

* During this artillery preparation for the first time Canadian guns were registered by the use of wireless communication with ground observers.[71]

the hill, with deep old-style dug-outs, the enemy now used only as shelter from shellfire and rain; but in the eyes of the Canadian planners the position was far enough to the east to protect the artillery observation posts which they proposed to establish on the summit. The hard chalk subsoil, in which the men could quickly dig serviceable trenches, would lend itself to early consolidation against the inevitable counter-attack, which must be made under close observation and for this the Canadian artillery would be well prepared.

The Germans were expected to accept the temporary loss of their lightly held forward position and to fight the main defensive battle from machine-gun posts and shell-holes immediately to the rear, counter-attacking with fresh troops from assembly areas in and about Cité St. Auguste. To meet this latter threat heavy and divisional artillery would shell probable lines of advance from these areas, while aerial observers watched for German troop concentrations farther back.* As far as possible Hill 70 was to be "a killing by artillery".[75] The main assault was to be supported by nine field brigades—five with the 1st Division on the left, and four with the 2nd Division. Their barrage would be supplemented by the fire of 160 machine-guns. Rehearsals for the attack, carried out on ground resembling the actual battlefield, repeated the tactics that had proved successful at Fresnoy. There was emphasis on immediately mopping up the captured area and bringing forward the machine-guns—48 with each assaulting brigade—as soon as the objective was taken. Each machine-gun position would then become the centre of a platoon strongpoint manned by at least 25 infantrymen.[76]

The two assaulting divisions each had two brigades forward—from north to south the 3rd, 2nd, 5th and 4th—totalling ten battalions. Their objective was marked off in depth in three stages. The assaulting battalions would take the enemy's front trenches in their first stride. The Blue Line ran along the German second position, on the crest of the hill. The Green, the final objective, marked the enemy's third line, on the lower reverse slope, some 1500 yards from the starting position. From north to south it followed in succession "Hugo" and "Norman" Trenches and "Nun's Alley", their chalky course showing a dead white on air photographs. Opposite the 2nd Division's right flank the Green Line inclined south-west along "Commotion" Trench, to bend sharply westward along "Chicory". In the centre, where the 2nd Brigade had the greatest distance to cover, the intermediate Red Line formed a chord to the curve of the final objective.[77]

The assault went in at 4:25 on the morning of 15 August, just as dawn was breaking. Special companies of the Royal Engineers began firing drums of burning oil into Cité Ste. Elisabeth and at other selected targets in order to supplement the artillery fire and build up a smoke-screen. The 18-pounders, 102 to each division, laid down their rolling barrage "with beautiful accuracy". Four hundred

* In the event, No. 43 Squadron R.F.C. rendered fine service in locating active batteries, reporting German troop movements and strafing "a large number of targets of all descriptions", while No. 16 cooperated "most effectually" with the artillery.[74]

yards ahead 4.5- and 6-inch howitzers fired a jumping barrage, while still further forward known enemy strongpoints were blasted by heavy howitzers*.[79]

The Germans holding Hill 70 were the 26th and 165th Regiments of the 7th Infantry Division. On the previous night, in anticipation of the Canadian attack, they had moved their reserve battalions up to Mortar Wood (600 yards north-east of Cité St. Auguste) and to the brickworks at the south-west corner of the Cité. They had detected the assembly of our troops at 3:00 a.m., and three minutes after zero their artillery brought down defensive fire at widely scattered points. Our counter-batteries were ready, however, and quickly neutralized the German guns. Under cover of the barrage and the thick oil smoke the Canadians advanced rapidly, overwhelming trench garrisons as they went. In the more difficult sector on the right the brigades of Major-General Burstall's 2nd Division made their way through the debris of Cité St. Edouard and Cité St. Laurent without losing pace. Within twenty minutes, both divisions were on the Blue Line, having covered an average distance of 600 yards. Another twenty minutes passed while the 18th and 21st Battalions of the 4th Brigade made of Chicory Trench a defensive flank facing the northern edge of Lens; the 20th then resumed the advance through the ruins of Cité Ste. Elisabeth to secure the remainder of Commotion Trench. To the right of centre; the 5th Brigade passed the 24th and 26th Battalions through the 25th and 22nd to overrun Cité St. Emile and take Nun's Alley. In spite of heavy machine-gun fire from Cité St. Auguste and the adjacent brickworks, the 2nd Brigade closed with the Red Line—the 7th Battalion on the left and the 8th on the right. The 3rd Brigade continued its advance to Hugo Trench with its three original assault battalions (the 15th, 13th and 16th) remaining forward.[80]

The careful planning that had gone into the operation was again reflected in the second phase, which met with little more opposition than the first. Brig.-Gen. Tuxford's battalions suffered some casualties from machine-guns in Bois Hugo before bombers closed in on these from the flanks. A medium trench mortar with all-round traverse fell to the 15th Battalion; 500 rounds which lay beside it were subsequently fired into the north-east end of Bois Hugo. By 6:00 a.m. the 2nd Brigade was at the intermediate Red Line, and in the other brigade sectors the Green Line was in Canadian hands.[81]

In Major-General Macdonell's sector there remained the 2nd Brigade's advance to its Green Line objective, which included Norman Trench and a large chalk quarry abreast of the northern outskirts of Cité St. Auguste. After a halt of twenty minutes prescribed by the artillery time-table Brig.-Gen. Loomis sent the 7th and 8th Battalions forward in this final phase. Unfortunately, during the delay the oil smoke-screen had largely cleared and the enemy had been able to rally his remaining garrison. Machine-gun and rifle fire swept the eastern slope of

*The G.O.C. Royal Artillery, Canadian Corps, Brig.-Gen. E. W. B. Morrison, was much concerned over the shortage and worn condition of his heavy guns. Many batteries had been withdrawn for the offensive in the north, and only 164 heavy pieces of various calibres remained. Before the operation the Corps Commander obtained the First Army's undertaking to maintain 75 per cent of these guns in action. Worn guns were used only when bursts of very intense fire with limited accuracy were needed against German units advancing in depth.[78]

Hill 70, slowing the advance to "individual rushes from shell-hole to shell-hole", in which all benefit of the barrage was lost. Only the flank companies of the two battalions reached their objectives. The 7th, on the left, found the quarry toughly garrisoned and well covered by enfilading machine-guns. Rifle grenadiers of one of the attacking companies wiped out a strongpoint manned by thirty Germans, and then covered a second company's assault from the northern flank. Knocking out a machine-gun post at the entrance, the latter rushed into the quarry, and seized close to fifty prisoners, setting up posts which they were able to hold until the early afternoon. The remainder of the battalion was forced to retire up the slope to the Red Line, being joined on the Brigade right by the 8th Battalion, whose attack had lost momentum and petered out in the shell-holes.[82]

On General Currie's right flank a diversionary operation mounted by the 4th Canadian Division at Lens had proved its worth. As the main attack went in, 200 gas bombs were projected on to enemy strongpoints and dug-outs opposite Avion, while artillery and machine-guns not involved at Hill 70 fired the conventional barrage. The simulated assault by the 12th Brigade on the divisional right drew much more retaliatory fire than did the main operation. Four hours later, on the 2nd Division's immediate right, the 11th Brigade pushed strong fighting patrols towards the centre of Lens, preparing to reinforce and exploit their success should the enemy relax his hold of the town. But the Germans were not ready to abandon Lens, and a renewal of local counter-attacks across the 4th Division's front drove the Canadian patrols back to the city's outskirts.[83]

German Counter-Attacks

On the main front the Canadians lost no time in constructing strongpoints all along the Blue Line and setting up Vickers guns as planned. Thus they were ready when between seven and nine o'clock on the morning of the 15th the enemy, using his immediate reserves, mounted local attacks at four points in the captured part of the Green Line. Through the good work of our forward artillery observers on the crest, who could now overlook the German preparations, each attempt was broken up before it was well started. Renewed efforts later in the morning with units drawn from flanking regiments met the same fate. One captured German officer reported that his regiment while marching up had been caught in concentration after concentration, and that it was completely spent before it was engaged by Canadian infantry—a striking tribute to the concept which had been gaining force since Vimy that the artillery must seek to *paralyze* the enemy, thereby enabling the infantry to close with him.[84] The enemy reinforced rapidly. As the day wore on, the eight battalions opposing the two Canadian Divisions were joined by seven more belonging to the 4th Guard and 185th Divisions.[85]

Enemy accounts of the battle indicate that the German plan of defence had provided only for immediate counter-blows—to catch the Canadians before they had time to consolidate. The additional forces that hurriedly assembled opposite Hill 70 were ordered to deliver their counter-attacks at 11:00 a.m., but these were delayed until early afternoon. What developed, instead of a well coordinated operation, was merely a large-scale resumption of the morning's efforts—a series of disorganized local assaults. Four waves of infantry, marching across the open "through fountains of earth sent up by the heavy shells" and then "through a hail of shrapnel and machine-gun bullets", were all but annihilated.[86] A frontal attack on the 2nd Brigade from Cité St. Auguste similarly failed. On the right flank of the 2nd Division, the enemy succeeded in re-entering Chicory Trench; but by 6:40 the position was again ours.

In the meantime, at about half-past one, Brig.-Gen. Loomis had ordered the 7th and 8th Battalions, supported by the 1st and 2nd Divisional Artilleries, to storm the 800-yard section of the Green Line still uncaptured. But the combined fighting strength of these units had been reduced to about 200, making the prospect of success on so wide a front extremely dubious. Necessary regrouping delayed the operation, which was to have started at 4:00 p.m.; and after two successive postponements it was cancelled. The barrage, however, was fired at 6:00 p.m. as planned, and had the effect of breaking up a further strong counter-attack that was threatening. As they turned in flight many Germans were cut down by the infantry's Lewis gun and rifle fire.[87] Throughout the evening the Germans persisted in their counter-attacks, but each time our artillery overwhelmed them. At one time all the guns of the Canadian and the 1st British Corps were firing defensive tasks along the front of the three Canadian divisions. Casualties on both sides were heavy. The day's operations had cost the Canadians 1056 killed, 2432 wounded and 39 taken prisoner. (In the 7th Battalion many lives were saved by the tireless and heroic efforts of one of the regimental stretcher-bearers, Private M. J. O'Rourke, whose "most conspicuous bravery and devotion to duty" won him the Victoria Cross.)[88] The number of enemy dead and wounded is not known, but by 9:00 p.m. on the 15th some 350 German prisoners had been counted; 24 hours later the number taken in both days' fighting was reported as 970.[89]

The second morning of the battle, 16 August, was relatively quiet, with only a few attempts by small enemy parties to approach our lines. At four in the afternoon the 2nd Brigade launched its postponed attack, the fresher 5th and 10th Battalions replacing the 7th and 8th. Despite fierce German resistance, in little more than an hour the whole of the Green Line was in Canadian hands. In the chalk quarry the 10th Battalion killed a hundred of the enemy and took 130 prisoners, while in Norman Trench the 5th Battalion captured fifty prisoners and eight machine-guns. By half-past five the latter battalion had used up all its ammunition and grenades and its two assaulting companies were down to less than ten men. Forced to fall back on the Red Line, the battalion partially reoccupied its objective but was unable to re-establish contact with the 2nd Division's left flank. The 10th Battalion, despite a temporarily open right flank, grimly hung on to its ground in the face of repeated counter-attacks.

Then occurred one of the many acts of heroism that illumine the dark pages of war. With all wires cut, communication between the 10th Battalion's company and battalion headquarters could be maintained only by runner. To ensure one urgent message being delivered, two runners had to venture back through an intense barrage. One was killed; but the other, Private Harry Brown, his arm shattered, doggedly struggled through to complete his mission before collapsing unconscious on the dug-out steps. He died of his wounds and received posthumously the Victoria Cross.[90] That night the 1st Brigade relieved the 3rd Brigade on the divisional left, and on the following night took over the 2nd Brigade's sector as well.[91]

Minor Canadian actions on the 17th met varying success. At the boundary between the 2nd and 4th Divisions a morning attempt by the 4th and 11th Brigades to eliminate an enemy salient between Cité Ste. Elisabeth and Lens failed; but in the evening bombing parties of the 5th Brigade occupied a section of Norman Trench, whose retention by the Germans had left an 80-yard gap between adjacent flanks of the 1st and 2nd divisions.[92]

As had been foreseen, determined German counter-attacks continued. The night of 17th-18th saw the beginning of a further series directed mainly against the chalk quarry. The enemy sought to wear down our artillery's resources by sending up false S.O.S. signals or provoking our infantry to call for unnecessary fire.[93] At the same time the Germans shelled batteries of the 1st and 2nd Field Brigades with the recently introduced "Yellow Cross" or mustard gas—a vesicant or blistering liquid which they had first used in Flanders during July.[94] The Canadian gunners suffered heavily. When the droplets of gas fogged the goggles of their respirators, some who removed their face-pieces in order to maintain accurate fire became casualties. Many were put out of action while replenishing ammunition, and there were instances of men with clothes sprinkled by the harmful liquid contaminating others in gas-proof dug-outs. In some cases it took a day or more for the gas to take effect; but by noon on 21 August the two artillery brigades had suffered 183 casualties from this bombardment.[95] Ironically, the 5th and 10th Battalions, retiring to billets in Les Brebis for a badly needed rest, were caught in the shelling and several became gas casualties.[96]

The enemy's pressure persisted. At 11:30 p.m. (on the 17th) large numbers of Germans advancing towards the chalk quarry were stopped some 100 yards out by the Lewis guns and rifles of the 4th Battalion. Another strong attack three hours later met the same fate, as did a third attempt at 4:15 on the morning of 18 August.[97] This last attack coincided with one against Chicory Trench on the 2nd Division's right flank by elements of the 55th Reserve Infantry Regiment (on loan to the 11th Reserve Division).[98] Only one company managed to close with the defences, and it was promptly driven off. Sergeant Frederick Hobson of the 20th Battalion, a veteran of the South African War, played a major part in repulsing one Germany party. He seized a Lewis gun whose crew had been put out of action and with it engaged the enemy at short range. When the weapon jammed, Hobson, who was not a Lewis gunner, ordered a survivor of the gun crew to remedy the stoppage, and, though wounded, attacked the enemy single-handed with bayonet and clubbed rifle. A rifle shot laid him low, but by that time the Lewis gun was back in action and reinforcements were coming up. Hobson's heroic action won him a posthumous Victoria Cross.[99]

Still another attack came at 5:00 a.m. (on the 18th), this time north of the chalk quarry. It fell mainly on two companies of the 2nd Battalion astride Bois Hugo. German bombers, with other men using flamethrowers, penetrated the more northerly position but were soon driven out. Elsewhere the enemy was pounded by artillery, raked by machine-gun and rifle fire at closer range, and finally brought to a halt right on the parapet by grenades. Both Canadian company commanders were killed; one, Major O. M. Learmonth (of the company south of the wood), earned the Victoria Cross. Though severely wounded he stood on the parapet directing the defence and hurling grenades at the approaching Germans. Several times he caught enemy bombs and threw them back with deadly effect. When he could no longer fight because of his wounds, he continued to instruct his junior officers in the conduct of the battle. So spirited a defence by the 2nd Battalion drove back the enemy and held the position intact; further threatened attacks were broken up by artillery fire.[100]

"It was altogether the hardest battle in which the Corps has participated", General Currie wrote of the events of 15-18 August in his personal diary.

> There were no fewer than twenty-one counter-attacks delivered, many with very large forces and all with great determination and dash . . . Four German divisions were accounted for, viz. 7th, 8th, 11th and 4 Guards Reserve [*sic*].* Our casualties so far about 5600 but in my opinion the enemy casualties must be close to 20,000. Our gunners, machine-gunners and infantry never had such targets, FOO's could not get guns for all their targets . . . It was a great and wonderful victory. G.H.Q. regard it as one of the finest performances of the war...

After the opening day of the battle the scale of Canadian casualties had dropped off considerably. From 16 to 18 August the actual numbers were 449 killed (including seven by gas), 1378 wounded by fire, 487 gassed non-fatally, and two taken prisoner.

The Attacks on Lens, 21 August

For the next two days, after the enemy had launched a final unsuccessful attack against the quarry, things were quieter along the Canadian Corps front. Although the gap between the 1st and 2nd Divisions had been closed, the Canadian position there was none too secure. Accordingly it was decided to abandon Norman Trench, drawing the front line back 300 yards to "Noggin" Trench, midway between the original Red and Green Lines. Meanwhile the 4th Division slightly advanced its posts on the outskirts of Lens and extended its front northward to include the Béthune road.

* German reports show that actually elements of five German divisions were engaged: the 7th, 185th and 220th Divisions, the 4th Guard Division and the 11th Reserve Division.[101]

Reproduced by Army Survey Establishment

Compiled and drawn by Historical Section G.S.

General Currie had decided on the 18th to clear up the situation in front of Lens on the lower southern slope of the hill. The 2nd and 4th Divisions would be used. The former's objective included, from left to right, the 500-yard section of Nun's Alley between Commotion Trench and Nabob Alley; "Cinnabar" Trench—a well-dug position just west of the main road leading out to Cité St. Auguste; and "Combat" Trench, which angled back south-westward to the fork of the Béthune and La Bassée roads. On the right of the Béthune road the 4th Division was to attack south-eastward into Lens in the direction of the Arras road, which was guarded by the line of "Aloof", "Aconite" and "Alpaca" Trenches. In all, 3000 yards of the enemy's front line would be occupied—from Eleu dit Leauvette to a point east of Cité St. Emile. The operation was scheduled for the morning of 21 August, the principal tasks north and west of Lens being divided between the 6th Brigade, on the left, and the 10th on the right. Holding the enemy line from north to south were two battalions of the 4th Guard Division, two battalions from the 220th Division, and one and a half from the 1st Guard Reserve Division (which was in the process of relieving the 11th Reserve Division). Six additional German battalions, or their equivalent, were in support.[102]

There would be no dearth of supporting guns. Brig.-Gen. Ketchen was assigned the 2nd Divisional Artillery, assisted by the 1st Division's guns; Brig.-Gen. Hilliam had the support of the 4th Divisional Artillery augmented by four British batteries and the Royal Canadian Horse Artillery. (The R.C.H.A. Brigade had been on loan to the 1st Division from the Cavalry Brigade, which was with the British Cavalry Corps in Flanders.) Before the attack the Canadian Corps Heavy Artillery—the 1st Canadian and two British heavy groups—fired destructive shoots on the trenches north of Lens and towards the centre of the city, much of which already lay in ruins. During the operation the "heavies" and "super-hows" shelled Lens continually, inflicting heavy casualties on the German infantry crowded in the cellars and ruined buildings of the city. To mislead the enemy the 1st Divisional Artillery and one of the British heavy groups also laid down a feint barrage north of the intended objective.[103]

Zero hour was at 4:35, while it was still dark, but whether by chance or design the enemy anticipated the assault. At about four o'clock he began to shell the Canadian positions, and just before zero he attacked the 6th Brigade's left flank with a Guard battalion. Both forces met between their respective objectives, and desperate bayonet fighting ensued.[104] The spearhead of the blow fell on the 29th Battalion's left-hand company at the northern end of the sector of assault, but was beaten off in bitter fighting. Meanwhile the Canadian battalion's right-hand company pushed forward to Cinnabar Trench, suffering crippling losses at it crossed the open fields. All the officers were killed or wounded, whereupon the company-sergeant-major, W.O. II Robert Hanna, assumed command and led a party against a German strongpoint that three assaults had failed to capture. He personally killed four of the defenders, seizing the position and silencing its machine-gun. He then made good a portion of Cinnabar Trench and held it against repeated counter-attacks. Such spirited leadership and daring brought Hanna the Victoria Cross.[105]

Although the 29th Battalion was able to repel the Guard battalion's counter-attack, it did not gain all its own objectives. With the help of the supporting 28th Battalion, most of Nun's Alley and the north-east end of Cinnabar Trench were cleared and consolidated, but at noon the enemy still held four to five hundred yards of Cinnabar; and his retention of several small trenches off Nabob Alley rendered most precarious the Canadian positions about the important junction of Nabob, Cinnabar and Nun's Alley.[106]

On Brig.-Gen. Ketchen's right the 27th Battalion, attacking on the north-western edge of Lens, was having its own troubles. The Battalion had to traverse some 500 yards of open ground, beyond which the 4th Guard Division was holding positions of considerable strength. The defenders had the advantage of deep cellars, immune to all but heavy artillery fire, and hidden communication trenches for moving up reinforcements and supplies. When machine-gun fire stopped the advance, the difficulty of digging in the rubble made it virtually impossible for the Canadians to consolidate their gains. To make matters worse, the 10th Brigade's 50th Battalion, on the right, was unable to keep abreast and provide the flank protection expected of it. Nevertheless the 27th succeeded in taking all but the central part of its objective—500 yards of Cinnabar Trench immediately south-west of its junction with Combat and "Conductor" Trenches.[107]

The 10th Brigade also had a story of limited achievement to tell. While assembling for the attack the 50th Battalion on the left flank had suffered more than a hundred casualties from shellfire—and it was necessary to make a last-minute change in the assaulting companies. A feint attack the day before against Aloof Trench, half way to the objective, had put the enemy in this sector on the alert, and on the 21st as the 50th's leading companies neared the German line they met the most intense artillery and machine-gun fire. Only three small parties, the largest of not more than twenty men, reached their goal, the junction of the Béthune and La Bassée roads. What was left of the rest of the battalion was back at the starting position within ninety minutes. Eventually the groups at the objective, unable to link up with one another or with either of the flanking battalions, also had to retire. Few got back alive.[108]

The 46th Battalion, assaulting in the centre, had been heavily shelled throughout the preceding night. In one forward company all officers became casualties and had to be replaced. Despite this and the 50th Battalion's setback on the left, the 46th reached its goal.[109] On the Brigade right the 47th Battalion escaped the shelling but then fought a bitter all-day battle, in which German machine-guns reaped a heavy harvest. By evening one company had gained the Arras road, and later that night the battalion had all its objectives. In the course of the day's fighting a former bayonet-fighting instructor in the Russian Army, Corporal Filip Konowal of the 47th, attacked one particularly troublesome machine-gun, killed the crew and captured the gun. In the same action this intrepid soldier entered single-handedly into two other attacks, killing several Germans; and in a minor operation next day he knocked out another machine-gun. "For most conspicuous bravery and leadership", Konowal was awarded the Victoria Cross, the sixth to be won by Canadians in the Hill 70-Lens fighting.[110]

As the day wore on the situation north and north-east of the Béthune road worsened. Communications between the 6th Brigade's forward units and General Ketchen's headquarters had broken down at the beginning of the attack and could not be restored; the intermediate areas were under heavy shellfire, and it was all but impossible to coordinate the further actions of the two battalions and the artillery. Nevertheless, with the "heavies" having their effect on the German defences, the 29th Battalion was ordered to attack the uncaptured portion of Cinnabar Trench with the support of trench mortars. Zero hour was to have been 2:30 p.m.; but by then the 4th Guard Division, reinforced by a battalion of the 220th Division, had resumed their counter-attacks with renewed vigour. Instead of carrying out the intended attack both the 29th Battalion and the 27th had to be withdrawn in the late afternoon to their original lines, leaving outposts desperately clinging to insecure positions in Nabob Alley and Conductor and Combat Trenches.[111]

It had been a difficult and costly day. In these operations the advancing forces had run beyond the advantages conferred by the ground. Canadian casualties on 21 August numbered 1154—346 killed or fatally wounded, 728 wounded by fire, 74 by gas, and six taken prisoner. On the other side of the ledger the sight of many German dead gave indication of considerable losses inflicted on the enemy. Between midday on 20 August and mid-morning of the 22nd some 200 captured Germans entered the Corps cage or the Casualty Clearing Station.[112]

The Green Crassier and Aloof Trench, 21-25 August

The 4th Division's efforts continued. The enemy's retention of Aloof Trench created a nasty salient in Major-General Watson's line, and on the evening of 21 August the 50th Battalion again attacked, with three parties attempting to bomb the position from the flanks. Only the group working in from the south achieved any success. A further attack planned for the 22nd failed to materialize, "because of a misunderstanding", says the battalion account. Nevertheless that night a prearranged plan to exploit what success the 10th Brigade had already gained was put into effect. The 44th Battalion, kept until now in brigade reserve, was given the assignment.[113] It was to be a costly and unprofitable task.

The objective of the 44th Battalion was a large heap of mine refuse, known at the Green Crassier, which stood between the railway station and the Canal de Lens, about a thousand yards east of the Lens-Arras road and some 350 beyond the right of the 10th Brigade's present position. Its capture would advance the Canadian front line so that it encircled Lens on three sides. Though such a threat might help to precipitate a German withdrawal from the city, it seems to have been insufficiently realized that to thus drive a narrow wedge into the enemy's positions would leave the 44th Battalion with dangerously exposed flanks.

The route assigned the battalion was dominated on the left by the Fosse St. Louis. This was one of the many pithead installations which abounded in the area. Contrary to a report that the position was free of enemy, the ruined buildings were thick with Germans, who were reinforced from large underground tunnels as the fight proceeded. The enemy was holding the Fosse St. Louis and the Green Crassier with two battalions of the 64th Reserve Infantry Regiment (1st Guard Reserve Division).[114] On discovering the true situation the Commanding Officer of the 44th Battalion had to split his force, sending two platoons to attack the Fosse and one company against the Crassier. Since the main effort would be made in depth and on a narrow front, the Commanding Officer detailed one and a half companies for support and mopping-up roles, for success would depend on proper consolidation and the prompt arrival of supplies and reinforcements.[115] (The fourth company, whose assistance would have been most welcome, was on loan to the 46th Battalion and could not be recalled in time.)

Zero hour was at 3:00 a.m. on the 23rd, and the start line the Lens-Arras road. The attackers followed the barrage forward in good order, and in half an hour the leading company had scaled the steep sides of the Crassier and taken up positions among the shattered debris of dump cars and torn up tracks that covered the plateau. But the platoons assaulting the Fosse St. Louis came under continuous machine-gun fire, and it was not until 8:30, after much bitter fighting, that they gained a footing in the buildings. This proved only temporary, and the Fosse changed hands several times that day. On one occasion the Canadians suffered heavily when the German defenders withdrew into the tunnels below and brought down heavy artillery fire over the whole area. When all reserves of the 64th Reserve Infantry Regiment had been committed against the Canadians, the Germans employed a company from the 1st Guard Reserve Regiment and a battalion of the 190th Infantry Regiment (of the 220th Infantry Division).[116] In the end the hotly disputed position was back in the enemy's possession.[117]

With the coming of daylight on the 24th the Canadians on top of the Crassier found themselves isolated, for though the supporting company had secured Alpaca Trench, which provided communication forward from the Arras road, this ended short of the Crassier and the enemy's heavy fire prevented any passage of the intervening gap. As the morning passed strong enemy parties, supported by fire from artillery, trench mortars and machine-guns, repeatedly counter-attacked the Crassier from all sides. The Canadians fought back desperately from shell-holes and from trenches hastily scraped in the coal slack, but in the end bombs gave out and ammunition ran low. By late afternoon the last 44th men on the Crassier had been killed or captured and the Germans were in full possession. In its heroic but fruitless efforts the battalion had suffered 257 casualties. These included 23 killed and 118 missing, of whom 70 were taken prisoner on the Green Crassier and seventeen at the Fosse St. Louis.[118] No further attack was made on the Fosse and the Crassier, and these strongholds remained in the enemy's hands until his general retirement at the end of the war.

Next day, 25 August, brought a more successful Canadian effort. In an attempt to improve its position on the 10th Brigade's left the 50th Battalion finally launched its attack against the north half of Aloof Trench at 2:00 a.m. After a bombardment by the 1st Canadian and the 63rd British Heavy Groups, the usual field artillery barrage was successfully replaced by one using Stokes mortars and large numbers of rifle grenades. This effectively beat down all opposition except for some machine-gun fire. At a cost of only half a dozen wounded, the 50th secured and consolidated Aloof Trench and during the day pushed patrols eastward almost to the objectives originally set for the assault on 21 August.[119]

With this satisfactory anticlimax Canadian operations at Lens virtually ended. Already by the morning of 23 August, the 3rd Division had relieved the 1st and 2nd on Hill 70; and on the night of the 24th-25th, the 11th Brigade took over from the 10th at Lens. The last few days of August, all September and the beginning of October, were relatively quiet, devoted mainly to preparations for a further offensive. General Horne wished to complete the capture of Lens and seal off the retreat of its defenders by making converging advances south-east from Hill 70 and north-east from Eleu towards the high ground at Sallaumines. The 4th Canadian Division was briefed for the latter role, but the operation did not materialize. Desirable though it was to divert the enemy's attention from Flanders by maintaining pressure here, the First Army lacked sufficient resources for the task.

Yet the capture of Hill 70 and the subsidiary attacks on Lens, costly as they were, had achieved the desired results, even though much of the town was still in the wrong hands. The fighting in the period 15-25 August had cost the Canadians 9198 casualties. But the Canadian effort had contributed towards wearing down the enemy: General Currie's forces had badly mauled five German divisions.[120] The Canadian success confronted Crown Prince Rupprecht with serious reinforcement problems. The possibility of a new battle breaking out at some other point on his Army Group's front jeopardized the scheme for exchanging fresh divisions with battle-worn formations in Flanders. A discerning German military historian has thus summed up the situation:

> Even though we soon succeeded in sealing off the local penetration at Lens, the Canadians had attained their ends. The fighting at Lens had cost us a considerable number of troops which had to be replaced. The entire preconceived plan for relieving the troops in Flanders had been upset. One had to reckon with a continuation of the attack by the Canadian divisions. Crown Prince Rupprecht therefore refrained from attempting immediately to recapture the lost ground at Lens, which would have required strong new forces and promoted the very intentions of the opponent.[121]

Topographically Hill 70 was no Vimy Ridge, yet it did not again change hands during the war. The tactical advantage that its possession gave to the Allies may well have brought it immunity from attack in the German offensive of 1918.

The eyes of the Canadians were now to turn northward, where before many weeks passed they were to be engaged on another battlefield, familiar to many of them from days before the Corps was formed.

CHAPTER X

PASSCHENDAELE, OCTOBER-NOVEMBER 1917

(See Map 9 and Sketches 43-45)

The Background to Third Ypres

PASSCHENDAELE, a typical crossroads village in Flanders, has given its name to an entire campaign; though officially the designation belongs only to the two last of eight battles known collectively as "Ypres 1917", or "Third Ypres". In this series of operations, which began at the end of July, the role of the Canadian Corps comprised the diversionary efforts in the Lens area already described and the four attacks between 26 October and 10 November which constituted the Second Battle of Passchendaele.[1] Because of the wide notoriety attained by these battles and the bitter and prolonged controversy which they occasioned the reasons for the decision to undertake them merit careful consideration.

At a meeting of French and British military leaders held in Paris on the day preceding the inter-Allied conference of 4-5 May (above, p. 278), Field-Marshal Haig had reached agreement with the French Chief of the General Staff, General Pétain, that the Allies could not hope to break through on the Western Front until the Germans had been further worn down. To this end the French were to continue their present offensive on the Aisne, if possible, while the British (who were then engaged in the Third Battle of the Scarpe) prepared to attack towards Cambrai. Should a lack of manpower compel Pétain to abandon the offensive, he would strive to contain the enemy by attacking elsewhere on a smaller scale and Haig would strike "in the north". In either event the French were to relieve six British divisions. That evening, however, Lloyd George expressed his doubts to Haig that the French would put forth a serious effort; and indeed at the first formal meeting next day the French C.G.S. revealed that the army's confidence in its leaders and in the Government was undermined. Pétain's statement had a dampening effect on the proceedings, though at the time its full significance was not realized.[2]

The larger strategical picture was far from clear. The Entente had lost a minor ally in December 1916 with the crushing of Rumania. It is true that on 6 April the United States had entered the war, brought in by Germany's having embarked upon a ruthless policy of unrestricted submarine warfare. But though American destroyers were already in European waters, there was little hope of effective military intervention before 1918. The Russian Revolution in mid-March had introduced a new complication. Despite the new socialist government's announced determination to go on fighting, British Intelligence foresaw the probability of a Russian secession from the war.[3] Fearing that Germany would strike on the Eastern Front while Russia was still disorganized, the Western Allies felt constrained to keep their own front active. Furthermore, maintaining pressure in the West would encourage the Italians to attack the Austrians, and thereby forestall an Austro-German counter-offensive. Above all it was important to prevent a German counter-offensive on the Western Front. In short, the enemy must not be allowed to rest his armies or to score a land victory anywhere while awaiting the results of his submarine campaign.

The Paris Conference closed with official unanimity that the Allies could not end the war in 1917. At the same time it was thought possible to ward off any German attempt at a decisive counter-offensive by launching a series of attacks with limited objectives. Such efforts could be covered by an overwhelming artillery barrage—a form of tactics strongly urged by Pétain as a result of the Nivelle débacle. Allied strength would thus be conserved for an all-out effort with American aid in 1918.[4] Privately, however, most of the delegates were inclined to interpret the new policy in their own way. The French had grave misgivings about any form of attrition that might further reduce their strength. The British Prime Minister, unaware of the serious weakness of the French Army, insisted that it was no good putting the full strength of the British Army into the attack "unless the French did the same".[5]

The First Sea Lord, Admiral Jellicoe, was obsessed with the notion that the enemy must be deprived of his submarine bases on the Belgian coast that summer. Despite the emphasis that had been placed on limited attacks, Jellicoe's concern was promptly seized on by Haig as a major consideration, even while the Nivelle offensive was still in progress. "I feel sure that you realize the great importance to all the Allies of making a great effort to clear the Belgian coast this summer", Sir Douglas wrote Nivelle on 5 May, in urging that the French take over a portion of his front. Brushing aside the black day of failures on 3 May, Haig outlined his plan to continue to wear out the enemy on the Arras-Vimy battlefront by local thrusts. These efforts would be preliminary to a well-mounted attack by sixteen divisions with adequate artillery against the Messines-Wytschaete ridge early in June. Capture of the high ground here would secure the right flank and prepare the way "for the undertaking of larger operations at a subsequent date directed towards the clearance of the Belgian coast".[6]

By the middle of May, as we have seen, the French attacks on the Aisne had ceased. Yet though the Arras battles had been planned only as subsidiary to the Nivelle offensive, the Paris decisions made it necessary to continue them at least until the British launched their attack on Messines Ridge. But, as already noted (above, p. 243), the French forces were unreliable because of virtual mutiny in their ranks. Fortunately the Germans were ignorant of the true situation, and thus missed an opportunity of taking advantage of the French weakness by launching a strong counter-attack across the Aisne opposite Paris.* The Crown Prince proposed such action, but the German High Command estimated that to attack here would require 30 divisions, and only 23 were available. Indeed eight of these were then on their way to Flanders, where already a British offensive was expected.[9]

Haig's Early Plans

Despite all efforts by French and British military leaders to conceal the state of the French forces, some word of the mutinies appears to have reached the British War Cabinet before 12 May. This prompted Lloyd George to remind Haig that the War Cabinet's support of his policy was only "on express condition that the French also play their full part as agreed upon at our Conference".[10] But Sir Douglas, engrossed in plans for his long-cherished northern offensive, does not appear to have been greatly concerned about French capabilities. At a private meeting with Haig at Amiens on 18 May, General Pétain objected to the distant aims of the British plan as contrary to the policy of attacks with limited objectives. The British Commander-in-Chief thereupon restated his intention in terms of successive limited attacks, adding that "as the wearing-down process continues, advanced guards and cavalry will be able to progress for much longer distances profiting by the enemy's demoralization until a real decision is reached".[11]

Pétain did not share Haig's optimism†. He would have preferred the British to take over more line, but he regarded as Sir Douglas' own business how the latter chose to implement the policy of limited objectives, providing that the French line was not further stretched as a result.[13] He refused to extend the French front to within a suggested eighteen miles south-east of Arras; instead, six French divisions would work with the British and Belgian forces in the main offensive while French local attacks at Malmaison (in Champagne), Verdun and elsewhere would serve a diversionary purpose. That evening Sir Douglas wired the War Cabinet that the necessary French support for his offensive was assured.[14]

Since January 1916, when Haig had first ordered planning to begin on operations to clear the Flemish coast, the scheme for an offensive north of the River Lys had undergone many revisions. The version that was officially adopted

* The French War Minister, Paul Painlevé, later revealed that for a time there were between Soissons (on the Aisne) and Paris only two divisions which he considered reliable.[7] Painlevé was responsible for maintaining order in the capital, and he probably had in mind the necessity of using for this purpose two cavalry divisions stationed north-east of the city. These had not taken part in the offensive of 16 April and their morale was therefore relatively unimpaired.[8]

† Two days later Pétain expressed to the British liaison officer at his headquarters, General Sir Henry Wilson, the opinion that "Haig's attack towards Ostend was certain to fail". And on 2 June General Foch, Pétain's successor as C.G.S., asked Wilson who it was who wanted Haig to go on "a duck's march through the inundations to Ostend and Zeebrugge"—a plan which he denounced as "futile, fantastic and dangerous". "So Foch is entirely opposed to this enterprise," Sir Henry noted in his dairy, "Jellicoe notwithstanding."[12]

and used until the first week of May 1917 as a basis for detailed planning was produced in February of that year. The nature of the terrain dictated that the main effort must be made north-eastward from the Ypres area; for south of a two-mile-wide belt of sand dunes along the coast the way was blocked by an inundated area extending along the lower Yser from Nieuport to Steenstraat—the work of Belgian engineers who had let in the sea in seeking to stem the German advance in 1914. The Germans had to be expelled from their prolonged tenure of the ridge which stretched from Gheluvelt northward through Passchendaele to Staden (on the Elverdinghe-Thourout railway). Once this had been cleared, Haig foresaw "opportunities for the employment of cavalry in masses".[15]

A prerequisite to pursuing the enemy off the high ground east of Ypres, however, was the capture of the spur which extended to the south—the Messines-Wytschaete Ridge. The original pattern of Haig's projected operations was thus an initial assault against this ridge by the Second Army on a front of nearly ten miles from St. Yves (adjoining Ploegsteert Wood) to Mount Sorrel; with a simultaneous attack by the Second and Fifth Armies east and north-east from the front Mount Sorrel-Steenstraat, following the direction of the Ypres-Roulers and the Elverdinghe-Thourout railways. To avoid dissipating artillery over so wide a frontage, Haig assigned the capture of the high ground immediately opposite Ypres to massed tanks, attacking without gun support. When the offensive had advanced about ten miles (or sooner if the enemy were demoralized), a corps of the Fourth Army would launch an attack along the coast from Nieuport, co-ordinated with a landing at three points in the Middelkerke area by a specially trained division embarked at Dunkirk.

The decisions reached at Paris on 4-5 May modified these plans. On the 7th, Haig announced to his Army Commanders that the operations would be split into two phases. The attack on the Messines-Wytschaete Ridge would take place on the conclusion of the Arras battle, about 7 June, and the "Northern Operation", to clear the Belgian coast, some weeks later.[16]

The preliminary bombardment of Messines began on 21 May.* On 2 June, five days before the attack, Haig received from a French liaison officer the first clear intimation of the French mutinies. What with the disturbances themselves and the granting of long-overdue leave as a measure to restore good order and morale, Pétain's forces would be unable to attack either as soon as promised or in the same strength. Concerned that the War Cabinet might oppose his plans in these circumstances, Haig decided to treat the matter as a military secret and proceed at least with the Messines operation without further consulting London.[18]

*Strong recommendations made by General von Kuhl, Crown Prince Rupprecht's Chief of Staff, that the Germans should withdraw from their exposed positions on the forward slope to a more readily defended switch-line behind the ridge were not insisted upon by Rupprecht because of the unanimous opposition of the local commanders. General von Kuhl charged later that Rupprecht's adherence to army custom instead of ordering a withdrawal was a mistake and the cause of one of the worst tragedies to befall German armies.[17]

The battle opened at 3:10 a.m. on 7 June with the explosion of the nineteen great mines (above, p. 282) on a frontage of some eight and a half miles.* These mines—some 465 tons of explosive[20]—had been placed under the German front line, mainly during 1916, by British and Dominion sappers. As the crest of the ridge blew skyward, nine divisions of the Second Army assaulted, supported by a powerful barrage which employed all the Army's field and medium guns. Demoralized by the long preparatory bombardment, stunned by the mine explosions and further shaken by the barrage, the surviving Germans were at first helpless. Practically the whole ridge was in British hands by nine o'clock that morning. The enemy then rallied, but was unable to redeem his losses. By 5:30 a.m. on the 11th all but one of the Second Army's original objectives had fallen.[21]

The successful termination of the battle on 14 June underlined the need for an early decision on the next step to be taken. General Plumer's Second Army now occupied a position overlooking the southern end of the German-held Passchendaele Ridge, which in turn commanded the ground across which Haig planned to launch his main offensive. Plumer wanted to exploit his recent success by immediately attacking with two corps towards the Gheluvelt plateau. But General Gough, to whose Fifth Army Haig had assigned the main role in the coming offensive, advised against any such preliminary operation, preferring to include it in his own tasks. Haig thereupon approved postponement of the attack and transferred the two corps to Gough's command. A great opportunity for exploitation was thus lost; had it been seized upon, the indescribable miseries experienced later at Passchendaele might well have been avoided.

After Messines the views of the War Cabinet and General Headquarters in the field steadily diverged. The successful outcome of the battle encouraged Haig to press for the "Northern Operation". In an appreciation to the War Cabinet dated 12 June he warned of the depressing effect that any relaxation of effort would have on the French, who "at the moment are living a good deal on the hope of further British successes". German discontent had "already assumed formidable proportions", and would grow worse as the failure of the submarine campaign became realized. If the War Cabinet provided him with "sufficient force" (a term which Haig defined as bringing up to and maintaining at establishment divisions then at his disposal), and if there was no extensive transfer of German troops from the Russian front, he thought it probable that the Belgian coast could be cleared that summer and "the defeats on the German troops entailed in doing so might quite possibly lead to their collapse".[22]

Haig appended to his appreciation an estimate of German resources prepared by his Intelligence Section, G.H.Q. (whose head, Brig.-Gen. John Charteris, was prone to under-estimate enemy strengths and over-estimate enemy losses).[23] The 400,000 casualties which the enemy was stated to have suffered on the

* One mine was fired by the 1st Canadian Tunnelling Company and four by the 3rd.[19] The operations of Canadian tunnellers are dealt with further in Chapter XVI.

Western Front during April and May* were believed to have reduced the strength of 104 of the 157 German divisions in that theatre by an average of 40 per cent. It was estimated that even in the event of a Russian collapse not more than 20 divisions could be moved from East to West. From these and other "definite facts" it was deduced that "given a continuance of the existing circumstances . . . and . . . of the effort of the Allies" Germany might well be forced to conclude a peace on Allied terms before the end of 1917.[25]

A less optimistic view was taken by the Director of Military Intelligence at the War Office, Brig.-Gen. G. M. W. Macdonogh, who held that the enemy's divisions had not suffered any serious decrease in fighting power, and that a Russian secession would indeed allow Germany to outmatch Allied rifle and gun strength on the Western Front. From his Intelligence the C.I.G.S. had advised the War Cabinet "that offensive operations on our front would offer no chance of success; and our best course would be to remain on the defensive, strengthen our positions, economize our reserves in manpower and material, and hope that the balance would be eventually redressed by American assistance."[26]

On 19 June Haig, accompanied by the C.I.G.S. (General Robertson), presented his case to a special Cabinet Committee on Policy which the Prime Minister had formed on 8 June.† Using a large relief map he demonstrated that an advance of only 25 miles along the coast would achieve the capture of Ostend and Zeebrugge. Once British troops reached the Scheldt there was a hope that the Netherlands might come into the war and join in a drive eastward to expel the Germans from Belgium. But Lloyd George, alarmed that the British would be fighting virtually single-handed at the outset, gloomily forecast no more than a small initial success. To him the immediate aim was simply to keep the enemy occupied while the Allies prepared for a victorious advance in 1918. As an "Easterner" he saw two possible courses—either a series of local wearing-down attacks on the Western Front, or a strong offensive on the Italian front designed at knocking Austria out of the war.[27]

The discussions continued on the 20th. Admiral Jellicoe, called in for his opinion, "dropped a bombshell" by declaring that because of the shipping losses inflicted by the enemy's submarines,‡ Britain must either capture Zeebrugge before the end of the year or accept defeat![29] Haig, for one, could not have been too much surprised. On the way over from France on 17 June he had travelled with the commander of the Dover anti-submarine patrol, Vice-Admiral Sir Reginald Bacon, whom he found "wholeheartedly with us", having "urged in writing to the Admiralty the absolute necessity of clearing the Belgian Coast before winter".[30] "No one present shared Jellicoe's view," Sir Douglas noted, "and all

* The German Official History gives 384,000 casualties on the Western Front (not including lightly wounded) in the months April, May and June 1917.[24]

† It was composed of the Prime Minister, Lord Curzon (Lord President of the Council), Lord Milner (Minister without Portfolio), Mr. Bonar Law (Chancellor of the Exchequer) and General Smuts. The secretary was Colonel Hankey, Secretary of the War Cabinet.

‡ In the first five months of 1917 the British Merchant Navy had lost 572 ships grossing 1,718,201 tons.[28]

seemed satisfied that the food reserves in Great Britain are adequate."[31] Nevertheless the First Sea Lord's pronouncements carried considerable weight—undue weight, for soon the convoy system belatedly adopted by the Admiralty, was to reduce Allied shipping losses considerably.

On the 21st the Prime Minister read a 5000-word statement setting forth the War Committee's attitude towards Haig's proposals. "His object", recorded Haig in his diary that day, "was to induce Robertson and myself to agree to an expedition being sent to support the Italians. It was a regular lawyer's effort to make black white!" In reply both Haig and Robertson submitted detailed memoranda refuting point by point the arguments raised by the Prime Minister. Finally the War Committee reached a partial decision. Though Lloyd George, Bonar Law and Lord Milner remained hostile to the project, they hesitated to overrule the Generals on a matter of strategy. The Prime Minister expressed the Committee's misgivings, but allowed preparations for the offensive to go on.[32]

It was not until 21 July, when the preliminary bombardment for the "Northern Operation" had been in progress for five days, that the War Cabinet gave formal approval for the Commander-in-Chief to carry out the plan which he had presented to the War Policy Committee. This sanction carried a proviso, however, that should the Flanders project not succeed Haig must be ready to send guns and troops to Italy for an offensive against Austria.[33] Haig protested the lack of confidence shown in this qualified approval, and on 25 July was assured of the War Cabinet's "whole-hearted support".[34]

The Summer Operations in Flanders

The long delay between the success at Messines and the opening of the Flanders offensive arose largely from Haig's transfer of the principal role to the Fifth Army. During 1916 and early 1917 planning for the operation had been in the hands of General Sir Henry Rawlinson, Commander of the Fourth Army, and General Plumer, whose Second Army had been defending the Ypres Salient for two and a half years. But at the end of April, as we have seen, Haig had given command of the northern offensive, including the landing force, to General Sir Hubert Gough, a cavalryman who was imbued with "the cavalry spirit" that favoured pushing forward at all costs. He was thus more in sympathy with the C.-in-C.'s tactical views than were the other army commanders, who felt that the advance should be made by a succession of infantry battles. Unfortunately the change meant that Plumer's extensive knowledge of the Ypres sector was not to be utilized, and valuable time was to be used up as Gough familiarized himself with the situation and redrew the plans for the venture.

The elaborate programme of regrouping and concentration for the offensive began at the end of May, when General Gough relinquished to the Third Army the Bullecourt sector south of Arras and moved north to take over a front of six and a half miles which included Boesinghe in the north and Mount Sorrel in the south. With the transfer of the Second Army's two left corps (the 2nd and 8th)

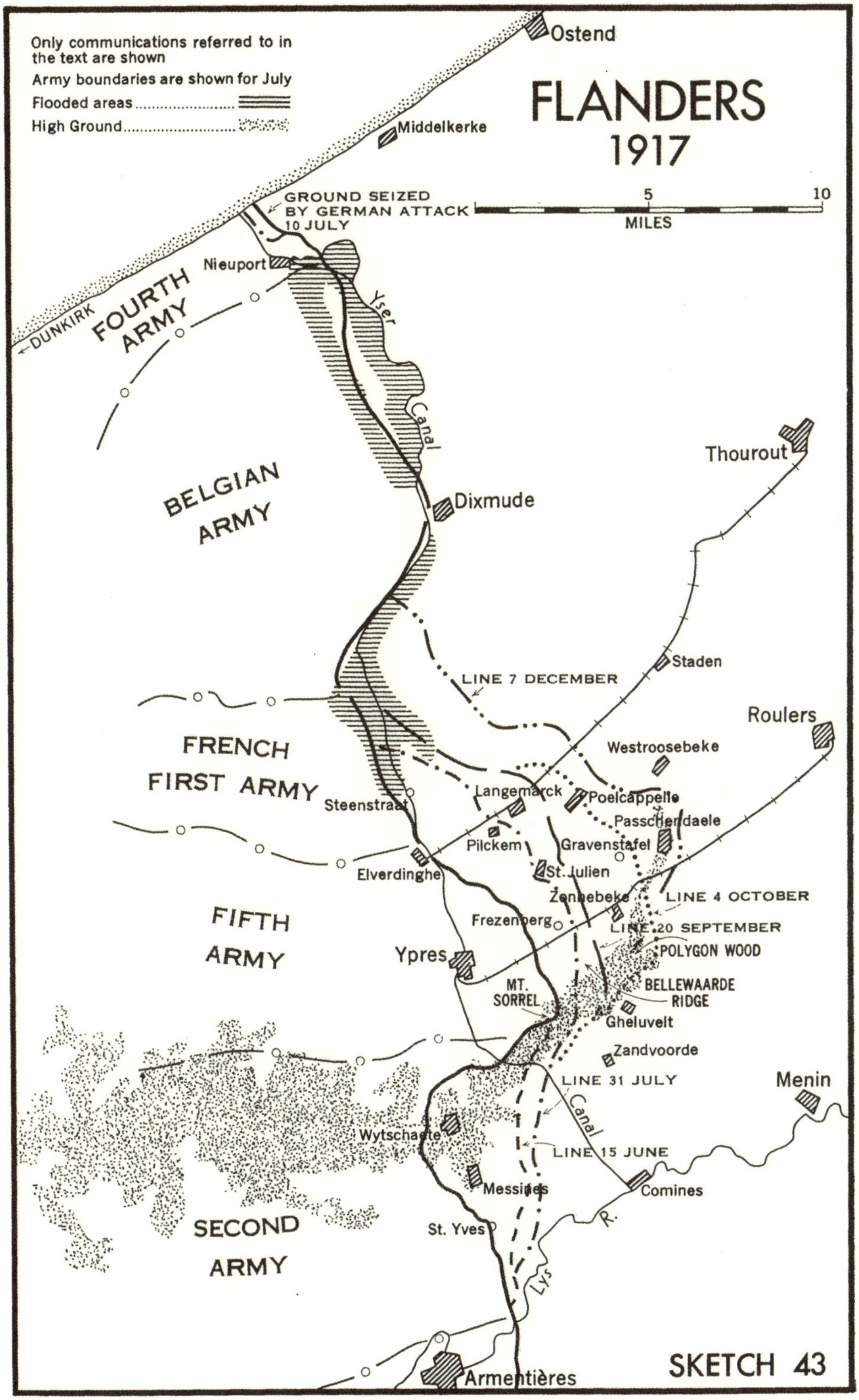
Only communications referred to in the text are shown
Army boundaries are shown for July
Flooded areas
High Ground
FLANDERS
1917
5
10
MILES
Ostend
Middelkerke
GROUND SEIZED BY GERMAN ATTACK 10 JULY
Nieuport
DUNKIRK
FOURTH ARMY
Yser
Canal
BELGIAN ARMY
Dixmude
Thourout
LINE 7 DECEMBER
Staden
Roulers
FRENCH FIRST ARMY
Westroosebeke
Steenstraat
Langemarck
Poelcappelle
Passchendaele
Pilckem
Gravenstafel
Elverdinghe
St. Julien
Zonnebeke
LINE 4 OCTOBER
FIFTH ARMY
Frezenberg
LINE 20 SEPTEMBER
POLYGON WOOD
Ypres
MT. SORREL
BELLEWAARDE RIDGE
Gheluvelt
Zandvoorde
LINE 31 JULY
Menin
Canal
Wytschaete
LINE 15 JUNE
Messines
Comines
R.
SECOND ARMY
St. Yves
Lys
Armentières
SKETCH 43

to Gough's command, the Fifth Army by late July numbered six army corps of seventeen divisions. There was a wholesale shifting of artillery as the entire British front was combed for guns for the Fifth Army. The Second Army gave up more than half of its heavy howitzers and concentrated almost half of its remaining pieces on its northern flank in order to support the right of the main offensive. Gough received three tank brigades, each of 72 tanks, and together with the Second Army could count on air support from 406 aircraft and eighteen kite balloon sections. On the Fifth Army's left, between Boesinghe and Nieuport, the offensive would be covered (from south to north) by the French First Army with six divisions, and six Belgian divisions under King Albert. Although Gough's responsibilities had originally included the operations along the coast, a modification in plan placed this sector, between Nieuport and the sea, under General Rawlinson's Fourth Army, which was to mount its offensive with the 15th Corps, of five divisions.[35]

The concentration in Flanders considerably weakened the remainder of the British front, as other armies contributed formations to the Fifth Army. By the end of July the Second Army on Gough's right had been reduced to twelve divisions; General Sir Henry Horne's First Army had the same number to hold 34 miles of front from the Lys to the Scarpe; and in the southern sector the Third Army, under General Sir Julian Byng, had only fifteen divisions (including two in G.H.Q. reserve) to guard 37 miles of front.[36]

But this reduction in strength outside of Flanders was matched by a general thinning out of the opposing forces. The deliberate Allied preparations had made it obvious to the enemy that large-scale operations were pending. Since the end of May Army Group Crown Prince Rupprecht had reckoned with the possibility that these would not take the form of a mere subsidiary attack in the Ypres-Wytschaete area, but rather of a major offensive against the entire front in Flanders.[37] As we have noted (above, p. 282,*n.*), the feint attacks towards Lens and Lille failed to divert the enemy's attention from the northern scene. The German Fourth Army in Flanders was reinforced—the Sixth Army sending ten divisions north in June alone. Five days after the Messines battle Colonel von Lossberg, who was now recognized as the leading exponent of the defensive battle, was appointed the Fourth Army's Chief of Staff. He brought with him his system of a deep defence, which dispensed with deep dug-outs and relied on counter-attack by special "intervention divisions" (*Eingreif-Divisionen*), each echeloned back some two to four thousand yards in readiness "to strike the enemy in the midst of his assault".[38]

Twice during July Haig was compelled unwillingly to postpone the opening of the offensive for three days—at the request first of General Gough, because of losses in guns and the late arrival of heavy artillery, and then of General Anthoine, the Commander of the French First Army, who demanded more time to complete his counter-battery preparation. The delay, besides giving the enemy more time to reinforce and to strengthen his defences, prolonged the bombardment which had begun on 16 July. The ground was therefore more cratered than

EVACUATION BY TRAMWAY

With the enforced assistance of German prisoners, Canadian soldiers wounded at Vimy Ridge are brought back by tram. Each push-truck carries four stretchers.

FORWARD SUPPLY ROUTE

Plank roads laid by Canadian troops behind their lines carry heavy traffic forward for the advance after the capture of Vimy Ridge.

A ROYAL VISIT

King George V tours the Vimy battlefield in July 1917. His Majesty is accompanied by General Horne, Commander of the First Army, and (at centre) Lieut.-General Sir Arthur Currie, who has just been appointed to command the Canadian Corps.

THE GREEN CRASSIER

This photograph, taken in the spring of 1919, shows the ground over which the 44th Battalion attacked on 23 and 24 August 1917 in its valiant but vain attempt to capture the great pile of mine refuse which two German battalions were holding as a formidable strongpoint in the southern outskirts of Lens. The steep-sided Green Crassier with its shattered pithead installations is seen at the right. In the centre are the ruined buildings of the Fosse St. Louis.

it need have been, so that the tanks were fatally obstructed, and later, when the rains came, the shattered soil more readily disintegrated into mud.

The long-heralded assault was finally launched at sunrise on 31 July. The Fifth Army attacked with nine divisions forward, flanked by two French divisions on the left, and five divisions of the Second Army on the right. At first things went well, and by 1:00 p.m. the formations attacking between the railways had advanced some two miles across Pilckem Ridge and retaken much of the ground lost in the spring of 1915, including the ruins of Frezenberg and St. Julien—names deeply engraved in Canadian military history. But having overrun the German forward zone with relative ease, capturing more than 6000 prisoners, the assaulting divisions were forced to ground by heavy observed artillery and machine-gun fire. Casualties mounted steadily, and during the afternoon German counter-attacks drove the centre back 2000 yards. On the right the Second Corps, advancing astride the Menin Road towards the strongly defended Gheluvelt Plateau, had reached Bellewaarde Ridge, but elsewhere was far short of even its first objective.[39]

Heavy rain which began falling on the evening of the 31st continued for four days and brought operations to a standstill. By 2 August the Battle of Pilckem Ridge was over. Sir Douglas Haig's report to the War Cabinet of "highly satisfactory" fighting and losses "slight for so great a battle" was using the standard of the Somme rather than Vimy or Messines. It had cost 31,850 casualties to advance the front line to a maximum depth of 3000 yards. The nine assaulting divisions, by nightfall of the 31st less than half way to the first day's objectives, had lost from 30 to 60 per cent of their fighting strength and were in no condition to continue the planned advance to the Passchendaele Ridge.[40] Much had been expected of the tanks, which were fighting their first action since being organized as the Tank Corps.* Small detachments had given the infantry useful support, but long before any opportunity had arisen for their main role of a break-through on to the Gheluvelt Plateau, nearly half the tanks available had been knocked out or ditched.

The Battle of Pilckem Ridge was followed on August 16-18 by the Battle of Langemarck, which produced slight ground gains from St. Julien north, but virtually nothing in the vital central sector. August proved to be the wettest in four years. By the end of the month Sir Douglas could report advances of up to three miles. "I am well satisfied . . ." he wrote to the War Cabinet on the 21st, "although the gain of ground would have been much more considerable but for the adverse weather conditions." Yet the enemy was being worn down, and the C.-in-C.'s purpose of drawing German strength to the Flanders front was being effected. How great was the requirement for divisions at the battle front in Flanders may be seen from the fact that in the first three weeks of the battle (31 July to 20 August) seventeen German divisions were used up.[41] "Our wastage had been so high", wrote Ludendorff later, "as to cause grave misgivings, and

* The Heavy Branch Machine Gun Corps became the Tank Corps on 27 July 1917.

exceeded all expectation."[42] At the beginning of September Haig noted with satisfaction in his diary that the result of the pressure at Ypres had appeared in the slackening of the German efforts on the Chemin des Dames, and the weak resistance to a French attack at Verdun towards the end of August. "The French Army has consequently had the quiet time desired by General Pétain in which to recover from the Nivelle offensive."[43]

Haig Revises his Plans

The situation was, however, by no means as satisfactory as Haig's reassuring reports would seem to convey. The first four weeks of the offensive had cost the British 68,000 casualties, more than 3400 of them officers. Against the C.-in-C.'s report of the excellent spirits of his troops[44] must be set the statement of the British Official Historian that "apart from actual losses, the discomfort of the living conditions in the forward areas and the strain of fighting with indifferent success had overwrought and discouraged all ranks more than any other operation . . . in the War. . . . Discontent was general."[45] In view of the Fifth Army's failure to make any appreciable headway Haig decided on 25 August to transfer the weight of his effort from the unprofitable low ground on the left to the ridges bounding the salient to the south-east. This involved switching the main offensive to the Second Army and giving back to General Plumer's command the sector held by the 2nd Corps between the Ypres-Roulers railway and the Ypres-Comines Canal. From this frontage the Second Army, abandoning the tactics of an attempted major break-through, would launch a succession of attacks, each with strictly limited objectives, to capture the southern half of the Passchendaele Ridge. Plumer was given three weeks to make his preparations.[46] The coastal operation* was postponed until the suitable October tides, and was subsequently abandoned.[48]

The Flanders campaign on which Haig had set such high hopes had declined, in effect, into a "step by step" affair.

The break in hostilities and the campaign's conspicuous lack of success so far gave the Cabinet Committee an opportunity of reviewing the situation. Called to London for a conference on 4 September, Sir Douglas Haig heard a proposal from the Prime Minister to limit operations on the Western Front for the rest of 1917 and to support the Italian offensive against Austria, which (according to General Cadorna, the Chief of the Italian General Staff) could not be continued without more heavy artillery. Earlier in the year the Italians had received thirteen British and twelve French heavy batteries.[49] General Foch had come to London to negotiate the transfer of 100 heavy guns from the French First Army in Flanders, to Italy— "the *political* effect of a success there", Haig quotes him, "would be greater . . . than one in Flanders".[50]

* On 10 July a "spoiling attack" by the German 3rd Marine Division between Nieuport and the sea had wiped out the small British bridgehead over the Yser. It was the first use by the enemy of shells containing dichlorethyl sulphide ("Yellow Cross") mustard gas.[47]

Haig was anxious to have adequate French artillery support on his flank in the forthcoming operations, but on 7 September he agreed with Pétain to send some 100 guns to Italy immediately and replace them with other French artillery in time for Plumer's offensive, scheduled to begin on 20 September.[51] On the eve of this attack Sir Douglas was moved to write in his diary, ". . . the French Army has not only ceased to be able to take the offensive on a large scale, but, according to Pétain's opinion, its discipline is so bad that it could not withstand a determined German offensive."[52] These remarks, interpreted out of context, have prompted an official reconstruction of a supposed visit that day by General Pétain to ask that the Flanders offensive be continued.* The only visit recorded in the relevant entry in Haig's diary, however, is one by the British Secretary of State for War, Lord Derby, who mentioned a revival of the idea of an Allied headquarters in France (above, p. 238). "It seems to be an effort of the French to retain control of operations", the British Commander-in-Chief wrote—and then went on to discuss the condition of the French forces.

There is no contemporary evidence of the Pétain visit. An examination of the complete Haig diary reveals that nowhere after 7 June 1917 does the C.-in-C. record having received a request from the French to continue the Flanders offensive. It is true that on 30 June 1917 General Anthoine, Commander of the French First Army, had brought Haig a message from Pétain which declared that "*les facteurs moraux du moment actuel*" made it imperative that the Flanders offensive be assured of complete success; and Anthoine had reiterated the point when Haig returned his visit on 2 July.[54] The consideration so important to French morale was not that there must be offensive action (whether for its own sake or to forestall a German offensive), but that the proposed attack, *if mounted,* must succeed. In other words, what Pétain wrote to Haig—and French experience of unsuccessful offensives surely justified his so doing—was an appeal not for action but for caution. On the day after his letter was delivered to Haig, Pétain, as recorded by the British C.-in-C. in his diary entry for 1 July, "told Robertson that he is in full agreement with me regarding my proposed operations in France and Belgium".[55] It would seem reasonable to believe that if on 30 June Pétain had deemed it necessary to goad Haig into action, he would not next day find himself merely "in full agreement" with him.

Pétain himself has denied making any such appeal in September,[56] and no record of any such action is to be found in French official historical sources.[57] Indeed there was little need at this stage for Pétain to insist on further British action, for he had seen Haig on 7 September and had been told that the battle would be renewed on the 20th.[58] The French Army had recovered from the moral crisis through which it had passed at the end of May and early in June. It had attacked brilliantly at Verdun on 20 August, inflicting on the Germans

*The British Official Historian has recorded: "On the 19th September, the French Commander-in-Chief was again imploring that the offensive in Flanders should be continued without further delay. During this special visit to British Headquarters he assured Sir Douglas Haig that . . . he had not a man on whom he could rely . . . ."

what their Official History termed "a very severe setback".[59] It was now preparing for a second offensive at Malmaison in order to secure a better position on the Chemin des Dames, and, as we shall see, this was also to be successful.

Pétain did not again visit Haig until 6 October.* Two days later in a long appreciation to the C.I.G.S. as to the future British role, Sir Douglas spoke confidently of the contribution that French forces might be expected to make. "Despite the comparative inactivity of the French", he wrote, "the enemy has so far shown that he does not consider it safe to weaken himself to any considerable extent in front of them." Haig estimated the 100 French divisions expected to be available by the spring as being "fully equal to an equivalent number of German divisions". The existing French formations were staunch in defence and would carry out useful local offensives, though, in Haig's opinion, they "would not respond to a call for more than that".[61] The appreciation noted that Germany and her allies relied "practically entirely on the invincibility of the German armies to secure for them favourable terms of peace". It therefore rejected the idea that Germany could be defeated by operations against her allies in other theatres, and concluded by urging "unhesitatingly the continuance of the offensive on the Western Front, with all our strength, as the correct role of the British forces".[62]

September brought a period of cloudless skies, and on the higher ground dust replaced the mud of late August. But General Plumer was busy regrouping, and three weeks of excellent campaigning weather were lost. The offensive was resumed on the 20th with the Second Army's attack against the Gheluvelt Plateau, the Fifth Army advancing on the left. The keynote of Plumer's well planned tactics was concentration. After an unusually heavy artillery bombardment lasting seven days two Australian and two British divisions attacked astride the Menin Road behind a tremendous barrage, each on a narrow frontage of 1000 yards. The objective was only 1500 yards away, and the depth of the reserves gave the attack double the weight used by the Second Army on 31 July. The Battle of the Menin Road Ridge, as it was named, was completely successful. It was followed by the successes of Polygon Wood (midway between Zonnebeke and Gheluvelt), launched on 26 September,† and Broodseinde (half a mile east of Zonnebeke), on 4 October. The latter, a triumph for Australian and New Zealand forces, included the capture of Gravenstafel Ridge, where Canadians had fought in April 1915. An advance of 4000 yards in two weeks produced a salient which extended to 10,000 yards east of Ypres. But the Second Army was still seven miles from Roulers and the Fifth more than eleven miles from Thourout.

* A memorandum written by the French General Staff for the Minister of War concerning the state of the French Army at the end of September 1917 expressed concern that a reverse might provoke anew the dangerous crisis through which the army had passed in May and June[60]. There is no evidence that Haig was informed of the contents of this memorandum.

† In this battle a Canadian, Lt.-Col. P. E. Bent, D.S.O., who had enlisted in the British Army in 1914, fell while leading elements of the 9th Leicestershire in a counter-attack near Polygon Wood on 1 October. He was posthumously awarded the Victoria Cross.[63]

Objectives that were to have been captured on July 31, the opening day of the offensive, were still untaken. One of General Gough's divisions had a foothold in Poelcappelle at the foot of the ridge, but the village of Passchendaele on the crest was still a mile from Plumer's foremost troops. Rain began falling on the night of 4 October and continued intermittently for the next three days. In the low ground west of the Passchendaele Ridge three months of constant shelling had blocked the watercourses that normally provided drainage, and the myriad shell-holes held water like the pores of some great sponge. To cross the valley of the upper Steenbeek and its tributaries was to proceed through "a porridge of mud".[64]

Haig's plans called for another series of three successive blows, to begin about 10 October, but on the evening of the 7th his two army commanders told him that because of the change in the weather they favoured closing down the campaign. Yet the C.-in-C. was impressed with the importance of gaining the Passchendaele-Westroosebeke sector of the main ridge in order that his men might winter on the more easily drained high ground, and his determination to secure this objective was fortified by his conviction of the need to divert German reserves from the French front, as well as from the Russian and Italian theatres.[65] So the struggle continued in ground conditions so bad as to be previously equalled only at the battles of the Somme. An attack on 9 October (the Battle of Poelcappelle) gained hardly any ground and cost the three assaulting divisions (the 2nd Australian, 66th and 49th) nearly 7000 casualties.[66] General Plumer however believed that the day's fighting had secured a sufficiently good jumping-off line for a successful attack on Passchendaele, at the conclusion of which the ridge would be handed over to the Canadian Corps, due to arrive from the Lens sector.

The assault through the mud was made on 12 October by the 2nd Anzac Corps. Hitherto undisclosed belts of wire that were discovered too late for destruction by artillery presented a formidable barrier to the attackers. In heavy rain—"our most effective ally", noted Crown Prince Rupprecht in his diary[67]—the 3rd Australian and New Zealand Divisions made a limited and costly advance to within 2500 yards of Passchendaele. One isolated Australian party, which subsequently withdrew, actually reached what remained of the village and found it temporarily abandoned.[68]

The First Battle of Passchendaele had petered out in the mud. Next day a G.H.Q. Conference at Cassel decided that further attacks should be postponed until an improvement in the weather permitted the construction of roads to bring forward artillery for a prolonged bombardment.

The Canadians at Passchendaele

Of a total of sixty British and Dominion divisions on the Western Front at the end of October, all but nine were sooner or later engaged in the Flanders offensive.[69] The first intimation that Canadian troops would be employed there came on 2 October 1917, when Field-Marshal Haig ordered the First Army to withdraw two Canadian divisions into G.H.Q. reserve;[70] and next day General Currie noted in his diary that two divisions which had just come out of the line "might go north". By 5 October the C.-in-C. had reached a decision to employ the full Canadian Corps of four divisions; on the 9th he issued orders for its transfer from the First to the Second Army.[71]

An entry in Haig's diary suggests that he had contemplated assigning the Corps to the Fifth Army, the change to the Second Army being made on the recommendation of his Chief of Staff, Lieut.-General Kiggell, "because the Canadians do not work kindly" with General Gough.[72] Currie had, in fact, expressed the hope that his Corps would not be required to fight with the Fifth Army. He later reported having told General Horne that several of Gough's divisional commanders had expressed to him their dissatisfaction with their Army Commander's conduct of the Third Battle of Ypres up to that time, and that his own lack of confidence arose from his experiences with Gough* at the Somme in 1916.[74] Contrary to an impression conveyed by General Currie the assignment of the Corps to the Second Army did not pose any problem of boundaries.[75] It will be recalled (above, p. 308) that the inter-army boundary had been moved north late in August when General Plumer took over responsibility for the main offensive action. The 2nd Anzac Corps, which Currie relieved, was already in the Second Army's sector, having fought all its October battles under General Plumer's command.

A Second Army directive of 13 October ordered the G.O.C. Canadian Corps to "submit plans for the capture of Passchendaele as soon as possible".[76] General Currie little relished committing his Corps in an attempt to resuscitate a campaign that was already played out.[77] Only three reasons for continuing the offensive could now be considered at all valid—to give indirect assistance to the forthcoming French attack in Champagne, to keep the enemy occupied during the preparations for Cambrai (below, p. 333), and to establish a suitable winter line on the 165-foot high Passchendaele-Westroosebeke ridge.

The front line which the Canadians took over from the 2nd Anzac Corps on 18 October ran along the valley of the Stroombeek between Gravenstafel Ridge and the heights about Passchendaele. It was virtually the same front as that which they had held in April 1915 before the gas attack. The right hand boundary was the Ypres-Roulers railway, from which the line slanted north-westward for 3000 yards, crossing the main Ypres-Zonnebeke-Passchendaele road about a mile south-west of Passchendaele. This road, and the parallel one to the north passing through Gravenstafel, were the only landmarks by which the relieving Canadians who had fought at Ypres in 1915 could orient themselves. Hardly a trace remained of the villages of St. Jean, Wieltje and Fortuin; and the disappearance of remembered woods and farm-houses had reduced the countryside to an unrecog-

* Later that year Haig was to draw Gough's attention to the number of divisions which "had hoped that they would not be sent to the Fifth Army to fight". This attitude Haig blamed on Gough's staff rather than on the Army Commander himself.[73]

nizable waste of ridge and hollow. Opposite the left half of the Corps sector a spur of high ground extended south-eastward from the main ridge through the hamlet of Bellevue, carrying the road from Gravenstafel forward to Mosselmarkt (1000 yards north-west of Passchendaele). This route and the Zonnebeke road, which followed the crest of the main ridge, provided the only practical approaches to Passchendaele; between these two defiles the Canadian front was split by the valley of the Ravebeek, which from the outskirts of Passchendaele ran down into the Stroombeek. Disrupted by shellfire, the water course was now a bog, in places half a mile wide, and without bridging impassable even to infantry. Altogether nearly half the area in front of Passchendaele was covered with water or deep mud. The continuous shelling by both sides had prevented any clearing up of additions made by the recent operations to the rotting debris of three years of war. "Battlefield looks bad", noted General Currie in his diary on the 17th. "No salvaging has been done and very few of the dead buried."

There was much to be accomplished, Sir Douglas Haig having impressed upon the Commander of the Second Army that the attack should not start until General Currie was satisfied that his preparations were complete.[78] The problem of artillery was serious. Currie's G.O.C. Royal Artillery, Brig.-Gen. E. W. B. Morrison, "had a rude awakening" when a personal reconnaissance prior to taking over the Corps front revealed extensive gun shortages. Of 250 "heavies" to be taken over *in situ* from the Australians he could find only 227, and of these 89 were out of action.[79] Even worse was the condition of the field artillery. Of 306 18-pounders on paper, less than half were in action, and many of these were "dotted about in the mud wherever they happened to get bogged". The guns, probably because of the extreme problems of mobility, were badly bunched, being sited mainly in two clusters of heavies and two of 18-pounders, thereby furnishing the enemy with irresistible targets. Nor had the Australians been able to send their disabled pieces back for repair, for their provost authorities had ordered that no guns could use the roads for fear of blocking traffic. Morrison's aim was to push three brigades of field artillery forward of the line Zonnebeke-St. Julien and to bring up 6-inch howitzers and 60-pounders for counter-battery work against the more distant German guns which were at present out of range. He wanted also to get the heavy guns forward, including some super-howitzers "which were useless back near Ypres".[80]

To effect these moves required an extensive programme of road building. The sodden ground offered little foundation for roads, defence work or gun platforms. Haig had noted in his diary on 13 October that light engines on the 60-centimetre railways had sunk half-way up the boilers in the mud, the track having completely disappeared. Beginning 17 October, Canadian sappers and the four Canadian Pioneer Battalions in France (2nd, 107th, 123rd and 124th) joined the Royal Engineers with the Second Army. Henceforth there was a daily average of ten field companies, seven tunnelling companies and four army troops companies, assisted by two infantry and seven pioneer battalions, at work setting up battery positions and repairing and extending existing plank roads* for moving the guns and supplying the batteries and ammunition dumps.[82] While this was going on Brig.-Gen. Morrison obtained permission to use the roads to the rear for getting disabled guns back for repair.[83] An improvement in the weather made for better working conditions, but allowed the enemy to hinder progress with night bombing and shelling, which included the firing of shells containing "Yellow Cross" gas (above p. 308,*n.*) and "Blue Cross" (diphenyl chlorarsine) sneezing gas.[84] The latter penetrated respirators, which the resulting sneezing and vomiting compelled the men to remove, thereby bringing exposure to the more harmful vesicant.

It was Haig's intention that the Canadian Corps should gain possession of the area about Passchendaele village by three attacks with limited objectives, delivered at intervals of three or more days. The Fifth Army would mount subsidiary operations on General Currie's left, with the 1st Anzac Corps advancing to protect the Canadian right flank. When Currie submitted his provisional outline plan on 16 October, he felt that the necessary engineer and artillery preparations could be completed in time to launch the first attack on the 24th; but next day, as it became apparent that getting sufficient artillery forward would take longer than expected, he recommended a postponement to the 29th. But the C.-in-C. was anxious to avoid unnecessary delay, particularly as the French attack at Malmaison was due to start on the 23rd. After Plumer had re-examined the situation with Currie, the initial Canadian attack was reset for the 26th, a prior demonstration by the French First and British Fifth Armies being timed to assist the French effort. The dates for the subsequent phases were tentatively given as 30 October and 6 November.[85]

There is ample evidence of Currie's skilled and forceful generalship and the efficiency of his well organized staff in the smoothness and despatch with which the preparations for the Canadian assault were carried to completion. A good start on the necessary liaison and reconnaissance had been made by Canadian representatives at Australian corps and divisional headquarters and by advance parties from Canadian brigade and battalion headquarters. As early as the 17th the assaulting units had all available details of the German defences. As intelligence officers and infantry and artillery observers working in joint observation posts recorded new enemy work, or work that had previously escaped notice, the gunners carried out the required destructive shoots. "... I am convinced that this reconnaissance and close liaison between the artillery, the infantry units, and the staff", General Currie stressed in his report on the action, "is vital to the success of any operation."[86]

Indeed, the forthcoming operations of the Canadian Corps were to demonstrate forcefully the effective use which from Vimy onward was made of the

* Between two draining trenches planks of elm or beech, nine feet long, one foot wide and 2½ inches thick, were laid across "runners" (four or five planks placed lengthwise to form the base of the track) and spiked in position, with a protecting curb of half-round pine logs. From the middle of October to mid-November a total of two miles of double plank road and more than 4000 yards of heavy tramline were constructed in the Canadian Corps area—at a cost of more than 1500 casualties.[81]

artillery in providing the massive support needed by the infantry, whether in attack or in defence, in order to assure success in battle and the avoidance of undue casualties. By September 1917 the arrival of the 5th Canadian Divisional Artillery in France had brought the strength of the Canadian Corps Artillery to a total of some 350 field and heavy guns and about 20,000 men. Not all these were available for Passchendaele. The artillery of the 5th Division received a more gradual battle inoculation in the Lens area by providing relief for the artillery of British divisions. Remaining fire power, nonetheless, was formidable.

The method of employing the fire power which the Corps Commander had at his disposal had been brought to a high standard of efficiency; and in the large-scale offensive operations to which the Canadians were committed in the last two years of the war, the work of the artillery was to be the framework on which each battle was planned. The ultimate object of the gunners was at all times to help the attacking infantry and tanks get forward. The barrages fired for this purpose had to be supplemented by other tasks—destroying the enemy's wire, harassing his defences, and neutralizing his artillery fire by an effective counter-battery programme. In these activities British artillery enjoyed a decided advantage over the enemy because of superior organization: British artillery fought on a corps level, while the German artillery was organized on a divisional basis. This centralization of control at the higher level made possible considerable flexibility in delivering a heavy weight of fire on any desired portion of the front and then quickly switching to some other section.[87]

Artillery plans provided for a continuing service of support to the infantry throughout the entire operation. For the initial barrage it was customary for all the field and part of the heavy batteries to fire their tasks in accordance with a plan issued by the G.O.C. Royal Artillery (the senior artillery officer in the corps) and coordinated with the fire of flanking corps. Detailed planning and close liaison between artillery and infantry were required to ensure that the advancing lines—or "lifts"—of the barrage were kept just ahead of the attacking troops. Heavy artillery not engaged in this work was usually employed in harassing the enemy's lines of retreat, his reserves and other targets selected by the intelligence section of Heavy Artillery Headquarters. As the attack progressed and the final line of the barrage was reached it was customary for a portion of the field artillery to revert to the control of the division and move forward in direct support of its infantry. The remainder of the field artillery would come into corps reserve while the "heavies" which had been employed in the barrage would also move forward to a position from which they could deal with the enemy's artillery as soon as it again came into action.[88]

As the method of employing artillery underwent continual development, the principle of massive, closely coordinated support for the infantry was the constant goal of General Currie, who, in the words of a subsequent commander of the Canadian Corps Heavy Artillery, "consistently sought to pay the price of victory in shells and not in the lives of men".[89]

The Defenders' Changed Tactics

Facing the Canadians were three regiments of the 11th Bavarian Division, of "Group Ypres". Each had one battalion forward, a second in support and a third in reserve.[90] Their disposition was in accordance with a concept of defence not previously employed by the enemy.

It will be recalled that the weight of Allied artillery fire on the German forward areas at the Somme in 1916 had forced the enemy to abandon the defence of fixed lines in favour of a more elastic battle procedure (above, p. 239). Under this new doctrine the front line and the entire zone forward of the main line of resistance were relatively lightly held by independent groups and machine-guns disposed in chequered patterns. These were expected to survive even the fiercest bombardment and subsequently decide the issue by pinning down or crippling the attack at the critical moment. Moreover, as long as the Allies concentrated their heavy fire on the forward zone, the German supporting elements and reserves were able to move up almost unscathed to deliver an effective counter-blow.[91]

By September 1917, however, the British had developed appropriate counter-tactics. Their big attacks were no longer planned to be executed in one continuous sweep towards a distant goal, but rather as a quick succession of limited advances, followed by immediate consolidation while fresh troops moved through towards the next objective. At the same time artillery fire drenched the German zone of approach, so that the German supporting elements could no longer strike while the assaulting forces were still off balance. Nor could German reserve divisions arrive in time to be effective, since it was impossible for them to organize their attack within range of the bombardment without suffering damaging casualties. The British successes achieved by these methods at Menin Road Ridge and Polygon Wood in September convinced the enemy that it was again his turn to introduce new tactics.

At German high-level conferences on 27 and 29 September it was decided to return to a denser occupation and firmer defence of the forward area, holding back the reserve divisions for a deliberate counter-attack on the second or third day. The machine-guns of the support and reserve battalions were taken to the forward zone and grouped in 4 and 8-gun batteries with the purpose of smothering the attack as early as possible. To assure quick intervention, the support and reserve battalions were moved closer to the front, and in order to free more men for fighting in the forward zone the protection of the artillery positions of each regiment in the line was taken over by an infantry battalion moved up from the reserve division. The changes were seen primarily as a matter of timing, the first counter-attack being advanced, the deliberate counter-attack set back in time. Overlooked in the stress of the moment was the fact that these revisions inherently were a return to the tactics which had failed at the Somme.

Several divisional commanders had protested in vain against this massing of strength in the forward zone, and the desperate difficulties experienced in the

Broodseinde battle on 4 October proved them right. With their best weapons deployed and quickly destroyed in the forward zone, the supporting elements could not fight effectively, and being closer to the front than heretofore they were hit heavily by British artillery fire. Moreover, it had not been possible to hold back the reserve divisions, which from sheer necessity had been committed prematurely and piecemeal.

New tactics were needed. As early as June 1917, when it was becoming increasingly difficult to replace the casualties of the big battles, General Ludendorff had suggested the introduction of a "Forefield". It was not until 7 October, however, that the Fourth Army issued orders in that sense. Henceforth the foremost line of craters would be covered only by scattered outposts and a few light machine-guns. From 500 to 1000 metres farther back—depending on the ground—would be the forward edge of a main line of resistance.* German guns were to be registered on the foremost line of craters; and when a large-scale attack was imminent the outposts might be withdrawn, allowing the artillery fire to move forward and backward in accordance with the movements of the assaulting forces.

This was the pattern of defence awaiting the Canadian attack. The Germans were satisfied that the use of a "forefield" furnished a solution to their defence problems.[92] Subsequent operations seemed to show that short of attack this was the best possible method of defence, and they made no further changes of consequence.

At Passchendaele most of the German machine-gun crews in the "forefield" had their weapons in small lengths of trench sheltered from the weather by canvas or corrugated iron, and moved them to the nearest shell-hole for firing; others were in inter-supporting circular shelters of reinforced concrete, each of which could accommodate 30 men. Because the wet ground made dug-outs impossible these shelters were built above the ground. Their appearance after shellfire had shaken off the earthen camouflage or destroyed the farm buildings inside which they had been constructed gave them the name "pillboxes". From the Canadian lines dozens of these could be seen dotted across the muddy fields and on the crests of the ridges. Shellfire had overturned some and caused others to tilt drunkenly, but nothing less than a direct hit from an eight-inch howitzer could smash their five-foot-thick walls.[93] Behind the main line of resistance battalion and regimental reserves had little or no cover; but farther to the rear the counter-attack divisions, one behind each front-line division, with which it was interchanged every four to six days, were more fortunate in finding some accommodation in iron or concrete shelters.[94]

The changes in the German defence system posed special problems for the artillery supporting the attackers. Not only would the conventional preliminary bombardment be extremely wasteful, and make the ground even more difficult

* Called by the Germans the "Flanders Line I", it ran almost due north from Broodseinde to Staden. The sector south of the Ravebeek had been breached by the Australian attack on 4 October, but opposite the Canadian left it was still in German hands, linking together strongpoints at Laamkeek, Bellevue and Wolf Copse.

than it already was, but by sacrificing surprise it would invite retaliation. Yet to reduce the preparatory fire would benefit the enemy more than the attacking troops. From the experience of the Second Army a compromise emerged. It was decided to expose the entire front to harassing fire combined with feint barrages, while paying special attention to all pillboxes and identified wire. Like all compromise policies this one had its drawbacks, but it was adhered to with variations for the remainder of the offensive.[95]

The Attack of 26 October

The interposition of the Ravebeek swamp meant that General Currie had to plan a two-pronged attack for 26 October. He assigned to the 3rd Canadian Division the wider sector on the left, which included the sharply rising ground of the Bellevue spur. The main objective, designated the "Red Line", was 1200 yards distant. From Friesland, at the edge of the swamp, it ran almost due north to Vapour Farm at the corps boundary. The advancing troops would halt for one hour at an intermediate "Dotted Red Line". Securing this line would involve the reduction of several German pillboxes about Bellevue, on the crest of the spur. The 3rd Division's advance would be made on a two-brigade frontage—the assaulting battalions being the 4th C.M.R. of the 8th Brigade, and the 43rd and 58th Battalions of the 9th. In the more restricted ground south of the Ravebeek the 4th Division would attack with the 10th Brigade's 46th Battalion, which, by occupying advanced positions before the start of the offensive, would have to fight forward less than 600 yards to its part of the Red Line. Its principal initial target was Decline Copse, which straddled the Ypres-Roulers railway. This tangle of shattered tree trunks was strongly held by Bavarians, who had good protection in shelters and dug-outs in the deep railway cutting.[96]

General Currie had assured the Corps attack sufficient depth by allotting the remaining units of the 8th, 9th and 10th Brigades in support, while the 7th and 11th Brigades were being held in divisional and the 12th in corps reserve. In army reserve were the 1st and 2nd Divisions. The arrival of Canadian divisional artilleries had considerably brightened the picture for Brig.-Gen. Morrison. He now had at his disposal 210 18-pounders, 190 howitzers and 26 heavy guns. These included the 3rd, 4th, 9th and 10th Field Brigades C.F.A., the 1st and 2nd Canadian Heavy Batteries, and the 2nd, 5th and 9th Canadian Siege Batteries. There were two New Zealand field brigades; the remaining nine field brigades and 47 heavy or siege batteries were British.[97]

Getting the assaulting troops up to the front line was in itself an exacting task. No communication trenches could cross the swampy ground, and the only means of approach forward of the roads and light railways were narrow duckwalks which wound between the shell-holes and were in places submerged knee-deep in mud. Men and pack animals slipping off these tracks were in danger of drowning.[98] Because of the harsh physical demands of such a trip, in order that the soldiers might be as fresh as possible for the attack, and to give the officers some knowledge of the ground over which the attack would go, the leading battalions entered the support line four days before the battle, the 3rd Division units spending half of this time in the front line. The weather had unexpectedly turned fine on the 15th, but nowhere save in a few captured pillboxes was life comfortable. The majority of the troops huddled in shell-holes covered with their rubber groundsheets.

In an attempt to wear down the enemy and mislead him as to the actual time of the forthcoming attack, for four days previously the hostile front was swept morning and afternoon by a full barrage which employed guns of all calibres from 18-pounders to 9.2-inch howitzers.[99] Then on the night of 25-26 October, the 46th Battalion crept forward to an assembly area just behind outposts of the 50th Battalion, which was holding the right of the Corps front. North of the Ravebeek the three 3rd Division battalions girded themselves to attack from their present positions.[100]

During the night the weather broke. The attack went in at 5:40 a.m. under a wet mist that changed to rain lasting all day. The barrage, edging forward in lifts of 50 yards every four minutes, moved slowly enough for the infantry to keep well up while negotiating the encumbering mud. South of the Ravebeek the 46th Battalion, attacking astride the Passchendaele road, captured all its objectives on the main ridge, as did an Australian battalion on its right. Between the road and the railway one of the Canadian companies even pushed 250 yards beyond its target.[101] Across the Ravebeek, however, the 3rd Division was less fortunate. On General Lipsett's right the two battalions of the 9th Brigade found the German wire well cut by the preliminary bombardment and within an hour were clearing out the Bellevue pillboxes, sending a steady stream of prisoners to the rear. But at the Dotted Red Line they came under heavy artillery fire that the enemy was bringing down on his abandoned positions, and by nine o'clock the brigade as a whole was falling back towards its starting line.[102]

There was one saving feature. When general failure in the centre of the Corps front resulted in a partial retirement on both flanks, Lieut. Robert Shankland, D.C.M., of the 43rd Battalion, who had reinforced his own platoon with elements of other companies and two detachments of the 9th Machine Gun Company, managed to maintain a small but important footing on the Bellevue spur, just north of the Mosselmarkt road. On the right the 46th Battalion had to pull in its forward posts and throw back a defensive left flank to the edge of the Ravebeek; on the far left the 4th C.M.R., which in bitter fighting had captured Wolf Copse and secured the 8th Brigade's part of the Dotted Red Line, dropped back 300 yards to link up with the 63rd (Royal Naval) Division, the Fifth Army's right flanking formation.

With Shankland's party holding on grimly in captured pillboxes and shell-holes, Brig.-Gen. Hill's 9th Brigade prepared a further attack. Towards noon a company of the supporting 52nd Battalion plugged the gap between his little band and the main body, while other companies went on to complete the capture of the Bellevue spur. Then working southward they successfully engaged one pillbox after another. Infantry sections created a diversion with their rifle grenades and Lewis guns, allowing smaller parties to work their way round to the blind side to throw in their hand grenades. By these means the defences of the Flanders Line I which had stopped the 2nd Anzac Corps on 5 and 12 October were finally overcome. By mid-afternoon the 52nd had captured Bellevue and Laamkeek, thereby taking a firm grasp on the intermediate objective; by 6:20 next morning the 9th Brigade had consolidated its gains and established outposts only 300 yards short of the Red Line. Lieut. Shankland's was the first of three Victoria Crosses won by the 3rd Division that day. The other winners were Capt. C. P. J. O'Kelly, M.C., who led his company of the 52nd Battalion in capturing six German pillboxes and 100 prisoners; and Private T. W. Holmes of the 4th C.M.R., who single-handed knocked out two machine-guns, captured a pillbox and took nineteen prisoners.[103]

On the Canadian right, due to a series of misunderstandings as much as to enemy pressure—though there were counter-attacks on both sides of the Ravebeek, and the 46th Battalion's positions were under steady enfilade fire from Germans still holding out at Laamkeek—Decline Copse, the common objective of the 4th Canadian and 1st Australian Divisions, was gradually abandoned. Such was the mistake of not assigning the Copse to a single formation. Advanced posts and then company positions were withdrawn to form defensive flanks, and when relieving companies took over less than their prescribed positions, the Germans promptly moved back in. It took the 44th Battalion, attacking astride the railway under heavy machine-gun fire, to restore the situation on the night of 27-28 October. The following evening, fifty to a hundred members of the enemy's 238th Division (which had relieved the Bavarians) penetrated the Copse position, but elements of the 44th and 85th Battalions quickly joined forces and expelled the Germans with grenade and bayonet.[104]

It had been a satisfying but costly beginning. On 26, 27 and 28 October the Canadians had suffered 2481 casualties, including 585 killed, 965 wounded and eight taken prisoner on the first day. They had killed many Germans and captured 370. Though not completely successful, the operation had placed the attackers on higher, drier, ground and in a good tactical position to deliver the next blow. But first a major job of housekeeping was required. To ensure the delivery of ammunition, rations and other supplies to the forward troops, engineers and pioneers set to building a track of planks, corduroy and fascines in each brigade sector, to carry brigade mule-trains, 250 strong. At great hazard by day and considerable exertion by night, these preparations were completed in time to strike a further blow on the 30th.

The Assault is Renewed, 30 October

In this next phase (the seventh in the series that had started on 20 September) Field-Marshal Haig hoped to complete the advance to the Red Line and to gain a base for the final assault on Passchendaele. This was the Blue Line objective, some 600-700 yards east of the Red Line. To secure it would mean taking the strongly held Crest Farm, just north of the Passchendaele road, and in the northern sector the hamlet of Meetcheele, up the Bellevue spur, and the Goudberg area between the Mosselmarkt road and the Corps left boundary. The Corps was to link up on the left at Vapour Farm with the Fifth Army, which would be advancing with the 63rd and 58th Divisions on either side of the swamps of the Lekkerboterbeek; and on the right with the 1st Anzac Corps at the railway line south of Vienna Cottage.[105]

The attack began at 5:50 a.m. on 30 October, in clear but very cold and windy weather which blew up rain in the afternoon. As on the 26th, some 420 guns and howitzers crashed out their support of the Canadian Corps. On the right, the 4th Division, augmenting its strength for its widening front, assaulted with three battalions of Brig.-Gen. MacBrien's 12th Brigade—the 85th, 78th and 72nd. The 3rd Division had the 7th and 8th Brigades forward, the assaulting units from right to left being Princess Patricia's Canadian Light Infantry, the 49th Battalion and the 5th C.M.R.[106]

It took the enemy eight minutes to reply with heavy artillery and machine-gun fire, and by that time the Canadians were well on their way. On General Watson's right (where this time the railway line was included within the Canadian boundary),[107] the 85th Battalion, though losing half its strength in casualties, knocked out all the strongpoints in its path, turning captured machine-guns on the fleeing Germans.[108] The 78th Battalion quickly gained its objectives east of the Passchendaele road and settled down to some effective sniping of small parties of Germans attempting to reorganize a line of defended shell-holes. On the divisional left the 72nd Battalion captured Crest Farm and then sent patrols beyond the Blue Line into Passchendaele, which they found the Germans evacuating. Later these were pulled back to assist in reorganization. By 8:30 a.m. General Watson could report all objectives taken between the railway and the Ravebeek, although north-west of Crest Farm the Blue Line was so badly flooded that consolidation had to be carried out short of the original goal. Owing to the failure of the 3rd Division's right flank to keep abreast, however, the 72nd Battalion was obliged to drop its left flank back along the Ravebeek.[109]

North of the Ravebeek the 3rd Division's attack had got off to a good start. During the night, before the main attack opened, the P.P.C.L.I. had captured "Snipe Hall", a particularly troublesome pillbox at the edge of the swamp, which had held up the 9th Brigade on 26 October. From here their assaulting companies struggled forward through the mire to take Duck Lodge, the battalion's intermediate objective. The storm of fire that lashed the Patricias from enemy posts farther up the valley brought heavy casualties. At the end of an hour they had lost almost all their junior officers. On the left of the main road the 49th Battalion, even harder hit, kept level by capturing Furst Farm, 600 yards west of the Meetcheele crossroads. It was reported that in the advance there was little bayoneting by either side but that it was a great day for snipers. German marksmen accounted for many of the Canadian casualties, but the day's success owed much to the accuracy of Canadian riflemen in covering their comrades' advance against German machine-gun nests and pillboxes.[110]

The best progress on the 8th Brigade's front was made by the left-hand companies of the 5th C.M.R. The Mounted Rifles had difficulty getting through the swampy ground in Woodland Plantation, north of the Bellevue ridge, but by seven o'clock brigade observers could report enemy parties in retreat, joining large numbers who were seen withdrawing in disorder and without equipment along the roads running north from Crest Farm and Mosselmarkt.[111]

By mid-afternoon of the 30th the 3rd Division was well up on the Blue Line on the extreme left, but on the right flank the 465th Infantry Regiment was still holding a small salient about Graf House.* The P.P.C.L.I.'s main accomplishment had been the storming of the fortified positions guarding the Meetcheele crossroads, an achievement largely made possible by the extreme heroism of two men. When the battalion's left companies were halted in their ascent of the ridge by fire from a machine-gun sited in a pillbox beside the main road, Lieut. Hugh Mackenzie, D.C.M. (a Patricia officer who was serving with the 7th Machine Gun Company) and Sergeant G. H. Mullin, M.M., a regimental sniper, led an attack on the position. Mackenzie was killed while drawing the enemy's fire, but Mullin went on to capture the pillbox single-handed, shooting its two machine-gunners with his revolver, and forcing the garrison of ten to surrender. Both won the Victoria Cross.[114]

To the left of the Canadian Corps, the 63rd (R.N.) and 58th Divisions, operating on lower and muddier ground, made only slight progress. For a time the 8th Canadian Brigade found itself with both flanks open, but, with the timely use of 5th C.M.R. reserves and companies of the 2nd C.M.R., Brig.-Gen. Elmsley re-established contact with only minor losses of ground. The success of the Mounted Rifles was in no small measure due to the sterling leadership of a company commander, Major G. R. Pearkes, who seized and held Vapour Farm and Source Farm against a series of local counter-attacks, keeping the 5th C.M.R. battalion headquarters informed of the situation by carrier pigeon. It was difficult indeed to reinforce these key positions astride the inter-Corps boundary, isolated as they were by the swampy source of a stream that ran north-westward into the Lekkerboterbeek.[115]

When, late that afternoon, the Canadian advance appeared to have reached its limit and reports of large numbers of Germans concentrating north of Mosselmarkt pointed to a major counter-attack, General Currie gave orders to Major-General Lipsett for the 3rd Division to consolidate what it had won, pushing out posts where possible, and to patrol rather than attempt to occupy the bog between the 7th and 8th Brigades. There was some question as to whether Major Pearkes' position could be maintained, for the Naval Division had been unable to reach its Source Farm objective. Reasoning that were these

* Facing the Canadians on 30 October were, from north to south, the 465th, 464th and 463rd Regiments of the 238th Infantry Division.[112] The intervention division was the 39th Infantry Division, which had replaced the exhausted 11th Bavarian Infantry Division in that role on the previous afternoon.[113]

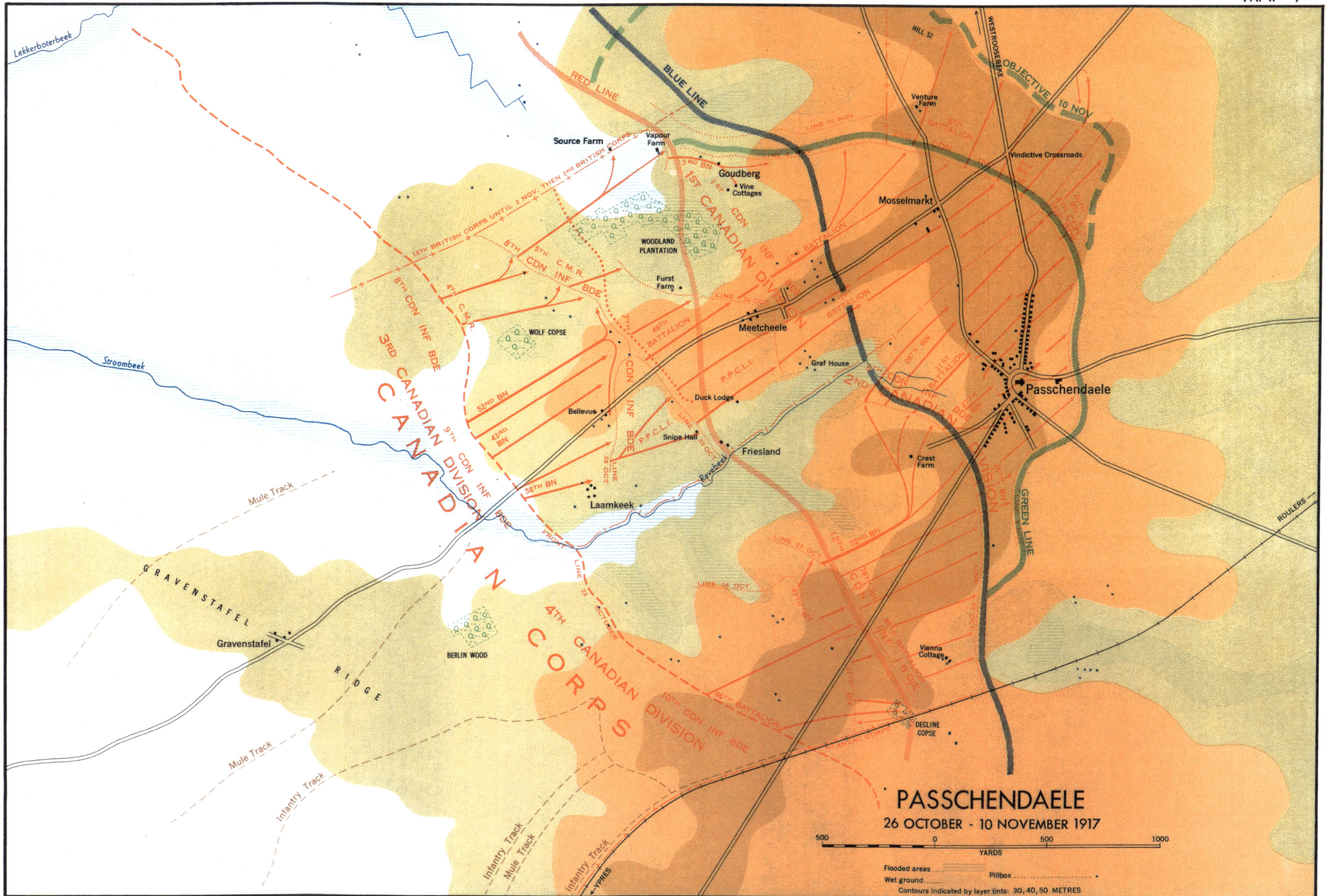

Reproduced by Army Survey Establishment
Compiled and drawn by Historical Section G.S.

gains relinquished they would only have to be retaken before the assault on Passchendaele, Currie with General Plumer's concurrence issued orders at 7:00 p.m. that every effort should be made to hold the line. That evening the 2nd Canadian Mounted Rifles, augmented by a company of the 1st, took over the 5th C.M.R.'s holdings. The night passed without further counter-attacks.* For his gallantry and leadership Major Pearkes, who already wore the M.C. and was later to win the D.S.O., was awarded the Victoria Cross—the third to go to the 3rd Canadian Division that day.[117]

The step by step battle was gradually accomplishing its purpose. In this second attack towards Passchendaele the Canadian Corps had achieved gains of up to a thousand yards on a 2800-yard front.[118] The cost had been high. The day's casualties had been almost as many as for the previous three-day attempt—884 killed, 1429 wounded (including 130 gassed), and eight taken prisoner.

The Capture of Passchendaele, 6 November

As early as 18 October General Currie had gained General Plumer's agreement that there should be a pause of seven days at the Blue Line, to give time for inter-divisional reliefs and to ensure that when operations were resumed the Fifth Army could help by advancing along its whole front rather than merely forming a protective flank for the Canadian attack.[119] This latter requirement was nullified, however, on 31 October, when G.H.Q. ordered the Second Army to take over a section of General Gough's front adjoining the Canadians, so that the battle might proceed under a single command. On 2 November, Plumer relieved the 18th with the 2nd Corps—though when the battle was re-joined the latter would do no more than provide the Canadians with artillery support. On the right of the Canadian Corps the 1st Anzac, 9th and 8th Corps, all under Plumer's command, were to simulate attacks along a four-mile front extending south to Zandvoorde (which lay midway between the Menin Road and the Ypres-Comines Canal).[120]

In the opening days of November the 1st and 2nd Divisions moved forward by rail from their reserve area east of Cassel to take over from the 3rd and 4th Divisions respectively. An uncomfortable three-hour train journey brought them to the ruined station of Ypres, whence they marched to battalion areas in the desolated salient. These reliefs were completed by the morning of 5 November. During the night of the 5th-6th, the assault units moved into their jumping-off positions. All were in place by 4:00 a.m.

General Currie's plan called for an attack in two stages (the eighth and ninth phases of the autumn battle)—the former to secure the village of Passchendaele, and the latter four days later, to seize the crest of the main ridge

*Corps Intelligence counted four battalion counter-attacks on the Canadian front during the morning of 30th. In the main, all were broken up by artillery and machine-gun fire a good distance from the Canadian positions.[116]

to the east. The Corps objectives for 6 November lay along the Green Line, a rough semicircle described about Graf House with a radius of 1000 yards. Besides Passchendaele it encompassed the hamlets of Mosselmarkt and Goudberg to the north-west. On the right the 2nd Division would send three battalions of the 6th Brigade (Brig.-Gen. Ketchen)—the 27th, 31st and 28th Infantry Battalions—against Passchendaele, while in the 1st Division's sector the 1st and 2nd Battalions would advance on either side of the Meetcheele-Mosselmarkt road. These 1st Brigade units would have farthest to go—about three-quarters of a mile. Covering the Corps right flank would be the 26th Battalion (5th Brigade), attacking Passchendaele from the south; on the left flank the 3rd Battalion was charged with a subsidiary operation against Vine Cottages, a strongpoint which the Germans were holding 350 yards south-east of Vapour Farm.[121]

The jumping-off line traversed large sections of swampy or flooded areas, especially in Major-General Macdonell's sector, where the only good footing was on the narrow Bellevue-Meetcheele spur. Farther forward, however, the ground was on the whole higher and drier than the Canadians had known in their previous attacks. On the right there were new opponents to be faced. The German 11th Division had arrived from the Champagne area only on 3 November to relieve the 39th Division between the Ypres-Roulers railway and the Mosselmarkt road. Opposite the 1st Canadian Division's left was a battalion of the 4th Division.[122]

At 6:00 a.m. on the sixth a powerful barrage, tremendously satisfying to the assaulting infantry, exploded across the front as the attack was launched under a clear sky that later became cloudy but shed no heavy rain. So quickly did the assaulting companies break out of their starting position that the enemy's retaliatory fire, opening a few minutes later, fell mainly behind the advancing troops. Afterwards prisoners reported that the infantry followed their barrage so closely that in most cases the Germans could not man their machine-guns before the attackers were on top of them.[123] Almost everywhere the attack went well. The 2nd Division encountered its chief opposition from pillboxes at the north end of Passchendaele, but less than three hours after zero the village that had so long been an Allied objective was securely in Canadian hands.

The 28th Battalion on the left had the hardest time. It came under heavy machine-gun fire early in the attack when it was struggling out of the Ravebeek valley, the men, according to a 6th Brigade report, "being knee deep, and in places waist deep in mud and water". Another troublesome if not serious factor was low-flying enemy aircraft. The visibility being too limited for much air fighting, pilots of both sides amused themselves by strafing each other's infantry. One ground target that received particular attention during the attack was the start line of the 31st Battalion, where German airmen mistook a row of greatcoats for troops.[124]

It was a satisfying day for the 6th Brigade. To the honour of being first into Passchendaele the 27th Battalion, on the Brigade right, could add the laurels won by one of its men, Private J. P. Robertson. His bravery in wiping out an enemy post cleared the way for his platoon to advance and earned him a posthumous Victoria Cross.[125]

On the 1st Division's front it was not the main assault but the subsidiary action on the left flank that produced the severer fighting. Here a company of the 3rd Battalion, isolated by swamp from the rest of Brig.-Gen. Griesbach's brigade, had a stubborn struggle with the defenders of Vine Cottages. In this action a member of the battalion, Corporal C. F. Barron, won the V.C. when he rushed and overcame three enemy machine-gun posts, turning one of the guns on the retreating enemy.[126] Captured machine-guns and forty prisoners, besides many German dead and wounded, testified to the bitterness of the resistance.

Elsewhere General Macdonell's forces encountered little trouble. Mosselmarkt was surprised and from its large pillbox there emerged in surrender four officers and 50 other ranks. Garrisons of well-camouflaged shell holes nearby put up more of a resistance before being overcome, but by eight o'clock the 1st Brigade had reached and consolidated the Green Line. On its right the 2nd Division beat off the only significant counter-attack of the day. The figure of a small loss of "under 700 men", which appeared in the enthusiastic entry which Sir Douglas Haig made in his diary concerning the operation, must have referred only to fatal casualties reported to him up to that time. Total Canadian casualties sustained during the assault and in shelling on the same day numbered 2238, of which 734 were killed or died of wounds. In all 464 captured Germans were admitted to the Corps cage or casualty clearing stations on 6 November and the following day.[127]

There was satisfaction for the Canadian Corps in having completed a highly successful attack in most difficult circumstances.* Classing it with the victory of Vimy Ridge, the Commander-in-Chief in his despatch referred to the accomplishment as one "by which for the second time within the year Canadian troops achieved a record of uninterrupted success".

On the day after the capture of Passchendaele General Currie gave orders for the ninth and final phase of the battle to be launched on 10 November.[129] This was to gain the remaining high ground north of the village in the vicinity of Vindictive Crossroads and Hill 52. The road junction was 1000 yards north of Passchendaele on the highway to Westroosebeke, Hill 52, half a mile beyond the crossroads, was the highest point on the northern end of the Passchendaele Ridge. With these goals in possession the Canadians would have complete observation over German positions to the north-east. The frontage of the Canadian attack was considerably narrowed, as the Second Corps on the left took over responsibility for the Goudberg spur. Currie entrusted the main thrust to the 2nd Canadian Brigade (Brig.-Gen. Loomis), with a battalion of the 4th Brigade (Brig.-Gen. Rennie) cooperating on the right.

* Continuous wave wireless sets received their first practical testing in operational conditions during the attack and proved entirely satisfactory. Up to this time commanders had been dubious about relying on this method of transmitting messages, but henceforth they were "willing to consider wireless as an integral part of the general scheme of communication".[128]

More German reliefs had taken place since the fighting on 6 November. Prisoners later reported that units had become so disorganized and intermingled during the recent operations that they could not identify the sectors of the line which they were holding. Opposite the Canadians now from north to south there were parts of three regiments of the 4th Division and one from the 44th Reserve Division, which had replaced the 11th Division on 9 November.[130] From the unsystematic pattern of their defences and the indifferent morale of several Germans who had already been taken prisoner, the enemy do not seem to have considered the area attacked as vital ground. This was later borne out by their generally light resistance to the attack. Officers in a group of eleven who were taken in one dug-out were obviously embarrassed when questioned as to the circumstances of their capture.

It was raining heavily when the 7th and 8th Battalions jumped off from positions north and north-east of Mosselmarkt on 10 November, shortly after six o'clock. By 7:30 a.m. both units were on the first objective, only 500 yards away; but to secure its goal the 7th Battalion on the right had to push on another 300 yards to quell troublesome German machine-guns in a nearby trench. At this stage the 10th Battalion, coming forward from brigade reserve, took over the whole of the 2nd Brigade's front, advancing the line to the final objective. On the left of the Canadians the 1st British Division's advance ran into difficulties when a German counter-attack got between two diverging battalions. Caught by the enemy's fire against their inner flanks both units suffered heavily and withdrew. As a result the 8th Canadian Battalion, which had overrun Venture Farm, capturing four 77-mm. guns, was forced to plug the gap by throwing back a left flank.[131]

The frontage of the Anglo-Canadian attack, narrow enough to begin with and reduced by three-fifths by the failure on the left, allowed the enemy to concentrate an unusual weight of artillery against the new line. In all, the counter-batteries of five German corps were turned on the Canadian front.[132] ". . . Almost as bad as Pozières . . .", an Australian diarist was to note. "The night is simply vile—and the day too. . . . If the Canadians can hold on they are wonderful troops."[133] The shelling was especially heavy between nine o'clock and late afternoon; many German prisoners on the way back to the Canadian cage were killed by their own guns. Bad visibility hampered the operation of counter-battery staffs and observation aeroplanes, yet did not prevent enemy fighters from bombing and machine-gunning Canadian troops who were consolidating or bringing up supplies. During the afternoon a German counter-attack was turned back by the 20th Battalion's small-arms fire; another was broken up with artillery. But the Canadians held grimly on. To make their newly-won salient less vulnerable, they pushed forward outpost groups in shell-holes and short lengths of trenches well down the eastern slope of the ridge. Their fighting that day had cost the Canadians losses of 1094, including 420 killed.

This attack on 10 November brought to an end the long drawn-out Third Battle of Ypres. Though Haig had hoped to have the entire Passchendaele-Westroosebeke ridge as a winter position, the line was still half a mile short of Westroosebeke village. But the Cambrai operation was only ten days off. Five British divisions had gone or were soon to go to Italy—in the face of strong protests from the C.-in-C.—and three others might be required. The extension of the line across the Somme to meet the French request would reduce the British offensive effort by four more divisions. Accordingly by 15 November the Commander-in-Chief had decided that "any further offensive on the Flanders front must be at once discontinued, though it is important to keep this fact secret as long as possible."[134] On 14 November the gradual relief of the Canadian divisions began, and on the 20th General Currie resumed command of the former Lens-Vimy front. During its stay in the north the Canadian Corps had suffered 15,654 battle casualties.

Passchendaele in Retrospect

What is the true appraisal of Passchendaele? The attempted break-through had failed, and Haig had been forced to settle for an advance of only four and a half miles. The enemy still held the Belgian ports; and five months later he recovered all the ground taken from him, and more. Can the Flanders 1917 campaign therefore be considered even a limited success?

The popular answer has generally been, No. In the years following the war the British High Command, and Haig in particular, became the target of violent attacks by such prominent men as David Lloyd George and Winston Churchill, and in due course various military historians added their censure. "Grim, futile and bloody", are among the adjectives used by the British wartime premier in describing the Third Battle of Ypres.[135] They are matched by the Churchillian phrase labelling the venture "a forlorn expenditure of valour and life without equal in futility".[136]

The main indictments against Earl Haig are that he planned his offensive on ground that adverse weather would render impassable; and that he persisted in costly fighting long after any reasonable hope of success had disappeared. Haig's supporters argue, however, that the campaign had to be fought to take pressure off the French, and that it was justified from the standpoint of attrition, the claim being made that the German casualties far outnumbered those of the Allies.

If indeed Lord Jellicoe's gloomy prognostications (above, p. 303) materially influenced the War Cabinet's decision to sanction Haig's attempted "duck's march" to Ostend and Zeebrugge, the Admiralty's share in the responsibility for Third Ypres requires examination. There seems little doubt that the U-boat campaign of 1917 was allowed to exert a far greater influence than it should have done on the conduct of the land operations. It is true that in the first four months of unrestricted sinkings submarine flotillas based in Flanders accounted for nearly one-third of the tonnage destroyed. Yet it seems fairly obvious that had Ostend and Zeebrugge been captured, the U-boats based there would have continued to operate from German ports; the merchant sinkings could not be stopped by any land operation. Much of the blame for the success of the submarine campaign must rest with the Admiralty for its stubborn opposition to the convoy system,* which was introduced on a general scale only in July, after Lloyd George had paid a personal visit to the Admiralty to "take peremptory action".[138] The immediate result was a far greater reduction in shipping losses than the capture of the Flanders bases could have achieved.[139]

The question of Pétain's responsibility has already been introduced. The time of the request for Haig to exert pressure as a relief to the French was in the early summer, immediately after the French mutinies (above, p. 243). As previously noted, there is no contemporary record of a later request having been made. Yet the belief that the weakness of the French Army had brought such a demand from Pétain was to gain currency soon after the war, as Haig came under fire from critics who contended that the costly campaign had been needlessly prolonged. The Field Marshal stated to various individuals that he had been forced to attack and continue attacking in Flanders to prevent an irresistible German offensive against the demoralized French. In 1930 Sir Arthur Currie, writing to a correspondent who had drawn his attention to an article about the Passchendaele fighting in the French newspaper, *Le Temps,*† recalled that at the time of the Peace Conference in 1919 Haig had told him "why Passchendaele had to be taken". Haig gave as his first reason the need to prevent the Germans attacking the French, low spirited as they were because of the mutiny in the French army. He also wanted to secure the submarine bases on the Belgian coast. Then, referring to the existence of a peace party in France and one in England, and to the very severe fighting that the British Army had had, Haig expressed his determination to help restore both French and British morale by finishing the fighting of 1917 with a victory.[140]

A further example of these representations is a letter Haig wrote in March 1927 to Brig.-Gen. Charteris, his former Chief of Intelligence: ". . . the possibility of the French Army breaking up in 1917 *compelled me to go on attacking.* It was impossible to change sooner from the Ypres front to Cambrai without Pétain coming to press me not to leave the Germans alone for a week, on account of the *awful* state of the French troops."[141]

But explanations put forward a decade or more after that event cannot carry the conviction of entries made by Haig in his diary at the time of the battle. If indeed the C.-in-C. felt himself in the autumn of 1917 to be under French pressure to continue the offensive in Flanders, he should have been enlightened by a con-

* The Admiralty gave as its objections the difficulty of providing sufficient escort ships, the belief that merchant captains had not the necessary skill or navigational aids to manoeuvre and keep station in convoy formation, the reduction in the carrying power of vessels in convoy because of the fewer round voyages possible in a year, and above all, the greater target that the concentration of a large number of merchant ships would present to hostile submarines, particularly during the vulnerable period of dispersal from convoy.[137]

† The article, dated 7 February 1930, had been prompted by a press report of an Armistice Day speech delivered by a former Canadian divisional commander who had fought at Passchendaele. It read in part:

> Flanders . . . was an English battle, of which Passchendaele was the last event. It had nothing to do with the French morale. The part played in this battle by the First French Army shows, moreover, that the morale of the French soldiers was far from being, at this time, what certain Canadian generals describe in their speeches and articles . . .

versation he had with President Poincaré at Lillers on the eve of the Australian attack at Passchendaele. The President dumbfounded him, he wrote in his diary, by asking "when I thought the operation would stop! He was anxious to know because of taking over more line. I said we ought to have only the one thought in our minds, namely to attack."[142]

We turn to the melancholy balance-sheet of attrition. An assessment of the casualty figures of the opposing sides should help to furnish a measure of the Allied success or failure. Unfortunately, although each side produced numerous statements of its own and estimates of the other's losses, no common basis has been found on which to make an exact comparison.* The British Official Historian, using figures submitted to the Supreme War Council in February 1918, gives the total British losses (killed, wounded, captured and missing) from 31 July to 12 November as 244,897.[143] He has adjusted (with a liberality† that is hard to justify) German official figures of 217,000 for the Fourth Army's losses (21 July-31 December), to arrive at the "probability that the Germans lost about 400,000".[146]

It is difficult to accept these figures, which in assessing the defenders considerably higher losses than the attackers run contrary to normal experience. An official compilation published by the War Office in 1922 reversed the balance—thereby providing Haig's critics with welcome ammunition. It gave the casualties on the entire Western Front in the last six months of 1917 as 448,614 British and 270,710 German. For the period 31 July to 19 November the same source shows British losses as 324,140.[147] If these figures are further reduced to exclude losses on the so-called "quiet" sectors outside the main battle front, the result approximates the total given to the Supreme War Council in 1918. The addition of some 15,000 to cover the ten days of the preliminary bombardment (from 21 July) would raise this to about 260,000. Comparable figures for the German Fourth Army for 21 July to 10 November issued by Supreme Headquarters set the German losses at 202,000.[148] These two totals would appear to reflect the comparative cost to each side as accurately as it is possible to determine.

But the true measurement of attrition lies in determining which side could worse afford the losses it sustained. From this standpoint the Germans suffered the deadlier blow. Their Official History admits that "the battle had led to an excessive expenditure of German forces. The casualties were so great that they could no longer be covered, and the already reduced battle strength of battalions sank significantly lower."[149] It is here that the real reason for Haig's pertinacity may be found. Misinformed by the exaggerated reports of German losses fed to him by his Intelligence (reports which by contrast tended to minimize his

* Statistics, given generally by armies, do not conform to the exact battle front nor to exact time limits of the campaign. Furthermore, British and German returns differ in the method of accounting for wounded.

† Edmonds adds some 30 per cent to cover lightly wounded (though there is strong evidence that these were already included in the German figure)[144] and further increases the total to cover "several divisions [which] rendered their returns after they had left the Fourth Army" and other unspecified troops outside that Army.[145]

own casualties), Haig was convinced that German morale, both military and civilian, was on the verge of breaking. In June he had called on his army commanders for "one more great victory" that might "turn the scale finally".[150] In August (assuring the C.I.G.S. that "an occasional glance at our daily intelligence summaries would convince even the most sceptical of the truth of what I write") he contrasted "the poor state of the German troops" with the "high state of efficiency of our own men".[151] At the end of September he was "of the opinion that the enemy is tottering".[152] Eventually in October, when even Haig's usually over-optimistic chief of Intelligence, Brig.-Gen. Charteris, noted in his diary (on the 10th) "there is now no chance of complete success here this year",[153] the C.-in-C. was forced to lower his sights. By the time that the Canadians entered the battle the objective had become a limited one—the capture of the Passchendaele Ridge, or (as the month ended without this being accomplished) enough of it to secure a defensible position for the winter. Indeed, by then even the *name* Passchendaele was an objective in itself. Yet the achievement of these limited aims was denied Haig, as the demands of the Italian front compelled him to abandon the offensive.

The controversy over Passchendaele is not likely soon to end. Placed in its best light Haig's Flanders offensive must be regarded as a particularly intensive phase of the continuous battle in which the Allies engaged the Germans on the Western Front from the beginning of trench warfare to the end of the war. Yet though the 1917 campaign failed in the strategical concept that Haig had envisaged for it and deteriorated into a contest of exhaustion, this attrition produced important results.

The Somme, costly as it was to the Allies, began the destruction of the German army. Passchendaele carried the process a long step forward.

The Supreme War Council

Although Lloyd George had been able to impose on the Admiralty the Cabinet's wishes as to how the enemy should be fought at sea (above, p. 328), his attempts to overrule the High Command with respect to the land operations had been singularly unsuccessful. In the eyes of the British Prime Minister the principal cause of the failures of the last three years had been the refusal of the "Westerners" to regard all theatres of war as one vast battlefield having a single front against which, at any given moment, coordinated efforts could be directed at the point then most vital to the fortunes of the Alliance. There was little hope of achieving this recognition as long as a Commander-in-Chief in the field, imbued with the importance of his own particular sector, was influential enough to override those in the War Ministry who recommended a strategic policy contrary to his own. The solution seemed to lie in the formation of some inter-Allied body provided with a staff and an intelligence section which, "working together, would review the battlefield as a whole and select the most promising sector for concentrated action".[154] The War Cabinet would thus have an alternative source of advice to those confirmed "Westerners", Haig and Robertson. Towards the end of July 1917 General Foch, in an appreciation of what steps needed to be taken in the event of Russia's expected defection, had recommended obtaining unity of action "by means of a permanent inter-Allied military organ", which could facilitate the rapid movement of troops from one theatre to another.[155] When the French Premier, M. Painlevé, visited Lloyd George in London in October 1917, the two reached agreement to submit such a proposal to Italy and the United States.[156]

The arguments for the establishment of a central Allied control were reinforced by the situation on the Italian front during the late summer and autumn. It will be recalled that a condition of the British Cabinet's approval of the Flanders offensive had been that should it fail Haig would transfer guns and men to Italy. With the help of the batteries sent by Britain and France early in the summer, inconsiderable as this contribution was, General Cadorna had launched offensives in April and in August (the latter being numbered the Eleventh Battle of the Isonzo). Both petered out inconclusively, largely for lack of sufficient guns and heavy ammunition. Then, on 24 October, the Central Powers, having reinforced the Italian sector with a German army of six divisions (four of them from the Eastern Front), launched a vigorous offensive across the upper Isonzo. Using gas shells against which Italian respirators were ineffective, General Otto von Below's Fourteenth Army, flanked to the south by two Austrian armies, smashed through the Italian defences in a brilliantly conducted battle which took its name from the nearby town of Caporetto. With his left flank completely turned, Cadorna ordered a retreat to the River Tagliamento, forty miles to the rear. But the pursuit of the demoralized Italians continued to the line of the Piave, where von Below's forces halted, having advanced eighty miles from the Isonzo. They had captured an estimated 265,000 prisoners and their booty included more than 3000 guns.[157] The operation in Italy—gaining "fresh laurels", as Ludendorff put it, for "German leadership and German troops"—had "achieved all that could possibly be expected of it."[158]

The alarming reports of the Caporetto disaster brought the Italians speedy but belated help. Five British and six French divisions and army troops reached northern Italy between 10 November and 12 December. The transfer was carried out rapidly and efficiently, thanks to good administrative preparations made by General Foch, who had been sent to Italy in April to plan for just such an emergency. And it was Foch who prudently halted the first reinforcements well to the rear to avoid their being sacrificed by piecemeal committal into the general *mêlée*.[159]

The Caporetto disaster could not have come at a more opportune time for Lloyd George's designs. On 5 November representatives of the British, French and Italian governments met at Rapallo, near the French frontier, ostensibly to discuss further aid to Italy.[160] The Italian demands emphasized the need for

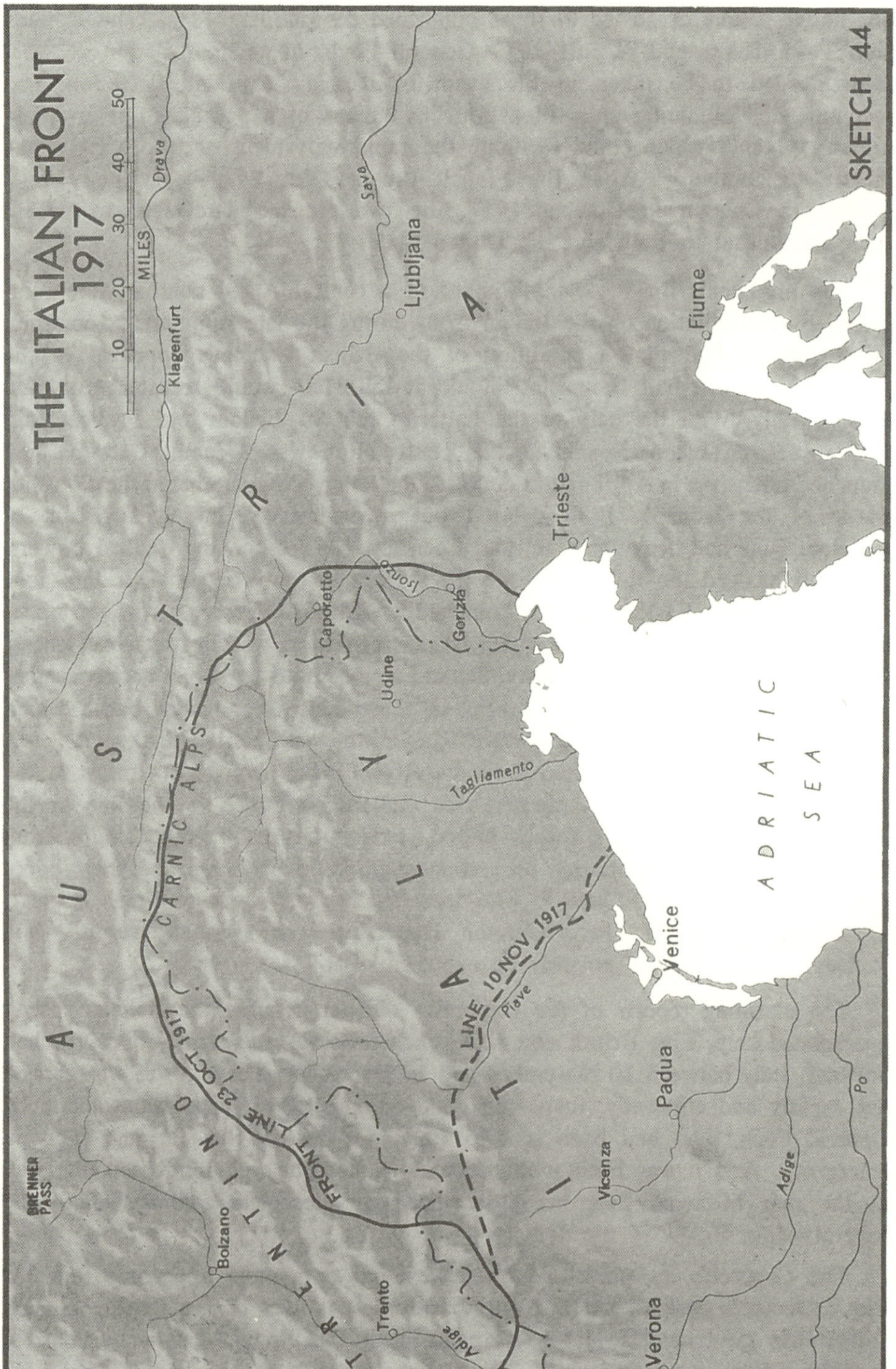
THE ITALIAN FRONT
1917
MILES
10 20 30 40 50
SKETCH 44
AUSTRIA
ITALY
TRENTINO
CARNIC ALPS
FRONT LINE 23 OCT 1917
LINE 10 NOV 1917
ADRIATIC SEA
BRENNER PASS
Bolzano
Trento
Verona
Vicenza
Padua
Venice
Udine
Caporetto
Gorizia
Trieste
Fiume
Ljubljana
Klagenfurt
Drava
Sava
Isonzo
Tagliamento
Piave
Adige
Po

consideration of strategic policy at an inter-Allied level. On the 7th* the conference voted the Supreme War Council into existence. It held its first session at Rapallo, subsequent meetings taking place at Versailles.

Initially the Council consisted of the leaders of the British, French and Italian Governments, or their representatives, and a general officer from each power as Permanent Military Representative. At the insistence of Lloyd George, who was determined that the new Council should be a free agent in making recommendations on Allied strategy, no country might have its Chief of Staff double as its Military Representative. He picked General Sir Henry Wilson, an "Easterner", to represent Britain. With Foch thus barred from membership on the Council, General Weygand became the French representative. By December the Council had come to include American political and military representation. While the Supreme War Council solved some of the British Prime Minister's problems of control, it fell far short of meeting the Allied need for an effective authority with power to act promptly and decisively in an emergency. At its best the Council was an organ for consultation and deliberation. It would take a tragic reverse on the Western Front in the following year to force Allied agreement on the creation of a Supreme Command.

Canadian Cavalry at Cambrai

From the collapse of the Italian front we return to the western theatre. The possibility of developing operations on the Cambrai front had been considered in April 1917, when the British Commander-in-Chief had ordered the Fourth and Fifth Armies to prepare plans for an attack in that sector (above, p. 272). The subseqent relief of those armies by the Third Army had transferred responsibility for such a project to General Byng. It remained in suspense during the prolonged Flanders offensive, but in mid-October Haig gave approval for preparations to proceed and for the necessary troops to be made available to train for an operation to be launched on 20 November.[161]

The design was a bold one—no less, if fully successful, than a rupture of the German front from St. Quentin, seventeen miles south of Cambrai, to the canalized River Sensée, five miles north of the city. It was Byng's intention to gain possession of the area lying between the Canal du Nord and the St. Quentin Canal,† bounded to the north by the Sensée. The southern end was closed by the Hindenburg Position, two strongly wired systems 500 yards or more apart, which angled north-westward for seven miles from Banteux to Havrincourt; and Byng meant to break through here. With this accomplished the whole German line west of the Canal du Nord would be endangered.[162]

This area of open, unscarred ground had been chosen because it was good tank country over which, for the first time in the war, armour might be used

*Meanwhile Russia's participation in the war was nearly ended. On 8 November the Bolsheviks seized the capital, Petrograd, and two weeks later Lenin asked the Germans for an armistice.

†The St. Quentin Canal followed the course of the Escaut (Scheldt) River, and was alternatively known as the Canal de l'Escaut.

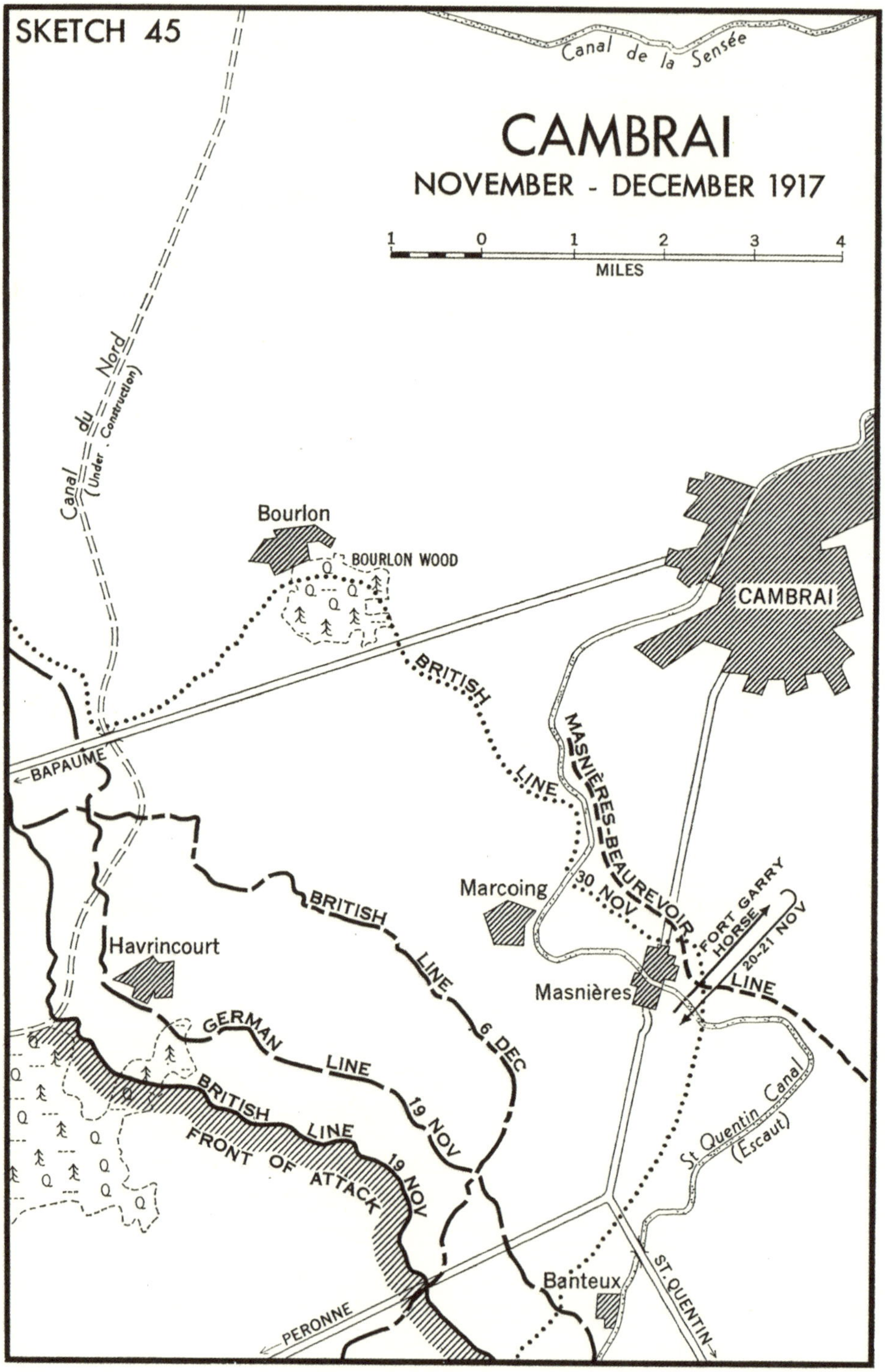
SKETCH 45
CAMBRAI
NOVEMBER - DECEMBER 1917
1 0 1 2 3 4
MILES
Canal de la Sensée
Canal du Nord
(Under Construction)
Bourlon
BOURLON WOOD
CAMBRAI
BRITISH LINE
MASNIÈRES-BEAUREVOIR LINE
30 NOV
BAPAUME
Marcoing
FORT GARRY HORSE
20-21 NOV
BRITISH LINE 6 DEC
Havrincourt
Masnières
GERMAN LINE 19 NOV
BRITISH LINE 19 NOV
FRONT OF ATTACK
St Quentin Canal
(Escaut)
Banteux
PERONNE
ST. QUENTIN

in more than "penny packets". The Army Commander planned to employ 300 tanks and five infantry divisions to smash through the Hindenburg Position between the canals, and to seize crossings over the eastward bend of the St. Quentin Canal at Marcoing and Masnières. As soon as the enemy's rear defences east of these places (the Masnières-Beaurevoir Line) had been breached, the Cavalry Corps, reverting to its normal role,* would pass through to sweep northward and isolate Cambrai from the east and to secure the passage over the River Sensée. In the meantime infantry reserves would capture Bourlon Wood, which covered a commanding spur north of the Bapaume-Cambrai road, and seize Cambrai itself. A junction with the cavalry at the Sensée would cut off the German front line troops to the west and expose them to attack from the rear.

While Haig's "great experiment" at Cambrai was the employment of massed armour to breach the enemy's defences, this was not the only tactical innovation in the battle. With the tanks counted on to flatten the hostile wire, it was possible to achieve surprise by omitting the usual preliminary bombardment. The enemy would not receive even the warning normally given by artillery ranging and registration; the guns would shoot by the map, taking advantage of improved techniques of survey and calibration.[164]

Cambrai was on the left wing of Army Group Crown Prince Rupprecht, in the area of General of Cavalry von der Marwitz's Second Army. The German formations on which the British attack would fall were the left wing of the 20th Landwehr Division, the entire 54th Division and the right wing of the 9th Reserve Division.[165] These divisions, however, were within easier reach of reinforcements than were the assaulting forces. The Germans little expected an offensive in this part of the theatre, which battle-weary troops brought down from the Passchendaele area called the "Flanders sanatorium". German regimental histories are agreed that measures had been taken to deal with local attacks expected for 20 or 21 November. But the scale of the assault came as a complete strategical surprise when it went in at daybreak on 20 November.[166]

The British Tank Corps had observed the utmost secrecy in assembling the armour at the forming-up line—in no case closer than a thousand yards from the enemy's outposts. First there was the roar of British aircraft flying low over the German positions, and then the unprecedented and awesome sight and sound of a long line of tanks rumbling forward. Simultaneously came the crash of a thousand guns opening fire, as wave after wave of infantry followed the tanks across no man's land. With few exceptions the defenders of the outpost zone surrendered or fled. Farther on there was opposition from isolated field batteries engaging tanks, and the infantry came under fire from machine-gun posts by-passed by the

* Towards the end of May 1917 the 2nd, 3rd, 4th and 5th (formerly 2nd Indian) Cavalry Divisions had been dismounted and assigned to a holding role north of the Somme. Here twenty-seven members of the Fort Garry and Lord Strathcona's Horse had won immediate awards in a 150-man raid on 8-9 July.[163]

armour. But by evening the Third Army had breached both Hindenburg systems,* having advanced from three to four miles on a six-mile front. German fire had knocked out 65 tanks, and 114 had broken down or become ditched. The assaulting troops had suffered about 4000 casualties.[168]

On the first day there had been little action for the five divisions of the Cavalry Corps. The village of Marcoing was cleared by the infantry shortly after midday, but at Masnières, 3000 yards to the east on the far bank, the enemy repelled efforts of the 88th Brigade to secure a bridgehead. Two companies crossed east of the village but were almost immediately pinned down by heavy fire. On the brigade left the Newfoundland Regiment fought its way across at the western outskirts of Masnières, but without artillery or tank support could make no headway against the well-manned Masnières-Beaurevoir Line and was forced to dig in.

Behind the armour and infantry wire-dragging tanks and pioneer parties had quickly cleared a track for the cavalry, and at 11:40 a.m. the 5th Cavalry Division, led by the Canadian Cavalry Brigade, began moving forward to the canal. Incorrect information led the Canadians' commander, Brig.-Gen. J. E. B. Seely, to believe that the 88th Brigade had gained its objective east of the canal, and accordingly about two o'clock he ordered the Fort Garry Horse forward. The road bridge in Masnières had collapsed under a tank that tried to cross, but with the assistance of local inhabitants a crossing suitable for cavalry was made at a lock 300 yards south-east of the village. By four o'clock "B" Squadron had begun riding towards a commanding ridge two miles north-east of Masnières. But by this time the early dusk of a November day was gathering, ending any prospect of passing a large body of mounted troops over the lock used by the Canadians.† Orders reached Seely to halt the movement of the Fort Garry Horse across the canal and to recall those already on the north bank.

But "B" Squadron was now out of touch and fighting a battle of its own. A short distance beyond Masnières the squadron commander was killed by machine-gun fire. Under the leadership of Lieut. Harcus Strachan the Canadians pushed on, overrunning a Germany battery and cutting down disorganized parties of enemy infantry. At dusk the squadron, reduced to some forty all ranks, took up a position in a sunken road a little over a mile from the canal and beat off German patrols. Strachan then stampeded the horses to divert the enemy's attention and led his men back on foot. Skirmishes with enemy parties on the return journey resulted in the taking of sixteen prisoners. Lieut. Strachan, who already wore the M.C., was awarded the Victoria Cross.[169] The only other cavalry to have engaged the enemy were some squadrons of the 1st Cavalry Division employed in clearing the west bank of the canal north of Marcoing.

*To help them cross the 12-foot wide Hindenburg trenches the tanks carried long fascines of tightly bound faggots. In making these Chinese labourers used 400 tons of brushwood and 12,000 feet of chain—the latter procured from all over England.[167]

†According to the British Official History, previous to the battle the Third Army circulated no details of the canal crossings eastward from Masnières. As a result a road bridge still intact less than a mile from the village was ignored by the cavalry.

From the second day onward the battle deteriorated into a race with German reinforcements, which the High Command and Crown Prince Rupprecht were hurrying in from the Fourth Army in Flanders.[170] There was no mounted action for the Canadian cavalry, but the Royal Canadian Dragoons and Lord Strathcona's Horse were placed in defensive positions west of the canal. The British attack reached its limit of success—a maximum advance of five miles—on the 23rd, with the capture of Bourlon Wood. But the impetus was lost, and the inability of the British Third Army, short of reserves, to gain ground northward spelled doom to the venture. On the 27th the enemy retook the wood. Three days later the German Second Army launched a powerful counter-attack in a determined effort to cut off the deep British salient. Supported by low-flying aircraft in unusually large numbers,* the Germans drove the British right wing back nearly three miles. With every reserve needed, once more the three Canadian cavalry regiments were called on to hold off the enemy.[172] The fighting petered out in a snowstorm in the first week of December. As Rupprecht directed the Second Army to consolidate "with a maintenance of activity", Haig ordered a further withdrawal from the uneconomical salient. This was carried out on the night of the 4th-5th, the British retaining much of the ground gained on 20 November but leaving in German hands five miles of their original line south of the Cambrai-Péronne road. In two weeks of fighting the British had suffered more than 44,000 casualties; the Germans gave their losses as 41,000.[173]

The results of the Battle of Cambrai were by no means as conclusive as the victorious ringing of church bells in Britain would seem to have implied. The British gains on the left flank did not greatly exceed the area of the ground which had been lost to the enemy on the southern flank. An official enquiry blamed the rawness and lack of training of the British infantry, and the British Official Historian extended censure to senior commanders who had failed to seize favourable opportunities for exploitation.[174] The Germans too had lost a great chance of annihilating the British right wing. According to Rupprecht the fault lay with the Second Army for missing its vital objectives by making its main thrust too far to the north.[175] Yet the Battle of Cambrai with its employment of massed tanks had set a new pattern in warfare, and its influence was to extend beyond 1918 into the operations of the Second World War.

The first day's fighting at Cambrai had cost the Fort Garry Horse eighty casualties, including a number of missing who may have later returned. At the end of November, during the main counter-attack, the enemy machine-gunned a train and shelled the lines of the 4th Battalion Canadian Railway Troops, inflicting a reported forty-five casualties (of 27 missing, the unit diarist expected that the majority would "probably turn up during the next few days").[176] The Strathconas suffered more than fifty casualties on the second day of the counter-attack.

* All German fighter units in the sector were temporarily commanded by von Richthofen who, now in the rank of *Rittmeister* (Captain of Cavalry), regularly commanded *Jagdgeschwader* (Fighter Wing) No. 1—four squadrons including the Baron's old unit, *Jagdstaffel* 11. Part of the responsibility of the "Circus" was to protect the strafing units.[171]

While the Germans were advancing, Brig.-Gen. Seely received an anxiously awaited "operational" helio signal—"Reference Canadian General Election now proceeding, please note your signal troop will vote as a unit and not with the Royal Canadian Dragoons"![177]

Winter 1917-1918

The General Election had intruded upon the scene some time earlier (see below, Chapter XI). On the eve of the final attack at Passchendaele the Commander-in-Chief received the following request from the Secretary of State for War:

> . . . Sir George Perley came to see me on behalf of the Canadians. As you know, there is to be a General Election in Canada in which the question of Conscription is the main feature and on Sir Robert Borden getting a majority for it depends practically the existence of the Canadian Divisions. Sir George knows that for the next 10 days or so you will have to employ Canadian Divisions but he asks whether they could be promised, unless some unforeseen military exigencies intervene, a rest behind the lines. It would give them time to recuperate when they could be visited and their votes secured. If you are able to make this promise Sir George Perley would very much like to come out and see the Corps Commander and tell him of your promise because he thinks it would hearten the men and do good from a conscription point of view and he will be able to inform Canada of your decision. He attaches great value to the effect that would have . . . .[178]

There is no evidence that this request affected in any way Haig's decision to end the Passchendaele offensive when he did—after which the relief of the Canadian Corps followed automatically.

On rejoining the First Army on 20 November in the relatively quiet Lens sector, the Corps had two divisions in the line—the 1st at Lens, the 2nd at Méricourt—each with four battalions forward.[179] Opposing them, on the German right was the 1st Guard Reserve Division, on the left, the 17th Division. Divisional reliefs followed at regular intervals. The policy for both sides was one of active defence, which meant as far as the Germans were concerned, sending out almost nightly raids. It was the familiar pattern of previous winters. On the night of 1-2 January three parties of the 17th Division, almost 100 strong, raided the 54th Battalion's position. They took four prisoners and left three of their own men in our hands. A fortnight later, in a 26-man raid near Lens, the 58th Battalion took eleven prisoners without a single Canadian casualty. The captives belonged to the 220th Division, which had relieved the 1st Guard Reserve on New Year's Eve.[180]

On the morning of 4 March the enemy attacked Aloof Trench, the 50th Battalion's hard-won objective of the previous August (above, p. 297), now held by the 21st Battalion. The Germans, 240 to 280 strong, from the 220th Division and a Bavarian assault battalion of Sixth Army troops, gained a small footing but were quickly counter-attacked and driven out, leaving behind many dead. Of several Canadian raids carried out that month, the most successful was that on the night of the 14th-15th by 156 of the 5th C.M.R. against German positions some two miles south-west of Méricourt. At a cost of 32 casualties to themselves, the

A DERELICT TANK IN FLANDERS MUD

In November 1917, when this photograph was taken, the condition of the ground made it impossible for the Canadians to use tanks at Passchendaele, though these had been employed there as late as September in support of British troops. A twisted tramline at the edge of a water-filled shell-hole adds to the desolation of the scene, and in the background the camera has caught a bursting German shell.

THE BELLEVUE SPUR

A German strongpoint on Bellevue Spur, overrun by the 9th Brigade on 26 October 1917, the opening day of the first Canadian attack at Passchendaele. This picture, taken some eighteen months later, shows temporary graves of Canadians who fell in the assault of the spur.

MACHINE-GUNS IN THE MUD, NOVEMBER 1917

During the fighting for Passchendaele members of the 16th Canadian Machine Gun Company (4th Division) take up positions in fresh shell-holes. It seems inevitable that these will soon fill with water like those in the foreground.

CANADIAN CAVALRY AT CAMBRAI

"B" Squadron of the Fort Garry Horse after its participation in the Third Army's massed tank attack on 20 November 1917. Leading the squadron is Lieut. Harcus Strachan, who won the V.C. in the action.

raiders killed an estimated 35 of the enemy (12th Reserve Division) and took 19 prisoners.[181]

These operations, each in itself of minor proportions, over the winter had taken a fairly substantial toll. Between 1 December 1917 and 21 March 1918 the Canadian Expeditionary Force suffered 3552 casualties, of which 684 were fatal.

CHAPTER XI

CONSCRIPTION

The Imperial War Cabinet

"UPON MY RETURN from England on May 15th, 1917, I speedily embarked upon an exceedingly stormy political sea, which was swept, from time to time, by gales of varying intensity and from many quarters." With these words Sir Robert Borden introduces in his *Memoirs* a chapter entitled "Conscription". To this subject we must now turn our attention.

The Canadian Prime Minister had gone to England at the invitation of the British Government to attend "a series of special and continuous meetings of the War Cabinet in order to consider urgent questions affecting the prosecution of the war, the possible conditions on which, in agreement with our Allies, we could assent to its termination, and the problems which will then immediately arise".[1] For the purpose of these meetings, Borden and the other Dominion Prime Ministers would be members of the War Cabinet, which at the time consisted of the Prime Minister (Mr. David Lloyd George) and four of his colleagues.* The enlarged sessions came to be known as the Imperial War Cabinet. An Imperial War Conference was to meet at the same time. Although Sir Robert had been in office for more than five years, he had not yet attended an Imperial Conference, the one scheduled for 1915 having been postponed. Having formerly protested that "statesmen of the British Isles" were arrogating to themselves the framing of war policy, without consulting the Dominions or even releasing relevant information to them, he welcomed the opportunity to go to London; and to allow him to do this the Canadian House of Commons adjourned its 1917 session from 7 February to 19 April.[2]

The meetings in the United Kingdom were delayed by the Australian Prime Minister's difficulties with the wartime election at home; it was not until 20 March that the new Imperial War Cabinet held its opening session. Next day the larger Imperial War Conference held its first meeting, and from then until 2 May deliberations of the two bodies continued, with meetings taking place usually on alternate

*** In addition to Mr. Lloyd George the following were members of the War Cabinet: Mr. Bonar Law (Chancellor of the Exchequer), Earl Curzon (Lord President of the Council), Viscount Milner and Mr. Arthur Henderson.**

days. Discussions at the Conference had very little to do with the conduct of the war, which was left almost entirely to the War Cabinet.[3] The Australian election campaign went on until 5 May 1917, and precluded the attendance of any representative from that Dominion; but South Africa, New Zealand, Newfoundland and India were all represented. Lloyd George, wrote Borden in his *Memoirs,* "had virtually answered the appeal or challenge of Sir Wilfrid Laurier in 1897: 'If you want our aid, call us to your councils'." He further noted that in the Imperial War Cabinet "Great Britain presided, but the Dominions met her on equal terms." He expressed his satisfaction that almost every question connected with the prosecution of the war had been under consideration by the Dominions. "We have been placed in possession of the confidential and secret reports of the Imperial General Staff and of the Commanders-in-Chief in the various theatres of operations as well as the naval advisers of the Admiralty."[4] At the same time the meetings had given the representatives of the British Government a much better appreciation of the Dominions' war effort than they could have learned from any number of telegrams and despatches. As summed up by the Secretary of the Imperial War Cabinet, "The great drain on the time and energy of the British Ministers, and the inconvenience of the overseas representatives in their prolonged absence from home and the dangers which they ran in passing through seas infested with submarines were felt to have been well worth while."[5]

The delay in holding the conferences permitted Borden to visit all the large Canadian camps in England. He also had ample opportunity to discuss with Sir George Perley matters concerning the Canadian Expeditionary Force. On 8 March, accompanied by Perley, the Prime Minister crossed to France, where before returning to England four days later, he met Currie, Haig, and Nivelle at their respective headquarters.

In France, Borden was impressed by the admirable spirit displayed by the troops. He reported that Haig and his staff "had afforded him every facility". The record reveals no promise to introduce conscription; and at this period it seems the Prime Minister had not abandoned hope of sufficient voluntary enlistment. On his return to London on 12 March Borden cabled Kemp: "I voice the feeling at the front when I appeal to the Canadian people to support with the most earnest effort the proposals which you are putting forward to stimulate and assist recruiting. A splendid response to those proposals is vitally necessary in order that the full strength of our Dominion in co-operation with the whole Empire shall be thrown into the struggle with the least possible delay."[6]

Borden had kept close touch with Canada, especially on the state of recruiting. As noted earlier (above, p. 218), Sir Sam Hughes, before his resignation, had committed Canada to a fifth division and had spoken of raising a sixth, and Borden himself had promised half a million men. After October 1916 there was no longer any intention of raising a sixth division (above, p. 231). In January 1917 the War Office had asked for the definite commitment of the 5th Division, but the difficulties of reinforcing five divisions had led to that formation's remaining in England for home defence. Telegrams from the Minister of Militia, ending with that of 30 April (above, p. 222), apprised Sir Robert of the meagre results from National Service lists and of the failure of the Home Defence Force Scheme. He was compelled to conclude that "any further effort for voluntary enlistment would provide . . . wholly inadequate results."[7]

On 3 May, King George V received members of the Conference at Windsor, and spoke of the meetings as "a giant stride on the road of progress and Imperial development". Two days later, the Canadian party sailed for home. Walter Long (the Colonial Secretary) accompanied Borden to Paddington Station to say good-bye, and gave his view that there should be no general election in either Great Britain or Canada during the war. He was told by Borden that there could be no further extension of the Canadian Parliament "except by practically unanimous consent". For this reason the Canadian Prime Minister might be "forced into an election".[8]

Borden's Decision

On 16 May Sir Robert returned to the Canadian House of Commons, bringing with him a gold mace from the Lord Mayor of London to replace that lost in the fire of 3 February 1916, when both chambers and the clock-tower of the parliament buildings had been destroyed. On the 18th he made a statement in the House regarding his recent visit to Europe, ending his speech with a review of the military situation, which had impressed him with its "extreme gravity". "The voluntary system", he asserted, "will not yield further substantial results", and for that reason "early proposals will be made . . . to provide, by compulsory military enlistment on a selective basis, such reinforcements as may be necessary to maintain the Canadian Army to-day in the field as one of the finest fighting units of the Empire. The number of men required will be not less than 50,000 and will probably be 100,000."[9]

It is convenient at this juncture to examine the reasons for Borden's apparent change in policy. He emphatically repudiated any suggestion that he was introducing conscription at the instigation of the British Government. "Some people afflicted with a diseased imagination have asserted that I took my present course at the request or dictation of the British Government . . . . The subject was never discussed between myself and any member of the British Government".[10] The record indicates nothing to the contrary. A letter to the Archbishop of Montreal in reply to a protest against the introduction of conscription is illuminating. Borden referred to his previous conviction that there need be no compulsion—though he reminded Archbishop Bruchési of his published statement to labour delegates in the previous December that he could give no assurance that conscription would not be resorted to if warranted. He had persisted in this belief up to his visit to England, but there, however, his eyes had been opened more fully. "What I saw and learned made me realize how much more critical is the position of the Allies and how much more uncertain is the ultimate result of the great struggle. . . ." In France, he had had "the privilege of looking into the eyes of tens of thousands of men at the front who look to us for the effort which will make their sacrifice serve the great purpose for which it was undertaken".[11]

There seems little doubt that Sir Robert confidently expected a creditable war effort by Canada to constitute a charter of full nationhood. Through Borden, Canada's autonomy within the Commonwealth* had been advanced—the last great step forward would be won for her on the field of battle. His visit to England undoubtedly enhanced his awareness of Allied needs in manpower, and before returning to Canada he was convinced that Canadian reinforcements for the front would not be forthcoming under the voluntary system. It was Canada's duty to provide men, for to have done otherwise would have been inconsistent with the determination to play a full part in the war and the peace that would follow. Thus, however reluctantly, Borden returned to Canada as the advocate of military conscription.

There were other factors. Based on population, Canada had sent proportionately fewer men into battle than had Great Britain, Australia, and New Zealand. Both Great Britain and New Zealand had already resorted to conscription, though Australia had rejected it by a referendum held in 1916. And at home Borden, who in the previous December had toured Canada to stimulate recruiting, was well aware of the bitterness of feeling on the part of English-speaking Canada provoked by what was generally regarded as the poor showing of French Canadians in enlistment figures.† In his *Memoirs* Borden was later to make allowance for the attitude of the Canadian of French descent, who, "thoroughly devoted to his people and his province and deeply attached to his family, his friends and neighbours", had a limited vision which sometimes "did not extend far beyond the boundaries of his parish". Contrary to expectations the Quebec peasant had little sympathy for the plight of the people of France, whose sufferings, he was being told, "were just retribution for the unholy spoliation and humiliation of the Church in France".[14]

Before presenting a measure to introduce compulsory military service, the Prime Minister was concerned with forming a coalition government that would accept conscription as a national necessity. Extension of the present parliamentary term by a party majority vote—which the British Government declared it would act on by placing the necessary amendment to the British North America Act before Parliament—Borden deemed unadvisable, as likely to undermine or destroy "the moral authority of the Government". On 6 June 1917 the leader of the

* The name "Commonwealth", replacing "Empire", had been given official use for the first time at the Imperial War Conference, when Sir Robert introduced a resolution calling for "full recognition of the Dominions as autonomous nations of an Imperial Commonwealth".[12]

† It is impossible to authenticate the various "statistics" concerning French-Canadian enlistments that were bandied about in the press and on the public platform during this period and since. In official military records all Canadian-born were treated alike as "Canadian". When attesting a man on enlistment into the Canadian Expeditionary Force no attempt was made to establish his nationality beyond recording the country of his birth. The only question on the Attestation Form bearing directly on this point read: "In what town, township or parish and in what country were you born?" Thus when Sir Robert Borden gave the House of Commons figures "furnished to me by the Department of Militia and Defence", showing that up to 31 March 1918 there had been despatched overseas, 147,505 Canadians born "of British descent", and 16,268 Canadian-born "of French descent", the accuracy of his information must be questioned.[13]

opposition, Sir Wilfrid Laurier, advised Borden that he could not accept conscription and would therefore not enter a coalition government adopting such a policy.[15]

Legislation for Compulsory Service

On 11 June Borden introduced his Military Service Bill. He explained that a section in the Militia Act of 1868 (retained in the Act of 1904) provided for compulsory military service outside, as well as within the Dominion, in a case of national emergency. All males who were British subjects between the ages of 18 and 60 were declared to be liable to service in the Militia, which the Governor in Council might place on active service "anywhere in Canada, and also beyond Canada, for the defence thereof." Though the law, as it stood, thus already gave the necessary compulsory powers, it provided only for levy by ballot—an indiscriminate method of selection which would deplete industries and agriculture of skilled workers. Borden demanded that the army should be reinforced by a process of selection "based upon an intelligent consideration of the country's needs and conditions". He emphasized the need for reinforcements. He pointed out that April and May had brought enlistments of 11,790 men, but that in those same two months Canadian casualties had numbered 23,939. During the next seven months at least 70,000 reinforcements would be needed to maintain four divisions in the field. The numbers to be raised under the bill would be limited to 100,000 men, between the ages of 20 and 45.[16]

When the bill came up for second reading, Laurier moved an amendment calling for a referendum to be taken on the issue. This was rejected by a vote in which the Government was supported by many Liberals and opposed by French-Canadian Conservatives. After a third reading, and passage through the Senate, the bill became law on 29 August.[17] As already noted (above, p. 284), while the matter was being discussed in the House, Borden used the appointment of Currie as Corps Commander to gain further public support for the bill's passage.[18] Needless to say, the contents of Currie's message urging that the necessary steps be taken to maintain the Corps at full strength were given full publicity in Canada.[19]

The provisions of the Military Service Act applied to all male British subjects in Canada between 20 and 45 years for the duration of the war and the period of demobilization. Men to be called up were at first placed in ten classes, later rearranged into six. The first to be summoned were young men, either unmarried or childless widowers, between the ages of 20 and 34. The final class included married men in the 40-44 age group and widowers in that age category with one or more children. These classes were to be called up from time to time by proclamation of the Governor in Council. Tribunals would be appointed to deal with individual claims to exemption and to hear appeals. The conditions of exemption were broad and liberal, and covered workers in essential war occupations, or certain specially qualified workers, those whose enrolment would result in serious hardship due to "financial or business obligations or domestic position, ill health or infirmity", and conscientious objectors. Among special classes exempted from war service were all clergy, and members of Mennonite or Doukhobor communities, who had been excused from bearing arms by Orders in Council passed in 1873 and 1898.[20]

On 17 July Borden moved a resolution to extend the term of the existing parliament for a year as foreshadowed at the opening of the session. He had no hope of unanimous assent, and the party majority which he achieved was useless for his purpose. A general election was inevitable.

The General Election of 1917

The government now introduced a bill of an extraordinary nature—the War-Times Election Bill—which, coupled with the Military Voters' Bill, prepared the ground for the impending election. Under the latter measure, which was passed on 31 August, military electors would now include all British subjects without age restriction, male or female, whether ordinarily resident in Canada or not, who were on active service in the Canadian forces, as well as recent residents of Canada who were serving in any forces of Britain or her Allies.[21] The War-Times Election Act, passed on 14 September after closure had been applied, gave the vote for the duration of the war and the period of demobilization to close women relatives* of persons, male or female, living or dead, who were serving or who had served outside of Canada in the Canadian or British forces. It disfranchised conscientious objectors and all citizens naturalized in Canada after 1902 if of alien enemy birth or extraction.[22]

Both these measures came under strong attack from the opposition. Sir Wilfrid Laurier emphatically declared that to enfranchise only women relatives of soldiers was unjust discrimination, and that the disfranchisement of former aliens who had been naturalized was a retrograde and German measure.[23] He accused the government of having created "a special electorate in view of an impending election".[24] In defence Borden argued that citizens whose origin, ties of kinship, and natural sympathies prevented them from being sent to fight "ought not to be called upon to pronounce judgement upon the issues . . . in this election".[25]

During August Borden had already decided to appeal to the country as the head of a Union Government. In proposing a coalition government having equal representation from both parties he was opening the doors to that section of the Liberal Party which supported compulsory military service. These were prominent Liberals who declared that they favoured National Government and the formation of a War Council, but thought a change of leadership essential. At a Conservative caucus on 29 August the Prime Minister expressed his willingness to retire altogether, or to serve under Sir George Foster or any other leader who could form a Union Government; but, led by Foster, the gathering pledged its firm adherence to Borden. With the Conservatives thus showing their solidarity the Liberals

*Wives, widows, mothers, sisters and daughters.

acquiesced. Parliament was dissolved on 6 October and five days later Union Government came into being with a strong cabinet drawn from the ranks of both parties. As the date for the general election approached, the Union Government issued a strongly worded appeal to the members of the C.E.F., declaring that the Military Service Act would be enforced "with vigour and promptitude".

Borden's personal election campaign in the Maritimes was interrupted on 6 December, when a French munitions ship collided with a Norwegian vessel and blew up in Halifax harbour. Large areas of both Halifax and Dartmouth were razed, and 1630 lives were lost. Appalled at the magnitude of the calamity to a city with which he had been associated for more than half his lifetime, Borden cancelled his public meetings and hurried to the distressed community. Canadians went to the polls on 17 December, and on the following day the result of the civil vote was announced. It was even then apparent that the Government had been sustained by an overwhelming majority.

In the voting overseas, the polls opened on 1 December and closed on the 17th. As we have seen (above, p. 338), in its efforts to secure every favourable vote, the Government had gone so far as to make an indirect approach to the Commander-in-Chief while a major battle was in progress. As might be expected the assistance of the Canadian Corps Commander was also sought. General Currie was not enthusiastic about the Corps "being bothered by an election",[26] and he was reluctant to send another message to the Canadian people urging conscription (above, p. 284).[27] He claimed that he had always striven to keep clear of politics, but, as he wrote to Perley on 10 December, "both sides seem determined to mix me up in it.* I do not consider it fair that in the propaganda issued by the Government my name should appear so prominently."[29]

Returns from overseas were not complete and officially issued until March 1918. Well over 90 per cent of the soldiers on active service cast their votes for the Union Government and conscription, bringing to 71 Borden's majority in the House. The Liberals won 82 seats—62 in Quebec, which also elected three Unionists.[30]

By the time the new parliament met on 18 March 1918, machinery for the enforcement of the Military Service Act had been set up under the control of the Department of Justice. A Military Service Sub-Committee, representing the Militia Department, was headed by the Chief of the General Staff, Major-General W. G. Gwatkin. On 3 September a Military Service Council, acting directly under the Minister of Justice, was created "to advise and assist in the administration and enforcement" of the Act. On 15 June 1918 its duties were taken over by the Military Service Branch (of the Department of Justice) under its Director, Lt.-Col. H. A. C. Machin. The Council appointed fifteen registrars or deputy registrars throughout Canada. To give everyone the opportunity of properly claiming exemption from compulsory service, local tribunals, to the number of 1387, were estab-

* Currie was much disturbed over opposition statements that he had been removed from the command of the Corps "owing to inefficiency and the excessive number of casualties at Passchendaele".[28]

lished, each composed of two members, one appointed by a parliamentary Board of Selection and the other by a County or District Judge. Appeals from their decisions could be carried to one of 195 appeal tribunals, each a judge, appointed in general by the Chief Justice of the province. Rulings of an appeal tribunal might be referred to the Central Appeal Judge, whose decision was final.[31]

The Department of Militia made an initial request for 25,000 men—a number with which it "could most conveniently deal"—and thereafter 10,000 each month. On 13 October 1917 a Royal Proclamation called on all men in Class 1 to register. By 10 November 1917, the final date fixed for registration and claims for exemption, 21,568 had reported for service and 310,376 had applied for exemption.[32] In Quebec, where Borden reported that "wholesale exemptions seemed to have been granted", unrest over conscription had steadily grown throughout the summer. On 2 June Archbishop Bruchési had again written to the Prime Minister, predicting disorders in Quebec if conscription should be persisted in; in August he warned, "We are nearing racial and religious war."[33] To his plea that the Military Service Act should not be enforced the Prime Minister remained adamant. "It is difficult", wrote Borden, "to understand why passion should be aroused in the Province of Quebec by a measure which does not in the least discriminate against that Province but applies equally to every Province of Canada .... I could not remain at the head of the Government and delay its enforcement." In four days recently 5500 Canadians had fallen in the vicinity of Lens. "I should feel that their blood and that of all others who have fought would be upon my head if the provisions of this law should remain unexecuted."[34]

The Operation of the Military Service Act

No serious disorder broke out until March 1918, when the effects of enforcement began to be felt in Quebec. The entry of the United States into the war in April 1917 had closed the door to a safe haven for escapees across the border; under agreements signed by Canada, Great Britain and the United States, absentee males of military age became subject to the conscription laws of the country in which they were residing.

Then came trouble. On 28 March Federal officers enforcing the Military Service Act in Quebec City were assaulted by a crowd, who released a young man who had been arrested for not having upon his person his certificate of exemption. Rioting continued on the following day, which was Good Friday, and the Military Service Registry office was destroyed by fire, together with all its records. About midday on 30 March the G.O.C. Military District No. 5 reported to the C.G.S. that matters were getting worse and he required 1000 men, in addition to the 890 available in Quebec, to cope with the situation. Shortly after the receipt of this message, the Cabinet directed the C.G.S. to move the required number of troops from Ontario to Quebec. Accordingly a mixed force of 700 men (from the 1st Central Ontario Regiment) was despatched to Quebec and arrangements were made to bring in a further 3000 troops from the west. The troops from Toronto began arriving by train on the afternoon of the 31st. On the previous day Major-General F. L. Lessard (Inspector General for Eastern Canada) had been instructed to proceed from Halifax to Quebec. The C.G.S. reported to the Minister of Militia (who was visiting in the United States) that Brig.-Gen. J. P. Landry, the G.O.C., was "doing all right but Lessard on account of local knowledge was ordered to Quebec." Lessard arrived in Quebec on 31 March and assumed command.[35]

There were further disorders on the Saturday night and on Easter Day, though these were less serious than had been expected. The mob broke into hardware stores in search of arms; soldiers were pelted with snowballs and pieces of ice; military picquets came under attack, and revolver shots were fired at a streetcar. The civil authorities were reluctant to read the Riot Act, but on General Lessard's arrival notices were posted warning the public against taking part in unlawful assemblies. Matters reached a climax on the evening of 1 April, when riots again broke out. Troops moving through the streets to break up gatherings of civilians were bombarded with ice and bricks and missiles of various kinds. Some of the rioters opened fire. The soldiers had displayed great steadiness and forbearance under grave provocation; now, after several of their number had been wounded, they were ordered to return the fire with rifles and machine-guns. Four members of the crowd were killed and many others injured; 58 were arrested. Order was restored by one o'clock in the morning, and by daybreak the troops had returned to barracks.[36] An Order in Council, passed on 4 April, strengthened the hands of the military authorities in dealing with the situation or any similar disturbances that might occur in the future. Happily no further incidents occurred.

The Quebec disturbances were thoroughly aired in Parliament. Opposition members criticized the government's use of the Order in Council to enforce its wishes, and the administration of the Military Service Act came under fire from both sides of the House. In general it seems fair to say that the riots of the Easter week-end arose from the tactless way in which the Act had been administered. Subsequently civil and church authorities in Quebec were active in bringing home to the people the futility and danger of any further demonstrations, and before long the Quebec riots passed into history.

Meanwhile across the Atlantic the war continued, and the Canadian Overseas Minister (Kemp) was experiencing some concern about the declining number of reinforcements arriving from Canada. On 27 March he had cabled the Minister of Militia (Mewburn) suggesting that 15,000 infantry and 200 cavalry reinforcements should leave for England by the end of April. But the Military Service Act was not producing men in sufficient numbers to meet such a demand and on 8 April Mewburn was forced to admit that the "trouble at Quebec has somewhat deranged plans". The best that could be done was to "hope" that 4900 men (including 1740 despatched on 25 March) would reach the United Kingdom during April or early in May. Kemp's reaction to this news could be anticipated, and the reply which he sent through the Prime Minister to the Minister of Militia and Defence on 12 April reflected his dissatisfaction and uneasiness:

> For your information reinforcements situation as follows—
>
> | | |
> |---|---|
> | Available in France .... | 9,000 |
> | Available in England .... | 4,100 in April |
> | | 10,400 in May |
> | | 3,300 in June |
>
> This will involve despatch of men overseas with only eight [instead of the usual twelve to fifteen] weeks' training which is most undesirable. Unless 15,000 infantry reinforcements arrive before May 1st practically no trained infantry reinforcements available after July 1st. Anticipated casualties will be heavy in immediate future and doubtful if number at present in sight will be sufficient to maintain infantry of Corps at establishment beyond June 1st.[37]

On the same day Borden received another message from Kemp stating that Lord Derby, the Secretary of State for War, was of the opinion that the general war picture was "very serious but not critical". Kemp was replying to a request which he had received from Borden on 11 April seeking "information as to conditions and probabilities" as "we are all terribly disturbed and depressed by the continuing success of the German drive".[38]

The contents of these communications, along with information from other secret reports, convinced Borden that the time had come to impress upon the Canadian people the gravity of the situation. Accordingly, on 12 April, he informed Lloyd George (in a message sent through the Governor General) that it would be helpful if the British Prime Minister could supply a statement which he might use at a secret session of the Canadian House of Commons to be held within a week. On the 15th of the month, Borden told Kemp that this session would be held on the 17th and asked for a comprehensive report on the Canadian reinforcement situation. Kemp replied the same day and on the 16th sent Borden a further message in which he noted that Currie was "very anxious over situation . . . Expects enemy may make heavy attack southeast Arras with a view of cutting off Canadian Corps." After giving the dispositions of the Canadian divisions in France the message went on: "Presume question you have to consider is whether Americans should be allowed to monopolize space for transport their troops or whether you should accelerate enlistment next Class under Act if unable to secure sufficient reinforcements under Class already called." Also on the 16th, Lloyd George passed Borden a detailed and up-to-date account of the British and Allied position. With this material before him the Canadian Prime Minister gave the secret session a long and revealing statement regarding conditions overseas. Having dealt with the deteriorating reinforcement situation he announced the Government's conclusion that, if the Canadian Corps was to be maintained as an effective fighting force, additional measures must be taken. One of the first of these was to be the cancellation of all exemptions granted under the Military Service Act.[39]

Although Borden had been confident that the "mere fact" of holding a secret session would "arouse our people", it is doubtful if the general public became really impressed until 19 April when, in an open session of the House of Commons, he again dealt with the matter.[40] On that day he tabled a "proposed" Order in Council which noted that, as there was "an immediate and urgent need of reinforcements for the Canadian Expeditionary Force and the necessity for these reinforcements admits of no delay", it was the intention to cancel exemptions already granted under the Military Service Act and to lower the age of the draft from 20 to 19. In addressing the House, the Prime Minister described the serious difficulties being encountered by the Allies and gave particulars of the contributions being made by the United Kingdom and the Dominions to the war effort. He dealt at length with Canada's role and gave the House statistics of the number of recruits obtained and sent overseas and the casualties suffered by the C.E.F.

Next the Prime Minister turned to the contents of the Order in Council. While admitting that the Military Service Act had been based upon the principle of exemption by tribunals, he pointed out that since it had been necessary to staff these with men having "no previous experience in any such task . . . naturally and inevitably the decisions of the various tribunals were attended with a great deal of inequality and sometimes with very marked injustice."* Because of these wholesale exemptions the results obtained by the Act had not been as satisfactory as anticipated. With regard to the reinforcement situation, he declared (citing Kemp): "The need is urgent, so urgent that without this Order in Council I do not believe we could provide them with reinforcements after the first day of July next, and if the attack comes, as it may come, within the next two weeks, we might be left without any reinforcements after the first day of June."[42]

To have amended the Military Service Act by the normal legislative process would have entailed more delay than the urgency of the reinforcement situation would seem to permit. But when the Prime Minister moved that the House of Commons should approve by resolution the proposed Order in Council, he was opposed by Sir Wilfrid Laurier, who in a bitter passage termed the resolution a wide departure from the "principle of constitutional government" and challenged the authority of "the Governor in Council to alter an Act of Parliament". Nevertheless, the House agreed to the resolution on the 19th and a similar resolution passed in the Senate the same evening.[43] The Order in Council having been approved by resolution of both Houses was dated 20 April and came into force. On 28 June 1918 the Supreme Court of Alberta ruled that the Order had not the force of law. A further Order in Council was therefore issued on 5 July ruling that the Order of 20 April should have effect despite adverse judicial decisions by any court;[44] when a test case was appealed to the Supreme Court of Canada on 18 July, four judges out of six upheld the Government.[45] The full effect of the new regulations was not apparent until June 1918, when 10,290 reinforcements proceeded overseas (in May the number had been 5202). During July 11,158 left Canada and this was increased to 13,977 in August.[46]

At this point some reference must be made to the documentation of draftees and the policies, not always in agreement, followed by H.Q., O.M.F.C. and

* The Report of the Military Service Branch reveals that for the whole country the number of claims for exemption was 93.7 per cent of the total registration, and that local boards allowed exemptions on more than 84 per cent of these claims.[41]

Militia Headquarters in Ottawa with respect to distinguishing between draftees and volunteers.

During October 1917 the Officer-in-Charge of Overseas Records recommended dispatching a message to Canada suggesting that either a distinguishing prefix letter or a special series of regimental numbers be allotted to draftees. The Adjutant General, O.M.F.C., was favourably impressed by the idea, but his views were not shared by the G.O.C. Canadians, who rejected the proposal in the following terms: "Not approved; policy unsound." General Turner was determined to discourage further attempts to separate volunteers from draftees and, in January 1918, a circular letter was sent to all commanding officers in the United Kingdom directing that, as "the reinforcements shortly arriving from Canada will be men who have enlisted under the new Military Service Act, the General Officer Commanding wishes you to take action which will ensure that all ranks under your Command will accord these reinforcements the same treatment and goodwill as has been extended to those who, in the past, enlisted under voluntary conditions. Any inclination to treat those reinforcements arriving in future in a manner that would harbour ill feeling is to be dealt with, at the outset, promptly and severely."[47]

No similar action was taken in Canada; on the contrary Militia Headquarters decided that it was desirable for purposes of administration to distinguish between men who enlisted voluntarily and those who had been drafted. Accordingly, in January 1918, a policy was adopted which saw volunteers continuing to be attested on the usual C.E.F. Attestation Paper (M.F.W. 23) and the introduction of a new form, "Particulars of Recruit Drafted under Military Service Act 1917" (M.F.W. 133), for use in the case of draftees. At the same time units were ordered to divide that part of their semi-monthly and monthly returns taking men on strength (or discharging them) into two sections: "voluntary enlistments" and "men obtained under the Military Service Act".[48]

Although no blocks of regimental numbers were set aside for the draftees, the majority of the men received numbers in the 3,000,000 and 4,000,000 series, which had been allotted to the Depot Battalions organized after the passage of the Military Service Act to receive infantry recruits and draftees. Yet these blocks did not become the exclusive property of draftees; some of the numbers were also issued to volunteers taken on the strength of Depot Battalions. At the same time, some draftees were given regimental numbers from other series.* The complications arising from this situation caused Militia Headquarters to direct that "In all correspondence with Headquarters relating to men drafted under the Military Service Act, the letter "D" should be prefixed to the regimental number of the man referred to."[50] Some Records Officers, misinterpreting the directive, began inserting the prefix before regimental numbers on the documents of draftees. In May 1918, however, on receiving complaints from Headquarters O.M.F.C. that

* The 2nd Depot Battalion, British Columbia Regiment, for example, was not allotted numbers within the 3,000,000 and 4,000,000 blocks, but was ordered to give draftees the unused numbers in a series originally allotted to reinforcement drafts (raised by the 30th B.C. Horse and the 50th, 88th and 102nd Regiments) which had been absorbed into the Depot Battalion during 1917.[49]

use of the prefix was contrary to the overseas policy of treating all soldiers alike, Militia Headquarters stopped this unauthorized practice.[51]

One of the major problems in enforcing the Military Service Act was that of dealing with the many defaulters. These included men who failed to register, or who defaulted a subsequent order to report for medical examination or for military duty, or became deserters. Nearly 28,000 men in Class 1 were offenders in one of these respects.[52] To seek out and apprehend so large a number was beyond the capabilities of the existing police force, and the temporary enlargement of the Dominion Police to permit the formation of a special plain clothes body was authorized for the purpose in January 1918.[53] In June this special force was transferred to the Department of Militia and Defence and became the Civil Branch of the Canadian Military Police Corps. The police were faced with a difficult task. In attempting to find men who had not registered they had to proceed without even the names of the culprits. Many defaulters went into hiding in the northern wilds of Ontario and the forested areas of Quebec and the Pacific Coast, where apprehension was expensive and slow. In the face of alarming statements concerning the situation in Quebec, the Director of the Military Service Branch was careful to point out that although registrars in that province had received many letters purporting to give information about unregistered defaulters, investigations had failed to disclose one actual case.[54]

On the grounds that delinquents under the Military Service Act had acted largely through ignorance or the bad advice of ill-disposed persons, on 2 August 1918 the Government granted an amnesty to all defaulters and deserters who would report on or before 24 August.[55] In all 5477 persons gave themselves up under this temporary amnesty, but when hostilities ended there were still some 20,000 Class 1 men who had neither reported nor been apprehended.[56] On 22 December 1919, when a general amnesty was proclaimed for all offenders under the Military Service Act, an estimated 15,000 were still at large, with about the same number serving prison sentences.[57]

It remains to examine the results of the Military Service Act—to answer the often-put question, "How many men did the Act make available for military service?" Statistics furnished by the two departments of the Government which were most closely concerned with the operation of the Act are at some variance; and interpretations which have from time to time been placed on these figures have tended to minimize the total number of men which the Act placed on the strength of the Canadian Expeditionary Force.

The table which appears as Appendix "E" to this volume compares the statistics provided by the Department of Justice and the Department of Militia and Defence. The table is based on the report made to the Minister of Justice by Lt.-Col. Machin, the Director of the Military Service Branch, and on a series of memoranda issued by the Militia Department. It is carefully documented, and for figures which have not appeared in published sources detailed explanations show how these were determined.

From a total of 401,882* of Class 1 registrations (no other classes were called up) a succession of deductions are made for one cause or another until the final net figure is reached. Colonel Machin's report shows that more than half the number who registered, or 221,949 men, were granted exemption on various grounds; a further 24,139 defaulted and were not apprehended; and 26,225 who were considered by the Military Service Branch of the Department of Justice to be "available for instant call" had not been called when hostilities ceased on 11 November 1918. These deductions left a total of 129,569 who reported for military service, of whom 8445 were permitted to enlist in British forces, leaving a net figure of 121,124 taken on strength the Canadian Expeditionary Force. (The comparable figure given by the Department of Militia and Defence is 124,588.)

But not all these men served. Some 16,000 were struck off strength upon being found medically unfit or otherwise eligible for exemption. They were "returned to Registrar's records" so that they might again be ordered to report for duty if changing circumstances made this necessary. Their departure left 108,288 men who were available for service with units of the C.E.F. By 11 November normal wastage, such as would apply equally to volunteers, had brought the discharge of 8637 of these, thereby reducing to 99,651 the number of drafted men on the strength of the C.E.F. when the war ended. This figure included 16,296 to whom the army had granted harvest or compassionate leave without pay, and whose leave had not expired. It is clear that any appraisal of the number made available by the Act must include these men; all were subject to recall from leave had the need for overseas drafts continued.

It will be remembered that the objective set the Military Service Act was the raising of a maximum of 100,000 reinforcements. An Order in Council issued on 10 August 1918 took pains to define reinforcements as "men ultimately selected and actually despatched for Overseas service". The order specified that the Act should continue to operate until it had produced and *despatched* from Canada "not less than one hundred thousand efficient soldiers for overseas service".[58] According to figures of the Department of Militia and Defence the number of draftees that proceeded overseas was 47,509, of whom 24,132 were taken on strength of units serving in France. There seems no doubt whatever that had the demand persisted, the objective of sending 100,000 draftees overseas would have been achieved. But the fighting in 1918 had not produced the heavy Canadian casualties that had been expected. Indeed it had become possible, in August of that year, to instruct registrars in all districts outside the province of Quebec to stop temporarily the call of men in order that Quebec might catch up. Then in October, when full scale call-ups were about to start again, the outbreak of the influenza epidemic halted proceedings in most districts.[59]

It must be concluded that while the administration of the Military Service Act was often inefficient and attended by many gross malpractices, the Act itself was neither a failure nor ineffective. Statistics show that it did produce the military results which it was designed to produce.

* For the source of this and other statistics cited see "References and Comments" to the table appearing in Appendix "E" (p. 552).

Administrative Changes Overseas

We now recross the Atlantic to see what changes took place in the administration of the Canadian forces overseas during the last two years of the war. A previous chapter has described the organization late in 1916 of the Headquarters Overseas Military Forces of Canada, and the appointment of Sir George Perley as Minister (above, p. 210). First for our present consideration is the appointment of a new Overseas Minister and the creation of an Overseas Military Council.

Before the general election of 1917, Sir George Perley had repeatedly urged Borden to remove what he considered the stigma of "Acting" from his title. "I have struggled so long with the little understood name of 'Acting High Commissioner' ", he wrote the Prime Minister in June, "that I should like to be actually appointed to that position before I quit. . . . In case of an election I shall have to decide whether to go home for it and if I have been of service over here I thought you might like to confirm my status here or so arrange that I need not continue to have a constituency to look after. . . .*[60]

Borden, confronted with the greatest political crisis of his career and troubled with ill health, did not reply until the first week in August. He warned Sir George that nothing could be settled with respect to changes in the government until after prorogation.[61] It seems likely that Perley, who was himself working under great strain and was not in good health, did not fully understand the difficulties confronting Borden and the Unionists. By September he had decided not to return to Canada for the election. He complained to Borden that his additional duties as Overseas Minister were too heavy to continue and suggested the solution was to "make me High Commissioner [and] appoint another Overseas Minister".[62] On 9 October, however, after a much needed holiday, he cabled Borden offering to continue as Overseas Minister lest a change "might prejudicially influence soldiers' vote".[63]

But the cable was four days too late—on 5 October Borden had arranged for Sir Edward Kemp to become Overseas Minister and Major-General S. C. Mewburn to take over the portfolio of Militia and Defence in Ottawa. Perley became High Commissioner. Though warned that "it may be necessary within six months or year to make different disposition", Sir George continued to occupy the post until 1922.[64]

The appointment of a new Overseas Minister provided a good opportunity to implement organizational changes which had been under study for some time. Not the least important of these was the formation, in May 1918, of an Overseas Military Council to "ensure more complete co-ordination in the administration of all parts of the Canadian Army".[65] The new Council bore little resemblance, either in composition or performance, to the Acting Sub-Militia Council established by Sir Sam Hughes in 1916 (above, p. 207). Formed "on

* Sir George was concerned that in an election based on the conscription issue his constituency of Argenteuil, in which nearly half the voters were French-Canadian, might be difficult to retain. His suggested solution was that Borden appoint him "to one of the vacant Ontario Senatorships".

the same principle and having the same functions as the Militia Council at Ottawa", its main purpose was to serve in an advisory capacity to the Overseas Minister.[66] It consisted of a chairman, vice-chairman, four members and two associate members; the Overseas Minister was allowed to fill all these positions at his own discretion.*[68] The membership of the Council changed very little throughout its existence, though in April 1919 two more members were added—Lieut.-General Sir Arthur Currie and Lt.-Col. T. Gibson, the Assistant Deputy Minister O.M.F.C.†[70]

The subjects with which the Overseas Military Council dealt were of such a varied nature "as not readily to admit of classification". A report on the Council's activities listed a wide range of matters receiving consideration: "organization and policies, financial and other arrangements with the British Government, expenditures of an extraordinary nature, the write-off or charge to individuals of losses of public property, pay and allowances, establishments of all units and formations, and confirmation of all promotions and appointments within the O.M.F. of C."[71]

The formation of the Overseas Military Council brought a change in designation of the appointment held by Sir Richard Turner. It will be recalled that in 1916 Turner had been named "General Officer Commanding Canadians" in the United Kingdom. General Turner's functions, however, extended beyond the administration of the Canadian Forces in the British Isles. The Overseas Minister required "not only a military advisor but also an executive military officer" who could give effect to whatever policies the Minister approved.[72] After considering the titles "General Officer i/c Administration, Overseas Military Forces of Canada" (proposed by the Deputy Minister) and "Chief of Staff" (Turner's own preference), Kemp settled upon "Chief of the General Staff" to describe Turner's appointment, and the War Office was so informed early in May.[73]

The Canadian Section, G.H.Q.

Meanwhile another important development in the administration of Canadian troops overseas was under consideration. This was the establishment of a Canadian Section at General Headquarters in France. The move had a dual significance. It established a close liaison between the O.M.F.C. and the British headquarters responsible for the tactical employment of Canadian troops; and it was an important step in the evolution of Canada's control over her own forces.

There had been a Canadian representative at General Headquarters since

*The original composition of the Council was as follows: Chairman, the Minister O.M.F.C., Sir Edward Kemp; Vice-Chairman, the Deputy Minister O.M.F.C., Colonel Walter Gow; Members, the Chief of Staff, Lt.-Gen. Sir Richard Turner, the Adjutant General, Maj.-Gen. P. E. Thacker, the Quartermaster General, Brig.-Gen. D. M. Hogarth, and the Accountant General, Col. W. R. Ward. The Associate Members were the Director General of Medical Services, Maj.-Gen. G. L. Foster, and the Paymaster General, Brig.-Gen. J. G. Ross. Major G. S. Harrington was the Secretary.[67]

†In October 1918 Gow resigned as Deputy Minister and Col. G. S. Harrington took his position. Harrington was replaced as Secretary to the Council by Capt. L. P. Sherwood.[69]

January 1915, when Sir Max Aitken was appointed to deal with "records generally appertaining to the Canadian Overseas Expeditionary Forces and particularly the reporting of all casualties occurring therein".[74] In September 1915 Aitken became officially known as "General Representative for Canada at the front", while continuing to perform essentially the same function. Sir Robert Borden saw Aitken's duties as giving "the public of Canada an account of the performances of the Canadian Troops.[75] Sir Max generally referred to his position as the "Canadian Eye-Witness", and for the period after September 1915 as the "Record Officer". On being created Baron Beaverbrook in January 1917 he relinquished the post of General Representative. In addition to his other duties he established the Canadian War Records Office and was one of the founders of the Canadian War Memorials Fund. Each of these deserves some mention.

The Canadian War Records Office was founded in January 1916, when Prime Minister Borden authorized Sir Max Aitken to spend $25,000 on the project.[76] As distinct from the Canadian Record Office, which was "the home of the bare facts of the civil and military career of every member of the forces", the War Records Office was "the home of the History of Canada's War". While the former compiled statistics and other records and registered the location of graves, the latter was concerned with the custody of documents giving "the story of what the army has done".[77]

Of the several sections into which the Canadian War Records Office was divided, one of the most important was the Historical Section. Besides being concerned with collecting, filing and referencing all documents of a historical nature it supplied a contemporary record of Canada's war effort. Sir Max himself wrote and published the first two volumes of *Canada in Flanders,* which appeared in 1916 and 1917.* Other publications included *Canada in Khaki* and the *Canadian War Pictorial.* Any "loss in accuracy" resulting from the contemporary nature of these accounts, Aitken considered, would be made up for by a "gain in vividness". Perhaps the most popular venture of this nature was the *Canadian Daily Record,* a daily newspaper for the troops in the field. By August 1917 its circulation had passed 12,500 copies.[78]

In January 1917 Lt.-Col. R. F. M. Sims succeeded Lord Beaverbrook as General Representative. A definition of his duties showed him representing the Overseas Minister in all matters at British General Headquarters, France; acting as liaison officer between the Minister, the War Office and the Canadian Corps; and providing a channel of direct communication on domestic matters between the Canadian Overseas Ministry in London and the Canadian Corps.[79] For carrying out these tasks the Canadian Representative had a staff of three officers and 22 other ranks. The inclusion in his establishment of three horses and eight motor cars arose from the necessity of providing transportation for the numerous high-ranking Canadian officials who from time to time came to visit the troops in France.[80]

*A third volume, written by Charles G. D. Roberts, was published in 1918.

Late in 1917 the Overseas Ministry initiated the move which was to bring the administration of Canadian forces more closely under Canadian control. A memorandum to the War Office in November stated that in future it was planned to have "all questions relating to appointments . . . promotions, transfers, exchanges, recalls and demands for officers, affecting the Canadian Forces in the Feld, pass from the senior officer of the Canadian formation concerned direct to the Canadian Representative, G.H.Q. for transmission to the Minister, O.M.F.C. . . . and not pass through the higher British commands with which the Canadian formations are serving". It was the Canadian view that decisions of the Overseas Minister should "be accorded the same significance in regard to the Canadian Force as similar communications from the War Office regarding British Forces."[81] In reply the War Office proposed a conference to arrange details, and Sir Douglas Haig suggested that the Minister of the Overseas Military Forces of Canada should go to France to discuss the matter.[82]

Both the conference and the visit to France were postponed while Canadian officials sought "a clear conclusion . . . as to what will best meet the needs of the situation from the Canadian standpoint."[83] A meeting of the heads of various branches in the O.M.F.C. at Argyll House on Tuesday 19 March 1918 decided that a Canadian Section at G.H.Q. was the best solution, and on 2 April Sir Edward Kemp and his chief administrative officers met War Office representatives and reached a general agreement. The solution, which contained three basic principles, was then embodied in a letter to Sir Douglas Haig. The Canadian authorities made it clear that they did not wish to interfere in military operations; the proposed changes would affect only the organization and administration of Canadian troops. On matters relative to military operations, including the allotment of reinforcements, establishments and senior appointments, the Canadians would be glad to have recommendations from G.H.Q. Finally, the duties of the Canadian Representative at G.H.Q. were to be taken over by the Officer-in-Charge of the Canadian Section.[84] Formation of the new organization was announced in June 1918, and the Section began functioning in July. It included representatives of the Adjutant General, the Quartermaster General, the Military Secretary, and the Medical, Chaplain and Pay services. Brig.-Gen. J. F. L. Embury was appointed Officer-in-Charge.

In the short period between its establishment and the Armistice, the Canadian Section proved its value. It provided a direct channel of communication between the Ministry, O.M.F.C. and G.H.Q., as well as a channel between these bodies and the heads of Canadian formations in the Field. Under direction from the O.M.F.C. Ministry it was responsible for supervising the various Canadian Administrative Services and Departments in the Field, and was empowered to take executive and administrative action regarding the control of personnel of the Canadian Forces in the Field. The Section did not cease to function with the Armistice. In dealing with the complex problems of demobilization its usefulness was again fully demonstrated.[85]

The Canadian War Memorials Fund

Intimately connected with the Canadian War Records Office, though not an integral part of it, was the Canadian War Memorials Fund. The Fund was established by Lord Beaverbrook at the end of 1916, with the approval of Sir George Perley and the Canadian Prime Minister.

The Committee formed to administer the Fund included besides Sir Max two prominent British newspaper proprietors, Lord Rothermere and Sir Bertram Lima. Lady Perley and Sir Edmund Walker (President of the Canadian Bank of Commerce) were later members of the Committee. The founders of the fund hoped to assemble a collection of paintings, photographs and moving-picture films which would give "a more vivid, truthful, and lasting impression than can be done even by the written word" respecting the efforts displayed by Canadians during the war.[86] A Photographic Section of the War Records Office had been formed in April 1916 with the appointment of the first official photographer to serve with the Canadian Corps in France. A cinematographic section followed in a few months.

Lord Beaverbrook's Committee at once set to work to put the War Memorials Fund on a sound financial basis. It borrowed a large number of official photographs from the Canadian War Records Office and had large and expensive enlargements made from them. These were placed on exhibition at the Grafton Galleries in London, and the showing was powerfully advertised by the newspapers controlled by Lords Beaverbrook, Rothermere and Northcliffe and Sir Bertram Lima. The enterprise was a tremendous success, and netted a considerable surplus over the cost of making the enlargements and staging the exhibition. With this money the Committee acquired paintings of Canadian War interest, which were exhibited to raise additional funds. Further revenue for the Fund came from the sales of *Canada in Khaki* and the first two volumes of *Canada in Flanders.* (The cost of printing and publishing the latter was borne personally by Lord Beaverbrook.) There was a small profit on the sale of official photographs to Canadian soldiers, and a greater one on similar sales to the press of the Allied countries. A number of interested individuals also contributed to the Fund.[87]

Under the auspices of the War Memorials Fund Lord Beaverbrook obtained permission from the Overseas Minister to appoint war artists and grant them honorary rank (not higher than that of major). Among those selected were two artists who were later to become members of the Canadian "Group of Seven"—A. Y. Jackson and F. H. Varley. The art which the Fund collected included the work of 108 artists. The most important acquisitions were four paintings—"The Death of Wolfe", by Benjamin West, presented by the owner, the Duke of Westminister; "Thayeadanegea" (Joseph Brant), by Romney; "Sir Alexander Mackenzie", by Sir Thomas Lawrence; and "Lord Amherst", by Reynolds. After the Armistice the Fund's holdings, described by Sir Edward Kemp as the "finest collection of war paintings and photographs of any of the Allied Nations", were transferred to Ottawa.[88]

Financial Agreements with the War Office

We conclude this chapter with a brief examination of Canada's contribution towards the cost of maintaining her forces overseas.

When on 1 August 1914 Canada tentatively offered to provide an overseas contingent in the event of war, the Dominion Government had suggested making "all necessary financial provision" for the "equipment, pay and maintenance" of such a force.[89] The British Government agreed to the suggestion, and in November 1914 the War Office issued provisional instructions for recovering expenditures incurred in meeting the requirements of Canadian troops while in the United Kingdom, but specified only such direct charges as the cost of clothing, stores, horses, hospital treatment and billeting. No charge was to be made for accommodation (other than billeting), barrack stores, hospital stores, or for transporting troops by land and sea after their arrival in Britain.[90]

Formal discussions between the two governments opened in March 1915, with the Canadians insisting that they defray the "entire cost in every particular of their own contingents".[91] It took the rest of 1915 and most of 1916 for the Acting High Commissioner, Sir George Perley, to draw up with the War Office an agreement which was finally approved on 24 January 1917.[92] It specified that Canada provide the pay, allowances and pensions of her troops and defray the cost of transporting them and material to the United Kingdom. There were two main changes from the provisional arrangement of November 1914. In addition to paying the actual cost of all supplies and stores issued in Great Britain, Canada would reimburse the British Government for transportation of Canadian troops and material on British railways. For all accommodation (whether in hutments or billets) and for barrack and hospital stores the British Government decided to make no charge.

At the same time the cost of maintaining Canadian forces in France was considered. Once troops crossed the Channel the adjustment could not be as simple or exact as in the United Kingdom, for it would obviously be impracticable to maintain a record of actual issues made to Canadians from numerous British Army depots on the Continent. The matter was solved by introducing a capitation rate. The War Office proposed a rate of six shillings per man per day. Of this amount, five shillings was reckoned as the average cost (excluding pay, allowances and pensions) of maintaining a British soldier in the field. It took into account rations, forage, fuel, clothing, and stores of all kinds; all ammunition except artillery; the replacement of small arms, guns, horses, mules, mechanical transport and wagons; and the transportation of troops from England to France and rail transportation on the Continent. The other shilling was to cover the cost of artillery ammunition used by Canadian forces (except for that fired by siege batteries being manned by Canadian personnel furnished at the request of the War Office).

This arrangement was subject to one reservation: the rate of six shillings would continue "unless conditions should so alter as to make it clearly unfair either to the Imperial or the Dominion Government".[93] In a very short time the British Government found it necessary to request a revision. On 2 March 1917 the War Office informed the Canadian High Commissioner that the one-shilling rate for artillery ammunition (which had been based on the average expenditure of shells up to the end of March 1916) was unrealistic.[94] Consumption by Canadian artillery units had risen from one shilling a day to 6s. 7d. for the three-month period 1 July-30 September 1916 (which included the Battle of the Somme with its tremendous artillery programmes). Sir George Perley was told that Australia and New Zealand had agreed to a revised rate of payment, and he was asked that Canada should not only increase its capitation rate for artillery ammunition, but that the new rate should be made retroactive to 4 November 1916 (the date of the War Office Letter which accompanied the memorandum presented to Canada on the 20th of that month).

There were prolonged negotiations between the two governments before settlement was reached on these two points. The British proposed the retention of the fixed five-shilling rate and the adoption of a variable rate for gun and howitzer ammunition which would depend upon the average daily Canadian consumption as revealed by quarterly returns.[95] Sir Robert Borden noted that this would add greatly to Canadian expenditures, but felt that since Australia and New Zealand had accepted the new arrangement, "we cannot decline".[96] Although in mid-July 1917 Sir George Perley considered that "the only point at issue" was whether such a revised rate should be made retroactive to the previous November,[97] it was not until March 1919 that Canada formally approved an increase. As to the effective date, Borden was distinctly hostile to the War Office's proposal that the revised rate should come into force on 4 November 1916. He insisted that any revision should date from 2 March 1917, the day on which the War Office "gave notice that new conditions had arisen".[98] This view found little favour with the British negotiators; on 29 June 1917 the Assistant Financial Secretary of the War Office pointed out to Sir George Perley that "the extent to which Canada would not pay her full share up to November last would be about three millions, and to March last another million [pounds]".[99]

The matter remained in deadlock. In the United Kingdom the responsibility for representing Canada's views on such questions passed from the Acting High Commissioner to the Overseas Minister (above, p. 355). As the months went by there were frequent discussions in London, and an intermittent exchange of cables with Ottawa. Meanwhile the War Office continued to furnish the Canadian Government with periodical returns on Canadian expenditures of artillery ammunition, and in January 1919 the Canadian Government appointed a committee of accountants to examine the correctness of these. This committee duly certified the British figures, and on 15 August 1919 the War Office was informed that Canada would accept these accounts as representing her "financial share of the cost of ammunition expended in France from March 2nd, 1917, to November 11th, 1918".[100] The Canadian refusal to antedate to November 1916 the revision of the capitation rates was a matter of some regret to the War Office. "On our first capitation rate settlement", wrote the Assistant Financial Secretary on

1 August 1919, "the Imperial Government lost a very considerable amount owing to our not having given formal notice to revise the figures in respect of gun ammunition until long after they were clearly inadequate."[101]

The daily rate per man charged for artillery ammunition varied from one shilling (February 1915 to 1 March 1917) to a high of 4s. 4¾d. (April-September 1918).[102] An attempt by the War Office to increase the five-shilling rate on general items of maintenance from 1 July 1918 was successfully opposed by Ottawa.[103] The Canadian authorities argued that any upward revision for the last four months of the war would be offset by a reduction from 11 November 1918 to the date when Canadian troops left France. Although the War Office declared that the British Government would lose "nearly a million" pounds,[104] the five-shilling rate remained unaltered. The Dominion agreed however to make certain subsidiary settlements of special claims connected with the capitation rate.

Altogether for the maintenance of her forces overseas (including expenditures for artillery ammunition) Canada paid the British Government $252,567,942.03.[105]

CHAPTER XII

THE GERMAN OFFENSIVES OF 1918

(See Map 10 and Sketch 46)

Relative Strengths of the Opposing Armies

As THE YEAR 1918 opened it was apparent to the members of the Entente that a crisis in the war was fast approaching. It is true that the disappointment of Cambrai had been to some extent offset by good news from the outer theatres of war. In Palestine General Allenby had more than wiped out the sting of Sir Archibald Murray's earlier defeats at Gaza by the brilliant campaign which carried his army from Beersheba to Jerusalem in six weeks. He entered the holy city, humbly on foot, on 11 December. In Mesopotamia, where General Sir Stanley Maude had captured Baghdad on 11 March 1917, the British force made some further advances at the end of the year, though it failed by a wide margin to take full advantage of the opportunities offered by the preoccupation of the Turks with General Allenby's Palestine operations.

But in Europe the outlook was less encouraging. The "October Revolution" earlier in the winter had brought the Bolsheviks to power under Lenin and Trotsky. A Russo-German armistice signed at Brest-Litovsk on 18 December was confirmed by a peace treaty in the following March. Early in 1917 the Allies had enjoyed numerical superiority over the Central Powers, but as a result of the heavy attrition of the summer and autumn fighting, and with Russia out of the war and the United States not yet effectively in, the balance had been reversed. It would be the middle of 1918 before the flow of American divisions would be great enough to tilt the scales in the right direction once more.*

Throughout the winter the Germans had been steadily transferring troops from Italy and the East, and by mid-February they had 178 divisions on the Western Front—two more than the number held a year earlier by the Allies, who now had the equivalent of only 173. Yet the Allies enjoyed greater overall strength, for in spite of the recent reduction of British infantry brigades from four to three battalions (above, p. 231), Allied divisions were generally larger than those of the enemy. The enemy forces in France and Belgium amounted to some 1,232,000 rifles, 24,000 sabres, 5500 heavy and 8800 field guns; as against, 1,480,000

* There were nine American combat divisions in France by the end of April. The next three months brought 20 more divisions. By the end of October the total arrivals numbered 42 divisions.[1]

Allied infantry, 74,000 cavalry, 6800 pieces of heavy and 8900 of field artillery.[2] In other infantry weapons the Germans held a distinct advantage. Each enemy division outnumbered its British counterpart 50 to 36 in trench mortars, and 350 to 64 in heavy or medium machine-guns, and held a heavy superiority in light machine-guns.[3] In air strength, taking the Western Front as a whole, the Allies outnumbered the enemy almost three to one (in the British sector 1255 aeroplanes to 1020 German; in the French, about 2000 to 470). The German air concentration in the actual area of the assault, however, gave the enemy a nominal superiority of nearly thirty per cent.[4]

The decision to reduce from twelve to nine the number of battalions in a British infantry division had been taken in January 5 on the recommendation of a Cabinet Committee on Manpower which saw the need to subordinate the demands of the army to those of the naval and air forces, the construction of ships, aeroplanes and tanks, and the production of food and timber. British divisions in the minor theatres (five in Italy, four in the Balkans, and fourteen—including six Indian divisions—in the Middle East) for the time being retained the four-battalion brigade, as did the divisions of the Dominions* (though in September Australia began reducing her brigades to three battalions). The British reorganization resulted in increasing the proportion of artillery and machine-guns to infantry, but unforeseen delays in putting the change into effect meant that when the Germans struck in March some brigade commanders were still unused to handling only three battalions.[6]

In January, as agreed between the British and French governments and approved by the Supreme War Council, the British line on the Western Front had been extended by 25 miles to a point five miles south of the Oise. This meant that in March British Armies (from south to north the Fifth, Third, First and Second) were holding 126 miles of front with a total of 59 divisions (including reserves and two Portuguese divisions) supported by 1640 heavy guns and 432 tanks. The French, whose front was now 300 miles long, had 97 divisions. The Belgians had ten divisions, the Americans five.[7] Early in December Haig had told his Army Commanders, "We must be prepared to meet a strong and sustained hostile offensive". How was this to be done?

Allied statesmen who recalled unsuccessful offensives when the odds had been nearly three to two in their favour, were slow to admit the possibility of a German break-through with lesser odds. The military members of the Supreme War Council, however, alarmed at the paucity of the existing British and French reserves—the latter amounting to 33-35 divisions—advocated creating a more adequate, international emergency force. A board composed of all four military representatives requested of the French, British and Italian commanders-in-chief a total of thirty divisions as a general reserve for the Western and Italian fronts, which would be treated as a single theatre. Italy offered six divisions, but for the Western Front Pétain and Haig preferred, in effect, to form a separate Franco-British

*As already noted (above, p. 232) the Canadian divisions in France increased each battalion by 100 men over establishment.

reserve. In the event of an attack on one the other pledged himself to render assistance in twelve hours. Mr. Lloyd George at first opposed this arrangement, which ran counter to his interest in the Italian theatre, but on 14 March, "in view of the apparent imminence of a large attack"[8], he reluctantly accepted it. The Supreme War Council, being merely an advisory body, could only do likewise.[9]

The British Prime Minister had at last rid himself of General Sir William Robertson, with whom his relations had never been happy. The new C.I.G.S. (as of 16 February) was General Sir Henry Wilson, whose place as British military representative at Versailles was taken by General Sir Henry Rawlinson, formerly commanding the Fourth Army.

The Offensive in Picardy, 21 March—5 April

The original plan for the German offensive had been laid the previous winter, when on 11 November—a significant date—Field-Marshal von Hindenburg's Chief of Staff, General Ludendorff, met at Mons with the chiefs of staff of the two army groups involved. Neither von Hindenburg nor any other commanders were present, and it is apparent that the German C.G.S. was content to leave the planning and conduct of the battle largely in Ludendorff's hands.[10] Ludendorff appreciated that the situation in Russia and Italy would, "as far as can be seen, make it possible to deliver a blow on the Western Front in the new year". Everything would be thrown into the one effort; he ruled out the possibility of a simultaneous large-scale offensive as a diversion. If possible the operation would be launched at the end of February or early March, in order that the British might be beaten before strong American forces arrived to turn the scale.[11]

Ludendorff's final decision was not made until 21 January 1918, but preparations to launch separate attacks near St. Quentin, Arras, Armentières and Ypres began at once.[12] During the winter German divisions underwent special training for the offensive. There was an overriding emphasis on the maintenance of momentum. Storm troops—whole battalions or smaller groups—were to by-pass opposition where they could not overcome it, accepting open flanks. Pockets of resistance would be dealt with by regimental or battalion reserves; counter-attacking tanks would be handled by artillery in rear. These tactics, to which no special name was given at the time, later came to be known as "infiltration".

In the form adopted on 21 January, the German plan called for an initial break-through to the Somme on both sides of Péronne; the German right wing would then wheel northward, rolling up the British flank. The attack, code-named "Michael", was to be launched on a 50-mile front by the Eighteenth Army of Crown Prince Wilhelm's Army Group in the sector from the Oise at La Fère to just north of St. Quentin, and from there to the Scarpe by the Second and Seventeenth Armies of Crown Prince Rupprecht's Group. These armies would employ 71 divisions, which by the third week in March had been brought up to a strength of 850 men per battalion* through ruthless reinforcement from other divisions,

* In addition each battalion had 130 men in its machine-gun company. Excluding these, the infantry strength of a German division was 7650, the total rifle strength being somewhat lower.[13]

at the expense of the latter's combat efficiency and mobility.[14] The actual assault would be carried out by 32 divisions, supported by some 2500 guns. Ludendorff planned that when Operation "Michael" had succeeded, "George" would be launched in the region of Armentières.

Both these planned blows would fall on British armies. "It need not be anticipated that the French will run themselves off their legs and hurry at once to the help of their Entente comrades", wrote the Eighteenth Army's Chief of Staff in mid-January.[15] Demonstrations designed to keep the French expecting an attack south of the Oise were assigned to Crown Prince Wilhelm's Group. Most of the front on which the German Eighteenth and Second Armies were to attack was thinly held by General Gough's Fifth Army, which because of the increased British commitment to General Pétain, with only twelve divisions was responsible for 42 miles of front from the boundary with the French Sixth Army northward to the Péronne-Cambrai road. Opposite the German Seventeenth Army and the Second Army's right wing General Byng's Third Army had fourteen divisions with which to defend a front of 28 miles.

Some thought had been given to strengthening the British defences, and during the winter work on these had to be carried out within the limitations of a shortage of manpower for labour. The front, support and reserve trenches had been converted to a German-pattern "forward zone", in which troops were placed in outpost groups and supporting posts sited to sweep intervening ground with rifle and machine-gun fire. Behind this forward zone, which was designed to delay the enemy's advance and to compel him to deploy, lay a "battle zone", consisting of a series of centres of resistance rather than continuous trench lines. It was here that the main defence would be made. What was to have been a "rear zone" had not materialized as more than a planned line, designated in some cases only by the removal of the turf to indicate its intended position.[16]

The British scheme of defence was based on the report of a committee of major generals charged with investigating German methods described in captured training manuals. Unfortunately the committee misinterpreted the enemy's pattern of defence. Whereas the Germans ensured mobility for their forward battalions by assigning only one-third of their battalions to man the strongpoints, leaving two-thirds in dug-outs available for immediate counter-attack where needed, the British tied up two-thirds or more of their strength in the defended localities. The result was that they were short of protective infantry to cover the intervening gaps or strike counter-blows. This produced a defence as rigid as the former system of holding continuous trench lines—and an almost complete absence of an effective counter-attack force.[17]

Limited as he was in manpower, Sir Douglas Haig apportioned his forces in keeping with the relative strategic importance of the sectors for which he was responsible. On the Second Army's front in the north, where loss of ground would compel the B.E.F. to fall back to the Channel coast, each division (excluding reserves) held an average of 3555 yards of front. The length of this frontage increased progressively southward, until in the Fifth Army, where

German gains could be considered least harmful, a division had 6555 yards to defend.[18]

On 10 March the Germans heavily bombarded the French defences in Champagne and mounted feint attacks on Verdun and Reims. On the same date British air observers reported large-scale troop movements by road and rail to the sector opposite the Fifth and Third Armies, and Intelligence at G.H.Q. noted that deserters' statements and the construction of large ammunition dumps confirmed the imminence of an offensive in the Arras-St. Quentin area. By the 19th it was evident that the enemy's preparations were practically complete, and the commander of the Fifth Army wrote home that the attack would probably be made on the 21st.[19]

On the expected day the enemy struck at dawn. At 4:40 a.m., in a dense fog, German high-explosive and gas shells began to fall all along the Fifth and Third Army fronts. While part of the First Army front also was bombarded as a deception, in general the Lens-Méricourt sector held by the Canadians escaped attention. The enemy did, however, launch an unusually strong raid on Hill 70, leaving behind a score of German dead and wounded. The main bombardment lasted a gruelling six hours, and played havoc with the British defended localities, as well as with formation headquarters and communications. When the assault came, strong battle groups penetrated deep through the thinly covered gaps, and fanning outward surrounded such strongpoints as still resisted. "Elastic defence" proved as foreign to the British nature as to the German a year earlier. At some points, parties of riflemen and machine-gunners valiantly attempting to hold their ground were overpowered; at others, small groups of Germans precipitated large-scale withdrawals. The end of the first day found the enemy in possession of the entire forward zone and part of the battle zone, having advanced to an average depth of three miles between the Oise and the Sensée. South of St. Quentin he had even broken right through the battle zone.[20]

Ludendorff's orders had been to exploit tactical success. As he told Crown Prince Rupprecht, "We chop a hole. The rest follows. We did it that way in Russia."[21] In the first three days the Eighteenth Army, on the German left, confronted by the weakest part of the British front, not only reached the Somme and the Crozat Canal (which linked the Somme to the Oise south-west of St. Quentin) but pushed beyond these objectives. The other two armies, however, had made slower progress and were in no position to roll up the British flank. Rather than follow up success where it occurred, accepting failure elsewhere, Ludendorff made the mistake of using up many of his reserves to redeem failures in the centre and on the right. He then introduced a new, dual aim—to split the British and French forces, and drive the British into the sea.[22]

Encouraged by the Eighteenth Army's success and by mistaken reports of favourable developments near Bapaume, on 23 March Ludendorff began to change the pattern of the entire operation. In the south the Eighteenth Army, hitherto mainly required to cover the flank of Rupprecht's two attacking armies, was now given its head and directed on the Chaulnes-Noyon area. In the north the Seventeenth Army would press towards St. Pol and Doullens; in the centre the

Second Army, with emphasis on its left, would continue advancing towards Amiens so as to separate the British and the French.[23]

For the next three days the German advance made rapid progress on almost the entire front of attack. Haig's southern wing seemed beaten; separation of the British from the French appeared imminent. Accordingly orders from the High Command late on 26 March signified a further widening of the operational aims. Increased importance was attached to the offensive against the French, where the Second and Eighteenth Armies would wheel to the left in a south-westerly direction. At the other end of the expanding operation the Seventeenth Army was to fan out north of the Somme, and while the Sixth Army readied itself to attack, the Fourth Army was to marshal its forces against the Belgians.[24] Could the Allies halt these impending drives?

Unity of Command for the Allies

Heavily outnumbered by the German strength arrayed against them, the Allied commanders searched desperately for reinforcements. In response to repeated requests by Sir Douglas Haig for French aid, Pétain ordered nine divisions to the British front between the second and fourth days of the offensive. Haig had asked for a concentration of 20 French divisions about Amiens, but on the evening of 24 March Pétain told him that no more could be spared. From north-west of Crépy, near Laon, the Germans had begun bombarding the French capital with a monster siege gun having a range of 75 miles, bringing the war unpleasantly close to the Parisians.[25] Convinced that the main blow was yet to come (in Champagne), and ordered by his government to "cover Paris at all costs", the French C.-in-C. was prepared to accept a gap between his own forces and the British. But Haig was convinced that the maintenance of a continuous front was and must remain a basic principle of Franco-British strategy. The Supreme War Council was powerless to resolve the deadlock, for neither French nor British would hand over to it the reserves which it demanded. In this crisis Haig asked the C.I.G.S. and the Secretary of State for War (now Lord Milner) to come to France.[26]

Privately to Sir Henry Wilson, and openly at a conference of French and British political and military leaders at Doullens on the 26th, Haig let it be known that he now favoured the appointment of General Foch as supreme commander in France. The French Premier, Georges Clemenceau, then proposed that Foch be charged with "the co-ordination of the action of the British and French Armies in front of Amiens".[27] Haig however realized the need of giving Foch complete authority over all operations in the West, and with the concurrence of Pétain the relevant terms were changed to read "Allied Armies on the Western Front".*

* On the eve of the conference the United States commander, General John Pershing, had offered Pétain four American divisions "equivalent in strength to eight French or British divisions" as a reserve. When Pétain objected that American troops were not yet experienced enough to form an American corps, two divisions (the 26th and the 42nd) relieved French divisions in quiet sectors of the line.[28]

Eight days later an Inter-Allied Conference, called to define Foch's powers further, entrusted him with "the strategic direction of military operations"; each C.-in-C. would remain "in full control of the tactical action" of his own armies. Thus unity of command was at last achieved, at least in the main theatre. Shortly afterwards Foch assumed the title of "Commander-in-Chief of the Allied Armies".[29]

On 25 March, as an immediate precaution against a breach between the British and French forces, Haig placed the Fifth Army, which was south of the Somme, under French command. To force a gap had been the German intention since 23 March, though the impending change of direction was not immediately noticeable. More apparent were the effects of the normal "diminishing force of the offensive". In six days the enemy had made a bulge 25 miles deep and 50 miles wide at the base; in the next ten days this increased by only thirteen miles on an ever-narrowing front. But astride the Scarpe a resolute and skilfully directed defence by the Third and First British Armies on 28 March had fought the Germans to a standstill. Ludendorff failed completely in his attempt to smash through the British line at Arras and regain the Vimy Ridge, though he attacked with 29 divisions against eight. (The comparative front line strengths were 13 German to six British divisions.) German authorities tend to attribute the final failure of their offensive to the use of poorly trained and under-disciplined troops. Ludendorff has been censured by some writers for not adhering to his original scheme nor consistently applying his doctrine of infiltration. According to von Kuhl, however, neither the individual army headquarters nor, on the whole, the troops were to be blamed for the failure. The real causes seem to be the developments which forced a diversion from the original plan and a shift of gravity towards the west and south-west. Since the objectives for the right wing (which required long advances towards the north-west) remained unchanged, the attack began diverging in three different directions with resultant dissipation of force.[30] However close the Germans came to reaching their goal, it must be concluded that their original plan was too ambitious and took too little account of their enemy's defensive capabilities.[31]

The operations in Picardy, variously called the March Offensive or the First Battles of the Somme, 1918, consisted of a number of large battles, the last of which ended on 5 April. By that time the Germans had swept forward from the line La Fère-St. Quentin to a new line which ran in a south-westerly direction from Lens to a point 40 miles west of La Fère. Péronne, Bapaume, Albert, Montdidier and Noyon had all been overrun, and the surge forward to the outskirts of Villers-Bretonneux, south of the Somme, meant that the important communications centre of Amiens, formerly nearly 40 miles inside British territory, was now less than ten miles behind the front. The fighting had cost the British 163,500 casualties, the French 77,000,[32] and the Germans 239,000*. The British figure includes Canadian casualties—618 in the three cavalry regiments, 144 in the 1st Motor Machine Gun Brigade, and 34 railway troops.

* The German calculation covers the period 21 March to 10 April, and includes the casualties of the five quiet days following the termination of the battle.[33]

Canadian Delaying Actions

As we have noted, the First Army's sector, in which the Canadian Corps was stationed, lay outside the area of the German attack. Canadian cavalry and machine-gunners, however, saw action. On the second day of the offensive, when the Fifth Army was under severe pressure, the British cavalry divisions had improvised dismounted units to reinforce General Gough's infantry; the Canadian Cavalry Brigade provided a dismounted brigade of 800 men.[34] The Canadians were employed in the area of the Crozat Canal, between the Somme and the Oise, where, on 23 March, they helped cover the retirement of the British 18th Division across the canal.[35] Falling back towards Noyon, the Dismounted Brigade came briefly in support of the French 6th Corps west of Chauny.

As the Allies continued to fall back there was still the greatest need for mounted troops to cover the retirement and fill important gaps in the line. Accordingly on 23 March a mounted detachment some 500 strong was formed from what was left of the 3rd Cavalry Division. The two British brigades provided 150 men each; the Canadian contribution was General Seely's brigade staff and 200 cavalrymen of his brigade. During the next four days the three squadrons operated in the northern half of the triangle formed by the Crozat Canal, the Oise and the Canal du Nord, helping to re-establish infantry lines that had broken and delivering small-scale counter-attacks on advanced German positions.[36]

On the evening of 27 March the Canadian brigade reassembled at Arsy, west of Compiègne, and was assigned to the 2nd Cavalry Division. Next day the Anglo-Canadian cavalry passed under command of the French First Army, which had just made successful local counter-attacks that enabled it to link up with the British right flank. In a further drive French troops, advancing with unexpected ease on Fontaine, a village eighteen miles south-east of Amiens, near Montdidier, took a number of "prisoners dressed like Canadians". One of the "captives" turned out to be Lieut. Harvey, V.C. (above, p. 242,*n.*), of the Strathconas! Sent forward some time beforehand on a mounted reconnaissance, Harvey and ten men had entered the village and driven out a greatly superior force of Germans.[37]

As German pressure in the direction of Amiens continued, the 2nd Cavalry Division again came under British command on 29 March in the sector adjoining the French left. When early next morning battalions of the 243rd German Division began occupying Moreuil Wood, a commanding position on the right bank of the River Avre only twelve miles south-east of Amiens, the 3rd and the Canadian Cavalry Brigades were at once sent to recapture it. French troops had already fallen back across the Avre. A mile and a quarter long from south to north and flaring to a width of nearly a mile at the northern end, the wood consisted mainly of ash trees. These were not yet in leaf, but close-growing saplings and heavy undergrowth made riding exceedingly difficult.[38] The Canadian brigade was first on the scene, and the assault was carried out in converging thrusts by three mounted squadrons of the Royal Canadian Dragoons, followed up by attacks—

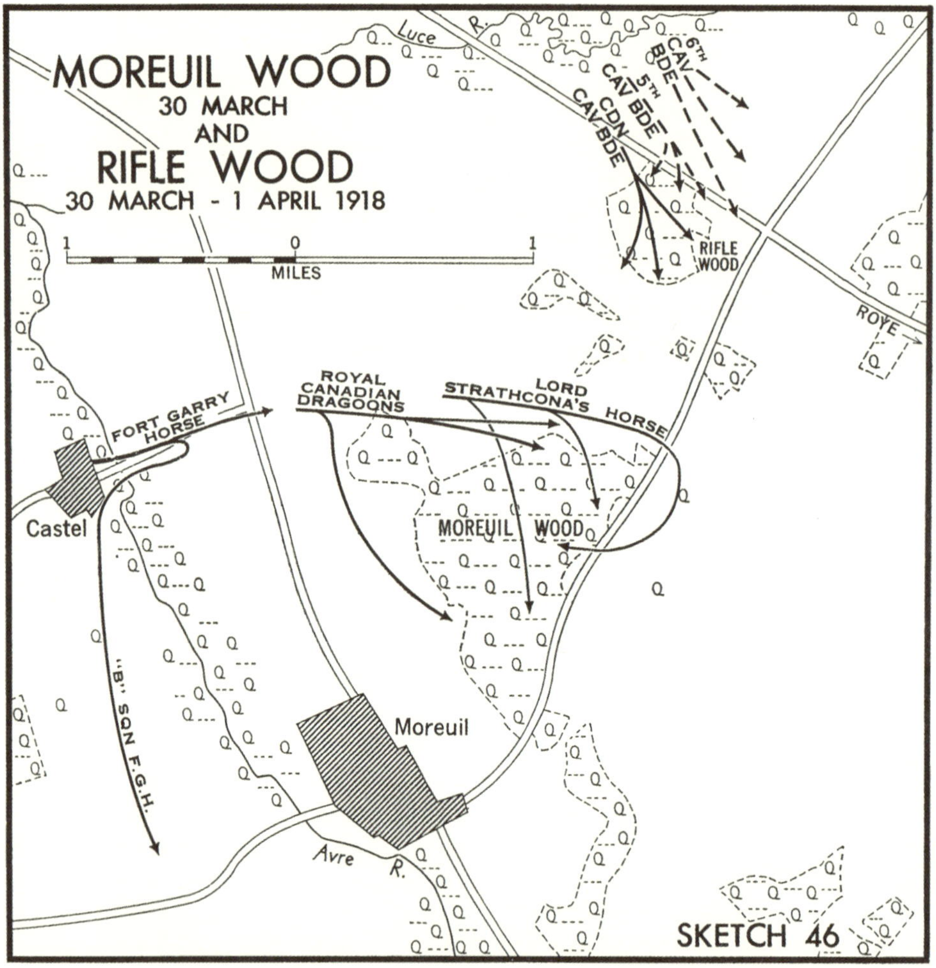

mounted and dismounted—by Lord Strathcona's Horse.* The German infantry resisted stoutly, but by 11:00 a.m., after a considerable amount of hand-to-hand fighting, the northern part of the wood was in Canadian hands. While one squadron of the Fort Garry Horse rode back across the Avre to bring the enemy under enfilade fire, a second joined in a dismounted advance through the remainder of the wood. By midday the wood was clear of Germans.[40]

The enemy soon counter-attacked. Reinforced by dismounted units of the 3rd Cavalry Brigade and a company of British infantry, the Canadians strove to maintain their position; though portions of the wood changed ownership more than once, and some lost ground was not recovered. That night the cavalry, having suffered many casualties, were relieved by three improvised battalions of the British 8th Division. On the 31st the enemy resumed his attacks, recapturing most

* Lieut. G. M. Flowerdew, mortally wounded while commanding a mounted squadron of the Strathconas in a gallant charge, was posthumously awarded the V.C.[39]

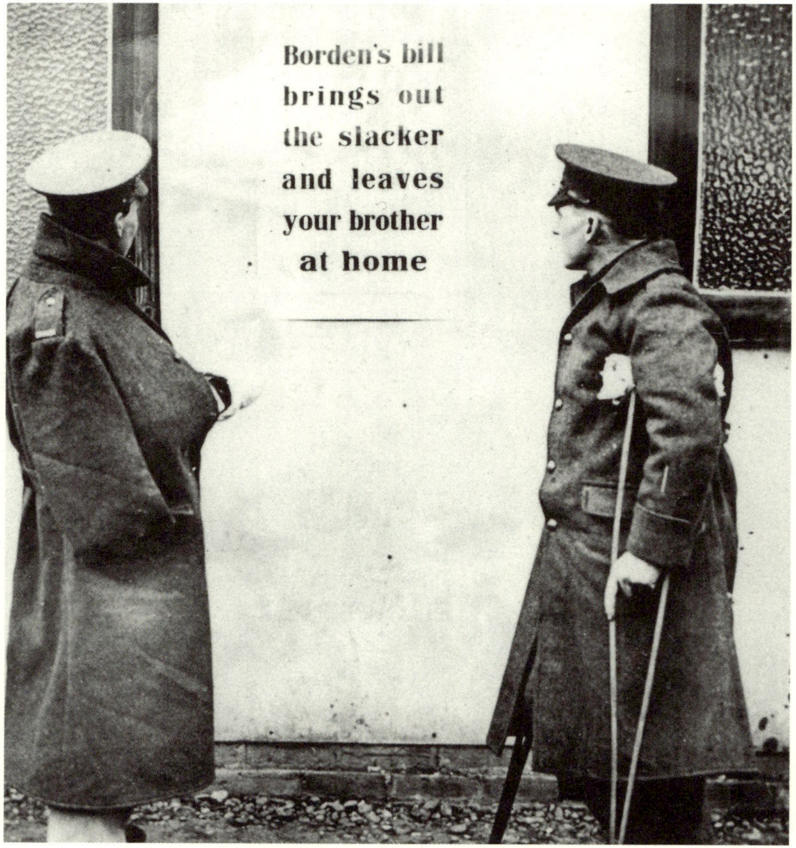

THE GENERAL ELECTION OF 1917

Patients at a Canadian hospital in England are urged to vote for Union Government—and conscription.

WINTER ON THE CANADIAN FRONT

In this picture, taken near Lens in February 1918, the hoarfrost accentuates the thick defensive barbed wire entanglements.

TRENCH ROUTINE

This photograph shows a quiet part of the line in the Canadian sector in February 1918. An officer keeps watch while sentries change over. Before retiring the "old" sentry cleans his rifle.

"THE MOTORS"

When the Germans launched their offensive in Picardy in the spring of 1918, the 1st Canadian Motor Machine Gun Brigade gave useful support to the British Fifth Army in the Amiens area. Here members of the Brigade carry out maintenance on their Vickers guns and their armoured cars.

of Moreuil Wood and occupying the smaller Rifle Wood, which lay a mile to the north beside the Amiens-Roye road. During the afternoon this was retaken, but only temporarily. A further attack that evening, the artillery support for which included two batteries of the R.C.H.A., partially restored the situation, but left Rifle Wood and all but the north-west corner of Moreuil Wood still in German hands. On the morning of 1 April dismounted units of the 2nd Cavalry Division attacked Rifle Wood in three waves. It was the third wave, consisting of 488 all ranks of the Canadian Cavalry Brigade, which entered and cleared the wood.[41]

Other Canadian forces to be actively involved in this first German offensive were the machine-gunners and some railway troops. The 1st Canadian Motor Machine Gun Brigade had been ordered from its positions at Vimy Ridge to the Fifth Army area on the second day of the initial battle. It moved without delay to Villers-Bretonneux (ten miles east of Amiens), whence its five batteries (above, p. 171,*n.*) were divided among three British Corps to aid in checking the enemy's advance and to fill dangerous gaps on the Army front.[42] The Fifth Army was virtually without support or reserves, and a large proportion of its artillery and machine-guns had been put out of action or captured. In these circumstances the arrival of the Canadian batteries with their 40 machine-guns was most timely aid, particularly as the mobility provided by their eight armoured cars greatly increased the effectiveness of their fire-power.[43]

An action typical of what the machine-gun units accomplished was that of "C" (Borden) and "B" Batteries, employed with the 7th Corps behind the Canal du Nord, north-west of Péronne. Early on the 24th the two batteries went into action about Cléry, on the north bank of the Somme, and for eight hours played a major role in holding up the German advance along the Péronne-Albert road. When they fell back that evening, covering an infantry withdrawal, the two batteries had only two guns left in action—manned by one officer and a small handful of men. Their casualties for the day numbered 47 all ranks.[44]

On the night of 25-26 March, when the threat to Amiens was becoming increasingly serious, General Gough ordered the disused Amiens Defence Line,* east of Villers-Bretonneux, to be put in order and manned by all available troops. To that end a force of some 3000 was raised. Composed mainly of British engineers, it included also 500 American railway troops, 400 officers and men of the 2nd Battalion Canadian Railway Troops, and a ten-gun battery organized from newly-arrived reinforcements for the 1st Canadian Motor Machine Gun Brigade. "Carey's Force", so called from the name of the divisional commander who took over command on the 24th, made a valuable contribution in establishing and holding its line of resistance until the night of 30-31 March, when Australian troops relieved it. By that time the number of machine-guns manned by the Canadians had risen to 32—their commander having "scraped up another sixteen from among stragglers and the infantry".[46] Although the Amiens Defence Line was never attacked in

* This position, extending south from the Somme to the River Luce, consisted of two lines about eight miles long, constructed by the French in 1915. The inner line was 11 miles and the outer (to which the name usually referred) 15 miles in front of Amiens. During 1917, to permit cultivation of the ground the wire had been removed and some of the trenches filled in.[45]

strength, the Railway Troops saw some minor action and were subjected to considerable shellfire.[47].

The whole of the Canadian Motor Machine Gun Brigade was eventually involved in the operations south of the Somme. On 26 March "A" and "B" Batteries moved up to Villers-Bretonneux, where their armoured cars, each mounting two Vickers guns, did valuable work patrolling the highways and side roads. Their role was specific—"to get in touch with the enemy, kill as many as possible and delay his advance".[48] On the 29th "C" Battery and the Eaton and Yukon batteries ("D" and "E"), had replaced the original Canadian machine-gun detachment in Carey's Force. On 6 April the newcomers supported Australian forces in a successful attack south-east of Villers-Bretonneux which resulted in regaining some ground and the capture of 200 Germans.[49] This ended the Canadian commitment with the Fifth Army. The assistance given by the Motor Machine Gun Brigade to General Gough's exhausted and disorganized divisions had been far out of proportion to the size of such a comparatively small unit. Its officers and men had been trained to fight on their own initiative—training which bore good results when orders could not reach them and headquarters of divisions and infantry brigades, continually on the move, could not be found.[50]

The Fighting in Flanders, 9-29 April

By the evening of 5 April Ludendorff "was forced to abandon the attack on Amiens for good".[51] Yet it was not immediately apparent to the Allies that Amiens was no longer threatened or where the next blow would fall. It was suspected that increased traffic northward, noticeable even before 21 March, might have been only a feint. By the second week of April, however, the Germans appeared to be in a position to strike anywhere north of the Scarpe. In fact Ludendorff intended to attack with his Sixth Army in the plain of the Lys between Armentières and La Bassée, and so draw the British reserves southward from Flanders, and then to deliver a blow with the Fourth Army against the weakened northern sector. The demands of the March battles farther south had already depleted the First and Second British Armies, who were holding the line with few reserves. Haig urgently requested French help, but Foch refused to send any reinforcements northward until the battle had started and the Germans had shown their hand.[52]

On 9 April the Germans struck. Fourteen divisions attacked on a twelve-mile front between Armentières and the La Bassée Canal. It was the first anniversary of the battle of Vimy Ridge, and early reports made Ludendorff's birthday more pleasant than the previous year's. The enemy advanced some three and a half miles, further penetration being stopped by his difficulty in keeping his supporting artillery within range, and by what Crown Prince Rupprecht called the "obstinate resistance" at Givenchy of a "particularly good" British division (the 55th).[53] But next to the 55th Division a Portuguese contingent, whose four tired brigades were long overdue for relief, fell back before the onslaught of four German divisions. The Fourth Army's attack that went in next day extended the battle front northward to the Ypres-Comines Canal. By the following morning both Armentières and Messines had fallen. Foch now ordered a French relief force of four infantry and three cavalry divisions (to be called the Tenth Army) to assemble behind Amiens; but he still refused to take over any British front or to move French formations northward. Recalling earlier British stands in front of Ypres he told Haig—who found him "most selfish and obstinate"—that the British could and must "hold on where they stood".[54] Events were to justify the Generalissimo's unwillingness to be argued into involving reserves in a running fight.

The German advance continued unevenly—the Fourth Army's attack gained impetus, while that of the Sixth Army lost momentum. On the 11th, a strong thrust put forward troops within five miles of Hazebrouck; and that evening Haig issued his famous Order of the Day: "With our backs to the wall and believing in the justice of our cause each one of us must fight on to the end. . . ." On 12 April the Germans contented themselves with local attacks, seeking to extend their gains in width rather than in depth, and from now on the offensive definitely lagged. With Ypres threatened General Plumer began to organize a main line of resistance on the more defensible western slope of the long Passchendaele ridge. By the 17th the eastern face of the ridge and much of the forward slope towards Ypres, all of which had been earlier bought with so much blood, had been abandoned to the enemy.[55] That day was marked by a costly repulse of German forces attempting to capture Mount Kemmel (five miles south of Ypres), the most easterly of the string of commanding heights reaching back to Cassel. North of Ypres an attack by General Sixt von Armin's Fourth Army had been stopped cold by the Belgians, fighting their first major battle since 1914.[56]

After the German setback there was a brief lull in the fighting on the ground, though not in the air. It was in this period that Captain von Richthofen scored his seventy-ninth and eightieth victories and fought his last battle.[57] He was shot down and killed in circumstances that still remain a subject of controversy.

On 19 April French troops of a newly-organized *Détachement d'Armée du Nord* began to relieve a British corps in the Mount Kemmel sector. Five days later Ludendorff temporarily turned his attention to the Somme. An assault by six divisions of the Second Army against the forces covering Amiens resulted in the capture of Villers-Bretonneux from the British and Moreuil from the French. In the former operation the Germans employed thirteen tanks to good effect—their first use of armour, apart from a few tanks in a mopping-up role on 21 March. Subsequently British tanks engaged them, and in the war's only armoured combat of any size knocked out one German tank and turned two others away.[58] Villers-Bretonneux was recovered next day in a counter-attack by British and Australian troops.

The last week of April saw the Germans return to the Flanders offensive (sometimes known as the Battles of the Lys), where they concentrated their efforts against the line of heights south of Ypres. On the 25th they stormed Mount Kemmel behind a particularly heavy bombardment and quickly overcame French resistance there. The final effort came four days later, when seven divisions of the

Fourth Army attacked on a ten-mile front from Ypres to the River Douve. Foch had brought the strength of the French-held sector up to seven divisions as well as providing strong artillery reserves. This time except for two small penetrations the Allied line held. With his Fourth and Sixth Armies so exhausted as to be extremely vulnerable to counter-attack, Ludendorff broke off the offensive. Once more a German advance had been halted in front of Ypres. Again the Channel ports were saved.

Much blood had been shed. The German losses in Picardy and Flanders (figures for both offensives were not divulged separately) totalled 348,300. Allied casualties for the same period totalled 330,000, the northern campaign having produced 76,300 British and 35,000 French casualties. The brunt of the battle had been borne by Haig's hard-pressed troops, and as a result of the continuous fighting, of the 61 British divisions in France (two had recently arrived from Palestine) only 48 were fit for battle. Eight had been reduced to mere skeletons, and in some cases would never be fully reconstituted.[59] General Pétain's forces were in better condition. As May began the French still had 103 divisions, all reinforced to full strength—63 in the line, including four in Flanders, and forty in reserve. Also under Pétain's command were two Italian divisions (received in the latter part of April) and three American divisions. The number of German divisions on the Western Front had been brought to 204 by further arrivals from Russia,[60] though Ludendorff was greatly worried about the lack of drafts to replace his losses. He angrily complained about the Government's failure to release exempted men and take "energetic action against deserters and shirkers".[61]

The initiative remained with the enemy. Now the great bulge of the German gains formed a right angle facing westward against the British and southward against the French, so that Ludendorff could strike equally well in two directions. The Germans were still hopeful of final victory; the Entente were still in danger of losing the war.

The German Advance to the Marne, 27 May—6 June

Before the fighting in Flanders and Picardy slowed to a halt Ludendorff had already set in motion plans for what he later styled "the second great German attack in France".[62] Before resuming operations in the north he determined on dealing a major diversionary blow across the Aisne towards the end of May, in order to compel the return of French reinforcements from Flanders. This would be followed about mid-June by a renewed attack against the British armies in the north, by that time denuded of their French reserves; while on the heels of the diversion in Champagne the Austro-Hungarian Army would launch an offensive on the Italian front.[63]

Secretly during May the German Seventh Army, which faced the French Sixth Army along the historic Chemin des Dames, increased its strength by 30 divisions with some 4000 guns, which had been placed at its disposal by the High Command. On the morning of 27 May 1918 the extreme left wing of the

German Eighteenth Army, all of the Seventh Army and the right wing of the First Army—38 divisions with 5263 guns of all calibres—stood deployed in three echelons on a 60-mile front reaching from south-east of Noyon to south-east of Reims.[64] Along the dozen miles of the Chemin des Dames, between Pinon and Craonne, the Germans had concentrated ten divisions. Holding the front line opposite them were one depleted British and two French divisions. The major tactical weakness of the French Sixth Army's position, partly dictated by the prestige value attached to the Chemin des Dames, was the placing of nearly half the available defending forces well forward on the ridge, with the unfordable rivers of the Aisne and the Vesle behind them. On his whole front the French Army Commander had only four of his sixteen divisions (eleven French and five British) in reserve.[65]

The attack was launched in the early hours of 27 May after a bombardment which, employing more than 40 batteries per mile of front, far surpassed in intensity any previous German effort that year. Ill-served by its intelligence services the French Army was taken completely by surprise. As the ten German divisions stormed the Chemin des Dames, five of them poured into the centre of the line and destroyed one French and the British division at a single blow. Nothing could stop the German onrush, which by nightfall had carried the centre of the Seventh Army to the Vesle on a nine-mile front. This advance of ten miles in a single day was without precedent in trench warfare.[66] By the end of the second day Soissons had fallen and the Germans held a pocket fifteen miles deep on a base of forty miles. Within a week they had reached the Marne at Château Thierry, though on the German left Reims remained untaken. Ludendorff had indeed exploited tactical success, though he was afterwards to admit that the attack had not been broken off early enough at all points.[67] The advance which was to have stopped at the Vesle had travelled forward to form a bulging salient thirty miles deep and on the average as many miles wide. Yet strategically the diversion had failed. Eventually accepting Haig's view that the real danger was still in the north, General Foch had not weakened his strategic reserve in Flanders in response to the German challenge in the south. In all, twenty-five French and two American divisions had been drawn into the battle between 28 May and 3 June, but all from Pétain's reserve. Both at the Somme and in Flanders the Allies had conserved and even increased their strength.[68]

Ludendorff's next effort was a westward extension of the Champagne diversion—an attack by the Eighteenth Army between Montdidier and Noyon. After two postponements due to the unexpected progress of the main diversion the operation was launched on 9 June, with eleven German divisions attacking west of the Oise and across its tributary, the Matz. On the first day the Germans broke through to a depth of six miles, but thereafter they were held to minor gains by the French Third Army, which with nine divisions forward, all well prepared for a German onslaught, was at less of a disadvantage than had been the case at the Chemin des Dames. General Foch promptly replied to Pétain's demand for reserves, and on the 11th a force of three French and two American divisions, strongly supported by tanks and aircraft, struck the German right flank. The counter-attack gained little ground, but it effectively stopped the enemy's advance. On the evening of the 12th Ludendorff called off the Eighteenth Army's attack, giving similar orders to the German Seventh Army, which had made little progress in a supporting effort launched that morning south-west of Soissons.[69]

The Last German Offensive, 15 July—6 August

"Again and again our thoughts returned to the idea of an offensive in Flanders", Ludendorff was to write of the summer of 1918.[70] How like Haig's sentiments of late 1916 and early 1917! But the German High Command had no illusions about the Allied strength in that sector, and in the hope of drawing off some of the reserves from the British front it ordered an attack on either side of Reims to be made in mid-July. This part of the front, from Château Thierry eastward to Verdun, had been left comparatively lightly held when Pétain, under public pressure to guard Paris, packed the bulk of his reserves along the forward arc of the German salient. The initial objective would be a crossing of the Marne. With this gained, the "battering train" of heavy artillery and trench mortars would be immediately transferred northward for a Flanders offensive (Operation "Hagen"), to begin in early August.[71] Any thought of going over to the defensive was ruled out by Ludendorff; for to adopt such a policy would make it easier for the Allies to concentrate their superior resources in war material on a single battlefield.[72]

But General Foch was also planning offensive operations. During June Allied attacks delivered on a scale of one or two divisions had revealed signs of feebleness in the enemy's resistance. The epidemic of influenza which was sweeping the world had reached the Western Front. Continuing through July and recurring in October, it was to cost the British forces nearly 16 per cent in casualties. The Germans, with their resistance lowered by inadequate diet, were greater sufferers. A toll of from 1000 to 2000 cases per division was reported, and the epidemic threatened postponement of the Flanders operations.[73] Encouraged by their preliminary successes, the French began preparing for a strong counter-offensive to be launched on 18 July against both sides of the German salient.[74]

By mid-July fifty divisions* of the German Crown Prince's Group of Armies, with the support of 6353 guns, stood ready to attack along the 75-mile front from the Argonne to Château Thierry, while some nine or ten depleted divisions under the Ninth Army Headquarters (which was brought in from Rumania) faced westward between the Oise and the Marne. Holding the line against this strong force, or preparing to launch converging counter-attacks from west and south-east, were close to 70 divisions in four French Armies (the Fourth, Fifth, Sixth and Tenth), including seven American, four British and two Italian divisions.[76] As

* Twelve divisions were in the first line west of Reims, fifteen east of Reims. Two more were held at Reims waiting to join the attack at a later moment, and 21 divisions were ready as second and third echelons.[75]

in their previous offensives, the Germans held vast superiority in artillery—1047 field batteries and 609 heavy guns to the Allied 360 field batteries and 408 heavy pieces.

In September 1914 the First Battle of the Marne had spoiled German hopes of quickly ending the war. Now, nearly four years later, the same river was again to mark the high tide of the enemy's progress towards Paris, and the battle waged along its banks was to be the last in which German forces would enjoy the initiative.

The Second Battle of the Marne began on the morning of 15 July with the usual heavy bombardment, which lost much of its effectiveness because the French, forewarned by captured Germans, had thinned out their front position, and were able to catch the opposing batteries with early fire. East of Reims the attackers suffered a staggering defeat at the hands of the French Fourth Army. It was a grave moment for the higher German commanders, who realized the far-reaching implications of the setback. Farther west, however, the German Seventh Army put six divisions across the Marne between Château Thierry and Epernay, capturing a bridgehead eight miles wide and four miles deep.[77] Fierce fighting followed, and General Pétain ordered preparations for the counter-offensive suspended in order that he might draw reserves from the assembling troops to reinforce his threatened front. But he was overruled by General Foch, who was confident that the German bridgehead, which was under constant heavy aerial bombing and artillery shelling, could be liquidated.[78]

In the early hours of 18 July the French Sixth and Tenth Armies struck with twenty-four divisions massed between Château Thierry and the Aisne, catching the enemy completely by surprise. By mid-afternoon these forces, which included four full-strength American divisions, had pushed the west face of the salient back four miles, and the Crown Prince had ordered the evacuation of the Marne bridgehead. First word of the French attack reached Ludendorff at the headquarters of Army Group Rupprecht, where the Chiefs of Staff of the Fourth and Sixth Armies were reporting to him on the preparations for the Flanders Offensive.

When subsequent messages indicated a grave deterioration of the situation, Ludendorff returned to his headquarters at Avesnes and in the evening requested General von Lossberg, the Fourth Army's Chief of Staff, to join him there. Next morning Lossberg examined the information on hand and advised Ludendorff that the Armies which had carried out the spring offensive should be withdrawn gradually to their starting positions. According to Lossberg the Field Marshal agreed in principle, but contended that for political reasons such a withdrawal was impossible.[79] It will be seen that a second great shock was required to make Ludendorff admit to himself the true nature of the situation and its serious implications (below, p. 407).

By 20 July the French Fifth and Ninth Armies had begun attacking west of Reims. Ludendorff's diversionary offensive had suddenly become for the Germans a grim defensive battle. The transfer of their heavy guns northward had started on the 18th. But these would not now be needed for Crown Prince Rupprecht's

Flanders offensive. Ludendorff, with no idea as to "how, if at all, we should be able to recover the initiative", had ordered Operation "Hagen" to be cancelled.[80] The Second Battle of the Marne dragged bloodily on for nearly three weeks, as both sides reinforced steadily. The Germans, fighting doggedly, were slowly driven back. By 7 August, when the battle ended, they had been forced behind the Vesle, where they were temporarily safe from French pressure. They had lost 29,000 prisoners and their overall casualties were estimated at 168,000.[81]

The great gamble of Ludendorff's offensives had failed. The million casualties suffered by the Germans since 21 March—casualties for which no adequate replacements were forthcoming—had enfeebled their armies at a time when they were soon to face their greatest test. Of the 201 German infantry divisions (or equivalent) on the Western Front at the beginning of August, 106 were unfit for battle—and ten were shortly to be broken up.[82] On the other hand the Entente not only slightly surpassed this strength numerically (130 front-line and 76 reserve infantry divisions), but more than matched their opponents in the quality of their formations. The British sector was considerably better off with its 53 divisions, most of them well rested during the summer, than it had been for many months. Thirty-six of these were in the front line. Haig's reserve included the Portuguese and four United States divisions. On the French front there were 84 divisions in the line (of which seven were American and three British), and 39 in reserve (including seven U.S., one British and two Italian divisions).[83]

The Canadian Corps on Defence and in Reserve, 21 March—30 July

Apart from the larger, and in the main, untried American and Belgian divisions, the strongest divisions in the entire theatre during the summer of 1918 were those of the Canadian Corps. Holding a seven-mile sector centred on Lens, at the right of the First Army's line, the Canadians had not been involved in the heavy fighting of March and April. At the time of the first German offensive the Corps had three divisions in the line—from north to south the 1st Division opposite Hill 70, the 4th in front of Lens, and the 3rd Division in the Avion-Méricourt sector. The 2nd Division was in the Corps training area at Auchel, eight miles west of Béthune.[84]

It was important ground that the Canadians were holding, for behind Lens and Vimy Ridge lay the only collieries that remained accessible in northern France and many key centres of communication that must be denied to the enemy. Accordingly the early months of 1918 saw much work done on the defences. Unusually fine weather assisted the completion of extensive works behind the main front-line system—250 miles of trench, 300 miles of wire entanglements, and 200 tunnelled machine-gun emplacements. Great care was taken in siting the artillery—on Vimy Ridge alone 72 new battery positions were built and ammunition stacked beside them. This pleased the French, who having good reason for attaching much importance to that particular sector sent a former Minister of War to inspect its defences.[85]

Scarcely had the Germans struck when demands reached General Currie to make Canadian formations available as reserves to hard-pressed British corps. On 23 March the 2nd Canadian Division was ordered into G.H.Q. reserve in the Mont St. Eloi area, and the 1st Division taken out of the line and placed in First Army reserve. As the 4th Division extended its left to cover Hill 70, at the other end of the Corps front the 3rd Division was called on to relieve a British division by taking over an additional 3000 yards in the Acheville-Arleux sector. By 25 March, the Corps was holding a 17,000-yard front with only two divisions. Next day, following a conference at Doullens between Earl Haig and his Army Commanders, orders came from General Horne that would detach the remaining Canadian divisions from General Currie's command and send his Corps Headquarters into reserve. Haig was imbued with the necessity of holding his ground in order to gain time for the French to come and support him. He hoped that his centre could resist enemy pressure which would cause his line to bulge, "thus extending our front as to risk its breaking. I therefore ordered Horne", he wrote in his diary, "to get three divisions of Canadians out and place them somewhere opposite the centre of Byng's line."[86] The Canadian sector was to be taken over by the two adjacent British Corps.

On the right the 13th Corps (the First Army's right-hand corps) assumed command of the 3rd Canadian Division at noon on the 27th; while north of the Souchez River the 46th Division of the 1st Corps was ordered to relieve the 4th Canadian Division, which would then pass into G.H.Q. reserve.[87] At the same time the 1st and 2nd Canadian Divisions were placed in General Byng's Third Army south of Arras—the former with the 17th Corps, astride the Arras-Cambrai road, and the latter on its immediate right in the Neuville-Vitasse sector of the 6th Corps' front.[88]

In the emergency of the German offensive Sir Arthur had agreed to the employment of Canadian divisions under British command "as required",[89] but he protested the orders which would remove all four divisions from his control. "I . . . offered suggestions", he states, "which to my mind would reconcile my claims (from the standpoint of Canadian policy) with the tactical and administrative requirements of the moment."[90] (Below, p. 381.) The effect of Currie's arguments was to leave his headquarters less than twenty-four hours without a front-line command. It was 10:15 a.m. on the 29th when the 1st Corps took over the remaining part of the Canadian Corps' front. But word had already come from the Army Commander that the 56th Division, which had been seriously weakened in the heavy fighting of 28 April, should be relieved in the Oppy-Gavrelle sector by the 4th Canadian Division, which would then, together with the 3rd Canadian Division on its left, return to Currie's command—the 13th Corps being pulled out of the line.[91] These reliefs were carried out expeditiously, and at 6:45 a.m. on the 30th the Canadian Corps resumed command of two of its divisions.[92]

Among Sir Arthur's suggestions to the First Army was one that the 1st Division (since 27 March with the Third Army) should relieve the 4th British Division astride the Scarpe, the inter-army boundary to be shifted southward accordingly. This adjustment was completed on 8 April, leaving the Canadian Corps holding a front of approximately 16,000 yards with three divisions. Currie also proposed that the 2nd Canadian Division, then holding some 6000 yards of the Third Army's line, should revert to his command as a reserve. But the additional burden suddenly imposed on the British forces by the second German offensive caused this move to be cancelled—indeed the 2nd Division was not to rejoin the Corps until 1 July. As the Battle of the Lys continued General Currie, with only three divisions at his disposal, was required to extend his front northward to free the 46th Division in the Lens-Hill 70 sector. Thus by mid-April the Canadian Corps was holding a front of more than 29,000 yards.[93]

Currie's protest created an unfortunate impression that long persisted—four strong divisions denied a share in the great defensive battles of March and April through his insistence that they fight only as a corps. The situation was not improved by the Canadian Commander's criticism of the performance of some of the British formations. On 14 April, he noted in his diary, "Army Commander called in afternoon, [and] resented any reflections on fighting ability of British Divisions."* Indeed General Horne (as recorded in the C.-in-C.'s diary) went so far as to suggest to Sir Douglas Haig that Currie was "suffering from a swollen head".[96] Haig's entry of 18 April draws an invidious comparison between Australian policy and that set forth by Currie:

> He wishes to fight only as a "Canadian Corps" and get his Canadian representative in London to write and urge me to arrange it! As a result, the Canadians are together holding a wide front near Arras, but *they have not yet been in the battle!* The Australians on the other hand have been used by Divisions and are now spread out from Albert to Amiens and one is in front of Hazebrouck.[97]

Three months later Haig was to remind Canada's Minister of Defence (Major-General S. C. Mewburn) that "the British Army alone and unaided by Canadian troops withstood the first terrific blow made by 80 German Divisions on March 21st until May 27th", and that he had been "on the point of employing Canadian Divisions in the battle" but had put them back into the line on receipt of "a wire . . . from the War office emphasizing the Canadian Government's desire to fight together".[98]

So much has been made of the incident that it may be useful to review from the relevant documents the sequence of events as they occurred. On 27 March 1918, following receipt of General Horne's orders, Currie made his formal representations to G.H.Q. in a letter to Lieut.-General Sir H. A. Lawrence, Haig's

* Currie's strictures had evidently not been confined to the pages of his diary, where for instance he had noted on 11 April, "Many British troops are not fighting well." General Pershing, who visited the Canadian Corps Headquarters on 20 April, has recorded that on that occasion "General Currie deplored the fact that the British had so easily given up Passchendaele Ridge, which the year before he had been told must be taken at all cost, and for which the Canadians made the tremendous sacrifice of 16,000 casualties."[94]

When he expressed these criticisms Currie could not have weighed carefully all the factors affecting the British performance during the initial German offensive. These have been well presented in a critical analysis of the situation by the British Official Historian. They include the overwhelming German superiority opposite the British Fifth Army, the recent reduction of British divisions to a nine-battalion structure, the weakening caused by a compelled extension to take over more front from the French, and the absence of a General Reserve.[95]

Chief of the General Staff. While not wishing "for a moment to make a single suggestion that would embarrass the Chief [Haig] in the slightest degree", Currie set forth clearly and reasonably the desire of the units of the Canadian Corps to fight side by side—a wish shared by the people of Canada. He argued that with one of its divisions "thrown in here and another there" the Corps had no chance to do its best. The letter concluded:

> From the very nature and constitution of the organization it is impossible for the same liaison to exist in a British Corps as exists in the Canadian Corps. My Staff and myself cannot do as well with a British Corps in this battle as we can with the Canadian Corps, nor can any other Corps Staff do as well with the Canadian Divisions as my own.
>
> I know that necessity knows no law and that the Chief will do what he thinks best, yet for the sake of the victory we must win, get us together as soon as you can.[99]

Currie sent a copy of this letter to Sir Edward Kemp, who replied on 30 March: "I note what you say about the Corps being divided. On Good Friday [29 March], however, I took the liberty of visiting Lord Derby and handing him a letter, copy of which I attach for your personal and confidential information."[100] In the communication to the Secretary of State for War Kemp, "without in any way presuming to interfere with the conduct of operations in France", pointed out that the efficiency of the Canadian Corps and its high morale were "undoubtedly due to the fact that it has been kept together as a unit under Lieut.-General Sir Arthur Currie, in whom the troops have unbounded confidence". If it were possible to continue this policy, it was felt that better results would be obtained than by breaking up the Corps to be used in smaller units at different points under new leadership. Kemp asked Lord Derby to convey this view to Haig as soon as possible.[101] This Lord Derby did in the War Office wire already referred to.

To keep Ottawa informed, on 2 April Kemp sent Sir Robert Borden a copy of his letter to Derby, together with a copy of Currie's letter to General Lawrence.[102] No reply came for a month, when on 3 May a cable from Borden rather abruptly warned Kemp that "any proposal to break up the Canadian Army Corps would be strongly resented in Canada and would have the most unfortunate effect upon public opinion." The cable was apparently inspired by a question asked in Parliament by Sir Sam Hughes concerning a rumour of such a proposal.[103] Sir Edward Kemp, who was about to leave for the front, at once cabled a reply to set Borden's mind at rest, stating that he had not heard of any intention to break up the Corps.[104]

In France Kemp found the Canadian Corps "in good condition". The 2nd Division was expected soon to rejoin the Corps. He lunched with Haig, who recorded in his diary that from some remarks which inadvertently fell from the Overseas Minister, "I could not help feeling that some people in Canada regard themselves rather as 'allies' than fellow citizens in the Empire".[105]

Final assurance was given in a letter to Kemp from Lord Milner. He had received a copy of Sir Robert Borden's cable, and he reiterated that there was no intention of breaking up the Canadian Corps. The result of continuously keeping the Corps together had proved so satisfactory that "even on purely military grounds—and apart entirely from the considerations of national sentiment", it would be the greatest possible mistake to pursue any other course. He pledged that if for any military reason the Corps became separated, it would be reunited again as soon as the emergency was over.[106]

Once during the period there had been prospects of offensive action for the Canadians. Late in April the Commander of the First Army had considered them for employment in a local counter-attack designed to forestall a renewal of the enemy's offensive on the Bailleul-Ypres front. The proposed operation, to be launched on a ten-mile front between Festubert and Robecq, was a northward thrust against the left of the enemy's Lys salient, with Merville and Estaires as the final objectives.[107] Planning for the scheme, which was given the code name "Delta", was already well advanced when on 3 May General Foch proposed that the Canadian Corps might be used in the very way that General Horne was intending. But the uncertain situation on either side of the First Army's sector made it impossible to provide relieving troops to free the Canadian Corps for "Delta", and on 8 May preparations for the operation were suspended.[108] Although "Delta" was subsequently cancelled, getting ready for the projected attack had been a useful exercise for all the Canadian arms and services, exerting, as reported by General Currie, "a most vivifying influence on the training of the Canadian Corps".[109]

The part played by the Canadian Corps during these critical weeks should not be minimized. "We are holding a 10 mile front with two divisions", noted Currie on the last day of March, "altogether too much, but owing to lack of men in British Army it cannot be helped. I am told we have 430,000 men in Mesopotamia. What a splendid place for a reserve!"[110] Extended almost to the breaking point and under the continued threat of an overwhelming attack, the Corps resolutely prepared to meet a German assault. As the Battle of the Lys progressed the Canadians found themselves in a dangerously deepening salient. To deceive the enemy regarding the frugality of their dispositions they "adopted a very aggressive attitude".[111] The artillery maintained a vigorous programme of harassing fire, supplemented by gas shells, while the infantry carried out numerous raids and patrols.* To meet the crying need for more infantry two provisional infantry brigades, with a total strength of about 8900 all ranks, were formed from personnel of the four Divisional Wings of the Canadian Corps Reinforcement Camp, the 1st Tunnelling Company, the field companies of the 5th Division, and certain other Canadian and attached British engineer units.[113]

General Currie was extremely concerned about his shortage of machine-guns, his resources in these weapons being quite inadequate to provide him with the defence in depth necessary to withstand an assault. He formed temporary Lewis and Hotchkiss gun detachments from personnel of the Canadian Light Horse and the Canadian Corps Cyclist Battalion. The arrival in France of the three

* In a large raid on the night of 27-28 April near Gavrelle in the 1st Division's sector, Lieut. G. B. McKean of the 14th Battalion personally accounted for eight Germans while capturing two trench blocks and destroying an enemy dug-out. McKean was awarded the V.C., and in the following September he won the Military Cross.[112]

MAP 10

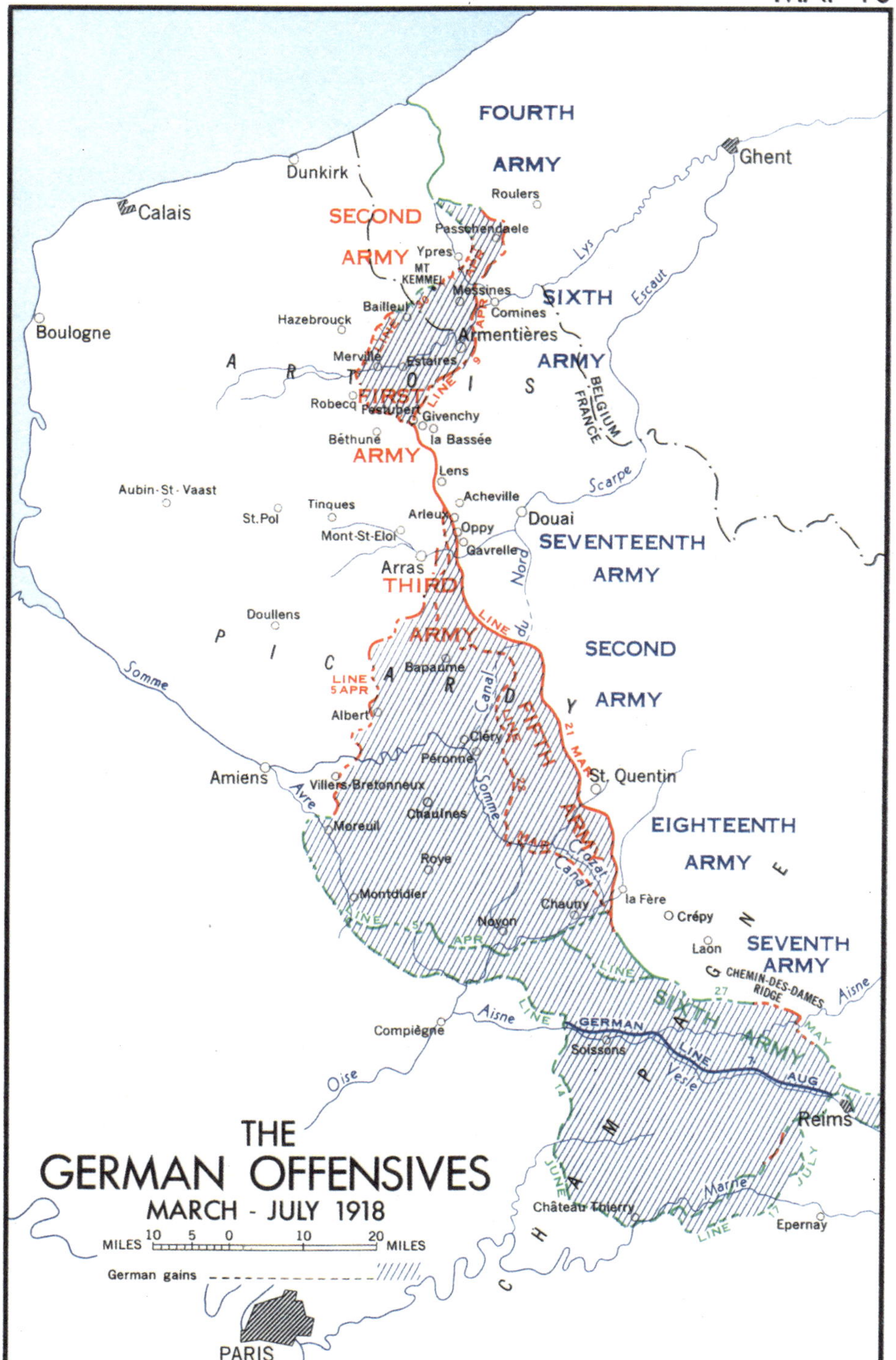

Reproduced by Army Survey Establishment

Compiled and drawn by Historical Section G.S.

machine-gun companies originally slated for the 5th Canadian Division and their allotment at the end of March to positions on Vimy Ridge helped the situation somewhat.[114] March had seen a reorganization of the Canadian Machine Gun Corps which grouped the machine-gun companies which had existed since November 1915 (four with each division) into four 2-company battalions, one with each infantry division. In April the Corps Commander added to each machine-gun battalion a third company of four batteries, manning these with fifty of the "best and brainiest men" from each infantry battalion. This fifty-percent addition to its strength in men and guns gave Canadian machine-gun battalions the organization with which they ended the war. The new establishment of 96 Vickers guns meant that the ratio of machine-guns to rifles within a Canadian division would once more match that of the British divisions, in which the relative gun power had been increased by the recent reduction in the number of infantry battalions.*

But the most significant fact about the new machine-gun battalions was the emphasis placed upon their employment as tactical units. A memorandum prepared by Brig.-Gen. Brutinel, Commander of the Canadian Machine Gun Corps, and issued by the Canadian Corps at the end of April, set forth the Corps policy with respect to machine-gun troops. The machine-gun service was to be regarded as a distinctive arm, intermediate between the infantry and the artillery, and with tactics of its own. Though there were occasions when M.G. companies or batteries might be temporarily attached to infantry brigades or battalions for duty, machine-gun battalions were divisional troops, under the command and tactical control of a Divisional Machine Gun Commander, whose position was closely analogous to that of the C.R.A. of a Division with respect to artillery.[116] This policy was far in advance of the existing G.H.Q. policy, which made each machine-gun battalion commander responsible to the G.O.C. of the Division for the discipline, administration and training of his battalion, but as yet gave him no tactical control. It was not until early in November that a G.H.Q. directive to the five British Armies on the Western Front authorized the adoption of the principles of command and tactical handling which had governed the activities of the Canadian Machine Gun Corps during the final six months of the war.[117]

During the first week of May the Canadian Corps (1st, 3rd and 4th Divisions) was relieved by five divisions of the 17th and 18th British Corps. The subsequent period in reserve gave General Currie the opportunity to carry out a reorganization of the Canadian Engineers, authority for which had been received on the day the Germans launched their March offensive. Under the existing system in the field the infantry had provided most of the labour for the small body of engineer "specialists"—giving rise to the motto, "engineers responsible for *quality* and infantry for *quantity*".[118] Unfortunately for both the quality and quantity of the work, the engineers had little control over the working parties provided by the infantry, and were themselves subject to dual control. Though in theory the commander of a field company was responsible to the C.R.E. for the task assigned in

* In a British division of nine battalions (9000 rifles) and 64 Vickers guns the proportion was one gun to 141 rifles. A Canadian division of twelve enlarged battalions (above, p. 232) would now have 96 Vickers to 13,200 rifles—a ratio of one to 138.[115]

a given brigade sector, in practice he was more under the orders of successive infantry brigadiers, each with his own idea of what work was required. The results were "confusion, lack of efficiency and waste of labour and material".[119]

To correct this situation Sir Arthur Currie expanded the three field companies then with each division into one Engineer Brigade, consisting of a Headquarters, three Engineer Battalions of 1000 men each, and a Pontoon Bridging and Transport Unit. He found the additional men required by disbanding the four Canadian Pioneer Battalions, the 1st and 2nd Tunnelling Companies, and the three field companies of the 5th Canadian Division Engineers. By the end of July organization of the new units was substantially completed, and all were ready for action when the big push came.[120] "I am of the opinion", Currie was to write later, "that much of the success of the Canadian Corps in the final 100 days was due to the fact that they had sufficient engineers to do the engineering work and that in those closing battles we did not employ the infantry in that kind of work. We trained the infantry for fighting and used them only for fighting."[121]

The period in reserve gave the Corps an opportunity of further expanding the Canadian machine-gun organization by reorganizing its Motor Branch. Existing motor machine-gun units were absorbed, together with the three machine-gun companies of the 5th Division, to form two motor machine-gun brigades*, each of five 8-gun batteries.[122] Added mobility was assured the new brigades by the establishment of a Canadian M.G. Corps Mechanical Transport Company for the administration and maintenance of its transport. The reorganization in May of the Machine Gun Wing of the Canadian Corps School at Aubin-St. Vaast into the Canadian Corps Machine Gun School, and the formation in June of a Machine Gun Wing of the Canadian Corps Reinforcement Camp, completed the changes in the organization of the Machine Gun Corps. At the end of the war its authorized strength had risen to 8771 all ranks.[123]

Dominion Day brought a welcome break in training. Since their arrival in France the Canadians had always made observance of the day one of the highlights of the year, and the 1918 celebration of the holiday topped all others. The 2nd Canadian Division had particular cause for rejoicing as it had just been relieved by the 3rd Division after 92 days continuously in the line. Nearly fifty thousand Canadian soldiers of all ranks gathered in perfect weather at Tincques, a village fourteen miles west of Arras, to witness or compete in the Corps' biggest sports day. As bands played and aeroplanes circled defensively overhead, the huge throng of khaki-clad spectators cheered the competitors in a full programme of track and field events. Among General Currie's distinguished guests were H.R.H. The Duke of Connaught, Sir Robert Borden and members of his cabinet, and General John J. Pershing, the American Commander-in-Chief. The 1st Canadian Division won top honours in track and field, and the 44th Battalion took the Corps soccer championship, in the final game beating the Engineers rather convincingly

* The new 1st C.M.M.G. Brigade was formed from "A" and "B" Batteries (of the original M.M.G. Brigade), the Borden M.M.G. Battery and the 18th C.M.G. Company (from the 5th Division); the 2nd C.M.M.G. Brigade comprised the Eaton and Yukon M.M.G. Batteries, and the 17th and 19th C.M.G. Companies (5th Division).

by a score of 75 to 8.[124] The Sappers, however, had the satisfaction of taking the Corps baseball championship, which was won by the 7th Battalion C.E. The memorable day came to a close with a performance by the "Volatiles", the 1st Divisional Concert Party, of their latest revue, "Take a Chance".

Next day the Prime Minister inspected units of the 1st and 4th Divisions, and on the following Saturday, 6 July, the 3rd Brigade, which had three Highland battalions (13th, 15th and 16th), acted as hosts to a Highland Gathering at Tincques to the Highland regiments of the British Army. All Highland battalions of the Canadian Corps were represented, as were most of the battalions of the 15th (Scottish), 51st (Highland) and 52nd (Lowland) Divisions. A day of competition in Highland games was climaxed by the playing of "Retreat" by the massed pipe bands of the 3rd Brigade and the visiting units—the marching of 284 pipers and 164 drummers providing a soul-stirring spectacle.[125]

The Canadian Corps' long period of rest and training came to end on 15 July, when it relieved the 17th Corps in the line. On the 18th, the same day that Ludendorff began moving his heavy guns northward from the Marne battle, the 2nd Canadian Division was withdrawn into G.H.Q. reserve in readiness for the attack threatening the Second Army in Flanders. The threat passed with the cancellation of Operation "Hagen", but on 20 July General Currie was advised of a new role that the Commander-in-Chief had in mind for the Canadian Corps. On the 27th the 3rd Division returned under Currie's command and three days later the Canadian Corps once more handed over to the 17th Corps.[126]

Since the beginning of the German offensive in March, the Canadians had suffered upwards of 9000 casualties. Of these 5690 had been sustained up to the time when the Corps withdrew into reserve (7 May), and they included losses by the Cavalry Brigade, the 2nd Division and other troops serving in British formations. There were 3998 casualties between 8 May and 7 August inclusive. To the 2nd Division came the honour of another Victoria Cross, won by Corporal Joseph Kaeble of the 22nd Battalion for repulsing an enemy raid virtually single-handed.*

On 22 July 1918 General Currie held a conference of divisional commanders to complete the plans for a Canadian attack against Orange Hill, east of Arras. Only the Corps Commander and a select few of his staff knew that such an operation would *not* take place and that the scheme was only a blind for an attack elsewhere. The discussions were conducted with the utmost realism and were highlighted by a particularly convincing and at times heated argument between General Currie and the G.O.C. 1st Division (who was not in the picture) over the allocation to the latter of (purely imaginary) tanks.

A week later Currie personally informed his divisional commanders of forthcoming offensive operations to be undertaken by the Canadian Corps on the Fourth Army front. Next day the Corps began to move with the utmost secrecy to a concentration area west of Amiens.

* On the evening of 8 June, when the enemy launched a strong raid near Neuville-Vitasse, Cpl. Kaeble, who was the sole survivor of a Lewis gun section in the front-line trenches, jumped over the parapet and swept the attackers with his fire. He stopped the advance of some 50 Germans against his post, and though mortally wounded continued firing as they withdrew.[127]

CHAPTER XIII

AMIENS, 8-11 AUGUST 1918

(See Map 11 and Sketches 47-49)

Prelude to the Offensive

ON 24 JULY, the seventh day of the French counter-attacks on the Marne, General Foch conferred with the Allied Commanders-in-Chief near Melun, twenty-five miles south-east of Paris. The situation on the Western Front gave cause for satisfaction. The German offensive east and west of Reims had been not only checked but turned from mere failure into costly defeat. For the first time since March 1918 the Allies enjoyed an overall superiority in the West—and each month a quarter of a million more American troops were arriving.

The moment had come for the Allies to assume and retain the initiative by turning from the defensive to the offensive. With a view to developing later operations as well as improving France's economic position, Foch proposed to Haig three limited offensives to free essential communications, to be followed by two more to liberate the northern coal-mining area and clear the Germans from the vicinity of Calais and Dunkirk. The Generalissimo was cautious in his optimism as to what these might accomplish. "How long these different operations will take and how far they will carry us", he set down in the memorandum which he presented to the conference, "cannot be determined now. Nevertheless, if the results at which they aim are attained before too late in the year, we can from now onwards look forward to an offensive to be launched at the end of the summer or during the autumn of such importance as will increase our advantages and leave no respite to the enemy."[1]

The first of these planned operations would continue the attacks then in progress, and was aimed at pushing the enemy farther back from the Paris-Chalons-Toul-Avricourt railway, an important lateral line running towards Strasburg. The second (scheduled for 10 August but shortly advanced to the 8th) was to be launched from the Amiens region to remove the threat posed by the Montdidier-Moreuil salient to the Paris-Amiens railway, another vital lateral. The third offensive, an attack on the St. Mihiel salient, was intended to free the eastern portion of the Paris-Avricourt line. Foch was emphatic that these operations and the two in the north should follow each other closely so as to disorganize the enemy's use of reserves and allow him no time to reorganize his forces.[2]

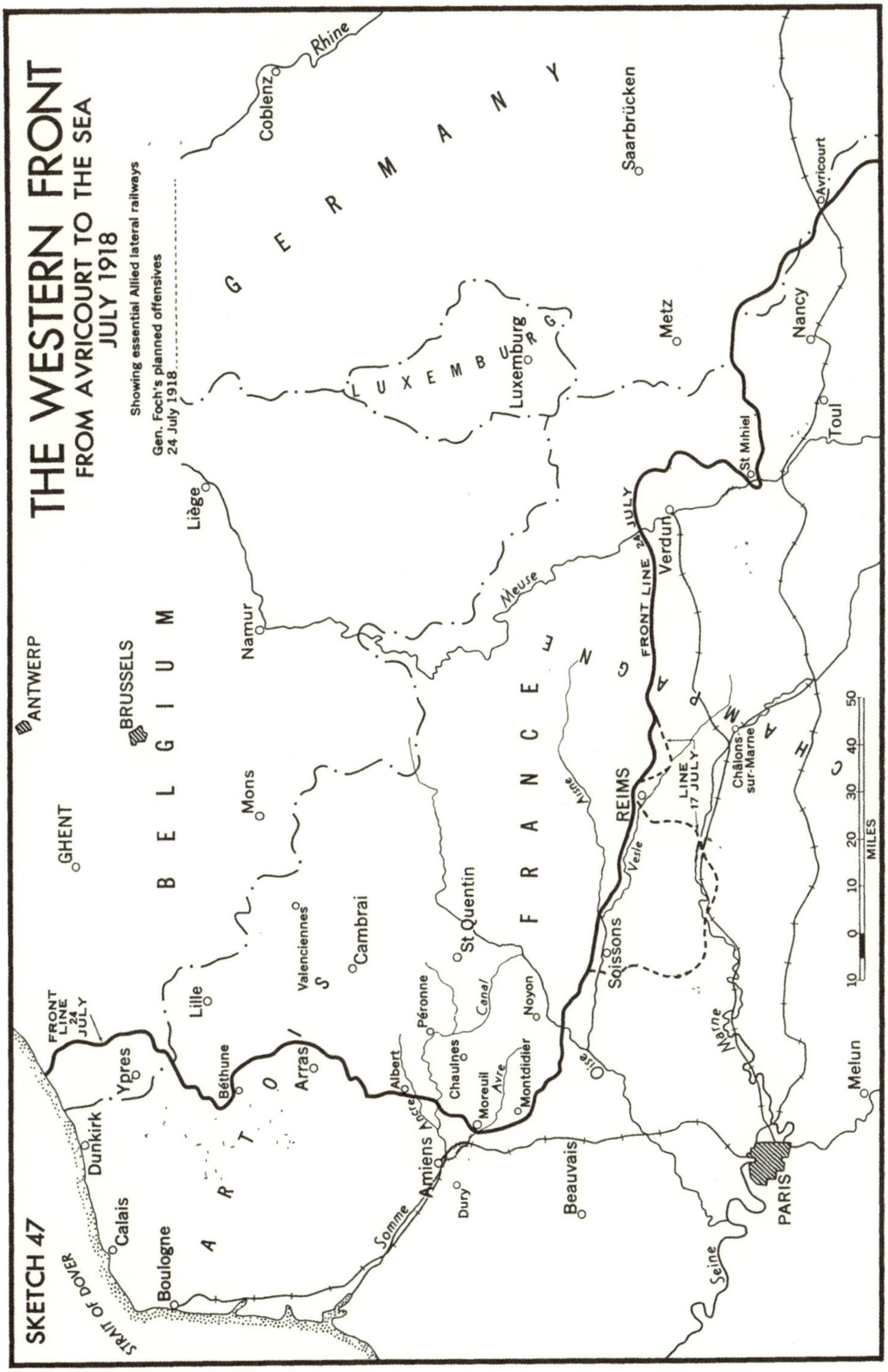
SKETCH 47
THE WESTERN FRONT
FROM AVRICOURT TO THE SEA
JULY 1918
Showing essential Allied lateral railways
Gen. Foch's planned offensives 24 July 1918
FRONT LINE 24 JULY
FRONT LINE 24 JULY
LINE 17 JULY
STRAIT OF DOVER
ANTWERP
BRUSSELS
GHENT
BELGIUM
GERMANY
LUXEMBURG
FRANCE
ARTOIS
CHAMPAGNE
Rhine
Coblenz
Saarbrücken
Metz
Luxemburg
Liège
Namur
Mons
Meuse
Avricourt
Nancy
Toul
St Mihiel
Verdun
REIMS
Vesle
Aisne
Châlons-sur-Marne
Marne
Soissons
Oise
Noyon
St Quentin
Canal
Péronne
Chaulnes
Albert
Ancre
Moreuil
Avre
Montdidier
Amiens
Somme
Dury
Beauvais
PARIS
Seine
Melun
Cambrai
Valenciennes
Lille
Arras
Béthune
Ypres
Dunkirk
Calais
Boulogne
10 0 10 20 30 40 50
MILES

The Marne counter-attack became a mere follow-up of a voluntary German retirement. It met no strong resistance, for the enemy abandoned Soissons and took up a new position on the north bank of the Vesle, content to hold his fire in the hope of being able soon to launch campaigns elsewhere, particularly against the British in Flanders and the French east and south-east of Reims. The German High Command expected an early revival of the French offensive now all but ended, to be followed by a series of thrusts in Flanders, between the Somme and the Oise, east of Reims, against the St. Mihiel salient, and farther south on the Lorraine front. These Allied efforts, in General Ludendorff's view, would take the form of isolated local attacks by troops who were "also tired, yet on the whole not less so than ourselves".[3] He did not foresee that the attacks which took place would develop into a mighty battle across the whole front.

General Foch issued his formal order for the Amiens operation on 28 July. The offensive, which was to be "pushed as far as possible in the direction of Roye", was to be carried out by the British Fourth Army and the French First Army, placed under Haig's command.[4] The Fourth Army (General Rawlinson), which had been reconstituted towards the end of the first German offensive, was in effect the old Fifth Army; a new Fifth Army (General Sir William Birdwood) had been formed on 23 May.[5] Besides his present forces—the Australian Corps and the 3rd Corps—Rawlinson would receive as reinforcement the Canadian Corps, then in reserve to the First Army.

To clear the way for the attack and at the same time give the impression of freeing French forces for operations elsewhere, at the beginning of August the Fourth Army's boundary with the French First Army was moved from the Amiens—Villers-Bretonneux—Chaulnes railway 7000 yards south to the Amiens-Roye-Noyon road. The change was effected without introducing any new formations into the front line, the British 3rd Corps, commanded by Lieut.-General Sir R. H. K. Butler, taking over all Australian positions north of the Somme and the Australian Corps (Lieut.-General Sir John Monash) extending itself as far as the new inter-army boundary. To the enemy this apparent weakening of the front gave no indication of an impending attack. He did not know that the Australians were acting as a screen behind which the Canadian Corps was to concentrate for a major role in the forthcoming offensive. As early as 20 July General Currie had been told of the C.-in-C.'s proposal to use the Canadian Corps in an attack by the French Army to free the Paris-Amiens railway; and on the 26th he learned that General Foch had modified these plans so as to include the French First Army on the right flank.[6] The order of battle for the attack would thus have from right to left two French corps between the Avre River and the Amiens-Roye road, the Canadian Corps between that road and the Amiens-Chaulnes railway, the Australian Corps between the railway and the Somme, and the 3rd Corps between the Somme and the Ancre. Getting the Canadians from the area of the First Army to the Fourth, and thence into their battle positions in the right half of the new Australian sector without disclosing their presence to the enemy posed major problems of security and administration.

"It is of the first importance", G.H.Q. emphasized in elaborating the Generalissimo's orders for the Amiens offensive, "that secrecy should be observed and the operation carried out as a surprise."[7] Instructions on "Secrecy" issued by the Fourth Army directed that on and after 1 August all movement of troops and transport in an easterly direction should take place by night, whether in the forward or back areas, except where daylight moves were absolutely necessary —the R.A.F. was to fly over the Army area and report any signs of abnormal military activity. In order to deceive the enemy as to Allied intentions work would continue on the construction and maintenance of rear lines of defence. Neither the Canadian Corps in its move southward nor divisions in reserve to the 3rd Corps would be permitted to open any wireless stations until after zero hour.[8] Reconnaissance of the German positions was rigidly restricted—"Nothing attracts attention to an offensive more than a large number of officers with maps looking over the parapet and visiting O.P.s."[9] (A party of staff officers from the Canadian Corps were attached to the Australian Corps to allow personal examination of the new area.) Since it was impossible to conceal the preparations for the attack from the troops who were to take part, further security instructions were ordered pasted in every individual's service and pay book. Under the emphatic heading, "KEEP YOUR MOUTH SHUT", these cautioned against loose talk before the offensive and directed that anyone having the ill fortune to be taken prisoner should supply no information beyond rank and name. Though the enemy might use threats, "he will respect you* if your courage, patriotism, and self-control do not fail."[11]

The projected local attack on Orange Hill, east of Arras, opposite the old Canadian sector, was cancelled; but at General Currie's suggestion the preparations for it were continued in the hope of deceiving the enemy.[12] On 27 July, to attract German attention to Flanders, the Royal Air Force was ordered to occupy additional aerodromes in the Second Army's area and to increase activity on that front until 6 August.[13] To the same end the 4th Canadian Mounted Rifles and the 27th Battalion, with certain signal and medical units, were ordered to Flanders on the 29th—ostensibly as an advanced party of the Canadian Corps. The signallers erected their sets and began a flow of dummy wireless traffic to aid in deceiving the enemy.[14] (These units rejoined the main body in its new location two days before the attack.)[15]

These measures were not completely effective. German Intelligence noted the presence of Canadian units with the Second Army, but evidently did not draw the desired conclusion. Prisoners taken in this period stated that the enemy expected an attack astride the Scarpe rather than in Flanders.[16] On 4 August, the German High Command, in notifying General von der Marwitz's Second Army of the disappearance of two Canadian divisions from the front line, pointed to the British Third or Fourth Army as a likely new location.[17] Yet if the enemy was not fully deceived, at least he was confused. A German

*Such an instance had been recorded some weeks earlier by the Royal Air Force. A German battalion commander had told his men to imitate the example of the pilot of a British single-seater forced down behind the enemy lines. He had refused to answer to questioning, even when threatened with shooting. The source of this report?—a German prisoner![10]

divisional staff officer captured by the 2nd Canadian Division on the first day of battle stated that while an attack had been expected, because of British air activity, it was not considered imminent.[18]

On 30 July the main body of the Canadian Corps began to move by train and bus from the Arras area to the concentration area south-west of Amiens. Rigid security restrictions continued. Even the senior A. & Q. staff officer was not notified of the destination until the 29th. As already noted, divisional commanders were informed on the same date, but they were warned not to discuss the matter with subordinates. The troops at first understood that they were going to the Ypres front, "where the Second Army expected a German attack"—a rumor reinforced by fictitious orders.[19] While the transfer of the Canadian Corps and other reinforcements for the Fourth Army was carried out with great secrecy—all trains were loaded and unloaded in darkness—false moves were staged by day, accompanied by much noise, dust and dummy wireless traffic, to a feigned concentration area some twenty miles north-west of Arras.[20] When it was no longer possible to conceal from the troops themselves the general direction in which they were going, they were "officially" informed that the Canadian Corps was in G.H.Q. reserve and might be called on to assist French forces on the Reims-Soissons front, or support either the French First Army or the British Fourth Army.*

During the first week of August nightly marches took the Canadian units from their billets in the concentration area towards their battle assembly positions. The nights were very dark, and to add to the difficulties the approach to the front was made through unfamiliar country and along very narrow roads. There was much congestion of wheeled traffic, which was restricted mainly to the Amiens-Roye and the Amiens-St. Quentin roads, the latter being shared with the Australian Corps. Problems of supply added to the administrative headaches.

The area which the Australians had taken over—soon to be the Canadian sector—was still organized as for French troops, for orders were that "nothing should be done in the area which might arouse the suspicion of the enemy".[22] (This emphasis on secrecy seems to have been misdirected, for, as already noted, the replacement of French by Australian troops was not intended to be a secret.) Storing ammunition at advanced refilling points could not begin in earnest until 3 August, and the nearest Fourth Army ammunition dump was so far away that lorries were unable to make more than one trip daily. Until the 5th or 6th, when the bulk of the heavy artillery transport arrived, there was a shortage of lorries; thereafter the problem was a scarcity of petrol. Fortunately, the weather prevented the enemy's air observers from detecting the abnormal traffic on the forward roads, yet permitted our bombers to fly over the area and cover the

* As not infrequently happens, the emphasis on secrecy was open to question. A Canadian brigade commander, protesting afterwards against the withholding of information from those responsible for planning, urged that in similar situations in the future battalion and company commanders be given a longer period in which to develop their plans and study their maps. He suggested that officers who could not be trusted to maintain secrecy were not fit to command battalions and companies.[21]

noise of tanks moving into position. Considering the tremendous amount of work to be done in such a brief time and under the limitations imposed by security, the administrative preparations went remarkably well. A slight shortage of small-arms ammunition and grenades had to be accepted. Some units, unable to get British grenades in time for the attack, drew from French sources.[23]

In the early hours of 4 August, the enemy raided posts held by the 4th Australian Division astride the Amiens-Roye road and made off with five prisoners. To the credit of the security measures taken by the Australian Corps and divisional staffs these captives gave no information. Even a hint dropped at this time could have turned the Amiens operation into a disaster. This was the future Canadian sector, in which the hand-over was scheduled to begin that evening and end on the night of the 6th-7th. The incident brought a postponement, lest a further raid should disclose the presence of Canadians in the line. Ultimately the relief of the forward troops did not take place until the 8th, within a few hours of zero.[24]

The Opposing Forces

Besides the raid on the 4th, other incidents in the four days preceding the offensive caused concern as to how much the enemy knew of Allied plans. On the afternoon of the 4th the German troops opposite the left of the British 3rd Corps abandoned their bridgehead west of the Ancre, and on the French First Army's front between Montdidier and Moreuil there were similar withdrawals across the Avre and the Rivière des Doms. In Flanders during the next three days the enemy retired 1500 yards on a ten-mile front. Meanwhile, on the morning of the 6th, in a local attack on a two-and-a-half-mile front between the Somme and the lower Ancre, the Germans made advances of up to 800 yards and took some 235 British prisoners. As it happened, the purpose of these moves was to eliminate salients or otherwise shorten the line. None was related to the forthcoming Franco-British operation; and according to the Germans themselves the prisoners taken on the 6th gave no hint of an impending offensive. The German attack on the Fourth Army's left, however, necessitated a change in the British start line and the fire plan. A counter-attack next day tired out troops who were to fight again on the 8th, and though it recovered part of the lost ground, the enemy was now very much more on his guard here.[25] Yet he could learn nothing on the Amiens front from aerial observation. When the weather was not adverse, the German flyers were driven back by superior Allied air strength.[26]

On the Fourth Army's right the French First Army, commanded by General Debeney, had in the line seven divisions which would be engaged on the opening day along an eight-mile front centred about Moreuil. As the battle developed additional formations would be brought in on the right flank; and it was Foch's intention that ultimately the French Third Army (General Humbert), on the south side of the German salient, would join in the attack. On General Rawlinson's own front there would be three Canadian divisions from just south of the Roye

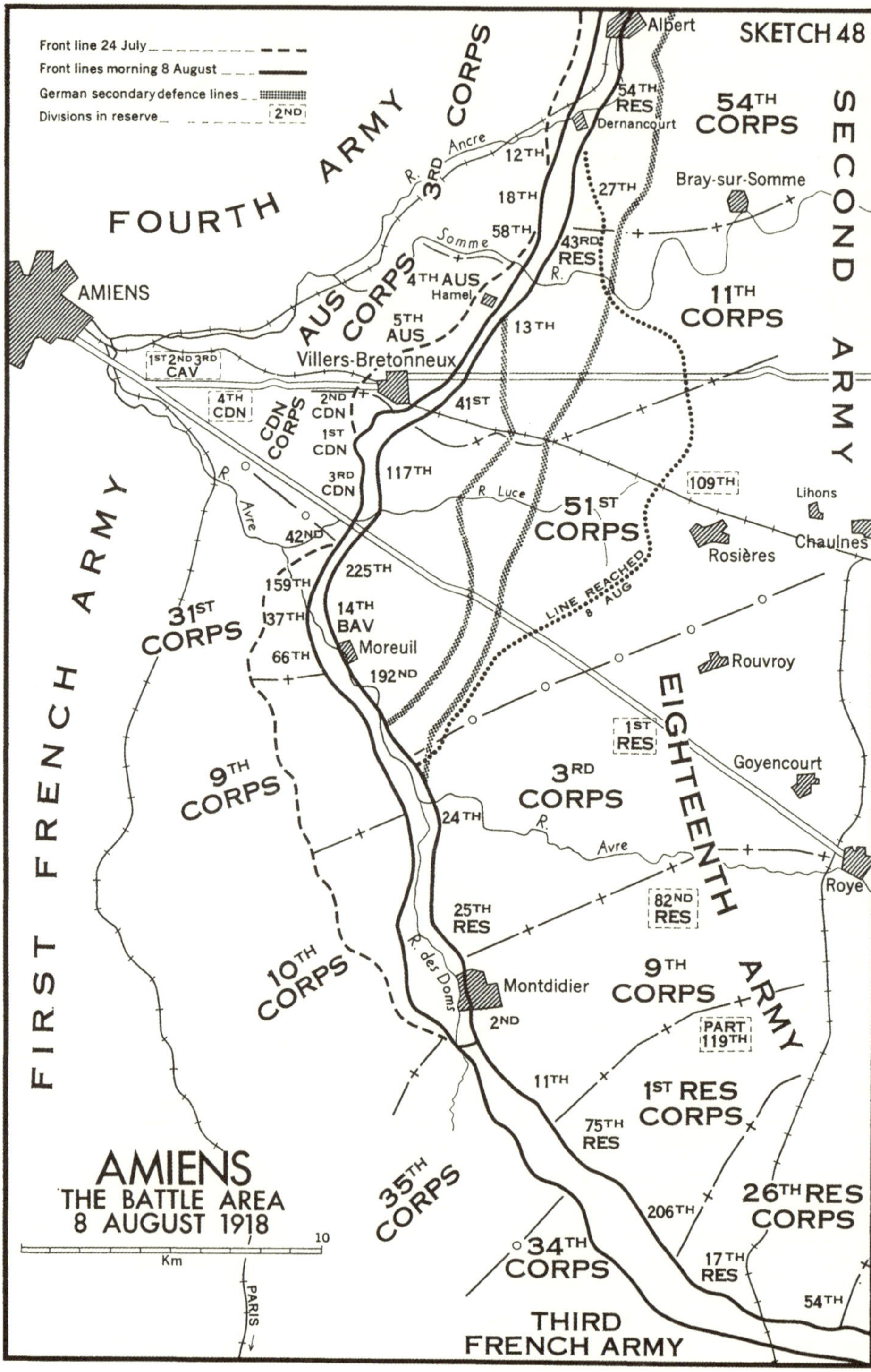
SKETCH 48
Front line 24 July
Front lines morning 8 August
German secondary defence lines
Divisions in reserve
2ND
Albert
Dernancourt
Bray-sur-Somme
AMIENS
Hamel
Villers-Bretonneux
Lihons
Chaulnes
Rosières
Moreuil
Rouvroy
Goyencourt
Roye
Montdidier
R. Ancre
Somme
R. Luce
R. Avre
R. des Doms
FOURTH ARMY
3RD CORPS
AUS CORPS
CDN CORPS
SECOND ARMY
54TH CORPS
11TH CORPS
51ST CORPS
3RD CORPS
EIGHTEENTH ARMY
9TH CORPS
1ST RES CORPS
26TH RES CORPS
FIRST FRENCH ARMY
31ST CORPS
9TH CORPS
10TH CORPS
35TH CORPS
34TH CORPS
THIRD FRENCH ARMY
LINE REACHED 8 AUG
1ST 2ND 3RD CAV
4TH CDN
2ND CDN
1ST CDN
3RD CDN
4TH AUS
5TH AUS
12TH
18TH
58TH
13TH
41ST
117TH
225TH
14TH BAV
42ND
159TH
37TH
66TH
192ND
24TH
25TH RES
2ND
11TH
75TH RES
206TH
17TH RES
54TH
54TH RES
27TH
43RD RES
109TH
1ST RES
82ND RES
PART 119TH
AMIENS
THE BATTLE AREA
8 AUGUST 1918
10
Km
PARIS

road to just north of the railway to Chaulnes; and between the railway and the Ancre River two divisions of the Australian Corps and three of the British 3rd Corps. In immediate reserve were three French, one Canadian and two Australian divisions—making a total of twenty-one Allied divisions opposing von der Marwitz's fourteen.

The Allied attack would have massive artillery support. The French had 780 field and 826 heavy or super-heavy guns, which gave them a field piece to every forty-five yards of front and a heavy to each forty-two yards. The Fourth Army had 1386 field guns and howitzers—twenty-nine yards' frontage per piece—and 684 heavies, one to each fifty-nine yards.[27] Whereas the Germans had few if any tanks opposite Amiens,* their opponents possessed 604 tanks of all types. The Fourth Army would employ 324 heavy fighting tanks and exploit with 96 "Whippet" medium tanks. (The standard fighting tank was now the Mark V, which, despite thicker armour than previous models, was somewhat faster—4.6 miles per hour as compared with 3.7—and more manoeuvrable. The Whippet, which weighed fourteen tons, was armed only with light machine-guns, and had an average speed of five miles per hour.) Seventy-two Whippets were allotted to French follow-up forces.[29]

In the air the Germans were considerably outnumbered. The British Fourth Army had available 800 machines—239 heavy bombers (day and night), 376 fighters, and 185 reconnaissance or fighter-reconnaissance planes—and the French First Army had a total of 1349 aircraft. His main air strength being in Champagne, the enemy had only 365 machines of all types opposite the British Fourth and French First Armies. This disparity was somewhat reduced, however, by the arrival of German air reinforcements on the first day of the operation.[30]

The front on which the British Fourth Army was to attack coincided exactly with that held by the German Second Army (General von der Marwitz). This army was the extreme left wing of Crown Prince Rupprecht's Group of Armies. On its left was the Eighteenth Army, forming with the Ninth Army the right wing of Crown Prince Wilhelm's Group of Armies. In anticipation of a renewed Allied effort in the sector held by these three armies a decision had been reached to combine them under a new Army Group Headquarters, to be commanded by General von Boehn (previously commanding the Seventh Army), with General von Lossberg as his Chief of Staff. The new arrangement became effective on 12 August. It had been Ludendorff's hope to hand von Boehn a well consolidated line. "Unfortunately", he wrote, "events were to prove me wrong."[31] The Second Army had ten divisions in the front line and four in reserve. In addition, the boundary with the Eighteenth Army (General von Hutier) ran north-eastward across the Amiens-Roye road, putting two of that army's reserve divisions (the 1st Reserve and the 119th) in the rear area of the Allied objective.[32]

General von der Marwitz judged only two of his divisions to be "fully battle fit", but a staff officer sent by Ludendorff to discuss with the Second Army

* They had a total of 40 tanks in the field—fifteen of German make and twenty-five captured from the Allies.[28]

defensive measures on the front Albert-Moreuil (the actual area attacked on 8 August) reported that it was necessary to relieve only two divisions that were very tired after a long period of service in the line.[33] The sector where the Canadians were to strike was manned by three divisions rated by their commander as "average"—from south to north the 225th and 117th Divisions, and part of the 41st Division. At the time of the attack the 117th had barely completed its relief of the 109th Division, a battle-worn formation of like calibre.[34]

Ludendorff seems to have been satisfied that the Second Army's defences were in reasonably good order, though he noted that von der Marwitz had fallen behind the Eighteenth Army in the construction of field works. Otherwise the lessons learned in the setback on 18 July had been put to good use—"the divisional fronts were narrow, artillery was plentiful and the trench system was organized in depth".[35] Marwitz's own headquarters expected only strong local attacks. Reports of the assembly of British tanks (which not even the most thorough deception programme could fully conceal) were attributed to "phantoms of the imagination or nervousness".[36] On 4 August, Ludendorff, more concerned about the morale of his own troops—many of whom were "depressed down to Hell"—than the possibility of a surprise attack, issued an order of the day in which he sought to dispel the feeling of apprehension with which many were reported to be viewing the possibility of an Allied offensive. He declared that the French owed their successes in the counter-offensive of 18 July to their tanks, and that these would not have been formidable if the German infantry had not allowed itself to be surprised, and had the artillery been sufficiently distributed in depth. This situation had been rectified on the Second Army's front by effecting a judicious organization in depth of infantry and guns. "Henceforward", he went on with grand assurance,

> . . . we can await every hostile attack with the greatest confidence. As I have already explained, we should wish for nothing better than to see the enemy launch an offensive, which can but hasten the disintegration of his forces . . . .[37]

The Plan of Battle

The pattern for the Amiens offensive had been set at Cambrai in the previous November. Since then the proper use of tanks in the attack had been strikingly demonstrated in a more recent and completely successful tank-infantry operation on a smaller scale on 4 July, when ten battalions of the 4th Australian Division had teamed up with sixty British tanks to capture the town of Hamel, between Villers-Bretonneux and the Somme[38]. In general the area of the forthcoming battle was well suited to the employment of armour. The country was a rolling plateau, with little relief in the French sector, but broken in the north by the valleys of tributaries of the Somme and the Avre. One of these, the Luce, had cut a wide trench nearly 200 feet deep that ran through the Canadian sector of attack. The Luce flowed generally down the line of the 1st Canadian Division's axis, its side branches cutting across the division's routes forward, and the river had to be crossed by the right wing of the 3rd Canadian Division before the battle opened. Only two crossings were available behind the start line: to construct other bridges or causeways would have risked betraying the Allied intentions.

Apart from a few woods and orchard-encircled villages that offered obvious defensive possibilities, the German positions south of the Somme consisted of little more than three lines of trench, poorly wired and without good shelters. Behind the front system adjoining no man's land, instead of the usual battle zone and rear zone, the enemy relied on the former French Amiens defences (above, p. 371,*n.*). The inner, or more westerly of these, crossing the front through Marcelcave, Demuin and Mézières, consisted of a series of disconnected posts dating from 1915; the outer line, which passed east of Harbonnières, Caix and Hangest, was well wired, but most of the wire was on the east side. Between these the enemy had constructed a length of trench in March 1918. The main strength of the defence proved to lie in a vast number of hidden machine-guns scattered in great depth across the front.[39]

The orders issued the Fourth Army by General Rawlinson on 6 August contemplated much more than the original intention of freeing the Paris-Amiens railway. At a conference on 5 August Sir Douglas Haig had impressed on his army and corps commanders that with General Foch's proposal to bring the French Third Army into the operation the battle would develop into one of considerable magnitude. There was to be less emphasis on consolidation and more on exploitation. Cambrai had taught the need for strong infantry reserves to follow up tank successes. To this end three British divisions were assembled in G.H.Q. reserve and held close behind the battle front in readiness to "maintain the fight and to take full advantage of any success gained".[40] The Outer Amiens Defence Line, seven miles distant, was now only an initial objective. It would be the Fourth Army's role to push forward as rapidly as possible a further eight miles to the line Roye-Chaulnes—roughly the old front line held by the British in the spring of 1917 before the German retreat to the Hindenburg Line. If the enemy could be thrust back towards Ham (thirteen miles beyond Chaulnes), the operations of the French driving north-eastwards from the Noyon-Montdidier front would be greatly facilitated.[41]

To the Canadian Corps fell the responsibility of striking the main blow on the Fourth Army's right. From its boundary with the French First Army the Corps start line crossed the Amiens-Roye road at Hourges, a village about nine miles from Amiens, and continued in a north-easterly direction for half a mile to the River Luce. It then turned north for 4500 yards before bending towards the east again to cut the Amiens-Chaulnes railway a mile beyond Villers-Bretonneux. The Corps task on the first day was to capture an intermediate objective (the Green Line) and to seize and hold the Red Line, which ran in a north-easterly direction from Mézières, south of the Roye road, to just west of Harbonnières (north of the railway). The Australian Corps would attack on the left of the Canadians, while north of the Somme the 3rd Corps, keeping its left on the Ancre, would occupy the north end of the old Amiens line and consolidate it as a defensive flank to the advance of the main forces farther south. The 2nd Canadian Division, on General Currie's left flank, had as an additional objective the Blue Line, which angled forward from the Red towards the village of Harbonnières (in the Australian sector).[42]

The infantry having done their job, it was planned that the Cavalry Corps would pass through at the Red Line to capture the Outer Amiens Defence Line, represented on the operations map by the Blue Dotted Line. For this purpose the 3rd Cavalry Division (which included the Canadian Cavalry Brigade) was placed directly under General Currie's command. There was special provision to give added strength on the Corps right, where greater resistance was expected (below, p. 405). The 4th Canadian Division, advancing from corps reserve at zero hour behind the two infantry divisions attacking on the right, was to pass through at the Red Line and either relieve the 3rd Cavalry Division in the Blue Dotted Line between the Roye road and Caix, or assist in the capture of that objective. The cavalry would then push forward to the line Roye-Chaulnes. Meanwhile, south of the Amiens-Roye road the French attack would develop from left to right as the Canadians advanced, with the 31st Corps directed on Hangest and the 9th Corps keeping contact on the right. The attack by General Debeney's right, south of Montdidier, was not due to start until 9 August.[43]

The time set for the assault by the Canadian and Australian Corps was 4:20 a.m. To aid surprise there would be no preliminary bombardment, the infantry counting on the barrage and the tanks to deal with the enemy wire and machine-guns. The French, however, having lost most of their heavy tanks on the Marne front in July had only a limited number of light tanks available for the forthcoming operation. Consequently surprise on their front would be sacrificed for an artillery bombardment of forty-five minutes, synchronized to begin with the opening of the Fourth Army's barrage at zero. Their assault would go in at 5:05.[44]

With so deep a penetration planned for the Canadians, the provision of adequate artillery support necessitated special arrangements. For the first two miles or more the assaulting battalions would have the benefit of the full weight of the barrage; thenceforth they would be assisted as far forward as possible by the heavy guns, and this support would be supplemented by batteries of field artillery (a brigade to each infantry division) leapfrogging forward to new positions in captured territory to keep the enemy within range. Altogether General Currie had at his disposal seventeen brigades of field artillery, nine heavy brigades, three batteries of 6-inch guns and one 12-inch howitzer battery—a total of 646 pieces. These included all the Canadian artillery units in France except the 1st and 2nd Brigades Canadian Garrison Artillery, which had remained with the First Army. The Royal Artillery provided a divisional artillery firing in the barrage, two heavy brigades on miscellaneous bombardment tasks, six heavy brigades on counter-battery, and four heavy batteries on long-range harassing fire.[45]

Each of the three assaulting Canadian divisions was allotted a battalion of 42 fighting tanks from the British 4th Tank Brigade. (The 4th Division, in corps reserve, received a 36-tank battalion.) These were distributed among the infantry brigades, and to ensure continuous armoured support a number were held back for committal after the first two objectives had been reached. Tanks were sub-allotted to battalions in sections of three, and an infantryman was detailed to ride in each tank to maintain liaison between the tank commander and the infantry.[46] There were also attached to each infantry division an average of six Mark IV supply tanks charged with delivering to the forward units trench-mortar and small-arms ammunition, drinking water, wire, stakes and picks and shovels. Each tank battalion had six supply tanks to bring petrol forward, and the Corps Chief Engineer was allotted six to carry additional equipment and stores to the final objective. Although numerous breakdowns caused serious delays in the early stages of the operation, the supply tanks later proved of great help in maintaining the advance.[47]

Air cooperation and support for the Canadians was provided by No. 5 (Corps Reconnaissance) Squadron R.A.F., which was attached to the Canadian Corps from July 1918 to the end of the war. The primary task of this and similar units on 8 August was the laying of smoke-screens at points beyond the artillery's range and supplementing the artillery smoke-screens with 40-pound phosphorus bombs. (There was a shortage of the 60-pound artillery smoke shells.) As things turned out a heavy morning mist that blanketed the whole area of attack was to reduce the need for a smoke-screen but also interfere with the provision of all forms of air support. Smoke bombs were nevertheless accurately dropped on the Canadian and Australian fronts and provided useful screening; and as the mist cleared away during the morning, patrols of the 5th Squadron flew over the battlefield trying to keep located the continually changing and always indefinite line where the foremost troops were in conflict with the enemy.[48]

In assigning his three assault divisions their positions General Currie placed the 1st Canadian Division in the centre, with the 2nd Division on its left and the 3rd on its right. The role of the 3rd Division, attacking astride the Amiens-Roye road, was one of special difficulty, not only because of the handicap imposed by the valley of the River Luce, but because of General Lipsett's responsibility to protect the Canadian right flank until the French, starting their advance at 5:05, should catch up. Accordingly the 3rd Division was given a somewhat narrower frontage for its initial attack, and its barrage would be furnished by six field artillery brigades as against four for each of the other infantry divisions.[49] A special international force was organized to provide liaison with the French. It consisted of a platoon of the 43rd Battalion and a detachment of some 30 men, with a machine-gun, from the French 42nd Division.[50]

Once the 3rd Division had made good its Red Line objective, the task of protecting the cavalry's right flank and providing liaison between cavalry and infantry was to be carried out by the "Canadian Independent Force", composed of the 1st and 2nd Motor Machine Gun Brigades, nine Lewis gun detachments of the Canadian Corps Cyclist Battalion and a section of two 6-inch trench mortars mounted on trucks. The Force, which was commanded by Brig.-Gen.

Brutinel, was to secure the Amiens-Roye road between the second and third objectives, and be ready to exploit further success.[51]

The Battle Opens, 8 August—The Assault by the 3rd Division

The night of 7-8 August was fine with no moon. There was a tense air of expectancy as the troops earmarked for the assault moved up under cover of darkness to their assembly area.* On the Canadian Corps right the 3rd Division relieved an Australian brigade at 2:00 a.m.; it was four o'clock, only twenty minutes from zero, before the last of General Lipsett's attacking units were in position. By that time a thick ground mist had begun to form in the valleys, blotting out visibility even after the sun had risen. The supporting tanks began to move forward at twelve minutes before zero from positions one thousand yards behind the front. To drown the hum of their engines—running as quietly as possible in second gear—the artillery maintained a normal harassing fire, and a large bombing plane droned noisily up and down above the forward trenches. Exactly at 4:20 the barrage opened with the thunder of more than nine hundred guns and immediately the assaulting infantry pressed forward.[54] In the Luce valley, where the mist was especially heavy, the Canadians were hard put to it to keep pace and direction. The enemy's barrage came down within a few minutes of zero, but thanks to the excellent counter-battery work of the British guns the German fire was generally erratic and not particularly damaging.

The 1st and 2nd Divisions were each attacking on a single brigade frontage, using a fresh brigade at successive lines of advance, but because the River Luce split the 3rd Division's front General Lipsett employed two brigades in the initial phase. He crowded three battalions of the 9th Brigade and a company of the 5th Tank Battalion into the narrow bridgehead south of the river about Hourges, while on his left flank the 8th Brigade assaulted with a single battalion up.

The leading battalions advanced well deployed so as to reduce the number of casualties from the enemy's fire. In general each was disposed in five waves at intervals of one hundred yards. Skirmishers in the foremost wave of two lines, thirty yards apart, helped guide the tanks. The next three waves consisted of well dispersed section columns in single file; and carrying parties brought up the rear. The infantry found themselves less heavily burdened than in former operations; for to meet the requirements of a prolonged yet rapid advance General Rawlinson's staff had devised a modified "fighting order"† which eliminated some unnecessary weight and distributed the rest more evenly.[55]

*Each division reported assembly completed by sending Corps Headquarters the code word "Llandovery Castle". Operational instructions for the attack issued by Canadian Corps Headquarters bore the initials "L.C."[52] The *Llandovery Castle*, a British merchant vessel serving as a Canadian hospital ship, had been torpedoed on 27 June 1918, while returning to England from Halifax. Of a Canadian crew and medical staff totalling 258 all ranks, only 24 survived. Among those who perished were the fourteen Canadian Nursing Sisters aboard.[53]

†This consisted of haversack, 250 rounds of ammunition (100 in bandoliers), gas mask, water bottle, "iron rations" (corned beef and biscuits), entrenching tool, two Mills bombs and two sandbags.

Brig.-Gen. D. M. Ormond's 9th Brigade achieved early and satisfying success. Taken completely by surprise the Germans allowed themselves to be overrun in their positions, many surrendering without firing a shot. In a little more than an hour the 43rd Battalion on the right had men in Rifle (or "Dodo") Wood, immediately south of the main road; but it was not until 7:30, after the 116th Battalion had overcome German resistance north of the road and tanks had worked their way southward among the shattered stumps cleaning out machine-gun posts, that the wood could be reported free of enemy. There were regimental claims of upwards of 40 machine-guns captured, and more than 250 German prisoners.[56] The tanks had found the going hard. Handicapped by lack of a detailed ground reconnaissance—which was forbidden in the interests of security—they were blinded by the dense mist and further impeded by the marshy ground. Many were late in starting and all found it virtually impossible to maintain direction and keep touch with the foot soldiers as tank-infantry co-operation largely broke down.[57]

By half-past seven the 9th Brigade had reached the Green Line. The 116th Battalion, suffering fairly heavy casualties, had captured Hamon Wood, between the Luce and the Roye road; and on the divisional left the 58th Battalion, working closely with its tanks, had fought its way into the village of Demuin on the south bank of the river.* The battalion then pressed on to occupy Courcelles, just before the Green Line.[59] North of the Luce, in Brig.-Gen. D. C. Draper's narrow sector, the 1st Canadian Mounted Rifles got well ahead of its tanks in the morning mist and in forty minutes had captured its first objective, Cemetery Copse, unaided. The tanks came up in time to help clear the nearby village of Hangard, moving on to form a bridgehead over the Luce at Demuin. The 2nd C.M.R. then passed through to complete the 8th Brigade's part in the first stage.[60]

These were exhilarating successes, but there was no time to lose if the momentum of the attack was to be maintained. While the 3rd Division's assaulting units had been winning their way to the Green Line, behind them the reserve infantry battalions of the 7th Brigade, moving up on a strict schedule, had filed over the Luce on duckboard bridges and marched forward in high spirits as they met an ever-increasing flow of German prisoners being shepherded to the rear. They passed through the 8th and 9th Brigades, and in jumping-off trenches at the far edge of Hamon Wood and to the north they formed up ready for the next phase of the operation.

Promptly at 8:20 the attack was resumed, Brig.-Gen. Dyer sending forward the 49th Battalion on the left, the 42nd in the centre, and The Royal Canadian Regiment on the right astride the Roye road. Progress was rapid. The 49th Battalion, meeting little opposition in its advance across the unfenced fields of standing grain, reached the Red Line at ten o'clock. In the centre the 42nd, having overrun two German batteries that were engaging it with point-blank

* In this attack an N.C.O. of the 58th Battalion, Corporal H. G. B. Miner, rushed three enemy posts—two of them single-handed—and turned a captured machine-gun on the enemy with telling effect. He was awarded the Victoria Cross, posthumously, having been mortally wounded at the third position.[58]

fire, crossed over the plateau of Hill 102 and arrived on its objective with four supporting tanks at 10:20. The last part of the advance, wrote the regimental historian, "was more or less of a route march enlivened by the sight of the panic-stricken enemy running in every direction".[61]

Meanwhile the R.C.R., proceeding with "something approaching the clock-like precision of a well rehearsed manoeuvre", was already on its objective, having cleared two woods with the assistance of the few surviving tanks.[62] On the Canadian Corps' right the Franco-Canadian liaison detachment, while maintaining contact between the 3rd Canadian and 42nd French Divisions' flanks, had contrived to clear a small copse south of Rifle Wood, taking thirty prisoners and a dozen machine-guns. On reaching the Green Line the original Canadian component rejoined its parent unit (the 43rd Battalion) and was replaced by a platoon from the R.C.R.

The 3rd Division had completed its assignment, though of its original 42 tanks only eight remained. The final infantry advance to the Blue Dotted Line on this part of the front was to be made by the 4th Canadian Division.

In German eyes the capture of the southern part of the Red Line had settled the fate of the 225th Division, except at Mézières, outside the Canadian right boundary. The official German report spoke of the loss of the entire artillery position and the virtual destruction of all the front line and support battalions. The division's reserve battalions, rushed in piecemeal, "had either been thrown back or had not got into action at all".[63] Towards 10:00 a.m., the faltering 225th Division was told that the 376th Regiment of the 109th Division was being placed under its command and sent to Cayeux. It would also receive the Regiment Bellmann, composed of the three resting battalions of the 192nd Division, being assembled in the wooded area south-east of Beaucourt. In addition the 1st Reserve Division from the neighbouring corps of the Eighteenth Army was moving forward astride the Roye-Amiens road with orders to stop any Canadian attacks in the Beaucort-Fresnoy area.[64]

The Advance on the Corps Left

We must now go back and examine the fortunes of General Currie's remaining assault divisions. The 1st Canadian Division, in the Corps centre, had been given the task of breaking through the wooded area north of the Luce and fighting forward from Hangard Wood on a decreasing frontage to the Outer Amiens Defence Line beyond Caix. In the later stages General Macdonell's forces would have to negotiate the valley of the Luce, which was flanked by a number of tree-clad ravines that gave the defender every advantage.

The initial phase was carried out by the 3rd Brigade (Brig.-Gen. Tuxford)—from right to left, the 16th, 13th and 14th Battalions. While the dense mist made infantry-tank cooperation difficult, it had the advantage of hiding the attackers from the German view, thereby substantially reducing the effectiveness of the enemy's fire. Disregarding threats from flank and rear, the Canadians

THE FIRST OF THE HUNDRED DAYS

As British Mark V tanks with infantry of the 3rd Canadian Division move forward through Hourges on 8 August 1918, they meet returning Canadian wounded and German prisoners.

AFTER AMIENS

German guns captured by the Fourth Army in the Amiens battle. Those in the foreground fell to the 2nd Canadian Division and the British 3rd Tank Battalion.

HAIG COMPLIMENTS CANADIANS

Presumably at the Field Marshal's request, troops of the 85th Battalion stand easy as Sir Douglas congratulates them on their performance during the Battle of Amiens.

CAVALRY AWAIT THE BREAK-THROUGH

A squadron of the Royal Canadian Dragoons on the Arras front pass German wounded during the September fighting.

pushed quickly ahead. Small detachments which became involved in local actions left the mopping up for succeeding waves. So rapid was the advance that the 3rd and 5th Battalions, which theoretically were not involved in this stage of the attack,* found themselves committed in sharp encounters with parties of Germans that had been by-passed. Twenty-five hundred yards from the start line fighting developed all along the trenches which formed the enemy's main line of resistance in front of his artillery positions.[65] It was here that Private J. B. Croak earned the first of two Victoria Crosses won that day by members of the 13th Battalion. Having attacked and captured a machine-gun nest single-handed, Croak, though badly wounded, later charged another German strongpoint and with the aid of other members of his platoon silenced three machine-guns, bayoneting or capturing their crews. Wounded a second time, he died just after the last resistance was overcome.[66] Equally courageous was Corporal H. J. Good, of the 13th, in disposing of three machine-guns and their crews, and then with the assistance of three comrades, assaulting and capturing a German battery of 5.9-inch guns and their entire crews.[67]

Beyond Aubercourt, where the division entered the Luce Valley, the speed of the advance quickened, for with the lifting of the fog the 3rd Brigade was able to get forward its supporting tanks (of the 4th Tank Battalion) to deal with troublesome enemy machine-guns. In a quarry on the river bank east of the village a party from the 16th Battalion aided by a tank flushed the regimental commander and headquarters staff of the 157th Regiment (117th Division).[68] The battalion crossed the Luce, and abreast of the 13th and 14th reached the Green Line by 8:15 a.m. Almost immediately the attacking battalions of Brig.-Gen. Griesbach's 1st Brigade leapfrogged the 3rd Brigade units and were on their way to the Red Line.[69]

In this second stage the advance of all three battalions followed the same pattern. On several occasions they were held up by the fire of German machine-guns advantageously sited on the high ridges or concealed in the small woods that interspersed the grain fields. Before their tanks caught up, the infantry had only the support of their own Lewis guns in dealing with these.† Canadian casualties were light, most of the losses coming from German artillery fire. By eleven o'clock the 2nd Battalion, south of the Luce, had reached its objective and established outposts on the high ground east of Cayeux. In the centre the 4th Battalion, advancing astride the river bed, cleared Cayeux without meeting much opposition; while on the Brigade left the 3rd Battalion, having run into trouble in the deep ravines that entered the Luce valley from the north, made good its portion of the Red Line by 11:30.[71]

By this time General Macdonell's front had narrowed considerably, so that the 2nd Brigade (Brig.-Gen. Loomis) was able to advance to the Blue Dotted Line

*The former was scheduled to take part in the advance from the Green to the Red Line; the latter was on loan to the 3rd Brigade as a reserve.

†So rapid had been the advance that the 2nd Brigade C.F.A., detailed to provide the 1st Division with mobile artillery support, could not keep the enemy in range. During the morning its guns were in action east of Morgemont Wood, and in the late afternoon the batteries moved up to the banks of the Luce at the Red Line.[70]

with only two battalions forward, each moving on a two-company front. The 7th Battalion, delayed by the absence of bridges over the Luce and the congestion caused by the long cavalry columns in their passage forward, came up through the 1st Brigade's right wing an hour and a half later. There was no longer any organized enemy resistance, though the assaulting companies had still to contend with isolated machine-gun nests and sniping from the more determined elements of the rapidly retreating enemy.[72] By half-past one the 10th Battalion, attacking north of the Luce, had worked through the village of Caix and captured its final objectives in the old Amiens Outer Line. An hour later the arrival of the 7th Battalion at the Blue Dotted Line completed the 1st Division's task.[73]

German losses had been very great. Thanks to the good work done by the heavy artillery supporting the Canadian attack, many troops of the 117th Division had been pinned in their shelters until overrun. Resting battalions, thrown in piecemeal, had suffered heavily in attempting to stand and even more severely in the subsequent retreat. Examination after the battle showed that the neutralization of German batteries had been very effective. The Canadians captured many batteries that had not fired a shot, although there were some cases of German gun crews being credited with firing until the last round before they deliberately destroyed their pieces. According to official German sources the 117th Division was virtually wiped out.[74] In an effort to bolster resistance opposite the centre of the Canadian front, the German Second Army was thrusting in the 119th Division, borrowed, like the 1st Reserve Division, from the neighbouring Eighteenth Army. Farther north the exhausted 109th Division, which, as we have noted, had been relieved by the 117th only a short time before, on the morning of the 8th, was rushed forward from corps reserve to Harbonnières, and thrown into action opposite the Canadian left. It was evening before the 119th Division arrived, but by 8:40 p.m. it could report having plugged the last gap in the Second Army's front, in the area Caix-Beaucourt.[75]

The advance of the 2nd Canadian Division on the Corps left on 8 August took place over more favourable ground than that assigned to the rest of the Corps. The rolling plateau, largely covered by grain crops, which in some places had already been harvested, afforded little cover to the enemy except in the villages and where an occasional wooded gully ran back from the River Luce. Of these villages, the one thought most likely to prove troublesome was Marcelcave, adjoining the Amiens-Chaulnes railway and just short of the Green Line objective. Since Marcelcave was out of range of most of the field artillery, a forty-five-minute bombardment by heavy guns was arranged to be fired while the infantry worked their way around on either side.[76] The divisional commander, Major-General Sir Henry Burstall, planned to use in order the 4th, 5th and 6th Brigades in the successive phases of the advance to the Blue Dotted Line.

When the assault went in at 4:20 a.m., with the 18th Battalion on the right and the 19th next to the railway, the mist, as it had done in other sectors, prevented the tanks (of the 14th Tank Battalion) from giving immediate support. Within half an hour, however, these were well on their way and doing a good job in helping to knock out hostile machine-guns. Early in its advance on the 4th Brigade's right a company of the 18th Battalion (which found its tank support "one of the finest features of the day") was able to aid the 14th Battalion (of the 1st Division) in the capture of Morgemont Wood, which lay south of the inter-divisional boundary. A number of machine-guns fell into Canadian hands, and by the time the 18th Battalion reached the Green Line, it had overrun a battery of 5.9-inch howitzers and another of 77-millimetre guns.[77]

In the meantime the progress of the 19th Battalion had been accelerated by the parallel advance along the railway of two companies of the 21st Australian Battalion, whose Lewis guns effectively cut down German opposition in front of the Canadians.[78] "Almost better than could be hoped for" was the way in which a 2nd Canadian Division report was to describe this cooperation by the Australians.[79] Entry into Marcelcave after the bombardment was relatively easy, though there was stiff fighting, in which the supporting 21st Canadian Battalion was involved, before the village was finally cleared. Farther along the railway lay the villages of Wiencourt and Guillaucourt, which were in the sector of the 148th Regiment—the left wing of the 41st Division—and at 8:20 a.m. the 5th Brigade (Brig.-Gen. J. M. Ross) passed through to deal with these in the second phase of the operation.[80]

The main opposition met by the 24th Battalion, on the Brigade left, and the 26th on the right, still came from scattered machine-gun posts, whose positions could not be sufficiently defined to be engaged by the artillery. It was difficult for the tanks to deal with these, as the mist had risen and the fighting had advanced out of range of protective smoke-screens. There were costly tank casualties from German batteries firing over open sights; and those that took evasive action by dodging about the country soon found themselves short of petrol. It took longer to clear Pieuret Wood and Snipe Copse, east and south-east of Marcelcave, than it did to secure Wiencourt, the first of the two villages in the 5th Brigade's path. A mile to the east fairly heavy fighting developed in and around Guillaucourt. The 18-pounders of the 5th Brigade Canadian Field Artillery, which had moved forward to Marcelcave, gave useful support, being supplemented by five German field-pieces captured in Pieuret Wood.[81]

It was about 2:15 p.m. when the 5th Brigade reached its Red Line objective. By half-past two the three batteries of the 5th Brigade C.F.A. had moved up to positions just west of Guillaucourt to support the final advance by the 6th Infantry Brigade. (Before the day ended every battery in the artillery brigade had taken up new positions at least five times in support of the rapidly advancing infantry.)[82] British units of the 1st Cavalry Division had taken the lead, and following them the 29th (on the left) and 31st Battalions crossed the Red Line at 4:30 p.m. Apart from some hostile shelling, opposition was negligible. The Canadian infantry passed through a British cavalry regiment a thousand yards short of the outer Amiens defences and, by early evening, were firmly established on the Blue Dotted Line. North of the railway, however, where the 15th Australian Brigade had not reached its objective, there remained a small pocket of resistance opposing the

Canadian left. That night a patrol of the 29th Battalion cleared up the trouble, capturing four machine-guns, so that contact with the Australians was restored next morning.[83]

For the Germans opposite this part of the Canadian Corps front operations of 8 August had been as costly as to their neighbours farther south. The 41st Division, facing the 2nd Canadian and 2nd Australian Divisions astride the railway, was officially reported as having sacrificed all its front and support battalions, "as well as the entire artillery down to trifling remnants" (in fact only three guns). Reserve units had been reduced to seven infantry and three machine-gun companies.[84]

Our account of the operations of the 1st and 2nd Divisions has taken us forward on the Corps left and centre to the Outer Amiens Defence Line. We left the 3rd Division at the Red Line, from where the attack on the Corps right was to be carried forward by the cavalry and by the 4th Canadian Division.

As the 7th Brigade dug in at the Red Line in the forenoon of 8 August, its troops were treated to the unusual but heartwarming sight of massed cavalry forming up for the attack. The Cavalry Corps (commanded by Lieut.-General Sir Charles Kavanagh) had begun moving off from its assembly area south-west of Villers-Bretonneux at about seven that morning, the 1st Cavalry Division on the left behind the 2nd Australian and 2nd Canadian Divisions, and the 3rd Cavalry Division (led by the Canadian Cavalry Brigade) on the heels of the 1st and 3rd Canadian Divisions.[85] The Canadian Cavalry Brigade, commanded by Brig.-Gen. R. W. Paterson, was accompanied by two companies of Whippet tanks—32 in all. The brigade crossed to the south bank of the Luce at Ignaucourt, and the right flank reached the Roye road shortly after 10:30 a.m. and established contact with Brutinel's armoured cars. Lord Strathcona's Horse then advanced astride the Roye road with the Royal Canadian Dragoons on their left. In the Canadian path lay the villages of Beaucourt-en-Santerre and Le Quesnel, roughly one-third and two-thirds of the distance to the Blue Dotted Line; the 7th Cavalry Brigade, moving up the valley of the Luce, would come in turn to Cayeux and Caix.

Moving across the inter-army boundary, the Strathcona advanced guard squadron encircled Fresnoy-en-Chaussée, and captured 125 prisoners there. Shortly afterwards, however, the enemy reoccupied the village. Beaucourt, which the Germans were already evacuating, presented no problem and yielded 300 prisoners; but in the wood to the east a stand by the Regiment Bellman was aided by fire from south of the Roye road, where the French had not yet secured Fresnoy. As a result Beaucourt Wood remained for the time in German hands.[86] A mile to the north, British cavalry were more fortunate in capturing Cayeux Wood after a short, sharp fight.[87]

In the meantime the 4th Canadian Division had begun passing through the 3rd at 12:40 p.m., about two hours behind the cavalry. On the right, next to the Amiens-Roye road, was the 11th Brigade (Brig.-Gen. Odlum), directed on Le Quesnel, with the 12th Brigade (Brig.-Gen. MacBrien) keeping pace on the left. About a mile east of the Red Line the leading battalions of the 11th

Brigade came up with the mounted units, in the vicinity of Beaucourt.[88] Each of the division's supporting tanks of the 1st Tank Battalion—the new Mark V Star, capable of transporting a score of men in addition to the crew—carried an infantry officer, a scout, and three machine-gun detachments (two Lewis, of three men each, and one Vickers, of five men)—thirteen men in all, besides the tank crew.[89] The plan was for the tanks to make straight for the Blue Dotted Line, where they would drop their passengers. Half would then remain forward while the others drove back to assist the main body of the infantry.[90]

But this scheme to transport foot-soldiers in tanks did not work out well. Jolted about in their cramped quarters, the men suffered severely from the unaccustomed heat and fumes from the engines; many became sick, and a number fainted. More than half of the infantry detachments were obliged to seek fresh air and follow on foot.[91] But there was worse to be faced than a lack of fresh air. A single German battery hidden a thousand yards south of Beaucourt Wood knocked out ten tanks. Eleven machines reached the objective; but because of unexpectedly strong German fire coming from north and east of Le Quesnel, seven of these picked up their infantry again and withdrew with them some 1500 yards.[92]

North of the Luce the British cavalry had reached the final objective by one o'clock. The greatest advances had been made in the centre, where the 6th, followed by the 2nd Cavalry Brigade, took advantage of the shelter afforded by the valleys of the Luce and one of its tributaries to reach the Blue Dotted Line. They had all but cleared the south bank of the river by half-past two, an hour before the left wing of the 4th Division's tank-infantry force arrived.[93] Over on the right in the sector of the French 31st Corps, thanks partly to the efforts of a platoon of the R.C.R. and elements of the Independent Force, the village of Mézières (a mile south-west of Beaucourt) was now in French hands. But trouble lay ahead of General Watson's right wing, for the German reoccupation of Fresnoy meant that Le Quesnel was now defended to a depth of more than a mile to west, south and east.[94]

Earlier that day German machine-guns in Beaucourt Wood had shown their superiority over Canadian sabres, and now these same guns were blocking the advance of the 11th Brigade and the right flank of the 12th. Three tanks detailed to help the 11th Brigade's 54th Battalion were set on fire or otherwise disabled. Without waiting longer for artillery or other support, the battalion commander personally led two platoons in a costly but partially successful attack on the wood. Aided by this action on their right flank the 102nd Battalion assaulted strongly and in hard fighting cleared the wood by half-past four, capturing 160 Germans. The 75th Battalion had passed through the 54th about an hour earlier; but the heavy machine-gun fire with which the Germans in Le Quesnel and Fresnoy were sweeping the flat fields forced the C.O. to rule out a frontal attack on the objective. Accordingly as night fell the brigade dug in a mile north-west of Le Quesnel. Events were to show that this was the only part of the entire Corps front where the first day's objective was not reached on the 8th.[95]

Facing considerably lighter opposition, Brig.-Gen. MacBrien's units had made better progress through country most of which had been swept by the cavalry. At first the 78th Battalion had met heavy fire from machine-guns north of Beaucourt Wood, but had overcome these with tank and artillery support. This success owed much to the achievement of "C" Company, commanded by Lieutenant J. E. Tait, M.C. Inspired by his courageous leadership in knocking out an enemy machine-gun post single-handed, his men captured twelve machine-guns and took a score of prisoners. (Tait, who was killed three days later, was posthumously awarded the V.C.)[96] A thousand yards from the final objective the 72nd Battalion passed through the 78th, and pressing forward by short platoon and section rushes, reached the Blue Dotted Line at 6:15. On the left the 38th Battalion made such good time that the 85th, assuming the lead in the final stages, was on its objective by half-past four.[97]

Little time was lost in the 4th Division's relief of the cavalry as the infantry began consolidating the day's gains. The 11th Brigade took over from the Canadian Cavalry Brigade about five o'clock, and an hour later the 7th Cavalry Brigade withdrew from the positions which it was holding jointly with the 12th Infantry Brigade in the Blue Dotted Line south of the Luce.[98] In their new stand Major-General Watson's infantry were covered by their own field artillery. The 3rd Brigade C.F.A., after completing its tasks in the opening barrage, had moved up to the Red Line during the afternoon; by eight that evening its batteries were deployed about Beaucourt, ready to fire a barrage on Le Quesnel. Plans made for an early morning attack on that village held good promise of fulfilment, for the menace to flanking enemy fire from across the French boundary had been removed in late evening when troops of the 31st Corps supported by light tanks captured Fresnoy.[99]

On General Currie's left, towards the Somme, the Australians had reached most of their objectives by 1:30 p.m., but progress on their extreme northern flank had been seriously handicapped by British reverses north of the river. The heavy fighting in which all the divisions of the 3rd Corps had been involved since the opening of the Germans' March offensive had taken a serious toll, resulting in a lack of experienced officers and N.C.O.s. to lead the young recruits brought up to fill the ranks of the stricken infantry units. On top of this the German attack of 6 August and the counter-attack of the 7th had brought further losses and disorganization. The result was that the 3rd Corps, fighting through some of the most difficult country on the entire Fourth Army's front, was unable to take much more than its first objective, a mile short of its final goal. Because of this the 4th Australian Division on the Corps left, after occupying the Amiens trenches, was compelled to withdraw its northern posts some 500 yards from the final objective.[100]

More far-reaching in its effect than the setbacks on the Fourth army's flanks was the failure to employ the cavalry to exploit the general success. Because of difficulties in transmitting orders* and an apparent reluctance by Cavalry Corps Headquarters to act without instruction from the Fourth Army a great opportunity was lost. Fighting ahead of the infantry in the final phases, by early afternoon of 8 August the cavalry had (except, on the extreme right, east of Le Quesnel) gained a footing in the Amiens Outer Defence Line across the whole of the Canadian Corps front. But there the advance had stopped. In the meantime, at 12:30 General Rawlinson's Major General, General Staff had sent instructions to the G.O.C. Cavalry Corps that the cavalry should not halt at the Blue Dotted Line, but push on eastward towards the general line Chaulnes-Roye. But it was 4:15 p.m. before such orders, relayed by Cavalry Corps Headquarters, reached the frequently moving headquarters of the 1st Cavalry Division. Attempts in the late afternoon to push patrols towards Chaulnes failed, for the Germans had dug in strongly along the line Rosières-Vrély, some two thousand yards east of the Blue Dotted Line. The 3rd Cavalry Division, as we have seen, had been checked in front of Le Quesnel. The 7th Cavalry Brigade on the divisional left, however, reached the Dotted Blue Line before three o'clock; but an attempt by the 2nd Cavalry Division to pass through and push on eastward failed. At 5:20 p.m. General Kavanagh ordered his 3rd Division to hold on to the line it had reached until the infantry came up.[101]

Although the day's operations by the Fourth Army and the French First Army had attained somewhat less than complete success, the enemy had suffered its greatest defeat since the beginning of the war.[102] From north of the Somme to south of Moreuil the German line had been thrown back as much as eight miles in the Canadian sector and up to seven on the Australian front. On the flanks the French had advanced a maximum of five miles, and the British two. The cost of all these gains had been remarkably light. The Fourth Army's casualties were approximately 8800, exclusive of tank and air losses. Canadian casualties totalled 3868—1036 killed, 2803 wounded, and 29 taken prisoner. The enemy admitted that his forward divisions between the Avre and the Somme had been "nearly completely annihilated", while his troops north of the Somme had "suffered severely". Official German figures gave the Second Army's casualties as "650 to 700 officers and 26,000 to 27,000 other ranks. . . . More than two-thirds of the total loss had surrendered as prisoners."† Allied forces had destroyed or seized more than 400 guns, many trench mortars and "a huge number of machine-guns".[104] The Canadian Corps was credited with capturing 5033 prisoners and 161 guns.[105]

"August 8th", Ludendorff was to write, "was the black day of the German Army in the history of this war."[106] German morale had been struck an irreparable blow. "Everything I had feared, and of which I had so often given warning",

* It had been impossible for cable layers to keep up with the rapid advance of the two leading cavalry divisions. Even Cavalry Corps Headquarters moved forward beyond the limit of voice transmission on the cable, and in communicating back to the Fourth Army and the Canadian and Australian Corps had to rely on telegraphed messages and wireless.

† British records show the total number of German prisoners to be about 15,000, which is less, not more than two-thirds of the Second Army's total casualties.[103]

he declared pessimistically, "had here, in one place, become a reality." No longer could he hope to resume the offensive or find any strategic expedient in which German forces might be employed to advantage. Even the Kaiser was now convinced that as a result of the failure of the German July offensive and the defeat on 8 August the war could no longer be won.[107] Indeed, on 10 August, when Ludendorff was reporting the disaster to the Kaiser, the latter had interjected: "We have reached the limits of our capacity. The war must be terminated."[108]

The Advance Slows Down, 9 August

"Having secured the old Amiens defence line . . ." the British G.H.Q. operation order for 9 August began, "the Fourth Army will push forward to-morrow and establish itself on the general line Roye—Chaulnes—Bray-sur-Somme—Dernancourt."[109] This line ran directly northward opposite the Canadian sector, angling to the north-west across the Australian and British fronts. To reach it would require an advance of nine miles on the Army right, but barely a mile on the extreme northern flank. On the right, the French were to continue to push eastward towards Roye, at the same time extending their sector of operations to their right by attacking on a sixteen-mile front reaching from Montdidier south-east to Autheil. The British cavalry would continue to operate on the Fourth Army's right flank in such a way as to assist the French advance, and—in the words of General Rawlinson's order of the 8th (untimed but probably issued late at night)—"to gain the objectives allotted to the Canadian Corps", the general line Roye—Hattencourt—Hallu. The Canadian right and left boundaries remained the Roye road and the Amiens-Chaulnes railway. General Currie and General Butler, G.O.C. 3rd Corps, were to select their own zero hours, and the Australian Corps in between would advance its flanks to conform with these timings.[110]

Surprise, of course, was out of the question. During the fighting on 8 August and throughout the following night, the Germans, reacting quickly, had brought up seven divisions from reserve. Elements of three of these were introduced opposite Canadian troops—from north to south the 119th Division at Rosières and Vrély, the 1st Reserve behind Le Quesnel, and the 82nd Reserve at the Franco-Canadian boundary. Other formations were on their way. The 261st Reserve Regiment (79th Reserve Division) arrived at Beaufort on the afternoon of the 9th; and the next day the 221st Division established itself astride the Roye road in the rear of the 1st and 82nd Reserve Divisions. Although British Intelligence had once rated two of these divisions "poor", all five were now considered to be of average calibre.[111]

An unfortunate change of mind at Fourth Army Headquarters was to cause considerable disruption to Canadian planning at the corps and divisional level, bringing back into action a tired division that had been heavily committed on the opening day of the battle, and, what was more serious, delaying the attack on 9 August for more than five hours, thereby giving the enemy that much additional

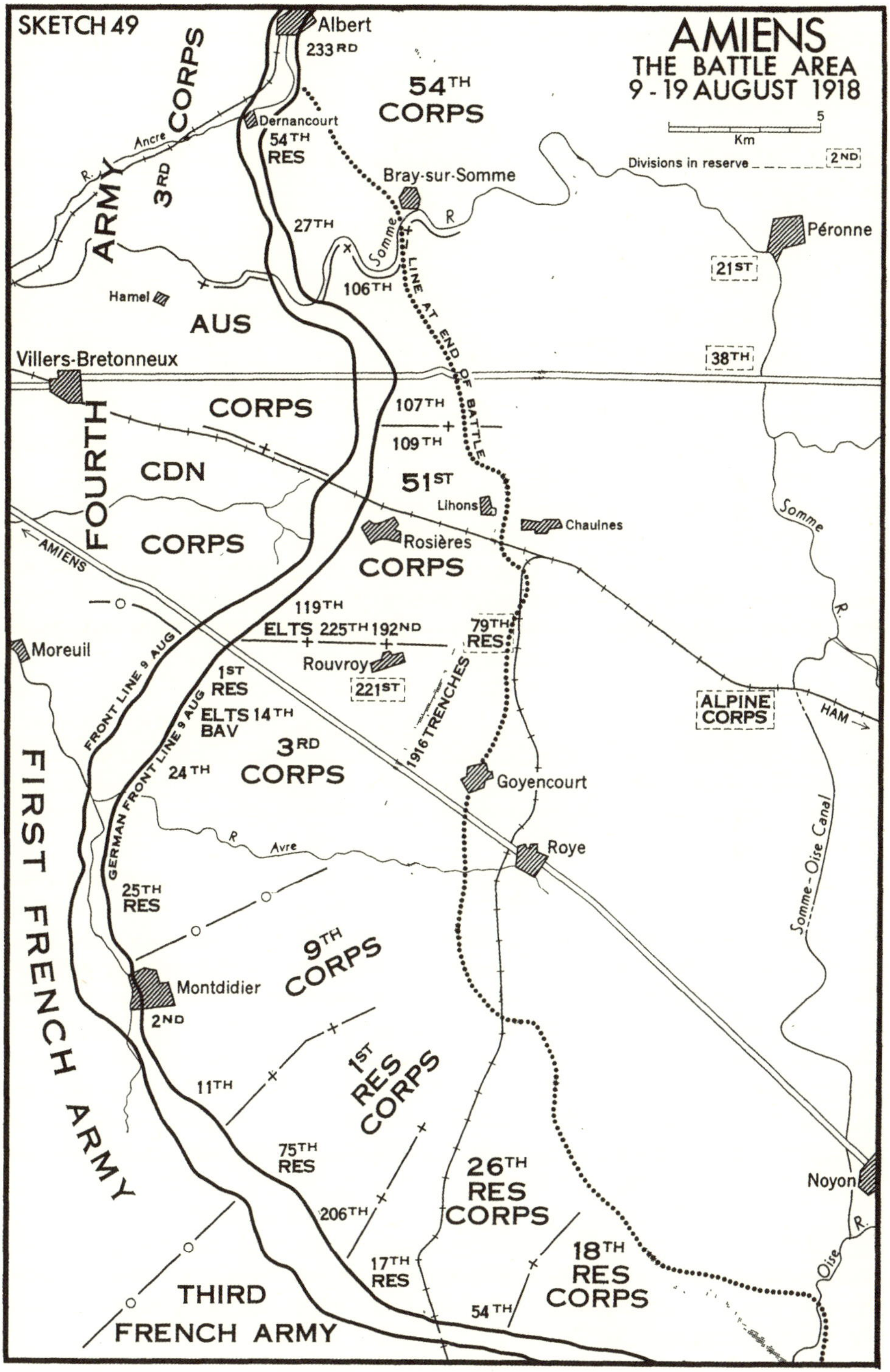
SKETCH 49
AMIENS
THE BATTLE AREA
9 - 19 AUGUST 1918
Km
5
Divisions in reserve
2ND
Albert
233RD
54TH
CORPS
Dernancourt
54TH
RES
Bray-sur-Somme
27TH
106TH
Somme
R
LINE AT END OF BATTLE
Péronne
21ST
38TH
3RD CORPS
ARMY
R. Ancre
Hamel
AUS
Villers-Bretonneux
CORPS
107TH
109TH
FOURTH
CDN
51ST
Lihons
Chaulnes
CORPS
Rosières
CORPS
AMIENS
Somme
R.
119TH
ELTS 225TH 192ND
79TH
RES
Moreuil
Rouvroy
221ST
1ST
RES
ELTS 14TH
BAV
FRONT LINE 9 AUG
GERMAN FRONT LINE 9 AUG
1916 TRENCHES
ALPINE
CORPS
HAM
24TH
3RD
CORPS
Goyencourt
FIRST FRENCH ARMY
R
Avre
Roye
Somme-Oise Canal
25TH
RES
9TH
CORPS
Montdidier
2ND
1ST
RES
CORPS
11TH
75TH
RES
26TH
RES
CORPS
Noyon
R.
206TH
17TH
RES
18TH
RES
CORPS
Oise
54TH
THIRD
FRENCH ARMY

time to bolster his resistance. At 4:30 on the afternoon of the 9th General Rawlinson came to General Currie's advanced headquarters at Gentelles (three miles southwest of Villers-Bretonneux). Currie was away visiting divisional headquarters, but the Army Commander informed the Canadian Corps B.G.G.S., Brig.-Gen. N. W. Webber, a British officer, that he was making the 32nd Division from army reserve available for operations with the Canadian Corps next day. On the strength of this decision plans were completed for the 1st and 2nd Canadian Divisions to attack at 5:00 a.m. on a front of one brigade each, while on the Corps right, after the 4th Division had cleared the corner next to the Roye road, the British division would pass through to advance on a two-brigade front.

But General Rawlinson's staff apparently felt that the situation was too satisfactory to warrant committing the Army's second-line divisions yet.[112] At 6:30 p.m. Brig.-Gen. Webber received a wire from General Rawlinson's M.G.G.S. (the Army Commander's chief executive officer), cancelling the order respecting the 32nd Division, and calling him back to Dury to receive further instructions by telephone. Because of blocked roads it was half-past eight by the time Webber reached Dury, where he learned that the M.G.G.S. was "very irate with Army Comdr for daring to give away 32nd Divn and with myself [Webber] for aiding and abetting".[113] The countermanded order meant that the 3rd Division, which had been relieved only that afternoon, had to be brought forward again to undertake the role intended for the 32nd Division. General Currie's headquarters worked through the night preparing fresh orders, which, because of the unreliability of wires forward had to go out by despatch-rider and motor car. They did not reach the divisions until four or five in the morning, by which time the original zero hour had been postponed to 10:00 a.m. on the 9th.

The immediate task set down in General Currie's new orders was for the 4th Division to secure Le Quesnel and the southern end of the Blue Dotted Line, after which the three remaining Canadian Divisions would continue their attacks.[114] The 3rd Division's advance would be adjacent to the Roye road, keeping touch with the French on the right—its sector included the villages of Folies and Bouchoir. The 1st Division in the Corps centre was directed on Beaufort, Warvillers and Rouvroy; on its left the 2nd Division had to capture Rosières and Vrély, before pushing on towards Méharicourt and Chilly.[115] In the 4th Division's sector the 75th Battalion began its attack at 4:30 a.m. For a time machine-gun fire from Le Quesnel and the high ground to the south held up the advance; but within an hour the battalion had successfully stormed these positions and driven the Germans from the village. There was more fighting in the adjoining Le Quesnel Woods, and at noon the extreme right of the objective, beside the Roye road, was still in German hands. Farther north bombing parties and tanks had by 11:00 a.m. reduced an enemy pocket between the 75th Battalion and the 87th, which had come up on the left, and sealed other gaps in the line, but not without the loss of two of the five supporting tanks, knocked out by an anti-tank gun.[116]

Revised orders for the day's operations issued by General Currie's advanced headquarters half an hour before the 4th Division's attack confirmed that the Canadian objectives would be considerably short of the Roye line—on the right as much as four miles short. The amended zero hour of 10:00 a.m. had to be postponed for a number of reasons.[117] Enemy rearguards still occupied the right of the Outer Amiens Defence Line, where the 3rd Division was to pass through the 4th. The front of the tired 3rd Division was reduced to that of a single brigade and the 1st and 2nd Divisions had to shift to the right, taking wider frontages. As they side-stepped, a bombardment from German heavy guns hindered the readjustment. Neither division found it possible to get its troops into their new positions before 11:00. A second postponement to permit the necessary regrouping of artillery was followed by a third and fourth, as details of the original plan had to be hastily modified. There were similar delays across the entire army front, and in the Canadian Corps only the 6th Brigade on the left got away at eleven o'clock, without its supporting tanks. For most of the Canadian brigades it was past one o'clock before any advance began, and the 3rd Division, attacking with only the 8th Brigade, did not resume operations until 2:00 p.m.[118] By that time French troops south of the Roye road had advanced past Le Quesnel, to make this flank more secure.[119]

Over on the Corps left, the 6th Brigade's expectation of stubborn resistance was well-founded. As the 29th and 31st Battalions advanced side by side up the long slope towards Rosières they were met by a hail of bullets from machine-guns sited in the village and along the Rosières-Vrély road. They had also to face a counter-barrage of shrapnel and high explosive from the enemy's artillery, while the whole brigade front was swept with enfilade fire from the unprotected flanks. An agonizing hour was to pass before five tanks came forward, and with no mist to shield them these made good targets for hostile guns and anti-tank rifles. Three were soon out of action. After an enforced pause the infantry fought doggedly forward again, and with better results because of help on either flank.[120] By noon the 5th Brigade had begun its attack on General Burstall's right, while an advance by the Australians along the railway was easing the pressure from the north.[121] The surviving tanks, assisted by trench-mortar detachments, took out one machine-gun nest after another, enabling the 31st Battalion, on the brigade right, to work around the south side of Rosières. There was aid too from overhead, as British aircraft bombed and machine-gunned German posts. By 1:15 p.m., the battalion, helped by the last remaining tank before it too was knocked out, had cleared its half of the village, while the 29th Battalion was mopping up on the left.[122]

The 5th Brigade, attacking with the 22nd and 25th Battalions, soon found that a report by a contact patrol of the R.A.F. that the Germans were retiring in disorder from Vrély was premature. From the outskirts of the village came a hail of machine-gun bullets that made an advance over the open ground out of the question. Instead small scouting parties followed by Lewis guns worked their way forward along ditches and sunken roads to outflank the enemy posts and take them with enfilade fire. By such tactics Vrély was secured, and soon after three o'clock the 5th Brigade, joined at last by its tanks, was continuing eastward on Méharicourt.[123] At about the same time, a direct hit by an enemy shell on Brigade Headquarters killed the brigade-major and the liaison officer from the division, and seriously wounded Brig.-Gen. Ross. Lt.-Col. T. L. Tremblay, C.O. of the 22nd Battalion, took over the brigade.[124]

North of Rosières the Australians had made a corresponding advance which enabled the 6th Brigade to resume its attack. Within the hour the 29th Battalion had driven the Germans from a sugar factory 1000 yards to the east. The 27th and 28th Battalions then went into the lead. Helped by its tanks the 5th Brigade quickened its pace. Shortly before five, the capture of Méharicourt by the 22nd Battalion completed a hard day of fighting, which had brought the French-Canadian unit its second V.C. of the war. On the morning of 8 August, when the 22nd Battalion was engaged in mopping-up operations west of Wiencourt, Lieutenant Jean Brillant, M.C., had rushed and captured a troublesome enemy machine-gun post. Though wounded he continued in action, and during the attack on Vrély next day he led a party of two platoons in an assault which resulted in the capture of fifteen machine-guns and 150 prisoners. He was again wounded, but he refused to leave his company, and shortly afterwards organized a charge against a German four-inch gun that was engaging the battalion over open sights. Again he was wounded, this time mortally. In the words of the citation that accompanied the award of the Victoria Cross to Brillant, throughout the day his wonderful example had "inspired his men with an enthusiasm and dash which largely contributed towards the success of the operations".[125]

The 1st Division reached its reduced objectives without much difficulty. The 2nd Brigade, operating on the 5th Brigade's right, had to side-step 2500 yards to the south before jumping off. It advanced largely unsupported by either tanks or artillery. The 8th Battalion met its most serious resistance from machine-guns firing out of Hatchet Wood and small copses beyond. On its right, the 5th Battalion found the ground, which was very flat, and masked with growing crops, well suited to section rushes covered by machine-gun fire. During the day's advance the Victoria Cross was won by three gallant non-commissioned officers of the brigade—Sergeant R. L. Zengel, M.M., of the 5th Battalion, and Corporal F. C. Coppins and Lance-Corporal Alexander Brereton of the 8th. In earning this high award each man at great personal risk boldly attacked and silenced one or more German machine-gun posts, thereby saving his comrades from heavy casualties.[126] The village of Warvillers in the right of the brigade sector was occupied without much opposition, and as the assaulting battalions neared the Méharicourt-Rouvroy road shortly before dusk, they received valuable if belated assistance from tanks of the 4th Tank Battalion, and from whippets on loan from the 1st Cavalry Division.[127]

In the southern half of General Macdonell's sector, it was 1:15 p.m. (9 August) when the 1st Brigade attacked, the 1st Battalion (on the right) passing through the left of the 11th Brigade north-west of Le Quesnel. Throughout the operation Brig.-Gen. Griesbach's brigade was assisted by three batteries of Vickers from the

MAP 11

THE BATTLE OF AMIENS
8 - 18 AUGUST 1918
MILES
Contours indicated by layer tints: 40, 60, 80, 100 metres
Line reached at midnight (French front in green)
Line of Outposts
Objectives
Infantry advances, Canadian Corps front
Cavalry advances Canadian Corps front
Trench systems
Final line (19 August)
CANADIAN CORPS
AUSTRALIAN CORPS
31ST FRENCH CORPS
1916 FRONT LINES
INTERNATIONAL FORCE
3RD CAVALRY DIVISION
GREEN LINE
RED LINE
BLUE DOTTED LINE
OUTER AMIENS DEFENCE LINE
Villers-Bretonneux
Gentelles
Marcelcave
Harbonnières
Wiencourt
Guillaucourt
Hangard
Aubercourt
Courcelles
Demuin
Hourges
Ignaucourt
Cayeux
Caix
Rosières-en-Santerre
Lihons
Chaulnes
Vrély
Meharicourt
Maucourt
Chilly
Hallu
Warvillers
Beaufort
Le Quesnel
Beaucourt-en-Santerre
Mézières
Moreuil
Fresnoy-en-Chaussée
Hangest-en-Santerre
Arvillers
Folies
Bouchoir
Le Quesnoy
Rouvroy-en Santerre
Fouquescourt
Hattencourt
Fransart
La Chavatte
Parvillers
Damery
Fresnoy-les-Roye
Goyencourt
Erches
Andechy
La Cambuse
AMIENS
PERONNE
ROYE

1st Battalion Canadian Machine Gun Corps; though on this day, as on 8 August, the advance proved too rapid for the machine-gunners to give effective close support. Not that the brigade's progress was free of delays and diversions. On the left the 2nd Battalion repeatedly came under fire from old British trenches on either side of Beaufort. After supporting tanks had broken this resistance the infantry quickly cleared the village. The 1st Battalion was obliged for its own good to take Folies, south of the divisional boundary, and hold it with a small force until the 3rd Division came abreast. The 4th Battalion then passed through, and by half-past five the brigade had secured most of the Rouvroy-Folies road. Part of Rouvroy, where both the 2nd and 4th Battalions had gained a hold, was still in German hands. Brig.-Gen. Griesbach then ordered his remaining reserve, the 3rd Battalion, into an evening attack, and by 9:20 the village had been cleared of Germans. Both the 1st Division and the 2nd, which had halted on a line 500 yards east of Méharicourt, pushed posts well forward during the night.[128]

On General Currie's extreme right the 8th Brigade's forward battalions passed through the 11th Brigade shortly after 2:00 p.m. Led by three tanks of the 5th Tank Battalion the 4th Canadian Mounted Rifles headed south-eastward from Le Quesnel towards Folies, achieving good results by sections making short rushes.[129] Fifty minutes later the 5th C.M.R., next to the Amiens-Roye highway, set out with four tanks, its objective the village of Bouchoir, three miles down the road. By 4:15 the 4th C.M.R. had linked up with the 1st Division in Folies and, according to the reports of returning wounded, was "meeting little resistance and . . . getting ahead fast." But the progress of the 5th C.M.R. was being delayed by enemy machine-guns which still covered the Roye road immediately south-east of Le Quesnel. South of the road French forces were held up at Arvillers, and the 5th C.M.R. were preparing to form a defensive flank with a detachment of Brutinel's Independent Force, before attacking the town. A beet-sugar factory at the junction with the side road to Arvillers was the scene of stiff fighting before the enemy withdrew under the impetus of a tank-infantry attack. Full kit, including rolled greatcoats, on enemy dead along the Roye road gave evidence of the recent arrival of German reinforcements.[130]

Bouchoir fell to the 5th C.M.R. at five o'clock, and shortly afterwards the Germans were reported retiring from Arvillers. A platoon of the Mounted Rifles entered from the north and held the village until French troops arrived about seven o'clock. Meanwhile the 4th C.M.R. had reached an old British trench line running from Bouchoir through Rouvroy to Méharicourt.[131] It marked the edge of the area of defences occupied before the 1916 Battles of the Somme. Though the trenches were badly broken down, enough wire remained to enable the Germans to make of them very formidable machine-gun positions. East of Arvillers a gap between the Canadian Corps and the French First Army was filled by British cavalry and light tanks, together with elements of the Canadian Independent Force.[132] The French First Army's offensive on the 9th had been notably lacking in results, and more than once Marshal Foch urged General Debeney to quicken his pace, and to push the 31st Corps forward "with drums beating on Roye".[133] That night the French resumed their advance and established firm contact with the Canadian right flank in front of Bouchoir.

Though the first day's impetus had not been maintained, on this second day of the battle the Canadians had made advances of up to four miles, their French neighbours doing slightly less. The average gain for the Fourth Army was three miles—about half the distance to Roye and Chaulnes, the objectives originally prescribed for the second day. The advance had lacked the clockwork precision of the opening day. There had been too much countermanding of orders with a resulting disunity that had led to brigades attacking at different times and under different conditions. Fortunately the defence was similarly uneven, and the enemy made no serious attempt to counter-attack. Nevertheless resistance had been stronger than expected, and was becoming still stronger. Canadian casualties for 9 August numbered 2574, about two-thirds of the previous day's total. On the other hand the Australian Corps between the Amiens-Chaulnes railway and the Somme, more heavily engaged than on the opening day of the battle, had doubled its casualties with a figure of 1310.[134]

As new German reserves arrived by train, bus and lorry, to be thrown piecemeal into the battle, the remnants of the formations battered by the Allied attacks—on the Canadian front the 41st, 117th and 225th Divisions—were gradually withdrawn. As a result of these movements, by the afternoon of 9 August the thirteen divisions of the British Fourth Army were facing thirteen German divisions and part of a fourteenth. These comprised the remnants of eight divisions in the line on 8 August and five newly inserted divisions, of which two had been exhausted previously and had been awaiting removal.[135] There were German fears that the British Fourth Army's penetration into the front of the Second Army would outflank the Eighteenth Army, opposite the French. Accordingly late on the ninth, after a long telephone consultation with Ludendorff, Army Group Rupprecht ordered the commander of the Eighteenth Army to withdraw some half dozen miles.[136] On the home front the German communique for 9 August, reporting that "the enemy had broken in south of the Somme on a broad front", spread panic among the German people and their allies. From Vienna the senior German representative at Austro-Hungarian Headquarters urged Ludendorff to tone down further admissions of defeat "if not on account of the German public, then for the sake of our Allies".[137]

The End of the Battle, 10-11 August

There could be little hope that August 10, the third day of the battle, would result in any further spectacular gains, though Field-Marshal Haig's orders to his armies prescribed the untaken objectives of the previous day—the line Roye-Chaulnes-Bray-Dernancourt. The enemy was still reinforcing his front. During the day four fresh divisions appeared opposite the Canadian Corps—the 221st Division astride the Amiens-Roye road; the 121st between it and Hattencourt; the

Alpine Corps* between Hattencourt and Hallu; and the 38th Division in the vicinity of Chaulnes.[130]

For these formations arriving so precipitately in the battle area there was little of the normal take-over of defended positions; yet they were fortunate in finding ground that was in itself a physical obstacle to a rapid advance by their opponents. A belt three miles wide pitted with shell-holes and befouled with tangles of barbed wire and the remains of old trenches overgrown with long concealing grass marked the position of the former Allied and German front lines before the German retirement to the Hindenburg Line in the spring of 1917. Here the new arrivals set up their machine-guns, ready to offer determined resistance to attackers who had not yet fully realized that the operation had suddenly reverted from open pursuit almost to the old pattern of trench warfare.†

General Currie's orders to the Canadian Corps set the hour of the renewed advance at 8:00 a.m. The 4th Division would relieve the 1st and 2nd Divisions in the left half of the Corps sector, now divided into two divisional sectors only. On the right the 3rd Division would be replaced by the British 32nd Division, which had finally been placed at Currie's disposal during the afternoon of the 9th.[141]

Before the 3rd Division was relieved, the 8th Brigade completed some unfinished business from the previous day. This was an attack on Le Quesnoy, a small hamlet two thousand yards east of Bouchoir. About midnight, three companies of the 2nd C.M.R. were lorried by the Independent Force to an assembly area near Bouchoir, and the attack went in at 4:20 a.m. By 6:30 the Canadians had captured the village, but soon had to break up a number of local counterattacks.[142] During the morning the 1st C.M.R., trailing the 2nd into Le Quesnoy, occupied old British trenches to the north-east. Meanwhile the French First Army, following up the withdrawal of the German Eighteenth Army, had found Montdidier in ruins. Troops on the left of the 31st Corps entered Erches, abreast of the Canadians.[143]

The Canadian Corps resumed its advance at 9:30 on the 10th, the 32nd British Division (Major-General T. S. Lambert) passing through the 1st and 3rd Divisions, its two assaulting brigades directed on Parvillers and Damery. Pending the arrival of its own artillery—delayed until 10:30 a.m. by night bombing—the British division was supported by the 5th Canadian Divisional Artillery. On its left, the 4th Division, taking over the sectors of the 1st and 2nd (which passed into corps reserve), began to move forward at 10:15. On General Watson's right flank the immediate objective of the 10th Brigade, commanded by Brig.-Gen. R. J. F. Hayter, a British officer, was the village of Fouquescourt; the 12th Brigade had to take Maucourt and Chilly.[144]

It was soon found that the Eighteenth Army's withdrawal in the French sector had not been matched on the front held by the German Second Army. Prisoners

* The Alpine Corps was actually only on the establishment of one division.[139]

† The location of these trenches was unknown to the assaulting battalions; large-scale maps showing the trench systems were not available in time for the advance beyond the Blue Dotted Line.[140]

captured by the 3rd Canadian Division during the morning of the 10th spoke of orders to hold at all costs a line (the old pre-Hindenburg Line position) on the western edges of Andechy (in the French sector), Damery, Parvillers and Fouquescourt. A subsequent order given at 8:15 a.m. by the 51st Corps for a retirement by the 221st, 79th Reserve and 119th Divisions to positions on either side of Hattencourt, was countermanded by 10:30 by General von der Marwitz as fresh reinforcements arrived. It appears that during the night of 9-10 August the Second Army had reported in a pessimistic sense. Next morning, however, a newly designated Army Chief of Staff appeared, and in accordance with the views of higher command authorities issued orders for an immediate counter-attack on the entire Army front with a resolute follow-up.[145]

The Germans were able to hold most of this line throughout the day. By midday they had checked the advance on all parts of the Corps sector, the 32nd Division and the right wing of the 4th Canadian Division being held up on the old British front and support lines. South of the Roye road units of the French First Army had been halted at Andechy.[146] That afternoon a squadron of the Fort Garry Horse captured the village and turned it over to the French,[147] but the latter were unable to go much farther. As might have been expected when horsemen are ordered to charge defended entrenchments, other attempts by the cavalry to advance brought little but casualties.[148] The Fort Garrys lost that day 45 all ranks and 112 horses.

During the morning the 32nd Division's right brigade captured La Cambuse, on the main road, and Square Wood (half a mile west of Parvillers). The left flank reached a point about half a mile west of Fouquescourt. As the day wore on the British units beat off sharp counter-attacks but could gain no more ground. There was particularly bitter fighting in the Bois-en-Equerre, from which all attempts to reach Damery, 1000 yards to the east, were hurled back. Ordering his troops to consolidate, General Lambert reported to Canadian Corps headquarters the need for fresh troops and careful artillery preparation before trying a further advance.[149]

Troops of the 10th Canadian Infantry Brigade could make little progress through the wire and trenches of the old Somme defences east of the Méharicourt-Rouvroy road. Shortly after noon as they approached the next lateral road joining Maucourt and Fouquescourt, heavy machine-gun fire from both villages checked the 44th Battalion on the right and the 46th on the left. At the same time the 12th Brigade's 72nd Battalion was meeting resistance from Maucourt; while on Brig.-Gen. MacBrien's left the 85th Battalion was under fire from north of the railway, where Lihons was still to be taken by the Australians. The 72nd drove the Germans out of Maucourt into nearby Chilly without much difficulty, but there was stiff fighting in the latter village before it was finally in Canadian hands, shortly after 12:30.[150]

With Maucourt in possession the 10th Brigade was able to establish a line east of the Fouquescourt road early in the afternoon, though Fouquescourt itself was still stoutly defended. General Watson was concerned about this situation on his right flank, where the attacking troops were confronted with the serious obstacle of well-manned trenches and uncut wire. Accordingly the guns of the 3rd Brigade C.F.A. and the 179th Brigade Australian Field Artillery were brought forward to deal with the German defences. With this support the 44th Battalion, attacking across an open field swept by machine-gun fire, forced an entry into Fouquescourt and in severe fighting drove out the defenders. By six o'clock the 44th had dug in just east of the village, the 47th Battalion coming up to extend the line to the left.[151] Meanwhile in the 12th Brigade's sector, the 78th Battalion had passed through the 72nd to take a temporary hold on Hallu; but next to the railway the 38th Battalion, under heavy fire from Lihons on the open left flank, had reached only the Chilly-Lihons road. During the evening the 72nd Battalion was called on to beat off a strong German counter-attack coming in on Chilly from the north-east. The enemy had vigorously resisted Australian attempts to take Lihons, and at the end of the day's fighting General Monash's right was nearly three miles behind the Canadian left, which echeloned back towards it. Things had gone better north of the Somme, where the old Amiens Defence Line was reached on a broad front and an American regiment fighting with the British 3rd Corps pushed forward almost to Bray.[152]

On the evening of 10 August General Rawlinson and General Debeney relayed to their respective armies orders issued by G.H.Q. for a resumption of the offensive next day. In view of the hardening of the enemy's resistance these appeared most optimistic. The French were to attack at dawn, their objective being the line of the Somme-Oise canal, which ran northward from Noyon, passing eight miles east of Roye.[153] The Fourth Army's task was to push forward to the long southward bend of the Somme between Ham and Péronne, and establish bridgeheads on the far bank. The Canadian Corps objective was the stretch of river between Offoy (three miles west of Ham) and St. Christ, eight miles downstream.[154] When orders reached the Cavalry Corps that it was to spearhead the Canadian advance, the Corps B.G.G.S. drove post-haste to Army Headquarters to remonstrate that the enemy's resistance was now very strong and that the ground over which the proposed advance was to be made was quite impassable for cavalry in any large numbers.[155]

There is evidence of a growing divergence of opinion between Sir Douglas Haig and Marshal Foch as to the wisdom of continuing the Amiens offensive, though this was not to come into the open for a few more days. Nevertheless a passive resistance to the Generalissimo's orders was beginning to manifest itself on the 11th. In the course of the morning General Rawlinson telephoned General Currie to say that he did not wish the attack of the 32nd Division pressed very strongly if that would entail heavy losses. Currie, who recognized the inadvisability of trying to progress mainly by infantry fighting, recommended that operations should be slackened to give time to organize a set-piece attack on a broad front. Shortly after midday he cancelled a proposed attack by the 4th Division.[156] Before the day ended Rawlinson, after seeing Sir Douglas Haig at Villers-Bretonneux, told his corps commanders that the C.-in-C. had approved the Fourth Army's offensive being discontinued for the time being. It would not be resumed until it had the support of all available artillery and an increased number of tanks.[157] Rawlinson left it to the discretion of corps commanders to make local improvements in the line which they were then holding.[158] As a general offensive, the Battle of Amiens* ended on 11 August. The operations of the next three days were only local actions carried out in preparation for a renewal of contemplated large-scale attacks, both British and French, on the 15th and 16th. For reasons to be shown presently (below, p. 422) these did not materialize.

Some adjustments were made in the Canadian front line. Hallu, which marked the most easterly point reached by any formation of the Fourth Army, was given up. During the previous night and on the morning of the 11th the 4th Canadian Division had beaten off three counter-attacks launched against the village by the Alpine Corps,[159] and with the cancellation of a further advance it was not practical to maintain such an exposed position. The 78th Battalion was withdrawn, and both the 4th Division and the British 32nd consolidated a line which ran along the western outskirts of Damery and Parvillers, passing to the east of Chilly.[160] During the night of 11-12 August the two formations were relieved by the 2nd and 3rd Canadian Divisions respectively.

A Lull in the Fighting

The next eight days saw no large-scale action on the Allied front. During the 12th, 13th and 14th, the 3rd Canadian Division, which had taken over the Corps right, was engaged in clearing the maze of enemy trenches between Fouquescourt and Parvillers. Except for the penetration south-west of Damery made by the 32nd Division on 11 August, the Germans still held the whole of their former trench network between the Roye road and Fouquescourt. By means of patrol encounters and local trench fighting, units of the 7th Brigade, working in close cooperation with the 9th Brigade on their right, slowly pushed forward to close in on Parvillers from both flanks.* On the 14th the P.P.C.L.I. gained an entry but could not occupy the village in the face of violent enemy reaction.[162] Parvillers was finally secured on the 15th and held against counter-attack by the R.C.R. and the 116th Battalion (now commanded by Lt.-Col. G. R. Pearkes, V.C.).[163]

On the same day the 52nd Battalion entered Damery, which had been the main centre of resistance in front of the 9th Brigade. The ease with which the village was taken pointed to a possible German ruse, which materialized in the afternoon with a violent shelling of Damery followed by an attack from two battalions of the 60th Regiment of the 121st Division. From positions to which they

* In these operations two men of the 7th Brigade won the V.C. Sgt. Robert Spall of the P.P.C.L.I. won a posthumous award when with great heroism he held off with his Lewis gun a German counter-attack outside Parvillers on 13 August, enabling his platoon to withdraw safely from an isolated position. Pte. Thomas Dinesen (42nd Battalion) earned the coveted decoration by his sustained bravery and leadership during ten hours of hand-to-hand fighting on 12 August which ultimately resulted in the capture of more than a mile of enemy trenches north of Parvillers.[161]

had temporarily withdrawn east of the village companies of the 52nd Battalion broke up the advancing waves, mowing down large numbers of Germans as they marched forward in massed formation. The enemy was driven back in disorder, leaving behind him some 200 prisoners and a great number of dead and wounded.[164]

Having lost Damery, the enemy found the Bois-en-Z, north of the Roye road, untenable; it was soon afterwards occupied by French forces. The 3rd Division was now relieved by the 1st and went into reserve, General Macdonell taking over command of the sector at midday on the 16th. The improvement of the French position prompted a further advance by the left wing of the 31st Corps, in which the Canadian Corps cooperated. On 16 August, as the French launched an attack on Goyencourt, only two miles from Roye, General Currie ordered the 1st Canadian Division to push forward to Fresnoy-les-Roye and La Chavatte, with the 2nd Division (which had relieved the 4th Division on the 12th and 13th) assisting on the left. Accordingly that afternoon, on General Burstall's front, the 19th Battalion, reinforced by companies of the 18th and the 20th, occupied Fransart, between Fouquescourt and Hattencourt.[165] But in the 1st Division's sector three attempts by the 13th Battalion to get into La Chavatte failed in spite of substantial artillery support, nor could strong patrols penetrate to Fresnoy-les-Roye, both places being well within the enemy's main position. Not until the morning of the 17th, when 4th Brigade patrols had cleared troublesome trenches north of La Chavatte, could the 13th Battalion secure that village.[166] Attempts to reach Fresnoy were abandoned. On the 19th, the 4th Division, having replaced the 2nd Division on the Corps left, improved its position in a minor operation north of Chilly. During the afternoon the 87th Battalion won back some of the ground lost earlier by the Division east of the Chilly-Lihons road and held its gains against four counter-attacks that night.[167]

This virtually ended active operations by the Canadian Corps east of Amiens. Roye and Chaulnes, which had marked the Fourth Army's objectives since the opening of the battle on 8 August, were not to fall to French forces for another eight days. As General Currie's formations began moving to new fields of endeavour they could look back with satisfaction on their recent achievements. Between 8 and 13 August the Corps had met and defeated elements of fifteen German divisions, completely routing four. By the 20th it had penetrated up to fourteen miles on a frontage which had widened from 7500 to 10,000 yards—an area of 67 square miles—and had liberated 27 villages. Captures included more than 9000 prisoners, nearly 200 guns of various calibres, and over a thousand machine-guns and trench mortars.[168] "This magnificent victory has been won", General Currie told the Corps in a special order on 13 August, "because your training was good, your discipline was good, your leadership was good." At the same time he warmly thanked staffs and supporting arms and services for their "splendid support and cooperation". These successes had been gained at a cost of 11,822 Canadian casualties (for the period 8 to 20 August). The greater part of this total, 9074, had been incurred on the four opening days of the offensive—3868 of them on 8 August.

Tank and Air Support, 8-11 August

Some German writers, possibly with a view to defending the prestige of their own troops, have been inclined to attribute the Allied success on 8 August largely to the tanks. Yet far from constituting a "massed tank" attack—such a use of armour had not been planned—the operation owed its success principally to the work of the infantry and the machine-gunners, valuably supported by the artillery, which throughout the course of the battle achieved and maintained a "definite ascendancy over the enemy's batteries."[169]

This is not to deny that the presence of the armour enabled the advance to proceed more rapidly than would otherwise have been the case. It may be argued that the tanks, which were hampered early in the operation by fog and battle smoke, might have been used more profitably if they had been held back until later in the day; yet it is certain that their employment in the early stages kept down the Fourth Army's infantry losses, which increased substantially as the number of supporting tanks diminished. The French, attacking without tanks, suffered far more heavily in proportion.[170]

The general pattern had been for small groups of armour and individual tanks to deal with enemy machine-gun nests and other local resistance that was holding up the advance of the infantry. The 4th Canadian Division's novel use of tanks to carry machine-gun teams forward appears to have exerted little influence on the battle, and the unfortunate experience of the riders was to make the idea of "armoured infantry" singularly repulsive to all foot-soldiers.[171] The combination of medium tanks and cavalry proved equally unpromising. Their top speed of 8.3 miles an hour cut by more than half by ground conditions, the Whippets could not keep up with the horses when the latter were not being fired on; under fire, the cavalry could not follow the tanks. In isolated instances, however, medium tanks and armoured cars carried out independent offensive tasks with heartening results.*[173] Whatever chance the mismated cavalry-Whippet force might have had of taking the Blue Dotted Line and exploiting beyond it depended largely on maintaining the momentum of the advance—and that hope, as we have noted, was dashed by the misunderstanding at Cavalry Corps Headquarters on the opening day of the battle (above, p. 407).

Between 8 and 15 August the Cavalry Corps suffered 887 casualties in personnel and lost 1800 horses;[174] the Canadian Cavalry Brigade reported losses of twelve officers and 233 men in the first four days of the offensive.[175] The toll on the armour was heavy indeed—only 145 tanks were fit for battle on the second day. After the opening day direct hits from German guns accounted for the great majority of the losses. Thirty-nine machines were knocked out on 9 August, and thirty more on the 10th.[176] Of 99 fighting tank casualties sustained between the 8th and the 13th by the 4th Tank Brigade (which was supporting

* Armoured cars, exploiting success on the Australian front, shot up an advanced corps headquarters and captured the German defence plan for 25 miles of the Hindenburg Line. Although evidently prepared early in 1917 and not kept up to date, the document was useful in directing the subsequent bombardment of that position on to vital centres of defence.[172]

the Canadian Corps), 80 resulted from enemy fire while only 19 broke down or were ditched.[177]

The role assigned to the Royal Air Force for the opening day of the battle had been one of interdiction—early morning attacks against the enemy's aerodromes on the Fourth Army front and evening and night bombing of the railway stations at Péronne and Chaulnes.[178] But a more attractive and profitable target appeared in the bridges over the Somme, with the result that no serious bombing of railway communications took place until the morning of the 10th. There were hopes that if the bridges, which served as gateways to and from the field of battle, could be put out of action, the Germans west of the Somme would be isolated. In all, on 8 August the R.A.F. made 205 bombing flights and dropped twelve tons of bombs in fruitless attempts to destroy the Somme spans. Forty-five British aeroplanes were shot down and 52 more rendered unserviceable. The bridges remained intact.[179]

Attacks on the bridges continued in full force day and night until 13-14 August and thereafter took place intermittently. As opposition from German fighter craft increased it became necessary to transfer R.A.F. fighters from a bomb-carrying role to that of escort to the heavy bombers. Even after a total of 700 flights against them, the bridges were all still quite usable. There seems little doubt that a strict adherence to the original plan of attacking rail centres of communication would have brought greater profit. Yet though the bombing had failed in its object, some justification might be argued that it had forced the German air forces to fight under conditions not of their own choice, and there was consolation that the Allied losses in bomber crews were matched by the enemy's loss of some of his finest pilots.[180] On 10 August Germany lost her leading ace when Lieutenant Erich Loewenhardt (53 victories) collided with a comrade. Three days later Lieutenant Baron Lothar von Richthofen* (40 victories) received a wound which kept him from active duty for the remainder of the war.[182]

The enemy's air service, though initially outnumbered, had reacted quickly to the Allied attack. As the morning fog of 8 August cleared, German fighter squadrons were ordered to abandon their customary high-flying defensive tactics in order to give all possible protection to their artillery observation and contact patrol machines. Soon, as they made contact with British bombers and fighters (carrying 25-pound bombs), the protection of the Somme bridges became their primary concern. Additional fighter units, including elements of the Richthofen Circus, were brought in and all squadrons were kept in the air as long as possible.[183] In the new 125-m.p.h. Fokker D VII biplane the enemy possessed a magnificent weapon, without which, according to one German writer, "the tenacious and successful [air] resistance offered in the final months of the war would have been impossible."[184]

*A younger brother of the late Captain Manfred von Richthofen, and acting commander of Fighter Wing No. 1. The second regular commander was Captain Wilhelm Reinhard (accidentally killed early in July) and the third and last, Lieut. Hermann Göring.[181]

After Amiens

Although by 13 August the Allied offensive had been definitely checked, the German leaders could no longer doubt that the initiative had passed from their hands. On that date, at a conference held at Spa with Field-Marshal von Hindenburg, Reichschancellor Count von Hertling and the Foreign Secretary, Admiral von Hintze, in attendance, Ludendorff, while opposing any voluntary surrender of ground,* admitted "that it was no longer possible to force the enemy to sue for peace by an offensive". Since the defensive alone could hardly achieve that object, the war would have to be ended by diplomatic means.[185] Hindenburg, on the other hand, derived some comfort from the fact that "the enemy had once more failed to extract all possible advantages from his great initial successes" and that German armies were "still standing deep in the enemy's country."[186] Next day, at a Crown Council presided over by the Kaiser, His Majesty ordered peace negotiations to be opened through the King of Spain or the Queen of the Netherlands.[187] It was also about this time that orders were issued calling off large-scale air attacks planned against the British and French capitals by German bombers using thousands of one-kilogram incendiary bombs. While it was proclaimed to the world that these cities were being spared on humanitarian grounds, there seems little doubt that the inevitability of a German defeat was the main reason for the cancellation of the attacks. Throughout the war British and French planes dropped some 14,000 bombs on German soil. A British plan to attack Berlin, however, failed to materialize owing to insufficient aircraft capable of such a mission.[188]

In the meantime Allied plans on the Western Front were undergoing revision. As early as the evening of 11 August, as German resistance stiffened, Marshal Foch had shown himself willing to modify objectives and consider alternatives to further offensive operations on the Amiens front. At that time large-scale operations were due to be resumed on the 15th. But on the 13th General Debeney asked for and received a day's postponement of the assault by his army; and next morning General Rawlinson was given the same extra time in which to complete his preparations.[189] Sir Douglas Haig has revealed in his diary that he shared Rawlinson's misgivings about attacking the well-prepared Roye-Chaulnes defences and that he was resolved that the French First and British Fourth Armies should merely "keep up pressure on that front" in order to hold the enemy's attention, while he prepared to strike elsewhere with the British First and Third Armies.[190]

There is no doubt that Rawlinson was considerably influenced by representations made to him by General Currie, upon whose forces the burden of a major share of a renewed offensive must fall. At a meeting on the morning of 14 August the Army Commander showed Haig a letter (accompanied by air photographs taken the previous day of the German positions) in which Currie set forth the

* General von Lossberg, now chief of staff to General von Boehn (commanding the Ninth, Eighteenth and Second Armies), had failed in repeated attempts to persuade Ludendorff to put all available reserves immediately to work on repairing the Hindenburg Line with a view to a withdrawal to that position.

arguments against renewing an operation which would "cost a great many casualties" without obtaining adequate results. He suggested that if the attack were found to be absolutely necessary it should be postponed in order to allow time to "recover the element of surprise." He recommended that an alternative, and better, course would be to withdraw the Canadian Corps from the line, and after resting it for a few days employ it on the Arras front in a surprise attack in the direction of Bapaume. An advance in this sector coupled with an attack by the French from their present line, might well force the enemy to abandon his positions west of the Somme without the necessity of a frontal assault.[191]

This last suggestion was in keeping with Haig's own ideas. An exchange of letters with Foch on the 14th brought no agreement about postponing operations at the Somme,[192] and that evening a telegram from the Generalissimo asked Haig "once more to maintain the date already set."[193] The Field Marshal, however, had made up his mind to limit the Somme attack to a series of set stages, and on the afternoon of the 15th he pressed his arguments at Foch's advanced headquarters at Sarcus (twenty miles south-west of Amiens). "I spoke to Foch quite straightly", his diary records, "and let him know that *I was responsible to my Government and fellow citizens for the handling of the British forces.*"[194] Foch's resistance had already been weakened when he learned from General Debeney that morning that the projected attack on Roye "would certainly be difficult", and even if mounted would leave the French forces too weak to maintain it. "I definitely came around to the opinion of Field-Marshal Sir Douglas Haig", he wrote in his *Memoirs,* and he agreed that the Amiens offensive should not be pressed.[195]

A new operation order issued by British G.H.Q. directed the Third Army, which was holding a nineteen-mile front north of Albert, without delay to "press the enemy back energetically in the direction of Bapaume"; the Fourth Army while continuing its preparations for an attack would be prepared to follow up any German withdrawal towards the Somme. Farther north the First Army would take advantage of any German retirement to exert pressure south-eastward from the Arras sector; under favourable conditions, it would attack Monchy-le-Preux and Orange Hill. The latter, it will be recalled, had been the proposed target of the cancelled Canadian attack at the end of July (above, p. 389).[196]

In a letter confirming his acceptance of Haig's proposals Marshal Foch made it clear that he was depending on the British operations to be developed with sufficient impetus to ensure a resumption of the thrust south of the Somme. He went on to thank Sir Douglas for his cooperation, which had completely freed the Amiens area and the Paris-Amiens railway. For an offensive north of the Aisne (below, p. 425) he was now going to transfer the French First Army from Haig's command back to Pétain's group of armies.[197] Accordingly the Franco-British boundary was shifted northward to the Amiens-Chaulnes railway, and the relief of the Canadian Corps by French troops began on 19 August.[198]

On the night of 19-20 August the 2nd Canadian Division began moving northward by bus and train to rejoin the First Army in the Arras sector, followed the next night by the 3rd Division. A number of days were to elapse before the 1st and

4th Divisions made the move. General Currie closed his Headquarters at Dury on the 22nd. During the day he called on a number of senior commanders and had the satisfaction of being told by General Byng that the Canadian performance at Amiens was "the finest operation of the war".[199]

CHAPTER XIV

THROUGH THE HINDENBURG LINE TO CAMBRAI

(See Maps 12 and 13 and Sketches 50 and 51)

The Expanding Allied Offensive

On 21 August Sir Douglas Haig received a visit from the British Minister of Munitions, Mr. Winston Churchill, who assured him that the supply of gas, large-calibre shells, and tanks for the armies in France was being speeded up considerably. This was gratifying news, but when Churchill reported that the General Staff in London saw the following July as being the decisive period of the war, the C.-in-C. told him forcibly that every effort should be made to get a decision in the present autumn. The Germans were being outlasted and beaten. "If we allow the enemy a period of quiet", declared Sir Douglas, "he will recover, and the 'wearing out' process must be recommenced."[1]

The success of the Amiens offensive had convinced Haig that the time had come for an all-out effort against the enemy—who was "feeling that this is the beginning of the end for him".[2] In the C.-in-C.'s opinion bold action should replace unenterprising caution. He told his army commanders to emphasize to their subordinates the changed conditions under which they must now fight. It was no longer necessary "to advance step by step in regular lines as in the 1916-17 battles. All Units must go straight for their objectives, while Reserves should be pushed in where we are gaining ground."[3]

The first move in the Allied scheme to extend the stalled Amiens offensive on both wings was made on the southern flank on 20 August, when the French Tenth Army of General Mangin struck northward from the Aisne between Compiègne and Soissons with twelve divisions. An advance of nearly five miles in two days carried the assault to the river Oise between Noyon and Chauny. On the 21st the French Third Army (General Humbert) on Mangin's left resumed operations with some success, while on the same day north of Albert the British Third Army initiated Sir Douglas Haig's share in the renewed offensive. General Byng's forces struck a telling blow on the 23rd, when a two-mile advance towards Bapaume netted 5000 prisoners from General Otto von Below's badly shaken Seventeenth Army. This achievement was matched on Haig's right flank, where the Fourth Army had taken up the battle astride the Somme and the 1st Australian Division had shattered two German divisions on the southern bank.[4] The next two days saw some slight progress on both the Third and Fourth Armies' fronts, and on 26 August an expansion of the battle into the First Army's sector brought the Canadian Corps once more into action. (See Sketch 51 on p. 455.)

The period of rest and refitting that would normally follow participation in such extensive operations as the Amiens battle was denied the Canadians; for in these last hundred days of the war each major offensive so rapidly succeeded its predecessor that unprecedented demands had to be made on the stamina of the forces employed. Back under General Horne's command in its former position east of Arras, the Canadian Corps was confronted by a series of formidable defence positions which the enemy was holding in strength. Immediately in front of the Canadians, about Monchy-le-Preux, were the old British trenches lost in the German offensive of March 1918, and to the east of these lay the enemy's former front line. This was backed up, two miles east of Monchy, by the so-called Fresnes-Rouvroy line, which was actually an extension south of the Scarpe of the original line joining Rouvroy (south-east of Lens) to Fresnes (north-east of Arras). Another mile to the east the approaches to Cambrai were blocked by the strongest position of all—the Drocourt-Quéant line (the southermost portion of the *Wotan I-Stellung*), which, extending northward from the Hindenburg Line (*Siegfried-Stellung*) at Quéant, had been constructed by the Germans to contain any Allied advance into the Douai plain. Still farther east, crossed by the main road at Marquion, was the unfinished Canal du Nord, connecting the Somme Canal with the Sensée Canal. Though not yet extensively fortified it formed in conjunction with the Sensée marshes a major obstacle.

On 22 August General Currie outlined to his divisional commanders his plans for an attack eastward astride the Arras-Cambrai road. The Canadian Corps had been given the task of forcing the Drocourt-Quéant line south of the Scarpe and advancing to the line of the Canal du Nord. Having thus broken the hinge of the Hindenburg system the Corps was to swing southward and sweep down behind that formidable position in order to deny the Germans opposing the Third Army a rallying ground.[5] On Currie's right the 17th Corps, operating on the Third Army's northern flank, was under orders to cooperate with the Canadian Corps, attacking south-eastward along both sides of the Hindenburg position.[6]

General Currie's was an important and a difficult assignment. The enemy's main defence positions, supplemented by various subsidiary switches and strongpoints, were among the strongest on the Western Front. The ground was pocked with the scars of 1917 and early 1918, and in the litter of old trenches and fortifications German engineers had found ready-made positions which they had considerably strengthened. Furthermore, topography was on the side of the Germans. The battle area spread over the north-eastern slopes of the Artois Hills, whose summits about Monchy were over three hundred feet above the valley-bottoms of the Scarpe and the Sensée. The latter river, flowing generally eastward, together with its tributaries had dissected the hills into numerous deep valleys. The intervening ridges and high points, often mutually supporting, the enemy had fortified with a skill that demonstrated his mastery in military engineering.

The Germans' general defensive plan at this time was to give up ground in the region of the Lys and Ypres salients and to fight a determined rearguard action in the Somme area. Ludendorff overruled the views of those staffs (in particular Crown Prince Wilhelm's) that favoured a major voluntary retirement into the Hindenburg and adjoining defence systems.[7] His purpose was by means of a gradual fighting withdrawal to wear out the Allied forces before they reached the Hindenburg position, thus gaining time to reorganize behind that formidable defence line. The defences about the Arras-Cambrai road in the Monchy area would form the pivot of any German retirement south of the Scarpe, while the security of Prince Rupprecht's northern armies also depended on retaining them.

These positions became the initial Canadian objective. With the enemy expecting attack, except for the actual hour of assault, surprise was clearly impossible. It would be a case of launching successive frontal, grinding assaults against well-established lines manned by tenacious, alert troops.

The Battle of the Scarpe 1918, 26-30 August

The front taken over by the 2nd and 3rd Canadian Divisions on reaching the Arras sector extended from Neuville-Vitasse north to the River Scarpe, a mile west of Fampoux. Three high features, all held by the Germans, dominated the landscape to the east. Three miles away Monchy-le-Preux, so fiercely fought for in previous encounters, stood on its own hill north of the Cambrai road; while ranged like twin bastions in front of it were the long ridge of Orange Hill reaching up towards the Scarpe and Chapel Hill lying astride the highway.

The 1st and 4th Canadian Divisions did not arrive from the Fourth Army until 25 and 28 August respectively, and in the meantime the 51st (Highland) Division formed part of the Canadian Corps, providing flank protection north of the river. General Currie's plan for the first phase of the offensive called for simultaneous attacks by the British division on the left, the 3rd Canadian Division between the Scarpe and the Cambrai road, and the 2nd on the right covering as far as the inter-army boundary, which ran eastward from Neuville-Vitasse. They were to secure a north-south line just west of Monchy-le-Preux, exploiting thence as far east as possible. The 51st Division, given no definite objective, was to capitalize on any success south of the Scarpe by pushing troops along the northern bank. For gun support General Currie could call on fourteen brigades of field* and nine of heavy artillery. Nine tanks from the 3rd Tank Brigade were allotted to each of the Canadian divisions, but as a result of the losses to armour at Amiens these were not to be used ahead of the infantry unless definite resistance demanded their employment.[9] The boundary between the Canadian divisions was the Cambrai road almost as far as Chapel Hill, where it swung eastward to place the hill in the 2nd Division's sector of

* These included in addition to the artillery of the 2nd and 3rd Canadian Divisions that of the 15th, 16th and 39th Divisions and three army brigades.[8]

operations. Monday, 26 August, was fixed as the day of assault, and zero hour, originally at dawn, was advanced to 3:00 a.m. in hope of confusing the enemy.[10]

There were preliminary operations along the Corps southern boundary in conjunction with advances made by the Third Army. In a daylight raid on 23 August, the 31st Battalion captured a sugar factory south of Neuville-Vitasse, and on the following evening gained partial control of the town, which was still in German hands.[11] German sources reveal that Neuville-Vitasse was evacuated early on the morning of 24 August. The decision not to undertake a protracted defence was reported to have been taken by the German 39th Infantry Division because "the commitment of the Canadians, the best British troops, had been recognized".[12] Bright, moonlit nights preceding 26 August and a favourable weather forecast raised meteorological hopes which proved vain. Heavy showers fell at intervals throughout the night of the 25th-26th, and General Currie noted in his diary that "it was none too bright at zero hour."[13]

In order to meet an Allied attack in the event of the Somme operations being extended northward the Germans had concentrated three divisions astride the Scarpe. Facing the Canadian Corps on 26 August were the 48th Reserve Division north of the Scarpe, the 214th Division from the river to south of the Arras-Cambrai road, and the 39th Division in the Neuville-Vitasse sector. They were ready for action. Their artillery was arranged to counter an assault and their resting battalions had been moved forward to their battle positions.[14]

The attack started on time. The opening artillery and machine-gun barrage was reported as admirable. The 2nd Division attacking south of the road made fine progress. At first the Germans, surprised by the early hour of the assault, offered little resistance, so that the advancing infantry had no need to call on the tanks for help. While the 6th Brigade, under Brig.-Gen. A. H. Bell, pushed out a defensive flank on the Corps right and mopped up the Neuville-Vitasse area, the 4th Brigade (Brig.-Gen. R. Rennie) making the main assault, drove rapidly through the enemy's outpost zone, encountering very little resistance. Shortly after 6:00 a.m. the 20th Battalion captured Chapel Hill, 2500 yards west of Monchy. By this time day had broken, making it easier for the tanks to support the infantry closely. But it also allowed the enemy good observation from high ground about Monchy; and his field artillery put a number of the tanks out of action. By 7:30, the 21st Battalion was approaching the outskirts of Guémappe, where it ran into heavy fire coming from Monchy, a mile to the north.

A mid-morning shift in the forward boundary of the First and Third Armies (partly in order to aid the Fourth Army by exerting more pressure in a south-easterly direction) had repercussions on the Canadian front. The 2nd Division, hitherto attacking eastward, was ordered to shift its axis of advance to the south-east, and to capture the high ground across the Cojeul River south-east of Wancourt. General Burstall gave the task to the 6th Brigade, assigning as objective the ruins of Wancourt Tower, 1200 yards south of Guémappe. At 4:40 p.m. the 27th and 28th Battalions crossed the dry river bed and attacked the ridge, supported by an effective barrage fired by the 5th and 6th Brigades C.F.A., which had moved forward of Neuville-Vitasse.[15] As the attackers topped the rise from the Cojeul valley they were heavily hit. The crest of the ridge was thick with uncut wire and swept by machine-gun fire from outposts of the Hindenburg Line over towards the right, which the British 52nd Division, making a parallel attack on the Third Army's left flank, had not yet reached. The two battalions were forced to dig in at dusk short of their final objective; but early next morning in a silent attack they secured Egret Trench on the German forward slope, thereby gaining a good jumping-off line for operations on the 27th.[16]

Meanwhile on the Corps left, where the approach of the 3rd Division was dominated by Orange Hill, rising sixty feet above the surrounding countryside, General Lipsett's plan was to turn the position by an attack along the southern bank of the Scarpe. The 8th Brigade (Brig.-Gen. D. C. Draper), employing in the assault three battalions of the Canadian Mounted Rifles, found the German opposition lighter than expected. The 4th C.M.R. advanced along the river bank and outflanked Orange Hill. It was followed by the 2nd C.M.R., which, turning sharply to its right, took the hill from the north. The 1st and 5th C.M.R. then passed through to left and right respectively, to attack Monchy from the north and the west; by 7:40 the village was in Canadian hands.* Shortly afterwards the 7th Brigade (Brig.-Gen. H. M. Dyer) pushed through to attack with The Royal Canadian Regiment and the P.P.C.L.I. a number of enemy-held woods east of Monchy.[18] The change in the 2nd Division's axis had led to the withdrawal of the 4th Brigade south of the Arras-Cambrai road. As a temporary measure two machine-gun batteries of General Brutinel's Canadian Independent Force were dispatched down the road to cover the gap.[19] The 42nd Battalion was then put in on the 20th Battalion's former front, where it evicted the enemy from its heavily-wired trenches south of Monchy.[20]

North of the Scarpe the 51st (Highland) Division had kept pace with little difficulty, pushing its line forward to secure the chemical works north of Roeux and establish patrols on the west side of Gavrelle.[21] By dusk the Canadian line, well inside the old German front trench system, ran from west of Pelves, on the south bank of the river, passing 1000 yards east of Monchy-le-Preux to include Guémappe and Wancourt Tower.[22] Powerful counter-attacks developed from the direction of the Bois du Vert and Jigsaw Wood, which the enemy was holding as outposts to his Fresnes-Rouvroy line. These were launched by two regiments of the German 35th Division, moved forward from the Drocourt-Quéant Line with orders to retake Monchy. The German effort was smashed, but it had succeeded in preventing any further Canadian advance on the 26th.[23]

General Currie's orders for the next day directed both Canadian divisions to attack in two stages to break through the Fresnes-Rouvroy Line. The 51st Division would continue pushing forward along the north bank of the Scarpe. In the opening stage, the 3rd Division was to overcome the troublesome Bois du

* This quick success by the 8th Brigade was not achieved without some difficult fighting, in the course of which Lieut. C. S. Rutherford, M.C., M.M., of the 5th C.M.R., was awarded the V.C. for "most conspicuous bravery, initiative and devotion to duty". During the advance, Rutherford captured some 70 prisoners and silenced several enemy machine-guns single-handed.[17]

Vert and Bois du Sart and establish a line through Boiry-Notre-Dame. At the same time the 2nd Division was to secure the ground on its front lying between the Cojeul and the Sensée River, two miles beyond, and having captured the villages of Chérisy and Vis-en-Artois in the Sensée valley, advance its line a further 2000 yards to the east. The 3rd Division was given as subsequent objectives Etaing and Dury, and the 2nd the village of Cagnicourt. To achieve these final goals would involve an advance of approximately five miles through heavily defended positions. Before the offensive opened on 26 August it had been Currie's intention to assault with only one brigade a day on each divisional front, in order that divisions could remain in action for three days without relief. But the vigour of the German resistance had spoiled this plan, and the G.O.C. had to warn the 1st Canadian and 4th British Divisions that they must be prepared to relieve the 2nd and 3rd Canadian Divisions on the evening of the 27th.[24]

Heavy rain fell during the night of the 26th-27th, and the slippery ground added to the difficulties of assembly. It was still raining when the 9th Brigade, which had not previously been committed in the battle, attacked at 4:55 a.m. through the 42nd Battalion north of the Cambrai road. The 52nd Battalion cleared the Bois du Vert, and the 58th the Bois du Sart; but the 116th Battalion, moving through the 52nd against Boiry-Notre-Dame, was halted by the hail of machine-gun fire coming from Artillery Hill and Jigsaw Wood to the north.[25] The newly-arrived 35th German Infantry Division was defending the Boiry area with, from south to north, the 61st, 176th and 141st Infantry Regiments.[26] On the left Pelves remained untaken, and the only additional advance that day on the divisional front was on the southern flank, where the 43rd Battalion joined in the 4th Brigade's attack on Vis-en-Artois.

Owing to the late arrival of the 5th Brigade from the rear, the 2nd Division did not begin the day's operations until ten o'clock. On the left the 4th Brigade advanced along the valley of the Cojeul, paralleling the Arras-Cambrai road. The 18th Battalion, with assistance from the 43rd Battalion north of the road, occupied Vis-en-Artois without much difficulty, but ran into damaging enemy fire at the Sensée. It took persistent fighting all afternoon to gain a small bridgehead over the narrow stream.[27] Farther south the 5th Brigade, advancing down the western slope of Wancourt Tower Ridge, received useful aid from supporting tanks and from batteries of the 2nd Canadian Machine Gun Battalion in dealing with hostile posts. On the right the 26th Battalion was over the Sensée by noon, and shortly afterwards the 24th and 22nd Battalions, having captured Chérisy, crossed above and below the village. They met stiff resistance on the far side, and on instructions from Corps Headquarters not to attempt too much in the face of heavy opposition, General Burstall ordered the 2nd Division to make good its line along the Sensée's east bank and to secure the bridge on the Arras-Cambrai road.[28] The increased German resistance encountered beyond Chérisy came from units of the 26th Reserve Division, which shortly after midday on 27 August had assumed command in the Rémy area. On its left, opposing the extreme right of the Canadian Corps, was the 21st Reserve Division.[29] On Burstall's right the 52nd Division had kept up by capturing Fontaine les Croisilles east of the Sensée. North of the Scarpe, the 51st Division reported taking the commanding Greenland Hill, opposite Pelves, but the afternoon brought a counter-attack and dusk found the line still west of the height. The proposed relief of the 2nd and 3rd Canadian Divisions was postponed, and both were ordered to continue the advance on 28 August with the object of breaching the Fresnes-Rouvroy line and capturing Cagnicourt, Dury and Etaing.[30]

The fighting on the 28th, a day warm and bright after much rain during the night, was extremely bitter and accompanied by heavy losses. On the previous afternoon General Lipsett had reorganized his front, both to sort out units that had got mixed up in the close fighting of the 26th and 27th, and because he wanted to assault the Fresnes-Rouvroy Line in strength, with all three of his brigades attacking abreast. He placed the 8th Brigade between the Arras-Cambrai road and the Cojeul River, the 9th north-westward to the Bois du Sart, and the 7th from there to the Scarpe. He planned to smother the German machine-gun nests with an immense concentration of artillery fire—a procedure which proved highly successful.

At eleven o'clock Brig.-Gen. Ormond's 9th Brigade attacked on a 1000-yard front with four battalions* covered by all the artillery of the 3rd Division. The three leading units pierced the Fresnes-Rouvroy line between Boiry and the Cojeul River and then the 52nd and 58th Battalions swung north to secure Boiry and Artillery Hill beyond. As the division's guns turned next on the German positions opposite the 8th Brigade, the 43rd Battalion and the 5th C.M.R. stormed the high ground between the Cojeul and the Sensée known as "Seventy Ridge". They captured the ridge and Rémy Wood beyond, but could not take the village of Haucourt, just across the Sensée. In the 7th Brigade's sector Princess Patricia's Canadian Light Infantry and the 42nd Battalion drove stoutly resisting Germans of the 141st Regiment out of Jigsaw Wood, and on the extreme left flank the 49th Battalion occupied Pelves, which the enemy had evacuated during the night.[31]

An equally fine effort by the 2nd Canadian Division in the general direction of Cagnicourt was less rewarding. The attack started half an hour after midday, behind a rolling barrage of field artillery which followed a morning bombardment by the heavy guns. The 5th Brigade, using the same three battalions as on the previous day, carried the major part of the operation. On the left the 4th Brigade, exhausted from two days of extremely heavy fighting, could muster only what amounted to a composite battalion from its four battalions—the reserve consisting mainly of headquarters details, batmen and cooks. In spite of the determination of all ranks to take the so-called Fresnes-Rouvroy line, the obstacle of uncut wire covered by intense machine-gun fire proved too much for troops that were mentally and physically worn out not only from fighting but from a serious shortage of sleep during the preceding eight days.[32] Although the 22nd and 24th Battalions got into the German front line during the afternoon, a counter-attack about 9:00 p.m. forced them back practically to their starting line.

* The 52nd, 58th and 116th Battalions, and the 4th C.M.R. The last unit was temporarily under command from the 8th Brigade in exchange for the 43rd Battalion, which could not be disengaged.

Casualties for the day were heavy, and brought the total reported by the 2nd and 3rd Divisions in the three days' fighting to 254 officers and 5547 other ranks.[33] The 22nd Battalion had lost all its officers, and the 24th Battalion was also grievously stricken. Major Georges Vanier (a future Governor General of Canada), who had taken command of the decimated 22nd Battalion on the previous day, lost his right leg in the action.[34] Lt.-Col. W. H. Clark-Kennedy, the 24th's C.O., amalgamated the remnants of both battalions and, in spite of a serious wound, continued to direct his forces against the German lines. His heroic and distinguished leadership in this and the previous day's fighting brought him the Victoria Cross.[35] The German High Command had been anxiously watching that sector of the Seventeenth Army between Bapaume and the Scarpe where the divisions of the 2nd Bavarian Corps were under critical pressure. Thus it was that although great deeds are often overlooked in the glum atmosphere of impending defeat, the German communique of 29 August did not fail to extol the valiant defence put up by the Württemberger regiments astride the Arras-Cambrai road on 28 August.[36]

The 2nd and 3rd Canadian Divisions were now thoroughly tired. During the night of 28-29 August the 2nd was relieved by the 1st Division, and the 3rd Division by the 4th British Division, which had been placed under General Currie's command, pending the arrival of the 4th Canadian Division from the Amiens front. In order better to protect his left flank, which he considered particularly sensitive about Pelves because of the lag in the advance north of the Scarpe, General Currie placed Brig.-Gen. Brutinel in charge of a composite brigade*, strong in machine-guns, assigning it to the 4th British Division to guard against counter-attacks from the direction of Hamblain.[38]

As the formations which had been relieved moved to locations west of Arras for an all too brief period of recuperation, they could take pride in having got the Corps operation away to an excellent start. In three days of the bitterest kind of fighting, over difficult, broken country beset with a maze of stoutly held trenches, the two Canadian divisions had advanced more than five miles on an ever-widening front and had seized an important part of the enemy's strong Fresnes-Rouvroy defence system, capturing more than 3300 prisoners and a vast quantity of booty that included 53 guns and 519 machine-guns.[39]

Ahead loomed a bigger task—the conquest of the Drocourt-Quéant Line (which we shall hereafter frequently refer to as the D-Q Line). On the afternoon of the 28th General Currie notified General Horne that because of the setback that day at the Fresnes-Rouvroy line it would not be possible to attack the next defence system before 31 August at the earliest.[40]

Plans for Attacking the D-Q Line

It was essential first to secure a firm jumping-off line. This meant completing the capture of the Fresnes-Rouvroy line and the Vis-en-Artois Switch (which from

* Brutinel's Brigade, as it was called, consisted of the 1st Canadian Motor M.G. Brigade, the 101st M.G. Battalion (less one company) and the Canadian Cyclist Battalion.[37]

Vis-en-Artois angled south-eastward to join the D-Q Line a mile west of Cagnicourt), besides taking other strongly defended localities. While the heavy artillery concentrated on cutting enemy wire in front of the D-Q Line, and the engineers assembled bridging material that would be needed to cross the Sensée and the Canal du Nord, the Canadian Corps carried out a number of minor operations on 29 August which considerably bettered the Canadian position. In the northern sector Brutinel's Brigade, still under the orders of the 4th British Division, advanced the line nearly one thousand yards by seizing Bench Farm and Victoria Copse, north of Boiry-Notre-Dame, with the Canadian Corps Cyclist Battalion establishing posts right up to the Scarpe. The rest of the division captured Rémy and Haucourt, and occupied the Fresnes-Rouvroy trench system as far south as the Sensée River. The Canadian front was considerably shortened as command of the 51st Highland Division and the 11th Division (which during the day relieved Brutinel's Brigade) passed to the 22nd Corps. For the time being, at least, General Currie would no longer have to worry about a long northern flank.[41]

There was further progress on the 30th, the chief gains resulting from a skilfully planned operation carried out with daring by the 1st Canadian Brigade. Taking advantage of the 17th Corps' capture of Hendecourt, which lay behind the Fresnes-Rouvroy Line, General Macdonell devised with Brig.-Gen. Griesbach, the Commander of the 1st Brigade, a scheme to turn the flank of the enemy position by attacking northward from Third Army territory. Reaching their assembly positions by a night march, the 1st and 2nd Battalions assaulted at 4:40 a.m. behind an ingenious barrage that rolled from right to left across the divisional front. They caught the garrison completely by surprise and rapidly mopped up the line northward.* At the same time the 3rd Battalion attacked frontally a mile south of Vis-en-Artois and with bomb and bayonet began clearing the German trenches southward. By 7:00 a.m. it had gained touch with its sister battalions in the vicinity of Upton Wood, which lay in the angle between the two German switch-lines. There the Canadians held on all day under heavy fire. They drove off a German counter-attack, and after dark the 1st Battalion cleared Upton Wood, capturing 50 prisoners and five machine-guns.[43]

North of the Cambrai road the 4th British Division, attacking that afternoon across the Sensée River, advanced one thousand yards east of Rémy through the Bois Soufflard and got troops into Eterpigny.[44]

At a conference between Generals Horne and Currie on 30 August the date for the assault of the Drocourt-Quéant Line was again postponed. Both commanders recognized the line as the backbone of the enemy's resistance and it seemed wise "not to attack it until we are ready, and then to go all out." On the following day the First Army issued the order for the Canadian Corps to attack the position on 2 September and exploit rapidly forward to seize crossings over the Canal du Nord on a five-mile front between Sains-lez-Marquion

* According to a German account the 1st and 2nd Battalions of the 121st Reserve Regiment were wiped out. Only 50 men escaped; the remaining survivors, including the two battalion headquarters, became prisoners. The parent formation, the 26th Reserve Division, completely exhausted, was withdrawn next day.[42]

and Palluel and capture the high ground beyond. The 3rd Tank Brigade, an armoured car battalion and a regiment of cavalry were placed under General Currie's command for the task.[45]

While these plans were developing, and work proceeded on the tremendous task of repairing and extending roads and light railways behind the front, the 1st Canadian and 4th British Divisions continued to improve their positions. Six-inch howitzers of the corps heavy artillery maintained their steady pounding of the wire of the D-Q defences. In a surprise dawn attack on the 31st, the 8th Battalion seized the Ocean Work, a strongpoint in the German trenches south of Haucourt which had held out on the previous day.[46] The British division, having secured Eterpigny, advanced level with the Canadians. Fighting continued throughout the night, while the 4th Canadian Division moved the 12th Brigade into the front line between the 1st Canadian and 4th British Divisions.

These successes ensured that when the main assault went in there would be no costly delay in having to deal with intervening obstacles. Yet another bid for a good jumping-off place was made on the morning of 1 September, when the 2nd and 3rd Brigades captured the Crow's Nest, an enemy strongpoint on a high bluff which overlooked a large section of the D-Q defences. The attack, carried out by the 5th Battalion, flanked on the right by the 14th and on the left by the 12th Brigade's 72nd Battalion, began at 4:50 a.m. and achieved quick success. Retaining the position, however, proved to be more difficult in the face of three stubborn though vain and costly counter-attacks which were made during the day. The Canadians captured 200 prisoners, the enemy leaving behind more than 140 dead, besides nine light trench mortars and upwards of 80 machine-guns.[47]

The Drocourt-Quéant Line was one of the most powerful and well organized German defence systems. It consisted of a front and a support line, both abundantly provided with concrete shelters and machine-gun posts and protected by dense masses of barbed wire. The Buissy Switch, connecting the D-Q Line with the Hindenburg support system, was constructed on the same solid principles. The two lines joined along the forward slope of Mont Dury (which filled the space between Dury and the Cambrai road), the switch-line angling south-eastward to pass in front of Villers-lez-Cagnicourt and Buissy. In general the front D-Q line was sited either on a crest or a forward slope in order to provide a good field of fire—the support system being on a reverse slope.[48] Next to the problem of capturing the village of Dury, which was incorporated in the D-Q Line itself, one of the most challenging tasks to the attackers was the necessity of crossing Mont Dury. Advancing infantry would be exposed to fire from machine-guns sited on its forward slopes; while covering the crest and rear slope were more guns well disposed in depth, and farther back the advanced batteries of the German field artillery.

That the formidable nature of the position now to be attacked was fully realized by the War Cabinet in London was demonstrated by a personal telegram which the Chief of the Imperial General Staff sent to Sir Douglas Haig on 29 August. Associating the D-Q Line with the Hindenburg Line General Wilson

CANADIAN SIGNALLERS NEAR DURY

A group of despatch riders of the 12th Infantry Brigade's Signal Section momentarily relax behind the lines. At the upper left of the photograph, which was taken in September 1918, are mounted troops attached to assist in delivering despatches in country where the roads have been destroyed.

ARTILLERY ON THE MOVE

These 18-pounders of a Canadian field brigade are being brought forward, on 26 September 1918, to support the attack on Bourlon Wood. In the foreground are engineers of the 4th Canadian Division with British and German wounded.

ACROSS THE CANAL DU NORD

This photograph of the unfinished canal was taken near Moeuvres on 27 September 1918, during the Bourlon Wood operation. The infantry moving up belong to a unit of the 4th Canadian Division.

BRIDGING THE CANAL DU NORD

Canadian Engineers construct an Inglis bridge over a flooded portion of the Canal du Nord near Marquion. A temporary span replaces a demolished bridge on the right, and on the left is a floating bridge for the passage of horse transport only.

warned the C.-in-C. that "the War Cabinet would become anxious if we received heavy punishment in attacking the Hindenburg Line without success". This discouraging communication Sir Douglas kept to himself; his plans and orders remained unchanged.[49]

General Currie planned to make his main attack with the 1st Canadian Division on the right having two brigades abreast, the 4th in the centre on a single brigade front, and on the left flank—beside the Sensée marshes—the 4th British Division on a frontage of 2500 yards. Late in the afternoon of 31 August, however, the British G.O.C. (Major-General T. G. Matheson) told the Corps Commander that because of heavy losses in the preliminary fighting he could assault with only one brigade. Accordingly at the last minute the 4th Canadian Division took over half the British Division's frontage.[50]

It was Currie's intention to break the German line at what was probably its most critical point, the Arras-Cambrai road, and then swing outward to roll up the German defences to north and south. He designated his objectives by four phase lines. Capture of the first two would bring the attackers within striking distance of the Canal du Nord. These were the Red Line, passing through Dury and west of Cagnicourt, inside the D-Q support line; and the Green Line, which ran along the dominating ground approximately 1200 yards west of the Canal du Nord. The remaining objectives were on high ground east of the Canal.[51] In corps reserve for the operation were the 1st British Division and Brig.-Gen. Brutinel's mobile group, now re-formed as the Canadian Independent Force (Brutinel's Brigade having been disbanded on 31 August). Six companies of Mark V tanks were allotted on the basis of two companies to each attacking division. If necessary the tanks were to advance before zero to ensure that the maximum number reached the first line of wire before the infantry. To drown out the noise of their engines arrangements were made with the 1st Brigade R.A.F. for twin-engine aircraft to fly over the area on the eve of the assault. An elaborate artillery barrage would carry the infantry forward to the first objective in three lifts.[52]

South of the Arras-Cambrai road the 1st Division, next to the 57th British Division of the Third Army, planned to assault with the 3rd Brigade on the right and the 2nd on the left. With Cagnicourt taken, the 1st Brigade, in reserve during the initial assault, was to leapfrog the two leading brigades immediately east of the Buissy Switch and capture the villages of Buissy and Baralle.[53] General Macdonell would temporarily have an open right flank; for the 57th Division, having no supporting tanks, would make no frontal attack. Instead it would station its assaulting brigades behind the 3rd Canadian Brigade ready to pass through and swing to the right after the Canadians had breached the D-Q line.[54] The 4th Canadian Division, in the centre, had to change its plan of attack, as we have seen, by increasing its frontage to the north. This imposed a difficult task on the 10th Brigade, which had to march ten miles into the new area, relieve a British brigade and take up its assembly positions, all in the hours of darkness preceding the attack. On the right of General Watson's front the 12th Brigade was to advance over Mont Dury to gain the first objective, where the 11th Brigade would pass through; on the left, the 10th Brigade was ordered to capture Dury and exploit eastward.[55]

On the Corps left the 4th British Division was given only three successive objectives. Its advance in the initial stages would by-pass Etaing on the left. Etaing itself was included only in the Division's final phase line, which ran along the south bank of the Sensée as far as Oisy-le-Verger.[56] It was the role of the Independent Force, as soon as the Red Line had been gained, to push rapidly down the Arras-Cambrai road and attempt to seize crossings over the Canal du Nord.[57]

Fighting for advantageous jumping-off lines continued along the Corps front almost to zero hour. Sensing the coming offensive, the enemy launched violent counter-attacks throughout the afternoon and evening of 1 September, particularly against the junction of the two Canadian divisions. The Germans persistently tried to push the forward edge of their outpost zone, already one mile deep in places, farther from their main trenches. The 12th Infantry Brigade astride the Cambrai road was hard beset, and its 72nd and 85th Battalions had to fight vigorously to retain their positions for the main operation.[58]

Assault and Capture, 2-3 September

A dark night, free from rain, preceded the attack. It was after midnight before every battalion commander had issued his operation order, and by the time all the assaulting troops were in their assembly trenches dawn was not far off. Its arrival coincided, as planned, with zero hour, and with it came the tremendous crash that opened the barrage.

On the Corps' southern flank three battalions led the 1st Division's attack—the 16th and 13th Battalions on the right opposite Cagnicourt, with the 7th Battalion of the 2nd Brigade on their left. The two 3rd Brigade units pushed forward quickly up the long slope to the enemy wire. They met little resistance at first, the Germans surrendering in large numbers. By 7:30 a.m. the 13th Battalion had captured its section of the D-Q support line. Shortly afterwards the 14th Battalion passed through to take Cagnicourt, where it surprised and captured in the village cellars enough Germans to make a full battalion.[59] The men of the 14th then seized the Bois de Loison east of the village and in a quick dash across 2000 yards of open country reached their final objective in the Buissy Switch directly in front of the village of Buissy.

On Brig.-Gen. Tuxford's right progress was slower. The 16th Battalion, suffering heavily from machine-gun fire coming in across the open southern flank, lost the supporting barrage and had to storm weapon posts which the enemy was quick to re-man in his front line. Among many acts of bravery performed that day two stood out at this stage of the operations. Lance-Corporal W. H. Metcalf, M.M., an American serving with the 16th Battalion, calmly walked across bullet-swept ground guiding a tank and directing its fire against German strongpoints which were holding up the infantry's advance. Later, after the battalion had broken through the main D-Q position, only to be halted in front of the support line, the Commanding Officer, Lt.-Col. Cyrus W. Peck, went forward through bursting shells and withering machine-gun fire to make a personal reconnaissance, and to compel roaming tanks to protect his open flank. He then reorganized his battalion and led them on to their objective. Both Metcalf and Peck won the Victoria Cross*—one of the very few occasions in the war when a battalion twice earned the coveted award in a single day.[61] Pushing through the 16th Battalion at the Red Line, the 15th, suffering crippling casualties, fought slowly forward to the Bois de Bouche, some 3000 yards short of the Buissy Switch, which here angled sharply to the south-east. Here the survivors consolidated as the 3rd Battalion came up from reserve. At 6:00 p.m. British infantry finally arrived to seal off the open flank which had proved so costly to the Canadians.[62]

On the 2nd Brigade's front the 5th Battalion was still engaged in hand-to-hand fighting for the jumping-off line when the 7th Battalion passed through to assault. Aided greatly by the shrapnel barrage and the supporting tanks the 7th had little difficulty in capturing and mopping up the D-Q line in its sector. At eight o'clock the 10th Battalion took over the lead at the Red Line. Up to this stage the tanks had kept well to the fore, knocking out one enemy post after another. East of the D-Q Line, however, they began falling victim to the German artillery fire. Soon the 10th Battalion was halted by the intense fire that came from machine-guns and trench mortars in the Buissy Switch in front of Villers-lez-Cagnicourt. In dogged fighting the battalion had by late afternoon established a line east of the village. One more effort was to be made. An artillery barrage called down at 6:00 p.m. on the German positions eased the situation, and the weary Canadians pushed forward again to capture the Buissy Switch by 11:00 p.m.

In the meantime the 4th Canadian Division was fighting its own hard battle. At the start the 12th Brigade on the right had to contend with an enemy pocket along the Arras-Cambrai road; and its supporting tanks arrived too late to help here. The leading battalions—from right to left the 72nd, the 38th and the 85th—found the D-Q trenches, as expected, heavily wired and strongly garrisoned. Nevertheless the Red Line, east of the support line, was reached on schedule. But as the 72nd and 38th Battalions crossed the long, exposed crest of Mont Dury they met the full force of the German machine-gun fire. From the objective, a sunken road joining Dury to the Cambrai road, German reinforcements swept the bare slopes with bullets, while on the right the 72nd Battalion was also caught in enfilade fire from the direction of Villers-lez-Cagnicourt.[63] In spite of mounting casualties the Canadians, aided by good work on the part of the tanks, pushed on grimly and by mid-morning they had captured and cleared the sunken road.

The 10th Brigade's initial assault on the divisional left was led by the 47th and

* It is a measure of the bitter fighting on both sides that no less than seven Victoria Crosses were won by Canadians on this day. The others who received this highest award for their courage were Captain B. S. Hutcheson, C.A.M.C. (attached to the 75th Battalion); Sgt. A. G. Knight, 10th Battalion; Pte. C. J. P. Nunney, D.C.M., M.M., 38th Battalion; Pte. W. L. Rayfield, 7th Battalion; Pte. J. F. Young, 87th Battalion.[60]

50th Battalions. Wire, largely intact, imposed serious delay as it had to be cut by hand. The two battalions occupied the main line trenches, allowing the 46th Battalion to leapfrog them and advance on the support line, which ran through the centre of Dury. There was particularly vicious fighting for the village, which was taken only after a flanking movement by the 46th had overcome a strong-point on the southern outskirts, capturing some 120 prisoners and nine machine-guns.[64] With the fall of Dury, the brigade's objective line at the sunken road was secured by 7:30 a.m.

The second phase of the attack began soon after eight, when the 78th Battalion, until now held in reserve, attempted to push forward on the right of the 10th Brigade. But it could make little headway against the storm of machine-gun fire coming out of Villers-lez-Cagnicourt and from a sugar-beet processing plant at the crossroads north-east of the village. A mile east of the sunken road, on a ridge extending from Buissy to Saudemont, German artillerymen were firing over open sights. By nine o'clock the 78th had been brought to a halt 200 yards east of the sunken road. Attempts by the 11th Brigade to exploit the 12th Brigade's gains east of Mont Dury were equally fruitless. By mid-afternoon all brigades on the divisional front reported their advance held up. Armoured cars from the Independent Force made several unsuccessful attempts to reach the lateral Villers-Saudemont road;* the Force had to confine its efforts to firing at enemy positions with machine-gun detachments posted on either side of the main Cambrai road.[66] On the Canadians' left the 4th British Division was able to capture its part of the D-Q system, but did not take Etaing until the following morning.

Although the Canadian Corps had not achieved all the objectives set (rather optimistically) for the attack, the results of 2 September were nevertheless eminently satisfactory. The Drocourt-Quéant Line had been assaulted and overrun on a frontage of seven thousand yards. In addition, the 1st Division had captured the Buissy Switch and the villages of Villers-lez-Cagnicourt and Cagnicourt. Some German formations in the forward line on 2 September had yielded quickly, but the Canadians had met resolute opposition from regiments of the 1st and 2nd Guard Reserve Divisions and the 3rd Reserve Division.[67]

That evening General Currie issued orders for the three divisions under his command to continue the advance on the 3rd, in order to gain direct observation of all bridges over the Sensée River and the Canal du Nord.[68] During the night, however, the enemy withdrew on a wide front. Air patrols flying over the enemy lines on the morning of 3 September saw no Germans between the Cagnicourt-Dury Ridge and the Canal du Nord. At the same time the Third Army reported that it had occupied Quéant and Pronville without fighting and that everywhere the enemy was falling back. By noon the entire Canadian Corps front was in motion as a general advance began to the Green Line. Except for artillery fire, resistance was practically negligible. By evening the 1st Division, having occupied Buissy and

* Unfortunately claims to success came back without foundation. Because of these the artillery was not able to re-establish its neutralizing fire over a belt about 1000 yards wide astride the Arras-Cambrai road which it had been ordered to suspend for the Independent Force's advance. A serious consequence was the heavy unopposed German fire that met the Canadians attacking down the forward slopes from Dury.[65]

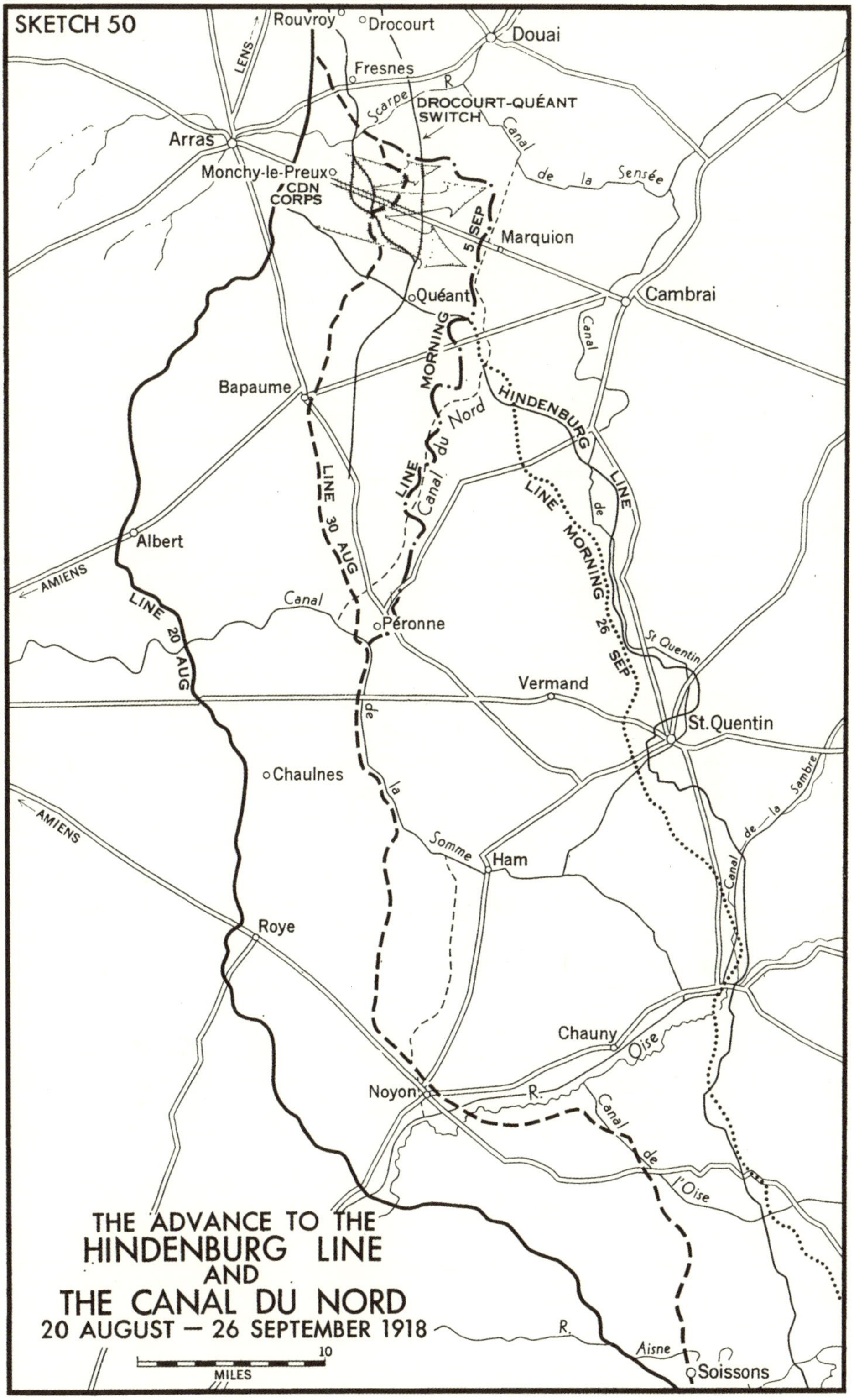
SKETCH 50
Rouvroy
Drocourt
Douai
LENS
Fresnes
R.
Scarpe
DROCOURT-QUÉANT SWITCH
Canal
de la Sensée
Arras
Monchy-le-Preux
CDN CORPS
5 SEP
Marquion
Cambrai
Quéant
Canal
MORNING
Bapaume
HINDENBURG LINE
Canal du Nord
LINE
LINE 30 AUG
LINE MORNING 26 SEP
de
Albert
AMIENS
Canal
LINE 20 AUG
Péronne
St Quentin
Vermand
St.Quentin
de
Chaulnes
la
Canal de la Sambre
AMIENS
Somme
Ham
Roye
Chauny
Oise
Noyon
R.
Canal de l'Oise
THE ADVANCE TO THE HINDENBURG LINE AND THE CANAL DU NORD
20 AUGUST – 26 SEPTEMBER 1918
R.
Aisne
Soissons
10
MILES

Baralle, had swept across the open fields to the west bank of the Canal du Nord. The 4th Canadian Division pushed quickly ahead, liberating the villages of Rumaucourt, Ecourt St. Quentin, Saudemont and Récourt. It reported the east bank of the Canal strongly held and all bridges destroyed. The 4th British Division cleared along the Sensée Canal, occupying the village of Lécluse. By nightfall the Canadian Corps controlled all ground west of the Canal du Nord between Sains-lez-Marquion and the Sensée. The formations which had broken the D-Q position had earned their relief, and during the hours of darkness the new line was taken over from north to south by the 1st British and the 3rd and 2nd Canadian Divisions.[69]

In reviewing the Corps' success General Currie had special praise for the 1st Canadian Division. In his diary he assessed as "one of the finest performances in all the war" its achievement in assaulting and capturing both the Fresnes-Rouvroy and the Drocourt-Quéant lines—a total penetration of nearly five miles. "It is a question", he wrote on 3 September, "whether our victory of yesterday or of August 8th is the greatest, but I am inclined to think yesterday's was."[70] Few would disagree with Sir Arthur. The Corps' success in destroying the hinge of the German defence system had not only made it possible for the Third Army to advance; the repercussions were to be felt along the whole front from Ypres to the Oise.

The German withdrawal had followed what von Hindenburg described as one of the "disagreeable decisions" forced upon the High Command in the first week of September.[71] About midday on the 2nd he had issued orders for the Seventeenth Army to retire that night behind the Sensée and the Canal du Nord, and on its left the Second Army to withdraw into the Hindenburg Position next night. Farther south the Eighteenth and Ninth Armies were to follow in succession, which meant that by 9 September the whole salient won in the March fighting would be abandoned. In the north the Sixth and Fourth Armies fell back between Lens and Ypres, giving up without a fight the Lys salient seized in the previous April.[72]

All this came as a result of the German defeat. The High Command had made every effort to throw back the attacking forces, stationing seven divisions opposite the Canadian Corps and the Third Army's left. From these the Corps captured approximately 6000 unwounded prisoners between 1 and 4 September.[73] In achieving their success the Canadians suffered between 1 and 3 September casualties of 297 officers and 5325 other ranks.

There followed a lull in Canadian operations. As a result of the advance the left flank of the Corps had again become very long; accordingly at midnight on 4-5 September command of the 1st British Division and its sector passed to the G.O.C. 22nd Corps. To the south the Third Army was still fighting its way through the outworks of the Hindenburg Line.

Fashioning the Next Blow

A mile south-east of Dury, at the highest point where the Drocourt-Quéant system crossed the Arras-Cambrai road, stands the Canadian Memorial to the soldiers who broke through that famous defence line. In the centre of a small park surrounded by holly hedge and maple trees a simple square block of stone carries the inscription beginning, "The Canadian Corps 100,000 strong. . . ." From its base one looks westward towards Arras over the terrain so gallantly captured by the Canadian divisions. To the south-east lie other battlefields. Seven miles away, to the right of the straight road reaching down to Cambrai, the observer can discern on a clear day the high mound of Bourlon Wood silhouetted against the sky. To the Canadians dug in on the Dury ridge in September 1918 this was a significant landmark, for they knew that between the wood and themselves lay the next major barrier in their path—the Canal du Nord.

Any operation to cross so formidable an obstacle as the Canal du Nord required much careful planning and preparation. To General Currie a frontal assault from his existing positions seemed out of the question. Not only was there the obstacle of the canal itself; on the far side marshes extended north and south of the Arras-Cambrai road, and these the enemy could cover by machine-gun fire from trench systems to the rear. Furthermore the high ground to the east gave the Germans full command of the canal approaches. It was not an encouraging prospect.[74] In the meantime what had been taken must be held. This presented no great problem, for having flooded the Sensée marshes and destroyed the canal bridges, the enemy had prevented himself from taking effective offensive action against the Canadians. By Currie's orders captured trenches were reversed and rewired and organized into an outpost line of resistance, a battle zone, and a rear zone—though no extensive fortifications were constructed. Until fighting began again the Canadians made the most of the opportunity to "reorganize, refit and rest."[75]

Except for patrol clashes and outpost fighting the quiet period on the Canadian front continued until 27 September. The term is relative only—there were few days when the count of battle casualties fell below 100. Because of the losses sustained by troops holding the canal bank, on the 16th Currie ordered the front line moved far enough back to escape the enemy's dominating machine-guns, while retaining control of the canal approaches with Canadian fire.[76] During this period the Corps lost the services of Major-General Lipsett, who had commanded the 3rd Division since 1916. He was succeeded by Major-General F.O.W. Loomis, formerly commanding the 2nd Brigade. General Lipsett, a British officer (who had been one of Currie's pre-war instructors), was given command of the British 4th Division on 1 October, but shortly afterwards he was killed while making a reconnaissance. General Loomis' promotion led to a number of changes in the command of infantry brigades. The 2nd Brigade was taken over by Brig.-Gen. R. P. Clark, the 4th by Brig.-Gen. G. E. McCuaig, the 6th by Brig.-Gen. A. Ross and the 7th by Brig.-Gen. J. A. Clark.

As the Germans on a wide front extending from the Scarpe to the Aisne fell back to the Hindenburg Line, Allied planners prepared for an assault on this most formidable of all the enemy's defensive systems. To avoid the risk of finding all the German reserve massed against the Allied onslaught, General Foch insisted on extending the front and the scope of the offensive. His directive of 3 September outlined the future course of the campaign. There was to be a general offensive on the entire front from the Meuse to the English Channel, with four great hammer-strokes delivered at crucial points. The British Armies were to attack towards Cambrai and St. Quentin; the French centre would continue to push the enemy beyond the Aisne; in the south the American Army was to reduce the troublesome St. Mihiel salient and then join with the French Fourth Army in a drive towards Mézières; while on the northern flank King Albert of Belgium was to lead a combined force in an offensive in Flanders, directed on Ghent and Bruges.[77] No longer were the Allied leaders seeking to knock out the enemy by battering him at his strongest point while absorbing tremendous punishment in the attempt. The great dull blows rained on the enemy from 1915 to 1917 by the lethargic heavyweight, "leading with his chin", now became the subtle crippling punches of a skilled boxer, elusive and wary, but crowding his opponent towards defeat. Successive attacks at different but closely related points, quickly begun and suddenly ended, were the mark of this strategy, described by Foch as *"Tout le monde à la bataille!"*[78]

Sir Douglas Haig met the commanders of the First, Second and Third Armies at General Byng's headquarters on 15 September. He explained his intention of launching a joint operation towards Cambrai by the First and Third Armies. General Horne was to seize Bourlon Wood and cover the Third Army's left as it advanced on Cambrai, and then extend this protection along the Scarpe and the Scheldt as far as Valenciennes. The capture of Bourlon Wood was assigned to the Canadian Corps, which would then form a defensive flank for operations farther south by establishing a general front from the north-eastern outskirts of Cambrai to Aubencheul-au-Bac on the Sensée Canal, for which purpose Currie would be given the 11th British Division.[79]

But first the obstacle of the Canal du Nord had to be overcome. Faced with broken bridges and flooded marshland, the 2nd Division after much careful reconnaissance reported that the canal was "practically impassable by any force larger than a platoon without considerable preparation."[80]

The outbreak of war had halted construction on the Canal du Nord, leaving the work at varying stages of completion. The naturally swampy area which the Germans had flooded extended from Sains-lez-Marquion northward across the Arras-Cambrai road; but southward along the 4000-yard stretch between Sains-lez-Marquion and Mœuvres the ground was firm and the canal itself was dry. The bank on the far side was strongly held by machine-guns, and immediately to the east the enemy had built his "Canal du Nord Defence Line". Air photographs revealed that its main strength lay in its dense barricade of wire; the trenches were not expected to give much protection from heavy bombardment. About a mile farther to the east and roughly paralleling the canal was the well-wired Marquion Line, which from the eastern outskirts of Marquion ran south for four miles to join the Canal Line at the Cambrai-Bapaume road. Bourlon Wood on its dominating hill a mile behind the Marquion Line—flanked by the village of Bourlon on the north-west edge and Fontaine-Notre-Dame to the south-east—was difficult to assess

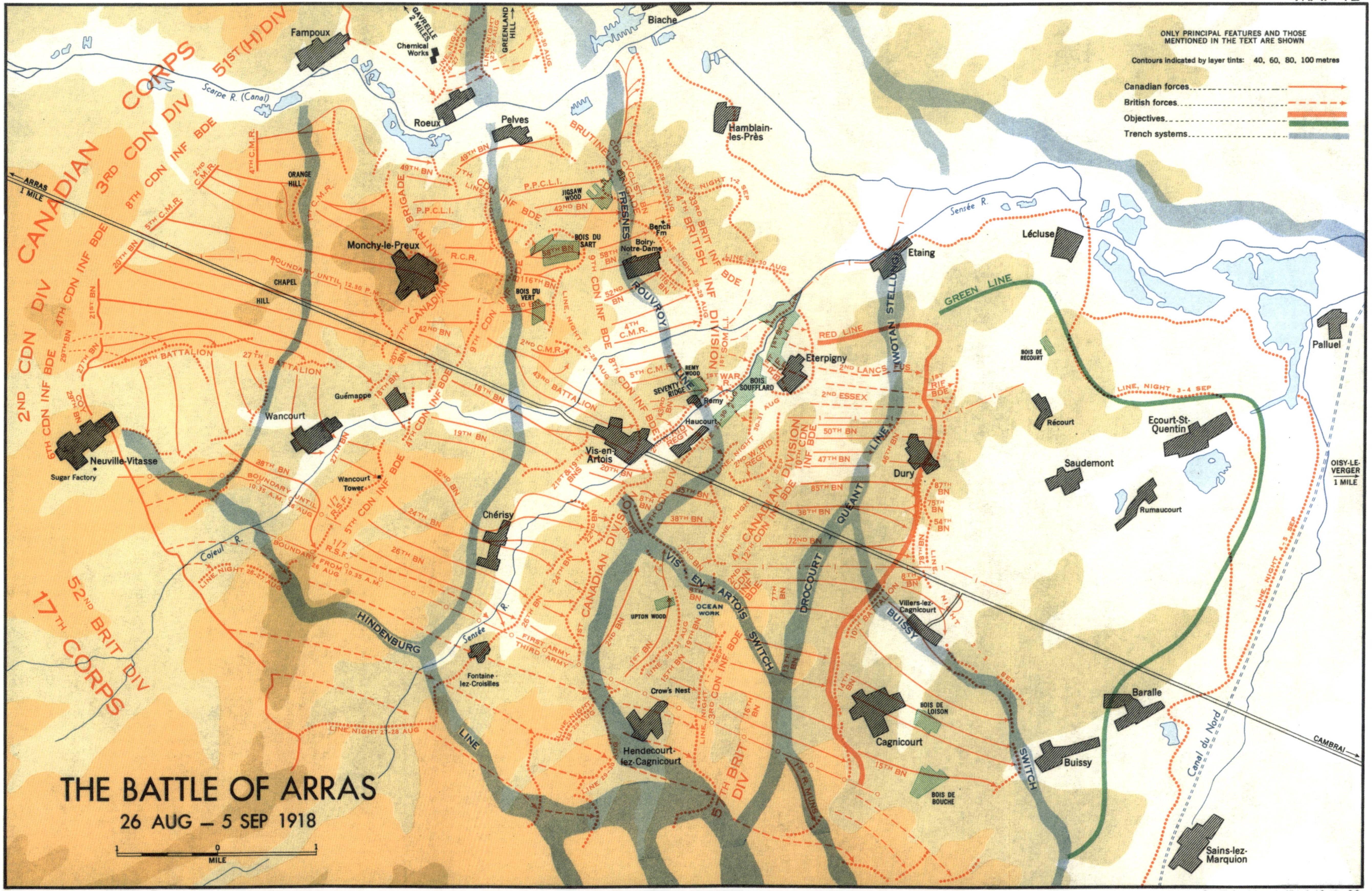
THE BATTLE OF ARRAS
26 AUG – 5 SEP 1918
ONLY PRINCIPAL FEATURES AND THOSE MENTIONED IN THE TEXT ARE SHOWN
Contours indicated by layer tints: 40, 60, 80, 100 metres
Canadian forces
British forces
Objectives
Trench systems
MILE
CANADIAN CORPS
51ST (H) DIV
3RD CDN DIV
2ND CDN DIV
17TH CORPS
52ND BRIT DIV
Fampoux
Biache
Roeux
Pelves
Hamblain-les-Prés
Monchy-le-Preux
Scarpe R. (Canal)
Sensée R.
Lécluse
Etaing
Palluel
Eterpigny
GREEN LINE
RED LINE
Récourt
Ecourt-St-Quentin
Saudemont
Rumaucourt
Dury
Guémappe
Wancourt
Neuville-Vitasse
Sugar Factory
Vis-en-Artois
Chérisy
Fontaine-lez-Croisilles
Hendecourt-lez-Cagnicourt
Cagnicourt
Villers-lez-Cagnicourt
Baralle
Buissy
Sains-lez-Marquion
Canal du Nord
HINDENBURG LINE
DROCOURT QUEANT LINE
WOTAN STELLUNG
BUISSY SWITCH
VIS EN ARTOIS SWITCH
FRESNES ROUVROY LINE
ARRAS 1 MILE
CAMBRAI
OISY-LE-VERGER 1 MILE
Crow's Nest
Upton Wood
Ocean Work
Bois de Loison
Bois de Bouche
Bois du Sart
Bois du Vert
Jigsaw Wood
Orange Hill
Chapel Hill
Wancourt Tower
Remy
Haucourt
Boiry-Notre-Dame
Bench Fm
Chemical Works
Gavrelle 2 Miles
Greenland Hill
Cojeul R.
FIRST ARMY
THIRD ARMY
4TH BRIT DIV
4TH CANADIAN DIVISION
1ST CANADIAN DIVISION
5TH BRIT DIV
LINE, NIGHT 3-4 SEP
LINE, NIGHT 27-28 AUG

MAP 13
THE CANAL DU NORD
AND CAMBRAI
27 SEP – 11 OCT 1918
Palluel
Sensée R.
DOUAI
Aubencheul-au-Bac
MARCOING LINE
Fressies
Hem Lenglet
Canal de la Sensée
Canal de l'Escaut (Schelde)
Lieu-St-Armand
NOYELLES 1 MILE
Ecourt-St-Quentin
Oisy-le-Verger
Rumaucourt
22ND CORPS
56TH BRITISH DIVISION
56TH BRITISH DIVISION
11TH BRITISH DIVISION
LINE NIGHT 9-10 OCTOBER
Estrun
Avesnes-le-Sec
Paillencourt
Abancourt
Bantigny
Epinoy
Sauchy-Cauchy
Sauchy-Lestrée
MARQUION LINE
Canal du Nord
LINE REACHED BY PATROLS 29TH & 31ST BNS 9 OCT
Cuvillers
Blécourt
Iwuy
Thun-l'Evêque
Thun-St-Martin
Eswars
ARRAS
Baralle
Marquion
Haynecourt
Sancourt
11TH BRIT DIV
BLUE LINE
2ND CANADIAN DIVISION
49TH BRIT DIVISION
SAULZOIR 3 MILES
Erclin R.
Chapel
Ramillies
Naves
4TH CDN BRIGADE
GREEN LINE
RED LINE
1ST CDN DIVISION
Sains-lez-Marquion
La Maison Neuve
Pilgrims Rest
Sailly
Tilloy
Morenchies
Pont d'Aire
Escaudoeuvres
Avesnes-lez-Aubert
Cagnoncles
Raillencourt
Inchy-en-Artois
Bourlon
Ste Olle
Neuville-St-Remy
3RD CDN DIVISION
CAMBRAI
Bourlon Wood
4TH CDN DIV
Moeuvres
Fontaine-Notre-Dame
Canal de l'Escaut
Proville
FIRST ARMY
THIRD ARMY
LE CATEAU
17TH CORPS
52ND BRIT DIV
63RD BRIT DIV
57TH DIV
24TH BRITISH DIVISION
BAPAUME
Awoingt
Niergnies
1000 0 1000 2000 3000 4000 5000
YARDS
Contours indicated by layer tints: 40, 60, 80, 100 METRES
Canadian forces
British forces
Intermediate objectives
German defence lines
Reproduced by Army Survey Establishment
Compiled and drawn by Historical Section G.S.

from air photographs because of the foliage still on its magnificent oak trees. These were some of the few to be found in Northern France and were not yet shattered by gunfire. But the ground between the wood and the Marquion Line was dotted with old excavations, dug-outs and shelters, all of them potential machine-gun sites. The grim fighting of the previous November gave warning that here there might be serious trouble. The last prepared defence line before Cambrai was the Marcoing defence system, which was based for much of its length on the Canal de l'Escaut, passing east of Fontaine to cut the Arras road at Raillencourt.[81]

General Currie planned to carry out in two phases the task assigned him. First would come the passage of the canal and the capture of Bourlon Wood and the high ground to the north about Pilgrim's Rest and La Maison Neuve (a farm beside the Arras-Cambrai road). In the second phase the Corps would seize bridges over the Canal de l'Escaut, north-east of Cambrai, and establish a firm line reaching across to the Canal de la Sensée.[82] Because the Canal du Nord was impassable in the northern portion of the Canadian front, on Currie's recommendation the Corps boundary was extended 2600 yards to the south to include the dry section opposite Inchy-en-Artois. While this change would permit a crossing in an unflooded area, it introduced the difficult problem of moving the whole Corps through a narrow defile before fanning out on a battle front that would rapidly expand to 9700 yards.[83]

The first phase was to be a set piece attack between Sains-lez-Marquion and the army boundary, with the 1st Division on the left on a two-brigade front, and the 4th with a single brigade on the right. In the second phase the front would be widened, as the 11th British Division moved up on the left of the 1st Division and the 3rd Canadian Division on the right of the 4th. Depending on the possibilities which then presented themselves, all four divisions were to push resolutely forward, the 3rd maintaining contact with the Third Army's left flank. The 2nd Division was to remain in corps reserve throughout the operation.[84]

The familiar "Red", "Green" and "Blue" lines marked three intermediate objectives for the first phase. From the northern outskirts of Sains-lez-Marquion the Red Line swung south-east to follow the Marquion Defence Line across the Canadian front. The Green Line, about 1500 yards to the east, included Marquion, Bourlon village and the western edge of Bourlon Wood. A further 2000 yards to the east the Blue Line crossed the Cambrai road near La Maison Neuve to pass behind Pilgrim's Rest on the crest of its hill and thence along the eastern outskirts of Bourlon Wood to the army boundary opposite Fontaine-Notre-Dame. Attainment of the Blue Line was vital to the success of the whole operation, for Bourlon Wood provided the key to the capture of Cambrai. It was a task full of difficulties.*

The sloping ground on either side of the canal, which gave the enemy good observation of the entire Canadian front, complicated the concentration of troops

* General Currie reveals that General Byng, the Commander of the Third Army, came to see him a few days before the attack and read over the plans drawn up by the Canadian Corps Staff. Byng considered the plans were the best under the circumstances, but his remark to Currie was, "Old man, do you think you can do it?"[85]

for the attack. On 23 September General Currie ordered all movement east of a line through Neuville-Vitasse carried out during hours of darkness. But the vast scale of preparations for the offensive made some daylight movement by road unavoidable; and enemy air reconnaissance could not fail to notice evidence of the increase in horselines, vehicle parks and camps of all descriptions, which, as the 2nd Division later reported, had made the bare and treeless area behind the front lines "as populous as Coney Island on July 4th".[86]

The alteration in the Corps front and the penetration which the attack was expected to achieve posed special problems to the artillery. The restricted area of the assault meant that in order to give the infantry assembly room batteries had to be kept well to the rear and sited in depth. In the first phase the 4th Division would have to advance more than 4000 yards to reach its final objective, the capture of which, as well as the success of the second phase, depended on a quick advance by the artillery. A solution was worked out to ensure support at all times on the moving front. Six of the ten field brigades supporting the 4th Infantry Division fired the barrage to the Red Line. At zero hour the other four limbered up and closely followed the attacking infantry to the canal, arriving in time to take part in the barrage for the Green Line. As the outranged brigades in the rear dropped out of the barrage, two moved up to the canal to join in the barrage to the final objective, while two more established a standing barrage on the west side of Bourlon Wood. The remainder then came forward to cross the canal, which by that time (zero plus four hours) had been made passable by the Engineers. This arrangement worked out most satisfactorily, the infantry reporting the barrage as being "very good".[87] Sains-lez-Marquion, which was to be by-passed and then assaulted from the rear, required a specially planned barrage. When the village was attacked, the supporting fire would creep backward towards the canal.[88]

A unique feature of the planned artillery support was the preparation of what was indeed a rolling barrage programme fired by heavy artillery. Inner limits of fire and timings followed the principle of a rolling barrage by field guns, except that the successive lifts varied from 500 to 1500 yards at different points, according to the speed with which the infantry was expected to advance. A large number of barrage maps on a scale of 1:40,000 were printed and distributed both to the heavy artillery and the attacking infantry.[89] Arrangements were also made for a comprehensive machine-gun barrage. All the Corps engineer resources, including sappers and pioneers of the 11th British Division, were placed at the disposal of the Chief Engineer, Major-General W. B. Lindsay, as special arrangements were made for the rapid construction of vital bridges over the canal immediately the attack had been mounted.[90] In achieving these tasks the new engineer reorganization (above, p. 384) decidedly proved its worth.

While preparations for the offensive went forward in the First Army's sector, to the south other Allied armies were closing up to the main Hindenburg position. Beginning on 12 September came two weeks of bitter fighting by the French First and the British Third and Fourth Armies as they wrestled the enemy out of the old Allied fortifications which the Germans had converted into outworks to his main defence line.* The failure of the German Second Army to repel the Fourth Army's advance brought the removal of General von der Marwitz from the command.[91] Meanwhile on 12 and 13 September at St. Mihiel, between the Meuse and the Moselle, United States forces vindicated General Pershing's repeated demands that the Americans be allowed to fight as a national army. In a few hours the inexperienced yet eager American divisions excised a salient sixteen miles deep which had troubled the Allied line for four years.[92]

The enemy's stubborn resistance during the September fighting had brought heavy casualties to both sides, and on 21 September Haig received another warning from the Secretary of State for War that the unsatisfactory recruiting situation in the United Kingdom made it necessary to guard against needless dissipation of the strength of the British Armies in France. The Commander-in-Chief was fully aware of the possible cost of attacking the formidable Hindenburg Line, as well as of the political effects that an unsuccessful attempt would have, both in Britain and in Germany. But having carefully weighed these considerations against the advantages to be gained by the proposed operations, Haig was convinced "that the British attack was the essential part of the general scheme, and that the moment was favourable. Accordingly", he wrote in his subsequent despatch, "I decided to proceed with the attack."[93]

The Canal du Nord and Bourlon Wood, 27 September

The night of 26-27 September was tense with expectation. There was no preliminary barrage and the air was still. In the crowded assembly areas infantry were closely bunched with artillery and machine-guns, brought forward this far in readiness for a rapid advance. Apprehensive that a counter preparation by German artillery might come down on their dangerously dense numbers, the troops waited impatiently for zero. Rain began to fall and the cold ground became slippery, adding to the difficulties expected in the coming assault. Morning arrived overcast and dark, but the rain had stopped.[94] Then, at 5:20 a.m., came a myriad of flashes from the guns in the artillery areas followed by the crash of bursting shells over the enemy positions.

On the Corps right, troops of the 10th Brigade, hugging their artillery cover, quickly crossed the canal† on a two-battalion front between Inchy and Moeuvres. They overcame resistance from the Canal du Nord Line, and established themselves on Red according to schedule. The 11th and 12th Brigades, leading the 4th Division's attack on the right and left respectively, pushed forward but almost immediately met trouble from the south. Opposing General Watson's formations was the German 187th Infantry Division, with its 188th Infantry

* In the area between St. Quentin and the Bapaume-Cambrai road the Third Army fought the Battle of Havrincourt (12-18 September), and the Fourth Army the battle of Epehy (17-18 September).

† This part of the Canal du Nord was only partially excavated. The western bank was from 10 to 12 feet high, the eastern 4 to 5 feet. The canal was about 40 yards across.[95]

Regiment directly west of Bourlon Wood, flanked to north and south respectively by the 186th and 187th Regiments.* Farther south was the dismounted 7th Cavalry Division; unused to infantry tactics they were quickly defeated.[97] The 52nd Division, attacking on the Third Army's flank, had not achieved the same initial success as the 4th Division, and as a result the Canadian right suffered many casualties from enfilade fire.

In stiff fighting the 87th Battalion gained an entry into the southern part of Bourlon village by 9:45 a.m., and the 54th, passing through, skirted the north end of Bourlon Wood to reach the far side. The slower advance of the British troops to the south compelled the 102nd Battalion to form a defensive flank beside the Bapaume road and defeated the plan to encircle the wood from the south. This left the 54th in a pronounced salient, suffering mounting casualties. The battalion pushed on towards Fontaine-Notre-Dame, finally coming to a halt about 7:00 p.m. just west of the village, the 75th and 87th Battalions coming up on its left. Farther north the 12th Brigade also had stiff fighting throughout the day. The 85th and 38th Battalions, heavily hit by shelling and machine-gun fire during their advance, cleared their part of the Marquion trench system, allowing the 78th and 72nd Battalions to gain all but the extreme right of its Blue Line objective. It took a fresh attack mounted at 8:00 p.m. by the 78th Battalion to overcome the final pocket of resistance.[98]

In the course of the 4th Division's operations on 27 September two subalterns had won the Victoria Cross. Lieutenant G. T. Lyall of the 102nd Battalion, and Lieutenant S. L. Honey, D.C.M., M.M., 78th Battalion, through their skilful leadership and courage in dealing with German strongpoints both significantly contributed to the capture of Bourlon Wood. Like many another recognition for brave deeds in the war, Lieutenant Honey's award came posthumously.[99]

On the Corps left the 1st Division's success paid tribute to careful planning and well-directed and determined execution. Two guns of the 1st Battery C.F.A. gave the 1st Brigade a good start by moving in front of Inchy-en-Artois and firing point-blank into enemy positions along the canal. Thus aided, the 4th Battalion, having crossed the dry bed with little difficulty, was able to jump ahead to the north-east and capture its assigned portion of the Marquion Line. Here the 1st Battalion pushed through as planned and secured the Green Line in short order. The 2nd and 3rd Battalions now assumed the lead, only to be stopped by heavy fire from the embanked railway which curved north from Bourlon. With the aid of a timely flanking attack by the 72nd Battalion they overcame this resistance and swept on to the Blue Line.[100] The action of the Commander of the 3rd Battalion's left support company, Lieutenant G. F. Kerr, M.C., M.M., in rushing single-handed a German strongpoint near the Arras-Cambrai road played an important part in the 1st Brigade's advance. Kerr, who captured four machine-guns and 31 prisoners, was awarded the Victoria Cross.[101]

* The 188th Infantry Regiment reported 27 September as "the blackest day of the Regiment . . . at the end of the day only a little band of men was left . . . on this day we buried all our hopes for victory".[96]

The 2nd Brigade's role was to follow the 1st up to the Marquion Line and then extend to the left to capture the central portion of the Blue Line on the divisional front. By two o'clock the 7th Battalion was firm on its objective midway between Marquion and Haynecourt. During the afternoon the 5th Battalion went on to occupy Haynecourt and push patrols almost to the main Cambrai-Douai road. On the left, units of the 11th British Division passed through, headed for Epinoy. By the end of the day (27 September) patrols of the 10th Battalion—which had passed through the 5th just east of Haynecourt—were approaching the Marcoing Line, coming first to a heavy belt of uncut wire covered by enemy machine-guns. With mounting casualties the infantry cut the wire and pushed forward; but confronted by a second wire barrier, which marked the line itself, and with darkness approaching, the battalion consolidated on the east side of the Douai-Cambrai road.[102]

On General Macdonell's left the 3rd Brigade had the important task of driving northward beyond the Canal du Nord and capturing in turn the villages of Sains-lez-Marquion and Marquion, thereby freeing the eastern bank to permit crossings by the 11th Division. Leading the 3rd Brigade's advance the 14th Battalion crossed south of Sains-lez-Marquion, and swinging north behind the village, quickly captured its part of the Red Line. Four supporting tanks rendered good service in crushing wire barricades and in mopping up the village, but mechanical difficulties kept them from advancing past the Red Line.[103] From Chapel Corner, south-east of Marquion, the German opposition, which had wavered before the initial rush of the 14th, rallied with heavy fire to stop the 13th Battalion, which was following up the initial assault. It took a joint effort by the 13th and 15th Battalions with tank assistance to clear Marquion. The 15th continued northward across the Arras road, mopping up the area east of the canal. By 2:00 p.m. it was firm at the Blue Line, just south of Sauchy-Lestrée.[104]

Both Canadian divisions had received useful help from the tanks—each being supported by a company (of eight tanks) from the 7th Tank Battalion. The four allotted to each assaulting brigade successfully crossed the dry canal under cover of an artillery smoke-screen. Later they contributed to their own concealment by means of smoke dischargers fitted to their exhausts. During the day they gave good service in crushing wire entanglements and silencing with their fire enemy machine-gun posts. Of the sixteen tanks engaged in the first phase of the operation five fell victim to German fire.[105]

About midday, when the 3rd Infantry Brigade had completed its assigned task of clearing the east bank of the canal, units of the 11th Division crossed at four places between Sains-lez-Marquion and the highway and moved smoothly into place on the left of the 1st Division to start the second phase of the attack. The advance to the north and north-east continued without serious interruption, and by dusk Epinoy and Oisy-le-Verger were in British hands.[106]

On the whole the day had gone very well. That night Currie wrote in his diary: "Today's success jeopardizes the hold of the enemy on the Quéant-Drocourt system north of the Scarpe, and he may be expected to fall back to Douai." With the obstacle of the Canal du Nord overcome there was hope that Cambrai might soon be captured, and that the fall of Douai would follow.[107] But gains had been limited on the Corps right, where the 4th Canadian Division, suffering from an open flank because of the slow progress of the British formations farther south, had been unable to start the second phase of the operation. During the night of 27-28 September, however, the Germans fell back. With his divisions ejected from their lines and lying unprotected in the open fields from Epinoy to Ribécourt, General von Below gave orders for a withdrawal to the far side of the Sensée between Arleux and Aubigny, and to the "Hagen" position running southward from Aubigny through Marcoing.[108]

The Marcoing Line and the Fighting Towards Cambrai, 28 September-1 October

On the evening of the 27th General Currie issued orders for the advance to continue throughout the night and following day in an effort to work around the north side of Cambrai and keep the enemy from setting up a defensive line west of the city. The 3rd Division was ordered to relieve all troops of the 4th Division within its own assigned boundaries for the second phase, and to capture Fontaine-Notre-Dame as soon as possible. In addition, Brutinel's Brigade* was warned to be prepared to exploit success, and the 2nd Division, in corps reserve, was readied for quick advance.[110]

It was impossible in fact for the 3rd Division to take over its portion of the line while Fontaine-Notre-Dame was still under enemy fire. Accordingly, late on 27 September it was decided that General Loomis' brigades, instead of relieving the 11th Brigade, would use its positions as a jumping-off place from which to attack Fontaine and force the Marcoing Line.[111] The two brigades, on the left the 7th (commanded by Brig.-Gen. J. A. Clark, who had succeeded Brig.-Gen. Dyer on 12 September) and the 9th Brigade on the right, launched their attack at 6:00 a.m. on the 28th. Led by The Royal Canadian Regiment, the 7th Brigade started well, reporting the capture of the Marcoing front line by 8:50 a.m. But thereafter progress slowed as the R.C.R. encountered dogged resistance in the Marcoing support line, where the Germans were determined to postpone capture of Cambrai and the crossings of the Canal de l'Escaut. The stiffest opposition came from the 26th (Württemberg) Reserve Division and some Guard units. This was the division that one month earlier had delayed the Canadians north and south of the Cambrai road (above, p. 430). In the meantime it had been reorganized, rested, and visited in the various bivouac areas by Field-Marshal von Hindenburg.[112]

Mid-morning found The Royal Canadian Regiment pinned down under heavy fire from the front and from Sailly on the left flank. The P.P.C.L.I. was thrust

* The Canadian Independent Force had been withdrawn from the line on the evening of 4 September and shortly afterwards disbanded. Brutinel's Brigade, however, was re-formed on 19 September on a semi-permanent basis.[109]

into the action, and by early afternoon both battalions had secured the Marcoing position between the Arras and Bapaume roads.[113] The R.C.R. action had been highlighted by the heroism of an officer, Lieutenant M. F. Gregg, M.C.,* which won him the Victoria Cross. With the advance held up by thick, uncut wire, he crawled forward alone to reconnoitre, subsequently leading his men through a small gap to force their way into the German trench. The enemy counter-attacked in force, and, when bombs ran short, Gregg though wounded, returned alone under terrific fire for a further supply. Wounded a second time, he re-organized his reduced numbers and led them on to clear the enemy trenches.[114]

In the meantime the 9th Brigade had had limited success. While the 102nd Battalion (loaned by the 4th Division) covered the open right flank with fire from the southern edge of Bourlon Wood, the 43rd Battalion entered and secured Fontaine and by 9:00 a.m. was half a mile south-east of the village. Continuing resistance from the Marcoing Line dictated a fresh attack by both brigades in the angle between the Arras-Cambrai and Bapaume-Cambrai roads. But there was delay in completing plans for an artillery barrage and in bringing up ammunition, and the operation had to be postponed from 3:00 p.m. until seven that evening.

Brig.-Gen. Clark had been given the task of carrying the Cambrai-Douai road and the railway beyond. It proved to be a costly assignment. On the brigade left Princess Patricia's Canadian Light Infantry advanced 2000 yards to the north-east before running into unmapped wire in front of the Douai road. From the railway embankment and the high ground north of Tilloy German fire raked the Patricias caught in the wire, forcing a slight withdrawal with heavy losses.[115] On the right the 49th Battalion, also heavily opposed, could get only as far as the northern outskirts of Ste. Olle—a suburb on the Arras road. On the 9th Brigade's front the 58th Battalion broke through the enemy's defences, allowing the 116th late at night to close up to Ste. Olle.[116]

North of the highway the 10th Brigade had carried most of the 4th Division's action on 28 September. The 47th and 50th Battalions attacked at 6:00 a.m., the advance going well enough as far as the outskirts of Raillencourt, where the Marcoing Line crossed the Arras-Cambrai road. Both the village and the trenches were strongly garrisoned, with German reserves in Cambrai ready to oppose any drive to encircle the city on the north. Raillencourt was taken in stiff fighting and then the 44th and 46th Battalions passed through as planned, the former clearing the adjoining village of Sailly. But heavy shelling halted their advance short of the Douai road. Throughout the day the 44th Battalion, depleted by heavy casualties suffered on the 27th in the assault of the Canal du Nord, fought off a series of vicious counter-attacks, receiving stout assistance from the Vickers guns of the 2nd Machine Gun Battalion. It was nevertheless compelled to fall back to the light railway east of Sailly.[117]

As we have noted, the success of the 1st Division on 27 September had

* Later, Brigadier Milton Gregg, who from 1947 to 1957 held successively the portfolios of Fisheries, Veterans Affairs and Labour in the Dominion Cabinet.

placed it well in advance of the 3rd and 4th Divisions. Its plan of attack for 28 September called for the 2nd Brigade to continue the divisional advance to the north-east. Zero hour, at the request of the 2nd, was delayed from 6:00 a.m. until nine in order that the troops on the right might close up level with the 1st Division. But the postponement accomplished nothing. When the 10th Battalion attacked from the Douai road the 4th Division was still lagging behind. The battalion struck heavy uncut belts of wire covered by enemy fire and was stopped practically in its tracks. Efforts throughout the day to cut the wire by heavy artillery shoots failed. The infantry made no significant advance here,[118] and similarly on the Corps northern flank the 11th British Division could report few gains.

The 29th was another day of hard fighting which gained little ground. On the Corps' right the 3rd Division had all brigades heavily engaged. The 9th Brigade sent its 58th Battalion across the army boundary to assist units of the 57th British Division clear the Marcoing line towards the Canal de l'Escaut. The 116th Battalion fought all morning to get into Ste. Olle. With the help of a bombardment from a supporting field battery the 116th captured the troublesome suburb about noon and pushed a company forward to the junction of the Arras and Bapaume roads.[119] In the centre the 8th Brigade, with orders to secure bridgeheads over the canal in the northern part of the city, at first could make little headway, both the 1st and 2nd Canadian Mounted Rifles being held up by fire from Ste. Olle, which was then still untaken. After its fall the two C.M.R. battalions were able to fight* forward to the outskirts of Neuville St. Rémy, a suburb astride the Douai road, west of the canal. On the divisional left the 7th Brigade's attack with the 49th and 42nd Battalions got to the Douai-Cambrai road opposite Tilloy, but was stopped there by machine-gun fire.[121]

Things were not much better on the 4th Division's front. General Watson continued the attack with the 12th Brigade, directing it on Sancourt and Blécourt to the north-east. On the right the 38th Battalion crossed the Cambrai-Douai road, only to be halted by fire from the railway embankment. The 78th Battalion passed through in the afternoon but was similarly stopped. Farther north the 72nd Battalion had better fortune; after taking some 250 prisoners and 20 machine-guns in Sancourt it gained a foothold at the railway. One small party reached Blécourt and with great audacity, having mounted a Lewis gun in the village square, began rounding up prisoners in the nearby buildings, withdrawing with some eighty to the railway. But there had been no parallel advance on either flank, and in the face of heavy artillery fire and threatened counter-attacks the 72nd was forced to fall back almost to the Cambrai-Douai road.[122] To the north neither the 1st Canadian nor the 11th British Division had achieved any significant success. General Macdonell was holding practically the same positions that his

* During this action, described by the 2nd C.M.R.'s regimental historian as "the most desperately fought engagement of the war for our battalion", one of the company commanders, Captain John McGregor, M.C., D.C.M., won the Victoria Cross. Single-handed he silenced a nest of German machine-guns that were holding up his company's advance, killing four of the gunners and taking eight prisoners.[120]

troops had captured on 27 September; further progress would be difficult until the British had captured the commanding ground north-east of Epinoy.[123]

The fighting on this Sunday had been exceedingly bitter, costing 2089 Canadian casualties;* and the enemy's determined defence had made the results disappointing. General Currie was convinced however that each day's attack by the Canadian Corps forestalled a German counter-attack, and he gave orders for the battle to be continued on the 30th.[125] The new operation was planned in two phases. On the Corps right the 3rd and 4th Divisions were to attack at 6:00 a.m. to seize bridge-heads over the Canal de l'Escaut, respectively at Ramillies and Eswars, north-east of Cambrai. With this accomplished, the 1st Canadian and 11th British Divisions would drive north-eastward, the former to capture the village of Abancourt, east of the Douai railway, and the latter directed towards Fressies, at the Sensée Canal.[126]

Right from the start the 4th Division encountered trouble. It had been planned that the attack should go in under a barrage of heavy artillery, which would include a smoke-screen along the Canal de l'Escaut and the "Batigny† Ravine", which extended north-eastward from Sancourt to the Sensée. (This was actually a valley with gently sloping sides, in which were located the villages of Sancourt, Blécourt and Bantigny. At Bantigny it was 1000 yards wide and about 40 feet deep.) But the promised smoke-screen failed, leaving the 11th Brigade's attack fully exposed to the enemy's guns on the high ground south of Abancourt. The 75th Battalion, in the lead, lost the majority of its officers and N.C.Os. Together with the 54th and 87th Battalions, also badly hit, it was withdrawn to the railway line—which was to represent the division's net gain for the day.[127] Initially the 3rd Division, attacking with the 7th Brigade, had better fortune. The P.P.C.L.I. pushed rapidly through Tilloy and on their left the R.C.R. reached the chapel that stood midway along the Blécourt-Tilloy road. But machine-gun fire that poured into their open northern flank from the direction of Blécourt forced a retirement almost to the railway, though the Patricias were able to retain their grasp on Tilloy.[128] The first phase having failed, there was no action by the 1st Canadian and the 11th British Divisions. The day's unsuccessful operations had left the crossings of the Canal de l'Escaut as far away as ever.

That afternoon (30 September) the Corps Commander held a conference at Major-General Watson's headquarters and ordered an attack for 1 October by all four divisions in line across the whole front. Divisional objectives remained essentially the same as for the 30th; the 2nd Division and Brutinel's Brigade were to be prepared, however, to move through the 3rd Division and cross the canal, exploiting success north-east of Cambrai. During the night of 30 September-

* Among the wounded was Hon. Lt.-Col. F. G. Scott, the senior Protestant Chaplain of the 1st Division, who had served for more than three and a half years on the Western Front. His contribution to the welfare of the troops was typical of the devoted service rendered by the padres in the field. "The men loved him", a former brigade commander was to write, ". . . for in hours of misery, help and comfort radiated from this undaunted soul."[124] Whether in an officers' mess or in a trench issuing candy or smokes, or conducting a burial behind the lines, Canon Scott was equally at home. Although he had many times been advised, and even ordered, to keep out of dangerous places, he always insisted on sharing the risks and hardship with the soldiers whom he called his "boys".

† So spelled on contemporary maps, although running through the village of Bantigny.

1 October the 56th Division, of the 22nd Corps, took over the northern part of the 11th British Division's front.[129]

Rain set in during the night, and slippery roads delayed the despatch riders delivering barrage maps and orders to all the batteries across the Corps front. Nevertheless promptly at 5:00 a.m. under Corps control a heavy creeping barrage extending from Neuville St. Rémy to north of Epinoy set the attack in motion. It was the beginning of a day of intense artillery activity, during which the guns supporting the Canadian Corps were to fire 7000 tons of ammunition.[130] Although successful in the initial stages of the operation, later in the day the 1st Division suffered the most severe reverse of any of the divisions engaged under General Currie's command. It attacked with the 1st and 3rd Brigades—both of which had been in reserve since the battle opened on 27 September. On the right the 3rd Brigade, led by the 13th Battalion, quickly pushed through Sancourt and took Blécourt, in spite of growing machine-gun fire from the direction of Abancourt. The 16th and 14th Battalions leapfrogged the 13th east of Blécourt and occupied Cuvillers and Bantigny, pushing patrols farther forward. But as enfilade fire from the left flank increased, it became apparent that these positions were untenable—three times the enemy counter-attacked the 14th Battalion in Bantigny—and both units had to retire. Nor could the 13th Battalion retain Blécourt, in spite of efforts by the 15th Battalion to reinforce it. With the coming of darkness the Brigade was forced to withdraw west of the village, having lost 29 officers and 618 other ranks.[131]

The German resistance had come mostly from the left flank, where the 1st Brigade, itself hampered by the 11th Division's lack of progress to the north, had been unable to keep pace with the 3rd. Attacking north of the Batigny Ravine, the 1st and 4th Battalions had been thwarted in attempts to free Abancourt* by the heavy fire coming from in front of the British Division. That formation, assigned the task of protecting the 1st Division's left, had been halted by heavy uncut wire almost before it began to advance. The two Canadian battalions were pinned down all day at the line of the railway. The 1st Brigade's 388 casualties brought to more than a thousand the losses sustained by the 1st Division on 1 October.[133]

Although it fought well, the 1st Division's inability to secure its objectives seriously affected the operations of the 4th and 3rd Divisions to the south. The 11th Brigade again led the 4th Division's attack—its objective the canal crossings at Eswars. From a start line just south of Sancourt the 102nd Battalion advanced to the road joining Ramillies with Cuvillers. Taking over on the right, the 87th pushed patrols eastward towards Eswars. Prisoners poured in, the identification of a large number of regiments and battalions being evidence that the enemy had thrown in strong reserves to resist the Canadians. But by this time the 1st Division had begun to withdraw, and it further appeared that the 3rd Division to the right would be unable to secure Ramillies.† With General Watson's con-

* In the fight for Abancourt Sgt. W. Merrifield of the 4th Battalion wiped out single-handed two enemy machine-gun emplacements, thereby winning the Victoria Cross.[132]

† Not the Ramilies of Marlborough's campaigns, which was ten miles north of Namur.

currence Brig.-Gen. Odlum abandoned the attempt to take Eswars in order to hold what he had gained. Backed by the 12th Brigade's 85th Battalion he succeeded in maintaining a salient south and east of Cuvillers.[134]

On the extreme right Major-General Loomis had planned for the 9th Brigade to carry out the 3rd Division's operations in two phases—to capture first the high ground some 1000 yards east of Tilloy, and then to wheel to the right and seize bridgeheads over the canal at Ramillies and the nearer Pont d'Aire. The 43rd and 52nd Battalions captured the ridge at comparatively little cost, securing some 350 prisoners. But as they changed course to descend to the canal both battalions were struck by withering machine-gun fire coming from the woods on the far bank opposite Morenchies. An attempt to maintain the advance by passing the 58th and 116th Battalions through failed, the two units being forced to dig in half-way down the hill. Furthermore, the division's left flank was in the air because of the check to the 4th Division. Help came here from the 27th Battalion (2nd Division), which moved up from reserve to a position on the spur north-east of Tilloy. Though heavy German counter-attacks late in the day from the direction of Pont d'Aire drove in the 9th Brigade's advanced posts, the main line held. On General Loomis' right flank the 8th Brigade had established posts along the bank of the canal from the army boundary to the northern outskirts of Neuville St. Rémy.[135]

The day's gains, though far short of what had been hoped for, represented an advance of about a mile. The only significant achievement had been the winning of the high ground east of Tilloy, which gave observation of the valley of the Escaut and the city of Cambrai. The Canadian units, many of which had been fighting continuously since 27 September, were extremely tired. In these circumstances to persist in operations against such strong opposition was inviting failure, and on the afternoon of 1 October General Horne ordered Currie to "maintain and consolidate positions gained by today's fighting and reorganize in depth".[136] That night the 2nd Division took over the front between the Cambrai-Arras railway and the northern outskirts of Blécourt, relieving the 4th Division, most of the 3rd and part of the 1st.

In the five days' fighting that had just ended the Canadian Corps had fulfilled its mission of protecting the flank of the Third and Fourth Armies. In doing so it had severely punished the German formations opposing it, capturing more than 7000 prisoners and 205 guns. In addition to these losses inflicted upon the enemy the Corps had breached the last organized defence system before Cambrai and gained a position from which an assault of the canal crossings could be launched with good prospect of success.[137] But almost a week was to pass before Cambrai was freed.

The enemy had shown ample proof of his unwillingness to yield the approaches to Cambrai without stiff resistance. Evidence shows that some units fought bitterly and skilfully until reduced to little bands of exhausted men. According to information from Canadian Intelligence Reports and from the record of a great many German regimental histories, during the last four days of September the Germans employed in the Canadian Corps sector nine full divisions and parts of three others. The initial assault on 27 September hit from north to south the 12th and 187th Divisions and the 7th Cavalry Division (dismounted). On the same day three more divisions were partly committed in fruitless counter-attacks or delaying actions—the 22nd and 207th Divisions and the 1st Guard Reserve Division. All were fully involved by the 28th, as was an "intervention" division, the tough 26th Reserve Division, sent in to fight piecemeal at various trouble spots. On 29 September, as the Canadians were striving to push forward north of Cambrai, the 234th Division appeared in the line; and on the 30th the 220th Division was brought in. In the general area about Abancourt the enemy's resistance had been bolstered on 29 September by the insertion of the 141st Regiment, of the 35th Division. Small elements of the 49th Reserve Division and the 18th Reserve Division also appeared in that sector.

As the successive Allied blows hit the Germans from Verdun to the sea, the High Command frantically shuffled its forces from one trouble spot to another. By the end of the first week of October all but three of these dozen divisions had been withdrawn in varying stages of exhaustion and new formations were approaching the combat area.

On other parts of the Western Front the four-fold offensive set in motion by Marshal Foch had started well, though in general the enemy's stout resistance had reduced the hoped-for pace of the Allied advance. The first blow had been struck on the right on 26 September, when the American First Army and the French Fourth Army attacked the great German salient along its southern face between Reims and Verdun. In spite of the difficulties confronting the Americans in penetrating the forests of the rugged Argonne country, by 3 October the two armies had driven the enemy back seven miles, and German reinforcements were hastening to the area.[138] Attacking on the 27th, the Third Army, covered as we have seen by the operations of the Canadian Corps forming the First Army's right wing, had broken through the Hindenburg Line south-west of Cambrai to reach the St. Quentin Canal and draw level with the Fourth Army farther south. All this was preliminary to General Rawlinson's attack, for which his Fourth Army had been allotted the bulk of the available tanks, and a heavy share of the supporting guns. Early on the 29th the Fourth Army, which included two American divisions, joined in the attack, and by nightfall had penetrated three miles into the main Hindenburg defences north of St. Quentin.[139]

In the meantime the offensive by the Belgian Army and the British Second Army in Flanders had opened auspiciously on 28 September. In spite of heavy rain the first two days' fighting won back the whole of the Messines-Passchendaele ridge, for possession of which so much blood had been expended in earlier battles. Opposite Ypres the advance progressed more than nine miles, and with the old churned-up battlefield behind them the Anglo-Belgian forces seemed to be in good position to speed forward and turn the enemy's northern flank. But now operations came to a halt, for staffs unused to open warfare could not cope with the difficulty of supplying the attacking troops across the trackless mud of the war-torn ground.[140] From the southern flank of the Allied offensive came simi-

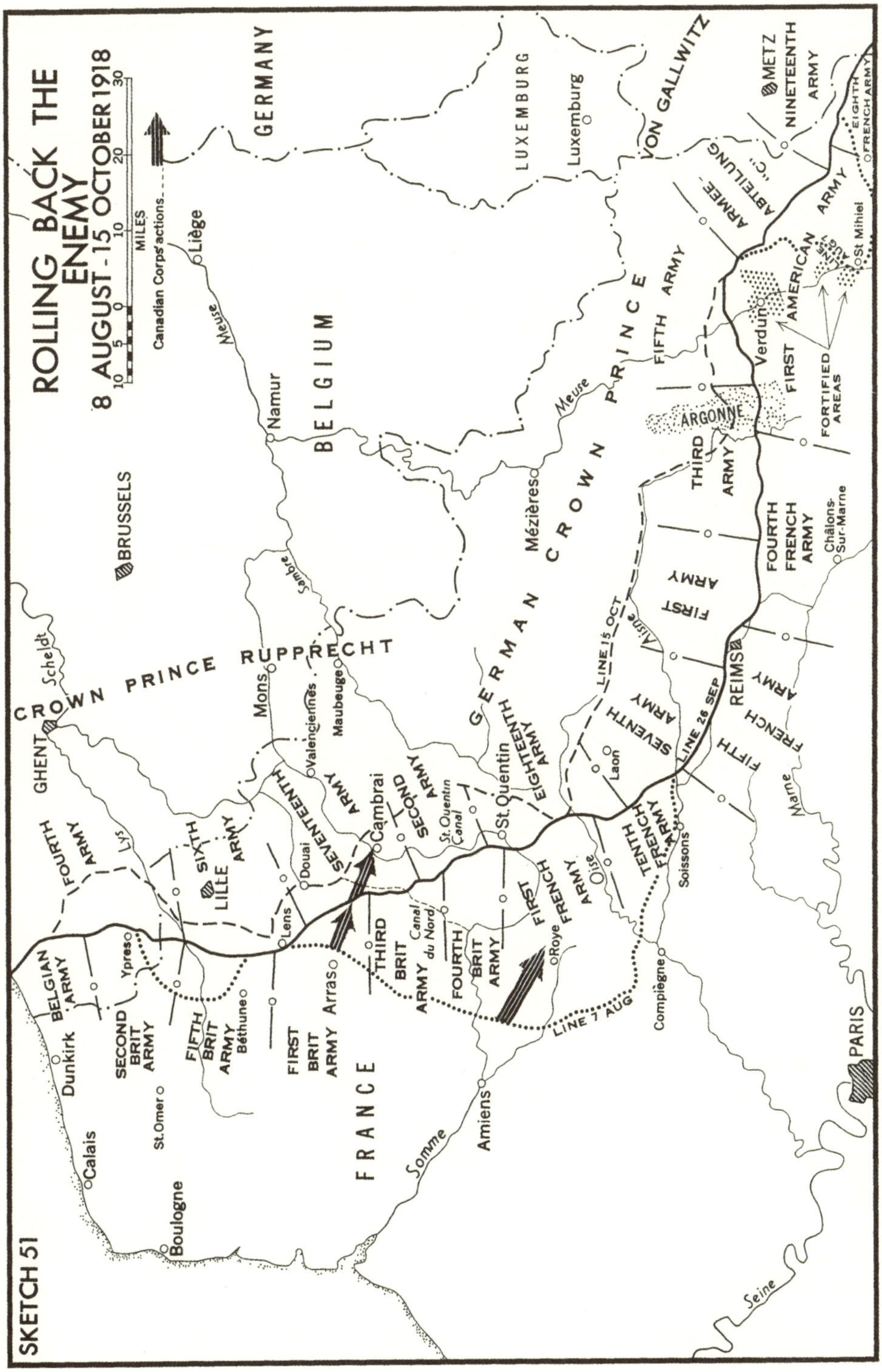
SKETCH 51
ROLLING BACK THE ENEMY
8 AUGUST - 15 OCTOBER 1918
MILES
10 5 0 10 20 30
Canadian Corps' actions
GERMANY
LUXEMBURG
Luxemburg
BELGIUM
BRUSSELS
Liège
Namur
Meuse
Sambre
Scheldt
Lys
Mons
GHENT
CROWN PRINCE RUPPRECHT
GERMAN CROWN PRINCE
VON GALLWITZ
METZ
NINETEENTH ARMY
ARMEE - ABTEILUNG "C"
FIFTH ARMY
THIRD ARMY
FIRST ARMY
SEVENTH ARMY
EIGHTEENTH ARMY
SEVENTEENTH ARMY
SIXTH ARMY
FOURTH ARMY
SECOND ARMY
BELGIAN ARMY
SECOND BRIT ARMY
FIFTH BRIT ARMY
FIRST BRIT ARMY
THIRD BRIT ARMY
FOURTH BRIT ARMY
FIRST FRENCH ARMY
TENTH FRENCH ARMY
FIFTH FRENCH ARMY
FOURTH FRENCH ARMY
EIGHTH FRENCH ARMY
FIRST AMERICAN ARMY
FORTIFIED AREAS
ARGONNE
Verdun
St Mihiel
Mézières
Châlons-Sur-Marne
REIMS
Laon
Soissons
Compiègne
Aisne
Oise
Marne
Seine
PARIS
LINE 15 OCT
LINE 26 SEP
LINE 7 AUG
St. Quentin
St. Quentin Canal
Canal du Nord
Cambrai
Valenciennes
Maubeuge
Douai
LILLE
Lens
Arras
Roye
Amiens
Somme
Béthune
Ypres
Dunkirk
Calais
St. Omer
Boulogne
FRANCE

lar reports of blocked communications that were holding up the American offensive west of the Meuse. Impatiently Haig wrote in his diary on 1 October: "What very valuable days are being lost! All this is the result of inexperience and ignorance on the part of the Belgian and American Staffs* of the needs of a modern attacking force."[141]

The Capture of Cambrai, 8-9 October

Between 2 and 8 October there was little action in the Canadian Corps' sector. The remainder of the 1st and 4th Divisions moved into reserve, leaving the front held, from north to south, by the 11th British, and the 2nd and 3rd Canadian Divisions. On 6 October plans for further reliefs were abruptly cancelled as orders came for a further attempt to seize Cambrai in conjunction with the Third Army, which had succeeded in crossing the Canal de l'Escaut south of the city advantage of any opportunities to exploit eastward.[143]

The operation was to be carried out in two phases. In the first phase the Third Army's 17th Corps, advancing from the south, was to capture the Niergnies-Awoingt Ridge, immediately south-east of Cambrai, while the Canadian Corps staged an artillery demonstration. With this phase completed the 2nd Canadian Division was to force a passage over the canal between Morenchies and Ramillies, and establish a line on the high ground behind Escaudoeuvres, joining hands with the British Corps. The 3rd Division on the right of the 2nd would then cross the canal and establish bridgeheads in Cambrai, while Brutinel's Brigade took advantage of any opportunities to exploit eastward.[143]

The 2nd Division was faced with the problem of attacking down the same exposed slopes which had cost the 3rd such heavy casualties a week before. The lack of cover clearly dictated a night assault, which would be launched at 9:30 p.m. on the day on which the 17th Corps reached its Awoingt objective. Major-General Burstall planned that the 6th Brigade should lead off by capturing Ramillies. For the remainder of the operation it would form a left flank guard reaching back to the Batigny Ravine. The 5th Brigade was to take the bridges at Morenchies, Pont d'Aire and a swing bridge at the bend of the canal immediately south of Ramillies, and establish a good bridgehead about Escaudoeuvres on the east bank. The 4th Brigade would then advance through the 5th to make contact with the 17th Corps. Full precautions were taken to seal off the left flank from German attack. The 1st Motor Machine Gun Brigade, under command of the 4th Division, was detailed to assist the 6th Brigade in maintaining its guard. During the night of 7-8 October British engineers projected 1000 drums of lethal gas—phosgene and chlorpicrin—into the Batigny Ravine to deny it to the enemy as as assembly area.[144] Units of the 6th Brigade pushed out a screen of posts between Blécourt and Cuvillers.[145]

* The same criticism might have been made concerning the staffs of all the Allied armies at that time (see below, p. 468).

The Third Army's attack went in on the morning of 8 October. While initial reports of the action were encouraging it soon became clear that the progress of the 17th Corps was falling short of expectation. At about 5:00 p.m. the 2nd Division was warned that regardless of whether Awoingt had been captured or not, the canal might have to be forced that night. When confirming orders came three hours later, General Burstall decided to carry out only the first stage of the operation—the capture of a bridgehead at Escaudoeuvres.

The night was very dark and broken by sudden, cold showers and gusts of wind. Troops of the 2nd Division, wearing arm bands of white calico for identification, attacked at 1:30 a.m. The assault was a complete surprise and caught the enemy in the midst of preparing for a withdrawal.[146] It was indeed the beginning of a large-scale retirement across the whole front from the Oise to the Scarpe as the German Eighteenth, Second and Seventeenth Armies began falling back towards the Hermann Line.[147] Construction of this position behind the two northern Groups of Armies had been ordered on 6 September, after the first big Allied offensive, but the required labour was not available before the last days of September. The Hermann Line branched off from the Flanders II Line (which ran from the Belgian coast at Nieuport to east of Roulers). It passed immediately west of Tournai, Valenciennes and Le Cateau, following successively stretches of the Scheldt, its tributary the Selle, and the upper Oise, before joining the Hunding-Brunhild position, constructed in 1917.[148] Prisoners taken by the Canadians in the early hours of 9 October confirmed that the initial retirement of the Seventeenth Army was to a line midway between Cambrai and Valenciennes, running east of the Canal de l'Escaut from Iwuy south through the villages of Naves and Cagnoncles.[149]

The 27th Battalion quickly captured Ramillies. Early morning patrols of the 29th and 31st Battalions found Blécourt, Batigny and Cuvillers unoccupied. By mid-morning all three places were firmly in Canadian hands.[150] Meanwhile the leading troops of the 5th Brigade with parties of engineers attached had rushed the bridges at Pont d'Aire, where the canal split into several channels. The job of preventing the demolition of the main bridge at this point was assigned to a party of the 4th Battalion Canadian Engineers, led by Captain C. N. Mitchell. While the Canadians worked to render harmless the explosive charges attached to the girders, Mitchell held at bay an enemy party attempting to rush the bridge from the far bank, killing three and capturing twelve. For this heroic act, which preserved the vital bridge from destruction, Mitchell was awarded the Victoria Cross.[151] It was still dark when the infantry crossed the canal by two hastily installed footbridges on cork floats and established a firm bridgehead on the far bank. The 25th Battalion captured Escaudoeuvres, and with the 22nd and 26th Battalions began mopping up the north-eastern outskirts of Cambrai.[152]

On the Canadian right flank the 4th and 5th C.M.R., leading the 3rd Division's attack, had advanced through Neuville St. Rémy and crossed the canal on partly demolished bridges to enter Cambrai itself. Chief opposition came from spasmodic enemy shelling, and except for small German rearguards the Canadians found the city deserted. Parties from the 4th Battalion C.E. immediately began constructing new bridges for wheeled traffic and guns to go forward, and clearing the streets of booby-traps and mines. Evidence of pillage and wanton destruction by the retreating Germans met the Canadians as they advanced. For some days they had seen columns of smoke rising from Cambrai, and it was now apparent that the enemy had determined to destroy the city by fire. But the rapid progress of the Canadians defeated these plans. Piles of combustible material were found unignited, and detachments of engineers extinguished the fires which were raging in many areas. General Loomis made a formal entry into Cambrai at 11:00 a.m., and by midday the 3rd Division had established a line of posts along the eastern outskirts. In the evening troops of the 24th British Division moving up from the south joined hands with the 2nd Division. The 3rd Division's front was pinched out, allowing its units to retire for a rest well-deserved after twelve days of continuous fighting.[153] On the Canadian Corps' northern flank the 11th British Division, after being held up at Abancourt, by evening had reached and occupied Paillencourt, 5000 yards to the north-east.

Early morning air reconnaissance on the 9th showed that the Germans had withdrawn from the angle between the Sensée and Escaut Canals, blowing bridges as they went. At first there was little except occasional shelling to impede the progress of the 2nd Division, clearing north-eastward astride the Canal de l'Escaut. On the right the 5th Brigade advanced on Naves, while the 6th kept pace along the west bank of the canal. The situation was one of the rare occasions when it seemed that mobile forces might be profitably employed. Brutinel's Brigade was ordered forward and the Canadian Light Horse received directions to push ahead and seize successive objectives of high ground north-west of Naves and on the far side of the Selle.

The participation by the cavalry was short lived. The leading squadron, riding up the Cambrai-Iwuy road, got on to the first objective but was held there by machine-gun fire converging from Iwuy and from Naves. The attempt to exploit across the Selle was abandoned and the cavalry withdrawn, having suffered casualties of a dozen men and 47 horses.[154] By the end of the day the 6th Brigade had occupied Eswars and reached Thun l'Evêque just beyond, though the latter village remained in German hands. At dusk the 26th Battalion ran into heavy machine-gun fire coming from behind strong wire defences west of Naves, and the 5th Brigade's units were forced to dig in for the night.[155]

General Horne's orders to the Canadian Corps for 10 October were to continue clearing between the canals and covering the Third Army's left flank. From the opposition which the Canadians encountered it was evident that the Germans were determined to hold as long as possible their link between the Selle and the Scheldt. During the morning the 31st Battalion occupied the village of Thun l'Evêque. Across the canal other units of the 6th Brigade took Thun St. Martin but could advance no further towards Iwuy. On the divisional right the 4th Brigade had no trouble in clearing Naves, and the 19th Battalion attacked across the dry bed of the Erclin River, just south of Iwuy. The crossing was made under cover of fire provided by the 2nd Battalion C.M.G.C. On General Currie's northern flank the 11th British Division cleared Estrun at the junction of the canals. Farther west along the Sensée patrols reached the outskirts of Hem Lenglet, and the village was taken later that night.[156]

The End of the Battle

The relief of the Canadian Corps began during the evening of 10 October, when the 49th British Division took over the southern portion of the 2nd Division's front. But before leaving this part of the line the Canadians were to strike the enemy one more blow. The straightforward plan for operations on the 11th called for an advance of some 6000 yards. On General Currie's right flank the 49th Division was directed to establish a bridgehead over the Selle at Saulzoir. The 2nd Division was to take Iwuy and advance on the villages of Avesnes-le-Sec and Lieu St. Armand, which stood on a ridge overlooking the river. The 4th Brigade, on the right, would then continue north-eastward to Noyelles and cross the Selle in that area. The 11th British Division, on the left flank, was ordered to clear the ground between the Iwuy-Denain railway and the Escaut Canal as far north as Bouchain.[157]

When the 4th and 6th Canadian Brigades attacked at 9:00 a.m. on the 11th, a vigorous reply from the enemy's artillery and machine-guns warned that the day would be one of hard fighting. The 6th Brigade met particularly heavy resistance from Iwuy, which was held by units of the 10th Ersatz Division, and it was past midday before the 28th Battalion, assisted by the 31st, finally cleared the sprawling village. It was during this operation that Lieutenant W. L. Algie, a young subaltern of the 20th Battalion, which was suffering heavy casualties on the 4th Brigade's exposed left flank, led a small party of volunteers across the brigade boundary to rush two German machine-guns and clear the east end of the village. He was killed while bringing up reinforcements, and was awarded the Victoria Cross posthumously.[158] About mid-morning as the 4th Brigade, keeping line with the British brigades on its right, reached the high ground south-west of Avesnes-le-Sec, the Germans counter-attacked with some half dozen tanks accompanied by infantry. British and Canadian troops were driven back distances of up to a mile. A battery of field artillery was rushed forward to deal with the tanks, and the guns of the 2nd C.M.M.G. Brigade, already in the line, halted the German infantry with a stream of bullets at ranges of less than 400 yards. During the afternoon both divisions launched a second attack, which regained much of the lost ground. As the day ended the 2nd Division was well established on the forward slope of the Iuwy spur. But the enemy's defences along the Selle were still intact.[159]

At 5:00 p.m. on 11 October General Currie handed over command of the Corps front to the G.O.C. 22nd Corps. For the Canadians it was the end of the Arras-Cambrai battle. Their record from 26 August to 11 October was an imposing one. In 47 days the Corps had fought forward 23 miles against very strong resistance. The opposing forces had been identified as belonging to as many as

31 German divisions, though many of these formations were already badly depleted. Under Currie's firm direction the Corps had functioned well and smoothly; its casualties were many, but by First World War standards not excessive in the light of their task. The total officially reported killed, wounded and missing between 22 August and 11 October numbered 1544 officers and 29,262 other ranks. In achieving its victory the Corps had captured 18,585 prisoners, together with 371 guns and nearly 2000 machine-guns. Besides depriving the enemy of the great distributing centre of Cambrai, the Canadians had liberated 54 towns and villages standing on more than 116 square miles of French soil.[160]

Altogether this was impressive testimony to the professional efficiency of the Canadian soldier and his leaders.

CHAPTER XV

THE FINAL ADVANCE, 12 OCTOBER-11 NOVEMBER

(See Maps 14 and 15 and Sketches 52 and 53)

The Enemy Faces Defeat

THE ALLIED VICTORIES of September and early October had badly shaken the enemy. Attempts to hide these serious defeats had met with little success. To the war-weary German people the revelation of weak and useless allies, depleted manpower reserves, and now a series of reverses on the Western Front, came as a sharp contrast to what their General Staff had promised them.

It was impossible for the German High Command to cheer itself by pointing to success in other theatres. On 29 September, the same day that the British Fourth Army smashed through the centre of the Hindenburg Line, came the news that Bulgaria, its army in Macedonia beaten by a Franco-Serbian offensive launched by General d'Esperey two weeks earlier, had signed an armistice with the Allied powers. As a result, Turkey was left to stand alone, beset by enemies advancing on all sides. While Allenby's cavalry pursued the routed Turks through Syria to Aleppo, the Salonika force threatened from Macedonia. On 30 October a new Turkish government accepted armistice terms. Germany's strongest and closest ally, Austria-Hungary, was showing disturbing symptoms of collapse. On 16 October the Hungarian Diet demanded the recall of "our Hungarian Army" from the Italian front—a demand which the Italian success at Vittoria Veneto on 24 October rendered superfluous.

Within and without Germany a series of crises became a chain of disasters. At a Council of War held at Spa on 29 September Ludendorff and von Hindenburg demanded an immediate armistice.[1] Further bad news from the Western Front in the next two days precipitated action, and on 2 October the High Command's liaison officer with the Reichstag told party leaders, "we cannot win the war".[2] German and Austrian notes were sent to President Wilson on 4 October requesting an armistice. Both Ludendorff and von Hindenburg were emphatic that Wilson's fourteen points "were to serve as the basis for the discussion of peace terms, but were not to be regarded as conditions imposed on us by the enemy".[3] It was a vain hope. It soon became clear that the Allied terms in effect amounted to unconditional surrender. This Ludendorff would not accept.

Meanwhile, on 13 October, the British C.-in-C. had been warned by the C.I.G.S., General Sir Henry Wilson, that President Wilson's fourteen points in no sense represented the terms of an armistice; and that until these had been laid down "and agreed to by the enemy, the operations now going on should be continued with all the vigour you consider safe and possible".[4] Thus while negotiations proceeded the Allies maintained their powerful offensive on the Western Front. But if one side was determined to keep up the pressure, no less was the other anxious to avoid any appearance of lessening its resistance. The German Groups of Armies were warned by Hindenburg on 12 October that the degree to which they might expect favourable armistice terms would depend on their success "in holding the forces together, in retaining possession of conquered territory and in inflicting damage on the enemy".[5]

The Last Cavalry Action

Before accompanying the Canadian Corps in its final operations of the war, we must turn back briefly to view the last action in which Canadian cavalry were engaged. This was the employment of the Canadian Cavalry Brigade with General Rawlinson's Fourth Army in the advance to the Selle River. The fighting took place south-west of Le Cateau on 9 October, the day on which the Canadian Corps captured Cambrai.

As already noted, increasing Allied pressure had forced the Germans to withdraw to the Hermann Position, which in the sector opposite the Third and Fourth Armies ran south from Valenciennes to Le Cateau. In falling back the enemy left a series of rearguards in a line approximately three miles east of his former positions. When British infantry encountered these early on the 9th they found a series of strong little centres of resistance which effectively slowed the advance, and allowed the German retirement to proceed without serious hindrance.[6]

On the afternoon of 8 October General Rawlinson had alerted the Cavalry Corps to "be prepared to take advantage of any break in the enemy's defence".[7] The Canadian Cavalry Brigade, which had seen no fighting since the Battle of Amiens, was concentrated with the rest of the 3rd Cavalry Division about seven miles north of St. Quentin, on the left flank of the Fourth Army. On the morning of the 9th the 66th Division, operating next to the boundary between the Fourth and Third Armies, had as successive objectives the village of Maretz, two miles away, and the road joining Bertry and Maurois, some three miles farther on and about the same distance short of the Selle. Advancing through heavy fog, the infantry encountered no enemy until they reached the eastern edge of Maretz. Here they came under machine-gun fire from German rearguards in the Bois de Gattigny and in Clary, which lay in Third Army territory. The defenders were members of the 72nd Regiment (8th Division) and the 413th Regiment (204th Division).[8]

It was decided to make an organized attack, in which the 3rd Cavalry Division was called on to participate. Its G.O.C., Major-General A. E. W. Harman, planned to move forward astride the old Roman road which ran straight as an arrow

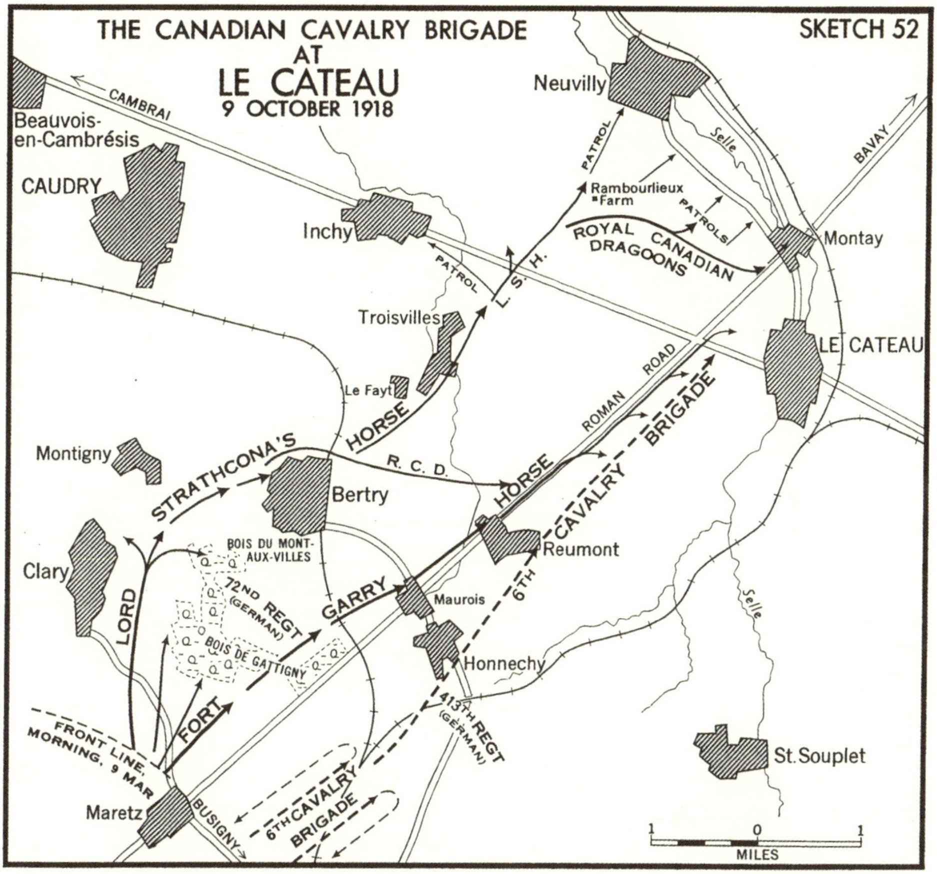

north-eastward from Maretz to Bavai. He placed the 6th Cavalry Brigade on the right of the road and the Canadian Brigade on the left. The Fort Garry Horse, with four machine-guns and a battery of the R.C.H.A. attached, led the Canadian advance. Lord Strathcona's Horse was given the task of protecting the left flank and reconnoitring out to the line Montigny-Inchy-Neuvilly.[9]

The Cavalry Brigade, commanded by Brig.-Gen. R. W. Paterson, moved forward at 9:30 a.m. Soon after crossing the lateral Clary-Maretz road both regiments met machine-gun fire from the same German positions that had stopped the infantry.[10] A spirited charge over 1500 yards of open ground by Lord Strathcona's Horse cleared out the enemy rearguard near Clary. Then, in the face of scattered shelling and machine-gun fire from Montigny on their left, the Strathconas worked their way around the edge of the Bois du Mont-aux-Villes—a northern extension of the Bois de Gattigny.[11]

Meanwhile the Fort Garry Horse, supported by the attached R.C.H.A. battery, had attacked the Gattigny Wood. While one troop of the regiment successfully charged the machine-guns in the southern half of the wood—though losing more than half its men in this attempt—a squadron galloped through a gap between the northern and southern halves of the wood to take the same objective in flank. With the assistance of infantry of the South African Brigade (of the 66th Division) in mopping up, the Bois de Gattigny was cleared shortly after 11:00 a.m. The encounter had yielded approximately 200 prisoners, a 5.9-inch howitzer and about 40 machine-guns.[12]

Success at the Bois de Gattigny and the Bois du Mont-aux-Villes prompted General Harman to make his next objectives Maurois on the Roman road and the neighbouring village of Honnechy a thousand yards to the south. He planned to encircle the latter place with a flanking move by the 6th Cavalry Brigade, while the Canadian Brigade came in on Maurois from the north. But when Brig.-Gen. Paterson went forward to relay these orders to the Fort Garry Horse he found that they had already taken Maurois. On the Canadian left the Strathconas had worked their way into Bertry.[13]

At 1:00 p.m. the 6th Cavalry Brigade reported that it had not been able to advance beyond the Busigny-Maretz road. At the same time the Fort Garrys were being held up on the Maurois-Bertry lateral. The next village on the Roman road was Reumont, only three miles from Le Cateau and the Selle. Paterson now ordered a squadron of the Royal Canadian Dragoons to swing wide to the left around Bertry to take the high ground north of Reumont. The reserve squadron of the Fort Garrys would make a smaller swing to enter Reumont from the north-west. Again the Strathconas were to provide flank protection by pushing north-east from Bertry to Troisvilles. All the guns of the R.C.H.A. Brigade, including an attached battery of 4.5-inch howitzers, were grouped in a valley 1000 yards west of Maurois to give the cavalry covering fire.

The neatly planned little operation was entirely successful. While dismounted Fort Garry troopers forced their way into Reumont, the Dragoons reached their objective in time to cut off a detachment of the retiring enemy. On the left the Strathconas were beyond Troisvilles shortly after 4:00 p.m. During the afternoon enemy guns and transport had been seen moving along the Cambrai-Le Cateau road, which crossed the path of the Canadians about a mile beyond Troisvilles. While the Fort Garry Horse retired into reserve the Dragoons and the Strathconas were ordered to cut this line of retirement as soon as possible.[14]

As night fell the Dragoons pushed forward to Montay, less than a mile from Le Cateau, and during the hours of darkness R.C.D. troopers patrolled the Montay-Neuvilly road along the west bank of the Selle.[15] On the left the Strathconas sent patrols into Inchy on the Cambrai road. Other patrols found the Germans still strongly holding Neuvilly, east of the river. In the meantime the relief of the 6th Cavalry Brigade by a cyclist battalion had left the Canadian right flank open from Reumont to Le Cateau until two squadrons of the Fort Garry Horse were brought forward to fill the gap. Enemy shelling during the night caused several casualties to both the Fort Garrys and the Strathconas, but daylight brought an end to the Canadians' operation. They were relieved by the 7th Cavalry Brigade and withdrew west of Troisvilles.[16]

In advancing approximately eight miles on a front over three miles wide, the Canadians had captured more than 400 prisoners and many weapons, and by disrupting enemy attempts at demolition they had materially aided the infantry's progress. The Brigade reported a total of 168 men and 171 horses killed, wounded and missing.[17]

It was gratifying that this last action by Canadian cavalry was successful. Mounted troops had too frequently met with frustration during the war. The introduction of machine-guns and tanks meant the end of their arm as a useful offensive weapon. This was particularly true on the Western Front, where the concentration of machine-guns and rifles was far greater than in other theatres. Nevertheless many Allied commanders either failed to recognize this trend or refused to believe it. Time and again cavalry was massed for a break-through which never occurred. On the comparatively few occasions when active employment came it was often misdirected. Horses were impeded and horribly injured by barbed wire, and their riders' sabres proved futile against enemy bullets. In assessing the work of the cavalry it must be recognized that the greatest contribution was that made by those squadrons which served dismounted in the trenches.

The Pursuit from the Sensée

When the Canadian Corps exchanged places with the fresher 22nd Corps during the second week of October, it found itself in the centre of General Horne's First Army, with the 7th Corps on its left, north of the Scarpe. Opposite was the German Seventeenth Army, which with the Second Army on its left formed the left wing of Prince Rupprecht's Group of Armies. The progressive shortening of the front had made the Army Group Headquarters Boehn redundant.[18] On 9 September the Ninth Army had reverted to the command of Army Group Wilhelm[19] and von Boehn's Army Group was dissolved on 8 October. Next day command of the Second Army returned to Army Group Rupprecht.[20]

The 1st Canadian Division had come temporarily under the 22nd Corps in this sector on 7 October, taking up positions behind the Trinquis Brook (which ran from Biache-St. Vaast to the Sensée below Etaing) and behind the Sensée for three miles east of Etaing. By the 11th the division had made its way across both waterways. It formed the left of the holding which General Currie took over on that date. The whole Corps front extended in a south-easterly direction from the Scarpe River, just east of Vitry-en-Artois, to Palluel. From there it followed the southern bank of the Sensée Canal to the junction with the Canal de l'Escaut, turning south to a point on the Escaut north-west of Iwuy. In the centre, lying for the most part before the obstacle of the Sensée, the 56th and 11th British Divisions had remained relatively quiet while the 1st Division moved forward. On the right the 2nd Canadian Division had continued the attacks begun on 9 October, but on a somewhat shortened front.[21]

There had been several attempts by units of the 1st Division to push across the Trinquis and the Sensée while the 3rd and 4th Canadian Divisions were still engaged about Cambrai. An existing bridgehead over the Trinquis near Sailly-en-

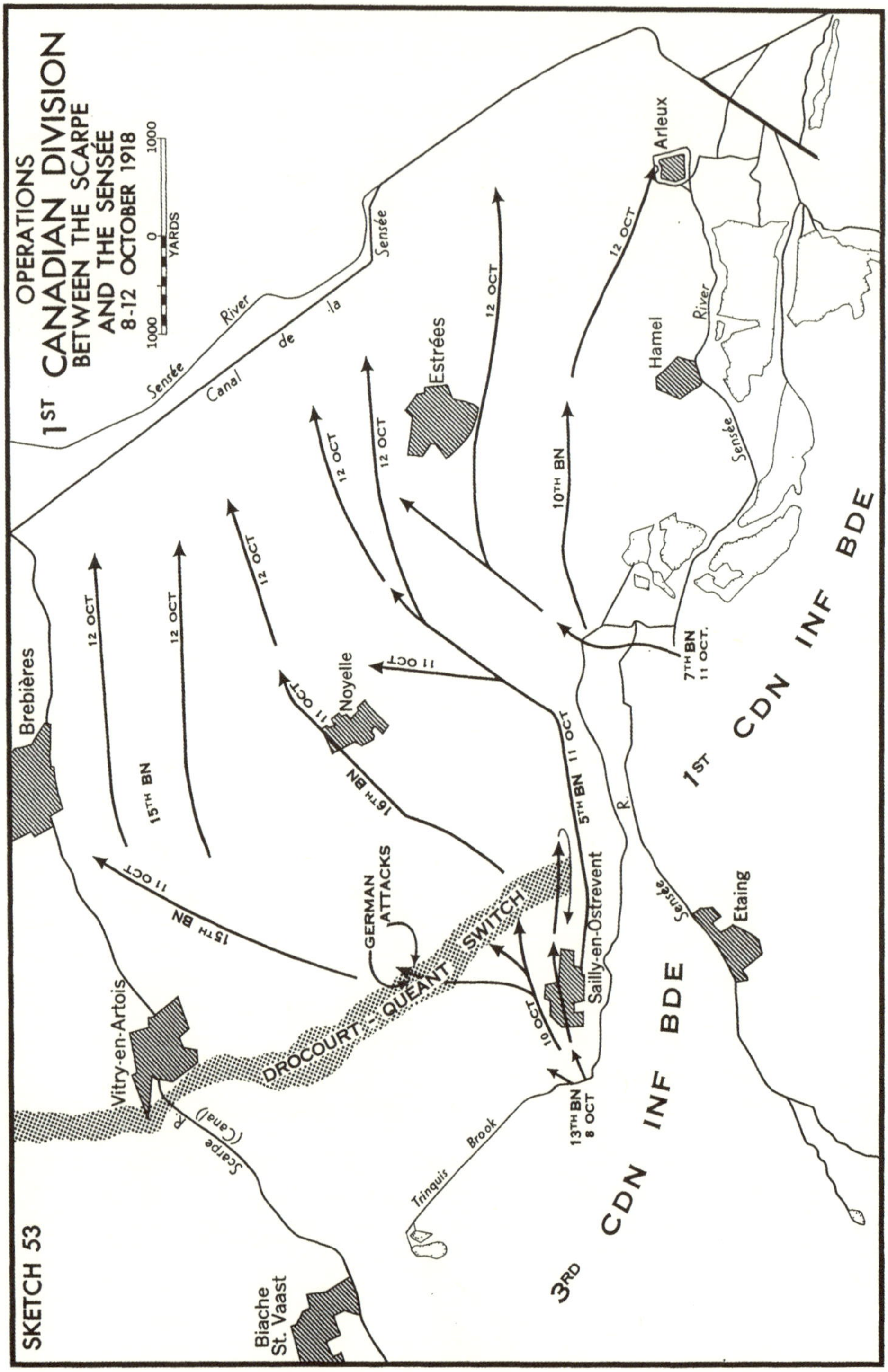
SKETCH 53
1ST CANADIAN DIVISION
OPERATIONS
BETWEEN THE SCARPE
AND THE SENSÉE
8-12 OCTOBER 1918
1000 0 1000
YARDS
Sensée River
Canal de la Sensée
Arleux
Hamel
River
Sensée
Estrées
Brebières
Noyelle
Vitry-en-Artois
Sailly-en-Ostrevent
Etaing
Biache St. Vaast
Scarpe R. (Canal)
Trinquis Brook
R. Sensée
DROCOURT - QUEANT SWITCH
GERMAN ATTACKS
15TH BN
16TH BN
5TH BN
10TH BN
7TH BN 11 OCT.
13TH BN 8 OCT
10 OCT
11 OCT
12 OCT
1ST CDN INF BDE
3RD CDN INF BDE

INTO CAMBRAI

A patrol of the 3rd Canadian Division crosses the devastated square of Cambrai, 8 October 1918. The retreating Germans have left many parts of the city ablaze.

THE MARCH OF LIBERATION

A thanksgiving ceremony marks the freeing of Denain by the 4th Canadian Division, 19 October 1918. The Prince of Wales stands between Sir Arthur Currie and his artillery commander, Brig.-Gen. Morrison, and at the right is the divisional commander, Major-General David Watson.

ENTERING VALENCIENNES

This photograph, taken under fire, shows the entry of the 10th Brigade into the western outskirts of Valenciennes, 1 November 1918.

MONS, 11 NOVEMBER 1918

After the 7th Canadian Brigade has cleared the town of Germans, the pipes of the 42nd Battalion play through the flag-bedecked streets.

Ostrevent was enlarged by a "Chinese Attack"* on 8 October, a false attack designed to determine the enemy's probable reaction to a genuine assault. Early on 10 October patrols of the 3rd Brigade, which held the left of the line, explored the possibility of piercing the positions still occupied by the enemy north of the Sensée. Members of the 13th Battalion crossed the Trinquis and penetrated well north of Sailly before being forced to withdraw with some 60 casualties.[23] South-east of Etaing patrols of the 2nd Brigade were less successful. When next day an attack by the 8th Corps on the Canadian left found the enemy in retreat, both brigades at once tried again to advance over the two rivers. Crossing on footbridges they moved steadily ahead, meeting only slight resistance from isolated machine-gun posts. Vitry-en-Artois was passed, and by dusk the new line ran from a point on the Scarpe about 1000 yards west of Brébières, south to Noyelle, Estrées and Hamel. On the 12th the advance continued unopposed, and by evening the 1st Division had pivoted on its right flank until the whole front faced the Canal de la Sensée. The two-day gain along the south bank of the Scarpe had been more than five miles.[24]

As noted in the previous chapter, the evening of 11 October found the 2nd Canadian Division forming General Currie's right flank about Iwuy (above, p. 459). The Germans shelled the village heavily that night as arrangements were completed for the 51st Division to relieve the Canadians as far west as the Iwuy-Denain Railway. Next morning the 5th Canadian Brigade joined in the British division's attack, and by mid-afternoon the 24th Battalion had pushed beyond Hordain, while patrols were advancing on Bouchain. During the evening of the 12th General Burstall extended his frontage westward almost to Aubencheul-au-Bac, taking over the area previously held by the 11th British Division.[25] This left the Corps front held by the 1st Canadian, the 56th British and the 2nd Canadian Divisions.

Across the entire front extended a water barrier, much of it swampy and impassable. General Horne's orders were to keep close touch with the enemy and cross the obstacle if means could be found to do so. Until then all corps were to "concentrate effort on reorganization of formations, and on restoring communications; and improving arrangements for supply". Fighting was to be limited to patrolling, raiding and firing test barrages.[26]

During the night of 12-13 October the 56th Division constructed a floating bridge across the Sensée Canal at Aubencheul and early on the 13th attacked Aubigny-au-Bac on the north bank.† The British troops captured the village and with it more than 200 prisoners from the 234th Infantry Division. The threat of strong enemy counter-attacks from the direction of Arleux, three miles to the west, indicated that further advance would not be profitable, and at dusk the bridgehead was abandoned, though the bridge itself remained in position, covered by our fire.[28] On the 14th patrols of the 1st Division pushed across the canal near Ferin, but once again the enemy's retaliation was too strong for a permanent bridgehead.[29]

* This consisted of making conspicuous preparations for an attack, culminating in a rolling barrage moving from in front of the outpost line toward the enemy's positions.[22]

† The crossing reversed the direction of the famous passage of the Sensée marshes by the Duke of Marlborough on 5 August 1711, when he led an army over a narrow causeway from Aubigny to Aubencheul to pierce the French "Ne Plus Ultra" lines.[27]

Prisoners' statements indicated that the Germans were preparing for a large-scale withdrawal. The Allied advance in Flanders had forced the German Fourth Army back across the Lys on 15 October, and next day the High Command ordered the Sixth and Seventeenth Armies to conform by retiring into the Hermann Line.[30] In the meantime on 16 October the 4th Canadian Division relieved the 56th British Division, whose continuous operations had left its troops too weak to carry out a vigorous pursuit of the enemy. Three Canadian divisions thus had the responsibility for twenty miles of front, and General Currie's scheme of having "two Divisions in and two out" was interrupted.[31] Next day the Germans began their retreat.

It had been the practice for the 1st Division to fire an artillery barrage along its front each morning as a test for the presence of the enemy. On 17 October there was no sign of the usual retaliation. Even as patrols were preparing to investigate, word came from the Fifth Army to the north that the Germans were retiring all along the front. The 1st and 2nd Brigades immediately crossed the Sensée Canal and pushed rapidly north-eastward. By dusk the 1st Division was established well beyond the Douai-Cambrai road, with patrols in the Douai suburb of Sin-le-Noble and in the villages of Dechy and Roucourt. Douai was found abandoned by the enemy.[32] To the south and east, where the German withdrawal was to be much more deliberate, the 4th and 2nd Divisions were opposed at the water barrier by heavy machine-gun fire. Not until the former's 87th Battalion had crossed the canal in the 1st Division's sector and cleared eastward along the far bank could troops of the 4th Division gain a footing at Aubigny-au-Bac from which the advance could proceed.[33] The enemy's artillery was subjecting the 2nd Division's front to more than normal harassing fire, but after dark patrols of the 6th Brigade crossed the Sensée at Pont Rade (in the bend of the canal north of Paillencourt). Shortly after midnight the engineers had bridges over the canal at Pont Rade and Hem Lenglet, and by daybreak on the 18th the 2nd Division held a firm bridgehead covering these.[34]

To increase the speed of the pursuit the 1st and 4th Divisions each received a squadron of the Canadian Light Horse, a company of the Canadian Cyclist Battalion, two medium machine-gun batteries and two armoured cars.[35] It was most important that the advance should be rapid enough to maintain contact with the retreating Germans, yet it proved almost as difficult to keep up with the enemy as to fight him. In the days that followed supply became a major problem. As the Germans withdrew, their engineers systematically demolished bridges and with their mines cratered roads and railways, thereby increasing tremendously the difficulty of maintaining the ever-lengthening supply lines. The problem was intensified by the large numbers of liberated but hungry civilians to be fed. On the 20th General Currie was to note in his diary, "Our Higher Authorities do not seem well enough organized to push their railheads forward fast enough." Yet it was hardly to be expected that after three years of siege warfare staffs would be fully prepared to handle a war of movement. Long marches and wet chilly weather added to the fatigue of troops who could take little rest.

The advance continued. In contrast to the shattered communities of the war-torn areas, the towns and villages abandoned by the Germans were relatively undamaged. The Canadians now found themselves in a new role—that of liberators. When on 18 October troops of the 1st Division entered Pecquencourt, six miles east of Douai, they were greeted by 2000 civilians whom the retiring enemy had left without food; before they departed the Germans had combed the countryside bare of cattle, sheep, pigs and poultry. It was the beginning of a series of liberations which before Valenciennes was reached was to bring to 70,000 the number of people released from the German yoke.[36] Against the administrative problems thus created must be set the warmth of the welcome the Canadians received. French tricolours, long hidden, appeared as if by magic along the route of the marching troops, who were greeted with embraces, cheers and shouts of "Vive la France!" As one regimental historian put it: "It was the first time they had ever really felt like 'heroes' and 'saviours of democracy', as flowery pens of the day were wont to describe hard and cynical fighting men."[37]

Pecquencourt was only one of a dozen places occupied by the Canadians on 18 October, and on the 19th they took nearly forty more communities, including the large industrial town of Denain, on the north bank of the Canal de l'Escaut.[38] The day's advance of 12,000 yards was the longest made by Canadians on any single day during the war. The Corps front was narrowing, for the boundary with the 22nd Corps ran almost due north toward Bouchain before turning north-east; and during the night of 19-20 October the 4th Canadian and 51st British Divisions came together just west of Denain, pinching out the 2nd Division, which went into corps reserve.[39]

There were still occasions when stiff resistance was encountered. On the 20th the 1st Division occupied Wallers, the last town of any size before reaching the large Forêt de Vicoigne. To one battalion at least German machine-gun and artillery fire brought its last fatal casualties of the war.[40] Before night fell the division had gained a line running along the western edge of the Forêt de Vicoigne, which the 1st and 3rd Brigades cleared next day. By the morning of 21 October General Macdonell's troops, who had been engaged in continuous operations since the battle of the Canal du Nord, had reached the St. Amand-Valenciennes road. The 3rd Division now came forward from reserve in the Quéant area, where on 15 October, in the presence of H.R.H. the Prince of Wales, the G.O.C. First Army, Sir Arthur Currie, and other senior officers, it had sadly buried its former commander, Major-General L. J. Lipsett (above, p. 441). Relief was completed on 22 October and the 1st Division left the line for the last time in the war.[41]

On the right the 4th Division had kept pace. There were occasional troublesome rearguards to dislodge, and these became more numerous as the Canadians neared the turn of the Escaut Canal, where their passage to Valenciennes was blocked. At the waterway the Corps came to a halt. To the north lay the Forêt de Raismes, an expanse some four miles square thinly covered with hardwood trees and some conifers. The 3rd Division's first task was to clear this area of enemy. Most of this was done on 22 October thanks to the good work of the

7th and 9th Brigades, which in fifteen hours made their way through the woods a maximum distance of some 7000 yards.[42] By evening on 23 October the Canadian front line stretched for eight miles along the Canal de l'Escaut from the Corps southern boundary to Fresnes, whence it slanted back toward the German-held village of Odomez, where the right wing of the British 8th Corps was closing to the Canal du Jard.[43]

A Pause at the Escaut

The Canadian line was now to remain stabilized for several days while preparations were made for capturing Valenciennes. Both flanking formations of the First Army—the 8th Corps to the north and the 22nd on the south—were well behind the Canadians. The former had been delayed by difficulties of supply and by German demolitions, while the 22nd Corps was held up by resistance along the Ecaillon River, which entered the Escaut four miles south-west of Valenciennes.[44]

On 21 October General Horne had ordered that bridgeheads over the Escaut would be secured wherever possible but that no attempt should be made to cross the canal in strength.[45] The resulting period of rest was not unwelcome. The rapid change from static trench fighting to the open warfare of September and October had sorely taxed human resources and material. Long forced marches and many hours of lost sleep had taken their toll of physical energy. Getting supplies forward continued to be a major problem despite the sustained efforts of the engineers, aided by squads of already weary infantry toiling to repair roads and bridges.[46] A considerable amount of transport was tied up in distributing army rations to the hungry population. Particularly hard pressed during this last phase of the war were the medical services who, in addition to the unaccustomed problems created by open warfare, now had to care for large numbers of civilian sick and wounded. Canadian hospitals for these unfortunates were established in Auberchicourt, Somain and Denain, while in smaller centres special dressing stations were reserved for civilians.[47]

During this period the 4th Division made several attempts to send patrols across the Escaut by boat, footbridges and over the debris of destroyed bridges. Orders that Valenciennes itself was not to be bombarded because of the large numbers of French civilians in the city made it extremely difficult to clear enemy machine-guns and snipers from the houses overlooking the canal.[48] From what probing the patrols could accomplish and from the statements of prisoners it was clear that the enemy was preparing to make a determined stand at Valenciennes. In selecting the city as a key-point in the Hermann Line the Germans had chosen well. The Escaut Canal provided an effective water barrier against attack from the west and the north. The enemy had heavily wired both banks of the canal and fortified the east bank with a well-planned trench system. In addition, he had loop-holed the walls of the city's houses and factories and armed them with machine-gun posts. By cutting gaps in the canal dykes and opening sluice gates the Germans had inundated the country on both sides of the Escaut. West and south-west of Valenciennes the flooded area was several hundred yards wide, and to the north, in the wide angle between the Escaut and the Condé-Mons Canals, the water spread over many square miles.[49]

Nature had further favoured the Germans in defending them against any attempt to capture Valenciennes from the south. The prominent wooded height of Mont Houy, east of the bend in the Escaut, rose to a height of 150 feet above the canal and completely dominated the southern approaches to the city. Behind it a long ridge overlooking the valley of the Rhonelle stream reached northward to Valenciennes, and along this the enemy had constructed a line of wire and trenches to add artificial strength to an already difficult natural position. Beyond this a second line of trenches, on which less work had been done, ran in a south-easterly direction from Aulnoy, a village 2500 yards south of Valenciennes, to Preseau and along the high ground east of the Rhonelle.[50]

Fully alert to the opportunities which Valenciennes offered for checking the Allied advance, the German Seventeenth Army was holding this section of the Hermann position with five divisions—though all were considerably reduced in numbers. On 1 November the flooded front opposite the Canadian left was being defended by the 234th Division between Condé and Bruary; the 220th Division (the 25th Division was in process of relieving it) held most of Valenciennes and northward to Bruay. The enemy had packed the bulk of his strength in the Mont Houy area, where three infantry divisions—the 6th, 35th and 214th—stood guard between the southern outskirts of the city and Aulnoy.[52]

Mont Houy Captured—Valenciennes Liberated

Resistance south of the Escaut continued as the 22nd Corps fought to come abreast of the Canadians. By the evening of 26 October the 51st Division, having forced a crossing of the Ecaillon, had reached a line along the outskirts of Famars, where the Highlanders could look down into the deep valley of the Rhonelle. But attempts to advance farther were thwarted by very heavy fire from Mount Houy and from German batteries about Saultain, on the high plateau south-east of Valenciennes.[52]

On 27 October General Horne called Sir Arthur Currie and the commander of the 22nd Corps to his advanced headquarters at Auberchicourt, and discussed means by which Valenciennes might be taken. With a frontal attack or an enveloping movement from the north out of the question, Mont Houy was obviously the key to the city. Operations were planned to take place in three stages. On the far side of the Escaut Canal the 51st Division of the 22nd Corps would attack north-eastward on 28 October and capture Mount Houy, advancing as far as the sunken road (forming part of the "Red" line objective) which joined Le Poirier Station (at the canal) and Aulnoy. The 4th Canadian Division would then move through the 51st and continue the attack between the Escaut and the Rhonelle with the object of gaining the "Blue" line, which ran from

Preseau to the southern outskirts of Valenciennes. Finally, on 1 November, the 4th Division would capture the high ground east of Valenciennes so as to outflank the city and enable the remainder of the Canadian Corps to cross the Escaut from the west. The objective in this phase was the "Green" line, which from the north-east corner of Valenciennes curved in a southerly direction behind the Saultain ridge.[53]

At 5:15 a.m. on the 28th a battalion of the 51st Division attacked Mont Houy with the support of nine British brigades of field artillery, five 6-inch howitzer and nine 60-pounder batteries.[54] Despite strong opposition the Highlanders gained the hill, but could not hold it. The Germans were determined to retain possession of so favourable a position for observation, and in the early afternoon they launched a counter-attack which drove the British battalion back over the top of Mont Houy. Nightfall found the 154th Brigade of the 51st Division holding most of the southern slope of the hill, and on either flank Le Poirier Station and the village of Famars.[55] This was considerably short of the Red line, where the 10th Canadian Brigade was to have relieved the British Brigade on the night of 28-29 October.[56]

During the night the 3rd Canadian Division took over some of the 4th Division's front, but General Currie recommended that the relief of the 51st Division be delayed 24 hours, though General Watson, G.O.C. 4th Division, was willing to make the change-over. At 5:00 p.m. on the 28th, however, General Horne issued instructions that the Canadian Corps would carry out the relief as ordered, provided that the 51st Division held Mont Houy. It was to be left to the "commanders of the troops on the spot" to make the decision.[57] When night fell on the 28th it was clear that most of the hill was still in German hands, and so the relief was postponed.* Throughout 29 October the tired Highlanders fought off repeated counter-attacks. That night the right of the 51st Division was relieved by the 49th Division, and the left, from Famars to Poirier Station, by the 10th Canadian Infantry Brigade.

The plan for taking Mont Houy and Valenciennes had been revised. Orders from G.H.Q. called for the Fourth, Third and First Armies, in conjunction with the First French Army, to be prepared to resume the main offensive on 3 November, and it was urgent that Valenciennes should be captured in order to secure the left flank of this large-scale operation.[60] The capture of the Blue and sub-

* Afterwards the M.G.G.S. of the First Army criticized General Horne's insistence that the 51st Division should not be relieved until it had reached the objective which the Army's plan had rigidly imposed. He also questioned the Canadian Corps' rather inflexible interpretation of these orders, suggesting that the tired British division should have been relieved before the attack took place at all, in order that such an assault might have the support of Canadian artillery west of the Escaut. Had the British and the Canadian command adapted themselves more readily to the changing situation, suggests the M.G.G.S., "24 hours would have been saved".[58]

The flexibility of action suggested by this critic may well have been just what this phase of the war demanded, but his view was challenged several years later by the former G.O.C. Canadian Corps Heavy Artillery. General McNaughton defended the Canadian refusal to make a premature relief, comparing the situation on 28 October with that which had existed in June 1916 at the St. Eloi Craters (when the Canadian Corps disastrously took over from the 5th Corps in the middle of a battle). Postponement of the assault on Mont Houy, he said, gave the Canadian Heavy Artillery a "full and proper opportunity to do our work free from the hysteria of a suddenly improvised attack."[59]

MAP 14

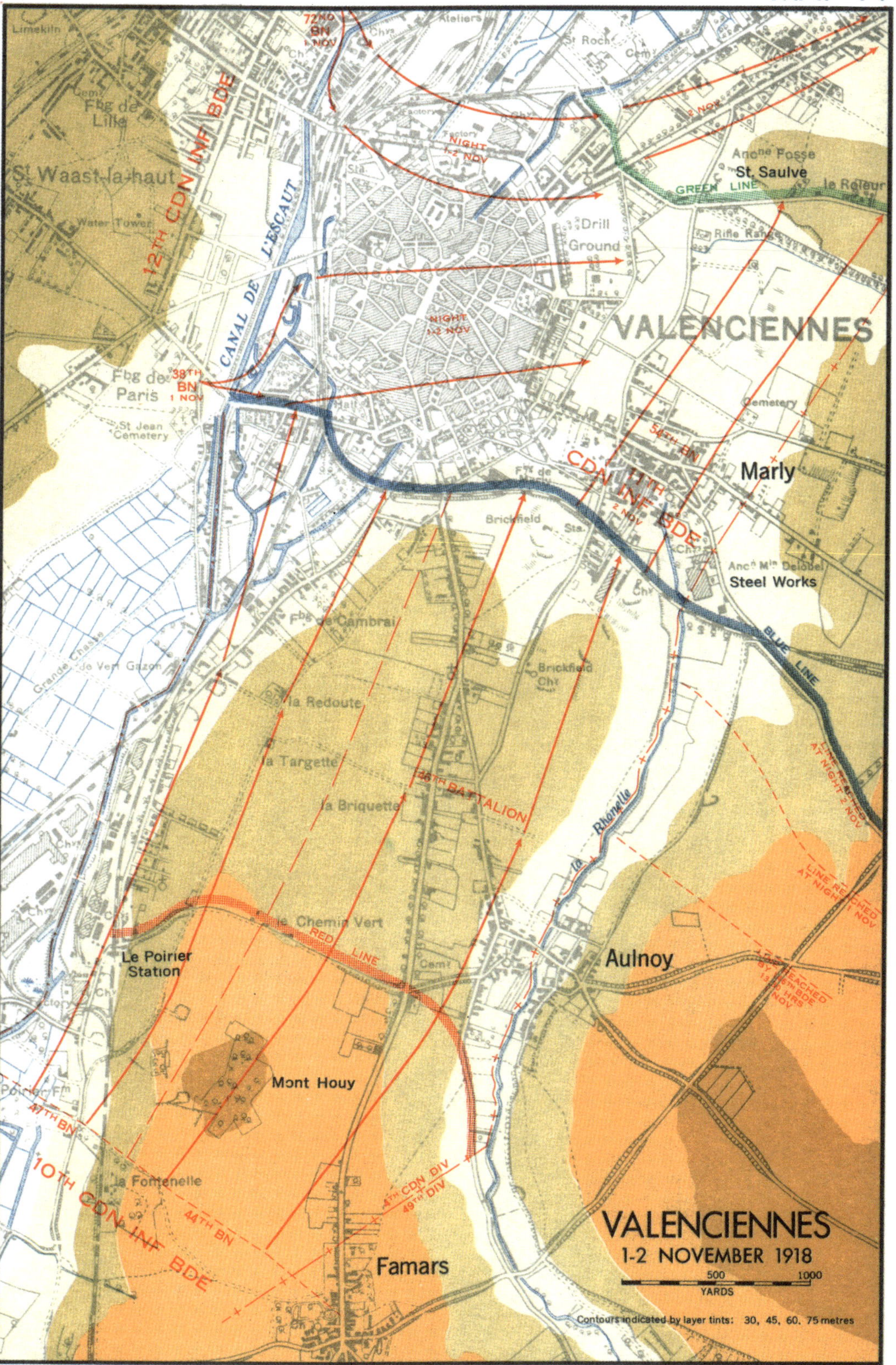

Reproduced by Army Survey Establishment

Compiled and drawn by Historical Section G.S.

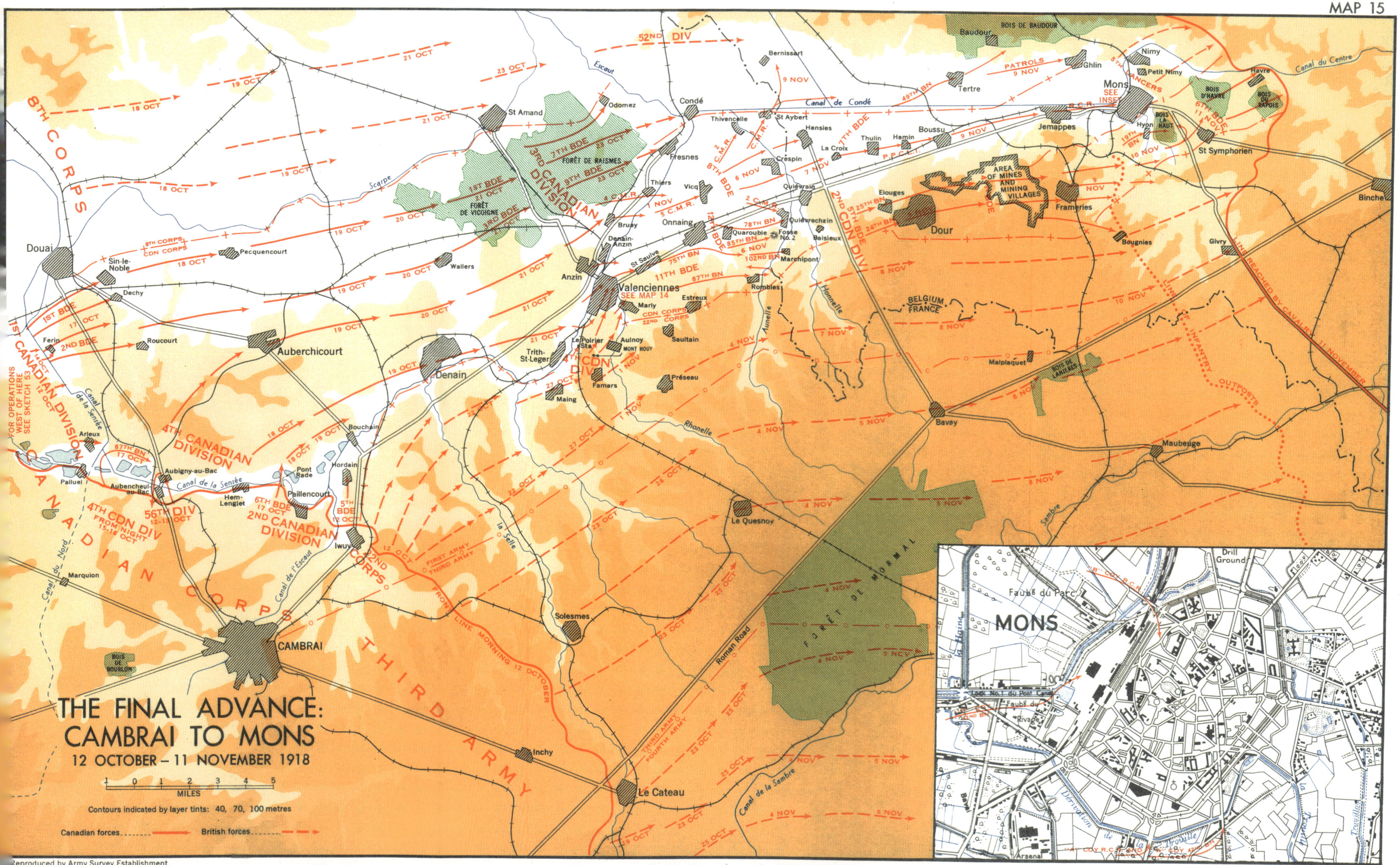

Reproduced by Army Survey Establishment

sequent exploitation to the Green line was now to be carried out as a single operation with massive artillery support, the 10th Canadian Brigade cooperating with the 49th Division on the right. While the 10th Brigade (commanded since 28 October by Brig.-Gen. J. M. Ross) assaulted Valenciennes from the south and moved around the east side, the 12th was to establish bridgeheads over the Escaut from the west and mop up the city. Farther to the north the 3rd Division prepared to cross the canal at the same time. The new plan was geared for an assault early on 1 November.[61]

Arrangements for the attack were complicated by the many civilians remaining in Valenciennes. As far as possible the city was spared from heavy artillery fire, and only such defended positions as the industrial centre of Marly and its steel works, which were known to be full of enemy troops, came under bombardment. Because its left wing, on the west side of the Escaut Canal, had advanced so far forward, the Canadian Corps was able to arrange a rather unique artillery barrage on the Mont Houy position. Eight field and six heavy artillery brigades supported the 10th Infantry Brigade in its attack. Three field brigades sited south of the Escaut, near Maing, supplied the frontal creeping barrage; one gave oblique fire from the left bank near Trith St. Leger; the other two were near La Sentinelle, west of the Cambrai-Valenciennes road, furnishing enfilade fire. Unable through lack of suitable bridges to cross the Escaut, the heavy artillery remained on the left bank in a position to bring oblique, enfilade and even reverse fire (deliberately arranged for moral effect) on the area of the attack. Some three and a half brigades were employed on counter-battery work, the remainder bringing down fire on houses which were suspected of containing machine-gun nests.[62] Three batteries of 4.5-inch howitzers fired an intense smoke-screen to cover the attack, and the normal artillery barrage was supplemented by the fire of twelve batteries of the 1st and 4th Canadian Machine Gun Battalions firing in close support or in enfilade from north of the canal.[63] On no other occasion in the whole war was a single infantry brigade to be supported with such a weight of gunfire.

The weather, which seemed constantly to be in opposition to Canadian plans, held true to form. Throughout the preceding night and the day of attack, frequent showers caused the soldiers much discomfort. There was no preliminary bombardment on the morning of 1 November, and promptly at 5:15 a.m. the infantry of the 10th Brigade began to advance behind a deluge of shrapnel, machine-gun bullets and high explosive shell that swept down on the enemy from front and flank and rear. The German artillery was prompt to retaliate, but its fire rapidly dwindled under the accurate counter-bombardment of the Canadian guns.

The 44th Battalion pushed over Mont Houy without difficulty, and on the left the 47th took Le Poirier Station. The Red objective was achieved on schedule and by 6:30 the right battalion was passing Aulnoy. German soldiers of the 35th and 214th Divisions, stupefied by the overpowering barrage, surrendered in large numbers. On the Brigade right the 46th Battalion leapfrogged the 44th Battalion as planned and with the 47th it reported the Blue line reached at 10:20. As the infantry moved into the outskirts of Valenciennes, considerable opposition developed on the right flank and along the front of the 146th Brigade (49th Division).

Heavy machine-gun fire came from the southern edge of the city, and the garrison of the steel works near Marly, veterans of the German 6th Division, fought back vigorously. In the course of the afternoon the brigade commander, Brig.-Gen. J. M. Ross, brought up the 50th Battalion to reinforce the 46th Battalion and to hold the brigade's right flank. Six batteries of machine-guns from the 4th Battalion C.M.G.C. were disposed facing east, but the fire from Marly continued to be strong.[64]

The last V.C. of the war awarded to a Canadian was won by Sergeant Hugh Cairns, D.C.M., of the 46th Battalion, for his conspicuous bravery during the day's action. When an enemy machine-gun suddenly opened fire on his platoon, Cairns seized a Lewis gun and ignoring the German bullets rushed the post single-handed, killing the crew of five, and capturing the gun. Later he repeated this daring act, accounting for 30 more of the enemy and two machine-guns. On a third occasion, though wounded, he led a small party to outflank and capture German machine-guns and field guns which were holding up the advance. His achievements ended during the mopping up of Marly, when he was severely wounded while disarming a party of Germans that his patrol had forced to surrender. Throughout the entire operation he showed the highest degree of valour and bold leadership. He died next day from his wounds.[65]

Encirclement of Valenciennes and penetration into the city continued. During the morning of 1 November the 12th Brigade and the 3rd Division had both established bridgeheads over the Escaut, the infantry crossing by means of collapsible boats and cork float bridges. By noon the 12th Brigade, on the immediate left of the 10th, had the greater part of the 38th and 72nd Battalions east of the canal and patrols had pushed well into the heart of the city.[66] The 3rd Division's initial crossing was made by a party of the 4th Canadian Mounted Rifles from the industrial area of Denain-Anzin, immediately north of Valenciennes. A long stretch of the canal was under enemy observation from a high mine dump outside Thiers, so that the battalion had to wait until darkness to secure crossings east of Bruay and opposite Thiers.[67]

On 2 November General Currie recorded in his diary: "The operation yesterday was one of the most successful the Corps has yet performed." The capture of the Mont Houy position and the advance on Valenciennes had been skilfully planned and well executed. Though the enemy still clung to the city and held firm his strong position near Marly, the day for him was one of disaster. The Canadians had taken nearly 1800 prisoners, and more than 800 enemy dead were counted in the battle area. Canadian losses numbered 80 killed and some 300 wounded. Careful coordination in employing a tremendous weight of artillery* in very close support of minimum numbers of infantry had achieved victory at a very low cost.

The majority of the enemy's casualties had come from the barrage. As for the remainder, it is probable that in different circumstances the proportion of enemy captured to those killed might have been larger. Regimental histories and various

* The G.O.C. Canadian Corps Heavy Artillery later contrasted the weight of 2149 tons of shells expended from noon on 31 October to noon on 2 November with the 2800 tons fired by both sides in the whole South African War.[68]

official and semi-official sources reveal that the Canadians' hostility towards the Germans was intensified during the closing stage of the war when they saw the conditions of oppression under which the civilians whom they liberated had existed. One battalion noted, of its prisoners, that "it was impossible to avoid taking so many as they surrendered in batches of from 20 to 50".[69] That some of the Canadian troops should apparently have indulged in unnecessary killing in the heat of action was regrettable but to a certain extent understandable. General Currie, when told that "the ground was simply littered with German dead", wrote in his diary: "I know that it was not the intention of our fellows to take many German prisoners as, since they have lived amongst and talked to the French people here, they have become more bitter than ever against the Boche."[70]

During the night of 1-2 November the 11th Brigade relieved the 10th. The 54th Battalion attacked Marly before dawn, only to find that most of the Germans had withdrawn from the village.[71] During the night the two battalions of the 12th Brigade, which had met strenuous opposition during the afternoon, were able to push through Valenciennes with no great difficulty as the Germans evacuated the city. Both units reported themselves on the eastern outskirts by 8:30 a.m. By nightfall on the 2nd the Brigade had secured St. Saulvé, a mile up the Mons road.[72] On the Canadians' right a determined German garrison in the steel works held up the 49th Division until mid-afternoon of the 2nd, when a battalion of the 148th Brigade successfully rushed the position. Heavy fire from the direction of Saultain halted the British advance at the Preseau-Marly road.[73]

Meanwhile the 3rd Division was with difficulty working its way across the flooded area north of Valenciennes. Often the only line of advance lay along a railway embankment or some sodden ridge which was swept by fire from German machine-guns and snipers. Despite these handicaps, the 8th Brigade managed by nightfall on 2 November to draw level with the 12th on its right. Because of the length of the front which General Loomis was holding in such adverse conditions, he was glad during the night of 2 November to hand over to the 52nd British Division the portion of his line north of Fresnes.[74]

Sir Douglas Haig had postponed by one day the set-piece attack by the four Allied Armies ordered for 3 November. On the morning of the 3rd, however, when it was clear that the enemy had retired from the Escaut leaving only weak rearguards, he cancelled the offensive. He ordered a general advance, telling divisions to act vigorously on their own initiative so as to keep the Germans from establishing a firm line. The 22nd Corps was given an initial objective ten miles away, and the Canadian Corps ordered to cover the British left. By nightfall on the 3rd, Canadian patrols of the 4th Division had pushed forward to the Estreux-Onnaing road, three miles east of Valenciennes, without making contact with the enemy.[75]

The Advance to Mons

The battle for Valenciennes was the last major prearranged attack in which the Canadian Corps was engaged. The week of campaigning that remained was to see no large action, as the enemy was kept continually on the move. Only twice was the daily advance less than a mile.

In these last few days of the war the Canadians encountered a new type of fighting. The need to maintain mobility was paramount, but the changing nature of the countryside made this a difficult task. Since the pursuit started in mid-October operations for the most part had been over flat or gently rolling country intersected by many rivers and streams. Now there were as many streams as before, but these flowed more swiftly and their valleys were more deeply cut. Numerous villages and isolated clusters of houses dotted the countryside, the number increasing after the Belgian frontier was crossed. The ground was thickly timbered and dotted with small plantations and hedged enclosures. Altogether it was the type of terrain in which a determined enemy, with time to prepare his defences, might have made a prolonged stand, costly to the attacker. But from Verdun to the sea the Germans were falling back under Allied pressure, and the speed of the Canadian pursuit was to be governed not so much by the strength of the enemy's resistance as by the pursuers' powers of maintenance. Under instructions from the First Army each division was now acting more independently of its corps headquarters, seeking its own opportunities to push towards its general objectives while cooperating with its flanking formations.[76]

Most of the roads were in miserable condition; and those that were paved were wide enough for lorry traffic in only one direction. As the Canadians sought to maintain contact with the enemy it was only with the greatest difficulty that the heavy artillery could maintain its support of the advancing infantry brigades. Reconnaissance patrols from Valenciennes located routes by-passing the maze of cratered road junctions, and on occasion the artillery's own engineers filled in key craters to allow the passage of the heavy guns. By such means the C.C.H.A. kept three brigades forward in continual touch with the attacking infantry.

The problem of maintaining the pursuit, already complicated by German demolitions, ever-lengthening supply lines, and inadequate communications, was intensified by bad weather. Rain fell constantly. There was only one day between 1 and 11 November on which some sector of the Canadian Corps front did not report precipitation.[77] The muddy roads slowed cyclists and mounted orderlies, and the poor visibility prevented signalling by flag or helio. To add to the difficulties of communications the civilians, fearful of the enemy's mines, appeared to mistake every piece of wire along the road for some sort of demolition fuze, and were continually cutting the Canadian telephone lines.[78] As the advance continued and town after town was liberated, rumours of the approaching cease fire were traded incessantly. For four long years men had looked forward anxiously to the termination of hostilities, and now it appeared that the end was really in sight. The First Army reported that morale was "never higher".

The enemy's retirement in front of the 4th Division during the night of 3-4 November took him back behind the Aunelle River, where he began digging in immediately east of the stream, which constituted the French-Belgian boundary across the Canadian path. Intelligence reports and aerial photographs of new field works indicated that the Germans intended to make a stand here. Accordingly Canadian action on the 4th was confined to repeated artillery barrages on the enemy's line, as plans were drawn for the 4th Division to attack next day. In conjunction with the flanking 3rd Canadian and 56th British Divisions it was hoped to secure crossings over both the Aunelle and the Grande Honnelle about 500 yards to the east. The enemy's continued shuffling of his depleted formations had brought the 187th Division in front of the Canadians. In fairly stiff fighting on 5 November the 12th Brigade took the village of Quarouble, with the 78th Battalion, but the 85th was halted by the German 188th Regiment's defence of a large heap of mine refuse (beside Fosse No. 2) west of the Aunelle. On the right the 87th Battalion (11th Brigade) captured Rombies and crossed the river, only to be thrown back by a German counter-attack.[79]

A further attempt to reach the Grande Honnelle succeeded on 6 November. The 85th Battalion captured Fosse No. 2 while Quievrechain fell to a joint attack by the 78th Battalion and the 2nd C.M.Rs. The 102nd Battalion took Marchipont and exploited forward to Baisieux. By nightfall the division controlled both the Petite and Grande Honnelle Rivers along its whole front. This action ended the last tour of front-line service for the 4th Division. During the night of 6-7 November it was relieved by the 2nd Division for what proved to be the beginning of the final Canadian effort.[80]

The 3rd Division to the north had, in the meantime, been threading its way forward through the heavily flooded area north of the Valenciennes-Mons road, led by the 8th Brigade. Vicious fighting took place on 4 November in front of the mining town of Vicq. The enemy was using as an observation post a big mine dump on the western outskirts of the town. Protected on the north by floods and on the west and south by wire and machine-gun posts, this strongpoint proved a difficult nut to crack. Vicq was defended by two battalions of the 115th Regiment of the 25th Division—one of the relatively few German divisions still rated first class in 1918.[81] The 5th Canadian Mounted Rifles, assaulting across flat fields devoid of cover, suffered numerous casualties before they gained a footing on the dump—only to be driven off by the Germans' incessant machine-gun and artillery fire. That night Canadian and British gains farther south compelled the enemy to fall back from Vicq, and in the early morning of the 5th the 5th C.M.R. entered the town. On 6 November the 8th Brigade again attacked, capturing Crespin and establishing crossings over the Aunelle and Honnelle Rivers. On the northern flank, however, the enemy was holding Condé and the Condé-Mons Canal in strength. To ensure the security of the Corps left the 3rd Division was ordered to press its attack northward. For this purpose there was a partial relief of the 8th Brigade on 7 November. The 7th Brigade took over the front astride the Mons road, while the 8th continued for a time to operate with two battalions on the northern flank.[82]

The Canadians were now in Belgian territory. As they crossed the international boundary the troops were impressed by the changed conditions which they encountered. Many of the villages through which they had passed on the French side of the border had been badly battered by war, and four years of enemy occupation had left their grim mark upon the undernourished inhabitants. By contrast, a short distance away in Belgium, there was evidence that German animosity had been less pronounced. Buildings appeared to be relatively undamaged, the shop windows offered a wider range of commodities, and more able-bodied men were seen in the streets. The welcome given the Canadians by the Belgian civilians was as warm as that which they had received in France. Amid scenes of gaiety and holiday-making they were hailed as liberators and greeted with cheers, handshakes and kisses and offerings of coffee, wine and beer.

The renewal of the advance by the British Fourth, Third and First Armies marked the beginning of a continuous drive towards the German frontier on a wide front. On 4 November the Fourth Army forced the Sambre-Oise Canal east of Le Cateau, while on its left the Third Army captured Le Quesnoy. North of the Canadian Corps' sector the First Army's left wing was making slower progress because of the inundated country about the Mons-Condé Canal. Farther north still there was little motion yet by the Fifth and Second Armies, which were still held up west of the Escaut by the enemy's Hermann Position. The main drive in the south was being made by the United States First Army,* which with assistance from the French Fourth Army on its left was pressing north-eastward along the west bank of the Meuse with a view to outflanking the German positions between the Aisne and the Meuse.[83] By 6 November American troops were in sight of Sedan.[84]

The German leaders were in a quandary. Negotiations for an armistice had been going on for some time, and in order to maintain its bargaining position the High Command was anxious to avoid any large-scale withdrawals. On 24 October when framing an order to the German Army (promulgation of which was, however, stopped by the government) von Hindenburg had interpreted Allied demands for unconditional surrender as "a challenge to continue our resistance with all our strength".[85] But another major defeat in the field would be a greater evil. Accordingly on the afternoon of 4 November the German High Command had reluctantly ordered a general retirement to the Meuse-Antwerp position, which ran from Verdun and Sedan northward through Charleroi to the Dutch border west of Antwerp.[86]

In the centre of the First Army's front the Canadian advance was gaining momentum. On the morning of the 7th the 8th Brigade occupied La Croix and Hensies, north of the main road, the Germans having abandoned both places the previous night. The 52nd British Division took Condé during the night of the 7th-8th, and next day the 2nd and 5th C.M.R. cleared Thivencelle and St. Aybert. That evening the 5th C.M.R. crossed the Canal de Condé under cover of darkness and gained a firm footing on the north bank. They pushed northward, and by mid-afternoon on the 9th were in touch with the 52nd British Division south-east of Bernissart. By this time the P.P.C.L.I., leading the advance between the canal and the Mons road, had forged rapidly ahead, taking in succession the villages of Thulin, Hamin and Boussu. To cover the open left flank the 49th Battalion made a long forced march to cross the canal on the afternoon of the 9th. Swinging

* A Second American Army had been formed on 12 October and put into the line on the right of the First, between the Meuse and the Moselle.

eastward through Tertre, the battalion threw a screen of patrols northward into the Bois de Baudour and as far forward as Ghlin, only two miles north-east of Mons. They established posts which were taken over on 10 November by units of the 52nd Division.[87]

Meanwhile the 7th Brigade was closing in on Mons. By the evening of 9 November the Patricias, "very, very tired" from their continuous marching, had reached the outlying suburb of Jemappes, where they were relieved by The Royal Canadian Regiment, which took over the whole 7th Brigade front. The R.C.R. planned to attack Mons from north, west and south by separate company groups, but heavy mist, poor communications and strong enemy fire on the morning of the 10th made it clear that the regiment would not be able to carry this out unaided.[88] At 8:30 a.m. Brig.-Gen. Clark ordered the 42nd Battalion to take over the brigade's right flank south of the Canal de Condé. The day was spent in a series of unsuccessful attempts by two companies of the 42nd to work their way into the city.[89]

We must turn now to what had been happening on the southern part of the Canadian Corps' front. On the relief of the 4th Division by the 2nd Division, Major-General Burstall put the 5th Brigade into the lead, instructing them "to act with the utmost boldness". Brig.-Gen. Tremblay's infantry were supported by two machine-gun companies and by batteries of the 2nd Canadian Divisional Artillery and a British brigade of field artillery. To provide flexibility in the pursuit, Burstall organized into a separate force—ready to push through the infantry if opportunity offered—the 2nd C.M.M.G. Brigade, a company of the Canadian Corps Cyclists and two squadrons of the Canadian Light Horse. With good foresight the force also included two sub-sections of engineers of the 6th Battalion C.E., carrying with them in lorries about seven tons of timber for road and bridge repair.[90] There was delay at the Honnelle River, which the heavy rains had made unfordable, but by nightfall on the 7th the 5th Brigade had advanced three miles to Elouges, which the 25th Battalion occupied in a mixture of street fighting against enemy die-hards and warm welcome from the civilian inhabitants. Next day the 24th Battalion took Dour, but with other units of the brigade ran into difficulties in the maze of mine dumps north-east of the town. Broken bridges and mine craters on the roads kept the Independent Force from making any useful headway.[91]

The 2nd Division's path now lay through densely populated mining country, in which one village spread into the next. But the latest German retirement had left these places undefended, and when the 4th Brigade passed through the 5th on the morning of 9 November, its progress as far as Frameries, a town three miles south-west of Mons, was practically a route march. Then machine-gun fire from the front and the right flank forced a deployment. By nightfall, however, the brigade had reached a line which from the village of Bougnies, four miles south of Mons, angled north-westward to the boundary with the 3rd Division on the Frameries-Mons road.[92]

That night the Canadian Corps issued orders for the capture of Mons on the following day.

The Capture of Mons

The ancient frontier town of Mons, dating back to Roman days, had experienced many sieges during its troubled history. Its latest association with fighting had come in August 1914, when the small British Expeditionary Force encountered and engaged for one day the advancing German right wing on the Condé Canal before falling back towards Paris and the Marne. For four years Mons had remained in German hands. It was a valuable asset to the enemy, for the finest coal in Belgium was to be found in the nearby mines, which unlike those destroyed or flooded by the Germans on the French side of the frontier, had been kept in vigorous production. This time there would be no siege; Mons was as far as possible to be spared damage. General Currie planned to take the city by an encircling manoeuvre. He ordered the 2nd Division, moving around the southern outskirts, to occupy the high ground to the east, while the 3rd Division captured the northern suburb of Nimy and infiltrated into the heart of the city.[93]

Fighting on 9 November had yielded only scant gains in comparison with the advances of previous days. As the Canadians completed the occupation of one village they would be held up by machine-gun fire from the next. In their retirement on the night of the 6th-7th the Germans had fallen back to a line running north and south through Mons, and attempts by the 2nd Canadian Division on 10 November to push around the southern edge of the city met spirited reminders that the enemy was still there. The main centres of resistance were in the dominant Bois la Haut—a wooded hill some 2000 yards south-east of Mons rising abruptly more than 350 feet above the surrounding country—and the village of Hyon, immediately west of this height.[94] Here strong rearguards were covering the planned retirement to the Antwerp-Meuse line, which began during the afternoon. Despite prisoners' reports of this intended withdrawal, machine-gun fire was still coming from Mons and the neighbouring villages, and at 10:00 p.m. the Canadian Corps gave instructions that the objectives of 11 November remained the same as for the 10th.[95]

During the night the 19th Battalion occupied Hyon, but the enemy in the Bois la Haut held out until 3:15 a.m. By that time the 3rd Division was well into Mons (below, p. 481) and hostile fire was rapidly dwindling. By 8:00 a.m. the 4th Brigade had crossed the Mons-Givry road and was at the village of St. Symphorien, on the main road from Mons to Charleroi.[96]

The whole of Mons lay within the 3rd Division's sector, and the task of entering the city was assigned to the 7th Brigade. The difficulty facing both the R.C.R. and the 42nd Battalion was to force crossings over the almost continuous water barrier which the Canal du Centre and the Dérivation de la Trouille formed around Mons, those watercourses having once constituted the moats of the ancient fortress. Enemy machine-guns sited in the outlying houses covered all approaches and made an assault virtually impossible during daylight, for orders from Corps Headquarters expressly forbade any shelling of Mons, not excepting German machine-gun posts. Immediately south of the Condé Canal there was a break in the water barrier, and here the commander of the 42nd Battalion decided to attempt an entry. He planned to work his troops through the city and thus cut off troublesome machine-guns, the majority of which were concentrated on his right flank.[97]

It was about 11:00 p.m. on 10 November when platoons of the 42nd, crossing the railway yards under the covering fire of Lewis guns, entered the city and began clearing eastward. As German machine-gunners on the southern edge of Mons fell back, a second company of the 42nd with an attached R.C.R. company crossed the Dérivation Canal on a hastily improvised plank bridge and moved northward into the town. The third entry of the night was made at 2:00 a.m.* by a company of the R.C.R. at the north-west corner of Mons. Farther north on the battalion left another R.C.R. company, having cleared the village of Ghlin and a troublesome nearby mine dump, crossed the Canal du Centre to secure the suburbs of Nimy and Petit Nimy.[99]

What German troops were the last to oppose the Canadians? During the final few days of the campaign the remnants of the German divisions on the whole were retreating towards the Antwerp-Meuse line obliquely to the Canadian axis of advance. This divergence in direction, and the enemy's practice of retiring his divisions through one another, meant that the leading Canadian units were meeting a succession of rearguards from many German formations. At the beginning of the month the enemy picture was still fairly simple; during the period 1-8 November an average of 250 captives from each of seven German divisions were admitted to the Canadian Corps Prisoner of War Cage. But as the hour of the armistice drew closer and fighting dwindled, admissions to the Corps Cage fell to an average of less than seven stragglers from each of fifteen different divisions.[100]

From the scanty information about this period available from German sources, and after eliminating a number of divisions known to have left the sector, it appears certain that German resistance south of Mons in the Hyon-Bois la Haut area was furnished by the rearguards of the 206th Infantry Division.[101] The parting shots north of Mons were probably fired by elements of either the 28th Reserve Division or the 4th Ersatz Division. Withdrawing directly through the city itself were the 62nd and 63rd Regiments of the 12th Infantry Division. Early on the 10th these forces were thinned out to battalion strength, the 2nd Battalion, 62nd Regiment taking over its regimental sector. At midnight this battalion withdrew also, leaving behind the 8th Company, which remained in the western part of Mons until dawn was approaching on 11 November.[102]

* A spirited controversy later developed between the R.C.R. and the 42nd Battalion over who was first to reach the centre of Mons. In the city's "Golden Book" the signature of Lieut. W. M. King (an officer of the R.C.R. company attached to the 42nd) appears before those of the 42nd Battalion's Lieuts. L. H. Biggar and J. W. Cave. Biggar, however, disputed this evidence, averring that he signed well down on the page so that a suitable inscription could subsequently be inserted above. The weight of testimony by the Burgomaster of Mons and members of his council favours the R.C.R. claimant.[98]

By daybreak troops of both battalions of the 7th Brigade had freed Mons of any remaining Germans. At about seven o'clock the 42nd Battalion's pipe band played its way into the city and, according to the unit's war diary, "created tremendous enthusiasm". By eleven that morning the pursuit had carried forward some five miles to the north-east. In the 3rd Division's sector the 5th Lancers—a regiment which had fought at Mons in 1914—reached St. Denis, while on the right the infantry of the 2nd Division had entered Havre and cleared the Bois du Rapois.[103]

Along the whole Western Front all the Allied armies were on the march, keeping apace or ahead of the First Army's advance. In the last few days German opposition had generally come from only artillery and machine-guns. A retreating division was rarely represented by more than an infantry battalion with perhaps a cavalry squadron and a few cyclists. In the north the Allied forces had shaken themselves loose from their long immobility. By the night of 10 November the Belgian Army had liberated Ghent. The French Sixth Army and the British Second and Fifth had crossed the Scheldt. On General Horne's right the Third Army had captured Maubeuge, with the Fourth keeping level. The Americans had reached the vital railway line at Mézières. In Lorraine two French Armies of 31 divisions were poised for a massive attack to be launched on the 14th.[104] Like an overwhelming tidal wave the Allied forces were surging forward, driving all before them.

At 6:30 a.m. on the 11th a message reached Canadian Corps Headquarters to the effect that hostilities would cease at eleven o'clock that morning.[105] This information was relayed to subordinate formations and units as rapidly as possible, but in some cases it did not reach the front-line troops until 9:00 a.m.[106] The delay in transmission was of little consequence as there was virtually no fighting after Mons had been cleared.

Considering the resistance put up by the German machine-gunners, the capture of the city had been achieved with very few casualties. The 3rd Division gave its total losses for both 10 and 11 November as 9 officers and 107 other ranks killed, wounded and missing.[107] The 2nd Division's reported total for the period 7 to 11 November inclusive was 22 officers and 343 other ranks.[108] Official post-war calculations of Canadian killed, wounded and missing, including casualties from gas, show a total of 18 officers and 262 other ranks for the final two days of operations. Careful research made at General Currie's request revealed that on 11 November itself there were one fatal and 15 non-fatal casualties.*

* The question of the number of casualties incurred by the Canadian Corps in the taking of Mons received considerable publicity some nine years after the war, when the publication by an Ontario newspaper of an editorial charging "deliberate and useless waste of human life" in the capture of the town led Sir Arthur Currie to initiate an action for libel against the editor and the publisher. At the trial responsible and informed testimony established that the attack on Mons was both justifiable and necessary, the Corps Commander's task being to press the enemy as hard as he could until ordered to stop. There was documentary evidence that Mons was completely cleared by six o'clock—some time before the cease-fire order was received. It was further shown that General Currie had given explicit orders that there should be no large-scale attack and that as far as possible casualties and losses were to be avoided. The court awarded Sir Arthur damages and costs.[109]

The Armistice

During the latter part of October and early November the negotiations to bring a suspension of hostilities had been rapidly moving to their climax. On 16 October the Germans learned with dismay that President Wilson would turn over to the Allied military and naval experts the task of setting the conditions of an armistice. On the day before Ludendorff resigned, Marshal Foch asked his commanders-in-chief for their views regarding the terms that should be imposed. Haig was inclined to be moderate, and to grant Germany conditions which she could accept. Surprisingly, the American Pershing demanded the same strict treatment for Germany as did Pétain, whose country had suffered most at German hands. The terms worked out by Foch were stern and different only in small degree from Pershing's.[110] To Ludendorff and von Hindenburg it had become clear that what they had fondly hoped might be a "peace of justice" was in fact to be a "peace of violence".[111] Such an exaggerated view could only have been arrived at by conveniently putting out of mind the pitiless terms meted out to France in 1871 at the conclusion of the Franco-Prussian War.

Within Germany meanwhile conditions became steadily more chaotic. On 29 October, two days after the German Government had agreed to President Wilson's latest demands, the German Admiralty in a desperate gesture to avoid humiliation ordered the fleet to put to sea. The sailors mutinied, and at the same time revolution was sweeping quickly through the entire Rhineland. On 9 November the Kaiser abdicated, taking refuge in Holland, and Germany became a Republic.

Foch received the German Armistice Commission on November 8 in a carriage of his special train on a siding in the Forest of Compiègne. The German plenipotentiaries were headed by a civilian, Matthias Erzberger, a Reichstag deputy who had been prominent in the peace negotiations between Germany and Russia. The German General Staff had withdrawn its representative at the last moment in order to demonstrate its dissociation from responsibility for accepting the severe Armistice terms. Foch was attended by his Chief of Staff, General Maxime Weygand, and by the British representative, Admiral Sir Rosslyn Wemyss. Uncompromisingly Weygand read the Allied conditions, startling the German delegation with their strictness. Given 72 hours to accept, the Germans made some ineffectual attempts to lessen the severity of the terms, but gained only a few minor concessions of detail. At 5:00 o'clock on the morning of the 11th the delegates affixed their signatures. Six hours later all hostilities ceased.[112]

Germany bound herself to evacuate the territory which she had invaded, as well as the provinces of Alsace and Lorraine, taken from France in 1871. She agreed to repatriate citizens of Allied nations and all Allied prisoners of war, without immediate reciprocity, and to hand over vast stocks of war material, including 5000 guns and 25,000 machine-guns. Her navy was to surrender all its submarines, and such surface vessels as the Allies designated would be interned. Finally Germany would evacuate the left bank of the Rhine and bridgeheads behind it, to be held by Allied occupation forces until the peace terms had been met.[113]

Once the excitement of the moment had passed, the Canadian soldiers who had fought so hard and long to end the war accepted the news of the Armistice with the impassive, seemingly unconcerned silence that is the outward sign of deep feeling or emotional exhaustion. Battalion diarists write of utterly unusual quietness settling over the war-ravaged countryside of France and Belgium. Veterans who remembered Ypres, Vimy, and the horrors of Passchendaele found it hard to believe that more was no longer expected. Thoughts of home and civilian life, previously too disturbing to engage in, came back slowly and with difficulty.

Allied forces had returned to Mons. It was the end of the journey.

CHAPTER XVI

OUTSIDE THE CORPS

(See Sketches 54 and 55)

THE RECORD of Canada's participation in the First World War, while largely the story of the Canadian Corps on the Western Front, would not be complete without some account of the part played by other components of the nation's armed forces. Of some 150,000 Canadian troops in France and Belgium at the time of the Armistice, nearly 40,000 were outside General Currie's command. Other Canadians were serving or had served elsewhere in various roles—military, naval and air. We have noted, for instance, that the future Canadian province of Newfoundland had been represented at Gallipoli and subsequently in the main theatre on the Western Front.

Some of these Canadian contributions have been described already. Earlier chapters have dealt with such matters as the dispatch of Canadian garrisons to the West Indies, and the operations of Canadian cavalry serving with British formations. Allusions made from time to time to the part played by the air services in specific operations will provide a background to a section of the present chapter dealing with Canadians who fought in the air. Other sections will cover the activities of groups of Canadians who were given special employment in various parts of the world. All made worth-while contributions.

Railway Troops on the Western Front

It was natural that Canada, where in the years immediately preceding the war more new railways had been built than anywhere else in the British Empire, should be called on to play a leading role in providing troops for the construction and operation of railways on the fighting fronts. The force of Canadian railway troops which served in France and Belgium was the largest body of Canadians on the Western Front not under the command of the Canadian Corps. Composed for the most part of men beyond the normal military age, the Canadian Railway Battalions were perhaps the most colorful of all units.

In the pre-war discussions that took place between the British and the French military staffs, the French undertook to man and control the entire railway service. They would be responsible for "the work of construction, repair, maintenance, traffic management and protection, not only in French territory but beyond the frontier".[1] When war broke out it first seemed that this arrangement might work out satisfactorily, since France appeared to have an ample supply of railway troops and a well-planned system for employing them. A British railway company which landed at Le Havre in mid-August 1914 was faced with lack of employment, and there was soon a proposal to transfer from it men of other than railway trades to replace casualties in field units.[2]

Then came the Battle of the Marne, and the subsequent advance to the Aisne. French and British forces found themselves as much as eighty miles beyond their railheads—a gap which French railway units vainly tried to close while, not by their own choice, British repair troops remained idle. Finally on 17 September 1914 the French Government accepted British assistance, though with certain reservations. The French staff still had a number of railway units of their own available, and hoped to use as unskilled labour prisoners of war and Belgians or Italians. At this stage of the war they seemed concerned about keeping their own railway repair arrangements neat and tidy by avoiding the complications that might arise from accepting British assistance.[3]

Early in October 1914 the War Office issued a call for additional railway troops.* When interested Canadians learned of this from the press and offered their services to their own government, Ottawa asked the British authorities to substantiate the newspaper reports, asserting that "Canada can supply the want probably better than any other country." While the Army Council expressed its appreciation of the offer, it was not prepared to take advantage of it at that time. "When accepted", the British reply concluded, "a railway corps should be organized on military basis [as opposed to civilian 'gangs'] through principal Canadian railways."[5] Finally on 21 January 1915 the Army Council sent word that it would be glad to have a corps of Canadian railwaymen. "Skilled construction men are wanted . . . please telegraph what numbers can be provided and on what conditions."[6]

On 2 February the Canadian Government replied that it could provide at its own expense a corps of 500 or more railwaymen for construction work; officials of the Canadian Pacific Railway were cooperating in the organization of the unit.[7] Mobilization of the Canadian Overseas Railway Construction Corps—two companies and a regimental headquarters—began at Saint John, N.B., recruiting being completed by 15 May. The men were all experienced construction workers employed by the C.P.R., and each had to pass a test as to his technical ability. By 15 May recruiting was completed, except to make up for discharges—approximately 100 out of some 670 attested—and to form a ten per cent reserve. The unit sailed

* In October Lord Kitchener sent Brig.-Gen. Sir Percy Girouard to France to report on the railway situation. Sir Percy, a distinguished Canadian-born Royal Engineer Officer, had made an outstanding contribution in the construction of railways for military purposes in the Sudan and South African campaigns. Out of his recommendations came the appointment of a permanent International Railway Commission on which the French, British and Belgian General Headquarters were represented. One of its main concerns was the provision and maintenance of rail transportation in Belgian territory.[4]

for England on 14 June and arrived on the 25th. Exactly two months later it landed in France.[8]

Between the last week of August and the beginning of October 1915 the Corps served with the Belgian forces, laying light track for 60-centimetre tramways. It also worked on siege-gun and machine-gun emplacements for the Royal Marines.[9] There was a sudden break in this employment when on 5 October the Canadian unit was withdrawn to England for transfer to Salonika. That move, however, did not materialize. Returning to France on 2 November, the Canadians were assigned to the British Second Army Lines of Communication for work in the Reninghelst area south of Poperinghe. Here they constructed sidings and maintained standard-gauge railway track that had been laid by British railway troops.[10]

In most sectors of the virtually static front the existing railheads were a dozen miles or more behind the front lines. Ammunition and supplies and engineer stores were commonly transported over this gap by lorry to a refilling point and thence by horse transport. The volume of traffic on the roads was tremendous. It has been calculated that at the Battle of the Somme an average of 1934 tons had to be removed from the railheads daily for each mile of the Fourth Army's front. The roads suffered heavily from this tonnage, particularly in wet weather, and damage from shelling increased the problems of keeping them in repair. One solution was to reduce the use of mechanical transport by providing railheads within reach of horse transport.[11] Such a programme was launched on an experimental basis in January 1916, the railheads being advanced to within some three miles of the front.[12]

But a further problem remained. When because of bad roads and shellfire the horse transport could not reach troops in the trenches, the last stage of moving supplies from the railhead had to be performed by manual labour or by pack animals. To remedy this situation, early in 1916 authority was given in cases of extreme necessity to construct 60-centimetre tramlines linking up the standard-gauge railheads with the trenches. The advantages of tramways, used with trolleys which were mostly pushed by hand, sometimes drawn by mules and only occasionally pulled by small locomotives, had been recognized more generally by the Canadian than the British forces. In the Canadian Corps two Tramway Companies composed of Canadian engineer personnel, under the C.R.E. Corps Troops, constructed, maintained, and operated tramways until the end of the war. There had been no wide-scale adoption of tramways, however, for while such a system was obviously well suited to supplying a stable front, it received little consideration from G.H.Q., which took the view that the war would soon revert to one of movement. By 1917 there was conviction that all railway resources should be concentrated on the standard-gauge lines that would be needed when the expected general advance started.[13]

In order to extend and maintain rail communications farther forward, more and more railway troops were required. There was no lack of response in Canada, as private individuals willing to raise railway units submitted their offers to the Governor General, the Minister of Militia, the Prime Minister, the Premier of British Columbia, as well as direct to the British authorities. Expansion overseas was rapid. In May 1916, the War Office asked Canada to furnish another railway construction unit approximately 1000 strong. Recruits drawn from skilled railway workers across the country were organized into the 239th Overseas Railway Construction Battalion, commanded by Lt.-Col J. W. Stewart. From the Chief of the Imperial Staff came congratulations to the Militia Department on the "promptitude you have shown in raising Jack Stewart's Railway Construction Battalion", a message whose apparent informality was doubtless prompted by General Sam Hughes' practice of referring to proposed units by the names of the individuals* offering or organizing them.[15] Before the unit could sail, however, Stewart was called to the United Kingdom at the request of the War Office, to be sent to France as Deputy Director of Light Railways.

By April 1917 there were five new Canadian railway units in France. The 1st Canadian Construction Battalion (which had crossed the Channel in October 1916) and the 127th Infantry Battalion (from Bramshott to France in January 1917) were reorganized as the 1st and 2nd Battalions Canadian Railway Troops. The 239th was renamed the 3rd Battalion Canadian Railway Troops, and proceeded from England to France in March. The 4th and 5th Battalions were formed at the C.R.T. Depot at Purfleet, in Essex, and reached France in February.

It was then decided to increase the number of battalions to ten. As more units arrived from Canada they were sent to Purfleet. By the end of June the 6th, 7th, 8th and 10th Battalions had been formed at the Depot. The 9th Battalion came from reorganization of the 1st Pioneer Battalion, in France since March 1916. In November the 11th and 12th Battalions were raised from Canadian labour battalions in France, and the 13th came into being at Purfleet in March 1918. April 1917 saw the arrival in France of the first of three specialist Canadian railway operating companies. A railroad shop company formed at the C.R.T. Depot in March 1918 arrived in France in April.†[16]

When they reached France the Canadian Railway Troops Battalions came under the command of Brig.-Gen. Stewart, who at the beginning of 1917 had been appointed Deputy Director General Transportation (Construction) at G.H.Q. In March 1917 he established the administrative headquarters of the Canadian Railway Troops at G.H.Q. British Armies in France, where it remained completely apart from the Canadian Corps. The following May saw a reorganization in which the original Overseas Railway Construction Corps and the four independent companies joined the thirteen battalions under the Headquarters, Canadian Railway Troops, the whole being redesignated the Corps of Canadian Railway Troops, under the command of Brig.-Gen. Stewart.[17] Towards the end

* As when the Acting High Commissioner for Canada in official correspondence with the Prime Minister writes of a "regiment" offered by "Big Jim McDonald"![14]

† These four units were the 13th Light Railway Operating Company, the 58th Broad Gauge Railway Operating Company, the 69th Wagon Erecting Company and the 85th Engine Crew Company.

of August, as we shall see, a C.R.T. bridging company was formed for service in the Middle East. By the time of the Armistice the strength of the Corps, including 3364 railway troops in the United Kingdom, had risen to 19,328.[18]

From the moment of their arrival in France the Canadian railway units found plenty to do. The German withdrawal to the Hindenburg Line meant that new track—of both standard and narrow gauge—had to be pushed forward. The work was carried out with remarkable speed, despite the hindrance of appalling weather and enemy demolitions. In preparation for the Arras-Vimy offensive in the spring of 1917 Canadian railway units laid steel up to the forward trenches; and as the infantry of the Canadian Corps advanced over Vimy Ridge, close on their heels tramways were pushed forward over the newly consolidated ground. Later that year Canadian construction units laboured under the dreadful conditions in the Ypres Salient before Passchendaele, when on the Second and Fifth Army fronts alone the number of breaks in the light railway lines caused by enemy shellfire averaged one hundred a day.[19]

From 1917 to the end of the war all light railway construction and maintenance on the British front was carried out by Canadian troops, assisted by attached labour. During the German offensives of 1918 railway units were diverted to the necessary reorganization of the L. of C. and to the construction of a rear defence system. The 2nd Battalion C.R.T., it may be recalled, assumed an infantry holding role (above, p. 371). The ready ability of the railway troops to undertake this commitment was a vindication of the policy laid down by the Canadian military authorities—that every Canadian engaged at the front on work of a technical nature must first be trained as a fighting soldier. All British railway, labour and other troops assigned to the defences came under the orders of General Stewart. At one point seven Canadian railway battalions and sixty British units—a total of 22,400 all ranks—were so employed.[20] The 2nd Canadian Battalion, working day and night under heavy shelling, maintained lines linking the British and French systems, making it possible to remove much valuable rolling stock which otherwise would have been destroyed or abandoned. To salvage valuable stocks of timber from the advancing Germans, the Canadians dumped the logs into the canals, forming them into rafts on which they carried to safety large quantities of steel rails, telephone poles and railway ties.[21] By the late summer of 1918 Canadian railwaymen were heavily involved in preparing for the great Amiens offensive which opened on 8 August. They continued to play an important role in the subsequent operations which eventually brought victory to the Allies.

Between April 1917 and the end of 1918 Canadian units laid 1169 miles of broad-gauge line and 1404 miles of light track. In the final year of the war the number of men employed on railway construction averaged nearly eight thousand daily. At the same time an average of more than four thousand were busy every day on maintaining lines already built. We have noted that in certain sectors the Canadian railway troops were under fire for protracted periods. The 10th Railway Battalion, for example, which was in the Ypres Salient, was never out of range of shellfire from the time of the Messines action in June 1917 until the end of the Passchendaele fighting. From 1 April 1917 to the end of the war the Corps of Canadian Railway Troops suffered 1977 casualties.[22]

Repairing Bridges in Palestine

One of the important contributions made by Canadian Railway units in France was to raise a bridging unit for service in the Middle East. The 1st Bridging Company C.R.T. was formed in August 1918 in response to a request by General Sir Edmund Allenby, who, it will be recalled, had relinquished the command of the Third Army in France to command the Egyptian Expeditionary Force in Palestine.[23]

We have already noted the successful offensive against the Turks at the end of 1917. By the late summer of 1918 the E.E.F. held a front stretching from the Mediterranean coast to the Jordan River on a line ten miles north of Jaffa and the Dead Sea. General Allenby was soon to resume the offensive, and it seemed certain that the enemy would attempt by means of railway demolitions to hinder a pursuit into Syria. The rate of Allenby's future progress would depend largely upon his ability to use two existing railway systems. One of these lines ran south-east from Haifa, on the Mediterranean coast, to the Jordan valley, thence northward to the Sea of Galilee (Lake of Tiberias). To the east of Palestine the Hejaz line from Medina passed generally northward through Der'a to Damascus and Aleppo. The two systems were linked by a Turkish line which ran eastward from a tributary of the Jordan, the Yarmuk, to Der'a. Particularly vulnerable were the bridges in the Yarmuk Valley, where the Turkish railway crossed and recrossed the deep gorge on spans which were so long and difficult of approach that the British staffs had previously estimated that their destruction of one of these—when the line was a supply route to the Turkish forces in Palestine—would isolate the enemy from his base for a fortnight.[24] It was in anticipation of the need for bridging operations here that the request was made for the Canadian unit. Personnel for the 1st Bridging Company (256 all ranks) were drawn mainly from Canadian railway battalions in France. Under the command of Major A. P. Linton, the company sailed from Marseilles on 20 September 1918.[25]

The great offensive for which Allenby had been preparing throughout the summer of 1918 opened on 19 September. Within a week he had inflicted a sweeping defeat on the enemy at Megiddo, and demoralized remnants of the Turkish armies were streaming northward into Syria. On the 27th the E.E.F. began to advance on Damascus, the Syrian capital. Brilliant destructive work on the Hejaz railway by Lt.-Col. T. E. Lawrence ("Lawrence of Arabia") and his Arab auxiliaries so delayed the retreat of the bulk of the Turkish army that it had no time in which to organize a defence of Damascus. The city fell on 1 October.[26] Allenby now had to restore railway communications between Jerusalem and Damascus, to which end the 1st Bridging Company, arriving in

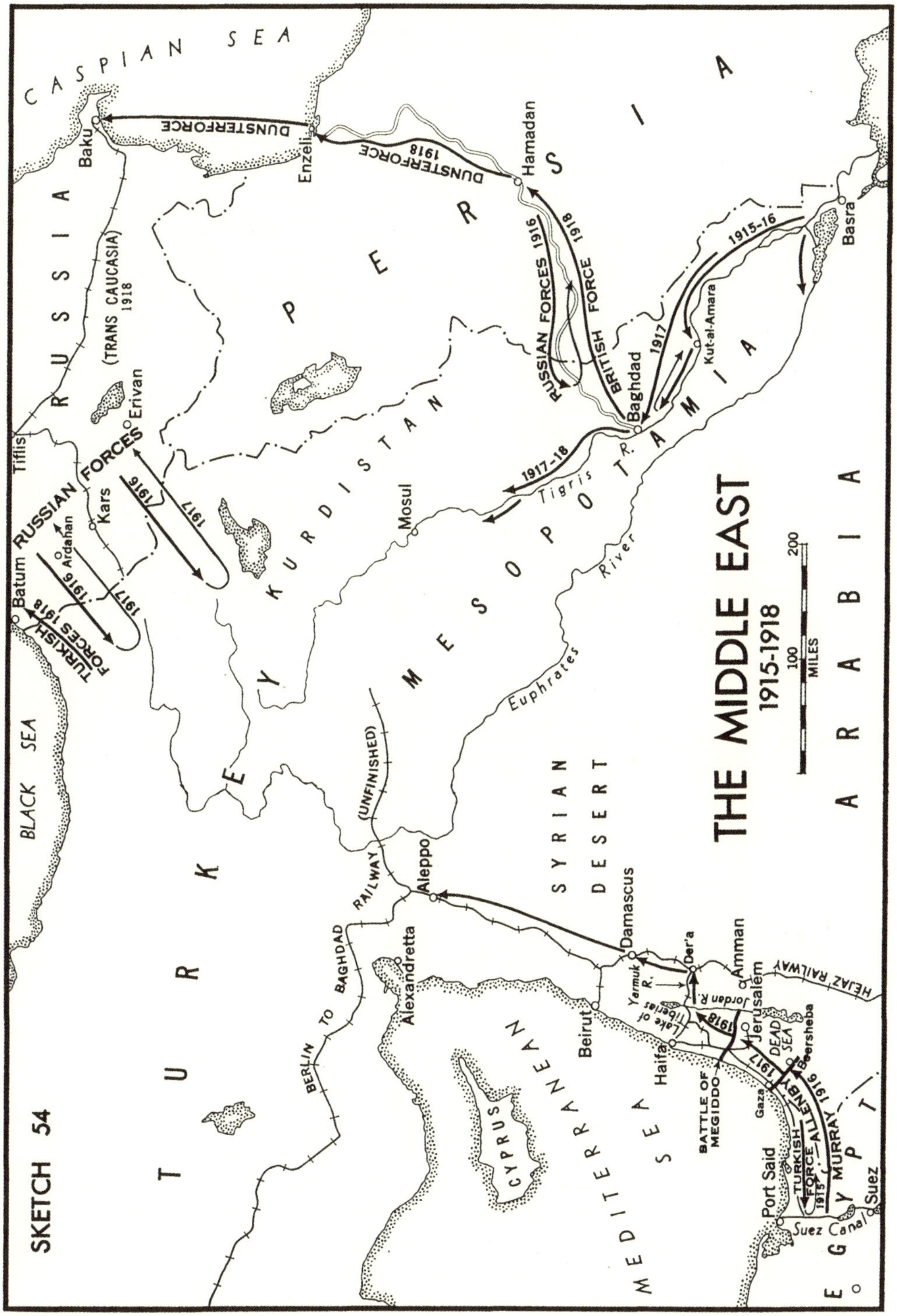
SKETCH 54
THE MIDDLE EAST
1915-1918
MILES
100
200
CASPIAN SEA
BLACK SEA
MEDITERRANEAN SEA
DEAD SEA
RUSSIA
(TRANS CAUCASIA)
1918
PERSIA
TURKEY
KURDISTAN
MESOPOTAMIA
SYRIAN DESERT
ARABIA
EGYPT
CYPRUS
Baku
Enzeli
Hamadan
Tiflis
Erivan
Kars
Ardahan
Batum
Mosul
Baghdad
Kut-al-Amara
Basra
Aleppo
Alexandretta
Beirut
Damascus
Der'a
Amman
Haifa
Jerusalem
Beersheba
Gaza
Port Said
Suez
Suez Canal
Tigris R.
Euphrates River
Yarmuk R.
Jordan R.
Lake of Tiberias
DUNSTERFORCE
DUNSTERFORCE 1918
RUSSIAN FORCES 1916
BRITISH FORCE 1918
RUSSIAN FORCES
TURKISH FORCES 1918
1915-16
1917
1917-18
1916
1918
BATTLE OF MEGIDDO
ALLENBY
MURRAY
TURKISH FORCE 1915
BERLIN TO BAGHDAD RAILWAY
(UNFINISHED)
HEJAZ RAILWAY

Palestine on 2 October, was promptly ordered to the Yarmuk valley. The second and third bridges above the junction with the Jordan were found to have been partly destroyed by the retreating Turks. Work on both spans began on the 7th.[27]

Operating conditions could scarcely have been more unpleasant. The valleys of the Jordan and the Yarmuk were among the most unhealthy places in Palestine. Temperatures of 100° in the shade continued week after week, rising at times to over 120°. Because of the great depth of these valleys and the enormous amount of evaporation from the Dead Sea, the air was heavy with moisture. Screened from any breeze by the high valley walls, the atmosphere was hot and stagnant, producing in the troops who worked there an extraordinary lassitude and sense of helplessness. The movement of transport stirred up dust from the powdered soil, and dun-coloured clouds would hang for long periods in the overcharged air. Hostile insects added to the pestiferous nature of the surroundings. In the dry parts were scorpions, six-inch centipedes and stinging spiders, and where the ground was swampy—mosquitoes.[20] The Canadian bridging company was soon crippled by malaria and other environmental ailments. Some men were hit by the influenza epidemic which was sweeping every theatre of operations. In many cases this was followed by pneumonia. For one week in October not more than six men were able to work at any one time. Nevertheless, with the aid of 560 men of the Egyptian Labour Corps, the unit pushed its task to completion; by 26 October supplies could be sent all the way to Damascus by rail.[29]

On that date British forces entered Aleppo and advanced eight miles beyond towards Alexandretta. The campaign was all but over; four days later Turkey signed an armistice. Now, with the problems of moving refugees and liberated prisoners of war, and supplying foodstuffs to whole populations on the verge of starvation, there was much work to be done on bridging and restoring and improving the railways. The 1st Bridging Company was transferred to Hama, south of Aleppo, where it carried on its work from the beginning of November 1918 to February 1919. In March the unit sailed for England, to join the C.R.T. Depot. Although the 1st Bridging Company had not come under fire during its tour of duty in the Middle East, it had suffered seven fatal casualties—five by disease, two accidental.[30]

With the Mesopotamian Expeditionary Force

During the First World War approximately 4000 Canadians and British subjects residing in Canada and the United States were enrolled in the Royal Engineers, or seconded to that Corps, for work on inland waterways and docks. Early in September 1916 some thirty members of the Canadian Pioneer Training Depot in England with experience of water transportation in British Columbia were discharged from the C.E.F. and sent to the Mesopotamian Expeditionary Force for such duties. Some served at the inland port of Basra at the head of the Persian

Gulf; others operated barges on the Tigris and the Euphrates. Their assignment lasted for the duration of the war and for some months afterwards.[31]

Another group of Canadians were destined to play much more of a combatant role in Mesopotamia. The manner of their becoming involved was directly related to British policies in the Middle East at that time. Ever since Turkey had entered the war on the side of the Central Powers, Britain had recognized the need to prevent German exploitation of Caspian oil. The British were furthermore acutely interested in the Persian, Caucasian and Caspian regions for other strategic reasons, for an advance there by the Central Powers would not only affect the campaign in Mesopotamia, but would seriously threaten the security of India's hinterland. Berlin-Batum-Baku was a more dangerous enemy route to the Indian frontier than Berlin-Baghdad. Following an Allied Conference in Paris in December 1917 at which it was decided to establish unofficial relations with the Bolsheviks, Britain took as her sphere of responsibility the Cossack territories, Armenia, the Caucasus and the territory east of the Caspian Sea. (Later North Russia was tacitly added.)[32]

After the Bolshevik Revolution Russia's political control over the Trans-Caucasus disappeared and anarchy among the Russian troops brought the collapse of military control. Under the influence of the Georgians, politically the most mature of the peoples in the region, an independent Trans-Caucasian republic was formed in November 1917, to include Georgians, Armenians and Tartars, despite religious differences and traditional animosities. In March 1918 came the Brest-Litovsk Treaty, which ceded the districts of Batum, Kars and Ardahan to Turkey. Outside influences then made themselves felt. The Turks advanced and, ignoring the terms of the treaty, began to seize the whole Caucasus region. They were opposed by Germany, who was determined to control Baku and its oilfields. Beset by the rival influences of Turkey and Germany, the newly formed Trans-Caucasian republic collapsed and was split up. At the western base of the Caucasus isthmus an independent Armenian republic of Erivan was proclaimed in May under Turkish protection; to the east a Tartar republic under the Turks, to include Baku, was established in the same month. To the north Georgia welcomed a German expeditionary force as protection from Turkish invasion and on 12 June German troops occupied Tiflis. Baku was the only Bolshevik stronghold, and on this the Turks were advancing in defiance of the Germans.[33]

The nearest British troops were small parties in Persia and the army in Mesopotamia, and their problems were already sufficiently complex. First, the 630-mile road which ran from Baghdad north-eastward through Hamadan to Enzeli on the Caspian Sea must be kept open against Turkish incursions from the west. This would be no easy task, for the route lay through a devastated, famine-stricken area and over a succession of mountain ranges; and the attitude of the local tribes, especially the Jangalis on the south-western shores of the Caspian, was uncertain and threatening. Furthermore, the advance of Bolsheviks (and Austrian prisoners of war freed by them) into the area east of the Caspian had to be checked lest they join with hostile elements there to present a serious threat to Afghanistan and

India. Finally, if the Eastern Front was to be restored, the Caspian and its shipping must be under Allied control, and this meant that Baku had to be taken and defended against the Turks.[34]

It was clear at the beginning of 1918 that sufficient British forces were not available from any theatre for dispatch to this area. The only solution seemed to be to organize a local defensive force from Georgians, Armenians, Assyrians, and Russian volunteers. To this end, in mid-January 1918 the War Office authorized a British Mission to be sent to the Caucasus. At its head was Major-General L. C. Dunsterville, an English officer who had served with distinction in campaigns in the Far East and who added to his linguistic accomplishments a keen friendship with the Russians. (Rudyard Kipling had already immortalized him as the "Stalky" of his tales of English public school life.) Dunsterville arrived in Baghdad from India on 18 January with orders to proceed to Tiflis as British representative to the Trans-Caucasian Government. It was foreseen that he would need 150 officers and 300 N.C.Os., who would be used to organize the required local defence forces.[35]

To "Dunsterforce", as the new force was named, Canada contributed fifteen officers up to the rank of lieutenant colonel and 26 N.C.O.s.,* of "strong character, adventurous spirit, especially good stamina, capable of organizing, training, and eventually leading, irregular troops".[36] All came from the Canadian Corps (although three who were medically unfit were replaced in England), leaving the Western Front for England on 13 January. Officers below the rank of captain were made acting captains, while junior N.C.Os. and men became acting sergeants. In London the Canadian contingent joined others from the British, Australian, New Zealand, and South African forces, and to this cross-section of the British Empire were added a party of a dozen Russian officers and one Persian. The aim, they were told, apart from training and leading, was to protect the Baku oilfields, to operate against the Turks from the east, and "to hold the Batum-Tiflis-Baku-Krasnovodsk† line to Afghanistan"—all in all, an ambitious programme.[37]

It was not until 2 March that the contingent from the Western Front, including the Canadians, reached Basra. Here the long voyage up the River Tigris to Baghdad began, all parties assembling in camps south of that city by the end of March. The journey passed pleasantly enough for the Canadians, for many of the officers and members of the crews of the river craft were British Columbians (above, p. 492). Reunions were numerous and heartwarming.[38]

Meanwhile Dunsterville had left Baghdad with a small staff at the end of January, hoping to be in Baku—then under the control of the Trans-Caucasian government—a fortnight later. At Hamadan, some 250 miles north-east of Baghdad, he was delayed by bad weather and the necessity of undertaking local famine relief. The swift onrush of events which followed Brest-Litovsk found

* A list of the Canadian Officers and N.C.Os. who served with Dunsterforce appears as an appendix to the first instalment of "Canadians in Dunsterforce", an article by Capt. W. W. Murray in the *Canadian Defence Quarterly* (January 1931).

† Krasnovodsk, an important port on the east side of the Caspian Sea opposite Baku, was the western terminus of the Central Asiatic Railway.

him still at Hamadan; chaotic conditions prevailing in the Caucasus precluded his onward journey to Baku en route to Tiflis. He was ordered to remain in Persia, where he began to organize and train local levies, at the same time putting tribesmen unfit for military service to work on improving the roads.[39] The situation was far from reassuring. Local brigands robbed and murdered without hindrance along the lonely passes. Demoralized Russians wandered at will throughout the area. Famine stalked the land. Jangali tribesmen, Austrian-trained and German-led, were astride the road to Enzeli, while a hundred miles to the west, in the mountains of Kurdistan, the operations of a Turkish army threatened the line of communication.[40]

Into this maelstrom the Canadians marched, joining Dunsterville at Hamadan during the early part of July. Little time was lost in dispersing them with the rest of Dunsterforce to placate distant tribes, train local levies, supervise road construction, and police the road between Baghdad and Hamadan.[41] Together with local forces, a brigade was being formed at Hamadan from Christian Assyrians who had fled thither following a massacre by Turks and Kurds in Kurdistan which took more than 40,000 lives. The protective rearguard which was hastily improvised from Dunsterforce to assist the Assyrians to reach Hamadan included seven Canadians.[42]

On 20 July a Jangali force of some 2500 attacked a 300-man British detachment near Enzeli. The attackers were beaten off, and thereafter communications to Enzeli remained undisturbed. Five days later General Bicharakoff, the pro-Allied commander of the Red Army in the Caucasus, assisted by a few officers and four armoured cars from Dunsterforce, staged a successful *coup d'état* in Baku. A new government, terming itself Centro-Caspian, handed over supreme military command to Bicharakoff, who at once asked for British aid, and sent transports to Enzeli to pick up the first instalment of troops. In front of Baku approximately 6000 local troops, mostly Armenians, were holding a line twelve miles long. They were poorly organized, had few officers and were utterly lacking in discipline, while their positions were badly placed. Nevertheless, heartened by the presence of a British detachment which reached Baku by sea from Enzeli on 4 August, local forces repulsed a Turkish attack on the 5th. Other reinforcements intended for Baku had to be diverted to meet a Turkish advance from Kurdistan which threatened to cut the lines of communication to Enzeli; though it was possible in mid-August to increase the British force at Baku to two battalions. General Dunsterville himself arrived from Enzeli on 18 August.[43] Among those associated with the defence of Baku were five Canadian officers* of Dunsterforce.[44]

In their determination to capture Baku the Turks struck again on the 26th. Four separate attacks were repulsed by a British battalion, but support by local

* Of these, one acted as paymaster, field cashier and "chancellor of the Baku exchequer", another was placed in charge of all machine-gun troops in the area, a third became Inspector of Infantry, a fourth assisted in arranging for supplies and a fifth commanded an Armenian battalion. A sixth Canadian was dispatched by sea on a mission to a British force operating on the eastern shores of the Caspian.

troops faded and a fifth assault brought heavy British casualties and the loss of some ground. In the main, further attacks in the last two days of August were resisted only by British troops, who were forced to give up more ground.[45] The Canadian captain commanding one of the Armenian battalions suddenly found himself without any men—all had bolted at the first sight of the enemy![46] General Dunsterville now had some 900 British troops, including a field battery, and about a thousand Russians on whom he could rely. The enemy was employing 6000 regulars and 8000 irregulars, while the city itself swarmed with sympathizers and agents.[47]

During the early part of September the question of evacuating Baku was under continuous examination. The War Office concurred in a recommendation by the C.-in-C. Mesopotamia that British troops be withdrawn, but some improvement in the local situation induced Dunsterville to promise the Baku government that he would remain with them as long as possible. By 12 September the British forces in Baku had been reinforced to three battalions, and 500 more Russians had arrived with ten machine-guns. Forewarned of a coming Turkish attack, Dunsterville hastened his defensive preparations. He was satisfied that the Turks could be held, if the irregulars showed the will to fight. But his reservations were amply justified. Attacking in force on 14 September the Turks broke right through an Armenian battalion at the most defensible part of the line. Dunsterville's position soon became hopeless. Only by the efforts of its own rearguards was the British force able to extricate itself. On the night of 14-15 September it withdrew in two armed ships, being forced to sail under the guns of the Red fleet. One transport was fired on, but the force got through to Enzeli without loss of life. Three days later, General Dunsterville was recalled and his mission ordered disbanded.[48]

Dunsterforce had failed to reach Tiflis or to create the Caucasian force required to hold the line between Batum, Tiflis and Baku. But the Baku oil did not fall into German hands. The Turks, foreseeing the loss of their Arabian provinces and looking to the occupation of the Caucasus as compensation, took control of the oil fields in September, though only for a matter of weeks. On 30 October the armistice with Turkey provided for the reoccupation of Baku by the Allies, and on 17 November a British force from North Persia took over the city. In the meantime, wildly exaggerated rumours about the strength of Dunsterforce had been sufficient to hold a Turkish army immobile in Kurdistan, thereby protecting the British flank in Mesopotamia and discouraging hostile penetration eastward. Though Dunsterville's enterprise had not achieved all that had been hoped for it, it had attained a measure of success in the important delay which it had imposed on the enemy.[49]

Canadian casualties in the Dunsterforce operations had been remarkably light—only one man had been wounded. On the disbandment of the force Canadian personnel were offered similar employment in Mesopotamia, North Persia and Siberia. About one-third accepted; the remainder chose to return to their original units.[50]

The Eastern Mediterranean

While no Canadian troops fought in the Eastern Mediterranean (Newfoundland was then not part of Canada), five Canadian hospitals operated in that theatre during the Gallipoli campaign and for some time afterwards. A total of some 450 officers (including nursing sisters) and about 1000 men served during the period 1915-1917.[51] The hospitals were dispatched by Major-General G. C. Jones, the Canadian Director of Medical Services, in response to an urgent request from the Director General of the [British] Army Medical Services.

The first units to go were Nos. 1 and 3 Canadian Stationary* Hospitals, which opened on the island of Lemnos during August 1915 for the treatment of patients from Gallipoli. After the evacuation of the Gallipoli peninsula four months later, both hospitals left Lemnos. No. 1 moved to Salonika in March 1916, where it remained until returning to England in August and September of the following year. No. 3 was transferred to France in April 1916. In the meantime two general hospitals had gone directly to Salonika: No. 4 (University of Toronto) General Hospital opened there in November 1915, while No. 5 opened a month later. Both returned to England late in the summer of 1917. A fifth Canadian hospital, No. 7 (Queen's University) General (which was sent out as No. 5 Stationary), opened in Cairo during August 1915, with 400 beds. The following January it became a General Hospital with 1040 beds. Three months later it left Egypt, to reopen in France in April 1916.[53]

It was at Mudros, on the island of Lemnos, that the greatest hardships were experienced. The site assigned to the two hospitals had been previously occupied by a camp of Egyptian labourers. It had primitive sanitary provisions and only a most precarious water supply. Dust and flies abounded; food was scarce and "unsuitable for the personnel, impossible for patients".[54] By September, ninety-five per cent of the hospital staff had developed acute enteritis, while the wards were crowded with cases of amoebic diseases from Gallipoli. With autumn came heavy rains and floods which caused extreme discomfort until tents were replaced by huts in October. The lack of fresh vegetables brought an outbreak of scurvy in November, while the intense cold at the end of that month led to frostbite —four hundred cases were admitted in one week.[55] Nor was respite obtained after the move to Salonika, for there malaria hit sixty per cent of the unit.[56]

In these circumstances the Officer Commanding No. 1 Stationary Hospital requested in September 1916 that his unit be returned to the United Kingdom. His letter reached England at a time when the Canadian Medical Services were under fire from the Minister of Militia. A special Inspector General (Colonel H. A. Bruce), who had been appointed (in July 1916) by the Minister to make

* Early in the war an infantry division was normally served by two general and two stationary hospitals. The latter were designed as "resting places on the lines for sick and wounded casualties on the way to the base". Later, as lines of communication shortened, stationary hospitals became small general hospitals. Bed capacities varied, general hospitals having about twice the capacity of stationary hospitals. Paradoxically the latter, being smaller, were more mobile.[52]

a tour of inspection of "all the Canadian Hospitals and Medical Institutions to which the Canadian Government in any way contributes", produced a report on 20 September which violently attacked the administration under Major-General Jones. It proposed that the Medical Services be completely reorganized.[57]

One of the principal recommendations of the Bruce report was the segregation of Canadian sick and wounded in Canadian hospitals,[58] and particular mention was made "of the mistake in judgement" in sending No. 4 General Hospital to the Mediterranean instead of acquiring buildings at Shorncliffe and staffing them with the personnel of the Canadian hospital. Bruce seems to have been unaware that at the time of the British request for the hospital, Shorncliffe Military Hospital was in fact largely Canadian in personnel, both patients and staff.[59]

The whole question of sending medical units into areas where no Canadian troops were engaged led to considerable controversy. At the time when the units were dispatched to the Mediterranean by Major-General Jones, General Carson had been informed of the move and in turn, the Minister of Militia and Defence. Nevertheless, in December 1915, Colonel Hughes asked Carson, "Why has Jones sent so many Canadian doctors to Servia?"[60]* And in a speech delivered in Toronto on 9 November 1916, only two days before his resignation (above, p. 211), the Minister made the unfounded allegation that "thousands of Canadians had lost months, and sometimes a year, in hospitals not under Canadian control, when they should have been back in the trenches".[61]

A letter written in September 1916 by the British Director General, Army Medical Service to General Jones amply vindicated the latter's actions:

> I had not any hospitals at that moment ready, and I called upon you for assistance. You gave me . . . Hospitals. As events proved, these saved the situation. They were good hospitals, containing good officers. . . . I shall always be indebted to you for the help you gave me at a time when I was very pressed. . . . The only alternative was to send home wounded in transports, which might have been sent to the bottom of the sea . . . if you had refused the help I asked. . . . You were quite entitled to refuse to send Canadian Hospitals where there were not Canadian Troops. . . . I am very glad you did not.[62]

In January 1917, the War Office acted on a recommendation by Colonel Bruce (who briefly replaced Major-General Jones as D.M.S.) that the hospitals should be withdrawn.[63] All three units were brought back to England during August and September 1917, their equipment being taken over by the British units which replaced them.[64] For the equipment of No. 4 Canadian General Hospital, which had been provided by the University of Toronto, the British Government reimbursed the University.[65]

Altogether eight Canadian General Hospitals and ten Stationary Hospitals (as well as three small Forestry Corps Hospitals) served overseas outside of the United Kingdom during the First World War. By November 1918 their total bed

* At the beginning of the war the form "Servia" was used more commonly than "Serbia". The Canadian hospitals to which Hughes alluded were, of course, at Salonika, in Greece.

RAILWAY CONSTRUCTION

Under the supervision of Canadian Railway Troops, Chinese labourers load earth for use in building a broad-gauge line in the Hazebrouck area, March 1918.

Photograph courtesy Mrs. Gerald Marryat, formerly Nursing Sister Helen Fowlds, No. 1 Stationary Hospital.

A KEROSENE SHAMPOO

Canadian nursing sisters with No. 1 Stationary Hospital at Lembet Camp, Salonika, wash their hair with kerosene to get rid of lice. The incident points up the discomforts attendant upon the primitive sanitary arrangements with which medical personnel had to contend in the Eastern Mediterranean.

CANADIAN TIMBERMEN

Men of the Canadian Forestry Corps at work in a British forest load timber under the eyes of a group of touring journalists.

CANADIAN FIGHTER PILOTS

Members of a largely Canadian squadron of the Royal Air Force with their Sopwith Camels. Although some months have passed since the formation of the R.A.F., the squadron commander, Major Raymond Collishaw, is still in naval uniform.

capacity had reached more than 13,500.[66] Not the least significant of this contribution to the common cause was that made by the five units whose destiny took them to the Eastern Mediterranean.

The Canadian Forestry Corps

Canadian forestry units are said to have "helped to defeat the submarine . . . more surely than a fleet of ships".[67] So enthusiastic a claim might be hard to substantiate, but the statement contains a considerable amount of truth.

British pre-war timber imported chiefly from Russia, Scandinavia and North America was valued at some forty million pounds sterling each year. The war brought an increased demand for lumber, but, because of U-boat sinkings, there was a steadily diminishing merchant fleet to carry it. The prior demands of munitions, food, forage and other essentials upon the depleted shipping made it impossible for Britain to continue to import Canadian timber on a sufficiently large scale to meet her war requirements. It was necessary therefore to begin felling English forests and converting them into lumber. A British inquiry, in January 1916, whether Canada could supply expert timbermen to produce lumber in the United Kingdom[68] was followed a month later by an urgent request from the Secretary of State for the Colonies to the Governor General for 1500 skilled lumbermen. The War Office suggested that Canada might enlist in the C.E.F. a battalion of lumbermen, to be dispatched to the United Kingdom in small companies.[69]

In response to this appeal the Minister of Militia authorized the formation of the 224th Forestry Battalion, C.E.F. By the end of May close to 1600 all ranks had been sent across the Atlantic and timber operations had begun in Great Britain's historic forests. France too had made certain of her forests available for the production of timber. But the situation remained serious. The shortage of shipping was still acute, and there was not enough skilled labour to produce all the timber required. Again in May, the British Government turned to Canada, this time for an additional "2000 lumbermen with plant".[70] In November 1916 the Army Council asked for 5000 more,[71] and before the end of the year a small Canadian forestry detachment was operating in France. The transfer of skilled Canadian woodsmen across the Atlantic continued throughout the war, and the Armistice found 12,127 Canadian foresters in France and 9967 in England.[72]

Canada bore the cost of initial equipment, pay, allowances and pensions, and transportation for the foresters to England, while Great Britain paid for accommodation, rations, maintenance and additional machinery and tools purchased in the United Kingdom.[73] As timber operations expanded, organization kept pace. To provide flexibility in administration Canadian forestry battalions were reorganized into companies of six officers and 164 other ranks. Formation of the Canadian Forestry Corps had been authorized on 7 November 1916, and a forestry directorate was set up at G.H.Q. in France and became effective on 2 April 1917.[74] Brig.-Gen. Alexander McDougall (the original commander of the 224th Forestry Battalion) was appointed G.O.C. Canadian Forestry Corps and Director General of Timber Operations, Great Britain and France. Before the war ended forestry operations in France were spread from the English Channel to the Jura mountains bordering on Switzerland, and from the Belgian to the Spanish frontiers.

By September 1917 Sir Douglas Haig was able to report that his armies had become "practically self-supporting" where timber was concerned; between May and October of that year forestry units provided more than three-quarters of a million tons of lumber.[75] It was during this period that a Canadian mill at La Joux set a record which, in the words of the officer commanding the Jura Group C.F.C., "cannot be obtained by any of the older firms in the Ottawa Valley, under the best civilian organization"—160,494 feet board measure in nineteen hours' running time.[76] Units in Britain managed to fill a sudden and particularly important demand for lumber on 20 March 1918, eleven days ahead of schedule; of a required 40,000 tons, 34,000 had been produced by Canadian foresters.[77]

Another task undertaken by Canadian forestry units from the autumn of 1916 onward was the construction of airfields for the Royal Flying Corps. Nine Canadian companies, especially organized for this employment, prepared more than a hundred sites in France and England. In France the work included erecting Nissen huts and hangars and the construction of emplacements for anti-aircraft guns.[78]

As was the case with other arms and services, the work of the Canadian forestry units in France was disrupted by the German offensive of March 1918. All forestry personnel were issued arms, both for their own protection and for the training of some 800 of their number as potential infantry reinforcements. Of these 800 men, 500 were reallocated to the Canadian Corps early in October.[80] Earlier in the year 314 Russo-Canadians, deemed unsuitable for combat duty in view of the Russian collapse, were transferred to the Forestry Corps.[81] In all the Canadian forestry operations attached labour played an important part. Companies on either side of the Channel employed British and prisoner-of-war labour. Those in France —56 companies when the war ended—used Chinese labour as well. Units in England and Scotland were liberally augmented by Finnish and Portuguese personnel.[82]

At the time of the Armistice 101 Canadian Forestry Companies, with a total strength (including attached personnel) of 31,447, were at work in France and Britain. Forestry operations were continued in France until mid-February 1919 and in Britain until early July. There was cause for pride that 70 per cent of the timber used by the Allied armies on the Western Front had been produced by the Canadian Forestry Corps. The statistics were impressive. Although Britain's consumption of timber had increased with the demands of war, her timber imports had fallen from 11,600,000 tons in 1913 to little more than half that amount in 1916; for 1918 the figure was only two million tons. It was calculated that the shipping space thereby released was sufficient to carry food for 15,000,000 people.[83]

To this extent had the Canadian Forestry Corps contributed to the failure of the submarine campaign.

Canadian Tunnelling Companies

A group of Canadian engineers who saw relatively little of their fellow Canadians during the war were the officers and men of the Canadian Tunnelling Companies. The demand that led to their being organized was slow in coming. In the early months of the war, as the Western Front became static, both sides revived various features of siege warfare, including underground mining as an offensive expedient. There was a growing appreciation of the need for some means of blowing up the enemy's trenches before launching an attack on them, or of cratering no man's land so as to provide advanced positions from which machine-guns and bombers could add surprise in such operations. The Germans early took the lead; and after they had exploded two mines under the British trenches late in 1914 British commanders requested special units for mining and counter-mining.[84]

In the beginning mining sections were attached to engineer field companies, drawing the men from former coal miners and other underground workers. The first Canadian tunnellers in France were organized in brigade mining sections, each consisting of one officer and thirty men. It was intended that these sections would reduce the load being borne by two Royal Engineer Tunnelling Companies which operated on the Canadian front during the summer of 1915. In the winter of 1915-16 these sections were formed into a single unit, the 3rd Tunnelling Company, Canadian Engineers, which in mid-January 1916 assumed responsibility for all mining in the Canadian Corps area south of Ypres. Later in the year it moved to the Lens district, coming under the 4th British Division to work on the tunnels at Hill 70. Meanwhile in response to a request from the British government, two other tunnelling companies had been raised at home. The 1st Tunnelling Company, recruited from miners in Central and Eastern Canada, reached France in February 1916; the 2nd (from Alberta and British Columbia) arrived in March.[85]

By the autumn of 1916, a total of 33 British and Dominion tunnelling companies were operating on the Western Front. A fourth Canadian tunnelling company had been disbanded in England and its personnel divided among the existing three. From the beginning of 1916 all mining activities were placed under the coordination of a Controller of Mines at G.H.Q. This meant that tunnelling companies, both from the United Kingdom and overseas alike, were separated from their corps and employed as army troops.[86] For this reason it is not at all easy to distinguish between the achievements of Canadian tunnellers and those of their British and Australian counterparts. Furthermore, the proportion of infantry and other labour, both military and civilian, attached to the tunnelling companies varied widely at different times, and this ruled out the possibility of assessing the Canadian contribution on the basis of the relative strengths employed. So far did individuals become removed from their own units that it is related that on more than one occasion a Canadian tunneller, emerging after a relief had taken place on the surface, was suspected by the relieving troops of being a deserter, if not indeed an enemy agent!

The tunnellers' life was hard, lonely and full of uncertainty. They faced all the risks of civil mining, many of the normal dangers of warfare, and certain hazards peculiar to military mining—such as breaking into an enemy gallery or being intruded upon by German tunnellers (with a resultant exchange of grenades, pistol shots and knife thrusts), or being blown up by an enemy charge exploded beneath their own workings. Frequently they were in danger of being trapped in their tunnels. Such an incident occurred at Mount Sorrel on 2 June 1916 (above, p. 149), when parties of the 2nd Tunnelling Company were cut off by a German attack. Many were killed or captured; indeed the Company's total reported losses on that and the following day were 96 all ranks, not counting 20 attached infantry.[87] Reference has already been made (above, p. 154) to a happier instance of close and successful cooperation between the 1st Tunnelling Company and Canadian infantry that took place in July that same year at The Bluff, when the 7th Battalion was saved from a probably heavy toll of casualties, and the tables were turned on the attacking Germans.

Towards the end of 1916 there was a distinct falling-off in mining activity on both sides. This was due largely to the recall of 125,000 German miners to industry—50,000 more followed in May and June 1917—and the concern of the British General Staff about the numbers of men employed underground. From then on the British policy was that, except for certain major offensive schemes still in progress, the work of the sappers should be confined to "absolutely necessary defensive measures".[88] The change in German defensive tactics (above, p. 239) which placed the new main lines of resistance usually outside the range of mining activity further limited the role of our tunnelling companies. The emphasis accordingly shifted to what might be termed "administrative" rather than "operational" tunnelling—the construction of dug-outs and subways leading to the front trenches. There was also a tendency, from the summer of 1917 onward, to use tunnellers more and more above ground as field engineers.

The great year for mining was 1916, when the British on the Western Front blew 750 mines and their opponents 696. The corresponding figures for 1917 were 117 and 106. Less than two months after Messines, "the greatest mining enterprise of the war",* British tunnelling companies were reduced in number and strength. By the time the Germans launched their first offensive in 1918, some 27 tunnelling companies were being employed on the construction of dug-outs on the British front.[89]

The two special brigades organized by Lieut.-General Currie in the spring of 1918 to bolster the Canadian defences of Vimy Ridge against the expected German attack included the 1st Canadian Tunnelling Company, along with British engineer units (above, p. 382). All were given a refresher course in musketry and drill and were assigned to the defence of specified localities.[90] As we have seen, the enemy attack passed the Canadians by, and the tunnelling units carried on with their tasks of preparing demolitions and constructing new defence lines.

* As we have seen (above, p. 302), the 1st and 3rd Canadian Tunnelling Companies fired some of the Messines mines.

At times there was a call to man trenches alongside the infantry. In June, when the Germans again threatened, the larger part of the 3rd Tunnelling Company, engaged in working on dug-outs in the Hazebrouck area, was ordered into the trenches to meet an expected attack, which once again failed to materialize.[91]

When General Currie reorganized the Canadian Engineers in the summer of 1918 (above, p. 384), the 1st and 2nd Tunnelling Companies were disbanded, and their members—approximately 1100 all told—distributed evenly among the new engineer battalions.[92] But the 3rd Tunnelling Company, which at the time was in the Ypres area supporting the 16th French Corps of the Second Army, could not then be released to the Canadian Corps. For the rest of the war and later, this Canadian unit remained virtually an orphan, performing a variety of tasks in Flanders and Northern France. October 1918 found it near the Belgian border building railway bridges with a battalion of Canadian Railway Troops. It was not until 6 February 1919 that the long-lost 3rd Tunnelling Company finally returned to Canadian command, to take its place in the repatriation queue.

Canadians in the Air Services

In two World Wars Canadian airmen made an outstanding contribution to victory. In the 1914-1919 conflict those achievements were all the more significant because of their lowly beginnings. Although by August 1914 five and a half years had elapsed from the February day when J. A. D. McCurdy lifted the "Silver Dart" in flight over the frozen surface of the Bras d'Or Lake at Baddeck Bay, the outbreak of war found Canada without any organized military flying service. After that history-making flight the Militia Council had expressed its intention of doing "everything in its power to facilitate the work of experiments in aerial navigation". As noted in Chapter I (above, p. 13), in August 1909 members of the Militia Council witnessed a number of test flights at Petawawa. But in 1910 the Treasury Board rejected an application by the Department of Militia and Defence for a grant of $10,000 (a later request for $5,000 was also turned down) to assist McCurdy and his partner, F. W. Baldwin, "to pursue their studies" in aviation and also train selected army officers to fly. A recommendation to include funds for a similar purpose in the 1911-1912 estimates did not get past the Militia Council. Early in 1912, the Chief of the General Staff, expressing the opinion that a military organization which did "not keep pace with the latest scientific developments must be hopelessly left behind by organizations which are alive to that necessity", sought authority for a start on a modest programme suggested by the War Office in answer to a Canadian request for advice. But the Minister would not approve of any such steps being taken, "neither towards training nor purchase of aeroplanes".[93] Government policy remained the same until war came: "No funds available".

On 25 August 1914 Colonel Sam Hughes cabled Lord Kitchener an offer to send aviators with the First Contingent. Kitchener asked for six, but only two could be provided. They were organized into a short-lived provisional "Canadian Aviation Corps" at Valcartier, and with one aeroplane, purchased in the United States, they accompanied the First Contingent to England. One aviator almost immediately returned to civil life in Canada. The other, Lieutenant W. F. Sharpe, underwent instructional training in France, but was killed on 4 February 1915 while making his first solo flight in England. Their American aircraft never left the ground.[94] In 1915 the Army Council suggested that Dominion air units be formed, but the Canadian authorities did not then consider a separate programme to be in the best interests of their country or the Empire. It was not until 1918 that the tremendous developments in flight made it apparent that an air force would be essential to Canada's post-war military organization and would also spur the development of commercial aviation. Accordingly steps were taken to create a small air force for overseas and a naval air service for home defence—but not in time for either to become operational.[95]

While Canada had no active air service of her own during the war, she was represented in practically every theatre of operations, even in German East Africa, by pilots, observers and mechanics serving in the Royal Air Force and its naval and military predecessors (above, p. 132,*n.*).[96] Officers were seconded from the Overseas Military Forces of Canada; other ranks were discharged from the Canadian forces and re-enrolled as British airmen (either as cadets or non-flying personnel); and in many cases cadets were enlisted by the British authorities in Canada, their status being the same as if they had enrolled in the United Kingdom.[97] Through these channels 22,802 Canadians are known to have entered the British air services. Nevertheless, as the number of Canadians in the R.A.F. by November 1918 was only 500 less than this, and fatal officer casualties alone totalled almost a thousand, it is clear that many more must have found their way in by other avenues—direct entry of civilians in the United Kingdom, for example, or transfer from other Imperial forces.[98]

Canadian airmen distinguished themselves most as fighter pilots. Ten of the 27 leading "aces"* in the R.A.F. were Canadians. Each was credited with 30 or more victories, the Canadians having between them accounted for 238 enemy aircraft. Indeed, the third and fifth top aces of the war were Canadians—Major W. A. Bishop with 72 victories, and Major Raymond Collishaw with 60.[100] The highest score of all was Captain Manfred von Richthofen's 80. In second and fourth place stood Lieutenant Réné Fonck (France) with 75 victories[101] and Lieutenant Ernst Udet (Germany) with 62.[102] A British airman, Major Edward Mannock, is widely credited with 73 victories, though the figure given in the announcement of his posthumous Victoria Cross is 50.

Bishop, originally a cavalry officer in the 2nd Canadian Division, began his career as a fighter pilot in March 1917.[103] He scored perhaps half his victories flying a French Nieuport Scout, which had a top speed of less than a hundred miles an hour and was armed with a single Lewis gun on the top wing. Some British machines of the period were about ten miles an hour faster and had a

* The French term "*as*" signified five or more aerial victories.[99]

synchronized Vickers fixed more conveniently on the cowl; contemporary German fighters carried two cowl machine-guns.[104] On the morning of 2 June 1917 Captain Bishop attacked a German aerodrome near Cambrai single-handed. When two machines took off in succession to meet the attack, Bishop sent one crashing to the ground, the other into a tree. Two more planes then rose simultaneously. The Canadian shot one down, used up the rest of his ammunition on the other, and then returned to his home field. For this intrepid action Bishop received the Victoria Cross—the first ever awarded a Canadian airman.[105]

The enemy's practice of improvising massed fighter formations, introduced by von Richthofen at the end of April, continued through the spring and early summer of 1917, when certain groupings became permanent. In the meantime other units besides Richthofen's predominantly red *Jagdstaffel* 11 had adopted garish colour schemes.[106] There were certain obvious advantages to both sides. "I was glad", wrote Bishop in describing an encounter with Richthofen's unit, "the Germans were scarlet and we were silver . . . no need to hesitate about firing when the right colour flitted by your nose." Some R.F.C. pilots wanted to paint their own machines, but these "budding notions were frowned upon by the higher officers of the Corps".[107] In that regard the Royal Naval Air Service appears to have been more liberally minded. As a flight lieutenant in one of several naval squadrons then attached to the R.F.C., Raymond Collishaw led an all-Canadian flight of five Sopwith triplanes painted black.[108] From the summer of 1917 onward, the Flying Corps and later the Air Force showed a preference for khaki aircraft; personal markings, "gaudy colours on wheels, cowlings, etc.", were forbidden.[109] Nevertheless former naval squadrons of the R.A.F. retained something of their brilliant plumage. A month after the amalgamation we find one such unit still sporting red noses.[110]

An interim answer to the massing of German fighters, as we have seen, had been to put up more British flights. But while the enemy learned to control still larger formations with less loss of striking power, the British found the necessary number of flights increasingly difficult to handle. Accordingly, early in 1918, British fighter squadrons were gradually converted from primarily administrative into tactical units—still only three flights of five or six aircraft, but designed to fight as a squadron and to work with other squadrons.[111] In short, the final answer to the "Circus" was something not unlike it. This tendency to imitate each other's tactical organization was paralleled in another field. Although Allied fighter models of 1916 pattern were superior to the early 1917 Albatros in manoeuvrability and climbing power, it was not until the middle of that summer, when the Scout Experimental 5 (one Vickers and one Lewis gun) and the Sopwith Camel (two Vickers) became available in quantity, that British airmen could match the Germans in speed and firepower. The enemy then turned partly from the 125-m.p.h. Albatros D V to the slower but more manoeuvrable Pfalz D III biplane and Fokker triplane.[112] Early models of the 1918 Fokker biplane were barely faster than the German fighters of the previous spring. What became the standard D VII model (above, p. 421) realized perhaps the happiest combination of speed (125 m.p.h.) and agility, supplemented by easy handling, an exceptional rate of climb, and the ability to "hang on its propeller" and pepper the underside of an opponent.[113] Its British equivalent in all round fighting performance, the Sopwith Snipe, appeared only in the last few weeks of hostilities, and then not in significant numbers.[114]

It was in a Snipe that Major W. G. Barker, formerly a machine-gunner in the 1st Canadian Mounted Rifles, fought an heroic single-handed combat against an overwhelming number of enemy scouts in the vicinity of Valenciennes.* On the morning of 27 October 1918 he shot down an enemy two-seater (his 47th victory) at the unusual height of 21,000 feet. He then came under fire from a Fokker D VII "standing on its tail" and was wounded. A spinning fall brought Major Barker into the midst of fifteen Fokkers. He attacked three of these, accounting for at least one. Wounded a second time, he lost consciousness. As he spun down to another enemy formation, Barker rallied and sent one D VII down in flames. He was again wounded, and at 12,000 feet he found himself attacked by two more Fokkers, one of which he shot down at less than ten feet. Eventually he crashed behind his own lines, escaping with a broken nose. Already a three-time winner of the Military Cross, and twice awarded the Distinguished Service Order and the Italian Cross of Valour, Major Barker now received the Empire's highest decoration.[116]

Fittingly enough, Canada's remaining air V.C., 2nd Lieut. A. A. McLeod, represented those who flew the less publicized multi-purpose two-seater aircraft. While carrying out a bombing and strafing mission east of Albert on 27 March 1918, McLeod was attacked by eight Fokker triplanes. The Canadian pilot's skilful manoeuvring enabled his observer to drive off three triplanes, but a fourth Fokker set the British aircraft on fire. Climbing out on the lower wing, Lieutenant McLeod maintained control of the machine, sideslipping to keep the flames on the other side while his observer carried on the fight. Both men were wounded a number of times before their plane crashed in no man's land. McLeod dragged his companion away from the burning wreckage, and despite ground fire and his own condition—he was now wounded a sixth time—got him to a place of relative safety. The observer recovered with the loss of a leg, but Lieutenant McLeod died later in hospital of influenza.[117]

Another high-scoring Canadian ace with the R.A.F. was Major Collishaw. He served as a Squadron Commander with No. 3 Naval Squadron, which was redesignated No. 203 Squadron R.A.F.† when the R.N.A.S. was merged with the Flying Corps at the beginning of April 1918. After hostilities had ceased in the West, Collishaw led an oversize squadron of scouts and bombers in South Russia.

* The commander of the Canadian Corps Heavy Artillery (Lt.-Col. A. G. L. McNaughton), who watched this "stimulating incident" from his advanced headquarters between Bellevue and Valenciennes, reported its immense moral effect upon the many thousands of British and Canadian troops who witnessed the spectacle from their positions in the trenches and the support areas. "The hoarse shout, or rather the prolonged roar, which greeted the triumph of the British fighter [it was only learned afterwards that he was a Canadian], and which echoed across the battle front was never matched . . . on any other occasion."[115]

† Always largely Canadian in personnel, at the end of the war all its pilots were Canadians.[118]

Of his 62 flying officers 53 were Canadians. He subsequently commanded an R.A.F. detachment in Persia. During the summer of 1918 Collishaw and Bishop, both of whom finished the war in the rank of lieutenant colonel, were transferred to London to take part in the organization of the future Canadian Air Force.

Of some 290,000 all ranks in the Royal Air Force at the end of the war, approximately 24 per cent of the officers and six per cent of the other ranks—a total of 6623 officers and 15,679 cadets and men—came from Canada.[119] The Book of Remembrance in the Peace Tower at Ottawa records the names of a further 1563 who fell in action, were killed accidentally or died from other causes. Besides the three Victoria Crosses to which we have referred, Canadian airmen were awarded more than 800 decorations.

Newfoundland at War

When the First World War broke out, Newfoundland, the Empire's oldest colony, was quick to respond to the call to arms. Recruiting for foreign service and home defence began on the island within a week. It was natural that many should seek service at sea. Early in September 100 Naval Reservists joined the complement of H.M.C.S. *Niobe*; in all, Newfoundland supplied 1964 Naval Reservists during the war. On land the colony's main military contribution was in infantry and forestry troops.* When the war ended some six thousand officers and men had proceeded overseas or were in training on the island. Other Newfoundlanders served in various arms of the British and Canadian forces.[120]

A Newfoundland detachment of two infantry companies, numbering 537 all ranks, sailed to the United Kingdom in October 1914 with the Canadian Contingent. By the end of the year Newfoundland's offer was increased to that of a full battalion, and between February and April 1915 three drafts of close to 250 men each brought the unit up to strength. Organization was completed in May under the name, the Newfoundland Contingent. Leaving behind a rear party, which was to become a draft-finding unit, the battalion embarked for Gallipoli, via Egypt, in August. On 19 September it landed at Suvla, and was assigned to the 88th Brigade, 29th British Division.[121] As the Newfoundlanders were not involved in any major operations in the Gallipoli theatre, battle losses were not excessive—the unit diary records 87 casualties. Among the wounded was the commanding officer, Lt.-Col. R. de H. Burton, a British regular.[122] The 29th Division returned to Egypt in January 1916, and two months later sailed for France. There the Newfoundland battalion was to become the 1st Newfoundland Regiment.

On 1 July, the first day of the Somme offensive (above, p. 162), the 29th Division attacked the German line on a two-brigade front near Beaumont Hamel, a village about a mile north-west of the bend in the Ancre. Although the 86th

* In 1917 the Newfoundland Patriotic Association raised a forestry battalion, 500 strong. Composed of trained woodsmen who had either been rejected as medically unfit or were over the age limit for military service, the corps was employed in Scotland until the end of the war, cutting down a forest on the Duke of Atholl's estate near Perth.

Brigade was soon cut to pieces by machine-gun fire, strong parties of the 87th, on its left, were reported to be advancing on the enemy's support line. Misled by such reports, the divisional commander committed his reserve brigade, the 88th. The 1st Newfoundland Regiment was to have attacked in conjunction with the 1st Battalion Essex Regiment on the right, but the "complete congestion of the trenches with the bodies of dead and dying"[123], prevented the latter unit from advancing on time. Ordered to carry the first line of enemy trenches the Newfoundlanders assaulted independently at 9:05 a.m. on a 1000-yard front. Because of the small number of gaps in the wire, the men had to bunch; and every gap was covered by machine-guns which the enemy had manned as soon as the artillery barrage slackened. Men dropped, dead or wounded, at every yard. Nevertheless the survivors pressed on towards objectives 650 to 900 yards distant, and a few were reported to have succeeded in hurling their bombs into the enemy's trench, if not actually gaining an entry.[124] Shortly after 10:00 a.m., by which time the Essex on the right had attacked with no better success, the divisional commander called off further attacks. The Newfoundland Regiment's casualties that day numbered 684, of which 310 were fatal.[125]

Towards mid-October the Regiment was engaged in the Battle of the Transloy Ridges (above, p. 180). On the 12th the unit, now only 385 strong, stormed and held German entrenchments just north of Gueudecourt.[126] Its next major operation after the Somme came with the Third Army in the First Battle of the Scarpe, in April 1917. On the night of the 13th-14th the 29th Division relieved another British formation astride the Arras-Cambrai road, and the 88th Brigade was ordered to launch an attack east of Monchy-le-Preux, which had been wrested from the Germans on 11 April. Assaulting along with the 1st Battalion Essex Regiment on the morning of the 14th, the Newfoundland Regiment gained its objective, a hill some 1500 yards east of Monchy. But there had been no flanking advance, and the two battalions soon found themselves heavily counter-attacked from three sides by units of the 3rd Bavarian Division. They were overwhelmed by sheer weight of numbers, and only a handful from each battalion managed to get back to Monchy. There the Newfoundland battalion headquarters, led personally by the C.O., Lt.-Col. J. Forbes-Robertson, heroically withstood every German attempt to capture the village. Once again, the Newfoundland Regiment had been virtually cut to pieces. Its casualties that day numbered 17 officers and 468 other ranks.[127]

The Newfoundlanders moved north to Belgium towards the end of June 1917 to take part in Haig's "northern offensive". In the Battle of Langemarck (16 August) the 29th Division attacked as the left flank of the Fifth Army, next to the French First Army. From the Steenbeek the 88th Brigade, operating north of the Ypres-Staden railway, advanced about a thousand yards and made good all its objectives.[128] The Newfoundland battalion killed a "large number of Germans" and captured four machine-guns, at a cost of 103 casualties. Less successful and almost twice as costly a battle for the Newfoundlanders was Poelcappelle, on 9 October. The Regiment again took all its objectives astride the Staden railway, but counter-attacks nullified much of the gains.[129]

Returning to France in mid-October, the Newfoundlanders rejoined General Byng's Third Army for the offensive against Cambrai. It was the 88th Brigade which on 20 November seized the bridgehead at Masnières through which the Canadian Cavalry Brigade attempted to exploit (above, p. 336). Stopped by the strong defences of the Masnières-Beaurevoir Line the Newfoundland battalion dug in, suffering 248 casualties in the first two days.[130] For eleven days the 29th Division held its vulnerable salient about Masnières, withstanding frequent German counter-attacks, before it was ordered to withdraw on 4 December. Recognition of the "magnificent and resolute determination" shown by the Newfoundlanders in these operations came in the following February, when His Majesty the King granted the title of "Royal" to the Newfoundland Regiment. The granting of such an honour during hostilities was unique in the First World War.[131] At the time of the first German offensive in 1918 the 1st Royal Newfoundland Regiment was billeted in Flanders. It did not come under attack in March but was involved in some heavy defensive fighting in the Battles of the Lys in mid-April.[132]

At the beginning of May, the Newfoundlanders severed their long connection with the 29th Division, and until mid-September served as G.H.Q. troops, providing guards and work parties. They did not rejoin the 88th Brigade but were assigned to the 28th Brigade of the 9th (Scottish) Division, which on 20 September took over trenches in front of Ypres. The Regiment now numbered about 650 all ranks, half of them reinforcements who had yet to see action. Towards the end of the month the British Second Army and Belgian forces on its left mounted the first of a series of attacks towards the Lys.[133] In six days the 9th Division broke through the German Flanders Position and advanced almost ten miles.[134]

After a delay in the offensive while supply services were reorganized, the Second Army surged forward again on 14 October. On that day 94 machine-guns and eight field guns fell into Newfoundland hands.[135] Four of the field guns were accounted for by one platoon. The capture owed much to the heroism of seventeen-year-old Private Thomas Ricketts, who with his section commander outflanked the hostile battery, having braved heavy machine-gun fire in order to bring up more ammunition for the Lewis gun which he was manning. He was awarded the Victoria Cross—the youngest winner of the honour from this side of the Atlantic.[136] An advance of nearly seven miles in two days brought the 9th Division to the Lys north of Courtrai, and on 17 October the 28th Brigade crossed the river.[137] The Regiment was in reserve during the crossing but had some hard fighting as the advance continued. On 27 October, as the Second Army closed up to the Scheldt on a narrowing front, the 9th Division was relieved, and the Newfoundlanders were withdrawn to billets for much-deserved rest. "No parade", reads the entry for 11 November in the unit diary, "owing [to] Germans signing Armistice."

The Newfoundlanders' long service overseas had taken a heavy toll. Of some six thousand who had joined the regiment or served with other British forces, 3720 were killed, wounded or captured. In addition 179 Newfoundland sailors had been lost at sea. It was a contribution to victory of which Newfoundland might be justly proud.

Canadians in Northern Russia

The remaining two sections of this chapter deal with Canadian participation in military undertakings which continued long after the Armistice.

While their comrades in the United Kingdom were enjoying their final leave before embarking for home, Canadian contingents were still serving in widely separated theatres in Europe and Asia. The employment of these forces, with the sanction of the Canadian Government, had come as a result of the situation which developed in Russia after the Bolshevik Revolution. As we shall see, Allied intervention in Northern Russia first took the form of what has been described as "a hasty improvisation . . . to prevent the Germans from winning the war in France";[138] later, after Brest-Litovsk, operations were part of an attempt to hold off Bolshevik attacks until White Russian forces could be built up sufficiently to stand alone.

When the Russian Revolution broke out early in 1917, and for some time afterwards, the Western Allies had entertained hopes that Russia could be kept in the war against the Central Powers. By the end of the year, however, any such prospects were rapidly disappearing, and these vanished on 3 March 1918 when the Bolsheviks, who had overthrown Kerensky's Socialist Government in the previous November, signed the peace treaty of Brest-Litovsk with Germany and Austria. With their commitments in the east thus materially reduced, the Germans could now transfer large bodies of troops to the Western Front. Furthermore, a German Army of 55,000 men under General von der Goltz was in Finland ostensibly to counteract Bolshevik troops which had invaded that country in January 1918. This German force seemed to be in a position to seize the ice-free port of Murmansk, out of which during 1917 a small British squadron had been operating against enemy submarines. Conversion of this port into a base for U-boats would create a serious threat to British shipping.[139]

Primarily in order to forestall this possibility Great Britain, at the invitation of the Soviet Government, landed a force of 150 marines at Murmansk in April 1918, and 370 more in May. The question of Allied intervention in Northern Russia had been placed before the Supreme War Council at Versailles. The internal political and military situation in Russia was still chaotic, and the Western Powers could not make up their minds to which side they should direct their negotiations. A large Czech corps was then half way across Siberia working towards Vladivostok. Composed of Czechs from Russia and Czech and Slovak deserters from the Austrian armies, it was the only large military group in Russia which was still a disciplined unit. It had grown from some 30,000 strong to more than twice that figure. Might not an Allied landing in Northern Russia encourage this corps to turn back and reopen hostilities on the Eastern Front? Furthermore,

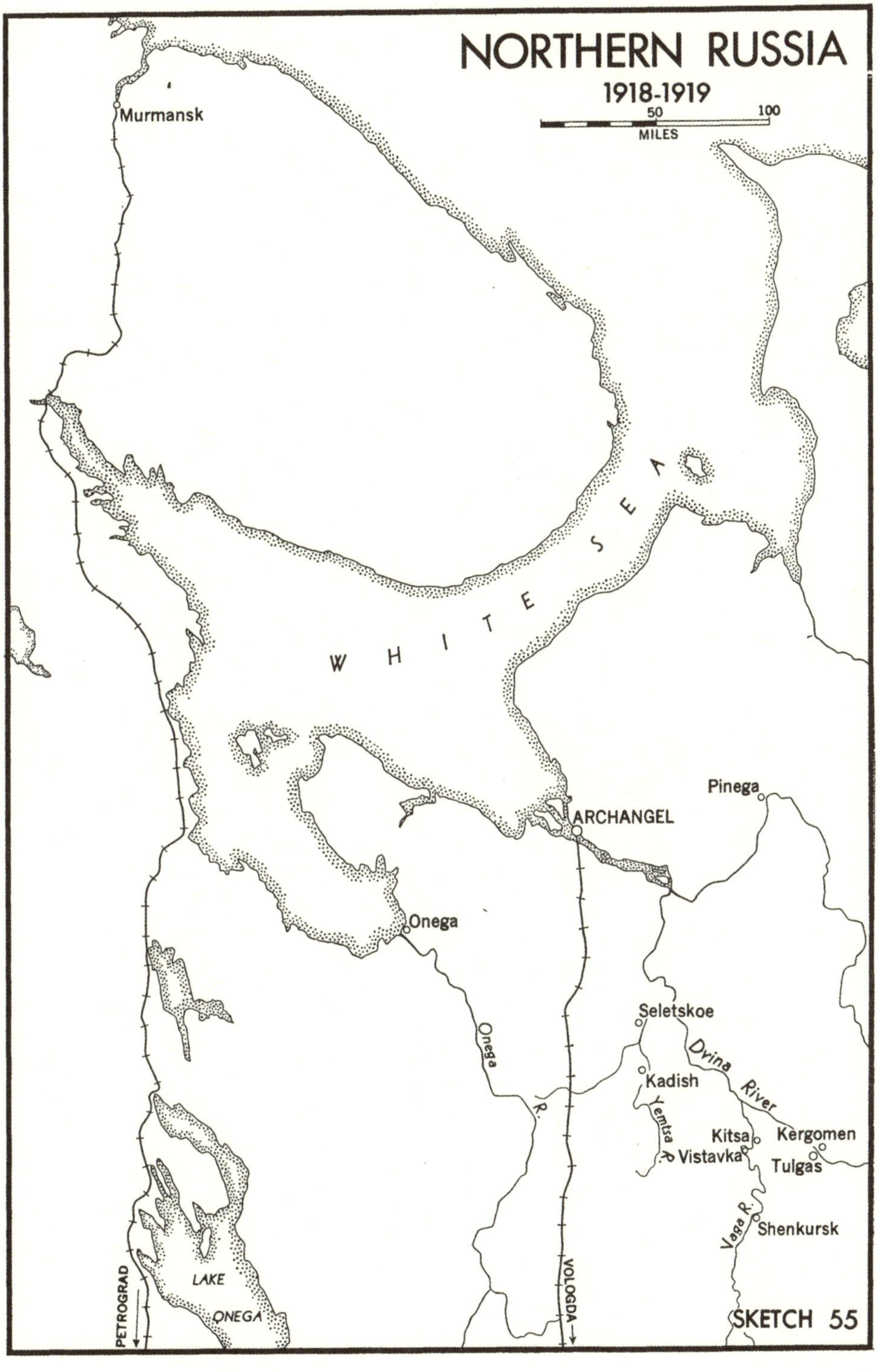
NORTHERN RUSSIA
1918-1919
50
100
MILES
Murmansk
WHITE SEA
Pinega
ARCHANGEL
Onega
Onega R.
Seletskoe
Dvina River
Kadish
Yemtsa R.
Kitsa
Kergomen
Vistavka
Tulgas
Vaga R.
Shenkursk
LAKE
ONEGA
PETROGRAD
VOLOGDA
SKETCH 55

large dumps of military equipment supplied by the Allies for Russia's use when she was still in the war. were reported to be at the White Sea port of Archangel, in imminent danger of falling into German hands. Accordingly, on 3 June the Supreme War Council sanctioned the dispatch under British command of expeditions to Murmansk and Archangel, 370 miles to the south-east.[140]

The Murmansk force, bearing the code-name "Syren", commanded by Major-General C. M. Maynard, consisted of 600 British infantry, a machine-gun company, and a half-company of Royal Engineers. The intended role at Archangel was to muster anti-Bolshevik forces into trained formations, and to this task was assigned a British Mission ("Elope") not to exceed 500 all ranks, under Major-General F. C. Poole. Both forces reached Murmansk on 23 June escorted by an Allied naval squadron; and since Archangel was then in Bolshevik hands, the "Elope" Mission landed with "Syren". On 31 July a naval force carrying British and French troops attacked Archangel, and with the aid of an anti-Bolshevik uprising, captured the town. This made it possible to transfer the "Elope" party to Archangel during August. Within two months a large area of Northern Russia had been freed of Bolsheviks, and land communications were restored with General Maynard's force along the Murmansk-Petrograd (later Leningrad) Railway. The military objectives, both at Murmansk and Archangel, had been achieved with few casualties.[141] By this time, however, events following the Brest-Litovsk treaty had radically changed the political picture. At first the harsh terms of the pact had shocked the Bolsheviks into seeking Allied aid. But no real support was forthcoming, and soon the Reds were frowning upon any intervention which might precipitate further German incursions. In May 1918 the inauguration of formal German-Soviet relations removed the German threat to the new regime in Russia. The Bolsheviks now decided to resist further Allied landings, and after the capture of Archangel any semi-official relations that had existed between Great Britain and the Soviet Government came to an abrupt end.[142]

In mid-May, when the composition of the "Elope" Mission was first considered, the War Office had suggested a Canadian contribution of five officers and eleven N.C.Os., none of whom needed to be fit for general service.[143] On 27 May the Overseas Minister, Sir Edward Kemp, gave Canadian concurrence. The required personnel were obtained from units stationed in England, and sailed with the force in June.[144]

When in July 1918 the question of reinforcing the "Syren" force arose, Canada was asked if she could provide an infantry battalion, since troops with experience of a rigorous climate were required. Unlike the suggestion for a Canadian contribution to "Elope", this request was for men who were fit for general service; but because of the urgent need which then existed for Canadian reinforcements in the western theatre, the invitation was declined.[145]

On 30 July the War Office made a further request for eighteen Canadian officers and 70 N.C.Os., to be included in a special mobile force which was being formed in the Murmansk area from Allied contingents and local levies. There was a requirement for infantry, machine-gun and artillery personnel, first to serve as instructors, and later for regimental or administrative duties in the units to be raised. This time the Canadian Government agreed. On 17 September 92 officers and N.C.Os.—all volunteers—commanded by Lt.-Col. J. E. Leckie, sailed from Leith, Scotland, for Murmansk.[146]

One more request came for Canadian troops to serve in Northern Russia. On 3 August Canada was asked to provide two field artillery batteries for the Allied contingents in Archangel. Again the Canadian Government concurred, and the 16th Brigade, C.F.A., consisting of the 67th and 68th Batteries under the command of Lt.-Col. C. H. L. Sharman, was formed of volunteers from the Canadian Reserve Artillery and left Dundee for Archangel on 20 September. The strength of the Brigade was eighteen officers and 469 other ranks, almost all of whom had seen service on the Western Front.[147]

Both at Murmansk and Archangel the Allied forces were by now of very mixed composition. Contingents were drawn from Britain, the United States, Italy, France and Canada. In both areas these troops were joined by anti-Bolshevik Russians; and at Murmansk, Finns and Karelians worked with the Allies, as did a group of Serbians who had fought their way north from Odessa.* The size of the locally recruited Russian forces fluctuated considerably as there were many defections, but the total Allied strength at Murmansk and Archangel never exceeded 35,000 men. In all Canada contributed to this theatre just under 600 officers and other ranks.[149]

Lack of space precludes a full account of operations in both the Murmansk and Archangel theatres. Because of the small number of Canadians at Murmansk, our account of the North Russian operations will deal principally with the latter theatre. The Canadian field brigade reached Archangel on 1 October and disembarked two days later. Major-General W. E. Ironside, who was to succeed General Poole, arrived in the same convoy. Although the local population was apathetic and evinced no desire to fight, Ironside found that Allied troops had pursued the Bolsheviks after their expulsion from Archangel far enough "to make elbow-room for the enlistment of as many Russians as possible during the winter". In the face of stiffening Bolshevik resistance, Poole's force was consolidating for defence.[150] Five Allied columns had been pushed into the interior of the country. One had reached a point a hundred miles along the Vologda Railway, which ran due south from Archangel. Another was upstream of the confluence

* The size of the various contributions by nationalities was estimated in December 1918 to be as follows:[148]

	Murmansk	*Archangel*
British and Canadian	6832	6293
American	—	5302
French	731	1686
Italian	1251	—
Serbian	1220	—
Russian and other locally raised troops	4441	2715
TOTALS	14,475	15,996

of the Dvina and Vaga Rivers, south-east of Archangel, with forces on both these waterways. Progress of this column, which had advanced about 260 miles from Archangel, had been aided by a monitor of the Royal Navy. Despite the growing distance between these two main columns (which consisted of British, French, American and Russian troops), both were under the single command of a British officer, Brig.-Gen. R. G. Finlayson. Two smaller columns protected the flanks of the column on the railway, one on the Yemtsa River to the east and the other at Onega on the White Sea to the west. A fifth small column was at Pinega, sixty miles east of Archangel.[151]

There was no continuous front; in fact the Vologda railway column was operating on a front of little more than a thousand yards. Communications between the isolated columns were extremely difficult, for the forest-covered ground was swampy in early and late summer and under deep snow in the winter. Except for the column on the railway, all supplies had to be brought forward by water and cart. The troops lived uncomfortably in blockhouses protected by barbed wire, and the effect which the approaching Arctic winter would have on men and weapons was unpredictable. One thing was certain—with ice shutting off Archangel from the rest of Europe all winter, for several months the force would have to subsist on what it had been able to accumulate while the rivers were still open.[152]

On assuming command on 14 October General Ironside placed the two main columns under separate commanders, and attempted to raise additional troops locally. In an effort to recruit more Russians, he visited the jails of Archangel during October and began to expand into a battalion a company of the Slavo-British Allied Legion under Captain R. C. Dyer, one of the Canadian instructors. This unit was later known as the "Dyer Battalion" in honour of its commander, who subsequently died as a result of exposure on the Dvina front.[153]

The 16th Brigade C.F.A. was temporarily divided. Three officers and 26 men joined the Vologda railway column, to man an armoured train. The balance of the brigade, consisting of the 67th Battery and a portion of the 68th, ascended the Dvina by barge as far as the junction with the Vaga River. The 68th Battery was not complete, having left the guns of one section at Dundee; and now a party was detached to Seletski in support of American infantry operating on the Yemtsa River, between the River Dvina and the railway. This group did not rejoin the brigade until December, and one section was left in the Seletski area until April. The 67th Battery was detailed to the Dvina River, and the truncated 68th Battery went to Shenkursk, the most southerly defended town on the Vaga. Lt.-Col. Sharman was appointed C.R.A. of the Dvina Force, which comprised groups on both rivers.[154]

Forces on the Dvina and the Vaga were badly outnumbered. Mid-October found the 67th Battery deployed with one section on the left bank of the Dvina in the village of Tulgas, and one on the opposite bank at Kergomen. The total strength of the group of which they formed a part was between 900 and 1000. The Canadian gunners were manning six 18-pounder field guns and one naval

5.1-inch gun mounted on an old iron barge. Opposing these were a score or more of armed craft, including several gunboats mounting 6-inch and 4.1-inch naval guns, three batteries of field guns, and approximately 3500 Bolshevik troops. Worse than the disparity in numbers was the fact that the Canadians were hopelessly outranged. Their naval gun kept the enemy at a respectful distance until 20 October, when its barge was sunk by a Bolshevik naval gun. Thereafter the enemy craft were able to approach and shell the Canadians, while remaining well out of range of the 18-pounders. Even the Bolshevik field guns outdistanced the Canadian guns. The appearance of river ice on 24 October forced the enemy to withdraw his boats and gave some respite until 10 November, when mild weather again permitted gunboats to come into action. It was a prelude to a Bolshevik attack on Tulgas the next day.[155]

Although 11 November 1918 brought a cessation of hostilities on the Western Front, for the Canadian artillerymen on the Dvina River the date marked the beginning of a period of bitter fighting. At daybreak the Bolsheviks opened their bombardment, following it at eight o'clock with a frontal infantry attack. The guns of the Canadian battery's right section immediately went into action in support of the infantry. An hour later, some 600 Bolsheviks pushed through the woods in the rear of the Canadian guns, and were only discovered by the section's drivers when 200 yards distant. Having temporarily checked the advance by rifle fire, the drivers fell back to the gun-pits. Their action gave warning to the gun crews, who ran one gun out of its pit, reversed it, and opened up on the enemy. A platoon of the Royal Scots was sent to assist the gunners, and throughout the remaining hours of daylight the little force held the enemy at bay. Late in the afternoon, when dusk permitted a second gun to be reversed, the enemy withdrew into the woods, leaving behind 60 dead and wounded. Two Canadians and ten Royal Scots had been killed.

The bravery and determination shown by the Canadians that day in saving their guns earned them a Military Cross, three Distinguished Conduct Medals and three Military Medals. Attempts to capture Tulgas continued until 15 November, when the enemy, admitting failure, retired to his previous positions.[156] Protecting their gun positions with defensive wire, the battery settled in for the winter. The arrival in January of a section of 4.5-inch howitzers and of two 60-pounders on 3 April at last put the Bolsheviks within range.[157]

Meanwhile, the Seletski detachment of the 68th Battery had seen constant action, though there were no major operations until 30 December. On that date two companies of the 339th U.S. Infantry Regiment, supported by a company of the French Foreign Legion, drove the Bolsheviks out of Kadish, a town at the river-crossing on the Yemtsa River about twenty miles above Seletski. When the Bolsheviks counter-attacked in force next day, two sections of the Canadian detachment were instrumental in driving off the enemy.[158] Early in January the Canadian gunners who had been manning the armoured train with the Vologda railway column moved over to the River Vaga to rejoin the 68th Battery at Shenkursk.[159]

The Bolsheviks now decided to launch a general offensive to drive the Allies out of Archangel, and on 19 January a strong force attacked American and Russian troops at Shenkursk. The enemy was in greatly superior strength, and on the 25th, when the town was practically surrounded, the garrison retreated to a new defensive position at Kitsa, thirty miles to the north. The long march down the Vaga was a stiff ordeal for the Canadian battery, but they brought their guns through safely.[160]

The enemy did not follow up the capture of Shenkursk. There is evidence that his success had raised his morale to a high level, while that of the Allies was correspondingly lowered.[161] The force at Kitsa had not much to cheer about. The cold was intense; the Arctic nights were depressingly long, with twenty hours of darkness out of each twenty-four. Above all the troops were dispirited by the seeming purposelessness of their mission in Northern Russia. With the signing of the Armistice on 11 November the original aims of the expedition had disappeared—the Allied operations had become only a phase of the Russian Civil War. There were clamorous outcries in the British press for the soldiers' return. Yet by the middle of January General Ironside had received no clear orders.[162] The Interventionist Powers had no agreed policy on the Russian Civil War, but on 4 March the British War Cabinet decided to press the Allied Representatives to agree to the early evacuation of Northern Russia.[163] A general review of the situation which the War Office sent Ironside at the end of April 1919 still left him without definite instructions, but made it clear that his main objective was to be "a peaceful evacuation of all Allied forces before the coming winter".[164]

Meanwhile, the uncertainty and futility of their situation led to disaffection among the Allied troops. On 26 February, a British battalion sent from Murmansk to reinforce Ironside's force refused to proceed to the front. The trouble was quickly suppressed, and the battalion marched the same day;[165] but at the beginning of March a company of French Colonials made a similar refusal.* A further incident occurred at the end of the month when an American company disobeyed orders to return to its forward position.[167]

During February neither the 67th nor the 68th Battery was involved in any serious engagement. After the loss of Shenkursk, Kitsa had become the Allied advance post on the River Vaga. On 1 March, the 68th fought well in the defence of Vistavka, an outpost of Kitsa, and on the 9th the same battery helped repulse a stronger Bolshevik attack. The Seletski detachment rejoined this battery during April. In March, the 67th Battery, still in position at Tulgas and Kergomen on the Dvina, handed over the Tulgas side of the river to a White Russian battery which had been in training with the force. On 25 April, however, the Russian infantry defending Tulgas mutinied, killing seven of their officers, and surrendered their positions to the Bolsheviks. It was a source of great satisfaction to the 67th Battery that the Russian battery which it had "mothered" did not join the muti-

*In a letter to the C.G.S. in April 1919, Colonel Sharman reported that one section of the Canadian Artillery Brigade had temporarily refused to obey orders. No details were given, and the War Diaries of Brigade Headquarters and the 67th and 68th Batteries for the period are missing.[166]

neers, but came over to the Canadians, bringing its guns with it. Nevertheless the loss of Tulgas, only 2500 yards away and on higher ground, made the Canadian position at Kergomen most precarious. The enemy used every means, including his river flotilla, to capture the place, but the clearing of the ice enabled two British gunboats mounting 6-inch guns to arrive from Archangel. Joint efforts by land and water forced the Bolsheviks back, and Tulgas was recaptured on 18 May.[168]

On that same day Sir Robert Borden addressed the British Secretary of State for War, Mr. Winston Churchill, insisting that the Canadians should be withdrawn from Northern Russia without delay. Two previous requests in March had elicited the information that this would not be possible before the early summer because of ice. In his letter of 18 May, the Canadian Prime Minister pointed out that the port of Archangel was now open to navigation and emphasized that "the demobilization of the Canadian Corps and the withdrawal of Canadian troops from Siberia [below, p. 522] render any further continuance of our forces at Archangel absolutely impracticable".[169] The Canadian request brought prompt action. At the end of May and early in June a relieving British force of two brigades, each with a battery of howitzers, arrived from England. The 16th Field Brigade held a farewell parade at Archangel on 11 June, when a number of Russian military decorations were awarded to officers and men; it embarked the same day for England. By September 1919 all the remaining Canadians at Murmansk and Archangel had been evacuated.[170]

The Canadians left Russia with a tribute from General Ironside that "over and over again the C.F.A. had saved the force from destruction". In the course of the campaign the Canadian casualties had been comparatively light—eight killed and sixteen wounded.[171] The remaining intervention forces did not linger long after the Canadians had gone; by 12 October all British troops were out of Northern Russia.[172]

Intervention in Siberia

The area about the White Sea was not the only sphere of Allied intervention in Russia. We have already noted (above, p. 494) the part played by British and other forces in the Trans-Caucasus region; and in December 1918 French troops landed at Odessa and moved into the Crimea and the Ukraine.[173] Before the war against the Central Powers ended, Allied contingents had entered Siberia. More than 4000 Canadians represented the Dominion in this venture, which kept them on active service until the summer of 1919.

To account for the presence of Canadians in Siberia it is necessary to trace briefly the course of events after the Bolshevik Revolution. The signing of the treaty of Brest-Litovsk, which followed the suspension of hostilities between Russia and Germany, had the effect of throwing Russia open to German domination. Grain from the Ukraine, oil and minerals from the Caucasus and the Caspian were now within the grasp of the Germans. With these resources, and by penetrating into Siberia, they hoped to circumvent the Allied blockade of their country; moreover the capture of the port of Vladivostok would give them very considerable military stores which had been supplied for Russian use against the Central Powers, and which, it was reported, were still stock-piled there. These were disturbing prospects for the Allies, who had, above all, to reckon with the wholesale transfer of German forces from the Eastern to the Western Front at a time when the weight of the American entry into the war had not been appreciably felt.[174]

On the other hand the Allies had some grounds for optimism on the Russian scene. The truce and peace treaty had produced widespread unfavourable reaction in Russia; the Cossacks on the Don had raised counter-revolutionary standards, and the mass of the Siberian people, who were generally content with their ordered existence under the old regime, had little leaning towards the Bolshevik system. As we have seen, Murmansk and Archangel were open to Allied shipping, and in the Caucasus movements were afoot to bar entry by the Central Powers to the Caspian. Finally, the pro-Allied Czech Corps, widely dispersed, lay along the line of the middle Volga and at Vladivostok, though the country between was still in Bolshevik hands.

The plain task of the Allies was to reconstitute the Eastern Front and to withhold Russian supplies from Germany. The Military Representatives of the Supreme War Council accordingly recommended as early as 23 December 1917 that all national troops in Russia who were determined to continue the war should be fully supported.

There were two approaches through which the Supreme War Council might supply help to anti-Bolshevik forces in Russia—the northern ports of Russia in Europe, and across the eastern frontiers of Siberia. The latter seemed to offer the better opportunity, especially as Japan, an Allied power and the only one with troops available for intervention in force, was close at hand, ready and willing to oppose incursions by the Central Powers into Eastern Russia. There was the risk, however, that a Japanese invasion might unite the mass of the Russian people with the Bolsheviks, causing them to throw in their lot openly with the enemy.[175] For this reason, it was deemed essential that intervention should be by more than one of the Allied Powers.

When in December 1917 Japan and the United States were asked for their views, Japan favoured intervention (but without American participation). President Wilson opposed any action, either jointly with Japan, or by the Japanese alone. Months passed with the issue undecided, until the Bolsheviks, at German instigation, sought to disarm the Czechs in Russia. The Czechs, who had been guaranteed safe passage through Russia, resisted this attempted treachery with violent counter-attacks. By 6 June 1918 they were in possession of the Trans-Siberian Railway from a hundred miles west of the Ural Mountains eastward to Krasnoyarsk in central Siberia—a distance of more than 1500 miles. On the 28th one of their detachments seized Vladivostok, and by 13 July the advance of their main force towards the Pacific had reached Irkutsk, beside

Lake Baikal.[176] No link had yet been established between Irkutsk and Vladivostok.

On 2 July 1918 a further appeal to President Wilson by the Supreme War Council was successful. The President, apprehensive that the victorious Czechs were in imminent danger of being annihilated by hordes of German and Austrian former prisoners of war whom the Bolsheviks had set free, proposed the dispatch of an international force "to restore and preserve the communications of the Czechs". Three days later the United States announced its decision for a limited intervention in Siberia. It was finally agreed that Britain and the United States should each send 7000 troops, and that Japan should provide a force* capable of effectively aiding the Czech Corps then at Irkutsk.[178]

A week after the American announcement the War Office asked the Canadian Prime Minister if Canadian troops could be made available for service in Siberia. It had learned, unofficially, that two battalions of discharged soldiers could be raised in Canada—a procedure quite in keeping with the Allied policy of not diverting "any appreciable body of troops from the Western Front".[179] Sir Robert Borden, who was in London at the time, examined the suggestion and, for reasons not wholly military, found himself favourably disposed to the dispatch of a small Canadian force to Siberia. "Intimate relations with that rapidly developing country", he wrote, "will be a great advantage to Canada in the future. Other nations will make very vigorous and determined efforts to obtain a foothold and our interposition with a small military force would tend to bring Canada into favourable notice by the strongest elements in that great community."[180]

Accordingly, on 12 July the C.G.S. in Ottawa was directed to organize a brigade headquarters, two battalions of infantry, a battery of field artillery, a machine-gun company, and certain other troops. In Siberia a British battalion was to join this force, and come under Canadian command.[181] The contingent, including the British unit, would be known as the Canadian Siberian Expeditionary Force, and would represent the British Empire among the Allied military expeditions operating in Siberia.[182] The Cabinet approved the idea in principle, and on 12 August a Privy Council instruction[183] was signed authorizing the dispatch of the troops.† The month's delay between the British request and final Canadian acceptance had made the War Office impatient; but its attempt to expedite the matter through the Governor General brought an angry cable from Borden, "No reply shall be sent to the British Government's message except through me."[185]

* In the end the Japanese landed more than 70,000 men, justifying this by claiming that the Americans had exceeded their assigned total through the addition of some 2,000 administrative troops.[177]

† The approved contingent, nearly 5000 strong, consisted of Headquarters Canadian Expeditionary Force (Siberia), H.Q. 16th Infantry Brigade, a base headquarters, and the following major units: "B" Squadron R.N.W.M.P. (Cavalry), 85th Battery C.F.A., 16th Field Company C.E., 6th Signal Company, 259th and 260th Infantry Battalions, 20th Machine Gun Company, No. 1 Company Divisional Train, No. 16 Field Ambulance, No. 11 Stationary Hospital, No. 9 Ordnance Detachment.[184]

It had been hoped that sufficient men could be raised by voluntary enlistment, but when this was not found possible some personnel drafted under the Military Service Act had to be employed.[186] During the late summer and early autumn the Canadian Brigade was concentrated on the West Coast in readiness for dispatch to Vladivostok,[187] but it was not until 11 October that an advance party of 680 all ranks sailed from Vancouver with the force commander, Major-General J. H. Elmsley, a former commander of the 8th Canadian Infantry Brigade in France.[188] The Canadian troops were to be under the over-all control of the Allied Commander-in-Chief, the Japanese General Otani. General Elmsley, however, had the right to appeal to the War Office against any order which in his opinion might imperil the safety of his force. He was authorized to correspond directly with Canada without reference to the War Office or any outside body; no appeal could be decided against him without the approval of the Canadian Government.[189]

While the Canadians were on their way to Siberia, Allied intervention there was actively proceeding. A British battalion from Hong Kong had advanced inland with French and Italian units to the vicinity of Omsk, where they were acting as a stabilizing influence on the anti-Bolshevik forces in Western Siberia. The Americans, arriving from the Philippines, were still near the coast, engaged in guarding military stores and forwarding supplies to the Czechs. The Japanese had advanced to Lake Baikal, but refused to have anything to do with operations farther west.[190] What was to be the Canadian role? Borden held the sound opinion that the disposition and employment of troops should be left to Elmsley's judgement,[191] but on 11 November, before further Canadian troops could be sent, the General Armistice was signed. In its wake a wave of opposition to further participation in Russian affairs swept across Canada.

"All our colleagues", Sir Thomas White, the Acting Prime Minister, wrote to Borden in the United Kingdom, "are of opinion that public opinion here will not sustain us in continuing to send troops many of whom are draftees under Military Service Act and Order in Council now that the war is ended." He pressed for a return to Canada of all the Canadian forces in Siberia as soon as the situation permitted.[192] Indeed, with the collapse of Germany, every military argument for intervention had disappeared. Yet in the face of militant Bolshevism, anti-Bolshevik armies and administrations which had grown up under the shelter of Allied forces required support and protection.

Borden's reply was made on 20 November. He had ascertained that the War Office did not intend to commit British or Canadian forces in an offensive campaign. Nevertheless, it was believed that their presence in Siberia would have an important stabilizing influence and help to prevent the country from lapsing into anarchy; for this reason the British were adding another battalion to the one already sent. Furthermore they would assist in training the White armies of the new anti-Bolshevik Government which had been set up at Omsk under Admiral A. V. Kolchak. Experience seemed to have shown that Russian troops would "melt away" without the moral support of an Allied contingent, no matter how small.[193] Borden therefore favoured the retention of Canadian troops in Siberia until the spring. He further recommended that "the additional forces originally arranged for should proceed to Siberia for the purposes indicated, as well as for economic considerations which are manifest".[194]

But the Canadian Cabinet again demurred. Many members were opposed to any continuation of the venture; and in any case it was not practicable to send only volunteers, as this would involve breaking up units ready to sail.[195] Yet Borden had given the British Government a definite undertaking, and he declared that Canada's "position and prestige would be singularly impaired by deliberate withdrawal from definite arrangement under these conditions". Nevertheless, he left the decision to the Privy Council,[196] which considered it on the 27th. On that day Borden advised the Acting Prime Minister that he had discussed the whole question at the War Office. The British attitude was reasonable. If the force must be withdrawn, it was hoped that General Elmsley, his staff, and fifty or a hundred instructors, would be permitted to remain. The question was now up to Council to decide, which it did in favour of proceeding with the expedition as originally planned, save that personnel would be permitted to return to Canada within one year of the signing of the Armistice. The matter, White advised Borden, was now closed.[197]

It was not long before the Cabinet had serious second thoughts about this decision. It was concerned that a possible clash of interests between the Americans and Japanese might lead to trouble. In such a case Canadian sentiment would almost certainly align itself with the United States, while Britain, bound by Anglo-Japanese Alliance, would be in the opposite camp and might request Canadian neutrality. The War Office was therefore notified that the Dominion Government would not permit its troops "to engage in military operations, nor, without its express consent, to move up country", pending clarification of British policy. Unless their mission were made clear, it might be necessary to withdraw the Canadians altogether.[198] Borden was justifiably exasperated at this vacillation. He explained to White that some few days earlier the British had practically understood that Canadians would be withdrawn, and then had come Council's decision to proceed. He went on to say that Council was armed with details of political and economic conditions. They were aware of the military situation. They, then, should judge, and with that he virtually washed his hands of the matter.[199] Meanwhile the War Office had lost patience and directed a forthright reply to the C.G.S., General Gwatkin. Because of the Canadian Government's latest restrictions the War Office felt obliged to recommend to the War Cabinet that the two British battalions should be withdrawn to Vladivostok and that the Canadians who had already sailed for the Far East should be returned to Canada. Those *en route* might be recalled by wireless, and no more should be sent.[200] Nevertheless, no immediate steps were taken by Ottawa to bring back the 1100 Canadians who had reached Siberia, nor were the ships carrying the 2700 men who formed the bulk of the force recalled.[201]

The restrictions imposed by Ottawa placed Major-General Elmsley in a most embarrassing position. He protested vigorously against any Canadian withdrawal.[202] Hamstrung as he was, there was little for him to do with his troops, whose oft-expressed sentiment was "Home or Fight!" The head of the British Military Mission in Siberia, Major-General Alfred Knox, was anxious to have the Canadians at Omsk, where they would help form "a tangible Allied force at the front".[203] This move Elmsley could in nowise make; and there were heated exchanges between the two generals. "If they [the Canadians]"; wrote Knox on 27 December, "only think of playing the American-Japanese sitting game in the Far East, I honestly don't see much use in their coming at all."[204]

And so the Canadian Siberian Expeditionary Force was held at Vladivostok, where officers and men were quartered in Russian barracks some twelve miles from the harbour. A small staff of eight officers and 47 other ranks was sent to Omsk to administer the two British battalions there.[205] The troops found the climate at Vladivostok pleasant enough—much like that of Eastern Canada. But the city itself, with its normal population of 40,000 almost quadrupled by refugees of many nationalities, was a centre of corruption and vice. There was little to do except routine training; though voluntary auxiliary services working with the Canadian Red Cross and the Y.M.C.A. provided some amenities. There were occasional football games with the crews of British naval vessels in port, and baseball games with the Americans.[206] The sole operational task given the Canadians came in April 1919, when General Otani called for a small Allied column to suppress an insurgent Bolshevik force in a village some thirty miles north of Vladivostok. General Elmsley sent a company of the 259th Battalion as the Canadian contribution, but by the time the force was ready to attack, the Bolsheviks had retired. When the Canadians got back to Vladivostok without having fired a shot, their disappointment was somewhat alleviated by the issue to them, on Otani's instruction, of 96 bottles of wine, 18 bottles of whiskey and three casks of saké.[207]

By the end of 1918 it had become obvious to Sir Robert Borden that Canada was unlikely to reap any economic advantages from intervention in Siberia. Accordingly, as a way out of the impasse in which the Allies found themselves, he suggested at a meeting of the Imperial War Cabinet on 30 December that an international conference be held to arbitrate the Russian Civil War.[208] This proposal came to nothing, for the White Russians, refusing "to confer on an equal basis with traitors, murderers and robbers",[209] indignantly rejected the invitation to attend. At the end of January the Canadian Government decided to demobilize the troops awaiting shipment in British Columbia, and early in February Borden informed Lloyd George of his intention to recall the Canadians from Siberia about April. He reiterated his determination to do this when the Russian situation was discussed at the Peace Conference between 13 and 17 February, despite the urgings of Lord Balfour and Mr. Churchill, who foresaw disastrous consequences resulting from any general Allied withdrawal.[210] But

Sir Robert remained firm, and the British Government had no alternative but to acquiesce in the Canadian decision.[211]

The first Canadian party to leave Vladivostok embarked on 21 April 1919, and the last sailed on 5 June.[212] As the organized body of troops withdrew, Churchill made one final appeal for Canadian volunteers "to co-operate with the volunteer detachments which compose our various missions to the loyal Russian armies".[213] A few volunteers from Canadian units in Siberia did remain with the British force, but by the autumn of 1919 the British contingent of approximately 2000 men, having lost Canadian administrative support, was withdrawn.[214]

In spite of the Allied intervention, the actual fighting in Russia was left to the Russians. During the spring of 1919 White Russian armies under Admiral Kolchak and General Denikin achieved a series of successes; in May Lenin was forced to tell his Revolutionary Military Council, "If we don't conquer the Urals before winter I think the destruction of the Revolution is inevitable."[215] By the end of June less than one-sixth of Russia remained in Bolshevik hands. But that was the zenith of White Russian achievements. In July they lost the Urals to the Bolsheviks, and in October an advance on Moscow was halted 250 miles from the capital. During the following winter the Bolsheviks drove Kolchak's forces from one stronghold after another. In March 1920 British warships covered the evacuation of troops to the Crimea, the only territory still in White Russian hands. As it became clear that the anti-Bolshevik cause was doomed, all the Allied contingents withdrew from Siberia except the Japanese, who remained in Vladivostok and the adjacent coastal area for two more years. The Czechs were safely evacuated and crossed Canada en route to Europe in June 1920.[216]

As an aggressive enterprise, the intervention in Siberia must be regarded as a complete failure. No armed help had been given to the anti-Bolshevik forces—in fact when the White Russians were making their best showing, the Canadian contingent was being withdrawn. Allied policy was singularly lacking in effectiveness and no concerted measures materialized. Yet it is possible to claim certain far-reaching indirect results. Intervention had delayed for many months the ultimate Bolshevik victory. Preoccupation with the internal struggle prevented the diversion of men and munitions to foment political, social and economic disorders in countries outside of Russia. Thus there was time for Finland, the Baltic States and Poland to establish their independence. The frontier of Bolshevism was held from advancing westward until after the Second World War.

CHAPTER XVII

AFTER THE ARMISTICE

The March to the Rhine

ALTHOUGH the signing of the Armistice brought an end of fighting for most Canadians, new duties lay ahead. Several months were to elapse before the majority of Canada's overseas forces returned to their homeland. For some, indeed, there were tasks which would engage them in operations in more remote fields than any where Canadians had previously served during the war.

Immediately after the conclusion of hostilities steps were taken to concentrate the formations of the Canadian Corps as far forward as possible in preparation for the forthcoming march to the Rhine. The 3rd Division was centred in Mons; the 2nd was on its right, east of Frameries; and the 1st and 4th were in the rear about Jemappes and Paturages, west and south-west of Mons respectively. The sector thus held by the Canadians was about five miles wide.[1] In accordance with the terms of the Armistice the leading troops stood fast on the final cease-fire line, and examining posts were placed on all roads to restrict the east-west movements of civilians. No fraternization or other intercourse with the enemy was allowed, nor were the Germans permitted to approach the Canadian lines. "I ordered commanders to pay the strictest attention to discipline and smartness", wrote General Currie, "and especially the well-being of their men."[2]

The Armistice had provided that Allied troops would advance to the left bank of the Rhine and occupy a series of bridgeheads on the right bank at the principal crossing-places, each bridgehead having a radius of thirty kilometres.[3] British forces were allotted a bridgehead which centred upon Cologne, and extended along the river from Düsseldorf to south-east of Bonn. Under the plan which was originally approved the Second and Fourth Armies would occupy the British bridgehead. The Canadian Corps on the right and the 2nd British Corps on the left would lead the Second Army's advance. The selection of their Corps to take part in the occupation was a distinction that the Canadians prized highly.[4] The 1st and 2nd Divisions (the senior formations of the Corps) would be in the Canadian van, followed later by the 3rd and 4th Division.[5]

On Sunday, 17 November, a day of thanksgiving, representatives of Canadian units attended special services in the Mons churches. In honour of the liberating troops the city's carillon played "O Canada". At nine o'clock on the following morning, leading units of the 1st and 2nd Canadian Divisions crossed the outpost lines and commenced the march to the Rhine. Each division proceeded in three brigade columns, on separate routes. Those of the 1st Division on the left, had Cologne as the destination; the 2nd Division on the right headed towards Bonn. A cavalry screen advanced one day's march ahead of the leading infantry, and each column provided its own close protection, in which it was assisted by cavalry and cyclists attached from Corps Troops. The whole 250-mile march was conducted under operational conditions, and all military precautions were taken against surprise. To ensure a smooth take-over from the enemy the country had been divided into zones. The Germans had orders to deposit war material at selected places in each zone and to withdraw from the area the day before the Allies entered it.[6] Before the 3rd and 4th Divisions could set out, however, supply difficulties necessitated a change in the general plan for the advance. The almost complete destruction of all railways and roads in the old battle areas made it impossible to maintain two armies on the move and at the same time provide for the Belgian civilian population. Accordingly the Second Army now went forward alone. The Canadian occupation force was reduced to the 1st and 2nd Divisions, together with Corps Headquarters and some Corps Troops already on the march. The 3rd and 4th Divisions, with the 8th Army Brigade Canadian Field Artillery and the 1st and 3rd Brigades Canadian Garrison Artillery, were transferred to the 4th Corps, of the Fourth Army. They remained billeted in Belgium until moving back to England, on the way to demobilization.[7]

Meanwhile, the marching divisions made frequent halts to permit the Germans to evacuate zones as planned. They encountered no enemy troops but saw much evidence of their passing. The wreckage of a great fighting machine was everywhere at hand. In accordance with the terms of the Armistice the Germans had assembled, usually in or near the villages and towns, huge parks of guns and dumps of munitions and other war equipment. Miles upon miles of laden barges had been left tied up on the canals, and the roadways were littered with helmets, discarded army clothing, and even weapons.[8] The march through Belgium was in general a triumphal progress, particularly for the leading battalions. The inhabitants of the various communities through which the Canadians passed where Germans had been in occupation were warm in their welcome and expressed their gratitude in many ways. In other places the populace was more restrained, for no soldiers of any nationality were wanted. At Nivelles, a town twenty miles north-east of Mons, which the 16th Battalion reached on 21 November, there was not only the luxury of warm billets and soft feather beds, but "eight thousand bottles of wine were dug up from the chateau grounds."[9] In marked contrast was the cool reception afforded the Canadians after they had crossed the German border. Here the only spectators in view were children with close cropped heads who stared curiously from the roadside. Their elders remained discreetly out of sight, peering through half closed doors or shuttered windows at the marching columns.[10]

The weather was generally good until 25 November, the day the leading troops reached the Meuse at Namur; but thereafter it rained daily, and this, together with the heavy traffic, caused roads to deteriorate rapidly. There was no move on the 26th, and on the following day, since side roads could no longer be used, each division was compelled to march in two columns. The Corps advance, which had been due east to Namur, now continued to the south-east. Boundaries between divisions were rearranged so that each would have one first-class road. Leaving the Meuse at Andenne, the 2nd Division, destined for Bonn, was directed south-east to the German frontier at Beho, a village some six miles south-east of Vielsalm. The 1st Division, some ten miles to the north, followed a parallel route to reach the frontier at Petit Thier, three miles north-east of Vielsalm.[11]

Owing to the lack of suitable billets among the sparsely inhabited hills of the Ardennes and the Eifel district, on and after 28 November each division moved in only one column. Brigade groups, each covering between eight and ten miles of road space, were separated usually by one day's march. The long hours of marching over cobblestones or through heavy mud were taking a toll in blistered feet, and the continual drizzling rain had an added depressing effect. The difficulties of bringing forward supplies were increasing, for railhead was still west of Valenciennes, more than a hundred miles away. On 28 November rations did not reach the 1st Division until some of the units were already on the march—breakfastless. On the 29th a repetition of the situation caused the 1st Division's march for that day to be cancelled. Only by securing additional lorries and utilizing the vehicles of the Canadian Machine Gun Corps was it possible to remedy the trouble sufficiently to permit the advance to continue on 30 November.[12]

Nevertheless despite rain, the hilly country, and short rations, the men's spirits remained remarkably high. A Special Order of the Day issued by General Currie called on the troops to remain "a close-knitted army in grim, deadly earnest", and to give German agents scattered through the country no opportunity of reporting any weakness or "evidence of disintegration of your fighting power". To that end the highest standard of discipline was insisted on, whether on the march or at the halt. "In short", the order continued, "you must continue to be, and appear to be, that powerful hitting force which has won the fear and respect of your foes and the admiration of the world."[13] Magnificently the Canadians responded. With bayonets fixed and flags flying the leading troops crossed the German frontier at nine o'clock on the morning of 4 December, the 1st Division at Petit Thier and the 2nd at Beho. During the following days the other units entered Germany, the pipes of the Highland battalions appropriately skirling "Blue Bonnets over the Border".[14]

From now on much of the route lay through heavily forested country which presented the marchers with a succession of steep hills and narrow valleys. Many of the men had blistered feet as a result of footgear which was becoming badly worn, yet units continued to cover twenty or more miles a day with no one dropping out.[15]

The day set for crossing the Rhine by the Allies was 13 December. The occasion was considered to be of greater significance than the crossing of the German frontier, and for several preceding days the Canadians were concentrated on the left bank opposite Cologne and Bonn, as far forward as possible. In these positions all units busied themselves with traditional "spit and polish" to ensure that with brass gleaming and equipment and clothing in the best possible condition all ranks would present a faultless appearance on the important day. On the 12th the British 1st Cavalry Brigade, which had come under General Currie's command on 1 December, crossed at Bonn to establish control posts within the bridgehead.[16]

The morning of the 13th dawned dark and wet, and a steady rain poured down throughout the day. The 1st Division crossed the Rhine* by South Bridge at Cologne, marching past the G.O.C. Second Army, General Sir Herbert Plumer, while crowds of Germans lining the streets of the city silently watched the steel-helmeted Canadians swing by in full battle order. At the bridge at Bonn, General Currie, "after a very comfortable night in His Majesty's bed",† witnessed the crossing and took the salute of the 2nd Division, which marched past in an impressive column that extended for eighteen miles. Here the civilian spectators were fewer in numbers, and equally undemonstrative. What was a memorable day for the Canadians could only be one of humiliation for the people whose armies they had helped to vanquish.[18]

Once across the Rhine the Canadian units unfixed bayonets and marched at ease to their assigned towns and villages, where comfortable billets had been arranged for them. The two divisions were disposed in depth for the defence of the southern sector of the Cologne-Bonn bridgehead, where their area of responsibility encompassed ground on the east or right bank of the Rhine, including the city of Bonn itself. Units proceeded to establish control posts on the roads and railways leading into the bridgehead, and to place guards on the various dumps of German stores. In general these duties were not arduous; the chief difficulty came in enforcing the military regulation which forbade movement of civilians between the occupied area and territory still under German control.

With military duties reduced to a minimum, efforts were made to provide opportunities for all to partake in sport. There was time also to begin preparing the men for their return to civil life. Education, in many cases interrupted by the war, received special attention. Battalions ran their own schools, finding teachers from their own ranks to instruct the men in elementary subjects. In this they were helped by text-books prepared and printed under the auspices of the Khaki University. The Khaki University of Canada, which originated as a project of the National Committee of the Canadian Y.M.C.A.,[19] had begun to function in England and France in the autumn of 1917, but the German offensive of the

* The honour of leading the 1st Division over the Rhine was given to the 3rd Brigade. The toss of a coin gave the 14th Battalion the proud privilege of leading the Brigade column across the river.

† At Bonn, Sir Arthur occupied the Kaiser's suite in the Palais Schaumburg, home of the German Emperor's youngest sister.[17]

following spring had halted the work in France. During 1918 Khaki Colleges were established in fourteen different locations in the United Kingdom, and in September of that year the Khaki University of Canada was formally authorized as a branch of the General Staff of the O.M.F.C., with control over all existing educational organizations overseas. The Central College of the Khaki University, in Ripon, Yorkshire, offered matriculation courses and the first two years of a university arts course, and in these were enrolled the more advanced soldier students from the United Kingdom and France. In addition some 300 graduate students and undergraduates of at least two years' university standing at home were sent to various universities in Great Britain.[20] These were enrolled for the two academic terms commencing 1 October 1918 and 1 February 1919.[21]

While the Canadians were still in Germany, they heard official denial of a rumour that the battalions of the Corps would be broken up and individuals shipped home for demobilization following a priority based on length of overseas service and marital status. Whatever views Canadian soldiers may have held about the desirability of following a "first over, first back" policy of demobilization, General Currie considered that it was important for the troops to return to Canada as formed units. As part of the Army of Occupation the Corps had to function as a fully organized formation, and he was concerned that to withdraw men on an individual basis could result in a breakdown of the administrative services of the Corps. The Army could not carry on in a bearable fashion without its clerks and cooks; yet their relatively sheltered role—they suffered far fewer casualties than, for instance, the infantry—meant that most of these administrative personnel had long service credits which would give them high priority in any competitive scheme of individual repatriation. Above all was the value of maintaining morale by keeping the men, as long as possible, in the units in which they had fought. Currie's views had been communicated to Ottawa on 11 November, with a strong supporting recommendation from Sir Edward Kemp, the Overseas Minister.[22] But the Privy Council had rejected the proposal on the grounds that it would "entail great additional expense, dislocate railway transportation, confuse administrative arrangements and throw on Militia, Re-establishment and Labour Departments an intolerable burden of work and responsibility".[23] Sir Robert Borden, who was in the United Kingdom at the time, then took up the cudgels on Currie's behalf, and asked the Acting Prime Minister, Sir Thomas White, to have the matter reconsidered.[24]

The Canadian Cabinet was not inclined to alter its decision, and on 23 November White reiterated its views to Sir Robert, venturing the belief that General Currie would find these "convincing".[25] On the same day the Corps Commander held a conference at Mons, attended by all available divisional and brigade commanders and heads of services and branches. A free discussion of demobilization brought unanimous agreement that "from every point of view it was desirous to demobilise the Corps by Units and not by categories".[26] Borden's reply to Ottawa two days later cited the example of Australia, which was returning its troops as units under their own officers. He warned his colleagues in the Cabinet of the bitter resentment which Canadian soldiers would feel "if units which have fought so magnificently and earned world-wide distinction in keen competition with each other are scrambled into one mass and returned to Canada".[27] Upon the receipt of this message the Canadian Cabinet gave in. On 29 November the Minister of Militia notified Borden that, subject to certain conditions (e.g., limiting the sanction to combatant units of the Corps), the Privy Council had concurred in deferring to General Currie's wishes.[28]

Garrison Duty in Belgium

The Canadians' occupation role in Germany lasted well into the New Year. A timely snowfall on the night of 24 December enabled all units to celebrate the white Christmas to which so many were accustomed at home. The traditional turkey and accompanying luxuries might be missing (they arrived later), but resourceful messing officers ably backed by expert battalion cooks saw to it that all enjoyed a Christmas dinner worthy of the name.

First to leave for Belgium were the 13th, 14th and 16th Battalions of the 1st Division, who entrained on 5 January 1919.[29] The 1st Division completed its move on 18 January, and next day the relief of the 2nd Division began.[30] Corps Troops followed and the arrival of the Canadian Corps Cyclist Battalion back in Belgium on 6 February completed the withdrawal of the Canadians from the Army of Occupation.[31] In Belgium the 1st Division occupied an area around Huy, midway between Namur and Liège, while the 2nd Division went to the neighbourhood of Auvelais, ten miles west of Namur.[32] The remaining divisions of the Corps had already moved from the Mons area to other parts of Belgium. In the middle of December the 4th Division had gone to billets in small towns and villages in the Wavre-Jodoigne district, about 25 miles south-east of Brussels. At the end of the year the 3rd Division had marched westward from Nivelles to the Tournai-Lille area, where it remained during most of January.[33]

In Belgium, as in Germany, despite the natural impatience of officers and men to return to their homeland, the time passed quickly, as all were kept busy. Units continued a programme of training, principally to maintain physical fitness; there were educational classes for those who needed them; there was more opportunity for recreation, and all ranks took part in various forms of sport. Contributing tremendously to the morale of the troops were the shows staged by the Dumbells, the popular 3rd Division Concert Party.* Small groups of men were transferred from one unit to another in order to benefit individuals whose home in Canada was at some distance from the dispersal area to which the bulk of their unit would

* The original Dumbells concert party was organized in 1916 from serving soldiers of the 3rd Division by Capt. Merton Plunket, a Y.M.C.A. entertainment officer. They gave their first performance near Poperinghe, and continued to entertain Canadian front-line troops until June 1919. Their repertoire included current music-hall songs, dances, impersonations, and skits based on army life. Their biggest production overseas was a full-dress presentation of H.M.S. *Pinafore,* which played for 32 days to packed houses in Mons after the Armistice.

be going (see below, p. 531). The exacting task of documentation began, it being the responsibility of divisional commanders that every soldier be documented before embarking from France.

When demobilization first began it was expected in Ottawa that Canadian troops on the Continent would sail direct from a French port to Canada. Such an arrangement would allow the British authorities to utilize all transportation facilities in France and the English Channel for demobilizing British armies and repatriating liberated prisoners of war, while continuing to supply the Army of Occupation in Germany. But the great majority of the Canadians had relatives or friends in the United Kingdom whom they wished to see before returning to Canada. Because of the difficult situation regarding transportation it was wholly impracticable to grant them leave to the British Isles, for this would mean providing them with passages in both directions so that they might subsequently sail from France. Accordingly General Currie made strong representations that all Canadian troops should return to England and embark from there to Canada. It was not until 23 January, after the Corps Commander had gone to London and personally put his case before the British Adjutant General and the Secretary of State for War, that the Canadian view prevailed.[34]

During January a Canadian Embarkation Camp, capable of accommodating 6000 men, was established at Le Havre, through which all units and formations of the Corps returned to England. As the senior division, the 1st Division would normally have been first to go, but since neither it nor the 2nd Division could be released from occupational duty, General Currie nominated the 3rd Division to head the Corps move.[35] Units of the division began arriving at Le Havre on 2 February, the P.P.C.L.I. and the R.C.R. being in the vanguard. Clearance was swift and smooth.[36] The Channel crossing took about ten hours, the troops, numbering about 1000 a day, disembarking at Weymouth, in Dorset. Transfer of the 1st Division commenced on 19 March, and the move of the 2nd and 4th Divisions followed in that order.

It was mid-April when the last of the 4th Division's units reached England. The units of the four divisions went to Concentration Camps at Bramshott or Witley. Corps troops, and troops outside the Corps, went to other Concentration Camps—at Seaford, Ripon, Shorncliffe, Purfleet and Sunningdale.[37] Soldiers whose dependents were to accompany them back to Canada concentrated at Buxton. Kirkdale was the centre at which the Medical Services prepared invalids and convalescents for the voyage.

Demobilization

Discussion of the procedure to be followed in demobilization had begun at the end of 1916, and from then to the end of the war there had been two years of careful planning by the Department of Militia and Defence and the Overseas Military Forces of Canada to ensure that when the time came, the return to Canada should be carried out speedily, that the transportation provided

CANADIANS AT VLADIVOSTOK

Members of the Canadian advance party to Siberia march in an Allied peace parade in Vladivostok on 15 November 1918.

OVER THE RHINE

In pouring rain the headquarters staff of the 2nd Division, led by the G.O.C., Major-General Sir Henry Burstall, approaches the saluting base on the Bonn bridge, where General Sir Arthur Currie stands ready to take the salute, 13 December 1918.

THE DUMBELLS

The 3rd Division Concert Party, the all-soldier show that did a sterling job of boosting the morale of Canadian troops in the trenches. In this picture Captain Al Plunkett, brother of the producer, is second from the left; the two female impersonators are, left to right, Privates Alan Murray and Ross Hamilton.

Reproduced by permission of the National Gallery of Canada

"THE *OLYMPIC* WITH RETURNED SOLDIERS"

The *Olympic,* famed troopship of the First World War, carried 70,000 Canadian soldiers safely across the Atlantic to the United Kingdom. Here the artist portrays her arrival at Halifax early in 1919. From a painting by Arthur Lismer, A.R.C.A.

should be as comfortable as possible, and that the troops should receive a "fair deal" in the priority in which they sailed. The Canadian decision to demobilize its overseas troops was taken immediately after the signing of the Armistice, and a week later the Cabinet authorized demobilization of C.E.F. units then in Canada.[38]

The original estimate that at least eighteen months would be required to bring back all overseas troops proved excessive. Two-thirds of the overseas force reached home within five months, and before a year had passed repatriation was virtually completed. On 13 November 1918 the British Ministry of Shipping advised the Canadian Government that ships would be available to move 50,000 troops each month; and in spite of strikes which cancelled individual sailings, shipping was never a real problem. But during the winter of 1918-1919 Canadian railways could handle less than 25,000 troops in a month; and even when disembarkation could take place at the St. Lawrence ports, with a resulting shorter rail haul, the capacity of the vessels available considerably exceeded that of the troop trains. Wisely the Militia Department called for expert assistance from the Minister of Railways and the presidents of the three major railway systems. High officials of the companies formed a railway demobilization committee which was able to increase the monthly carrying capacity to a total of 45,000 troops.[39]

With the exception of the Canadian Corps, which, as we have seen, was returned by units, the principle of "first in, first out" was adopted. The full duration of the war was divided into seventeen three-month periods, with two service groups assigned to each. The first seventeen consisted of married men, the last seventeen of single, the married groups having priority over the single. Thus while the guiding principle for release was the order of enlistment, men who had families dependent on them took precedence over single men.

Each soldier had the right to choose his destination in Canada. In order that each might be demobilized at a point near this destination, twenty-two Dispersal Areas were set up in Canada by subdividing the existing eleven Military Districts. At the concentration camps established in the United Kingdom troops from the continent, as well as those already in England, were regrouped and distributed among twenty-two wings, each matched to a Dispersal Area in Canada. From these camps units of the Canadian Corps entrained direct for the port of embarkation, but for troops outside the Corps a large staging camp was organized at Kinmel Park, thirty miles from Liverpool.[40] Only the 3rd Division (which headed the Corps move) and Corps Troops were not regrouped, but returned to Canada in the units in which they had fought.

At the concentration camps the soldier completed his documentation and received his final medical and dental clearances. His kit deficiencies were replaced, his pay account adjusted, and he filed his application for his War Service Gratuity. He was then granted demobilization leave of from eight days to two weeks. On his return he received his Last Pay Certificate and was posted to an embarkation company to await sailing.[41] In all, the average soldier spent about a month in England. There were some cases when for compassionate reasons individuals returned home in advance of normal sailings. Unfortunately, though these were few, they were a cause of dissatisfaction to soldiers who did not understand the circumstances involved. Furthermore, for considerations of economy and to keep ships filled, certain untrained drafts were sent back to Canada soon after their arrival in the United Kingdom.

These modifications to the policy of "first over, first back", aggravated by disappointment brought about by the cancellation of individual sailings, were at the root of some of the rioting which occurred at several Canadian camps. Men were being brought home as fast as the available ships and trains could move them, but not as rapidly nor in the order in which some desired to come. There was resentment over the fact that the 3rd Division—which included many Military Service Act men with comparatively little service—was given precedence over the other divisions. Unfortunately not enough effort appears to have been given to explain the reasons for the delays, unavoidable as they were.[42] In all, between November 1918 and June 1919, there were thirteen instances of riots or disturbances involving Canadian troops in England.

The most serious of these occurred at Kinmel Park on 4 and 5 March 1919, when dissatisfaction over delays in sailing precipitated rioting by upwards of 800 soldiers which resulted in five men being killed and 23 wounded. Seventy-eight men were arrested, of whom 25 were convicted of mutiny and given sentences varying from 90 days' detention to ten years' penal servitude. At Witley, on the night of 14-15 June, a small group of dissidents started trouble by trying to free some soldiers arrested for persisting in playing Crown and Anchor in defiance of previous regulations curbing widespread gambling in the camp. The disturbance spread to canteens and the civilian area. On the following night the Garrison Theatre was burned and nearly all the civilian shops in the area were destroyed. Similarly at Epsom on 17 June, the indiscipline of a small minority was to blame when a civilian police station was stormed, one policeman was killed and seven others injured.[43]

On 20 June, 1919, Lieut.-General Sir R. E. W. Turner, V.C., Chief of the General Staff, O.M.F.C., published a Special Order of the Day warning all troops of their individual responsibility to quell such disturbances. He made clear in no uncertain terms that the incidents that had occurred were acts of mutiny, and that to remain a passive spectator in such a situation was to side with the mutineers.[44] The order appeared to have a good effect upon the troops; at any rate, there were no further disturbances. The outbreaks had been regrettable, particularly as there seems little doubt that the unrest which produced them might have been considerably lessened had more publicity been given to explaining the reasons for having to modify the plans for demobilization.

Despite attempts by the Canadian Government to discourage the discharge of soldiers in the United Kingdom, 15,182 men signed away their right to free transportation home and remained in England. This total, added to 7136 who had already been discharged there before the Armistice, meant that in all some 22,000 Canadian soldiers entered civil life in the United Kingdom.[45]

In Canada demobilization proceeded smoothly and expeditiously. On the arrival of a troopship at a port of disembarkation, the Clearing Services* welcomed the soldiers and their dependents—an estimated 54,000 relatives accompanied the returning troops—and arranged for their transportation inland to the Dispersal Areas. Immigration officers worked closely with the military authorities, so that an average train, carrying about five hundred troops, could be loaded in thirty minutes. Spirits were high as the trains rolled rapidly westward; those with only one night on board found in the excitement of nearing home little time for sleep. The heartwarming reception given by cheering crowds as the train drew into its destination was repeated in cities all across Canada. In many cases the returning unit would form up outside the railway station for its last march—a proud parade through thronged streets to the place of dismissal. Then came the last order by the Commanding Officer. The men turned right and broke off—and another unit of the Canadian Expeditionary Force passed into history.[47]

The final stages of demobilization were quickly effected. The soldier turned in his arms and equipment (retaining his clothing and steel helmet), had his medical history sheet signed, and received his war badge, his cheque and his discharge certificate. The careful documentation carried out in England and on the ships now paid off, as men passed through the dispersal station at the rate of about six every minute.[48] Every soldier who had been overseas for six months and everyone who had served in Canada for a full year received a gratuity based on his length of service and the rate of pay of his rank. (For overseas service, single privates received payments which varied from $420—for three years' service or more—to $210 for service of less than a year.)[49]

Those veterans who wanted to establish themselves on the land were assisted with long-term loans; in this way the Soldier Settlement Board withdrew more than 30,000 soldiers from the general labour market and directed them into agriculture. For the disabled, there were pensions and medical treatment and opportunities for vocational training. Up to the end of 1919, a total of 91,521 pensions had been granted, amounting to some $22,500,000 annually. At the same time 8000 soldiers were receiving medical treatment, while more than 23,000 were enrolled for vocational training.[50] In such manner did a grateful country attempt in some measure to repay its debt to those who had served and survived.

Conclusion

We have tried in these pages to tell something of the part played by Canadian soldiers in what came to be known as the first of the total wars. The narrative has been made as factual as possible, recording without embellishment or excessive detail their achievements and their disappointments. Yet if the reader finds nothing

* The Clearing Services, organized as a separate command in July 1918, had control of the Clearing Depots (which replaced the earlier Discharge Depots) at Halifax, Quebec, Saint John and Montreal.[46]

to inspire him in this story of as gallant a band as ever bore arms in the service of their country, the fault is the author's alone.

In their four years away from their homeland Canadian troops earned the reputation of being tough, resourceful fighters, well trained and well commanded. There has not been lacking testimony from senior Allied commanders that in the latter part of the war no other formation on the Western Front surpassed the Canadian Corps as a superb fighting machine. "Whenever the Germans found the Canadian Corps coming into the line", wrote Lloyd George in his *War Memoirs,* "they prepared for the worst".[51] Much of its success the Corps owed to the fact that while other British corps headquarters saw divisions frequently enter and leave their command, the Canadian Corps was in the unique position of being able to preserve its composition unchanged. The effect was more than an *esprit* arising from a sense of national pride. The men who made up its units were heartened by the comradeship that comes from shared experiences in the face of difficulty and danger, whether the result be reverse or triumph. Their morale was high, and they endured grievous hardships and bitter setbacks with a dogged optimism and irrepressible cheerfulness. They were further strengthened by the confidence which they had in their leaders—a confidence that they would not suffer needless sacrifice through being committted in unsound tactics that had already been tested and found wanting. Added to these various contributing factors was a careful coordination at the staff level under the Corps Commander's personal direction, the result of which was a unity and sense of mutual reliability in the Corps which enabled it to function as an efficient and well-balanced team.

The Canadian Corps was fortunate in its leaders. To Sir Julian Byng must go much of the credit for laying the foundations of the Corps' *esprit* and its splendid fighting efficiency. The Corps reached the peak of its performance under the command of Sir Arthur Currie, whose organizing genius and unflagging efforts were constantly directed towards improving and maintaining the standard of his troops' performance. Currie was particularly determined that Canadians should be spared unnecessary casualties, and it was ever his object to exploit gun power to the limit for the purpose of saving infantrymen's lives.[52] The Somme had brought home to the British General Staff the need for reorganizing the artillery of the British armies, and the work begun along these lines by General Byng, then commander of the Canadian Corps, had been amplified and extended by his successor. By 1917 the organization of the Canadian Corps Artillery and its ancillary services had reached an advanced stage that artilleries of other formations on the Western Front were unable to match to the end of the War. In awarding Currie much of the credit for this, the former Commander of the Corps Heavy Artillery points to the Corps Commander's sympathetic attitude towards the Canadian gunners, to whom he "gave the necessary means and encouragement to surmount the difficulties which from time to time faced us".[53] There developed a close and comprehensive system of cooperation between the artillery and the infantry. Living up to their motto to shoot the "ultimate round", Canadian gunners were unsparing in their expenditure of ammunition to provide adequate assistance to the assaulting infantry. "I know of no organization in the history of War", wrote General McNaughton in 1929, "which was able to produce such a high ratio in shell to troops, nor any in which the price paid for victory was lower in personnel".[54]

As the war progressed, the sense of national unity which permeated the Canadian Corps became stronger and stronger. At the unit level there was manifested a strong regimental spirit—a determination on the part of the individual not to let the Battalion or one's comrades down which contributed tremendously to the fighting efficiency and high state of discipline of the Corps. Yet more binding than the narrow loyalty to regiment or geographical locality, this broader patriotism, fostered by comradeship, confidence and pride of accomplishment, grew with each successive achievement by Canadian arms. The men of the various units from every province in Canada who fought at Vimy Ridge and at Passchendaele and in the battles of the Hundred Days, fought not as Maritimers, or British Columbians, or representatives of Quebec or Ontario or the Prairie Provinces. They fought as Canadians, and those who returned brought back with them a pride of nationhood that they had not known before.

What was the extent of the national military effort, and the price of the Canadian achievement? The records show that 619,636 Canadian men and women served with Canada's army in the First World War. (Canadian naval forces numbered some ten thousand; and about 24,000, many of whom came from the Canadian Expeditionary Force, fought with the British air forces.) The sacrifice in lives was heavy. Of those who did not return 51,748 Canadian soldiers and nursing sisters were killed in action or died of their wounds. The addition of 7796 who died of disease or injury, or who were accidentally killed, brings the total of fatal army casualties to 59,544 all ranks. For all services the total was 60,661, or 9.28 per cent of all who enlisted.* The total number of Canadian army casualties of all categories in all theatres was 232,494 (see Appendix "C").

Nearly one of every ten Canadians who fought in the First World War did not return to the homeland. More than fifty thousand sleep in the war cemeteries of France and Belgium. Others found their final earthly resting place in graves in the United Kingdom, in the Near East, in North Russia and Siberia, or on native Canadian soil. Some were lost at sea. Few members of the Canadian Expeditionary Force were soldiers by profession; the Force was largely an army of citizen soldiers. From every walk of life they came to render their service, and those who did not return left their country the poorer from their loss.

Yet the contribution of these men and women was great, for they gave of their best—they gave all that they had. In the post-war years, on the November day set apart to honour them, their comrades in arms—a diminishing band as the passage of time took its toll—would gather in communities large and small

* In the Second World War fatal casualties numbered 41,992, or 3.86 per cent of the total enlisted.

across the land to relive together well-remembered experiences of those adventu ous days, and to renew the solemn pledge to their fallen brethren:

> "They shall not grow old, as we that are left grow old;
> Age shall not weary them, nor the years condemn.
> At the going down of the sun and in the morning
> We will remember them."

APPENDICES

APPENDIX "A"

PERSONS HOLDING PRINCIPAL APPOINTMENTS

Officers are shown with rank and decorations as of the day on which they relinquished the appointments concerned. Names of officers who held acting appointments or were detailed temporarily to command are not shown unless they were subsequently confirmed in the appointments or held them for a period of thirty days or more. No distinction is made between honorary, acting and confirmed ranks.

An asterisk denotes officers of the British Army serving with the Canadian forces.

CANADA

Minister of Militia and Defence

Lt.-Gen. The Hon. Sir Sam Hughes, K.C.B.	10 Oct. 11 — 14 Nov. 16
Hon. Sir A. E. Kemp, K.C.M.G.	23 Nov. 16 — 11 Oct. 17
Maj.-Gen. The Hon. S. C. Mewburn, C.M.G.	12 Oct. 17 — 1 Jan. 20

Deputy Minister of Militia and Defence

Maj.-Gen. Sir E. Fiset, K.C.M.G., D.S.O.	22 Dec. 06 — 31 Mar. 24

Chief of the General Staff

*Maj.-Gen. W. G. Gwatkin, C.B., C.M.G.	1 Nov. 13 — 14 Nov. 19

Adjutant General

Brig.-Gen. V. A. S. Williams†	1 Dec. 12 — 31 Dec. 18
Maj.-Gen. W. E. Hodgins (acting)	1 Jan. 15 — 7 Sep. 17
Maj.-Gen. S. C. Mewburn, C.M.G. (acting)	8 Sep. 15 — 11 Oct. 17
Maj.-Gen. R. J. Gwynne (acting)	17 Oct. 17 — 31 Dec. 17
Maj.-Gen. E. C. Ashton, C.M.G. (acting to 1 Jan. 19)	1 Jan. 18 — 17 Aug. 20

Quartermaster General

Maj.-Gen. Sir D. A. Macdonald, K.C.M.G., I.S.O.	15 Nov. 04 — 31 Oct. 17
Maj.-Gen. J. L. Biggar, C.M.G.	1 Nov. 17 — 30 Jun. 20

Master General of the Ordnance

Maj.-Gen. T. Benson	1 Mar. 13 — 31 Mar. 16
*Maj.-Gen. H. M. Elliot, C.M.G.	1 Apr. 16 — 31 Mar. 20

† Although not employed as such from 20 Aug. 14, Williams held the appointment until 31 Dec. 18.

UNITED KINGDOM

Minister of Overseas Military Forces of Canada†

Hon. Sir G. H. Perley, K.C.M.G.	31 Oct. 16 — 11 Oct. 17
Hon. Sir A. E. Kemp, K.C.M.G.	12 Oct. 17 — 29 Feb. 20‡

Deputy Minister, Overseas Military Forces of Canada

Col. W. Gow	29 Jan. 17 — 28 Oct. 18
Col. G. S. Harrington, V.D.	29 Oct. 18 — 29 Feb. 20

Chief of the General Staff§

Lt.-Gen. Sir R. E. W. Turner, V.C., K.C.B., K.C.M.G., D.S.O.	5 Dec. 16 — 31 Jul. 19
Maj.-Gen. J. H. MacBrien, C.B., C.M.G., D.S.O.	1 Aug. 19 — 29 Feb. 20

Adjutant General

Maj.-Gen. P. E. Thacker, C.B., C.M.G.	5 Dec. 16 — 15 Aug. 19

Quartermaster General

Brig.-Gen. A. D. McRae, C.B.	4 Dec. 16 — 18 Feb. 18
Maj.-Gen. D. M. Hogarth	19 Feb. 18 — 12 Dec. 19

Director General of Medical Services

Maj.-Gen. G. C. Jones, C.M.G.	21 Sep. 14 — 12 Oct. 16
Col. H. A. Bruce	13 Oct. 16 — 30 Dec. 16
Maj.-Gen. G. C. Jones, C.M.G.	31 Dec. 16 — 8 Feb. 17
Maj.-Gen. G. La F. Foster, C.B.	9 Feb. 17 — 29 Feb. 20

CANADIAN CORPS

General Officer Commanding

*Lt.-Gen. Sir E. A. H. Alderson, K.C.B.	13 Sep. 15 — 28 May 16
*Lt.-Gen. Hon. Sir J. H. G. Byng, K.C.B., K.C.M.G., M.V.O.	29 May 16 — 8 Jun. 17
Lt.-Gen. Sir A. W. Currie, G.C.M.G., K.C.B.	9 Jun. 17 — 8 Aug. 19

Brigadier-General, General Staff

*Brig.-Gen. C. H. Harington, D.S.O.	13 Sep. 15 — 4 Jun. 16
*Brig.-Gen. P. P. de B. Radcliffe, C.B., D.S.O.	5 Jun. 16 — 7 Apr. 18
*Brig.-Gen. N. W. Webber, C.M.G., D.S.O.	8 Apr. 18 — 27 Oct. 18
*Brig.-Gen. R. J. F. Hayter, C.B., C.M.G., D.S.O.	28 Oct. 18 — 15 Aug. 19

Deputy Adjutant and Quartermaster General

*Brig.-Gen. T. B. Wood, C.M.G.	14 Sep. 15 — 15 Jun. 16
*Brig.-Gen. G. J. Farmar, C.B., C.M.G.	19 Jun. 16 — 26 Feb. 19
Brig.-Gen. E. de B. Panet, C.M.G., D.S.O.	27 Feb. 19 — 11 Jul. 19

General Officer Commanding Royal Artillery

Brig.-Gen. H. E. Burstall, C.B.	13 Sep. 15 — 14 Dec. 16
Maj.-Gen. Sir E. W. B. Morrison, K.C.M.G., C.B., D.S.O.	18 Dec. 16 — 17 May 19

Chief Engineer

Brig.-Gen. C. J. Armstrong, C.M.G.	13 Sep. 15 — 6 Mar. 16
Maj.-Gen. W. B. Lindsay, C.B., C.M.G., D.S.O.	7 Mar. 16 — 11 Jul. 19

General Officer Commanding, Canadian Machine Gun Corps

Brig.-Gen. R. Brutinel, C.B., C.M.G., D.S.O.	28 Oct. 16 — 18 Apr. 19

† Principal appointments in the United Kingdom prior to 31 October 1916 are given in Chapter VII.

‡ H.Q., O.M.F.C., London, closed this date.

§ "General Officer Commanding, Canadian Forces in the British Isles" from December 1916 to April 1918.

General Officer Commanding, Heavy Artillery
*Brig.-Gen. A. C. Currie, C.M.G. 8 Apr. 16 — 22 Jan. 17
*Brig.-Gen. R. H. Massie, C.B., C.M.G. 23 Jan. 17 — 21 Oct. 18
Brig.-Gen. A. G. L. McNaughton, C.M.G., D.S.O. 22 Oct. 18 — 4 May 19

5th Divisional Artillery
Brig.-Gen. W. O. H. Dodds, C.M.G. 23 Jan. 17 — 26 May 17
Lt.-Col. A. T. Ogilvie 27 May 17 — 1 Jul. 17
Brig.-Gen. W. O. H. Dodds, C.M.G., D.S.O. 2 Jul. 17 — 30 Dec. 18
Lt.-Col. A. T. Ogilvie, D.S.O. 31 Dec. 18 — 15 Mar. 19
Brig.-Gen. G. H. Ralston, D.S.O. 16 Mar. 19 — 10 Jun. 19

1st CANADIAN DIVISION

General Officer Commanding
*Lt.-Gen. E. A. H. Alderson, C.B. 29 Sep. 14 — 12 Sep. 15
Maj.-Gen. A. W. Currie, C.B. 13 Sep. 15 — 8 Jun. 17
Maj.-Gen. Sir A. C. Macdonell, K.C.B., C.M.G., D.S.O. 9 Jun. 17 — 22 May 19

1st Infantry Brigade
Brig.-Gen. M. S. Mercer, C.B. 29 Sep. 14 — 21 Nov. 15
Brig.-Gen. G. B. Hughes, C.M.G., D.S.O. 25 Nov. 15 — 13 Feb. 17
Brig.-Gen. W. A. Griesbach, C.B., C.M.G., D.S.O. 14 Feb. 17 — 25 Feb. 19
Brig.-Gen. G. E. McCuaig, C.M.G., D.S.O. 26 Feb. 19 — 14 Apr. 19

2nd Infantry Brigade
Brig.-Gen. A. W. Currie, C.B. 29 Sep. 14 — 12 Sep. 15
*Brig.-Gen. L. J. Lipsett, C.M.G. 14 Sep. 15 — 15 Jun. 16
Brig.-Gen. F. O. W. Loomis, C.M.G., D.S.O. 4 Jul. 16 — 31 Dec. 17
Brig.-Gen. J. F. L. Embury, C.M.G. 1 Jan. 18 — 15 Mar. 18
Brig.-Gen. F. O. W. Loomis, C.B. C.M.G., D.S.O. 16 Mar. 18 — 12 Sep. 18
Brig.-Gen. R. P. Clark, C.M.G., D.S.O., M.C. 6 Oct. 18 — 12 May 19

3rd Infantry Brigade
Brig.-Gen. R. E. W. Turner, V.C., C.B., D.S.O. 29 Sep. 14 — 11 Aug. 15
Brig.-Gen. R. G. E. Leckie, C.M.G. 12 Aug. 15 — 17 Feb. 16
Brig.-Gen. G. S. Tuxford, C.B., C.M.G., D.S.O. 13 Mar. 16 — 22 May 19

1st Divisional Artillery
Brig.-Gen. H. E. Burstall, C.B. 29 Sep. 14 — 12 Sep. 15
Brig.-Gen. H. C. Thacker, C.B., C.M.G., D.S.O. 13 Sep. 15 — 22 May 19

2nd CANADIAN DIVISION

General Officer Commanding
Maj.-Gen. S. B. Steele, C.B., M.V.O. 25 May 15 — 16 Aug. 15
Maj.-Gen. R. E. W. Turner, V.C., C.B., D.S.O. 17 Aug. 15 — 26 Nov. 16
Maj.-Gen. Sir H. E. Burstall, K.C.B., C.M.G. 15 Dec. 16 — 22 May 19

4th Infantry Brigade
*Brig.-Gen. L. G. F. M. Lord Brooke, C.M.G., M.V.O. 25 Jun. 15 — 16 Nov. 15
Brig.-Gen. R. Rennie, C.B., C.M.G., M.V.O., D.S.O. 17 Nov. 15 — 11 Sep. 18
Brig.-Gen. G. E. McCuaig, C.M.G., D.S.O. 14 Sep. 18 — 25 Feb. 19
Brig.-Gen. R. Rennie, C.B., C.M.G., M.V.O., D.S.O. 26 Feb. 19 — 12 May 19

5th Infantry Brigade
Brig.-Gen. D. Watson, C.B. 1 Sep. 15 — 21 Apr. 16
Brig.-Gen. A. H. Macdonell, C.M.G., D.S.O. 22 Mar. 16 — 22 Jul. 17
Brig.-Gen. J. M. Ross, D.S.O. 23 Jul. 17 — 9 Aug. 18
Brig.-Gen. T. L. Tremblay, C.M.G., D.S.O. 10 Aug. 18 — 9 May 19

6th Infantry Brigade

Brig.-Gen. H. D. B. Ketchen, C.M.G.	25 Jun. 15 — 20 Apr. 18
Brig.-Gen. A. H. Bell, C.M.G., D.S.O.	21 Apr. 18 — 1 Oct. 18
Brig.-Gen. A. Ross, C.M.G., D.S.O.	2 Oct. 18 — 18 May 19

2nd Divisional Artillery

Brig.-Gen. H. C. Thacker	25 Jun. 15 — 27 Sep. 15
Brig.-Gen. E. W. B. Morrison, D.S.O.	2 Oct. 15 — 17 Dec. 16
Brig.-Gen. H. A. Panet, C.B., C.M.G., D.S.O.	18 Dec. 16 — 25 Jun. 19

3RD CANADIAN DIVISION

General Officer Commanding

Maj.-Gen. M. S. Mercer, C.B.	24 Dec. 15 — 2 Jun. 16
*Maj.-Gen. L. J. Lipsett, C.B., C.M.G.	16 Jun. 16 — 12 Sep. 18
Maj.-Gen. F. O. W. Loomis, C.B., C.M.G., D.S.O.	13 Sep. 18 — 11 Apr. 19

7th Infantry Brigade

Brig.-Gen. A. C. Macdonell, C.M.G., D.S.O.	22 Dec. 15 — 17 Feb. 16
Brig.-Gen. F. O. W. Loomis, D.S.O.	16 Mar. 16 — 5 May 16
Brig.-Gen. A. C. Macdonell, C.B., C.M.G., D.S.O.	6 May 16 — 8 Jun. 17
Brig.-Gen. H. M. Dyer, C.M.G., D.S.O.	29 Jun. 17 — 11 Sep. 18
Brig.-Gen. J. A. Clark, C.M.G., D.S.O.	12 Sep. 18 — 30 Apr. 19

8th Infantry Brigade

Brig.-Gen. V. A. S. Williams	28 Dec. 15 — 2 Jun. 16
Brig.-Gen. J. H. Elmsley, C.M.G., D.S.O.	19 Jun. 16 — 25 May 18
Brig.-Gen. D. C. Draper, C.M.G., D.S.O.	26 May 18 — 11 Apr. 19

9th Infantry Brigade

Brig.-Gen. F. W. Hill, C.M.G., D.S.O.	7 Jan. 16 — 25 May 18
Brig.-Gen. D. M. Ormond, C.M.G., D.S.O.	26 May 18 — 19 Feb. 19

3rd Divisional Artillery

Brig.-Gen. J. H. Mitchell, D.S.O.	20 Jun. 16 — 18 Nov. 17
Lt.-Col. H. G. Carscallen, D.S.O.	20 Nov. 17 — 28 Dec. 17
Brig.-Gen. J. S. Stewart, C.M.G., D.S.O.	29 Dec. 17 — 5 Jan. 19
Brig.-Gen. G. H. Ralston, D.S.O.	6 Jan. 19 — 11 Mar. 19

4TH CANADIAN DIVISION

General Officer Commanding

Maj.-Gen. Sir D. Watson, K.C.B., C.M.G.	25 Apr. 16 — 23 Jun. 19

10th Infantry Brigade

Brig.-Gen. W. St. P. Hughes, D.S.O.	16 Jun. 16 — 17 Jan. 17
Brig.-Gen. E. Hilliam, C.M.G., D.S.O.	18 Jan. 17 — 11 Nov. 17
*Brig.-Gen. R. J. F. Hayter, C.M.G., D.S.O.	4 Dec. 17 — 27 Oct. 18
Brig.-Gen. J. M. Ross, C.M.G., D.S.O.	28 Oct. 18 — 23 Jan. 19

11th Infantry Brigade

Brig.-Gen. F. O. W. Loomis, D.S.O.	16 May 16 — 3 Jul. 16
Brig.-Gen. V. W. Odlum, C.B., C.M.G., D.S.O.	4 Jul. 16 — 23 Jun. 19

12th Infantry Brigade

*Brig.-Gen. L. G. F. M. Lord Brooke, C.M.G., M.V.O.	11 May 16 — 11 Sep. 16
Brig.-Gen. J. H. MacBrien, C.M.G., D.S.O.	20 Sep. 16 — 12 Dec. 18
Brig.-Gen. J. Kirkcaldy, C.M.G., D.S.O.	13 Dec. 18 — 5 Jun. 19

4th Divisional Artillery

Brig.-Gen. C. H. Maclaren, D.S.O.	20 Jun. 17 — 7 Nov. 17
Brig.-Gen. W. B. M. King, C.M.G., D.S.O.	27 Nov. 17 — 2 Jun. 19

SERVING OUTSIDE CANADIAN CORPS

Canadian Cavalry Brigade

*Brig.-Gen. The Rt. Hon. J. E. B. Seely, C.B., D.S.O.	28 Jan. 15 — 19 Jun. 17
Lt.-Col. R. W. Paterson	23 Jun. 17 — 22 Aug. 17
*Brig.-Gen. The Rt. Hon. J. E. B. Seely, C.B., C.M.G., D.S.O.	23 Aug. 17 — 20 May 18
Brig.-Gen. R. W. Paterson, C.M.G., D.S.O.	21 May 18 — 20 May 19

APPENDIX "B"

CANADIAN UNITS IN FRANCE AND BELGIUM, NOVEMBER 1918

This list is compiled largely from an Order of Battle attached to Headquarters Canadian Corps Circular Letter A.118-3, 22 November 1918. The complete roll is too long to be reproduced here. It has been necessary to omit formation headquarters and numerous small units, although all made important contributions to efficiency.

ARMY, CORPS, ETC., TROOPS

Cavalry

- Royal Canadian Dragoons
- Lord Strathcona's Horse (Royal Canadians)
- Fort Garry Horse
- Canadian Light Horse
- R.N.W.M.P. Squadron

Artillery

- R.C.H.A. Brigade
- 8th Army Brigade C.F.A.
  - 24th Field Battery
  - 30th Field Battery
  - 32nd Field Battery
  - 43rd Howitzer Battery
  - 8th Army Bde. Ammunition Column
- "E" Anti-Aircraft Battery
- Corps Heavy Artillery
- 1st Brigade C.G.A.
  - 1st Siege Battery
  - 3rd Siege Battery
  - 7th Siege Battery
  - 9th Siege Battery
- 2nd Brigade C.G.A.
  - 1st Heavy Battery
  - 2nd Heavy Battery
  - 2nd Siege Battery
  - 4th Siege Battery
  - 5th Siege Battery
  - 6th Siege Battery
- 3rd Brigade C.G.A.
  - 8th Siege Battery
  - 10th Siege Battery
  - 11th Siege Battery
  - 12th Siege Battery
- 5th Divisional Artillery
  - 13th Brigade C.F.A.
    - 52nd Field Battery
    - 53rd Field Battery
    - 55th Field Battery
    - 51st Howitzer Battery
  - 14th Brigade C.F.A.
    - 60th Field Battery
    - 61st Field Battery
    - 66th Field Battery
    - 58th Howitzer Battery
  - 5th Div. Ammunition Column

Engineers

- 1st to 5th Army Troops Companies
- Anti-Aircraft Searchlight Company
- 3rd Tunnelling Company
- Corps Survey Section
- 1st Tramways Company
- 2nd Tramways Company

Machine Gun Corps

- 1st Motor M.G. Brigade
- 2nd Motor M.G. Brigade

Army Service Corps

- Corps Troops M.T. Company
- 1st to 4th Div. M.T. Companies
- Engineers M.T. Company
- Motor Machine Gun M.T. Company
- 5th Div. Artillery M.T. Detachment
- 5th Divisional Train Detachment

Medical Corps

- Nos. 1 to 3 General Hospitals
- Nos. 6 to 8 General Hospitals
- No. 2 Stationary Hospital
- No. 3 Stationary Hospital
- Nos. 7 to 10 Stationary Hospitals
- Forestry Corps Hospitals (6)
- Nos. 1 to 4 Casualty Clearing Stations
- No. 7 (Cavalry) Field Ambulance
- No. 14 Field Ambulance

Railway Troops

- Canadian Overseas Railway Construction Corps
- 1st to 13th Battalions

Labour

- 1st to 4th Infantry Works Coys.
- 5th to 9th Area Employment Coys.

Miscellaneous

- Canadian Cyclist Battalion
- Corps Signal Company
- Corps Reinforcement Camp
- Corps Schools
- Forestry Companies (58)

COMPOSITION OF DIVISIONS

1st Division

1st Brigade C.F.A.
- 1st Field Battery
- 3rd Field Battery
- 4th Field Battery
- 2nd Howitzer Battery

2nd Brigade C.F.A.
- 5th Field Battery
- 6th Field Battery
- 7th Field Battery
- 48th Howitzer Battery

1st Div. Ammunition Column

1st Brigade Cdn. Engineers
- 1st, 2nd and 3rd Battalions

1st Div. Signal Company

1st Infantry Brigade
- 1st Battalion
- 2nd Battalion
- 3rd Battalion
- 4th Battalion
- 1st Trench Mortar Battery

2nd Infantry Brigade
- 5th Battalion
- 7th Battalion
- 8th Battalion
- 10th Battalion
- 2nd Trench Mortar Battery

3rd Infantry Brigade
- 13th Battalion
- 14th Battalion
- 15th Battalion
- 16th Battalion
- 3rd Trench Mortar Battery

1st Bn. Cdn. Machine Gun Corps

1st Divisional Train C.A.S.C.

Nos. 1, 2 and 3 Field Ambulances

1st Div. Employment Company

2nd Division

5th Brigade C.F.A.
- 17th Field Battery
- 18th Field Battery
- 20th Field Battery
- 23rd Howitzer Battery

6th Brigade C.F.A.
- 15th Field Battery
- 16th Field Battery
- 25th Field Battery
- 22nd Howitzer Battery

2nd Div. Ammunition Column

2nd Bde. Cdn. Engineers
- 4th, 5th and 6th Battalions

2nd Div. Signal Company

4th Infantry Brigade
- 18th Battalion
- 19th Battalion
- 20th Battalion
- 21st Battalion
- 4th Trench Mortar Battery

5th Infantry Brigade
- 22nd Battalion
- 24th Battalion
- 25th Battalion
- 26th Battalion
- 5th Trench Mortar Battery

6th Infantry Brigade
- 27th Battalion
- 28th Battalion
- 29th Battalion
- 31st Battalion
- 6th Trench Mortar Battery

2nd Bn. Cdn. Machine Gun Corps

2nd Divisional Train C.A.S.C.

Nos. 4, 5 and 6 Field Ambulances

2nd Div. Employment Company

3rd Division

9th Brigade C.F.A.
- 31st Field Battery
- 33rd Field Battery
- 45th Field Battery
- 36th Howitzer Battery

10th Brigade C.F.A.
- 38th Field Battery
- 39th Field Battery
- 40th Field Battery
- 35th Howitzer Battery

3rd Div. Ammunition Column

3rd Bde. Cdn. Engineers
- 7th, 8th and 9th Battalions

3rd Div. Signal Company

7th Infantry Brigade
- The Royal Canadian Regiment
- Princess Patricia's Canadian Light Infantry
- 42nd Battalion
- 49th Battalion
- 7th Trench Mortar Battery

8th Infantry Brigade
- 1st Canadian Mounted Rifles Bn.
- 2nd Canadian Mounted Rifles Bn.
- 4th Canadian Mounted Rifles Bn.
- 5th Canadian Mounted Rifles Bn.
- 8th Trench Mortar Battery

9th Infantry Brigade
- 43rd Battalion
- 52nd Battalion
- 58th Battalion
- 116th Battalion
- 9th Trench Mortar Battery

3rd Bn. Cdn. Machine Gun Corps

3rd Divisional Train C.A.S.C.

Nos. 8, 9 and 10 Field Ambulances

3rd Div. Employment Company

4th Division

3rd Brigade C.F.A.
- 10th Field Battery
- 11th Field Battery
- 12th Field Battery
- 9th Howitzer Battery

4th Brigade C.F.A.
- 13th Field Battery
- 19th Field Battery
- 27th Field Battery
- 21st Howitzer Battery

4th Div. Ammunition Column

4th Bde. Cdn. Engineers
- 10th, 11th and 12th Battalions

4th Div. Signal Company

10th Infantry Brigade
- 44th Battalion
- 46th Battalion
- 47th Battalion
- 50th Battalion
- 10th Trench Mortar Battery

11th Infantry Brigade
- 54th Battalion
- 75th Battalion
- 87th Battalion
- 102nd Battalion
- 11th Trench Mortar Battery

12th Infantry Brigade
- 38th Battalion
- 72nd Battalion
- 78th Battalion
- 85th Battalion
- 12th Trench Mortar Battery

4th Bn. Cdn. Machine Gun Corps

4th Divisional Train C.A.S.C.

Nos. 11, 12 and 13 Field Ambulances

4th Div. Employment Company

APPENDIX "C"

APPOINTMENTS, ENLISTMENTS, STRENGTH AND CASUALTIES—CANADIAN EXPEDITIONARY FORCE

(Four Tables)

TABLE 1: APPOINTMENTS AND ENLISTMENTS BY MONTHS, 1914–1920

Month	1914			1915			1916			1917			1918*			1919			1920		
	Off	N/S	ORs	Off	N/S	ORs	Off	N/S	ORs	Off	N/S	ORs	Off	N/S	ORs	Off	N/S	ORs	Off	N/S	ORs
January	—	—	—	324	43	9,363	1,002	108	28,185	238	66	6,690	194	44	19,099	20	4	710	—	—	53
February	—	—	—	460	43	8,211	1,024	75	26,638	186	19	5,311	105	68	8,910	22	15	601	1	—	27
March	—	—	—	318	41	9,002	932	21	33,960	143	159	4,886	67	41	9,505	10	1	730	1	—	8
April	—	—	—	321	225	7,094	681	88	20,200	143	126	4,492	216	109	14,436	10	—	478	—	—	13
May	—	—	—	310	53	7,539	735	52	14,572	152	166	6,211	422	31	38,336	15	1	391	—	—	5
June	—	—	—	436	49	10,465	502	58	10,059	89	42	5,298	642	71	24,041	5	2	413	—	—	—
July	—	—	—	465	75	14,819	364	64	7,961	93	38	3,515	173	73	17,305	—	2	320	—	—	—
August	1,117	9	20,838	494	16	17,357	319	73	6,597	94	18	2,902	91	27	10,289	2	—	184	—	—	—
September	454	95	9,531	464	29	16,229	318	22	5,717	102	11	3,559	95	16	5,441	—	—	326	—	—	—
October	132	10	5,152	427	40	12,410	255	27	5,262	108	36	4,814	178	9	24,506	4	—	218	—	—	—
November	449	2	13,015	711	29	17,282	259	49	5,540	84	83	9,284	68	15	1,375	—	—	114	—	—	—
December	290	2	8,048	1,102	32	22,581	209	61	4,930	90	46	4,317	25	4	394	—	—	56	—	—	—
TOTALS	2,442	118	56,584	5,832	675	152,352	6,600	698	169,621	1,522	810	61,279	2,276	528	153,637	88	25	4,541	2	—	106
	59,144			158,859			176,919			63,611			156,441			4,554			108		
GRAND TOTAL: 1914 to 1920																18,762	2,854	598,020			
																619,636					

*Includes 142,588 men enlisted under the provisions of the Military Service Act.

TABLE 2: STRENGTH AT END OF EACH MONTH FROM 30 SEPTEMBER 1914 TO 30 NOVEMBER 1919

Months	1914			1915			1916			1917			1918			1919		
	Officers	Other Ranks	All Ranks	Officers	Other Ranks	All Ranks	Officers	Other Ranks	All Ranks	Officers	Other Ranks	All Ranks	Officers	Other Ranks	All Ranks	Officers	Other Ranks	All Ranks
January	—	—	—	2,815	63,151	65,966	10,226	208,034	218,260	16,790	286,359	303,149	18,539	301,650	320,189	18,401	291,365	309,766
February	—	—	—	3,299	70,191	73,490	11,364	231,704	243,068	17,181	286,977	304,158	18,485	304,721	323,206	17,404	260,994	278,398
March	—	—	—	3,631	77,564	81,195	12,343	261,851	274,194	17,458	287,127	304,585	18,485	307,773	326,258	15,684	212,608	228,292
April	—	—	—	4,110	81,352	85,462	13,115	277,009	290,124	17,802	283,494	301,296	18,954	314,331	333,285	13,680	171,152	184,832
May	—	—	—	4,445	86,454	90,899	13,916	285,936	299,852	17,815	285,369	303,184	19,228	344,757	363,985	11,334	120,089	131,423
June	—	—	—	4,926	95,321	100,247	14,424	288,087	302,511	17,872	287,160	305,032	19,851	359,833	379,684	9,301	84,106	93,407
July	—	—	—	5,504	108,659	114,163	14,897	290,026	304,923	18,231	287,402	305,633	19,861	368,177	388,038	6,759	46,279	53,038
August	Not available			6,059	124,218	130,277	15,450	290,793	306,243	18,179	285,035	303,214	19,895	362,280	382,175	4,979	27,213	32,192
September	1,674	30,289	31,963	6,572	138,330	144,902	15,556	286,055	301,611	18,387	285,220	303,607	19,677	354,334	374,011	3,281	17,133	20,414
October	1,816	35,385	37,201	7,055	147,828	154,883	15,718	282,894	298,612	18,273	285,454	303,727	19,629	351,592	371,221	2,436	12,441	14,877
November	2,251	47,905	50,156	7,799	162,674	170,473	16,162	282,787	298,949	18,213	288,577	306,790	20,048	342,726	362,774	1,996	9,569	11,565
December	2,481	55,033	57,514	8,961	182,693	191,654	16,421	283,516	299,937	18,182	288,947	307,129	19,403	323,245	342,648	—	—	—

TABLE 3: FATAL CASUALTIES BY THEATRE AND CATEGORY 1914–1920

THEATRE OF OPERATIONS	DEATHS DUE TO ENEMY ACTION										Died of Disease or Injury, Killed in Accidents, etc.		TOTAL DEATHS ALL CAUSES	
	Killed in Action		Missing and Presumed Dead		Died of Wounds		Died at Sea		TOTAL					
	Off	ORs	Off	ORs	Off	ORs	Off	O	Off	ORs	Off	ORs	Off	ORs
France and Belgium	1,775	33,148	156	4,273	583*	11,411*	—	—	2,514	48,796	91	1,815	2,605	50,611
Prisoners of War	—	—	—	—	18	247	—	—	18	247	5	98	23	345
United Kingdom	—	30†	—	—	—	—	—	—	—	30	197	2,490	197	2,520
Near East (Palestine, etc.)	2	—	1	—	—	—	—	—	3	—	4	12	7	12
North Russia	—	6	—	—	1	—	—	—	1	6	—	1	1	7
Siberia	—	—	—	—	—	—	—	—	—	—	1	15	1	15
At Sea	—	—	—	—	—	—	28	ı05	28	105	6	142	34	247
Canada, Bermuda, St. Lucia	—	—	—	—	—	—	—	—	—	—	121	2,798	121	2,798
TOTALS BY CATEGORY	1,777	33,148	157	4,273	602	11,658	28	105	2,564	49,184	425	7,371	2,989	56,555
													59,544 All Ranks	

*Includes those dying of wounds after transfer to United Kingdom (37 officers, 833 other ranks) and Canada (3 officers, 47 other ranks).

†As a result of enemy air raids.

TABLE 4: NON-FATAL CASUALTIES BY ARM OF SERVICE AND CATEGORY 1914–1920

ARM OF SERVICE	NON-FATAL BATTLE CASUALTIES									Ordinary Non-Fatal Casualties: Injuries, etc.			TOTAL NON-FATAL CASUALTIES		
	Wounded			Gassed			TOTAL								
	Off	ORs	Total	Off	ORs	Total	Off	ORs	Total	Off	ORs	Total	Off	ORs	Total
Infantry	4,223	102,593	106,816	206	6,784	6,990	4,429	109,377	113,806	345	11,090	11,435	4,774	120,467	125,241
Cavalry	78	1,338	1,416	2	50	52	80	1,388	1,468	23	570	593	103	1,958	2,061
Artillery	392	5,876	6,268	57	1,723	1,780	449	7,599	8,048	65	2,944	3,009	514	10,543	11,057
Engineers	233	4,428	4,661	29	1,062	1,091	262	5,490	5,752	62	1,480	1,542	324	6,970	7,294
Signals	14	227	241	2	76	78	16	303	319	9	203	212	25	506	531
Machine Gun	204	3,519	3,723	38	762	800	242	4,281	4,523	15	653	668	257	4,934	5,191
Army Service Corps	9	363	372	—	76	76	9	439	448	19	823	842	28	1,262	1,290
Army Medical Corps	113	949	1,062	11	248	259	124	1,197	1,321	44	445	489	168	1,642	1,810
Railway Troops	43	1,087	1,130	5	247	252	48	1,334	1,382	23	1,064	1,087	71	2,398	2,469
Forestry Corps	3	20	23	—	3	3	3	23	26	18	754	772	21	777	798
Chaplain Service	23	—	23	3	—	3	26	—	26	12	—	12	38	—	38
Cyclists	8	165	173	—	52	52	8	217	225	3	65	68	11	282	293
Works and Employment Coys.	5	392	397	—	63	63	5	455	460	—	396	396	5	851	856
Miscellaneous	141	47	188	3	6	9	144	53	197	92	254	346	236	307	543
TOTAL FRANCE AND BELGIUM	5,489	121,004	126,493	356	11,152	11,508	5,845	132,156	138,001	730	20,741	21,471	6,575	152,897	159,472
OTHER THEATRES	7	94	101	5	59	64	12	153	165	549	12,764	13,313	561	12,917	13,478
TOTAL ALL THEATRES	5,496	121,098	126,594	361	11,211	11,572	5,857	132,309	138,166	1,279	33,505	34,784	7,136	165,814	172,950

APPENDIX "D"

INFANTRY BATTALIONS WHICH SERVED WITH THE CANADIAN CORPS, SHOWING SUBSIDIARY TITLES (WHERE APPLICABLE) AND PLACES OF MOBILIZATION OR ORGANIZATION

Battalion	Subsidiary Title	Place of Mobilization or Organization
1st	(Western Ontario)	Valcartier Camp, P.Q.
2nd	(Eastern Ontario)	Valcartier Camp, P.Q.
3rd	(Toronto Regiment)	Valcartier Camp, P.Q.
4th	(Central Ontario)	Valcartier Camp, P.Q.
5th	(Western Cavalry)	Valcartier Camp, P.Q,
7th	(1st British Columbia Regiment)	Valcartier Camp, P.Q.
8th	(90th Rifles)	Valcartier Camp, P.Q.
10th	(Canadians)	Valcartier Camp, P.Q.
13th	(Royal Highlanders of Canada)	Valcartier Camp, P.Q.
14th	(Royal Montreal Regiment)	Valcartier Camp, P.Q.
15th	(48th Highlanders of Canada)	Valcartier Camp, P.Q.
16th	(The Canadian Scottish)	Valcartier Camp, P.Q.
18th	(Western Ontario)	London, Ont.
19th	(Central Ontario)	Toronto, Ont.
20th	(Central Ontario)	Toronto, Ont.
21st	(Eastern Ontario)	Kingston, Ont.
22nd	(French Canadian)	St. Jean, P.Q.
24th	(Victoria Rifles of Canada)	Montreal, P.Q.
25th	(Nova Scotia Rifles)	Halifax, N.S.
26th	(New Brunswick)	Saint John, N.B.
27th	(City of Winnipeg)	Winnipeg, Man.
28th	(Northwest)	Winnipeg, Man.
29th	(Vancouver)	Vancouver, B.C.
31st	(Alberta)	Calgary, Alta.
38th	(Ottawa)	Ottawa, Ont.

INFANTRY BATTALIONS WHICH SERVED WITH THE CANADIAN CORPS, SHOWING SUBSIDIARY TITLES (WHERE APPLICABLE) AND PLACES OF MOBILIZATION OR ORGANIZATION—*Concluded*

Battalion	Subsidiary Title	Place of Mobilization or Organization
42nd	(Royal Highlanders of Canada)	Montreal, P.Q.
43rd	(Cameron Highlanders of Canada)	Winnipeg, Man.
44th	(Manitoba)[1]	Winnipeg, Man.
46th	(South Saskatchewan)	Moose Jaw, Sask.
47th	(British Columbia)[2]	New Westminster, B.C.
49th	(Edmonton Regiment)	Edmonton, Alta.
50th	(Calgary)	Calgary, Alta.
52nd	(New Ontario)	Port Arthur, Ont.
54th	(Kootenay)[3]	Vernon, B.C.
58th	(Central Ontario)	Niagara-on-the-Lake, Ont.
60th	(Victoria Rifles of Canada)[4]	Montreal, P.Q.
72nd	(Seaforth Highlanders of Canada)	Vancouver, B.C.
73rd	(Royal Highlanders of Canada)[5]	Montreal, P.Q.
75th	(Mississauga)	Toronto, Ont.
78th	(Winnipeg Grenadiers)	Winnipeg, Man.
85th	(Nova Scotia Highlanders)	Halifax, N.S.
87th	(Canadian Grenadier Guards)	Montreal, P.Q.
102nd	(North British Columbians)[6]	Comox, B.C.
116th	(Ontario County)	Uxbridge, Ont.
The Royal Canadian Regiment		Halifax, N.S.
Princess Patricia's Canadian Light Infantry		Ottawa, Ont.
1st Bn. Canadian Mounted Rifles		................*See* note 7
2nd Bn. Canadian Mounted Rifles		
4th Bn. Canadian Mounted Rifles		
5th Bn. Canadian Mounted Rifles		

Notes: [1] Redesignated "44th (New Brunswick) Battalion", August 1918.

[2] Redesignated "47th (Western Ontario) Battalion", February 1918.

[3] Redesignated "54th (Central Ontario) Battalion", August 1917.

[4] Replaced by 116th Bn. in April 1917; men of the 60th Bn. were transferred to other battalions serving in the field.

[5] Disbanded in April 1917 and replaced by 85th Bn; men of the 73rd Bn. were transferred to other battalions serving in the field.

[6] Redesignated "102nd (Central Ontario) Battalion" in August 1917.

[7] 1st Bn. C.M.R. organized in France from personnel of 1st and 3rd Regts. C.M.R., which had been mobilized at Brandon, Man. and Medicine Hat, Alta. respectively; 2nd Bn. C.M.R. organized in France from personnel of 2nd and 3rd Regts. C.M.R., mobilized at Victoria, B.C. and Medicine Hat respectively: 4th Bn. C.M.R. organized in France from personnel of 4th and 6th Regts. C.M.R., mobilized at Toronto, Ont. and Amherst, N.S. respectively; 5th Bn. C.M.R. organized in France from men of the 5th and 6th Regts. C.M.R., mobilized at Sherbrooke, P.Q. and Amherst respectively.

APPENDIX "E"

THE RESULTS OF THE MILITARY SERVICE ACT

(Reconciliation of Statistical Data Issued by the Departments of Justice and Militia and Defence.)

Status of Men		Department of Justice[1]	Department of Militia and Defence[2]
Class 1 Registrations		401,882[3]	No Comparable Figures, as Men under Civil Authorities until Taken on Strength of the C.E.F.
Granted exemption from service on Agricultural, Occupational, Medical, etc., grounds		221,949	
Liable for Military Service		179,933[4]	
Unapprehended defaulters	24,139[5]		
Available 11 Nov 1918 but not called	26,225[6]		
	50,364	50,364	
Reported for Military Service		129,569	
Permitted to enlist in British Forces (e.g., R.A.F., Royal Engineers Inland Water Transport)		8,445[7]	
Taken on strength Canadian Expeditionary Force		121,124	124,588[8]
Performed no military service and struck off strength ("Returned to Registrar's Records") upon being found medically unfit, eligible for exemption, or liable for non-combatant service only		16,108[9]	16,300[10]
Available for service with C.E.F. units		105,016	108,288
Discharged prior to 11 Nov 1918 for miscellaneous reasons		8,637[11]	8,637[12]
On strength C.E.F. 11 Nov 1918 (includes 16,296 draftees on *unexpired* harvest or compassionate leave of absence without pay)		96,379	99,651[13]
Proceeded overseas			47,509[14]
Taken on strength units in France			24,132[15]

REFERENCES AND NOTES

The following detailed documentation gives the sources of the statistics in the preceding table and explains how certain conclusions are reached.

---

1. *Report of the Director of the Military Service Branch to the Honourable The Minister of Justice on the Operation of the Military Service Act, 1917* dated 1 March 1919, *Canada Sessional Papers* No. 246, 1919; hereafter M.S.B. Report.

2. *Memorandum Respecting Work of the Department of Militia and Defence No. 5—From January 1, 1918, to October 31, 1918; Memorandum Respecting Work of the Department of Militia and Defence No. 6—From November 1, 1918, to October 31, 1919;* hereafter *Memorandum No. 5.* Files of the Department of Militia and Defence now held in the Public Archives of Canada.

3. M.S.B. Report, p. 94 (Table 1, column 6).

4. *Ibid.*, pp. 3 (para 2), 117 (Table 21, column 2), 119 (Table 23, column 3).

5. *Ibid.*, pp. 4 (para 2), 38 (para 2).

6. *Ibid.*, pp. 3 (para 4), 117 (Table 21, column 3).

7. M.S.B. Report (p. 117—Table 21, column 9) gives the number as 7673. However, after the Report was published in March 1919, the Military Service Branch of the Department of Justice reached the conclusion that 8445 men had been permitted to join British units. This information was passed to officials of the Department of Militia and Defence and a reference to the change appeared in *Memorandum No. 6* (p. 45), which was distributed some months after the M.S.B. Report.

8. Statement dated 24 February 1942 (prepared by the Officer i/c Records, National Defence Headquarters, for the Private Secretary to the Minister of National Defence) on H.Q. 64-1-24 (FD 196) Vol. 32.

9. M.S.B. Report, pp. 3 (para 3), 117 (Table 21, column 5).

10. *Memorandum No. 5*, p. 11, para 12 (b). Most of these men were taken on strength under the provisions of the Order in Council (P.C. 962) of 20 April 1918, which directed the Minister of Militia and Defence to order every man in Class 1 (20-22 years of age) to report for military service irrespective of any exemption granted or claimed. In December 1918 an Order in Council noted that "there is a considerable number of men belonging to Class 1 under the Military Service Act who were ordered to report for duty and did report, but who could not, by reason of low category, non-liability to combatant service or otherwise, be usefully employed in the Canadian Expeditionary Force; and that such men were struck off strength and returned to the Registrar's Records instead of being discharged, in order that, if changing circumstances rendered it advisable, they might again be ordered by the Registrar to report for duty." The same Order in Council (P.C. 3051), which was dated 11 December 1918, ordered that the men concerned be discharged with effect from the day upon which they were struck off strength.

11. Department of Militia and Defence figure inserted to maintain continuity.

12. This figure, which will not be found in published sources, has been arrived at as follows:

(a) *Memorandum No. 5* (p. 11, para 12) states that 24,933 men were on leave of absence without pay "or subsequently discharged". As the *Memorandum* is concerned with the period 1 January to 31 October 1918, it would appear that those "subsequently discharged" must have been released on or before 31 October 1918.

(b) *Memorandum No. 6* (p. 45, para 3 of the "Special Section") repeats the statement regarding the 24,933 draftees and (in para 7 of the "Special Section") notes that "At the signing of the Armistice there were 10,296 on 'compassionate leave' while in addition there were some 6000 on harvest leave".

(c) Thus it is established that some 16,296 of the 24,933 were on either compassionate or harvest leave on 11 November 1918. It therefore seems reasonable to conclude that the remaining 8637 had been discharged prior to the signing of the Armistice and probably before the end of October 1918.

13. In view of the wide-spread use of another figure (83,355), the appearance of 99,651 in this place needs elaboration.

(a) The figure of 83,355 originates in a statement in the final report of the Military Service Sub-Section, Department of Militia and Defence (which was reproduced on page 45 of *Memorandum No. 6*) that "the number of men obtained under the Military Service Act was 83,355". A table supporting this figure shows the numbers obtained from each Province. However, a statement following the table is generally overlooked or ignored. This reveals that in addition to the 83,355 "there also were 24,933 on leave without pay under the Orders in Council relating to compassionate leave and hardship cases, or subsequently discharged—making a total of 108,288."

(b) It is thus obvious that 108,288 potential reinforcements were taken on strength of the C.E.F. Of these, 8637 were discharged prior to 11 November 1918 (see note 12 above) for reasons which would also be applicable to volunteers. Another 16,296 were on compassionate (10,296) and harvest (6000) leave of absence without pay when the war ended.

(c) It is difficult to find merit in any suggestion that these 16,296 draftees were granted indefinite leave of absence without pay and that they could not be recalled from leave and placed in the reinforcement stream. The record shows that they were not granted indefinite leave of absence—in the first instance they were granted thirty days' leave, and from time to time this was extended as the exigencies of the service permitted. The actual status of the men is best described on page 3 (para 4) of *Memorandum No. 5*:

> In Canada, on 31st October 1918, there were in various draft-producing units about 20,000 men; in addition, a considerable number of men who had been called to the colours had been allowed harvest leave, so that the number of men available for reinforcement (had the need for drafts continued, and the necessity arisen for recalling those absent on leave), would have been nearly 35,000.

(d) The necessity for recalling the men did not however arise, and since (according to *Memorandum No. 6*, p. 45) "practically none of them had served beyond having received their call under the Military Service Act and reported", authority was obtained to effect their discharge as quickly and inexpensively as possible. Under the provisions of C.E.F. Routine Order 1357, dated 25 November 1918, each of the 16,296 men was given the option of proceeding to a Depot Battalion and being discharged in the normal manner or signing a release form (waiving all rights of compensation) and mailing it to the Depot Battalion. *Memorandum No. 6* (pp. 37 and 39) shows that eighty-five per cent of the draftees used the form and in return received a receipt which was equivalent to a Discharge Certificate.

14. Statements appearing on Militia and Defence file HQ 1064-30-6, vol. 8.

15. H.Q. 683-1-12, vol. 13 (copy on Historical Section file Hist 5-2-1), Information supplied Director of Staff Duties (for Minister of National Defence) by Director Historical Section in November 1944. In 1927 the compilation of personnel and medical statistics by means of the Hollerith (machine records) system was completed without any record having been made of the number of draftees who proceeded to France from England. It was not then considered desirable to undertake the formidable task of re-examining thousands of service documents to obtain this single piece of information. In 1944, when an estimate of the numbers involved was urgently required, it was decided to rely upon entries appearing in Part II Orders of units which served in France. Fortunately during 1923 and 1924 the Historical Section, when dealing with the award of Battle Honours, had carried out a painstaking survey of Part II Orders and had compiled lists showing the regimental number of every man who served in France. This research revealed that 24,132 of the soldiers serving in the field bore regimental numbers appearing in either the 3,000,000 or 4,000,000 series of numbers. It was assumed that these blocks had been set aside for the exclusive use of draftees.

In accepting this figure of 24,132 as the best available count of draftees who served in the field, it must be emphasized that it is only an approximation. As noted in Chapter XI (page 351), there were instances of volunteers' receiving numbers from these blocks and of draftees' being given numbers appearing in other series of regimental numbers. These exceptions tended to cancel out each other, and it seems safe to assume that this figure would not greatly differ from one obtained by an examination of every service document.

APPENDIX "F"

BATTLES AND OTHER ENGAGEMENTS IN WHICH CANADIAN FORCES PARTICIPATED

FRANCE AND FLANDERS: 1915-18

Dates shown are those during which Canadian troops were present and do not necessarily cover the full period of the battle. An asterisk has been placed before the names of battles and actions in which the only Canadian forces present were detached units or sub-units, e.g., Batteries, Tunnelling Companies, etc. This list uses the official names contained in the Report of the Battles Nomenclature Committee, 1921.

I. TRENCH WARFARE 1915

*BATTLE OF NEUVE CHAPELLE	10 March
Action of St. Eloi	14-15 March
THE BATTLE OF YPRES, 1915	
GRAVENSTAFEL RIDGE (The Gas Attack)	22-23 April
ST. JULIEN	24 April-4 May
FREZENBERG RIDGE	8-13 May
BELLEWAARDE RIDGE	24-25 May
*BATTLE OF AUBERS RIDGE	9 May
BATTLE OF FESTUBERT	17-25 May
Second Action of Givenchy, 1915	15-16 June
THE BATTLE OF LOOS	25 September-8 October
*Action of Bois Grenier	25 September
*Actions of the Hohenzollern Redoubt	13-19 October

II. TRENCH WARFARE 1916

Actions of St. Eloi Craters	27 March-16 April
BATTLE OF MOUNT SORREL	2-13 June

III. THE ALLIED OFFENSIVE 1916

THE BATTLES OF THE SOMME, 1916	
*ALBERT, 1916 (Capture of Montauban, Mametz, Fricourt, Contalmaison and la Boisselle)	1-13 July
BAZENTIN RIDGE	14-17 July
*Attack at Fromelles	19 July
Attacks on High Wood	20-25 July
POZIERES RIDGE (Fighting for Mouquet Farm)	1-3 September
*GUILLEMONT	3-6 September
*GINCHY	9 September
FLERS-COURCELETTE	15-22 September
THIEPVAL RIDGE	26-29 September
LE TRANSLOY RIDGES (Capture of Eaucourt l'Abbaye)	1-18 October
ANCRE HEIGHTS (Capture of Regina Trench)	1 October-11 November
THE ANCRE, 1916 (Capture of Beaumont Hamel)	13-18 November

IV. THE ADVANCE TO THE HINDENBURG LINE 1917

German Retreat to the Hindenburg Line	24-29 March

V. THE ALLIED OFFENSIVE 1917

THE BATTLE OF ARRAS, 1917
- VIMY RIDGE .... 9-14 April
- *FIRST SCARPE, 1917 .... 9-14 April
- *SECOND SCARPE, 1917 .... 23-24 April
- Attack on la Coulotte .... 23 April
- ARLEUX .... 28-29 April
- THIRD SCARPE, 1917 (Capture of Fresnoy) 3-4 May

Affairs south of the Souchez River .... 3-25 June
Capture of Avion .... 26-29 June
BATTLE OF HILL 70 .... 15-25 August
*THE BATTLE OF MESSINES, 1917 (Capture of Wytschaete) .... 7-14 June
THE BATTLES OF YPRES, 1917
- *PILCKEM RIDGE .... 31 July-2 August
- *LANGEMARCK, 1917 .... 16-18 August
- *MENIN ROAD RIDGE .... 20-25 September
- *POLYGON WOOD .... 26 September-3 October
- *BROODSEINDE .... 4 October
- *POELCAPPELLE .... 9 October
- *FIRST PASSCHENDAELE .... 12 October
- SECOND PASSCHENDAELE .... 26 October-10 November

BATTLE OF CAMBRAI, 1917
- The Tank Attack .... 20-21 November
- *Capture of Bourlon Wood .... 23-28 November
- The German Counter-Attacks .... 30 November-3 December

VI. THE GERMAN OFFENSIVES 1918

THE FIRST BATTLES OF THE SOMME, 1918
- ST. QUENTIN .... 21-23 March
- *Actions at the Somme Crossings .... 24-25 March
- *FIRST BAPAUME .... 24-25 March
- *ROSIERES .... 26-27 March
- *FIRST ARRAS, 1918 .... 28 March
- *AVRE .... 4 April

*Capture of Hamel .... 4 July
THE BATTLES OF THE LYS
- *ESTAIRES (First Defence of Givenchy, 1918) .... 9-11 April
- *MESSINES, 1918 (Loss of Hill 63) .... 10-11 April
- *HAZEBROUCK .... 12-15 April
- *BAILLEUL (Defence of Neuve Eglise) .... 13-15 April
- *FIRST KEMMEL RIDGE .... 17-19 April

*Action of La Becque .... 28 June

VII. THE ADVANCE TO VICTORY 1918

THE BATTLE OF AMIENS .... 8-11 August
Actions round Damery .... 15-17 August
THE SECOND BATTLES OF THE SOMME, 1918
- *ALBERT, 1918 .... 21-23 August
- *SECOND BAPAUME .... 31 August-3 September

THE SECOND BATTLES OF ARRAS, 1918
- SCARPE, 1918 (Capture of Monchy-le-Preux) .... 26-30 August
- DROCOURT-QUEANT CANAL .... 2-3 September

THE BATTLES OF THE HINDENBURG LINE	
*HAVRINCOURT	12 September
*EPEHY	18 September
CANAL DU NORD (Capture of Bourlon Wood)	27 September-1 October
ST. QUENTIN CANAL	29 September-2 October
BEAUREVOIR LINE	3-5 October
CAMBRAI, 1918 (Capture of Cambrai)	8-9 October
*BATTLE OF YPRES, 1918	28 September-2 October
Pursuit to the Selle	9-12 October
*BATTLE OF COURTRAI	14-19 October
*BATTLE OF THE SELLE	17-25 October
BATTLE OF VALENCIENNES (Capture of Mont Houy)	1-2 November
BATTLE OF THE SAMBRE	4 November
Passage of the Grande Honnelle	5-7 November
Capture of Mons	11 November

OTHER THEATRES OF WAR

MACEDONIA 1915-17. DARDANELLES 1915-16.
EGYPT AND PALESTINE 1915-16, 1918.
NORTH WEST PERSIA AND CASPIAN 1918-19.
MURMAN 1918-19. ARCHANGEL 1918-19. SIBERIA 1918-19.

ABBREVIATIONS

A.A. .... Anti-Aircraft
A.A. & Q.M.G. .... Assistant Adjutant and Quartermaster General
A.C.I. .... Army Council Instruction
A.D.M.S. .... Assistant Director of Medical Services
A.G. .... Adjutant General
A.H.Q. .... Army Headquarters
A.I.F. .... Australian Imperial Force
Anzac .... Australian and New Zealand Army Corps
Appces/Appx. .... Appendices/Appendix
Arty. .... Artillery
Aux. .... Auxiliary

Bde. .... Brigade
B.E.F. .... British Expeditionary Force
B.G.G.S. .... Brigadier General, General Staff
B.G.S. .... Brigadier, General Staff
B.M. .... Brigade Major
Bn. .... Battalion
B.O.H. .... British Official History
Brig.-Gen. .... Brigadier-General
Brit. .... British
Bty. .... Battery

C.A.M.C. .... Canadian Army Medical Corps
Capt. .... Captain
Cav. .... Cavalry
C.B. .... Companion of the Order of the Bath
C.B.S.O. .... Counter Battery Staff Officer
C.C.H.A. .... Canadian Corps Heavy Artillery
Cdn. .... Canadian
C.E. .... Canadian Engineers
C.E.F. .... Canadian Expeditionary Force
C.F.A. .... Canadian Field Artillery
C.F.C. .... Canadian Forestry Corps
C.G.A. .... Canadian Garrison Artillery
C.G.S. .... Chief of the General Staff
C.I.G.S. .... Chief of the Imperial General Staff
C.-in-C. .... Commander-in-Chief
C.M.G. .... Companion of the Order of St. Michael and St. George
C.M.G.C. .... Canadian Machine Gun Corps
C.M.M.G. .... Canadian Motor Machine Gun
C.M.R. .... Canadian Mounted Rifles
C.O. .... Commanding Officer
Comd. .... Commander
Col. .... Colonel
C.O.R.C.C. .... Canadian Overseas Railway Construction Corps
Cpl. .... Corporal
C.R.A. .... Commanding Royal Artillery
C.R.E. .... Commanding Royal Engineers
C.R.T. .... Canadian Railway Troops
C.W.N.S. .... Canadian War Narrative Section
C.W.R.O. .... Canadian War Records Office

D.A. .... Dominion Arsenal
D.A. & Q.M.G. .... Deputy Adjutant and Quartermaster General
D.C.M. .... Distinguished Conduct Medal
D.D. .... Deputy Director

D.H.S. (D. Hist.) .... Director Historical Section
Div. .... Division
D.L.I. .... Durham Light Infantry
D.M. .... Deputy Minister
D.M.I. .... Director Military Intelligence
D.M.S. .... Director of Medical Services
D.N.D. .... Department of National Defence
D.N.S. .... Director of Naval Service
D.O.C. .... District Officer Commanding
D-Q Line .... Drocourt-Quéant Line
D.S.O. .... Companion of the Distinguished Service Order

E.E.F. .... Egyptian Expeditionary Force
Engrs. .... Engineers

F.G.H. .... Fort Garry Horse
F.O.H. .... French Official History
F.O.O. .... Forward Observation Officer

G.C.M.G. .... Knight Grand Cross of the Order of St. Michael and St. George
Gen. .... General
G.H.Q. .... General Headquarters
G.O. .... General Order
G.O.C. (-in-C.) .... General Officer Commanding (-in-Chief)
G.O.H. .... German Official History
Gov. Gen. .... Governor General
G.S. .... General Staff
G.S.O. I, II and III .... General Staff Officer, 1st, 2nd or 3rd Grade

H.M.C.S. .... His Majesty's Canadian Ship
H.M.S. .... His Majesty's Ship
How. .... Howitzer
H.Q. .... Headquarters
H.T. .... Horse Transport

Inf. .... Infantry
I.S.O. .... Imperial Service Order

K.C.B. .... Knight Commander of the Order of the Bath
K.C.M.G. .... Knight Commander of the Order of St. Michael and St. George

L/Cpl. .... Lance Corporal
Lieut. or Lt. .... Lieutenant
L. of C. .... Line(s) of Communication
Lt.-Col. .... Lieutenant-Colonel

Maj. .... Major
M.C. .... Military Cross
M.D. .... Military District
M.G. .... Machine Gun
M.G.G.S. .... Major General, General Staff
M.G.R.A. .... Major General, Royal Artillery
M.M. .... Military Medal
M.M.G. .... Motor Machine Gun
M.S.B. .... Military Service Branch
M.T. .... Mechanical Transport
M.V.O. .... Member of the 4th or 5th Class of the Royal Victorian Order

N.C.O. .... Non-Commissioned Officer
N.P.A.M. .... Non-Permanent Active Militia
N.R.E.F. .... North Russia Expeditionary Force

O.C. .... Officer Commanding
O.M. .... Overseas Minister
O.M.F.C. .... Overseas Military Forces of Canada
O.P. .... Observation Post
O.S. .... Overseas

P.A.C. .... Public Archives of Canada
P.C. .... Privy Council
P.P.C.L.I. .... Princess Patricia's Canadian Light Infantry
Pte. .... Private

R.A. .... Royal Artillery
R.A.F. .... Royal Air Force
R.C.A.F. .... Royal Canadian Air Force
R.C.D. .... Royal Canadian Dragoons
R.C.H.A. .... Royal Canadian Horse Artillery
R.C.R. .... The Royal Canadian Regiment
R.E. .... Royal Engineers
R.F.A. .... Royal Field Artillery
R.F.C. .... Royal Flying Corps
R.H.C. .... Royal Highlanders of Canada
R.G.A. .... Royal Garrison Artillery
Reinf. .... Reinforcement(s)
R.N. .... Royal Navy
R.N.A.S. .... Royal Naval Air Service
R.N.W.M.P. .... Royal North-West Mounted Police
R.O. .... Routine Order

Sec. .... Secretary or Section
Sgt. .... Sergeant
S.O.S. .... Struck off strength
Sqn. .... Squadron
Stat. .... Stationary

Tel. .... Telegram
Trg. .... Training

U. of T. .... University of Toronto

V.C. .... Victoria Cross
V.D. .... Volunteer Officers' Decoration or Colonial Auxiliary Forces Officers' Decoration

W.D. .... War Diary
W.O. .... War Office

Y.M.C.A. .... Young Men's Christian Association

REFERENCES

(Unless otherwise specified all files cited are those of the Department of National Defence, in the custody of the Public Archives of Canada. All numbered formations and units referred to are Canadian unless otherwise indicated.)

CHAPTER I

Canada at War

1. Szogyeny to Berthold, 5 Jul 14, cited in S.B. Fay, *The Origins of the World War* (New York, 1928), II, 203-4.
2. G.N. Tucker, *The Naval Service of Canada* (Ottawa, 1952), I, 398.
3. Fay, *The Origins of the World War*, II, 529.
4. Winston S. Churchill, *The World Crisis 1911-1918* (London, 1938), I, 161.
5. *The Origins of the World War*, II, 545.
6. Col. C. P. Stacey, *Six Years of War* (Ottawa, 1955), 49.
7. R. MacGregor Dawson, *The Government of Canada* (Toronto, 1947), 60.
8. This cable and others cited are contained in the collection of "European War Prints", held by the Historical Section.
9. *Debates, House of Commons*, 12 Jan 10.
10. *Minutes of Proceedings of the Colonial Conference, 1907* (Cd. 3523, London, 1907), 100.
11. J. Castell Hopkins, *The Canadian Annual Review of Public Affairs, 1914*, 143.
12. Annual Reports of the Militia Council, 1906-1913.
13. *Regimental Establishments of the Canadian Militia including Establishments of the Permanent Force for 1914-1915*, 24-5.
14. *Department of Militia and Defence for the Dominion of Canada Report for the Year ended 31st December, 1898*, 38.
15. *Report of the Department of Militia and Defence for the Dominion of Canada for the Year ended December 1902*, 6. *Report of the Militia Council for the Dominion of Canada for the Fiscal Year ending March 31, 1916*, 18.
16. Appendix A to *The Regulations and Orders for the Militia of Canada, 1904*, 205.
17. Army Order No. 41 of 1904.
18. *Colonial Conference 1902 . . . Minutes of Proceedings and Papers laid before the Conference*, 210, 261.
19. *Minutes of Proceedings of the Colonial Conference, 1907* (Cd. 3523, London, 1907), vi.
20. Sessional Paper No. 29a-1910, 37.
21. *Report on the Military Institutions of Canada by General Sir Ian Hamilton, G.C.B., D.S.O., Inspector-General of the Overseas Forces* (Ottawa, 1913).
22. *Debates, House of Commons*, 4 Dec 12.
23. *Report of the Militia Council for the Dominion of Canada for the Fiscal Year ending March 31, 1915*, 7.
24. Compiled from "Regimental Establishments . . . 1914-1915".
25. C. P. Stacey, *The Military Problems of Canada* (Toronto, 1940), 71.
26. "Memorandum on the General Naval Situation", 20 Aug 12, reproduced in Tucker, *The Naval Service of Canada*, I, Appx. VIII.
27. Col. A. F. Duguid, *Official History of the Canadian Forces in the Great War 1914-1919, General Series*, vol. I (Ottawa, 1938), Appx. 11, "Note on the Overseas Mobilization Scheme 1911-1912".
28. "Report No. 1 of the Committee on Canadian Defence, 1898 Defence Scheme", microfilm copy held by the Historical Section.
29. "Canadian Defence Committee—Recommendations—1898", microfilm copy held by the Historical Section.
30. Governor General to Colonial Office, 18 Apr 03, Public Archives of Canada (hereinafter P.A.C.), G.10, Vol. 34.
31. Memorandum 1 Aug 12, on Dept. of Naval Service file 1019-1-2. D.M.I. draft memo (n.d.), *ibid.*
32. P.A.C., Maj.-Gen. Gwatkin's Papers.
33. Stacey, *Six Years of War*, 9.
34. Letter, G. J. Desbarats to Sir Joseph Pope, 9 Dec 13, on D.N.S. file 1019-1-2.
35. P.A.C., Borden Papers, O.C. 208(1), 20967.
36. P.C. 2049, 4 Aug 14.
37. Tucker, *The Naval Service of Canada*, I, 241-2, 264-9.
38. Tel., Sec. of State for Colonies to Gov. Gen., 4 Aug 14, European War Print No. 40.
39. Tels., Sec. of State for Colonies to Gov. Gen., 6 and 7 Aug 14, *ibid.*, Nos. 84 and 121.

Chapter II

Forging the Weapon

1. P.C. 2067, 6 Aug 14.
2. *Debates, House of Commons,* 26 Jan 16.
3. A.G. to O.C. 5 Div. [Cdn. Militia], 31 Jul 14, M.D. No. 5 file 5-D s/016.
4. A.G. Memo, 13 Aug 14, on H.Q. 593-1-5, vol. 3.
5. Col. S. J. A. Denison, G.O.C. 4th Division, to Secretary, Militia Council, 20 Aug 14.
6. *Debates, House of Commons,* 26 Jan 16.
7. Tel., Sec. of State for Colonies to Gov. Gen., 10 Aug 14, European War Print No. 169.
8. P.A.C., Borden Papers, O.C. 208(1), 21131.
9. *Ibid.*
10. Tel., Gov. Gen. to Sec. of State for Colonies, 17 Aug 14, European War Print No. 282.
11. *Debates, House of Commons,* 23 Jan. 16.
12. Gov. Gen. to Sec. of State for Colonies, 17 Aug 14, European War Print No. 282.
13. Brig.-Gen. C. F. Winter, *Lieutenant-General The Hon. Sir Sam Hughes* (Toronto, 1931), 53.
14. *The Canadian Annual Review,* 1914, 201.
15. *Debates, House of Commons,* 26 Jan 16.
16. Duguid, 79.
17. *Memoranda Respecting Work of the Department of Militia and Defence, European War, 1914-15,* 55-7, Report by Acting Minister of Militia and Defence, 22 Sep 14.
18. Hughes to Prime Minister, 13 May 15, in *Debates, House of Commons,* 30 Jan 17.
19. "Evidence taken before the Public Accounts Committee during the Session 1915", 483, reproduced in Duguid, Appx. 113.
20. Papers on H.Q. 593-2-6, vol. 1.
21. Duguid, 87.
22. Telegram to Special Representative of the Minister of Militia and Defence, 9 Feb 15, Carson file 4-10-14.
23. G.O.C.-in-C. British Forces in France to War Office, 12 Feb 16, on H.Q. 130-19-2-3.
24. Toronto *Telegram,* 14 Nov 16.
25. Letter, Carson to Lt.-Col. F. A. Reid, 14 May 15, Carson file 8-5-37.
26. Letter, Perley to Kitchener, 29 Aug 14, P.A.C., Perley Papers, vol. 1.
27. Tel. Borden to Perley, 29 Aug 14, *ibid.*
28. Supplement to *The London Gazette,* 27 Oct 14.
29. Report of Chief Embarkation Officer to Secretary Militia Council, 10 Oct 14, reproduced in Duguid, Appx. 131.
30. A. J. Gorrie to Lt.-Col. Price, 6 Oct 14, reproduced in Duguid, Appx. 130.
31. *Royal Commission Concerning Purchase of War Supplies and Sale of Small Arms Ammunition, Evidence,* vol. 1, 329.
32. Sir Julian Corbett, *History of the Great War, Naval Operations* (London, 1920), I, 204.
33. Churchill, *The World Crisis 1911-1918,* I, 258.
34. Sir Andrew Macphail, *History of the Canadian Forces, 1914-1919—Medical Services* (Ottawa, 1925), 26.
35. J. Castell Hopkins and Rev. J. Renison, *Canada at War: A Record of Heroism and Achievement, 1914-1918* (Toronto, 1919), 101.
36. C. D. Spittal to Carson, 3 Oct 14, Carson file 8-5-8.
37. W.O. to G.O.C. Southern Command, 27 Nov 14 (192).
38. Borden to Perley, received 9 Oct 14, P.A.C., Perley Papers, vol. 2.
39. Winter, *Lieutenant-General The Hon. Sir Sam Hughes,* 90.
40. G.O. 175, October 1914.
41. Duguid, 126-7.
42. P.A.C., Borden Papers, O.C. 183(1), 14752-3.
43. *Ibid.,* 14775-6.
44. P.A.C., Borden Papers, O.C. 183(1), 14733, Carson to Hughes, 31 Dec 14; and 14789-90, Perley to Borden, 25 Jan 15.
45. Brig.-Gen. Sir J. E. Edmonds, *Military Operations, France and Belgium, 1914* (Volume II of *British Official History of the Great War*) (London, 1925), 3. (Hereinafter referred to as B.O.H.)
46. Carson to Hughes, Carson file 8-5-8, vol. 2.
47. C. E. W. Bean, *The Story of Anzac* (Volume I of *The Official History of Australia in the War of 1914-1918*) (Sydney, 1933), 110-11.
48. Hopkins and Renison, *Canada at War,* 117.
49. Documents on O.S. files E-7-1 and E-36-1.
50. First Canadian Contingent Orders, Nos. 924, 1103 & 1160, of 18, 29 Jan and 2 Feb 15 respectively.
51. Letter, Borden to Perley, 6 Feb 15, P.A.C., Perley Papers, vol. 2.
52. B.O.H., *1914,* I, 9.
53. Gerhard Ritter, *Der Schlieffenplan—Kritik eines Mythos* (Munich, 1956), 13.
54. *Ibid.,* 145-60.
55. Reichsarchiv, *Der Weltkrieg 1914-1918* (Berlin, 1925-1944), I, 55. (Hereinafter referred to as G.O.H. (German Official History).)
56. *Ibid.,* 69.
57. Ritter, *Der Schlieffenplan—Kritik eines Mythos,* 149.
58. G.O.H., I, 62.
59. Von Hindenburg, *Out of My Life* (London, 1920), 81.

60. Brig.-Gen. E. L. Spears, *Liaison, 1914* (London, 1930), 267.
61. Sewell Tyng, *The Campaign of the Marne 1914* (London, 1935), Appx. X.
62. Etat-Major de l'Armée, Service Historique, *Les Armées françaises dans la Grande Guerre* (Paris, 1922-1938) Tome II, Cartes, No. 26. (Hereinafter referred to as F.O.H. (French Official History).)
63. Winston S. Churchill, *The World Crisis, 1911-1918*, (London, n.d.) II, 462-3.
64. *Ibid.*, 472.
65. Kitchener to Sir John French, cited in B.O.H., *1915*, I, 61.
66. Churchill, *The World Crisis*, II, 528.
67. Foreign Office Telegram cited in *ibid.*, 529.
68. C. F. Aspinall-Oglander, *Military Operations, Gallipoli* (London, 1929), I, 68.
69. B.O.H., *1915*, I, 66.

CHAPTER III

The Battles of Ypres, 1915

1. Despatch to Secretary of State for War, 5 Apr 15, *The Despatches of Lord French* (London, 1917), 249.
2. 1st Cdn. Div. Memorandum, Principles of Defence, 4 Mar 15 (270). (In this and in future references the bracketed number identifies the appendix to Duguid, *Official History of the Canadian Forces in the Great War 1914-1919*, which reproduces this source either whole or in part.)
3. F.O.H., Tome II, Annexe 890 (279).
4. *Ibid.*, Annexe 917 (280).
5. *Ibid.*, Annexes 927, 979, 1108 (281-3).
6. 1st Cdn. Div. Operation Order No. 5, 9 Mar 15 (285).
7. G. C. Wynne, *If Germany Attacks, The Battle in Depth in the West* (London, 1940), 30-1, 35.
8. H.Q. 1st Cdn. Div. Artillery Instruction, 9 Mar 15, Appx. 4 to War Diary.
9. B.O.H., *1915*, I, 149.
10. *Ibid.*, 151-4.
11. *Ibid.*, 159-60. F.O.H., Tome II, 691-3.
12. 5th Corps Operation Order No. 9, 11 Apr 15, Appx. 6a to W.D., G.S., 1st Cdn. Div., 1 Apr-4 May 15 (309).
13. "Report on Condition of Trenches" by O.C. 2nd Field Company C.E., 21 Apr 15, in Appx. I to W.D., [1st] Cdn. Div. Engrs., May 1915 (334).
14. 1st Cdn. Div. Scheme of Defence, 17 Apr 15, Appx. 14 to G.S. Diary, 1 Apr-4 May 15 (330a).
15. W.D., 1st Inf. Bde., 20, 21 Apr 15.
16. G.O.H., VIII, maps 1 & 2.
17. General Erich von Falkenhayn, *General Headquarters 1914-1916 and its Critical Decisions* (London, 1920 [?]), 65.
18. *Ibid.*, 84.
19. Account reproduced in B.O.H., *1915*, I, 188-90.
20. *Die deutsche Kriegführung und das Völkerrecht*, cited in *ibid.*, 194.
21. G.O.H., VIII, 37.
22. Von Falkenhayn, 47.
23. V. Lefebvre, *The Riddle of the Rhine: Chemical Strategy in Peace and War* (New York, 1937), 36, 155-6. A. M. Prentiss, *Chemicals in War* (New York, 1937), 148-50.
24. G.O.H., VIII, 38.
25. *Ibid.*, VII, 63-4.
26. Général Ferry, "Ce qui s'est passé sur l'Yser" (*La Revue des Vivants*, Paris, July 1930), 899-900 (318).
27. 5th Corps Summary of Information No. 45, 15 Apr 15, 1st Cdn. Div. H.Q. file, folder No. 11, file 3 (322).
28. F.O.H., Tome II, Annexe 1392.
29. Ferry, "Ce qui s'est passé sur l'Yser", 899-900.
30. Letter, General Ilse (C.G.S. Fourth Army) to Reichsarchiv, 16 Nov 31, in G.O.H., VIII, 39. G.O.H., VII, 64.
31. 1st Cdn. Div. Message A.A. 645, 22 Apr 15 (339).
32. Prentiss, *Chemicals in War*, 663. R. Hanslian, *Der Chemische Krieg*, 3rd revised ed. (Berlin, 1937), I, 77-8, 87.
33. 3rd Bde. Message B.M. 738, 22 Apr 15, in 1st Div. Field Messages, Appx. 34 to G.S. Diary, 1 Apr-4 May 15 (342).
34. 1st Cdn. Div. Report on Operations, 22 April-4 May 1915, Appx. 1 to G.S. Diary.
35. W.D., 10th Bn., 22 Apr 15.
36. 3rd Bde. Message B.M. 741, 22 Apr 15 (351). 1st Cdn. Div. Messages G. 522, G. 2, 1st Div. Field Messages (358, 359).
37. 1st Cdn. Div. Messages G.A. 16, 17, *ibid.* (382, 385).
38. G.O.H., VIII, 40-1.
39. *Ibid.*, 40.
40. Supplement to *The London Gazette*, 22 Jun 15.
41. 3rd Bde. Message to 10th and 16th Bns. and 3rd Bde., C.F.A., 10:47 p.m., 22 Apr 15, 1st Div. Field Messages (388).
42. W.Ds., 10th and 16th Bns., 22 Apr 15.
43. 1st Cdn. Div. Message G. 30, 23 Apr 15 (404).
44. 1st Cdn. Div. Message G.A. 21, 23 Apr 15 (425).
45. Liaison message to 1st Cdn. Div., G.B. 169, 23 Apr 15 (442).
46. 1st Bde. Message, B.M. 806, 23 Apr 15, 1st Div. Field Messages (460).

47. B.O.H., *1915*, I, 198.
48. *Ibid.*, 201.
49. 1st Cdn. Div. Message G.A. 33, 23 Apr 15 (486).
50. 45th (French) Div. Orders G.B. 175, 23 Apr 15, 1st Div. Field Messages (485).
51. 13th Bde. Message B.M. 128, 23 Apr 15, *ibid.* (497).
52. B.O.H., *1915*, I, 205-6.
53. F.O.H., Tome II, Annexe 1430, Putz to Foch, Report for 23 April.
54. Duguid, 284.
55. G.O.H., VIII, 42-3.
56. *Ibid.*, 44.
57. B.O.H., *1915*, I, 216.
58. W.D., 8th Bn., 24 Apr 15.
59. 3rd Cdn. Arty. Bde. Message to 3rd Inf. Bde., 24 Apr 15, Field Messages, 3rd Inf. Bde., 21 Apr-8 May 15, Turner Papers (526).
60. 3rd Bde. Message B.M. 400, 24 Apr 15, 1st Div. Field Messages (542).
61. B.O.H., *1915*, I, 219.
62. Supplement to *The London Gazette*, 22 Jun 15.
63. 1st Cdn. Div. Message G. 80, 24 Apr 15 (557).
64. 1st Cdn. Div. Message G. 369, 24 Apr 15 (566).
65. Supplement to *The London Gazette*, 13 May 19.
66. Diary of Operations, 22 Apr-5 May 15, Appx. "A" to W.D., 3rd Inf. Bde., April-May 1915.
67. 1st Cdn. Div. Message G.A. 50, 24 Apr 15 (580).
68. 3rd Bde. Message 818, 24 Apr 15, Field Messages, 3rd Inf. Bde. (586).
69. 27th Div. Message G.C. 2, 24 Apr 15, *ibid.* (600).
70. 3rd Bde. Message Z. 329, 24 Apr 15, *ibid.* (631).
71. Letter to Director Historical Section, date not shown, Currie Papers, Drawer J-1, "Canadian Official War History".
72. Currie to 1st Cdn. Div., 3:30 p.m., 24 Apr 15, H.Q.C. 4950.
73. Note 71, above.
74. 1st Cdn. Div. Message 53, 4:35 p.m., 24 Apr 15 (612).
75. G.H.Q. Message O.A. 959, 24 Apr 15, Appx. 23 to B.O.H., *1915*, I.
76. Letter to General Smith-Dorrien, cited in *ibid.*, 233.
77. Note from General Foch to Sir John French, *ibid.*, 233-4.
78. 5th Corps Message G.A. 416, 24 Apr 15, 1st Div. Field Messages (619).
79. 1st Cdn. Div. Operation Order No. 10, 24 Apr 15, 1st Cdn. Div. H.Q. file, folder No. 15, file 1 (627).
80. 5th Corps Message G.A. 417, 24 Apr 15, 1st Div. Field Messages (634).
81. 1st Cdn. Div. Message G. 92, 25 Apr 15 (640).
82. 10th Bde. Message B.M. 1, 25 Apr 15, 1st Div. Field Messages (654).
83. G.O.H., VIII, 44.
84. 1st Cdn. Div. Message G.A. 58, 25 Apr 15 (659).
85. 10th Bde. Message to 2nd Bde., about 3:15 p.m., 25 Apr 15, Field Messages, 2nd Inf. Bde., April-May 1915, Urquhart Papers (670a). 27th Div. Message G.R. 488, 25 Apr 15, 1st Div. Field Messages (670).
86. H.Q. 650-52-7, vol. 2, Observations by Director Historical Section on B.O.H., 19 Nov 25.
87. 1st Cdn. Div. Message G. 13, 25 Apr 15 (674).
88. Supplement to *The London Gazette*, 22 Jun 15.
89. Second Army Operation Order No. 8, 26 Apr 15, Appx. 26 to B.O.H., *1915*, I.
90. Cdn. Div. Operation Order No. 12, 26 Apr 15 (684).
91. B.O.H., *1915*, I, 261.
92. F.O.H., Tome II, Annexe 1461.
93. B.O.H., *1915*, I, 273.
94. C.G.S. to Second Army, 2:15 p.m., 27 Apr 15, Appx. 30 to *ibid.*
95. General Smith-Dorrien to Lieut.-Gen. Sir William R. Robertson, 27 Apr 15, Appx. 29 to *ibid.*
96. G.H.Q. Message O.A. 976, 27 Apr 15, Appx. 31 to *ibid.*
97. Field-Marshal Sir William Robertson, *Soldiers and Statesmen 1914-1918* (London, 1926), I, 57.
98. F.O.H., Tome II, Annexe 1466.
99. 1st Cdn. Div. Message G. 96, 28 Apr 15 (694).
100. W.D., P.P.C.L.I., 28 Feb 15 and Appx. XIV. Ralph Hodder-Williams, *Princess Patricia's Canadian Light Infantry 1914-1919* (Toronto, 1923), I, 30-4.
101. B.O.H., 1915, I, 310-11. G.O.H., VIII, 47-8.
102. W.D., P.P.C.L.I., 8 May 15.
103. B.O.H., *1915*, I, 317.
104. *Ibid.*, 339-40.
105. Communique issued by the War Office to the Press, 24 Apr 15 (701a).
106. B.O.H., *1915*, I, 355.
107. All casualty figures, except where otherwise stated, have been supplied by War Service Records.

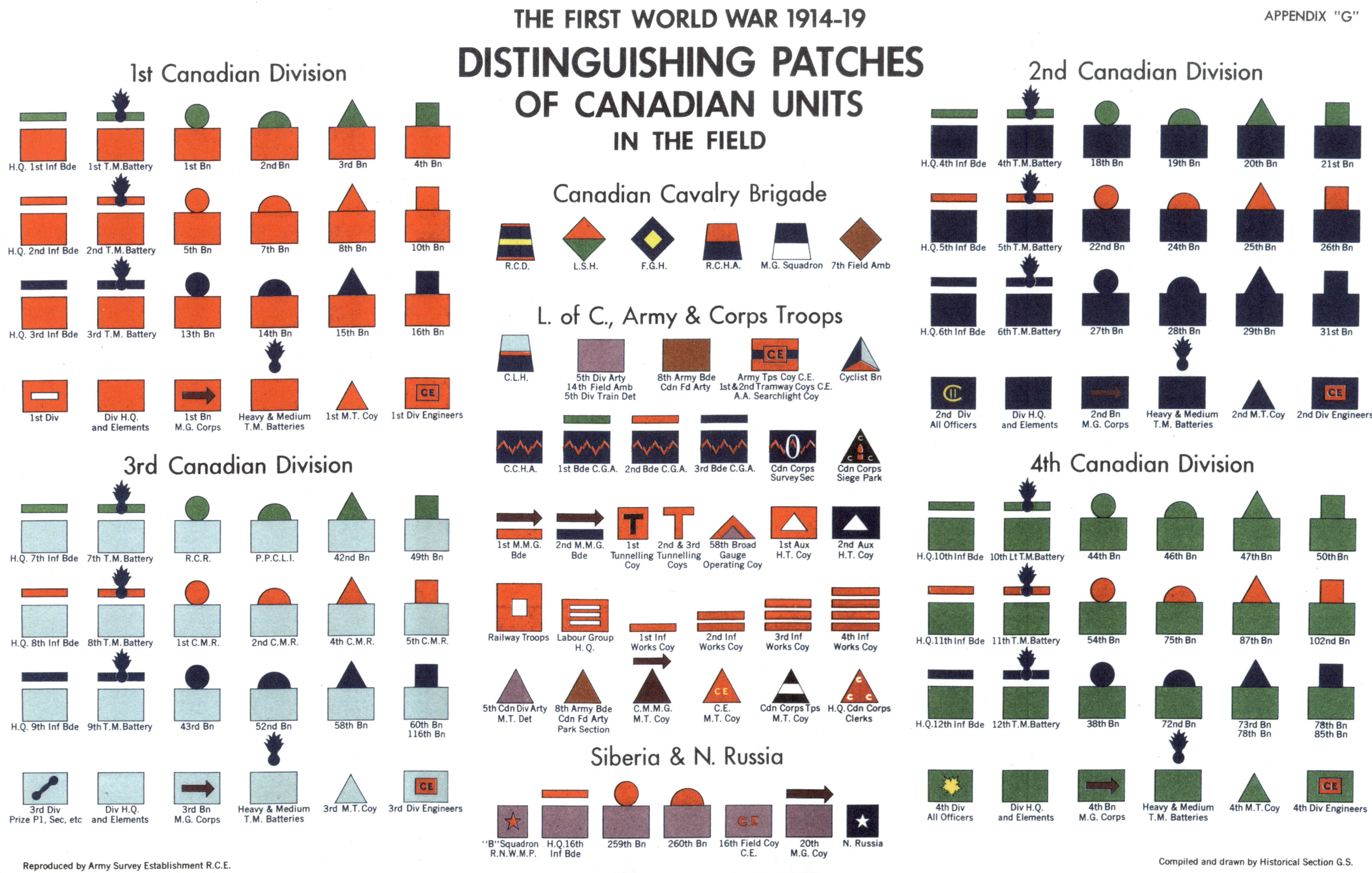

APPENDIX "G"
THE FIRST WORLD WAR 1914-19
DISTINGUISHING PATCHES OF CANADIAN UNITS IN THE FIELD
1st Canadian Division
H.Q. 1st Inf Bde
1st T.M.Battery
1st Bn
2nd Bn
3rd Bn
4th Bn
H.Q. 2nd Inf Bde
2nd T.M.Battery
5th Bn
7th Bn
8th Bn
10th Bn
H.Q. 3rd Inf Bde
3rd T.M. Battery
13th Bn
14th Bn
15th Bn
16th Bn
1st Div
Div H.Q. and Elements
1st Bn M.G. Corps
Heavy & Medium T.M. Batteries
1st M.T. Coy
CE
1st Div Engineers
3rd Canadian Division
H.Q. 7th Inf Bde
7th T.M.Battery
R.C.R.
P.P.C.L.I.
42nd Bn
49th Bn
H.Q. 8th Inf Bde
8th T.M.Battery
1st C.M.R.
2nd C.M.R.
4th C.M.R.
5th C.M.R.
H.Q. 9th Inf Bde
9th T.M.Battery
43rd Bn
52nd Bn
58th Bn
60th Bn 116th Bn
3rd Div Prize P1, Sec, etc
Div H.Q. and Elements
3rd Bn M.G. Corps
Heavy & Medium T.M. Batteries
3rd M.T. Coy
CE
3rd Div Engineers
Canadian Cavalry Brigade
R.C.D.
L.S.H.
F.G.H.
R.C.H.A.
M.G. Squadron
7th Field Amb
L. of C., Army & Corps Troops
C.L.H.
5th Div Arty 14th Field Amb 5th Div Train Det
8th Army Bde Cdn Fd Arty
CE
Army Tps Coy C.E. 1st & 2nd Tramway Coys C.E. A.A. Searchlight Coy
Cyclist Bn
C.C.H.A.
1st Bde C.G.A.
2nd Bde C.G.A.
3rd Bde C.G.A.
Cdn Corps Survey Sec
Cdn Corps Siege Park
1st M.M.G. Bde
2nd M.M.G. Bde
T
1st Tunnelling Coy
2nd & 3rd Tunnelling Coys
58th Broad Gauge Operating Coy
1st Aux H.T. Coy
2nd Aux H.T. Coy
Railway Troops
Labour Group H.Q.
1st Inf Works Coy
2nd Inf Works Coy
3rd Inf Works Coy
4th Inf Works Coy
5th Cdn Div Arty M.T. Det
8th Army Bde Cdn Fd Arty Park Section
C.M.M.G. M.T. Coy
CE
C.E. M.T. Coy
Cdn Corps Tps M.T. Coy
H.Q. Cdn Corps Clerks
Siberia & N. Russia
"B" Squadron R.N.W.M.P.
H.Q. 16th Inf Bde
259th Bn
260th Bn
CE
16th Field Coy C.E.
20th M.G. Coy
N. Russia
2nd Canadian Division
H.Q. 4th Inf Bde
4th T.M.Battery
18th Bn
19th Bn
20th Bn
21st Bn
H.Q. 5th Inf Bde
5th T.M.Battery
22nd Bn
24th Bn
25th Bn
26th Bn
H.Q. 6th Inf Bde
6th T.M.Battery
27th Bn
28th Bn
29th Bn
31st Bn
2nd Div All Officers
Div H.Q. and Elements
2nd Bn M.G. Corps
Heavy & Medium T.M. Batteries
2nd M.T. Coy
CE
2nd Div Engineers
4th Canadian Division
H.Q. 10th Inf Bde
10th Lt T.M.Battery
44th Bn
46th Bn
47th Bn
50th Bn
H.Q. 11th Inf Bde
11th T.M.Battery
54th Bn
75th Bn
87th Bn
102nd Bn
H.Q. 12th Inf Bde
12th T.M.Battery
38th Bn
72nd Bn
73rd Bn 78th Bn
78th Bn 85th Bn
4th Div All Officers
Div H.Q. and Elements
4th Bn M.G. Corps
Heavy & Medium T.M. Batteries
4th M.T. Coy
CE
4th Div Engineers
Reproduced by Army Survey Establishment R.C.E.
Compiled and drawn by Historical Section G.S.

CHAPTER IV

Festubert and Givenchy, 1915

1. F.O.H., Tome III, 38-43. Brig.-Gen. Sir J. E. Edmonds, *A Short History of World War I* (Oxford, 1951), 93-4.
2. B.O.H., *1915,* II, 7-8, 11.
3. *Ibid.*, 13.
4. Wynne, *If Germany Attacks,* 43-6.
5. B.O.H., *1915,* II, 41.
6. *Ibid.*
7. *Ibid.*, 29, 39.
8. *Ibid.*, 43. G.O.H., VIII, 60.
9. G.H.Q. Message O.A. 157, 13 May 15, Appx. 10 to W.D., G.S., 1st Cdn. Div., May 1915.
10. 1st Corps Operation Order No. 83, 14 May 15, Appx. 11 to *ibid.*
11. Robert Blake (ed.), *The Private Papers of Douglas Haig, 1914-1919* (London, 1952), 93.
12. G.H.Q. letter, 14 May 15, cited in B.O.H., *1915,* II, 51.
13. Appx. 13 to W.D., G.S., 1st Cdn. Div., May 1915.
14. G.O.H., VIII, sketches 4 and 6.
15. 1st Corps Message, G.245, 17 May 15, Appx. LXVI to W.D., G.S., 1st Army Corps, May 1915, (744).
16. B.O.H., *1915,* II, 69.
17. 1st Corps Message, G. 268, 18 May 15, Appx. 14 to W.D., G.S., 1st Cdn. Div., May 1915.
18. 7th Div. Operation Order No. 13, 18 May 15 (749).
19. W.D., 16th Bn., 18 May 15.
20. British W.D. Extracts, "Artillery—Festubert", Folder 13, W.D., 12th Bde. R.G.A., 18 May 15. Arty Folder 8, 41st Bde. R.F.A. Message, 3:38 p.m., 18 May 15.
21. 14th Bn. Message, 5:15 p.m., 18 May 15, in Turner Papers, "Festubert".
22. H. M. Urquhart, *The History of the 16th Battalion (The Canadian Scottish)* (Toronto, 1932), 75-7.
23. History of 57th Infantry Regiment, 76 (782c).
24. British W.D. Extracts, W.D., First Army, G.S., May 1915, First Army Report on Operations, 22-31 May 15.
25. Letter, Lt.-Col. G. W. Gordon Hall to Director Historical Section, 20 Mar 37, on H.Q. 683-1-30-5, vol. 5.
26. G.O.H., VIII, 72.
27. 1st Cdn. Div. Operation Order No. 16, 20 May 15, Appx. 9 to W.D., 2nd Inf. Bde., May 1915 (769).
28. W.D., 15th Bn., 20 May 15.
29. Copies of Festubert trench map in Appx. 28 to W.D., G.S., 1st Cdn. Div., May 1915.
30. W.D., 10th Bn., 20 May 15. O.C. 10th Bn. to G.O.C. 2nd Cdn. Bde., 10:00 p.m., 20 May 15 (774).
31. History of 91st Reserve Infantry Regiment, 165-6 (782c).
32. W.D., 10th Bn., 22 May 15.
33. Note 25, above.
34. British W.D. Extracts, First Army, G.S., May 1915, First Army Weekly Report on Operations, 22-31 May 15.
35. W.D., G.S., 1st Corps, 23 May 15.
36. W.D., 3rd Bn., May 1915, Appx. II. 1st Cdn. Bde., to 1st Cdn. Div., Message B.M. 154, 25 May 15 (784).
37. J. E. B. Seely, *Adventure* (London, 1931), 221.
38. B.O.H., *1915,* II, 75.
39. First Army Weekly Report on Operations, 22-31 May 15.
40. R.C.D. Narrative of Operations, 24-27 May 15, Appx. 8 to W.D., Seely's Detachment, May 1915. Seely's Detachment to 1st Cdn. Div., 27 May 15, Appx. 22 to W.D., G.S., 1st Cdn. Div., May 1915 (792).
41. Supplement to *The London Gazette,* 10 Jul 15.
42. British W.D. Extracts, G.S. 91(a), First Army to G.H.Q., 4 Jun 15, Appx. "A" to W.D., G.S., First Army, June 1915.
43. B.O.H., *1915,* II, 79.
44. Cdn. War Narrative Section, "German Divisions Encountered", 14. History of 134th (Saxon) Regiment, 22.
45. 4th Corps Operation Order No. 21, 31 May 15, Appx. 27 to W.D., G.S., 1st Cdn. Div., May 1915 (802).
46. 1st Cdn. Div. Operation Orders Nos. 23 and 24 (803 and 813).
47. Note by Brig.-Gen. Burstall on 1st Cdn. Div. Draft Operation Order 23, Appx. 7 to W.D., G.S., 1st Cdn. Div., June 1915 (810).
48. Cdn. Div. Arty. to 1st Cdn. Div., 10 Jun 15, Appx. 11 to *ibid.*, (811).
49. Cdn. Div. Arty. to 1st Cdn. Div., 17 Jun 15, Appx. 17 to *ibid.*, (821).
50. M.52, 1st Bde. C.F.A. to Cdn. Div. Arty. 15 Jun 15, Appx. 15 to *ibid.*, (815).
51. 1st Bn. Narrative of Operations, 15 Jun 15, Appx. I to Unit W.D., June 1915.
52. Supplement to *The London Gazette,* 23 Aug 15.
53. W.D., 3rd Bn., 16 Jun 15.
54. B.O.H., *1915,* II, 97.
55. G1531, Instructions by H.Q. 3rd Corps re Defence Lines Ploegsteert Front, 14 Jun 15 (828).
56. G1740, B.G.G.S. 3rd Corps to Cdn. Div.,

1 Jul 15, Appx. 1 to W.D., G.S., 1st Cdn. Div., July 1915 (829).
57. W.Ds., 13th Bn., 9, 13 Jul 15; and 4th Bn., 31 Aug 15.
58. W.D., 1st Cdn. Motor Machine Gun Bde., July 1915.
59. W.Ds., 1st Cdn. Div. Artillery, 7 Aug 15; P.P.C.L.I., 8 Aug 15; R.C.H.A., 8 Aug 15.
60. European War Print No. 836.
61. Gov. Gen. to Sec. of State for Colonies, 18 Oct 14, European War Print No. 912 (157).
62. P.C. 2831, 7 Nov 14. Gov. Gen. to Sec. of State for Colonies, 21 Nov 14, European War Print No. 1217 (161).
63. Sec. of State for Colonies to Gov. Gen., 31 Oct 14, file 593-3-1 (159).
64. Correspondence on H.Q. 593-3-12, vols. 1 & 2, and H.Q. 32-1-210, October & November 1915.
65. A.G. to O.C. 5th Div., Quebec, 30 Oct 14 on file H.Q. 32-1-210.
66. Table of Infantry, Pioneer and C.M.R. Units C.E.F. . . . authorized prior to 15 Sep 15 (734).
67. W.D., G.S., Cdn. Corps, 3 Oct 15.
68. Macphail, *The Medical Services,* 39.
69. Militia Order No. 257 (715a).
70. "History of the Canadian Machine Gun Corps, C.E.F." (in MS), by Maj H. T. Logan and Capt. M. R. Levey, vol. I, 13-17, 24-5, 31, 33.
71. Kitchener to Hughes, 11 Mar 15, on file H.Q. 593-3-25, vol. 1, docket 339.
72. H.Q. 593-2-51, A.G. to Col. J. C. MacDougall, 9 Feb 15.
73. P.A.C., Borden Papers, O.C. 190, 15652-4.
74. *Debates, House of Commons,* 30 Jan 17.
75. Perley Papers, vol. 4, Perley to Borden, 11 Jun 15.
76. *Ibid.,* 22 Jun 15.
77. *Ibid.,* Kitchener to Perley, 24 Jun 15.
78. Hughes to Lougheéd, 26 Jul 15, Carson file 6-T-4.
79. H.Q. 413-2-15, in folder Org. & Adm. Cdn. Training Division.
80. Memo to all Units 2nd Division, 10 Sep 15, Appx. "B" to G.S. Diary, September, 1915.
81. "Note on the Landing and Move Forward of 2nd Canadian Division", Appx. 20 to Duguid, II (draft).
82. Bean, *The Story of Anzac,* 117-19.
83. Carson file, 8-5-8.
84. Cited in Message, Sir John French to Kitchener, 27 Apr 15, Perley Papers, vol. 3.
85. Carrick to Minister of Militia and Defence, 27 Apr 15, Appx. 4 to Duguid, II (draft).
86. Carson file, 8-1-5.
87. Henry Borden (ed.), *Sir Robert Laird Borden: His Memoirs* (Macmillan, 1938), 1, 523.
88. European War Prints, vol. 3, No. 306.
89. "The Growth and Control of the Overseas Military Forces of Canada" (8).
90. 1st Div. Routine Orders, 13 Sep 15, Appx. 13 to G.S. Diary. W.D., 2nd Cdn. Bde., 20 Sep 15.
91. "Monthly Return of Strength, Canadians in France", compiled by Statistical Dept., O.M.F.C.
92. W.D., G.S., Cdn. Corps, October 1915, Special Intelligence Report, 7 Oct 15. History of 17th Bavarian Regiment, 34. History of 18th Bavarian Regiment, 99.
93. W.D., G.S., Cdn. Corps, October 1915, Operation Order No. 3, 23 Sep 15.
94. Aspinall-Oglander, *Military Operations, Gallipoli,* I, 58.
95. John F. O'Flaherty, "The Royal Newfoundland Regiment" (MS copy held by Historical Section).
96. Aspinall-Oglander, *Gallipoli* (London, 1932), II, 484.
97. B.O.H., *1915,* II, 128.
98. *Ibid.,* 116-17.
99. Churchill, *The World Crisis,* III, 854-6.
100. B.O.H., *1915,* II, 129.
101. GHQ General Instructions for Commanders of Armies and GHQ Reserve, 18 Sep 15, Appx. 15 to B.O.H., *1915,* II.
102. B.O.H., *1915,* II, 267-70.
103. F.O.H., Tome III, 459, 463.
104. B.O.H., *1915,* II, 272-81, 299, 305.
105. W.D., G.S., Cdn. Corps, 25 Sep 15, and Corps Summary of Operations, 22-30 Sep 15.
106. Report of Manufacture of Smoke Bombs, by Capt. J. B. Dunbar, 13 Oct 15, Cdn. Corps G.S. file No. 17, folder 86.
107. B.O.H., *1915,* II, 392. G.O.H., IX, 98.
108. C.R.M.F. Cruttwell, *A History of the Great War, 1914-1918* (Oxford, 1936), 165.
109. B.O.H., *1915,* II, 393.
110. *Ibid., 1916,* I, 156.
111. M.G.G.S. Second Army Memorandum, 28 Oct 15, Cdn. Corps G.S. file No. 23, folder 3.
112. B.O.H., *1915,* I, 31-4 and *1916,* I, 156.
113. "Organization and Execution of a Raid", Appx. 6 to B.O.H., *1916,* I, 42-5.
114. Urquhart, *The History of the 16th Battalion (The Canadian Scottish),* 112.
115. Report by Brig.-Gen. Lipsett, 17 Nov 15, Appx. 17 to W.D., G.S. 1st Cdn. Div., November 1915.
116. *Ibid. Histories of Two Hundred and Fifty-One Divisions of the German Army which Participated in the War 1914-1916* (Washington, 1920), 610.
117. 1st Div. Arty. Operation Order No. 32, 14 Nov 15, Appx. 14 to G.S. Diary, November 1915.
118. Reports by 5th and 7th Bns., Appx. 17 to W.D., G.S., 1st Div., November 1915. B.O.H., *1916,* I, 156.
119. "Summary of Minor Offensive Operation Night 14-15 Dec 15", in Appendix III/2 to W.D., G.S., Cdn. Corps, December 1915.
120. W. W. Murray, *The History of the 2nd Canadian Battalion in the Great War* (Ottawa, 1947), 75.

121. W.D., A. & Q., Cdn. Corps, 6 Nov 15.
122. General Routine Order No. 1235, 29 Oct 15, Appx. 5 to W.D., D.D.M.S. Cdn. Corps, October 1915.
123. Appendices 7 & 8 to *ibid.*, November 1915.
124. Macphail, *The Medical Services,* 62-3, 88-9, 118-19.
125. *Ibid.*, 269.
126. *Ibid.*, 269-70. D.M.S. (London) file 5-7-6, vol. I, "Diseases Miscellaneous". "Report on Frostbite", 1 Cdn. Stationary Hospital, 30 Dec 15, *ibid.*
127. W.A. Steel, "Wireless Telegraphy in the Canadian Corps in France" (*Canadian Defence Quarterly*, July 1929), 445.
128. W.D., 5th Inf. Bde., 25 Dec 15.
129. W.Ds., G.S., Cdn. Corps, 25 Dec 15, and 3rd Div., 22-28 Dec. 15.
130. Perley Papers, vol. 4, Telegram, Aitken to Hughes, 29 Nov 15.
131. *Ibid.*, Hughes to Aitken, 30 Nov 15.
132. *Ibid.*, vol. 5, Bennett to Borden, 7 Dec 15.
133. *Ibid.*, vol. 4, Borden to Perley, 2 Dec 15.
134. *Ibid.*, Bonar Law to Perley, 31 Dec 15.
135. *Ibid.*, vol. 5.
136. *Ibid.*, Bennett to Borden, 7 Dec 15.

CHAPTER V

The St. Eloi Craters and Mount Sorrel, 1916

1. B.O.H., *1916,* I, 3.
2. *Ibid.*, 4, 7.
3. Erich von Falkenhayn, *Die Oberste Heeresleitung 1914-1916* (Berlin, 1920), 164-8.
4. G.O.H., X, 2, 9.
5. B.O.H., *1916,* I, 55-6.
6. *Ibid.*, 45-6.
7. *Ibid.*, 242.
8. H.A. Jones, *The War in the Air* (Oxford, 1928), II, 149-51.
9. *Ibid.*, 156-7.
10. *Ibid.*, 158-61. John R. Cuneo, *The Air Weapon 1914-1916,* vol. II of *Winged Mars* (Harrisburg, 1947), 230 4.
11. B.O.H., *1916,* I, 18-19, 23-4, 193.
12. 121/Overseas/720 (S.D. 2), 24 Jun 15 (847).
13. Carson to Hughes, 26 Nov 15, on Carson file 8-5-8B.
14. Statement "A" attached to memo, G.H.Q. to Second Army, 4 Jan 16, Cdn. Corps G.S. files, 99 (1).
15. P.C. 1593, 8 Jul 15.
16. "The Growth and Control of the Overseas Military Forces of Canada" (8).
17. Notes on Personnel of 3rd Canadian Division, H.Q. 650-52-7, vol. 5.
18. Canadian Conference, 28 Apr 16, on Carson file 8-1-106A.
19. Cdn. Corps G.S. files, 99(1-a).
20. "Formations and Units Ledger", held by Historical Section.
21. *Canada in the Great World War,* III (Toronto, 1919), 233.
22. Summary of Operations, 22-31 Jan 16, Appx. III/2 to W.D., G.S., Cdn Corps, January 1916.
23. *Ibid.*
24. Lord Beaverbrook, *Canada in Flanders* (London, 1917), II, 68.
25. B.O.H., *1916,* I, 162-72. History of 124th Regiment, 44-7.
26. W.D., G.S., Cdn. Corps, 15-16 Feb. 16.
27. *Work of Royal Engineers in the European War, 1914-1919—Military Mining* (*Chatham,* 1922), 24.
28. B.O.H., *1916,* I, 177-9.
29. *Ibid.*, 179, 185.
30. *Canada in Flanders,* II, 94.
31. History of 213th Reserve Regiment, 367-8.
32. B.O.H., *1916,* I, 182-4.
33. *Ibid.*, 185, 192. History of 213th Reserve Regiment, 366.
34. 27th Bn., "Summary of Operations with reference to the Recent Operations", 12 Apr 16, Appx. 3 to W.D., 27th Bn., April 1916.
35. W.Ds., 27th and 31st Bns., 4 Apr 16.
36. "The Fight for the Craters", account by Lt.-Col. D.E. Macintyre, formerly 28th Battalion and Staff Captain (Intelligence) H.Q. 6th Cdn. Inf. Bde., G.A.Q. 5-67.
37. Report on 2nd Canadian Division's Operations at St Eloi, 3-16 April 1916, para 10, Appx. "C" to G.S. Diary.
38. *Ibid.*, paras 10-11.
39. *Ibid.*, para 14.
40. Report by Brig.-Gen. H.D.B. Ketchen, Appx. 1 to 2nd Div. Report.
41. W.D., 6th Inf. Bde., 6 Apr 16. 2nd Div. Report, paras 16-23. "The German Account of the St Eloi Fighting". B.O.H., *1916,* I, 191-3. History of 214th Reserve Regiment, 187-93.
42. Photographs—St Eloi Area, March and April 1916, G.A.Q. 13-10. 2nd Div. Report, para 27.
43. 6th Inf. Bde. Report, 12 Apr 16. Appx. 1 to 2nd Div. Report.
44. 2nd Div. Report, para 31.
45. B.O.H., *1916,* I, 189-90.
46. 2nd Cdn. Div. Directive to 4th Cdn. Inf. Bde., G. 571, 8 Apr 16, Appx. 162 to W.D., G.S., 2nd Div., April 1916.
47. 2nd Div. Report, paras 32-42.
48. Appx. 182 to G.S. Diary, April 1916
49. "St Eloi Craters—Report on Operations", General Turner's Papers, G.A.Q. 13-10, folder, I, Part II, fol. 000747.
50. B.O.H., *1916,* I, 191, 193.
51. Letter, Sir Richard Turner to Col. A.F. Duguid. 7 Aug 30, H.Q. 650-52-7, vol. 5.

52. Aitken to Hughes, 26 Apr 16, P.A.C., Borden Papers, O.C. 183(2), 14955-7. Haig's Diary, 21 Apr 16.
53. 2nd Cdn. Div. Memo, G. 685, 12 Apr 16, 2nd Cdn. Div. H.Q. file, folder 20, file 7.
54. B.O.H., *1916*, I, 191.
55. Summary of Operations, Appx. III/2 to W.D., G.S., Cdn. Corps, April-May 1916.
56. Haig's Diary, 23 Apr 16.
57. Aitken to Hughes, 26 Apr 16, transcript of sender's copy furnished Director Historical Section by Lord Beaverbrook. (A copy of the text received in Ottawa substitutes the word "nominally" for "disastrously", makes the "Canadian Divisions" singular), P.A.C., Borden Papers, O.C. 183(2), 14955-7.
58. Hughes to Aitken, Borden to Aitken and Perley, 26 Apr 16, P.A.C., Borden Papers, O.C. 183(2).
59. Editorial, *Canadian Defence Quarterly*, January 1928, 131-3.
60. Adolf Deutelmoser, *The 27th Infantry Division in the World War 1914-18* (Stuttgart, 1925), 39. History of 120th Regiment, 34.
61. B.O.H., *1916*, I, 229-30. Account of Operations by Canadian Corps, June 1 to June 8, 1916, file 1-A-1, 16-6-13, vol. 2, 1-3.
62. *Canada in Flanders*, II, 173.
63. History of 120th Regiment, 36.
64. S. G. Bennett, *The 4th Canadian Mounted Rifles 1914-1919* (Toronto, 1926), 19-20.
65. Lt.-Gen. Sir A. C. Macdonnell, "Mount Sorrel and Hooge", H.Q. 650-52-7, vol. 5.
66. History of 120th Regiment, 36. History of 125th Regiment, 118.
67. Maj.-Gen. A.G.L. McNaughton, "The Development of Artillery in the Great War" (*Canadian Defence Quarterly*, January, 1929), 171.
68. History of 125th Regiment, 120.
69. W.D., P.P.C.L.I., 2 Jun 16. Hodder-Williams, *Princess Patricia's Canadian Light Infantry, 1914-1919*, I, 123, 135-6.
70. *The 27th Infantry Division in the World War 1914-18*, 40.
71. W.Ds., 10th and 52nd Bns., 3 Jun 16.
72. Account of Operations by Canadian Corps, 12.
73. *Ibid.*, 17-19.
74. *The 27th Infantry Division in the World War 1914-18*, 40.
75. W.Ds., 28th and 31st Bns., 6 Jun 16.
76. *Canada in Flanders*, II, 219-20.
77. B.O.H., *1916*, I, 239-40.
78. Summary of Operations, 1st Cdn. Div., 8-15 Jun 16, Appx. 15 to G.S. Diary.
79. B.O.H., *1916*, I, 241.
80. W.D., A. & Q., 1st Cdn. Division, 17 Jun 16. Cdn. Corps Summaries of Operations, 2-14 Jun 16, Appx. III/2 to G.S. Diary.
81. *The 27th Infantry Division in the World War 1914-18*, 40.
82. W.D., G.S., Cdn. Corps, 18 Aug 16.
83. *Ibid.*, 14, 18 Aug 16.
84. *The War in the Air*, II, 179-80.
85. Appendix III/5 to W.D., G.S., Cdn. Corps, August 1916.
86. "Distinguishing Markings", G.A.Q. file 11-76. 3rd Cdn. Div. R.O. 939, 5 Sep 16 and R.O. 1839, 23 May 17.
87. W.D., A. & Q., Cdn. Corps, June 1916.
88. General A. G. L. McNaughton to Director Historical Section, 22 Jun 61.
89. Alderson to Gwatkin, 6 Feb 16, cited in Appx. 111 to Duguid.
90. Appx. 111 to Duguid.
91. Lt.-Col. S. S. Weatherbie to Col. C. P. Stacey, 31 Jan 57.
92. Undated and unaddressed, 1st Div. file 1-B-1.
93. Report by Sir John French, 23.
94. C.-in-C. to War Office, 12 Jun 15 (111).
95. Alderson to Gwatkin, 6 Feb 16, *ibid.*
96. Hughes to Alderson, 7 Mar 16, *ibid.*
97. "Lieut.-Gen. Sir Edwin Alderson, K.C.B., A Brave Commander who was Sacrificed to the Ross Rifle" (*The Khaki Call*, February 1928).
98. Appx. 111 to Duguid.
99. Cdn. Corps memo G. 654, 2 May 16, Carson file 4-5-13B, *ibid.*
100. Haig to the War Office, 28 May 16, *ibid.*
101. Bonar Law to Governor General, 11 Jul 16, *ibid.*

Chapter VI

The Battles of the Somme, July-November 1916

1. British General Staff Weekly Summary, 29 Jun 16, cited in Robertson, *Soldiers and Statesmen*, I, 268.
2. "Operations of 1916", Appx. "A" to Haig's *Private Papers.*
3. B.O.H., *1916*, I, 31.
4. Haig's *Private Papers*, 145.
5. Edmonds, *A Short History of World War I*, 177-9.
6. Wynne, *If Germany Attacks*, 101-3.
7. Crown Prince Rupprecht von Bayern, *Mein Kriegstagebuch*, ed. Frauenholz (Mittler, Berlin, 1929), 3 vols., I, 482.
8. G.O.H., X, 42, 348-9.
9. B.O.H., *1916*, I, 250, 268-9, 300-1.
10. *Ibid.*, 483, 485-6, 488.
11. W.D., Cdn. Cav. Bde., 14 Jul 16.
12. "Special Report to C.I.G.S., 1 Aug 16", quoted in B.O.H., *1916*, II, 232.
13. *Ibid.*, 230.

14. Hindenburg, *Out of My Life*, 123, 163. General Ludendorff, *My War Memories* (London, n.d.), 2nd ed., I, 239.
15. G.O.H., X, 422.
16. *Ibid.*, 675-6.
17. O.A.D. 116, "G.H.Q. Plans for a Mid-September Offensive", Appx. 16 to B.O.H., *1916*, II.
18. C.E.W. Bean, *The A.I.F. in France, 1916* (Volume III of *The Official History of Australia in the War of 1914-1918*), 853-61. W.D., G.S., 1st Cdn. Div., 5-8 Sep 16.
19. Supplement to *The London Gazette*, 26 Oct 16.
20. B.O.H., *1916*, I, 293.
21. O.A.D. 116, 19 Aug 16, "G.H.Q. Plan for a Mid-September Offensive", Appx. 16 to *ibid.*, II.
22. Maj.-Gen. Sir E.D. Swinton, *Eyewitness* (London, 1932), 186-7.
23. B.O.H., *1916*, II, 248-9.
24. *Ibid.*, 296.
25. *Ibid.*, I, 288.
26. "Training of Divisions for Offensive Action", 8 May 16, Appx. 17 to *ibid.*
27. Cdn. Corps Operation Order No. 46, 13 Sep 16, Appx. 11/10 to G.S. Diary, September 1916. Summary of Operations, Appx. VI to *ibid.*
28. Cdn. Corps Intelligence Summary, 15 Sep 16, Appx. V to *ibid.*
29. Report on Operations of Tanks, 15.9.16, Appx. VII to *ibid.*
30. *Ibid.* B.O.H., *1916*, II, 364.
31. Churchill, *The World Crisis*, III, 1052.
32. Report on Operations of Tanks, 15.9.16.
33. J.H. Boraston (ed.), *Sir Douglas Haig's Despatches* (London, 1920), 42.
34. Col.-Gen. Heinz Guderian, *Die Panzerwaffe* (Stuttgart, 1943), 2nd ed., 53-4.
35. Summary of Operations, Appx. VI to W.D., G.S., Cdn. Corps, September 1916.
36. 5th Inf. Bde. memorandum to 22nd, 25th and 26th Bns., 22 Sep 16, Appx. 28a to Bde. Diary.
37. Joseph Chaballe, *Histoire du 22e Bataillon canadien-français, 1914-1919* (Montreal, 1952), 204. Appx. 28a to W.D., 5th Inf. Bde., September 1916.
38. Bennett, *The 4th Canadian Mounted Rifles, 1914-1919*, 32-4.
39. History of the Canadian Machine Gun Corps C.E.F., I, 35.
40. B.O.H., *1916*, II, 348.
41. Supplement to *The London Gazette*, 26 Oct 16.
42. Cdn. Corps Summary of Operations, 15-22, 22-29 Sep 16. W.Ds., G.S. 1st Cdn. Div. and 1st Bn., 22 Sep 16.
43. Haig's *Despatches*, 42.
44. B.O.H., *1916*, II, 392.
45. Cdn. Corps Operation Order No. 55, 24 Sep 16, and Message G. 277 of same date.
46. Kim Beattie, *48th Highlanders of Canada, 1891-1928* (Toronto, 1932), 180.
47. R.C. Featherstonhaugh, *The Royal Montreal Regiment, 14th Battalion C.E.F., 1914-1925* (Montreal, 1927), 117.
48. B.O.H., *1916*, II, 395-8.
49. *If Germany Attacks*, 130.
50. W.D., 14th Bn., 26-27 Sep 16. C.E.F. Historical Summary, 3rd Infantry Brigade.
51. C.E.F. Historical Summary, 2nd Infantry Brigade.
52. B.O.H., *1916*, II, 399, 407-8.
53. W.D., G.S., 2nd Cdn. Div., 27 Sep 16.
54. W.D., 3rd Inf. Bde., 27 Sep 16.
55. Report on Cavalry Operation, night of 27th-28th September 1916, Appx. C-6 to W.D., Cdn. Corps Cavalry Regt., September 1916.
56. W.D., 19th Bn., 28 Sep 16.
57. W.Ds., 24th and 25th Bns., 28 Sep 16.
58. B.O.H., *1916*, II, 413, 420-1. W.D., G.S., 3rd Cdn. Div., 29 Sep 16.
59. W.D., 7th Inf. Bde., 30 Sep 16.
60. Haig's *Despatches*, 45.
61. Letter of 23 Sep 16, cited in B.O.H., *1916*, II, 392.
62. *Ibid.*, 427.
63. W.D., G.S., Cdn. Corps, 1 Oct 16.
64. Report on Operations, 27 Sep-3 Oct 16, Appx. "A" to W.D., 8th Inf. Bde., October 1916.
65. 5th Brigade Operation Order No. 87, 30 Sep 16.
66. "J.A.H.", *Les Poilus Canadiens, Le Roman du Vingt-Deuxième Bataillon Canadien-Français* (n.p., 1918), 30.
67. O.C. 22nd Bn, to H.Q. 5th Inf. Bde., Appx. 1 to Bde. Diary, October 1916.
68. O.C. 25th Bn. to G.O.C. 5th Cdn. Inf. Bde., 5 Oct 16, *ibid.*
69. W.Ds., 5th Inf. Bde. and G.S., Cdn Corps, 1 Oct 16.
70. 5th Inf. Bde. Summary of Operations, Appx. 5 to Bde. Diary, October 1916.
71. Reserve Army to Cdn. Corps, 5 Oct 16, Appx. 1/12 to G.S. Diary, October 1916.
72. B.O.H., *1916*, II, 450-1.
73. Supplement to *The London Gazette*, 22 Oct 18.
74. Resumé of Events, 9 Oct 16, Appx. 9 to W.D., 3rd Inf. Bde., October 1916.
75. Narrative of Attack on Regina Trench, Appx. "A" to W.D., 9th Inf. Bde., October 1916.
76. Appx. 3 to W.D., R.C.R., October 1916.
77. Report by Lt.-Col. W. A. Griesbach, O.C. 49th Bn., 12 Oct 16, appended to Bn. Diary, October 1916.
78. W.Ds., 7th and 9th Inf. Bdes., 8 Oct 16.
79. S.G. 66/43, 10 Oct 16, on Cdn. War Records Office file 214, folder 6.
80. B.O.H., *1916*, II, 566.
81. Maj.-Gen. A. G. L. McNaughton, "The Development of Artillery in the Great War" (*Canadian Defence Quarterly*, January 1929), 163.
82. Artillery Instruction No. 38, 4 Oct 16, and No. 39, 5 Oct 16, Appx. "A" to W.D., G.O.C. R.A. Cdn. Corps, October 1916.

83. Artillery Instructions by G.O.C. R.A. Cdn. Corps, 10 Oct 16, in *ibid.*
84. W.D., H.Q., C.C.H.A., 1-14 Oct 16.
85. Report to G.O.C. 7th Inf. Bde., 12 Oct 16, Appended to W.D., 49th Bn., October 1916.
86. Report, 1st Cdn. Div. to Cdn. Corps, 12 Oct 16, C.W.R.O. file 214, folder 3.
87. *Ibid.*
88. B.O.H., *1916*, II, 453-4.
89. C.-in-C. Report to C.I.G.S., 7 Oct 16, cited in *ibid.*, 456-7.
90. Information compiled from G.O.H., X and XI.
91. B.O.H., *1916*, II, 456-7.
92. *Ibid.*, 458.
93. *Ibid.*, 459.
94. Haig's *Private Papers*, 173.
95. W.D., G.S., 4th Cdn. Div., 3 Sep 16. Summary of Operations, Second Army, 31 Aug-7 Sep, and 14-21 Sep 16.
96. W.D., G.S., 4th Cdn. Div., 3, 5 Sep 16. Stühmke, History of 26th Infantry Division, Part II, 36-9 and Sketch 3. G.O.H., XI, Map 2. *Histories of 251 Divisions of the German Army*, 97.
97. W.D., G.S., 4th Cdn. Div., 8, 16 Sep 16.
98. Bean, *The A.I.F. in France, 1916*, 882. Report on Raids carried out by 4th Cdn. Div., Appx. "A" to G.S. Diary, September 1916.
99. W.D., G.S., 4th Cdn. Div., 17 Sep 16.
100. Bernard McEvoy and Capt. A. H. Finlay, *History of the 72nd Battalion Seaforth Highlanders of Canada* (Vancouver, 1920), 24-5.
101. 4th Cdn. Div. Operation Orders No. 8, 10 Oct 16, and No. 12, 15 Oct 16.
102. W.D., G.S., 4th Cdn. Div., 13-20 Oct 16.
103. Report on Operations conducted 21-10-16, Appx. "K" to W.D., 11th Inf. Bde., October 1916.
104. B.O.H., *1916*, II, 463-4.
105. Appx. "C" to W.D., 10th Inf. Bde., October 1916.
106. Intelligence Report, 26 Oct 16, Appx. "C3" to *ibid.*
107. W.D., 44th Bn., 25 Oct 16.
108. Letter to Overseas Minister of Militia, 20 Mar 17, file GAQ 13-7.
109. Appx. 1 to W.D., 10th Bde. C.F.A., October 1916.
110. W.Ds., 3rd, 10th and 12th Bdes. C.F.A., October 1916.
111. Haig's *Private Papers*, 176.
112. Operations on Night 10/11th November, Appx. "A" to W.D., G.S., 4th Cdn. Div., November 1916.
113. W.D., 3rd Cdn. Div. Arty., 10 Nov 16.
114. Report on Operation, Appx. "C"-1 to W.D. 10th Inf. Bde., November 1916. History of 106th Regiment, 107. History of 107th Regiment, 293-7. History of 2nd Guard Reserve Regiment, 77.
115. Appx. 1 to W.D., 3rd Cdn. Div. Arty., November 1916.
116. E. S. Russenholt, *Six Thousand Canadian Men—Being the History of the 44th Battalion Canadian Infantry 1914-1919* (Winnipeg, 1932), 58.
117. B.O.H., *1916*, II, 478.
118. Ludendorff, *My War Memories*, I, 290.
119. B.O.H., *1916*, II, 510.
120. *Ibid.*, 513.
121. Operations 4th Canadian Division, November 18th, 1916, Appx. "C" to G.S. Diary, November 1916.
122. *Ibid.* Report of Operations conducted by Brig.-Gen. Odlum, Comd. 11th Inf. Bde., 18 Nov 16, Appx. 3 to Bde. Diary, November 1916.
123. B.O.H., *1916*, II, 517-19.
124. *Ibid.*, 515-16.
125. 4th Div. Report (above, note 121).
126. B.O.H., *1916*, II, 536.
127. "Lessons to be derived from Operations on the Somme", 23 Dec 16, Cdn. Corps G.S. file 1, folder 44.
128. Russenholt, *Six Thousand Canadian Men*, 46.
129. B.O.H., *1916*, II, 529.
130. Letter, Col. Duguid to Senator F. B. Black, 24 Apr 34, H.Q. 54-21-1-208.
131. Haig's *Despatches*, 51.
132. Haig's *Private Papers*, 152.
133. *The World Crisis*, III, 1057.
134. *War Memoirs of David Lloyd George*, (London, 1936) VI, 3414.
135. G.O.H., XI, 41.
136. *Ibid.*, X, Appx. 3 and XI, Appx. 4.
137. B.O.H., *1916*, I, x.
138. Colonel the Lord Sydenham of Combe *et al*, *The World Crisis by Winston Churchill, A Criticism* (London, n.d.), 54-5.
139. B.O.H., *1916*, II, xvi and 553.
140. G.O.H., XI, 103-4.
141. *Ibid.*
142. *My War Memories*, I, 304.
143. Jones, *The War in the Air*, II, 323.
144. Edmonds, *Short History*, 150.
145. *The War in the Air*, II, 324.

Chapter VII

Behind the Front

1. European War Print No. 2 (Item 170).
2. Tel., Militia, Ottawa, to Thompson, London, n.d., H.Q. 593-2-51. Carson to MacDougall, 15 Aug 16, Carson file 6-Mc-153.
3. P.C. 107, 15 Jan 15.
4. Letter to Perley, 21 Jan 15, P.A.C., Borden Papers, O.C. 225, 22830.
5. Carson to G.O.C. Southern Command, 18 Feb 15, Carson file 8-5-10.

6. Carson to Minister, 23 Feb 15, *ibid.*
7. H.Q. 593-2-51. Carson file 8-5-10.
8. Carson file 8-1-28, 2 Jul 15.
9. War Office to C.-in-C., 15 Jul 15, Cdn. Section G.H.Q. 3rd Echelon file 14-1-21, folder 3, A86.
10. Carson file 8-1-28.
11. H.Q., O.M.F.C. file 10-8-22, copy of message, Hughes to Lougheed, 25 Jul 15.
12. Hughes to Lougheed, 28 Jul 15, Carson file 8-5-10.
13. Carson file 8-5-43.
14. Carson to Hughes, 15 Nov 15, *ibid.*
15. Carson file 8-5-10-B.
16. Carson to Hughes, 15 Dec 15, Carson file 8-1-55.
17. Letter to Borden, 9 May 15, P.A.C., Perley Papers, vol. 1.
18. P.A.C., Borden Papers, O.C. 183(2), 14863, 14868.
19. *Ibid.*, 14903.
20. Lord Beaverbrook's Papers, copy in possession of Historical Section.
21. Memo to Deputy Minister, 1 Apr 16, H.Q.C. 54-21-5-7, vol. 2.
22. P.A.C., Sir Edward Kemp's Papers, Acting Minister of Militia, "Inventory of Clothing in England and Canada". P.A.C., Borden Papers, O.C. 378(1), 35632-4.
23. H.Q., O.M.F.C. (Argyll House) file 0-153-33, vol. 1.
24. MacDougall to Aitken, 19 Apr 16, Carson file 6-Mc-153. Borden Papers, O.C., 183(3), 15044-6.
25. *Debates, House of Commons,* 28 and 30 Mar 16.
26. Borden Papers, O.C. 318(1), 35679-80.
27. Borden's *Memoirs,* II, 563-4.
28. Borden Papers, O.C. 318(1), 35721-3.
29. *Canadian Gazette,* 3 Aug 16, 430. Borden Papers, O.C. 318(1), 35683.
30. Borden Papers, O.C. 318(1), 35704; O.C. 190, 15821.
31. Correspondence in *ibid.*, O.C. 318(1), 35725.
32. Carson file, "Minutes of the Acting Sub-Militia Council for Overseas Canadians, London, England; September 5, 1916 to October 18, 1916".
33. Borden Papers, O.C. 318(1), 35727.
34. *Thid.*, O.C. 318(2), 35779.
38. Correspondence in *ibid.*, 35785.
36. Carson file 8-1-106.
37. Hughes to Carson, 8 Oct 16, *ibid.*, 8-1-106A.
38. Minutes of the Acting Sub-Militia Council.
39. Borden Papers, O.C. 318(2), 35810-13.
40. *Ibid.*, 35808-9.
41. H.Q. 54-21-1-64, Hughes to Boudreau, 23 Oct 16.
42. Borden Papers, O.C. 318(2), 35835-7.
43. *Ibid.*, 35838.
44. Copies of correspondence in Montreal *Gazette,* 17 Nov 16.
45. Borden Papers, O.C. 318(2), 35852.
46. *Ibid.*, 35847. P.C. 2656, 31 Oct 16.
47. Borden Papers, O.C. 318(2), 35868-9.
48. *Ibid.*, 35881.
49. *Ibid.*, 35884-5.
50. *Ibid.*, 35887.
51. Perley Papers, vol. 7, letter dated 6 Nov 16.
52. P.A.C., Turner Papers.
53. H.Q., O.M.F.C. 10-8-7, memo dated 14 Jun 17.
54. Adam Shortt, *Early Economic Factors of the War Upon Canada* (New York, 1918), 10-11.
55. *Canadian Annual Review, 1914,* 195-6.
56. P.C. 2831/1914; P.C. 1593/1915; P.C. 2559/1915.
57. H.Q. 1982-1-42, vol. 1.
58. H.Q. 1982-1-46, vol. 5.
59. Borden Papers, O.C. 313(1), 34611.
60. H.Q.C. 1591, vol. 2, Letter to Under Secretary of State for External Affairs, 25 Nov 15.
61. P.C. 36/1916.
62. *Memorandum (No. 3) Respecting the Work of the Department of Militia and Defence from February 1 to December 31, 1916,* H.Q. 54-21-1-20, vol. 2.
63. Statistics from Machine Records Section, Adjutant General's Branch.
64. Currie Papers, Currie to Hon. H. G. Brewster, Premier of British Columbia, 27 Jan 18.
65. Perley Papers, vol. 5, R. B. Bennett to Borden, 7 Dec 15.
66. Borden's *Memoirs,* I, 529.
67. *Debates, House of Commons,* 17 Jan 16.
68. H.Q. 1982-1-42, vol. 3, fol. 283.
69. *Canadian Annual Review, 1916,* 303.
70. Toronto *Globe,* 5 Jan 16. Winnipeg *Free Press,* 5 Jan 16.
71. Hughes to Borden, 5 Jul 16, quoted in *Debates, House of Commons,* 19 Jun 17.
72. Borden's *Memoirs,* I, 494.
73. *Debates, House of Commons,* 17 Jan 16.
74. Sir Thomas White, *The Story of Canada's War Finance* (Montreal, 1921), 30-1.
75. Note 71, above.
76. *Canadian Annual Review, 1914,* 217; *1915,* 193.
77. Perley Papers, vol. 5.
78. Borden Papers, O.C.A. 149, 77912.
79. *Ibid.*, 77915
80. *Ibid.*, O.C. 318(1), 35703.
81. Statistics from Machine Records Section, Adjutant General's Branch.
82. Borden Papers, O.C. 194, vol. 1, 16569.
83. *Ibid.*, 16573.
84. *Ibid.*, 16581.
85. *Ibid.*, 16618.
86. H.Q. 1982-1-42, vol. 3.
87. Manitoba *Free Press,* 17 Apr 16, *ibid.*
88. *Canadian Annual Review, 1916,* 630.
89. Borden Papers, R.F.B. 963(1).
90. Militia Order No. 340 of 12 Jul 15, and No. 72 of 14 Feb 16.
91. Report by R. B. Bennett in *Debates, House of Commons,* 20 Sep 17.
92. *Debates, House of Commons,* 20 Sep 17.

93. H.Q. 1982-1-71, vol. 2, Reports, M.D. No. 5 and M.D. No. 10, 2 Aug 17.
94. H.Q. 54-21-8-41, A.G. to Director General of National Service, 21 Mar 17.
95. O. D. Skelton, *Life and Letters of Sir Wilfrid Laurier* (Toronto, 1921), II, 462.
96. H.Q., M.D. No. 4 file 4 D. 25-2-1, vol. 1.
97. Currie Papers, file on "Corps Matters", Currie to McBain, 12 Dec 16.
98. H.Q.C. 1883, Kemp to Borden, 22 Dec 16.
99. Borden Papers, O.C. 317(2), 35563.
100. *Debates, House of Commons,* 3 May 17.
101. Documents on H.Q. 593-2-1, vol. 1, H.Q. 593-7-1 and H.Q. 593-7-2.
102. Carson file 8-5-10.
103. Cdn. Trg. Div., Shorncliffe, Routine Order No. 2565/1915.
104. H.Q.C. 1591, vol. 1, Troopers to Minister of Militia, 26 Apr 15.
105. *Ibid.*, A.G., to Officers Commanding Divisions and Districts.
106. "Drafts Despatched Overseas" (734).
107. H.Q.C. 1591, vol. 3, C.G.S. to A.G., 3 Jun 16.
108. Cdn. Routine Order No. 1535, 26 May 17.
109. Carson file 8-1-106, Minutes of "Canadian Conference", 28 Apr 16.
110. Cdn. Routine Order, No. 163, 5 Jan 17.
111. Overseas Minister's files, "Report of the Adjutant General's Branch, O.M.F.C., 20 Feb 17".
112. Overseas Minister's file 10-8-17. W.D., 3rd Cdn. Pioneer Bn., May 1917. Cdn. Corps G.S. file, "Organization and Establishment of Pioneer Battalions".
113. Overseas Minister's file 10-8-17.
114. L.M. Gould, *From B.C. to Baisieux, Being the Narrative History of the 102nd Canadian Infantry Battalion* (Victoria, 1919), 63.
115. Overseas Minister's file 10-8-17, Currie to Perley, 29 Aug 17.
116. Correspondence on M.D. No. 3 file 26-5-1, vol. 1.
117. War Office to Colonial Office, 28 May 15 (848).
118. Under Secretary of State for External Affairs to the Governor General's Secretary, 28 Sep 15, *ibid.*
119. M.D. No. 3 file 26-5-1, vol. 1. R.C. Fetherstonhaugh, *McGill University at War, 1914-1918, 1939-1945* (Montreal, 1947), 16-18.
120. M.D. No. 4 file 48-9-1, vol. 1.
121. Hodder-Williams, *Princess Patricia's Canadian Light Infantry, 1914-1919,* I, 83. W.D., P.P.C.L.I., 9 Jun 16.
122. M.D. No. 4 files 48-6-1, 48-7-1, 48-8-1, 48-9-1.
123. Strength Return dated 31 Aug 16, on Cdn. Sec. G.H.Q. file E-38-5, vol. 2.
124. Cdn. Corps Directive A-24-0-48, dated 5 Sep 17, on file GAQ 1-6.
125. A.G., G.H.Q. to H.Q. Cdn. Corps, 5 Dec 17, on Cdn. Sec. G.H.Q. file E-38-5, vol. 3.
126. Minutes of the Acting Sub-Militia Council, 13 Oct 16. Carson file 8-1-130.
127. Minutes of Acting Sub-Militia Council, 13 and 18 Oct 16.
128. Letter dated 10 Nov 16, on H.Q.C. 1883.
129. H.Q., O.M.F.C. (Argyll House) file 0-241-33, vol. 1.
130. *Ibid.*, vol. 3.
131. B.O.H., *1918,* I, 50-5.
132. Currie to the Overseas Minister of Militia, 7 Feb 18, Currie Papers, file 7, Drawer 1801.
133. *Ibid.*
134. H.Q., O.M.F.C. (Argyll House) file 0-210-33.
135. Letter, Kemp to Wilson, 21 Jun 18, Borden Papers, OC 494.
136. "Organization of the Canadian Corps in the Field", Currie Papers, folder 2, Drawer 1801.

CHAPTER VIII

The Battle of Vimy Ridge, 9-14 April 1917

1. W.D., G.S., Cdn. Corps, 21-28 Oct 16.
2. W.D., G.O.C., R.A., Cdn. Corps, 26, 31 Oct 16
3. Report on Operations, Appx. "B" to W.D., 8th Inf. Bde., December 1916.
4. 4th Brigade Report on Operation, 17 Jan 17, 4th Bde. files, folder 22, vol. 7.
5. Appx. 8 to *ibid.* W.Ds., 20th and 21st Bns., 4th Field Coy. C.E., 17 Jan 17. G.O.H. XI, Sketch 15. History of 22nd Regiment, 140-3.
6. Report by Lt.-Col. R. D. Davies (O.C. Raiding Parties), 13 Feb 17, in Appx. "B-2" to W.D., 10th Inf. Bde.
7. W.Ds., 44th and 72nd Bns., 1, 2 Mar 17. G.O.H., XII, 185. History of 261st Reserve Regiment, 51.
8. "Resolutions of the Chantilly Conference", 16 Nov 16, Appx. 1 to B.O.H., *1917,* I.
9. F.O.H., Tome V, vol. I, 151-2.
10. Nivelle to Haig, 21 Dec 16, *ibid.*, Annexe 332. (For translation see Appx. 2 to B.O.H., *1917,* I.)
11. B.O.H., *1917,* I, 20-1.
12. Letter, O.A.D. 262, Haig to Nivelle, 6 Jan 17, Appx. 7 to *ibid.*
13. *War Memoirs of David Lloyd George,* III, 1434-5.
14. Haig's *Private Papers,* 188.
15. Appx. 8 to B.O.H., *1917,* I.

16. Haig's Diary, Entries for 16 and 18 Jan 17.
17. Appx. 18 to B.O.H., *1917*, I. Haig's *Private Papers*, 200.
18. Haig's *Private Papers*, 201.
19. French Fifth Army, G.S. 3rd Sec. No. 2043-3, 30 Apr 15, cited in Wynne, *If Germany Attacks*, 148.
20. G.O.H., XII, 38-9.
21. Ludendorff, *My War Memories, 1914-1918*, I, 386-7.
22. *If Germany Attacks*, 156-7.
23. Fritz von Lossberg, *Meine Tätigkeit im Weltkriege, 1914-1918* (Berlin, 1939), 277. G.O.H., XI, 17.
24. *My War Memories*, I, 387.
25. G.O.H., XII, 61-3, and XI, Map 2a.
26. B.O.H., 1917, I, 91.
27. *My War Memories*, II, 404-5.
28. G.O.H., XI, 514-16; XII, 64.
29. *Ibid.*, XII, 143-5, and Map 6.
30. B.O.H., *1917*, I, 486.
31. G.O.H., XII, Appx. 18 (map). F.O.H., Tome V, vol. I, Cartes 35 and 60.
32. F.O.H., Tome V, vol. II, Annexes 1914 and 1917.
33. G.O.H., XII, 410.
34. Edmonds, *Short History*, 222.
35. F.O.H., Tome V, vol. II, 192-5, 206.
36. "Canadian Corps Scheme of Operations for Battles of Arras", G. 266, 5 Mar 17, on Cdn. Corps file S. 156/31/1.
37. Reported by Lt.-Col. D. E. Macintyre, formerly Bde. Maj. 4th Inf. Bde.
38. B.O.H., *1916*, I, 2.
39. G. 295, Cdn. Corps to Divisions, 23 Dec 16, on Cdn. Corps file S. 156/31/1, vol. 1.
40. G. 208, Byng to First Army, 19 Dec 16, on *ibid.*
41. G.O.H., XII, 211.
42. *If Germany Attacks*, 170-1.
43. G.O.H., XII, Appx. 9 (map). Reichsarchiv, *Die Schlachten des Weltkrieges*, vol. 28, *Die Osterschlacht bei Arras 1917*, I, 22-6, 34-6, 40.
44. G.O.H., XII, Appx. 8 (map).
45. *Histories of 251 Divisions of the German Army*, 43, 273, 538.
46. B.O.H., *1917*, I, 317, and Sketches 7, 11.
47. First Army No. G.S. 529/12(a), Comments on Canadian Corps Scheme of Operations, 8 Mar 17, on Cdn. Corps file S. 156/31/1, vol. 1.
48. "Report on Operations of Canadian Corps against Vimy Ridge", Corps G.S. file, folder 51, file 5, p. 3.
49. Comments on Canadian Corps Scheme of Operations.
50. CCHA B.M. 121/6, Arrangement of Counter Battery and Siege Groups, 7 Apr 17, on S. 340/3, vol. 2.
51. Corps Report on Operations, p. 5. B.O.H., *1917*, I, 306-7.
52. War Office, *Text Book of Ammunition* (London, 1936), 163-4.
53. B.O.H., *1917*, I, 307.
54. Maj.-Gen. A. G. L. McNaughton, "Counter Battery Work" (*Canadian Defence Quarterly*, July 1926), 380-91. McNaughton, "The Development of Artillery in the Great War" (*ibid.*, January 1929), 160, 171.
55. Diary of Lt.-Col. D. E. Mcintyre, B.M. 4th Cdn. Inf. Bde., 19 Feb 17.
56. Cdn. Corps G. 776, Instructions to Divisions, 22 Mar 17, on S. 156/31/1, vol. 1.
57. *If Germany Attacks*, 166-7. H. M. Urquhart, Arthur Currie, *The Biography of a Great Canadian* (Toronto, 1950), 141-3.
58. Lt.-Col. Macintyre's Diary, 5 Apr 17.
59. *Die Osterschlacht bei Arras 1917*, I, 30.
60. *Ibid.*, 29-32.
61. Cdn. Corps Weekly Summaries of Operations, Appx. III to G.S. Diary, March-April 1917.
62. O. G. Thetford and E. J. Riding, *Aircraft of the 1914-1918 War* (Harleyford, 1954), 31, 74.
63. Jones, *The War in the Air*, III, 340-4. C.B.S.O. Cdn. Corps Artillery Report on Capture of Vimy Ridge (n.d.), folder 8, file 4, Part F, p. 4.
64. Lt.-Col. Macintyre's Diary, 17 March 17.
65. Bruce Robertson, ed., *Von Richthofen and the Flying Circus* (Letchworth, Herts, 1958), 44-5.
66. W. A. Bishop, *Winged Warfare* (London, 1918), 126-7.
67. Col. A. F. Duguid, "Canada on Vimy Ridge" (*The Canada Year Book, 1936*), 58.
68. Brigade reports on operations.
69. History of the Canadian Machine Gun Corps, C.E.F., II, 12.
70. Unit W.Ds., particularly Appendix to W.D., 14th Bn., April 1917.
71. Supplement to *The London Gazette*, 8 Jun 17.
72. Corps Report on Operations.
73. Supplement to *The London Gazette*, 8 Jun 17.
74. W.Ds., G.S., 2nd Cdn. Div., and 2nd and 3rd Inf. Bdes., 9 Apr 17.
75. History of 263rd Reserve Regiment, 116, 119.
76. Narrative of Operations, Appx. 601 to W.D., G.S., 3rd Cdn. Div., April 1917.
77. W.D., G.S., Cdn. Corps, Message from 1st Cdn. Div., 7:30 a.m., 9 Apr 17.
78. W.D., 21st Cdn. Bn., 9 Apr 17.
79. W.D., 25th Cdn. Bn., 9 Apr 17.
80. W.D., G.S., Cdn. Corps, 9 Apr 17.
81. *Die Osterschlacht bei Arras 1917*, I, 40.
82. Report on Operations, 15 Apr 17, Appx. "D" to W.D., 7th Inf. Bde., April 1917.
83. 28th Bn. Narrative of Operations, 8-11 Apr 17, Appx. "D" to Unit Diary.
84. B.O.H., *1917*, I, 335.
85. Duguid, "Canada on Vimy Ridge", 57.
86. Corps Report on Operations.
87. Narrative of Offensive, Appx. to W.D., 27th Bn., April 1917.
88. *Ibid.*
89. W.D., G.S., Cdn. Corps, 9 Apr 17.
90. "Battle of Arras, Considerations of Probable Action after the Attack on Vimy

Ridge, First Army, 28th March 1917", Appx. 29 to B.O.H., *1917*, I.
91. *Ibid.*, 333.
92. Cavalry Corps Instructions, 1 Apr 17 and amendments, Appx. 31 to *ibid.*
93. Message from First Army, 3:50 p.m., W.D., G.S., Cdn. Corps, 9 Apr 17.
94. B.O.H., *1917*, I, 333.
95. Messages of 4:50 and 6:00 p.m. in Corps War Diary.
96. Report by O.C. Cdn. Light Horse, Appx. "C" to W.D., Cdn. Light Horse, April 1917.
97. *Die Osterschlacht bei Arras 1917*, I, 64.
98. W.D., G.S., Cdn. Corps, Messages from 2nd Cdn. Div., 6:20 and 7:15 p.m., 9 Apr 17.
99. B.O.H., *1917*, I, 354-5. *Die Osterschlacht bei Arras 1917*, I, 92.
100. B.O.H., *1917*, I, 311, 362-8, 353-5. G.O.H., XII, 198.
101. Corps Report on Operations.
102. 4th Div. Report on Operations, Appx. "B" to W.D., April 1917.
103. Brigade and Unit Accounts of Operations.
104. G.O.H., XII, 214-15, 236-8.
105. 4th Div. Report on Operations.
106. 12th Brigade Report on Operations, Appx. 5 to Bde. Diary. April 1917. Supplement to *The London Gazette*,. 8 Jun 17.
107. Report on Operations, 46th Cdn. Inf. Bn., April 9th to April 15th 1917, appended to Unit Diary.
108. Report on Operations of the 10th Cdn. Inf. Bde. on Vimy Ridge, Appx. "A-1" to Bde. Diary, April 1917.
109. 12th Brigade Report on Operations.
110. Corps Report on Operations, 17.
111. First Army Order No. 103, 5 Apr 17, W.D., G.S., Cdn. Corps, April 1917.
112. Cdn. Corps Order G. 165, 2 Apr 17, on S. 156/31/1.
113. *Die Osterschlacht bei Arras 1917*, I, 142 *ff*. G.O.H., XII, Appx. 10 (map).
114. *Die Osterschlacht bei Arras 1917*, I, 142. G.O.H., XII, 231.
115. Report on Operations, Appx. "A-1" to W.D., 10th Inf. Bde., April 1917.
116. B.O.H., *1917*, I, 344*n*.
117. G.H.Q. letter O.A.D. 279, 15 Jan 17, on Cdn. Corps file S. 156/31/5 "Gas and Smoke". B.O.H., *1917*, I, 345.
118. B.O.H., *1917*, I, 345*n*.
119. Corps Report on Operations.
120. Rupprecht, *Mein Kriegstagebuch*, II, 138.
121. B.O.H., *1917*, I, 349, 352. G.O.H., XII, 230.
122. Corps Report on Operations.
123. Cdn. Corps Operation Order G. 589, 14 Apr 17.
124. B.O.H., *1917*, I, 236.
125. *If Germany Attacks*, 180. G.O.H., XII, 203, 289.
126. *My War Memories*, II, 421.
127. B.O.H., *1917*, I, Sketches 9 & 10.
128. G.H.Q. letter O.A.D. 350, 26 Mar 17, Appx. 26 to *ibid.*
129. C. E. W. Bean, *The A.I.F. in France*, 1917 (Volume IV of *The Official History of Australia in the War of 1914-1918*), 343.
130. B.O.H., *1917*, I, 368.
131. *Ibid.*, 273, 378.
132. G.O.H., XII, 230. Edmonds, *Short History*, 231.
133. G.O.H., XII, Appx. 9 (map). Lossberg, *Meine Tätigkeit im Weltkriege*, 280, 287.
134. G.O.H., XII, 210, 220, 232, 244-5, and Appx. 27.
135. First Army G.S. 557, 12 Apr 17, Appx. VII to W.D., G.S., Cdn. Corps, April 1917.
136. "Canada on Vimy Ridge", 59.
137. G.O.H., XII, 234-6.
138. *Ibid.*, 237.
139. *Ibid.*, 200-1.
140. *Ibid.*, 202. General Hermann von Kuhl, *Der Weltkrieg, 1914-1918*, 2 vols. (Weller, Berlin, 1930), II, 85-6.
141. *Meine Tätigkeit im Weltkriege*, 288.
142. *My War Memories*, II, 430.
143. G.O.H., XII, 255.

CHAPTER IX

The Capture of Hill 70, 1917

1. Cdn. Corps Operation Order No. 110, 21 Apr 17, Appx. II/18 to G.S. Diary, April 1917.
2. G.O.H., XII, Map 10.
3. Edmonds, *Short History*, 234-5. G.O.H., XII, 251.
4. B.O.H., *1917*, I, 413-23. G.O.H., XII, 248, Maps 8, 11, 12.
5. G.O.H., XII, 247.
6. B.O.H., *1917*, I, 425-6. Wynne, *If Germany Attacks*, 246-8.
7. B.O.H., *1917*, I, 423.
8. "Instructions for the Attack on Arleux, No. 2", in 2nd Bde. Report on Operation, Appx. 6 to Bde. Diary, May 1917. History of 73rd Fusilier Regiment, 103-4.
9. History of 76th Regiment, 132.
10. 2nd Bde. Report on Operation. *If Germany Attacks*, 248-9. Cdn. Corps Summary of Operations, 26 Apr-3 May, Appx. III/1 to G.S. Diary, May 1917.
11. B.O.H., *1917*, I, 427.
12. *Ibid.*, III, 4.
13. *Ibid.*, I. 427-8 and Appendix 51.

14. Ibid., 430-1. *If Germany Attacks,* 249.
15. B.O.H., *1917,* I, 431.
16. *Ibid.,* 453-4. *If Germany Attacks,* 250.
17. B.O.H., *1917,* I, 440, 450.
18. Jones, *The War in the Air,* II, 368-71.
19. Artillery Order No. 23, 2 May 1917, Appx. 1-6 to W.D., G.O.C., R.A., Cdn. Corps, May 1917.
20. W.D., 1st Inf. Bde., 3 May 17.
21. 2nd Bn. Report, Appx. II/5 to Unit Diary, May 1917. Murray, *The History of the 2nd Canadian Battalion in the Great War,* 180.
22. G.O.H., XII, Appx. 28.
23. 31st Bn. Report, Appx. "B-4" to Unit Diary, May 1917.
24. 27th Bn. Report, Appx. "D" to Unit Diary, May 1917.
25. Supplement to *The London Gazette,* 27 Jun 17.
26. 27th Bn. Report.
27. *Ibid.* B.O.H., *1917,* I, 450-3. G.O.H., XII, 257, 259, Map 12.
28. *The War in the Air,* III, 371-4. 1st Bn. Report on Operations 1-2 to 4-5 May 1917, Appx. A to Unit Diary. 6th Inf. Bde. Report on Operations of 3 May 1917, Appx. 23 to Bde. Diary.
29. W.D., G.S., Cdn. Corps, 5 May 17.
30. History of 19th Bavarian Regiment, 281.
31. W.Ds., 19th and 29th Bns., 7 and 8 May 17.
32. *If Germany Attacks,* 252-3, B.O.H., *1917,* I, 521, 523. G.O.H., XII, 260, 262.
33. B.O.H., *1917,* I, 521. W.D., 4th Inf. Bde., 9 May 17.
34. O.A.D. 434, 7 May 17, cited in B.O.H., *1917,* II, 23-5.
35. *The War in the Air,* V, 19-27.
36. "Methods Suggested for the Preventing of Air Raids in the United Kingdom", 15 Jun 17, Appendix IV to *ibid.*
37. Edmonds, *Short History,* 298.
38. W.D., G.S., Cdn. Corps, May 1917, Appx. I/4, "Withdrawal of Field and Heavy Artillery from Cdn. Corps".
39. First Army Order No. 122, 27 May 17, and First Army No. G.S. 604/14(A), 14 Jun 17, Appx. I/3 to W.D., G.S., Cdn. Corps, June 1917.
40. Cdn. Corps Operation Order No. 119, Appx. II/15 to G.S. Diary, May 1917.
41. W.Ds., G.S., Cdn. Corps and 4th Cdn. Div., 10th Inf. Bde., 5-11 May 17.
42. Brigade and Unit Reports, Appx. "C" to W.D., 10th Inf. Bde., June 1917.
43. Cdn. Corps Summary of Operations, 31 May-7 June 1917, Appx. III/1 to G.S. Diary, June 1917.
44. First Army Order No. 125, 5 Jun 17, Appx. I/3 to W.D., G.S., Cdn. Corps, June 1917.
45. Cdn. Corps Summary of Intelligence, 9 and 10 Jun 17, Appx. IV to G.S. Diary, June 1917. Cdn. Corps Summary of Operations, 7-14 Jun 17, Appx. III/2 to *ibid.* History of 10th Reserve Regiment, 131-5.
46. Reports on operation appended to W.Ds., 7th and 11th Inf. Bdes., June 1917.
47. G.O.H., XII, 267-70. Lossberg, *Meine Tätigkeit im Weltkriege, 1914-1918,* 292-3.
48. W.D., G.S., Cdn. Corps, 10 Jun 17.
49. B.O.H., *1917,* II, 87-8. G.O.H., XII, 471-2.
50. "Memorandum on the Present Situation and Future Plans written for the War Cabinet by the Commander-in-Chief, 12th June 1917", Appx. XII to B.O.H., *1917,* II.
51. First Army No. G.S. 604/14(A), 14 June 1917, Appx. I/3 to W.D., G.S., Cdn. Corps, June 1917.
52. *Ibid.*
53. W.D., G.S., 3rd and 4th Cdn. Divs., 28 Jun 17. 3rd Div. Summary of Intelligence, 28-29 Jun 17, Appx. 773 to G.S. Diary, June 1917.
54. B.O.H., *1917,* II, 113-14 and Sketch 8.
55. Currie Papers, entry in diary, 6 Jun 17.
56. P.A.C., Overseas Minister's files, folder 348, drawer A38.
57. P.A.C., Perley Papers, vol. 9.
58. *Ibid.*
59. P.A.C., Overseas Minister's files.
60. *Ibid.*
61. Cdn. Routine Order 1981, 13 Jul 17.
62. P.A.C., Perley Papers, vol. 9.
63. *Debates, House of Commons,* 26 Jun 17.
64. First Army Order No. G.S. 658/1(a), 7 Jul 17, Appx. I/1 to W.D., G.S., Cdn. Corps, July 1917.
65. First Army Order No. 137, 10 Jul 17, Appx. I/2 to *ibid.,* and entry for 16 Jul 17.
66. First Army No. G.S. 658/4(a), 10 Jul 17, Appx. I/3 to *ibid.* Currie Diary, 10 Jul 17.
67. Cdn. Corps G. 39/25-15-1, 11 Jul 17, Appx. II/3 to G.S. Diary, July 1917.
68. First Army No. G.S. 658/13(a), 13 Jul 17, Appx. I/4 to W.D., G.S., Cdn. Corps, July 1917.
69. Cdn. Corps Operation Order No. 139, 17 Jul 17, Appx. II/10 to *ibid.*
70. 116th Bn. Report, Appx. 18 to W.D., 9th Inf. Bde., July 1917. G.O.H., XII, Appx. 26.
71. W. A. Steel, "Wireless Telegraphy in the Canadian Corps in France" (*Canadian Defence Quarterly,* October 1928), 51.
72. Cdn. Corps Summaries of Operations, 2, 9, 16 Aug 17, Appendices III/1-3 to G.S. Diary, August 1917.
73. B.O.H., *1917,* II, 222.
74. First Army reports cited in *The War in the Air,* IV, 170-2.
75. Comments by General A. G. L. McNaughton on draft B.O.H., 18 May 46, file H.Q. 650-52-7, vol. 8.
76. B.O.H., *1917,* II, 220-2. Cdn. Corps Operation Orders Nos. 140, 26 Jul 17 and 141, 14 Aug 17, Appx. II to G.S. Diary, August 1917.
77. Cdn. Corps Operation Order No. 140.
78. Maj.-Gen. Sir Edward Morrison, "Vimy and Hill 70" (*Toronto Star Weekly,* 21 Apr 28). General A. G. L. McNaughton to Director Historical Section, 25 Apr 61.
79. W.Ds., G.S. Cdn. Corps, 2nd and 3rd Inf.

Bdes., 15 Aug 17. Morrison, "Vimy and Hill 70".
80. *Ibid.* History of 165th Regiment, 150-7, and Sketch 11. History of 26th Regiment, 704-5.
81. "Vimy and Hill 70". 15th Bn. Report on Operations, Appx. "A" to Unit Diary, August 1917.
82. 2nd Bde. Report, 14-17, Appx. 10 to Bde. Diary, August 1917.
83. W.D., G.S., 4th Cdn. Div., 15 Aug 17, Appx. "A", Report on Operation: Appx. "B", 4th Div. Operation Order No. 49, 14 Aug 17. W.Ds., 11th and 12th Inf. Bdes., 15 Aug 17.
84. "Vimy and Hill 70".
85. B.O.H., *1917*, II, 225.
86. History of 5th Foot Guard Regiment, 338-41. History of 5th Guard Grenadier Regiment, 406-11. History of 65th Regiment, 248-52.
87. Cdn. Corps Summary of Operations, 9-16 Aug 17, Appx. III/3 to G.S. Diary, August 1917. 2nd Bde. Report, 17, 19. "Capture of Hill 70", 8, Appx. 2 to W.D.. 1st Div. Artillery, August 1917.
88. Supplement to *The London Gazette*, 6 Nov 17.
89. Cdn. Corps Summaries of Intelligence, 15 and 16 Aug 17, Appendices IV/6 and 7 to G.S. Diary, August 1917.
90. W.Ds., G.S., Cdn. Corps and 1st Div., 2nd Inf. Bde., and 5th and 10th Bns., 16 Aug 17. Supplement to *The London Gazette*, 17 Oct 17.
91. 1st Cdn. Div. Report on the Hill 70 & Puits 14 Bis Operation, 1st Div. files, folder 25, vol. 2.
92. W.D., G.S., Cdn. Corps, 17 Aug 17. 1st Div. Summary of Operations, Appx. 15-a to G.S. Diary, August 1917.
93. 1st Cdn. Div. Report on the Hill 70 & Puits 14 Bis Operation.
94. B.O.H., *1917*, II, 119.
95. "Capture of Hill 70", 9-10 (note 87, above).
96. 2nd Bde. Report, 27.
97. 4th Bn. Report, Appx. 2 to Unit Diary, August 1917.
98. B.O.H., *1917*, II, 228*n*. History of 156th Regiment, 215.
99. "Summary of Information—Lens", 18 Aug 17, Appx. 18 to W.D., 4th Inf. Bde., August 1917. Supplement to *The London Gazette*, 17 Oct 17.
100. 2nd Bn. Report, Appx. II/13 to Unit Diary. Supplement to *The London Gazette*, 8 Nov 17.
101. *Die Schlachten and Gefechte des Grossen Krieges* (Compiled by the German General Staff) (Berlin, 1919), 302. *Histories of 251 Divisions of the German Army*, 693.
102. W.D., G.S., 4th Cdn. Div., 21 Aug 17. 2nd Div. Operation Order No. 146, 19 Aug 17. Corps Summary of Intelligence, 22 Aug 17. History of 64th Reserve Regiment, 115.
103. Artillery Order No. 65, 18 Aug 17, Appx. 28 to G.O.C., R.A., Cdn. Corps Diary. "Vimy and Hill 70".
104. "Operations of the 4th Canadian Division", Appx. "A" to G.S. Diary, August 1917. 2nd Div. Summary of Operations, 19-22 Aug 17, Appx. 863 to G.S. Diary, August 1917.
105. 6th Bde. Narrative, Appx. 50 to Bde. Diary, August 1917. 29th Bn. Report, Appx. 6 to Unit Diary. Supplement to *The London Gazette*, 8 Nov 17.
106. 6th Bde. Narrative.
107. *Ibid.* W.D., 27th Bn., 21 Aug 17.
108. W.D., 50th Bn., 21 Aug 17, and Appx. "J", Report on Operations 17-26 Aug 17. 10th Inf. Bde. Summary of Operations, 17-18 to 25-26 Aug 17, Appx. C-3 to Bde. Diary, August 1917.
109. Special Summary of Operations, 21 Aug 17, Appx. No. 7 to W.D., 46th Bn., August 1917. 10th Bde. Summary of Operations.
110. W.D., 47th Bn., 22-3 [should read 21-2] Aug 17. Supplement to *The London Gazette*, 26 Nov 17. (Correct date of casualty from War Service Records.)
111. W.D., 6th Inf. Bde., 21 Aug 17 and Appx. 50, Brigade Narrative of Operations.
112. Cdn. Corps Summary of Intelligence, 22 Aug 17, 2, Appx. IV/11 to Corps Diary, August 1917.
113. "Operations of the 4th Canadian Division" (note 104, above).
114. Report on the Attack of the Green Crassier by the 44th Canadian Infantry Battalion, August 23rd 1917, Appx. C3 to W.D. 6th Inf. Bde., August 1917.
115. General Notes by C.O. 44th Bn., 26 Aug 17, Appx. "C" to W.D., 10th Inf. Bde., August 1917.
116. History of 64th Reserve Regiment, 116.
117. 44th Bn. Report on the Attack of the Green Crassier.
118. W.D., 44th Bn., 24 Aug 17. Russenholt, *Six Thousand Canadian Men*, 112.
119. W.Ds., 50th Bn. and C.C.H.A., 25 Aug 17. 50th Bn. Report, Appx. "J" to Unit Diary, August 1917.
120. B.O.H., *1917*, II, 230.
121. Von Kuhl, *Der Weltkrieg, 1914-1918*, II, 123.

Chapter X

Passchendaele, October-November 1917

1. *Report of the Battles Nomenclature Committee as Approved by the Army Council* (London, 1921), 20.
2. B.O.H., *1917*, II, 22. Haig's *Private Papers*, 226-7.
3. B.O.H., *1917*, II, 98.
4. F.O.H., Tome V, vol. I, 787 ff.
5. *War Memoirs of David Lloyd George*, III, 1560-1.
6. Haig's *Private Papers*, 228-9.
7. Paul Painlevé, *Comment j'ai nommé Foch et Pétain* (Paris, 1923), 143.
8. Chef du Service Historique, Paris, to Director Historical Section, 22 May 59.
9. B.O.H., *1917*, II, xvi, 25. G.O.H., XII, 556-66.
10. Telegram, C.I.G.S. to C.-in-C., cited in Haig's *Private Papers*, 230.
11. B.O.H., *1917*, II, 27.
12. Sir Charles E. Callwell, *Field-Marshal Sir Henry Wilson, Bart: His Life & Diaries* (London, 1927), I, 359.
13. General Wilson's diary, 20 May 17, *ibid*, 354. Basil Collier, *Brasshat: A Biography of Field-Marshal Sir Henry Wilson* (London, 1961), 286.
14. B.O.H., *1917*, II, 27-8. Haig's *Private Papers*, 232.
15. B.O.H., *1917*, II, 131.
16. *Ibid*., 25.
17. G.O.H., XII, 431-2. Von Kuhl, *Der Weltkrieg, 1914-1918*, II, 113-14. Sendtner, *Rupprecht von Wittelsbach. Kronprinz von Bayern* (Munich, 1954), 286-7.
18. B.O.H., *1917*, II, 29-30. Haig's *Private Papers*, 234-5.
19. W.Ds., 1st and 3rd Tunnelling Coys., C.E., 7 Jun 17.
20. *The Work of the Royal Engineers in the European War, 1914-19, Military Mining*, Plate XVIII.
21. B.O.H., *1917*, II, 71-5, 86.
22. Appx. XII to *ibid*.
23. "Note on the Strategic Situation with Special Reference to the Present Condition of German Resources and Probable German Operations", 11 Jun 17, *ibid*.
24. G.O.H., XIII, 22.
25. Note 23, above.
26. B.O.H., *1917*, II, 98.
27. *War Memoirs of David Lloyd George*, IV, 2151-2. Haig's Diary, 19 Jun 17.
28. Sir Archibald Hurd, *Official History of the Great War: The Merchant Navy* (London, 1929), III, Appx. "C".
29. *War Memoirs of David Lloyd George*, IV, 2162.
30. Haig's Diary, 17 Jun 17.
31. *Ibid*., 20 Jun 17.
32. *Ibid*., 21-22 Jun 17. B.O.H., *1917*, II, 103-4. *War Memoirs of David Lloyd George*, IV, 2185.
33. Haig's *Private Papers*, 246.
34. B.O.H., *1917*, II, 106.
35. *Ibid*., 108-10.
36. *Ibid*., 111.
37. G.O.H., XII, 444.
38. Reichsarchiv, *Schlachten des Weltkrieges*, vol. 27, *Flandern 1917*, 120.
39. B.O.H., *1917*, II, 150-9, 170-3, Sketches 13-16.
40. *Ibid*., 177-9.
41. *Der Weltkrieg, 1914-1918*, II, 130.
42. Ludendorff, *My War Memories, 1914-1918*, II, 480.
43. Haig's *Private Papers*, 252.
44. Haig's report of 2 September 1917, cited in Leon Wolff, *In Flanders Fields—The 1917 Campaign* (Toronto, 1958), 164.
45. B.O.H., *1917*, II, 209.
46. Second Army Operation Order No. 4, 1 Sep 17, Appx XXI to *ibid*.
47. *Ibid*., 119-21. G.O.H., XIII, 56-7. R. Hanslian, *Der Chemische Krieg*, I, 26.
48. B.O.H., *1917*, II, 209.
49. *Ibid*., *Italy 1915-1919*, 31.
50. Haig's *Private Papers*, 252-3.
51. *Ibid*.
52. *Ibid*., 255.
53. B.O.H., *1917*, II, 235.
54. F.O.H., Tome V, vol. II, 653 and letter, Anthoine to Pétain, 2 Jul 17, Annexe 621.
55. Haig's *Private Papers*, 242.
56. Correspondence supplied to Director Historical Section by Capt. B. H. Liddell Hart, 3 Feb 60.
57. Chef du Service Historique to Deputy Director Historical Section, 20 May 59.
58. F.O.H., Tome V, vol. II, 689-90.
59. G.O.H., XIII, 108.
60. Painlevé, *Comment j'ai nommé Foch et Pétain*, 215.
61. "Role of the British Forces should Russia fall out of the War", 8 Oct 17, Appx. I to B.O.H., *1918*, I.
62. *Ibid*.
63. Supplement to *The London Gazette*, 11 Jan 18.
64. B.O.H., *1917*, II, 325, 327.
65. *Ibid*., 325-6.
66. *Ibid*., 334.
67. Rupprecht, *Mein Kriegstagebuch*, II, 271.
68. Bean, *The A.I.F. in France, 1917*, 917-18.
69. B.O.H., *1917*, II, 352, 386-7.
70. O.A.D. 646, 2 Oct 17, in Haig's Diary.
71. Haig's *Private Papers*, 257. O.A. 191/1, 9 Oct 17, in Appx. "A" to G.H.Q. (G.S.) War Diary, October 1917.
72. Haig's *Private Papers*, 257.
73. *Ibid*., 272.

74. Letter, Currie to Livesay, 26 Jan 33, Currie Papers, drawer J-1.
75. *Ibid.* Urquhart, *Arthur Currie, The Biography of a Great Canadian*, 172.
76. G. 744, Appx. 1/7/0 to W.D., G.S., Cdn. Corps, October 1917.
77. Note on Canadian Participation at Passchendaele, attached to letter, Duguid to Edmonds, 20 Nov 45, HQ 650-52-7, vol. 8.
78. B.O.H., *1917*, II, 347.
79. Brig.-Gen. E.W.B. Morrison, "Operations of the Canadian Corps during October 1917", p. 2, in Morrison Papers, folder 2.
80. *Ibid.*, p. 4.
81. "Passchendaele—Causes of Success and Failure", Cdn. Corps G. 724/27-3 to Second Army, 20 Nov 17.
82. *History of the Corps of Royal Engineers* (Chatham, 1952), V, 313, 323.
83. Morrison, "Operations of the Canadian Corps".
84. B.O.H., *1917*, II, 347.
85. Cdn. Corps Operation Order No. 159, 23 Oct 17. Notes on Conference, 13-18 Oct 17, Cdn. Corps G.S. file S 2520-1, vol. 1.
86. "Passchendaele—Causes of Success and Failure".
87. Maj.-Gen. A.G.L. McNaughton, "The Development of Artillery in the Great War" (*Canadian Defence Quarterly*, January 1929), 162-3.
88. *Ibid.*, 168.
89. McNaughton to Director Historical Section, 25 Apr 61.
90. G.O.H., XIII, 89. History of 3rd Bavarian Regiment, 114. History of 22nd Bavarian Regiment, 84.
91. *Flandern 1917*, 27-8.
92. G.O.H., XIII, 88, 91, *et al.*
93. Morrison, "Operations of the Canadian Corps".
94. History of 126th Infantry Regiment, 257-9.
95. "Cdn. Corps Artillery Report on Passchendaele Operations, Oct. 17th to Nov. 18th 1917", 4-5.
96. Cdn. Corps Operation Order No. 159, 23 Oct 17, IV.
97. Cdn. Corps Order of Battle, 26 Oct 17.
98. Russenholt, *Six Thousand Canadian Men*, 118-19.
99. W.D., G.S., 3rd Cdn. Div., October 1917, Appx. 1 to 3rd Cdn. Div. G 532, "Instructions for Offensive No. 2", 20 Oct 17.
100. W.D., G.S., Cdn. Corps, October 1917, Appendix II/14, Notes on Corps Commander's Conference at H.Q. 4th Div., 14 Oct 17. *Ibid.*, Appendix II/28, B.G.G.S. memo, 23 Oct 17.
101. W.D., G.S., 4th Cdn. Div., October 1917, Appx. "A", "Passchendaele Attack, Phase I".
102. W.D., G.S., 3rd Cdn. Div., October 1917, Appx. 971, "Narrative of First Stage of Operations against Passchendaele Ridge".
103. Supplement to *The London Gazette*, 18 Dec 17, 11 Jan 18.
104. 4th Div. Report on Passchendaele (Phase 1, Appx. "A" to G.S. Diary, October 1917. History of 22nd Bavarian Regiment, 84. History of 464th Regiment, 106.
105. Second Army Operation Order No. 10, 27 Oct 17, Appx. 1/20 to Corps Diary.
106. Cdn. Corps Report (G.S. file, unnumbered), vol. 5, 30 Oct 17.
107. Cdn. Corps Operation Order No. 161, 28 Oct 17.
108. Joseph Hayes, *The Eighty-fifth in France and Flanders* (Halifax, 1920), 91.
109. 4th Div. Narrative, Appx. "B" to G.S. Diary, October 1917. W.D., 12th Bde., 30 Oct 17.
110. R. Hodder-Williams, *Princess Patricia's Canadian Light Infantry, 1914-1919*, (Toronto, 1923), I, 260.
111. 3rd Div. Narrative of Operations, Appx. 938 to G.S. Diary, October 1917.
112. History of 464th Regiment, 105-20.
113. History of 126th Infantry Regiment, 262.
114. Supplement to *The London Gazette*, 11 Jan and 13 Feb 18.
115. 5th C.M.R. Summary of Operations, Appx. "G" to Unit Diary, October 1917.
116. Cdn. Corps Summary of Intelligence, 30 Oct 17, Appx. IV/12 to G.S. Diary.
117. Supplement to *The London Gazette*, 11 Jan. 18.
118. Map S. 21, Cdn. Corps Report, vol. 5.
119. Second Army to Cdn. Corps, G. 894, 16 Oct. 17, and G. 8, 18 Oct 17, Appces. I/9 and I/11 to Corps Diary, October 1917.
120. Second Army to Canadian Corps, G. 771, 31 Oct 17, Appx. I/25 to *ibid.*
121. 2nd Cdn. Div. Operation Order No. 160, 7 Nov 17, Appx. 922 to G.S. Diary, November 1917. 1st Cdn. Div. Report on Passchendaele Ridge Operations, 4-12 Nov 17, Appx. 10 to G.S. Diary, November 1917.
122. 1st Cdn. Div. Report, 24. History of 10th Grenadier Regiment, 213-19. History of 51st Regiment, 204-8. History of 49th Regiment, 235-41.
123. 2nd Div. "Summary of Operations, 6 p.m. 2/11/17 to 6 p.m. 8/11/17."
124. Jones, *The War in the Air*, IV, 211-12. 6th Bde. Narrative, Appx. 11 to Bde. Diary, November, 1917.
125. Supplement to *The London Gazette*, 11 Jan 18.
126. *Ibid.*
127. Cdn. Corps Summaries of Intelligence, 6, 7 Nov 17, Appendices IV/4 and IV/5 to G.S. Diary.
128. Major W. A. Steel, "Wireless Telegraphy in the Canadian Corps in France", Part II (*Canadian Defence Quarterly*, July 1930), 462.
129. Cdn. Corps Operation Order No. 167, 7 Nov 17.
130. 1st Cdn. Div. Report, 24. *Flandern 1917*, 153-6. History of 49th Regiment, 243-5. History of 208th Regiment, 75-6.
131. 1st Cdn. Div. Report.

132. H.Q. 650-52-7, vol. 8, Extracts from MSS by Brig.-Gen. E.W.B. Morrison.
133. *The A.I.F. in France, 1917,* 935.
134. Haig's *Private Papers,* 267.
135. *War Memoirs of David Lloyd George,* IV, 2110.
136. Churchill, *The World Crisis, 1911-1918,* IV, 1177.
137. Sir Henry Newbolt, B.O.H., *Naval Operations,* V, 7-8.
138. *War Memoirs of David Lloyd George,* III, 1162-7.
139. Capt. S. W. Roskill, R.N., "The U-Boat Campaign of 1917 and Third Ypres" (*Journal of the Royal United Service Institution,* November 1959), 441.
140. Undated letter, Currie to D'Arcy McGreer, in answer to letter of 8 Feb 30, in Currie Papers, Drawer J-1, (1809).
141. Cited in Alfred Duff Cooper, *Haig* (London, 1935), II, 134.
142. Haig's *Private Papers,* 260.
143. B.O.H., *1917,* II, 361.
144. B. H. Liddell Hart, "The Basic Truths of Passchendaele" (*Journal of the Royal United Service Institution,* November 1959), 436.
145. B.O.H., *1917,* II, 363.
146. "The Basic Truths of Passchendaele", 437.
147. *Statistics of the Military Effort of the British Empire During the Great War, 1914-1920* (London, 1922), 326-7, 361.
148. Note 144, above.
149. G.O.H., XIII, 97.
150. Circular Letter to Army Commanders, in Haig Papers, cited by Michael Howard in *Journal of the Royal United Service Institution,* February 1960, 108.
151. Haig to Robertson, 13 Aug 17, cited in *ibid.*
152. Haig's Diary, 28 Sep 17, cited in *ibid.*
153. Brig.-Gen. J. Charteris, *At G.H.Q.* (London, 1931), 259.
154. *War Memoirs of David Lloyd George,* IV, 2342-4.
155. Colonel T. Bentley Mott (translator), *The Memoirs of Marshal Foch* (London, 1931), 257.
156. B.O.H., *1918,* I, 29-30.
157. *Ibid., Italy 1915-1919,* 58, 102. G.O.P., XIII, 226, 231 and Appx. 28a.
158. Ludendorff, *My War Memories,* II, 502.
159. B. H. Liddell Hart, *Foch, The Man of Orleans* (Boston, 1932), 250.
160. B.O.H., *1918,* I, 30-1.
161. *Ibid., 1917,* III, 5-9.
162. Cambrai 1917, The Third Army Plan, 13 Nov 17, Appx. I to *ibid.*
163. *Ibid.,* I, 532. Cdn. Cavalry Bde. Report, Appx. "A" to Bde. Diary, July 1917.
164. B.O.H., *1917,* III, 10-13.
165. *Der Weltkrieg, 1914-1918,* II, 225. G.O.H., XIII, Appendices 10 and 11.
166. *Der Weltkrieg, 1914-1918,* II, 226-7.
167. B.O.H., *1917,* III, 15.
168. *Ibid.,* 88, 90.
169. Supplement to *The London Gazette,* 18 Dec. 17. W.Ds., Cdn. Cav. Bde. and Fort Garry Horse, 20 Nov 17.
170. G.O.H., XIII, 129-36.
171. *The War in the Air,* IV, 245. Robertson, *Von Richthofen and the Flying Circus,* 86-7.
172. W.Ds., Cdn. Cavalry Bde. and Units, 30 Nov, 1 Dec 17.
173. B.O.H., *1917,* III, 273. G.O.H., XIII, 143, 146.
174. Edmonds, *Short History,* 272.
175. *Mein Kriegstagebuch,* II, 297-300.
176. W.D., 4th Bn. Cdn. Railway Troops, 30 Nov 17.
177. Detailed Performance Cdn. Cav. Bde., G.A.Q. file 9-4, pp. 4-5. Seely, *Adventure,* 283-4.
178. Haig's *Private Papers,* 266-7.
179. W.D., G.S., Cdn. Corps, 18-20 Nov 17.
180. *Ibid.,* 2, 14 Jan 18. Cdn. Corps Summary of Operations, week ending 3 Jan. History of 2nd Guard Reserve Regiment, 188-9. *History of 251 Divisions of the German Army,* 277, 694.
181. W.D., G.S., Cdn. Corps, March 1918, Appx. III/1, Summary of Operations 28 Feb-7 Mar 18. History of 51st Regiment, 226.

CHAPTER XI

Conscription

1. *The War Cabinet Report For the Year 1917* (London, 1918), 6.
2. Borden's *Memoirs,* II, 622, 626, 662.
3. M. Ollivier, *Colonial and Imperial Conferences* (Ottawa, 1954), II, 171.
4. Borden's *Memoirs,* II, 666, 679.
5. Lord Hankey, *The Supreme Command, 1914-1918* (London, 1961), II, 662-3.
6. P.A.C., Borden Papers, Memoir Notes, vol. V, 1917-1918.
7. Borden's *Memoirs,* II, 698.
8. *Ibid.,* 757.
9. *Debates, House of Commons,* 18 May 17.
10. *Ibid.,* 11 Jun 17.
11. Borden to Archbishop Bruchési, 31 May 17, P.A.C., Borden Papers, Memoir Notes, vol. V, 1917-1918.
12. *The War Cabinet Report For the Year 1917,* 9.
13. *Debates, House of Commons,* 19 Apr 18.

14. Borden's *Memoirs*, II, 612-13.
15. Borden Papers, Memoir Notes, vol. V, Borden to Governor-General, 7 Jun 17, 2160-1.
16. *Debates, House of Commons*, 11 Jun 17.
17. *Ibid.*, 18 Jun, 5 and 24 Jul 17.
18. Perley Papers, vol. 9.
19. *Debates, House of Commons*, 26 Jun 17.
20. *The Military Service Act*, 1917, Canadian Statutes 7-8, George V, Chap. 19.
21. *Ibid.*, Chap. 34.
22. *Debates, House of Commons*, 6 Sep 17. Canadian Statutes 7-8, George V, Chap. 39.
23. *Debates, House of Commons*, 10 Sep 17.
24. *Ibid.*, 19 Mar 18.
25. Borden's *Memoirs*, II, 711-12.
26. Letter to Perley, 3 Dec 17, Currie Papers, Drawer 1801.
27. Currie Diary, 4 Dec 17.
28. Letter to Perley, 10 Dec 17, Currie Papers, Drawer 1801.
29. *Ibid.*
30. Borden Papers, Memoir Notes, vol. V. 1917-1918, 2219.
31. *Report of the Director of the Military Service Branch to the Honourable the Minister of Justice on the Operation of the Military Service Act, 1917* (Ottawa. 1919), 2, 5.
32. H.Q. 1064-30-6, vol. 1, Minutes of Military Service Council meeting 1 Sep 17. *The Canadian Annual Review, 1917*, 349-51.
33. Borden Papers, Memoir Notes, vol. V. 1917-1918, 2114.
34. *Ibid.*, 2122-4.
35. H.Q. 17-152-2, vol. 1, "Calling out Militia in Aid to Civil Power". Correspondence and Reports on H.Q.C. 2358, vol. 1.
36. H.Q.C. 2358, vol. 1. Borden Papers. Memoir Notes, vol. V, 1917-1918, 2347, 2350-1.
37. O.M. file 10-8-21.
38. Borden Papers, O.C. 516.
39. *Ibid.*, R.L.B. 2. *Debates, House of Commons*, 17 Apr 18.
40. Borden's *Memoirs*, II, 799-901.
41. *Report of the Director of the Military Service Branch*, 94, 96.
42. *Debates, House of Commons*, 19 Apr 18.
43. *Ibid. Debates of the Senate*, 19 Apr 18.
44. P.C. 1697, 5 Jul 18.
45. P.C. 1795, 17 Jul 18.
46. H.Q. 683-1-12, vol. 13, Historical Section to Library of Parliament, 28 Nov 44 (Statistics compiled by Historical Section in November 1944 from Machine Records).
47. Correspondence on H.Q., O.M.F.C. file E-12-33.
48. C.E.F. Routine Order No. 46 dated 12 Jan 18.
49. Notes on Historical Section file Hist 5-2-1. H.Q., M.D. No. 11 file 99-4-16, vol. 2.
50. C.E.F. Routine Order No. 106 dated 26 Jan 18.
51. H.Q., O.M.F.C. file E-12-33.
52. *The Canadian Annual Review, 1918*, 472.
53. P.C. 54, 8 Jan 18.
54. *Report of the Director of the Military Service Branch*, 23.
55. P.C. 1931, 1 Aug 18.
56. *Report of the Director of the Military Service Branch*, 24, 74.
57. *The Canadian Annual Review, 1919*, 25.
58. P.C. 1953, 10 Aug. 18.
59. *Report of the Director of the Military Service Branch*, 3.
60. Perley to Borden, 24 Jun 17, Perley Papers, vol. 9, 261.
61. Borden to Perley, 7 Aug 17, *ibid.*, 267.
62. Perley to Borden, 14 Sep 17, *ibid.*, 274B.
63. Perley to Borden, 9 Oct 17, *ibid.*, 279A.
64. Borden to Perley, 13 Oct 17, Perley Papers, vol. 9, 281A. "Short Biography of Perley". *ibid.*
65. *Canadian Daily Record*, No. 424, 28 May 18.
66. *Debates, House of Commons*, 27 May 19.
67. "Report Covering the Constitution and Activities of the Overseas Military Council of Canada", n.d., O.M. file 10-8-49.
68. P.C. 885, 11 Apr 18.
69. P.C. 878, 26 Apr 19.
70. P.C. 913, 1 May 19.
71. Note 67, above.
72. Memorandum, Gow to Kempt, 14 Mar 18, Kemp Papers, vol. 162, T-7.
73. Turner to Kemp, 29 Apr 18, *ibid.* Kemp to Maj.-Gen. Lynden-Bell, 9 May 18, *ibid.*
74. P.C. 29, 6 Jun 15.
75. *Debates, House of Commons*, 20 Mar 18.
76. Report of C.W.R.O., 11 Jan 17, O.M. file 10-8-11A.
77. Reports—The Origin of Records 1915 to 1918, H.S. 40-1-6.
78. Reports, C.W.R.O., 22 Aug 17, H.S. 40-1-2.
79. Perley to War Office, 25 Jan 17, O.M. file 10-8-1.
80. "Establishment Canadian Representatives at G.H.Q., France", O.M. file 10-8-1.
81. A/Deputy Minister O.M.F.C. to War Office, 27 Nov 17, O.M. file 10-8-7.
82. Haig to War Office, 26 Jan 18, *ibid.*
83. Deputy Minister to War Office, 14 Mar 18, *ibid.*
84. War Office to Haig, 16 Apr 18, *ibid.*
85. "Canadian Section G.H.Q.", Currie Papers, J-6, 2, pp. 8-9.
86. Report of C.W.R.O., 31 Aug 19, Appx. 1, O.M. file 10-8-11A.
87. Report by Maj. W. Watkins, Fund Secretary to Col. H. C. Osborne, 2 Jul 19, D.H.S. 7-1A.
88. *Debates, House of Commons*, 27 May 19. Report of C.W.R.O., 7.
89. Gov.-Gen. to Sec. of State for the Colonies, 1 Aug 14, European War Print No. 1, Item 8.
90. H.Q. 54-21-23-13, vol. 1.
91. Gov.-Gen. to Sec. of State for Colonies, 26 Apr 15, *ibid.*, vol. 2.
92. P.C. 40, 24 Jan 17.
93. H.Q. 54-21-23-13, vol. 2.

94. O.M. file 10-2-13, vol. 1.
95. H.Q. 54-21-23-13, vol. 2.
96. Borden to Sir George Foster, 22 Mar 17, Borden Papers O.C. 415, 43605.
97. O.M. file 10-2-13, vol. 1.
98. Perley to Harris, 4 Jun 17, *ibid.*
99. Harris to Perley, 29 Jun 17, *ibid.*
100. W.D., Dept. of the General Auditor, O.M.F.C. (1 Jan 18-31 Oct 19). Kemp to Harris, 15 Aug 19, O.M. file 10-2-13, vol. 5 (July 1919-April 1920).
101. Harris to Kemp, O.M. file 10-2-13, vol. 5, *ibid.*
102. A.D.M. to Minister, 20 Mar 50, H.Q.C. 8215, F.D. 205.
103. B. B. Cubitt to Secretary O.M.F.C., 26 Jun 18, O.M. file 10-2-13, vol. 3.
104. Harris to Kemp, 1 Aug 19, *ibid.*, vol 5 (July 1919-April 1920).
105. H.Q. 54-21-23-13, vol. 2.

CHAPTER XII

The German Offensives of 1918

1. Edmonds, *Short History*, 278.
2. Capt. Peter E. Wright, *At the Supreme War Council* (London, 1921), 50. L. Gehre, *Die Deutsche Kräfteverteilung während des Weltkrieges* (Berlin, 1928), Appendix.
3. Edmonds, *Short History*, 276.
4. Jones, *The War in the Air*, IV, 350 and Appx. XVI.
5. B.O.H., *1918*, I, 54.
6. *Ibid.*, 51-5. *War Memoirs of David Lloyd George*, V, 2638-9.
7. Edmonds, *Short History*, 279-80. Wright, *At the Supreme War Council*, 50.
8. Haig's *Private Papers*, 292.
9. *Ibid.*, 289-92. B.O.H., *1918*, I, 80-90.
10. Lossberg, *Meine Tätigkeit im Weltkriege, 1914-1918*, 315.
11. G.O.H., XIV, 53.
12. *Ibid.*, 75, 77.
13. *Ibid.*, 27.
14. *Ibid.*, 41-7, 85-92, 516.
15. B.O.H., *1918*, I, 145-6.
16. *Ibid.*, 123-5.
17. Capt. G. C. Wynne, "Pattern for Limited Nuclear War" (*Journal of the Royal United Service Institution*, February 1958), 41.
18. B.O.H., *1918*, I, 254-5.
19. *Ibid.*, 110.
20. "Pattern for Limited Nuclear Warfare" (note 17, above), 42. W.D., G.S., Cdn. Corps, 22 Mar 18. B.O.H., *1918*, II, 479-84.
21. Rupprecht, *Mein Kriegstagebuch*, II, 372*n*.
22. Von Kuhl, *Der Weltkrieg, 1914-1918*, II, 330.
23. *Ibid.* G.O.H., XIV, 166.
24. G.O.H., XIV, 201-2.
25. *Ibid.*, 160 and map 6.
26. B.O.H., *1918*, II, 475. Haig's *Private Papers*, 297.
27. B.O.H., *1918*, I, 542.
28. "Final Report of General John J. Pershing" in *United States Army in the World War 1917-1919*, XII (Washington, 1948), 33. F.O.H., Tome VI, Annexe 668 to vol. I, "Summary of Meeting between General Pershing and General Petain at French G.H.Q., 25 March 1918".
29. B.O.H., *1918*, II, 114-15.
30. *Der Weltkrieg*, II, 340-1.
31. B.O.H., *1918*, II, 462-3.
32. Edmonds, *Short History*, 297.
33. G.O.H., XVI. 255*n*.
34. W.D., Cdn. Cavalry Bde., 22 Mar 18.
35. B.O.H., *1918*, I, 333.
36. Appx. "F" to W.D., Cdn. Cavalry Brigade, March 1918, "Narrative of Operations, 3rd Cavalry Division Detachment".
37. Lt.-Col. C. E. Connolly, "The Action of the Canadian Cavalry Brigade at Moreuil Wood and Rifle Wood—March and April, 1918" (*Canadian Defence Quarterly*, October 1925), 8-10.
38. B.O.H., *1918*, II, 89.
39. Supplement to *The London Gazette*, 24 Apr 18.
40. Narrative of Operations, 2nd Cav. Div., 30 Mar-1 Apr 1918. History of 122nd Fusilier Regiment, 239-42.
41. Connolly, "Moreuil and Rifle Wood", 10-15. B.O.H., *1918*, II, 89-90. 2nd Cav. Div. Narrative. Zimmermann, *Die Englische Kavallerie in Frankreich im März und April 1918* (Berlin, 1935), 52-4.
42. W.D., 1st C.M.M.G. Bde., 22-24 Mar 18.
43. History of the Canadian M.G. Corps, II, 202.
44. *Ibid.*, 157-60. B.O.H., 1918, I, 414.
45. B.O.H., *1918*, I, 506-7.
46. Appx. 23 to W.D., 1st C.M.M.G. Bde., March 1918.
47. B.O.H., *1918*, I, 507; and II, 45, 95, 456. W.D., 2nd Bn. Cdn. Railway Troops, 28-31 Mar 1918. Summary of Operations, 1st C.M.M.G. Bde., 22 Mar-10 Apr 18, Currie Papers, Drawer 1793, Folder 18.
48. Appx. 14 to W.D., 1st C.M.M.G. Bde., March 1918.
49. History of the Canadian M.G. Corps, II, 204.
50. Summary of Operations, 1st C.M.M.G. Bde.
51. Ludendorff, *My War Memories*, II, 600. G.O.H., XIV, 253-4.
52. B.O.H., *1918*, II, 154-5. F.O.H., Tome VI, vol. I, 434.

53. *Mein Kriegstagebuch,* II, 375, quoted in B.O.H., 1918, II, 192.
54. Haig's *Private Papers,* 302. F.O.H., Tome VI, vol. I, 441, B.O.H., *1918,* II, 247.
55. B.O.H., *1918,* II, 316, 337, Sketches 22-25.
56. *Ibid.,* 355-6, Cyril Falls, *The Great War* (New York, 1959), 339. G.O.H., XIV, 287.
57. W.D., *Jagdgeschwader* No. 1, 20-21 Apr 18.
58. B.O.H., *1918,* II, 389-92. Capt. B.H. Liddell Hart, *The Tanks: The History of the Royal Tank Regiment* (London, 1959), I, 167.
59. B.O.H., *1918,* II, 490. Kabisch, *Ergänzungen zu Streitfragen des Weltkrieges,* 426, cited in *ibid. Ibid.,* III, 25, 168-9.
60. *Ibid.,* 20 and 26. *Der Weltkrieg,* II, 298.
61. Edmonds, *Short History,* 317. *My War Memories,* II, 611.
62. *My War Memories,* II.
63. *Ibid.* B.O.H., *1918,* III, 27-8. Regele, *Feldmarschall Conrad,* (Vienna, 1955), 399.
64. G.O.H., XIV, Apprx. 38h, 39c and 18 (map). *Der Weltkrieg,* II, 357.
65. B.O.H., *1918,* III, 38 and Sketch 2.
66. *Ibid.,* 48. Falls, *The Great War,* 344.
67. *My War Memories,* II, 631.
68. Edmonds, *Short History,* 321-2.
69. B.O.H., *1918,* III, 181-2. G.O.H., XIV, 393-411.
70. *My War Memories,* II, 639.
71. *Ibid.* B.O.H., *1918,* III, 214-15, 251-2. G.O.H., XIV, 446-56.
72. *My War Memories,* II, 640.
73. *Mein Kriegstagebuch,* II, 420.
74. B.O.H., *1918,* III, 215.
75. G.O.H., XIV, 447 and Appces. 22 and 38i.
76 *Ibid.,* 440, 447, 467. Edmonds, *Short History,* 330-1.
77. *Der Weltkrieg,* II, 381. B.O.H., *1918,* III, 229, 233.
78. B.O.H., *1918,* III, 233.
79. *Meine Tätigkeit im Weltkriege,* 343-7.
80. *My War Memories,* II, 675.
81. B.O.H., *1918,* III, 305.
82. *Ibid.,* IV, 7, 8.
83. *Ibid.,* 4, 5, and Map 2.
84. *Report of the Ministry, Overseas Military Forces of Canada, 1918* (hereinafter *Report of O.M.F.C.*), 129.
85. *Ibid.,* 107.
86. Haig's Diary, 26 Mar 18.
87. Canadian Corps Operation Order 187, 27 Mar 18, Appx. II/47 to Corps Diary.
88. *Report of O.M.F.C.,* Sketch No. 5.
89. B.O.H., *1918,* II, 30*n.,* 2.
90. *Report of O.M.F.C.,* 112.
91. Canadian Corps G. 170/19-14, 28 Mar 18, Appx. II/57 to Corps Diary.
92. G. 203, 30 Mar 18, Appx. II/68 to *ibid.*
93. *Report of O.M.F.C.,* 112-14, 116.
94. John J. Pershing, *My Experiences in the World War* (New York, 1931), II, 3.
95. B.O.H., *1918,* II, 456-88.
96. Haig's *Private Papers,* 303.
97. *Ibid.,* 303-4.
98. *Ibid.,* 319.
99. P.A.C., Kemp Papers, Canadian Corps, C. 25.
100. Kemp to Currie, 30 Mar 18, *ibid.*
101. Kemp to the Earl of Derby, 29 Mar 18, *ibid.*
102. Kemp to Borden, 2 Apr 18, *ibid.*
103. Borden's *Memoirs,* IV, 774. *Debates, House of Commons,* 1 May 18.
104. Kemp to Borden, 3 May 18, P.A.C., Kemp Papers.
105. Cable, Kemp to Borden, 7 May 18, *ibid.* Haig's Diary, 5 May 18.
106. Milner to Kemp, 6 May 18, P.A.C., Kemp Papers.
107. B.O.H., *1918,* III, 18.
108. First Army G.S. 1183/11, 8 May 18.
109. *Report of O.M.F.C.,* 124.
110. Currie Diary, 31 Mar 18.
111. *Report of O.M.F.C.,* 116.
112. Supplement to *The London Gazette,* 28 Jun 18.
113. *Report of O.M.F.C.,* 118.
114. *Ibid.,* 115.
115. History of the Canadian Machine Gun Corps, I, 150-1.
116. *Ibid.,* 230, 232.
117. O.B./407, 2 Nov 18, *ibid.*
118. Col. H.F.H. Hertzberg, "The Reorganization of the Engineering Troops of a Canadian Division—Great War 1914-18" (*Canadian Defence Quarterly,* July 1924), 41.
119. *Ibid.*
120. *Ibid.*
121. Currie to Mr. McGillicuddy [first page of this letter missing], Currie Papers, Drawer J-1, Folder, The War—A.W.C.'s Comments.
122. History of the Canadian Machine Gun Corps, I, 192, 203.
123. *Ibid.,* 219.
124. Russenholt, *Six Thousand Canadian Men,* 153.
125. Urquhart, *The History of the 16th Battalion (The Canadian Scottish),* 265.
126. *Report of O.M.F.C.,* 123-7, 130.
127. Supplement to *The London Gazette,* 16 Sep 18.

Chapter XIII

Amiens, 8-11 August 1918

1. "Memorandum by General Foch read at the Conference held by the Commander-in-Chief of the Allied Armies, 24th July, 1918", Appx. XX to B.O.H., *1918,* III.
2. B.O.H., *1918,* IV, 2-4.
3. Ludendorff, *My War Memories,* II, 678.
4. B.O.H., *1918,* IV, 3.
5. *Ibid.,* III, 194. War Office, *Order of Battle* (London, 1945), Part 4, 105, 119.
6. *Report of O.M.F.C.,* 129.
7. G.H.Q. Operation Order, O.A.D. 900/3, 29 Jul 18, Appx. II to B.O.H., *1918,* IV.
8. Fourth Army G.S. Instructions, 31 Jul, 1 and 4 Aug 18, Appx. VI to *ibid.*
9. *Ibid.*
10. R.A.F. Communique No. 10, 3-9 Jun 18.
11. B.O.H., *1918,* IV, 16 and note.
12. *Report of O.M.F.C.,* 128.
13. Jones, *The War in the Air,* VI, 433.
14. W. A. Steel, "Wireless Telegraphy in the Canadian Corps in France" (*Canadian Defence Quarterly,* October 1930), 84.
15. *Report of O.M.F.C.,* 130.
16. B.O.H., *1918,* IV, 27.
17. *Die Schlachten des Weltkrieges,* vol. 36, *"Die Katastrophe des 8 August 1918",* 19-20.
18. Corps Commander's Log, 8-14 Aug 18 (in Currie Papers, Drawer 1802, Folder 3 (b)), 11.
19. *Report of O.M.F.C.,* 129-30.
20. *Ibid.,* 131. B.O.H., *1918,* IV, 21.
21. "3rd Inf. Bde. Report on Operations of 8-9 Aug 18", Appx. 10A to Bde. Diary.
22. *Report of O.M.F.C.,* 131.
23. *Ibid.,* 131-2.
24. C. E. W. Bean, *The A.I.F. in France, 1918* (Volume VI of *The Official History of Australia in the War of 1914-1918*), 511-12. *Report of O.M.F.C.,* 137.
25. B.O.H., *1918,* IV, 27-8.
26. *Ibid.,* 37.
27. *Ibid.,* 22-3, 523-4.
28. C.W.N.S., "Intelligence, Canadian Corps Battle Fronts, Period Aug. 8th to Nov. 11th 1918", 18.
29. Liddell Hart, *The Tanks,* I, 155-6, 177. J. F. C. Fuller, *The Decisive Battles of the Western World* (London, 1955), III, 285.
30. *The War in the Air,* VI, 434-6, 442.
31. G.O.H., XIV, 571, Appx. 25 (map), Appx. 36b. *My War Memories,* II, 678.
32. G.O.H., XIV, 554 and Appx. 25 (map).
33. *My War Memories,* II, 679.
34. *Die Katastrophe,* 26-7, 136, Maps 1 and 2. History of 2nd Grenadier Regiment, 434. History of 11th Grenadier Regiment, 220-1.
35. *My War Memories,* II, 679.
36. *Die Katastrophe,* 17-19.
37. B.O.H., *1918,* IV, 38. G.O.H., XIV, 539.
38. B.O.H., *1918,* III, 198-208.
39. *Ibid.,* IV, 10-12.
40. G.H.Q. Operation Order of 5th August, 1918, Appx. VIII to *ibid.*
41. Fourth Army Operation Orders of 6th August, 1918, Appx. IX to *ibid.*
42. L.C. [*Llandovery Castle*] Instructions, No. 1, Appx. II-71 to Corps G.S. Diary, August 1918.
43. *Ibid.* F.O.H., Tome VII, vol. I, 176-7, and Annexe 492.
44. Cdn. Corps Message G. 275/2523-4, 6 Aug 18, Appx. II-20 to G.S. Diary. F.O.H., Tome VII, vol. I, 176.
45. C.W.N.S., "R.A. Canadian Corps, 8 Aug 18" (in "Artillery-Amiens"); "The Battle of Amiens", V-ii, 1, V-i, 3.
46. L.C. Instructions No. 2, 4 Aug 18, Appx. II-72 to Corps G.S. Diary.
47. 4th Tank Bn. Report, "Supply Tanks".
48. *The War in the Air,* VI, 437-40. "5th Sqn. R.A.F. Narrative of Operations, 8 Aug to 11 Nov 18", 3-4.
49. L.C. Instructions No. 1, 6.
50. "3rd Cdn. Div. Report on Operations between the Avre and the Somme between Aug 8th and Aug 16th, 1918", Appx. "C" to G.S. Diary.
51. "Canadian Independent Force Summary of Operations, 8-10 Aug 18", i, Appx. VII to W.D., G.O.C. Cdn. M.G. Corps, August 1918. L.C. Instructions No. 1, Appx. IV, 4.
52. Cdn. Corps Operation Order No. 220, 7 Aug 18, Appx. II/22 to G.S. Diary.
53. Macphail, *The Medical Services,* 241. Hurd. *The Merchant Navy,* III, 333.
54. B.O.H., *1918,* IV, 43, 62, 77.
55. *Ibid.,* 18.
56. W.D., 43rd Bn., 8 Aug 18 and Appx. "A".
57. B.O.H., *1918,* IV, 45.
58. Supplement to *The London Gazette,* 26 Oct 18.
59. 3rd Div. Report, 6. W.D., 9th Inf. Bde., 8 Aug 18.
60. W.D., 8th Inf. Bde., 8 Aug 18.
61. C.B. Topp, *The 42nd Battalion, C.E.F. Royal Highlanders of Canada* (Montreal, 1931), 213.
62. R.C. Fetherstonhaugh, *The Royal Canadian Regiment, 1883-1933* (Montreal, 1939), 330. "7th Cdn. Inf. Bde. Report on Operations undertaken South-East of Amiens 8-16 Aug 1918", Appx. 8 to Bde. Diary.
63. *Die Katastrophe,* 155.
64. *Ibid.,* 155, 184-5. History of 3rd Reserve Regiment, 162-5.
65. "1st Cdn. Div. Report on Amiens Operations 8-12 Aug 1918", II, 1-3, 6.
66. Supplement to *The London Gazette,* 27 Sep 18.
67. *Ibid.* R.C. Fetherstonhaugh, *The 13th Bat-*

talion Royal Highlanders of Canada, 1914-1919 (Montreal, 1925), 252-3.
68. *Die Katastrophe,* 141. History of 157th Regiment, 292.
69. 1st Div. Report, II, 9, 10.
70. W.D., 2nd Bde. C.F.A., 8 Aug 18.
71. 1st Div. Report, II, 1-5.
72. *Ibid.*, 6.
73. W.Ds., 7th and 10th Bns., 8 Aug 18.
74. *Die Katastrophe,* 116-22, 147. B.O.H., *1918,* IV, 89.
75. *Die Katastrophe,* 173, 191-4. History of 46th Regiment, 420. History of 58th Regiment, 233.
76. "2nd Canadian Division Report on Operations Carried out during Period 13th March 1918 to 11th November, 1918", 8.
77. W.Ds., 4th Inf. Bde. and 18th Bn., 8 Aug 18.
78. Bean, *The A.I.F. in France, 1918,* 533.
79. 2nd Div. Report, 9.
80. "Narrative of Operations by 4th Cdn. Inf. Bde. on 8 Aug 1918", Appx. 10 to Bde. Diary. *Die Katastrophe,* Maps 1 and 2, 116-24.
81. "5th Cdn. Inf. Bde. Narrative of Operations, 8-10 Aug 1918", Appx. 4 to Bde. Diary, 2-3.
82. W.D., 5th Bde. C.F.A., 8 Aug 18.
83. "6th Cdn. Inf. Bde. Narrative of Operations, 8-10 Aug 1918", Appx. 18 to Bde. Diary, 3-4. 2nd Div. Report, 11. *The A.I.F. in France, 1918,* 662.
84. *Die Katastrophe,* 122-3.
85. C.W.N.S., "Cav. Corps Narrative of Operations, 8-12 Aug 1918", 1-2.
86. "Cdn. Cav. Bde. Narrative of Operations, August 8th to August 11th, 1918", Appx. "E" to Bde. Diary. History of 183rd Regiment, 97-9. History of 192nd Regiment, 135-42.
87. Cavalry Corps Narrative, 2, and Appx. "B".
88. "11th Cdn. Inf. Bde. Narrative of Operations 8-9 Aug 1918", Appx. 11 to Bde. Diary.
89. "4th Cdn. Div. Narrative of Operations, Battle of Amiens 8-13 Aug 1918", Appx. 1 to G.S. Diary, 19.
90. C.W.N.S., "1st Tank Bn. Narrative", in "Whippets and Tanks, Amiens".
91. 4th Div. Narrative, 8.
92. 1st Tank Bn. Narrative.
93. B.O.H., *1918,* IV, 54-6.
94. *Ibid.*, 60. 7th Bde. Report, 3. "Summary of Operations Canadian Independent Force 8-10 Aug 1918", Appx. VII to W.D., G.O.C. Cdn. M.G. Corps, August 1918.
95. 4th Div. Narrative, 5-6. "54th Bn. Report on Operations of August 1918", Appx. "N" to Unit Diary. Report by C.O. 102nd Bn., 13 Aug 1918, Appx. "B" to Bn. Diary.
96. 78th Bn. Report on Operations 8-12 Aug 18, Appx. V to Unit Diary. Supplement to *The London Gazette,* 24 Sep 18.
97. "12th Cdn. Inf. Bde. Report, Llandovery Castle Operation 8-13 Aug 1918", Appx. 20 to Bde. Diary, and unit reports.
98. C.W.N.S., Cavalry Corps Narrative, Appx. "B".
99. Map "C", Field Artillery Barrage, in W.D., 3rd Bde. C.F.A., August 1918. B.O.H., *1918,* IV, 60.
100. *Ibid.*, 73, 82. *The A.I.F. in France, 1918,* 594.
101. Cavalry Corps Narrative, 3.
102. *Die Katastrophe,* 196.
103. B.O.H., *1918,* IV, 89, note 2.
104. *Die Katastrophe,* 196-7. Lossberg, *Meine Tätigkeit im Weltkriege,* 354.
105. B.O.H., *1918,* IV, 58.
106. *My War Memories,* II, 679.
107. *Ibid.*, 684-5.
108. Von Kuhl, *Der Weltkrieg, 1914-1918,* II 409.
109. O.A.D. 900/20, Appx. X to B.O.H., *1918,* IV.
110. Appx. XI to *ibid.*
111. C.W.N.S., "Intelligence, Canadian Corps Battle Fronts, Period Aug. 8th to Nov. 11th 1918", Sec. I, 4-6. G.O.H., XIV, 556. *Die Katastrophe,* 171-2, 183-4. History of 41st Regiment, 279-80. History of 45th Regiment, 218-19. History of 60th Reserve Regiment, 170-3.
112. B.O.H., *1918,* IV, 87.
113. Letter, Brig.-Gen. N. W. Webber to Brig.-Gen. J. E. Edmonds, 8 May 39, G.A.Q. 5-85.
114. Cdn. Corps Operation Order, 8:55 p.m., 8 Aug 18, Appx. II/24 to G. S. Diary.
115. Cdn. Corps Op. Order, G. 15, 10:30 p.m., 8 Aug 18, in 1st Div. Report of Operations, 2.
116. 4th Div. Narrative, 8-9. 4th Tank Bde. Report, 2. B.O.H., *1918,* IV, 94.
117. Appx. II/27 to W.D., G.S., Cdn. Corps, August 1918.
118. 1st Div. Report, IV, 1-4. 2nd Div. Report, 14. 3rd Div. Report, 8.
119. B.O.H., *1918,* IV, 116.
120. H. C. Singer, *History of the Thirty-First Battalion, C.E.F.* (n.p., 1939), 359.
121. 2nd Div. Report, 14.
122. 6th Bde. Narrative of Operations, 6.
123. 2nd Div. Report, 15.
124. W.D., 5th Inf. Bde., 9 Aug 18.
125. Supplement to *The London Gazette,* 27 Sep 18.
126. *Ibid.*
127. 1st Div. Report, IV, 4-5. B.O.H., *1918,* IV, 99-100.
128. 1st Div. Report, IV, 1-3. 2nd Div. Report, 16. Appx. VI/2 (Map "B") to W.D., G.S., Cdn. Corps, August 1918.
129. "4th C.M.R. Narrative of Events, 9 Aug 18", Appx. 1 to Unit Diary. Bennett, *The 4th Canadian Mounted Rifles 1914-1919,* 120-1.
130. "Summary of Operations, 8-10 Aug 18", Appx. 3 to W.D., 5th C.M.R., August 1918. Staff Capt. Intelligence Reports, W.D., 8th Inf. Bde., 9 Aug 18.

131. W.D., 8th Inf. Bde., 9 Aug 18. 5th C.M.R. Summary of Operations.
132. B.O.H., *1918,* IV, 98.
133. F.O.H., Tome VII, vol. I, 182. See also B.O.H., *1918,* IV, 115-16.
134. *Ibid.,* 158-9.
135. *Ibid.,* 117. G.O.H., XIV, 554-6. *Die Katastrophe,* 171-91 and Maps 1 and 2. History of 59th Reserve Regiment, 241. History of 45th Regiment, 223.
136. Rupprecht, *Mein Kriegstagebuch,* II, 436.
137. Bloem, *Der Weltkrieg,* II, 227-8, cited in B.O.H., *1918,* IV, 118.
138. G.O.H., VIII, 18; IX, Appx. 2, note 2.
139. B.O.H., *1918,* IV, 139. Information from Histories of 41st, 45th, 60th, 94th and 95th Regiments, Body Regiment and Bavarian Jäger Regiment.
140. 12th Bde. Report, 6.
141. B.O.H., *1918,* IV, 120.
142. 2nd C.M.R. Report on Operations, 8-10 Aug 18, Appx. "B" to Unit Diary.
143. B.O.H., *1918,* IV, 123, 138.
144. *Ibid.,* 123. *Report of O.M.F.C.,* 139.
145. G.O.H., XIV, 560-1. B.O.H., *1918,* IV, 139.
146. B.O.H., *1918,* IV, 123, 125-6.
147. W.D., Fort Garry Horse, 10 Aug 18.
148. B.O.H., *1918,* IV, 126.
149. *Ibid.,* 124-5. 32nd Div. Narrative of Operations, 9-11 Aug 18.
150. 4th Div. Narrative, 11-12.
151. *Ibid.,* 11.
152. B.O.H., *1918,* IV, 130.
153. F.O.H., Tome VII, vol. II, Annexe 605.
154. Appx. XV to B.O.H., *1918,* IV.
155. Cavalry Corps Narrative.
156. 4th Div. Narrative, 13. *Report of O.M.F.C.,* 140.
157. B.O.H., *1918,* IV, 145-6, 152.
158. Appx. XVI to *ibid.*
159. History of Body Regiment, 111.
160. 4th Div. Narrative, 12-14. Cdn. Corps Message, noon 11 Aug 18. B.O.H., *1918,* IV, 145.
161. Supplement to *The London Gazette,* 26 Oct 18.
162. P.P.C.L.I. Narrative of Operations, 11-15 Aug 18, Appx. 1 to Diary. *Report of O.M.F.C.,* 140.
163. Field Messages, 11-28 Aug 18, Appx. 2 to W.D., P.P.C.L.I., August 1918.
164. Operations in front of Damery and Capture of Damery, 15 Aug 18, Appx. 7 to W.D., 52nd Bn., August 1918. History of 60th Regiment, 249.
165. 4th Bde. Narrative.
166. 3rd Bde. Report.
167. *Report of O.M.F.C.,* 140. W.D., 87th Bn., 19 Aug 18. History of 94th Regiment, 268.
168. Special Order by Lt.-Gen. Currie, 13 Aug 18, Currie Papers, 1793 (2), last page. *Report of O.M.F.C.,* 140-1.
169. B.O.H., *1918,* IV, 156-7.
170. *The Tanks,* I, 184-5.
171. *Ibid.,* 180.
172. *Ibid.,* 183. B.O.H., *1918,* V, 96.
173. *The Tanks,* I, 181-4. Fuller, *The Decisive Battles of The Western World,* III, 287, 290-2.
174. B.O.H., *1918,* IV, 158.
175. Cdn. Cavalry Bde. Narrative, 6.
176. *The Tanks,* I, 184.
177. 4th Tank Bde. Report, 7.
178. B.O.H. *1918,* IV, 34, 35.
179. *The War in the Air,* VI, 442, 445.
180. *Ibid.,* 446, 452-4, 457-8.
181. Karl Bodenschatz, *Jagd in Flanderns Himmel* (Munich, 1940), 112-13.
182. *Ibid.,* 129-30. W.D., *Jagdgeschwader* No. 1, 10, 13 Aug 18.
183. *The War in the Air,* VI, 442-3. W.D., *Jagdgeschwader* No. 1, 8 Aug 18.
184. Martin Sommerfeldt, *Hermann Göring: Ein Lebensbild,* 33, quoted in *The War in the Air,* VI, 445.
185. *My War Memories,* II, 686.
186. Hindenburg, *Out of My Life,* 395-6.
187. *My War Memories,* II, 689.
188. *The War in the Air,* VI, 152, 174, 455-6.
189. B.O.H., *1918,* IV, 167-8. Telegram, Foch to Haig, 14 Aug 18, F.O.H., Tome VII, vol. I, Annexe 657.
190. Haig's *Private Papers,* 323.
191. G. 153/2524-4, H.Q. Cdn. Corps to Fourth Army, 13 Aug 18, in Currie Papers.
192. Haig to Foch, 14 Aug 18, Annexe 658 to F.O.H., Tome VII, vol. I. Foch to Haig, 14 Aug 18, *Annexe* 656 to *ibid.*
193. Annexe 657 to *ibid.*
194. Haig's *Private Papers,* 323-4.
195. *The Memoirs of Marshal Foch* (London, 1931), 446-7.
196. O.A.D. 907/2, 15 Aug 18, Appx. XIX to B.O.H., *1918,* IV.
197. F.O.H., Tome VII, vol. I, Annexe 672.
198. B.O.H., *1918,* IV, 171.
199. Currie Diary, 22 Aug 18.

Chapter XIV

Through The Hindenburg Line to Cambrai

1. Haig's *Private Papers,* 324.
2. *Ibid.*
3. Note to Army Commanders, 22 Aug 18, cited in *ibid.,* 324.
4. B.O.H., *1918,* IV, 232-5.
5. Currie Diary, 19-22 Aug 18. H.Q. Cdn. Corps G 512/2525-4, "Future Policy of Operations", 25 Aug 18, Appx. II-50 to G.S. Diary, August 1918.
6. B.O.H., *1918,* IV, 298.

7. *Ibid.*, 311. G.O.H., XIV, 581.
8. B.O.H., *1918*, IV, 306.
9. 2nd Cdn. Div. Report on Operations 13 Mar-11 Nov 18, 23.
10. Cdn. Corps Operation Order No. 228, 24 Aug 18, Appx. II-46 to G.S. Diary, August 1918.
11. 2nd Div. Report, 24.
12. History of 132nd Regiment, 393-4.
13. Currie Diary, 26 Aug 18.
14. C.W.N.S., "Intelligence, Canadian Corps Battle Fronts, Period Aug. 8th to Nov. 11th 1918", Section II, 2. History of 221st Regiment, 260. History of 132nd Regiment, 388 and Sketch 54.
15. 2nd Div. Report, 27.
16. W.D., 6th Inf. Bde., 26-27 Aug. 18. Battalion accounts of operations appended to Unit Diaries.
17. Supplement to *The London Gazette*, 15 Nov 18.
18. "3rd Cdn. Div. Report on Operations, Aug 26th to Aug 28th, 1918", Appx. "C" to G.S. Diary, August 1918, 4.
19. "Summary of Operations Cdn. Independent Force, 26 to 27 Aug 18", Appx. "A" to W.D., G.O.C. Canadian Machine Gun Corps, August 1918.
20. W.D., 7th Inf. Bde., 26 Aug 18.
21. First Army, "Report on Operations 26th August-11th November", 3.
22. 3rd Div. Report, 5. 2nd Div. Report, 28.
23. History of 176th Regiment, 273-4, 282.
24. Appx. II-52 to W.D., G.S., Cdn. Corps, August 1918.
25. "9th Cdn. Inf. Bde. Narrative of Operations 25-30 Aug 18", Appx. 28 to Bde. Diary, August 1918.
26. History of 176th Regiment, 274-7 and Sketch 49.
27. W.Ds., 18th and 43rd Bns., 27 Aug 18.
28. 2nd Div. Report, 31-2.
29. History of 26th Reserve Division, Part II, 62-3, 70-1 and Sketch 11.
30. W.D., G.S., Cdn. Corps, 27 Aug 18, Appx. II-57.
31. 3rd Div. Report, 6.
32. 2nd Div. Report, 33-5.
33. *Ibid.*, 36. 3rd Div. Report, 7.
34. Chaballe, *Histoire du 22ᵉ Bataillon canadien-français*, 376-7.
35. Supplement to *The London Gazette*, 14 Dec 18.
36. History of 26th Reserve Division, II, 64. History of 121st Reserve Regiment, 75.
37. Cdn. Corps Operation Order G. 642, 27 Aug 18, Appx. II-57 to G.S. Diary, August 1918.
38. Currie Diary, 28 Aug 18.
39. 2nd and 3rd Div. Reports.
40. "First Army Notes on Conference held at Canadian Corps Hqrs.", 28 Aug 18, C.E.F. Records D-136, 1.
41. First Army Report on Operations, 7. W.D., G.S., Cdn. Corps, 29 Aug 18.
42. History of 121st Reserve Regiment, 75-6.
43. "1st Cdn. Div. Report on Arras Operations, Drocourt-Quéant Line, Aug 28-Sep 4 1918", II, 1-2, Appx. to G.S. Diary, August 1918.
44. First Army Report on Operations, 8.
45. "Notes on Conference at Canadian Corps, Corps Headquarters, 30th August 1918". First Army Order No. 262, Appx. I-16 to W.D., G.S., Cdn. Corps, August 1918.
46. W.D., 2nd Inf. Bde., 31 Aug 18.
47. 1st Div. Report, II, 5.
48. "4th Cdn. Div. Report on Operations Scarpe, Sept 2nd-Sept 4th 1918", Appx. 1 to G.S. Diary, September 1918. B.O.H., *1918*, IV, 396.
49. Haig's *Private Papers*, 325.
50. Currie Diary, 31 Aug 18. Appx. 20 to W.D., G.S., 4th British Div., September 1918.
51. Cdn. Corps Operation Order No. 234, 31 Aug 18, Appx. II-1 to G.S. Diary, September 1918.
52. *Ibid.*
53. "Drocourt-Quéant Instructions No. 1", Appx. "B" to 1st Cdn. Div. Report on Arras Operations.
54. B.O.H., *1918*, IV, 404.
55. 4th Cdn. Div. Report.
56. "Narrative of Operations of 4th Division 26 Aug-4 Sep 18", Appx. 20 to G.S. Diary, September 1918.
57. Cdn. Corps Operation Order No. 234.
58. 12th Cdn. Inf. Bde. Report, Scarpe Operation, Appx. 14 to Bde. Diary, September 1918.
59. Fetherstonhaugh, *The Royal Montreal Regiment, 14th Battalion, C.E.F., 1914-1925*, 241.
60. Supplement to *The London Gazette*, 15 Nov, 2 Dec, 14 Dec, 1918.
61. *Ibid.*, 15 Nov 18.
62. 1st Div. Report. Beattie, *48th Highlanders of Canada, 1891-1928*, 364.
63. W.Ds., 72nd, 85th and 38th Bns., 2 Sep 18. 4th Div. Report.
64. 46th Bn. Report on Operations, 2-4 Sep 18, Appx. 20 to Unit Diary, September 1918.
65. Comments to author by General A.G.L. McNaughton, 21 Aug 61.
66. History of the Canadian M.G. Corps, III, 590.
67. History of 2nd Guard Reserve Regiment, 237-44. History of 91st Reserve Regiment, 424-9. History of 2nd Grenadier Regiment, 453-8.
68. G. 944 and G. 950, 2 Sep 18, Appces. II-15 and II-17 to W.D., G.S., Cdn. Corps, September 1918.
69. First Army Report on Operations. Divisional Reports already cited. W.D., G.S., Cdn. Corps, 3-4 Sep 18.
70. Currie Diary, 3 Sep 18.
71. Von Hindenburg, *Out of My Life*, 398.
72. First Army Report on Operations, 14. B.O.H., *1918*, IV, 414. Von Kuhl, *Der Weltkrieg, 1914-1918*, II, 430.
73. W.D., G.S., Cdn. Corps, 4 Sep 18.

74. Currie Diary, 4 Sep 18.
75. Cdn. Corps "Future Policy", 5 Sep 18, Appx. II-37 to G.S. Diary, September 1918.
76. W.D., G.S., Cdn. Corps, 16 Sep 18.
77. F.O.H., Tome VII, vol. I, Annexe 938.
78. Liddell Hart, *Foch, the Man of Orleans*, 356.
79. First Army Instructions for Operations No. G.S. 1427/1, Appx. I-13 to W.D., G.S., Cdn. Corps, September 1918.
80. "Cdn. Corps G.S., Operations", file 2526-4, drawer C-11, folder 76.
81. "Cdn Corps R.A., Operations", in Intelligence file, I.G. 562, drawer C-22, folder 42.
82. Cdn. Corps B.W. [Bourlon Wood] Instructions No. 1, 23 Sep 18, Appx. II-63 to G.S. Diary, September 1918.
83. *Report of O.M.F.C.*, 157.
84. Cdn. Corps B.W. Instructions No. 1.
85. Letter, Sir Arthur Currie to F. H. Underhill, 17 Sep 20, in Currie Papers, J-1, Historical, the War, A.W.C.'s Comments.
86. "Narrative of Operations of 2nd Cdn. Divisional Artillery, 27 Sep - 1 Oct 18", in file 8, drawer C-27, folder 42.
87. Maj.-Gen. E. W. B. Morrison, "Artillery Notes on Operations of the Canadian Corps, September 27th to October 1st, 1918".
88. "Cdn. Corps R.A., Operations", in file 11, drawer C-27, folder 42. *Ibid.*, file 10, drawer C-27, folder 48.
89. "Artillery Notes on Operations of the Cdn. Corps".
90. B.W. Instructions No. 2, 25 Sep 18, Appx. II-73 to W.D., G.S., Cdn. Corps, September 1918.
91. B.O.H., *1918*, IV, 496. G.O.H., XIV, 604.
92. *Final Report of General John J. Pershing* (1 Sep 19), Pt II, 584-9.
93. Haig's *Despatches*, 278.
94. Currie Diary, 27 Sep 18.
95. "Cdn. Corps R.A., Operations", in Intelligence file, I.G. 477, drawer C-22, folder 42.
96. History of 188th Regiment, 308-9.
97. History of 2nd Guard Reserve Regiment, 251-2. History of 26th Regiment of Dragoons, 83-4.
98. C.W.N.S., "4th Cdn. Div. Report, Cambrai Operations, Sept 27th - Oct 1st, 1918".
99. Supplement to *The London Gazette*, 14 Dec 18, 6 Jan 19.
100. "2nd Bn. Report on Operations 26-28 Sep 18", Appx. 11/II to Unit Diary, 1st Cdn. Div. Report on Canal du Nord.
101. Supplement to *The London Gazette*, 6 Jan 19.
102. W.D., 10th Bn., 27 Sep 18.
103. "14th Bn. Narrative of Bourlon Wood Operations", Appx. 13 to Unit Diary, September, 1918.
104. W.D., 3rd Inf. Bde., 27 Sep 18.
105. C.W.N.S., "Report by 7th Tank Bn."
106. W.D., G.S., 11th Brit. Div., 27 Sep 18.
107. Currie Diary, 27 Sep 18.
108. G.O.H., XIV, 615-16.
109. History of the Canadian M.G. Corps, III, 590, 597.
110. Cdn. Corps Messages G. 860 and 870, 27 Sep 18, Appces. II-80, 81 to G.S. Diary, September 1918.
111. C.W.N.S., "3rd Canadian Division Report on Cambrai Battle September 27th - October 10th", 5.
112. History of 26th Reserve Division, II, 73-83.
113. W.D., 7th Inf. Bde., 28 Sep 18.
114. Supplement to *The London Gazette*, 6 Jan 19.
115. "Operations of P.P.C.L.I., 27 Sep - 1 Oct 18", Appx. "C" to Unit Diary, September 1918.
116. 3rd Div. Report, 6-7.
117. 4th Div. Report, 8-9.
118. "1st Cdn. Div. Report on Canal du Nord, Bourlon Wood and Cambrai Operations, Sep 27th-Oct 2nd, 1918", Appx. to G.S. Diary.
119. "9th Cdn. Inf. Bde. Narrative of Operations", Appx. 7 to Bde. Diary, September 1918. E. P. S. Allen, *The 116th Battalion in France* (Toronto, 1921), 83.
120. Supplement to *The London Gazette*, 6 Jan 19. Lt.-Col. Chalmers Johnston, *The 2nd Canadian Mounted Rifles* (Vernon, B.C., n.d.), 70.
121. 3rd Div. Report, 7, 8.
122. 4th Div. Report, 10.
123. W.D., G.S., 11th Brit. Div., 29 Sep 18. 1st Div. Report, III, 3-4.
124. Seely, *Adventure*, 234.
125. Currie Diary, 30 Sep, 1 Oct 18.
126. W.D., G.S., Cdn. Corps, September 1918, Appx. II-87.
127. "Narrative of Operations of 11th Cdn. Inf. Bde. against Bourlon Wood", Appx. 1 to Bde. Diary, February 1919.
128. 3rd Div. Report, 9.
129. First Army Message G. 669, 30 Sep 18, Appx. I-2 to W.D., G.S., Cdn. Corps, October 1918.
130. "Artillery Notes on Operations of the Canadian Corps". Currie to Capt. Alistair Fraser, 7 Dec 18, Currie Papers, Drawer J, Historical, the War, A.W.C.'s Comments.
131. W.D., 3rd Inf. Bde., 1 Oct 18. "Narrative of Events, 30 September - 2 October 1918", Appx. 4 to *ibid.*
132. Supplement to *The London Gazette*, 6 Jan 19.
133. 1st Cdn. Inf. Bde. Report, "The Attack on Abancourt", Appx. 3 to Bde. Diary, October 1918.
134. "Narrative on Operations of 11th Cdn. Inf. Bde. against Bourlon Wood", Appx. 1 to Bde. Diary.
135. 3rd Div. Report, 9-11.
136. First Army Message G. 690, Appx. 1-5 to W.D., G.S., Cdn. Corps, October 1918.
137. First Army Report on Operations, 35.

138. *United States Army in the World War 1917-1919,* IX, 186.
139. B.O.H., *1918,* V, 46, 51, 111.
140. *Ibid.,*. 83.
141. Haig's *Private Papers,* 329.
142. First Army Order No. 275, 6 Oct 18, Appx. I-14 to W.D., G.S., Cdn. Corps, October 1918.
143. Cdn. Corps Operation Order No. 242, 7 Oct 18, Appx. II-28 to *ibid.*
144. "Operations Special Companies R.E.", drawer C-11, folder 78.
145. 2nd Div. Report, 46-7.
146. *Ibid.,* 47-8.
147. G.O.H., XIV, 647.
148. *Ibid.,* 592-3, 610 and Appx. 27a.
149. *Ibid.,* 647. "Intelligence, Canadian Corps Battle Fronts, 2-8 Oct 18", Sec. V, 2.
150. "The Sixth Canadian Infantry Brigade Narrative of Operations, Battle of Cambrai", Appx. 25 to Bde. Diary, October 1918
151. Supplement to *The London Gazette,* 31 Jan 19.
152. 2nd Div. Report, 48-9.
153. 3rd Div. Report, 12-13.
154. Appx. "D" to W.D., Cdn. Light Horse, October 1918.
155. "26th Bn. History of Operations, 9 Oct 18". Appx. "B-5" to Unit Diary. 2nd Div. Report, 50.
156. 2nd Div. Report, 51-2. W.D., G.S., Cdn. Corps, 10 Oct 18.
157. 2nd Div. Report, 53.
158. Supplement to *The London Gazette,* 31 Jan 19.
159. 2nd Div. Report, 54-5. W.D., G.S., Cdn. Corps, 11 Oct 18.
160. *Report of O.M.F.C.,* 168.

CHAPTER XV

The Final Advance, 12 October – 11 November 1918

1. G.O.H., XIV, 632-3.
2. Ludendorff, *My War Memories,* II, 725.
3. *Ibid.,* 730.
4. Haig's *Private Papers,* 331-2.
5. Cited in B.O.H., *1918,* V, 268.
6. *Ibid.,* 212.
7. *Ibid.,* 213.
8. History of 413th Regiment, 140-1.
9. "Canadian Cavalry Brigade Narrative of Operations for period 8th-10th October 1918", 1, Appx. "D" to Bde. Diary, October 1918.
10. "Narrative of Operations Fort Garry Horse, 9-10-18", Appx. "A" to Unit Diary, October 1918.
11. "Narrative of Operations Lord Strathcona's Horse (R.C.) 9/10/18", Appx. 1 to Unit Diary, October 1918.
12. "Narrative of Operations F.G.H." ("Cdn. Cav. Bde. Narrative"), 2, Appx. "D" to Bde. Diary, October 1918.
13. "Cdn. Cav. Bde. Narrative", 3.
14. *Ibid.*
15. W.D., R.C.D., 9 Oct 18.
16. "Cdn. Cav. Bde. Narrative", 4.
17. *Ibid.*
18. Von Kuhl, *Der Weltkrieg 1914-1918,* II, 474.
19. G.O.H., XIV, 596.
20. *Ibid.,* 647. *Rupprecht, Mein Kriegstagebuch* II, 456.
21. W.D., G.S., Cdn. Corps, 11-12 Oct 18.
22. "Instruction regarding a 'Chinese' Attack, 7 Oct 18", Appx. 6 to W.D., G.S., 1st Cdn. Div., October 1918.
23. "Report on Operations at Sailly-en-Ostrevent, 10 Oct 18", Appx. G to W.D., 13th Bn., October 1918.
24. C.W.N.S., "Report on Operations of 3rd Cdn. Inf. Bde. Sailly-en-Ostrevent to Sensée Canal October 5th to October 12th, 1918". "Itinerary of 1st Canadian Division from July 31st to October 23rd, 1918", in G.S. Diary, October 1918.
25. "2nd Cdn. Div. Narrative of Operations from March 13th to Nov. 11th 1918", 56-7.
26. Message GS 1447/8, First Army to Cdn. Corps, 15 Oct 18, Appx. I-34 to W.D., G.S., Cdn. Corps, October 1918.
27. G.W.L. Nicholson, *Marlborough and the War of the Spanish Succession* (Ottawa, 1955), 146-9.
28. C.W.N.S., "Operations by 56th Division October 10th-October 16th".
29. W.D., G.S., 1st Cdn. Div., 14 Oct 18.
30. G.O.H., XIV, 652-3. *Mein Kriegstagebuch,* 460-3.
31. Currie Diary, 10 Oct 18. Appx. II-58 to W.D., G.S., Cdn. Corps, October 1918.
32. W.D., G.S., 1st Cdn. Div., 17 Oct 18.
33. W.D., G.S., Cdn. Corps, 17 Oct 18.
34. 2nd Div. Narrative.
35. W.D., G.O.C. Cdn. M.G. Corps, 17-18 Oct 18.
36. W.D., G.S., Cdn. Corps, 18 Oct 18. *Report of O.M.F.C.,* 174.
37. Beattie, *48th Highlanders of Canada 1891-1928,* 388.
38. *Report of O.M.F.C.,* 174.
39. W.D., G.S., Cdn. Corps, 20 Oct 18.
40. *48th Highlanders of Canada 1891-1928,* 390.
41. "Itinerary of 1st Cdn. Div.", 11. C.W.N.S., "3rd Canadian Division Report on Operations Forêt de Raismes-Mons, Oct 22nd to Nov. 11th 1918", 2. W.D., A.A. & Q.M.G., 3rd Cdn. Div., 15 Oct 18.
42. 3rd Div. Report, 3.

43. W.D., G.S., Cdn. Corps, 23 Oct 18.
44. First Army "Report on Operations 26th August-11th November 1918", V, 55.
45. First Army Order No. 282, 21 Oct 18, Appx. I-45 to W.D., G.S., Cdn. Corps, October 1918.
46. "Report on Operations of 3rd Bde. C.E.", in 3rd Div. Report.
47. A. E. Snell, *The C.A.M.C. With the Canadian Corps During the Last Hundred Days of the Great War* (Ottawa, 1924), 207.
48. "4th Cdn. Div. Report, Valenciennes Operations Oct. 27th to Nov. 6th", 4.
49. First Army Report on Operations, V, 58.
50. 4th Div. Report, 4. Maj.-Gen. Sir W. H. Anderson, "The Operations Round Valenciennes by the First Army, October-November, 1918" (*Canadian Defence Quarterly*, April 1925), 289-90.
51. C.W.N.S., "Intelligence, Cdn. Corps Battle Fronts, 8 Aug - 11 Nov 18", Sec. 7, Map 1 (confirmed from German regimental histories).
52. First Army Report on Operations, V, 57.
53. "Notes on Conference of Corps Commanders held at First Army Headquarters on 27 October 1918", Appx. I-54 to W.D., G.S., Cdn. Corps, October 1918.
54. Maj.-Gen. A. G. L. McNaughton, "The Capture of Valenciennes" (*Canadian Defence Quarterly*, April 1933), 281.
55. First Army Report on Operations, V, 60.
56. Valenciennes Instructions No. 1, 28 Oct 18, Appces. I and II to 4th Div. Report.
57. First Army Report on Operations, V, 60.
58. "The Operations Round Valenciennes by the First Army", 293.
59. "The Capture of Valenciennes", 281.
60. "The Operations Round Valenciennes by the First Army", 293.
61. 4th Div. Report, Appx. IV.
62. First Army Report on Operations, V, 63. "The Capture of Valenciennes", 284-6.
63. 4th Div. Report, 5. "The Capture of Valenciennes", 285.
64. 4th Div. Report, 7. C.W.N.S., "10th Cdn. Inf. Bde. Narrative of Operations, Second Battle of Valenciennes", 9.
65. Supplement to *The London Gazette*, 31 Jan 19.
66. 4th Div. Report, 7.
67. 3rd Div. Report, 5.
68. "The Capture of Valenciennes", 293.
69. "50th Bn. Report of Operations 7 Oct - 2 Nov 17", Appx. 30 to 4th Div. Report.
70. Currie Diary, 1 Nov 18.
71. W.D., 11th Inf. Bde., 2 Nov 18.
72. "12th Cdn. Inf. Bde. Report, Valenciennes Operation, 16 Oct-6 Nov 18", Appx. 18 to 4th Div. Report.
73. First Army Report on Operations, V, 64-5.
74. 3rd Div. Report, Appx. 1, "Aeroplane photographs", 4-6.
75. First Army Report on Operations, V, 65. 4th Div. Report, 9.
76. First Army Report on Operations, VI, 67-8.
77. "Weather Reports, 1917 and 1918".
78. 2nd Div. Narrative, 65.
79. History of 188th Regiment, 99.
80. 4th Div. Report, 9-10.
81. History of 115th Regiment, 210 and Sketch 23. *Histories of 251 Divisions of the German Army*, 354.
82. 3rd Div. Report, 7.
83. *The Memoirs of Marshal Foch*, 514.
84. Falls, *The Great War*, 414.
85. G.O.H., XIV, 672-3.
86. *Ibid.*, 699 and Appx. 27a (map).
87. 3rd Div. Report, 8-9.
88. "The Royal Canadian Regiment, Operations November 9th, 10th, 11th, 1918", Appx. 2 to Unit Diary, November 1918.
89. "Narrative of Operations, 42nd Canadian Battalion, R.H.C., November 9th-11th", Appx. to Unit Diary, November 1918.
90. 2nd Div. Narrative, 62.
91. "Narrative of Operations 5th Cdn. Inf. Bde., Nov 5 to Nov 11, 1918", Appx. 28 to Bde. Diary, November 1918.
92. W.D., 4th Inf. Bde., 9 Nov 18.
93. Cdn. Corps Operation Order No. 254, Appx. II-27 to G.S. Diary, November 1918.
94. 2nd Div. Narrative, 67-8.
95. *Ibid.*
96. *Ibid.*, 68.
97. Appx. "A" to W.D., 42nd Bn., November 1918.
98. "Correspondence re R.C.R. first to enter Mons", G.A.Q. 5-34.
99. "R.C.R. Operations, 9, 10, 11, Nov 18", Appx. 2 to Unit Diary, November 1918.
100. C.W.N.S., "Cdn. Corps Intelligence, Notes on German Divisions", Periods 1-8 Nov 18 and 9-13 Nov 18.
101. History of 359th Regiment, 79. History of 4th Reserve Ersatz Regiment, 216-17.
102. Information from Histories of 214th and 109th Reserve and 23rd and 62nd Regiments.
103. 3rd Div. Report, 10. 2nd Div. Narrative, 69.
104. B.O.H., *1918*, V. 559. F.O.H. Tome VII, vol. II, 336-7.
105. Cdn. Corps Message G. 121, 11 Nov 18, Appx. II-33 to G.S. Diary, November 1918.
106. W.Ds., P.P.C.L.I., R.C.R., 11 Nov 18.
107. 3rd Div. Report, Details of Casualties.
108. 2nd Div. Narrative, 69.
109. Supreme Court of Ontario, "Currie v. Wilson and Preston Trial", Currie Papers, J-9.
110. Haig's *Private Papers*, 336. *United States Army in the World War 1917-1919, The Armistice Agreement and Related Documents* (Washington, 1948), X, 20-4.
111. *My War Memories*, II, 756.
112. B.O.H., *1918*, VI, 567-8.
113. *United States Army in the World War 1917-1919*, X, 52-6.

CHAPTER XVI

Outside the Corps

1. B.O.H., *Transportation on the Western Front 1914-1918* (London, 1937), 13.
2. *Ibid.*, 54.
3. *Ibid.*, 56-7.
4. *Ibid.*, 77-8, 94.
5. Telegram, Governor General to Secretary of State for Colonies, 10 Oct 14, and reply, 22 Oct, European War Print No. 4.
6. H.Q. file 600-10-18, vol. 1, fol. 87.
7. *Ibid.*, fol. 93.
8. "Historical Record of Cdn. Overseas Railway Construction Corps", 1, on G.A.Q. file 8-37.
9. *Ibid.*, 2-3. W.D., C.O.R.C.C., 25 Aug-30 Sep 15.
10. "Historical Record", 3-4. W.D., C.O.R.C.C., 31 Oct-30 Nov 15.
11. B.O.H., *Transportation on the Western Front*, 156-7.
12. Letter, Lt.-Col. C.W.P. Ramsey to Lt.-Col. F.L. Wanklyn, 23 Jan 16, H.Q. file 600-10-18, vol. 4, fol. 150.
13. B.O.H., *Transportation on the Western Front*, 160-1.
14. Perley to Prime Minister, 1 May 15, H.Q. file 600-10-22, fol. 12.
15. Telegram, Militia from C.I.G.S., 2 Jun 16, H.Q. file 600-10-36, vol. 1, fol. 16.
16. Historical Sketch of the Formation of Canadian Railway Troops", 1-4, on G.A.Q. file 8-38.
17. B.O.H., *Transportation on the Western Front*, 386.
18. *Report of O.M.F.C.*, 360-1.
19. *Ibid.*, 358.
20. Ibid., 357-9. B.O.H., *Transportation on the Western Front*, 386-7.
21. "Other Information Concerning Canadian Railway Troops", supplied by D.D.; C.R.T. for Ministry O.M.F.C., 19 May 18, G.A.Q. file 8-38.
22. W.D., 2nd Bn. C.R.T., March 1918. *Report of O.M.F.C.*, 362. Miscellaneous information provided by Headquarters C.R.T. for Ministry of O.M.F.C., 15 Feb 19, G.A.Q. file 8-38.
23. *Report of O.M.F.C.*, 23.
24. B.O.H., *Military Operations, Egypt and Palestine*, II (London, 1930), 400, 439, 461-6.
25. Historical Section G.S., "1st Bridging Company, Canadian Railway Troops".
26. B.O.H., *Military Operations, Egypt and Palestine*, II, 468, 567, 588-9.
27. W.D., 1st Bridging Coy., 2-7 Oct 18. Report of Maj. A.P. Linton, 9 Oct 18, H.S. 6-E-1.
28. B.O.H., *Military Operations, Egypt and Palestine*, II, 422-3.
29. *Ibid.*, 597, 600. "1st Bridging Company, C.R.T."
30. B.O.H., *Military Operations, Egypt and Palestine*, II, 616-17, 622. "1st Bridging Company, C.R.T."
31. Letter, Acting D.M. Militia and Defence to Mil. Secretary to Governor General, 12 Jan 19. Memo, E. Pye to Executive Officer, Historical Section, 10 Sep 51 on D.H.S. file D-4-27. Letter R. W. Gornall to Director Historical Section, 17 Mar 31, G.A.Q. 10-28(2).
32. R.W. Sellen, "The British Intervention in Russia 1917-1920" (*The Dalhousie Review*, Fall 1960).
33. B.O.H., *The Campaign in Mesopotamia 1914-1918*, IV (London, 1927), 111, 171, 177.
34. *Ibid.*, 105-6.
35. *Ibid.*, 102-5.
36. "The Dunsterforce", on G.A.Q. file 10-28 (2).
37. *Ibid.*
38. *Ibid.* Capt. W.W. Murray, "Canadians in Dunsterforce", I (*Canadian Defence Quarterly*, January 1931), 214-15.
39. B.O.H., *The Campaign in Mesopotamia*, IV, 106-7, 116, 119.
40. Murray, "Canadians in Dunsterforce", I, 215-16.
41. "The Dunsterforce".
42. "Canadians in Dunsterforce", II (*Canadian Defence Quarterly*, April 1931), 380-1.
43. B.O.H., *The Campaign in Mesopotamia*, IV, 200-4, 210-21.
44. "Canadians in Dunsterforce", V (*Canadian Defence Quarterly*, January 1932), 233. *Ibid.*, III, 489-90.
45. B.O.H., *The Campaign in Mesopotamia*, IV. 223-9.
46. "Canadians in Dunsterforce", V, 235.
47. B.O.H., *The Campaign in Mesopotamia*, IV, 232.
48. "Canadians in Dunsterforce", V, 232-9, 243-9.
49. *Ibid.*, 207-10, 323, 330.
50. "The Dunsterforce".
51. Macphail, *The Medical Services*, 295-8. Letter, D.M.S. to Carson, 21 Dec 15, Carson file 8-4-26.
52. *The Medical Services*, 119-20.
53. *Report of O.M.F.C.*, 396-7.
54. *The Medical Services*, 296.
55. *Ibid.*, 297.
56. Letter, O.C. No. 1 Cdn. Stationary Hospital to D.M.S. Salonika, 22 Sep 16, Carson file 8-4-63.
57. Col. H.A. Bruce, *Report on the Canadian Army Medical Service* (London, 1916), 5, 84.
58. *Ibid.*, 84.
59. Memorandum, A D.M.S. Canadians, Shorn-

cliffe Area to D.M.S. Canadian Contingents, London, 4 Oct 16, in Jones's Interim Reply to Bruce Report, Bruce Papers, vol. 2. *The Medical Services*, 141-2.
60. Letter, Jones to Carson, 21 Dec 15, Carson file 8-4-26. Letter, Jones to Carson, 9 Nov 15, *ibid.*, 8-4-22. Telegram, Minister to Carson, 20 Dec 15, *ibid.*, 8-4-26.
61. *The Medical Services*, 196.
62. Letter, Keogh to Jones, 14 Sep 16, on D.M.S. (London) file 30-3-1, vol. 1.
63. Letter War Office to Secretary, H.Q., C.E.F., 7 Jan 17; letter D.M.S. [Canadian] to War Office, 16 May 17; both on D.M.S. (London) file 30-4-4, vol. 1.
64. W.D., No. 1 Stat. Hospital C.A.M.C., 16 Aug, 3 Sep 17.
65. Letter, President U. of T. to Chief Accountant, Dept. of Militia, 24 Dec 18, H.Q. file 54-21-15-86.
66. *Report of O.M.F.C.*, 396-7
67. L. Amy, *The Camera with the Canadian Forestry Corps in Great Britain* (London, n.d.), 3.
68. Telegram, Perley to Borden, 11 Jan 16, H.Q. file 54-21-23, vol. 1.
69. European War Print No. 26, Item 22A, 15 Feb 16.
70. Telegram, Secretary of State for Colonies to Governor General, 19 May 16, *ibid.*, No. 27, Item 114B.
71. Letter, Secretary War Office to Perley, 30 Nov 16, Carson file 8-1-134.
72. *Report of O.M.F.C.*, 369-70.
73. A.C.I. 414, 8 Mar 17, O.M. file 0-9-12.
74. C.F.C. Orders, 14 Nov 16. H.Q. Canadians letter, No. A.G. 7-1-10, 7 Nov 16. W.D., H.Q. Cdn. Forestry Corps, 18 Mar-2 Apr 17.
75. Haig's *Despatches*, 144.
76. Memos to D.D. Forestry and Timber Operations, 3 and 6 Aug 17, O.S. file 0-53-32, vol. 2, fols, 141-2.
77. Letter, Derby to Kemp, 12 Apr 18, quoted in C. W. Bird and Lieut J. B. Davies, *The Canadian Forestry Corps: Its Inception, Development and Achievements* (London, 1919), 13.
78. "Note on Canadian Forestry Corps Aerodrome Construction Companies", Appx. 23 to Duguid II, Chap. XIII.
79. *Report of O.M.F.C.*, 368.
80. *Ibid.*, W.D., H.Q., C.F.C., 2-4 Oct 18.
81. W.D., A. & Q. Cdn. Corps, 5 Mar 18. W.D., H.Q. C.F.C., March-April 1918.
82. *Report of O.M.F.C.*, 369-70.
83. *Ibid.* "Canadian Forestry Corps", MacBrien Papers, vol. 2.
84. *Work of the Royal Engineers in the European War, 1914-19: Military Mining*, 1.
85. W.D., 1st Cdn. Tunnelling Coy., February 1916. W.D., 2nd Cdn. Tunnelling Coy., April 1916.
86. *Military Mining*, 2-6.
87. Appendices 1 and 2 to W.D., 2nd Tunnelling Coy. C.E., June 1916.
88. *Military Mining*, 14-15.
89. *Ibid.*, 17-19.
90. *Report of O.M.F.C.*, 118.
91. W.D., 3rd Cdn. Tunnelling Coy., June 1918.
92. W.Ds., 1st Tunnelling Coy., 11 Jul 18; 2nd Tunnelling Coy., 7 Jul 18.
93. Documents on file H.Q. 6978-4, vol. 1.
94. Duguid, I, 73. General H.D.G. Crerar to author, 26 Jan 62, HQC 1456-1-3.
95. Air Historian, "History of the R.C.A.F." (1962), Part 3, Sections 1 and 3. *Report of O.M.F.C.*, 349.
96. "History of the R.C.A.F.", Part 3, Section 2.
97. *Report of O.M.F.C.*, 345-6.
98. Letter, D.M. Militia Service to Maj. George W. Le Mar, 10 Jun 29, D.H.S. file 4-8, vol. 2. Liaison Officer R.C.A.F. to Secretary D.N.D., 26 Mar 35, G.A.Q. file 10-20J.
99. F. M. Cutlack, *The Australian Flying Corps in the Western and Eastern Theatres of War 1914-1918* (Volume VIII of *The Official History of Australia in the War of 1914-18*), 445.
100. "History of the R.C.A.F.", Part 3, section 2.
101. Memo, Chef du Service Historique de l'Armée de l'Air to Director Historical Section, 10 Aug 60.
102. Bruce Robertson (ed.), *Air Aces of the 1914-1918 War* (Letchworth, Herts, 1959), 42, 84, 196.
103. Bishop, *Winged Warfare*, 1, 29.
104. A. J. L. Scott, *Sixty Squadron R.A.F.* (London, 1920), 27-9. J. M. Bruce, *British Aeroplanes, 1914-18* (London, 1957), 552-68.
105. Jones, *The War in the Air*, IV, 129.
106. Robertson, *Von Richthofen and the Flying Circus*, 58, 65.
107. *Winged Warfare*, 126, 151.
108. G. A. Drew, *Canada's Fighting Airmen* (Toronto, 1931), 76-7.
109. R.F.C. letter, CRFC 1693G, 15 Aug 17.
110. *British Aeroplanes*, 578. Notation on Combat Report of Lieut. M. S. Taylor, No. 209 Sqn. R.A.F., 2 May 18.
111. *The War in the Air*, IV, 286-7.
112. *British Aeroplanes*, 445-57, 573-93. Thetford and Riding, *Aircraft of the 1914-1918 War*, 27, 32, 50, 61, 96. *Sixty Squadron R.A.F.*, 27-9, 43*n*.
113. *The War in the Air*, VI, 445. *Aircraft of the 1914-1918 War*, 51.
114. *British Aeroplanes*, 607-14. *Aircraft of the 1914-1918 War*, 37.
115. Letter, General A. G. L. McNaughton to author, 20 Feb 62.
116. *The War in the Air*, VI, 542-3.
117. *Ibid.*, IV, 333-4.
118. "History of the R.C.A.F.", Part 3, Section 2. Drew, *Canada's Fighting Airmen*, 88.
119. Liaison Officer R.C.A.F. to Secretary D.N.D., 26 Mar 35. Air Historical Section, *R.C.A.F. Log Book, A Chronological Outline of the Origin, Growth and Achieve-*

ment of the Royal Canadian Air Force (Ottawa, 1949), 10.

120. P. T. McGrath and C. Lucas, "Newfoundland", in Lucas, *The Empire at War*, II, 299, 301, 311, 317-18. The War Office, *Statistics of the Military Effort of the British Empire during the Great War 1914-1920*, 363.
121. J.F. O'Flaherty, "The Royal Newfoundland Regiment", 9-10.
122. W.D., Newfoundland Contingent, 20 Sep 15-7 Jan 16.
123. B.O.H., *1916*, I, 436.
124. *Ibid.* W.D., 1st Nfld. Regt., 1 Jul 16.
125. Statement at end of W.D., 1st Nfld. Regt., July 1916.
126. W.D., 1st Nfld. Regt., 12 Oct 16.
127. B.O.H., *1917*, I, 291-2.
128. *Ibid.*, II, 201 and Sketch 19.
129. *Ibid.*, 336. W.D., 1st Nfld, Regt., 16 Aug, 9 Oct 17.
130. W.D., 1st R. Nfld. Regt., 20-21 Nov 17.
131. Letter, Haig to Woodruffe, 4 Feb 18 (quoted in W.D. entry, 8 Feb 18).
132. *Ibid.*, 21 Mar, 13-14 Apr 18.
133. *Ibid.*, 1-11 May, 11-21 Sep, 28 Sep 18.
134. B.O.H., *1918*, V, 66, 77 and sketches 8 and 9.
135. W.D., 1st R. Nfld. Regt., 14 Oct 18.
136. Supplement to *The London Gazette*, No. 31108, 6 Jan, 19.
137. B.O.H., *1918*, V, 275, 286, Sketch 22. W.D., 1st R. Nfld. Regt., 15, 20 Oct 18.
138. Edmund Ironside, *Archangel 1918-1919* (London, 1953), 192.
139. *Ibid.*, 17.
140. Leonid I. Strakhovsky, *Intervention at Archangel* (Princeton, 1944), 2-3.
141. Ironside, *Archangel*, 17-21.
142. Sellen, "The British Intervention in Russia, 1917-1920".
143. "Proceedings of Conference" (n.d.), O.M. F.C. (G.S.) file A-77-33.
144. Brig.-Gen. H.F. McDonald to C.G.S., O.M.F.C., 31 May 18, *ibid.* C.G.S., O.M.F.C. to Minister, O.M.F.C., 24 Feb 19, O.M.F.C. (G.S.) file 0-10-36, vol. 1.
145. Correspondence on O.M.F.C. (G.S.) file A-77-33. Kemp to Borden, 1 Aug 18, Borden Papers, O.C. 518(1).
146. War Office to O.M.F.C., 30 Jul 18; C.G.S., O.M.F.C. to Minister, 24 Feb 19; both on O.M.F.C. (G.S.) file 0-10-36. Borden to Kemp. 2 Aug 18, Borden Papers, O.C. 518(1).
147. Correspondence on O.M.F.C. (G.S.) file 0-10-36. *Report of O.M.F.C.*, 21-2.
148. Tel. from War Office, London, to C.G.S. Ottawa, 9 Dec 18, "Archangel Party", file 4-20.
149. Director of Records, Vital Statistics Ledger, 40.
150. *Archangel*, 27-8.
151. Ibid., 27-8, 31, 118. *N.R.E.F., 16th Brigade C.F.A.* (Toronto, n.d.), 6.
152. *Archangel*, 29-30, 32.
153. *Ibid.*, 33, 35, 43-5. Strakhovsky, *Intervention at Archangel*, 196.
154. *N.R.E.F., 16th Brigade C.F.A.*, 6-8, 30.
155. *Ibid.*, 17.
156. *Ibid.*, 17, 19. Leonid I. Strakhovsky, "The Canadian Artillery Brigade in North Russia, 1918-1919" (*The Canadian Historical Review*, June 1958), 135-6. W.D., 16th Bde. C.F.A., 2 Dec 18.
157. *N.R.E.F., 16th Brigade C.F.A.*, 19, 21, 23.
158. *Ibid.*, 34. Strakhovsky, "The Canadian Artillery Brigade in North Russia", 140.
159. *N.R.E.F., 16th Brigade C.F.A.*, 49-50.
160. "The Canadian Artillery Brigade", 140-1.
161. *Archangel*, 66, 86, 91. "The Canadian Artillery Brigade", 141.
162. Archangel, 106.
163. Winston S. Churchill, *The Aftermath* (New York, 1949), 248.
164. *Archangel*, 129.
165. *Ibid.*, 112.
166. Colonel Sharman to C.G.S., 13 Apr 19, cited in "Precis of Correspondence relative to North Russian Force" prepared for Sir Robert Borden, 17 May 19, Borden Papers, O.C. 518(2).
167. *Intervention at Archangel*, 162-3.
168. *N.R.E.F., 16th Brigade, C.F.A.*, 12, 23, 25-9.
169. Letters, Borden to Churchill, and Borden to Lloyd George, 18 May 19, Borden Papers, O.C. 518(2).
170. *N.R.E.F., 16th Brigade C.F.A.*, 12. "Canadian 'Syren' Party", G.H.Q. file 10-28.
171. Information from Director of Records, Vital Statistics Ledger.
172. Letter from C.G.S. to Ministry of O.M.F.C., 26 Aug 19, H.Q. file 4-21, "Murmansk Force (Syren Party)", D.H.S. folder 15. Tel. from Churchill to C.G.S., 21 Jul 19, Borden Papers, O.C. 518(2).
173. Churchill, *The Aftermath*, 168-9.
174. Lloyd George, *War Memoirs*, VI, 3157-8. *The Aftermath*, 78, 80-1.
175. *War Memoirs*, VI, 3176. *The Aftermath*, 82.
176. *War Memoirs*, VI, 3172.
177. *Ibid.*, 3192.
178. *The Aftermath*, 88.
179. Director of Military Operations (Maj.-Gen. P. de B. Radcliffe, formerly B.G.G.S. Cdn. Corps) to President of the Privy Council, 9 Jul 18, Borden Papers, O.C. 518(1).
180. Borden to Mewburn, 13 Aug 18, *ibid.*
181. Minister of Militia and Defence to C.G.S., 12 Jul 18, *ibid.*
182. C.I.G.S. to Elmsley, 10 Sep 18, "Siberian E.F. 1919", folder 17, file 1.
183. P.C. Instruction 1983. Minister of Justice to Prime Minister, 28 Jul 18, Borden Papers, O.C. 518(1). "Mobilization Generally. C.E.F. in Siberia", C.E.F. (Siberia) file 762-12-7, vol. 1.
184. Establishments—C.E.F. (Siberia), D.A.A.G. 3 File.
185. Borden to White, 25 Jul 18, Borden Papers, O.C. 518(1).

186. Minister of Militia and Defence to Prime Minister, 13 Aug 18, *ibid.*
187. C.G.S. to G.O.C. Mil. Dist. No. 11, 28 Nov 18, "Organization Rolls, C.E.F. Siberia", D.A.A.G. 3 File.
188. G.O.C. M.D. No. 11 to Secretary, Militia Council, Ottawa, 11 Oct 18, *ibid.*
189. C.I.G.S. to Elmsley, 10 Sep 18, "Siberian E.F. 1919", folder 17, file 1.
190. British General Staff Appreciation of Siberian Situation, 22 Nov 18, Borden Papers, O.C. 518(1).
191. Prime Minister to Militia and Defence, 13 Aug 18, *ibid.*
192. White to Borden (through Kemp), 14 Nov 18, *ibid.*
193. Borden to White, 20 Nov 18, *ibid.* British G.S. Appreciation, 22 Nov 18, *ibid.*
194. Borden to White, 20 Nov 18, *ibid.*
195. White to Borden, 22 Nov 18, *ibid.*
196. Borden to White, 24 Nov 18, *ibid.*
197. White to Borden, 27 Nov 18; and reply, same date. White to Borden, 29 Nov 18, *ibid.*
198. C.G.S. to War Office, 22 Dec 18, *ibid.*
199. War Office to C.G.S., 4 Jan 19; repeated to Gen. Elmsley, *ibid.*
200. Borden to White, 9 Dec 18, *ibid.*
201. War Office to C.G.S., 4 Jan 19, repeated to Gen. Elmsley, *ibid.*
202. C.G.S. to War Office, 10 Jan 19, *ibid.*
203. Knox to Elmsley, "Notes on the present military situation in Siberia", 27 Nov 18, "Siberian E.F. 1919", folder 17, file 2.
204. Knox to Elmsley, 27 Dec 18, *ibid.*, file 3.
205. W.D., Force H.Q., C.E.F. (Siberia), 8 Dec. 18.
206. C. F. Clingan, "The Canadian Expeditionary Force, Siberia", file G.A.Q. 10-29.
207. W.D., 16th Inf. Bde., February - April 1919. Reports by W. E. Playfair, Official Correspondent in Siberia, H.Q., C.E.F. (Siberia) file 49. W.D. 16th Inf. Bde., April 1919, "B" Company Diary, appended.
208. Minutes of Imperial War Cabinet, 30 Dec 18, P.A.C., Borden Papers, Box 333.
209. William H. Chamberlin, *The Russian Revolution, 1917-1921* (New York, 1935), II, 158.
210. Borden to White, 17 Feb 19, Borden Papers, O.C. 518(2).
211. Churchill to Borden, 17 Mar 19, *ibid.*
212. "Canadian Expeditionary Force—Siberia," H.Q. file 4-18.
213. Churchill to Borden, 1 May 19, Borden Papers, O.C. 518(2).
214. C.G.S. to War Office, 24 Mar 19, A-88, folder 19. *The Aftermath*, 256.
215. Chamberlin, *The Russian Revolution*, 188-91, 242-4.
216. *Ibid.*, 164. Secretary Immigration and Colonization to Prime Minister, 4 Jun 20, Borden Papers, O.C. 518(2).

CHAPTER XVII

After the Armistice

1. "Interim Report on the Operations of the Canadian Corps during the Year 1918", *Report of O.M.F.C.*, 186.
2. *Ibid.*, 185.
3. *United States Army in the World War 1917-1919*, X, 53.
4. Currie Papers, Currie to Lt.-Col. R. Watson, 10 Dec 18.
5. Currie Diary, 16 Nov 18.
6. *Report of O.M.F.C.*, 186.
7. *Ibid.*, 189.
8. *Ibid.*, 187. Singer, *History of the 31st Battalion C.E.F.*, 436-7.
9. Urquhart, *The History of the 16th Battalion (The Canadian Scottish)*, 325.
10. Fetherstonhaugh, *The 13th Battalion Royal Highlanders of Canada*, 308.
11. *Report of O.M.F.C.*, 190.
12. *Ibid.*, 190-1. R. C. Fetherstonhaugh, *The 24th Battalion, C.E.F. (Victoria Rifles of Canada), 1914-1919* (Montreal, 1930), 275.
13. "Special Order of the Day", 25 Nov 18., G.A.Q. file 4-15.
14. *The 13th Battalion Royal Highlanders of Canada 1914-1919*, 308. *The History of the 16th Battalion (The Canadian Scottish)*, 327. Beattie, *48th Highlanders of Canada, 1891-1928*, 398.
15. *History of the 31st Battalion C.E.F.*, 440.
16. *Report of O.M.F.C.*, 192.
17. Currie Diary, 12 Dec 18.
18. *Report of O.M.F.C.*, 192.
19. C. W. Bishop, *The Canadian Y.M.C.A. in the Great War* (Toronto, 1924), 342-3.
20. *Report of O.M.F.C.*, 478.
21. *The Canadian Y.M.C.A. in the Great War*, 343.
22. Kemp to Mewburn, 11 Nov 18, P.A.C. file M.G. 27, series 11, D 9.
23. Mewburn to Kemp, 16 Nov 18, *ibid.*
24. Borden to White, 18 Nov 18, *ibid.*
25. White to Borden, 23 Nov 18, *ibid.*
26. *Report of O.M.F.C.*, 189.
27. Borden to White, 25 Nov 18, P.A.C. file M.G. 27.
28. Mewburn to Borden, 29 Nov 18, *ibid.*
29. W.D., G.S. Cdn. Corps, 5 Jan 19.
30. W.D., G.S., 2nd Cdn. Div., 19 Jan 19.
31. W.D., G.S. Cdn. Corps, 6 Feb 19.
32. W.D., G.S., 1st Cdn. Div., 12-13 Jan 19. W.D., G.S., 2nd Cdn. Div., 26 Jan 19.

33. W.D., G.S., 3rd Cdn. Div., 14 and 30 Dec 18.
34. Currie Diary, 17 and 23 Jan 19.
35. *Ibid.*, 13 Dec 18.
36. Department of Militia and Defence, *The Return of the Troops: A Plain Account of the Demobilization of the Canadian Expeditionary Force* (Ottawa, 1920).
37. *Ibid.*, 48.
38. *Ibid.*, 11-12.
39. *Ibid.*, 12-13.
40. *Ibid.*, 18-19, 48. Hist. Sec. folder, "Demobilization C.E.F. 1919" (n.d.), 7-9.
41. *The Return of the Troops*, 19-20.
42. White to Kemp, 12 Mar 19, Borden Papers, O.C. 567.
43. "Disturbances in Canadian Camps and Areas in Great Britain, 1918-1919", in Hist. Sec. folder, "General Demobilization".
44. *Ibid.* Routine Orders, O.M.F.C., (London, 1919), Special Order of the Day, 20 June 1919.
45. *The Return of the Troops*, 24.
46. *Ibid.*, 66.
47. Accounts in various regimental histories.
48. *The Return of the Troops*, 20.
49. *Ibid.*, 29, 152.
50. *Ibid.*, 29, 148-51.
51. Lloyd George, *War Memoirs*, VI, 3367.
52. Maj.-Gen. A. G. L. McNaughton, "The Development of Artillery in the Great War" (*Canadian Defence Quarterly*, January 1929), 164.
53. *Ibid.*
54. *Ibid.*, 170.

INDEX—PART I

GENERAL

A

B

C

D

E

F

G

H

I

J

K

L

M

N

O

P

Q

R

S

T

U

V

W

Y

Z

INDEX—PART II

FORMATIONS, UNITS AND CORPS

A. CANADIAN FORCES

B. BRITISH AND ALLIED FORCES

BRITISH (UNITED KINGDOM) FORCES

Air Force

Army

Navy

COMMONWEALTH AND EMPIRE FORCES

(OTHER THAN UNITED KINGDOM AND CANADA)

Australian

Indian

New Zealand

South African

ALLIED FORCES

Belgian

Czechoslovak

French

United States

C. GERMAN FORCES

Air Services

Army

Note: German divisions and regiments not otherwise described are regular infantry formations.